D0142276

Examples and Applications

Four carefully crafted feature types prove the practical uses of theory and how to apply it to a variety of situations in business, government, and everyday life.

 **Application** boxes and in-text examples found throughout the text show how useful the microeconomic toolbox is.

Figure It Out exercises are worked-out problems that outline how to identify and use the tools necessary for problem solving. The "*" next to the Figure It Out titles below indicates an online tutorial providing interactive assistance for each step of the problem.

Freakonomics boxes show some surprising ways economic analysis can illuminate not only common phenomena, but also things not normally thought to be within the economist's purview. New for the Third Edition are in-class activities designed to reinforce the connection between chapter concepts and the Freakonomics story.

A⁺ Make the Grade boxes offer practical advice for learning microeconomics.

Microeconomics

THIRD EDITION

Austan Goolsbee
The University of Chicago Booth School of Business

Steven Levitt
The University of Chicago

Chad Syverson
The University of Chicago Booth School of Business

worth publishers
Macmillan Learning
New York

Senior Vice President, Content Strategy: Charles Linsmeier
Program Director, Social Sciences: Shani Fisher
Program Manager: Sarah Seymour
Senior Developmental Editors: Valerie Raymond, Bruce Kaplan
Editorial Assistant: Amanda Gaglione
Marketing Manager: Clay Bolton
Marketing Assistant: Steven Huang
Director of Media Editorial and Assessment, Social Sciences: Noel Hohnstine
Media Editor: Stephany Harrington
Senior Assessment Editor: Joshua Hill
Director, Content Management Enhancement: Tracey Kuehn
Senior Managing Editor: Lisa Kinne
Senior Content Project Manager: Kerry O'Shaughnessy
Project Managers: Linda DeMasi & Ronald D'Souza, Lumina Datamatics, Inc.
Senior Workflow Project Manager: Paul Rohloff
Executive Permissions Editor: Robin Fadool
Director of Design, Content Management: Diana Blume
Design Services Manager: Natasha Wolfe
Cover Designer: John Callahan
Art Manager: Matthew McAdams
Production Supervisor: Robert Cherry
Media Project Manager: Andrew Vaccaro
Composition: Lumina Datamatics, Inc.
Printing and Binding: King Printing Co., Inc.
Cover Photo: malerapaso/E+/Getty Images

Library of Congress Control Number: 2019946723

ISBN-13: 978-1-319-10556-3
ISBN-10: 1-319-10556-4

© 2020, 2016, 2013 by Worth Publishers
All rights reserved.

Printed in the United States of America
3   4   5   6   24   23   22   21

Worth Publishers
One New York Plaza
Suite 4600
New York, NY 10004-1562
www.macmillanlearning.com

From Austan

To Aden, Addison, and Emmett

From Steve

To the next generation of economists, whose wisdom will shape the future

From Chad

To my wife Genaya and my children Claire, Adam, Victoria, and Gabrielle

From all

And to the University of Chicago, where people don't just study economics, they live it, breathe it, eat it, and sleep it. The world of economics would never be the same without you, and neither would we.

About the Authors

Lumina Foundation

Austan Goolsbee is the Robert P. Gwinn Professor of Economics at the University of Chicago Booth School of Business, where he joined the faculty in 1995. From 2009 to 2011, he served in Washington as a Member and then Chairman of the Council of Economic Advisers and the youngest member of the President's Cabinet. He is a past Alfred P. Sloan Fellow and Fulbright Scholar. He earned bachelor's and master's degrees from Yale University and a PhD in economics from Massachusetts Institute of Technology.

Beth Rooney

Steven Levitt is the William B. Ogden Distinguished Service Professor of Economics at the University of Chicago, where he directs the Becker Center on Chicago Price Theory. He earned a bachelor's degree from Harvard University and his PhD from Massachusetts Institute of Technology. He has taught at the University of Chicago since 1997. In 2004, Levitt was awarded the John Bates Clark Medal, and in 2006, he was named one of *Time* magazine's "100 People Who Shape Our World." He co-authored a series of books on popular economics starting with *Freakonomics* and is also part of the *Freakonomics* podcast.

JasonSmith.com

Chad Syverson is the Eli B. and Harriet B. Williams Professor of Economics at the University of Chicago Booth School of Business. He joined the Chicago faculty in 2001. His research spans several topics, with a particular focus on the interactions of firm structure, market structure, and productivity. He is an editor of the *Journal of Political Economy*, has served on multiple National Academies committees, and is a research associate of the National Bureau of Economic Research. He earned bachelor's degrees in economics and mechanical engineering from the University of North Dakota, and a PhD in economics from the University of Maryland.

The Story of Microeconomics:
Our Vision

We believe that microeconomics should inspire and excite students with its elegance and usefulness, and that a textbook should support this goal.

The three of us have been friends for a long time. So why would we risk that friendship to embark on such a difficult task as writing a textbook together? We wanted to bring a different perspective to the presentation of intermediate microeconomics. We teach in economics departments and in business schools, and we are active empirical microeconomics researchers. Our experiences made us want to write a textbook that could show students how realistic theory can be if used in practical settings and make clear how economists use data and empirical analysis to test and refine theories.

For all three editions we've provided a visual cue to our approach to microeconomics: We put a Swiss Army knife on the cover of the book. The Swiss Army knife contains many tools that you can use to accomplish many varied tasks. This is how we view microeconomics:

- It introduces tools that are **fundamental** to all forms and extensions of economics, and

- It is extremely **useful** for making decisions in business, government, and everyday life.

We want to help each student grow from someone who has learned some economic principles to someone who can apply the tools of economic analysis to real situations, as economists do. And in envisioning and writing this book we wanted to deal effectively with two questions we hear regularly from students about the micro course:

Do people and firms really act as theory suggests?

All microeconomics texts present the standard tools and theory of economics, and all have examples. However, they often expect students to take on faith that these theories work. They do not always show effectively that these theories can be used in specific and practical ways.

Furthermore, continued reductions in the cost of collecting and analyzing data have led to a radical shift in microeconomics, and current texts have not fully kept up with the dramatic rise of empirical work in applied microeconomics research. Undergraduates and business school students will find microeconomics compelling if it not only explains the theory, but also demonstrates how to use it, and provides real-world data to back it up. We show students the reality behind the theory in our plentiful and up-to-date examples. We have developed and selected events, topics, and empirical studies with a clear eye toward *how* economists use real data to test and refine ideas.

How can someone use microeconomic theory in a practical way?

Students often view the intermediate microeconomics course as abstract and theoretical. Because this course requires a high degree of effort from students, they should know why and how the material they learn will be useful. Without that knowledge, they will be bored and unmotivated. So we wanted to write a book of **useful economics.** When done the right way, economics *is* extremely useful: useful for business, useful for policy, useful for life. Our book shows students how to take the tools they learn and *do* something with them.

The Story of the Third Edition:
What's Retained and What's New

We are happy to have heard positive and constructive feedback on the second edition. As such, the overall structure and pedagogical features have been retained, while examples have been thoroughly updated.

A Leaner Text

There's an old joke about someone not having enough time to write a short letter, so they wrote a long one instead. Well, after three editions, we've had enough time to write a shorter book. We figured out where we could slim down the text without losing the essence of the material. All told, this edition is about 10% shorter than the second. We have been able, despite this, to present clearly and fully the core material of a rich microeconomics course. We did not do this by sacrificing any of the real-world, tools-based focus that is the hallmark of the book. Indeed, we hope that by presenting certain things more concisely, we will actually make the material easier to absorb. At the same time, we have also left plenty of flexibility for instructors and students to dive deeper into more specific topics as desired.

Real World, Real Life

Microeconomics provides examples that offer unusual perspectives on the seemingly ordinary. We have been gratified by the overwhelmingly positive response to the many ways in which we integrated real-life, up-to-date, and, above all, interesting examples and *Applications* into our presentation. Instructors especially appreciated our extensive inclusion of empirical examples. All told, we have over 200 examples (20% of them new in this edition), *Applications,* and *Freakonomics* boxes that illustrate how useful the microeconomic toolbox is in illuminating and understanding all aspects of economics and life.

Our *Freakonomics* boxes, in particular, show how (in often surprising ways) economic analysis can illuminate not only common phenomena but also things not normally thought to be within the economist's purview.

For a complete list of these features, please look at the pages inside the front cover.

Application: Toxic Algae in Florida

Periodically, warm water temperatures and excess agricultural runoff will cause a bloom of toxic algae, known as a "red tide" (or "green slime"), to form on the Gulf coast of Florida. As a result of increasing water temperatures, the algae blooms have become more frequent over time and sometimes stretch hundreds of miles and persist for multiple months. When they arrive, they smell awful and lifeguards often must wear respirators to avoid getting lung infections. Masses of fish die and wash up on the shores. Thousands of tourists cancel their planned vacations on the Gulf.

When the governor of Florida declares the red tide an official natural disaster, Florida's Economic Development Committee will try to compensate merchants for the damage done by the disaster. They then design surveys to analyze the issue. What they're trying to compute is, simply put, the loss in producer surplus.

To compute the loss, they ought to estimate a supply and a demand curve, and then contemplate any shift in demand. Such a shift is illustrated in **Figure 3.5**. Prices and quantities decrease in response to a red tide event—just as the model suggests. Before the red tide, producer surplus is the area below the equilibrium price and above the supply curve, or $A + B + C$ in the graph.

Figure 3.5   "Red Tide" Damage in Florida

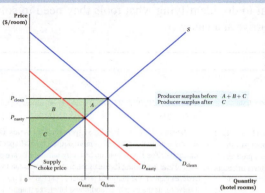

Producer surplus before $A + B + C$
Producer surplus after C

After a toxic algae bloom in Florida, the demand curve for hotel rooms from people visiting the Gulf Coast shifts inward, from D_{clean} to D_{nasty}. During the time when the Gulf's waters are clean, the equilibrium hotel room price and quantity are P_{clean} and Q_{clean}, respectively, and the producer surplus is the total shaded area, $A + B + C$.

Once the waters become nasty, the equilibrium price and quantity fall to P_{nasty} and Q_{nasty}, and the producer surplus is reduced to the area C. The area $A + B$ represents the loss in producer surplus to the local hotels.

Application: Perfect Price Discrimination in Tuition

Although you might not have realized it, you may have experienced something close to perfect price discrimination when you decided to go to college. Families in the United States applying for college financial aid are required to submit the Free Application for Federal Student Aid (FAFSA). This form requires them to report complete information about their family assets and income along with the student's assets and income. While this information is used by the government to determine how much subsidized federal aid a student is eligible for, it also gives the college an almost perfect understanding of each student's willingness to pay. This allows schools to produce an individually tailored financial aid plan that might supplement federal aid. But that is just another way of saying that they charge a different tuition price to each student, depending on how much they think the student can afford.

Economist Ian Fillmore has shown that this price discrimination has huge effects on the market.[1] He estimates that the actual tuition paid at selective universities is almost $1,000 per year higher than it would be if schools couldn't use family financial information to determine financial aid (i.e., the student's effective price). However, as noted above, these price increases are partly counteracted by efficiency gains that (almost) perfect price discrimination allows. Fillmore demonstrates that colleges use high tuition rates paid by students from wealthy and high-willingness-to-pay families to subsidize students from poorer, low-willingness-to-pay families. This allows students from families with fewer financial resources to attend selective schools they would be priced out of if those schools had to charge all students the same price. In the end, whether you are a net gainer or loser from giving colleges your and your family's financial information depends on what exactly that information is. ■

FREAKONOMICS

How Uber Took the Taxi Industry by Storm

Every time a snowstorm hits New York City, people get a lesson in market equilibrium. Traffic becomes snarled. People's tempers flare. And taxis are virtually impossible to find. Yet riders with ride-share companies like Uber can summon one with almost no wait time.

You would think such commuters might be happy that Uber can deliver them home even as the massive New York taxi system fails. But they usually aren't, because in such circumstances Uber prices go up—a lot.

Snowstorms create a supply and demand nightmare for taxi drivers. They are unable to adjust their prices. The city regulates the rate and fees taxis may charge, and to make money, drivers must complete many trips. When road conditions are bad, the amount a taxi driver can earn plunges (plus the risk of an accident goes up). Often, it's just not worth it for taxi drivers to remain on the streets and many head back to the garage. Demand is high and supply is low. The price needs to rise, but it can't.

Uber, on the other hand, can adjust its prices to match supply and demand. Everyone that wants to ride at the market price can do so because two events occur: Some consumers are not willing to pay the higher price, and they drop out of the market. Some Uber drivers who would not

have wanted to drive at regular prices pick up passengers at the higher fare. By choosing a high enough price, Uber equilibrate supply and demand, even in extreme circumstances like a snowstorm. The problem for Uber, however, is that the equilibrium price sometimes turns out to be high. Passengers' Twitter feeds then blow up.[*]

These passengers seem to forget a basic principle of equilibrium. As one of the drivers responded to the many complaints:

I hope everyone realizes that, as a Driver, if there wasn't any surge pricing, I'd just stay home in a snow storm. There would be no drivers and then everyone would be complaining about how they waited 30 minutes for a cab to pick them up to take them 6 blocks.

If Uber doesn't raise prices, there wouldn't be enough Ubers, just like there aren't enough taxis.

But the cold logic of economic equilibrium can make for some serious black eyes in terms of public relations. Uber's automated surge-pricing algorithm raised prices dramatically when demand escalated following a bomb threat in New York City and violent mass attacks in London and Sydney. If you wanted to get away from the threat of death, it cost you 4 times the regular price.

Today, Uber has learned from the bad publicity. It still uses surge pricing but imposes caps so that prices don't soar too high for consumers in critical situations. And to ensure that drivers keep driving under such circumstances, Uber continues to pay drivers the high rates they'd normally charge consumers. In other words, Uber takes a loss on rides in extreme-weather events, because its executives have determined that the long-run benefits of this policy outweigh the short-run costs.

That's a different kind of equilibrium.

[*]Jose Martinez, "Uber Prices Are Surging Because of Snow and People Aren't Happy," November 16, 2018, https://www.complex.com/life/2016/11/uber-prices-are-surging-because-of-the-snow-and-people-arent-happy/uber-surge-6.

Good luck finding a cab when the snow starts falling in New York City.

FREAKONOMICS

Memories of Mutton

You've probably never eaten mutton and you're probably glad. Mutton is the meat of mature sheep. It's stronger in flavor than lamb, gamier, with a considerably chewier consistency. Even mutton's supporters admit that it is an acquired taste. There was a time, however, when more mutton was consumed than turkey, cheese, cocoa, or rice! Why did mutton disappear? The answer is one that you would never guess.

The man who spelled doom for mutton went by the name of Wallace Hume Carothers. Carothers was a small, bespectacled man who lived in Wilmington, Delaware. He didn't care much about mutton; his passion was complex chemical compounds, especially a class of molecules known as polyamides. He worked obsessively, sometimes to the point where he had to be institutionalized. Indeed, his great discovery in February 1935 came shortly after his release from a mental hospital.

Carothers didn't discover a substitute for mutton. Nor did he discover something bad about mutton that drove it out of fashion. Rather, his discovery was nylon.

Nylon was a miracle fabric that revolutionized women's fashion. The demand for nylon skyrocketed. By the 1940s, "nylon riots"—at which hundreds to thousands of women lined up at department stores in the hope of procuring nylon stockings—became commonplace. In a single incident,

40,000 women queued outside a store in Pittsburgh for the chance to buy 1 of only 13,000 pairs of stockings!

More and more women switched to nylon stockings, abandoning wool ones. The demand for wool plunged, driving down its price. In response, farmers raised many fewer sheep. Farmers had never exclusively raised sheep for mutton; they raised them for their wool. Being able to sell the slaughtered animals as mutton simply generated a bit of profit on the side. Fewer sheep meant there was now little mutton to be had. This scarcity might have transformed it into a rare delicacy. For whatever reason, that never happened. Nowadays in the United States, mutton is most commonly reserved for dog and cat food.

The impact of one market on another is exactly what we mean by general equilibrium. But the effects of general equilibrium are not always as subtle as the link between mutton and nylon. Just a few years after nylon was introduced, a new material called polyester hit the streets, which held up better than nylon against water, most chemicals, light, and heat. Nylon's dominance was soon eclipsed by that of polyester, which today is 10 times more prevalent in the marketplace. While mutton lovers may have believed justice was served when nylon fell from its place of preeminence, nylon's decline did not signal the return of mutton. Polyester, like nylon, was a substitute for wool, meaning there was even less mutton to go around.

Helping Students Succeed

Figure It Out exercises

We have been especially pleased with the overwhelmingly positive responses from instructors *and* students alike to our efforts to help students hone and improve their problem-solving abilities. As we were writing the first two editions, reviewers, focus group participants, and class testers continually told us that their students have difficulty translating what they have learned into the ability to solve problems *using* what they have learned. To address this problem, each chapter has several *Figure It Out* exercises. These detailed, worked-out problems patiently and completely walk students through analyzing exactly what a problem asks them to do, identifying what tools they need to solve the problem, and using those tools to arrive at an answer.

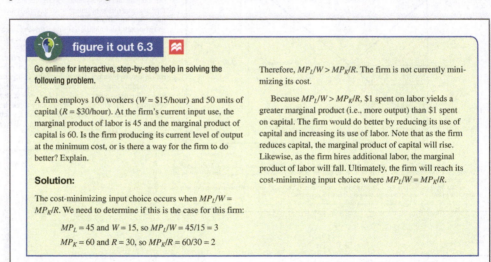

figure it out 6.3

Go online for interactive, step-by-step help in solving the following problem.

A firm employs 100 workers ($W = \$15$/hour) and 50 units of capital ($R = \$30$/hour). At the firm's current input use, the marginal product of labor is 45 and the marginal product of capital is 60. Is the firm producing its current level of output at the minimum cost, or is there a way for the firm to do better? Explain.

Solution:

The cost-minimizing input choice occurs when $MP_L/W = MP_K/R$. We need to determine if this is the case for this firm:

$MP_L = 45$ and $W = 15$, so $MP_L/W = 45/15 = 3$

$MP_K = 60$ and $R = 30$, so $MP_K/R = 60/30 = 2$

Therefore, $MP_L/W > MP_K/R$. The firm is not currently minimizing its cost.

Because $MP_L/W > MP_K/R$, $1 spent on labor yields a greater marginal product (i.e., more output) than $1 spent on capital. The firm would do better by reducing its use of capital and increasing its use of labor. Note that as the firm reduces capital, the marginal product of capital will rise. Likewise, as the firm hires additional labor, the marginal product of labor will fall. Ultimately, the firm will reach its cost-minimizing input choice where $MP_L/W = MP_K/R$.

End-of-Chapter Problem Sets

There are over 350 problems, more than in the second edition, 30% of which are new to this edition. There are problems for every chapter section, and they also coordinate with the chapter's *Figure It Out* exercises. If students have worked through the *Figure It Outs*, they will be successful in tackling the solutions to each problem. Each problem set was reviewed by instructors to ensure its validity and usefulness in testing the chapter's coverage.

Make the Grade Essays

Make the Grade essays point out common pitfalls that students may encounter, help them navigate through the finer points of microeconomic theory, and present practical advice on topics that frequently trip up students during homework and tests.

 make the grade

Holding the rest of the world constant

As you have probably seen in your previous economics courses, economists often use simplifying assumptions in their models to make the world an easier place to understand. One of the most important assumptions we use time and time again in this text is *ceteris paribus*—that is, "all else is equal." For example, suppose you are contemplating your friend Max's demand for an ice cream cone and considering how his demand is affected by an increase in the price of an ice cream cone. To see this

impact, you need to hold constant everything else that may influence Max's decision: the amount of money he has, the outside temperature, the prices of other things Max buys, even his preferences for ice cream itself. This "all else equal" assumption then allows you to focus on the factor that you are interested in, the *price* of an ice cream cone.

It is easy to get tripped up on this assumption when you're asked to dissect an application or an example, so be careful! Don't read more into a scenario than the facts you are given, and don't drive yourself crazy by dragging into the problem all kinds of hypothetical situations beyond those provided in the problem you are analyzing (e.g., what if Max is lactose intolerant? what if it's a cold, windy day? or what if Max just lost his job?).

It is also important to remember that the "all else equal" assumption applies, in addition, to the goods we are considering. When we talk about a particular good, we assume that all units of that good are the same; that is, we hold all the characteristics of the good constant. This means that when we talk about ice cream cones, we are talking about cones of a particular size and quality. Do not think that the price of an ice cream cone has risen if the ice cream inside it is now a premium brand, or if the same ice cream now comes in a chocolate-dipped waffle cone. By introducing either of those changes, you're changing the nature of the good itself, not just its price. By allowing something other than the cone's price to change, you would be violating the "all else equal" assumption.

M. Unal Ozmen/Shutterstock; wildarrow/iStock/Getty Images

Things are not held constant between these two cones.

Words and Pictures

Outstanding presentation in an economics text depends on two main factors. We have ensured that our book delivers on each one.

■ We use **straightforward and accessible writing** without sacrificing rigor. Powerful, complex, and useful ideas should not be conveyed in abstract, dry, or complicated language.

■ Almost as important as a clear verbal explanation is a **clear graphical presentation.** Through color, clear labels, and detailed explanatory captions, each graph complements our words and provides students with a powerful tool for deeper understanding.

How We Deal with Math

Math is a powerful tool for economic analysis, and we want students of every skill level to be able to use it effectively. We have provided a text that will work for a diverse population of students and encourage them to use their math skills to unlock the potential of economic analysis. Our versatile text and its accompanying resources will allow you to use our book in a course with a standard algebraic and geometric focus or in one that relies more on calculus.

Our clear, accessible verbal and graphical presentations are supported by thorough, step-by-step explanations. The whys and wherefores of each step in the mathematical development of concepts are always clearly explained, and allow even math-shy students to easily understand how the use of math can enhance and simplify economic analysis. The main text uses algebra and geometry, but our in-text and online calculus appendices and accompanying resources allow calculus to be integrated easily into our book's presentation of theory, practice, and application.

Math Review Appendix

Most students entering this course will benefit from a math review, whether it is a review of basic algebra or of calculus. A *Math Review Appendix* at the back of the book provides the review necessary to prepare students for the math they will use throughout the text.

Calculus

The calculus is presented in appendices that employ the same conversational tone and intuitive approach as the text and include examples and *Figure It Out* problems (which are often the same as the algebra-based ones in the chapter). In this way, students can see how the calculus analysis buttresses the algebraic analysis. To give students an opportunity to practice what they have learned, each appendix includes problems that require the use of calculus.

To connect the material presented in the chapter with that in the calculus appendices, we have placed marginal notes in the chapter. These notes direct students to the appropriate appendix, and explain specifically how calculus will be used to understand the concepts. We hope these notes will encourage students familiar with calculus to utilize it on their own.

In-text and Online Calculus Appendices (* indicates an online appendix)

Chapter 2:   *The Calculus of Equilibrium and Elasticities*

Chapter 3:   *The Calculus of Consumer and Producer Surplus*

Chapter 4:   The Calculus of Utility Maximization and Expenditure Minimization

                  The Mathematics of Utility Functions

Chapter 5:   The Calculus of Income and Substitution Effects

                  The Calculus of Demand

Chapter 6:   The Calculus of Cost Minimization

                  The Calculus of Production Functions

Chapter 7:   The Calculus of a Firm's Cost Structure

                  The Calculus of a Firm's Cost Structure Expanded

Chapter 8:   *The Calculus of Long-Run Competitive Equilibria*

Chapter 9:   The Calculus of Profit Maximization

Chapter 10: *The Calculus of Price Strategies*

Chapter 11: *The Calculus of Cournot and Differentiated Bertrand Competition Equilibria*

Chapter 12: *The Mathematics of Mixed Strategies in Game Theory*

How Our Book Is Organized

Here is a brief snapshot of the chapters in the book with a bit of discussion on particular subjects that received some special attention or might be different from what you would find in other books. We consider Chapters 1–11 the core chapters that most instructors will teach. The remaining chapters, 12–18, can be taught independently of one another.

Chapter 1, Adventures in Microeconomics: We open the book with a brief introductory chapter and a story about the markets for making and for buying coffee to entice and excite students about the study of microeconomics. Through an *Application,* a *Theory and Data* section, and a *Freakonomics* box, we show students right away how microeconomic tools are useful, not just in the study of economics and business, but in everyday life.

Chapter 2, Supply and Demand: In Chapters 2 and 3, we lay a solid foundation by going deeply into supply and demand before moving on to consumer and producer behavior. Most microeconomics texts separate the presentation and the application of this simple yet powerful model. Presenting the entire model at the beginning makes logical sense, and we (and those who have used our book) have experienced success with this approach in classes.

Chapter 2 presents the basics of the supply-and-demand model. Of particular note is the section Key Assumptions of the Supply and Demand Model, which exemplifies the care and clarity with which we develop and explain microeconomic theory.

Chapter 3, Using Supply and Demand to Analyze Markets: In Chapter 3, we use the supply-and-demand model to analyze extensively consumer and producer surplus, price and quantity regulations, and taxes and subsidies. We believe that the earlier these concepts are introduced and the more completely they are explained, the easier it is to use them throughout the course. Chapter 3 is designed to be flexible: You can pick and choose which topics to cover and emphasize.

Chapter 4, Consumer Behavior: How do consumers decide what and how much to consume given the enormous variety of goods and services available to them? We begin this crucial chapter by clearly laying out, in one section, the assumptions we make about consumer behavior. Actual tests among professors consistently showed this approach as being especially helpful for their students.

Chapter 5, Individual and Market Demand: Here we show how consumer preferences are used to derive market demand. Section 5.3, Consumer Responses to Price Changes: Substitution and Income Effects, takes extra care in explaining this topic, which students often find challenging. Abundant applications and a discussion of pitfalls to avoid make this material particularly accessible and interesting.

Chapter 6, Producer Behavior: How do companies decide which combination of inputs to use in production, and how does this decision affect production costs? We begin this chapter by clearly laying out the Simplifying Assumptions about Firms' Production Behavior. Later in the chapter, we devote a complete section to the role technological change plays in firms' productivity over time. Several applications and examples bring this material alive for students.

Chapter 7, Costs: Cost curves illustrate how costs change with a firm's output level and are crucial in deriving market supply. Because opportunity costs and sunk costs are often difficult concepts for students to master, we take extra care at the start of Chapter 7 to distinguish these concepts and illustrate the role they play in decision making. Our examples engage students so that they can better understand the often challenging concepts in this chapter.

Chapter 8, Supply in a Competitive Market: This chapter begins our coverage of market structure, and it uses real-life industries such as the Texas electricity industry to explain how competitive markets work. We clearly, carefully, and patiently explain a firm's shutdown decision, a topic that students often find confusing.

Chapter 9, Market Power and Monopoly: This chapter begins with a thorough discussion of the origins of market power and how having such power affects a firm's production and pricing decisions. We bring the concept of monopolistic market power to life using examples of real firms with near-monopoly power, such as Durkee-Mower, Inc.; the firm that makes Marshmallow Fluff; and Dr. Brown's, a manufacturer of specialty sodas. Abundant applications further engage students' interest.

Chapter 10, Pricing Strategies for Firms with Market Power: This practical chapter will appeal especially to business students. We thoroughly discuss the many ways in which a firm can take advantage of pricing power, and we clearly describe which pricing strategies are useful in which situations.

Chapter 11, Imperfect Competition: This chapter looks at oligopolies and monopolistically competitive firms. Unlike perfectly competitive and monopolistic firms, these firms must consider their competitors' actions and strategize to maximize their profits.

Chapter 12, Game Theory: The tools of game theory can be used to explain strategic interactions among firms and to predict market outcomes. Students will find our game theory analysis (presented in one chapter for better comprehension) easy to follow and understand. Varied topics from penalty kicks in soccer to airlines' responses to threats of entry show the usefulness of game theory not just in business, but also in everyday decision making.

Chapter 13, Factor Markets: This chapter covers many features of factor markets. To make the concepts more concrete, we use the labor market as an example in much of the development, but we also discuss the unique features of other factor markets. Factor demand and supply are built up from the individual firm or worker level, and then aggregated to an industry equilibrium.

Chapter 14, Investment, Time, and Insurance: Understanding the role of risk and uncertainty over time helps individuals and firms make better economic decisions about investments and insurance. We clearly explain how current costs, future payoffs, time, and uncertainty play a fundamental role in the many decisions firms and consumers face every day. Reviewers especially appreciated our coverage of all these topics in one concise chapter.

Chapter 15, General Equilibrium: We explain intuitively the concepts of general equilibrium, using an extension of the supply-and-demand framework. We also explain the connections among exchange, input, and output efficiencies and tie them to the Welfare Theorems.

Chapter 16, Asymmetric Information: After discussing in earlier chapters what conditions must hold for markets to work well, we look at situations in which markets might not work well. Chapter 16 shows how market outcomes are distorted when information is not equally shared by all potential parties in a transaction. As always, a variety of examples, from auto insurance to credit cards to pirates, shows students that concepts learned in microeconomics are useful in many areas of life.

Chapter 17, Externalities and Public Goods: This chapter continues our examination of market failure by looking at what happens to market outcomes when transactions affect people who are neither the buying nor the selling party, and what happens when a good's benefits are shared by many people at the same time. Our coverage makes clear to students why externalities occur and how they can be remedied.

Chapter 18, Behavioral and Experimental Economics: The recent growth of behavioral economics poses a challenge to traditional microeconomics because it questions whether people actually behave the way traditional theory predicts they will. This question presents any intermediate microeconomics book with a conundrum because embracing behavioral economics seems to undermine the methods learned in the book. Our chapter on behavioral economics explains how to think rationally in an irrational world. If some people make irrational economic decisions (and we present the behavioral evidence of situations in which they tend to make mistakes), other market participants can use this irrationality to their advantage.

Everything you need for **Microeconomics**

SaplingPlus is the first system to support students and instructors at every step, from first point of contact with new content to demonstrating mastery of concepts and skills. It is simply the best support available for intermediate microeconomics.

Classroom Activities

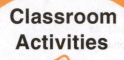

Foster student curiosity and understanding through the new Freakonomics Activity, compatible with iClicker.

Test Bank

Multiple-choice and short-answer questions to help instructors assess students' comprehension, interpretation, and ability to synthesize.

Developing Understanding

Animated Graphing Tutorials narrate graphical concepts, Figure It Out activities pair problems with video solutions, and LearningCurve Quizzes identify knowledge gaps, then nudge students to fill those gaps through an enhanced e-Book, videos, and interactives.

Assessment

Homework Assignments- with an intuitive approach to graphing-offer multi-part questions and targeted feedback.

For more information on Sapling Plus, visit www.macmillanlearning.com.

Engaging Students with Technology

The technology for this new edition has been developed to spark student engagement and improve outcomes while offering instructors flexible, high-quality, research-based tools for teaching this course.

SaplingPlus

SaplingPlus combines powerful multimedia resources with an integrated e-book and the robust problem library of Sapling Learning, creating an extraordinary new learning resource for students. Online activities help students get better grades with targeted instructional feedback tailored to the individual. It saves instructors time preparing for and managing a course by providing personalized support from a PhD or master's level colleague trained in Sapling's system.

LearningCurve Adaptive Quizzing

Embraced by students and instructors alike, this incredibly popular and effective adaptive quizzing engine offers individualized question sets and feedback tailored to each student based on correct and incorrect responses. Questions are hyperlinked to relevant e-book sections, encouraging students to read and use the resources at hand to enrich their understanding.

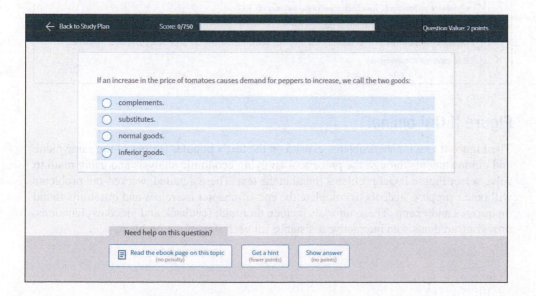

Animated Graphing Tutorials

Based on key figures from the text, the narrated Animated Graphing Tutorials walk students through important graphical concepts of intermediate microeconomics. These assignable activities are also accompanied by multiple-choice assessment with feedback.

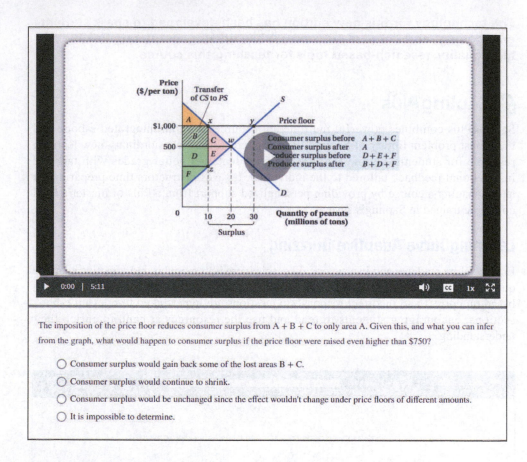

The imposition of the price floor reduces consumer surplus from A + B + C to only area A. Given this, and what you can infer from the graph, what would happen to consumer surplus if the price floor were raised even higher than $750?

○ Consumer surplus would gain back some of the lost areas B + C.

○ Consumer surplus would continue to shrink.

○ Consumer surplus would be unchanged since the effect wouldn't change under price floors of different amounts.

○ It is impossible to determine.

Figure It Out online!

The Figure It Out online problems expand on the text's popular feature of the same name and guide students through the process of applying economic analysis and using math to solve select Figure It Out problems found in the text. These detailed, worked-out problems will better prepare students to complete the end-of-chapter exercises and questions found on quizzes and exams. These tutorials include thorough feedback and video explanations, providing students with interactive assistance for each step of the problem.

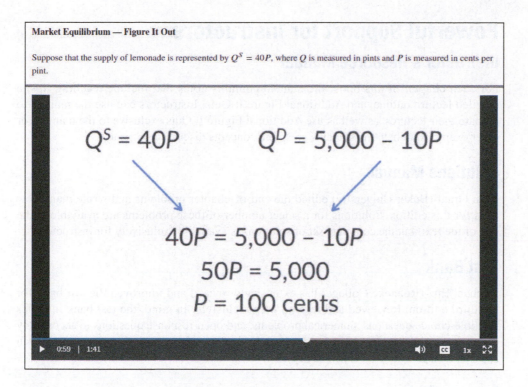

Market Equilibrium — Figure It Out

Suppose that the supply of lemonade is represented by $Q^S = 40P$, where Q is measured in pints and P is measured in cents per pint.

Math and Graphing Video Tutorials

The math and graphing video tutorials are a helpful tool for students to review basic mathematical concepts and how to apply them. Additionally, there are tutorials that cover more advanced math and graphing concepts specific to intermediate microeconomics. These tutorials contain video explanations, as well as multiple-choice assessments to help the students apply the concepts learned in the videos.

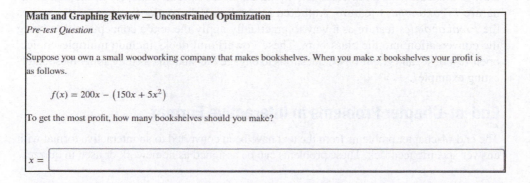

Math and Graphing Review — Unconstrained Optimization

Pre-test Question

Suppose you own a small woodworking company that makes bookshelves. When you make x bookshelves your profit is as follows.

$$f(x) = 200x - (150x + 5x^2)$$

To get the most profit, how many bookshelves should you make?

$x =$

Online Calculus Appendices, Figure It Outs, and End-of-Chapter Problems

In addition to the five in-text appendices, ten additional calculus appendices are available online for students and instructors. These appendices include examples and Figure It Out problems, which are often the same as the algebra-based ones in the chapter. These interactive problems also contain feedback to help students better understand each step in the calculus problems.

Powerful Support for Instructors

Instructor's Resource Manual

For each chapter of this book, the manual contains notes that include teaching tips, a detailed lecture outline, and Additional Figure It Outs. Instructors can use the manual to prepare their lectures, as well as use Additional Figure It Outs exclusive to the manual for other examples to help the students grasp the concepts discussed in the text.

Solutions Manual

Alan Grant (Baker University) edited the end-of-chapter problems and wrote many new ones for this edition. Solutions for a select number of these problems are available at the end of the text, but the complete set of solutions is available exclusively for instructors.

Test Bank

Michael Enz (Roanoke College) has extensively revised and improved the test bank for the third edition. Reviewed and revised with inclusivity in mind, the test bank includes multiple-choice questions, numerical problems, and open-response questions to accompany each chapter. Additionally, there is a separate bank of calculus questions to accompany each appendix chapter.

Lecture Slides

The lecture slides have been revised for the third edition. They feature accessible and interactive graphs that show how the graphs change. These updated slides provide a concise review of the concepts discussed in the chapters.

Freakonomics In-Class Activity

New to this edition is an in-class activity based on the unique examples in the text's signature *Freakonomics* feature. Authored by Andrea Valenzuela, this new activity uses the *Freakonomics* feature as a way to practically apply the text's concepts and to bring the conversation into the classroom. These PowerPoint decks include multiple-choice, open-response, and graph-based questions to engage the students as they apply these interesting examples.

End-of-Chapter Problems in Interactive Format

The end-of-chapter problems from the text have been converted to an interactive format with answer-specific feedback. These problems can be assigned as homework or used in quizzes.

Asymmetric Information — End of Chapter Problem

Harry is dating Sally. Because he is devastated at the thought of being dumped, he spends considerable resources making himself attractive to her: expensive haircuts, ballroom dancing classes, a gym membership, and so on. Harry's marginal cost of making himself attractive to Sally is given by MC in the graph below. Sally, of course, appreciates his efforts: The marginal benefit Harry receives from his efforts (which account for the probability of being dumped) is shown as MB.

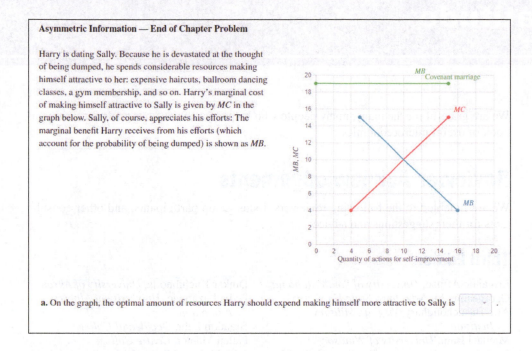

a. On the graph, the optimal amount of resources Harry should expend making himself more attractive to Sally is ⬚.

Graphing Questions

Powered by improved graphing capabilities, multistep questions paired with helpful feedback guide students through the process of problem solving. Students are asked to demonstrate their understanding by simply clicking, dragging, and dropping a line to a predetermined location. The graphs have been designed so that students' entire focus is on moving the correct curve in the correct direction, virtually eliminating grading issues for instructors.

Practice Quizzes

Designed to be a study tool for students, practice quizzes are curated for each chapter with questions from the test bank. These quizzes allow for multiple attempts as students familiarize themselves with chapter content.

How to Use Calculus

These brief explanations describe how the calculus appendices cover using calculus for the concepts presented in the text. These synopses describe how calculus Figure It Outs and appendix content differ from the main text and explain how calculus can be used as an alternate tool to understand the concepts in this course.

With Gratitude

We are grateful for the many, many people who helped us achieve our goals for writing a book of useful microeconomics.

Reviewer Acknowledgements

We are indebted to the following reviewers, focus group participants, and other consultants for their suggestions and advice:

Third Edition

Ermanno Affuso, *University of South Alabama*
Georgeanne M. Artz, *Iowa State University*
Atin Basuchoudhary, *Virginia Military Institute*
Michael Batu, *University of Windsor*
Ergin Bayrak, *University of Southern California*
Kenneth Chiso Fah, *Ohio Dominican University*
Finn Christensen, *Towson University*
Monica Deza, *University of Texas at Dallas*
Aaron Finkle, *University of Maryland*
Daniel Gottlieb, *Washington University*
Christian Helmers, *Santa Clara University*
Jack W. Hou, *California State University, Long Beach*
Michael P. Kelsay, *University of Missouri, Kansas City*
Jennifer L. Kohn, *Drew University*

Dinkar Kuchibhotla, *University of Akron*
Fedja Lazarevic, *University of Alberta, Edmonton*
Brandon Lehr, *Occidental College*
Patten Mahler, *Centre College*
John Mukum Mbaku, *Weber State University*
Andrew Nowel, *North Carolina State University*
Inge O'Connor, *Syracuse University*
Tomson Ogwang, *Brock University*
Pamela Schmitt, *United States Naval Academy*
John Tauras, *University Illinois at Chicago*
Russell E. Triplett, *University of North Florida*

Second Edition

Olugbenga Ajilore, *The University of Toledo*
Richard Anderson, *Texas A & M University*
Nestor Arguea, *The University of West Florida*
Don Bumpass, *Sam Houston State University*
Joni Charles, *Texas State University*
Anoshua Chaudhuri, *San Francisco State University*
Isaac Dilanni, *University of Illinois, Urbana-Champaign*
Isabel Galiana, *McGill University*
Robert Gazzale, *University of Toronto*
Julie Gonzalez, *University of California, Santa Cruz*
Merlin Hanauer, *Sonoma State University*
Geoffrey Jehle, *Vassar College*
Carrie Kerekes, *Florida Gulf Coast University*
Jim Leady, *Notre Dame*
Ata Mazaheri, *University of Toronto*
Richard McGrath, *Armstrong State University*

Felix Munoz-Garcia, *Washington State University*
Michael Nuwer, *State University of New York–Potsdam*
Birikorant Okraku, *Kettering University*
Peter Orazem, *Iowa State University*
Nathan Perry, *Colorado Mesa University*
Tricia Petras, *The Ohio State University*
Spencer Phillips, *The University of Virginia*
Manu Raghav, *De Pauw University*
Reza Ramazani, *St. Michael's College*
Dan Saros, *Valparaiso University*
Mark Tendall, *Stanford University*
Paola Valenti, *Columbia University*
Bruce Watson, *Harvard University*
Colin Wright, *Claremont McKenna College*
Janice Yee, *Worcester State University*
Haiphong Zhou, *Western Michigan University*

First Edition

Senyo Adjibolosoo, *Point Loma Nazarene University*
David Anderson, *Centre College*
Anthony Andrews, *Governors State University*
Georgeanne Artz, *Iowa State University*
Kevin Beckwith, *Salem State University*
Scott Benson, *Idaho State University*
Tibor Besedes, *Georgia Institute of Technology*
Volodymyr Bilotkach, *Newcastle University*
David Black, *University of Delaware*
Victor Brajer, *California State University–Fullerton*
John Brock, *University of Colorado–Colorado Springs*
Keith Brouhle, *Grinnell College*
Bruce Brown, *California State Polytechnic University–Pomona*
Byron Brown, *Michigan State University*
Donald Bumpass, *Sam Houston State University*
Paul Byrne, *Washburn University*
Benjamin Campbell, *The Ohio State University*
Bolong Cao, *Ohio University*
Shawn Carter, *Jacksonville State University*
Fwu-Ranq Chang, *Indiana University–Bloomington*
Joni Charles, *Texas State University–San Marcos*
Ron Cheung, *Oberlin College*
Marcelo Clerici-Arias, *Stanford University*
John Crooker, *University of Central Missouri*
Carl Davidson, *Michigan State University*
Harold Elder, *University of Alabama*
Tisha Emerson, *Baylor University*
Michael Enz, *Framingham State University*
Brent Evans, *Mississippi State University*
Haldun Evrenk, *Boston University*
Li Feng, *Texas State University*
Chris Ferguson, *University of Wisconsin–Stout*
Gary Fournier, *Florida State University*
Craig Gallet, *California State University–Sacramento*
Linda Ghent, *Eastern Illinois University*
Alex Gialanella, *Manhattanville College*
Lisa Giddings, *University of Wisconsin–La Crosse*
Kirk Gifford, *Brigham Young University*
Darrell Glaser, *United States Naval Academy*
Tuncer Gocmen, *Shepherd University*
Jacob Goldston, *University of South Carolina*
Julie Gonzalez, *University of California–Santa Cruz*
Darren Grant, *Sam Houston State University*
Chiara Gratton-Lavoie, *California State University–Fullerton*

Thomas Grennes, *North Carolina State University*
Philip Grossman, *Monash University*
Steffen Habermalz, *Northwestern University*
Jennifer Hafer, *University of Arkansas*
James Halteman, *Wheaton College*
David Hammes, *University of Hawaii at Hilo*
Mehdi Haririan, *Bloomsburg University*
Daniel J. Henderson, *University of Alabama*
Paul Hettler, *California University of Pennsylvania*
Tia Hilmer, *San Diego State University*
Gary Hoover, *University of Alabama*
Jack Hou, *California State University–Long Beach*
Greg Hunter, *California State University–Pomona*
Christos A. Ioannou, *University of Southampton*
Miren Ivankovic, *Anderson University*
Olena Ivus, *Queen's University*
Michael Jerison, *State University of New York–Albany*
Bruce K. Johnson, *Centre College*
Daniel Johnson, *Colorado College*
Leo Kahane, *Providence College*
Raja Kali, *University of Arkansas*
Pari Kasliwal, *California State University–Long Beach*
John W. Keating, *University of Kansas*
Russell Kellogg, *University of Colorado–Denver*
Chris Kennedy, *George Mason University*
Rashid Khan, *McMaster University*
Vasilios D. Kosteas, *Cleveland State University*
Carsten Lange, *California State Polytechnic University, Pomona*
Jeffrey Larrimore, *Georgetown University*
Sang Lee, *Southeastern Louisiana University*
Daniel Lin, *American University*
Qihong Liu, *University of Oklahoma*
Jeffrey Livingston, *Bentley University*
Kristina Lybecker, *Colorado College*
Guangyu Ma, *State University of New York–Buffalo*
Teny Maghakian, *University of California–Merced*
Arindam Mandal, *Siena College*
Justin Marion, *University of California–Santa Cruz*
Timothy Mathews, *Kennesaw State University*

Ata Mazaheri, *University of Toronto–Scarborough*

John McArthur, *Wofford College*

Naranchimeg Mijid, *Central Connecticut State University*

Lijia Mo, *Kansas State University*

Myra Moore, *University of Georgia*

Tamah Morant, *North Carolina State University*

Thayer Morrill, *North Carolina State University*

Felix Munoz-Garcia, *Washington State University*

Kathryn Nantz, *Fairfield University*

Pascal Ngoboka, *University of Wisconsin–River Falls*

Hong V. Nguyen, *University of Scranton*

Michael Nieswiadomy, *University of North Texas*

Matthew J. Notowidigdo, *The University of Chicago*

Constantin Ogloblin, *Georgia Southern University*

Alex Olbrecht, *Ramapo College of New Jersey*

Heather O'Neill, *Ursinus College*

June O'Neill, *Baruch College, City University of New York*

Patrick O'Neill, *University of North Dakota*

Alexei Orlov, *Radford University*

Lydia Ortega, *San Jose State University*

Emily Oster, *The University of Chicago*

Orgul Ozturk, *University of South Carolina*

Alexandre Padilla, *Metropolitan State University of Denver*

James Payne, *University of South Florida*

Anita Alves Pena, *Colorado State University*

Marie Petkus, *Centre College*

Jeremy Petranka, *University of North Carolina–Chapel Hill*

Barry Pfitzner, *Randolph-Macon College*

Brennan Platt, *Brigham Young University*

James Prieger, *Pepperdine University*

Samuel Raisanen, *Central Michigan University*

Rati Ram, *Illinois State University*

Ryan Ratcliff, *University of San Diego*

Marie Rekkas, *Simon Fraser University*

Michael Reksulak, *Georgia Southern University*

Malcolm Robinson, *Thomas More College*

Juliette Roddy, *University of Michigan–Dearborn*

Brian Rosario, *American River College*

Nicholas Rupp, *East Carolina University*

Robert Rycroft, *University of Mary Washington*

Shane Sanders, *Western Illinois University*

Sudipta Sarangi, *Louisiana State University*

Tom Scheiding, *Cardinal Stritch University*

Helen Schneider, *University of Texas–Austin*

Barbara Schone, *Georgetown University*

Kathleen Segerson, *University of Connecticut*

Quazi Shahriar, *San Diego State University*

Carl Shapiro, *University of California–Berkeley*

Alexandre Skiba, *University of Wyoming*

Rachael Small, *University of Colorado at Boulder*

Christy Spivey, *University of Texas–Arlington*

Kevin Stange, *University of Michigan*

Lee Stone, *State University of New York–Geneseo*

David Switzer, *St. Cloud State University*

Ellen Szarleta, *Indiana University–Northwest*

Kerry Tan, *Loyola University Maryland*

Gwendolyn Tedeschi, *Manhattan College*

Jeremy Thornton, *Samford University*

Irene Trela, *Western University*

Regina Trevino, *Loyola University–Chicago*

Brian Trinque, *University of Texas–Austin*

Victoria Umanskaya, *University of California–Riverside*

Michael Vaney, *University of British Columbia*

Jennifer VanGilder, *Ursinus College*

Jose Vazquez, *University of Illinois at Urbana-Champaign*

Annie Voy, *Gonzaga University*

Bhavneet Walia, *Western Illinois University*

Joann M. Weiner, *The George Washington University*

Jeanne Wendel, *University of Nevada–Reno*

Benjamin Widner, *New Mexico State University*

Keith Willet, *Oklahoma State University*

Beth Wilson, *Humboldt State University*

Catherine Wolfram, *University of California–Berkeley*

Peter Wui, *University of Arkansas–Pine Bluff*

Erik Zemljic, *Kent State University*

Faculty Advisers

We owe an enormous debt to Linda Ghent, Eastern Illinois University, our consulting faculty editor, a talented economist, and gifted teacher. So much of this book, from text to features to graphics, reflects her imprint. Her devotion to and belief in this book from its inception to its completion have been invaluable and it has been a real pleasure working with her.

Alan Grant, Baker College, produced end-of-chapter questions that don't just test the material in the book, but enhance it. We would also like to thank Alan for his vigilant and eagle-eyed accuracy checking of the entire book. The book is cleaner, easier to read, and more understandable because of his careful work. Alan could spot an awkward turn of phrase or a typo half a mile away, and we're all better off for it.

Scott Houser, Colorado School of Mines, and Anita Pena, Colorado State University, shaped the calculus program for the book and with Skip Crooker and Kristina Lybecker, developed many of the resources needed to make this book useful for a broad range of instructors and students.

Publisher Acknowledgments

We owe a great deal of thanks to the many hardworking and creative people who have helped bring this book into existence.

Craig Bleyer, then Publisher of the economics list at Worth, started us down this road with a knock on Austan's door many years ago. Over the course of three editions, each member of our book team brought unique talents and perspective to the work. Our able and accomplished Program Manager at Worth, Sarah Seymour, managed this project with great expertise, humor, and devotion. Keeping the project on track required her heroic (and heroically patient) efforts.

The efforts of our Developmental Editor, Valerie Raymond, show up in the third edition in far too many places to count. She was able to master a rare combination of two traits: persistence about the mission of putting together a readable and student-focused text, and patience in working with us to do just that. We don't know quite how she pulled it off, but are thankful for the results.

We are grateful to the many people at Worth who provided the knowledge and support needed to get this book into your hands. Tracey Kuehn and Lisa Kinne provided essential direction, from the earliest planning stages to the very end. Kerry O'Shaughnessy saw our manuscript through the production process with superior attention to detail and resourcefulness in the wake of missed deadlines here and there (and there and there and there!). Thanks, too, to our compositors, Linda DeMasi and Ronald D'Souza at Lumina Datamatics, who are responsible for the text's clear flow. And, we are grateful for the careful eye of Patti Brecht, our copyeditor. Design Services Manager Natasha Wolfe deserves credit for the book's eye-catching design. Robin Fadool worked tirelessly to find interesting and entertaining photos for many of the chapters.

Intermediate microeconomics is a hands-on course for instructors and students, and there is a great need for quality instructional and learning tools to enhance their experiences in and out of the classroom. Thanks to Mathieu Carlson, Meredith Crane, and Joe Nowakowski who were instrumental in developing our strong assessment program. Our Media Editor, Stephany Harrington, and our Assessment Editor, Joshua Hill, have worked to provide innovative tools for both instructor and student. We are especially grateful to Stephany and Joshua for turning the plans for a truly useful media and supplements program into reality. The resources they and their colleagues, have delivered will enhance the course experience of instructors and students.

Final Thoughts

Heartfelt thanks to our families for their continued support of our work (especially when we are too busy to let them know how much we appreciate it).

Ultimately, any text is only a tool and a complement to what students learn in the classroom and from one another. We hope that this text will help you to start them on that journey to using economics.

Austan Goolsbee   **Steven Levitt**   **Chad Syverson**

Brief Contents

Contents

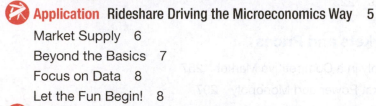

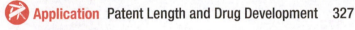

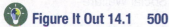

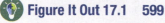

Adventures in Microeconomics

It is morning in Peru's Selva Alta hills, and the sun has been up for a few hours. Rosa Valencia looks admiringly at the coffee plants she's grown. The coffee plants' fruits, called *cherries* because of the red hue they take on when ripe, are ready for harvest. Rosa's workers handpick the fruit and carry it to the outbuilding where it is processed. There, other workers sort the cherries, then remove the fruits' flesh to expose the two seeds—the coffee beans—inside. The beans are washed and prepared for drying and roasting.

That same morning, about 5,000 miles away in Seattle, Washington, home of Starbucks, Lauren Russell grapples with a physics problem. She's at her favorite coffee shop, a block off campus, for her mid-morning break. Sitting on the table next to her book is her usual, a skinny cappuccino. Every few moments, between calculations, Lauren takes a sip and savors the deep, rich flavor of the coffee.

Lauren and Rosa have never met each other, and likely never will. Yet, their morning routines are connected to each other because the two women are part of the same market, the market for coffee. Lauren's taste in drinks connects her to Rosa, who provides a critical input for that drink. Both women benefit from this connection: Rosa profits from growing coffee, and Lauren gets a cappuccino at a price she is willing to pay. This is microeconomics at work.

The ripe coffee "cherry" and savory cappuccino are two sides of the same market.

Marshall Ikonography/Alamy

Peerawat Chotikanokrat/EyeEm/Getty Images

1.1 Microeconomics (and What It Can Teach Us about Rosa and Lauren)

Rosa and Lauren's connection is the consequence of a large number of decisions and transactions that combine to make Rosa believe that growing coffee is worth her time and effort, and make Lauren feel that her skinny cappuccino is worth the money. This book investigates those many decisions and transactions, and how they interact in markets.

We will look at these decisions through the framework of *micro*economics. **Microeconomics** is *the branch of economics that studies the specific choices made by consumers (like Lauren) and producers (like Rosa)*. In contrast, *macro*economics looks at the world through a wider lens and is a description of the larger, complex system in which consumers and firms operate. Macroeconomics takes hundreds of millions of individual producers and consumers like Rosa and Lauren, and tries to describe and predict the behavior and outcome of the combined total of their individual decisions. In this book, we steer clear of the macroeconomic questions.

microeconomics The branch of economics that studies the specific choices made by consumers and producers.

Although the basic outline and content of this course are similar to those of the principles of a microeconomics course, there are some important differences. First, we incorporate mathematics into our models along with graphs. At its heart, economics is concerned with resource allocation, so we want to be able to create precise models that can be solved for optimal quantities. For example, we often want to know exactly how much of a good a consumer will want to consume to maximize her happiness (utility) given that she has limited income. We also want to model how a firm maximizes its profit when choosing its output level and the amounts of inputs it uses to make that quantity of output. Although graphs and verbal explanations are helpful, using math allows us to better quantify these economic agents' decisions.[1]

Second, in intermediate microeconomics, the level of analysis is deeper than in principles. We don't take relationships such as the law of demand or the law of supply for granted. We examine the details of *why* the relationships exist and when they don't apply.

Finally, intermediate microeconomics has a greater policy focus than the principles of microeconomics course. Understanding the economic behavior of consumers and producers is the key to developing appropriate policies. We can also use this deeper knowledge to attempt to predict how various policies (proposed or in place) alter individuals' and firms' incentives and change their behaviors.

Learning the Tools of Microeconomics

theories and models
Explanations of how things work that help us understand and predict how and why economic entities behave as they do.

What sorts of tools will we learn to use as we explore the study of microeconomics? We always start with **theories and models,** *explanations of how things work that help us understand and predict how and why economic entities (consumers, producers, industries, governments, etc.) behave as they do.* To learn the intricacies of the theories and models, we use the tools of graphs and mathematics.

We then use the theories and models to look at how people and firms actually behave in real life (including some seemingly noneconomic situations). The interaction between microeconomic theory and the events, decisions, and empirical data from the real world lies at the heart of microeconomics. Each chapter includes the following sections that illustrate this interaction:

- *Application* sections help us understand theory at work by showing how microeconomics can be used to inform economic decision making in a variety of interesting, real-world situations. Want to know about the effect of toxic algae in Florida? Or, whether or not animals care about fairness? Or, how and why consumers and producers act as they do in the markets for housing, movies, electricity generation, corn, music, and avocados? Some applications delve into the specifics like these of how consumers and producers act in real life. Other applications look at current microeconomic research to see how the data gathered by microeconomists inform and test the predictions of theory across a wide range of topics, such as golf tournaments, plumbers' reputations, the use of gym memberships, and a patent's duration of time and cancer drug development.

- *Freakonomics* essays reveal the surprising ways in which economic analysis provides a unique perspective for exploring a huge variety of phenomena in the world around us. These essays look at topics as diverse as a homemade toaster and why fishermen love their cell phones. Such stories give us a framework for thinking about the economic phenomena that surround us.

---

[1] For students who might need a review of basic mathematical tools, an end-of-book appendix provides such a review. Although we use only algebra throughout the chapters, several chapters also include appendices that show you how the use of simple calculus skills (such as taking a first derivative) can greatly simplify the analysis.

FREAKONOMICS

Thomas Thwaites's Toaster

Thomas Thwaites must really like toast.

Not content simply to buy a toaster to make his toast, Thomas Thwaites set out on a mission to make a toaster from scratch. He started with the raw materials, gathering copper, mica, nickel, and oil (to make plastic), some of which he extracted himself from abandoned mines in the English countryside. He even built his own version of a microwave smelter in order to smelt the iron ores needed for the toaster's grill and spring. In the end, his homemade contraption was indeed capable of making toast about as well as any cheap toaster sold in stores. If you factor in time, effort, and money spent, Thwaites's toaster cost thousands of times more to make than a store-bought version.

It should not have come as a surprise to Thwaites that making a toaster from scratch would be hard work, at least not if he knows anything about economics. Think about the goods and services you've consumed so far just *today,* and all the different materials, technology, workmanship, and coordination that went into making them. The modern economy is nothing short of miraculous. All of us—Thwaites included—have become completely dependent on the market's amazing ability to deliver a nearly infinite variety of products to us at a tiny fraction of the cost and effort it would cost us to produce them ourselves.

Compared to other things we use as consumers, a toaster is fairly simple. Imagine trying to build a computer or an automobile completely from scratch, starting from the rawest materials. Even making your own dinner, if you had to grow the food, would be life-consuming.

No doubt Thomas Thwaites's toaster experiment taught him—the hard way—about the modern economy. If his goal is to learn economics, we suggest a different approach the next time he gets a craving, say, for ice cream. Rather than raising cows, growing sugarcane, and hand harvesting vanilla beans, we suggest he visit his local convenience store and enjoy some store-bought ice cream while he finishes reading Chapter 2 of this book.

Thomas Thwaites

Thomas Thwaites's Toaster Project
A very expensive custom-built toaster.

Using the Tools of Microeconomics

An old joke tells of a tourist looking for a famous concert venue in New York City, who asks a local, "How do you get to Carnegie Hall?" "Practice, practice, practice," the New Yorker replies. So it is with microeconomics. Practice with using the tools of microeconomics is how you get good at it, and there's plenty of help on this front as you progress through this book.

■ In each chapter, you will find several worked out problems titled *Figure It Out* (see p. 23 for an example). These problems are typical of the problems you will encounter in your homework sets, quizzes, and exams, and they appear throughout the chapters to illustrate how to translate your understanding of theory, graphs, and mathematics into successful problem-solving skills. Each Figure It Out shows you, step-by-step, how to understand what, exactly, a problem is asking you to do, and then how to solve it using the tools you've just learned.

■ At the end of each chapter, you will find a set of *Problems* to solve. The variety of problems will prepare you well for applying the tools you've learned to new situations, scenarios, and dilemmas. You should try to solve as many of these problems as you can,

Holding the rest of the world constant

As you have probably seen in your previous economics courses, economists often use simplifying assumptions in their models to make the world an easier place to understand. One of the most important assumptions we use time and time again in this text is *ceteris paribus*— that is, "all else is equal." For example, suppose you are contemplating your friend Max's demand for an ice cream cone and considering how his demand is affected by an increase in the price of an ice cream cone. To see this

impact, you need to hold constant everything else that may influence Max's decision: the amount of money he has, the outside temperature, the prices of other things Max buys, even his preferences for ice cream itself. This "all else equal" assumption then allows you to focus on the factor that you are interested in, the *price* of an ice cream cone.

It is easy to get tripped up on this assumption when you're asked to dissect an application or an example, so be careful! Don't read more into a scenario than the facts you are given, and don't drive yourself crazy by dragging into the problem all kinds of hypothetical situations beyond those provided in the problem you are analyzing (e.g., what if Max is lactose intolerant? what if it's a cold, windy day? or what if Max just lost his job?).

It is also important to remember that the "all else equal" assumption applies, in addition, to the goods we are considering. When we talk about a particular good, we assume that all units of that good are the same; that is, we hold all the characteristics of the good constant. This means that when we talk about ice cream cones, we are talking about cones of a particular size and quality. Do not think that the price of an ice cream cone has risen if the ice cream inside it is now a premium brand, or if the same ice cream now comes in a chocolate-dipped waffle cone. By introducing either of those changes, you're changing the nature of the good itself, not just its price. By allowing something other than the cone's price to change, you would be violating the "all else equal" assumption.

M. Unal Ozmen/Shutterstock; wildarrow/iStock/Getty Images

Things are not held constant between these two cones.

and for selected problems, you can check your answers with the solutions provided in the back of the text. If you get stuck on a problem, go back through the Figure It Out examples to review the steps you should take to solve for the correct answer.

■ In many chapters, you will find a *Make the Grade* box with hints and explanations about how to successfully navigate the sometimes confusing path through microeconomic theory and its application. Read these boxes carefully before exams and quizzes to help you avoid some common mistakes that students often make in the intermediate micro course.

1.2 This Book (and How Rosa and Lauren Would See It)

We begin our investigation of microeconomics with an overview of how the preferences of consumers like Lauren (the demand side of a market) combine with the decisions of firms like Rosa's coffee plantation (the supply side) to determine the quantity sold and price of goods such as coffee (Chapters 2 and 3). We explore, for example, why consumers' and suppliers' responses to price changes differ, and how these differences affect what happens when consumer preferences or production technologies change. And we see how the benefits of a market transaction, such as buying a cappuccino, are split between consumers like Lauren and producers like the coffee shop and Rosa.

Consumers' and Producers' Decisions

After taking this overview, the next section of the book digs a lot deeper into each side of the market, starting with consumers' decisions (Chapters 4 and 5). What determines whether Lauren has coffee instead of tea, or if she goes to a shop other than Starbucks, or does something else entirely? If Lauren becomes richer, will her choices change? We answer the question of how consumers decide which goods, and how much of each, to consume in the face of the enormous number of goods and services they are offered. Then we see how adding up these decisions across all consumers gives us the total market demand curve.

After investigating consumer behavior in detail, we explore producers' decisions (Chapters 6 and 7). For example, how do companies like Rosa's plantation decide which combination of inputs such as agricultural machinery (capital) and workers (labor) to use in production? As it turns out, those types of decisions for firms are similar in many respects to the decisions consumers make when deciding what products to buy. Once we've described firms' input mix choices, we look at how these affect their costs of production. We pay particular attention to how these costs change with a firm's output level, as embodied in firms' cost curves. If Rosa doubles her production, for example, will her total costs double, more than double, or less than double? We focus on cost movements as a firm's output changes because they are crucial in determining what a market's supply curve looks like.

 ## Application: Rideshare Driving the Microeconomics Way

In microeconomics, we focus in large part on two key economic players: consumers (buyers) and producers (firms). We all have ample experience as consumers. Every time we go to the supermarket or the college bookstore, we are consumers. This makes it easier to grasp the economic intuition of the consumer's problem. It's often more difficult to understand producers and the issues they face because the majority of us will make far fewer production decisions over our lifetimes.

When we think about production, big firms like Procter & Gamble or United Airlines might come to mind. But there are also many small producers who face the same fundamental decisions that confronted by the world's largest corporations. Let's look at the production decisions a car driver for a ridesharing service faces.

Suppose you are interested in working for one of these alternatives to taxicabs. The first decision you need to make is which ridesharing company to affiliate with. Uber and Lyft are the two biggest companies, so many drivers consider these to be their principal options. Uber is larger and aims to be slightly more upscale (the business requires the driver to have a newer-model car, offers limo/sedan services and the like); Lyft sells itself as fun and cool, with drivers sometimes greeting customers with fist bumps. You must decide at which company you are likely to make more income. Both companies will take a share of each fare you receive and charge you different mandatory fees (for instance, for a company-specific phone on which you must take all customer calls). You might try to work for both companies, switching between the two based on the fares you expect to receive.

BUST A COMMUTE.

⬇ 🚗 DOWNLOAD & RIDE   lyft

Deciding whether to join Uber or Lyft is only one of many decisions you will make.

Once you're signed up, you need to determine the quality and frequency of service you will provide. There are many variables to consider, from whether to work nights and weekends to whether to engage your passengers in conversation or play the radio instead. Your customers' experiences will influence your ratings as a driver and the probability that you get more business in the future. You will also face some decisions about the longer term. An Uber driver, for instance, may choose to purchase a high-end vehicle and obtain a chauffeur's license to qualify as an UberBlack driver, with the potential to earn substantially higher wages. Although you can decide to chat up one customer and not the next with little impact, you cannot so easily trade in your loaded limo should you decide a chauffeur's life is not profitable enough for you. Here, you will have to consider how the rideshare company may fare in the future to decide if buying a high-end car would be a worthwhile investment.

These examples of the many production decisions you'll face all share a basic principle: They require you to determine whether the costs (financial, time, or effort) of your decision will bring in enough additional revenue to make your choice worthwhile. As you will see in this text, the tools of microeconomics let you and all producers frame the decisions in a way that makes it clearer what the better choice is.

The microeconomics of production decisions may not come as easily to you as the microeconomics of consumer decisions, but understanding the production side of things will help you make more informed and perhaps wiser choices should you find yourself running your own or someone else's business. ■

Market Supply

The book's next section compares many possible configurations through which firms supply output to markets. We start with the canonical case of perfect competition (Chapter 8). In a perfectly competitive market, all firms take the market price as given (they don't have any ability to choose the price at which they can sell their products) and decide how much they want to produce. This is close to Rosa's case. The international coffee market is large and supplied by coffee growers all over the world, so how much coffee Rosa decides to put on the market is not going to noticeably affect its market price. In a perfectly competitive industry, supply reflects the aggregation of the cost curves of Rosa and every other coffee grower, and industry supply combines with market demand to determine price and quantity movements over both the short and long runs.

After perfect competition, we move to the other extreme: monopoly (Chapter 9). When only one firm supplies a good to a market, the situation differs in several ways from perfect competition. Key is that the firm now has the ability to choose the price at which it sells its products. We see that this ability implies that if Rosa were a monopolist selling to the world's coffee consumers, she would choose to produce less than a competitive industry would—even if she had the capacity needed to produce more. This is because limiting the amount she produces raises the price at which she could sell her coffee. We see why governments might want to (and sometimes do) step into such situations using antitrust laws. Next, we discuss other ways monopolists use their pricing power (Chapter 10). This includes ways to charge higher prices to consumers with a greater willingness to pay, or combining products together and selling them as a single bundle to consumers.

In the book's final look at forms of a market's supply side, we investigate oligopolies (Chapter 11). Oligopolies exist when multiple firms interact strategically in the same market. In such markets, firms have some ability to choose their prices, but their fortunes are determined, in part, by the actions of the other firms in the market. (They dish it out as well as they take it, though: Their own actions also impact other firms.) These sorts of situations are common; few firms are either pure monopolists or perfectly competitive price takers. Strategic interactions among firms raise all sorts of interesting questions that we can analyze using the tools of game theory (Chapter 12). For example, how might we expect a firm like Lauren's favorite coffee shop, say, to respond to a new coffeehouse opening across the street?

Beyond the Basics

After these detailed looks at the basics of markets' supply and demand sides, we study several specific subjects in the final section of the book. The economic concepts covered here are present in many markets. In some applications, these concepts deepen our understanding of markets by supplementing the basic analytical structure we introduce in the first parts of the book. In other cases, the basic structure may be inadequate to grasp all the necessary elements of economic interactions, so these concepts will be absolutely necessary to understanding the behavior of particular markets.

The first specific topic we dig into is how factor markets operate (Chapter 13). Factors are inputs into production, such as labor, capital, and land. These markets interact with the decisions of producers like Rosa's plantation to determine where workers work and for what wage, and where factories are built.

Next, we look at the combined role of risk, uncertainty, and time in economic decision making (Chapter 14). These features are especially prominent in investment decisions—choices that typically involve paying an upfront cost with the hope of earning a future return—so these decisions are a focus of our exploration. Understanding risk, uncertainty, and time's interactions in investment choices helps us answer questions such as whether Rosa should invest in a new bean-drying facility, or whether Lauren should go to business school.

We then explore how markets are interconnected (Chapter 15). Changes in the supply or demand of one good can lead indirectly to similar or opposite shifts in other markets. After studying this interconnectedness, we are able to see how a supply disruption in China's tea-growing areas can raise the price at which Rosa will sell her coffee and the price that Lauren must pay for her cappuccino. Once we're able to tie markets together, we can analyze the conditions that must hold for an economy to operate efficiently. For example, are producers supplying the "right" mix of coffee and tea, and doing so at the lowest possible cost? Answering such questions allows us to determine whether markets are working to maximize the social benefit of a good or service.

After seeing what must hold for markets to work well, we look in detail at a series of situations in which markets might *not* work well. One set of situations involves markets in which information about tastes, costs, or product quality is not equally shared by all potential parties in a transaction (Chapter 16). For example, if Rosa wants to buy a used tractor for the plantation, she wouldn't know with 100% accuracy how well the tractor works before buying it, and she might be especially concerned that the current owner was selling the tractor precisely *because* it didn't operate up to par. How does this lack of accurate information affect her decision? Or, if Lauren wants to convince a potential employer she would be a hard-working employee before she gets the job, how might she do so?

A second set of situations in which markets may not operate efficiently includes transactions that affect people who are neither the buying nor the selling party, or markets in which a good's benefits are shared across many people at the same time (Chapter 17). An example would be Rosa's decision whether or not to apply pesticides to her crop. Doing so would not only affect the economics of her own operation, but would also have spillover effects on others. A neighboring coffee plantation might benefit from facing a smaller population of local insects, for instance. On the other hand, other neighbors, workers, and maybe coffee consumers could be harmed by the chemical pollution that pesticide use involves. What makes these situations interesting—and what causes markets to have difficulty delivering the socially optimal outcome—is that Rosa is likely to take into account the pesticide's impact on her own production when deciding whether to use it or not, but less inclined to consider its effects on neighboring farms, the local population, and coffee drinkers in Seattle.

The book concludes with an exploration of behavioral economics (Chapter 18). This study of the intersection of psychology and economics has become an increasingly prominent part of economic research. People often have deeply formed biases and social preferences that limit their ability to act in the completely rational, self-interested way that we often assume in economic analysis. If this is true, then our basic analytical structure—even when supplemented with knowledge of the deeper concepts discussed above—may be inadequate for explaining economic decision making.

Focus on Data

empirical Using data analysis and experiments to explore phenomena.

All these topics provide you with microeconomic tools to study the world around you. Over the past fifty years, this set of tools has expanded and changed. Microeconomics has evolved into a more **empirical** discipline, *using data analysis and experiments, and not just abstract theory, to explore economic phenomena.* The computing revolution made this change possible. As you'll see throughout this book, when the price of a good decreases, people consume more of it. This has been true of computing. Much more of modern-day economists' efforts toward understanding the economy center on data and measurement than they did years ago.

Let the Fun Begin!

By the end of your microeconomics course, you will have the resources necessary to examine the world as an economist does. We've already used microeconomic tools to broadly describe a very specific economic exchange between coffee producer Rosa and university student Lauren. But what's powerful about microeconomics is that it can be applied to any market, not just to a market like the one inhabited by Rosa and Lauren. You can use microeconomics to think rationally about any of the dozens of choices (economic and noneconomic) you face each day. By the end of your study of intermediate microeconomics, you'll not only *be able to* think like an economist—you'll see *how useful* it is.

 Application: The Benefits of Studying Economics

There are many reasons to study economics. Maybe you are one of the lucky few with a burning passion to understand economics. Or, maybe you just need an economics course to graduate. Either way, you will learn a set of tools in this class that will better equip you to make all sorts of decisions, not just economic ones. There's even evidence that if you become an economics major, it will make you richer.

Economists Dan Black, Seth Sanders, and Lowell Taylor analyzed the question of how much people earn depending on their choice of major.[2] They approached the question in typical economic fashion: with a sizable dataset and quantitative statistics. Using the National Survey of College Graduates combined with information from the U.S. Census, they found that economics majors earn almost 20% more than graduates with degrees in any of the other social sciences. (Accounting, finance, and marketing students do earn about the same as economics majors.) Music majors don't fare so well in salary terms: Their incomes are approximately 40% lower than those of economics majors.[3]

One thing you might worry about in this analysis is whether it is actually learning economics that leads to higher wages, or perhaps just that the kind of people who major in economics are different from, say, sociology majors, and would have earned more money, regardless of what they studied. To at least partially address that critique, Black, Sanders, and Taylor took a look at earnings within narrower career paths. For instance, looking only at students who go on to law school, they determined that those who studied economics as undergrads earn more than students with other majors—up to 35% more, in the case of former sociologists. An economics degree is similarly beneficial to those who eventually pursue an MBA.

We hope that you will be so enthralled by economics that you want to make it your focus. But if you are in it just for the money, you could do worse. ■

[2] Dan A. Black, Seth Sanders, and Lowell Taylor, "The Economic Reward for Studying Economics," *Economic Inquiry* 41, no. 3 (2003):365–377.

[3] While the data available for the study dated back a few years, these patterns have been quite consistent; see http://www.payscale.com/college-salary-report/majors-that-pay-you-back/bachelors.

Summary

1. **Microeconomics** relies on **theories and models** to study the choices made by individuals and firms. Intermediate microeconomics builds on the principles of microeconomics course by adding mathematical models to the examination of consumer and producer behavior. Practicing the mathematics underlying microeconomic theory is the key to becoming a skilled economist. In addition, intermediate microeconomics has a strong focus on policy and its effects on behavior. [**Section 1.1**]

2. Microeconomics looks at a variety of decisions made by consumers and producers as they interact in the markets for goods and services, and at the different market structures in which consumers and producers operate. A wide range of topics deepens our understanding of the microeconomics of consumer and producer interaction, including risk and uncertainty, the role of information, and the study of behavioral economics. In recent years, microeconomics has evolved from a discipline that relied primarily on theory to one based on **empirical** studies (data analysis and experiments). [**Section 1.2**]

Review Questions

1. What differentiates microeconomics from macroeconomics?

2. Name one instance in which you were a *consumer*.

3. How are consumption and production interconnected?

4. What tools do we use to study microeconomics?

5. Why has microeconomics evolved into an empirical discipline?

Supply and Demand

Today's computers are more than a trillion times more powerful, measured in terms of the number of mathematical operations they can do per second, than were the first commercially available computers. This mind-boggling increase in power has been put to use in virtually every corner of the economy, from entertainment to manufacturing to health care and everything in between.

One application of computing power also turns out to be one of the largest users of electric power, too: Bitcoin mining. Creating a new Bitcoin requires that it be "mined," which means using a computer to solve a complicated math problem. The supply of new Bitcoins is limited by the fact that the difficulty of the math problem grows with every mined Bitcoin. This requires more and more computing power—and the electricity needed to run them. Mining has now become so resource-intensive that almost all of it is done by large companies that run massive server farms employing processors designed specifically to solve mining's math problems. By some estimates, Bitcoin mining in 2018 was using over 0.3% of all electricity generated in the world. That's about as much electricity as the entire *countries* of Austria or Chile use. As a result, mining server farms often locate themselves in places like Iceland, where electricity is relatively cheap and cooling the massive server farms is easier.

Bitcoin is just one of a collection of cryptocurrencies that are similarly mined. Mining companies are willing to expend such massive amounts of resources because they believe they can make a profit as suppliers of a desired good: cryptocurrencies. This desire to buy—the demand for Bitcoin and other cryptocurrencies—arises from various reasons why consumers find them valuable.

In this chapter, we explore these forces, the two most powerful forces in economics: supply and demand. We answer the most fundamental question in economics: *How do consumers and producers interact in the market for a good or service to determine how much is sold and at what price?*

2.1 Markets and Models

Modern economies are amazingly complex. Producers from all over the world offer close to unlimited varieties of goods and services that consumers can purchase. A large supermarket will have more than 100 different kinds of cold cereal on the shelf. There are thousands of degree-granting colleges and universities. On any given day, millions of items are for sale on Amazon or eBay. With over 7 billion people in the world, each of them with different tastes and incomes, and tens of millions of businesses supplying goods and services, how do consumers decide what products, and how much of each, to buy? How do producers know what products to produce? And who decides at what price the products sell?

Answering these questions seems hopelessly complex. Indeed, if we tried to tackle them all at once, it *would* be hopeless. Instead, we follow the economist's standard approach: **Simplify the problem until it becomes manageable.**

supply The combined amount of a good that all producers in a market are willing to sell.

demand The combined amount of a good that all consumers in a market are willing to buy.

The *supply and demand model* represents the economist's best attempt to capture many of the key elements of real-world markets in a simple enough way that we can analyze it. **Supply** is *the combined amount of a good that all producers in a market are willing to sell*; **demand** is *the combined amount of a good that all consumers are willing to buy*. The idea of a "market" is central to economics.

What Is a Market?

In the strictest sense, a market is defined by the specific product being bought and sold (e.g., oranges or Bitcoin), a particular location (a mall, a city, or the Internet), and a point in time (January 4th). In principle, the buyers in a market should be able to find the sellers in that market, and vice versa, although it might take some work (what economists call "search costs") to make that connection.

In practice, the kinds of markets we talk about tend to be broadly defined. They might be broad in terms of the product (e.g., all groceries rather than just oranges), the location (often we consider all of North America or even the world as the geographic market), or the time period (annual sales rather than by day). These broader markets are often of more interest and result in more data to analyze, but as we will see, defining markets too broadly can make the assumptions of the supply and demand model less realistic. Thus, we face a tradeoff between studying small, less consequential markets that closely match the underlying assumptions and broader and more important markets that do not.

Key Assumptions of the Supply and Demand Model

There are four basic assumptions that underpin the supply and demand model (summarized in **Table 2.1** below). Although actual markets usually don't perfectly conform to all these assumptions, the supply and demand model has proven to be remarkably useful for thinking about how markets work.

1. **We restrict our focus to supply and demand in a single market.** The first simplifying assumption we make is to look at how *supply* and *demand* interact *in just one market* to determine how much of a good or service is sold and at what price it is sold. In focusing on one market, we won't ignore other markets completely—indeed, the interaction between the markets for different kinds of products is fundamental to supply and demand, and we'll discuss it in a later chapter. For now, however, we only worry about other markets if they influence the market we're studying and we ignore any impact of our market on other markets.

2. **All goods bought and sold in the market are identical.** We assume that all the goods bought and sold in the market are homogeneous, meaning they are identical, so a consumer is just as happy with any one unit of the good (e.g., a gallon of gasoline is

Table 2.1 The Four Key Assumptions Underlying the Supply and Demand Model

1. We focus on supply and demand in a single market.

2. All goods sold in the market are identical.

3. All good sold in the market sell for the same price, and everyone has the same information.

4. There are many producers and consumers in the market.

fairly homogenous regardless of the seller).[1] These are **commodities,** *goods that are traded in markets where consumers view different varieties of the good as essentially interchangeable.* Goods such as wheat, soybeans, crude oil, nails, gold, or #2 pencils are commodities. Custom-made jewelry, cars, the different offerings on a restaurant's menu, and wedding dresses are not commodities because the consumer typically cares a lot about specific varieties of these goods.

commodities Goods traded in markets where consumers view different varieties of the good as essentially interchangeable.

3. **All goods sold in the market sell for the same price, and everyone has the same information about prices, the quality of the goods being sold, and so on.** This assumption is a natural extension of the identical-goods assumption, but it also implies that there are no special or secret deals for particular buyers and no quantity discounts. In addition, everyone knows what everyone else is paying.

4. **There are many buyers and sellers in the market.** This assumption means that no one consumer or producer has a noticeable impact on anything that occurs in the market and on the price level in particular. This assumption also tends to be more easily justified for consumers than for producers. Think about your own consumption of bananas, for instance. Whether you stopped eating bananas altogether or quadrupled your banana spending, your decision would not affect the banana market as a whole. On the producer side, however, most bananas (and many other products) are produced by a few big companies. It is more likely that decisions by these firms about how much to produce or what markets to enter will substantially affect market prices and quantities. We're going to ignore that possibility for now and stick with the case of many sellers. Starting in Chapter 9, we analyze what happens in markets with one or a few sellers.

Notice that the assumptions of the supply and demand model are not completely realistic. Few of the markets in real life fully satisfy them. It turns out, however, that a strength of this model is that when some (or even most) of the specific assumptions of the model fail, it still manages to provide a good description of how markets work. No model is perfect, but the supply and demand model has survived the test of time and is the workhorse of economics. Developing a deep understanding of the basic supply and demand model is one of the most important economic tools you can have, even if it does not perfectly fit every market. Plus, economics isn't completely wedded to the most stringent form of the model. Much of the rest of this book, and the field of economics more generally, are devoted to examining how changing the model's assumptions influences its predictions about market outcomes.

Having made these assumptions, let's see how they help us understand how markets work, looking first at demand and then at supply.

2.2 Demand

Pike Place Market, one of the best-known public markets in the world, spans several blocks in the northwest corner of downtown Seattle. It has operated continually since 1907, and on any given day hosts hundreds of vendors selling everything from fish and meat to produce and flowers to crafts and antiques. Approximately 10 million people a year visit the market.

---

[1] Throughout this book, we often use the word "good" to mean both tangible goods, such as trucks, computers, jewelry, and so on; and services, such as haircuts, dog walking, financial planning, and so on. In this usage, anything a consumer values—tangible or not, concrete or abstract—is a good.

Factors That Influence Demand

Tomatoes are a popular item for shoppers at farmers' markets like Pike Place. All sorts of factors influence how many tomatoes consumers purchase there. Let's discuss the most important.

Price   The price of tomatoes is probably the most important consideration. Few consumers would pay $40 per pound for tomatoes, but many would pay $1 a pound.

The Number of Consumers   All else equal, the more people there are in a market, the greater the quantity of the good desired.

Consumer Income or Wealth   As a consumer becomes richer, she will buy more of most goods. Tomatoes (and clothes and cars and jewelry and porterhouse steaks) probably fall in that category for most people. Sometimes, however, when a consumer becomes richer, she buys less of a good. For example, she might buy a car and stop taking public transportation and might stay in nice hotels instead of youth hostels. The consumption of public transportation and hotels still responds to income or wealth, but in a different direction.

Consumer Tastes   A change in consumer preferences or tastes for tomatoes (for a given level of the consumer's income and tomato prices) will change the amount of tomatoes the consumer wants to purchase. Taste changes can be driven by all sorts of forces. For example, news about the health benefits of eating tomatoes would make many consumers want to eat more of them. News about salmonella being found in some tomato crops will make consumers reluctant. For other products, taste changes might arise due to a popular advertising campaign, fads, changes in demographics, and so on.

Prices of Other Goods   Produce vendors at Pike Place Market sell other goods such as onions and peppers that consumers can use to make their salads or top their burgers. *Goods that can be used in place of another good* are called **substitutes.** When the price of a substitute good falls, consumers will want to buy more of that substitute and less of the initial good. The lower the prices of onions and peppers relative to the price of tomatoes, the fewer tomatoes consumers will want to buy. We can also think of tomatoes in some other market (say, at another location, like a consumer's neighborhood grocery store) as substitutes for tomatoes at Pike Place Market. If grocery store tomatoes become cheaper, shoppers at Pike Place Market are going to want to buy fewer tomatoes there.

Vendors at Pike Place Market also sell goods that consumers like to use with tomatoes. *Goods that are often purchased and used in combination with a certain good* are called **complements.** When the price of a complement falls, consumers will want to buy more of it and also more of the initial good. There are some goods that people like to consume with tomatoes—basil, for instance, or mozzarella cheese. If basil prices fall, consumers are likely to want to buy more basil and with it buy *more* tomatoes as a result.

The prices of substitutes and complements both affect how much of a good consumers want to buy, but they have opposite effects. A price decrease in a good's substitute will cause consumers to want less of the good; a price decrease in a good's complement will cause consumers to want more of the good.

substitute A good that can be used in place of another good.

complement A good that is often purchased and used in combination with another good.

Demand Curves

In economics, "demand" is a catch-all word that captures the many different factors that influence the willingness of consumers to purchase a good. With so many factors influencing demand, it is difficult to wrap our minds around what would happen if all those various factors changed at the same time. We simplify the problem by considering what happens to the amount consumers demand when only a good's price changes, while everything else that determines consumer demand stays the same.

Graphical Representation of the Demand Curve

The result of this simplifying assumption is a **demand curve**, which is *the relationship between the quantity of a good that consumers demand and the good's price, holding all other factors constant.*[2] Price is on the vertical axis and quantity demanded is on the horizontal axis. **Figure 2.1** depicts a demand curve for tomatoes at the Pike Place Market.

demand curve The relationship between the quantity of a good that consumers demand and the good's price, holding all other factors constant.

The point about demand curves holding all factors other than price constant is so important that it is worth repeating it again: A demand curve is drawn under the assumption that there is no change in *any* of the other factors—such as consumers' incomes, tastes, or the prices of other goods—that might also affect how much of a good consumers buy at any given price. This means the demand curve in Figure 2.1 embodies the results of the following thought experiment: Show up at Pike Place Market some weekend and observe both the price of tomatoes and the amount consumers buy. Imagine we have magical powers that allow us to go back in time and replace the price tags on tomatoes at the market prices $1 per pound lower. Then let the weekend happen all over again—the same weather, the same visitors to the market, the same set of items on display, and so on; the only difference is that tomatoes are $1 per pound cheaper. What's the total amount of tomatoes consumers buy at this new price? Repeating this exercise over and over at different prices gives us a collection of price and quantity combinations that we call the demand curve.

The demand curve in Figure 2.1 exhibits a fundamental characteristic of demand curves: They slope downward.[3] This is another way of saying that, all else equal, the lower the price of a good, the greater the amount of it consumers will buy.

Figure 2.1 Demand for Tomatoes

The demand curve D_1 for tomatoes at Pike Place Market shows how the quantity of tomatoes that consumers want varies with the price of tomatoes. As the price of tomatoes decreases, consumers demand greater quantities of tomatoes, creating a downward-sloping demand curve. At a price of $5 per pound, consumers demand no tomatoes; at $4, $3, $2, and $1, consumers are willing to purchase 200, 400, 600, and 800 pounds of tomatoes, respectively.

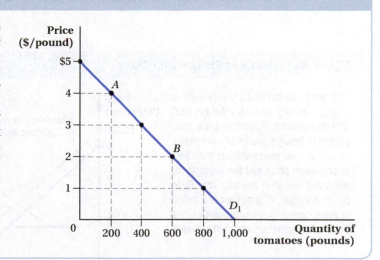

---

[2] Economists often draw demand curves as straight lines, and we do so as well throughout much of this book. This is just for convenience. As their name suggests, demand curves in reality are normally *curved*.

[3] An interesting but unusual exception to this is a Giffen good, which has an upward-sloping demand curve. We will discuss such goods in Chapter 5. Demand curves for regular (non-Giffen) goods can also sometimes be flat, as we discuss in the next section. We explore the deeper reasoning that explains why demand curves usually slope downward in Chapters 4 and 5.

Mathematical Representation of the Demand Curve We could also represent the demand curve in Figure 2.1 mathematically by the equation

$$Q = 1,000 - 200P$$

where Q is the quantity demanded (in pounds) and P is the price (in dollars per pound). This equation implies that every $1 per pound increase in price leads to a 200-pound decline in the quantity of tomatoes demanded. *The price at which quantity demanded equals zero, the vertical intercept of the inverse demand curve,* (here, it's $5) has a special name: the **demand choke price.** It is the price at which no consumer is willing to buy a good.

Sometimes economists turn this relationship around. An **inverse demand curve** is *a demand curve written in the form of price as a function of quantity demanded.* The inverse demand curve for tomatoes at Pike Place Market is $P = 5 - 0.005Q$. (We've simply rearranged the demand curve equation to put price in terms of quantity rather than the other way around.) It is sometimes easier to work with inverse demand curves, in part because demand curves are drawn with price on the vertical axis and quantity on the horizontal.

demand choke price The price at which quantity demanded is zero; the vertical intercept of the inverse demand curve.

inverse demand curve A demand curve written in the form of price as a function of quantity demanded.

Shifts in Demand Curves

A given demand curve such as D_1 in Figure 2.1 illustrates how the quantity demanded of a good changes as its price, *and only its price,* changes. *When one of the other (nonprice) factors that affect demand changes, the change affects the quantity of tomatoes consumers want to buy at every price.* For example, if there is an outbreak of salmonella poisoning, and public health officials believe that tomatoes may be the source of the outbreak, consumers' tastes will change. They will want fewer tomatoes at any given price than they did before, and the demand curve will shift down and to the left to D_2, as shown in **Figure 2.2**.[4] Mathematically, the demand curve D_2 corresponds to $Q = 500 - 200P$.

Figure 2.2   Shifts in the Demand Curve

The demand curve D_1 shifts with a change in any nonprice factor that affects demand. If tomatoes are suspected of being a source of salmonella, consumers will demand fewer tomatoes at any given price and the demand for tomatoes will shift inward, from D_1 to D_2. In contrast, if tomatoes are found to have cancer-fighting properties, the demand for tomatoes will shift outward, from D_1 to D_3.

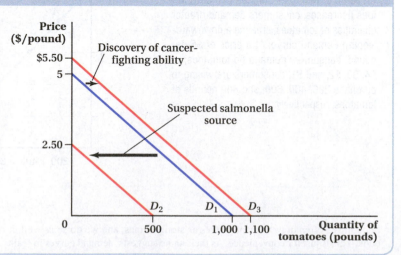

---

[4] When we use the word "shift," this includes not only parallel shifts of the demand curve, as shown in Figure 2.2, but also rotations (which change the steepness or slope of a demand curve). Later, we discuss what economic forces affect the slopes of demand curves.

Similarly, if scientists discover that tomatoes help prevent cancer, consumers may want to buy more tomatoes at any given price than they did before, and the whole demand curve for tomatoes will shift out to the right from D_1 to D_3 (Figure 2.2). Mathematically, the new demand curve D_3 is described by the equation $Q = 1,100 - 200P$. Note that we are shifting the demand curves in the simplest way—sliding them over with the same slope. In real markets, this doesn't need to be true. The new curve can change steepness, too, if demand becomes more or less sensitive to price.

The changes in the quantity demanded at every price that occur when nonprice factors change illustrate an essential distinction:

- **Changes in quantity demanded** are reflected in movements *along* a given demand curve (e.g., the move from point A to point B in Figure 2.1) and happen when a good's price changes but everything else stays constant.

- **Changes in demand** are reflected in a shift of a good's entire demand curve (e.g., the shifts from D_1 to D_2 and D_3 in Figure 2.2) and are caused by changes in any of the factors *other than price* that influence demand.

We treat prices differently than other factors that influence demand because price is a factor that also directly influences the supply of the good, so it is the critical element tying together supply and demand.

change in quantity demanded A movement *along* the demand curve that occurs as a result of a change in the good's price.

change in demand A shift of the entire demand curve caused by a change in a determinant of demand other than the good's own price.

2.3 Supply

We have outlined the demand half of the supply and demand model. What factors influence the other half, meaning the combined amount of a good that all producers in a market are willing to sell?

Factors That Influence Supply

Just as there are many factors that determine demand, there are factors that can determine supply. Let's discuss these again in the context of our Pike Place Market tomatoes example.

Price Just as it does with demand, price plays an important role in supply decisions. If farmers expect to be able to sell tomatoes at $40 a pound at Pike Place Market, they will bring loads of them. If they expect the price to be only $1 per pound, a much smaller quantity will be made available.

Suppliers' Costs of Production Suppliers' production costs will change when input prices and production technology change. There are many inputs a supplier must use to produce tomatoes and bring them to market, including land, tomato seeds, harvesting equipment, and gasoline needed to ship tomatoes to markets, to name just a few. If the prices of these inputs change, the suppliers' costs will change and will influence the quantity of tomatoes supplied to the market.

Similarly, changes in **production technology,** *the processes used to make, distribute, and sell a good,* such as tomatoes, will change the costs of production. The more efficient these processes are, the lower the costs to sellers of providing tomatoes for sale. Lower costs will raise sellers' willingness to supply tomatoes at a particular price.

production technology The processes used to make, distribute, and sell a good.

The Number of Sellers More farmers bringing tomatoes to Pike Place Market will raise the available supply.

Sellers' Outside Options Farmers who are busy selling tomatoes at Pike Place Market aren't selling some other product or selling tomatoes at some other place. A change in farmers' prospects for doing business in markets for other goods or in other markets for tomatoes can affect their willingness to supply tomatoes at Pike Place Market. These prospects depend on factors such as the prices of other goods the farmers might be growing and selling or tomato prices at markets other than Pike Place Market.

Supply Curves

Just as we introduced demand curves as a way of thinking in a more focused manner about demand, we can do the same for supply. **Supply curves** show *the relationship between the quantity supplied of a good and the good's price, holding all other factors constant.* Like demand curves, they capture the idea that factors influencing supply can be divided into two sets: (1) price and (2) everything else.

supply curve The relationship between the quantity supplied of a good and the good's price, holding all other factors constant.

Graphical Representation of the Supply Curve
Figure 2.3 depicts a supply curve for tomatoes at Pike Place Market. The vertical axis reflects the price of the good, and the horizontal axis is the quantity supplied. The supply curve in the figure slopes upward: Holding everything else equal, producers are willing to supply more of a good as its price rises.[5] Many firms experience increasing costs of production as their output rises. When this is the case, they need to earn a higher price in the market in order to induce them to produce more output.

Mathematical Representation of the Supply Curve
We can write the supply curve in Figure 2.3 mathematically as

$$Q = 200P - 200$$

supply choke price The price at which no firm is willing to produce a good and quantity supplied is zero; the vertical intercept of the inverse supply curve.

where Q is the quantity supplied (in pounds of tomatoes) and P is the price in dollars per pound. This indicates that holding everything else constant, for every dollar increase in price, the quantity of tomatoes supplied increases by 200 pounds. The **supply choke price** is *the price at which no firm is willing to produce a good and quantity supplied is zero;*

Figure 2.3   **Supply of Tomatoes**

The supply curve S_1 for tomatoes at Pike Place Market shows how the quantity of tomatoes supplied varies with the price. As the price of tomatoes increases, producers supply greater quantities of tomatoes, creating an upward-sloping supply curve. At a price of $1 per pound, producers supply no tomatoes; at $2, $3, $4, and $5, respectively, producers supply 200, 400, 600, and 800 pounds of tomatoes.

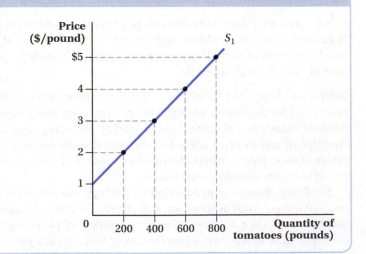

---

[5] We typically expect that supply curves slope upward, although in some cases (especially in the long run), they may be horizontal, and in others they might be perfectly vertical. We will discuss these special cases later.

the vertical intercept of the inverse supply curve. In this example, the supply choke price is $1. The **inverse supply curve** is *a supply curve written in the form of price as a function of quantity supplied.* Here, it's $P = 0.005Q + 1$.

Shifts in the Supply Curve

A given supply curve such as S_1 in Figure 2.3 illustrates how the quantity supplied of a good changes as its price, and only its price, changes.

When one of the other (nonprice) factors that affect supply changes, the change affects the quantity of tomatoes that suppliers want to sell at every price. For example, if someone invents a machine that can harvest tomatoes faster and at lower cost, producers who wanted to produce 600 pounds of tomatoes at $4 per pound will now be willing to supply 800 pounds of tomatoes at $4. Those who were willing to supply 200 pounds at $2 will now be willing to supply 400 at $2, and so on. Because producers supply more tomatoes at any particular price, the whole supply curve will shift out to the right from S_1 to S_2, as shown in **Figure 2.4**. The way we've drawn it, that additional quantity is 200 pounds at any price, though there's nothing that says all supply shifts must exhibit this pattern.[6] Mathematically, the supply curve S_2 is described by the equation $Q = 200P$.

Similarly, if a drought occurs, it will cost producers more to irrigate their fields. They will want to supply fewer tomatoes at any given price than they did before, and the supply curve will shift up and to the left, from S_1 to S_3. Mathematically, the supply curve S_3 corresponds to $Q = 200P - 600$. Analogous to demand curves, changes in quantity supplied at every price illustrate a distinction:

- **Changes in quantity supplied** are reflected in movements *along* a given supply curve and happen when a good's price changes but everything else stays constant.

- **Changes in supply** are reflected in shifts of the entire supply curve and are caused by changes in any factors *other than* the good's own price.

Supply curves isolate the effect of prices on supply just as demand curves isolate price effects on demand, and price is a factor that has a direct influence on both supply and

inverse supply curve A supply curve written in the form of price as a function of quantity supplied.

change in quantity supplied A movement *along* the supply curve that occurs as a result of a change in the good's price.

change in supply A shift of the entire supply curve caused by a change in a determinant of supply other than the good's own price.

Figure 2.4 Shifts in the Supply Curve

The supply curve S_1 shifts when any nonprice factor that affects supply changes. If a faster harvesting method is developed, the supply of tomatoes will shift outward, from S_1 to S_2. In contrast, if there is a drought, the supply of tomatoes will shift inward, from S_1 to S_3.

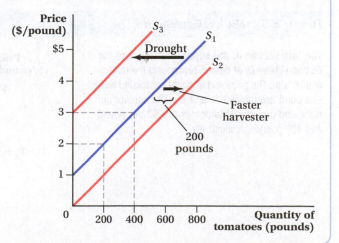

---

[6] Note that, just as with demand curves, there's no requirement that supply curves be linear. We just draw them as such for simplicity.

demand. Price is the critical element that ties together the two sides of a market. Price's roles in both the supply and demand sides of a market mean that prices can be adjusted freely to make the quantity demanded by consumers equal to the quantity supplied by producers. When this happens, we have a market in which everyone who wants to buy at the current price can do so, and everyone who wants to sell at the current market price can do so as well.

As we see in the next section, we can also use the supply and demand model to predict how changes in nonprice factors affect market outcomes. To get to the point where we *can* do that, however, we need to identify an initial market price and quantity sold. Treating price as special allows us to do just that.

2.4 Market Equilibrium

The true power of the supply and demand model emerges when we combine demand and supply curves. Both relate quantities and prices, so we can draw them on the same graph, with price on the vertical axis and quantity on the horizontal axis. **Figure 2.5** overlays the original demand and supply demand curves for tomatoes at Seattle's Pike Place Market. As a reminder, expressed as equations, the demand curve is $Q = 1,000 - 200P$ (with an equivalent inverse demand curve $P = 5 - 0.005Q$), and the supply curve is $Q = 200P - 200$ (with an inverse supply curve of $P = 1 + 0.005Q$).

market equilibrium The point where the demand and supply curves cross.

The point where the demand and supply curves cross is the **market equilibrium.** The equilibrium is labeled as point E on Figure 2.5. The **equilibrium price** P_e is *the* only *price at which quantity supplied equals quantity demanded.*

equilibrium price The only price at which quantity supplied equals quantity demanded.

The Mathematics of Equilibrium

What is the market equilibrium for our Pike Place Market tomatoes example? We can see from Figure 2.5 that the equilibrium price P_e is $3 per pound, and the equilibrium quantity Q_e is 400 pounds. But we can also determine these same quantities mathematically by using the equations for the demand and supply curves. Quantity demanded is given by $Q^D = 1,000 - 200P$ (we've added the superscript "D" to quantity just to remind us that this equation is the demand curve), and quantity supplied is $Q^S = 200P - 200$ (again, we've

---

Figure 2.5   **Market Equilibrium**

The intersection of the supply curve S_1 and the demand curve D_1 at point E represents the market equilibrium. The price and quantity associated with this point are labeled P_e and Q_e. The equilibrium price and quantity of tomatoes are $3 per pound and 400 pounds, respectively.

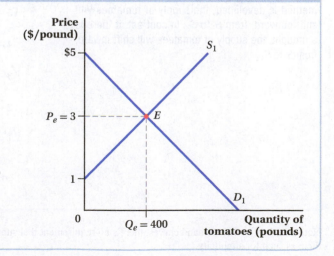

added an identifying superscript). We know that at market equilibrium, quantity demanded equals quantity supplied; that is, $Q_e = Q^D = Q^S$. Using the equations above, we have

$$Q^D = Q^S$$
$$1,000 - 200P = 200P - 200$$
$$1,200 = 400P$$
$$P_e = 3$$

At a price P of \$3 per pound, quantity demanded Q^D equals quantity supplied Q^S, so the equilibrium price P_e is \$3, as we observe in Figure 2.5. To find the equilibrium quantity Q_e, we plug this value of P_e back into the equation for *either* the demand or supply curve, because both quantity demanded and quantity supplied will be the same at the equilibrium price:

$$Q_e = 1,000 - 200P_e = 1,000 - 200(3) = 1,000 - 600 = 400$$

We just solved for the equilibrium price and quantity by using the fact that the quantity demanded equals the quantity supplied in equilibrium, and substituting the demand and supply curve equations into this equality. We could have obtained the same answer by instead using the fact that the price given by the *inverse* demand and supply curves is the same at the market equilibrium quantity. That is,

$$5 - 0.005Q_e = 1 + 0.005Q_e$$

Solving this equation gives $Q_e = 400$ pounds, just as before. Plugging $Q_e = 400$ back into either the inverse demand or supply equation indicates that the market price P_e is \$3 per pound, as expected.

Why Markets Move toward Equilibrium

When a market is in equilibrium, the quantity demanded by consumers and the quantity supplied by producers are equal at the market price. To see why equilibrium is a stable situation, think about what happens when price is not in equilibrium. If the current price is higher than the equilibrium price, there will be excess supply. If the price is lower, there will be excess demand.

Excess Supply With a price higher than the equilibrium price, call it P_{high} instead of P_e, as shown in **Figure 2.6a**, the quantity supplied, Q^S_{high}, is greater than the quantity

make the grade

Does quantity supplied equal quantity demanded in equilibrium?

Solving for the market equilibrium as we just did is one of the most common exam questions in intermediate microeconomics classes. The basic idea is always the same: Take the equations for the demand curve and the supply curve, solve for the equilibrium price, and then plug that equilibrium price back into either the supply curve or the demand curve (it does not matter which) to determine the equilibrium quantity. The solution is straightforward, but it is easy to make math errors under the time pressure of an exam, especially if the demand and supply curves take

on more complicated forms than the basic examples we deal with here.

A simple trick will ensure that you obtain the right answer, and applying it requires only a few seconds more. Take the equilibrium price that you get and plug it into *both* the demand and supply curves. If you don't arrive at the same answer when you substitute the equilibrium price into the supply and demand equations, you will know immediately that you made a math error along the way because the quantity demanded must equal the quantity supplied in equilibrium.

Figure **2.6**   Why P_e Is the Equilibrium Price

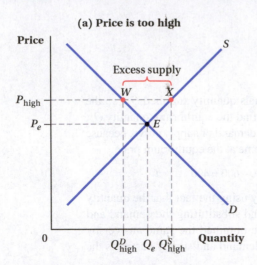

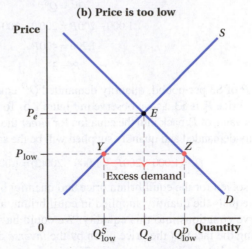

(a) Price is too high

(b) Price is too low

(a) At the price P_{high} above the equilibrium price P_e, producers supply the quantity Q_{high}^S, while consumers demand only Q_{high}^D. This results in an excess supply of the good, as represented by the distance between points W and X. Over time, price will fall and the market will move toward equilibrium at point E.

(b) At the price P_{low} below the equilibrium price P_e, producers supply the quantity Q_{low}^S, while consumers demand Q_{low}^D. This results in an excess demand for the good, as represented by the distance between points Y and Z. Over time, price will rise and the market will move toward equilibrium at point E.

---

demanded, Q_{high}^D. Producers come out of the woodwork wanting to sell at this high price, but not all producers can find willing buyers at that price. The excess quantity for sale equals $Q_{high}^S - Q_{high}^D$, the horizontal distance between the demand and supply curves at P_{high}. To eliminate this excess supply, producers need to attract more buyers, and to do this, sellers must lower their prices. As price falls, quantity demanded rises and quantity supplied falls until the market reaches equilibrium at point E.

Excess Demand   The opposite situation exists in Figure 2.6b. At price P_{low}, consumers demand a lot of the good when it's that cheap, Q_{low}^D, but that amount is more than producers are willing to supply, Q_{low}^S. To eliminate this excess demand, buyers who cannot find the good available for sale will bid up the price and enterprising producers will be more than willing to raise their prices. As price rises, quantity demanded falls and quantity supplied rises until the market reaches equilibrium at point E.[7]

Adjusting to Equilibrium   It is important to note that in the real world, equilibrium is a bit mysterious. In our stylized model, we're acting as if all the producers and consumers gather in one spot and report to a sort of auctioneer how much they want to produce or consume at each price. The auctioneer combines all this information, computes and announces the market-clearing price, and only then do all the sellers and

---

[7] Prices can sometimes remain at levels other than their equilibrium value for extended periods of time, especially if there are policy-based interventions in the market, such as price ceilings (maximum prices allowed by law) or price floors (minimum prices prescribed by law). We discuss these sorts of situations in Chapter 3.

figure it out 2.1

Go online for interactive, step-by-step help in solving the following problem.

Suppose that the demand and supply curves for a monthly cell phone plan with unlimited texts can be represented by

$$Q^D = 50 - 0.5P$$
$$Q^S = -25 + P$$

The current price of these plans in the market is $40 per month. Is this market in equilibrium? Would you expect the price to rise or fall? If so, by how much? Explain.

Solution:

There are two ways to solve the first question about whether the price will rise or fall. The first is to calculate the quantity demanded and quantity supplied at the current market price of $40 to see how they compare:

$$Q^D = 50 - 0.5P = 50 - 0.5(40) = 50 - 20 = 30$$
$$Q^S = -25 + P = -25 + 40 = 15$$

Because quantity demanded is greater than quantity supplied, we can tell that there is excess demand (a shortage) in the market. Many people are trying to purchase texting plans, but find them sold out because few suppliers want to sell at that price. Prices will rise to equalize quantity supplied and quantity demanded, moving the market to equilibrium.

Alternatively, we could start by solving for the market equilibrium price:

$$Q^D = Q^S$$
$$50 - 0.5P = -25 + P$$
$$1.5P = 75$$
$$P = \$50$$

The current market price, $40, is below the market equilibrium price of $50. (This is why there is excess demand in the market.) Therefore, we would expect the price to rise by $10. When the market reaches equilibrium at a price of $50, all buyers can find sellers and all sellers can find buyers. The price will then remain at $50 unless the market changes and the demand curve or supply curve shifts.

buyers make their deals at the announced market-clearing price. But few markets work this way in the real world. Real markets must rely on what the great eighteenth-century Scottish economist Adam Smith called the "invisible hand." Producers independently decide how much to produce of their products given the price at which they expect to be able to sell them, and consumers show up at stores, gas stations, or websites to buy the good. Sometimes producers might supply too much or too little in the short run, but through the market, these mistakes correct themselves. Economists typically assume that the market reaches equilibrium one way or another, without being too specific about the process.

The Effects of Demand Shifts

As we have learned, demand and supply curves hold constant everything else besides price that might affect quantities demanded and supplied. Therefore, the market equilibrium depicted in Figure 2.5 will hold only as long as none of these other factors change. If any other factor changes, there will be a new market equilibrium because either the demand or supply curve or both curves will have shifted.

Suppose the demand for tomatoes falls when, as in our previous example, a news story reports that tomatoes are suspected of being the source of a salmonella outbreak. The resulting change in consumer tastes causes the demand curve to shift in (i.e., to the left), as **Figure 2.7** shows, from D_1 to D_2.

How does the market equilibrium change after this demand shift? The equilibrium price and quantity both fall. The equilibrium quantity falls from Q_1 to Q_2, and the equilibrium

Figure 2.7   Effects of a Fall in the Demand for Tomatoes

After a salmonella outbreak, the demand for tomatoes decreases, causing a leftward shift of the demand curve from D_1 to D_2. This fall in demand results in a new equilibrium point E_2, which is lower than the initial equilibrium point E_1. The equilibrium quantity falls from Q_1 (400 pounds) to Q_2 (150 pounds), and the equilibrium price falls from P_1 ($3) to P_2 ($1.75).

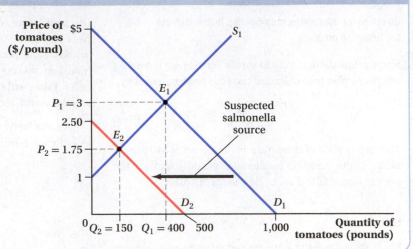

price drops from P_1 to P_2. The reason for these movements is that if prices stayed at P_1 after the fall in demand, tomato farmers would be supplying a much greater quantity than consumers were demanding. The market price must fall to get farmers to rein in their quantity supplied until it matches the new, lower level of demand.

We can solve for the new equilibrium price and quantity using the same approach we applied earlier, but using the equation for the new demand curve D_2, which is $Q = 500 - 200P$. (The supply curve stays the same.)

$$Q^D = Q^S$$

$$500 - 200P_2 = 200P_2 - 200$$

$$400P_2 = 700$$

$$P_2 = 1.75$$

So, the new equilibrium price is $1.75 per pound, compared to $3 per pound from before the demand shift. Plugging this into the new demand curve (or the supply curve) gives the new equilibrium quantity:

$$Q_2 = 500 - 200(1.75) = 150$$

The new equilibrium quantity is 150 pounds, less than half of what it was before the demand shift.

We could have just as easily worked through an example in which demand increases and the demand curve shifts out. Perhaps incomes rise or substitute produce items become more expensive. In the face of a stable supply curve, this increase in demand would shift the curve up to the right and cause both the equilibrium price and quantity to rise. At the previous market price, the new quantity demanded would be greater than sellers' willingness to supply. The price would have to rise, causing a movement along the supply curve until the quantities supplied and demanded are equal.

Shifts in Curves versus Movement along a Curve   This analysis highlights the importance of distinguishing between shifts in a demand or supply curve and movements along those curves. This distinction can sometimes seem confusing, but understanding it is

figure it out 2.2

Draw a supply and demand diagram of the market for peanuts.

a. Suppose that someone finds a cure for peanut allergies, so a set of people who formerly had to avoid peanut foods can now eat them. What will happen to the equilibrium price and quantity of peanuts?

b. Does this change reflect a change in demand or a change in quantity demanded?

Solution:

a. Peanuts are a substitute for other foods. If peanut allergies are cured so that more people can eat peanuts than before, the demand for peanuts will rise, and the demand curve will shift out to the right. As the figure shows, this shift will result in

a higher equilibrium price and quantity of peanuts purchased.

b. Because the allergy cure changes the appeal of peanuts at any given price, this is a change in the demand for peanuts.

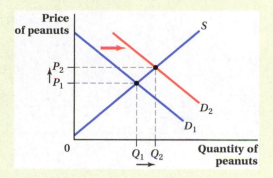

critical. We saw in Figure 2.7 what happens to a market when there is a change in consumers' tastes that makes them view a product more negatively. That change in tastes made consumers want to buy less of the product at any given price—that is, caused an inward *shift* in the demand curve. Remember, anything that changes how much consumers want to buy of a good at any particular price must shift the demand curve. At the same time, this change in tastes has no effect on how much producers wish to sell at any given price. It doesn't affect their costs of producing or their outside options. So, supply does not change, and the supply curve doesn't shift. However, the *quantity supplied* does change. It falls in response to the reduced demand. This change in quantity supplied is a movement *along* the supply curve. The only reason that the quantity supplied falls in this example is because the shift in the demand curve has made the equilibrium price lower, and at a lower price, suppliers produce less of the good. Therefore, a *shift* in the demand curve causes a movement *along* the supply curve to the new equilibrium.

The Effects of Supply Shifts

Now let's think about what happens when the supply curve shifts, but the demand curve does not. **Figure 2.8** shows the case in which the supply of tomatoes rises, shifting the supply curve out from S_1 to S_2. This shift implies that, at any given price, farmers are willing to sell a larger quantity of tomatoes than before. Such a shift would result from a reduction in farmers' input costs—for example, if seed prices fell. The logic of why a cost reduction increases quantity supplied at any given price is straightforward: If the farmers can make an average profit of, say, $1 per pound when the price is $3 per pound, then a $1 decrease in cost (which increases their profit) will lead farmers to offer more for sale. Note, however, that this cost change has no direct impact on the demand curve. Holding price fixed, consumers are no more or less willing to buy tomatoes than they were before.

> **Figure 2.8**   **Effects of an Increase in the Supply of Tomatoes**
>
> With cheaper fertilizer, farmers supply more tomatoes at every given price and the supply curve shifts outward from S_1 to S_2. The equilibrium quantity increases from Q_1 (400 pounds) at E_1 to Q_2 (600 pounds) at E_2, while the equilibrium price falls from P_1 ($3/pound) to P_2 ($2/pound).
>
>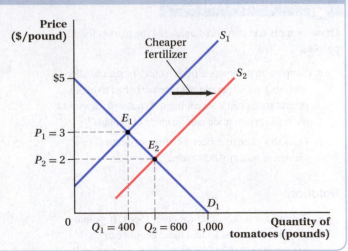

The supply curve has shifted from its original position S_1 (given by the equation $Q = 200P - 200$) to S_2 (given by the equation $Q = 200P + 200$). If the price stayed at the original equilibrium price P_1 after the supply shift, the amount of tomatoes that sellers would be willing to supply would exceed consumers' quantity demanded. Therefore, the equilibrium price must fall, as seen in the figure. This drop in price causes an increase in quantity demanded along the demand curve. The price drops until the quantity demanded once again equals the quantity supplied. The new equilibrium price is P_2, and the new equilibrium quantity is Q_2.

We can solve for the new equilibrium price and quantity using the equations for the original demand curve and the new supply curve:

$$Q^D = Q^S$$
$$1{,}000 - 200P_2 = 200P_2 + 200$$
$$400P_2 = 800$$
$$P_2 = 2$$

The cost drop and the resulting increase in supply lead to a fall in the equilibrium price from $3 to $2 per pound. This is intuitive: Lower farmers' costs end up being reflected in lower market prices. We can plug this price into either the demand or new supply equation to find the new equilibrium quantity:

$$Q_2 = 1{,}000 - 200(2) = 600$$
$$Q_2 = 200(2) + 200 = 600$$

The equilibrium quantity of tomatoes increases from 400 to 600 pounds in response to the increase in supply and the subsequent fall in the equilibrium price.

Again, we could go through the same steps for a decrease in supply. The supply curve would shift up to the left. This decline in supply would increase the equilibrium price and decrease the equilibrium quantity.

FREAKONOMICS

How Uber Took the Taxi Industry by Storm

Every time a snowstorm hits New York City, people get a lesson in market equilibrium. Traffic becomes snarled. People's tempers flare. And taxis are virtually impossible to find. Yet riders with ride-share companies like Uber can summon one with almost no wait time.

You would think such commuters might be happy that Uber can deliver them home even as the massive New York taxi system fails. But they usually aren't, because in such circumstances Uber prices go up — a lot.

Snowstorms create a supply and demand nightmare for taxi drivers. They are unable to adjust their prices. The city regulates the rate and fees taxis may charge, and to make money, drivers must complete many trips. When road conditions are bad, the amount a taxi driver can earn plunges (plus the risk of an accident goes up). Often, it's just not worth it for taxi drivers to remain on the streets and many head back to the garage. Demand is high and supply is low. The price needs to rise, but it can't.

Uber, on the other hand, can adjust its prices to match supply and demand. Everyone that wants to ride at the market price can do so because two events occur: Some consumers are not willing to pay the higher price, and they drop out of the market. Some Uber drivers who would not have wanted to drive at regular prices pick up passengers at the higher fare. By choosing a high enough price, Uber can equilibrate supply and demand, even in extreme circumstances like a snowstorm. The problem for Uber, however, is that the equilibrium price sometimes turns out to be very high. Passengers' Twitter feeds then blow up.*

These passengers seem to forget a basic principle of equilibrium. As one of the drivers responded to the mounting complaints:

> I hope everyone realizes that, as a Driver, if there wasn't any surge pricing, I'd just stay home in a snow storm. There would be no drivers and then everyone would be complaining about how they waited 30 mins for a car to pick them up to take them 6 blocks.

If Uber doesn't raise prices, there wouldn't be enough Ubers, just like there aren't enough taxis.

But the cold logic of economic equilibrium can make for some serious black eyes in terms of public relations. Uber's automated surge-pricing algorithm raised prices dramatically when demand escalated following a bomb threat in New York City and violent mass attacks in London and Sydney. If you wanted to get away from the threat of danger, it cost you 4 times the regular price.

Today, Uber has learned from the bad publicity. It still uses surge pricing but imposes caps so that prices do not soar too high for consumers in critical situations. And to ensure that drivers keep driving under such circumstances, Uber continues to pay drivers the high rates they'd like to charge consumers. In other words, Uber takes a loss on rides in extreme-weather events, because its executives have determined that the long-run benefits of this policy outweigh the short-run costs.

That's a different kind of equilibrium.

Caro / Marc Meyerbroeker/Newscom

Good luck finding a cab when the snow starts falling in New York City.

*Jose Martinez, "Uber Prices Are Surging Because of Snow and People Aren't Happy," November 15, 2018, https://www.complex.com/life/2018/11/uber-prices-are-surging-because-of-the-snow-and-people-arent-happy/uber-surge-6.

figure it out 2.3

Go online for interactive, step-by-step help in solving the following problem.

Suppose that the supply of orange juice is represented by $Q^S = 40P$, where Q is measured in pints and P is measured in cents per pint.

a. If the demand for orange juice is $Q^D = 5,000 - 10P$, what are the current equilibrium price and quantity?

b. Suppose that a severe frost in Florida raises the price of oranges and thus the cost of producing orange juice. In response to the increase in cost, producers reduce the quantity of orange juice supplied by 400 pints at every price. What is the new equation for the supply of orange juice?

c. After the frost, what will the equilibrium price and quantity of orange juice be?

Solution:

a. To solve for the equilibrium price, we need to equate the quantity demanded and quantity supplied:

$$Q^D = Q^S$$
$$5,000 - 10P = 40P$$
$$50P = 5,000$$
$$P = 100 \text{ cents}$$

To solve for the equilibrium quantity, we want to substitute the equilibrium price into either the demand curve or the supply curve (or both!):

$$Q_D = 5,000 - 10(100) = 5,000 - 1,000 = 4,000 \text{ pints}$$
$$Q^S = 40(100) = 4,000 \text{ pints}$$

b. If the quantity supplied of orange juice falls by 400 pints at every price, then the supply curve is shifting left (in a parallel fashion) by a quantity of 400 at each price:

$$Q_2^S = Q^S - 400 = 40P - 400$$

The new supply curve can be represented by $Q_2^S = 40P - 400$.

c. To solve for the new equilibrium, we would set $Q^D = Q_2^S$:

$$Q^D = Q_2^S$$
$$5,000 - 10P_2 = 40P_2 - 400$$
$$50P_2 = 5,400$$
$$P_2 = 108 \text{ cents}$$

Solving for equilibrium quantity can be done by substituting the equilibrium price into either the demand or supply equation:

$$Q^D = 5,000 - 10(108) = 5,000 - 1,080 = 3,920 \text{ pints}$$
$$Q^S = 40(108) - 400 = 4,320 - 400 = 3,920 \text{ pints}$$

As we would expect (see Table 2.2), the equilibrium price rises and the equilibrium quantity falls.

Summary of Effects

Table 2.2 summarizes the changes in equilibrium price and quantity that result when either the demand or supply curve shifts while the other curve remains in the same position. When the demand curve shifts, price and quantity move in the same direction. An increase in demand leads consumers to want to purchase more of the good than producers are willing to supply at the old equilibrium price. This will tend to drive up prices, which in turn induces producers to supply more of the good. The producers' response is captured by movement along the supply curve.

When the supply curve shifts, price and quantity move in opposite directions. If supply increases, the supply curve shifts out, and producers want to sell more of the good at the old equilibrium price than consumers wish to buy. This will force prices down, giving consumers an incentive to buy more of the good. Similarly, if supply shifts in, the equilibrium price has to rise to reduce the quantity demanded. These movements along the demand curve involve price and quantity changes in opposite directions because demand curves are downward-sloping.

Table 2.2 Effect of Shifts in Demand and Supply Curves in Isolation

Curve that Shifts	Direction of Shift	Impact on Equilibrium	
		Price	Quantity
Demand Curve	Out (increase in D)	↑	↑
	In (decrease in D)	↓	↓
Supply Curve	Out (increase in S)	↓	↑
	In (decrease in S)	↑	↓

Application: Supply Shifts and the Classic Video Game Crash

People love video games. Over half of households in the United States have at least one video game console, and many of these have multiple consoles. Sales of video game consoles and software were around $14.6 billion in the United States in 2017. To put that number in perspective, it is one-third more than 2017's total domestic box office haul of $11.1 billion.

Seeing these numbers, you'd never know that in the industry's early days, there was a point when many people declared video games a passing fad and a business in which it would be impossible to make a profit. Why did people say this? The problem wasn't demand. Early video games, from *Pong* to *Space Invaders* and consoles like the Atari 2600, were a huge hit and cultural touchstones. The problem was supply—way too much of it. In 1983 a set of factors combined to lead to a massive supply shift for the industry in North America that ended up crippling it for years.

Two primary factors led to the supply shift. Home video consoles, led by the Atari 2600 but also including popular machines from Mattel and Coleco, had taken off in the early 1980s. At this early point in the industry, console producers hadn't yet learned the best way to handle licensing arrangements with third-party game producers. As a result, just about anyone who wanted to could write a game title for a console. And just about everyone did. Even the pet food company Purina had a game. It publicized its Chuck Wagon brand dog food. (The game, *Chase the Chuck Wagon,* involved a dog chasing a chuck wagon through a maze.) In essence, there was a gold rush: Too many producers, each hoping to capture part of the fast-growing market, all entered at the same time, leading to a much larger total supply than any producer expected individually beforehand. The same phenomenon occurred in console production as well. Several

The discovery of a long-buried *E.T. the Extra-Terrestrial* Atari game after an excavation at a New Mexico landfill.

Juan Carlos Llorca/AP Images

companies made clones of Atari's market-leading console, and others produced their own machines and lines of games.

The leading console makers didn't help themselves with their own game-production decisions either. The most infamous failures were Atari's self-produced games *Pac-Man* and *E.T. the Extra-Terrestrial.* Atari management expected unprecedented sales for both, due to the extreme popularity of the arcade version of the former and the movie tied to the latter. In fact, Atari produced 12 million copies of *Pac-Man* even though there were only 10 million consoles in existence at the time, presuming that not only would just about every owner of a console buy the game, but also millions of others would purchase a console just to play the game. Both were rushed through production to take advantage of the holiday shopping seasons. The games were a mess, and quantity supplied well exceeded quantity demanded, even at the depressed prices in the market.

The sudden rush of producers to put product on the market created an outward shift in the supply curve—producers' behavior made clear that they were willing to produce more at any given price in early 1983 than they were just a couple years earlier, in early 1981. And while the demand for home video games had been trending upward as the technology diffused through households, the rush to produce new titles and consoles probably didn't have much of an effect on the demand curve. (In fact, because of the poor quality of the new games, it may have even shifted the demand curve inward.) It's reasonable to assume, then, that the demand curve was unmoved by the producer gold rush. The supply and demand model predicts the consequences of this supply shift on the market. A shift out in the supply curve in the face of constant demand will lead to an increase in quantity and a drop in prices, as shown in **Figure 2.9**. (These days, video game companies take more care in rolling out new games.)

That's exactly what happened in the video game industry. Price changes, in particular, were precipitous. Games that had been selling a year earlier at list prices of $35–$50 were being sold for $5 or even $1. Console prices fell by double-digit percentages as well. With games going at these rates, quantities increased somewhat, but nowhere near enough to make them profitable for their producers. Dozens of firms—console and games makers alike—went out of business. Atari, which until then had been a cash machine, ended up secretly burying hundreds of thousands of unshipped *E.T.* cartridges in a landfill in the New Mexico desert and was sold by its parent Warner Communications. It never

---

Figure 2.9   Effects of an Increase in the Supply of Video Games

In 1983 a sudden increase in the number of video game producers shifted the supply curve from S_{1981} to S_{1983}. At the equilibrium, the price of video games dropped from P_1 ($35) to P_2 ($5), while the quantity increased from Q_1 to Q_2.

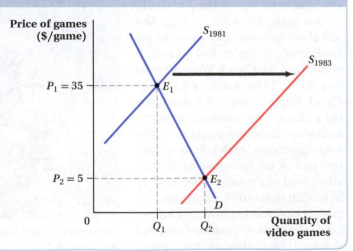

recovered. The carnage was so total that some retailers, figuring the market was hopeless, refused to stock games anymore. It essentially wiped out producers from the market for three to four years, an eternity in this fast-moving industry where technological races are seemingly never-ending. The dire situation finally turned around when a company known as Nintendo managed to convince retailers that its all-new 8-bit Nintendo Entertainment System would revitalize the moribund industry.

So, if you are wondering why, even today, Nintendo takes its time releasing games on the Switch, now you know the answer. ■

---

 make the grade

Did the curve shift, or was it just a movement along the curve?

A common type of exam question on demand and supply will involve one or more "shocks" to a market — changes in factors that influence demand or supply. Your job will be to sort out how those shocks affect demand and supply, and by extension, the equilibrium price and quantity in the market. Generally, the trickiest part of questions like these is figuring out whether changes in price and quantity are the result of moving along a given demand or supply curve, or whether the curves are shifting.

If you follow a few simple steps, this type of question need not be too difficult.

1. **Figure out what the shock is in any particular problem.** It is the change that causes a shift in either the supply curve, the demand curve, or both. There is a nearly infinite variety of shocks. A pandemic could wipe out a large number of consumers, a new invention might make it cheaper to manufacture a good, a different good that consumers like better might be introduced, or inclement weather may damage or kill off a large portion of a certain crop.

   Importantly, though, a change in either the price or the quantity of the good *in the market being studied* cannot be the shock. The changes in price and quantity in this market are the *result* of the shock, not the shock itself. Be careful, however: Changes in prices or quantities in some *other* market can serve as a shock to this market. If the price of chunky peanut butter falls, for example, that could be a shock to the market for grape jelly or the market for creamy peanut butter.

2. **Determine whether the shock shifts the demand or supply curve.**

   a. To figure out whether a shock shifts the demand curve and how the shock shifts it, ask yourself the following question: If the price of this good didn't change, would consumers want to buy more, less, or the same amount of the good after the shock? If consumers want more of the good at the same price after the shock, then the shock increases the quantity demanded at every price and shifts the demand curve out (to the right). If consumers want less of

the good at the same price after the shock, then the shock decreases demand and the demand curve shifts in. If consumers want the same amount of the good at the same price, then the demand curve doesn't move at all, and it's probably a supply shock.

   Let's go back to the grape jelly example. Our shock was a decline in the price of peanut butter. Do consumers want more or less grape jelly (holding the price constant) when peanut butter gets cheaper? The answer to this question is probably "more." Cheap peanut butter means consumers will buy more peanut butter, and because people tend to eat peanut butter and jelly together, consumers will probably want more jelly even if the price of jelly stays the same. Therefore, the decline in peanut butter's price shifts the demand for grape jelly out.

   b. To figure out whether a shock shifts the supply curve and how it shifts it, ask yourself the following question: If the price of this good didn't change, would suppliers want to produce more, less, or the same amount of the good after the shock? In the jelly example, a change in the price of peanut butter doesn't affect the costs of making jelly — it's not an input into jelly production. So, it's not a supply shock. An increase in the price of grapes, however, would be a supply shock in the market for grape jelly.

3. **Draw the market's demand and supply curves before and after the shocks.** In the jelly example, we would draw the original demand and supply curves, and then add the new demand curve (to the right of the initial demand curve) that results from the increase in the demand for jelly because of lower peanut butter prices. From this, it's easy to execute the final step, interpreting what impact the shock has on equilibrium price and quantity. For grape jelly, the increase in demand will result in a higher equilibrium price and quantity for jelly because the demand shift creates movement up and to the right along the jelly supply curve.

Practice following this approach; before long, manipulating demand and supply curves will become second nature.

figure it out 2.4

Last month, you noticed the price of asparagus rising, and you also noted that there was less asparagus being sold than in the prior month. What inferences can you draw about the behavior of the supply and demand for asparagus?

Solution:

We need to work backward to determine what could have happened to either supply or demand to lead to the change described in this question. Let's start with the change in price. The equilibrium price of asparagus is *rising*. This must mean one of two things: Either the demand for asparagus rose or the supply of asparagus fell. (If you have trouble seeing this, sketch a couple of quick figures.)

We also know that the equilibrium quantity of asparagus fell. A drop in the equilibrium quantity can only have two causes: either a decrease in the demand for asparagus or a

fall in the supply of asparagus. (Again, you may want to draw these scenarios to understand such results.)

Which shift leads to both a rise in equilibrium price and a fall in equilibrium quantity? It must be a decrease in the supply of asparagus, as shown in the figure.

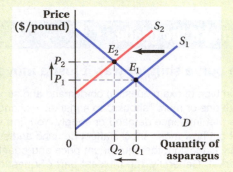

What Determines the Size of Price and Quantity Changes?

Thus far, the analysis in the chapter (summarized in Table 2.2) tells us about the *direction* in which equilibrium price and quantity move when demand and supply curves shift. But we don't know the size of these changes. In this section, we discuss the factors that determine how large the price and quantity changes are.

Size of the Shift   One obvious and direct influence on the sizes of the equilibrium price and quantity changes is the size of the demand or supply curve shift itself. The larger the shift, the larger the change in equilibrium price or quantity.

Slopes of the Curves   Even for a fixed-size demand or supply curve shift, the magnitudes of the resulting equilibrium price and quantity changes can vary. Specifically, the *relative* sizes of the price and quantity changes depend on the steepness of the demand and supply curves (**Figure 2.10**). If the demand curve shifts, then the slope of the supply curve determines whether the shift leads to a relatively large equilibrium price change and a relatively small equilibrium quantity change, or vice versa. If the supply curve shifts, it's the slope of the demand curve that matters.

This analysis raises an obvious question: What affects the slope of demand and supply curves? We discuss the economic forces that determine the steepness or flatness of demand and supply curves next.

Changes in Market Equilibrium When Both Curves Shift

Sometimes, we are faced with situations in which demand and supply curves move simultaneously. For example, **Figure 2.11** combines two shifts: decreases (inward shifts) in both supply and demand. Let's return to the tomato market at Pike Place Market and suppose that a big increase in oil prices occurs. This increase drives up the cost of production because harvesting and distribution costs rise for sellers. Increased oil prices also decrease the demand for tomatoes, because driving to the market becomes more expensive for consumers and so there are fewer people buying at any given price.

Figure 2.10 Size of Equilibrium Price and Quantity Changes, and the Slopes of the Demand and Supply Curves

(a) Demand curve shift with flatter supply curve

(b) Demand curve shift with steeper supply curve

(c) Supply curve shift with flatter demand curve

(d) Supply curve shift with steeper demand curve

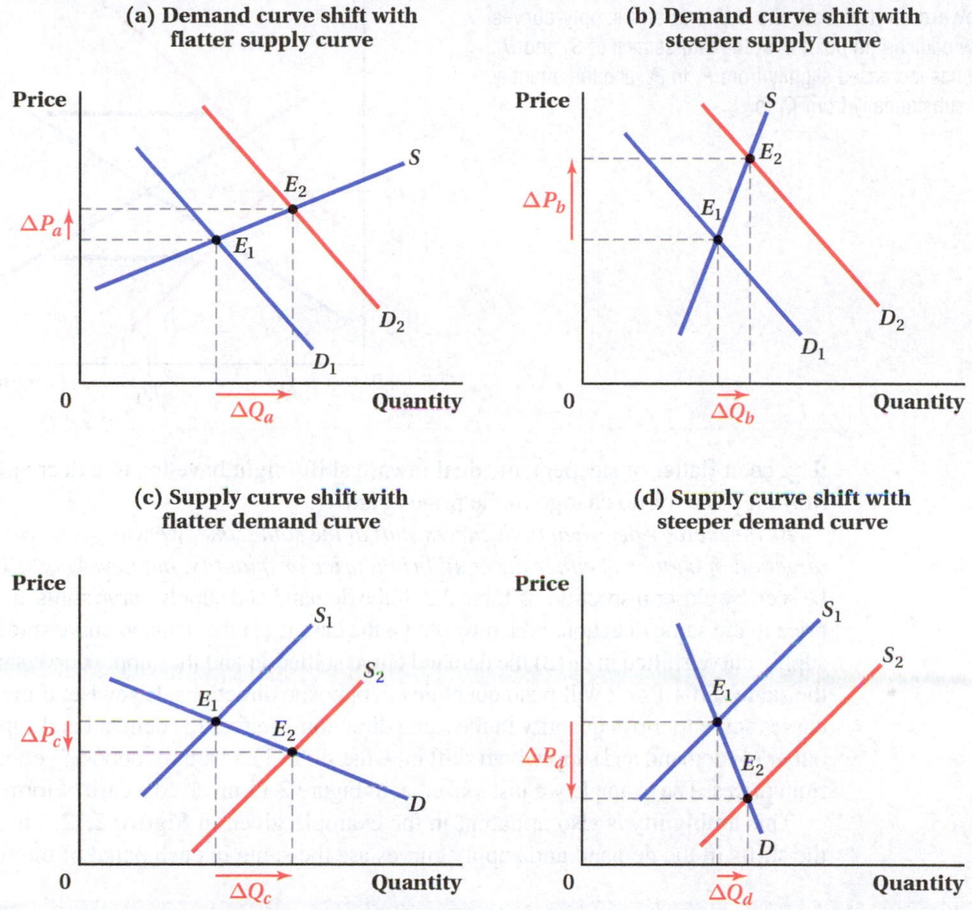

Panels a and b show the same shift in the demand curve, from D_1 to D_2. In panel a, the supply curve is relatively flat, while in panel b, it's relatively steep. When the demand curve shifts, if the supply curve is flat (panel a), the change in the equilibrium quantity (ΔQ_a) will be relatively large but the change in price (ΔP_a) will be small. When the supply curve is steep (panel b), the price change (ΔP_b) is large and the quantity change (ΔQ_b) is small. The same results hold for shifts in the supply curve. Panels c and d show the same supply curve shift, from S_1 to S_2. When the demand curve is relatively flat (panel c), a shift in supply from S_1 to S_2 will result in a relatively small decrease in equilibrium price ΔP_c and a relatively large increase in equilibrium quantity ΔQ_c. With a relatively steep demand curve (panel d), a shift in supply from S_1 to S_2 will result in a relatively large decrease in equilibrium price ΔP_d and a relatively small increase in equilibrium quantity ΔQ_d.

In this particular case, the simultaneous inward shifts in supply and demand have led to a substantial reduction in the equilibrium quantity and a slight increase in price. The reduction in quantity should be intuitive. The inward shift in the demand curve means that consumers want to buy less at any given price. The inward shift in the supply curve means that at any given price, producers want to supply less. Because both producers and consumers want less quantity, equilibrium quantity falls unambiguously, from Q_1 to Q_2.

The effect on equilibrium price is not as clear, however. An inward shift in demand with a fixed supply curve will tend to reduce prices, but an inward shift in supply with a fixed demand curve will tend to raise prices. Because both curves are moving simultaneously, it is unclear which effect will dominate, and therefore whether equilibrium price rises or falls. We have drawn the curves in Figure 2.11 so that the equilibrium price rises slightly, from P_1 to P_2. But had the demand and supply curves shifted by different amounts (or had

Figure **2.11**   Example of a Simultaneous Shift in Demand and Supply

The original equilibrium occurred at the intersection of D_1 and S_1, point E_1. An inward shift of both the demand and supply curves results in a new equilibrium point E_2 at the intersection of S_2 and D_2. At E_2, the price has increased slightly from P_1 to P_2, and the quantity has decreased substantially from Q_1 to Q_2.

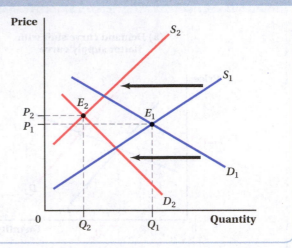

they been flatter or steeper), the dual inward shift might have led to a decrease in the equilibrium price, or no change in the price at all.

As a general rule, when both curves shift at the same time, we will know with certainty the direction of change of either the equilibrium price or quantity, but never both. This result can be seen by closer inspection of Table 2.2. If the demand and supply curve shifts are both pushing price in the same direction, which would be the case if (1) the demand curve shifted out and the supply curve shifted in or (2) the demand curve shifted in and the supply curve shifted out, then the same shifts 1 or 2 will push quantities in opposite directions. Likewise, if the shifts in both curves serve to move quantity in the same direction—either (3) demand and supply both shift out or (4) demand and supply both shift in—the shifts 3 and 4 have opposing effects on equilibrium prices. The example we just looked at in Figure 2.11 involved a case of form 4.

This ambiguity is also apparent in the example given in **Figure 2.12**. The directions of the shifts in the demand and supply curves are the same in each panel of the figure: Supply

Figure **2.12**   When Both Curves Shift, the Direction of Either Price or Quantity Will Be Ambiguous

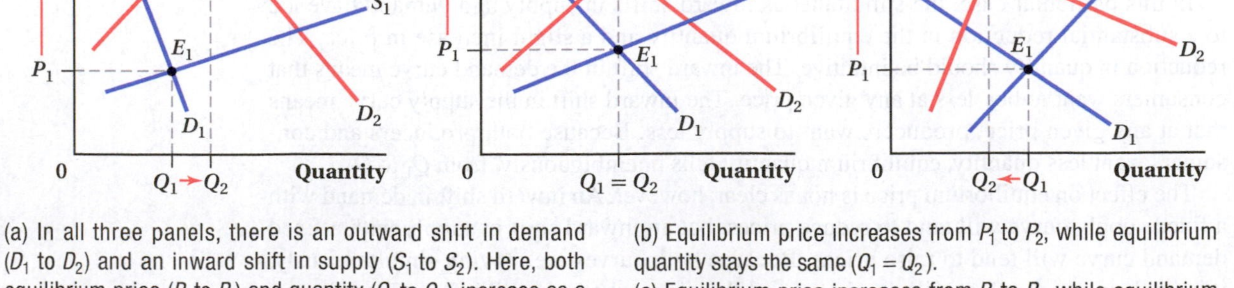

(a) In all three panels, there is an outward shift in demand (D_1 to D_2) and an inward shift in supply (S_1 to S_2). Here, both equilibrium price (P_1 to P_2) and quantity (Q_1 to Q_2) increase as a result.

(b) Equilibrium price increases from P_1 to P_2, while equilibrium quantity stays the same ($Q_1 = Q_2$).

(c) Equilibrium price increases from P_1 to P_2, while equilibrium quantity decreases from Q_1 to Q_2.

shifts inward from S_1 to S_2, and demand shifts outward from D_1 to D_2. Both these shifts will lead to higher prices, and this is reflected in the change in the equilibrium (from point E_1 to E_2). But, whether the equilibrium quantity rises, falls, or stays the same depends on the relative size of the shifts and the slopes of the curves. The figure's three panels show examples of each possible case. When examining a situation in which both supply and demand shift, you might find it helpful to draw each shift in isolation first, note the changes in equilibrium quantity and price implied by each shift, and then combine these pieces of information to obtain your answer.

2.5 Elasticity

Mathematically, the slopes of demand and supply curves relate changes in price to changes in quantity demanded or quantity supplied. Steeper curves mean that price changes are correlated with relatively small quantity changes. When demand curves are steep, this implies that consumers are not very price-sensitive and won't significantly alter their quantity demanded in response to price changes. Similarly, steep supply curves mean that producers' quantities supplied are not particularly sensitive to price changes. Flatter demand or supply curves, on the other hand, imply that price changes are associated with large quantity changes. Markets with flat demand curves have consumers whose quantities demanded change quite a bit as price varies. Markets with flat supply curves will see big movements in quantity supplied as prices change.

The concept of elasticity expresses the responsiveness of one value to changes in another (and here specifically, the responsiveness of quantities to prices). An **elasticity** is *the ratio of the percentage change in one value to the percentage change in another.* So, for example, when we talk about the sensitivity of consumers' quantity demanded to price, we refer to the **price elasticity of demand:** *the percentage change in quantity demanded resulting from a given percentage change in price.*

> **elasticity** The ratio of the percentage change in one value to the percentage change in another.
>
> **price elasticity of demand** The percentage change in quantity demanded resulting from a given percentage change in price.

Slope and Elasticity Are Not the Same

You might be thinking that the price elasticity of demand sounds a lot like the slope of the demand curve: how much quantity demanded changes when price does. Although elasticity and slope are certainly related, they're not the same.

The slope relates a change in one level (prices) to another level (quantity). The demand curve we introduced in the tomato example was $Q = 1{,}000 - 200P$. The slope of this demand curve is −200; that is, quantity demanded falls by 200 pounds for every dollar per pound increase in price.

There are two big problems with using just the slopes of demand and supply curves to measure price responsiveness. First, slopes depend on the units of measurement. If we measured tomato prices P in cents per pound rather than dollars, the demand curve would be $Q = 1{,}000 - 2P$, because the quantity of tomatoes demanded would fall by 2 pounds for every 1 cent increase in price. But the fact that the coefficient on P is now 2 instead of 200 doesn't mean that consumers are 1/100th as price-sensitive as before. Nothing has changed about consumers' price responsiveness in this market: The quantity demanded still falls by 200 pounds for each $1 increase in price. The change in the slope simply reflects a change in the units of P.

The second problem with slopes is that you can't compare them across different products. Suppose we were studying consumers' grocery shopping patterns and wanted to compare consumers' price sensitivity for tomatoes in the market at Pike Place Market to their price sensitivity for bunches of celery. Does the fact that consumers demand

100 fewer celery bunches for every 10-cent-per-bunch increase in price mean that consumers are more or less price-sensitive in the celery market than in the tomato market? The slope of the celery demand curve implied by these numbers is −10 (if we measure quantity demanded in bunches and price in cents per celery bunch). How could we ever compare this slope to the −200 slope for tomatoes?

Using elasticities to express responsiveness avoids these tricky issues, because everything is expressed in relative percentage changes. That eliminates the units problem (a 10% change is a 10% change regardless of what units the factor changing is measured in) and makes magnitudes comparable across markets.

The Price Elasticities of Demand and Supply

The price elasticity of demand is the ratio of the percentage change in quantity demanded to an associated percentage change in price. Mathematically, its formula is

Price elasticity of demand = (% change in quantity demanded)/(% change in price)

The price elasticity of supply is exactly analogous:

Price elasticity of supply = (% change in quantity supplied)/(% change in price)

To keep the equations simpler from now on, we'll use some shorthand notation. E^D will denote the price elasticity of demand, E^S the price elasticity of supply, $\%\Delta Q^D$ and $\%\Delta Q^S$ the percentage change in quantities demanded and supplied, respectively, and $\%\Delta P$ the percentage change in price. In this shorthand, the two equations above become

$$E^D = \frac{\%\Delta Q^D}{\%\Delta P} \quad \text{and}$$

$$E^S = \frac{\%\Delta Q^S}{\%\Delta P}$$

So, for example, if the quantity demanded of a good falls by 10% in response to a 4% price increase, the good's price elasticity of demand is $E^D = -10\%/4\% = -2.5$. There are a couple of things to note about this example. First, because demand curves slope downward, the price elasticity of demand is always negative (or more precisely, always nonpositive; in special cases that we discuss later, it can be zero). Second, because it is a ratio, a price elasticity can also be thought of as the percentage change in quantity demanded for a 1% increase in price. That is, for this good, a 1% increase in price leads to a −2.5% change in quantity demanded.

The price elasticity of supply works exactly the same way. If producers' quantity supplied increases by 25% in response to a 50% increase in price, for example, the price elasticity of supply is $E^S = 25\%/50\% = 0.5$. The price elasticity of supply is always positive (or again more precisely, always nonnegative) because quantity supplied increases when a good's price rises. And just as with demand elasticities, supply elasticities can be regarded as the percentage change in quantity in response to a 1% increase in price.

Price Elasticities and Price Responsiveness

Now that we've defined elasticities, let's use them to think about how responsive quantities demanded and supplied are to price changes.

When demand (supply) is very price-sensitive, a small change in price will lead to large changes in quantities demanded (supplied). That means the numerator of the elasticity expression, the percentage change in quantity, will be very large in magnitude compared to the percentage change in price in the denominator. For price elasticity of demand, the change in quantity will have the opposite sign as the price change, and the elasticity will be negative. But its magnitude (its absolute value) will be large if consumers are very responsive to price changes.

■ *Markets with large price elasticities of demand—where quantity demanded is sensitive to price differences—are those where consumers have a lot of ability to substitute away from or toward the good in question.* The demand for apples at the grocery store is probably fairly price-responsive because consumers have an array of other fruits they can buy instead if apple prices are high; if apple prices are low, they will buy apples instead of other fruits. The price elasticity of demand for apples might be something like −4: For every 1% increase in price, consumers' quantity demanded would fall by 4%.

■ *Markets with less price-responsive elasticities of demand—where quantity demanded is fairly unresponsive to price changes—are those where consumers have fewer options for substitution.* The demand for candy at the circus (certainly for the parents of small children) probably has a fairly small price elasticity of demand. In this case, the price elasticity of demand might be something like −0.3: for every 1% increase in price, quantity demanded would fall by 0.3%. (If you prefer, you could also express this as saying for every 10% price increase, quantity demanded would drop by 3%.)

■ *Markets with large price elasticities of supply—where the quantity supplied is sensitive to price differences—are those where it is easy for suppliers to vary their amount of production as price changes.* Perhaps they have a cost structure that allows them to make as many units as they'd like without driving up their per-unit costs too much. In the market for software, for example, if a program is wildly popular and drawing a high price, it's fairly easy for the game's producer to make additional copies available for download. So, the elasticity of supply might be quite large in this market, something like 12 (a 1% increase in price leads to a 12% increase in quantity supplied).

■ *Markets with low price elasticities of supply—where the quantity supplied is fairly unresponsive to price changes—are those where it is difficult to increase production.* This would occur in markets where it is costly for producers to vary their production levels, or it is difficult for producers to enter or exit the market. The supply curve for tickets to the Super Bowl might have a very low price elasticity of supply because there are only so many seats in the stadium. If the ticket price rises today, the stadium owners can't really put in additional seats. The supply elasticity in this market might be close to zero. It's probably slightly positive, however, because the owners could open some obstructed-view seats or make other temporary seating arrangements.

Application: Demand Elasticities and the Availability of Substitutes

We discussed how the availability of substitutes can affect the price elasticity of demand. When consumers can easily switch to other products or markets, they will be more responsive to changes in the price of a particular good. This means that, for any small rise in price, there will be a large decline in quantity demanded and the price elasticity of demand will be relatively large (in absolute value).

Table 2.3 presents some other elasticities estimated by economists for various goods. Larger groupings like "juice" or "beef" tend to have inelastic demand. The more narrowly defined the goods are (and so the more substitute products there are), the more elastic the

Table 2.3 Examples of Estimated Elasticities for Specific Goods

Product	Estimated Own-Price Elasticity of Demand
BROAD FOOD GROUPS	
Eggs	−0.06
Beef	−0.35
Fish	−0.39
Juice	−1.05
SPECIFIC BREAKFAST CEREALS	
Cap'N Crunch	−2.28
Froot Loops	−2.34
Kellogg's Corn Flakes	−3.38
Cheerios	−3.66
Shredded Wheat	−4.25
SPECIFIC AUTOMOBILES	
Jeep Grand Cherokee	−3.06
Cadillac Seville	−3.16
Toyota Corolla	−3.92

Source: For food data: K. S. Huang and B. Lin, *Estimation of Food Demand and Nutrient Elasticities from Household Survey Data,* Technical Bulletin 1887, Food and Rural Economic Division, Economic Research Service, U.S. Department of Agriculture, August 2000. For cereal data: Aviv Nevo, "Measuring Market Power in the Ready-to-Eat Cereal Industry," *Econometrica* 69, no. 2 (March 2001): 307–342. For automobile data: Steven Berry, James Levinsohn, and Ariel Pakes, "Differentiated Products Demand Systems from a Combination of Micro and Macro Data: The New Car Market," *Journal of Political Economy* 112, no. 1, Part 1 (February 2004): 68–105.

demand tends to be. Thus, the elasticity of beef is only −0.35, whereas the elasticity of Shredded Wheat brand breakfast cereal is −4.25.

In 2017, Amazon purchased grocer Whole Foods and, in a very public fashion, cut the price of many items at Whole Foods stores. This decision was quite notable, especially given that even regular customers were known to refer to the chain as "Whole Paycheck"! One possible interpretation of this price-cutting strategy was that Amazon believed demand for many of the products sold at Whole Foods was more elastic than previous management did. It viewed the many options consumers have when buying groceries as creating fairly elastic demand for groceries. This ease of substitutability, even among those consumers who might be predisposed to like Whole Foods' offerings, meant the high prices kept away many potential customers. By cutting prices, the theory goes, Amazon expected to make a lot more sales (highly elastic demand works both ways—high prices cause a big loss in quantity, but low prices create big gains in quantity).

Time will tell if Amazon's beliefs about the demand elasticity for groceries are accurate. In the meantime, though, Whole Foods customers won't be paying quite so much for their organic quinoa. ∎

Elasticities and Time Horizons

Often, a key factor determining the flexibility that consumers and producers have in responding to price differences, and therefore the price elasticity of their quantities demanded and supplied, is the time horizon.

In the short run, consumers are often limited in their ability to change their consumption patterns, but given more time, they can make adjustments that give them greater flexibility. A classic example of this is the market for gasoline. If a sudden price spike occurs, many consumers are essentially stuck having to consume roughly the same quantity of gas as they did before the price spike. After all, they have the same car, the same commute, and the same schedule as before. Maybe they can double up on a few trips, or carpool more often, but their ability to respond to prices is limited. For this reason, the short-run price elasticity of gasoline demand is relatively low; empirical estimates by economists who specialize in the market suggest that it is around −0.2. That is, for a 1% change in the price of gas, the quantity demanded changes by only −0.2% in the direction opposite the price change. Over longer horizons, however, individuals have greater scope to adjust their consumption. If the gas spike lasts, they can set up a permanent ride-sharing arrangement, buy a more efficient car, or even move closer to work. The long-run price elasticity of demand for gasoline is therefore much larger in magnitude; empirical studies typically find it to be something like −0.8. This means that in the long run, consumers can make four times the quantity adjustment to price changes they can make in the short run.

The same logic holds for producers and supply elasticities. The longer the horizon, the more options they have to adjust output to price changes. Manufacturers already producing at capacity might not be able to increase their output much in the short run if prices increase, even though they would like to. If prices stay high, however, they can hire more workers and build larger factories, and new firms can set up their own production operations and enter the market.

For these reasons, the price elasticities of demand and supply for most products are larger in magnitude (i.e., more negative for demand and more positive for supply) in the long run than in the short run. As we see in the next section, larger-magnitude elasticities imply flatter demand and supply curves. As a result, long-run demand and supply curves tend to be flatter than their short-run versions.

Classifying Elasticities by Magnitude

Economists have special terms for elasticities of particular magnitudes. *Elasticities with magnitudes (in absolute value) greater than 1 are referred to as* **elastic.** In the above examples, apples have elastic demand and software has elastic supply. *Elasticities with magnitudes less than 1 are referred to as* **inelastic**. The demand for circus candy and the supply of Super Bowl tickets are inelastic. *If the price elasticity of demand is exactly −1, or the price elasticity of supply is exactly 1, this is referred to as* **unit elastic.** *If price elasticities are zero—that is, there is no response in quantity to price changes—the associated goods are called* **perfectly inelastic.** Finally, *if price elasticities are infinite in magnitude (−∞ for demand, +∞ for supply)—the quantity demanded or supplied changes infinitely in response to any price change—this is referred to as* **perfectly elastic.**

Elasticities and Linear Demand and Supply Curves

As we discussed above, economists often use linear (straight-line) demand and supply curves, mostly for the sake of convenience. Because they are so common, it's worth discussing how elasticities are related to linear curves. Even more important, drawing this connection shows exactly how curves' slopes and elasticities, the two measures of price responsiveness we've been using, are related but still different.

elastic A price elasticity with an absolute value greater than 1.

inelastic A price elasticity with an absolute value less than 1.

unit elastic A price elasticity with an absolute value equal to 1.

perfectly inelastic A price elasticity that is equal to zero; there is no change in quantity demanded or supplied for any change in price.

perfectly elastic A price elasticity that is infinite; any change in price leads to an infinite change in quantity demanded or supplied.

We can rewrite the elasticity formula in a way that makes it easier to see the relationship between elasticity and the slope of a demand or supply curve. A percentage change in quantity ($\%\Delta Q$) is the change in quantity (ΔQ) divided by the original quantity level Q. That is, $\%\Delta Q = \Delta Q/Q$. Similarly, the percentage change in price is $\%\Delta P = \Delta P/P$. Substituting these into the elasticity expression from above, we have

$$E = \frac{\%\Delta Q}{\%\Delta P} = \frac{\Delta Q/Q}{\Delta P/P}$$

where E is a demand or supply elasticity, depending on whether Q denotes quantity demanded or supplied.

Rearranging terms yields

$$E = \frac{\Delta Q/Q}{\Delta P/P} = \frac{\Delta Q}{\Delta P} \cdot \frac{P}{Q}$$

or

$$E = \frac{1}{\text{slope}} \cdot \frac{P}{Q}$$

where "slope" refers to $\Delta P/\Delta Q$, the slope of the demand or supply curve in the standard price-versus-quantity space.

Elasticity of a Linear Demand or Supply Curve   Suppose we're dealing with the demand curve in **Figure 2.13**. Its slope is −2, but its elasticity varies as we move along it because P/Q does. Think first about the point A, where it intercepts the vertical axis. At $Q = 0$, P/Q is infinite because P is positive ($\$20$) and Q is zero. This, combined with the fact that the curve's (constant) slope is negative, means the price elasticity of demand is $-\infty$ at this point. The logic behind this is that consumers don't demand any units of the good at A when its price is $\$20$, but if price falls at all, their quantity demanded will become positive, if still small. Even though this change in quantity demanded is small in numbers of units of the good, the *percentage* change in consumption is infinite, because it's rising from zero.

As we move down along the demand curve, the P/Q ratio falls, reducing the magnitude of the price elasticity of demand. (Remember, the slope isn't changing so that part of the elasticity stays the same.) It will remain elastic — that is, have a magnitude larger than 1 — for some distance. Eventually, the absolute value of the elasticity will fall to 1, and at that point the demand curve is unit elastic. For the curve in Figure 2.13, this happens to be when $P = 10$ and $Q = 5$, because $E^D = -(1/2) \times (10/5) = -1$. This is labeled point B in the figure.[8] As we continue down and to the right along the demand curve, the magnitude of the elasticity will fall further and demand will become inelastic. At the point where the demand curve hits the horizontal axis (point C in the figure), price is zero, so $P/Q = 0$, and the price elasticity of demand is zero.

A similar effect happens as we move along a linear supply curve. Again, because the slope of the curve is constant, the changes in elasticity along the curve are driven by the price-to-quantity ratio. At the point where the supply curve intercepts the vertical axis, the quantity is 0 and P/Q is infinite. The price elasticity of supply is $+\infty$ at this point. The same logic holds as with the demand curve: For the smallest increase in price, the

---

[8] For a linear demand curve that intersects both the price and quantity axes, the point where the demand curve is unit elastic is always the midpoint. The curve's slope equals the price where it crosses the vertical axis (call this P_Y) divided by the quantity where it crosses the horizontal axis (call this Q_X), so 1 over the slope equals $-Q_X/P_Y$. The price-to-quantity ratio at the midpoint equals $(P_Y/2)/(Q_X/2)$, or simply P_Y/Q_X. The elasticity, which is the product of these two ratios, must therefore equal −1.

Figure 2.13   Elasticity of a Linear Demand Curve

The ratio between price and quantity (P/Q) and the magnitude of the elasticity of a demand curve decrease as we move down the curve. At point A, $Q = 0$, $P/Q = \infty$, and the price elasticity of demand is $-\infty$. Between points A and B, the demand curve is elastic with a price elasticity of demand less than -1 (greater than 1 in absolute value). At point B, the demand curve is unit elastic, or the price elasticity of demand equals -1. Between points B and C, the demand curve is inelastic with a price elasticity of demand greater than -1 (less than 1 in absolute value). At point C, $P = 0$, $P/Q = 0$, and the price elasticity of demand equals zero.

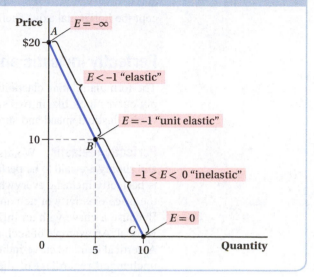

quantity supplied rises from zero to a positive number, an infinite percentage change in quantity supplied.

As we move up along the supply curve, the P/Q ratio falls. It's probably obvious that it must fall from infinity, but you might wonder whether it keeps falling, because both

---

  figure it out 2.5

The demand for gym memberships in a small rural community is $Q = 360 - 2P$, where Q is the number of monthly members and P is the monthly membership rate.

a. Calculate the price elasticity of demand for gym memberships when the price is $50 per month.

b. Calculate the price elasticity of demand for gym memberships when the price is $100 per month.

c. Based on your answers to (a) and (b), what can you tell about the relationship between price and the price elasticity of demand along a linear demand curve?

Solution:

a. The price elasticity of demand is calculated as

$$E = \frac{\Delta Q/Q}{\Delta P/P} = \frac{\Delta Q}{\Delta P} \cdot \frac{P}{Q}$$

Let's first calculate the slope of the demand curve. The easiest way to do this is to rearrange the equation in terms of P to find the inverse demand curve:

$$Q = 360 - 2P$$
$$2P = 360 - Q$$
$$P = 180 - 0.5Q$$

We can see that the slope of this demand curve is -0.5. We know this because every time Q rises by 1, P falls by 0.5.

Thus, we now know the slope and the price. To compute the elasticity, we need to know the quantity demanded at a price of $50. To determine this, we plug $50 into the demand equation for P:

$$Q = 360 - 2P = 360 - 2(50) = 360 - 100 = 260$$

Now we are ready to compute the elasticity:

$$E = \frac{1}{-0.5} \cdot \frac{50}{260} = \frac{50}{-130} = -0.385$$

b. When the price is $100 per month, the quantity demanded is

$$Q = 360 - 2P = 360 - 2(100) = 360 - 200 = 160$$

Plugging into the elasticity formula, we get

$$E = \frac{1}{-0.5} \cdot \frac{100}{160} = \frac{100}{-80} = -1.25$$

c. From (a) and (b), we can see that as the price rises along a linear demand curve, demand moves from being inelastic ($|-0.385| < 1$) to elastic ($|-1.25| > 1$).

P and *Q* are rising. It turns out that, yes, it must keep falling. Unlike with the demand curve, however, the *P/Q* ratio never falls to zero because the supply curve will never intercept the horizontal axis. Therefore, the price elasticity of supply won't drop to zero.

Perfectly Inelastic and Perfectly Elastic Demand and Supply

The formula relating elasticities to slopes also sheds some light on what demand and supply curves look like in two special but often discussed cases: perfectly inelastic and perfectly elastic demand and supply.

Perfectly Inelastic   We discussed above that when the price elasticity is zero, demand and supply are said to be perfectly inelastic. But what would a demand curve look like that is perfectly inelastic everywhere? A linear demand curve with a slope of $-\infty$ would drive the price elasticity of demand to zero because elasticity and slope are inversely related. Because a curve with an infinite slope is vertical, a perfectly inelastic demand curve is vertical. An example of such a curve is shown in **Figure 2.14a**. This makes intuitive sense: A vertical demand curve indicates that the quantity demanded by consumers is completely unchanged regardless of the price. Any percentage change in price will induce a 0% change in quantity demanded. In other words, the price elasticity of demand is zero.

Although perfectly inelastic demand curves don't really exist (after all, there are almost always possibilities for consumers and producers to substitute toward or away from a good as prices hit either extreme of zero or infinity), we might see some situations approaching them. For example, diabetics might have very inelastic demand for insulin. Their demand curve will be almost vertical if they will buy it at any price.

The same logic holds for supply: A vertical supply curve indicates perfectly inelastic supply and no response of quantity supplied to price differences. The supply of tickets for a particular concert or sporting event might also be close to perfectly inelastic, with a near-vertical supply curve, due to capacity constraints of the arena.

Figure 2.14   **Perfectly Inelastic and Perfectly Elastic Demand or Supply Curves**

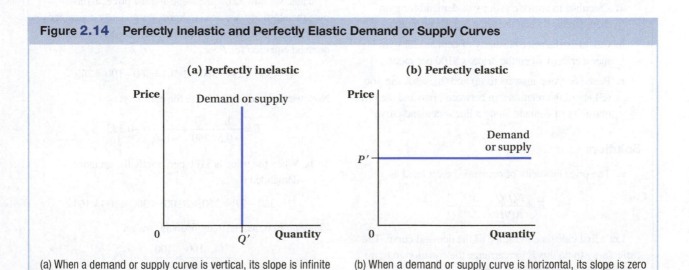

(a) When a demand or supply curve is vertical, its slope is infinite and it is perfectly inelastic. In other words, any change in price will result in a 0% change in quantity demanded or supplied.

(b) When a demand or supply curve is horizontal, its slope is zero and it is perfectly elastic. In other words, any change in price will result in an infinitely large change in quantity demanded or supplied.

One implication of perfect inelasticity is that any shift in the market's demand or supply curve will result in a change only in the market equilibrium price, not the quantity. That's because there is absolutely no scope for quantity to change in the movement along a perfectly inelastic demand curve from the old to the new equilibrium. Likewise, for perfectly inelastic supply, if there is a demand curve shift, all equilibrium movement occurs in price, not quantity.

Perfectly Elastic   When demand or supply is perfectly elastic, on the other hand, the price elasticity is infinite. This will be the case for linear demand or supply curves that have slopes of zero—those that are horizontal. An example of such a curve is shown in Figure 2.14b. This shape makes intuitive sense, too. As flat demand or supply curves imply large quantity responses to price changes, *perfectly* flat curves imply infinitely large quantity changes to price changes. If price is just above a horizontal demand curve, the quantity demanded will be zero. But if price fell just a bit, to below the demand curve, the quantity demanded would be infinite. Similarly, a small price change from above to below a horizontal supply curve would shift producers' quantity supplied from infinity to zero.

Small producers of commodity goods probably face demand curves for their products that are approximately horizontal. (We'll discuss this in depth in Chapter 8.) For instance, a small corn farmer can probably sell as many bushels of corn as she wants at the market price. If the farmer decided that the price was too low and insisted that she be paid more than the going rate, no one would buy her corn. Consumers could buy from someone else for less. Effectively, then, it is as if the farmer faces an infinite quantity demanded for her corn at the going price (or below it, if for some reason she's willing to sell for less) but zero quantity demanded of her corn above that price. In other words, she faces a flat demand curve at the going market price.

Supply curves are close to perfectly elastic in competitive industries in which producers all have roughly the same costs, and entry and exit are very easy. (We'll also discuss this point at greater length in Chapter 8.) These conditions mean that competition will drive prices toward the (common) level of costs, and differences in quantities supplied will be soaked up by the entry and exit of firms from the industry. Because of competition in the market, no firm will be able to sell at a price above costs, and obviously no firm will be willing to supply at a price below costs. Therefore, the industry's supply curve is essentially flat at the producers' cost level.

As opposed to the perfectly inelastic case, shifts in supply in a market with perfectly elastic demand will only move equilibrium quantity, not price. There's no way for the equilibrium price to change when the demand curve is flat. Similarly, for markets with perfectly elastic supply, demand curve shifts move only equilibrium quantities, not prices.

The Factors in "Everything Else"

We've been focusing on price elasticities to this point, and with good reason: They are a key determinant of demand and supply behavior and play an important role in helping us understand how markets work. However, they are not the only elasticities that matter in demand and supply analysis. Remember how we divided up all the factors that affected demand or supply into two categories: price and everything else? Well, each of those other factors that went into "everything else" has an influence on demand or supply that can be measured with an elasticity. The most commonly used of these elasticities measure the impact of two other factors on quantity demanded: the income elasticity of demand and the cross-price elasticity of demand.

The online appendix calculates and applies different demand and supply elasticities.

income elasticity of demand The ratio of the percentage change in quantity demanded to the corresponding percentage change in consumer income.

Income Elasticity of Demand

The **income elasticity of demand** is *the ratio of the percentage change in quantity demanded to the corresponding percentage change in consumer income* (I):

$$E_I^D = \frac{\%\Delta Q^D}{\%\Delta I} = \frac{\Delta Q^D}{\Delta I} \cdot \frac{I}{Q^D}$$

(Equivalently, it is the percentage change in quantity demanded associated with a 1% change in consumer income.)

Income elasticities describe how responsive demand is to income changes. Goods are sometimes categorized by the sign and size of their income elasticity.

inferior good A good for which quantity demanded decreases when income rises.

- *Goods with negative income elasticities* (consumers demand a lower quantity of the good when their income rises) are called **inferior goods.** This name isn't a comment on their inherent quality; it just describes how their consumption changes with people's incomes. (Note, however, that low-quality versions of many products are inferior goods by this economic definition.) Examples of likely inferior goods are bus tickets, youth hostels, and hot dogs.

normal good A good for which quantity demanded rises when income rises.

luxury good A good with an income elasticity greater than 1.

- *Goods with positive income elasticities* (consumers demand a higher quantity of the good when their income increases) are called **normal goods.** As the name indicates, most goods fit into this category.

- *Normal goods with income elasticities above 1* are sometimes called **luxury goods.** Having an income elasticity that is greater than 1 means the quantity demanded of these products rises at a faster rate than income. As a consequence, the share of a consumer's budget that is spent on a luxury good becomes larger as the consumer's income rises. (To keep a good's share of the budget constant, quantity consumed would have to rise at the same rate as income. Because luxury goods' quantities rise faster, their share increases with income.) Yachts, butlers, and fine art are all luxury goods.

We will dig deeper into the relationship between incomes and consumer demand in Chapters 4 and 5.

cross-price elasticity of demand The ratio of the percentage change in one good's quantity demanded (say, good *X*) to the percentage change in the price of another good *Y*.

Cross-Price Elasticity of Demand

The **cross-price elasticity of demand** is *the ratio of the percentage change in one good's quantity demanded (say, good* X) *to the percentage change in the price of* another *good* Y:

$$E_{XY}^D = \frac{\%\Delta Q_X^D}{\%\Delta P_Y} = \frac{\Delta Q_X^D}{\Delta P_Y} \cdot \frac{P_Y}{Q_X^D}$$

(To avoid confusion, sometimes the price elasticities we discussed above, which are concerned *with the percentage change in quantity demanded to the percentage change in the price of the* same *good*, are referred to as **own-price elasticities of demand.**)

own-price elasticities of demand The percentage change in quantity demanded for a good resulting from a percentage change in the price of that good.

When a good has a positive cross-price elasticity with another good, that means consumers demand a higher quantity of it when the other good's price rises. In other words, the good is a substitute for the other good: Consumers switch to the good when the other one becomes more expensive. Many pairs of goods are substitutes for one another—different brands of cereal, meals at restaurants versus dinners at home, colleges, and so on. Economist Aviv Nevo, who measured the elasticities for cereals mentioned above, also measured the cross-price elasticities of the cereals. He found that Froot Loops, for example, is a substitute for other kids' cereals, like Frosted Flakes and Cap'n Crunch ($E_{XY}^D = 0.131$ and 0.149, respectively). However, it is much less of

figure it out 2.6

Suppose that the price elasticity of demand for cereal is −0.75 and the cross-price elasticity of demand between cereal and the price of milk is −0.9. If the price of milk rises by 10%, what would have to happen to the price of cereal to exactly offset the rise in the price of milk and leave the quantity of cereal demanded unchanged?

Solution:

The first step will be to see what happens to the quantity of cereal demanded when the price of milk rises by 10%. We can use the cross-price elasticity to help us determine this. The cross-price elasticity for cereal with respect to the price of milk is equal to $\frac{\%\Delta Q_{cereal}}{\%\Delta P_{milk}} = -0.9$. Using the equation, we know that the denominator is 10 since the price of milk rose by 10%, so we get

$$\frac{\%\Delta Q_{cereal}}{\%\Delta P_{milk}} = \frac{\%\Delta Q_{cereal}}{10} = -0.9$$

$$\%\Delta Q_{cereal} = -9$$

Thus, when the price of milk rises by 10%, the quantity of cereal demanded falls by 9%.

Now we must consider how to offset this decline in the quantity of cereal demanded with a change in the price of cereal. In other words, what must happen to the price of cereal to cause the quantity of cereal demanded to *rise* by 9%? It is clear that the price of cereal must fall because the law of demand suggests that an inverse relationship exists between price and quantity demanded. However, because we know the price elasticity of demand, we can actually determine how far the price of cereal needs to fall.

The price elasticity of demand for cereal is

$$\frac{\%\Delta Q}{\%\Delta P} = -0.75$$

To offset the decline in cereal consumption caused by the rise in the price of milk, we need the percentage change in quantity demanded to be +9%. Therefore, we can plug 9% into the numerator of the ratio and solve for the denominator:

$$\frac{\%\Delta Q}{\%\Delta P} = -0.75$$

$$\frac{9}{\%\Delta P} = -0.75$$

$$\%\Delta P = \frac{9}{-0.75} = -12$$

The price of cereal would have to fall by 12% to exactly offset the effect of a rise in the price of milk on the quantity of cereal consumed.

a substitute for the more adult Shredded Wheat, which had a cross-price elasticity of only 0.020.[9]

When a good has a negative cross-price elasticity with another good, consumers demand less of it when the other good's price increases. This indicates that the goods are complements. Complements tend to be goods that are consumed together. If either of the goods within each pair were to become more expensive, consumers would buy not just less of that good itself, but also less of the other good in the pair. Milk and cereal are complements, as are tennis rackets and tennis balls, or computers and software.

2.6 Conclusion

This chapter introduced the concepts of supply and demand, two of the most important ideas in economics. Using the simplified supply and demand framework, we examined a variety of topics, including equilibrium price and quantity, the effects of shocks to supply and demand, and elasticities.

Nevertheless, the various cases we looked at in this chapter are, for the most part, simplified and abstract. In reality, measuring a market's demand and supply curves and

---

[9] Aviv Nevo, "Measuring Market Power in the Ready-to-Eat Cereal Industry," *Econometrica* 69, no. 2 (2001): 307–342.

determining the equilibrium price and quantity can be quite complicated. For example, firms hoping to make production decisions based on the types of analysis we've done here need to consider a wide range of data—prices, elasticities, demand curves, and so on—that are often not known. As a result, producers might rely on more trial-and-error practices than allowed for in our simplified model. Beginning with Chapter 6 and continuing through Part 3: Markets and Prices, we will talk more about situations that producers face in the real world and the production decisions that they must make, such as how much of a product to produce, how to produce it, and if they should enter a particular market at all. And we will see how these decisions are reflected in a firm's supply curve. In the meantime, the simplified supply and demand framework we've developed here provides a valuable structure for delving into a deeper analysis of markets and equilibrium price and quantity in upcoming chapters.

Summary

1. Economists use models to analyze markets. Models employ simplifying assumptions to reduce the incredible complexity of the real world so that general insights can be learned. The **supply and demand** model is one of the most used analytical frameworks in economics. This model makes several assumptions about the market that is being analyzed, including that all goods bought and sold in the market are identical, they are all sold for the same price, and there are many producers and consumers in the market. **[Section 2.1]**

2. Demand describes the willingness of consumers to purchase a product. There are many factors that affect demand, including price, income, quality, tastes, and availability of **substitutes and complements.** Economists commonly use the concept of a **demand curve,** which essentially divides these factors into two groups: price and everything else. A demand curve relates consumers' quantity demanded to the price of the good while holding every other factor affecting demand constant. A change in a good's price results in a movement along a given demand curve. If non-price factors change, the quantity demanded at every price changes and the whole demand curve shifts. **[Section 2.2]**

3. Supply describes the willingness of producers to make and sell a product. Factors that affect supply include price, available **production technologies,** input prices, and producers' outside options. **Supply curves** isolate the relationship between quantity supplied and price, holding all other supply factors constant. A change in a good's price results in a movement along a given supply curve. If nonprice factors change, the quantity supplied at every price changes and the whole supply curve shifts. **[Section 2.3]**

4. Combining demand and supply curves lets us determine the **market equilibrium** price, which is where quantity demanded equals quantity supplied. This equilibrium can be determined because demand and supply curves isolate the relationships between quantities and the one factor that affects both demand and supply: price. At the equilibrium, every consumer who wants to buy at the going price can, and every producer who wants to sell at the current market price can as well. **[Section 2.4]**

5. Changes in the factors (other than price) that affect demand or supply will change the market equilibrium price and quantity. Changes that increase demand and shift out the demand curve will raise **equilibrium price** and quantity in the absence of supply shifts; when the changes decrease demand and shift the demand curve in, price and quantity will fall. Changes that increase supply and shift out the supply curve, assuming no change in the demand curve, will increase equilibrium quantity and reduce price. Changes that decrease supply and shift in the supply curve decrease quantity and raise price. **[Section 2.4]**

6. If both supply and demand shift, either the effect on equilibrium price or the effect on equilibrium quantity will be ambiguous. If supply and demand move in the same direction, equilibrium quantity will follow, but the impact on price is unknown. On the other hand, if supply and demand move in opposite directions, equilibrium price will move in the same direction as demand (increase when demand rises, fall when demand decreases), but we cannot say with certainty what the effect on equilibrium quantity will be. **[Section 2.4]**

7. Economists typically express the sensitivity of demand and supply to various factors, but especially price, in terms of elasticities. An **elasticity** is the ratio of the percentage changes in two variables. The **price elasticity of demand** is the percentage change in quantity demanded for a 1% change in price, and the **price elasticity of supply** is the percentage change in quantity supplied for a 1% price change. **[Section 2.5]**

8. Other common demand elasticities measure the responsiveness of quantity demanded to changes in income and the prices of other goods. The **income elasticity of demand** is positive for **normal goods** and negative for **inferior goods.** The **cross-price elasticity of demand** is positive for substitutes and negative for complements. **[Section 2.5]**

Review Questions

1. There are four key assumptions underlying the supply and demand model. Name these assumptions.

2. Complements and substitutes of a given good affect the demand for that good. Define complements and substitutes.

3. What simplifying assumption do we make to build a demand curve? Why is the demand curve downward-sloping?

4. What is the difference between a change in quantity demanded and a change in demand?

5. What form do inverse supply and demand equations take? Why do economists often represent supply and demand using the inverse equations?

6. Why is the supply curve upward sloping?

7. What is the difference between a change in quantity supplied and a change in supply?

8. Define market equilibrium. What is true of the quantity supplied and demanded at the market equilibrium?

9. What happens when price is below the equilibrium price? Why?

10. In what direction will price and quantity move as a result of a demand shift?

11. In what direction will price and quantity move as a result of a supply shift?

12. Why is the direction of change of *either* price *or* quantity unknown when both supply and demand shift?

13. What happens to equilibrium price when supply and demand shift in the same direction? What happens to equilibrium quantity in the same situation?

14. What is the difference between an elasticity and slope?

15. We learned that economists have special terms for elasticities of particular magnitudes. Name the magnitudes for the following: inelastic, elastic, unit elastic, perfectly elastic, and perfectly inelastic.

16. Using the concept of income elasticity of demand, describe normal, luxury, and inferior goods.

17. Using the concept of cross-price elasticity of demand, describe substitutes and complements.

Problems
(Solutions to problems marked with an asterisk appear at the back of this book. Problems adapted to use calculus are available online.)

1. One assumption of the supply and demand model is that all goods bought and sold are identical. Why do you suppose economists commonly make this assumption? Does the supply and demand model lose its usefulness if goods are not identical?

2. List the assumptions of the supply and demand model. Then, for each assumption, give one example of a market in which the assumption is satisfied, and one example of a market in which that assumption is not satisfied. Is it reasonable to use the supply and demand model when assumptions are violated?

*3. The demand for organic carrots is given by the following equation:

$$Q_O^D = 75 - 5\,P_O + P_C + 2I$$

where P_O is the price of organic carrots, P_C is the price of conventional carrots, and I is the average consumer income. Notice how this isn't a standard demand curve that just relates the quantity of organic carrots demanded to the price of organic carrots. This demand function also describes how other factors affect demand—namely, the price of another good (conventional carrots) and income.

   a. Graph the inverse demand curve for organic carrots when $P_C = 5$ and $I = 10$. What is the choke price?

   b. Using the demand curve drawn in (a), what is the quantity demanded of organic carrots when $P_O = 5$? When $P_O = 10$?

   c. Suppose P_C increases to 15, while I remains at 10. Calculate the quantity demanded of organic carrots. Show the effects of this change on your graph and indicate the choke price. Has there been a change in the demand for organic carrots, or a change in the quantity demanded of organic carrots?

   d. What happens to the demand for organic carrots when the price of conventional carrots increases? Are organic and conventional carrots complements or substitutes? How do you know?

   e. What happens to the demand for organic carrots when the average consumer's income increases? Are carrots a normal or an inferior good?

*4. Out of the following events, which are likely to cause the demand for coffee to increase? Explain your answers.

   a. An increase in the price of tea

   b. An increase in the price of doughnuts

   c. A decrease in the price of coffee

   d. The Surgeon General's announcement that drinking coffee lowers the risk of heart disease

   e. Heavy rains causing a record-low coffee harvest in Colombia

5. How is each of the following events likely to shift the supply curve or the demand curve for fast-food hamburgers in the United States? Make sure you indicate which curve (curves) is affected and if it shifts out or in.

a.   The price of beef triples.

b.   The price of chicken falls by half.

c.   The number of teenagers in the economy falls due to an aging population.

d.   Mad cow disease, a rare but fatal medical condition caused by eating tainted beef, becomes common in the United States.

e.   The Food and Drug Administration publishes a report stating that a certain weight-loss diet, which encourages the intake of large amounts of meat, is dangerous to one's health.

f.   An inexpensive new grill for home use that allows consumers to make delicious hamburgers is heavily advertised on television.

g.   The minimum wage rises.

6.   The supply of wheat is given by the following equation:

$$Q_W^S = -6 + 4P_w - 2P_c - P_f$$

where Q_W^S is the quantity of wheat supplied, in millions of bushels; P_w is the price of wheat per bushel; P_c is the price of corn per bushel; and P_f is the price of tractor fuel per gallon.

a.   Graph the inverse supply curve when corn sells for $4 a bushel and fuel sells for $2 a gallon. What is the supply choke price?

b.   How much wheat will be supplied at a price of $4? $8?

c.   What will happen to the supply of wheat if the price of corn increases to $6 per bushel? Explain intuitively; then graph the new inverse supply carefully and indicate the new choke price.

d.   Suppose instead that the price of corn remains $4, but the price of fuel decreases to $1. What will happen to the supply of wheat as a result? Explain intuitively; then graph the new inverse supply. Be sure to indicate the new choke price.

7.   Bitcoin and other cryptocurrencies are demanded by those who wish to use them to complete transactions or those who wish to speculate on their future value. Bitcoins are supplied by thousands of competing miners who harness computing power to "dig" for Bitcoins by solving math problems. The more Bitcoins mined, the more difficult the math problems become.

a.   Use information in the chapter opener to explain why the supply curve of Bitcoins is likely to be upward-sloping.

b.   Increases in computing speed have, all else equal, made it easier for miners to mine Bitcoins. Draw a properly labeled graph showing how an increase in computing power affects the supply of Bitcoins.

c.   Suppose that the only change in the market for Bitcoins is the change described in (b). How would that change affect the equilibrium price and quantity of Bitcoins sold?

8.   In March 2002 the retail price of gasoline was $1.19 per gallon—exactly the same as it was in August 1990. Yet, total gasoline production and consumption rose from 6.6 million barrels per week in 1990 to 8.7 million barrels per week in 2002. Using the graph below, draw the appropriate shifts in the demand and supply curves to explain these two phenomena.

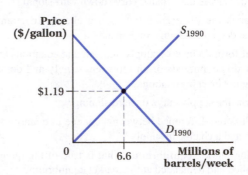

9.   When the demand for toilet paper increases, the equilibrium quantity sold increases. Consumers are buying more, and producers are producing more.

a.   How do producers receive the signal that they need to increase production to meet the new demand?

b.   Based on the facts given above, can you say that an increase in the demand for toilet paper causes an increase in the supply of toilet paper? Carefully explain why or why not.

*10.   Suppose the demand for towels is given by $Q^D = 100 - 5P$, and the supply of towels is given by $Q^S = 10P$.

a.   Derive and graph the inverse supply and inverse demand curves.

b.   Solve for the equilibrium price and quantity.

c.   Suppose that supply changes so that at each price, 20 fewer towels are offered for sale. Derive and graph the new inverse supply curve.

d.   Solve for the new equilibrium price and quantity. How does the decrease in supply affect the equilibrium price and quantity sold?

e.   Suppose instead that supply does not change, but demand decreases so that at each price, 25 fewer towels are desired by consumers. Solve for the new equilibrium price and quantity. How does the decrease in demand affect the equilibrium price and quantity sold? How do those changes compare to your response in (d)?

11.   The market for whisky in Scotland is described by the following demand and supply equations:

$$\text{Demand: } Q^D = 80 - P$$
$$\text{Supply: } Q^S = -40 + 2P$$

where P is the price of a liter of whisky and Q is the number of liters sold per week, in thousands. Suppose the Scottish government mandates a price of £60 per liter.

a. Is the market in equilibrium? Why or why not?

b. At the government's price, is there an excess demand or excess supply of whisky?

c. Suppose that the government decides to let the price of whisky be determined by the market rather than by the government. Based on your answer to (b), would you expect the price of whisky to increase, decrease, or stay the same? Explain your reasoning intuitively.

12. The inverse demand for carbon-steel chef's knives is given by $P = 120 - \frac{1}{2}Q^D$, where P is the price of a chef's knife and Q^D is the quantity of chef's knives desired per week, in thousands. The inverse supply of chef's knives is given by $P = 20 + 2Q^S$, where Q^S is the quantity of chef's knives offered for sale each week, in thousands.

a. Accurately graph the inverse supply and inverse demand curves, with P on the vertical axis and Q on the horizontal axis.

b. What are the buyers' and sellers' choke prices in your graph? How can you find those same choke prices by looking at the inverse demand and inverse supply equations?

c. Equate inverse demand and inverse supply to find the market equilibrium quantity of chef's knives sold. (*Hint:* In equilibrium, $Q^D = Q^S$, so you can replace both Q^D and Q^S with a generic letter Q.)

d. Plug the quantity you found in (c) into the inverse demand curve to solve for the equilibrium price. Then double-check your work by plugging that same quantity into the inverse *supply* curve.

13. In the United States, the biggest shopping day each year is "Black Friday," the day after Thanksgiving. Every Black Friday, the local branch of a major retailer makes this offer to the public: the first 100 54-inch HD flat-screen televisions sold will sell at the discounted price of $50 each. Customers line up before the store opens its doors to take advantage of this tremendous bargain.

a. In this scenario, what is the "price" of a 54-inch flat-screen television?

b. How would that "price" likely change if the retailer offered the first 500, instead of the first 100, televisions at $50 apiece? If only the first 50 were offered at the discounted price?

14. Determine the effects of the following events on the price and quantity of beer sold. Assume that beer is a normal good.

a. The price of wine, a substitute for beer, decreases.

b. The price of pizza, a complement to beer, increases.

c. The price of barley, an ingredient used to make beer, increases.

d. Brewers discover they can make more money producing wine than they can producing beer.

e. Consumers' incomes increase as the economy emerges from a recession.

*15. Suppose the demand for down pillows is given by $Q^D = 100 - P$, and that the supply of down pillows is given by $Q^S = -20 + 2P$.

a. Solve for the equilibrium price.

b. Plug the equilibrium price back into the demand equation and solve for the equilibrium quantity.

c. Double-check your work by plugging the equilibrium price back into the supply equation and solving for the equilibrium quantity. Does your answer agree with what you got in (b)?

d. Solve for the elasticities of demand and supply at the equilibrium point. Which is more elastic: demand or supply?

e. Invert the demand and supply functions (in other words, solve each for P) and graph them. Do the equilibrium point and relative elasticities shown in the graph appear to coincide with your answers?

16. In both the United States and France, the demand for haircuts is given by $Q^D = 300 - 10P$. But in the United States, the supply is given by $Q^S = -300 + 20P$, while in France, the supply is given by $Q^S = -33.33 + 6.67P$.

a. Graph supply and demand for haircuts for each country. (Use the same scale on each axis and graph carefully!)

b. Solve for the equilibrium price and quantity of a haircut in each country.

c. Suppose that the demand for haircuts in the United States increases by 100 units at each price, so the new demand is $Q^D = 400 - 10P$. Place this new demand curve in the appropriate graph, and solve for the new equilibrium price and quantity in the United States.

d. Suppose that, in a similar fashion, the demand for haircuts in France increases by 100 units at each price. Add the new demand curve for haircuts to the appropriate graph, and solve for the new equilibrium price and quantity.

e. Drawing on your answers to (c) and (d), comment on the following statement: "The impact of an increase in *demand* depends critically on the slope of the *supply* curve."

17. Suppose that budding economist Buck measures the inverse demand curve for toffee as $P = \$100 - Q^D$, and the inverse supply curve as $P = Q^S$. Buck's economist friend

Penny likes to measure everything in cents. She measures the inverse demand for toffee as $P = 10,000 - 100Q^D$, and the inverse supply curve as $P = 100Q^S$.

a. Find the slope of the inverse demand curve and compute the price elasticity of demand at the market equilibrium using Buck's measurements.

b. Find the slope of the inverse demand curve and compute the price elasticity of demand at the market equilibrium using Penny's measurements. Is the slope the same as Buck calculated? How about the price elasticity of demand?

18. Some policy makers have claimed that the U.S. government should purchase illegal drugs, such as cocaine, to increase the price that drug users face and therefore reduce their consumption. Does this idea have any merit? Illustrate this logic in a simple supply and demand framework. How does the elasticity of demand for illegal drugs relate to the efficacy of this policy? Are you more or less willing to favor this policy if you are told demand is inelastic?

*19. Suppose that Jo has an inverse demand for frogs' legs given by $P = 3/Q^D$, while Kyle's inverse demand for frogs' legs is given by $P = 4 - Q^D$. Graphs of each consumer's demand curve are shown below.

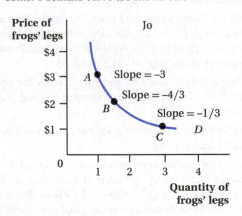

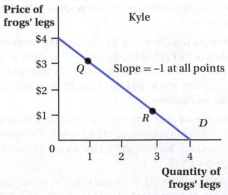

a. Show that Jo's demand for frogs' legs is unit elastic.

b. Show that Kyle's elasticity of demand for frogs' legs differs at different points on his demand curve.

c. Use your answers to (a) and (b) to comment on the difference between the slope of a demand curve and the elasticity of demand.

20. The cross-price elasticity of demand measures the percentage change in the quantity of a good demanded when the price of a different good changes by 1%. The income elasticity of demand measures the percentage change in the quantity of a good demanded when the income of buyers changes by 1%.

a. What sign might you expect the cross-price elasticity to have if the two goods are shampoo and conditioner? Why?

b. What sign might you expect the cross-price elasticity to have if the two goods are gasoline and ethanol? Why?

c. What sign might you expect the cross-price elasticity to have if the two goods are coffee and shoes? Why?

d. What sign might you expect the income elasticity to have if the good in question is hot stone massages? Why?

e. What sign might you expect the income elasticity to have if the good in question is Ramen noodles? Why?

f. What sign might you expect the income elasticity to have if the good in question is table salt? Why?

21. Which of the following cases will result in the largest decrease in equilibrium price? The largest change in equilibrium quantity? Verify your answers by drawing graphs.

a. Demand is highly inelastic; there is a relatively large increase in supply.

b. Demand is highly elastic; there is a relatively small increase in supply.

c. Supply is highly inelastic; there is a relatively small decrease in demand.

d. Supply is highly elastic and demand is very inelastic; there is a relatively large increase in supply.

Using Supply and Demand to Analyze Markets

overnments often enact policies that affect how markets work. The purpose of these policies can be to serve a particular constituency, to raise necessary tax revenue, or (as we'll see in Chapter 17) to correct a market failure. For example, every time gas prices rise above a level that the public will tolerate, some politicians call for a cap on gas prices (or at least an investigation). Opinion polls conducted at such times suggest people like that idea. Are they right? Whether changes in market conditions are the result of government market interventions or changes in any of the many factors that affect supply, demand, or both, we can use supply and demand analysis to figure out not only what happens to price and quantity, but also who benefits, who loses, and by how much.

In Chapter 2, we introduced supply and demand analysis. We learned about the economic decisions that supply and demand curves embody, and we defined what it means for a market to be in equilibrium. Now we put those tools to work. We show how to measure the total benefits that consumers and producers gain in any given market, and how these benefits change when supply or demand shifts. We also show how various government interventions into markets affect the well-being of consumers and producers.

3.1 Consumer and Producer Surplus: Who Benefits in a Market?

To understand the market impact of any policy, we need a way to measure the benefits consumers and producers obtain from participating in that market. Economists measure these benefits using the concepts of consumer and producer surplus.

Consumer Surplus

Consumer surplus is *the difference between the price consumers would be willing to pay for a good (as measured by the height of their demand curves) and the price they actually have to pay.* Consumer surplus is usually measured as an amount of money. Suppose someone with $1000 in his pocket is lost in the desert and extremely thirsty. He stumbles upon a convenience store, where he spots a bottle of water for sale. He would be willing to pay his entire $1,000 for it. Applying the concept of elasticity from Chapter 2, we can say his demand for a drink is almost perfectly inelastic: He will demand the one bottle of water almost regardless of its price. Let's say the store is asking $1 for the bottle of water. Mr. Thirsty was willing to pay $1,000 for the water but only had to pay the $1 market price. After the transaction, he has his drink *and* $999 left in his pocket. That $999 — the difference between what he was willing to pay and what he actually paid — is his consumer surplus.

We can take this one-person example and extend the consumer surplus to the demand curve for an entire market. For example, let's return to Pike Place Market but now consider the market for Honeycrisp apples. The market demand curve in **Figure 3.1** tells us how

consumer surplus The difference between the price consumers would be willing to pay for a good (as measured by the height of their demand curves) and the price they actually have to pay.

Figure 3.1 **Consumer Surplus:** The Difference between the Amount Consumers Are Willing to Pay and the Amount They Have to Pay

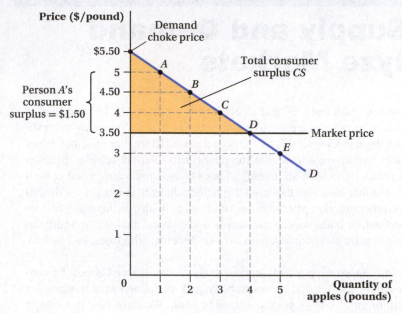

The market demand curve shows how many pounds of apples consumers are willing to buy at a given price. The consumer at point *A* is willing to pay $5 for 1 pound of apples; if we assume a market price of $3.50, this person has a consumer surplus of $1.50. Similarly, at the market price of $3.50, consumers at points *B* and *C* have consumer surpluses of $1 and $0.50 respectively. The person at point *D* is willing to pay the market price of $3.50 a pound, and thus, no consumer surplus exists for this individual.[1] The consumer at point *E* does not purchase any apples. The total consumer surplus, the total gains for each individual who buys apples—person *A*, person *B*, and so on—is the area under the demand curve and above the price, represented by the area of the shaded triangle *CS*. The base of the consumer surplus triangle is the quantity sold. The height of the triangle is the difference between the market price ($3.50) and the *demand choke price* ($5.50 per pound), the price at which quantity demanded is reduced to zero.[2]

many pounds of apples consumers are willing to buy at any given price. If every point along the market demand curve represents a different person's willingness to pay for a pound of apples, we can measure each person's consumer surplus just as we did for Mr. Thirsty.

In this Pike Place Market apple example, the demand curve represents a collection of consumers, each with a different willingness to pay for the good. Those with a high willingness to pay are located at the upper left portion of the curve; those with a lower willingness to pay are down and to the right along the curve. The same logic also applies to an individual's demand curve, which reflects his declining willingness to pay for each additional unit of the good. For instance, an apple buyer might be willing to pay $5 for the first pound

---

[1] Some years ago, there was an economist who was hired away by another university. As part of the deal to lure him, the new school gave him a big raise. When he arrived at the new university in the fall, his new dean said that the school was happy he had decided to come. The economist responded that if the university really was happy, then he hadn't asked for enough money. He wanted to leave the school with no consumer surplus.

[2] This kind of calculation involves two technicalities. First, the area is a triangle only if the demand curve is a straight line. We use straight-line demand curves here only because they are easy. Demand curves in real life are often curved so the consumer surplus area under the demand curve need not be a triangle. Second, calculating the total consumer surplus in dollars is only accurate if the marginal utility of income is constant. We discuss the idea of utility in Chapter 4. If a dollar of income is worth a lot more when income is low than when income is high, then we can't say for sure that all dollars of consumer surplus have the same impact on people's well-being.

of apples he buys, but only $4 for the second pound, and $3.50 for the third pound (maybe he has limited ability to store them, or just gets tired of eating apples after a while). If the market price is $3.50 per pound, he will buy 3 pounds of apples. His consumer surplus will be $1.50 for the first pound, $0.50 for the second, and zero for the third, a total of $2. Doing this calculation for all apple buyers and adding up their consumer surpluses will give the total consumer surplus of the same type shown in the triangular area in Figure 3.1.

Producer Surplus

Just as consumers gain surplus from engaging in market transactions, so do producers. **Producer surplus** is *the difference between the price producers actually receive for their goods and the cost of producing them (measured by the height of the supply curve).* The supply curve in the Pike Place apple market (**Figure 3.2**) tells us how many pounds of apples producers are willing to sell at any given price, and as we discussed in Chapter 2 and will explain in more detail in Chapters 7 and 8, this comes from the costs of producing the goods.

producer surplus The difference between the price producers actually receive for their goods and the cost of producing them (measured by the height of the supply curve).

Figure 3.2   Producer Surplus: The Difference between the Price Producers Receive for Their Goods and the Cost of Producing Them

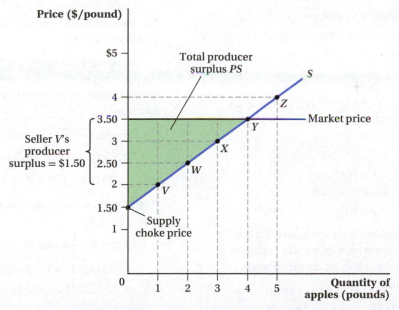

If we think of every point on the supply curve as representing a different apple seller, we see that Firm *V* would be willing to supply apples at a price of $2 per pound. Because it can sell apples at the market price of $3.50, however, it receives a producer surplus of $1.50.[3] Firm *W* is willing to sell apples for $2.50 per pound and so receives $1 of producer surplus, while Firm *X* receives $0.50 of producer surplus. Firm *Y*, which is only willing to sell a pound of apples for $3.50, receives no surplus. Firm *Z* is shut out of the market; the market price of $3.50 per pound is less than its willingness to sell ($4).

The total producer surplus for the entire market is the sum of the producer surplus for every seller along the supply curve. In this example with a linear supply curve, the sum equals the triangle above the supply curve and below the price, the area of the shaded triangle *PS*. The base of the triangle is the quantity sold. The height of the triangle is the difference between the market price ($3.50) and the *supply choke price*, the price at which quantity supplied equals zero. Here, the supply choke price is $1.50 per pound; no seller is willing to sell apples below that price.

---

[3] Resist the temptation to call producer surplus "profit." Although it seems natural to do this here, we will see in later chapters that the term "profit" has a precise meaning in economics, and it's not exactly this.

The supply curve in Figure 3.2 represents a collection of producers that differ in their willingness to sell. The same logic applies to an individual producer's supply curve in cases where the firm's cost of producing additional output rises with its output. In these cases, the firm must be paid more to sell additional units.[4] The firm's producer surplus is the sum of the differences between the market price and the minimum price the firm would need to receive to be willing to sell each unit.

 The online appendix uses integration to find consumer and producer surplus.

---

figure it out 3.1

Go online for interactive, step-by-step help in solving the following problem.

The demand and supply curves for candy bars in a midwestern city are given by

$$Q^D = 152 - 20P$$

$$Q^S = 188P - 4$$

where Q is measured in thousands of candy bars per day and P in dollars per candy bar.

a. Find the equilibrium price and quantity.

b. Calculate the consumer and producer surplus at the equilibrium price.

Solution:

a. Equilibrium occurs where $Q^D = Q^S$. Therefore, we can solve for equilibrium by equating the demand and supply curves:

$$Q^D = Q^S$$
$$152 - 20P = 188P - 4$$
$$156 = 208P$$
$$P = \$0.75$$

Therefore, the equilibrium price of a candy bar is $0.75. To find the equilibrium quantity, we need to plug the equilibrium price into either the demand or supply curve:

$Q^D = 152 - 20P$	$Q^S = 188P - 4$
$= 152 - 20(0.75)$	$= 188(0.75) - 4$
$= 152 - 15$	$= 141 - 4$
$= 137$	$= 137$

Remember that Q is measured in terms of thousands of candy bars per day, so the equilibrium quantity is 137,000 bars per day.

b. To calculate consumer and producer surplus, it is easiest to use a graph. First, we need to plot the demand and supply curves. For each curve, we can identify

two points. The first point is the equilibrium, given by the combination of equilibrium price ($0.75) and equilibrium quantity (137). The second point we can identify is the choke price. The choke prices for demand and supply can be determined by setting Q^D and Q^S equal to zero and solving for P:

$Q^D = 152 - 20P$	$Q^S = 188P - 4$
$0 = 152 - 20P$	$0 = 188P - 4$
$20P = 152$	$4 = 188P$
$P = \$7.6$	$P = \$0.02$

So, the demand choke price is $7.60 and the supply choke price is $0.02.

The demand and supply curves are graphed in the figure below. Consumer surplus is the area below demand and above the price (area A). Its area can be calculated as

$$CS = \text{area } A = \frac{1}{2} \times \text{base} \times \text{height}$$
$$= (0.5) \times (137,000 - 0) \times (\$7.60 - \$0.75)$$
$$= (0.5) \times 137,000 \times \$6.85 = \$469,225$$

Producer surplus is the area below price and above supply (area B):

$$PS = \text{area } B = \frac{1}{2} \times \text{base} \times \text{height}$$
$$= (0.5) \times (137,000 - 0) \times (\$0.75 - \$0.02)$$
$$= 0.5 \times 137,000 \times \$0.73 = \$50,005$$

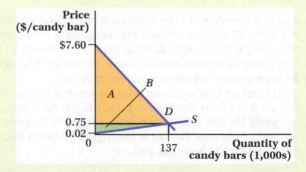

---

[4] We're also assuming here that the firm takes the market price as given. We'll discuss firms' supply behavior in this case and in the alternative case where a firm has price-setting power in Chapters 8 and 9.

Application: The Value of Innovation

Equipped with the concepts of consumer and producer surplus, we can analyze one of the most important issues in economics—the introduction of new products. Economists emphasize the importance of innovation and new goods in raising a society's standard of living. In any discussion of the value of innovation, we need a way to compute how much benefit a new product gives to consumers.

A simple suggestion for valuing a new product would be to just add up what people paid for it. However, that's wrong. Many consumers value the product at much more than the price they paid to get it. Consumer surplus measures the full benefit of the new product because it tells us how much consumers value the product *over and above* the price they pay.

A key factor in determining the amount of potential consumer surplus in a market for a new good is the steepness of the demand curve: All else equal, the steeper it is, the bigger the consumer surplus. That's because steep demand curves mean that at least some consumers (those on the upper-left-hand part of the demand curve) have very high willingness to pay for the good. You can see this on a price–quantity demand curve diagram. First, draw a horizontal line representing an equilibrium market price. Next, draw various demand curves with different slopes that intersect this price at the same point—that is, so the equilibrium quantity demanded is the same. You will see that the consumer surplus triangles are larger for steeper demand curves.

Let's look at eyeglasses as an example. Economist Joel Mokyr explained in his book *The Lever of Riches* that the invention of eyeglasses around the year 1280 allowed craftsmen to do detailed work for decades longer than they could before. If we think of glasses as a "new technology" circa 1280, we can visualize what the demand curve for glasses might have looked like. Because many people in 1280 would be quite blind without glasses, the demand curve was probably very steep—there was a set of individuals with a very high willingness to pay for glasses, and their demand wasn't particularly sensitive to prices. This steepness of the demand curve probably remained stable for several centuries, until contact lenses became widely available in the latter half of the twentieth century.

In Chapter 2, we learned that readily available substitute goods are likely to make demand more elastic. This is true of glasses, too: When contact lenses became available, the demand for glasses became more price elastic. How would this change in elasticity affect the consumer surplus people get from the existence of eyeglasses? **Figure 3.3** illustrates the answer.

Figure 3.3   Consumer Surplus and the Elasticity of Demand

Before contact lenses were available, consumer surplus was large because the demand for glasses D_1 was inelastic—if you wanted to see better, glasses were the only game in town. The consumer surplus was the area above the price and below D_1, or area $A + B$. Many people would be willing to buy glasses even if the price were much higher than P. (That's what having an inelastic demand means.)

When contact lenses became available, the demand for glasses became much more elastic, as shown by curve D_2. Even if just as many people bought glasses at the equilibrium price as before, a sharp rise in the price of glasses would have caused many people to stop buying them because now they had an alternative. The figure shows that the consumer surplus from glasses declines after contacts come on the market. The area below the new, flatter demand curve and above the price is only area B.

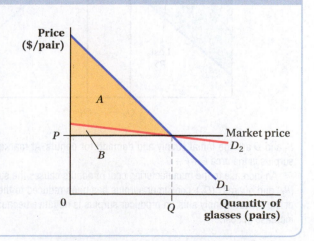

Remember that consumer surplus depends on the *most* that people would be willing to pay for the product. That maximum price goes down if alternatives are available. When alternative methods of vision correction are available, glasses are just another option rather than a virtual necessity, and the consumer surplus associated with them falls. If you're concerned this example implies that innovation destroys surplus, remember that the substitute goods create surpluses of their own. They have their own demand curves, and the areas under those curves and above the substitute goods' prices are also consumer surplus. For example, while the invention of contact lenses reduces the consumer surplus provided by glasses, it creates a lot of surplus in the new contact lens market. ■

The Distribution of Gains and Losses from Changes in Market Conditions

One nice thing about our definitions of producer and consumer surplus is that we can analyze the impact of any changes on either side of a market in a way that builds on the analysis we started in Chapter 2. There, we learned how shocks to supply and demand affect prices, quantity demanded, and quantity supplied. We can also show how these shocks affect the benefits producers and consumers receive in a market. **Figure 3.4** shows the

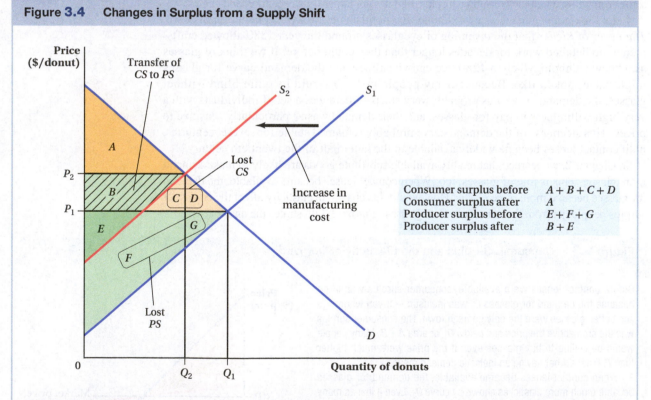

Figure 3.4   Changes in Surplus from a Supply Shift

Consumer surplus before	$A + B + C + D$
Consumer surplus after	A
Producer surplus before	$E + F + G$
Producer surplus after	$B + E$

S_1 and D are the initial supply and demand for donuts. At market price P_1, consumer surplus is the area $A + B + C + D$, and producer surplus is the area $E + F + G$.

An increase in the manufacturing cost of donuts causes the supply curve to shift leftward from S_1 to S_2. At the new equilibrium price (P_2) and quantity (Q_2), consumer surplus has been reduced to the area A. The new producer surplus is shown by $B + E$. The net effect of the inward supply shift on producer surplus is negative because downward-sloping demand means the price will rise less than the increase in cost.

initial supply and demand in the market for donuts. We see that at the market price P_1, the donut buyers' benefit from buying donuts is greater than the price they pay for the donuts (reflected in the consumer surplus area $A + B + C + D$). Similarly, the donut makers' benefit from making the donuts is greater than the price at which they sell the donuts (reflected in the producer surplus area $E + F + G$).

Now let's suppose that a shock hits the donut market. Because of a poor berry harvest, the price of jelly filling goes up (assuming that the donut filling actually has some real fruit in it!). When this shock hits, the cost of making donuts rises and suppliers are no longer willing to supply as many donuts at any given price. The supply of donuts falls, as reflected in the inward shift of the donut supply curve from S_1 to S_2. In response to the jelly shock, the equilibrium price of donuts rises to P_2, and the quantity of donuts bought and sold in the donut market falls to Q_2.

These changes affect both consumer and producer surplus. The higher equilibrium price and lower equilibrium quantity both act to reduce consumer surplus. Compared to triangle $A + B + C + D$ in Figure 3.4, triangle A is much smaller. For producer surplus, the lower equilibrium quantity that results from the supply shift reduces it, but this reduction is partially counteracted by the higher price. These opposing effects can be seen in Figure 3.4. Some of the producer surplus before the shift—specifically, the space $G + F$ between the old and new supply curve and below the demand curve—is lost. But the price increase shifts some of what was consumer surplus to producer surplus; this is area B. Because the equilibrium price rises less than the increase in cost (a consequence of downward-sloping demand), however, it must be that the increase in producer surplus from a higher price is less than the surplus lost due to higher costs. Therefore, the net effect on producer surplus of the inward supply shift is negative. These effects on consumer and producer surplus are reversed for outward supply shifts.

We can do a similar analysis for the effects of demand shifts. An inward shift in demand leads to a lower equilibrium price and quantity, both of which reduce *producer* surplus. The impact on consumer surplus, however, has opposing effects. Having a smaller equilibrium quantity reduces consumer surplus, but this reduction is counteracted by the drop in price. Similar to the supply shift case above (but in the opposite direction), the inward demand shift transfers to consumers part of what was producer surplus. We see these effects in the application that follows.

 ## Application: Toxic Algae in Florida

Periodically, warm water temperatures and excess agricultural runoff will cause a bloom of toxic algae, known as a "red tide" (or "green slime"), to form on the Gulf coast of Florida. As a result of increasing water temperatures, the algae blooms have become more frequent over time and sometimes stretch hundreds of miles and persist for multiple months. When they arrive, they smell awful and lifeguards often must wear respirators to avoid getting lung infections. Masses of fish die and wash up on the shores. Thousands of tourists cancel their planned vacations on the Gulf.

When the governor of Florida declares the red tide an official natural disaster, Florida's Economic Development Committee will try to compensate merchants for the damage done by the disaster. They then design surveys to analyze the issue. What they're trying to compute is, simply put, the loss in producer surplus.

To compute the loss, they ought to estimate a supply and a demand curve, and then contemplate any shift in demand. Such a shift is illustrated in **Figure 3.5**. Prices and quantities decrease in response to a red tide event—just as the model suggests. Before the red tide, producer surplus is the area below the equilibrium price and above the supply curve, or $A + B + C$ in the graph.

Figure 3.5   **"Red Tide" Damage in Florida**

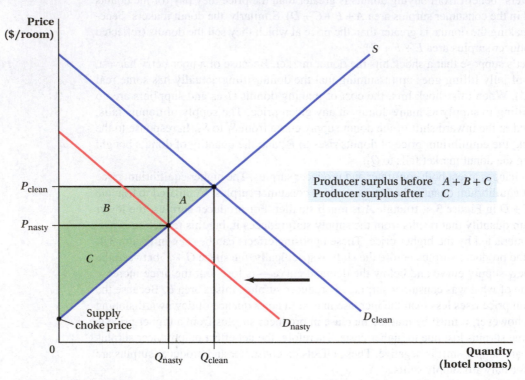

Producer surplus before $A + B + C$
Producer surplus after C

After a toxic algae bloom in Florida, the demand curve for hotel rooms from people visiting the Gulf Coast shifts inward, from D_{clean} to D_{nasty}. During the time when the Gulf's waters are clean, the equilibrium hotel room price and quantity are P_{clean} and Q_{clean}, respectively, and the producer surplus is the total shaded area, $A + B + C$.

Once the waters become nasty, the equilibrium price and quantity fall to P_{nasty} and Q_{nasty}, and the producer surplus is reduced to the area C. The area $A + B$ represents the loss in producer surplus to the local hotels.

After the tide, the area would just be C. The amount of producer surplus lost from the drop in demand would be A and B. The committee can figure that out with the information on how much price and quantity changed. Note that this involves not just the simple calculation of lost revenue, which would be $P_{clean} \times Q_{clean} - P_{nasty} \times Q_{nasty}$. They would also need to subtract the costs the producers saved by not having to produce such additional goods, which is the area under the supply curve between Q_{nasty} and Q_{clean}. ∎

---

    figure it out 3.2

A local tire market is represented by the following equations and in the diagram offered below:

$$Q^D = 3,200 - 25P$$
$$Q^S = 15P - 800$$

where Q is the number of tires sold weekly and P is the price per tire. The equilibrium price is $100 per tire, and 700 tires are sold each week.

Suppose an improvement in the technology of tire production makes them cheaper to produce so that sellers are willing to sell more tires at every price. Specifically, suppose that quantity supplied rises by 200 at each price.

a. What is the new supply curve?

b. What are the new equilibrium price and quantity?

c. What happens to consumer and producer surplus as a result of this change?

Solution:

a. Quantity supplied rises by 200 units at every price, so we simply add 200 to the equation for Q^S:

$$Q_2^S = 15P - 800 + 200 = 15P - 600$$

b. The new equilibrium occurs where $Q^D = Q_2^S$:

$$3,200 - 25P = 15P - 600$$
$$3,800 = 40P$$
$$P = \$95$$

We can find the equilibrium quantity by substituting the equilibrium price into either the supply or demand equation (or both):

$$Q^D = 3,200 - 25(95) \qquad Q_2^S = 15(95) - 600$$
$$= 8,200 - 2,375 \qquad\qquad = 1,425 - 600$$
$$= 825 \qquad\qquad\qquad = 825$$

The new equilibrium quantity is 825 tires per week. Notice that because supply increased, the equilibrium price fell and the equilibrium quantity rose just as we would predict.

c. The easiest way to determine the changes in consumer and producer surplus is to use a graph such as the one shown here. To calculate all the areas involved, we need to make sure we calculate the demand choke price and the supply choke prices before and after the increase in supply.

The demand choke price is the price at which quantity demanded is zero:

$$Q^D = 0 = 3,200 - 25P$$
$$25P = 3,200$$
$$P = \$128$$

The demand choke price is $128.

The supply choke price is the price at which quantity supplied is zero. Because supply is shifting, we need to calculate the supply choke price for each supply curve:

$$Q_1^S = 0 = 15P - 800 \qquad Q_2^S = 0 = 15P - 600$$
$$15P = 800 \qquad\qquad\qquad 15P = 600$$
$$P = \$53.33 \qquad\qquad\qquad P = \$40$$

The initial supply choke price is $53.33 but falls to $40 when supply increases.

With the choke prices and the two equilibrium price and quantity combinations, we can draw the supply and demand diagram.

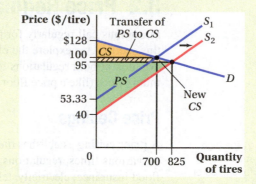

Consumer surplus: The initial consumer surplus is the area of the triangle below the demand curve but above the initial equilibrium price ($100):

$$CS_{\text{initial}} = \frac{1}{2} \times \text{base} \times \text{height}$$
$$= \frac{1}{2} \times (700 - 0) \times (\$128 - \$100)$$
$$= (0.5)(700)(\$28) = \$9,800$$

The new consumer surplus is the area of the triangle below the demand curve and above the new equilibrium price ($95):

$$CS_{\text{new}} = \frac{1}{2} \times \text{base} \times \text{height}$$
$$= \frac{1}{2} \times (825 - 0) \times (\$128 - \$95) = (0.5)(825)(\$33)$$
$$= \$13,612.50$$

So, after the outward shift in supply, consumer surplus rises by $3,812.50.

Producer surplus: The initial producer surplus is the area of the triangle below the initial equilibrium price and above the initial supply curve (S_1):

$$PS_{\text{initial}} = \frac{1}{2} \times \text{base} \times \text{height}$$
$$= \frac{1}{2} \times (700 - 0) \times (\$100 - \$53.33) = (0.5)(700)(\$46.67)$$
$$= \$16,334.50$$

The new producer surplus is the area of the triangle below the new equilibrium price and above the new supply curve (S_2):

$$PS_{\text{new}} = \frac{1}{2} \times \text{base} \times \text{height}$$
$$= \frac{1}{2} \times (825 - 0) \times (\$95 - \$40) = (0.5)(825)(\$55)$$
$$= \$22,687.50$$

The increase in supply also led to a rise in producer surplus by $6,353.

3.2 Price Regulations

Politicians call regularly for price ceilings on products whose prices have risen a lot. In this section, we explore the effects of direct government interventions in market pricing. We look at both regulations that set maximum prices (like a gas price ceiling) and minimum prices (like a price floor such as a minimum wage).

Price Ceilings

price ceiling The highest price that can be paid legally for a good or service.

A **price ceiling** establishes *the highest price that can be paid legally for a good or service.* At various times, regulations have set price ceilings for cable television, auto insurance, flood insurance, electricity, telephone rates, gasoline, prescription drugs, apartments, food products, and many other goods.

If the price ceiling is above market equilibrium price, it is nonbinding and will not hinder the free-market outcome. The more interesting case is when the price ceiling is lower than market equilibrium.

Suppose the city council of a college town passes a pizza price control regulation. With the intent of helping out the college's financially strapped students, the city council says no pizzeria can charge more than $8 for a pizza. Let's say the demand curve for pizzas in a month during the school year is described by the equation $Q^D = 20,000 - 1,000P$. The cheaper pizzas get, the more students will eat them, so the demand curve slopes downward. If the price were zero, 20,000 pizzas would be sold per month (the college in town isn't that big, and there are only so many meals a person can eat). The demand choke price is $20 per pizza — if the price were $20 per pizza, no pizzas would be sold.

Let's say the supply of pizzas is given by $Q^S = 2,000P - 10,000$. Supply slopes upward because when prices are higher, the local pizzerias make more pizzas. If the price is below $5, they make no pizzas. For each $1 increase in the price of a pizza after that, an additional 2,000 pizzas per month would be supplied.

Figure 3.6 graphs the supply and demand curves described by these two equations. The free-market equilibrium is at point *w*; that is, before price controls, the equilibrium price for a pizza is $10, and at that price, 10,000 pizzas are supplied and demanded. Given these baseline market conditions, we can study the impact of the price ceiling using the graph or the equations. Let's start with the graph.

Graphical Analysis   Before any price controls, the consumer surplus for pizza-eating students is given by the area below the demand curve and above the $10 free-market price, $A + B + C$. The producer surplus is the area above the supply curve but below the price, $D + E + F$.

When the city council implements the price control regulation, the highest price the pizzerias can charge is $8 per pizza, which is less than the market-clearing price of $10. At $8, students demand a total of 12,000 pizzas (point *y*). This quantity demanded is larger than the 10,000 pizzas demanded at the free-market equilibrium because the price ceiling price is lower than the free-market price. At an $8 price, however, pizzerias are only willing to supply 6,000 pizzas (point *x*). That is, there is **excess demand:** *The difference between the quantity demanded and the quantity supplied at a price ceiling.* There will be a large number of students frustrated that they cannot buy the number of pizzas they would like at the price ceiling.

excess demand The difference between the quantity demanded and the quantity supplied at a price ceiling.

Now consider how the price ceiling affects consumer and producer surplus. It's clear that the pizzerias are worse off. In the free market, they would have sold more pizzas (10,000 versus 6,000) at a higher price ($10 versus $8). The producer surplus after the price control law is everything below the capped price and above the supply curve; producer surplus shrinks from area $D + E + F$ to area F.

Figure 3.6 The Effects of a Price Ceiling

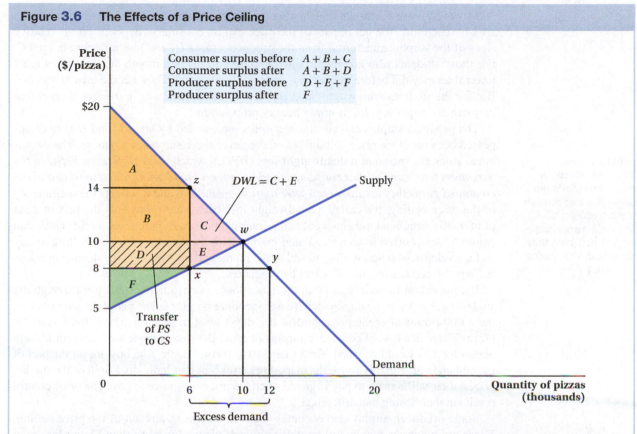

Consumer surplus before	$A + B + C$
Consumer surplus after	$A + B + D$
Producer surplus before	$D + E + F$
Producer surplus after	F

A price ceiling affects both producer and consumer surpluses. Before price controls in the pizza market, consumers pay $10 per pizza, and producers supply 10,000 pizzas per week at the equilibrium point *w*. Consumer surplus is the triangle $A + B + C$, and producer surplus is $D + E + F$. At the $8 price ceiling, pizzerias are only willing to supply 6,000 pizzas (point *x*), but consumers demand 12,000 pizzas (point *y*), creating excess demand. Because pizzerias are now selling fewer pizzas at a lower price, producer surplus is reduced to area *F*. The new consumer surplus is the area $A + B + D$, and the net gain to consumers is $D - C$. The shaded area $C + E$ is the deadweight loss created by the price ceiling.

The law was passed to benefit students by lowering pizza prices. But we can't actually say for sure whether they are better off as a result.[5] The consumer surplus with the price ceiling is the area below the demand curve and above the price, area $A + B + D$. The consumer surplus now includes area *D* because imposing price controls shifted that area from being part of producer surplus to being part of consumer surplus. We call area *D* a **transfer,** *surplus that moves from producer to consumer, or vice versa, as a result of a price regulation.*

transfer Surplus that moves from producer to consumer, or vice versa, as a result of a price regulation.

---

[5] The analysis of consumer surplus can become a bit complicated in situations with excess demand. Excess demand can create incentives for buyers to come into the market who wouldn't have even been interested in the product if not for the price ceiling, because these buyers hope to obtain the good at the low, controlled price and resell it to high-value buyers at a higher price. (This is why ticket brokers who have no interest in seeing a sold-out concert or game still try hard to obtain tickets to it.) How many such buyers come into the market, what they eventually resell the good for, and any additional costs of this reselling process all affect how much surplus is in the market and who obtains it.

However, fewer pizzas are bought after the price cap law, resulting in consumers losing area *C*. Therefore, the net impact of the price cap on consumers depends on the relative sizes of the surplus transferred from the producers (area *D*) and loss reflected in area *C*. For those students who are able to buy the 6,000 pizzas in a month at a price that is $2 lower than they did before the law was enacted, life is good. They get the area *D* transfer. But for the students who would have enjoyed 4,000 more pizzas in the free market that they can no longer buy, life is now a hungry proposition.

The producer surplus and consumer surplus represented by areas *C* and *E* have disappeared because of the price ceiling. No one receives these surpluses anymore. Their combined areas are known as a **deadweight loss (DWL),** which is *the difference between the maximum total surplus that consumers and producers could gain from a market and the combined gains they actually reap after a price regulation,* and it reflects the inefficiency of the price ceiling. It's called a deadweight loss because it represents the loss of a set of mutually beneficial, surplus-generating transactions (pizza purchases, in this case) that would have occurred in an unregulated market with a customer who was willing to buy and a producer who was willing to sell at the market price. Area *C* is the deadweight loss suffered by consumers; area *E* is lost by producers.

It's important to understand that there is a loss in consumer surplus even though the students get to keep the money they're not spending on pizza. The people missing out on the 4,000 pizzas after the price control law don't want to save the $10 — they want the pizza! There is a loss of consumer surplus because the pizzas those students would have gotten for $10 would be worth *more* than $10 to them. People who buy are on the part of the demand curve that is above the market price (except that individual right *at* the market price); their willingness to pay is greater than the price they have to pay. The price control results in their losing that difference.

Some producer surplus also becomes deadweight loss as a result of the price ceiling. There are pizzerias that would be willing to sell pizzas for more than $8 but less than the $10 equilibrium price. Once the $8 price ceiling is in place, pizzerias will pull 4,000 pizzas off the market because $8 is not enough to cover their costs of making those extra pizzas. So, both students and pizzerias benefited from transactions that took place before the price control; once the price ceiling is imposed, however, some of those transactions no longer take place and they lose those benefits.

Analysis Using Equations Now compare the free and regulated markets for pizzas using the supply and demand equations we described earlier. To determine the free-market equilibrium using the equations, we set quantity supplied equal to quantity demanded and solve for the market clearing price *P*:

$$Q^S = Q^D$$
$$2{,}000P - 10{,}000 = 20{,}000 - 1{,}000P$$
$$3{,}000P = 30{,}000$$
$$P = \$10$$

Plugging that price back into either the supply or demand equation gives an equilibrium quantity of 10,000 pizzas:

$$Q^S = 2{,}000P - 10{,}000 \qquad \text{or} \qquad Q^D = 20{,}000 - 1{,}000P$$
$$= 2{,}000(10) - 10{,}000 \qquad\qquad\quad = 20{,}000 - 1{,}000(10)$$
$$= 20{,}000 - 10{,}000 \qquad\qquad\qquad = 20{,}000 - 10{,}000$$
$$= 10{,}000 \qquad\qquad\qquad\qquad\quad = 10{,}000$$

---

deadweight loss (DWL) The difference between the maximum total surplus that consumers and producers could gain from a market and the combined gains they actually reap after a price regulation.

The consumer surplus in the free market is the triangle $A + B + C$. The area of that triangle is

$$CS = \frac{1}{2} \times (\text{base}) \times (\text{height})$$

$$= \frac{1}{2} \times (\text{quantity sold}) \times (\text{demand choke price} - \text{market price})$$

The demand choke price is the price at which $Q^D = 0$. In this case,

$$0 = 20{,}000 - 1{,}000(P_{DChoke})$$

$$1{,}000(P_{DChoke}) = 20{,}000$$

$$(P_{DChoke}) = \$20$$

The consumer surplus triangle is

$$CS = \frac{1}{2} \times (\text{quantity sold}) \times (P_{DChoke} - \text{market price})$$

$$= \frac{1}{2}(10{,}000)(\$20 - \$10)$$

$$= (5{,}000)(\$10) = \$50{,}000 \text{ per month}$$

(Remember that quantities are measured in pizzas per month, so the consumer surplus is measured in dollars per month.)

The producer surplus is the triangle $D + E + F$ in the graph. The area of that triangle is

$$PS = \frac{1}{2} \times (\text{quantity sold}) \times (\text{market price} - \text{supply choke price})$$

The supply choke price is the price at which quantity supplied is zero:

$$Q^S = 2{,}000P - 10{,}000$$

$$0 = 2{,}000(P_{SChoke}) - 10{,}000$$

$$P_{SChoke} = 10{,}000/2{,}000 = \$5$$

Plugging this price into the equation for producer surplus, we find

$$PS = \frac{1}{2}(\text{quantity sold}) \times (\text{market price} - P_{SChoke})$$

$$= (10{,}000)(\$10 - \$5)$$

$$= (5{,}000)(\$5)$$

$$= \$25{,}000 \text{ per month}$$

Now consider the impact of the price ceiling. The price of a pizza cannot rise to $10 as it did in the free market. The highest it can go is $8. We saw in the graphical analysis that this policy led to excess demand, the difference between the quantity demanded and the quantity supplied at the price ceiling (P_c):

$$Q_c^D = 20{,}000 - 1{,}000P_c \qquad\qquad Q_c^S = 2{,}000P_c - 10{,}000$$

$$= 20{,}000 - 1{,}000(8) \qquad\qquad\quad = 2{,}000(8) - 10{,}000$$

$$= 12{,}000 \qquad\qquad\qquad\qquad\qquad = 6{,}000$$

The excess demand is $12{,}000 - 6{,}000$ or 6,000 pizzas per month. This means that there are students ringing pizzerias' phones off the hook trying to order more pizzas, but whose orders the pizzerias won't be willing to fill at the new market price.

Next, we compute the consumer and producer surpluses after the price control is imposed. Producer surplus is area F:

$$PS_c = \frac{1}{2}(Q_c^S) \times (P_c - P_{SChoke})$$

$$= \frac{1}{2}(6{,}000)(\$8 - \$5)$$

$$= (3{,}000)(\$3) = \$9{,}000 \text{ per month}$$

which is just over one-third of the $25,000 of producer surplus pizzerias were making before the price ceiling. It is no wonder that producers fight against laws like this one.

The consumer surplus is now areas $A + B + D$. An easy way to figure out the value for this surplus is to add the area of triangle A to the area of the rectangles B and D. Triangle A has an area of

$$\text{Area of } A = \frac{1}{2}(Q_c^S) \times (P_{DChoke} - \text{price at point } z)$$

where the price at point z is the price at which quantity demanded equals the new quantity supplied of 6,000 pizzas. To determine this price, set $Q^D = Q_C^S$ and solve for the price:

$$Q^D = 20{,}000 - 1{,}000P_z = Q_c^S$$

$$20{,}000 - 1{,}000P_z = 6{,}000$$

$$20{,}000 - 6{,}000 = 1{,}000P_z$$

$$P_z = 14{,}000/1{,}000 = \$14$$

This means that, if the price of a pizza were actually $14, exactly 6,000 pizzas would be demanded. With this value for the price at point z, we can now calculate:

$$\text{Area of } A = \frac{1}{2}(Q_c^S) \times (P_{DChoke} - P_z)$$

$$= \frac{1}{2}(6{,}000)(\$20 - \$14)$$

$$= (3{,}000)(\$6)$$

$$= \$18{,}000 \text{ per month}$$

The area of rectangle B is

$$B = Q_c^S \times (P_z - \text{free-market price})$$

$$= (6{,}000)(\$14 - \$10)$$

$$= \$24{,}000 \text{ per month}$$

and the area of rectangle D (the transfer) is

$$D = Q_c^S \times (\text{free-market price} - P_c)$$

$$= (6{,}000)(\$10 - \$8)$$

$$= \$12{,}000 \text{ per month}$$

Adding these three areas, we find that total consumer surplus after the pizza price ceiling is $A + B + D = \$54{,}000$ per month.

Therefore, consumers *as a group* are better off than they were under the free market: They have $4,000 more of consumer surplus per month. However, this outcome hides a big discrepancy. Those students lucky enough to get in on the 6,000 pizzas for $8 rather than $10 are better off, but there are 4,000 pizzas that would have been available in the free market that are no longer being supplied. Students who would have consumed those missing pizzas are worse off than they were before.

What is the deadweight loss from the inefficiency of this price-controlled market outcome? The full DWL is the area of triangle $C + E$ in the figure, so

$$DWL = \frac{1}{2} \times (\text{free-market quantity} - Q_c^S) \times (P_z - P_c)$$

$$= \frac{1}{2}(10{,}000 - 6{,}000)(\$14 - \$8)$$

$$= \frac{1}{2}(4{,}000)(\$6)$$

$$= \$12{,}000 \text{ per month}$$

The Problem of Deadweight Loss   As we have seen, a price ceiling creates a deadweight loss. This deadweight loss is just that: lost. It's surplus that was formerly earned by consumers (C) or producers (E) that neither gets when there is a price ceiling. This analysis has shown that price ceilings and other mandates and regulations can come with a cost, even if they don't involve any direct payments from consumers or producers the way taxes do.

A natural way to think about the size of the deadweight loss is as a share of the transfer. Because the price control was designed to transfer surplus from pizzerias to students, the deadweight loss tells us how much money gets burned up in the process of transferring surplus through this regulation. In this case, the deadweight loss ($12,000) is just as large as the transfer. In other words, in the process of transferring income from pizzerias to students through the price ceiling, one dollar of surplus is destroyed for every dollar transferred.

This example illustrates the dilemma of using regulations to transfer income. If somehow the city council could get the producers to directly pay the consumers the amount $D - C$ without changing the price, the consumers would be just as happy as with the price control, because that's all they net in the deal after losing the deadweight loss. The producers would be better off as well. Rather than being left with just F, they would have their free-market producer surplus of $D + E + F$ minus their payment of $D - C$. The areas D in these two values cancel, leaving the pizzerias $E + F + C$, which is larger than the F in producer surplus they get under the price ceiling law. Deadweight loss occurs because the price-control regulation transfers income by changing prices, and price changes affect incentives and lead to inefficiency. Practically speaking, though, it's difficult to figure out how to organize the payment of $D - C$ without changing the price. A per pizza subsidy paid by pizzerias to students, for example, would have the same result as reducing the price and would thus have its own deadweight loss, as we describe in Section 3.5.

Importance of Price Elasticities   The elasticities of supply and demand are the keys to the relative sizes of the deadweight loss and the transfer. Consider two different pizza markets in **Figure 3.7**. In panel a, the curves are relatively inelastic and show little price sensitivity. In panel b, the relatively elastic supply and demand curves reflect a greater amount of price sensitivity. It's clear from the figure that if the same price-control rule is applied to both markets, the deadweight loss will be larger as a share of the transfer in the market with more elastic supply and demand.

The intuition behind this result is that the price ceiling's deadweight loss comes about because it keeps a set of sellers and buyers who would be willing to trade in the market at the free-market price from doing so. If the number of people in this set is small (in other words, the quantity after the regulation is close to the quantity before), then the deadweight distortion is small. That magnitude depends on how sensitive supply and demand are to prices. If supply and demand are relatively inelastic, the number of people and firms

Figure 3.7 Deadweight Loss and Elasticities

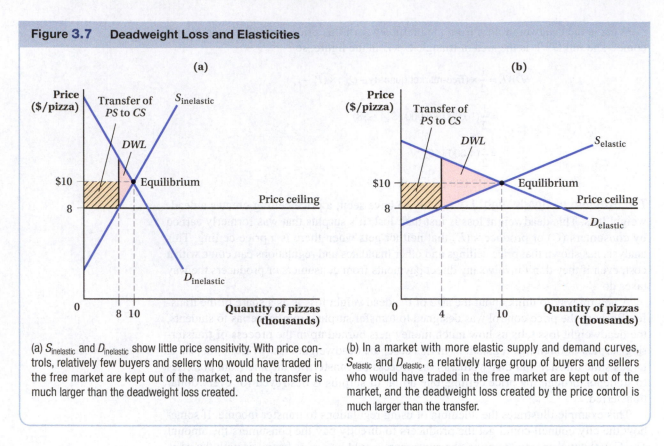

(a)

(b)

(a) $S_{inelastic}$ and $D_{inelastic}$ show little price sensitivity. With price controls, relatively few buyers and sellers who would have traded in the free market are kept out of the market, and the transfer is much larger than the deadweight loss created.

(b) In a market with more elastic supply and demand curves, $S_{elastic}$ and $D_{elastic}$, a relatively large group of buyers and sellers who would have traded in the free market are kept out of the market, and the deadweight loss created by the price control is much larger than the transfer.

changing their quantity demanded or supplied will be small, and the DWL will be small relative to the transfer. If supply and demand are relatively elastic, the number of people and firms who change their quantity demanded or supplied will be large.

Price Floors

price floor (or price support) A price regulation that sets the lowest price that can be paid legally for a good or service.

The other major type of price regulation is a **price floor** (sometimes called a **price support**), *a price regulation that sets the lowest price that can be paid legally for a good or service.*

Lawmakers around the world use price floors to prop up the prices of all sorts of goods and services. Agricultural products are a favorite. In the United States, the federal government began setting price supports for agricultural goods such as milk, corn, wheat, tobacco, and peanuts as early as the 1930s. The goal was to guarantee farmers a minimum price for their crops to protect them from fluctuating prices. Many of these price supports remain today. We will use the tools of consumer and producer surplus to analyze price floors just as we used them for price ceilings.

Let's look at the market for peanuts. The unregulated market for peanuts is shown in **Figure 3.8**. The equilibrium quantity of peanuts is 20 million tons, and the equilibrium price of peanuts is $500 per ton. The government decides that farmers should be getting more than $500 per ton for their peanuts, so it passes a regulation that peanuts must sell for no less than $1,000 per ton.

excess supply The difference between the quantity supplied and the quantity demanded at a price floor.

Immediately, we know there is going to be a problem. At the higher price, peanut farmers want to sell lots of peanuts—30 million tons. But at that price, quantity demanded is much lower—only 10 million tons. (Peanut butter sandwiches are just too expensive when peanuts cost $1,000 per ton.) This imbalance leads to **excess supply** in the

Figure 3.8   The Effects of a Price Floor

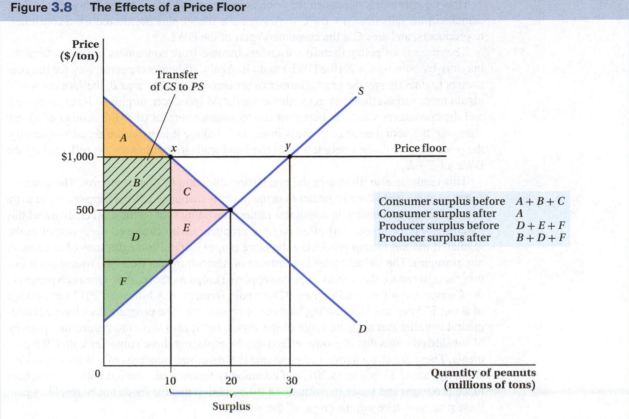

A price floor affects both producer and consumer surpluses. Before price controls in the peanut market, consumers pay $500 per ton, and producers supply 20 million tons of peanuts. Consumer surplus is the triangle $A+B+C$, and producer surplus is $D+E+F$. When a price floor of $1,000 per ton is put in place, peanut farmers supply 30 million tons of peanuts (point y), but consumers demand only 10 million tons of peanuts (point x), creating an excess supply of 20 million tons of peanuts. Consumer surplus is reduced to A. Producer surplus is now $B+D+F$, and the net gain to producers is $B-E$. The deadweight loss is $C+E$.

market: *the difference between the quantity supplied and the quantity demanded at a price floor*. This is indicated in the figure by the 20-million-ton difference between the quantity of peanuts supplied and the quantity demanded at the price floor.

The goal of the price floor policy is to help farmers, so we need to look at the producer surplus to know how well the policy accomplishes its goal. Before the regulation, producer surplus was the area $D+E+F$. After the regulation, prices go up for all the peanut farmers who are still able to find buyers, so producers gain area B as a transfer from consumers. The farmers sell 10 million tons of peanuts and receive $500 per ton more than they were receiving in the free market. But peanut growers lose some of their market. The reduction in quantity demanded from 20 million to 10 million tons knocks out producers who used to sell peanuts at market prices and made a small amount of producer surplus from it. This area E then becomes the producers' part of the deadweight loss (DWL) from the regulation.

Overall, the producers gain surplus of $B-E$. If supply and demand are sufficiently elastic (i.e., if both curves are flat enough), producers could actually be made *worse off* from the price floor that was put in place to help them. This is because area E — the producers' share of the DWL — may be larger than the transfer from consumers, area B. This outcome is another application of our discussion above about how the deadweight loss grows as the supply and demand curves become more elastic.

How do consumers fare when the price floor is enacted? You can probably guess: Consumer surplus falls from $A + B + C$ to A. Area B is the surplus transferred from consumers to producers, and area C is the consumers' part of the DWL.

The price floor policy therefore transfers income from consumers to peanut farmers, but only by burning $C + E$ (the DWL) to do it. Again, if there were some way for the consumers to directly pay the peanut farmers a set amount equal to area B, the farmers would obtain more surplus than they get with the regulation (producer surplus of B versus $B - E$), and the consumers would be better off too (consumer surplus of $A + C$ instead of A). By changing the actual price of peanuts instead of making a transfer unrelated to quantity, the price support distorts people's incentives and leads to inefficiency, as reflected by the DWL of $C + E$.

This analysis also illustrates the everlasting dilemma of price supports. The quantity supplied at the price floor is greater than the quantity demanded. What happens to the extra peanuts? They accumulate in containers rather than being sold on the market. To avoid this outcome, a government will often pay the producers who can't sell their output in the regulated market to *stop* producing the extra output (20 million extra tons of peanuts in our example). The United States Department of Agriculture, for example, oversees various programs to reduce the surplus of price-supported crops on the market. One such program, the Conservation Reserve Program (CRP), paid farmers $1.8 billion in 2017 (an average of about $77 per acre) for holding land out of production. The program does have environmental benefits that mitigate some of the losses, but it also serves to reduce the quantity of subsidized crops that is grown, effectively by replacing those subsidies with CRP payments. There are also a number of programs that distribute hundreds of millions of dollars annually (about $1 billion in 2017) of commodity foods—like peanut butter—to school lunch programs and needy individuals on the condition that the foods not be resold. Again, these programs take surplus crops off the market.

Another example of a price support is a minimum wage. Here, the "product" is labor and the "price" is the wage, but the analysis is the same. If the government tries to help college students save tuition money by mandating that all summer internships pay at least $40 an hour, the quantity of labor supplied for internships will be much greater than the quantity demanded. As a result, there will be a lot of unemployed intern-hopefuls who would have been working at the equilibrium wage.

Just as with our earlier examples, how many people a minimum wage adds to the number of unemployed (the excess quantity supplied in the price floor figure), the amount of income transferred to workers (the change in producer surplus), and the size of the deadweight loss all depend on the elasticity of labor supply and labor demand. The price floor's deadweight loss arises because a set of sellers and buyers who would be willing to trade in the market at the free-market price will not do so at the regulated price. When suppliers and demanders are relatively insensitive to price, the number of transactions that the price floor prevents from happening is relatively small, and therefore so is the deadweight loss. Large price elasticities imply a large number of destroyed transactions and a large deadweight loss relative to the transfer of income. If a price floor is set below the free-market equilibrium price, it is nonbinding, and will have no effect on the market, and will not create excess supply or deadweight loss.

3.3 Quantity Regulations

Sometimes, rather than regulating prices, governments impose quantity regulations. We discuss some of these regulations and analyze their effects on market outcomes in this section.

Quotas

A **quota** is *a regulation that sets the quantity of a good or service provided.* Quotas are occasionally used to force firms to produce a certain amount of a good (say, a vaccine in preparation for a flu epidemic), but more often they limit the amount of a good.

For example, countries wanting to limit imports but not wanting to publicly announce tariffs (taxes on imports) might put a quota on imports. The U.S. government imposes quotas on the amount of sugar that can be imported from various countries, for example.[6] In other circumstances, a government may limit the amount of fish people can catch or the production of milk.[7] France limits the amount of U.S. television shows that can be broadcast on TV. Singapore limits the number of cars that people can buy. London's Heathrow Airport limits the number of direct flights from U.S. airports. Zoning laws impose another type of quota. Most towns have zoning laws that limit what construction can take place in a certain area, such as limiting the number of tattoo parlors.

Let's consider as an example the impact of a quota on the amount of tattoo services that can be provided in the fictional town of River City, where a concerned town council wants to limit tattoos. Suppose the city's demand curve for tattoos is $Q_d = 2,500 - 20P$, and the supply curve is $Q_s = 100P - 3,500$, where the quantities demanded and supplied are both measured in the number of tattoos per year. We can analyze the effects of a quota on price and quantity by using graphs or equations.

Graphical Analysis In the free market, the equilibrium quantity of tattoos supplied and demanded in River City is 1,500 tattoos per year at a price of $50 per tattoo (**Figure 3.9**).

Suppose that River City's mayor believes tattoo shops are a blight on society, decides that people should get no more than 500 tattoos in a year in the city, and enforces this quota by requiring everyone who wants a tattoo to buy a tattoo permit before being inked.

The quota creates a regulatory bend in the supply curve so that it becomes vertical at the quantity of 500. In other words, no matter what the price of tattoos is, parlors cannot supply more than 500. When this happens, the supply curve becomes perfectly inelastic at 500, making the new supply curve S_2 look like the red line in Figure 3.9. Now the demand curve intersects supply at point z rather than at point x, and the price rises from $50 to $100. Consumer surplus falls from area $A + B + C$ to area A, which is the only area below the demand curve and above the post-quota price P_{quota}. The post-quota producer surplus is above the supply curve and below the new price. This area $B + D + F$ includes a surplus transfer B from consumers to producers. The area $C + E$ is the deadweight loss.

Analysis Using Equations The equilibrium price is the price that exists when quantity supplied equals quantity demanded:

$$Q^D = Q^S$$
$$2,500 - 20P = 100P - 3,500$$

quota A regulation that sets the quantity of a good or service provided.

---

[6] Legally, the current sugar quotas aren't completely binding. If a country goes over its quota allocation, it can still export sugar to the United States, but it must pay an additional tariff to do so. In practice, however, this tariff is so high that it all but eliminates shipments beyond the quota allocation.

[7] As we will see in Chapter 17 when we discuss externalities, governments may have their reasons for limiting the production of certain goods. For now, we just want to know what effects quotas have in a standard market situation.

Figure 3.9   The Effects of a Quota

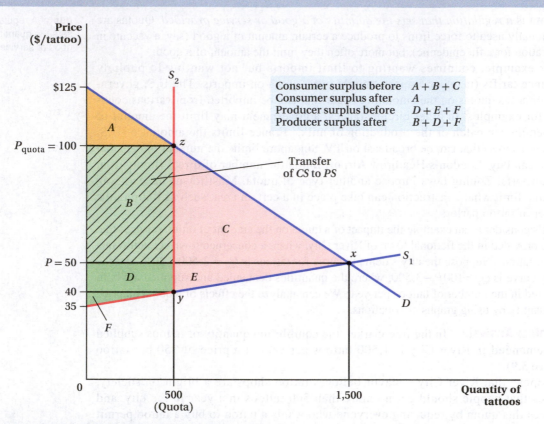

Consumer surplus before	$A + B + C$
Consumer surplus after	A
Producer surplus before	$D + E + F$
Producer surplus after	$B + D + F$

In the free market for tattoos in River City, producers supply 1,500 tattoos per year at a price of $50 per tattoo at the equilibrium (point x). Consumer surplus is $A + B + C$, and producer surplus is $D + E + F$. After the mayor of River City enacts a law requiring a permit to get a tattoo, the supply for tattoos becomes vertical at the quantity of 500 tattoos. At the new equilibrium (point z), producers supply 500 tattoos at the increased price of $100 per tattoo. Consumer surplus is reduced to A. Producer surplus is $B + D + F$, and the net gain to producers is $B - E$. The deadweight loss is $C + E$.

Solving for P and Q, we find

$$P = \$50$$
$$Q^D = 2{,}500 - 20(50) = 1{,}500 \quad \text{or} \quad Q^S = 100(50) - 3{,}500 = 1{,}500$$

At the free-market equilibrium price and quantity, the consumer surplus is

$$CS = \frac{1}{2} \times (\text{base}) \times (\text{height})$$

$$= \frac{1}{2} \times Q \times (P_{D\text{Choke}} - P)$$

The demand choke price $P_{D\text{Choke}}$ is the price at which $Q^D = 0$, which in this case is

$$Q^D = 2{,}500 - 20(P_{D\text{Choke}}) = 0$$
$$20 P_{D\text{Choke}} = 2{,}500$$
$$P_{D\text{Choke}} = \$125$$

Consumer surplus is therefore

$$CS = \frac{1}{2} \times Q \times (P_{DChoke} - P)$$

$$= \left(\frac{1}{2}\right)(1,500)(\$125 - \$50)$$

$$= (750)(\$75) = \$56,250$$

The producer surplus is the triangle $D + E + F$ in the graph. That triangle's area is

$$PS = \frac{1}{2} \times Q \times (P - P_{SChoke})$$

The supply choke price P_{SChoke} is the price at which quantity supplied is zero:

$$Q^S = 100(P_{SChoke}) - 3,500 = 0$$

$$P_{SChoke} = 3,500/100 = \$35$$

Producer surplus in the unregulated tattoo market is then

$$PS = \frac{1}{2} \times Q \times (P - P_{SChoke})$$

$$= \frac{1}{2} \times 1,500 \times (\$50 - \$35)$$

$$= (750)(\$15) = \$11,250$$

After the 500-tattoo quota is implemented, the supply curve is the same up to $Q_S = 500$, at which point it becomes perfectly inelastic (point y). The equilibrium price will be

$$Q^S = Q^D$$

$$500 = 2,500 - 20P_{quota}$$

$$P_{quota} = \$100$$

At this price, the consumer surplus is the area A:

$$CS = \frac{1}{2} \times Q_{quota} \times (P_{DChoke} - P_{quota})$$

$$= \left(\frac{1}{2}\right)(500)(\$125 - \$100)$$

$$= (250)(\$25) = \$6,250$$

This is dramatically reduced from the free-market surplus of $56,250. Sorry, River City tattoo fans.

The producer surplus is measured by the areas $B + D + F$. We can break out each of these areas separately:

$$\text{Area } F = \frac{1}{2} \times Q_{quota} \times (\text{price at point } y - P_{SChoke})$$

The price at point y is the price at which the quantity supplied is equal to the quota. It can be determined by setting $Q^S = 500$ and solving for P:

$$Q^S = 100(\text{price at point } y) - 3,500 = 500$$

$$100(\text{price at point } y) = 4,000$$

$$\text{Price at point } y = 4,000/100 = \$40$$

So, this means

$$\text{Area } F = \frac{1}{2} \times 500 \times (\$40 - \$35) = \$1,250$$

The rectangle B is

$$\text{Area } B = Q_{\text{quota}} \times (P_{\text{quota}} - P)$$
$$= 500(\$100 - \$50) = \$25,000$$

and the rectangle D is

$$\text{Area } D = Q_{\text{quota}} \times (P - \text{price at point } y)$$
$$= 500(\$50 - \$40) = \$5,000$$

Thus, the total producer surplus equals $F + B + D = \$31,250$.

Let's compare the quota outcomes to those of the free, unregulated River City tattoo market. Consumers are much worse off after the quota because their surplus has fallen from $56,250 to only $6,250. This decrease reflects, in part, the losses of the additional 1,000 people who would be willing to get a tattoo in River City in a free market but cannot with the quota in place. However, the loss in consumer surplus also reflects the fact that the quota increases the price of tattoos even for those people who get one. This price increase shrinks the gap between what they are willing to pay for the tattoo and the price they actually have to pay.

On the supply side, the tattoo parlors do just fine. They lose the producer surplus in area E when the quota is imposed, but the quantity restriction leads to much higher prices for their output—they get a huge transfer from consumers (area B), which makes their total producer surplus $31,250 under the quota instead of $11,250 without it. This gain could explain why the tattoo parlors may not complain about an ordinance that would reduce the total number of tattoos they could sell, although a non-economist might expect they would.

The quantity-restricting quota drives up the price of tattoos. In doing this, the quota transfers a bunch of surplus from tattoo buyers to tattoo parlors and creates a significant amount of deadweight loss (area $C + E$, which based on our calculations above totals $25,000 + $5,000 = $30,000$).

This analysis took on real-world relevance in 2019 when New York City imposed a quota on the number of ride-share drivers within city limits at companies like Uber and Lyft. Nominally, they applied the quota to reduce the amount of traffic and improve the quality of life for residents. The basic model suggests, though, that the main impact would be on the prices consumers will have to pay for rides. In fact, taxi companies lobbied hard for the rule, and it's easy to see why.

3.4 Taxes

Governments at all levels (local, state, federal) tax all kinds of things, and they do it in different ways. Sometimes, suppliers pay the tax. Stores in the United States collect sales taxes and send them to state revenue agencies, for example, just as producers in Canada and Europe collect and remit value-added tax (VAT). Sometimes the legal burden for collecting the tax falls on consumers, like "use taxes" that states levy on purchases their residents make in other states. In still other cases, the legal burden is shared. For instance, half of the U.S. federal payroll tax (which funds the Social Security and Medicare programs) is paid by employers before workers get their wages, and the other half is paid by workers through a deduction from their wages.

In this section, we use the supply and demand model to show a striking finding of economics: In a competitive market, it doesn't matter whether the buyer or the seller is required by law to actually pay the tax; the impact on consumers and producers is the same either way. The government could change the law to make consumers pay the sales tax instead of sellers, or to make employers pay the entire payroll tax. In a competitive market, nothing would change. The total impact of a tax on consumers and sellers depends only on the steepness of the supply and demand curves, not who has to pay. Before we can understand why this is true, however, we first need to look at how taxes affect a market.

Tax Effects on Markets

We start with a market that is in equilibrium and has no taxes, the market for movie tickets in Boston, Massachusetts. In the early 2000s, the mayor of Boston proposed adding a 50-cent tax to movie tickets to help balance a budget deficit. Many thought he proposed the tax because a large number of moviegoers in Boston are college students who live in the Greater Boston area but who are not Boston voters. Regardless of the motivation, if it had been enacted (the legislature killed the idea), the tax would have required theater owners to pay 50 cents per ticket to the government. Let's look at how such a change would affect the market for movie tickets using both graphs and equations.

Graphical Analysis   With no taxes, solving the model our usual way gives a free-market equilibrium price P_1 and quantity Q_1 and the resulting consumer and producer surpluses (**Figure 3.10**).

Figure 3.10   Effect of a Tax on Boston Movie Tickets

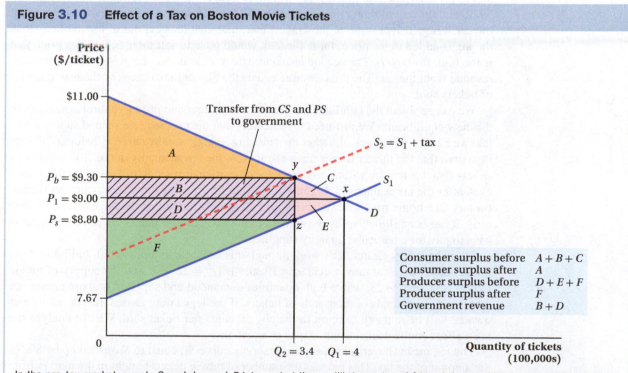

Consumer surplus before	$A + B + C$
Consumer surplus after	A
Producer surplus before	$D + E + F$
Producer surplus after	F
Government revenue	$B + D$

In the pre-tax market, supply S_1 and demand D intersect at the equilibrium price of $9 and the equilibrium quantity of 400,000 movie tickets. The consumer surplus is $A + B + C$, and the producer surplus is $D + E + F$. The addition of the $0.50 tax per movie ticket results in an upward shift of the supply curve from S_1 to S_2 by the amount of the tax and decreases the equilibrium quantity to 340,000 tickets. The resulting tax wedge creates two prices: $9.30, the price the buyer faces, and $8.80, the price the seller actually receives. The new consumer surplus is A, and the producer surplus is F. Area $B + D$ is government tax revenue, while area $C + E$ is the deadweight loss.

The tax is much like a 50-cent-per-ticket increase in the theaters' costs. We know from Chapter 2 that increases in production costs cause suppliers to supply a smaller quantity at any given price. Therefore, in response to the tax, the supply curve shifts up by the amount of the tax (50 cents) to S_2, and the equilibrium quantity of movie tickets sold falls to Q_2.[8]

But, taxes do something different from a typical supply shift: They drive a wedge between the price buyers pay (the market price) and the price that producers actually receive (the market price minus the tax). With a normal supply curve, the price at any point on the supply curve is the price a producer receives for selling its product. With a tax, the product sells for the price P_b (we denote the price the buyers pay with a "b"), but the sellers only receive P_s (we denote the price the seller receives with an "s"). This is the buyers' price minus the tax: $P_s = P_b - \text{tax}$. In other words, the buyers have to pay 50 cents more for any quantity, but the movie theaters don't get to keep the extra money — they receive only the higher price minus the tax.

Because of this wedge, the new equilibrium in the Boston movie market involves *two* prices. The first, point y, is the price ($9.30) the buyers pay at the theater that includes the 50-cent tax. Thus, $9.30 is the market price. The second, point z, is the price ($8.80) that the suppliers receive after taking the 50 cents out of the higher market price and sending it to the government.

There are two key things to note about the post-tax market equilibrium. First, the price of movie tickets increases, but not by the full 50 cents of the tax. You can see this in Figure 3.10. The size of the tax is reflected in the vertical distance between P_b ($9.30) and P_s ($8.80). The rise in the price of movie tickets, however, is the distance between $9.30 and the equilibrium price with no tax, $9.00. The reason for this discrepancy is that the tax wedge drives some of the highest marginal-cost theaters out of the market: Once the tax is added to the price, these theaters would have to sell their tickets at a price that is too high for buyers. The second characteristic to note is that the government generates revenue from the tax. The total revenue equals the 50-cent tax times Q_2, the new quantity of tickets sold.

We can apply all the familiar concepts from consumer and producer surplus analysis to this new equilibrium. We just need to remember that the tax creates a second supply curve that we have to keep track of, rather than moving a single supply curve as before. The supply curve that the theater owner cares about is S_1, the initial supply curve. The number of tickets that theaters are willing to supply at any particular price is still given by this curve, even after the tax is imposed, because the level of S_1 reflects the after-tax dollars theater owners take home from selling tickets. But the supply curve that the buyers actually face is S_2. It has been shifted up by the amount of the tax, because that is the price moviegoers have to pay for a particular quantity supplied.

To make things clearer, let's work through this example in more detail. In Figure 3.10, the demand curve for movie tickets in Boston is $Q^D = 22 - 2P$ and the supply of movie tickets is $Q^S = 3P - 23$, where both quantities demanded and supplied in these curves are measured in hundreds of thousands of tickets. If the legislature passes the tax, all theater owners will be required to remit to the city 50 cents per ticket sold. We can analyze the tax's effect on the market using graphs or equations.

The tax means buyers now face a new supply curve S_2, equal to S_1 shifted up by $0.50, the amount of the tax. This reduces the number of movie tickets bought in the market from 400,000 to 340,000. At that quantity, the price the buyers are paying rises from $9.00 to $9.30. Because the law requires suppliers (the theater owners) to pay the government a

---

[8] A tax expressed in percentage terms, such as a sales tax of 6%, is called an *ad valorem* tax (as opposed to a *specific tax* that is a set dollar amount, like the 50 cents per ticket here). An ad valorem tax version of this tax would shift the supply curve, but not by a fixed amount at every point. Instead, it would rotate the curve by a fixed percent around the point at which quantity supplied is zero.

50-cent tax for every ticket they sell, the suppliers don't get to keep $9.30; they get to keep only $8.80 = $9.30 − 0.50.

What happens to consumer and producer surplus changes after the tax. The new consumer surplus is smaller than before. In the no-tax market, consumer surplus was $A + B + C$. Now it is only A, the area below the demand curve but above the price that the buyers have to pay, $9.30.

The new producer surplus is also smaller than before. Before the tax, it was $D + E + F$. After the tax, it is only F, the area above the supply curve and below the price that the suppliers receive after they pay the tax, $8.80.

Imposing the tax reduces total producer and consumer surplus from area $(A + B + C) + (D + E + F)$ to just area $A + F$. Where has the surplus in areas B, C, D, and E gone? The area $B + D$ is no longer consumer *or* producer surplus; it is government tax revenue, the tax times the quantity sold after the tax is implemented. With a tax, there is no surplus transfer between producers and consumers, as we saw in earlier examples. Instead, both producers and consumers transfer some of their surpluses to the government. This tax revenue is then "returned" to consumers and producers in the form of government services, so it is not lost.

Areas C and E are the deadweight loss from the tax. They are surpluses that moviegoers and theater owners formerly got from buying and selling tickets at the competitive price. This surplus is gone now because consumers buy fewer tickets at the higher post-tax price and sellers supply fewer tickets at their lower post-tax price.

Just as in the price regulation cases, a natural way to look at the size of the deadweight loss is as a fraction of the surplus transfer. Beforehand, that transfer occurred from producers to consumers (for a price ceiling) or from consumers to producers (for a price floor). Now, it's from both to the government. The ratio in this case is the area $C + E$ to the area $B + D$, which is the DWL as a share of revenue.

Analysis Using Equations   The demand curve for movie tickets in Boston is $Q^D = 22 - 2P$ and the supply of movie tickets is $Q^S = 3P - 23$, where both quantities demanded and supplied in these curves are measured in hundreds of thousands of tickets. The no-tax market equilibrium equates quantity demanded and quantity supplied:

$$Q^D = Q^S$$
$$22 - 2P = 3P - 23$$
$$5P = 45$$
$$P_1 = 45/5 = \$9 \text{ per ticket}$$
$$Q^D = 22 - 2(\$9) = 4 \quad \text{or} \quad Q^S = 3(\$9) - 23 = 4$$

Therefore, before the tax, the equilibrium price is $9 and 400,000 tickets are sold.

The pre-tax consumer surplus is the triangle above the price and below the demand curve, as shown in Figure 3.10:

$$CS = \frac{1}{2} \times Q \times (P_{DChoke} - P_1)$$

Again, the choke price is found by determining the price that pushes the quantity demanded to zero:

$$Q^D = 22 - 2P_{DChoke} = 0$$
$$P_{DChoke} = \$11$$

In other words, this demand curve says that if tickets cost $11, no one will go to theaters in the city of Boston (perhaps because theaters in the suburbs are an attractive alternative).

Plugging the demand choke price into the *CS* formula gives a consumer surplus of

$$CS = \frac{1}{2}(400{,}000)(\$11 - \$9)$$
$$= \$400{,}000$$

The producer surplus is the triangle above the supply curve and below the price:

$$PS = \frac{1}{2} \times Q \times (P_1 - P_{SChoke})$$

The supply choke price is the price that moves quantity supplied to zero:

$$Q^S = 3P_{SChoke} - 23 = 0$$
$$P_{SChoke} = \$7.67$$

That is, at any price below $7.67 a ticket, no theaters would operate in Boston. Plugging this supply choke price into the *PS* formula gives a producer surplus of

$$PS = \frac{1}{2}(400{,}000)(\$9 - \$7.67)$$
$$= \$266{,}667$$

What happens to consumer and producer surplus under the mayor's 50-cent tax? Theaters must pay the state for each ticket they sell. This creates a dual-supply-curve situation. The supply curve for the theater owners is the same as the initial supply curve. The theater is still willing to supply whatever number of tickets the supply curve says at the market price. But now, the supply curve buyers face is shifted up by the amount of the tax: At each quantity, the tickets supplied to consumers now cost $0.50 more. The difference between the supply curve that the buyers face and the supply curve that the sellers face is the amount of the tax. In words, the theaters' supply curve says they would be willing to sell 400,000 tickets if they receive $9 per ticket (after the tax gets paid), but for theaters to get $9 per ticket, buyers would actually have to pay $9.50 per ticket because $0.50 of the tax needs to be paid out of the price received by the theaters. The prices that result for both the buyer and the seller are summed up in the equation $P_b = P_s + \$0.50$.

To solve for the post-tax quantity and prices, we substitute this expression, which links the two supply prices in our supply and demand equations:

$$Q^D = Q^S$$
$$22 - 2P_b = 3P_s - 23$$
$$22 - 2(P_s + 0.50) = 3P_s - 23$$
$$22 - 2P_s - 1 = 3P_s - 23$$
$$5P_s = 44$$
$$P_s = 44/5 = \$8.80$$

Therefore, the buyers face the following price:

$$P_b = P_s + 0.50 = \$8.80 + 0.50 = \$9.30$$

Now if we plug the buyers' price into the demand curve equation and the sellers' price into the supply curve equation, they will both give the same after-tax market quantity:

$$Q_2 = 22 - 2(9.30) = 3.4 \qquad \text{or} \qquad Q_2 = 3(8.80) - 23 = 3.4$$

Only 340,000 tickets will be sold once the tax is put into place.

The consumer surplus after a tax is the area below the demand curve but above the price that the buyers pay:

$$CS = \frac{1}{2}(340{,}000)(\$11.00 - \$9.30)$$
$$= \$289{,}000$$

The producer surplus is the area above the supply curve and below the price that the suppliers receive:

$$PS = \frac{1}{2}(340{,}000)(\$8.80 - \$7.67)$$
$$= \$192{,}667$$

(We've rounded $7.67 to the nearest cent above.)

So, the tax makes consumer surplus fall by $111,000 and producer surplus fall by $74,000 from their values in the no-tax market equilibrium. Some of that $185,000 in lost surplus flows to the government in the form of revenue from the tax, however. That revenue is equal to $0.50 per ticket times the number of tickets sold after the tax, or

$$\text{Revenue} = \$0.50 Q_2$$
$$= \$0.50(340{,}000) = \$170{,}000$$

Notice that the total amount of the lost surplus, $185,000, is more than the amount of revenue that the government generated, $170,000. The difference of $15,000 is the deadweight loss of the tax.

A different way to calculate DWL is to compute the area of the triangle whose base is the change in quantity and whose height is the amount of the tax:

$$DWL = \frac{1}{2} \times (Q_1 - Q_2) \times (P_b - P_s) = \frac{1}{2} \times (Q_1 - Q_2) \times \text{tax}$$
$$= \frac{1}{2}(400{,}000 - 340{,}000)(\$0.50) = \$15{,}000$$

That's about 9% of the revenue generated by the tax. In other words, this tax burns up about $1 of surplus in DWL for every $11 of revenue it generates.

Why Taxes Create a Deadweight Loss

Just as we showed in the case of price and quantity regulations, the main determinant of the DWL from a tax as a share of the revenue it generates is how much the quantity changes when the tax is added. The size of that change depends, in turn, on how sensitive supply and demand are to prices. The deadweight loss from pizza price controls, for example, came from consumers and suppliers who would like to trade at market prices and who would have earned surplus from doing so, but were prevented from engaging in these transactions by the price ceiling. With taxes, there are no forbidden transactions. The source of the deadweight loss is the same, however: People who would have bought tickets at the market price without a tax and would have gained some surplus from doing so but don't buy after the tax raises the prices too high. They get to keep their money, but they were previously able to buy something with it that gave them surplus. Likewise, movie theaters lose surplus because some would have shown movies at the pre-tax market price but find the after-tax price too low to justify operating. These lost surpluses are the DWL of the tax.

FREAKONOMICS

Unintended Consequences of a Tax on Garbage

South Norfolk is an idyllic area nestled in the eastern part of England. If you happened to visit after 2005, though, amidst the charming villages, cattle grazing in the fields, the occasional castle on a hill, you would have seen huge piles of garbage (the British call it "rubbish") strewn haphazardly along the side of the road.

It's not that South Norfolkians at that time were filthy slobs. Something else had gone terribly wrong. The government used simple economic tools to fight a problem. And those tools worked. Too well.

Collecting trash is the government's responsibility, and there is a cost associated with collecting trash and putting it in landfills. Governments usually pay for this cost by charging their citizens lump-sum fees; one payment buys any amount of trash removal someone needs, large or small. As a result of this practice of not taxing trash on the margin, people don't pay the full cost of the garbage they produce, and they sometimes produce too much. The obvious economic solution is to charge people by the amount of trash they generate. And this is exactly what the South Norfolk District Council aimed to do when it initiated the trial run of a new garbage pricing policy in 2005. The local government placed microchips in garbage bins, with plans to tax citizens by the weight of trash in the bins as measured by the microchips.

South Norfolk citizens soon realized that they could get around the potential tax by *fly-tipping,* that is, by throwing bags of trash out their car window while driving. Fly-tipping increased over 250% once the trial started. The District Council ended its trial in frustration. Other geographic locations, such as Charlottesville, Virginia, have experimented with a per-bag tax on trash, and in those jurisdictions, the number of bags of garbage produced plummeted by 37%, consistent with economic theory. But the pounds of trash collected only fell 14%. People had simply stuffed more in each bag they threw out. This is not such a bad result . . . it reduces government revenue, but doesn't cause any other problems.

Evasion of a trash tax doesn't always proceed so smoothly, however. Ireland recently introduced a pay-as-you-throw-away tax, and some people decided to try and avoid the tax by burning their trash. We know this because after the trash tax was imposed, the number of emergency room visits for burns sustained while lighting backyard fires more than doubled![*]

The broader lesson: People react strongly to strong incentives. They change their behavior not only in the way you want them to, but also in all sorts of other ways that you might prefer they don't. One of the characteristics that distinguishes good economic analysis from not-so-good analysis is thinking through all the different ways in which behavior might be affected when an incentive changes. So when you call for the next great rule, remember the piles of garbage alongside the roads of South Norfolk and imagine what kind of surprising, devious actions might be the response to your grand plans.

[*] S. M. Murphy, C. Davidson, A. M. Kennedy, P. A. Eadie, and C. Lawlor, "Backyard Burning," *Journal of Plastic, Reconstructive & Aesthetic Surgery* 61, no. 2 (2008): 180–182.

© roger ashford/Alamy

Fly-tipped garbage on a South Norfolk road.

Why a Big Tax Is Much Worse Than a Small Tax

An interesting result of this analysis is that it implies the inefficiency represented by the size of the deadweight loss gets much bigger as the size of a tax becomes larger. In the movie ticket tax example (Figure 3.10), we saw that the DWL from the tax was area $C + E$ and that the revenue generated was $B + D$. What would happen if the mayor decided to *increase* the ticket tax? How much more revenue and how much more DWL would this tax increase create?

Figure 3.11 illustrates the outcome for a general case. The larger tax reduces the quantity even further, from Q_2 to Q_3. In fact, if taxes become high enough, the increase in

Figure 3.11   The Effect of a Larger Tax on Boston Movie Tickets

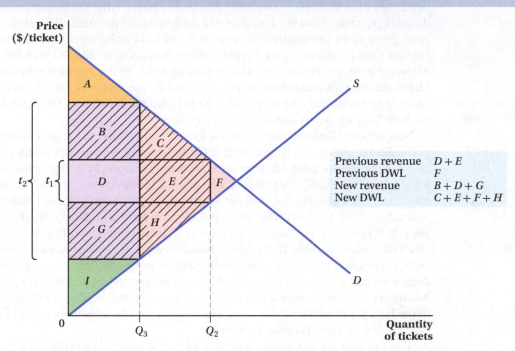

Previous revenue	$D + E$
Previous DWL	F
New revenue	$B + D + G$
New DWL	$C + E + F + H$

After an increase in the tax on movie tickets in Boston from t_1 to t_2, the tax wedge between the price consumers pay and the price movie theaters receive increases, while the quantity of movie tickets at the equilibrium (Q_3) decreases. Government revenue, which was area $D + E$ with a smaller tax, is now area $B + D + G$. However, the government loses area E, because some people stop buying movie tickets after the tax is raised. If we look at the DWL as a share of the revenue generated, it is clear that the *incremental* revenue generated by increasing this tax causes more inefficiency than the smaller tax did. Initially, the DWL was F, with a revenue gain of $D + E$. But the incremental DWL here is $C + E + H$, while the revenue gain is only $B + G - E$.

revenue per ticket from the tax will be more than offset by the reduction in the quantity of tickets sold, and there will be no revenue gain at all!

A general rule-of-thumb is that the DWL of a tax rises with the square of the tax rate.[9] That is, doubling the tax rate quadruples the DWL. All else equal, taxing 10 things at a low rate is better than taxing 5 things at zero and 5 things at a high rate. Because DWL rises with the square of the tax rate, the overall DWL will be larger with the 5 high rates than with the 10 low rates.

The Incidence of Taxation: The Payer Doesn't Matter

An important thing to note about the movie ticket example is that although we supposed that it would be the theater owners who were legally obligated to pay the 50 cents per ticket tax to the City of Boston, they don't bear the complete burden of the tax. Before the

[9] To see where this intuition comes from, notice that with linear supply and demand curves, the DWL from a tax is a triangle, with a height equal to the quantity reduction caused by the tax and a base equal to the tax. Because the supply and demand curves are linear, the quantity reduction is proportional to the tax. Specifically, it will be $\Delta Q = A * t$, where A is some number that depends on the slope of the demand and supply curves. Therefore, the area of the DWL triangle is $\frac{1}{2} * A * t * t = \frac{1}{2} * A * t^2$. This area is proportional to the square of the tax. For nonlinear demand and supply curves, this formula is only an approximation, but if they aren't too nonlinear, the intuition remains the same.

tax was introduced, the theater owners received $9 per ticket and moviegoers paid $9 a ticket. After the $0.50 tax, moviegoers pay $9.30 a ticket. After the theater owners submit their tax payment, however, they only end up with $8.80 per ticket. Therefore, of the 50 cents going to the government, 30 cents (60%) of it is coming out of consumers' pockets because their price went up by 30 cents. Movie theaters send along a check for taxes due to the government, but they are able to pass on much of that tax to consumers through higher prices. This means that the price realized by the suppliers goes down by only 20 cents. *Who* really *bears the burden of a tax* is called **tax incidence**. The incidence of this tax is 60% on the buyers and 40% on the suppliers.

tax incidence Who *really* bears the burden of a tax.

Now let's say Boston changed the rule for who pays the tax to the government. Instead of the theater sending the tax payment to the government, moviegoers would pay the tax, after buying their ticket at whatever price the theater charges, by dropping the money into a box labeled "TAXES." This changes who physically pays the tax. It does not alter the tax incidence. The equations below show why. In the tax formula, it doesn't matter whether you subtract the tax from what the supplier receives or add the tax to what the buyer pays. $P_s = P_b - \text{tax}$ is the same as $P_s + \text{tax} = P_b$. Having moviegoers drop 50 cents in a box when they attend a movie shifts their demand curves down by that amount. Given such a shift, the supplier has to charge less for the tickets to find the price that equates quantity demanded and supplied (now $8.80). Just as in the case where the theaters paid the tax, moviegoers end up paying a total of $9.30 to take in the movie. They've dropped 50 cents in the box, but effectively 20 cents of that tax was paid by theaters because of the lower market-clearing (pre-tax) price for tickets.

You can also see this same scenario at play in a graph. The original case where the theater pays the tax is shown in **Figure 3.12a**. When the buyers instead pay the tax, their quantity demanded depends on the full price, including the tax. But the price suppliers receive at this quantity demanded is only the price without the tax. To account for this

---

Figure 3.12   Tax Incidence

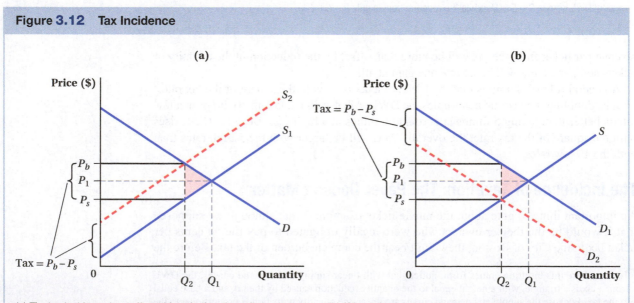

(a) The tax incidence is unaffected by whether the seller or buyer pays the tax. When the seller pays the tax, the supply curve shifts upward by the amount of the tax, $P_b - P_s$, from S_1 to S_2. The equilibrium quantity decreases from Q_1 to Q_2. The seller now faces price P_s at the equilibrium, while the buyer pays price P_b.

(b) When the buyer pays the tax, the demand curve shifts downward by the amount of the tax, $P_b - P_s$, from D_1 to D_2. The equilibrium quantity decreases from Q_1 to Q_2. As in panel a, the seller now faces price P_s at the equilibrium, while the buyer pays price P_b.

A⁺ make the grade

Did I measure deadweight loss correctly?

A few simple tricks will help you nail problems involving deadweight loss. First, whenever the quantity consumed falls as a result of a government policy, a deadweight loss occurs. (This isn't *exactly* correct; if externalities are present, government policies can actually improve market outcomes. We will learn more about externalities in Chapter 17.) If the quantity doesn't become distorted, no deadweight loss occurs. Second, the deadweight loss almost always takes the shape of a triangle, and moreover, that triangle points at the efficient market equilibrium with no market distortion. Why? Because deadweight loss measures the consumer and producer surplus destroyed. As we have seen, this loss in surplus grows as we move further and further away from the efficient equilibrium. The growing distance between the sides of the triangle reflects this fact.

difference, we shift down the demand curve by the amount of the tax, from D_1 to D_2 in Figure 3.12b. But the result hasn't changed: Quantity demanded is still Q_2, and the difference between the buyers' price and the sellers' price still equals the amount of the tax. Thus, the incidence of a tax does not depend on who is legally bound to pay it.

That's why a helpful way to picture taxes on a graph is to just forget about whether the tax is moving the supply curve up or the demand curve down. Instead, start from the initial no-tax equilibrium point and move left until the vertical space between the supply and demand curves is the amount of the tax. This gives you the right answer regardless of whether the tax is being legally applied to suppliers or buyers.

This point about tax incidence is fundamental. In almost all countries of the world, the government imposes payroll taxes on workers' wages. In the United States, it collects them to pay for Social Security and Medicare, but the rates are split evenly between workers and employers. In other words, if you earn wages of $1,000, you have to pay 7.65% of that in payroll taxes and the employer has to pay another 7.65% on its own.[10] Some people propose switching things so that employers would pay the 15.3% and workers would pay nothing. Others say only workers, not employers, should pay taxes. The analyses we've just completed suggest that such changes wouldn't make any difference. In a competitive market, the wage would adjust to the same level regardless of which side of the market is legally bound to pay the tax.

It turns out the only thing that matters about the economic effects of this tax is how elastic the supply and the demand for labor are. To see why, consider the two extremes.

Relatively Elastic Demand with Relatively Inelastic Supply   In a market characterized by relatively elastic demand and inelastic supply, buyers are very sensitive to price and the suppliers are not. Most labor economists tend to think of the labor market in this way: Labor supply is fairly inelastic (people work the same amount at different wage levels) and firms' demand for labor is fairly elastic. This market is illustrated in **Figure 3.13a**.

Applying the methods we've used throughout this section, we see that a payroll tax would be borne almost entirely by the workers—they are the supply curve of labor. With a tax, employers have to pay wages W_b that are a bit higher than wages without the tax, W_1. But after taxes, the workers receive a wage W_s that is much less than W_1. Therefore, workers are a lot worse off after the tax than employers. And we know from the discussion we just had on tax incidence that even if the government switched the payroll tax rules so that employers paid the entire amount, workers would not do any better. Their wages would fall almost as much as the employers' tax went up.

---

[10] FICA taxes apply only to "earned" income like wages and salaries. In 2017 the Social Security tax applied to the first $128,400 of wages per person. After that, only the Medicare part of the tax applied (that rate is 2.9% plus a 0.9% surcharge above a threshold income level). The limit is subject to increases from year to year, typically at a rate tied to inflation.

Figure 3.13 Tax Incidence and Elasticities

(a)

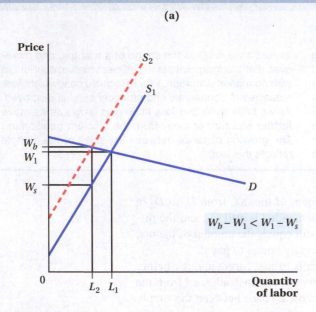

(b)

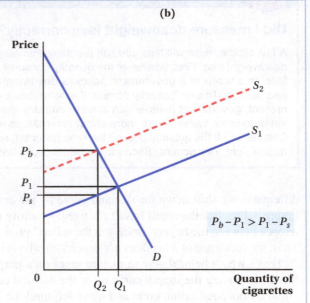

(a) In a labor market where demand is elastic and supply inelastic, we begin with supply curve S_1, demand D, and equilibrium price and quantity (W_1, L_1). The implementation of the tax, $W_b - W_s$, shifts the supply curve upward from S_1 to S_2 and decreases the equilibrium quantity of labor from L_1 to L_2. Because laborers in this market are not very sensitive to price and employers are, the effect of the tax on the wages laborers receive is much larger than its effect on the wage employers pay, $W_b - W_1 < W_1 - W_s$.

(b) In the market for cigarettes where demand is inelastic and supply elastic, we begin with supply curve S_1, demand D, and equilibrium price and quantity (P_1, Q_1). The implementation of the tax, $P_b - P_s$, shifts the supply curve upward from S_1 to S_2 and decreases the equilibrium quantity of cigarettes from Q_1 to Q_2. Because smokers in this market are not very sensitive to price and cigarette companies are, the effect of the tax on the price consumers pay is much larger than its effect on the price companies receive, $P_b - P_1 > P_1 - P_s$.

Relatively Inelastic Demand with Relatively Elastic Supply   Figure 3.13b shows a market characterized by relatively inelastic demand (buyers are not sensitive to price) and elastic supply (suppliers are very sensitive to price). In the market for cigarettes, for instance, many buyers are addicted to nicotine and buy a similar amount no matter how much the price goes up. Cigarette supply is more elastic. As you can see in the figure, consumers bear the burden of the tax in this case. A tax on cigarettes causes the buyers' price to rise from P_1 to P_b, almost the entire amount of the tax. Suppliers are only a bit worse off than they were before, because they can pass on the higher costs to the inelastic consumers.

We could do this entire analysis using equations, as we did in the movie ticket example. It turns out there is a general formula that will approximate the share of the tax borne by the consumer and the share borne by the producer. Not surprisingly, given what we've just discussed, these shares depend on elasticities:

$$\text{Share borne by consumer} = \frac{E^S}{E^S + |E^D|}$$

$$\text{Share borne by producer} = \frac{|E^D|}{E^S + |E^D|}$$

figure it out 3.3

Consider the demand and supply for cola in a market represented by the following equations:

$$Q^D = 15 - 10P$$
$$Q^S = 40P - 50$$

where Q is millions of bottles per year and P measures dollars per bottle. The equilibrium price of cola is $1.30 per bottle, and 2 million bottles are sold each year.

a. Calculate the price elasticity of demand and the price elasticity of supply at the equilibrium price and quantity.

b. Calculate the share of a tax that would be borne by consumers and the share borne by producers.

c. If a tax of $0.15 per bottle is imposed, what would be the expected price buyers will have to pay? What price will sellers receive after the tax?

Solution:

a. The formula for price elasticity of demand is

$$E^D = \frac{\Delta Q^D}{\Delta P} \times \frac{P}{Q^D}$$

From the demand curve, we can calculate $\frac{\Delta Q^D}{\Delta P}$. Each time P changes by 1 unit, Q^D falls by 10. Therefore,

$$\frac{\Delta Q^D}{\Delta P} = -10$$

Substituting into the formula for elasticity, we get

$$E^D = \frac{\Delta Q}{\Delta P} \times \frac{P}{Q} = -10 \times \frac{1.3}{2} = \frac{-13}{2} = -6.5$$

The formula for price elasticity of supply is

$$E^S = \frac{\Delta Q^S}{\Delta P} \times \frac{P}{Q^S}$$

From the supply curve, we can see that $\frac{\Delta Q^S}{\Delta P} = 40$. Note that each time P increases by 1 unit, Q^S rises by 40.

Thus, the price elasticity of supply is

$$E^S = \frac{\Delta Q^S}{\Delta P} = \times \frac{P}{Q^S} = 40 \times \frac{1.3}{2} = \frac{52}{2} = 26$$

b. The proportion of the tax borne by buyers will be

$$\frac{E^S}{E^S + |E^D|} = \frac{26}{26 + |-6.5|} = \frac{26}{32.5} = 0.8$$

The proportion of the tax borne by sellers will be

$$\frac{|E^D|}{E^S + |E^D|} = \frac{|-6.5|}{26 + |-6.5|} = \frac{6.5}{32.5} = 0.2$$

So, buyers will bear 80% of the tax and sellers will bear only 20% of the tax.

c. If there is a tax of $0.15 per bottle, buyers will bear 80% of the tax:

Increase in $P_b = (0.80)(\$0.15) = \$0.12$

The price buyers pay will rise from $1.30 per bottle (the original equilibrium price) to $1.42.

Sellers will bear the other 20% of the tax:

Decrease in $P_s = (0.2)(\$0.15) = \$0.03$

The price sellers receive will fall from $1.30 per bottle to $1.27.

If the price elasticity of supply (E^S) is infinite, the consumers' share is equal to 1; that is, consumers bear the whole burden when supply is perfectly elastic. If the absolute value of the price elasticity of demand ($|E^D|$) is infinite, the consumers' share of the tax burden is zero, and suppliers bear the whole burden of the tax.

3.5 Subsidies

A **subsidy** is *a payment by the government to a buyer or seller of a good or service*. It is, in essence, the exact opposite of a tax. In fact, when we analyze the effects of subsidies on markets, we can treat the subsidy as a negative tax. Thus, the price the buyer

subsidy A payment by the government to a buyer or seller of a good or service.

Figure 3.14   The Impact of a Producer Subsidy

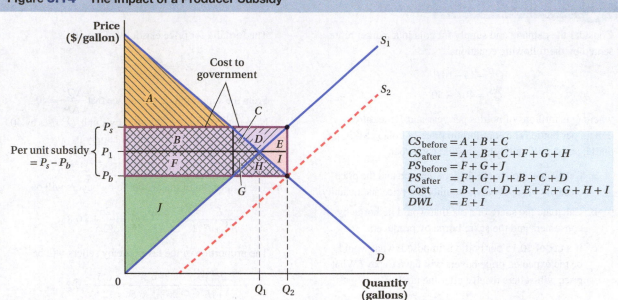

$CS_{before} = A + B + C$
$CS_{after} = A + B + C + F + G + H$
$PS_{before} = F + G + J$
$PS_{after} = F + G + J + B + C + D$
$Cost = B + C + D + E + F + G + H + I$
$DWL = E + I$

In the pre-subsidy market for gasoline, the supply curve S_1 intersects the demand curve D at the equilibrium price P_1 and equilibrium quantity Q_1. The consumer surplus is $A + B + C$, and the producer surplus is $F + G + J$. If the government gives fuel producers $1 for every gallon of gas–ethanol mix they sell, the supply curve shifts down by the amount of the subsidy, $P_s - P_b$, to S_2. The supply curve that buyers face is lower because the amount people pay to fill their tank is less than the amount the gas station receives, since the government is footing part of the bill (the effects of a tax are just the opposite). At the equilibrium, the quantity increases to Q_2, the price facing suppliers is P_s, and the price facing buyers is P_b. Consumer surplus is now $A + B + C + F + G + H$, and producer surplus is $F + G + J + B + C + D$. The cost of the subsidy is $B + C + D + E + F + G + H + I$, and the deadweight loss is $E + I$. Therefore, the costs associated with the subsidy are larger than the sum of the benefits to producers and consumers.

pays is *lower* than the price the supplier receives after the subsidy. If the government subsidizes gasoline by $1 per gallon, for example, then buyers might pay $3.50 per gallon at the pump, but gas stations receive $4.50 per gallon because they get to add the government dollar to the $3.50. This relationship is $P_b +$ subsidy $= P_s$, where P_b is the price the buyer pays (the market price) and P_s is the price the seller receives after the subsidy is paid.

Let's look at the effects of the U.S. government subsidy for the domestic production of ethanol, a corn-based fuel additive that can be mixed with gasoline (**Figure 3.14**). (A common rationale given for the subsidy is to reduce the dependence of the United States on imported oil, though not coincidentally, politicians from large corn-producing states have been the most vocal backers of the policy.) This ethanol subsidy would effectively be a subsidy on gasoline that is mixed with ethanol.

Before the subsidy was in place, consumer surplus was everything below the demand curve and above the price that consumers pay (P_1), area $A + B + C$ in Figure 3.14. After the subsidy, consumer surplus will change. But it will not get smaller, as in the case of a tax. It will get larger. The new consumer surplus is the area below the demand curve and above the price that the consumers have to pay (the new lower price, P_b). This is the old consumer surplus $A + B + C$ *plus* the new part $F + G + H$. This additional surplus comes from the lower price and the additional sales at that price.

figure it out 3.4

Suppose the demand for, and supply of, ethanol in a small town are as follows:

$$Q^D = 9{,}000 - 1{,}000P$$
$$Q^S = 2{,}000P - 3{,}000$$

where Q measures gallons per day and P represents price per gallon. The current equilibrium price is \$4, and the current equilibrium quantity is 5,000 gallons per day.

Now suppose that the government wants to create a subsidy of \$0.375 per gallon to encourage the use of ethanol.

a. What will happen to the price buyers pay per gallon, the price sellers receive per gallon, and the number of gallons consumed each day?

b. How much will this subsidy cost the government (and ultimately taxpayers)?

Solution:

a. Determining the prices that buyers and sellers face under a subsidy is done in a way similar to how we determined the prices for buyers and sellers in the presence of a tax. However, there is one big difference. Now, the price sellers receive is actually larger than the price paid by buyers (due to the subsidy):

$$P_s = P_b + \text{subsidy}$$

Now we know that in our problem,

$$P_s = P_b + 0.375$$

Remember that we need to start with the demand and supply equations in the following form:

$$Q^D = 9{,}000 - 1{,}000P_b$$
$$Q^S = 2{,}000P_s - 3{,}000$$

Once we have come up with these, we can substitute for P_s in the supply equation so that it becomes

$$Q^S = 2{,}000P_s - 3{,}000$$
$$Q^S = 2{,}000(P_b + 0.375) - 3{,}000 = 2{,}000P_b + 750 - 3{,}000$$
$$= 2{,}000P_b - 2{,}250$$

Next, we can equate Q^D and Q^S to solve for P_b:

$$9{,}000 - 1{,}000P_b = 2{,}000P_b - 2{,}250$$
$$3{,}000P_b = 11{,}250$$
$$P_b = 3.75$$
$$P_s = P_b + 0.375$$
$$P_s = 4.125$$

To solve for the quantity of ethanol sold after the subsidy is put in place, we can substitute P_b into the demand equation or substitute P_s into the supply equation. (It is a good idea to do both to check your work.)

$$Q^D = 9{,}000 - 1{,}000P_b = 9{,}000 - 1{,}000(3.75)$$
$$= 9{,}000 - 3{,}750 = 5{,}250$$
$$Q^S = 2{,}000P_s - 3{,}000 = 2{,}000(4.125) - 3{,}000$$
$$= 8{,}250 - 3{,}000 = 5{,}250$$

So, buyers will pay \$3.75 per gallon, sellers will receive \$4.125 per gallon, and 5,250 gallons will be sold each day. This can be seen in the figure below.

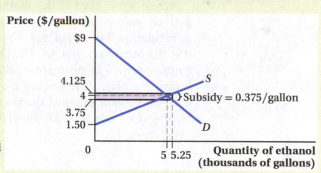

b. The cost of the subsidy will be the subsidy per gallon multiplied by the number of gallons sold:

Cost of subsidy = (\$0.375)(5,250) = \$1,968.75 per day

Before the subsidy, the producer surplus was everything above the supply curve but below the price the suppliers received (P_1), area $F + G + J$. After the subsidy, producer surplus gets bigger, too. The area above the producers' own supply curve S_1 and below the price that the suppliers receive (P_s) is now $F + G + J$ plus $B + C + D$. (We calculate producer surplus using the *producers'* supply curve (S_1) because this is the supply curve that the suppliers actually receive and embodies the suppliers' costs of production.)

Note that parts of the consumer and producer surplus areas overlap in this case (areas $B + C + F + G$) because both sides are getting more surplus than before. The only way this is possible, however, is if someone else foots the bill. In this case, it's the government. The subsidy costs money. The cost of the subsidy is the subsidy amount times the quantity produced, $Q_2 \times (P_s - P_b)$, which amounts to the rectangle $B + C + D + E + F + G + H + I$.

This isn't the only cost of the subsidy, however. Like any other price regulation, a subsidy also creates deadweight loss. It might seem odd at first that there would be DWL when both consumers *and* producers are better off after the subsidy. The key is to compare how much their surplus goes up to how much the subsidy costs the government. While consumer surplus went up by $F + G + H$ and producer surplus by $B + C + D$, total government outlays for the subsidy were $(F + G + H) + (B + C + D) + (E + I)$. Therefore, the subsidy's DWL is $E + I$. Society as a whole pays more for the subsidy than the added benefit it gives to consumers and producers. If somehow the government could just turn over the subsidy revenue to consumers and producers without changing the price, society would be better off. Changing the price gets some extra people to buy gas-ethanol mix who really were not interested in purchasing it before.

When we looked at the market interventions earlier in this chapter, the DWL derived from the surplus lost by people who would have bought if there were no tax or regulation, but do not buy when the tax is in place and the price is too high. Here, it is the other way around. The DWL comes from people who would *not* have made a purchase in a competitive market. They only make a purchase because the subsidy lowers the price. The amount they value the extra quantity is less than what it costs the government to move them to buy it. Some people say Christmas is inefficient for the same reason — people give gifts that cost about 15% more than the receivers value them.[11]

3.6 Conclusion

In this chapter, we took the supply and demand hammer and pounded every nail in sight. We saw how you can compute the consumer and producer surplus generated by transactions in a market, learned how to value new goods, and learned what deadweight loss is. We learned to use supply, demand, and total surplus to analyze industries and the ways in which they change in response to changes in the market, particularly to price and quantity regulations, taxes, and subsidies. Being able to do so much with such a simple model makes supply and demand the workhorse of microeconomics.

---

[11] Joel Waldfogel, "The Deadweight Loss of Christmas," *American Economic Review* 83, no. 5 (1993): 1328–1336. Leave it to an economist to point out the deadweight loss of Christmas!

Summary

1. **Consumer surplus** is the value that consumers receive from participating in market transactions. It is the difference between the most they would pay for something and the price they actually have to pay for it. On a supply and demand graph, consumer surplus is measured by the area under the demand curve and above the price. **Producer surplus** is the benefit that producers receive from participating in market transactions. It is the difference between what they sell their product for and the least they would be willing to receive to sell their product. On a supply and demand graph, producer surplus is measured by the area above the supply curve and below the price. **[Section 3.1]**

2. Using consumer and producer surplus, we can compute how shifts in supply and demand affect the well-being of customers and of companies. An inward shift in supply will cause consumer surplus to fall because of both the increase in the equilibrium price and the decrease in the equilibrium quantity. An outward shift in supply, on the other hand, raises consumer surplus. An inward shift in demand leads to a drop in producer surplus because it decreases both the equilibrium price and quantity. Outward demand shifts have the opposite effect. **[Section 3.1]**

3. If the government imposes a price regulation—either a maximum price or **price ceiling** like rent control or a minimum price or **price floor** like the minimum wage—the quantities supplied and demanded will differ at the market price, resulting in either **excess demand** or **excess supply** of the good. Such regulations also create a **deadweight loss (DWL)** that arises because some of the surplus-creating transactions that took place before the regulation was enacted do not occur in the regulated environment. A direct transfer of income from one side to the other without changing the price would be a more efficient way to help consumers and suppliers. Deadweight losses are largest when supply and demand are most elastic. **[Section 3.2]**

4. If the government introduces a regulation that mandates the provision of a given quantity of a good or service (a **quota**) this action will change the market and create a deadweight loss, just as a price regulation does. These actions do not create excess demand or supply, though, because prices are able to adjust and clear the market. **[Section 3.3]**

5. Taxes reduce output and raise price. In doing so, they reduce consumer and producer surplus but generate tax revenue. The revenue they generate is less than the damage they do to surplus, and the difference is the deadweight loss of the tax. The concept of **tax incidence** tells us who really bears the burden of a tax: It does not matter who actually pays a tax by law. All that matters is the elasticities of supply and demand. The more elastic side of the market will bear less of the burden because it can more easily shift away from the taxed good. **[Section 3.4]**

6. **Subsidies** increase both consumer and producer surplus relative to the free-market equilibrium. They still create a deadweight loss, though, because the outlay cost of the subsidy exceeds the amount by which it increases the surplus of the two groups. **[Section 3.5]**

Review Questions

1. Define consumer and producer surplus.

2. How does the demand choke price relate to consumer surplus?

3. How does the supply choke price relate to producer surplus?

4. How does a supply shift affect consumer and producer surplus in a given market? Consider both inward and outward shifts of the supply curve.

5. How does a demand shift affect consumer and producer surplus in a given market? Consider both inward and outward shifts of the demand curve.

6. What is a price ceiling? Why does a price ceiling create excess demand for (shortage of) a good?

7. What is a price floor? Why does a price floor create an excess supply of (surplus of) a good?

8. What is a deadweight loss? If the price elasticity of a good is large, would you expect the deadweight loss to be large or small?

9. When is a price ceiling nonbinding? When is a price floor nonbinding?

10. What is a quota? How does it differ from a price ceiling or a price floor?

11. What happens to the equilibrium price and quantity of a good when a tax is imposed on the good? Why does a tax create a wedge between the price the consumer pays and the price the producer receives?

12. How does a tax affect consumer and producer surplus? Why does a tax create a deadweight loss?

13. What is the tax incidence? What factors determine the tax incidence?

14. What is a subsidy?

15. How does a subsidy affect consumer and producer surplus?

16. Why does a subsidy create a deadweight loss?

Problems

(Solutions to problems marked with an asterisk appear at the back of this book. Problems adapted to use calculus are available online.)

1. Consider the demand for broadband Internet service, given as follows: $Q^D = 224 - 4P$, where Q is the number of subscribers in a given area (in hundreds) and P is the price in dollars per month. This demand relationship is illustrated in the diagram below. Assume that the price of broadband service is $25 per month. Determine the following, paying particular attention to the units in which quantity is denominated:

   a. The total number of subscribers at that price

   b. The total amount paid by subscribers for broadband service, area B

   c. The consumer surplus received by subscribers, area A

   d. The total value to consumers of the broadband service they received, areas A and B

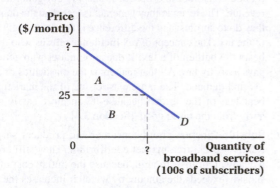

2. Consider the following diagram, which depicts the supply of broadband Internet service. The supply of broadband service is given by $Q^S = 12.5P - 150$, where Q is the quantity of services (in hundreds) and P is the price per month. Assume that the price of broadband service is $25 per month. Determine the following, paying particular attention to the units in which quantity is denominated:

   a. The total number of services providers will supply at that price

   b. The total amount received by producers for that service, areas D and E

   c. The producer surplus received by suppliers, area D

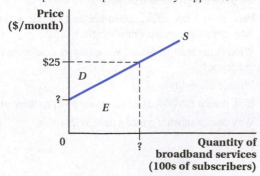

3. The annual demand for full-spectrum LED light bulbs in Fairbanks, Alaska, is estimated to be $Q^D = 20,000 - 1,000P$. The supply is estimated to be $Q^S = -12,000 + 3,000P$.

   a. Find the equilibrium price and quantity of LED light bulbs in Fairbanks, Alaska.

   b. Calculate the consumer and producer surplus at the equilibrium price.

   c. What is the total surplus created in the market for LED light bulbs?

4. Increases in demand generally result in increases in consumer surplus. But that's not always true. Illustrate a situation in which an increase in demand actually results in a *decrease* in consumer surplus. What conditions on the supply side of the market make this more likely to occur?

*5. The Ministry of Tourism in the Republic of Palau estimates that the demand for its scuba diving tours is given by $Q^D = 6,000 - 20P$, where Q is the number of divers served each month and P is the price of a two-tank dive. The supply of scuba diving tours is given by $Q^S = 30P - 2,000$. The equilibrium price is $160, and 2,800 divers are served each month. A new air route from Australia increases the number of dives demanded at each price by 1,000 per week.

   a. What is the equation for the new demand curve?

   b. What are the new equilibrium price and quantity?

   c. What happens to consumer and producer surplus as a result of the demand change?

6. In 1997, Sony introduced the DVD player, replacing the VHS videotape and shepherding in a new era of high-definition movie viewing. Soon, there were over 100 different player models competing. DVD became the standard, preferred way to watch movies at home; VHS movies became increasingly difficult to rent and/or purchase. Then, in 2010, Netflix introduced streaming video that allowed users to watch movies on their television or mobile device.

   a. Explain why the consumer surplus gained by those purchasing DVD players was likely to be quite high between 1997 and 2010.

   b. Describe how the introduction of streaming video likely altered the consumer surplus received by purchasers of DVD players after 2010.

   c. Do you believe the consumer surplus received by *movie viewers* increased or decreased after 2010? Explain.

7. Low-skilled workers operate in a competitive market. The labor supply is $Q^S = 10W$ (where W is the price of labor measured by the hourly wage) and the demand for labor is $Q^D = 240 - 20W$. Q measures the quantity of labor hired (in thousands of hours).

   a. What are the equilibrium wage and quantity of low-skilled labor working in equilibrium?

b.   If the government passes a minimum wage of $9 per hour, what will the new quantity of labor hired be? Will an excess demand or excess supply of labor exist? How large?

c.   What is the deadweight loss of a $9 minimum wage?

d.   How much better off does the $9 minimum wage make low-skilled workers (in other words, how much does producer surplus change), and how much worse off are employers?

e.   How would your answers to (c) and (d) change if the minimum wage was set at $11, rather than $9?

*8.   The diagram below illustrates the market for beef. Suppose that the government has instituted a price support program for beef by placing a price floor at $4.00 per pound. Under the program, any unsold beef will be purchased by the government and placed in long-term storage.

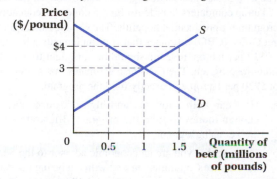

a.   What is the cost to consumers in lost surplus?

b.   What is the cost to taxpayers to purchase the unsold beef?

c.   How much producer surplus do sellers of beef gain?

d.   What is the loss to society of the beef program?

e.   The president of the National Cattleman's Association makes the following semi-extortionary offer to consumers: "Pay us $2.2 million per month forever and we'll lobby our congressmen to abandon the price support program." Should consumers pay the Cattleman's Association? Why or why not?

9.   The Reinheitsgebot is a set of laws established in the 1500s that regulate the production and sale of beer in Germany. Among its provisions, the edict set maximum prices that brewers could charge at various times of the year: "From Michaelmas to Georgi, the price for one [Bavarian Liter] is not to exceed one Pfennig Munich value." Cheap beer — this must be a great thing for consumers! Suppose that the demand for beer is given by $Q^D = 6,000 - 1,500P$, and the supply of beer is given by $Q^S = -1,000 + 2,000P$.

a.   Graph the supply and demand for beer carefully.

b.   Calculate the equilibrium price and quantity in a free market; then calculate consumer and producer surplus.

c.   How will a 1-Pfennig price ceiling affect the price paid by consumers for beer? How will it affect the quantity consumed?

d.   Calculate the consumer surplus received by beer drinkers and the producer surplus received by beer producers after the 1-Pfennig price ceiling is imposed.

e.   Does the price ceiling make society better off? Does it make beer producers better off? Does it make beer drinkers better off?

f.   Does a rule designed to make beer more affordable necessarily end up making consumers better off? Explain why or why not, drawing on the example given.

10.   You know that price ceilings are socially costly in that they create deadweight losses. But they may be costly in other ways, too. Suppose the government imposes a price ceiling of $1 per loaf on bread. Enumerate at least two ways in which this regulation will cause resources to be wasted beyond the deadweight loss it creates.

11.   Evaluate the truthfulness of each of the following statements:

a.   "If the demand for margarine is perfectly elastic, then a price ceiling in the market for margarine will definitely cause consumer surplus to increase."

b.   "The impact of a price ceiling on consumers' well-being depends only on the shape of the demand curve."

12.   Black markets are markets where items are sold in violation of government rules and regulations.

a.   Suppose that the government imposes a $1 per loaf price ceiling on bread sales, well below its free-market price. Explain how the existence of a black market for bread could potentially improve society's well-being.

b.   Suppose that the government establishes a $20 per bushel price floor in the market for corn. Explain how the existence of a black market for corn could potentially improve society's well-being.

13.   Noni is a tropical fruit grown in Hawaii and widely marketed as an herbal cure for various diseases. The market for Noni fruit is depicted in the graph below.

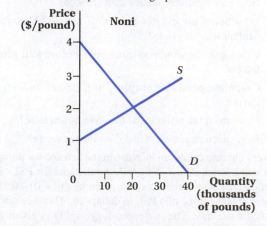

Concerned that Noni fruit may be habit-forming and produce adverse side effects, the U.S. Department of Agriculture (USDA) and the Food and Drug Administration (FDA) decide to reduce the quantity of Noni available by restricting production to 10,000 pounds monthly.

a. Alter the supply curve to show the impact of the quantity regulation on the market for Noni.

b. What will the market price of Noni be after the regulation goes into effect?

c. What will happen to consumer surplus as a result of the regulation?

d. "We, the producers of Noni fruit, stand united against these intrusive and unnecessary quantity restrictions. Until the dangers of Noni consumption are fully documented, we will fight for the freedom to produce all the Noni we want!" Given this public proclamation, do you expect Noni growers to fight hard against these regulations?

14. You are a USDA economist, and the Senate Finance Committee has come to you for advice. The government is considering bolstering its finances by imposing a tax on either salt or blue cheese. You know that the markets for salt and blue cheese are roughly the same size, although the demand for salt is highly inelastic, whereas the demand for blue cheese is highly elastic. Salt and blue cheese have similar supply elasticities. Which option do you recommend as the least costly choice?

*15. The demand for ice cream is given by $Q^D = 20 - 2P$, measured in gallons of ice cream. The supply of ice cream is given by $Q^S = 4P - 10$.

a. Graph the supply and demand curves, and find the equilibrium price and quantity of ice cream.

b. Suppose that the government legislates a $1 tax on a gallon of ice cream, to be collected from the buyer. Plot the new demand curve on your graph. Does demand increase or decrease as a result of the tax?

c. As a result of the tax, what happens to the price paid by buyers? What happens to the price received by sellers? How many gallons of ice cream are sold?

d. Who bears the greater burden of the tax? Can you explain why this is so?

e. Calculate consumer surplus both before and after the tax.

f. Calculate producer surplus both before and after the tax.

g. How much tax revenue did the government raise?

h. How much deadweight loss does the tax create?

*16. Every autumn brings an increase in the demand for pumpkin spice lattes (PSL). This fall, the demand for PSLs in a mid-sized midwestern town is given by $Q^D = 10 - 0.5P$, where P is the price of a PSL in dollars and Q is thousands of PSLs per day. The corresponding supply is given by

$Q^S = -5 + 2P$. The equilibrium price of a PSL is $6; the equilibrium quantity is 7,000.

a. Calculate the price elasticity of demand and the price elasticity of supply at the equilibrium price and quantity.

b. Eager to capitalize on the addictive nature of the PSL, the City Council decides to impose a $1 tax on pumpkin spice lattes. "We can use the proceeds to fund an espresso machine for City Hall!" they rave. Using your answer to (a), calculate the share of the tax borne by consumers of pumpkin spice lattes, and the share of the tax borne by sellers.

c. Determine the expected price buyers will have to pay after the tax is imposed. Then calculate the expected price sellers will receive after the tax.

17. The U.S. Senate is considering a bill that would tax the sale of laptop computers in order to fund a computer education program for presidential hopefuls. The Congressional Budget Office (CBO) estimates that if it implements a low tax of $12 per laptop, revenue should be sufficient to exactly fund the program. The CBO also estimates that a high tax of $230 per laptop will exactly fund the program.

a. How can both a low tax and high tax raise exactly enough money to fund the program? Illustrate your answer using a graph.

b. Suppose that you are an economic advisor to the Senate Finance Committee, tasked with analyzing the economic impact of the tax proposals. Which proposal do you recommend and why?

18. A tax increases the price paid by buyers and reduces the price received by sellers; it makes society worse off. In contrast, a subsidy reduces the price paid by buyers and increases the price received by sellers. True or false: Because a subsidy's effects are the opposite of a tax's effects, the subsidy must make society better off. Explain your reasoning.

19. The government believes that access to the Internet is essential in today's society, and to bolster access, it proposes subsidizing the purchase of mobile devices. The inverse demand for mobile devices is given by $P = 500 - 0.1Q^D$. The supply is given by $P = 200 + 0.1Q^S$.

a. Solve for the equilibrium price and quantity in this market, and calculate producer and consumer surplus.

b. Suppose the government offers a $100 per unit subsidy to sellers of mobile devices. Alter the equation for the inverse supply curve to reflect the subsidy.

c. With the subsidy in place, how many mobile devices will be sold? What will the price paid by buyers be? The price received by sellers?

d. What will the subsidy program cost the government? What will the net effect of the subsidy on total surplus in society be?

Consumer Behavior

The Korean electronics company Samsung manufactures smartphones. In the run-up to the holidays, it needs to add new features to the next version of its Galaxy phone to experience a big sales year. The features Samsung will include depend a great deal on consumer preferences: how long a battery must last, how much memory the phone offers, the type of camera wanted, how much they are willing to pay for a larger screen, and so on. Only by determining the answers to these questions can Samsung succeed in the marketplace.

This chapter is about one key question: How do consumers decide which products (and how much of each) to buy? The answer to this question is the building block for the demand curve in the basic supply and demand model, and understanding consumer behavior is a powerful tool with many applications.

We begin the chapter by discussing the nature of consumers' *preferences* (what they like and don't like) and how economists use the concepts of *utility* (a measure of a consumer's well-being) and *utility functions* to summarize their preferences. In addition, this chapter explores a concept you will continue to encounter: *constrained optimization*. When facing decisions, consumers try to do the best they can (to *optimize*) given the *constraints* they face, such as the amount of money they have to spend. To arrive at choices that will make them happiest, consumers must make tradeoffs in the smartest way possible. Such tradeoffs depend on a consumer's preferences, the amount of income the consumer has to spend, and the prices of goods. We combine these ideas to analyze how consumers behave: why people buy less of something when its price rises (i.e., why demand curves slope down), why people consume different goods as they grow wealthier rather than a lot more of the same things, and so on.

The set of techniques we will use to analyze consumers' constrained optimization problems will appear repeatedly, with slight modifications, throughout this book and in any economics courses you take in the future. Learn the techniques here and you can use them forever.

4.1 The Consumer's Preferences and the Concept of Utility

Consumers' preferences underlie every decision they make. Economists think of consumers as making rational choices about what they like best, given the constraints they face.

Assumptions about Consumer Preferences

Consumers make many choices every day about what to buy and what not to buy. These choices involve many different goods: Buy a giant bag of Twizzlers and walk home, or buy a bus ticket and leave a sweet tooth unsatisfied? Buy a new video game or get your car's oil changed? To understand how consumers form their preferences for all the possible goods and services they can buy, we need to make some simplifying assumptions. Specifically, we assume that all decisions about what to buy share four properties:

1. **Completeness and rankability.** We assume that consumers can make comparisons across all possible sets of goods. Economists use the term **consumption bundle** (or just *bundle*) to describe *any set of goods or services a consumer considers purchasing*. The assumption means that, given any two bundles, a consumer can decide which she prefers (or whether she is *indifferent*, meaning she likes them the same). This assumption is important because it means that we can apply economic theory to any bundle of goods we want to discuss. Whether the bundle includes sapphires and SUVs or movies, modern art, and marshmallows, the consumer can decide which bundle she likes better. Note, however, that this assumption does not tell us what kinds of bundles the consumer will like more than others. It just implies she is able to determine if one is better than the other.

> **consumption bundle** A set of goods or services a consumer considers purchasing.

2. **For most goods, more is better than less (or at least more is no worse than less).** In general, more of a good thing is good. If we like a car that will better ensure our safety in a crash, we would like that same car even more if it were even safer.[1]

3. **Transitivity.** For any three bundles of goods (call them *A*, *B*, and *C*), if a consumer prefers *A* to *B* and also prefers *B* to *C*, then she prefers *A* to *C*. If you prefer apples to oranges, and you prefer oranges to bananas, then transitivity implies that you must also prefer apples to bananas. Note that, as always, we are holding everything else constant when making these comparisons. Transitivity does *not* mean that you prefer apples to bananas in all situations—only that, at a given moment, you prefer apples to bananas. Transitivity imposes logical consistency on preferences.

4. **The more a consumer has of a particular good, the less she is willing to give up of something else to get even more of that good.** The idea behind this assumption is that consumers like variety. If you like powdered donuts and haven't had any lately, you might be willing to give up a lot to get some. You might be willing to pay a high price for a donut, wait in a long line for a donut, or trade away your last carton of milk for a good donut. On the other hand, if you've just polished off eight donuts in a row, you wouldn't pay as much for the ninth donut as you did for that first one.[2]

The Concept of Utility

Given these assumptions about preferences, we could create a list of all the consumer's preferences between any possible bundles for every decision. But because such a list would include billions of possible bundles, it would be basically useless as a decision aid. Instead, economists use the concept of utility and a mathematical description called a utility function to describe preferences more simply.

---

[1] There may come a point at which more of a good thing stops being better. Economists call this a *satiation point*. For instance, the first jelly bean may make us happy, but the 1,437th jelly bean might actually make us sick if we eat it, causing us to be worse off than had we eaten only 1,436. However, because people can sometimes save extra jelly beans for later on, trade them with someone else for something they want, or just give them away, satiation points tend not to be very important in practice.

   In addition, to keep things relatively simple, we assume that consumers can discard unwanted goods at no cost, a concept economists call "free disposal."

[2] In some special cases, this might not be true. Most people, for example, would prefer having a second water ski or a second basketball shoe to having one of each. But the likelihood of diminishing gains from adding quantity is almost always true and makes our analysis much simpler.

■ **Utility** *is a measure of how satisfied a consumer is.* For practical purposes, you can think of utility as a fancy word for happiness or well-being. It is important to realize that utility is *not* a measure of how rich a consumer is. Income may affect utility, but it is just one of many factors that do so.

■ A **utility function** *mathematically describes the relationship between what consumers actually consume and their level of well-being.* A function is a mathematical relationship that links a set of inputs to an output. For instance, if you combine the inputs eggs, flour, sugar, vanilla, butter, frosting, and candles in just the right way, you end up with the output of a birthday cake. In consumer behavior, the inputs to a utility

A scenic view is just one type of utility input that increases consumer well-being.

function are the different things that can give a person utility. Examples of inputs to the utility function include traditional goods and services like cars, candy bars, health club memberships, and airplane rides. But there are many other types of inputs to utility as well, including scenic views, a good night's sleep, spending time with friends, and the pleasure that comes from giving to charity. The output of the utility function is the consumer's utility level. By mapping the various bundles a consumer considers to an explicit measure of that same consumer's level of well-being, a utility function gives us a concise way to rank a consumer's bundles.

utility A measure of how satisfied a consumer is.

utility function A mathematical function that describes the relationship between what consumers actually consume and their level of well-being.

Utility functions can take a variety of mathematical forms. Let's look at the utility someone enjoys from consuming combinations of Junior Mints and KitKats. Generically, we can write this utility level as $U = U(J, K)$, where $U(J, K)$ is the utility function and J and K are, respectively, the number of Junior Mints and KitKats the consumer eats. An example of a specific utility function for this consumer is $U = J \times K$. In this case, the consumer's level of utility equals the product of the number of Junior Mints and KitKats she eats. But it could instead be that the consumer's utility equals the total number of Junior Mints and KitKats eaten. In that case, the utility function is $U = J + K$. Yet another possibility is that the consumer's utility is given by $U = J^{0.7} K^{0.3}$. Because the exponent on Junior Mints (0.7) is larger than that on KitKats (0.3), this utility function implies that a given percentage increase in Junior Mints consumed will raise utility more than the same percentage increase in KitKats.

These are just a few examples from the large variety of possible utility functions we could imagine consumers having for these or any other combination of goods. At this point in our analysis of consumer behavior, we don't have to be too restrictive about the form any particular utility function takes, and it's sort of arbitrary to choose one here. Just remember, utility functions represent consumers' preferences. They are supposed to represent what people actually like. And they have to conform to our four assumptions about preferences (rankability and completeness, more is better, transitivity, and variety is important).

Marginal Utility

One of the most important concepts related to utility functions is **marginal utility,** *the extra utility a consumer receives from a 1-unit increase in consumption.*[3] Each good in a utility function has its own marginal utility. Using the Junior Mints and KitKats utility function, for example, the marginal utility of Junior Mints, MU_J, would be

$$MU_J = \frac{\Delta U(J,K)}{\Delta J}$$

marginal utility The extra utility a consumer receives from a 1-unit increase in consumption.

[3] Marginal utility can be calculated for any given utility function.

where ΔJ is the small (1-unit) change in the number of Junior Mints the consumer eats and $\Delta U(J, K)$ is the change in utility she gets from doing so. Likewise, the marginal utility of consuming KitKats is given by

$$MU_K = \frac{\Delta U(J,K)}{\Delta K}$$

Later in this chapter, we see that marginal utility is the key to understanding the consumption choices a person makes.

Utility and Comparisons

One important point about utility and the four assumptions about preferences with which we started our discussion is that they allow us to rank all bundles of goods for a particular consumer, but they do not allow us to determine how much more a consumer likes one bundle than another. In mathematical terms, we have an *ordinal* ranking of bundles (we can line them up from best to worst), but not a *cardinal* ranking (which would allow us to say by exactly how much a consumer prefers one bundle to another). We say this because the units with which we measure utility are essentially arbitrary and made up.

An example will make this clearer. Let's say we define our measurement of consumer utility in a unit we call a "util." And let's say we have three bundles: *A*, *B*, and *C*, and a consumer who likes bundle *A* the most and bundle *C* the least. We might then assign these three bundles values of 8, 7, and 6 utils, respectively. The difficulty is that we just as easily could have defined consumer utility in terms of "bootles" and assigned the bundles values of 8, 7, and 2 bootles (or 19, 17, and 16 tootles; you get the idea), and this would still perfectly describe the situation. You can say that you like something better, but how can you describe how happy it makes you, according to some objective measuring tape? Because there is no real-world unit of measure, like a dollar, gram, or inch, with which to measure utility, we can shift, stretch, or squeeze a utility function without altering any of its observable implications, as long as we don't change the ordering of preferences over bundles.[4] With ordered rankings, we can still provide answers to the important questions about how consumers behave and how this behavior results in a downward-sloping demand curve.

The thing we can't do, though, is make *interpersonal comparisons* of utility, meaning one person's utility to some other person's. We can say Person A and Person B both like KitKats more than Junior Mints, but we can't say who likes KitKats more and hence should purchase all of them, or if we should divide the candies evenly. Questions like this relate to what is called **welfare economics,** *the area of economics concerned with the economic well-being of society as a whole,* which we discuss later in this book. For now, however, we focus on the preferences of one consumer at a time.

Just as important as the assumptions we make when analyzing utility functions are the assumptions that we do *not* make. For one, we do not impose particular preferences on consumers. People like what they like. Some people like ferrets more than dogs as pets. As long as they follow the four preference assumptions, we don't make judgments on what is valuable. Even if the expressed preference is a ticket to go see Justin Bieber, preferences are just a description of what makes people happy. We also don't require that preferences

welfare economics The area of economics concerned with the economic well-being of society as a whole.

---

[4] In mathematical parlance, these order-preserving shifts, squeezes, or stretches of a utility function are called *monotonic* transformations. Any monotonic transformation of a utility function will imply exactly the same preferences for the consumer as the original utility function. Consider our first example of a utility function from consuming Junior Mints and KitKats, $U = J \times K$. Suppose that it was $U = 8J \times K + 12$ instead. For any possible bundle of Junior Mints and KitKats, this new utility function will imply the same ordering of the consumer's utility levels as would the old function. (You can put in a few specific numbers to test this.) Because the consumer's relative preferences don't change, she will make the same decisions on how much of each good to consume with either utility function.

remain constant over time. Someone may prefer sleeping to seeing a movie tonight, but tomorrow indicate the opposite preference.

The concepts of utility and utility functions are general enough to account for a consumer's preferences over any number of goods and the various bundles into which they can be combined. As we build our model of consumer behavior, however, we focus on a simple case where a consumer buys a bundle with only two goods, though the ideas still apply in more complicated situations.

4.2 Indifference Curves

As we discussed in the previous section, the right way to think about utility is in relative terms; that is, in terms of whether one bundle of goods provides more or less utility to a consumer compared to another bundle. An especially good way of understanding utility is to consider when a consumer is **indifferent,** *the special case in which a consumer derives the same level of utility from each of two or more consumer bundles.*

Consider the case of renting an apartment where there are two "goods" you must choose between: the size in square feet and the number of friends living in the same building. Michaela wants a large apartment, but also wants to be able to easily see her friends. **Figure 4.1a** graphs three bundles (apartments) that offer Michaela the same utility from different size/friend combinations: a 750-square-foot apartment in a building where 5 of her friends live; one only 500 square feet big in a building where 10 friends reside; a more generous-sized, 1,000-square-foot apartment for which Michaela would be willing to make do with only 3 friends nearby. These are not the only three bundles that would give Michaela

indifferent The special case in which a consumer derives the same level of utility from each of two or more consumption bundles.

➡️ The online appendix explores the mathematics of monotonic transformations of utility functions.

Figure 4.1   Building an Indifference Curve

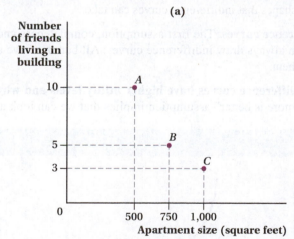

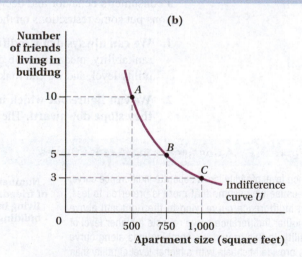

(a) Because Michaela receives utility from both the number of friends in her apartment building and the square footage of her apartment, she is equally happy with 10 friends in her building and a 500-square-foot apartment, or 5 friends in her building and a 750-square-foot apartment. Likewise, she is willing to trade off 2 more friends in her building (leaving her with 3) to have a 1,000-square-foot apartment. These are three of many combinations of friends in her building and apartment size that make her equally happy.

(b) An indifference curve connects all bundles of goods that provide a consumer with the same level of utility. Bundles *A*, *B*, and *C* provide the same satisfaction for Michaela. Thus, the indifference curve represents Michaela's willingness to trade off between friends in her apartment building and the square footage of her apartment.

the same level of utility; there are many different bundles that will accomplish this goal—an infinite number of bundles, in fact, if we ignore that it might not make sense to have access to a fraction of a friend (or maybe it does?).

indifference curve The combination of all the different consumption bundles that provide a consumer with the same utility.

The combination of all the different bundles of goods that give a consumer the same utility is called an **indifference curve.** In Figure 4.1b, we draw Michaela's indifference curve, which includes the three points shown in Figure 4.1a. Notice that it contains not just the three bundles we discussed, but many other combinations of square footage and friends in the building. Also notice that it always slopes down: Every time a friend moves from Michaela's building, she would need more square footage to remain indifferent. (Equivalently, we could say any apartment with less space would require more friends in the building to keep her equally well off.)

For each level of utility, there is a different indifference curve. **Figure 4.2** shows two of Michaela's indifference curves. Which corresponds to the higher level of utility? The easiest way to figure this out is to think like Michaela. One of the points on the indifference curve U_1 represents the utility Michaela would get if she had 5 friends in her building and a 500-square-foot apartment. Curve U_2 includes a bundle with the same number of friends and a 1,000-square-foot apartment. By our "more is better" assumption, indifference curve U_2 must make Michaela better off. We could have instead held the apartment's square footage constant and asked which indifference curve had more friends in the building, and we would have found the same answer. Any indifference curve that is closer to the origin (zero units of both goods) than another curve has a lower utility (we learn below that they can't cross). Michaela's utility is higher at every point on U_2 than at any point on U_1.

Characteristics of Indifference Curves

Generally speaking, the positions and shapes of indifference curves can tell us a lot about a consumer's behavior and decisions. However, our four assumptions about utility functions put some restrictions on the shapes that indifference curves can take.

1. **We can always draw indifference curves.** The first assumption, completeness and rankability, means that we can always draw indifference curves: All bundles have a utility level, and we can rank them.

2. **We can figure out which indifference curves have higher utility levels and why they slope downward.** The "more is better" assumption implies that we can look at

---

Figure 4.2   A Consumer's Indifference Curves

Each level of utility has a separate indifference curve. Because we assume that more is preferred to less, an indifference curve lying to the right and above another indifference curve reflects a higher level of utility. In this graph, the combinations along curve U_2 provide Michaela with a higher level of utility than the combinations along curve U_1, the curve closer to the origin (zero units of both goods). Michaela will be happier with a 1,000-square-foot apartment than a 500-square-foot apartment, holding the number of friends living in her building equal at 5.

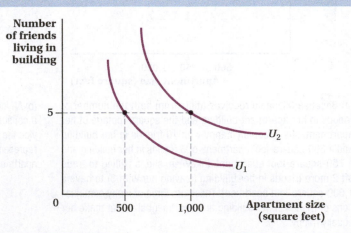

a set of indifference curves and figure out which ones represent higher utility levels. This can be done by holding the quantity of one good fixed and seeing which curves have larger quantities of the other good. This is exactly what we did when examining Figure 4.2. The assumption also implies that indifference curves never slope upward. If they did, this would mean that a consumer was indifferent between a particular bundle and another bundle with more of *both* goods. There's no way this can be true if more is always better.

3. **Indifference curves never cross.** The transitivity property implies that indifference curves for a given consumer can never cross. To see why, suppose our apartment-hunter Michaela's hypothetical indifference curves intersect with each other, as shown in **Figure 4.3.** The "more is better" assumption implies she prefers bundle E to bundle D, because E offers both more square footage and more friends in her building than does D. Now, because E and F are on the same indifference curve U_2, Michaela's utility from consuming either bundle must be the same by definition. And because bundles F and D are on the same indifference curve U_1, she must also be indifferent between *those* two bundles. But here's the problem. Putting this all together means she's indifferent between E and D because each makes her just as well off as F. We know that can't be true. After all, she must like E more than D because it has more of both goods. Something has gone wrong: We violated the transitivity property by allowing the indifference curves to cross. Intersecting indifference curves imply that the same bundle (the one located at the intersection) offers two different utility levels, which can't be the case.

4. **Indifference curves are convex to the origin (i.e., they bend toward the origin in the middle and away at the edges).** The fourth assumption of utility—the more you have of a particular good, the less you are willing to give up of something else to get even more of that good—implies something about the way indifference curves are curved. Specifically, it implies they will be convex to the origin; that is, the middle will bend in toward the origin as if the origin is tugging on the indifference curve, trying to pull it in.

To see what this curvature means in terms of a consumer's behavior, think about what the slope of an indifference curve means. Again, we'll use Michaela as an example. In **Figure 4.4,** at point A where the indifference curve is steep, Michaela is willing to give up a lot of friends to get a few more square feet, because she already has a lot of friends in the building but little space. At point B where the indifference curve is relatively flat, Michaela has a large apartment but few friends around, so she now would require a large amount of space in return for a small reduction in friends to be left equally satisfied.

Figure 4.3   A Consumer's Indifference Curves Cannot Cross

Indifference curves cannot intersect. Here, Michaela would be indifferent between bundles D and F and also indifferent between bundles E and F. The transitivity property would therefore imply that she must also be indifferent between bundles D and E. But this can't be true, because more is preferred to less, and bundle E contains more of both goods (more friends in her building and a larger apartment) than D.

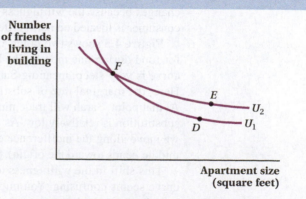

Figure 4.4   Tradeoffs along an Indifference Curve

If the indifference curve is steep, as it is at point *A*, Michaela is willing to give up a lot of friends to get just a few more square feet of apartment space. It isn't just coincidence that she's willing to make this tradeoff at a point where she already has a lot of friends in the building but a very small apartment. Because she already has a lot of one good (friends in the building), she is willing to relinquish quite a bit of it in order to gain more of the other good (apartment size) she doesn't have much of. On the other hand, where the indifference curve is relatively flat, as it is at point *B*, the tradeoff between friends and apartment size is reversed. At *B*, the apartment is already big, but Michaela has few friends around, so she now needs to receive a great deal of extra space in return for a small reduction in friends to be left as well off.

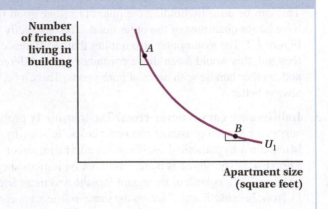

Because tradeoffs between goods generally depend on how much of each good a consumer would have in a bundle, indifference curves are convex to the origin. Except for some extreme cases where the indifference curves become completely flat lines or bend all the way into right angles (which we will discuss later in the chapter), all the indifference curves we draw will have this shape.

The Marginal Rate of Substitution

Indifference curves are all about tradeoffs: How much of one good will a consumer give up to get a little bit more of another good? The slope of the indifference curve exactly captures this tradeoff idea. Economists have a particular name for the slope of an indifference curve: the **marginal rate of substitution of *X* for *Y*** (MRS_{XY}), *the rate at which a consumer is willing to trade off or substitute exactly 1 unit of good* X *(the good on the horizontal axis) for more of good* Y *(the good on the vertical axis) and feel equally well off, with utility held constant:*

marginal rate of substitution of *X* for *Y* (MRS_{XY}) The rate at which a consumer is willing to trade off one good (the good on the horizontal axis, *X*) for another (the good on the vertical axis, *Y*) and still be left equally well off.

$$MRS_{XY} = -\frac{\Delta Y}{\Delta X}$$

(A technical note: We put a negative sign in front of the slope so that we can refer to MRS_{XY} as a positive number. The slope of the indifference curve will be a negative number on its own because the curve slopes downward.) The word "marginal" indicates that we are talking about the tradeoffs associated with small changes in the composition of the bundle of goods—that is, changes at the margin. It makes sense to focus on marginal changes because the willingness to substitute between two goods depends on where the consumer is located on her indifference curve.

Figure 4.5 shows two points on an indifference curve that reflects Sarah's preferences for food during one month. She lives on lattes and burritos. At point *A*, the indifference curve is very steep, meaning Sarah will give up multiple burritos to get one more latte. Here, the marginal rate of substitution is relatively high. The reverse is true at point *B*. At that point, Sarah will trade multiple lattes for one more burrito, so the marginal rate of substitution is relatively low. As a result of this change in Sarah's willingness to trade as we move along the indifference curve, the indifference curve is convex to the origin (the middle bends toward the origin).

This shift in the willingness to substitute one good for another along an indifference curve seems confusing. You might be more familiar with thinking about the slope of a straight line (which is constant) than the slope of a curve (which varies at different points

Figure 4.5   The Slope of an Indifference Curve Is the Marginal Rate of Substitution

The marginal rate of substitution measures the willingness of a consumer to trade one good for the other. It is measured as the negative of the slope of the indifference curve at any point. At point *A*, the slope of the curve is –2, meaning that the MRS is 2. This implies that, for that given bundle, Sarah is willing to trade 2 burritos to receive 1 more latte. At point *B*, the slope is –0.5 and the MRS is 0.5. At this point, Sarah is only willing to give up 0.5 burritos to get another latte.

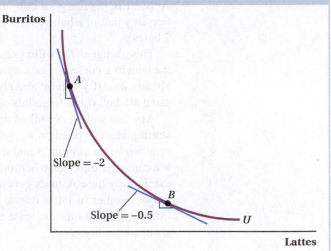

along the curve). Also, how can preferences differ along an indifference curve? After all, a consumer isn't supposed to prefer one point on an indifference curve over another, but now we're saying the consumer's relative tradeoffs between the two goods change as one moves along the curve. Let's address each of these issues in turn.

First, the slope of a curve, unlike a straight line, depends on where on the curve you are measuring the slope. To measure the slope of a curve at any point, draw a straight line that just touches the curve (but does not pass through it) at that point but nowhere else. This point where the line (called a tangent) touches the curve is called a tangency point. The slope of the line is the slope of the curve at the tangency point. The tangents that have points *A* and *B* as tangency points are shown in Figure 4.5. The slopes of those tangents are the slopes of the indifference curve at those points. At point *A*, the slope is –2, indicating that at this point Sarah would require 2 more burritos to forgo 1 latte. At point *B*, the slope is –0.5, indicating that at this point Sarah would require only half of a burrito to be willing to give up a latte. Second, although it's true that a consumer is indifferent between any two points on an indifference curve, that doesn't mean her relative preference for one good versus another is constant all along the curve. As we discussed above, Sarah's relative preference changes with the number of units of each good she already has.

Despite an intimidating name, the marginal rate of substitution makes sense. It tells us the relative value that a consumer places on obtaining one more unit of the good on the horizontal axis, in terms of the good on the vertical axis. You make this kind of decision all the time. Whenever you order off a menu at a restaurant, choose whether to fly or drive home for the holidays, or decide what brand of jeans to buy, you're evaluating relative values. As we see later in this chapter, when prices are attached to goods, the consumer's decision about what to consume boils down to a comparison of the relative value she places on two goods and the goods' relative prices.

The Marginal Rate of Substitution and Marginal Utility

Consider point *A* in Figure 4.5. The marginal rate of substitution at point *A* equals 2 because the slope of the indifference curve at that point is –2:

$$MRS_{XY} = -\frac{\Delta Y}{\Delta X} = -\frac{\Delta Q_{\text{burritos}}}{\Delta Q_{\text{lattes}}} = 2$$

In words, this means that in return for 1 more latte, Sarah is willing to give up 2 burritos. At point *B*, the marginal rate of substitution is 0.5, which implies that Sarah would sacrifice only half of a burrito for 1 more latte (or equivalently, she would sacrifice 1 burrito for 2 lattes).

This change in the willingness to substitute between goods at the margin occurs because the benefit a consumer gets from another unit of a good falls with the number of units she already has. If you have already amped up on caffeine after drinking 6 lattes but haven't eaten all day, you'd forgo lots of lattes to get a burrito.

Another way to see all of this is to think about the change in utility (ΔU) created by starting at some point on an indifference curve and moving a short distance along it. Suppose we begin at point *A* and then move just a bit down and to the right along the curve. We can write the change in utility created by that move as the marginal utility of lattes (the extra utility the consumer gets from a 1-unit increase in lattes, MU_{lattes}) times the increase in the number of lattes due to the move (ΔQ_{lattes}), plus the marginal utility of burritos (MU_{burritos}) times the decrease in the number of burritos ($\Delta Q_{\text{burritos}}$) due to the move. The change in utility is

$$\Delta U = MU_{\text{lattes}} \times \Delta Q_{\text{lattes}} + MU_{\text{burritos}} \times \Delta Q_{\text{burritos}}$$

where MU_{lattes} and MU_{burritos} are the marginal utilities of lattes and burritos at point *A*, respectively. Here's the key: Because we're moving along an indifference curve (so utility is constant at every point on it), *the total change in utility from the move must be zero.* If we set the equation equal to zero, we get

$$0 = \Delta U = MU_{\text{lattes}} \times \Delta Q_{\text{lattes}} + MU_{\text{burritos}} \times \Delta Q_{\text{burritos}}$$

Rearranging the terms slightly will allow us to discern an important relationship:

$$-MU_{\text{burritos}} \times \Delta Q_{\text{burritos}} = MU_{\text{lattes}} \times \Delta Q_{\text{lattes}}$$

$$-\frac{\Delta Q_{\text{burritos}}}{\Delta Q_{\text{lattes}}} = \frac{MU_{\text{lattes}}}{MU_{\text{burritos}}}$$

Notice that the left-hand side of this equation equals the negative of the slope of the indifference curve, or MRS_{XY}. We now can see a very significant connection: *The MRS_{XY} between two goods at any point on an indifference curve equals the inverse ratio of those two goods' marginal utilities:*

➡ The end-of-chapter appendix uses calculus to derive the relationship between the marginal rate of substitution and marginal utilities.

$$MRS_{XY} = -\frac{\Delta Q_{\text{burritos}}}{\Delta Q_{\text{lattes}}} = \frac{MU_{\text{lattes}}}{MU_{\text{burritos}}}$$

In more basic terms, MRS_{XY} shows the point we emphasized from the beginning: You can tell how much people value something by their choices of what they would be willing to give up to get it. The rate at which they give things up reveals the marginal utility of the goods.

We've now established the connection between a consumer's preferences for two goods and the slope of her indifference curves (the MRS_{XY}). They are the same thing. An indifference curve reveals a consumer's willingness to trade one good for another, or each good's relative marginal utility. We can flip this relationship on its head to see what the shapes of indifference curves tell us about consumers' utility functions. In the next two sections, we discuss two key characteristics of an indifference curve: how steep it is, and how curved it is.

The Steepness of Indifference Curves

Figure 4.6 presents two sets of indifference curves reflecting two different sets of preferences for concert tickets and MP3s. In panel a, the indifference curves are steep. In panel b, they are flat. (These two sets of indifference curves have the same degree of curvature

Figure 4.6   Steepness of Indifference Curves

(a) Steep Indifference Curves

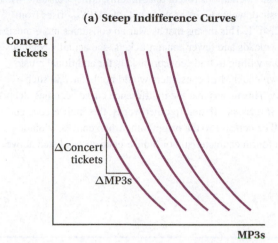

(b) Flat Indifference Curves

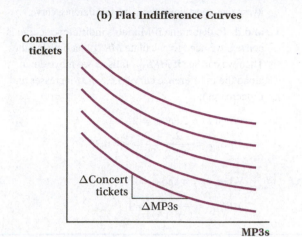

Because the MRS measures the willingness of the consumer to trade one good for another, we can tell a great deal about preferences by examining the shapes of indifference curves. (a) Indifference curves that are relatively steep indicate the consumer is willing to give up a large quantity of the good on the vertical axis to get another unit of the good on the horizontal axis.

Here, the consumer is willing to give up a lot of concert tickets for some additional MP3s. (b) Relatively flat indifference curves imply that the consumer would require a large increase in the good on the horizontal axis to give up a unit of the good on the vertical axis. The consumer with flat indifference curves will give up a lot of MP3s for one additional concert ticket.

so we don't confuse steepness with curvature.) When indifference curves are steep, as in panel a, consumers are willing to give up a lot of the good on the vertical axis (concert tickets) to get a small additional amount of the good on the horizontal axis (MP3s). The opposite is true in panel b, which shows flatter indifference curves. These relationships are just another way of restating the concept of the MRS_{XY} that we introduced earlier.

---

 figure it out 4.1

Go online for interactive, step-by-step help in solving the following problem.

Mariah consumes music downloads (M) and concert tickets (C). Her utility function is given by $U = 0.5M^2 + 2C^2$, where $MU_M = M$ and $MU_C = 4C$.

a. Write an equation for MRS_{MC}.

b. Would bundles of ($M = 4$ and $C = 1$) and ($M = 2$ and $C = 2$) be on the same indifference curve? How do you know?

c. Calculate MRS_{MC} when $M = 4$ and $C = 1$ and when $M = 2$ and $C = 2$.

d. Based on your answers to question b, are Mariah's indifference curves convex? (*Hint*: Does MRS_{MC} fall as M rises?)

Solution:

a. We know that the marginal rate of substitution MRS_{MC} equals MU_M/MU_C. We are told that $MU_M = M$ and $MU_C = 4C$. Thus, $MRS_{MC} = \dfrac{MU_M}{MU_C} = \dfrac{M}{4C}$.

b. For bundles to lie on the same indifference curve, they must provide the same level of utility to the consumer. Therefore, we need to calculate Mariah's level of utility for the bundles of ($M = 4$ and $C = 1$) and ($M = 2$ and $C = 2$):

When $M = 4$ and $C = 1$, $U = 0.5(4)^2 + 2(1)^2 = 0.5(16) + 2(1) = 8 + 2 = 10$

When $M = 2$ and $C = 2$, $U = 0.5(2)^2 + 2(2)^2 = 0.5(4) + 2(4) = 2 + 8 = 10$

Each bundle provides Mariah with the same level of utility, so they must lie on the same indifference curve.

c. and d. To determine if Mariah's indifference curve is convex, we need to calculate MRS_{MC} at both bundles. Then we can see if MRS_{MC} falls as we move down along the indifference curve (i.e., as M increases and C decreases):

When $M = 2$ and $C = 2$,

$$MRS_{MC} = \frac{2}{(4)(2)} = \frac{2}{8} = \frac{1}{4} = 0.25$$

When $M = 4$ and $C = 1$,

$$MRS_{MC} = \frac{4}{(4)(1)} = \frac{4}{4} = 1$$

These calculations reveal that, holding utility constant, when music downloads rise from 2 to 4, the MRS_{MC} rises from 0.25 to 1. This means that as Mariah consumes more music downloads and fewer concert tickets, she actually becomes *more* willing to trade concert tickets for additional music downloads! Most consumers would not behave in such a way. This means that the indifference curve becomes steeper as M rises, not flatter. In other words, this indifference curve will be concave to the origin rather than convex, violating the fourth characteristic of indifference curves listed above.

 Application: Indifference Curves for Breakfast Cereal

Many people can't start the day without a bowl of cereal. Surveys suggest that more than 90% of families in the United States buy breakfast cereal during the course of a year, and total annual cereal sales exceed $10 billion. Hundreds of different kinds of cereal fill grocery store shelves throughout North America.

Economists have studied the cereal market and how people decide what cereal to buy. Their findings give us some direct estimates of indifference curves.

Economist Aviv Nevo once looked at 25 leading cereal brands in 65 cities.[5] He gathered information on the characteristics of the cereals in terms of sugar, calories, fat, fiber, mushiness, and so on, and treated each cereal like a bundle of these characteristics. (An analysis of products using their attributes is called *hedonic analysis,* and economists have done hedonic analyses of cars, computers, houses, and many other kinds of products.)

Nevo computed the implied marginal rates of substitution for these different product attributes by comparing the demand for different cereals at different prices. Let's take his results on two of the "goods" people consume when buying cereal—sugar and fiber. Both have a value and both cost money to produce, so consumers must make tradeoffs between them when choosing what cereal to buy.

We can use Nevo's results to compute a direct estimate of the MRS of fiber for sugar for different kinds of people. Holding everything else equal, Nevo found that a 50-year-old consumer (let's call him Ricardo) with an income one-third above the national average has an MRS of 1.24. To remain indifferent between his current cereal and a new cereal with 1 less gram of fiber, Ricardo requires 1.24 grams of additional sugar in the new cereal (to sweeten the deal). He clearly likes taking in fiber at breakfast.

The MRS differs for other kinds of people, however. A 20-year-old consumer (let's call him David) with income about one-third below the national average has a much lower taste for fiber. According to Nevo's measurements, David's MRS of fiber for sugar is only 0.57. For David to remain indifferent between his current cereal and a new cereal with 1 less gram of fiber, he requires only 0.57 grams of additional sugar. He likes sugar more and is thus more willing to give up fiber to get it.

---

[5] Aviv Nevo, "Measuring Market Power in the Ready-to-Eat Cereal Industry," *Econometrica* 69, no. 2 (2001): 307–342.

Figure 4.7   Older and Younger Adults' Preferences for Breakfast Cereal

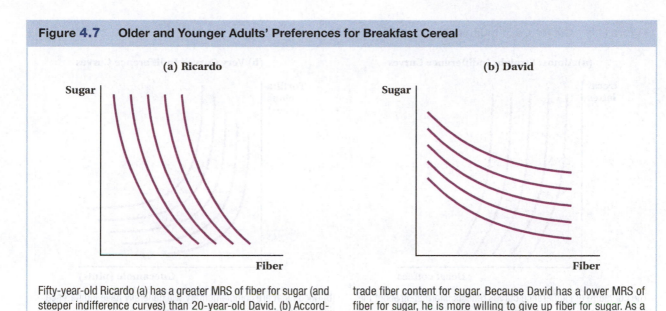

Fifty-year-old Ricardo (a) has a greater MRS of fiber for sugar (and steeper indifference curves) than 20-year-old David. (b) Accordingly, Ricardo is more likely to want his fiber and less willing to trade fiber content for sugar. Because David has a lower MRS of fiber for sugar, he is more willing to give up fiber for sugar. As a result, his indifference curves are flatter.

We know that the MRS of fiber for sugar is the ratio of marginal utilities, MU_{fiber}/MU_{sugar}. Ricardo's ratio is greater than David's because he is willing to give up more sugar in exchange for fiber. Ricardo's indifference curves (**Figure 4.7a**), when drawn with fiber on the horizontal axis and sugar on the vertical axis, are therefore steeper than David's indifference curves (Figure 4.7b). Something about 50-year-olds makes them more likely to prefer high-fiber cereals than high-sugar cereals; 20-year-olds prefer just the opposite. Because they have different tastes in cereal, the marginal rates of substitution and, in turn, the slopes of the indifference curves look different for older adults and younger adults.

This result probably also explains why the people buying Kellogg's Honey Smacks (with 20 grams of sugar and 1.3 grams of fiber per cup) likely aren't the same people purchasing Kashi's GoLean (with 6 grams of sugar and 10 grams of fiber per cup). ■

The Curvature of Indifference Curves: Substitutes and Complements

The steepness of an indifference curve tells us the rate at which a consumer is willing to trade one good for another. The curvature of an indifference curve also has a meaning. If indifference curves between two goods are almost straight, as in **Figure 4.8a,** a consumer (let's call him Evan) is willing to trade about the same amount of the first good (here, decaf coffees) to get the same amount of the second good (decaf lattes), regardless of whether he has a lot of lattes relative to coffees or vice versa. Stated in terms of the marginal rates of substitution, the MRS of coffees for lattes doesn't change much as we move along the indifference curve. In practical terms, it means that the two goods are close substitutes for each other in Evan's utility function. That is, the relative value a consumer places on two substitute goods will not change much depending on the amounts he has of one good versus the other. (It's no coincidence that this example features two goods that many consumers would consider to be close substitutes for each other.)

➡ The online appendix looks at the relationship between the utility function and the shape of indifference curves.

Figure 4.8   Curvature of Indifference Curves

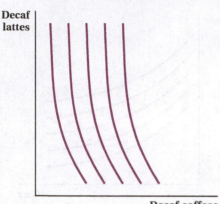

(a) Almost Straight Indifference Curves

Decaf lattes

Decaf coffees

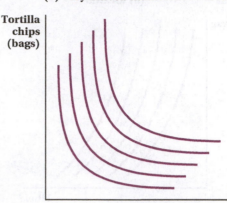

(b) Very Curved Indifference Curves

Tortilla chips (bags)

Guacamole (pints)

The curvature of indifference curves reflects information about the consumer's preferences between two goods, just as its steepness does. (a) Goods that are highly substitutable (such as decaf lattes and decaf coffees) are likely to produce indifference curves that are relatively straight. This means the MRS does not change much as the consumer moves from one point to another along the indifference curve.

(b) Goods that are complementary will generally have indifference curves with more curvature. For example, if a consumer has many tortilla chips and little guacamole, he will be willing to trade many tortilla chips to get some guacamole. If a consumer has a lot of guacamole and few tortilla chips, he will be less willing to trade chips for guacamole.

On the other hand, for goods such as tortilla chips and guacamole that are complements as in Figure 4.8b, the relative value of one more pint of guacamole will be much greater when you have a lot of chips and not much guacamole than if you have 10 pints of guacamole but no chips. In these types of cases, indifference curves are sharply curved, as shown. The MRS of guacamole for chips is very high on the far left part of the indifference curve (where the consumer does not have much guacamole) and very low on the far right (when the consumer is awash in guacamole). The intuition behind the meaning of the curvature of indifference curves may be easier to grasp if we focus on the most extreme cases: perfect substitutes and perfect complements.

perfect substitute A good that a consumer can trade for another good, in fixed units, and receive the same level of utility.

Perfect Substitutes   **Perfect substitutes** are *goods that a consumer can trade for another good, in fixed units, and receive the same level of utility.* **Figure 4.9** offers an example of two goods that might be perfect substitutes: 12-ounce bags of tortilla chips and 3-ounce bags of tortilla chips. If all the consumer cares about is the total amount of chips, then she is just as well off trading 4 small bags of chips for each large bag, regardless of how many of either she already has.[6] These kinds of preferences produce linear indifference curves, and utility functions for perfect substitutes take on the general form $U = aX + bY$, where a indicates the marginal utility of consuming one more unit of X and b indicates the marginal utility of consuming one more unit of Y. This is precisely the situation shown in Figure 4.9. Two goods that are perfect substitutes have indifference curves that are straight lines. In this case, the consumer is willing to trade one 12-ounce bag of tortilla chips for four 3-ounce bags of tortilla chips no matter

---

[6] You could think of reasons why the different-sized bags might not be *perfect* substitutes—multiple small bags, for instance, might be more convenient to bring to the office for lunch. But, regardless, they're close to perfect substitutes.

Figure 4.9 Indifference Curves for Perfect Substitutes

For perfect substitutes, the indifference curves are straight lines with a constant slope, in this case equal to −1/4, which means that the MRS_{XY} is also constant and equal to 1/4. We can't actually say what values a and b take here, only that their ratio is 1 to 4 — that is, $a/b = 1/4$. The indifference curves in this example would be the same if $a = 1$ and $b = 4$ or if $a = 40$ and $b = 160$, for instance. This is another demonstration of the point we made above: A transformation of a utility function that does not change the order of which goods the consumer prefers implies the same preference choices.

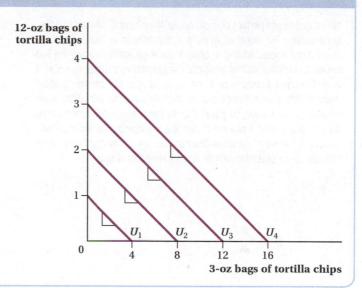

how many of each she currently has, and the consumer's preference for chips does not change along the indifference curve. The MRS is constant in this case.

Another form of perfect substitution might arise if a product has attributes that a consumer does not care about at all. For instance, it may not matter to some people if a bottle of water is branded Aquafina or Dasani. Their indifference curves when comparing Aquafina and Dasani water would therefore be straight lines. On the other hand, other consumers who *do* care about such features would not view the goods as perfect substitutes, and their indifference curves would be curved.

It is crucial to understand that two goods being perfect substitutes does *not* automatically imply that the consumer is indifferent between single items of the goods, one-for-one. In our tortilla chip example above, for instance, the consumer likes a big bag a lot more than a small bag. That's why she would have to receive 4 small bags, not just 1, to be willing to trade away 1 large bag. The idea behind perfect substitutes is only that the tradeoff the consumer is willing to make between the two goods — that is, the marginal rate of substitution — doesn't depend on how much or little she already has of each, but is instead constant at every point along an indifference curve.

Perfect Complements

Perfect complements are *goods from which the consumer receives utility dependent on its being used in a fixed proportion with another good.* **Figure 4.10** shows indifference curves for right and left shoes, which are an example of perfect complements (or at least something very close to it). Compare point A (2 right shoes and 2 left shoes) and point B (3 right shoes and 2 left shoes). Although the consumer has one extra shoe at point B, there is no matching shoe for the other foot, so the extra shoe is useless to her. She is therefore indifferent between these two bundles, and the bundles are on the same indifference curve. Similarly, comparing points A and C in the figure, we see that an extra left-footed shoe provides no additional utility if it isn't paired with a right-footed shoe, so A and C must also lie on the same indifference curve. However, if you add an extra left shoe *and* an extra right

perfect complement A good from which the consumer receives utility dependent on its being used in a fixed proportion with another good.

Figure 4.10 **Indifference Curves for Perfect Complements**

When goods are perfect complements, they have L-shaped indifference curves. For example, at point A, the consumer has 2 left shoes and 2 right shoes. Adding another right shoe while keeping the left shoes constant does not increase the consumer's utility, so point B is on the same indifference curve as point A. In like manner, adding another left shoe will not increase the consumer's utility without an additional right shoe, so point C is on the same indifference curve as points A and B. Because shoes are always consumed together, 1 right shoe and 1 left shoe, the consumer's utility rises only when she has more of both goods (a move from point A to point D).

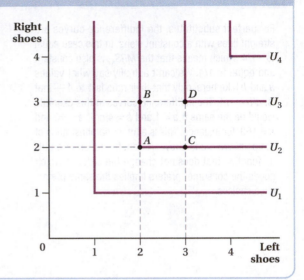

---

shoe (point D compared to point A), then the consumer is better off. That's why D is on a higher indifference curve.

Perfect complements lead to distinctive L-shaped indifference curves. Mathematically, this can be represented as $U = \min\{aX, bY\}$, where a and b are again numbers reflecting how consuming more units of X and Y affects utility. This mathematical structure means a consumer reaches a given utility level by consuming a minimum amount of each good X and Y. To be on the indifference curve U_2, for instance, the consumer must have *at least* 2 left shoes and 2 right shoes. The kink in the indifference curve is the point at which she is consuming the minimum amount of each good at that utility level.[7]

This L-shape is the most extreme case of curvature of indifference curves. It is at the other extreme from the straight-line indifference curves that arise with perfect substitutes, and its shape produces interesting results for MRS_{XY}. At the horizontal part of the indifference curve, MRS_{XY} equals zero, while on the vertical portion, the marginal rate of substitution is infinite. As we've noted, indifference curves more generally will fall somewhere in between the shapes of the indifference curves for perfect substitutes and perfect complements, with some intermediate amount of curvature.

Different Shapes for a Particular Consumer One final point to make about the curvature of indifference curves is that even for a particular consumer, indifference curves may take on a variety of shapes depending on the utility level. They don't all have to look the same.

---

[7] The proportion in which perfect complements are consumed need not be one-for-one, as in the case of our left- and right-shoe example. Chopsticks and Chinese buffet lunches might be perfect complements for some consumers, for example, but it's likely that they will be consumed in a proportion of 2 chopsticks to 1 buffet.

Figure **4.11**   The Same Consumer Can Have Indifference Curves with Different Shapes

Indifference curves for a consumer can take on a variety of shapes, depending on the utility level. For example, at low levels of utility, bananas and strawberries may be substitutes and the consumer may just want to buy something to give her calories, not caring whether it is a banana or strawberry. This means that the indifference curve will be close to linear, as is the case of U_A. But, at higher levels of utility, the consumer may prefer a variety of fruit. This means that she will be willing to give up many bananas for another strawberry when she has a lot of bananas, but is not willing to do so when she only has a few bananas. Here, the consumer's indifference curve will have more curvature, such as U_B.

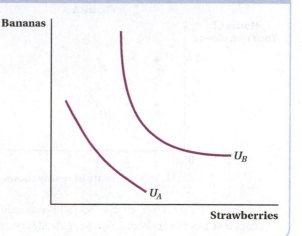

For instance, indifference curve U_A in **Figure 4.11** is almost a straight line. This means that at low levels of utility, this consumer considers bananas and strawberries almost perfect substitutes. If all she is worried about is getting enough calories to survive (which might be the case at really low utility levels like that represented by U_A), she's not going to be picky about the mix of fruit she eats. Indifference curve U_B, on the other hand, is very sharply curved. This means that at higher utility levels, the two goods are closer to perfect complements. When this consumer has plenty of fruit, she will likely prefer some of each fruit rather than a lot of one or the other. Remember, however, that even as the shapes of a consumer's indifference curves vary with her utility levels, the indifference curves will never intersect.

figure it out 4.2

Ming can watch hours of videos on YouTube (Y) or hours of reality shows (R) on TV. Watching more YouTube makes Ming happier, but he really doesn't care about reality shows—good or bad. Draw a diagram showing a set of Ming's indifference curves for hours of YouTube and hours of reality shows. (Put reality shows on the horizontal axis.) What is Ming's MRS_{RY} when he is consuming 1 unit of each good?

Solution:

The easiest way to diagram Ming's preferences is to consider various bundles of reality shows and YouTube, and determine whether they lie on the same or different indifference curves. For example, suppose he watches 1 hour of reality TV and 1 hour of YouTube. Plot this in

Figure A as point A. Now suppose he watches 1 hour of reality TV and 2 hours of YouTube. Plot this as point B. Because watching more hours of YouTube makes Ming happier, point B must lie on a higher indifference curve than point A.

Next, try another point with 2 hours of reality TV and 1 hour of YouTube. Call this point C. Compare point A with point C. Point C has the same number of hours of YouTube as point A, but provides Ming with more reality TV. Ming neither likes nor dislikes reality TV, however, so his utility is unchanged by having more reality TV available. Points A and C must therefore lie on the same indifference curve. This would also be true of points D and E. Economists often refer to a good that has no impact on utility as a "neutral good."

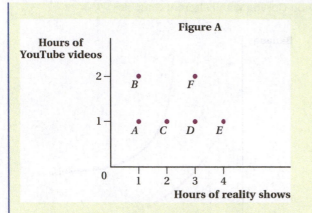

Figure A

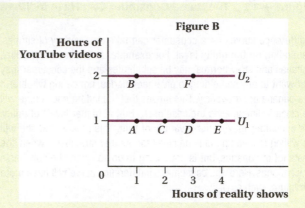

Figure B

Looking at Figure A, we see that there will be an indifference curve that is a horizontal line going through points A, C, D, and E. Will all the indifference curves be horizontal lines? Let's consider another bundle to make sure. Suppose that Ming watches 3 hours of reality TV and 2 hours of YouTube, as at point F. It is clear that Ming will prefer point F to point D because he gets more YouTube. It should also be clear that Ming will be equally happy between points B and F; the same number of hours of YouTube are available to him, and reality shows have no effect on his utility. As shown in Figure B, points B and F lie on the same indifference curve (U_2) and provide a greater level of utility than the bundles on the indifference curve below (U_1).

To calculate the marginal rate of substitution when Ming is consuming 1 unit of each good, we need to calculate the slope of U_1 at point A. Because the indifference curve is a horizontal line, the slope is zero. Therefore, MRS_{RY} is zero. This makes sense; Ming is not willing to give up any YouTube to watch more reality TV because reality TV has no impact on his utility. Remember that MRS_{RY} equals MU_R/MU_Y. Because MU_R is zero, MRS_{RY} will also equal zero.

 Application: Indifference Curves for "Bads"

Let's look at some real-life data on house prices. A research paper by Steven Levitt and Chad Syverson looked at how houses' sale prices vary depending on their characteristics.[8] Their analysis, like Nevo's work on breakfast cereals, uses hedonic regressions. Although the extent to which these types of analyses directly measure utility functions is controversial among economists, the details of that argument are not important to understanding our basic point here: Some products or services are the opposite of "goods." *Goods or services that provide a consumer with negative utility* are called **bads**.

bad A good or service that provides a consumer with negative utility.

Using regression techniques to compare otherwise similar houses (e.g., those having the same architectural style, the same type of siding material, and even located on the

---

[8] Steven Levitt and Chad Syverson, "Market Distortions When Agents Are Better Informed: The Value of Information in Real Estate Transactions," *Review of Economics and Statistics* 90, no. 4 (2008): 599–611.

Figure 4.12 Indifference Curves for a "Bad"

An economic "bad" is a product that reduces a consumer's utility. This homebuyer's utility from a house falls as the age of the house increases. Therefore, to keep her utility constant, we must provide the homebuyer with more bedrooms if we increase the house's age. This leads to upward-sloping indifference curves. Indifference curve U_2 provides more utility than U_1 because (holding the number of bedrooms constant) bundle B contains an older house than bundle C, making the homebuyer worse off. Alternatively, bundles A and C contain houses of the same age, but the house in bundle C has more bedrooms. Thus, the homebuyer is better off at point C (on U_2) than at point A (on U_1).

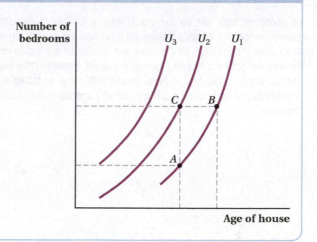

same city block), Levitt and Syverson found that an extra bedroom adds about 5% to the sale price of a house. Central air-conditioning adds about 7% to a house's price, a "state-of-the-art kitchen" almost 8% more, and a fireplace brings in another 4%. The correlation between each of these amenities and the sale price of the house suggests that homebuyers are willing to pay for them. In other words, the number of bedrooms, central air, a state-of-the-art kitchen, and a fireplace are all "goods" (they just happen to be sold as pre-made bundles in the form of houses).

But Levitt and Syverson also uncovered a characteristic that had a negative effect on a house's price, at least up to a point: its age. Again, comparing otherwise similar houses, they found that a house between 6–10 years old sold for 9% less than one that was built less than 6 years ago. Houses 11–25 years old, in turn, had sale prices that were 6% lower than those recorded for 6- to 10-year-old houses. There was another 3% drop in price for houses that were between 11–25 and 26–50 years old. (For houses older than that, prices stopped dropping and even rose slightly, suggesting that eventually "age" may be regarded as a strong selling point.) Therefore, at least for houses less than 50 years old, age is a "bad"; all else equal, buyers receive lower utility from an older house than they would from an otherwise comparable but newer one.

The indifference curves for bundles of age (a bad) and bedrooms (a good) are shown in **Figure 4.12.** We see that the indifference curves slope upward, not downward. Why? Let's first consider bundles A and B, which lie on the same indifference curve, U_1. A homebuyer who does not like old houses needs more bedrooms for the utility of bundle B (greater age, more bedrooms) to equal that of bundle A (younger age, fewer bedrooms). Bundle C has more space than bundle A but is the same age, so C must be preferred to A. Indifference curves that lie higher (more space) and to the left (not as old) indicate greater levels of utility.

Although bads would seem to violate our assumption that more is better, we can always just redefine the age factor as "newness," the *absence* of age and newness is a regular good, and our indifference curves for newness versus bedrooms then slope downward. Graphing our homebuyer's indifference curves in terms of how new a house is — the opposite of

Figure 4.13   Indifference Curves for the Absence of a "Bad"

An economic "bad" can be converted into a "good." By changing the economic bad of a house's "increased age" into the economic good of a house's "newness," we can have two goods that our homeowner desires and produce typical downward-sloping, convex indifference curves. The homebuyer's utility increases with either an increase in the number of bedrooms in a house or an increase in the house's newness.

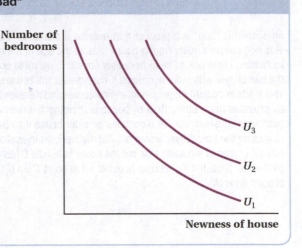

age—produces the standard, downward-sloping indifference curves we've been working with, as in **Figure 4.13.** ■

4.3 The Consumer's Income and the Budget Constraint

In the preceding sections, we analyzed how a consumer's preferences can be described by a utility function, why indifference curves are a convenient way to think about utility, and how the slope of the indifference curve—known as the marginal rate of substitution—captures the relative utility that a consumer derives from different goods at the margin. Our ultimate goal in this chapter is to understand how consumers maximize their utility by choosing a bundle of goods to consume. Because consumers have a limited amount of money and because goods are not free, consumers must make tradeoffs when deciding how much of each good to consume. The decision depends on not only the utility consumers get from each good, but also how much money they have to spend and the prices of the goods. We have to analyze the interaction among all these factors.

We must start with some assumptions (again, to keep things simple, we focus on a model with only two goods). We assume three things:

1. Each good has a fixed price, and any consumer can buy as much of a good as she wants at that price if she has the income to pay for it. We can make this assumption because each consumer is only a small part of the market for a good, so her consumption decision will not affect the equilibrium market price.

2. The consumer has a fixed amount of income available to spend.

3. For now, the consumer cannot borrow or save. Without borrowing, she can't spend more than her income in any given period. With no saving, it means that unspent money is lost forever, so it's use it or lose it.

budget constraint A curve that describes the entire set of consumption bundles a consumer can purchase when spending all income.

To incorporate prices and the consumer's income into our model of consumer behavior, we use a **budget constraint,** *a curve that describes the entire set of consumption bundles a consumer can purchase by spending all income.* For instance, let's go back to the example of Sarah and her burritos and lattes. Suppose Sarah has an income of

Figure 4.14   The Budget Constraint

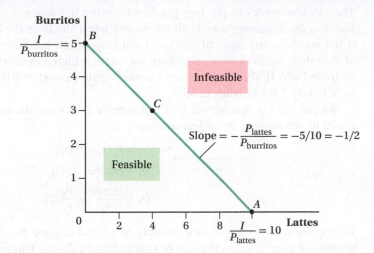

The budget constraint demonstrates the options available to a consumer given her income and the prices of the two goods. Income is $50 in this example; the price of burritos is $10 and the price of lattes is $5. The horizontal intercept is the quantity of lattes the consumer could afford if she spent all of her income (I) on lattes, I/P_{lattes}. The vertical intercept is the quantity of burritos she could afford if she spent all of her income on burritos, $I/P_{burritos}$. Given this, the slope of the budget constraint is the negative of the ratio of the two prices, $-P_{lattes}/P_{burritos}$.

$50 to spend on burritos (which cost $10 each) and lattes ($5 each). **Figure 4.14** shows the budget constraint corresponding to this example. The number of lattes is on the horizontal axis; the number of burritos is on the vertical axis. If Sarah spends her entire income on lattes, then she can consume 10 lattes (10 lattes at $5 each is $50) and no burritos. This combination is point A in the figure. If instead Sarah spends all her money on burritos, she can buy 5 burritos and no lattes, a combination shown at point B. Sarah can purchase any combination of burritos and lattes that lies on the straight line connecting these two points. For example, she could buy 3 burritos and 4 lattes. This is point C.

The mathematical formula for a budget constraint is

$$\text{Income} = P_X Q_X + P_Y Q_Y$$

where P_X and P_Y are the prices for 1 unit of goods X and Y (lattes and burritos in our example), and Q_X and Q_Y are the quantities of the two goods. The equation simply says that the total expenditure on the two goods (the per-unit price of each good multiplied by the number of units purchased) equals the consumer's total income.

Any combination of goods on or below the budget constraint that the consumer has the income to purchase (i.e., any point between the origin on the graph and the budget constraint, including those on the constraint itself) is a **feasible bundle**. *Any combination of goods above or to the right of the budget line that the consumer cannot afford to purchase* is an **infeasible bundle**. These bundles are beyond the consumer's reach even if she spends her entire income. Figure 4.14 illustrates the feasible and infeasible bundles for the budget constraint $50 = 5Q_{lattes} + 10Q_{burritos}$.

The budget constraint in Figure 4.14 is straight, not curved, because we assumed Sarah can buy as much as she wants of a good at a set price per unit. Whether buying the first latte or the tenth, we assume the price is the same. As we see later, if the goods' prices change with the number of units purchased, the budget line will change shape depending on the amount of the goods purchased. That's an unusual case, though.

feasible bundle Any combination of goods on or below the budget constraint that the consumer has the income to purchase.

infeasible bundle Any combination of goods above or to the right of the budget line that the consumer cannot afford to purchase.

The Slope of the Budget Constraint

The relative prices of the two goods determine the slope of the budget constraint. Because the consumer spends all her money when she is on the budget constraint line, if she wants to buy more of one good and stay within her budget, she has to buy less of the other. Relative prices pin down the rate at which purchases of the two goods can be traded off. If she wants to buy 1 more burrito (a cost of $10), for example, she'll have to buy 2 fewer lattes at $5.

We can see the equivalence between relative prices and the slope of the budget constraint by rearranging the budget constraint:

$$\text{Income} = P_X Q_X + P_Y Q_Y$$

$$P_Y Q_Y = \text{Income} - P_X Q_X$$

$$Q_Y = \frac{\text{Income}}{P_Y} - \frac{P_X}{P_Y} Q_X$$

The equation shows if Q_X—the quantity purchased of good X—increases by 1 unit, the quantity of good Y, or Q_Y, that can be bought falls by P_X/P_Y. This ratio of the price of good X relative to the price of good Y is the negative of the slope of the budget constraint. It makes sense that this price ratio determines the slope of the constraint. If good X is expensive relative to good Y (i.e., P_X/P_Y is large), then buying additional units of X will mean you must give up a lot of Y and the budget constraint line will be steep. If good X is relatively inexpensive, you don't have to give up a lot of Y to buy more X, and the constraint line will be flat.

We can use the equation for the budget constraint (Income = $P_X Q_X + P_Y Q_Y$) to find its slope and intercepts. Using the budget constraint ($50 = 5Q_{\text{lattes}} + 10Q_{\text{burritos}}$) shown in Figure 4.14, we get

$$50 = 5Q_X + 10Q_Y$$

$$10Q_Y = 50 - 5Q_X$$

Dividing each side by 10—the price of Q_Y—yields a slope of $-1/2$:

$$Q_Y = 5 - \frac{1}{2}Q_X$$

As we noted earlier, if Sarah spends all of her income on lattes, she will buy 10 lattes (the x-intercept), while she can purchase 5 burritos (the y-intercept) using all of her income. These relative prices and intercepts are illustrated in Figure 4.14.

As will become clear when we combine indifference curves and budget constraints in the next section, the slope of the budget constraint plays an important role in determining which consumption bundles maximize consumers' utility levels.

Factors That Affect the Budget Constraint

Because relative prices determine the slope of the budget constraint, changes in relative prices will change its slope. **Figure 4.15a** demonstrates what happens to our example budget constraint if the price of lattes doubles to $10. The budget constraint rotates clockwise around the vertical axis. Because P_X doubles, P_X/P_Y doubles, and the budget constraint becomes twice as steep. If Sarah spends all her money on lattes, then the doubling of the price of lattes means she can buy only half as many lattes with the same income (the 5 lattes shown at A', rather than 10 lattes as before). If, on the other hand, she spends all her money on burritos (point B), then the change in the price of a latte doesn't affect the bundle she can consume. That's because the price of burritos is still the same ($10). Notice that after the price increase, the set of feasible consumption bundles is smaller: There are now fewer combinations of goods that Sarah can afford with her income.

If instead the price of a burrito doubles to $20, but that of a latte remains stable at the original $5 price (Figure 4.15b), the budget constraint's movement is reversed: It rotates counterclockwise around the horizontal axis, becoming half as steep. If Sarah wanted to buy only lattes, this wouldn't affect the number of lattes she could buy. If she wants only burritos, now she can obtain only half as many (if you could buy a half a burrito; we'll assume you can for now), at bundle B'. Notice that this price increase also shrinks the feasible set of bundles just as the lattes' price increase did. Always remember that when the price *rises,* the budget constraint rotates *toward* the origin. When the price *falls,* it rotates *away* from the origin.

Now suppose prices are stable but Sarah's income falls by half (to $25). With only half the income, Sarah can buy only half as many lattes and burritos as she could before (Figure 4.15c). If she spends everything on lattes, she can now buy only 5. If she buys only burritos, she can afford 2.5. But because relative prices haven't changed, the tradeoffs between the goods haven't changed. To buy 1 more burrito, Sarah still has to give up 2 lattes. Thus, the slope of the budget constraint remains the same.

Note that had both prices doubled while income stayed the same, the budget constraint would be identical to the new one shown in Figure 4.15c. We can see this more

---

Figure 4.15   Effects of Price or Income Changes on the Budget Constraint

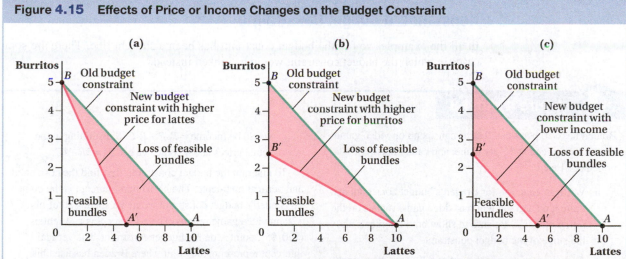

(a) When the price of lattes increases, the horizontal intercept (I/P_{lattes}) falls, the slope ($-P_{lattes}/P_{burritos}$) gets steeper, the budget constraint rotates toward the origin, and the consumer (Sarah) has a smaller set of latte and burrito combinations from which to choose. The higher price for lattes means that she can buy fewer lattes, or if she purchases the same number of lattes, she has less money remaining to buy burritos.

(b) When the price of burritos increases, the vertical intercept ($I/P_{burritos}$) falls, the slope ($-P_{lattes}/P_{burritos}$) gets flatter, the budget constraint rotates toward the origin, and again, Sarah has a smaller choice set. The higher price for burritos means that she can buy fewer burritos or, for a given purchase of burritos, she has less money available to buy lattes.

(c) When Sarah's income falls, both the horizontal and vertical intercepts fall and the budget constraint shifts in. The horizontal intercept is lower because income I falls; thus, (I/P_{lattes}) falls. The same holds for the vertical axis. Because the movement along both axes is caused by the change in income (the reduction in I is the same along both axes), the new budget constraint is parallel to the initial budget constraint. Had both prices doubled while income stayed the same, the budget constraint would be the same.

clearly if we plug in $2P_X$ and $2P_Y$ for the prices in the slope-intercept format of the budget constraint:

$$Q_Y = \frac{\text{Income}}{2P_Y} - \frac{2P_X}{2P_Y}Q_X$$

$$Q_Y = \frac{1}{2}\left(\frac{\text{Income}}{P_Y}\right) - \frac{P_X}{P_Y}Q_X$$

In both the figure and the equation, this type of change in prices decreases the purchasing power of the consumer's income, shifting the budget constraint inward. The same set of consumption bundles is feasible in either case. If Sarah's income had increased rather than decreased (or the prices of both goods had fallen in equal proportions), the budget constraint would have shifted out, not in. Its slope would remain the same, though, because the relative prices of burritos and lattes would not have changed.

We've now considered what happens to the budget constraint in two situations: when income changes while prices stay constant and when prices change, holding income constant. If prices and income both go up proportionally (e.g., all prices double and income doubles), then the budget constraint doesn't change at all. You have double the money but everything costs twice as much, so you can only afford the same bundles you could before. You can see this mathematically in the equation for the budget constraint above: If you multiply all prices and income by any positive number (call it k), all the ks will cancel out, leaving you with the original equation.

Nonstandard Budget Constraints

In all the examples so far, the budget constraint has been a straight line. There are some cases in which the budget constraint would be kinked instead.

figure it out 4.3

Braden has $20 per week that he can spend on video game rentals (R), priced at $5 per game, and candy bars (C), priced at $1 each.

a. Write an equation for Braden's budget constraint and draw it on a graph that has video game rentals on the horizontal axis. Be sure to show both intercepts and the slope of the budget constraint.

b. Assuming he spends the entire $20, how many candy bars does Braden purchase if he chooses to rent 3 video games?

c. Suppose that the price of a video game rental falls from $5 to $4. Draw Braden's new budget line (indicating intercepts and the slope).

Solution:

a. The budget constraint represents the feasible combinations of video game rentals (R) and candy bars (C) that Braden can purchase given the current prices and his income. The general form of the budget constraint

would be Income $= P_R R + P_C C$. Substituting in the actual prices and income, we get $20 = 5R + 1C$.

To diagram the budget constraint, first find the horizontal and vertical intercepts. The horizontal intercept is the point on Braden's budget constraint where he spends all of his $20 on video game rentals. The x-intercept is at 4 rentals ($20/$5), point A on his budget constraint. The vertical intercept represents the point where Braden has used his entire budget to purchase candy bars. He could purchase 20 candy bars ($20/$1) as shown at point B. Because the prices of candy bars and video game rentals are the same no matter how many Braden buys, the budget constraint is a straight line that connects these two points.

The slope of the budget constraint can be measured by the rise over the run. Therefore, it is equal to $\frac{\Delta C}{\Delta R} = -\frac{20}{4} = -5$. We can check our work by recalling that the slope of the budget constraint is equal to the negative of the ratio of the two prices or $-\frac{P_R}{P_C} = -\frac{5}{1} = -5$. Remember that the slope of the budget constraint shows the rate at which Braden is able to exchange candy bars for video game rentals.

b. If Braden currently purchases 3 video game rentals, that means he spends $15 (= $5 × 3) on them. This leaves $5 (= $20 − $15) for purchasing candy bars. At a price of $1 each, Braden purchases 5 candy bars.

c. When the price of a video game rental falls to $4, the vertical intercept is unaffected. If Braden chooses to spend his $20 on candy bars, at a price of $1, he can still afford to buy 20 of them. Thus, point B will also be on his new budget constraint. However, the horizontal intercept increases from 4 to 5. At a price of $4 per rental, Braden can now afford 5 rentals if he chooses to allocate his entire budget to rentals (point C). His new budget constraint joins points B and C.

The slope of the budget constraint is $\frac{\Delta C}{\Delta R} = -\frac{20}{5} = -4$.

Note that this equals the inverse price ratio of the two goods $\left(-\frac{P_R}{P_C} = -\frac{4}{1} = -4 \right)$.

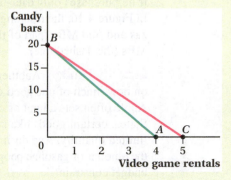

Quantity Discounts

Suppose Alex spends his $100 weekly income on pizzas and data usage on his phone. A pizza costs $10; if he spends everything on pizzas, he can buy 10. If the price of phone data is constant at 10 cents per MB, he can buy up to 1 GB (1,000 MBs) of data (**Figure 4.16**). The budget constraint in the case where data use costs a constant 10 cents per MB is given by the solid section of the line running from zero MBs and 10 pizzas up to 1,000 MBs and zero pizzas.

Phone plans often offer quantity discounts on data. With a quantity discount, the price the consumer pays per unit of the good depends on the number of units purchased. If Alex's

Figure 4.16   **Quantity Discounts and the Budget Constraint**

When the price of phone data is constant at 10 cents per MB, Alex's budget constraint for megabytes of data and pizza has a constant slope, as represented by the solid line. If the phone company offers a quantity discount on data, however, Alex's budget constraint will be kinked. Here, Alex's data plan charges 10 cents per MB for the first 600 MBs per month and 5 cents per MB after that, resulting in the kink at 600 MBs shown by the dashed line. The triangle above the initial budget constraint and below the dashed line represents the set of MBs of data and pizza combinations Alex can afford under the new pricing scheme that he could not have purchased at a constant price of 10 cents per MB.

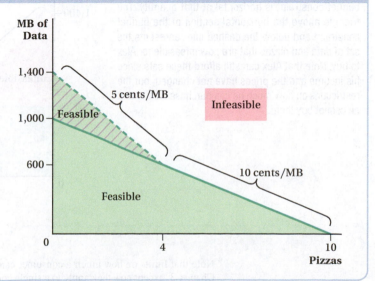

calling plan charges 10 cents per MB for the first 600 MBs per month and 5 cents per MB after that, his budget constraint will have a kink. In particular, because data usage gets cheaper above 600 MBs, the actual budget constraint has a kink at 600 MBs and 4 pizzas. Because the price of the good on the *y*-axis (data usage) becomes relatively cheaper, the constraint rotates clockwise at that quantity, becoming steeper. To find where the budget constraint intercepts the vertical axis, we have to figure out how many MBs Alex can buy if he purchases only data. This total is 1,400 MBs [(600 × $0.10) + (800 × $0.05) = $100]. In Figure 4.16, the resulting budget constraint runs from 10 pizzas and zero MBs to 4 pizzas and 600 MBs (part of the solid line) and then continues up to zero pizzas and 1,400 MBs (the dashed line).

Quantity Limits   Another way a budget constraint can be kinked is if there is a limit on how much of one good can be consumed. When the newest iPhone model comes out, Apple often sets a limit of one per customer. Similarly, during World War II in the United States, certain goods like sugar and butter were rationed. Each family could buy only a limited quantity. And during the oil price spikes of the 1970s, gas stations often limited the amount of gasoline people could buy. These limits have the effect of creating a kinked budget constraint.[9]

Suppose that Alex's carrier or the government (or maybe his parents) expressly capped Alex's weekly data usage at 600 MBs per week. In that case, the part of the budget constraint beyond 600 MB becomes infeasible, and the constraint becomes horizontal at 600, as shown by the solid line in **Figure 4.17**. Note that neither Alex's income nor any prices have changed in this example. He still has enough money to reach any part in the area below the dashed section of the budget constraint that is labeled infeasible. He just isn't allowed to spend it. Consequently, for the flat part of the budget constraint, he will have unspent money left over. As we see in the next

---

Figure 4.17   Quantity Limits and the Budget Constraint

When there is a limit on how much of a good a person can consume, a budget constraint will be kinked. When Alex is limited to 600 MBs of data per week, his budget constraint is horizontal at that quantity. The triangle above the horizontal section of the budget constraint and below the dashed line represents the set of data and pizzas that are now infeasible for Alex to buy. Note that Alex can still afford these sets since his income and the prices have not changed, but the restrictions on how much he can purchase dictate that he cannot buy them.

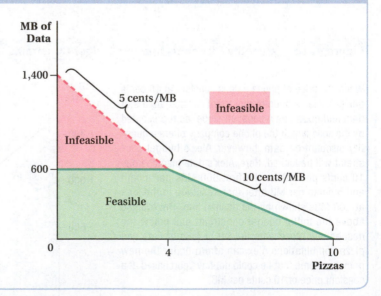

---

[9] Note that limits on how much a consumer can purchase are a lot like the quotas we learned about in Chapter 3, except now they apply to a single consumer, rather than to the market as a whole.

section, you will never actually want to consume a bundle on the flat part of the budget constraint. (You might want to see if you can figure out why yourself, before we tell you the answer.)

4.4 Combining Utility, Income, and Prices: What Will the Consumer Consume?

We now have in place all the pieces necessary to figure out what a consumer will buy. We know the consumer's preferences for bundles of goods from the utility function and its associated indifference curves. We know the consumer's budget constraint and which bundles are feasible given her income and the goods' prices.

FREAKONOMICS

Do Traffic Jams Lead to Divorce?

There are lots of reasons why couples get divorced. Traffic jams are not typically something we expect to be at the top of that list. In Beijing, however, bad traffic is leading to divorces, but you would never guess the reason why.

Beijing has some of the worst traffic in the world. As the Chinese economy grew, so did the demand for automobiles. The resulting traffic jams and air pollution became so severe that in 2011 government officials realized they had to take action. A committee was formed to find a solution to traffic congestion. It came up with a plan many considered excellent: The city would limit the number of new license plates issued each month. Without an official license plate, you could not drive a car, so this policy would bring a halt to the mounting number of automobiles. It was further decided that, to give all of Beijing's residents a fair chance, the license plates would be awarded by lottery, held on the 26th of each month.

VCG/Getty Images

Did the new policy work? Definitely not as government officials had hoped, and for reasons any economist could have predicted. It dramatically reduced the supply of new license plates and kept the price of a new plate low should you happen to win the lottery. The number of consumers who wanted a license plate at that reduced price was far greater than the number available, making the chance of winning the lottery low. Knowing that, people who didn't even own a car at that point entered the lottery anyway. If they were lucky enough to win, they could hold onto their new plates until ready to actually purchase a car. The likelihood of winning the lottery was so low—1 in 1,907—that not many people had to worry about winning a license plate before they were able to use it!

When government policies prevent a market from reaching equilibrium, consumers find ways to get around the policy. A black market in license plates soon sprung up. Another solution was for Beijing residents to buy a car in another province and then just transport it to the city (even though that action was illegal, and the police could fine you 100 to 200 RMB, or $15 to $30, each time they stopped you).

There is only one legal way to transfer a license plate from one person to another in Beijing: through marriage. If, say, a wife wins the lottery, she is allowed to give that license plate to her husband. How badly did some people want license plates? Well, it turns out some happily married couples decided to get a divorce. One of the partners would then pay a lottery winner to marry him (or her), transfer the license plate, immediately seek a divorce, and then remarry the original spouse!

This is how bad traffic—combined with government policies that do not respect the power of supply and demand—could lead someone to get divorced not just once, but twice.

Solving the Consumer's Optimization Problem

As we mentioned in the introduction to this chapter, the choice of how much to consume (like so many economic decisions) is a *constrained optimization* problem. There is something you want to maximize (utility, in this case), and there is something that limits how much you can get (the budget constraint, in this case). And as we will see in the next chapter, the constrained optimization problem forms the basis of the demand curve.

Before we try to solve this constrained optimization problem, think about what makes it tricky: We must compare some things measured in dollars (like income and prices) to other things measured in imaginary units that don't translate into dollars (like utils of utility). How can you know whether you're willing to pay $3 to get an extra unit of utility? Well, you can't, really. What you can figure out, however, is whether spending an extra dollar on, say, golf balls gives you more or less utility than spending an extra dollar on something else, like AAA batteries. It turns out that figuring out this choice using indifference curves and budget constraints makes solving the consumer's optimization problem straightforward.

Look at the axes we use to show indifference curves and budget constraints. They are the same: The quantity of some good is on the vertical axis, and the quantity of some other good is on the horizontal axis. That's important because it means we can display indifference curves and the budget constraint for two goods in the same graph, making the consumer's problem easier to solve.

Figure 4.18 presents an example that shows a combination of indifference curves and a budget constraint. Remember, the consumer wants to get as much utility as possible from consuming the two goods, subject to the limits imposed by her budget constraint. What bundle will she choose? The bundle at point *A*. That's the highest indifference curve she can reach given her budget line.

Why is *A* the utility-maximizing consumption bundle? Compare point *A* to another feasible bundle, such as *B*. Point *B* is on the budget constraint, so the consumer could afford it. However, because *B* is on a lower indifference curve (U_1) than *A* is (U_2), bundle *B* provides less utility than *A*. Bundles *C* and *D*, too, are feasible but worse than *A* in terms of utility provided because they are on the same indifference curve as *B*. The consumer

Figure 4.18   The Consumer's Optimal Choice

The consumer's optimal consumption bundle occurs at the point of tangency between her budget constraint and her indifference curve, shown here at point *A*. The consumer can afford the consumption bundles represented by points *B*, *C*, and *D*, but these are on a lower indifference curve (U_1) than is point *A* (U_2). Point *E* is on a higher indifference curve (U_3), but it lies outside the consumer's budget constraint and is thus infeasible.

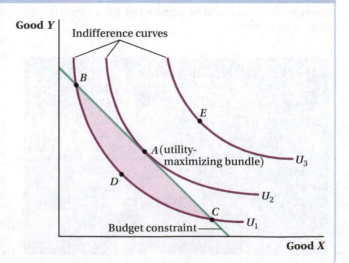

would love to consume bundle E because it's on an indifference curve (U_3) that corresponds to a higher utility level than U_2. Unfortunately, she can't afford E. It's outside her budget constraint. Basically, the consumer reaches for the sky but can only get as high as the budget constraint will allow.

A look at the consumer's optimal consumption bundle A in Figure 4.18 shows that it has a special feature: The indifference curve, U_2, touches the budget constraint once and only once, exactly at A. Mathematically speaking, U_2 and the budget constraint are tangent at point A. As long as the original assumptions we made about utility hold, no other indifference curve we can draw will have this feature. Any other indifference curve will not be tangent, and therefore will cross the budget constraint twice or not at all. If you can draw another indifference curve that is tangent, it will cross an indifference curve shown in Figure 4.18, violating the transitivity assumption. (Give it a try—it is a useful exercise.)

This single tangency is not a coincidence. It is a requirement of utility maximization. To see why, suppose an indifference curve and the budget constraint never touched. Then no point on the indifference curve is feasible, and by definition, no bundle on that indifference curve can be the way for a consumer to maximize her utility given her income.

Then suppose the indifference curve crosses the budget constraint twice. This implies there must be a bundle that offers the consumer higher utility than any on this indifference curve and that the consumer can afford. For example, the shaded region between indifference curve U_1 and the budget constraint in Figure 4.18 reflects all the bundles that are feasible and provide higher utility than bundles B, C, D, or any other point on U_1. That means no bundle on U_1 maximizes utility; there are other bundles that are both affordable *and* offer higher utility. This means that only at a point of tangency are there no other bundles that are both (1) feasible and (2) offer a higher utility level. This tangency is the utility-maximizing bundle for the consumer.

Mathematically, the tangency of the indifference curve and budget constraint means that they have the same slope at the optimal consumption bundle. This has an important economic interpretation. In Section 4.2, we defined the negative of the slope of the indifference curve as the marginal rate of substitution, and we discussed how the MRS_{XY} reflects the ratio of the *marginal utilities* of the two goods. In Section 4.3, we saw that the slope of the budget constraint equals the negative of the ratio of the *prices* of the two goods. Therefore, the fact that the consumer's utility-maximizing bundle is at a tangency between an indifference curve and the budget constraint gives us this key insight: *When the consumer spends all her income and maximizes her utility, her optimal consumption bundle is the one at which the ratio of the goods' marginal utilities exactly equals the ratio of their prices.*

This economic idea behind utility maximization can be expressed mathematically. At the point of tangency,

$$\text{Slope of indifference curve} = \text{Slope of budget constraint}$$
$$-MRS_{XY} = -MU_X/MU_Y = -P_X/P_Y$$
$$MU_X/MU_Y = P_X/P_Y$$

Why are the marginal utility and price ratios equal when the consumer maximizes her utility level? If they were not equal, she could do better by shifting consumption from one good to the other. To see why, let's say Meredith is maximizing her utility over bottles of Gatorade and protein bars. Suppose bottles of Gatorade are twice as expensive as protein bars, but she is considering a bundle in which her marginal utilities from the two goods *are not* 2 to 1 as the price ratio is. Say she gets the same amount of utility at the margin from another bottle of Gatorade as from another protein bar so that the ratio of the goods' marginal utilities is 1. Given the relative prices, she could give up 1 bottle of Gatorade and buy 2 more protein bars, and doing so would let her reach a higher utility level. Those 2 extra protein bars are worth twice as much in utility terms as the lost bottle of Gatorade.

Now suppose that a bottle of Gatorade offers Meredith 4 times the utility at the margin as a protein bar. The ratio of Meredith's marginal utilities for Gatorade and protein bars (4 to 1) is higher than the price ratio (2 to 1), so she could buy 2 fewer protein bars in exchange for 1 more bottle of Gatorade. Because the Gatorade delivers twice the utility lost from the 2 protein bars, Meredith will be better off buying fewer protein bars and more Gatorade.

It is often helpful to rewrite this optimization condition in terms of the consumer's marginal utility per dollar spent:

$$\frac{MU_X}{MU_Y} = \frac{P_X}{P_Y} \Rightarrow \frac{MU_X}{P_X} = \frac{MU_Y}{P_Y}$$

→ The end-of-chapter appendix uses calculus to solve the consumer's utility-maximization problem.

Here, the utility-maximization problem can be restated as finding the consumption bundle that gives the consumer the most bang for her buck. This occurs when the marginal utility per dollar spent (MU/P) is equal across all goods. If this is not the case, the consumer can improve her utility by adjusting her consumption of good X and good Y.[10]

 figure it out 4.4

Go online for interactive, step-by-step help in solving the following problem.

Suppose Antonio gets utility from consuming two goods, burgers and fries. His utility function is given by

$$U = \sqrt{BF} = B^{0.5}F^{0.5}$$

where B is the number of burgers he eats and F the servings of fries. Antonio's marginal utility of a burger $MU_B = 0.5B^{-0.5}F^{0.5}$, and his marginal utility of an order of fries $MU_F = 0.5B^{0.5}F^{-0.5}$. Antonio's income is \$20, and the prices of burgers and fries are \$5 and \$2, respectively. What are Antonio's utility-maximizing quantities of burgers and fries?

Solution:

We know that the optimal solution to the consumer's maximization problem sets the marginal rate of substitution—the ratio of the goods' marginal utilities—equal to the goods' price ratio:

$$MRS_{BF} = \frac{MU_B}{MU_F} = \frac{P_B}{P_F}$$

where P_B and P_F are the goods' prices. Therefore, to find the utility-maximizing quantities of burgers and fries, we set the ratio of marginal utilities equal to the goods' price ratio and simplify:

$$\frac{MU_B}{MU_F} = \frac{P_B}{P_F}$$

$$\frac{0.5B^{-0.5}F^{0.5}}{0.5B^{0.5}F^{-0.5}} = \frac{5}{2}$$

$$\frac{0.5F^{0.5}F^{0.5}}{0.5B^{0.5}B^{0.5}} = \frac{5}{2}$$

$$\frac{F}{B} = \frac{5}{2}$$

$$2F = 5B$$

$$F = 2.5B$$

This condition tells us that Antonio maximizes his utility when he consumes fries to burgers at a 5 to 2 ratio. We now know the ratio of the optimal quantities, but do not yet know exactly what quantities Antonio will choose to consume. To figure that out, we can use the budget

---

[10] Interestingly, the same consumer utility-maximization problem can be solved as a cost-minimization problem instead and it will give exactly the same answer. In this case, a consumer tries to minimize the cost of reaching a target level of utility. Economists call this the "dual" to the utility-maximization problem. The appendix to this chapter gives the mathematics behind both approaches and shows why they yield the same answer.

constraint, which pins down the total amount Antonio can spend, and therefore the total quantities of each good he can consume.

Antonio's budget constraint can be written as

$$\text{Income} = P_F F + P_B B, \text{ or}$$

$$B = \frac{\text{Income}}{P_B} - \frac{P_F}{P_B} F$$

Substituting in the values from the problem gives

$$B = \frac{20}{5} - \frac{2}{5} F$$

$$B = 4 - 0.4F$$

Now we can substitute the utility-maximization condition $F = 2.5B$ into the budget constraint to find the quantity of burgers Antonio will consume:

$$B = 4 - 0.4F$$
$$B = 4 - 0.4(2.5B)$$
$$B = 4 - B$$
$$2B = 4$$
$$B = 2$$

And because $F = 2.5B$, then $F = 5$.

Therefore, given his budget constraint, Antonio maximizes his utility by consuming 2 burgers and 5 servings of fries.

Implications of Utility Maximization

The marginal-utility-ratio-equals-price-ratio result has another implication for the economy as a whole that can initially be surprising. Even if two consumers have very different preferences between two goods, they will have the *same* ratio of marginal utilities for the two goods in equilibrium, because utility maximization implies that the MRS for each of them will equal the ratio of the prices, and that ratio is the same for both of them.[11]

This might seem odd. First of all, we have said that you can't compare utility levels across people. Second, even if you could—if, say, Jack consumes 9 packs of gum and 1 iTunes download, while Meg consumes 9 downloads and only 1 pack of gum—it would seem that Jack likes gum a lot and would therefore be willing to pay more for another pack of gum (and a lot less for iTunes) than Meg.

That would be true *if both Jack and Meg had to consume the same bundle,* but they don't. They can choose how much of each good they want to consume. Because Jack likes gum a lot, he will consume so much of it that he drives down his marginal utility until, by the time he and Meg both reach their utility-maximizing consumption bundles, they will both end up placing the same relative marginal utilities on the two goods. This outcome occurs because the relative value they place on any two goods (on the margin) comes from the relative prices. Because Meg and Jack face the same prices, the goods they consume will end up with the same relative marginal utilities.

Figure 4.19 depicts this very situation. To keep the picture simple, let Jack and Meg have the same incomes. Because they also face the same relative prices, their budget constraints are the same. Jack really likes gum relative to iTunes downloads, so his indifference curves tend to be flat: He has to be given a lot of iTunes to make up for any loss of gum. Meg feels the opposite. She has to receive quite a bit of gum to make up for relinquishing an iTunes download, so her indifference curves are steep. Nevertheless, both Jack and Meg's utility-maximizing bundles are on the same budget line, and they will pick consumption points where their marginal rates of substitution at those bundles are the same (and match the relative prices). We've drawn the indifference

[11] Technically, this is true only of consumers who are consuming a positive amount of both goods, or who are at "interior" solutions in economists' lingo. We'll discuss this issue in the next section.

Figure 4.19 Two Consumers' Optimal Choices

Although they have the same budget constraint, Jack and Meg have different relative preferences and, therefore, different optimal consumption bundles. Because Jack likes gum relative to iTunes downloads, his indifference curve (U_J) is flat and he consumes much more gum than iTunes at his optimal consumption bundle at point J. Meg's indifference curve (U_M) is much steeper and reflects her relative preference for iTunes downloads over gum; her utility-maximizing bundle is shown at point M. Although their consumption bundles are different, the MRS is the same at these points.

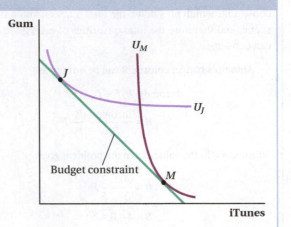

curves for Jack (U_J) and Meg (U_M) so that they are tangent to the budget line and therefore contain the utility-maximizing bundle.

Even though Jack and Meg have the same MRS_{XY}, the amounts of each good they consume are different. Jack, the gum lover, maximizes his utility by choosing a bundle (J) with a lot of gum and not many iTunes downloads. Meg's optimal consumption bundle (M), on the other hand, has a lot of iTunes downloads and little gum. Again, both consumers end up with the same MRS in their utility-maximizing bundles because each consumes a large amount of the good for which he or she has the stronger preference. By behaving in this way, Jack and Meg drive down the relative marginal utility of the good they prefer until their marginal utility ratio equals the price ratio.

Note that these two indifference curves cross. Although earlier we learned that indifference curves can never cross, the "no crossing" rule applies only to the indifference curves of one individual. Figure 4.19 shows indifference curves for two different people with different preferences, so the *transitivity* rule we talked about before doesn't hold. If you like gum more than iTunes, and your friend likes iTunes more than, say, coffee, that doesn't imply you have to like gum more than coffee. So, the same consumption bundle (say, 3 packs of gum and 5 iTunes downloads) can offer different utility levels to different people.

A Special Case: Corner Solutions

Up to this point, we have analyzed situations in which the consumer optimally consumes some of both goods. This assumption usually makes sense if we think that utility functions have the property that the more you have of a good, the less you are willing to give up of something else to get more. Because the first little bit of a good provides the most marginal utility in this situation, a consumer will typically want at least *some* amount of a good.

Depending on the consumer's preferences and relative prices, however, in some cases a consumer will not want to spend any of her money on a good. *A utility-maximizing bundle located at the "corner" of the budget constraint where the consumer purchases only one of two goods* is called a **corner solution**. (Its name derives from the fact that the optimal consumption bundle is at the "corner" of the budget line, where it meets the axis.) *A utility-maximizing bundle that contains positive quantities of both goods* (like the cases we've looked at so far in this chapter) is called an **interior solution**.

Figure 4.20 depicts a corner solution. Greg, our consumer, has an income of $240 and is choosing his consumption levels of mystery novels and Bluetooth speakers. Let's say a hardcover mystery novel costs $20, and a Bluetooth speaker costs $120. Because speakers are more expensive than mystery novels, Greg can afford up to 12 mysteries but only 2 speakers. Nonetheless, the highest utility that Greg can obtain given his income is bundle *A*, where he consumes all speakers and no mystery novels.

How do we know *A* is the optimal bundle? Consider another feasible bundle, such as *B*. Greg can afford it, but it is on an indifference curve U_1 that corresponds to a lower utility level than U_2. The same logic would apply to bundles on any indifference curve between U_1 and U_2. Furthermore, any bundle that offers higher utility than U_2 (i.e., above and to the right of U_2) isn't feasible given Greg's income. So, U_2 must be the highest utility level Greg can achieve, and he can do so only by consuming bundle *A*, because that's the only bundle he can afford on that indifference curve.

In a corner solution, then, the highest indifference curve touches the budget constraint exactly once, just as with the interior solutions we discussed earlier. The only difference with a corner solution is that bundle *A* is not a point of tangency. The indifference curve is flatter than the budget constraint at that point (and everywhere else). That means Greg's MRS—the ratio of his marginal utility from mystery novels relative to his marginal utility from Bluetooth speakers—is *less* than the price ratio of the two goods rather than equal to it. In other words, even when he's consuming no mysteries, his marginal utility from them is so low, it's not worth paying the price of a book to be able to consume one. The marginal utility he'd have to give up with fewer speakers would not be made up for by the fact that he could spend some of his money on novels.

corner solution A utility-maximizing bundle located at the "corner" of the budget constraint where the consumer purchases only one of two goods.

interior solution A utility-maximizing bundle that contains positive quantities of both goods.

↪ The online appendix further explains the mathematics of corner solutions.

Figure 4.20 A Corner Solution

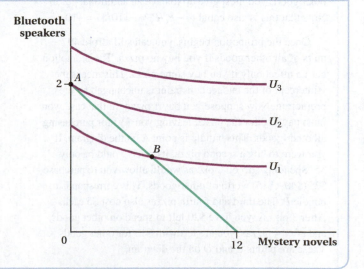

A corner solution occurs when the consumer spends all his money on one good. Given Greg's income and the relative prices of mystery novels and Bluetooth speakers, Greg is going to consume two speakers and zero mystery novels at his optimal consumption bundle (*A*). All other feasible consumption bundles, such as point *B*, correspond to indifference curves with lower utility levels than the indifference curve U_2 at point *A*. Greg cannot afford consumption bundles at a higher utility level, such as U_3, with his current income.

figure it out 4.5

A pizza chain recently offered the following special promotion: "Buy one pizza at full price and get your next three pizzas for just $5 each!" Assume that the full price of a pizza is $10, your daily income is $40, and the price of all other goods $1 is per unit.

a. Draw budget constraints for pizza and all other goods that reflect your situations both before and during the special promotion. (Put the quantity of pizzas on the horizontal axis.) Indicate the horizontal and vertical intercepts and the slope of the budget constraint.

b. How is this special offer likely to alter your buying behavior?

c. How might your answer to (b) depend on the shape of your indifference curves?

Solution:

a. To draw your budget constraint, you need to find the combinations of pizza and all other goods that are available to you before and during the promotion. The starting place for drawing your budget constraint is to find its x- and y-intercepts.

Before the promotion, you could afford 4 pizzas a day ($40/$10) if you spent all of your income on pizza. This is the x-intercept (Figure A). Likewise, you could afford 40 units of all other goods per day ($40/$1) if you purchased no pizza. This is the y-intercept. The budget constraint BC_1, shown in Figure A, connects these two points and has a slope of $-40/4 = -10$. This slope measures the amount of other goods you must give up to have an additional pizza. Note that this is also equal to $-P_x/P_y = -\$10/\$1 = -10$.

Once the promotion begins, you can still afford 40 units of all other goods if you buy no pizza. The promotion has an effect only if you buy some pizza. This means the y-intercept of the budget constraint is unchanged by the promotion. Now suppose you buy 1 pizza. In that case, you must pay $10 for the pizza, leaving you $30 for purchasing all other goods. This bundle is point A on the diagram. If you were to buy a second pizza, its price would be only $5. Spending $15 on 2 pizzas would allow you to purchase $25 ($40 − $15) worth of other goods. This corresponds to bundle B. The third and fourth pizzas also cost $5 each. After 3 pizzas, you have $20 left to spend on other goods, and after 4 pizzas, you are left with $15 for other goods. These are points C and D on the diagram.

A fifth pizza will cost you $10 (the full price) because the promotion limits the $5 price to the next 3 pizzas you buy.

That means if you choose to buy 5 pizzas, you will spend $35 on pizza and only $5 on other goods, as at bundle E. Now that you have again purchased a pizza at full price, you are eligible to receive the next 3 at the reduced price of $5. Unfortunately, you only have enough income for one more $5 pizza. Therefore, if you would like to spend all of your income on pizza, you can buy 6 pizzas instead of just 4.

As a result of the promotion, then, your x-intercept has moved out to 6, and your budget line has pivoted out (in a somewhat irregular way because of all the relative price changes corresponding to purchasing different numbers of pizzas) to reflect the increase in your purchasing power due to the promotion (budget constraint BC_2).

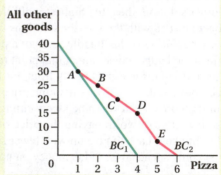

Figure A

b. It is likely that the promotion will increase how much pizza you consume. Most of the new budget constraint lies to the right of the initial budget constraint, increasing the number of feasible bundles available to you. Because more is preferred to less, it is likely that your optimal consumption bundle will include more pizza than before.

c. If your indifference curves are very flat, you have a strong preference for other goods relative to pizza. For example, look at U_A (Figure B). The slope of this indifference curve is relatively small (in absolute value). This means that the marginal rate of substitution of pizza for other goods is small. If your indifference curves look like this, you are not very willing to trade other goods for more pizza, and your optimal consumption bundle will likely lie on the section of the new budget constraint that coincides with the initial budget constraint. The promotion would cause no change in your consumption behavior; pizza is not a high priority for you, as indicated by your flat indifference curve.

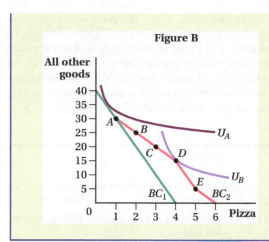

Figure B

On the other hand, if your indifference curves are steeper, like U_B, your marginal rate of substitution is relatively large, indicating that you are willing to forgo a large amount of other goods to consume an additional pizza. Then this promotion will, more than likely, cause you to purchase additional pizzas.

4.5 Conclusion

In this chapter, we looked at how consumers decide what to consume. This decision combines two characteristics of consumers, their preferences (embodied in their utility functions) and their income, and one characteristic of the market, the goods' prices.

We saw that a consumer maximizes her utility from consumption when she chooses a bundle of goods such that the marginal rate of substitution between the goods equals their relative prices. That is, in this bundle the ratio of the goods' marginal utilities equals their price ratio. Equivalently, the goods' marginal utilities per dollar spent are equal. If this property didn't hold, a consumer could make herself better off by consuming more of the good with the high marginal utility per dollar and less of the good with the low marginal utility per dollar.

Summary

1. **Utility** is the economic concept of consumers' happiness or well-being, and the **utility function** is the construct that relates the amount of goods consumed (the inputs) to the consumer's utility level (the output). There are properties that we expect almost all utility functions to share: the completeness, rankability, and transitivity of utility bundles; that having more of a good is better than having less; and that the more a consumer has of a particular good, the less willing she is to give up something else to get more of that good. **[Section 4.1]**

2. Consumers' preferences are reflected in their **indifference curves,** which show all the combinations of goods over which a consumer receives equal utility. The set of properties imposed on utility functions imply some restrictions on the shapes of indifference curves. Namely, indifference curves slope downward, never cross for a given individual, and are convex to the origin. **[Section 4.2]**

3. The negative of the slope of the indifference curve is the **marginal rate of substitution of good X for good Y** (***MRS**_{XY}$). It reflects how much of one good a consumer would need to give up in order to have an additional unit of another good. The MRS is the ratio of the marginal utilities of the goods in the utility function. **[Section 4.2]**

4. Consumer preferences lead to differences in the steepness and curvature of indifference curves. If a consumer views two goods as **perfect substitutes** or **perfect complements,** their indifference curves will be shaped like straight lines and right angles, respectively. **[Section 4.2]**

5. The consumer's decision about how much of each good to consume depends on not only utility, but also how much money that person has to spend (her income) and the prices of the goods. In analyzing the role of income in consumption decisions, we assume the following: Each good has a fixed price, and any consumer can buy as much of a good as she wants at that price if the consumer has sufficient income to pay for it; the consumer has some fixed amount of income to spend; and the consumer cannot save or borrow.

   The **budget constraint** captures both a consumer's income and the relative prices of goods. The constraint shows which **consumption bundles** are **feasible** (i.e., affordable given the consumer's income) and which are **infeasible.** The slope of the budget constraint is the negative of the ratio of the prices of the two goods ($-P_X/P_Y$). **[Section 4.3]**

6. The consumer's decision is a constrained optimization problem: to maximize utility while staying within her budget constraint. The utility-maximizing solution is generally to consume the bundle of goods located where an indifference curve is tangent to the budget constraint. At this optimal point, the consumer's marginal rate of substitution—the ratio of the consumer's marginal utilities from the goods—equals the goods' relative price ratio.

A **corner solution,** where the optimal quantity consumed of one good is zero, can occur when a consumer's marginal utility of a good is so low compared to that good's relative price that she is better off not consuming any of that good at all. In such cases, the MRS does not equal the price ratio even though the consumer is at the utility-maximizing consumption bundle. **[Section 4.4]**

Review Questions

1. We make four assumptions about preferences: completeness and rankability, "more is better," transitivity, and consumers' desire of variety. Briefly describe each assumption.

2. What does the term "utility" mean? How does utility relate to a utility function?

3. Define "indifference curve." What does an indifference curve tell us about the consumer?

4. We learned that the slope of the indifference curve is called the marginal rate of substitution of X for Y. What does the MRS_{XY} tell us about a consumer's preferences between two goods?

5. Why does the slope of the indifference curve vary along the curve? What does this variability tell us about consumers' preferences?

6. What does a steep indifference curve indicate about a consumer's preferences? What does a flat indifference curve say?

7. When are two goods perfect substitutes? What does the indifference curve look like, or what is its *curvature*?

8. When are two goods perfect complements? What does the indifference curve look like?

9. In addition to utility, what other factors determine how much of a good to buy?

10. Describe the three assumptions we make when incorporating income into our model of consumer behavior.

11. What is a budget constraint?

12. What determines the slope of a budget constraint? What situation would change the slope of a budget constraint?

13. What do we call the bundle represented by the point of tangency between the consumer's indifference curve and her budget constraint?

14. At the point of tangency, what is true about the ratio of the goods' marginal utilities and the ratio of their prices?

Problems

(Solutions to problems marked with an asterisk appear at the back of this book. Problems adapted to use calculus are available online.)

1. Which assumption about consumer preferences does each of the following individuals violate?

   a. Adam likes basketball more than football; football more than baseball; and baseball more than basketball.

   b. Christina prefers prune juice to orange juice but cannot decide how she feels about grapefruit juice.

   c. Blake likes superhero comic books but prefers 5 comic books to 10 comic books.

2. By assumption, individual preferences must be transitive so that if A is preferred to B, and B is preferred to C, then A is preferred to C. Suppose that Marsha, Jan, and Cindy individually have transitive preferences over three goods: oranges, apples, and pears. If Marsha, Jan, and Cindy were to vote on whether to name oranges, apples, or pears the "fruit of the month," show that it is possible the preferences for the *group* might *not* be transitive.

3. The following table displays the total utility U(X) that corresponds to the number of units of X consumed by three different consumers (Auon, Barbara, and Camira), holding everything else constant:

Auon		Barbara		Camira	
U(X)	X	U(X)	X	U(X)	X
10	2	10	2	10	2
14	3	10	3	12	3
16	4	10	4	15	4
17	5	9	5	19	5
17.5	6	8	6	24	6

   a. Compute the marginal utility of X for each of the three consumers at each level of X.

   b. Based on the data in the table, can you tell whether any of these consumers are violating any of the standard assumptions about preferences?

   c. Is it possible that any of these three consumers have the same preferences, and that columns for the three consumers differ only because of the arbitrary units that are used to measure utility? Explain.

4. Juliette and Andrew regularly go to the movies, where they like to consume popcorn and slushies. At the movies, Juliette's utility function is given by $U_J = \sqrt{P \times S}$, where P is the number of cups of popcorn and S is the number of slushies she consumes. Andrew's utility function is given by $U_A = P + S$.

a. Compute the utility Juliette and Andrew receive from the following combinations of popcorn and slushies:

Units of Popcorn	Units of Slushies	Juliette's Utility	Andrew's Utility
1	1		
2	2		
3	3		

b. Suppose that Juliette and Andrew are each consuming 2 popcorns and 2 slushies. Who gets the most happiness from their movie snacks?

c. Suppose that Juliette has consumed 2 popcorns and 3 slushies. What is the marginal utility Juliette will receive if she eats another cup of popcorn? What is the marginal utility she will receive if she drinks another slushie?

d. When Andrew is consuming 1 popcorn and 1 slushie, another popcorn will bring increase his utility by 1 unit. (Verify this!) When Andrew is consuming 8 popcorns and 1 slushie, another popcorn will again increase his utility by 1 unit. Which assumption of consumer preferences might Andrew's particular utility function violate? Does Juliette's utility function appear to violate that assumption, too?

5. Draw two indifference curves for each of the following pairs of goods. Put the quantity of the 1st good on the horizontal axis and the quantity of the 2nd good on the vertical axis.

a. Paul likes pencils and pens, but does not care which he writes with.

b. Rhonda likes carrots and dislikes broccoli.

c. Emily likes hip-hop iTunes downloads and doesn't care about heavy metal downloads.

d. Michael only likes dress shirts and cufflinks in 1 to 2 proportions.

e. Carlene likes pizza and shoes.

f. Steven dislikes both fish and potatoes.

*6. Suppose that John is indifferent between consuming bundle A, which consists of 4 apples and 1 peach, and bundle B, which consists of 4 peaches and 1 apple. If John were given the choice between bundle A and bundle C, which contained 3 peaches and 2 apples, which should he pick? (*Hint:* Draw an indifference curve or two.)

*7. A consumer's utility function is given by $U = XY$, where $MU_X = Y$ and $MU_Y = X$.

a. What is the utility derived from 1 unit of X and 2 units of Y? What is the utility derived from 2 units of X and 1 unit of Y? What is the utility derived from 5 units of X and 2 units of Y?

b. How does the consumer rank the following bundles?

Bundle	Quantity of X	Quantity of Y
A	2	2
B	10	0
C	1	5
D	3	2
E	2	3

c. Graph an indifference curve that shows the bundles of X and Y for which $U = 6$. Then graph a second indifference curve for bundles of X and Y for which $U = 8$. Is the "more is better" assumption satisfied for X and Y?

8. Suppose John's utility function is $4XY$, where X is consumption of beer and Y is consumption of pizza. For this utility function, the marginal utility of X is given by $MU_X = 4Y$; the marginal utility of Y is given by $MU_Y = 4X$.

a. Suppose $Y = 3$. Calculate John's utility for $X = 2$, 3, 10, and 11. For a given level of Y, does good X display diminishing marginal utility?

b. Suppose $X = 3$. Calculate John's utility for $Y = 2$, 3, 10, and 11. For a given level of X, does good Y display diminishing marginal utility?

c. Find three different bundles containing X and Y that give John 48 utils of satisfaction. Plot the three bundles and connect them with an indifference curve. What happens to the marginal rate of substitution between X and Y as consumption of X increases?

d. Does the principle of diminishing MRS depend on the diminishing marginal utility of X and Y?

9. Carmen is a writer who enjoys writing with both pencils and pens. Her utility function for pencils and pens is given by $U = 4X + 2Y$, where X is the number of pencils she has and Y is the number of pens. Carmen currently has 2 pencils and 4 pens.

a. Calculate Carmen's current utility.

b. What is the marginal utility of an additional pencil, MU_X? An additional pen, MU_Y?

c. Find two other bundles of pencils and pens that would give Carmen the same level of satisfaction she currently has, and connect the dots to create an indifference curve. Does the indifference curve have a special shape? Why might it have this shape?

d. The marginal rate of substitution (MRS) is measured as the slope of an indifference curve. Calculate the

MRS at Carmen's current consumption level. Does it equal the ratio of marginal utilities, MU_X/MU_Y?

10. Joey likes macaroni well enough and really loves cheese. Phoebe likes cheese well enough, but really loves macaroni. Below are two sets of indifference curves for two different consumers. Determine which set of indifference curves belong to Joey, and which belong to Phoebe.

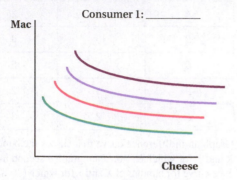

Consumer 1: _____

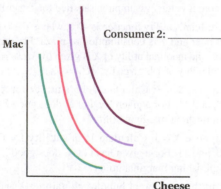

Consumer 2: _____

11. José gets satisfaction from both music and fireworks. José's income is $240 per week. Music costs $12 per CD, and fireworks cost $8 per bag.

    a. Graph the budget constraint José faces, with music on the vertical axis and fireworks on the horizontal axis.

    b. If José spends all his income on music, how much music can he afford? Plot a point that illustrates this scenario.

    c. If José spends all his income on fireworks, how many bags of fireworks can he afford? Plot a point that illustrates this scenario.

    d. If José spends half his income on fireworks and half his income on music, how much of each can he afford? Plot a point that illustrates this scenario.

    e. Connect the dots to create José's budget constraint. What is the slope of the budget constraint?

    f. Divide the price of fireworks by the price of music. Have you seen this number before while working on this problem, and if so, where?

    g. Suppose that a holiday bonus temporarily raises José's income to $360. Draw José's new budget constraint.

    h. Indicate the new bundles of music and fireworks that are feasible, given José's new income.

12. John enjoys ordering out for pizza and renting movies online. He makes $30 each week at a part-time job. If movies cost $2 per rental and pizza costs $7.50 per slice, graph John's budget constraint. Then illustrate the effects of each of the following events:

    a. John's mother finds a coupon good for 1 free pizza at a local chain and gives it to John.

    b. The company from which John rents movies sponsors a holiday week promotion: Rent the first 5 movies at their regular price, and all movies after the fifth are half off.

    c. John's favorite pizzeria increases the price of a slice from $7.50 to $10.

13. Sydney earns $100 from his YouTube videos each week; he spends it all on concert tickets and paintball.

    a. If concert tickets cost $20 each and paintball admission is $10 per session, graph Sydney's budget constraint.

    b. Suppose Sydney's YouTube haul increases to $200 per week. Graph Sydney's new budget constraint.

    c. Suppose Sydney's YouTube income remains steady at $100, but the price of concert tickets decreases to $10 and the price of paintball to $5. Graph Sydney's new budget constraint.

    d. Is there a fundamental difference between a doubling of income and a halving of prices? Explain.

    e. Would there be a difference in feasible bundles if the price of concert tickets was cut to $10, but the price of paintball remained the same?

14. During World War II, gasoline sold for a remarkable $0.20 per gallon. Suppose that Rosie works part-time and earns an average of $4 each week to spend on gasoline and food, which costs $0.50 per serving.

    a. Graph Rosie's budget constraint, putting gasoline on the vertical axis and food on the horizontal axis.

    b. During World War II, ordinary citizens were allowed to purchase only 3 gallons of gasoline each week. Show the effects of this quantity restriction on Rosie's budget constraint.

15. Caitlin spends her money on tuition and books. One credit hour of tuition costs her $320; each book costs her $200.

    Currently, the marginal utility of a credit hour to Caitlin is 80; the marginal utility of another book is 40.

    a. Is Caitlin maximizing her utility?

    b. Should Caitlin buy more books and enroll in fewer credit hours?

16. André gets utility from playing laser tag and reading books. Each week, André spends his entire $100 paycheck on both goods. One hour of laser tag costs $20; a book costs $10.

    a. Graph André's budget constraint. Put books on the horizontal axis and hours of laser tag on the vertical axis.

b. When André maximizes his utility, he buys 6 books. Carefully add an indifference curve to your graph to reflect André's utility-maximizing bundle of books and laser tag.

c. When André maximizes his utility, how many hours of laser tag does he play?

d. When André maximizes utility, the marginal utility he receives from playing an extra hour of laser tag is 12 utils. How much utility must André get from reading another book?

*17. For Maahir, shampoo and conditioner are perfect complements. He likes to use 1 squirt of shampoo and 1 squirt of conditioner each time he washes his hair.

a. Draw a set of indifference curves for Maahir that illustrate the utility he derives from using shampoo and conditioner.

b. Assume that shampoo costs $4 and conditioner costs $2. Construct a budget constraint for Maahir and describe his purchasing habits. What is his optimal bundle likely to look like? (*Hint:* Assume some level of income for Maahir.)

c. Suppose that prices change so that shampoo costs $2 and conditioner costs $4. What is likely to happen to Maahir's optimal bundle as a result? Explain.

d. How would your answer to (c) change if Maahir used 2 squirts of shampoo and 1 squirt of conditioner each time he washed his hair?

18. Suppose that there are only two goods, books and coffee. Justine gets utility from both books and coffee, but her indifference curves between them are concave rather than convex to the origin.

a. Draw a set of indifference curves for Justine.

b. What do these particular indifference curves tell you about Justine's marginal rate of substitution between books and coffee?

c. What will Justine's utility-maximizing bundle look like? (*Hint:* Assume some level of income for Justine and some prices for books and coffee; then draw a budget constraint.)

d. Compare your answer to (c) to real-world behaviors. Does the comparison shed any light on why economists generally assume convex preferences?

*19. Chrissy spends her income on fishing lures (*L*) and guitar picks (*G*). Lures are priced at $2, while a package of guitar picks costs $1. Assume that Chrissy has $30 to spend and her utility function can be represented as $U(L,G) = L^{0.5}G^{0.5}$. For this utility function, $MU_L = 0.5L^{-0.5}G^{0.5}$ and $MU_G = 0.5L^{0.5}G^{-0.5}$.

a. What is the optimal number of lures and guitar picks for Chrissy to purchase? How much utility does this combination give her?

b. If the price of guitar picks doubles to $2, how much income must Chrissy make to maintain the same level of utility?

20. A popular cellular telephone provider offers its customers the following pay-as-you-go data plan: The first 4 gigabytes of data cost $10 each; each gigabyte of data after that costs $20.

a. Suppose the typical data customer has $100 to spend on either phone use or chocolate bars, which cost $1 each. Graph the typical customer's budget constraint.

b. Add an ordinary-looking (downward-sloping, convex to the origin) set of indifference curves to the graph, to represent the preferences of the typical customer. How many gigs of data is the typical customer likely to use?

c. Does your answer to (b) depend critically on the steepness or flatness of the typical customer's indifference curves? Explain.

21. Cherise considers movies and concerts to be perfect substitutes. When Cherise maximizes her utility, what will the optimal bundle of movies and concerts probably look like? Explain your reasoning by drawing a graph that includes her indifference curves and a hypothetical budget constraint.

22. Economist Joel Waldfogel may be America's biggest Grinch. He bemoans what he calls the "deadweight loss of Christmas" created when people give gifts (such as ugly sweaters) the recipients would rarely, if ever, buy for themselves.

a. Draw a graph with a budget constraint showing affordable bundles of a composite good costing $1 and ugly sweaters. (You may assume some level of income and a price for ugly sweaters.)

b. Cheryl might get some utility from an ugly sweater, but is currently spending all of her income on the composite good. Add an indifference curve that reflects Cheryl's situation. What must her indifference curves look like?

c. Suppose Cheryl receives a gift of 1 ugly sweater from a coworker. Show the effect of the gift on Cheryl's budget constraint. Where on the constraint is Cheryl likely to maximize her utility?

d. Waldfogel suggests that the world might be a happier place if instead of giving ugly sweaters, people simply gifted an equivalent amount of cash. Draw the budget constraint Cheryl would face if this was the case. Add an indifference curve or two to show what happens when Cheryl maximizes her utility. Does the cash gift make her happier than the sweater?

23. Consider Joey and Phoebe, our mac and cheese lovers from Problem 10. Comment on the following statement: *Because Joey really loves cheese, when he maximizes his utility, he will be willing to give up more mac to get another cheese than Phoebe will.*

Chapter 4 Appendix:
The Calculus of Utility Maximization and Expenditure Minimization

In the chapters you've read so far, you've probably noticed that we use several different approaches when explaining microeconomic theories and applications. One method is mainly intuitive: Tell a story to illustrate an economic concept or discuss the logic of a model and its implications. This method of economic analysis goes back to Adam Smith and the invisible hand. A second method is the graphical approach. You only have to say "supply and demand" to conjure up a simple but powerful representation of a market. Finally, you've seen some simple mathematical models such as the algebraic representations of supply and demand curves in Chapter 2 and the consumer's budget constraint in Chapter 4. Each of these approaches provides a different window into understanding economic concepts.

Those of you who are familiar with calculus have yet another way to approach microeconomics. The tools of calculus are a natural fit with economics, and most economic models are formally derived using calculus. For some people (especially economists), it's easy to become so caught up in the math that the real economic ideas get lost. We don't want you to fall into that trap. That's why we present the calculus as a supplement to the intuition that we develop in the chapter. The calculus appendices provide an additional set of tools to examine the economic decisions and interactions discussed in the chapter. The logic of the models and the intuition from the chapter are still here in the calculus, only in another form.

So, don't think of the calculus that we explore in the appendices as a substitute for the logic, graphs, and algebra we use to explain microeconomics in the chapters. Instead, think of these techniques and the calculus as complements. As you learn more about microeconomics, you will find that each of these different approaches to understanding microeconomics may be more or less useful depending on the circumstances.

Consumer's Optimization Problem

One of the topics for which calculus provides additional insight is consumer behavior. Let's start by recalling the answer to the consumer's problem that we derived graphically in the chapter before seeing how we can get there using calculus. A consumer maximizes her utility $U(X,Y)$ when

$$MRS_{XY} = \frac{MU_X}{MU_Y} = \frac{P_X}{P_Y}$$

You may have noticed that to solve the optimization problem in the chapter, we just gave you the consumer's marginal utilities of goods X and Y — we didn't actually solve for them. This is because solving for the marginal utilities requires more than just the algebra and geometry we've relied on so far. Calculus allows us to derive the marginal utilities directly from the consumer's utility function. After determining the values of the marginal utilities, we can calculate the marginal rate of substitution. Calculus also provides us with another way to solve the consumer's problem — the Lagrangian — which yields some important insights into utility maximization.

The Marginal Rate of Substitution and Marginal Utility

In the chapter, we develop the connection between the marginal rate of substitution and marginal utility by thinking about how utility from each good changes as the consumer moves a little bit along one of her indifference curves. Here, we work in the opposite direction by starting with utility and seeing how we can use calculus to find the MRS. In this way, we examine what happens when we make small changes to the consumption bundle.

Take the consumer who has utility for goods X and Y, $U(X,Y)$. Any of the consumer's indifference curves show how the consumer trades off good X for good Y while keeping utility constant. We can choose any one of these indifference curves and call its level of utility $\overline{U}$:

$$U(X,Y)=\overline{U}$$

We are interested in how the utility from each good changes as we change the quantities of X and Y. So, we will totally differentiate the utility function, setting the total change in utility, dU, equal to zero because we are holding the level of utility constant:

$$dU = \frac{\partial U(X,Y)}{\partial X}dX + \frac{\partial U(X,Y)}{\partial Y}dY = 0$$

$$\frac{\partial U(X,Y)}{\partial X}dX = -\frac{\partial U(X,Y)}{\partial Y}dY$$

$$MU_X dX = -MU_Y dY$$

$$\frac{MU_X}{MU_Y} = -\frac{dY}{dX}$$

The right-hand side of this equation, $-dY/dX$, is the negative of the slope of the indifference curve or the marginal rate of substitution. Therefore,

$$MRS_{XY} = \frac{MU_X}{MU_Y}$$

Utility Maximization

The ratio of the marginal utilities is one piece of the puzzle—the preferences side. To finish the consumer's optimization, we need to relate consumer preferences to the prices of the goods and the consumer's income. Let's start by looking at a consumer whose utility function is the standard Cobb–Douglas functional form, $U(X,Y)=X^{\alpha}Y^{1-\alpha}$, where $0<\alpha<1$, and whose income is $I = P_X X + P_Y Y$. This consumer's utility-maximization problem is written formally as

$$\max_{X,Y} U(X,Y) = X^{\alpha}Y^{1-\alpha} \text{ subject to (s.t.) } I = P_X X + P_Y Y$$

This is known as a *constrained optimization problem,* in which $U(X,Y)$ is the objective function and $I = P_X X + P_Y Y$ is the constraint. In other words, how much utility the consumer can get is *constrained* by how much income she has to spend. In the chapter, we solved the same constrained optimization problem graphically with the objective of reaching the highest indifference curve while staying on the budget constraint.

If this were an unconstrained maximization problem, finding the optimal combination of variables would be fairly straightforward: Take the partial derivatives of the objective function with respect to each of the variables, set them equal to zero, and solve for the variables. But the presence of the budget constraint complicates the solution of the optimization problem (although without the constraint there wouldn't even be a finite solution to the utility-maximization problem because in an unconstrained world, the consumer consumes infinite amounts of each good).

There are two approaches to solving the consumer's utility-maximization problem using calculus. The first relies on what we already demonstrated in this chapter: At the optimum, the marginal rate of substitution equals the ratio of the two goods' prices. First, take the partial derivatives of the utility function with respect to each of the goods to derive the marginal utilities:

$$MU_X = \frac{\partial U(X,Y)}{\partial X} = \frac{\partial (X^\alpha Y^{1-\alpha})}{\partial X} = \alpha X^{\alpha-1} Y^{1-\alpha}$$

$$MU_Y = \frac{\partial U(X,Y)}{\partial Y} = \frac{\partial (X^\alpha Y^{1-\alpha})}{\partial Y} = (1-\alpha) X^\alpha Y^{-\alpha}$$

Next, use the relationship between the marginal utilities and the marginal rate of substitution to solve for MRS_{XY} and simplify the expression:

$$MRS_{XY} = \frac{MU_X}{MU_Y} = \frac{\alpha X^{\alpha-1} Y^{1-\alpha}}{(1-\alpha) X^\alpha Y^{-\alpha}} = \frac{\alpha}{(1-\alpha)} \frac{Y}{X}$$

Find Y as a function of X by setting MRS_{XY} equal to the ratio of the prices:

$$\frac{\alpha}{(1-\alpha)} \frac{Y}{X} = \frac{P_X}{P_Y}$$

$$Y = \frac{(1-\alpha)P_X}{\alpha P_Y} X, \text{ where } \frac{(1-\alpha)P_X}{\alpha P_Y} \text{ is a constant}$$

Now that we have the optimal relationship between Y and X, substitute the expression for Y into the budget constraint to solve for the optimal consumption bundle:

$$I = P_X X + P_Y \left[\frac{(1-\alpha)P_X}{\alpha P_Y} \right] X$$

$$I = P_X X \left[1 + \frac{(1-\alpha)}{\alpha} \right] = P_X X \left[\frac{\alpha}{\alpha} + \frac{(1-\alpha)}{\alpha} \right] = \frac{P_X}{\alpha} X$$

$$X^* = \frac{\alpha I}{P_X}$$

$$Y^* = \frac{(1-\alpha)P_X}{\alpha P_Y} \left(\frac{\alpha I}{P_X} \right) = \frac{(1-\alpha)I}{P_Y}$$

You can see that the resulting optimal bundle $\left(\frac{\alpha I}{P_X}, \frac{(1-\alpha)I}{P_Y} \right)$ is dependent on all three pieces of the consumer's problem: the consumer's relative preferences $(\alpha, 1-\alpha)$, the consumer's income I, and the goods' prices (P_X, P_Y).

Utility Maximization Using the Lagrangian

The first approach to finding the optimal consumption bundle is precisely the method we used in the chapter; the only difference is that we used calculus to derive the marginal utilities and then solved for the marginal rate of substitution. A second approach introduces something known as the Lagrange multiplier, or λ. The Lagrangian is a technique for transforming a constrained optimization problem into an unconstrained problem by combining the objective function and the constraint into one equation. λ is a variable that multiplies the constraint.

Suppose, for example, that the objective function is $f(x,y)$ and the constraint is $g(x, y) = 0$. The Lagrangian equation is

$$\mathcal{L}(x, y, \lambda) = f(x, y) + \lambda[g(x, y)]$$

Now maximize the equation by taking the partial derivatives of the equation with respect to x, y, and λ, and set them equal to zero. Partial derivatives in this form are known as first-order conditions, or FOC:

$$\frac{\partial \mathcal{L}}{\partial x} = \frac{\partial f(x, y)}{\partial x} + \lambda \frac{\partial g(x, y)}{\partial x} = 0$$

$$\frac{\partial \mathcal{L}}{\partial y} = \frac{\partial f(x, y)}{\partial y} + \lambda \frac{\partial g(x, y)}{\partial y} = 0$$

$$\frac{\partial \mathcal{L}}{\partial \lambda} = g(x, y) = 0$$

So, we have three equations and three unknowns and can solve the system of equations. Note that the third first-order condition is simply the constraint.

Let's see how the Lagrangian can be applied to our consumer facing the utility-maximization problem:

$$\max_{X,Y} U(X, Y) = X^\alpha Y^{1-\alpha} \text{ s.t. } I - (P_X X + P_Y Y) = 0$$

(Notice that we wrote the budget constraint so that it is equal to zero—this is important for how we set up the Lagrangian.) This equation can be rewritten in Lagrangian form as

$$\max_{X,Y,\lambda} \mathcal{L}(X, Y, \lambda) = X^\alpha Y^{1-\alpha} + \lambda(I - P_X X - P_Y Y)$$

Take the first-order conditions (FOCs):

$$\frac{\partial \mathcal{L}}{\partial X} = aX^{\alpha-1}Y^{1-\alpha} - \lambda P_X = 0$$

$$\frac{\partial \mathcal{L}}{\partial Y} = (1-\alpha)X^\alpha Y^{-\alpha} - \lambda P_Y = 0$$

$$\frac{\partial \mathcal{L}}{\partial Y} = I - P_X X - P_Y Y = 0$$

Embedded in these three first-order conditions are the same three pieces of information we've seen before: the marginal utilities of X and Y, the goods' prices, and the consumer's income.

The Lagrange multiplier λ is in the first two first-order conditions. So, solve each of these equations for λ:

$$\lambda = \frac{\alpha X^{\alpha-1}Y^{1-\alpha}}{P_X} = \frac{(1-\alpha)X^\alpha Y^{-\alpha}}{P_Y}$$

How can we interpret this Lagrange multiplier? First, recognize that the numerators are the marginal utilities of X and Y. In other words, at the optimum, $\lambda = \frac{MU_X}{P_X} = \frac{MU_Y}{P_Y}$. Therefore, λ is the exchange rate between utility and income—an additional dollar of income allows the consumer to purchase additional goods that generate λ more units of utility. We can also see this in the Lagrangian: If income increases by $1, maximum utility increases by λ units. In other words, λ measures the marginal utility of income. For example, let's say that λ is 0.5. Then, if you gain $1 more in income, you'll gain 0.5 units of utility.

Note that this expression for λ is the optimization condition in terms of the consumer's marginal utility per dollar spent that we derived in the chapter. We can rearrange this to get exactly what we showed graphically in the text—that the marginal rate of substitution equals the ratio of the prices:

$$\frac{MU_X}{MU_Y} = MRS_{XY} = \frac{P_X}{P_Y}$$

We can then solve for (X^*, Y^*) exactly as we did in the first approach, starting by finding Y as a function of X using the equality from the first two conditions:

$$\frac{\alpha X^{\alpha-1}Y^{1-\alpha}}{P_X} = \frac{(1-\alpha)X^{\alpha}Y^{-\alpha}}{P_Y}$$

$$\frac{Y^{1-\alpha}}{Y^{-\alpha}} = \frac{(1-\alpha)P_X}{\alpha P_Y}\frac{X^{\alpha}}{X^{(\alpha-1)}}$$

$$Y = \frac{(1-\alpha)P_X}{\alpha P_Y}X$$

Using the last first-order condition, we can plug this value for Y into the budget constraint:

$$I - P_X X - P_Y Y = 0$$

$$I = P_X X + P_Y \frac{(1-\alpha)P_X}{\alpha P_Y}X$$

$$I = P_X X \left[1 + \frac{(1-\alpha)}{\alpha}\right]$$

$$I = P_X X \left[\frac{\alpha}{\alpha} + \frac{(1-\alpha)}{\alpha}\right]$$

$$I = \frac{P_X}{\alpha}X$$

$$X^* = \frac{\alpha I}{P_X}$$

$$Y^* = \frac{(1-\alpha)P_X}{\alpha P_Y}\left(\frac{\alpha I}{P_X}\right) = \frac{(1-\alpha)I}{P_Y}$$

---

 figure it out 4A.1

Let's revisit Figure It Out 4.4. Antonio gets utility from burgers (B) and fries (F) in the form

$$U(B, F) = \sqrt{BF} = B^{0.5}F^{0.5}$$

His income is $20, the price of burgers is $5, and the price of fries is $2.

Find Antonio's optimal consumption bundle.

Solution:

To find the optimal consumption bundle, we need to solve the consumer's utility-maximization problem:

$$\max_{B,F} U = B^{0.5}F^{0.5} \text{ s.t. } 20 = 5B + 2F$$

The solution in the chapter uses the approach in which we solve for the MRS_{BF} from the marginal utilities. If instead we use the Lagrangian, we begin by writing Antonio's constrained optimization problem and then solve for the first-order conditions:

$$\max_{B,F,\lambda} \mathcal{L}(B, F, \lambda) = B^{0.5}F^{0.5} + \lambda(20 - 5B - 2F)$$

FOC:

$$\frac{\partial \mathcal{L}}{\partial B} = 0.5B^{-0.5}F^{0.5} - 5\lambda = 0$$

$$\frac{\partial \mathcal{L}}{\partial F} = 0.5B^{0.5}F^{-0.5} - 2\lambda = 0$$

$$\frac{\partial \mathcal{L}}{\partial \lambda} = 20 - 5B - 2F = 0$$

Use the first two conditions to solve for λ:

$$0.5B^{-0.5}F^{0.5} = 5\lambda$$

$$\lambda = 0.1B^{-0.5}F^{0.5}$$

$$0.5B^{0.5}F^{-0.5} = 2\lambda$$

$$\lambda = 0.25B^{0.5}F^{-0.5}$$

Set the two expressions for λ equal to each other and solve for F as a function of B:

$$\lambda = 0.1B^{-0.5}F^{0.5} = 0.25B^{0.5}F^{-0.5}$$

$$0.1F^{0.5}F^{0.5} = 0.25B^{0.5}B^{0.5}$$

$$F = (10)0.25B = 2.5B$$

So, for every burger Antonio consumes at the optimum, he will consume 2.5 orders of fries. Substitute $F = 2.5B$ into the third condition (the consumer's budget constraint) and solve for the optimal bundle (B^*, F^*):

$$20 = 5B + 2F$$

$$20 = 5B + 2(2.5B)$$

$$20 = 10B$$

$$B^* = 2 \text{ burgers}$$

$$F^* = 2.5B = 2.5(2) = 5 \text{ orders of fries}$$

This is where we stopped when we solved Antonio's constrained optimization problem using the first approach we presented in this appendix. But using the Lagrangian, we can also solve for one more variable: the marginal value of Antonio's income, λ, when Antonio is maximizing his utility.

$$\lambda = 0.1B^{-0.5}F^{0.5} = 0.1(2)^{-0.5}(5)^{0.5} \approx 0.16$$

Therefore, Antonio's utility increases by 0.16 units of utility for every extra dollar of income he has.

Expenditure Minimization

As we saw in the chapter, utility maximization—where you take income as given and find the combination of goods that will give you the greatest utility—is only one way to look at the consumer's optimization problem. Another is expenditure minimization, in which you start with a level of utility and find the cheapest bundle that achieves that utility level. In many ways, expenditure minimization is less intuitive—in real life, you probably do face a set income, but no contract you sign will ever specify your utility. But, ultimately, expenditure minimization leads to the same answer. What is more, the expenditure-minimization technique is extremely useful in the appendices for Chapters 5 and 7. In particular, this technique makes a lot more sense in the context of the producer's cost-minimization problem in Chapter 7.

Let's demonstrate the equivalence of utility maximization and expenditure minimization using Antonio's utility function from the Figure It Out in the chapter and the Lagrangian method (the first approach is identical to that for utility maximization except that you plug into the utility constraint instead of the budget constraint in the last step). We write out Antonio's expenditure-minimization problem given a constant utility of $\sqrt{10}$ or $10^{0.5}$, the utility at his optimal consumption bundle from the utility-maximization problem above:

$$\min_{B,F} I = 5B + 2F \text{ s.t. } 10^{0.5} = B^{0.5}F^{0.5}$$

or

$$\min_{B,F,\lambda} \mathcal{L}(B, F, \lambda) = 5B + 2F + \lambda(10^{0.5} - B^{0.5}F^{0.5})$$

As before, solve for the first-order conditions:

$$\frac{\partial \mathcal{L}}{\partial B} = 5 - \lambda 0.5B^{-0.5}F^{0.5} = 0$$

$$\frac{\partial \mathcal{L}}{\partial F} = 2 - \lambda 0.5 B^{0.5} F^{-0.5} = 0$$

$$\frac{\partial \mathcal{L}}{\partial \lambda} = 10^{0.5} - B^{0.5} F^{0.5} = 0$$

Then solve for λ in the first two conditions:

$$\lambda 0.5 B^{-0.5} F^{0.5} = 5$$

$$\lambda = 10 B^{0.5} F^{-0.5}$$

$$\lambda 0.5 B^{0.5} F^{-0.5} = 2$$

$$\lambda = 4 B^{-0.5} F^{0.5}$$

Set the two expressions for λ equal to each other and solve for F as a function of B:

$$\lambda = 4 B^{-0.5} F^{0.5} = 10 B^{0.5} F^{-0.5}$$

$$4 F^{0.5} F^{0.5} = 10 B^{0.5} B^{0.5}$$

$$F = 2.5 B$$

Now substitute F as a function of B into the utility constraint:

$$10^{0.5} = B^{0.5} F^{0.5} = B^{0.5} (2.5 B)^{0.5} = (2.5)^{0.5} B^{0.5} B^{0.5}$$

$$B^* = \left(\frac{10}{2.5}\right)^{0.5} = 4^{0.5} = 2$$

$$F^* = 2.5 B^* = 2.5(2) = 5$$

This optimal bundle of goods costs Antonio

$$5 B^* + 2 F^* = 5(2) + 2(5) = \$20$$

the minimum expenditure needed to achieve $10^{0.5}$ units of utility.

Expenditure minimization is a good check of our cost-minimization problem because it should yield the same results. In this case, as with utility maximization, Antonio purchases 2 burgers and 5 orders of fries for a cost of $20 and a total utility of $10^{0.5}$.

Problems

1. For the following utility functions,

   - Find the marginal utility of each good.

   - Determine whether the marginal utility decreases as consumption of each good increases (i.e., does the utility function exhibit diminishing marginal utility in each good?).

   - Find the marginal rate of substitution.

   - Discuss how MRS_{XY} changes as the consumer substitutes X for Y along an indifference curve.

   - Derive the equation for the indifference curve where utility is equal to a value of 100.

   - Graph the indifference curve where utility is equal to a value of 100.

   a. $U(X,Y) = 5X + 2Y$

   b. $U(X,Y) = X^{0.33} Y^{0.67}$

   c. $U(X,Y) = 10 X^{0.5} + 5Y$

2. Suppose that Maggie cares only about chai and bagels. Her utility function is $U = CB$, where C is the number of cups of chai she drinks in a day, and B is the number of bagels she eats in a day. The price of chai is $3, and the price of bagels is $1.50. Maggie has $6 to spend per day on chai and bagels.

   a. What is Maggie's objective function?

   b. What is Maggie's constraint?

   c. Write a statement of Maggie's constrained optimization problem.

   d. Solve Maggie's constrained optimization problem using a Lagrangian.

3. Suppose that there are two goods, X and Y. The price of X is $2 per unit, and the price of Y is $1 per unit. There are two consumers, A and B. The utility functions for the consumers are

$$U_A(x, y) = x^{0.5} y^{0.5}$$

$$U_B(x, y) = x^{0.8} y^{0.2}$$

Consumer A has an income of $100, and Consumer B has an income of $300.

a. Use Lagrangians to solve the constrained utility-maximization problems for Consumer A and Consumer B.

b. Calculate the marginal rate of substitution for each consumer at his or her optimal consumption bundles.

c. Suppose that there is another consumer (let's call her C). You don't know anything about her utility function or her income. All you know is that she consumes both goods. What do you know about C's marginal rate of substitution at her optimal consumption bundle? Why?

4. Katie likes to paint and sit in the sun. Her utility function is $U(P,S)=3PS+6P$, where P is the number of paint brushes and S is the number of straw hats. The price of a paint brush is $1 and the price of a straw hat is $5. Katie has $50 to spend on paint brushes and straw hats.

a. Solve Katie's utility-maximization problem using a Lagrangian.

b. How much does Katie's utility increase if she receives an extra dollar to spend on paint brushes and straw hats?

5. Suppose that a consumer's utility function for two goods (X and Y) is

$$U(X,Y)=10X^{0.5}+2Y$$

The price of good X is $5 per unit and the price of good Y is $10 per unit. Suppose that the consumer must have 80 units of utility and wants to achieve this level of utility with the lowest possible expenditure.

a. Write a statement of the constrained optimization problem.

b. Use a Lagrangian to solve the expenditure-minimization problem.

Individual and Market Demand

I n Chapter 4, we learned the basics of how consumers make choices: Preferences (embodied in the consumer's utility function and its associated indifference curves) along with income and market prices (both embodied in the consumer's budget constraint) pin down the consumer's utility-maximizing bundle of goods. Variations in preferences show up in the shapes of indifference curves, and variations in income and prices in the location and slope of the budget constraint. With that consumer choice framework, we can see exactly where the demand curves we used in Chapters 2 and 3 come from, when they shift, and how to add up individual consumers' demands to get market demand curves.

Because demand is half the story in any market, knowing what determines and drives consumer demand is crucial to understanding a number of issues, including:

■ why shifts in tastes affect prices,

■ the benefits that products offer consumers,

■ what happens to purchase patterns as consumers (or even entire countries) become wealthier,

■ how changes in the price of one good affect the demand for other goods, and

■ what factors determine consumers' responses to price changes.

Samsung's chief marketing officer, for example, needs to know all these things about smartphones when making the company's plans for a new model.

We start this chapter by looking at what happens to a consumer's choices when prices stay fixed but income goes up or down. This analysis involves finding the consumer's optimal bundle not just once for a particular income level (as we did in Chapter 4), but over and over for every possible amount of income.

Next, we determine how a consumer's chosen bundle changes as the price of one good in the bundle changes (holding the other prices and income constant). Analyzing how the quantity desired of a good changes as the price of that good changes maps out an individual consumer's demand curve for that good. We'll see that consumers' responses to price changes have two components: the change in relative prices caused by the price change and the change in the purchasing power of the consumer's income caused by the price change.

We then see how changes in the price of *other* goods affect the consumer's decision about how much of a particular good to consume. This effect can increase or decrease the quantity of a good demanded, depending on whether one good is a substitute for the other or if the two goods are consumed together.

After we explore all these features of an *individual's* choices, we show how total *market* demand responds to the same changes. Once this is done, we'll have arrived at a full understanding of what determines the market demand that we took as given in Chapters 2 and 3.

5.1 How Income Changes Affect an Individual's Consumption Choices

In Section 4.3, we learned how changes in income affect the position of a consumer's budget constraint. Lower incomes shift the constraint toward the origin; higher incomes shift it out. In this section, we look at the **income effect,** the *change in a consumer's consumption choices that results from a change in the purchasing power of the consumer's income*. To isolate this effect, we hold everything else constant during our analysis. Specifically, we mean that relative prices don't change and the consumer's preferences (reflected in the utility function and its associated indifference curves) stay the same. We just increase income and see what happens. **Figure 5.1** shows the effect of an increase in income on consumption for Eve, a consumer who allocates her income between vacations and tickets to basketball games. Her initial budget constraint BC_1 is tangent to the indifference curve U_1 at the optimal consumption bundle A. An increase in Eve's income is represented by the outward parallel shift of BC_1 to BC_2. Because the prices of the goods are unchanged, Eve can now afford to buy more vacations and basketball tickets, and her new utility-maximizing bundle is B, where indifference curve U_2 is tangent to BC_2.

Because U_2 shows bundles of goods that offer a higher utility level than those on U_1, the increase in income allows Eve to achieve a higher utility level. Because when we analyze the effect of changes in income on consumer behavior, we hold preferences (as well as prices) constant, indifference curve U_2 does not appear because of some income-driven shift in preferences. U_2 was always there even when Eve's income was lower. At the lower income, however, point B and all other bundles on U_2 (and any other higher indifference curves) were infeasible because she could not afford them.

income effect The change in a consumer's consumption choices that results from a change in the purchasing power of the consumer's income.

Normal and Inferior Goods

Notice how the new optimal bundle in Figure 5.1 involves higher levels of consumption for both goods. This result isn't that surprising; Eve was spending money on both vacations and basketball tickets before her income rose, so we might expect that she'd spend some of her extra income on both goods. Recall from Chapter 2 that economists call a *good for which consumption rises when income rises* a **normal good.** For a normal good, the income effect is positive. Vacations and basketball tickets are normal goods for Eve.

normal good A good for which consumption rises when income rises.

Figure 5.1   Consumer's Response to an Increase in Income When Both Goods Are Normal

Initially, Eve's budget constraint is BC_1 and the utility-maximizing consumption bundle occurs at point A, where indifference curve U_1 is tangent to BC_1. If the prices of vacations and basketball tickets remain unchanged, an increase in Eve's income means that she can afford more of both goods. As a result, the increase in income induces a parallel, outward shift in the budget constraint from BC_1 to BC_2. Note that, because we hold prices fixed, the slope of the budget constraint (the ratio of the goods' prices) remains fixed. The new optimal consumption bundle at this higher income level is B, the point where indifference curve U_2 is tangent to BC_2. At bundle B, Eve's consumption of vacations and basketball tickets rises from Q_v to Q_v' and Q_b to Q_b', respectively.

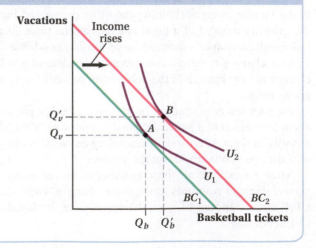

Figure 5.2 Consumer's Response to an Increase in Income When One Good Is Inferior

An increase in the consumer's income from BC_1 to BC_2 leads to more steak being consumed, Q_s to Q_s', but less macaroni and cheese. Note it isn't just that the quantity of mac and cheese *relative to* the quantity of steak falls. This change can happen even when both goods are normal (i.e., they both rise, but steak rises more). Instead, it is the *absolute* quantity of macaroni and cheese consumed that drops in the move from A to B, because Q_m' is less than Q_m. Note also that this drop is optimal from the consumer's perspective—B is her utility-maximizing bundle given her budget constraint BC_2, and this bundle offers a higher utility level than A because indifference curve U_2 represents a higher utility level than U_1.

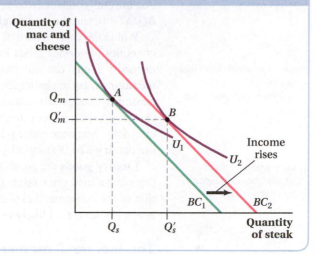

As "normal" suggests, most goods have positive income effects, but not all. *A good for which consumption decreases when income rises* is an **inferior good. Figure 5.2** presents an example in which one of the goods, macaroni and cheese, is inferior.

inferior good A good for which consumption decreases when income rises.

What kinds of goods tend to be inferior? Usually, they are lower-quality or otherwise less-desirable goods. Examples might include generic cereal brands, secondhand clothing, nights spent in youth hostels, and Spam (the grocery kind, not the junk e-mail kind, which probably isn't a good at all, but rather a "bad"). We do know that *every* good can't be inferior, however, because a consumer who gets more income has to spend it on *something* (remember, there is no saving in this model).

Whether the effect of an income change on a good's consumption is positive (consumption increases) or negative (consumption decreases) can vary with the level of income. A used car, for instance, is likely to be a normal good at low levels of income, and an inferior good at high levels of income. When income is very low, owning any car beats taking the bus, so as income increases, demand for used cars goes up. For people with a very high income, used cars are supplanted by new cars and the consumption of used cars falls. At that point, used cars are an inferior good.

Income Elasticities and Types of Goods

We've discussed how the income effect can be positive (as with normal goods) or negative (as with inferior goods). We can make further distinctions between types of goods by looking not just at the sign of the income effect, but at the *income elasticity* as well, which we discussed in Chapter 2. Remember that the **income elasticity** *measures the percentage change in the quantity consumed of a good in response to a given percentage change in income.* Formally, the income elasticity is

income elasticity The percentage change in the quantity consumed of a good in response to a given percentage change in income.

$$E_I^D = \frac{\%\Delta Q}{\%\Delta I} = \frac{\Delta Q/Q}{\Delta I/I} = \frac{\Delta Q}{\Delta I}\frac{I}{Q}$$

where Q is the quantity of the good consumed (ΔQ is the change in quantity), and I is income (ΔI is the change in income).

The first ratio in the income elasticity definition is the income effect shown in the equations above: $\Delta Q/\Delta I$, the change in quantity consumed in response to a change in income.

Therefore, the sign of the income elasticity is the same as the sign of the income effect. For normal goods, $\Delta Q/\Delta I > 0$, and the income elasticity is positive. For inferior goods, $\Delta Q/\Delta I < 0$, and the income elasticity is negative.

Within the class of normal goods, economists occasionally make a further distinction. The quantities of *normal goods with an income elasticity between zero and 1* (sometimes called **necessity goods**) rise with income, but at a slower rate. Because prices are held constant when measuring income elasticities, the slower-than-income quantity growth implies the *share* of a consumer's budget devoted to the good *falls* as income grows. Many normal goods fit into this category, especially consumer staples that everyone needs, like toothpaste, salt, socks, and electricity. Someone earning $1 million a year may consume more of these staples than a person earning $10,000 annually, but not 100 times more despite having 100 times the income.

Luxury goods are *goods with an income elasticity greater than 1*. Because their quantities consumed grow faster than income does, these goods account for an increasing fraction of the consumer's expenditure as income rises. First-class airline tickets, jewelry, and beach homes are all likely to be luxury goods.

necessity good A normal good for which income elasticity is between zero and 1.

luxury good A good with an income elasticity greater than 1.

The Income Expansion Path

Imagine repeating the analysis in the previous section for every possible income level, starting with 0. That is, for a given set of prices and a particular set of preferences, find the utility-maximizing bundle for every possible budget constraint, where each constraint corresponds to a different income level. Those optimal bundles will be located wherever an indifference curve is tangent to a budget line. In the examples above, bundles *A* and *B* were optimal at the two income levels.

Figure 5.3 shows how Meredith allocates her income between bus rides and bottled water. Points *A*, *B*, *C*, *D*, and *E* are the optimal consumption bundles at five different income levels that correspond to the budget constraints shown. Note that the indifference curves themselves come from Meredith's utility function. We have chosen these indifference curve locations just to illustrate that these points can move around in different ways.

Figure 5.3   Income Expansion Path

Meredith's income expansion path connects all the optimal bundles of bottled water and bus rides for each income level. Points *A, B, C, D,* and *E* are optimal consumption bundles associated with budget constraints BC_1 through BC_5. Where both bottled water and bus rides are normal goods, the income expansion path is upward-sloping. At incomes higher than that shown at the budget constraint BC_4 and to the right of bundle *D*, bus rides become inferior goods, and the income expansion path slopes downward.

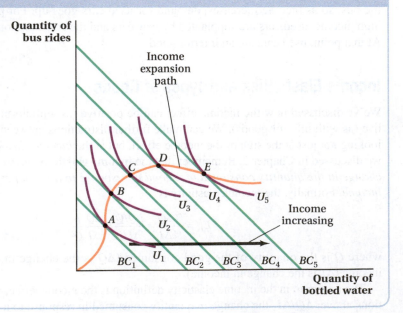

If we draw a line connecting all the optimal bundles (the five here plus all the others for budget constraints we don't show in the figure), it would trace out Meredith's **income expansion path,** *a curve that connects a consumer's optimal bundles at each income level.* This curve always starts at the origin because when income is zero, the consumption of both goods must also be zero.

income expansion path A curve that connects a consumer's optimal bundles at each income level.

When both goods are normal goods, the income expansion path will be positively sloped because consumption of both goods rises when income does. If the slope of the income expansion path is negative, then the quantity consumed of one of the goods falls with income while the other rises. The one whose quantity falls is an inferior good. Remember that whether a given good is normal or inferior can depend on the consumer's income level. In Figure 5.3, for example, both bus rides and bottled water are normal goods at incomes up to the level corresponding to the budget constraint containing bundle *D*. As income rises above that and the budget constraint continues to shift out, the income expansion path begins to curve downward. This outcome means that bus rides become an inferior good as Meredith's income rises beyond that level. We can also see from the income expansion path that bottled water is never inferior, because the path never curves back to the left.

The Engel Curve

The income expansion shows how consumer behavior changes in response to changes in income, but it has two important weaknesses. First, with just two axes, we can only look at two goods at a time. Second, although we can easily see the consumption quantities of each good, we can't discern the income level to which a particular point on the curve corresponds. The income level equals the sum of the quantities consumed of each good (which are easily seen in the figure) multiplied by their respective prices (which aren't listed). The basic problem is that when we talk about consumption and income, we care about three numbers—the quantities of each of the two goods and income—but we have only two dimensions on the graph through which to see them.

A better way to see how the quantity consumed of one good varies with income (as opposed to how the relative quantities of the two goods vary) is to take the information conveyed by the income expansion path and plot it on a graph with income on the vertical axis and the quantity of the good in question on the horizontal axis. Panel a of **Figure 5.4** shows the relationship between income and the quantity of bus rides from our example. The five points mapped in panel a of Figure 5.4 are the same five consumption bundles represented by points *A, B, C, D*, and *E* in Figure 5.3; the only difference between the figures is in the variables measured by the axes.

The lines traced out in Figure 5.4 are known as *Engel curves,* named for the nineteenth-century German economist Ernst Engel who first presented the data in this way. **Engel curves** *show the relationship between the quantity of a good consumed and a consumer's income*—bus rides and bottled water, in this case. If the Engel curve has a positive slope, the good is a normal good at that income level. If the Engel curve has a negative slope, the good is an inferior good at that income. In Figure 5.4a, bus rides are initially a normal good, but become inferior after bundle *D*, just as we saw in Figure 5.3. In panel b, bottled water is a normal good at all income levels and the Engel curve is always positively sloped.

Engel curve A curve that shows the relationship between the quantity of a good consumed and a consumer's income.

Whether income expansion paths or Engel curves are more useful for understanding the effect of income on consumption choices depends on the question. If we care about how the relative quantities of the two goods change with income, the income expansion path is more useful because it shows both quantities at the same time. On the other hand, if we want to investigate the impact of income changes on the consumption of each particular good, the Engel curve is best because it isolates this relationship more clearly. The two

Figure 5.4 Engel Curves Show How Consumption Varies with Income

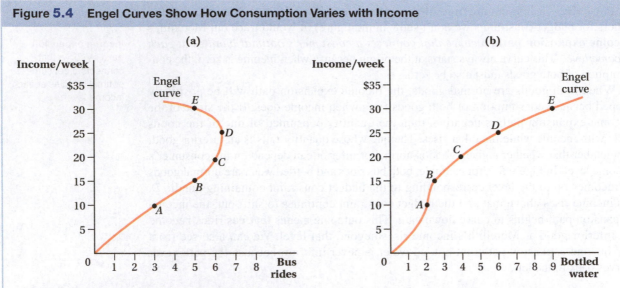

(a) In contrast to an income expansion path, an Engel curve compares the consumption of a single good to the consumer's income. As Meredith's income increases from $10/week to $25/week, her consumption of bus rides increases from 3 to a little over 6 bus rides. At income levels above $25/week, bus rides are inferior goods, and the number of bus rides she takes decreases.

(b) Bottled water is a normal good, so positively sloped, across all income levels shown here. At an income of $10/week at point A, Meredith consumes 2 bottles of water. At point E, Meredith's income is $30/week, and the number of bottles of water she buys increases to 9 per week.

curves contain the same information but display it in different ways due to the limitations imposed by having only two axes.

 ## Application: Engel Curves and Restaurants

Restaurants are perhaps the most common type of business in the economy. Cities have entire blocks full of them, and all but the smallest towns have at least one or two. According to the U.S. Bureau of Economic Analysis, Americans spend about $800 billion at eating and drinking establishments per year. That's about $2,500 per person. A recent Gallup survey found 60% of respondents had eaten in a restaurant the previous week, and 16% had done so 3 times or more. No wonder: People like to go out to eat, whether for convenience, for variety, or to socialize.

While food is a basic necessity, eating it in a restaurant is not. Eating meals at home is cheaper than eating out, so budgets are tight, we might expect people to eat more frequently at home. An increase in income should have the opposite effect as people substitute more toward eating out.

This intuition suggests that while spending on food might rise with income, spending on food in restaurants should rise faster. That's exactly what economists Mark Aguiar and Mark Bils determined in their study of how income shapes households' consumption decisions.[1] They estimated Engel curves for a number of different goods, among them food eaten at home and food consumed at restaurants. Food eaten at home had an income elasticity of about 0.4, so a 10% increase in income led to an increase in food consumed at home of 4%. Food consumed away from home, however, had an income elasticity of 1.3.

[1] Mark Aguiar and Mark Bils, "Has Consumption Inequality Mirrored Income Inequality?," *American Economic Review* 105, no. 9 (September 2015): 2725–2756.

Not only is this elasticity more than 3 times as large as that for food at home, it is above 1. Food consumed away from home is, therefore, a luxury good. These results are consistent with what the Gallup survey found, too: Only 44% of people from households with less than $30,000 in annual income had eaten out the previous week, while 72% of those from households with more than $75,000 in income had done so.

Aguiar and Bils weren't just concerned with how consumption changed with income across households; they also investigated the implications of those income responses over time. Their results imply, for example, that as average incomes have risen over time, spending on restaurant meals should have increased more than proportionately due to restaurant meals being a luxury good. That is, in fact, consistent with the long-run patterns in the data. The $800 billion ($2,500 per person) in annual restaurant spending we see today is much higher than it used to be. For example, total restaurant spending in the United States 50 years ago was only $175 billion (adjusted for inflation to today's dollars), less than one-fourth of what it is now. The population then was smaller, but not three-fourths smaller. Dividing by the population at the time suggests annual restaurant spending of $900 per person, just a bit over one-third its current level.

The high income responsiveness of food consumed outside the home has led to a long-run restaurant boom as Americans have become wealthier. So, the next time you get excited about checking out the new trattoria down the street, it's very likely that part of the reason the restaurant has opened is because of your higher income, and that of your neighbors, compared to your past counterparts. ■

---

figure it out 5.1

Annika spends all of her income on golf and pancakes. Greens fees at a local golf course are $10 per round. Pancake mix is $2 per box. When Annika's income is $100 per week, she buys 5 boxes of pancake mix and 9 rounds of golf. When Annika's income rises to $120 per week, she buys 10 boxes of pancake mix and 10 rounds of golf. Based on these figures, determine whether each of the following statements is true or false, and briefly explain your reasoning.

  a. Golf is a normal good, and pancake mix is an inferior good.

  b. Golf is a luxury good.

  c. Pancakes are a luxury good.

Solution:

  a. A normal good is one of which a consumer buys more when income rises. An inferior good is a good for which consumption falls when income rises. When Annika's income rises, she purchases more pancake mix and more rounds of golf. This means that both goods are normal goods for Annika. Therefore, the statement is *false*.

  b. A luxury good has an income elasticity greater than 1. The income elasticity for a good is calculated by dividing the percentage change in quantity demanded

by the percentage change in income. Annika's income rises from $100 to $120. Therefore, the percentage change in income is $\frac{\Delta I}{I} \times 100 = \frac{20}{100} \times 100 = 20$.

When Annika's income rises, her consumption of golf changes from 9 rounds to 10. Thus, the percentage change in the quantity of rounds demanded is $\frac{\Delta Q}{Q} \times 100 = \frac{1}{9} \times 100 = 11.1$. To calculate the income elasticity, we divide the percentage change in quantity by the percentage change in income, $\frac{11.1}{20} = 0.555$.

Golf cannot be a luxury good for Annika because the income elasticity is not greater than 1. Therefore, the statement is *false*.

  c. Again, we must calculate the income elasticity, this time for pancake mix. When Annika's income rises from $100 to $120 [a 20% rise as calculated in part (b)], Annika increases her purchases of pancake mix from 5 boxes to 10 boxes. Thus, the percentage change in the quantity of pancake mix demanded is $\frac{\Delta Q}{Q} \times 100 = \frac{5}{5} \times 100 = 100$. This means that the income elasticity of demand is $\frac{\%\Delta Q}{\%Q} = \frac{100}{20} = 5$. Because the income elasticity is greater than 1, pancake mix is a luxury good for Annika. Therefore, the statement is *true*.

5.2 How Price Changes Affect Consumption Choices

We now know how changes in income affect a consumer's choices, holding prices and preferences constant. In this section, we see what happens when the price of a good changes, holding income, preferences, and the prices of all other goods constant. *This analysis will tell us exactly where a demand curve comes from.*

At this point, it's useful to recall exactly what a demand curve is. We learned in Chapter 2 that although many factors influence the quantity a consumer demands of a good, the demand curve only isolates how the good's own price affects the quantity demanded while holding everything else constant. Changes in any other factor (such as income, preferences, or the prices of other goods) *shift* the demand curve.

Up to this point, it always seemed that demand curves slope downward because diminishing marginal utility implies that consumers' willingness to pay falls as quantities rise. That explanation is still correct as a summary, but it skips a step. A consumer's demand curve actually comes straight from the consumer's utility maximization. *A demand curve answers the following question: As the price of a good changes (while holding all else constant), how does the quantity of that good in the utility-maximizing bundle change?*

Deriving a Demand Curve

To see how a consumer's utility-maximizing behavior leads to a demand curve, let's look at a specific example. Caroline is deciding how to spend her income on two goods, 2-liter bottles of Mountain Dew and 1-liter bottles of grape juice, and we want to know her demand curve for grape juice. Caroline's income is $20, and the price of Mountain Dew is $2 per 2-liter bottle. We hold these other factors (income and price of Mountain Dew) and Caroline's preferences constant throughout our analysis. If we didn't, we would not be mapping out a single demand curve but would, instead, be shifting the demand curve around.

To build the demand curve, we start by figuring out the consumer's utility-maximizing consumption bundle at some price for grape juice. We can start with any price we want. Let's say $1 per liter bottle of grape juice to make it easy.

The top half of **Figure 5.5a** shows Caroline's utility-maximization problem. Her budget constraint reflects the combinations of bottles of Mountain Dew and bottles of grape juice that she can afford at the current prices. With an income of $20, she can buy up to 10 bottles of Mountain Dew at $2 per bottle if that's all she spends her money on, or up to 20 bottles of grape juice at $1 per bottle if she only buys grape juice. The slope of the budget constraint equals the negative of the price ratio P_G/P_{MD}, which is -0.5 in this case. The figure also shows the indifference curve that is tangent to this budget constraint. The point of tangency gives the utility-maximizing bundle. Given her income, her preferences, and the prices of the two drinks, Caroline's optimal quantities to consume are 3 bottles of Mountain Dew and 14 bottles of grape juice.

That yields 1 point on Caroline's demand curve for grape juice: At a price of $1 per liter, her quantity demanded is 14 bottles. The only problem is that the top panel of Figure 5.5a does not have the correct axes for a demand curve. Remember that a demand curve for a good is drawn with the good's price on the vertical axis and its quantity demanded on the horizontal axis. When we graphically search for the tangency of indifference curves and budget constraints, however, we put the quantities of the two goods on the axes. Thus, we'll create a new figure, shown in the bottom panel of Figure 5.5a, that plots the same quantity of grape juice as the figure's top panel, but with the price of grape juice on the vertical axis. Because the horizontal axis in the bottom panel is the same as that in the

Figure 5.5   Building an Individual's Demand Curve

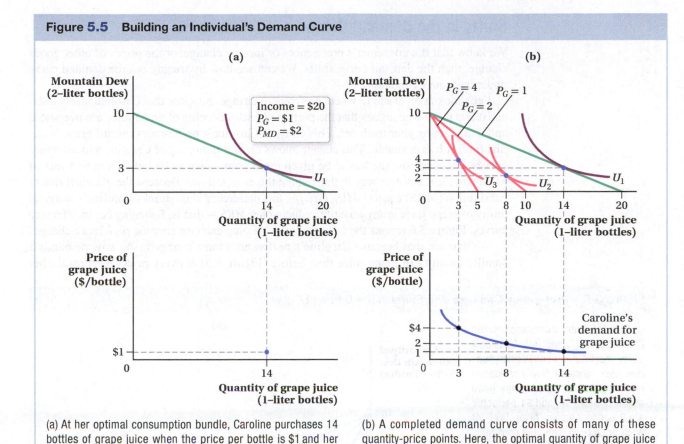

(a) At her optimal consumption bundle, Caroline purchases 14 bottles of grape juice when the price per bottle is $1 and her income is $20. The bottom panel plots this point on her demand curve, with the price of grape juice on the *y*-axis and the quantity of grape juice on the *x*-axis.

(b) A completed demand curve consists of many of these quantity-price points. Here, the optimal quantity of grape juice consumed is plotted for the prices $1, $2, and $4 per bottle. This creates Caroline's demand curve, as shown in the bottom panel.

top—the quantity of grape juice—we can vertically transfer that dimension of the figure directly from the top to the bottom panel.

To finish building the demand curve, we just repeat the process for different prices of grape juice. When the price changes, the budget constraint's slope changes, which reflects the relative prices of the two goods. For each new budget constraint, we determine the optimal consumption bundle by finding the indifference curve that is tangent to it. Preferences are constant, so the set of indifference curves corresponding to Caroline's utility function remains the same. The particular indifference curve that is tangent to the budget constraint will depend on where the constraint is, however. Each time we determine the optimal quantity consumed at a given price of grape juice, we identify another point on the demand curve.

Figure 5.5b shows this exercise for grape juice prices of $1, $2, and $4 per bottle. As the price of grape juice rises (holding fixed the price of Mountain Dew and Caroline's income), the budget constraint gets steeper, and the utility-maximizing quantity of grape juice falls. In our example, Caroline's optimal quantity of grape juice when it costs $2 per bottle is 8 bottles. When the price is $4, she consumes 3 bottles. These combinations of prices and quantities are plotted in the lower panel. These points are all on Caroline's demand curve for grape juice. Repeating this exercise for every possible grape juice price will trace out her whole demand curve, which we've drawn in the figure. Caroline's quantity demanded falls as price rises.

Shifts in the Demand Curve

We know that if a consumer's preferences or income change, or the prices of other goods change, then the demand curve shifts. We can see how by tracing out the demand curve under these new conditions.

Let's look at an example where preferences change. Suppose that Caroline meets a scientist at a party who argues that the purported health benefits of grape juice are overstated and that it stains your teeth red. This changes Caroline's preferences toward grape juice. She finds it less desirable. This change shows up as a flattening of Caroline's indifference curves, because now she has to be given more grape juice to be indifferent to a loss of Mountain Dew. Another way to think about this is as follows: Because the marginal rate of substitution (MRS) equals $-MU_G/MU_{MD}$, this preference shift shrinks Caroline's marginal utility of grape juice at any quantity, reducing her MRS—that is, flattening her indifference curves. **Figure 5.6** repeats the demand-curve building exercise after the preference change.

We can see that because Caroline's preferences have changed, she now demands a smaller quantity of grape juice than before (Figure 5.5) at every price. As a result, her

---

Figure 5.6 Preference Changes and Shifts in the Demand Curve

(a) With the flatter indifference curves (labeled U_1', U_2', and U_3'), Caroline's utility-maximizing consumption bundles have changed. Now her optimal consumption levels of grape juice at prices of $1, $2, and $4 per bottle are 9, 6, and 2 bottles, respectively. At each price level, she now consumes fewer bottles of grape juice.

(b) Because she purchases fewer bottles of grape juice at each price point, Caroline's demand curve for grape juice shifts inward from D_1 to D_2.

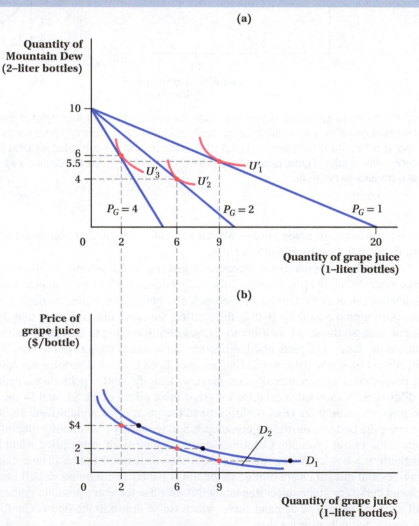

FREAKONOMICS

Even Animals Like Sales

If you think the laws of economics only apply to humans, think again. Monkeys, and even rats, behave in ways that would make you think they've taken intermediate micro.

Some of the most intensive testing of the economic behavior of animals was carried out by Yale economist Keith Chen and his co-authors on a group of Capuchin monkeys. As a first step, Chen introduced the monkeys to the concept of money. He gave them "money" in the form of metal washers that they could exchange for various types of foods including Jell-O, grapes, and Marshmallow Fluff (Capuchin monkeys *love* sweets).

After about six exasperating months, these monkeys finally figured out that the washers had value. Chen observed that individual monkeys tended to have stable preferences: Some liked grapes the best, others were fans of Jell-O. How did he learn this? He would give a particular monkey a coin and then offer that monkey a choice between a bowl of 3 Jell-O cubes and a bowl of 6 grapes and see which one the monkey chose.

Next, Chen did what any good economist would do: He subjected the monkeys to price changes! Instead of getting 3 Jell-O cubes for one washer, he would offer the monkey,

say, the choice between a single Jell-O cube per washer and a bowl of 6 grapes per washer. Thus, the relative price of Jell-O became 3 times as high. The monkeys responded exactly the way economic theory would predict, shifting their consumption away from the goods whose prices had risen.[*]

Perhaps it is not so surprising that monkeys, one of our closest relatives in the animal kingdom, would be sophisticated consumers. But there is no way rats understand supply and demand, is there? It seems they do. Economists Raymond Battalio and John Kagel equipped rats' cages with two levers, each of which dispensed a different beverage.[†] One of these levers gave the rat a refreshing burst of root beer. Rats, it turns out, love root beer. The other lever released quinine water. Quinine is a bitter-tasting substance initially used to treat malaria, and now used primarily to give vodka tonics their distinctive flavor. Rats are far less fond of quinine than they are of root beer, and they made that quite clear to the researchers by pressing the root beer lever far more often. Battalio and Kagel, like Chen, then explored changes in "prices" (how much liquid came out per press of the lever) and in the rats' budget constraint (how many times they could press the levers each day). Like monkeys (and humans), the rats consumed less of a drink when its relative price increased. Even more interesting is that when the rats were made very poor (i.e., allowed to press a lever only a few times per day), they shifted their consumption away from root beer toward quinine water. The researchers found that root beer is a luxury good for rats, and quinine water is an inferior good! Perhaps if the researchers had only mixed the quinine with a little bit of vodka, things would have been different. . . .

M. Keith Chen

Just like us?

[*]That wasn't the only humanlike behavior these monkeys exhibited when exposed to money — for the whole amusingly sordid story, see the epilogue to *SuperFreakonomics*.

[†]A description of the work by Battalio and Kagel may be found in Tim Harford, *The Logic of Life: The Rational Economics of an Irrational World* (New York: Random House, 2008), pp. 18–21.

demand curve for grape juice has shifted in from D_1 to D_2. This result demonstrates why and how preference changes shift the demand curve. Changes in Caroline's income or in the price of Mountain Dew also shift her demand curve. (We saw earlier how income shifts affect quantity demanded, and we investigate the effects of price changes in other goods in Section 5.4.) Remember, however, that for any *given* value of these factors on demand, the change in the quantity demanded of a good in response to changes in its own price results in a movement along a demand curve, not a shift in the curve.

The online appendix derives the demand curve directly from the utility function.

figure it out 5.2

Cooper allocates $200 of his weekly budget to entertainment. He spends all of this $200 on two goods: theater tickets (which cost $50 each) and movie tickets (which cost $10 each).

a. With theater tickets on the horizontal axis, draw Cooper's budget constraint, making sure to indicate the horizontal and vertical intercepts. What is the slope of the budget constraint?

b. Suppose that Cooper currently purchases 3 theater tickets per week. Indicate this choice on the budget constraint and mark it as point A. Draw an indifference curve tangent to the budget constraint at point A. How many movie tickets does Cooper buy?

c. Suppose that the price of a theater ticket rises to $80, and Cooper lowers his purchases of theater tickets to 2. Draw Cooper's new budget constraint, indicate his choice with a point B, and draw an indifference curve tangent to the new budget constraint at point B.

d. Once again, the price of a theater ticket rises to $100, and Cooper lowers his purchases of theater tickets to 1 per week. Draw his new budget constraint, show his choice on the budget constraint with a point C, and draw an indifference curve tangent to this new budget constraint at C.

e. Draw a new diagram below your indifference curve diagram. Use your answers to parts (b)–(d) to draw Cooper's demand for theater tickets. Indicate his quantities demanded at $50, $80, and $100. Is there an inverse relationship between price and quantity demanded?

Solution:

a. To start, we need to calculate the horizontal and vertical intercepts for Cooper's budget constraint. The horizontal intercept is the point at which Cooper spends all his income on theater tickets and purchases no movie tickets. This occurs when he buys $200/$50 = 4 theater tickets (Figure A). The vertical intercept is the point at which Cooper spends his entire income on movie tickets and buys no theater tickets. This means that he is buying $200/$10 = 20 movie tickets. The budget constraint connects these two intercepts. The slope of the budget constraint equals rise/run = −20/4 = −5.

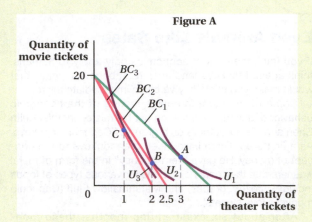

Figure A

Note that this slope is the negative of the ratio of the two prices: $= -\dfrac{P_{\text{theater tickets}}}{P_{\text{movie tickets}}} = -\$50/\$10 = -5$.

b. Maximum utility occurs where the indifference curve is tangent to the budget constraint. Therefore, point A should be the point where this tangency takes place. If Cooper purchases 3 theater tickets a week, he will spend $50 × 3 = $150, leaving him $200 − $150 = $50 to spend on movie tickets. Since movie tickets cost $10 each, he purchases $50/$10 = 5 movie tickets.

c. Cooper's budget constraint will rotate in a clockwise direction. The vertical intercept is not affected because neither Cooper's income nor the price of movie tickets changes. However, the price of theater tickets has risen to $80, and now if Cooper were to allocate his entire budget to theater tickets, he could afford only $200/$80 = 2.5 of them. This is the new horizontal intercept. If Cooper chooses to buy 2 theater tickets, he will have an indifference curve tangent to this budget constraint at that point (B).

d. The budget constraint will again rotate clockwise and the vertical intercept will remain unchanged. The new horizontal intercept will be $200/$100 = 2. Point C will occur where Cooper's indifference curve is tangent to his new budget constraint at a quantity of 1 theater ticket.

e. The demand curve shows the relationship between the price of theater tickets and Cooper's quantity demanded. We can take the information from our indifference curve diagram to develop three points on Cooper's demand curve:

Point	Price	Quantity of Theater Tickets Demanded
A	$50	3
B	$80	2
C	$100	1

We can then plot points A, B, and C on a diagram with the quantity of theater tickets on the horizontal axis and the price of theater tickets on the vertical axis

(Figure B). Connecting these points gives us Cooper's demand curve for theater tickets.

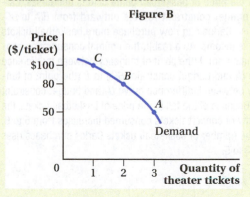

Figure B

5.3 Consumer Responses to Price Changes: Substitution and Income Effects

When the price of a good changes, the demand curve tells us how much consumption will change. That total change in quantity demanded, however, is a result of two distinct forces that affect consumers' decisions:

1. The **substitution effect** is the *change in a consumer's consumption choices that results from a change in the relative prices of two goods*—consumers wanting to buy more of the good that has become relatively cheaper and less of the relatively more expensive one.

2. The **income effect** is the *change in a consumer's consumption choices that results from a change in the purchasing power of the consumer's income.* A price shift changes the purchasing power of consumers' incomes—the amount of goods they can buy with a given dollar-level expenditure. If a good gets cheaper, for example, consumers are effectively richer and can buy more of the cheaper good and other goods. If a good's price increases, the purchasing power of consumers' incomes is reduced, and they can buy fewer goods.

substitution effect The change in a consumer's consumption choices that results from a change in the relative prices of two goods.

income effect The change in a consumer's consumption choices that results from a change in the purchasing power of the consumer's income.

The distinction between substitution and income effects is one of the most subtle concepts that you will come across in this entire book. Two factors make this topic difficult. First, we never observe these two effects separately in the real world, only their combined effects. As a consumer, you figure out how much to consume without knowing or determining how much of the change is due to income effects and how much is due to substitution effects. Separating the effects out is an artificial analytical tool—but it is useful. Second, the income effect occurs even when the consumer's *measured* income remains constant. If your income stays at $10,000 but the prices of all goods fall by half, you just doubled your income even though your measured income remained the same. The income effect refers to how rich you are in terms of purchasing power, not the number of dollar bills in your pocket.

In our overview, we demonstrate income and substitution effects using graphs. The appendix to this chapter describes these effects mathematically.

Figure 5.7 shows how one consumer, Carlos, who spends his income on attending music concerts and basketball games, reacts to a fall in the price of basketball tickets. This is just like the analysis we did in Section 5.2.

Figure 5.7 Effects of a Fall in the Price of Basketball Tickets

When the price of basketball game tickets decreases, Carlos's budget constraint rotates outward from BC_1 to BC_2 because Carlos can now purchase more basketball tickets with his income. As a result, the optimal consumption bundle shifts from A (the point of tangency between indifference curve U_1 and budget constraint BC_1) to B (the point of tangency between indifference curve U_2 and budget constraint BC_2). Because of the fall in the price of basketball tickets, the quantity of concert tickets consumed increases from 5 to 6, and the number of basketball tickets Carlos purchases rises from 3 to 5.

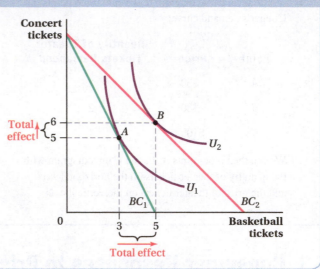

total effect The total change (substitution effect + income effect) in a consumer's optimal consumption bundle as a result of a price change.

Note that just as in Section 5.2, we figured out the optimal bundle without any reference to income or substitution effects. These overall changes in quantities consumed between bundles A and B are the **total effect,** the *total change (substitution effect + income effect) in a consumer's optimal consumption bundle as a result of a price change.* In the next sections, we break down the *total effect* into separate *substitution* and *income effects.* That is,

$$\text{Total Effect} = \text{Substitution Effect} + \text{Income Effect}$$

Breaking down the movement from A to B into income and substitution effects helps us understand how much of the total change in Carlos's quantity demanded occurs because Carlos switches what he purchases as a result of the reduction in the relative prices of the two goods (the substitution effect), and how much of the change is driven by the fact that the decrease in the price of basketball tickets gives Carlos more purchasing power (the income effect).

Note also that all the examples we work through involve a drop in the price of a good. When the price of a good increases, the effects work the same but in the opposite direction.

Isolating the Substitution Effect

Let's begin by isolating the substitution effect. This part of the change in quantities demanded is due only to the change in relative prices, not to the change in Carlos's buying power. To isolate the substitution effect, we need to figure out how many concert and basketball tickets Carlos would want to buy if, after the price change, there was no income effect, that is, if he had the same purchasing power as before the price change and felt neither richer nor poorer.

For Carlos to feel neither richer nor poorer, the *bundle he consumes after the price change must provide him with the same utility he was receiving before the price change; that is, the new bundle must be on the initial indifference curve U_1.*

The substitution-effect-only bundle on U_1 has to reflect the fact that the goods' relative prices have changed. Those new relative prices are seen in the slope of the new budget line BC_2. The problem is that a point of tangency doesn't exist between U_1 and BC_2 — as we can see in **Figure 5.8**. However, there *is* a point of tangency between U_1 and a budget line

Figure 5.8   Substitution and Income Effects for Two Normal Goods

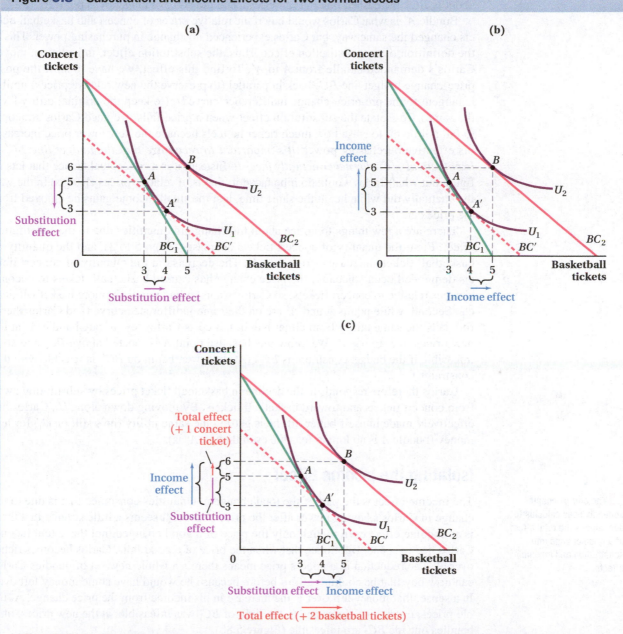

(a) The substitution effect is the change in quantities demanded due to the change in relative prices of basketball and concert tickets after the price of basketball tickets decreases. The budget constraint BC' is parallel to Carlos's new budget constraint BC_2 but tangent to his original utility level U_1. The point of tangency between BC' and U_1, consumption bundle A', is the bundle Carlos would purchase if relative prices changed but his purchasing power did not. *The change from bundle A to bundle A' along the initial indifference curve is the substitution effect.*

(b) The income effect is the change in quantities demanded due to the change in the consumer's purchasing power after the change in prices. When the price of basketball tickets decreases, Carlos can afford to purchase a larger bundle than he could before the price change. The change in the quantity of goods consumed from bundle A' to B represents the income effect.

(c) The total effect is the sum of the substitution and income effects. In this case, Carlos buys 1 more concert ticket and 2 more basketball tickets.

with the same slope (i.e., the same relative prices) as BC_2. The budget line we're talking about is BC', the dashed line in Figure 5.8a, and the point of tangency is point A'.

Bundle A' is what Carlos would buy if the relative prices of concert and basketball tickets changed the same way, but Carlos experienced no change in purchasing power. This is the definition of the substitution effect. Thus, the substitution effect, in isolation, moves Carlos's demanded bundle from A to A'. To find this effect, we have to shift the post-price-change budget line BC_2 back in parallel (to preserve the new relative prices) until it is tangent to the pre-price-change indifference curve U_1 (to keep the original utility level the same). To isolate the substitution effect when a price falls, we need Carlos's income to fall a little bit to erase how much richer he feels because the new lower price increases his effective purchasing power. *It's important to recognize that the budget line BC' is hypothetical—Carlos never actually faces it.* Instead, it is a conceptual device that lets us figure out what Carlos would do *if* he faced it; that is, if relative prices changed in the way they actually did while he, at the same time, lost the small income gains he enjoyed from the price cut.

There are a few things to notice about the change in quantities due to the substitution effect. First, the quantity of concert tickets decreases (from 5 to 3), and the quantity of basketball tickets increases (from 3 to 4). The decrease in the quantity of concert tickets demanded occurs because the price change has caused basketball tickets to become cheaper relative to concert tickets, so Carlos wants to buy relatively more basketball tickets. Second, while points A and A' are on the same indifference curve (and Carlos therefore gets the same utility from either bundle), it costs Carlos less to buy bundle A' at the new prices than to buy A. We know this because point A is located above BC' and so is infeasible if the budget constraint is BC'. (A', however, being on BC', is feasible with this constraint.)

Carlos therefore responds to the decline in basketball ticket prices by substituting away from concert tickets and toward basketball tickets. By moving down along U_1, Carlos has effectively made himself better off; he is getting the same utility (he's still on U_1) for less money (bundle A is no longer feasible even though A' is).

Isolating the Income Effect

➡ The end-of-chapter appendix uses calculus to decompose the total effect of a price change into substitution and income effects.

The income effect is the part of the total change in quantities consumed that is due to the change in Carlos's buying power after the price change. It seems a little strange that there is an income effect even though only the price of a good changed, not the actual income Carlos had to spend. But notice that when the price of a good falls, Carlos becomes richer overall. The reduction in a good's price means there's a whole new set of bundles Carlos can now buy that he couldn't afford before because he would have some money left over. In a sense, that money left over is the increase in his income from the price change. At the old prices, everything above and to the right of BC_1 was infeasible; at the new prices, only bundles outside BC_2 are infeasible (Figure 5.8b).

This increase in buying power allows Carlos to achieve a higher level of utility than he did before. The income effect is the change in Carlos's choices driven by this shift in buying power while holding relative prices fixed at their new level. Finding these income-effect consumption changes is easy once we've isolated the substitution effect. Remember that to find bundle A', we shifted the new budget constraint back in parallel until it was tangent to the original indifference curve. Doing that shift in reverse reflects the income effect exactly: It is the shift in consumption quantities (from bundle A' to B in Figure 5.8b) due to Carlos's ability to reach a higher indifference curve (U_2 instead of U_1) while holding relative prices fixed (BC_2 and BC' have the same slope).

A⁺ **make the grade**

Computing substitution and income effects from a price change

There are three basic steps to analyzing substitution and income effects. We start with the consumer at a point of maximum utility (Point *A*) where his indifference curve is tangent to his budget constraint.

1. When prices change, draw the new budget constraint (a price change rotates the budget constraint, altering its slope). Then find the optimal quantity at the point (Point B) where this new budget constraint is tangent to a new indifference curve.

2. Draw a new line that is parallel to the new budget constraint from Step 1 and tangent to the original indifference curve at Point *A'*. The movement along

the original indifference curve from Point *A* (the original, pre-price-change bundle) to this new tangency (point *A'*) is the substitution effect. This movement shows how quantities change when relative prices change, even when the purchasing power of income is constant.

3. The income effect of the price change is seen in the movement from point *A'* on the initial indifference curve to point B on the indifference curve at the new price. Here, relative prices are held constant (the budget lines are parallel) but the purchasing power of income changes.

In this particular example, the income effect led to increases in the quantities of both concert and basketball tickets. That means both goods are normal goods. In the next section, we offer an example in which one of the goods is inferior.

The Total Effects

Figure 5.8c shows the total effects of the decline in basketball ticket prices:

1. The quantity of concert tickets Carlos desires rises by 1 ticket from 5 in the initial bundle at point *A* to 6 in the final bundle at point *B*. (A decline of 2 caused by the substitution effect is counteracted by a rise of 3 caused by the income effect for a net gain of 1 concert ticket.)

2. The quantity of basketball tickets Carlos wants to buy rises by 2, from 3 in the initial bundle *A* to 5 in the final bundle *B*. (This is a rise of 1 caused by the substitution effect plus a rise of 1 caused by the income effect.)

What Determines the Size of the Substitution and Income Effects?

The size (and as we'll see shortly, sometimes the direction) of the total effect of a price change depends on the relative sizes of its substitution and income effects. So, it's important to understand what factors influence how large substitution and income effects are. We discuss some of the more important factors below.

The Size of the Substitution Effect   The size of the substitution effect depends on the degree of curvature of the indifference curves. You can see this in **Figure 5.9**. The figure's two panels show the substitution effects of the same change in the relative prices of concert and basketball tickets for two different indifference curve shapes. (We know it's the same relative price change because the budget constraints' slope changes by the same amount in both panels.) When indifference curves are highly curved, as in Figure 5.9a, the MRS changes quickly as one moves along them. This means any given price change won't alter consumption choices much, because one doesn't need to move far along the indifference

Figure 5.9   **The Shape of Indifference Curves Determines the Size of the Substitution Effect**

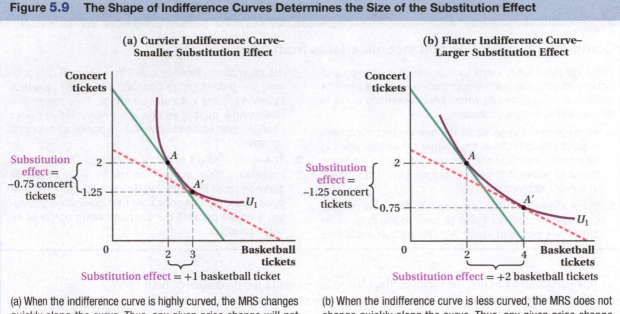

(a) When the indifference curve is highly curved, the MRS changes quickly along the curve. Thus, any given price change will not change consumption choices by much. Here, the original consumption bundle *A* is 2 basketball tickets and 2 concert tickets. After a change in prices, the new optimal consumption bundle is *A′*, and Carlos now demands 1.25 concert tickets and 3 basketball tickets.

(b) When the indifference curve is less curved, the MRS does not change quickly along the curve. Thus, any given price change affects consumption choices more strongly. At the new optimal consumption bundle *A′*, Carlos now demands 0.75 concert tickets and 4 basketball tickets.

curve to change the MRS to match the new relative prices. Thus, the substitution effect is small. This is unsurprising, because we learned in Chapter 4 that indifference curves have more curvature when two goods are not highly substitutable (yes, it seems kind of redundant to explain that goods have smaller substitution effects the worse substitutes they are, but there you have it).

When indifference curves are less curved, as in Figure 5.9b, the MRS doesn't change much along the curve, so the same relative price change causes a much greater substitution effect. The substitution from *A* to *A′* in panel b involves much larger changes in basketball and concert ticket consumption than that caused by the same relative price change in panel a.[2] Again, we can relate this to what we learned about the curvature of indifference curves in Chapter 4. Indifference curves with little curvature indicate that the two goods are close substitutes. Thus, it makes sense that a price change will lead to a much greater adjustment in the quantities in the consumer's preferred bundle.

The Size of the Income Effect   The size of the income effect is related to the quantity of each good the consumer purchases before the price change. The more the consumer was

---

[2] This logic also explains why perfect substitutes, the special case we discussed in Chapter 4 with perfectly straight indifference curves, have the largest substitution effects. There, a small relative price change can lead the consumer to shift from one corner solution to another—that is, from consuming all of one good, *A*, and none of the other good, *B*, to consuming only *B* and no *A*. (To see this, suppose all a consumer cares about is the number of potato chips he consumes, and he views 3-ounce and 12-ounce bags of chips as perfect substitutes. If the price of 12-ounce bags is less than 4 times the price of 3-ounce bags, he will only buy 12-ounce bags. But if the price of 12-ounce bags is just a bit more than 4 times the price of 3-ounce bags, he will only buy 3-ounce bags.) It's also why perfect complements, with their right-angled indifference curves, have no substitution effect; they are always consumed in constant proportion regardless of relative prices.

spending on the good before the price change, the greater the fraction of the consumer's budget affected by the price change. The price drop of a good that the consumer initially buys a lot of will leave him with more income left over than the price drop of a good with a smaller budget share (and a price increase will sap a greater share of the consumer's income). For example, think of how a change in the prices of food and pest control affect a typical homeowner. A typical consumer spends much more of his budget on food. There-fore, a change in the price of food will affect his income and alter his purchases by more than a similar change in the price of pest control. (At the extreme, if the consumer cur-rently purchases no pest control, a change in the price of pest control will have no effect on income at all.)

---

 figure it out 5.3

Go online for interactive, step-by-step help in solving the following problem.

Pavlo eats cakes and pies. His income is $20, and when cakes and pies both cost $1, Pavlo consumes 4 cakes and 16 pies (point A in Figure A). But when the price of pies rises to $2, Pavlo consumes 12 cakes and 4 pies (point B).

a. Why does the budget constraint rotate as it does in response to the increase in the price of pies?

b. Trace the diagram on a piece of paper. On your dia-gram, separate the change in the consumption of pies into the substitution effect and the income effect. Which is larger?

c. Are pies a normal or inferior good? How do you know? Are cakes a normal or inferior good? How do you know?

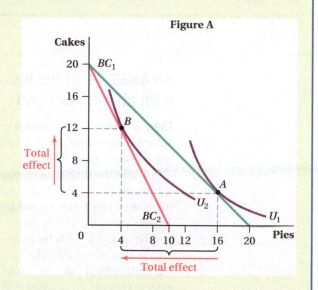

Solution:

a. The price of cakes hasn't changed, so Pavlo can still buy 20 cakes if he spends his $20 all on cakes (the y-intercept). However, at $2 per pie, Pavlo can now afford to buy only 10 pies instead of 20.

b. The substitution effect is measured by changing the ratio of the prices of the goods but holding utility constant (Figure B). Therefore, it must be measured along one indifference curve. To determine the substitution effect of a price change in pies, you need to shift out the post-price-change budget constraint BC_2 until it is tangent to Pavlo's initial indifference curve U_1. The easiest way to do this is to draw a new budget line BC' that is parallel to the new budget constraint (thus

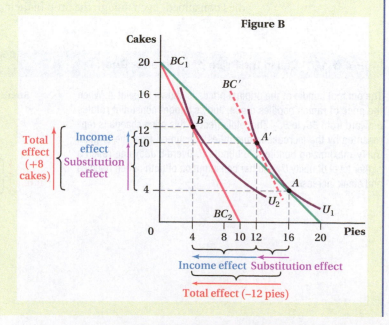

changing the ratio of the cake and pie prices) but tangent to U_1 (thus holding utility constant). Label the point of tangency A'. Point A' is the bundle Pavlo would buy if the relative prices of cakes and pies changed as they did, but he experienced no change in purchasing power. When the price of pies rises, Pavlo would substitute away from buying pies and purchase more cakes.

The income effect is the part of the total change in quantities consumed that is due to the change in Pavlo's buying power after the price of pies changes. This is reflected in the shift from point A' on budget constraint BC' to point B on budget constraint BC_2. (These budget constraints are parallel because the income effect is measured holding relative prices constant.)

For pies, the income effect is larger than the substitution effect. The substitution effect leads Pavlo to purchase 4 fewer pies (from 16 to 12), while the income effect further reduces his consumption by 8 pies (from 12 to 4).

c. Pies are a normal good because Pavlo purchases fewer pies (4 instead of 12) when the purchasing power of his income falls due to the price increase. However, cakes are an inferior good because the fall in purchasing power actually leads to a rise in cake consumption from 10 to 12.

An Example of the Income and Substitution Effects with an Inferior Good

Figure 5.10 provides another example of breaking out quantity changes into income and substitution effects. Here, however, one of the goods is inferior. The graph shows Judy's utility-maximizing bundles of steak and ramen noodles for two sets of prices.

To split the shift from bundle A to bundle B into its substitution and income effects, we follow the steps described in the previous section. To find the substitution effect, we shift the budget constraint inward from the price change until it is tangent to the original indifference curve U_1. This is shown by the dashed line BC' in **Figure 5.11a**.

The quantity shifts between bundle A' and bundle B, shown in **Figure 5.11b**, are due to the income effect. As before, this is the change in quantities consumed due to the shift in the budget lines from BC' to BC_2: Judy's increase in buying power while holding relative prices constant. Notice that now the income effect here *reduces* the quantity of ramen noodles consumed, even though the drop in their price makes Judy richer by expanding the set

Figure 5.10   Fall in the Price of an Inferior Good

The optimal bundle at the original prices is shown at point A. When the price of ramen noodles drops, Judy's budget constraint rotates outward from BC_1 to BC_2. The total effect of this price change is represented by the increase in quantities consumed from the original utility-maximizing bundle A to bundle B. Overall, Judy can reach a higher level of utility U_2 and her consumption of both ramen noodles and steak increases.

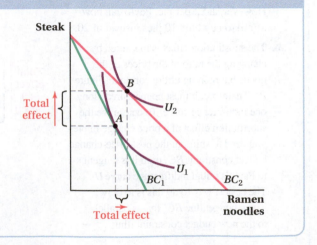

Figure **5.11**   Substitution and Income Effects for an Inferior Good

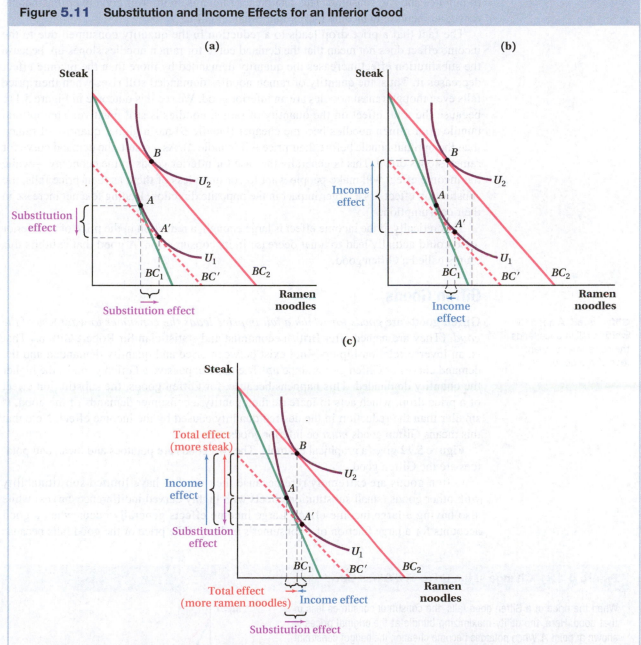

(a) BC' is the budget constraint parallel to BC_2, the budget constraint after the price change, and tangent to U_1, the consumer's utility before the price change. The point of tangency between BC' and U_1, consumption bundle A', is the bundle the consumer would purchase if relative prices changed but her purchasing power did not. The change from bundle A to bundle A' is the substitution effect. As before, the substitution effect leads Judy to purchase more of the good that has become relatively cheaper (ramen) and less of the other good (steak).

(b) The change in the quantity of goods consumed from bundle A' to B represents the income effect. Because ramen is an inferior good, the income effect leads Judy to decrease her consumption of ramen noodles, while her consumption of steak still increases. (c) The change in the quantity of goods consumed from bundle A to B represents the total effect. Since the substitution effect increases the quantity demanded by more than the income effect decreases it, Judy consumes more ramen noodles in the new optimal bundle B than in the original optimal bundle A.

of bundles she can consume. This just means ramen is an inferior good over this income range; an increase in income makes Judy want less of it.

The fact that a price drop leads to a reduction in the quantity consumed due to the income effect does not mean that the demand curve for ramen noodles slopes up, because the substitution effect increases the quantity demanded by more than the income effect decreases it. Thus, the quantity of ramen noodles demanded still rises when their price falls even though ramen noodles are an inferior good. We see this outcome in Figure 5.11c because the total effect on the quantity of ramen noodles is still positive: The optimal bundle after ramen noodles become cheaper (bundle *B*) has a higher quantity of ramen than the optimal bundle before their price fell (bundle *A*). As a result, the demand curve for ramen slopes down. This is generally the case for inferior goods in the economy—while the income effect will make people want to consume less of them as their price falls, the substitution effect has a larger impact in the opposite direction, leading to a net increase in their consumption.

Theoretically, if the income effect is large enough, a reduction in the price of an inferior good could actually lead to a net decrease in its consumption. A good that exhibits this trait is called a Giffen good.

Giffen Goods

Giffen good A good for which a fall in price leads the consumer to want *less* of the good.

Giffen goods are *goods for which a fall in price leads the consumer to want* less *of the good*. (They are named after British economist and statistician Sir Robert Giffen.) That is, an inverse relationship does not exist between price and quantity demanded and the demand curves of Giffen goods slope *up*! The more expensive a Giffen good is, the higher the quantity demanded. This happens because, for Giffen goods, the substitution effect of a price drop, which acts to increase the quantity a consumer demands of the good, is smaller than the reduction in the desired quantity caused by the income effect. Note that this means Giffen goods *must* be inferior goods.

Figure 5.12 gives a graphical example. The two goods are potatoes and meat, and potatoes are the Giffen good.

Giffen goods are extremely rare because they need to have limited substitutability with other goods (small substitution effects with highly curved indifference curves) while also having a large income effect. Large income effects generally occur when a good accounts for a large fraction of a consumer's budget. If the price of the good falls because

---

Figure 5.12   Change in the Price of a Giffen Good

When the price of a Giffen good falls, the consumer consumes less of that good. Here, the utility-maximizing bundle at the original prices is shown at point *A*. When potatoes become cheaper, the budget constraint rotates out from BC_1 to BC_2 and the optimal bundle shifts from *A* to *B*. Notice that in this case, when the price of potatoes decreases, the consumer purchases fewer potatoes, as reflected in the change in quantities consumed from bundle *A* to bundle *B*.

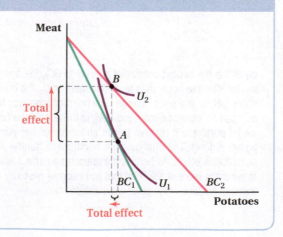

the consumer is already spending most of her income on it, she's likely to feel a larger bump in effective buying power than if the good were only a small share of her budget. Finding goods that are a huge share of the budget but do not have many substitutes is extremely rare.

 ## Application: Someone Actually Found a Giffen Good!

While Giffen goods are theoretically possible, like Bigfoot, they seem extremely rare in practice and typically disproven on further examination. An often cited example of a Giffen good is the potato in Ireland during the Irish famine of the mid-1800s. The story is that the famine-driven increase in potato prices drastically reduced the purchasing power of Irish families' incomes, shrinking the bundles of goods that they could afford because potatoes already consumed a very large fraction of a typical Irish family's meager cash income. The resulting income effect led to a decrease in the demand for other foods, such as meat, that were normal goods for Irish families and an increase in the demand for potatoes, an inferior good, that swamped any substitution effect. However, more recent reexaminations of the data by economists Gerald Dwyer and Cotton Lindsay, and later Sherwin Rosen in a separate study, found that even this canonical example proved not to be a Giffen good.[3]

For one thing, if potatoes were a Giffen good for individual households, then the total market demand curve for potatoes in Ireland should have also sloped up (quantity demanded would have increased as price increased). (We will learn about how individuals' demand curves add up to total market demand later in this chapter.) But that would mean the huge drop in supply due to the blight—about which there is no historical argument—should have led to lower potato prices. It didn't; when potatoes were available, they were sold at historically unprecedentedly high prices.

However, a recent policy experiment with extremely poor households in rural areas of China's Hunan province by Robert Jensen and Nolan Miller has produced what could be the most convincing documentation of a Giffen good to date.[4] Jensen and Miller subsidized the purchases of rice to a randomly selected set of such households, effectively lowering the price of rice that they faced. They then compared the change in rice consumption in the subsidized households to rice consumption in unsubsidized households of similar incomes and sizes.

Jensen and Miller found that the subsidy, even though it made rice cheaper, actually caused the households' rice consumption to fall. Rice was a Giffen good for these households. (Jensen and Miller conducted a similar experiment subsidizing wheat purchases in Gansu province and also found evidence that wheat was a Giffen good for some families, though the effect was weaker.) Rice purchases took up so much of these households' incomes that the subsidy greatly increased the households' effective buying power. The resulting income effect made them want to consume less rice in place of other foods for the sake of dietary variety. This income effect was large enough to outweigh the substitution effect. To oversimplify things a little, the households were initially buying enough rice to meet their caloric needs and spending their (nonexistent) leftover income on foods that added variety. When they could meet their caloric needs more cheaply, they used the

[3] Gerald P. Dwyer Jr. and Cotton M. Lindsay, "Robert Giffen and the Irish Potato," *American Economic Review* 74, no. 1 (1984): 188–192. Sherwin Rosen, "Potato Paradoxes." *Journal of Political Economy* 107, no. 6 (1999): S294–S313.

[4] Robert T. Jensen and Nolan H. Miller, "Giffen Behavior and Subsistence Consumption," *American Economic Review* 98, no. 4 (2008): 1553–1577.

now-freed-up income to buy variety foods—enough to replace some of the calories formerly supplied by rice.

Interestingly, Jensen and Miller also determined that while rice was a Giffen good for very poor households, it was not a Giffen good for the very poorest of the poor. Those extremely impoverished households basically ate only rice before the subsidy, and not really enough to meet their basic caloric needs at that. When rice became cheaper, they bought more in order to meet some basic level of healthy subsistence. Essentially, even the subsidy didn't raise their income enough to allow them to buy any other foods besides rice. ■

The online appendix takes a deeper look into income and substitution effects using the Slutsky equation.

5.4 The Impact of Changes in Another Good's Price: Substitutes and Complements

The two preceding sections showed how a change in the price of a good leads to a change in the quantity demanded of that same good. In this section, we look at the effects of a change in a good's price on the quantity demanded of *other* goods.

To examine what happens when the price of another good changes, we start, as before, with a fixed level of income, a set of indifference curves representing the consumer's preferences, and initial prices for the two goods. We compute the optimal consumption bundle under those conditions. Then, we vary one of the prices, holding everything else constant. The only difference is that as we vary that price, we focus on how the quantity demanded of the other good changes.

A Change in the Price of a Substitute Good

substitute A good that can be used in place of another good.

Figure 5.13 shows an example of the effects of a change in the price of a substitute good—in this case, Pepsi and Coke. As we learned in Chapter 2, when the quantity demanded of one good (Coke) rises when the price of another good (Pepsi) rises, the goods are **substitutes,** *goods that can be used in place of one another.* More generally, the quantity a consumer demands of a good moves in the same direction as the prices of its substitutes. The more alike two goods are, the more one can be substituted for the other, and the more responsive the increase in quantity demanded of one will be to price increases in the other. Pepsi and Coke are closer substitutes than milk and Coke.

Figure 5.13   When the Price of a Substitute Rises, Demand Rises

At the original prices, the consumer consumes 15 liters of Pepsi and 5 quarts of Coke at the utility-maximizing bundle *A*. When the price of Pepsi doubles, the consumer can only afford a maximum of 10 liters instead of 20 and the consumer's budget constraint rotates inward from BC_1 to BC_2. The maximum quantity of Coke the consumer can buy stays at 20 because the price of Coke has not changed. At the new optimal consumption bundle *B*, the consumer decreases his consumption of Pepsi from 15 to 5 quarts and increases his consumption of Coke from 5 to 10 liters. Since the quantity of Coke demanded rose while the price of Pepsi rose, Coke and Pepsi are considered substitutes.

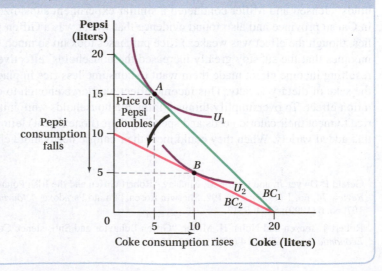

Figure 5.14   When the Price of a Complement Rises, Demand Falls

At the original prices, the consumer consumes 20 gallons of ice cream and 30 quarts of hot fudge at the utility-maximizing bundle A. When the price of ice cream increases, the consumer's budget constraint rotates inward from BC_1 to BC_2. At the new optimal consumption bundle B, the consumer decreases his consumption of ice cream from 20 to 15 gallons and likewise decreases his consumption of hot fudge from 30 to 20 quarts. An increase in the price of ice cream causes the consumer to demand not only less ice cream (this is the own-price effect we've studied so far in this chapter), but also less hot fudge, the complementary good.

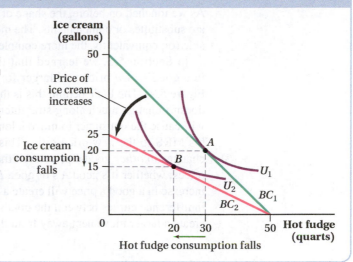

Changes in the prices of a good's substitutes lead to shifts in the good's demand curve. When a substitute for a good becomes more expensive, this raises the quantity demanded of that good at any given price level. As a result, the demand curve for the good shifts out (the demand for that good increases). When a good's substitutes become cheaper, the quantity demanded at any given price falls, and the good's demand curve shifts in.

When the quantity consumed of a good moves in the opposite direction of another good's price, they are **complements,** *goods that are purchased and used in combination with another good.* Complements are often goods that the consumer would use in tandem, like vanilla ice cream and hot fudge. **Figure 5.14** shows how an increase in ice cream's price leads to a decrease in the quantity demanded of hot fudge. If the price of a complement of a good increases, the quantity demanded of that good at every price decreases, and its demand curve shifts in. If the price of a complement of a good falls, the quantity demanded of that good rises at all prices and the demand curve shifts out. Changes in the price of a complementary good *shift* the demand curve for the other good. Changes in a good's own price cause a *move along* the same demand curve. The effects of price changes in substitute and complementary goods on demand are summarized in **Figure 5.15**.

complement A good that is purchased and used in combination with another good.

Figure 5.15   Changes in the Prices of Substitutes or Complements Shift the Demand Curve

When the price of a substitute good rises or the price of a complement falls, the demand curve for good X shifts out. When the price of a substitute good falls or the price of a complement rises, the demand curve for good X shifts in.

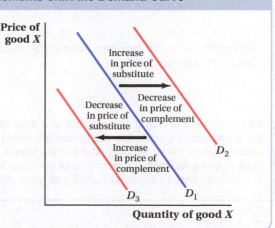

Indifference Curve Shapes, Revisited

As we touched on before, the shape of indifference curves is related to whether two goods are substitutes or complements. The more curved the indifference curve, the less substitutable (or, equivalently, the more complementary) are the goods.

In Section 5.3, we learned that the size of the substitution effect from a change in a good's *own* price was larger for goods with less-curved indifference curves (see Figure 5.9). The logic behind this is that, because the marginal rate of substitution (MRS) doesn't change much along straighter indifference curves, a given relative price change will cause the consumer to move a longer distance along his indifference curve to equate his MRS to the new price ratio. This logic holds true when it comes to the effects of changes in *other* goods' prices. All that matters to the substitution effect are the *relative* prices; whether it's good *A*'s or good *B*'s price that changes doesn't matter. Therefore, an increase in a good's price will create a larger movement toward a substitute good when the indifference curves between the goods are less curved. (A decrease in a good's price will create a larger movement away from the substitute good.)

A⁺ make the grade

Simple rules to remember about income and substitution effects

It is easy to get tripped up when you're asked to identify income and substitution effects. First, remember to always start your analysis on the indifference curve associated with the consumption bundle *before* the price change. If you want to know why consumption changed going from one bundle to the other, you must start with the initial bundle. Next, keep in mind the key distinctions between the two effects listed in the table below.

Substitution Effects	Income Effects
Involve comparisons of bundles that lie on the same indifference curve.	Involve comparisons of bundles that lie on two different indifference curves.
The direction of the effect on quantity consumed for a given change in the relative price of the good is unambiguous.	The direction of the effect on quantity consumed for a given change in the relative price of the good is ambiguous and depends on whether the good is normal or inferior.
If the good's relative price falls, the substitution effect causes the consumer to want more of it.	If the good is normal, then a fall in either its price or the price of the other good will cause the consumer to want more of it. (A drop in any price, even of another good, increases the effective income of the consumer.) If the good is inferior, then a price drop will cause the consumer to want less of it.
If the good's relative price rises, the substitution effect causes the consumer to want less of it.	If the good is normal, then a rise in either its price or the price of the other good will cause the consumer to want less of it. If the good is inferior, then a rise in either price will cause the consumer to want more of it.

Finally, remember that the total effect of a price change (for either good) on quantity consumed depends on the relative size of the substitution and income effects. If the price of one good falls, the quantities of both goods consumed may rise, or consumption of one good may rise and consumption of the other good may decline. But the quantities consumed of both goods cannot both decline, because this would mean the consumer would not be on her budget constraint.

Application: Movies in a theater and at home — substitutes or complements?

If you own a movie theater company, one of the most important issues you face for the long-run viability of your firm is whether watching a movie on a home theater system and seeing a film in your mulitplex are substitutes or complements. Improvements in home electronics like large-screen, high-definition TVs, streaming video, and compact surround sound audio systems have greatly reduced the price of having a high-quality movie-watching experience at home. A middle-class family today can buy a home theater system that a multimillion-aire could have only dreamed about a few decades ago. If movies on Netflix or some other streaming service at home are a substitute good for movies in a theater, this price reduction will reduce the number of people visiting their local multiplex and lead to some theaters going out of business. If movies at home are instead a complement, theater-going will increase and bring newfound growth to the movie exhibition business.

Either case is plausible in theory. On the one hand, if home electronics can better replicate the theater experience, people only want to see a movie once, and it's less costly to watch at home, they would be substitutes. On the other hand, if people become more interested in films, in general, because they watch more at home — perhaps even develop a movie habit, or get caught up in following certain actors or really like watching their favorite movie multiple times — they might be more likely to go see a movie in a theater than they would have beforehand, particularly if those theaters offer some component of the movie-watching experience that you can't get at home (audiences to laugh or scream along with, early film releases, a huge screen, greasy popcorn, etc.).

While things could go either way in concept, the data don't look promising for theater companies. **Figure 5.16** shows total U.S. box office sales receipts (inflation-adjusted to 2018 dollars) and the number of tickets sold per capita from 1980 to 2018.[5] Total box office revenues rose over the period, but it topped out in 2002 and ever since has bounced in the neighborhood of $11 billion. The data on the number of tickets sold per capita — you

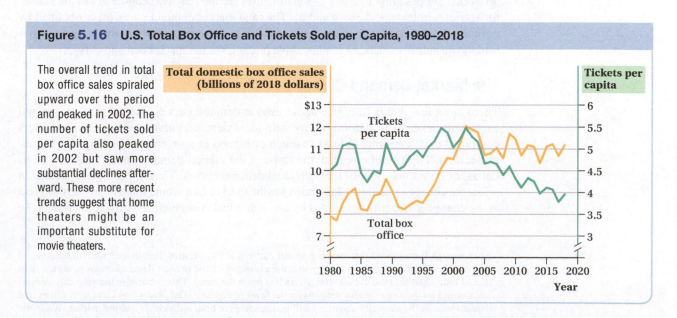

Figure 5.16   U.S. Total Box Office and Tickets Sold per Capita, 1980–2018

The overall trend in total box office sales spiraled upward over the period and peaked in 2002. The number of tickets sold per capita also peaked in 2002 but saw more substantial declines afterward. These more recent trends suggest that home theaters might be an important substitute for movie theaters.

[5] The data in this application are from www.boxofficemojo.com.

can think of this as the average number of times a person goes to see a movie during the year—also peaked in 2002, but since then there has been an even more pronounced drop than in total box office sales. Tickets per capita have recently fallen, down 25% since 2002 and even below their 1980 level.

The decrease in theater-going after 2002 suggests that watching movies at home is a substitute, because it coincides with the period of the increased availability of big-screen HDTVs, surround sound, and, more recently, streaming video services. One small bit of hope to hang onto if you're a theater owner is that the widespread diffusion of VCRs, DVD players, and early surround-sound systems in the 1980s and 1990s didn't permanently erode the movie exhibition industry. Revenues and tickets per capita both rose, indicating that they may have been complements to watching films in a theater. Maybe cheap, high-quality home theater systems and streaming video won't be that strong of a substitute. Then again, in 1946, before TVs were in most people's homes, over 4 billion movie tickets were sold in the United States when the population was about 140 million (less than half the population today). That's an average of over 28 movies a year per person! By 1956 attendance per person was half that. ∎

5.5 Combining Individual Demand Curves to Obtain the Market Demand Curve

When studying consumer demand, we're often more interested in the combined demand of all consumers, rather than just one consumer's demand. If a government wants to figure out how much revenue a tax on soda will raise, for example, it needs to look at the entire market demand for soda.

The market demand for a good is the sum of all the individual demand curves. That is, the market quantity demanded for a good at a particular price is the sum of every individual consumer's quantity demanded at that price. **Figure 5.17** shows graphically how this adding up works. Suppose first that you and your cousin are the only two consumers in the market for sets of wireless speakers (a and b). The total market demand curve (c) is obtained by summing *horizontally* each of the individual demand curves. Adding up the individual consumers' quantities demanded at all possible prices gives the market demand curve.

The Market Demand Curve

There are a few things to notice about market demand curves. First, a market demand curve will never be to the left of any individual demand curve, because all consumers combined must consume at least as much of a good at a given price as any single consumer does. For a similar reason, the slope of the market demand curve must also be as flat as, or flatter than, any of the individual demand curves. That is, for a given change in price, the change in quantity demanded for the market as a whole must be at least as great as the change in quantity demanded by any individual consumer.[6] Finally, if the price is so

---

[6] Even though the *slope* of the market demand curve is always flatter than that of individual demand curves, that doesn't necessarily imply that the *elasticity* of the market demand curve is higher than that of individual demand curves (though such is often the case). This is because the elasticity doesn't just depend on the slope; it also depends on the level of demand. The percentage change in prices (the denominator in the elasticity equation) will be the same for both individuals and the market. While the change in quantity will be smaller for individuals, the level of demand will be lower, too. If the level is small enough, the percentage change in quantities for the individual can be large enough to make individual demand as elastic as, or more elastic than, market demand.

Figure 5.17   Market Demand Curve

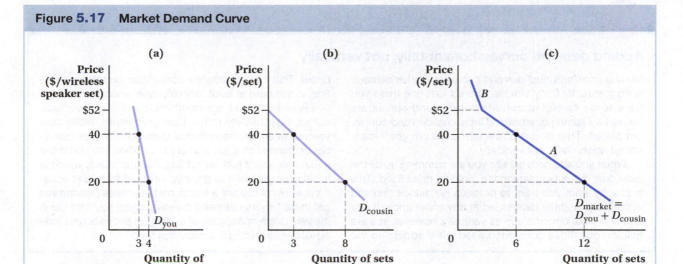

(a) Your individual demand curve D_{you} shows the number of sets of wireless speakers you would demand at each price. At a price of $40 per set, you demand 3 sets; at $20 per set, you demand 4 sets.
(b) Your cousin's individual demand curve D_{cousin} shows that he is more sensitive to price changes in speakers than you are. At a price of $40 per set, he similarly demands 3 sets, but when the price of a set of speakers is $20, he demands 8 sets.
(c) In a market consisting only of you and your cousin, the total market demand curve D_{market} is the sum of your demand curve D_{you}

and your cousin's demand curve D_{cousin}. At a price of $40 per set of speakers, you and your cousin each demand 3 sets, summing to 6 sets on D_{market}. When speaker sets cost $20 each, you demand 4 sets and your cousin demands 8, summing to 12 sets of speakers on D_{market}. At prices above $52, your cousin's quantity demanded is zero, so D_{market} overlaps with D_{you}, and therefore D_{market} is kinked at a price of $52. Market demand will always be flatter and will never be to the left of the individual demand curves.

high that only one consumer wants any of the good, the individual demand curve for that consumer will lie directly on top of the market demand curve at that price. At this point, the consumer *is* the market.

Using Algebra to Move from Individual to Market Demand

We can move from individual to market demand algebraically as well as graphically. The formulas for the two demand curves in Figure 5.17 are

$$Q_{you} = 5 - 0.05P$$
$$Q_{cousin} = 13 - 0.25P$$

To find the market demand for the speakers, we start by adding up the two individual demand curves—adding the Qs at a given P:

$$Q_{market} = Q_{you} + Q_{cousin} = (5 - 0.05P) + (13 - 0.25P)$$
$$Q_{market} = 18 - 0.3P$$

If we plug in the prices from Figure 5.17, they match the quantities in the figure as long as we are on the part of the curve labeled A, where quantities demanded by both you and your cousin are above zero. According to the equation, market demand when $P = \$40$ is $Q_{market} = 6$, which is what the figure shows, and when $P = \$20$, $Q_{market} = 12$, just as on the figure.

A⁺ make the grade

Adding demand curves horizontally, not vertically

Moving from individual demand curves to market demand is conceptually fairly simple. There's just one thing you have to be careful about. Market demand curves are derived by adding *quantities* of individual demand curves, not prices. That is, individual demands are graphically added horizontally, not vertically.

When you add horizontally, you are summing up all the individual quantities demanded, holding price fixed. This is exactly what you want to do because market demand is the total quantity demanded at any given price. If you add individual demand curves vertically, however, you are holding quantities demanded fixed while adding up the prices. That's a very different conceptual exercise and one that, in this case at least, doesn't really make any sense.

Likewise, if you are combining individual demand curves algebraically rather than graphically, make sure you've written out the individual demand curves as quantities demanded as a function of price. When you add those equations, you'll just be adding the quantities, which is again what you want to do. If you instead try to add equations where prices are a function of quantities (economists call these "inverse demand curves"), again you'll be doing the very different exercise of adding up prices across individuals while holding the quantities fixed.

We're not quite done yet, though. The prices at which you and your cousin will consume no speakers—the demand choke prices—are different. Yours is \$100; your cousin's is \$52. (You can check this by plugging these prices into the demand curves and verifying that the quantities demanded equal zero.) That means at prices above \$52, the market demand is only *your* demand because your cousin's quantity demanded is zero. There is no negative demand allowed. This isn't accounted for when we add together the two demand curves above, however, because at prices above \$52, the part of the market demand curve coming from the formula for Q_{cousin} is less than zero. Therefore, market demand is your demand, $Q = 5 - 0.05P$, for prices between \$52 and \$100 (quantity demanded is zero at prices higher than \$100), and is $Q = 18 - 0.3P$ (yours plus your cousin's) for prices below \$52. That is, the market demand has a kink at $P = \$52$.

 figure it out 5.4

Suppose that at a rural gas station in Toby Acres, there are only two customers, Johnny (who drives a 4×4 pickup) and Olivia (who drives a Prius). Johnny's demand for gasoline is $Q_J = 32 - 8P$, while Olivia's demand is $Q_O = 20 - 4P$, where Q is measured in gallons and P is the price per gallon.

a. Solve for the market demand equation for gasoline at Toby Acres.

b. Draw a diagram showing the market demand curve for gasoline at Toby Acres.

Solution:

a. The market demand curve is the horizontal sum of the buyers' demand curves. Remember that summing horizontally means adding up quantities demanded at each price. This means that we can get the market demand by adding Q_J and Q_O:

$$Q_{market} = Q_J + Q_O$$
$$= (32 - 8P) + (20 - 4P)$$
$$= 52 - 12P$$

But there is more to the story than solving for the summation of the two demand curves. Johnny is not willing to buy any gas if the price is greater than or equal to \$4 per gallon because that is his demand choke price:

$$Q_J = 32 - 8P$$
$$0 = 32 - 8P$$
$$8P = 32$$
$$P = \$4$$

So, once the price hits $4, only Olivia will be in the market. Her demand choke price is $5:

$$Q_O = 20 - 4P$$
$$0 = 20 - 4P$$
$$4P = 20$$
$$P = \$5$$

Thus, as long as the price is below $4 per gallon, the market demand for gasoline is the horizontal sum of the two buyers' demand curves. Between a price of $4 and $5, the market demand is simply the same as Olivia's demand. At a price greater than or equal to $5, quantity demanded is zero.

b. The figure here shows the market demand for gasoline in Toby Acres. Notice that the market demand curve is kinked as a result of the buyers' different choke prices.

Segment A is the section of demand below the price of $4 and is the horizontal summation of Johnny's and Olivia's demand for gasoline. Segment B is the segment of market demand where Olivia is the only buyer (since the price is above Johnny's demand choke price). At a price of $5 or above, quantity demanded is zero.

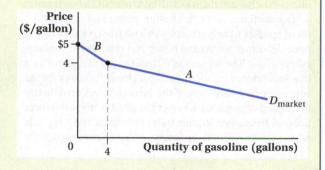

5.6 Conclusion

In this chapter, we used the consumer choice model of Chapter 4 to see where demand curves come from and what factors shift them. We studied how changes in various factors that drive consumer demand for a good—the consumer's income, the good's price, and the prices of other goods—affect the consumer's utility-maximizing bundle and, through this, the demand curve.

We broke down the response of a consumer's choices to a price change in a good into two components: the substitution effect and the income effect. The substitution effect reflects changes in quantities consumed due to the new relative prices of goods after the price change. The income effect reflects the fact that a price change affects a consumer's buying power, and this, in turn, changes the consumer's optimal consumption bundle.

We also saw how individuals' demand curves for a good are added up to create the market demand curve for that good.

This chapter ends our examination of the factors that determine consumer demand. In the next chapter, we move on to producer behavior and the supply side of markets.

Summary

1. Shifts in income holding prices constant are reflected in parallel shifts in the budget constraint and affect a consumer's demand curve. An **Engel curve** shows the relationship between income and the quantity of a good demanded. Whether an increase in income raises or reduces the quantity demanded of a good depends on the type of good. **Normal goods** are those for which demand increases with income. **Inferior goods** are those for which demand decreases with income. Within normal goods, goods with an **income elasticity** between zero and 1 (those whose share of expenditure rises more slowly than income rises) are called **necessity goods.** Goods with an income elasticity greater than 1 (those

whose share of expenditure grows faster than income) are called **luxury goods. [Section 5.1]**

2. The way in which changes in the price of a good affect the quantity demanded of that good is what creates the shape of the demand curve. We construct a consumer's demand curve by examining what happens to a consumer's utility-maximizing bundle as the price of one good changes, holding the price of the other good, income, and preferences fixed. Changes in income, holding preferences and prices constant, can shift the demand curve. Changes in preferences, holding income and prices constant, can shift the demand curve. **[Section 5.2]**

3. The **total effect** on the quantity demanded of a good in response to a change in its own price can be broken down into two components.

   The **substitution effect** causes the consumer to shift toward the good that becomes relatively cheaper and away from the good that becomes relatively more expensive. This shows up as a movement along the consumer's initial indifference curve, driven by the change in relative prices.

   The **income effect** occurs because a change in the price of a good changes the purchasing power of the consumer; a price drop increases purchasing power and expands the set of bundles a consumer may choose from, while a rise in price decreases purchasing power and reduces the consumer's options. The income effect shows up as a move to a new indifference curve, reflecting a change in utility for the consumer. The direction of the income effect on quantity demanded depends on whether the good is normal (where demand rises when income rises) or inferior (demand falls when income rises). If the income effect is large enough for inferior goods, it is theoretically possible for the quantity demanded of a good to rise when its price rises. However, these types of goods, called **Giffen goods,** are exceedingly rare in the real world. **[Section 5.3]**

4. Changes in the prices of other goods shift the demand curve for a good. Which way these cross-price effects shift demand depends on the nature of the relationship between the goods. Goods are **substitutes** if a price increase in one leads to an increase in demand for the other, due to consumers switching away from the now more expensive good and toward the substitute. Goods are **complements** if an increase in one's price causes demand for the other to fall. Complements are goods that are often consumed together. **[Section 5.4]**

5. Individuals' demand curves are aggregated to get total market demand. Market demand at a given price is the sum of all individual demands at that same price. Another way of saying this is that market demand is the horizontal (i.e., quantity) sum of individual demands. **[Section 5.5]**

Review Questions

1. Define the income effect. What variables do we hold constant in order to isolate the income effect?

2. What are the differences between normal goods, inferior goods, and luxury goods?

3. Both the income expansion path and the Engel curve show the effect of income on consumption choices. When might you choose to use the income expansion path? When might the Engel curve be more useful?

4. Describe how we can derive a consumer's demand curve from his indifference curves. Why would we expect the demand curve to slope downward?

5. Name at least three factors that can shift an individual's demand curve for pizza. Also describe the effect each factor has on demand (e.g., does it rise or fall?).

6. Define the substitution effect. How does it relate to the income effect?

7. Describe how to decompose the consumer's response to price changes into the substitution and income effects.

8. How do income and substitution effects differ between normal and inferior goods?

9. What is a Giffen good?

10. What are complements and substitutes?

11. If demand for one good increases when the price of another good falls, are the two goods complements or substitutes? What if the demand for one good decreases when the price of the other falls?

12. What can the shape of the indifference curve tell us about two goods?

13. How does the market demand relate to individual demand curves?

14. Why will a market demand curve always be at least as flat as a given individual demand curve?

Problems   (Solutions to problems marked with an asterisk appear at the back of this book. Problems adapted to use calculus are available online.)

1. Show, using indifference curves and budget constraints, that

   a. all goods can be normal, but

   b. all goods cannot be inferior.

2. Joelle consumes food and clothing. For incomes near her current income, her income expansion path is negatively sloped. Indicate whether each of the following statements is true or false, and provide a brief explanation why. (You may want to use a graph in formulating your explanation.)

   a. At current income levels, food must be an inferior good.

   b. At current income levels, clothing must be an inferior good.

   c. At current income levels, food and clothing must be inferior goods.

   d. At current income levels, either food or clothing must be an inferior good.

3. Suppose that, holding prices constant, Alice has preferences over the number of books she purchases that look like:

Income (thousands of dollars)	Optimal number of books purchased
5	5
10	6
15	20
20	25
25	26
30	10
35	9
40	8
45	7
50	6

a. Draw a smooth approximation of Alice's Engel curve for books, indicating the ranges over which books are inferior goods and over which they are normal goods.

b. A luxury good is a good that has an income elasticity greater than 1. Give the ranges in which books are luxury goods for Alice.

4. Suppose that Grover consumes two goods, cookies and milk. Grover's income expansion path is shown in the diagram below. Use the information in the diagram to explain whether each of the statements below is true or false. Provide an explanation for each answer.

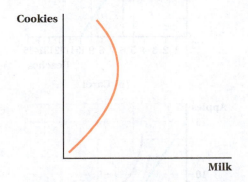

a. At low levels of income, both cookies and milk are normal goods for Grover.

b. As Grover's income grows, eventually cookies become an inferior good.

c. Draw, intuitively, the Engel curve for Grover's consumption of milk at various incomes.

d. Draw, intuitively, the Engel curve for Grover's consumption of cookies at various incomes.

5. College sophomore Martin enjoys attending sporting events and going to concerts. Because his scholarship pays for room and board, he spends all his income on these live events. Every once in a while, a doting aunt sends a cash gift to Martin; of course, he spends this additional sum on attending more sporting events and concerts.

a. True or false: Both sporting events and concerts are luxury goods for Martin. (*Hint:* Use the income elasticity of demand to determine the answer to this question.)

b. True or false: If concerts are a luxury good to Martin, sporting events must be an inferior good. Explain your answer, referring to the formula for the income elasticity of demand.

6. Chloe makes $500 per week and spends all her income on books and tea. Books cost $25 each, and Chloe buys 16 each week. Tea costs $5 per cup, and Chloe buys 20 cups. When Chloe's income falls to $450 per week, she cuts her consumption of books by 3 books and purchases 5 more cups of tea. Based on these figures, indicate whether each of the following statements is true or false, and briefly explain your reasoning.

a. Books are an inferior good.

b. Tea is a necessity.

c. Books are a luxury good and tea is an inferior good.

*7. Consider the following graph, which illustrates Tyler's preferences for DVD rentals and in-theater movie tickets:

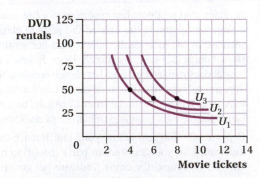

Suppose that DVD rentals always cost $1 and Tyler's income is $100 per week.

a. If the price of a movie ticket is $10, draw Tyler's budget line. Be very careful to draw to scale. How many movies does he see in the theater?

b. Begin to draw Tyler's demand curve for movies by creating a new set of axes with price on the vertical axis and the quantity of movies on the horizontal axis. Plot a point that shows how many movies Tyler demands when the price of movies is $10.

c. The movie theater changes the price of tickets to $12.50. Modify the graph provided to reflect this price change. Then add a point to your demand curve graph to show how many movies Tyler demands at a price of $12.50.

d. Tyler's mother gives him a discount card that allows him to purchase movie tickets for $7.50 each. Modify the graph provided to reflect this price change. Then add a point to your demand curve graph to show how many movies Tyler demands at a price of $7.50.

e. Connect the dots in the graph you created to complete Tyler's demand curve for movie tickets.

8. Juliette spends $48 each month on Oreo cookies (which cost $2 per package) and salt and vinegar chips (which cost $3 per bag).

   a. With chips on the horizontal axis, draw Juliette's budget constraint, making sure to indicate the horizontal and vertical intercepts.

   b. Suppose that at current prices, Juliette purchases 6 bags of chips each month. Draw an indifference curve tangent to Juliette's budget constraint consistent with this choice (assume Juliette is maximizing her utility). Label her chosen bundle with the letter A. How many packages of Oreos does Juliette buy?

   c. Suppose that the price of chips falls to $2 per bag, and Juliette increases her chip consumption to 8 bags each month. Draw Juliette's new budget constraint and indicate her chosen bundle with an appropriately drawn indifference curve. Label her utility-maximizing bundle with the letter B. (Be sure to determine the right quantities of both chips *and* Oreos!)

   d. A major chip producer has experienced a fire, and the disruption of supply has caused the price of chips to increase to $4. As a result, Juliette cuts her consumption of chips to 5 bags per month. Draw Juliette's new budget constraint and indicate her chosen bundle with an appropriately drawn indifference curve. Label her utility-maximizing bundle with the letter C. (Again, be sure to determine the right quantities of both chips *and* Oreos!)

   e. Draw a new diagram below your indifference curve diagram. Use your answers to parts (b)–(d) to draw Juliette's demand for chips. Indicate her quantities demanded at prices of $2, $3, and $4. Is there an inverse relationship between price and quantity demanded?

9. Armen lives in Washington State, where grapes are grown. Armen's twin Allen lives in New York, where grapes must be trucked in from Washington at a fixed cost of $0.20 per pound of grapes. Armen and Allen have identical tastes, but Armen tends to purchase lower-quality grapes and Allen tends to purchase higher-quality grapes. Use indifference curve analysis to explain this oddity.

10. Klaus cares only about how much he can write. Because a pen will write 7 miles of text and a pencil will write 35 miles of text, Klaus considers them perfect 5 to 1 substitutes. If the price of pens is given by P_{pen} and the price of

pencils is given by P_{pencil}, and if Klaus's income is given by Y, use indifference curve analysis to *derive* the demand curve for pencils.

11. Consider the following three graphs, which illustrate the preferences of three consumers (Bob, Carol, and Ted) regarding two goods, apples and peaches. Each consumer has an income of $30, and each consumer pays $2 for apples and $3 for peaches.

   a. Suppose that the price of peaches falls to $2. Draw a new budget line for each consumer and find the new optimal bundle of apples and peaches each would buy. How does the new quantity of peaches compare to the original quantity? Indicate the change in the first column of the table that follows (an increase of 1 unit might be denoted as a +1).

   b. For each consumer, determine the substitution effect of the price change by drawing a hypothetical budget line with the same slope as your new budget line, but just tangent to the consumer's original indifference curve. How much of a change in peach consumption does the substitution effect account for? Indicate that change in the second column of the same table.

(a) Bob

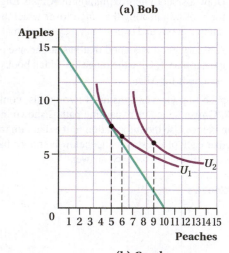

(b) Carol

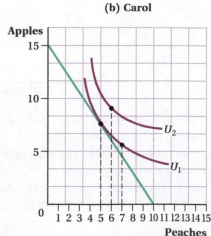

(c) Ted

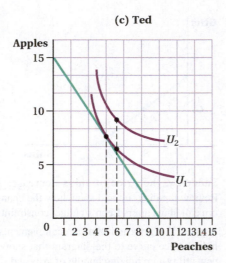

c. Now add in the income effect. Compare each consumer's peach consumption in (b) to his or her final peach consumption in (a). Indicate the difference in column 3 of the table below. Double-check your work to ensure that the last two columns add up to the number in the first column.

d. Do Bob, Carol, and Ted consider peaches normal, inferior, or income inelastic?

	Total Effect of Price Change	Substitution Effect of Price Change	Income Effect of Price Change
Bob			
Carol			
Ted			

*12. Suppose that Sonya faces an increase in the price of pasta, as depicted below, moving her from an optimal bundle of rice and pasta at A to an optimal bundle at B.

a. Trace a copy of this diagram. Graphically depict the substitution and income effect.

b. Which effect is strongest? How can you tell?

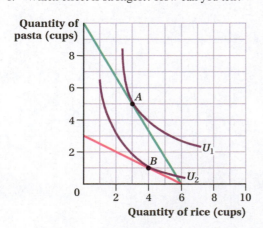

13. Brady, who has ordinary-shaped indifference curves, buys 16 ounces of salt each year. Even when the price of salt doubles, Brady continues to purchase exactly 16 ounces.

a. Use indifference curves and budget constraints to depict Brady's behavior graphically. Put salt on the horizontal axis and a composite good on the vertical axis.

b. True or False (and explain): Salt is neither inferior nor normal to Brady.

c. What is Brady's price elasticity of demand for salt?

d. What can we say about Brady's income elasticity of demand for salt?

e. What can we say about the substitution and income effects of a change in the price of salt?

14. Explain intuitively why any normal good cannot possibly be a Giffen good. (You may wish to illustrate your answer with a budget line/indifference curve graph.)

*15. At a price of $3 each, Yoshi (a typical New Yorker) drinks 200 44-ounce sodas each year. Concerned about burgeoning obesity, the mayor of New York proposes a $0.50 tax on such drinks. She then proposes compensating consumers for the price increase by mailing each resident a check for $100.

a. What will happen to Yoshi's consumption of soda? Show the result using an indifference curve diagram with soda on the horizontal axis and a composite good (price = $1) on the vertical axis.

b. Will Yoshi be better off, worse off, or indifferent to the change? Explain using your diagram.

c. In terms of revenue, will the government be better off, worse off, or indifferent to the proposal? Explain.

*16. Consider the following diagram, which illustrates Gaston's preferences for red beans and rice. Gaston has an income of $20. Rice costs $2 per serving.

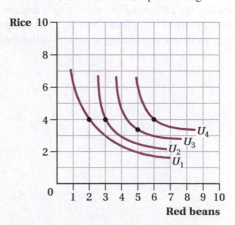

a. Derive Gaston's demand for red beans. Use prices of $2 and $4 in your analysis. Graph your results and connect the points you plotted to yield Gaston's demand for red beans.

b. Suppose that the price of rice increases to $3. Again, derive Gaston's demand for red beans using the same prices you used in part (a).

c. Does Gaston's demand for red beans increase or decrease as a result of the increase in the price of rice?

d. Does your answer to (c) indicate that red beans and rice are substitutes or complements?

17. Consider Liu's indifference curve indicated in the graph below:

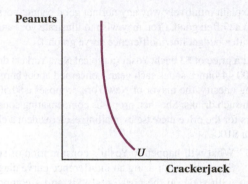

a. True or False (and explain): Peanuts and Crackerjack are clearly complements.

b. True or False (and explain): Peanuts and Crackerjack are clearly both normal goods.

18. True or False: If pizza and calzones are substitutes, then the substitution effect of a price change will be in a different direction than if pizza and calzones are complements. Explain using a diagram.

19. Consider the following diagram, which depicts various combinations of two goods: grits and shins. Leon is currently maximizing his utility at point A in the diagram.

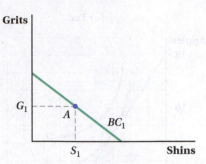

a. Suddenly, the price of shins decreases by half. Redraw the diagram and show how the change in the price of shins alters Leon's budget constraint.

b. Suppose that grits and shins are complements. Add an indifference curve to the diagram that shows Leon's new utility-maximizing bundle of grits and shins.

c. Redraw part (b), but this time assume that grits and shins are substitutes.

20. Reconsider Problem 8, in which you derived Juliette's demand for chips. In that problem, are chips and Oreos complements or substitutes?

21. You may have noticed that the market demand curve is always at least as flat as individual demand curve. Is market price elasticity of demand also always lower than individual price elasticity of demand? Why or why not?

22. Three students have different demands for doughnuts. Andre's demand is given by $Q = 5 - P$; Carlene's demand is given by $Q = 6 - 2P$; Cooper's demand is given by $Q = 4 - 0.5P$.

a. Derive the market demand curve for doughnuts algebraically.

b. Graph the market demand curve for doughnuts. Pay special attention to any kinks in the market demand!

Chapter 5 Appendix:
The Calculus of Income and Substitution Effects

We saw in this chapter that a price change in one good influences a consumer's consumption in two ways. The *substitution effect* is the change in a consumer's optimal consumption bundle due to a change in the relative prices of the goods, holding his utility constant. The *income effect* is the change in a consumer's optimal consumption bundle due to the change in his purchasing power. In the chapter, we solved for these two effects using a figure like the one below where good X is shown on the horizontal axis and good Y on the vertical axis. The consumer's original consumption bundle is A. Consumption bundle B is the optimal bundle after a decrease in the price of X, holding the price of Y constant. Finally, bundle A' shows what the consumer would buy if the price of X decreased but utility stayed the same as at bundle A (i.e., on indifference curve U_1). Graphically, the substitution effect is the change from bundle A to bundle A', the income effect is the change from A' to B, and the total effect is the sum of these two effects or the change from A to B.

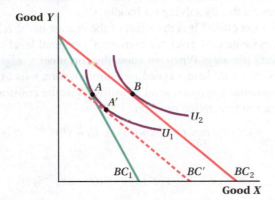

The graphical approach to decomposing the income and substitution effects can be a little messy. You have to keep track of multiple budget constraints, indifference curves, and their respective shifts. The calculus links the effects we observed in the graph to the techniques we learned for solving the consumer's problem in the Chapter 4 Appendix. Solving for these effects is a two-step process. We begin by finding the new consumption bundle B to solve for the total effect. Second, we solve for bundle A', which will allow us to identify both the substitution and income effects.

Let's start with a consumer with budget constraint $I = P_X X + P_Y Y$ (BC_1 in the graph) and a standard Cobb–Douglas utility function $U(X,Y) = X^\alpha Y^{1-\alpha}$, where $0 < \alpha < 1$. Point A in the figure is the solution to the constrained optimization problem:

$$\max_{X,Y} \ U = X^\alpha Y^{1-\alpha} \ \text{s.t.} \ I = P_X X + P_Y Y$$

In the Chapter 4 Appendix, we derived the solution to this particular utility-maximization problem, and found that the optimal bundle A is $\left(X_A = \dfrac{\alpha I}{P_X}, \ Y_A = \dfrac{(1-\alpha)I}{P_Y} \right)$.

Now suppose that the price of good X, P_X, decreases to P_X'. The consumer has the same utility function as before, but because of the price change, his budget constraint rotates outward to $I = P_X' X + P_Y Y$ (BC_2 on the graph). Once again, we rely on utility maximization to solve for the optimal bundle:

$$\max_{X,Y} \ U = X^\alpha Y^{1-\alpha} \ \text{s.t.} \ I = P_X' X + P_Y Y$$

Because we already know the generic solution to this problem, we can plug in the new price of X to find the new optimal bundle $B = \left(X_B = \dfrac{\alpha I}{P_X'}, \ Y_B = \dfrac{(1-\alpha)I}{P_Y} \right)$. This gives us the total effect of the price change on the consumer's consumption bundle—the difference between his new consumption bundle $\left(\dfrac{\alpha I}{P_X'}, \dfrac{(1-\alpha)I}{P_Y} \right)$ and his original consumption bundle $\left(\dfrac{\alpha I}{P_X'}, \dfrac{(1-\alpha)I}{P_Y} \right)$. Note that in this instance the change in the price of X does not affect the quantity of Y the consumer purchases. That the demand for each good is independent of changes in the price of the other good is a quirk of the Cobb–Douglas utility function. This result is not necessarily true of other utility functions.

The solution to the utility-maximization problem gives us the final bundle B. But we want to know more than just the total effect of the price change on the consumption bundle. We want to decompose this total effect into its two components: the substitution and income effects. We can do this by solving for bundle A'.

What is the substitution effect? It is the effect of the change in the relative price of two goods on the quantities demanded given the consumer's original level of utility. How can we solve for this effect? It's easy! When we know the consumer's original level of utility and the goods' prices, as we do here, expenditure minimization tells us the answer to the problem. Take the consumer's original level of utility U_1 as the constraint and set up the consumer's expenditure-minimization problem

$$\min_{X,Y} \ I = P_X' X + P_Y Y \ \text{s.t.} \ U_1 = X^\alpha Y^{1-\alpha}$$

as a Lagrangian:

$$\min_{X,Y,\lambda} \ \mathcal{L}(X,Y,\lambda) = P_X' X + P_Y Y + \lambda(U_1 - X^\alpha Y^{1-\alpha})$$

Write out the first-order conditions:

$$\frac{\partial \mathcal{L}}{\partial X} = P_X' - \lambda \alpha X^{\alpha-1} Y^{1-\alpha} = 0$$

$$\frac{\partial \mathcal{L}}{\partial Y} = P_Y - \lambda(1-\alpha) X^\alpha Y^{-\alpha} = 0$$

$$\frac{\partial \mathcal{L}}{\partial \lambda} = U_1 - X^\alpha Y^{1-\alpha} = 0$$

Solve for Y using the first two conditions:

$$\lambda = \frac{P_X'}{\alpha X^{\alpha-1} Y^{1-\alpha}} = \frac{P_Y}{(1-\alpha) X^\alpha Y^{-\alpha}}$$

$$P_X'(1-\alpha) X^\alpha Y^{-\alpha} = P_Y \alpha X^{\alpha-1} Y^{1-\alpha}$$

$$Y^{1-\alpha} Y^\alpha = \frac{(1-\alpha)}{\alpha} \frac{P_X'}{P_Y} X^\alpha X^{1-\alpha}$$

$$Y = \frac{(1-\alpha)}{\alpha} \frac{P_X'}{P_Y} X$$

Plug this expression for Y as a function of X into the constraint to solve for bundle A':

$$U_1 = X^\alpha Y^{1-\alpha} = X^\alpha \left[\frac{(1-\alpha)}{\alpha} \frac{P_X'}{P_Y} X \right]^{1-\alpha}$$

$$U_1 = X^\alpha X^{1-\alpha} \left[\frac{(1-\alpha)}{\alpha} \frac{P_X'}{P_Y} \right]^{1-\alpha} = X \left[\frac{(1-\alpha)}{\alpha} \frac{P_X'}{P_Y} \right]^{1-\alpha}$$

$$X_{A'} = U_1 \left[\frac{\alpha}{(1-\alpha)} \frac{P_Y}{P_X'} \right]^{1-\alpha}$$

Then plug this optimal value of X into the expression for Y as a function of X from above:

$$Y_{A'} = \frac{(1-\alpha)}{\alpha} \frac{P_X'}{P_Y} X_{A'} = \frac{(1-\alpha)}{\alpha} \frac{P_X'}{P_Y} U_1 \left[\frac{\alpha}{(1-\alpha)} \frac{P_Y}{P_X'} \right]^{1-\alpha}$$

To simplify, invert the third term and combine like terms:

$$Y_{A'} = \frac{(1-\alpha)}{\alpha} \frac{P_X'}{P_Y} U_1 \left[\frac{(1-\alpha)}{\alpha} \frac{P_X'}{P_Y} \right]^{\alpha-1}$$

$$Y_{A'} = U_1 \left[\frac{(1-\alpha)}{\alpha} \frac{P_X'}{P_Y} \right]^{\alpha}$$

Solving the consumer's expenditure-minimization problem at the new prices and original utility level gives us the third piece of the substitution/income effect puzzle: bundle A'.[7] Having these three bundles (A, A', and B) allows us to solve for the substitution and income effects. The substitution effect is the difference between the consumer's original bundle and what he would buy at the new prices but at the old utility level, the difference between A and A'. The income effect is the difference between what he would buy at the new prices and original utility and what he buys with his new income at the new prices, the difference between A' and B. The total effect is the sum of the substitution and income effects or the difference between A and B.

---

 figure it out 5A.1

A sample problem will make breaking down the total effect of a price change into the substitution and income effects even clearer. Let's return to Figure It Out 4.4, which featured Antonio, a consumer who purchases burgers and fries. Antonio has a utility function $U(B,F) = \sqrt{BF} = B^{0.5}F^{0.5}$ and income of $20. Initially, the prices of burgers and fries are $5 and $2, respectively.

a. What is Antonio's optimal consumption bundle and utility at the original prices?

b. The price of burgers increases to $10 per burger, and the price of fries stays constant at $2. What does Antonio consume at the optimum at these new prices? Decompose this change into the total, substitution, and income effects.

Solution:

a. We solved this question in the Chapter 4 Appendix, but the answer will be crucial to solving for the total, substitution, and income effects in part (b). When a burger costs $5 and fries cost $2, Antonio's original constrained optimization problem is

$$\max_{B,F} U = B^{0.5}F^{0.5} \text{ s.t. } 20 = 5B + 2F$$

We found that Antonio consumes 2 burgers and 5 orders of fries, and his utility for this bundle is $B^{0.5}F^{0.5} = 2^{0.5}5^{0.5} = 10^{0.5}$.

b. When the price of hamburgers doubles to $10 each, Antonio faces a new budget constraint: $20 = 10B + 2F$.

---

[7] One way to check our answer to bundle A' is to take the new prices, income, and utility function, and solve for the bundle using utility maximization. As we saw in the Chapter 4 Appendix, this approach will yield the same answer.

Antonio's new utility-maximization problem is

$$\max_{B,F} \; U = B^{0.5}F^{0.5} \text{ s.t. } 20 = 10B + 2F$$

Therefore, we should write his constrained optimization problem as a Lagrangian and solve for his new optimal bundle at the higher burger price:

$$\max_{B,F,\lambda} \; \mathcal{L}(B,F,\lambda) = B^{0.5}F^{0.5} + \lambda(20 - 10B - 2F)$$

$$\frac{\partial \mathcal{L}}{\partial B} = 0.5B^{-0.5}F^{0.5} - 10\lambda = 0$$

$$\frac{\partial \mathcal{L}}{\partial F} = 0.5B^{0.5}F^{-0.5} - 2\lambda = 0$$

$$\frac{\partial \mathcal{L}}{\partial \lambda} = 20 - 10B - 2F = 0$$

We use the first two conditions to solve for λ and then solve for F as a function of B:

$$\lambda = 0.05B^{-0.5}F^{0.5} = 0.25B^{0.5}F^{-0.5}$$

$$F^{0.5}F^{0.5} = 20(0.25)B^{0.5}B^{0.5}$$

$$F = 5B$$

and substitute this value for F into the budget constraint:

$$20 = 10B + 2F$$

$$20 = 10B + 2(5B)$$

$$20 = 20B$$

$$B^* = 1 \text{ burger}$$

$$F^* = 5B = 5(1) = 5 \text{ orders of fries}$$

In response to the increase in the price of burgers from \$5 to \$10, then, Antonio decreases his consumption of burgers and leaves his consumption of fries unchanged. Therefore, the total effect of the price change is that Antonio's consumption of burgers declines by 1 and his consumption of fries remains the same at 5.

Next, we use expenditure minimization to find the substitution and income effects. Remember that we want to find out how many burgers and fries Antonio will consume if the price of burgers is \$10 but his utility is the same as his utility when burgers cost \$5. His third constrained optimization problem is

$$\min_{B,F} \; I = 10B + 2F \text{ s.t. } 10^{0.5} = B^{0.5}F^{0.5}$$

We could solve using the Lagrangian as we did above, but instead let's use what we know about the solution to the consumer's optimization problem and set the marginal rate of substitution of burgers for fries equal to the ratio of their prices and solve for F as a function of B:

$$\frac{MU_B}{MU_F} = \frac{P_B}{P_F}$$

$$\frac{0.5B^{-0.5}F^{0.5}}{0.5B^{0.5}F^{-0.5}} = \frac{10}{2}$$

$$\frac{F}{B} = \frac{10}{2}$$

$$F = 5B$$

Now plug this value for F into the consumer's utility constraint:

$$10^{0.5} = B^{0.5}F^{0.5} = B^{0.5}(5B)^{0.5}$$

$$10^{0.5} = B(5^{0.5})$$

$$B' = \frac{10^{0.5}}{5^{0.5}} = 2^{0.5} \approx 1.4 \text{ hamburgers}$$

$$F' = 5B' \approx 5(1.4) \approx 7 \text{ orders of fries}$$

Antonio's expenditure-minimizing bundle for the new prices and the original utility is approximately 1.4 hamburgers and 7 fries compared to his original bundle of 2 hamburgers and 5 fries. As intuition would tell you, the desired consumption of burgers decreases when burgers become relatively more expensive, while the desired consumption of fries increases as fries become relatively less expensive—that's the substitution effect in action. In particular, Antonio's substitution effect is to consume 0.6 fewer burgers (1.4 − 2 burgers = −0.6 burgers) and 2 more orders of fries (7 − 5 orders of fries = 2 orders of fries).

While this bundle gives Antonio the same level of utility as the original bundle, he would have to spend about \$8 more to buy it [his original expenditure was \$20; his new one is \$10(1.4) + \$2(7) = \$28]. Remember, however, that Antonio doesn't actually purchase this \$28 combination of burgers and fries. It's just a step on the way to his final consumption bundle (1 hamburger, 5 orders of fries) that we got from the utility-maximization problem above. We can use this final bundle to find the income effect. Here, the income effect is to consume 0.4 fewer burgers (1 − 1.4 burgers = −0.4 burgers) and 2 fewer orders of fries (5 − 7 orders of fries = −2 orders of fries) because the increase in the price of burgers reduces Antonio's purchasing power. Notice that the quantity of both goods declines as his purchasing power declines. This means that, for Antonio, they are both normal goods.

In the end, the price change only changes Antonio's consumption of hamburgers: The total effect on his consumption bundle is 1 fewer burger (1 − 2 burgers = −1 burger), which is the sum of the substitution effect (−0.6 burgers) and the income effect (−0.4 burgers). On the other hand, the total effect on his consumption of fries is zero because the substitution effect (2 more orders of fries) and the income effect (2 fewer orders of fries) exactly offset one another.

Let's review what we've learned about decomposing the total effect of a price change into the substitution and income effects. To find the original bundle, we solve the utility-maximization problem at the original prices and income. We identify the substitution effect after a price change by solving the expenditure-minimization problem using the new prices with the original level of utility as the constraint. This tells us how a consumer's bundle responds to a price change while leaving the consumer with the same level of utility—the substitution effect. Finally, to find the income effect, we solve the utility-maximization problem using the new prices and the consumer's actual income. Comparing this bundle with the bundle we found using expenditure minimization tells us how consumption responds to the change in purchasing power that is caused by the price change, or the income effect.

Problems

1. Malachi only consumes 2 goods: DVD rentals and coffee. His utility function is

   $$U(R,C) = R^{0.75}C^{0.25}$$

   where R is the number of rentals and C is cups of coffee. Malachi has $16 in his pocket right now, and he plans to spend all of it on DVD rentals and coffee today.

   a. The price of one rental is $4 and the price of coffee is $2 per cup. Solve for Malachi's optimal bundle.

   b. Suppose that Malachi signs up for a membership that reduces the price of a rental to $2, while leaving his income unchanged. Find the substitution effect, the income effect, and the total effect of the decrease in the price of video rentals on Malachi's consumption of rentals and coffee.

   c. From your answer to part (b), are DVD rentals and coffee normal or inferior goods for Malachi? Explain.

2. Suppose that a consumer has utility given by $U(X,Y) = XY + 10Y$ and income of $100 to spend on goods X and Y.

   a. The prices of X and Y are both $1 per unit. Use a Lagrangian to solve for the optimal basket of goods.

   b. Suppose that the price of X increases to $5 per unit. Use a Lagrangian to solve for the new optimal basket of goods. Find the total effect of the price change on the consumption of each good.

   c. Use a Lagrangian to find the substitution effect of the increase in the price of good X on the consumption of each good. What income would the consumer need to attain the original level of utility when the price of X increases to $5 per unit?

   d. Find the income effect of the increase in the price of good X on the consumption of each good. Are the goods normal or inferior? Explain.

   e. Show that the total effect of the increase in the price of X is equal to the sum of the substitution effect and the income effect.

Producer Behavior

At the beginning of Chapter 4, we imagined being an executive at Samsung tasked with developing the next Galaxy smartphone for the market and deciding what features to add so consumers would find it the most desirable option. Suppose you've done your market analysis and selected the new features, but now must produce the phone. How many do you want to make? What mix of inputs are you going to use to do so? What is the size of your factory? How many employees does it have? How much glass? What will the manufacturing process for the phone cost? Suppose you've already produced the new Galaxy, and it is an even bigger hit than predicted. You now want to ramp up production. If you can't easily adjust the size of your factory, how much will its capacity limit your ability to make more phones, and how much will costs rise if you increase production levels?

Any producer of a good or service faces these types of questions and others like them. The next several chapters will examine the economics surrounding such questions and their answers. Chapters 4 and 5 were about consumer behavior, which determines the demand side of markets. With this chapter, we turn our attention to producer behavior, which drives the supply side of markets. As you'll see, there are a lot of parallels in the economics of consumers' and producers' decisions.

6.1 The Basics of Production

Before anyone can consume a good, someone must first produce it (duh). **Production** is the *process by which a person, company, government, or non-profit agency uses inputs to create a good or service for which others are willing to pay*. Production can take many forms. Some producers make **final goods**, *goods that are bought by consumers*.[1] Others make **intermediate goods**, *goods that are used to produce another good*, such as electricity, sugar, or advertising services. The range of products is so extensive that formulating a general model of production is difficult—not unlike building the model of consumer behavior in the previous two chapters. We begin our model of production by laying out the assumptions that economists typically adopt to simplify firms' decisions.[2]

Simplifying Assumptions about Firms' Production Behavior

To draw general conclusions about optimal production behavior in the messy real world, we need to make some simplifying assumptions. However, we do not want to assume away so much that the model stops being a useful way to understand

production The process by which a person, company, government, or non-profit agency uses inputs to create a good or service for which others are willing to pay.

final good A good that is bought by a consumer.

intermediate good A good that is used to produce another good.

[1] Throughout this book, we often use the word "good" to mean both tangible goods, such as trucks or computers, as well as services, such as haircuts or dog walking. In this usage, anything a consumer values—tangible or not, concrete or abstract—is a good.

[2] We use the word "firm" as a generic term for any producer. Many producers are firms, but the term can also mean persons, governments, or non-profit agencies that create products.

real-world behavior. In our attempt to model producer behavior in this chapter, we assume the following:

1. **The firm produces a single good.** If a firm sells many products, then the decisions it makes about each product can become intertwined in complicated ways. In the basic model of the firm, we can avoid these complications by assuming that the firm makes just one good.

2. **The firm has already chosen which product to produce.** The firms we study already know what they want to produce; we just decide how they can make it most efficiently. Deciding what to produce is an important aspect of a real firm's success, but that analysis is beyond the scope of what we analyze here. The branch of economics called *industrial organization* studies many aspects of firm behavior, including product choice.

3. For whatever quantity it makes, **the firm's goal is to minimize the cost of producing it.**

    Note the assumption is not to minimize cost completely, just for a given quantity level. The firm can always reduce its total production cost by producing nothing, so minimizing cost alone can't be the answer. In building our model, we want to analyze how a firm produces a specific quantity of output. (A firm's choice about the specific quantity of output to make depends on the characteristics of the market for its product, including the demand for the product and the number and type of its competitors. We will discuss firms' choices of output quantities in Chapters 8–11.)

    Second, cost minimization is necessary for the firm to maximize its profits, another standard assumption economists make about firm behavior. We can think of cost minimization as a first step in profit maximization. Remember, though, that we don't need to assume a firm is maximizing profits for it to be minimizing costs. Producers such as non-profits or governments might have priorities other than profits, but they would still want to minimize their costs; they gain nothing from wasting resources when producing.

4. **The firm uses only two inputs to make its product: capital and labor.** Capital encompasses the buildings, machinery, and raw materials needed to make the product. Labor refers to all the human resources (such as factory workers, salespeople, and CEOs) that are used to produce the firm's output. In building our model, we lump together all different kinds of capital under one single label and do the same for labor.[3]

5. **In the short run, a firm can choose to employ as much or as little labor as it wants, but it cannot rapidly change how much capital it uses. In the long run, the firm can freely choose the amounts of both labor and the capital it employs.** The **short run** is the *period of time during which one or more inputs into production cannot be changed*. **Fixed inputs** are *inputs that cannot be changed in the short run*; **variable inputs** are *inputs that can be changed in the short run*. The **long run**, then, is the *amount of time necessary for all inputs into production to be fully adjustable*; in the long run, all inputs are variable. The assumption here captures the fact that it takes time to put capital into use. For example, between acquiring permits and undertaking construction, it can take many years for an electric company to build a new power plant. During this time, the electric company's capital input is fixed, and we

short run In production economics, the period of time during which one or more inputs into production cannot be changed.

fixed inputs Inputs that cannot be changed in the short run.

variable inputs Inputs that can be changed in the short run.

long run In production economics, the amount of time necessary for all inputs into production to be fully adjustable.

---

[3] We can lump together different kinds of capital and labor in this way because we measure each input in common units that measure the productive ability of a given input. Economists call these units *efficiency units,* and they allow us to add up all the units across the various types of capital and of labor the firm employs. This simplifies our model by leaving the producer with only two inputs to purchase, labor and capital.

can consider this period (even though it might be several years long) as the short run in terms of the company's production decisions. In comparison, the electric company, and firms in general, can much more easily adjust worker hours by allowing employees to leave early or asking them to work overtime. Hiring new employees and putting them to work are also relatively easy. Even though companies must take the time to find and train these workers, such tasks do not usually take as long as building or integrating new capital.

6. **The more inputs the firm uses, the more output it makes.** This assumption is similar to the "more is better" assumption for consumers' utility functions that we discussed in Chapter 4. Here, the analogous implication for production is that if the firm uses more labor or capital, its total output rises.

7. **A firm's production exhibits diminishing marginal returns to labor and capital.** For a given amount of capital in the firm, each additional worker eventually generates less output than the one before. The same diminishing returns exist for adding capital for a given amount of labor. This assumption captures a basic idea of production: A mix of labor and capital is more productive than labor alone or capital alone. Capital helps workers to be productive and vice versa. Even hundreds of workers will make little progress digging if they have no shovels to dig with. Similarly, a large amount of fancy digging equipment will be of little benefit without people to operate it. The two inputs work best when combined in the right amounts.

8. **The firm can buy as many capital or labor inputs as it wants at fixed market prices.** Just as we assumed consumers could buy as much of any good as they wanted at a fixed price, we assume the firm can do the same for buying its capital and labor. Most firms are small relative to the markets for the inputs they use. Even the largest companies employ only a small fraction of an economy's workers. Furthermore, as long as the markets that produce a firm's inputs are reasonably competitive, even the largest firms can likely acquire as much capital and labor as they desire at a fixed price.

9. **If there is a well-functioning capital market (e.g., banks and investors), the firm does not have a budget constraint.** As long as the firm can make profits, it will be able to obtain the resources necessary to acquire the capital and labor it needs to produce. If a firm doesn't have the cash necessary to finance its input expenditures, it can raise funds by borrowing (or issuing stock). Outside investors should be willing to finance a firm's expenditures if they expect it to be profitable. Notice that this assumption about a firm's production does not have a counterpart in consumer choice theory. Consumers have a budget constraint that limits the maximum level of utility they can obtain.

You may have noticed that there are more simplifying assumptions for the production model than for the consumption model. This is because producer behavior is a bit more complicated. For example, we need to consider producer behavior in two time frames: the short run and the long run. The added levels of complication require us to simplify things a little more.

Production Functions

A firm's task is to turn capital and labor inputs into outputs. As noted above, we simplify things in our model of production so that we can get a better handle on the economics. Namely, our firm makes one product as its output and uses two inputs, capital and labor, to do so.

production function A mathematical relationship that describes how much output can be made from different combinations of inputs.

A **production function** is a *mathematical relationship that describes how much output can be made from different combinations of inputs*. It summarizes how a firm transforms these capital and labor inputs into output. A production function is just a formula that tells you how much output (which we label Q for quantity) you get as a function of the two inputs, capital (K) and labor (L):

$$Q = f(K, L)$$

In this production function, f is a mathematical function that describes how capital and labor are combined to produce the output. Production functions can take a form such as $Q = 10K + 5L$ in which the inputs are separate, or $Q = K^{0.5}L^{0.5}$ (a different way of writing that would be $\sqrt{KL}$) in which the inputs are multiplied together. They can also take many other forms depending on the technology a firm uses to produce its output.

The type of production function in which capital and labor are each raised to a power and then multiplied together (as in $Q = K^{0.5}L^{0.5}$ above) is known as a *Cobb–Douglas production function*. It is named after mathematician Charles Cobb and University of Chicago economist (and later, U.S. Senator) Paul Douglas. The Cobb–Douglas production function is one of the most common types of production functions used by economists because it usually describes actual production data reasonably well and it has handy mathematical properties.

6.2 Production in the Short Run

We start by analyzing production in the short run because it is the simplest case. Again, while the capital stock is fixed in the short run, the firm can choose how much labor to hire to minimize its cost of making the output quantity. **Table 6.1** shows some values of labor inputs and output quantities from a short-run production function. Here, we use the Cobb–Douglas production function and fix capital ($\overline{K}$) at 4 units, so the numbers in Table 6.1 correspond to the production function $Q = f(\overline{K}, L) = \overline{K}^{0.5}L^{0.5} = 4^{0.5}L^{0.5} = 2L^{0.5}$.

Figure 6.1 plots the short-run production function from Table 6.1. The plot contains the numbers in Table 6.1, but also shows output levels for all amounts of labor between 0 and 5 hours per week, as well as amounts of labor greater than 5 hours per week.

Even though capital is fixed, when the firm increases its labor, output rises. This reflects Assumption 6 above: More inputs mean more output. Notice, however, that the *rate* at which output rises slows as the firm hires more and more labor. This phenomenon of additional units of labor yielding less and less additional output reflects Assumption 7: The production function exhibits diminishing marginal returns to inputs. To see why there are

Table 6.1 An Example of a Short-Run Production Function

Capital, K	Labor, L	Output, Q	Marginal Product of Labor, $MP_L = \dfrac{\Delta Q}{\Delta L}$	Average Product of Labor, $AP_L = \dfrac{Q}{L}$
4	0	0.00	—	—
4	1	2.00	2.00	2.00
4	2	2.83	0.83	1.42
4	3	3.46	0.63	1.15
4	4	4.00	0.54	1.00
4	5	4.47	0.47	0.89

Figure 6.1   A Short-Run Production Function

This figure graphs the firm's continuous short-run production function using the values from Table 6.1. The production function's positive slope means that an increase in labor increases output. As the firm hires more labor, however, output increases at a decreasing rate and the slope flattens.

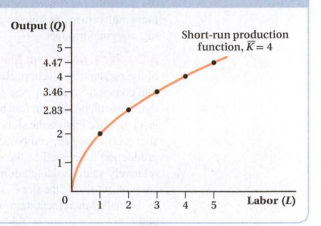

diminishing marginal returns, we need to understand just what happens when one input increases (labor) while the other input (capital) remains fixed. This is what is meant by an input's *marginal product.*

Marginal Product

The additional output that a firm can produce by using an additional unit of an input (holding use of the other input constant) is called the **marginal product**. In the short-run example in Table 6.1, the marginal product that is most relevant is the marginal product of labor because we are assuming that capital is fixed at 4. The marginal product of labor (MP_L) is the *change* in quantity (ΔQ) resulting from a 1-unit *change* in labor inputs (ΔL):

$$MP_L = \Delta Q/\Delta L$$

marginal product The additional output that a firm can produce by using an additional unit of an input (holding use of the other input constant).

The marginal product of labor for our short-run production function $Q = 4^{0.5} L^{0.5}$ is shown in the fourth column of Table 6.1. If a firm with this production function (in which capital is fixed at 4 units) uses 0 units of labor, it produces 0 units of output. (Perhaps the firm can't generate any output without someone to run the machines.) If it hires 1 unit of labor to combine with the 4 units of capital, it gets 2 units of output. Therefore, the marginal product of that first unit of labor is 2.00. With 2 units of labor (and the same 4 units of capital), the firm can produce 2.83 units of output, making the marginal product of the second unit of labor the change in output or $2.83 - 2.00 = 0.83$. With 3 units of labor, output rises by 0.63 to 3.46, so the marginal product of labor for that third unit is 0.63, and so on.

The **diminishing marginal product** of labor is the *reduction in the incremental output obtained from adding more and more labor*; it is embodied in our Assumption 7 and is a common feature of production functions. This is why the production function curve in Figure 6.1 flattens at higher quantities of labor. A diminishing marginal product makes intuitive sense. With a fixed amount of capital, then every time you add a worker, each worker has less capital to use. If a coffee shop has one espresso machine and one worker, she has a machine at her disposal during her entire shift. If the coffee shop hires a second worker to work the same hours as the first, the two workers must share the machine and may get in each other's way. With three workers per shift and still only one machine, the situation grows worse. A fourth worker may produce a tiny bit more output, but this fourth worker's marginal product will be smaller than the first's. The solution to this problem is for the coffee shop to buy more espresso machines—that is, add more capital. But we've assumed it can't do that in the short run. Eventually, in the long run, it can. We will look at what happens when a firm is able to change its capital level later in this chapter.

diminishing marginal product The reduction in the incremental output obtained from adding more and more labor.

Keep in mind, however, that diminishing marginal returns do not have to occur all the time; they just need to occur eventually. A production function could have increasing marginal returns at low levels of labor before running into the problem of diminishing marginal product.

A Graphical Analysis of Marginal Product   We can plot the marginal product in a graph of the production function. Recall that the marginal product is the change in output quantity that comes from adding one additional unit of input: $MP_L = \Delta Q / \Delta L$. $\Delta Q / \Delta L$ is the slope of the short-run production function in Figure 6.1. Thus, the marginal product of labor at a given level of labor input is the slope of the production function at that point. Panel a of **Figure 6.2** shows how the MP_L can be derived from our production function. At $L = 1$, the slope of the production function (i.e., the slope of the line tangent to the production function at $L = 1$) is relatively steep. Adding additional labor at this point will increase output by a substantial amount. At $L = 4$, the slope is considerably flatter, and adding more labor will boost output by a smaller increment than when $L = 1$. The marginal product of labor falls between $L = 1$ and $L = 4$, as we saw in Table 6.1. Panel b of Figure 6.2 illustrates the corresponding marginal product of labor curve. Because this production function exhibits diminishing marginal returns at all levels of labor, the marginal product curve is downward sloping.

A Mathematical Representation of Marginal Product   To find MP_L, we need to calculate the additional output obtained by adding an incremental unit of labor, holding capital constant. So, let's compute the firm's increase in output when it uses $L + \Delta L$ units of labor instead of L units (holding capital constant). ΔL is the incremental unit of labor. Mathematically, MP_L is

$$MP_L = \frac{\Delta Q}{\Delta L} = \frac{f(\overline{K}, L + \Delta L) - f(\overline{K}, L)}{\Delta L}$$

Applying this to our short-run production function ($\overline{K}^{0.5} L^{0.5} = 4^{0.5} L^{0.5} = 2L^{0.5}$) gives

$$Q = f(\overline{K}, L)$$

$$MP_L = \frac{2(L + \Delta L)^{0.5} - 2L^{0.5}}{\Delta L}$$

Figure 6.2   Deriving the Marginal Product of Labor

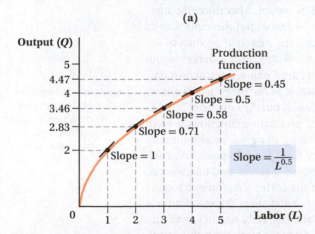
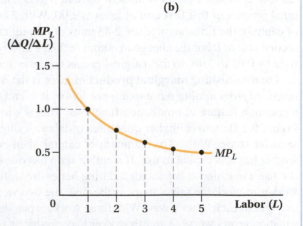

(a) The marginal product of labor is the slope of the production function. As the quantity of labor increases, the marginal product decreases, from $MP_L = 1$ when $L = 1$ to $MP_L = 0.45$ when $L = 5$, and the slope flattens.

(b) Using the production function in panel a, we can derive the marginal product of labor curve. The downward slope of the curve shows the diminishing marginal returns to labor.

To consider what happens as we let ΔL become really tiny involves some calculus. If you don't know calculus, however, here is the marginal product formula for our Cobb–Douglas production function: $MP_L = \dfrac{1}{L^{0.5}}$. The MP_L values calculated using this formula are shown in Figure 6.2. (These values are slightly different from those in Table 6.1: While the table sets $\Delta L = 1$, the formula allows the incremental unit to be much smaller. The economic idea behind both calculations is the same, however.)

➡ The end-of-chapter appendix explores the Cobb–Douglas production function using calculus.

Average Product

It's important to recognize that the *marginal* product is not the same as the *average* product. **Average product** is the *total quantity of output divided by the number of units of input used to produce it*. The average product of labor (AP_L), for example, is the quantity produced, Q, divided by the amount of labor L used to produce it:

average product The total quantity of output divided by the number of units of input used to produce it.

$$AP_L = Q/L$$

The average product of labor for our short-run production function is shown in the last column of Table 6.1. Notice that the average product of labor falls as labor inputs increase. This decline occurs because the marginal product of labor is less than the average product at each level of labor in the table, so each unit of labor added on the margin brings down labor's average product. An easy way to understand this scenario is to consider your grades in a hypothetical course. If your mid-semester average is 80% and you then take an exam and get 90%, your average will rise because the score on the last exam you took (the *marginal* exam) is greater than your previous average. If your exam score is 65%, however, your course average will fall because the marginal score is lower than the average score.

figure it out 6.1

The short-run production function for a firm that produces pizzas is $Q = f(\overline{K}, L) = 15\,\overline{K}^{0.25} L^{0.75}$, where Q is the number of pizzas produced per hour, $\overline{K}$ is the number of ovens (which is fixed at 3 in the short run), and L is the number of workers employed.

a. Write an equation for the short-run production function for the firm showing output as a function of labor.

b. Calculate the total output produced per hour for $L = 0$, 1, 2, 3, 4, and 5.

c. Calculate the MP_L for $L = 1$ to $L = 5$. Is MP_L diminishing?

d. Calculate the AP_L for $L = 1$ to $L = 5$.

Solution:

a. To write the production function for the short run, we plug $\overline{K} = 3$ into the production function to create an equation that shows output as a function of labor:

$$Q = f(\overline{K}, L) = 15\overline{K}^{0.25} L^{0.75}$$
$$= 15(3^{0.25})L^{0.75} = 15(1.316)L^{0.75} = 19.74L^{0.75}$$

b. To calculate total output, we plug in the different values of L and solve for Q:

$L = 0$	$Q = 19.74(0)^{0.75} = 19.74(0) = 0$
$L = 1$	$Q = 19.74(1)^{0.75} = 19.74(1) = 19.74$
$L = 2$	$Q = 19.74(2)^{0.75} = 19.74(1.682) = 33.20$
$L = 3$	$Q = 19.74(3)^{0.75} = 19.74(2.280) = 45.01$
$L = 4$	$Q = 19.74(4)^{0.75} = 19.74(2.828) = 55.82$
$L = 5$	$Q = 19.74(5)^{0.75} = 19.74(3.344) = 66.01$

c. The marginal product of labor is the additional output generated by an additional unit of labor, holding capital constant. We can use our answer from (b) to calculate the marginal product of labor for each worker:

$L = 1$	$MP_L = 19.74 - 0 = 19.74$
$L = 2$	$MP_L = 33.20 - 19.74 = 13.46$
$L = 3$	$MP_L = 45.01 - 33.20 = 11.81$
$L = 4$	$MP_L = 55.82 - 45.01 = 10.81$
$L = 5$	$MP_L = 66.01 - 55.82 = 10.19$

Note that, because MP_L falls as L rises, there is a diminishing marginal product of labor. This implies that output rises at a decreasing rate when labor is added to the fixed level of capital.

d. The average product of labor is calculated by dividing total output (Q) by the quantity of labor input (L):

$L = 1$	$AP_L = 19.74/1 = 19.74$
$L = 2$	$AP_L = 33.20/2 = 16.60$
$L = 3$	$AP_L = 45.01/3 = 15.00$
$L = 4$	$AP_L = 55.82/4 = 13.96$
$L = 5$	$AP_L = 66.01/5 = 13.20$

6.3 Production in the Long Run

In the long run, firms can change not only their labor inputs but also their capital. This difference gives them two important benefits. First, in the long run, a firm might be able to lessen the sting of diminishing marginal products. As we saw above, when capital is fixed, the diminishing marginal product limits a firm's ability to produce additional output by using more and more labor. If additional capital can make each unit of labor more productive, then a firm can expand its output more by increasing capital and labor inputs *jointly*.

Think back to our example of the coffee shop. If the shop adds a second worker per shift when there is only one espresso machine, the firm won't gain much additional output because of the diminishing marginal product of labor. Hiring still another worker per shift will cause output to barely budge at all. But if the firm bought another machine for each additional worker, output could increase with little drop in productivity. In this way, using more capital and labor at the same time allows the firm to avoid (at least in part) the effects of diminishing marginal products.

The second benefit of being able to adjust capital in the long run is that producers often have some ability to substitute capital for labor or vice versa. Firms can be more flexible in their production methods and in the ways they respond to changes in the relative prices of capital and labor. For example, as airline ticket agents became relatively more expensive and technological progress made automated check-in less so, airlines shifted much of their check-in operations from being labor-intensive (checking in with an agent at the counter) to being capital-intensive (checking in at an automated kiosk or at home online).

The Long-Run Production Function

In a long-run production function, the firm can adjust all of its inputs. The long-run production is the same production function we first introduced in Section 6.2: $Q = f(K, L)$, but rather than having a fixed level of $\overline{K}$ and choosing L (as we did for the short run), now the firm can choose the levels of both inputs.

We can also illustrate the long-run production function in a table. **Table 6.2** shows the relationship between output and inputs for our example production function $Q = K^{0.5}L^{0.5}$. The columns correspond to different amounts of labor; the rows denote different amounts of capital. The number in each cell is the quantity of output generated by the corresponding combination of inputs.

Table 6.2 An Example of a Long-Run Production Function

		Units of Labor, *L*				
		1	**2**	**3**	**4**	**5**
	1	1.00	1.41	1.73	2.00	2.24
Units of Capital, *K*	**2**	1.41	2.00	2.45	2.83	3.16
	3	1.73	2.45	3.00	3.46	3.87
	4	2.00	2.83	3.46	4.00	4.47
	5	2.24	3.16	3.87	4.47	5.00

In the fourth row of the table, where the firm has 4 units of capital, the values exactly match the short-run production function values from Table 6.1 that held K steady at 4 units. Table 6.2 adds to Table 6.1 other possible output quantities the firm could achieve once it can change its level of capital. One way to think about the long-run production function is as a combination of all the firm's possible short-run production functions, where each possible short-run function has a different fixed level of capital. Notice that for any given level of capital—that is, for any particular short-run production function—labor has a diminishing marginal product. For example, when capital is fixed at 5 units, the marginal product of labor of the first worker is 2.24, the MP_L of the second worker is $0.92 (= 3.16 - 2.24)$, the MP_L of the third worker is $0.71 (= 3.87 - 3.16)$, and so on.

6.4 The Firm's Cost-Minimization Problem

At the start of the chapter, we made several assumptions about a firm's production behavior. Assumption 3 states what is known as **cost minimization**, *a firm's goal of producing a specific quantity of output at minimum cost*. (How a firm determines that quantity is the subject of Chapters 8–11.) We call the challenge of producing a specific amount of a particular good as inexpensively as possible the firm's *cost-minimization* problem.

cost minimization A firm's goal of producing a specific quantity of output at minimum cost.

The firm's production decision is another *constrained optimization* problem. Remember from our discussion in Chapter 4 that these types of problems are ones in which an economic actor tries to optimize something while facing a constraint on her choices. Here, the firm's problem is a constrained *minimization* problem. The firm wants to minimize the total costs of its production. However, it must hold to a constraint in doing so: It must produce a particular quantity of output. That is, it can't minimize its costs just by refusing to produce as much as it would like (or refuse to produce anything, for that matter). In this section, we look at how a firm uses two concepts, *isoquants* (which reveal to the firm the quantity constraint it faces) and *isocost lines* (which tell the firm the various costs at which the firm can produce its quantity), to solve its constrained minimization problem.

Isoquants

With the consumer's utility function in Chapter 4, we looked at three variables: the quantities of the two goods consumed and the consumer's utility. Each indifference curve showed all the combinations of the two goods consumed that allowed the consumer to achieve a particular utility level.

Figure 6.3 Isoquants

Each isoquant shows the possible combinations of labor (L) and capital (K) that produce the output (Q) levels 1, 2, and 4 units.

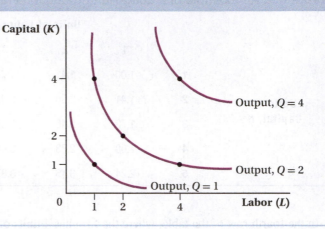

---

isoquant A curve representing all the combinations of inputs that allow a firm to make a particular quantity of output.

We can do the same thing with the firm's production function. We can plot as one curve all the possible combinations of capital and labor that can produce a given amount of output. **Figure 6.3** does just that for the production function we have been using throughout the chapter; it displays the combinations of inputs that are necessary to produce 1, 2, and 4 units of output. **Isoquants** are the *curves representing all the combinations of inputs that allow a firm to make a particular quantity of output.* (The Greek prefix *iso-* means "the same," and *quant* is a shortened version of the word "quantity.")

Just as with indifference curves, isoquants further from the origin correspond to higher output levels (because more capital and labor lead to higher output), isoquants cannot cross (because if they did, the same quantities of inputs would yield two different quantities of output), and isoquants are convex to the origin (because using a mix of inputs generally lets a firm produce a greater quantity than it could by using an extreme amount of one input and a tiny amount of the other).

The Marginal Rate of Technical Substitution

The slope of the isoquant plays a key role in analyzing production decisions because it captures the tradeoff in the productive abilities of capital and labor. Look at the isoquant in **Figure 6.4**. At point A, the isoquant is steeply sloped, meaning that the firm can reduce the amount of capital it uses by a lot while increasing labor only a small amount, and still maintain the same level of output. In contrast, at point B, if the firm wants to reduce capital just a bit, it will have to increase labor quite a bit to keep output at the same level. Isoquants' curvature and convexity to the origin reflect the fact that the capital–labor tradeoff varies as the mix of the inputs changes.

marginal rate of technical substitution ($MRTS_{XY}$) The rate at which the firm can trade input X for input Y, holding output constant.

The negative of the slope of the isoquant is called the **marginal rate of technical substitution ($MRTS_{XY}$)**, and it is the *rate at which the firm can trade input X for input Y, holding output constant.* It is the quantity change in input Y necessary to keep output constant if the quantity of input X changes by 1 unit. For the most part in this chapter, we will be interested in the MRTS of labor for capital or $MRTS_{LK}$, which is the amount of capital needed to hold output constant if the quantity of labor used by the firm changes.

If we imagine moving just a little bit down and to the right along an isoquant, the change in output—which we know must add up to zero because we're moving along an isoquant—equals the marginal product of labor times the change in the units of labor due to the move, plus the marginal product of capital times the change in the amount of capital. (This change in capital is negative because we're taking away capital when we move down

---

Figure 6.4 **The Marginal Rate of Technical Substitution**

The negative slope of the isoquant is the marginal rate of technical substitution of labor L for capital K. At point A, the marginal product of labor is high relative to the marginal product of capital, and a relatively small decrease in labor would require a large quantity of capital to hold output constant. At point B, the marginal product of labor is low relative to the marginal product of capital, and a relatively small decrease in capital would require a large quantity of labor to hold output constant.

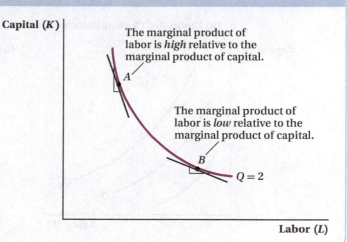

---

along the isoquant.) So we can write the total output change (which, again, is zero along an isoquant) as

$$\Delta Q = MP_L \times \Delta L + MP_K \times \Delta K = 0$$

If we rearrange this to find the slope of the isoquant, $\Delta K / \Delta L$, we have

$$MP_K \times \Delta K = -MP_L \times \Delta L$$

$$MP_K \times \frac{\Delta K}{\Delta L} = -MP_L$$

$$\frac{\Delta K}{\Delta L} = -\frac{MP_L}{MP_K}$$

$$MRTS_{LK} = -\frac{\Delta K}{\Delta L} = \frac{MP_L}{MP_K}$$

> ➡️ The end-of-chapter appendix derives the relationship between the marginal rate of technical substitution and marginal products.

Therefore, the $MRTS_{LK}$ at any point on an isoquant tells you the relative marginal products of capital and labor at that point.

The concepts underlying the marginal rate of technical substitution are the same as those of the marginal rate of substitution (MRS) for consumers (if you remember those!), which we learned about in Chapter 4. The two are so closely tied together, in fact, that the names are essentially the same—the word "technical" is tacked on to distinguish the producer case. Both the MRTS and MRS are about marginal tradeoffs. The MRS concerns a consumer's willingness to trade one good for another while still obtaining the same utility level. The MRTS concerns a firm's ability to trade one input for another while still producing the same quantity of output. The shape of the curves in both cases tells you the rate at which one good or input can be substituted for the other.

Substitutability   How curved an isoquant is shows how easily firms can substitute one input for another in production. For isoquants that are almost straight, as in panel a of **Figure 6.5**, a firm can replace a unit of one input (capital, e.g.) with a particular amount of the second input (labor) without changing its output level, regardless of whether it is already using a lot or a little of capital. Stated in terms of the marginal rate of technical substitution, $MRTS_{LK}$ doesn't change much as the firm moves along the isoquant. In this

> ➡️ The online appendix explores the relationship between the production function and the shape of isoquants.

Figure 6.5 The Shape of Isoquants Indicates the Substitutability of Inputs

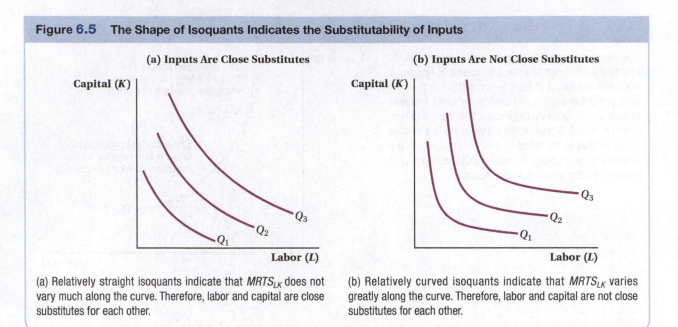

(a) Inputs Are Close Substitutes

Capital (K)

Labor (L)

(b) Inputs Are Not Close Substitutes

Capital (K)

Labor (L)

(a) Relatively straight isoquants indicate that $MRTS_{LK}$ does not vary much along the curve. Therefore, labor and capital are close substitutes for each other.

(b) Relatively curved isoquants indicate that $MRTS_{LK}$ varies greatly along the curve. Therefore, labor and capital are not close substitutes for each other.

case, the two inputs are close substitutes in the firm's production function, and the relative usefulness of either input for production won't vary significantly with how much of each input the firm is using.

Highly curved isoquants, such as those shown in panel b of Figure 6.5, mean that the $MRTS_{LK}$ changes a lot along the isoquant. In this case, the two inputs are poor substitutes. The relative usefulness of substituting one input for another in production depends a great deal on the amount of the input the firm is already using.

Perfect Substitutes and Perfect Complements in Production In Chapter 4, we discussed the extreme cases of perfect substitutes and perfect complements in consumption. For perfect substitutes, indifference curves are straight lines; for perfect complements, the curves are "L"-shaped right angles. The same holds for inputs: It is possible for them to be perfect substitutes or perfect complements in production. Isoquants for these two cases are shown in **Figure 6.6**.

If inputs are perfect substitutes as in panel a, the MRTS doesn't change at all with the amounts of the inputs used, and the isoquants are perfectly straight lines. This characteristic means the firm can freely substitute between inputs without suffering diminishing marginal returns. An example of a production function where labor and capital are perfect substitutes is $Q = f(K,L) = 10K + 5L$; 2 units of labor can always be substituted for 1 unit of capital without changing output, no matter how many units of either input the firm is already using. In this case, imagine that capital took the form of a robot that behaved exactly like a human when doing a task, but did the work twice as fast. Here, the firm can always substitute 1 robot for 2 workers or vice versa, regardless of its current number of robots or workers. This is true because the marginal product of labor is 5 (holding K constant, a 1-unit increase in L causes output to grow by 5). At the same time, holding L constant, a 1-unit rise in K will increase output by 10 units, making the MP_K equal to 10. No matter what levels of L and K the firm chooses, $MRTS_{LK} = MP_L/MP_K = \dfrac{5}{10} = \dfrac{1}{2}$.

If inputs are perfect complements, isoquants have an "L" shape. This implies that using inputs in any ratio outside of a particular fixed proportion—the ratio at the isoquants'

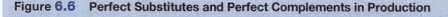

Figure 6.6   Perfect Substitutes and Perfect Complements in Production

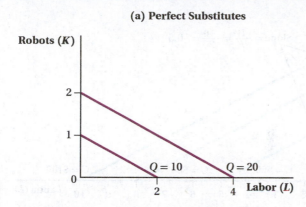

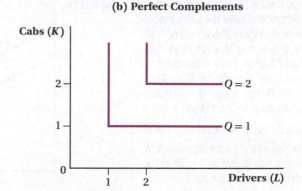

(a) Robots K and labor L are perfect substitutes. The isoquants are straight lines, and the $MRTS_{LK}$ does not change along the isoquant. In this case, 2 humans can substitute for 1 robot.

(b) Cabs K and drivers L are perfect complements. The isoquants are L-shaped, and the optimal quantity (K, L) for each output Q is the corner of the isoquant. In this case, 1 cab with 1 driver produces $Q = 1$, while 2 cabs with 2 drivers produce $Q = 2$.

corners—yields no additional output. Cars and drivers might be close to perfect complements in the production of taxi rides. Anything other than a 1 to 1 ratio of cabs to drivers is unlikely to produce any additional cab rides. If a company has 1 driver and 2 cabs, it will not be able to offer any more rides than if it had 1 driver and 1 cab. Nor could it offer more rides if it had 30 drivers and 1 cab. Therefore, the production function would be $Q = \min(L, K)$, where "min" indicates that output (Q) is determined by the minimum level of either labor (L) or capital (K). Of course, the cab company could offer more rides if it had 30 drivers *and* 30 cabs, because this would preserve the 1-to-1 driver-to-cab ratio.[4]

Isocost Lines

Up to this point in the chapter, we have focused on various aspects of the production function and how quantities of inputs are related to the quantity of output. That's only half of the story. As we discussed earlier, the firm wishes to minimize its costs of producing a given quantity of output. So, we need to add in the costs of those choices.

The key concept that brings costs into the firm's decision is the **isocost line**, a *curve that shows all the input combinations that yield the same cost.* As we saw earlier, *iso-* is a prefix meaning "the same," so "isocost" is a line that shows all the combinations of capital and labor that the firm can purchase for a given total expenditure. Mathematically, the isocost line corresponding to a total expenditure level of C is given by

isocost line A curve that shows all the input combinations that yield the same cost.

$$C = RK + WL$$

where R is the price (the *rental rate*) per unit of capital, W is the price (the wage) per unit of labor, and K and L are the number of units of capital and labor that the firm hires. It's best to think of the cost of capital as a rental rate in the same type of units as the wage (e.g., per hour, week, or year). Because capital is used over a long period of time, we can consider R as not just the purchase price of the equipment but also the economic user cost of capital. The user cost takes into account capital's purchase price, as well as its rate of depreciation and the opportunity cost of the funds tied up in its purchase (foregone interest).

[4] There is nothing special about a 1-to-1 ratio. Inputs can be perfect complements at other ratios as well.

Figure 6.7   Isocost Lines

Each isocost line shows all bundles of inputs that have the same cost to the firm. As you move farther from the origin, the isocost lines represent higher total expenditures, from cost $C = \$50$ to $C = \$80$ to $C = \$100$. For wage $W = \$10$ and rental rate $R = \$20$, the slope of the isocost lines is $-W/R$, or $-\dfrac{1}{2}$. Therefore, for every 1-unit increase in K, the firm has to give up 2 units of L in order to keep cost constant.

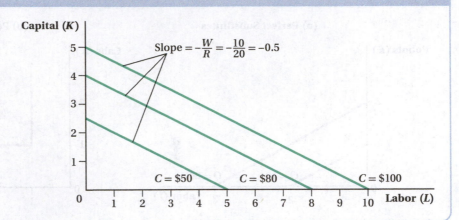

Figure 6.7 shows isocost lines corresponding to total cost levels of $50, $80, and $100 when the price of capital is $20 per unit and labor's price is $10 per unit. It is important to note two things about the figure:

■ First, isocost lines for higher total expenditure levels are further from the origin. This reflects the fact that, as a firm uses more inputs, total expenditure on those inputs increases.

■ Second, the isocost lines are parallel. They all have the same slope, regardless of what total cost level they represent.

To see why all the isocost lines in Figure 6.7 have the same slope, think about what that slope represents. We can rewrite the equation for the isocost line in slope-intercept form so that the value on the vertical axis (capital) is expressed as a function of the value on the horizontal axis (labor):

$$C = RK + WL$$
$$RK = C - WL$$
$$K = \frac{C}{R} - \frac{W}{R}L$$

This means that the y-intercept of the isocost line is C/R, while the slope is the (negative of the) inputs' price ratio, $-W/R$.

As is so often the case in economics, the slope tells us about tradeoffs at the margin. Here, the slope reflects the cost consequences of substituting one input for another. It indicates how much more of one input a firm could hire, without increasing overall expenditure on inputs, if the firm used less of the other input. If the isocost line's slope is steep, labor is relatively expensive compared to capital. If the firm wants to hire more labor without increasing its overall expenditure on inputs, it must use a lot less capital. (Or, if the firm chose to use less labor, it could hire a lot more capital without spending more on inputs overall.) If labor is relatively cheap compared to capital, the isocost line will be relatively flat. The firm could hire a lot more labor and not have to give up much capital to do so without changing expenditures.

Because of Assumption 8, the understanding that the firm can buy as much capital or labor as it wants at a fixed price per unit, the slopes of isocost lines are constant. That's why they are straight, parallel lines: Regardless of the overall cost level or amount of each input the firm chooses, the relative tradeoff between the inputs in terms of total costs is always the same.

Figure 6.8   When Labor Becomes More Expensive, the Isocost Line Becomes Steeper

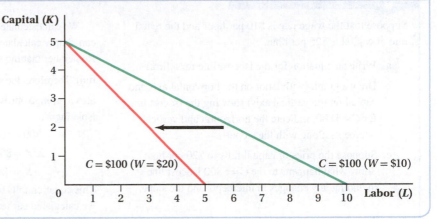

When the price of labor increases from $W = \$10$ to $W = \$20$ and the price of capital stays constant at $R = \$20$, the slope of the isocost changes from $-\frac{1}{2}$ to $-\frac{2}{2}$, or -1. The isocost line therefore becomes steeper, and the quantity of inputs the firm can buy for $100 decreases.

$C = \$100 \ (W = \$20)$

$C = \$100 \ (W = \$10)$

If these ideas seem familiar to you, it's because the isocost line is analogous to the consumer's budget line we learned about in Chapter 4. The consumer's budget line expressed the relationship between the quantities of each good consumed and the consumer's total expenditure on those goods. Isocost lines capture the same idea, except with regard to firms and their input purchases. We observed that the negative of the slope of the consumer's budget constraint was equal to the price ratio of the two goods, just as the negative of the slope of the isocost line equals the price ratio of the firm's two inputs.

Isocost Lines and Input Price Changes   Just like budget lines for consumers, when relative prices change, the isocost line rotates. In our example, say labor's price (W) rises from $10 to $20. Now if the firm only hires labor, it will only be able to hire half as much. The line becomes steeper as in **Figure 6.8**. The isocost line rotates because its slope is $-W/R$. When W increases from $10 to $20, the slope changes from $-\frac{1}{2}$ to -1, and the isocost line rotates clockwise and becomes steeper.

Changes in the price of capital also rotate the isocost line. **Figure 6.9** shows what happens to the $100 isocost line when the price of capital increases from $20 to $40 per unit, and the wage stays at $10 per unit of labor. If the firm hires only capital, it can afford half as much, so the slope flattens. A drop in the capital price would rotate the isocosts in the other direction.

Figure 6.9   When Capital Becomes More Expensive, the Isocost Line Becomes Flatter

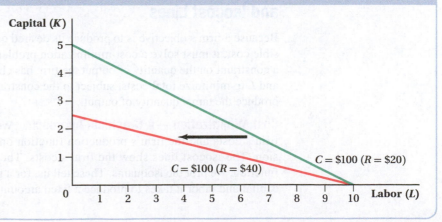

When the price of capital increases from $R = \$20$ to $R = \$40$ and the price of labor stays constant at $W = \$10$, the slope of the isocost changes from $-\frac{1}{2}$ to $-\frac{1}{4}$. The quantity of inputs the firm can buy for $100 decreases, and the isocost line becomes flatter.

$C = \$100 \ (R = \$40)$

$C = \$100 \ (R = \$20)$

figure it out 6.2

Suppose that the wage rate is $10 per hour and the rental rate of capital is $25 per hour.

a. Write an equation for the isocost line for a firm.

b. Draw a graph (with labor on the horizontal axis and capital on the vertical axis) showing the isocost line for $C = \$800$. Indicate the horizontal and vertical intercepts along with the slope.

c. Suppose the price of capital falls to $20 per hour. Show what happens to the $C = \$800$ isocost line including any changes in intercepts and the slope.

Solution:

a. An isocost line always shows the total costs for the firm's two inputs in the form of $C = RK + WL$. Here, the wage rate (W) is $10 and the rental rate of capital (R) is $25, so the isocost line is $C = 10L + 25K$.

b. We can plot the isocost line for $C = \$800 = 10L + 25K$. One easy way to do this is to compute the horizontal and vertical intercepts. The horizontal intercept tells us the amount of labor the firm could hire for $800 if it only hired labor. Therefore, the horizontal intercept is $\$800/W = \$800/\$10 = 80$. The vertical intercept tells us how much capital the firm could hire for $800 if it were to use only capital. Thus, it is $\$800/R = \$800/\$25 = 32$. We can plot these points on the graph below and then draw a line connecting them. This is the $C = \$800$ isocost line labeled C_1.

We can calculate slope in several different ways. First, we can simply calculate the slope of the isocost line as drawn. Remember that the slope of a line is $\Delta Y/\Delta X$ (i.e., rise over run). Therefore, the slope is $\Delta Y/\Delta X = -\dfrac{32}{80} = -0.4$. We can also rearrange our isocost line into slope-intercept form by isolating K:

$$800 = 10L + 25K$$
$$25K = 800 - 10L$$
$$K = (800/25) - (10/25)L = 32 - 0.4L$$

This equation tells us that the vertical intercept is 32 (which we calculated earlier) and -0.4 is the slope.

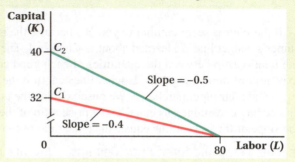

c. If R falls to $20, the horizontal intercept is unaffected. If the firm is only using labor, a change in the price of capital will have no impact. However, the vertical intercept rises to $\$800/R = \$800/\$20 = 40$ and the isocost line becomes steeper (C_2). The new slope is $-W/R = -\$10/\$20 = -0.5$.

Identifying Minimum Cost: Combining Isoquants and Isocost Lines

Because a firm's objective is to produce its desired quantity of output at the minimum possible cost, it must solve a cost-minimization problem: It must achieve an objective given a constraint on the quantity of output the firm has chosen to produce. It needs to choose K and L to minimize total costs, subject to the constraint that it involves enough K and L to produce the target quantity of output.

Cost Minimization—A Graphical Approach   We can combine information about the firm's costs and the firm's production function on the same graph to analyze its decision. The isocost lines show the firm's costs. Then to represent the firm's production function, we plot the isoquants. These tell us, for a given production function, how much capital and labor it takes to produce a fixed amount of output.

Figure **6.10**   Cost Minimization

The firm wants to minimize the cost to produce the quantity $Q = \overline{Q}$. Because A is on the isoquant, the firm can choose to use input combination A to produce $\overline{Q}$. However, A is not cost-minimizing because the firm can produce $\overline{Q}$ at a lower cost at any point below and to the left of the isocost C_A. Point B, located at the tangency between isocost C_B and the isoquant, is the firm's cost-minimizing capital and labor combination. Input combinations on C_C cost less than those on C_B, but are too small to allow the firm to produce $\overline{Q}$.

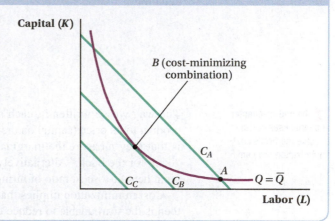

Before we work through a specific example, think about the logic of the firm's cost-minimization problem. The firm's objective is to minimize costs subject to the constraint that it has to produce a particular quantity of output, $\overline{Q}$. The cost-minimization part means the firm wants to be on an isocost line that is as close to the origin as possible (because isocost lines closer to the origin correspond to lower levels of expenditure) but still on the isoquant that corresponds to $\overline{Q}$. **Figure 6.10** shows the isoquant for the firm's desired output quantity $\overline{Q}$. The firm wants to produce this quantity at minimum cost, so it must decide on capital and labor levels. Suppose the firm is considering the level of inputs shown at point A, which is on isocost line C_A. That point is on the $Q = \overline{Q}$ isoquant, so the firm will produce the desired level of output. However, there are many other input combinations on the $\overline{Q}$ isoquant that are below and to the left of C_A. These all would allow the firm to produce $\overline{Q}$ but at a lower cost than input mix A. Only one input combination exists that is on the $\overline{Q}$ isoquant but for which there are no other input combinations that would allow the firm to produce the same quantity at a lower cost. That combination occurs at point B, on isocost C_B. There are input combinations that involve lower costs than B—for example, any combination on isocost line C_C—but these input levels are all too small to allow the firm to produce $\overline{Q}$.

The minimized total cost of producing a given quantity is where the isocost line is tangent to the isoquant. Point B is the point of tangency of the isocost line C_B to the $\overline{Q}$ isoquant. That's a lot like the tangency involved with optimal consumer behavior, too. Another important feature of the tangency result is that the isocost line and isoquant have the same slope at a tangency point (that's the definition of a tangency point). We know what these slopes are from our earlier discussion. The slope of the isocost line is the negative of the relative price of the inputs, $-W/R$. For the isoquant, the slope is the negative of the marginal rate of technical substitution ($MRTS_{LK}$), which is equal to the ratio of MP_L to MP_K. The tangency therefore implies that at the combination of inputs that minimizes the cost of producing a given quantity of output (like point B), the ratio of input prices equals the MRTS:

$$-\frac{W}{R} = -\frac{MP_L}{MP_K} \quad \text{or}$$

$$\frac{W}{R} = \frac{MP_L}{MP_K}$$

This condition has an important economic interpretation. Rearrange the terms in the equation:

$$\frac{W}{R} = \frac{MP_L}{MP_K}$$

$$MP_K \times W = MP_L \times R$$

$$\frac{MP_K}{R} = \frac{MP_L}{W}$$

➡️ The end-of-chapter appendix uses calculus to solve the firm's cost-minimization problem.

The way we've written it, each side of this equation is the ratio of an input's marginal product to its price (capital on the left, labor on the right). One way to interpret these ratios is that they measure the marginal product per dollar spent on each input, or the input's "bang for the buck." Alternatively, we can think of each of these ratios as the firm's marginal benefit-to-cost ratio of hiring an input.

Cost minimization implies that each input's benefit-to-cost ratio is equal because only then is the firm unable to reduce the cost of producing its current quantity by changing its input levels. For example, if the firm produced an input bundle where this wasn't true, if, say, $\frac{MP_K}{R} > \frac{MP_L}{W}$, then the firm's benefit-to-cost ratio for capital is higher than for labor. This would mean that the firm could replace some of its labor with capital while keeping its output quantity the same but reducing its total cost. Or if it wanted to, the firm could substitute capital for labor in a way that kept its total *cost* constant but raised its *output*. These options are possible because capital's marginal product per dollar is higher than labor's. If the sign of the inequality were reversed so $\frac{MP_K}{R} < \frac{MP_L}{W}$, the firm could reduce the cost of producing its current quantity (or raise its production without increasing cost) by substituting labor for capital because the marginal product per dollar spent is higher for labor.

Again, this logic parallels that from the consumer's optimal consumption choice in Chapter 4. There, at the optimal point, the marginal rate of substitution between goods equals the goods' price ratio. Here, the analog to the MRS is the MRTS (the former being a ratio of marginal utilities, the latter a ratio of marginal products), and the price ratio is now the input price ratio.

There is one place where the parallel between consumers and firms is slightly different. A firm doesn't have a budget constraint. That might sound odd. But the firm maximizes profit and if it doesn't have enough resources to pay for the inputs necessary to produce this quantity, then as long as the firm is profitable, someone should be willing to lend it the money (so long as well-functioning capital markets exist).

Input Price Changes

We've established that the cost-minimizing input combination occurs at the point of tangency between an isocost line and the isoquant that corresponds to the output quantity the firm wants to produce. A firm produces that level of output at the lowest cost when the marginal product per dollar spent is equal across all inputs. So let's consider what happens when input prices change.

A Graphical Representation of the Effects of an Input Price Change   We saw that differences in input costs show up as differences in the slopes of the isocost lines. A higher relative cost of labor (from an increase in W, decrease in R, or both) makes isocost lines steeper. Decreases in labor's relative cost flatten them. A cost-minimizing firm uses the input combination where the slope of the isocost line equals the slope of the isoquant. This requirement means that when the inputs' relative price changes, the point of tangency between the isocost line (now with a new slope) and the isoquant must also change. Input price changes

figure it out 6.3

Go online for interactive, step-by-step help in solving the following problem.

A firm employs 100 workers ($W = \$15$/hour) and 50 units of capital ($R = \$30$/hour). At the firm's current input use, the marginal product of labor is 45 and the marginal product of capital is 60. Is the firm producing its current level of output at the minimum cost, or is there a way for the firm to do better? Explain.

Solution:

The cost-minimizing input choice occurs when $MP_L/W = MP_K/R$. We need to determine if this is the case for this firm:

$MP_L = 45$ and $W = 15$, so $MP_L/W = 45/15 = 3$

$MP_K = 60$ and $R = 30$, so $MP_K/R = 60/30 = 2$

Therefore, $MP_L/W > MP_K/R$. The firm is not currently minimizing its cost.

Because $MP_L/W > MP_K/R$, \$1 spent on labor yields a greater marginal product (i.e., more output) than \$1 spent on capital. The firm would do better by reducing its use of capital and increasing its use of labor. Note that as the firm reduces capital, the marginal product of capital will rise. Likewise, as the firm hires additional labor, the marginal product of labor will fall. Ultimately, the firm will reach its cost-minimizing input choice where $MP_L/W = MP_K/R$.

cause the firm to move along the isoquant corresponding to the firm's desired output level to the input combination where an isocost line is tangent to the isoquant.

Figure 6.11 offers an example of this. The initial input price ratio gives the slope of isocost line C_1. The firm wants to produce the quantity $\overline{Q}$, so initially the cost-minimizing combination of inputs occurs at point A. Now suppose that labor becomes relatively more expensive (or equivalently, capital becomes relatively less expensive). This change causes the isocost lines to become steeper. With the steeper isocost lines, the point of tangency shifts to point B. Therefore, the increase in the relative cost of labor causes the firm to shift to an input mix that has more capital and less labor than before.

The implication of this outcome makes sense: If a firm wants to minimize its production costs and a particular input becomes relatively more expensive, the firm will substitute away from the now more expensive input toward the relatively less expensive one.

Figure 6.11   A Change in the Relative Price of Labor Leads to a New Cost-Minimizing Input Choice

When labor becomes relatively more expensive, the isocost line shifts from C_1 to C_2. With the steeper isocost line, the cost-minimizing input choice shifts from point A, with a high ratio of labor to capital, to point B, with a low ratio of labor to capital.

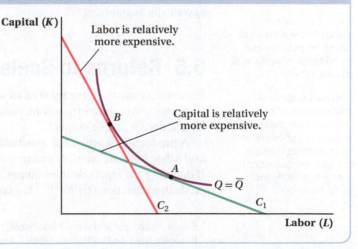

The online appendix derives the firm's demands for capital and labor.

This is why we sometimes observe different production methods used to make the same products. For example, if you spend a growing season observing a typical rice-farming operation in Vietnam, you will see dozens of workers tending small paddies tending plants one-by-one and using only basic farm tools. If you visit a rice farm in Texas, on the other hand, a typical day might involve a single farmer operating various types of large machinery that do the same tasks as the Vietnamese workers. Both farms sell rice to a world market. A key reason for the differences in their production methods is that the relative prices of capital and labor are very different. In Vietnam, labor is relatively cheap compared to capital. Therefore, the tangency of Vietnamese rice farms' isoquants and isocost lines occurs at a point like point *A* in Figure 6.11. At point *A*, a lot of labor and only a little capital are used to grow rice. In Texas, on the other hand, labor is relatively expensive. This implies steeper isocost lines for Texas farms, making their cost-minimizing input mix much more capital-intensive, as at point *B*.

Application: Robots Are Coming for Your Grandma (in a Good Way?)

The health-care sector, you have no doubt heard many times, is enormous. And it is still growing. The sector has been one of the largest sources of employment growth for over a decade.

But it's not just workers who are flooding to the sector. Capital is, too. For every employee working in the health-care industry, there are over $100,000 in buildings, equipment, and software capital, according to the U.S. Bureau of Economic Analysis. This capital–labor ratio has also been growing steadily as several changes in the economics and regulatory environment of the industry have made capital less expensive relative to labor than it formerly was. Real wages, in general, have been on the rise. The Affordable Care Act subsidized an industrywide shift to electronic medical record-keeping systems. And economists Daron Acemoglu and Amy Finkelstein showed that a policy change in the way Medicare pays hospitals for patient care made capital cheaper relative to labor. Hospitals responded by becoming more capital-intensive.[5]

The recent acceleration in applications of machine learning and artificial intelligence technologies has some people speculating that the capital-for-labor substitution will accelerate in the health-care sector. Beyond just having their rooms vacuumed by a Roomba or their coffee made in a Keurig, soon patients might see more of their actual medical care provided by machines. Next thing you know, Grandma will be complaining that her robot never calls anymore. ∎

returns to scale A change in the amount of output in response to a proportional increase in all the inputs.

constant returns to scale A production function for which changing the amount of capital and labor by some multiple changes the quantity of output by exactly the same multiple.

6.5 Returns to Scale

Economists use the term **returns to scale** to describe *a change in the amount of output in response to a proportional increase in all the inputs*. For instance, if you double the inputs, does it double output?

A production function has **constant returns to scale** if *changing the amount of capital and labor by some multiple changes the quantity of output by exactly the same multiple*. If doubling the inputs doubles output, that's constant returns to scale. Our Cobb–Douglas production function $Q = K^{0.5}L^{0.5}$ has constant returns to scale. You can see that in Table 6.2.

5 Daron Acemoglu and Amy Finkelstein, "Input and Technology Choices in Regulated Industries: Evidence from the Health Care Sector," *Journal of Political Economy* 116, no. 5 (2008): 837–880.

Output (Q) is 1 when $L = 1$ and $K = 1$. Doubling both of them to $L = K = 2$ doubles output, too: $Q = 2$. If you double labor and capital again to $L = K = 4$, then $Q = 4$.

A production function has **increasing returns to scale** if *changing all inputs by the same proportion changes output* more *than proportionately.* (Doubling capital and labor more than doubles output.) **Decreasing returns to scale** exist if *adjusting all inputs by the same multiple changes output by* less *than that multiple.* (Output does not fully double when inputs are doubled.)

We assumed earlier in the chapter that inputs have diminishing returns—their marginal products fall as firms use more of them. But returns to scale can still be constant or even increasing, even when there are diminishing returns to inputs. Marginal products refer to changes in *only one input while holding the other input constant,* but returns to scale are about changes in *all inputs at the same time.* In other words, diminishing marginal returns refer to short-run changes, while returns to scale are a long-run phenomenon because we are changing all inputs simultaneously.

Figure 6.12 demonstrates these returns to scale cases using isoquants. In the first panel, a doubling of inputs leads to the doubling of outputs, so the technology exhibits constant returns to scale. Similarly, the isoquants in panel b indicate increasing returns to scale, while decreasing returns to scale are shown in panel c.

> **increasing returns to scale** A production function for which changing all inputs by the same proportion changes output *more* than proportionately.
>
> **decreasing returns to scale** A production function for which adjusting all inputs by the same multiple changes output by *less* than that multiple.

Factors Affecting Returns to Scale

A number of factors determine a production function's returns to scale. In some ways, it is natural for a production function to have constant returns to scale. If a firm can replicate a production process, output should grow proportionately with inputs. A company with a factory that makes 1,000 cars a day using 3,000 units of labor and 4,000 units of capital

Figure 6.12   Returns to Scale

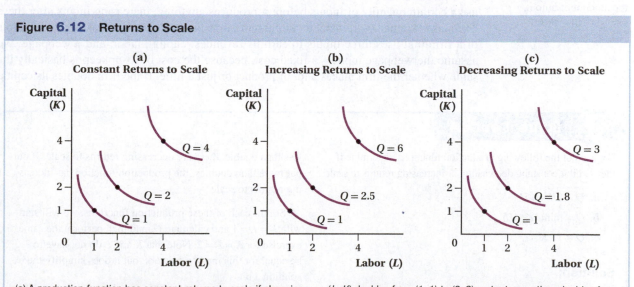

(a) A production function has constant returns to scale if changing the amount of capital and labor by some multiple changes output by exactly the same multiple. When the input combination (L, K) doubles from (1, 1) to (2, 2), output doubles from Q = 1 to Q = 2.

(b) A production function has increasing returns to scale if changing the amount of capital and labor by some multiple changes output by more than that multiple. When the input combination

(L, K) doubles from (1, 1) to (2, 2), output more than doubles from Q = 1 to Q = 2.5.

(c) A production function has decreasing returns to scale if changing the amount of capital and labor by some multiple changes output by less than that multiple. When the input combination (L, K) doubles from (1, 1) to (2, 2), output less than doubles from Q = 1 to Q = 1.8.

A⁺ make the grade

How to determine a production function's returns to scale

A common question on many intermediate micro exams asks if a production function exhibits constant, increasing, or decreasing returns to scale. If you approach this question in the right way, it will prove to be one of the easiest questions on which you will ever be tested.

Given a formula, first solve for the quantity when both capital and labor equal 1. Next, multiply the inputs by 2 and work out the quantity. If the total quantity doubles, the production function exhibits constant returns to scale. If it less than doubles, then the production function has decreasing returns to scale. More than doubles? You guessed it: increasing returns to scale.

Here is one last trick. If the production function is a Cobb–Douglas function, then all you need to do is add up

the exponents on the inputs. If these sum to 1, then the production function exhibits constant returns to scale. If they sum to more than 1, it indicates increasing returns to scale, and if they add up to less than 1, it shows decreasing returns to scale.

Say you're given the production function $Q = K^{0.3}L^{0.8}$. Solving using the first method gives you $Q = 1$ when $K = 1$ and $L = 1$, and $Q = 2^{0.3} 2^{0.8} = 2^{1.1}$ when $K = 2$ and $L = 2$. Since $2^{1.1}$ is greater than 2, this production function has increasing returns to scale. But this is a Cobb–Douglas function, so you could instead simply add the exponents $(0.3 + 0.8 = 1.1 > 1)$ and find the same result.

could build an identical factory across the street and have identical output. Double all its inputs, and it doubles its output. Adding a third identical factory and set of workers should again increase output in the same way.

But there are other influences that can push production functions toward increasing or decreasing returns to scale as well. For example, a common source of increasing returns to scale is a **fixed cost**, an *input cost that does not vary with the amount of output, even if output is zero.* (We will talk more about fixed costs in Chapter 7.) If the firm must use a certain quantity of inputs before it produces anything, increasing inputs after these fixed costs are paid will increase output more than proportionately. Consider the example of a firm that uses three inputs to earn its revenues: capital, labor, and a webpage. We assume the webpage input is a fixed cost, because the cost of its upkeep is basically the same whether the firm makes a lot of product or just a little. If the firm doubles its capital

fixed cost An input cost that does not vary with the amount of output, even if output is zero.

figure it out 6.4

For each of the following production functions, determine if they exhibit constant, decreasing, or increasing returns to scale.

a. $Q = 2K + 15L$

b. $Q = \min(3K, 4L)$

c. $Q = 15 K^{0.5}L^{0.4}$

Solution:

The easiest way to determine the returns to scale for a production function is to simply plug in values for L and K, calculate Q, and then double the input levels to see what happens to output. If output exactly doubles, the production function exhibits constant returns to scale. If output rises by

less than double, there are decreasing returns to scale. If output more than doubles, the production function has increasing returns to scale.

So, for each of these production functions, we will start with $K = L = 1$ and calculate Q, and then perform the same exercise for $K = L = 2$. Note that K and L do not have to be equal for this method to work, but it does simplify the solution a bit.

a. If $L = 1$ and $K = 1$, $Q = 2K + 15L = 2(1) + 15(1) = 2 + 15 = 17$.

If $L = 2$ and $K = 2$, $Q = 2K + 15L = 2(2) + 15(2) = 4 + 30 = 34$.

Since output exactly doubles when inputs are doubled, the production function exhibits constant returns to scale.

b. If $L = 1$ and $K = 1$, $Q = \min(3K, 4L) = \min(3(1), 4(1)) = \min(3, 4) = 3$.

If $L = 2$ and $K = 2$, $Q = \min(3K, 4L) = \min(3(2), 4(2)) = \min(6, 8) = 6$.

Because output exactly doubles when inputs are doubled, the production function exhibits constant returns to scale.

c. If $L = 1$ and $K = 1$, $Q = 15\,K^{0.5}L^{0.4} = 15(1)^{0.5}(1)^{0.4} = 15(1)(1) = 15$.

If $L = 2$ and $K = 2$, $Q = 15\,K^{0.5}L^{0.4} = 15(2)^{0.5}(2)^{0.4} = 15(1.414)(1.320) = 27.99$.

Because output less than doubles when inputs are doubled, the production function exhibits decreasing returns to scale.

and labor inputs while maintaining the same webpage, it will probably double its output. Because the firm is able to double its output without having to double all its inputs, it exhibits increasing returns to scale.

A firm can also see increasing returns to scale if it experiences **learning by doing**, *the process by which a firm becomes more efficient at production as it produces more output*. If a firm gets better at producing as it produces more output, then it may be able to produce the second batch of output using fewer resources than it required for the first batch. That is, it will be able to double its output without having to double its inputs.

Decreasing returns to scale are possible but should be unlikely in the long run for the same reason that constant returns to scale are natural. If inputs are measured properly and the firm has sufficient time to adjust all its inputs, the firm can just replicate its current production operation, allowing it to increase output by the same factor as inputs.

learning by doing The process by which a firm becomes more efficient at production as it produces more output.

6.6 Technological Change

When economists try to measure production functions using data from firms' operations, they often discover that output rises over time even though the firms might still be using the same amount of inputs. *An improvement in technology that changes the firm's production function such that it gets more output from the same amount of inputs* is referred to as **total factor productivity growth** (or sometimes **technological change**).

We can adjust a production function to allow for technological change. There are many possible ways to do this, but one easy approach is to assume the level of technology is a constant that multiplies the production function:

$$Q = Af(K, L)$$

where A is the level of total factor productivity, a parameter that affects how much output can be produced from a given set of inputs.

Let's now think about how technological change affects a firm's cost-minimization decisions. First, the firm's isocost lines don't change because the prices of the inputs remain fixed. Since A is part of the production function, however, it will affect the isoquants. An increase in A means that the same number of inputs will produce more output, so it also implies that the *same* output can be made with *fewer* inputs. Because an isoquant reflects the combinations of inputs that produce a given amount of output, higher values of A shift isoquants in (the good way — toward the origin).

total factor productivity growth (technological change) An improvement in technology that changes the firm's production function such that it gets more output from the same amount of inputs.

FREAKONOMICS

Why Indian Fishermen Love Their Cell Phones (It's Not from Instagram)

Few products are more cherished by American consumers than their phones. It's hard to imagine, as you lovingly caress your iPhone, that it was only a little over 25 years ago that the first cell phone, the Motorola DynaTAC 8000x, hit the consumer marketplace.* Weighing in at almost 2 pounds (almost 6 times the weight of the iPhone), it had a battery life of one hour. All the Motorola model did was make phone calls, and its sound quality was horrible. But at least it was expensive! Adjusting for inflation, the phone cost more than $9,000.

Of course, since the late twentieth century, astounding improvements have occurred in the technology of phones. When economists talk about technological progress, they mean changes in the production function. Compared to 30 years ago, we've gotten much better at taking a set of inputs (e.g., plastic, silicon, metal, the time of engineers and factory workers, etc.) and transforming them into cell phones.

Although it is natural to consider technological progress in terms of innovations in manufacturing, there are many other sources of such progress. Indeed, the cell phone is not just the beneficiary of technological progress — in some parts of the world, it is an important *source* of technological progress. Economist Robert Jensen has studied fishing villages in Kerala, a state on India's southern coast.[†] He looked at 15 markets where fishermen and consumers met to buy and sell the day's catch. If there were not enough buyers, the excess fish would go to waste because of the absence of refrigeration. If there were not enough sellers, some of the consumers walked away empty-handed.

Prices varied wildly in response to daily fluctuations in supply and demand, and up to 8% of fishermen had to let their fish go to waste because no demand existed.

Traditionally, fishermen would take their boats out to sea, make their catch, and face a guessing game as to which market to choose on any given day. Then cell phone coverage came to the area. Very quickly, fishermen began using cell phones, which allowed them to call ahead to determine which market would offer them the best prices for their fish. Better information led to better matching of buyers and sellers. There were rarely wasted fish; in fact, Jensen found that after cell phone use became commonplace, it was extremely rare for sellers not to find buyers for their fish. The figure here presents evidence of just how profoundly cell phones affected this market. It shows the fluctuation in fish prices over time in three areas in Kerala. Each colored line in the graph represents prices at one particular market. The introduction of cell phones was staggered across regions, and the points at which cell phones became available are denoted by the vertical lines near week 20 for Region I, week 100 for Region II, and week 200 for Region III.

Before cell phones, prices in each region were extremely volatile. Sometimes prices were almost as high as 14 rupees per kilogram on one beach, whereas at another beach on the same day, the fish were basically given away for free. From day to day, it was difficult if not impossible to predict which market would have the best price. The impact of cell phone use on the market was seen as soon as cell phone service became available in each area, although as you might expect, it took a few weeks for people to learn how to adjust and figure out how best to use this new technology. Roughly 10 weeks after the introduction of cell phones into this industry, though, the variation in prices across beaches in each of the three regions on a given day had shrunk dramatically.

A local fisherman uses a mobile phone as he works at Nariman Point in Mumbai, a commercial hub of India.

Prashanth Vishwanathan/Bloomberg via Getty Images

*The DynaTAC 8000x was the first cell phone available to the general public, but it was not the first cell phone produced or even to make a successful phone call. That distinction goes to a much heavier prototype dating back to 1973.

†Robert Jensen, "The Digital Provide: Information (Technology), Market Performance, and Welfare in the South Indian Fisheries Sector," *Quarterly Journal of Economics* 122, no. 3 (2007): 879–924. The figure is reproduced by permission of Oxford University Press and Professor Jensen.

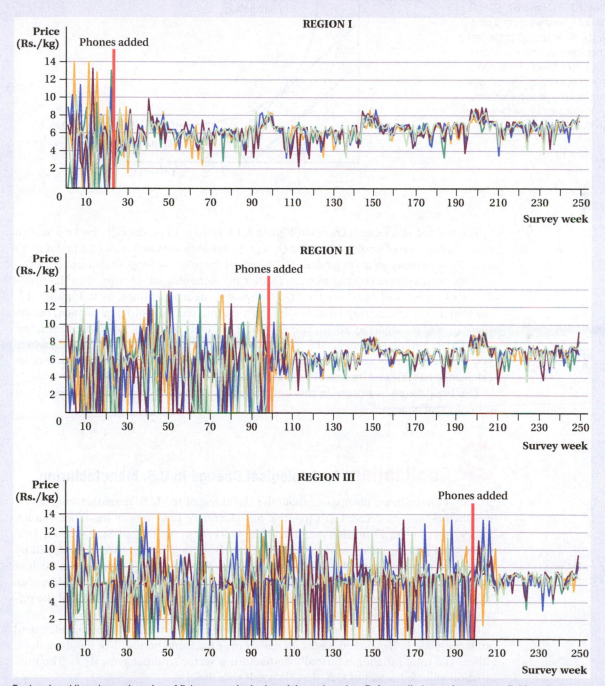

Each colored line shows the price of fish at a particular beach in each region. Before cell phones became available, prices were extremely volatile. After cell phones became available, as denoted by the vertical red lines, prices showed less variation.

Figure 6.13   The Impact of Technological Change

An improvement in technology shifts the isoquant $Q_1 = \overline{Q}$ inward to $Q_2 = \overline{Q}$. The new cost-minimizing input combination (L_2, K_2) is located at the tangency between Q_2 and the isocost C_2. (L_2, K_2) uses fewer inputs and is therefore cheaper than the original cost-minimizing input combination (L_1, K_1) located at the tangency between Q_1 and the isocost C_1.

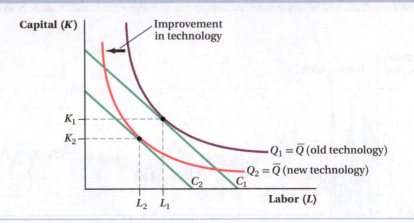

You can see this exact scenario in **Figure 6.13**. Before, to produce $\overline{Q}$, the firm needed some combination of inputs on isoquant $Q_1 = \overline{Q}$. Technology increases A and the firm doesn't need to use as many inputs to produce $\overline{Q}$. Therefore, the isoquant for $\overline{Q}$ shifts in, to $Q_2 = \overline{Q}$.

If the firm's desired output remains $\overline{Q}$ after the technological change, then the firm's choice of inputs will be where $Q_2 = \overline{Q}$ is tangent to its isocost lines, as in Figure 6.13. The initial cost-minimizing input combination (before the technological change) occurs where $Q_1 = \overline{Q}$ is tangent to isocost line C_1, that is, K_1 units of capital and L_1 units of labor. After the technological change, the optimal input combination becomes K_2 and L_2, where $Q_2 = \overline{Q}$ is tangent to isocost line C_2. Because the firm needs to use fewer inputs, technological change has reduced its cost of producing $\overline{Q}$.

The Freakonomics feature in this chapter offers a vivid description of the power of technological change.

 ## Application: Technological Change in U.S. Manufacturing

You might have heard discussion about the shrinking of the U.S. manufacturing sector over the past several decades. It's true that manufacturing employment has fallen—a lot. In 1997 there were 17 million manufacturing workers in the United States, about 18% of the total private-sector workforce. Of those, 10 million workers were employed by companies manufacturing **durable goods**—*goods that have long service lives*, such as appliances, airplanes, cars, metal and wood products, and electrical equipment. More than 20 years later, there were only 12.8 million manufacturing workers, about 9% of the private workforce, 8 million of whom were making durable goods.

durable good A good that has a long service life.

Given this trend, it might surprise you to find out that the total value of manufactured products made in the United States *increased* over the same period. Not by just a little, either. The total inflation-adjusted manufacturing sector's output grew 43%. The total inflation-adjusted output of U.S. durable goods rose 96%.

How is it possible for manufacturing employment to fall for an extended time while the sector's output grows? Well, in part, manufacturing firms shifted from using labor to using more capital. But much of the growth derived from the fact that technological change was faster in manufacturing than in the rest of the economy, particularly in durable goods manufacturing.

The total factor productivity of U.S. manufacturers grew 12% over 20 years, and that includes a big slide during the Great Recession. Durable goods manufacturers were able to produce 27% more output across 20 years. This meant that they could employ fewer workers and still experience the same total output growth. ■

6.7 The Firm's Expansion Path and Total Cost Curve

We've seen how a firm minimizes its costs at the optimal production quantity. We can now use this information to illustrate how the firm's production choices and its total costs change as the optimal production quantity changes.

Panel a of **Figure 6.14** shows sets of isoquants and isocost lines for a firm we'll call Ivor's Engines. The figure illustrates three isoquants and isocost lines, but remember that there are isoquants for every possible quantity level and isocost lines for every cost level. Recall that the combination of labor and capital that minimizes the cost of producing a given quantity of output is at the tangency of an isocost line and the isoquant corresponding to that output level. The figure shows three such tangencies. On the lower left, $Q = 10$ is the isoquant that corresponds to input combinations that allow Ivor's Engines to make 10 engines. This isoquant is tangent at point X to the $C = \$100$ isocost line, so $\$100$ is the lowest cost at which Ivor can build 10 engines. The isoquant representing input combinations that produce 20 engines, $Q = 20$, is tangent to the $C = \$180$ isocost line at point Y, indicating that Ivor's minimum cost for producing 20 engines is $\$180$. At point Z, the $Q = 30$ isoquant is tangent to the $C = \$300$ isocost line, so $\$300$ is the minimum cost of making 30 engines.

Figure 6.14 The Expansion Path and the Total Cost Curve

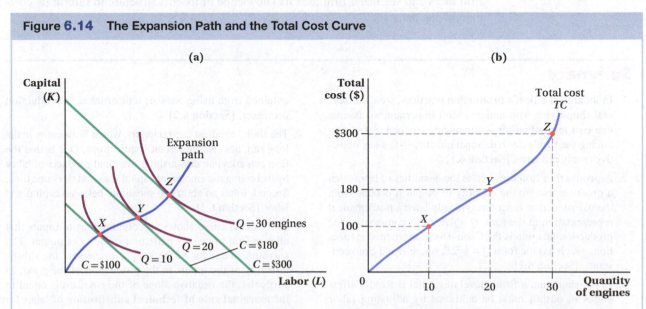

(a) The expansion path for Ivor's Engines maps the optimal input combinations for each quantity Q. Here, points X, Y, and Z are the cost-minimizing input combinations given output levels $Q = 10$, $Q = 20$, and $Q = 30$, respectively.

(b) The total cost curve for Ivor's Engines is constructed using the isocost lines from the expansion path in panel a. The cost-minimizing input combinations cost $\$100$, $\$180$, and $\$300$ at output levels $Q = 10$, $Q = 20$, and $Q = 30$, respectively.

expansion path A curve that illustrates how the optimal mix of inputs varies with total output.

total cost curve A curve that shows a firm's cost of producing particular quantities.

➡ The end-of-chapter appendix derives the firm's expansion path.

The line connecting the three cost-minimizing input combinations in Figure 6.14a (as well as all the other cost-minimizing isoquant–isocost line tangencies for output levels that are not shown) is the firm's **expansion path**, a *curve that illustrates how the optimal mix of inputs varies with total output.*

The expansion path shows the optimal input combinations at each output quantity. If we plot the total cost from the isocost line and the output quantity from the isoquants located along the expansion path, we have a **total cost curve**, a *curve that shows a firm's cost of producing particular quantities.* Panel b of Figure 6.14 gives these cost and quantity combinations for the expansion path in Figure 6.14a, including the three cost-minimizing points at 10, 20, and 30 units of output. The total cost curve is another way to show the information in the expansion path. Both the total cost curve and expansion path show how, when the firm is minimizing its cost of producing any given quantity, the firm's minimized cost changes when its output changes.

Note that the expansion path and total cost curve are for a given set of input prices (as reflected in the isocost lines) and a given production function (as reflected in the isoquants). As we saw earlier, if input prices or the production function changes, so will the cost-minimizing input combinations. Therefore, the expansion path and total cost curve will change, too. In Chapter 7, we use the total cost curve—as derived from the expansion path—in our discussion of a firm's cost functions.

6.8 Conclusion

Much like the consumer from Chapter 4 minimizes her expenditures of achieving a given utility level, a firm minimizes its costs of producing a given quantity of a good. These optimal production decisions that a firm makes trace out its total cost curve, which shows the costs of producing a given quantity. In Chapter 7, we will tackle the specific costs a firm faces and see that a firm uses its knowledge of its cost structure to inform its cost-minimizing behavior.

Summary

1. In looking at a firm's **production** practices, we made several simplifying assumptions. Most important, we assume that **cost minimization**—minimizing the total cost of producing the firm's desired output quantity—is a key objective of any producer. [**Section 6.1**]

2. A **production function** relates the quantities of inputs that a producer uses to the quantity of output it obtains from them. Production functions typically have a mathematical representation in the form $Q = f(K, L)$. A commonly used production function is the Cobb–Douglas production function, which has the form $Q = K^\alpha L^\beta$, where α and β are constants. [**Section 6.1**]

3. In the short run, a firm's level of capital is fixed. Differences in output must be achieved by adjusting labor inputs alone. We looked at properties of the production function including an input's **marginal** and **average product** (we focused on labor in this case, because capital is fixed). We saw examples of **diminishing marginal products** for labor, where the incremental output

obtained from using another unit of labor in production decreases. [**Section 6.2**]

4. The ability to adjust capital inputs, which firms enjoy in the long run, has two important implications. One is that the firm can alleviate diminishing marginal products of labor by increasing the amount of capital it uses at the same time. Second, it has an ability to substitute between capital and labor. [**Section 6.3**]

5. An isoquant curve shows all combinations of inputs that allow a firm to make a particular quantity of output. The curvature and slope of the isoquant represent the substitutability of the inputs in the production of the good. In particular, the negative slope of the isoquant is equal to the **marginal rate of technical substitution** of labor for capital. [**Section 6.4**]

6. An isocost line connects all the combinations of capital and labor that the firm can purchase for a given total expenditure on inputs. The relative costs of capital and labor determine the slope of the isocost line. [**Section 6.4**]

7. A firm aims to minimize its costs at any given level of output. The firm's cost-minimizing output occurs where the isocost line is tangent to the isoquant, or where the marginal rate of technical substitution is equal to the relative price of labor to capital. **[Section 6.4]**

8. **Returns to scale** is a property of production functions that describes how the level of output changes when all inputs are simultaneously changed by the same amount. Production functions can have returns to scale that are constant (if all inputs increase by a factor, output changes by the same factor); increasing (if all inputs increase by a factor, output changes by more than that factor); or decreasing (if all inputs increase by a factor, output changes by less than that factor). **[Section 6.5]**

9. When there is **technological change**, a production function changes over time so that a fixed amount of inputs can produce more output. This is reflected by a shift of a production function's isoquants toward the origin. **[Section 6.6]**

10. A firm's cost curves are derived from its **expansion path**, which uses isoquants and isocost curves to show how its input choices change with output. The **total cost curve** relates the costs tied to the isocost lines and the quantities tied to the isoquants that intersect the expansion path. **[Section 6.7]**

Review Questions

1. What are the differences between a firm's production in the short run and the long run?

2. What does a production function tell us?

3. What is the difference between fixed costs and variable costs?

4. What is the difference between the short run and long run?

5. If one isoquant is farther from the origin than another, does it represent a higher or lower level of output? Why can't two isoquants cross?

6. What is the marginal rate of technical substitution? What does it imply about an isoquant's shape?

7. What does the curvature of an isoquant imply about the two inputs, capital and labor?

8. What is an isocost line? What does its slope tell us about the relative cost of labor and capital?

9. How will a firm react to an increase in the price of one input relative to another?

10. When is a production function said to have constant returns to scale, increasing returns to scale, or decreasing returns to scale?

11. How does technological change affect a firm's output?

12. What is an expansion path and how does it relate to a firm's total cost curve?

Problems

(Solutions to problems marked with an asterisk appear at the back of this book. Problems adapted to use calculus are available online.)

1. For parts (a) to (d), determine which basic assumption of production is violated.

   a. The local coffee shop serves 400 customers per day with 8 employees, 420 with 9 employees, or 450 with 10 employees.

   b. The French government makes it very difficult for Antoine, a bakery owner, to hire new workers or fire existing workers. On the other hand, Antoine can instantly change the quantity of the ovens and mixers in his shop.

   c. Business is booming at Jordan's custom bicycle factory. When she increases the number of employees from 40 to 45, her production falls from 500 bikes per month to 480.

   d. Smartphone apps are all the rage . . . but finding skilled programmers is becoming more difficult. The more programmers Google (a large employer) hires, the more it must pay each programmer.

2. Complete the table below:

Labor Input	Total Product	Marginal Product	Average Product
0	0	—	—
1		70	
2	135		
3			63
4		51	
5			57
6	324		

3. Abel, Baker, and Charlie all run competing bakeries, where each makes loaves of bread.

   a. At Abel's bakery, the marginal product of labor is 15 and the average product of labor is 12. Would Abel's average product increase or decrease if he hired another worker?

   b. At Baker's bakery, the marginal product of labor is 7 and the average product of labor is 12. Would Baker's average product increase or decrease if he hired another worker?

   c. At Charlie's bakery, the MPL is −12. Does this mean her average product must also be negative?

   d. Based on your answers above, can you generalize the nature of the relationship between the average and marginal products of labor?

4. Nobody fixes more fender benders than Crazy Bob! At his auto body shop, the production function showing the number of cars repaired each year is $Q = 100\sqrt{KL}$, where K is the number of arc welding machines available and L is the number of employees. Currently, K is fixed at 9.

   a. Write an equation for Crazy Bob's short-run production function, showing output as a function of labor only.

   b. Calculate the total number of cars Bob can repair each year for $L = 1, 2, 3, 4$, and 5.

   c. Calculate the marginal product of labor for each of Bob's first five workers. Does the MP_L diminish?

   d. Calculate the average product of labor for Bob's first five workers. Is the MP_L greater than, equal to, or less than the AP_L at each level of employment? Why?

5. Jerusha, a woodworker, builds coffee tables using both labor (L) and tools (capital, or K). Her production function for coffee tables is a Cobb–Douglas production function: $Q = 4K^{0.5}L^{0.5}$.

   a. Can Jerusha build any coffee tables without tools?

   b. Can Jerusha completely mechanize coffee table production?

   c. Jerusha currently has 16 tools, and in the short run she can neither acquire more tools nor sell existing tools. Her woodshop is capable of holding up to 49 employees. What is Jerusha's short-run production function?

   d. Graph the production function you found in (c), with labor on the horizontal axis and output on the vertical axis. (*Hint:* Don't plot every possible amount of labor; instead, choose convenient levels of L that are perfect squares: 0, 1, 4, 9, etc.)

   e. Determine the average and marginal products of labor at each level of labor you worked with in (d). (*Hint:* To compute the marginal product of the 25th worker, you'll need to figure out how much Jerusha would produce with both 25 and 26 workers.)

f. Suppose that overnight, 7 of Jerusha's machines fail. Show what happens to the total, marginal, and average products of labor as a result.

6. The table below represents the production function for Hawg Wild, a small catering company specializing in barbecued pork. The numbers in the cells represent the number of customers that can be served with various combinations of labor and capital.

		Labor (L)					
		0	**1**	**2**	**3**	**4**	**5**	**6**
	1		100	132	155	174	190	205
	2		152	200	235	264	289	310
Capital (K)	**3**		193	255	300	337	368	396
	4		230	303	357	400	437	470
	5		263	347	408	457	500	538
	6		293	387	455	510	558	600

   a. Is this production function a short-run or long-run production function? How can you tell?

   b. Suppose that Hawg Wild employs 5 units of capital and 2 workers. How many diners will be served?

   c. Suppose that Hawg Wild employs 5 units of capital and 2 workers, but the owner Billy Porcine is considering adding his nephew to the payroll. What will the marginal product of Billy's nephew be?

   d. Notice that when Hawg Wild uses 1 unit of capital, the marginal product of the fifth unit of labor is 16. But when Hawg Wild uses 5 units of capital, the marginal product of the fifth unit of labor is 43. Does this production function violate the law of diminishing marginal product of labor? Why or why not?

   e. Suppose that Hawg Wild employs 5 units of capital and 2 workers, but the owner Billy Porcine is considering adding another meat smoker to the kitchen (which will raise the amount of capital input to 6 units). What will the marginal product of the smoker be?

   f. Hawg Wild employs 5 units of capital and 2 workers. Billy is considering the choice between hiring another worker or buying another smoker. If smokers cost $8 and workers $12, then at the margin, what is the most cost-effective choice for Billy to make?

7. Suppose that a firm's production function is given by $Q = K^{0.33}L^{0.67}$, where $MP_K = 0.33K^{-0.67}L^{0.67}$ and $MP_L = 0.67K^{0.33}L^{-0.33}$.

   a. As L increases, what happens to the marginal product of labor?

b. As K increases, what happens to the marginal product of labor?

c. Why would the MP_L change as K changes?

d. What happens to the marginal product of capital as K increases? As L increases?

*8. Consider the production function presented in the table below:

		Labor (L)					
	0	**1**	**2**	**3**	**4**	**5**	**6**
	1	100	200	300	400	500	600
	2	200	400	600	800	1,000	1,200
Capital **(K)**	**3**	300	600	900	1,200	1,500	1,800
	4	400	800	1,200	1,600	2,000	2,400
	5	500	1,000	1,500	2,000	2,500	3,000
	6	600	1,200	1,800	2,400	3,000	3,600

a. If the firm decides to employ 6 units of capital and 1 worker, what is its output?

b. What other combinations of capital and labor could be used to produce the same level of output you found in (a)?

c. Plot the combinations you determined in (a) and (b) on a graph, with labor on the horizontal axis and capital on the vertical axis. Connect the dots to form the production isoquant corresponding to 600 units of output.

9. Fetzer valves can be made in either China or the United States, but because labor in the United States is more skilled, on average, than labor in China, the production technologies differ. Consider the two production isoquants in the figure below. Each represents either the production technology for the United States or for China. Based on the *MRTS,* which production isoquant is more likely to represent the United States and which represents China? Explain.

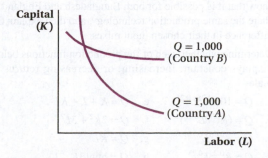

*10. Consider the production functions given below:

a. Suppose that the production function faced by a 30-weight ball bearing producer is given by $Q = 4K^{0.5}L^{0.5}$, where $MP_K = 2K^{-0.5}L^{0.5}$ and $MP_L = 2K^{0.5}L^{-0.5}$. Do both labor and capital display diminishing marginal products? Find the marginal rate of technical substitution for this production function. (*Hint: MRTS = MP_L/MP_K.*) Does this production function display a diminishing marginal rate of substitution?

b. Suppose that the production function faced by a 40-weight ball bearing producer is given by $Q = 4KL$, where $MP_K = 4L$ and $MP_L = 4K$. Do both labor and capital display diminishing marginal products? Find the marginal rate of technical substitution for this production function. Does this production function display a diminishing marginal rate of substitution?

c. Compare your answers to (a) and (b). Must labor and capital display diminishing marginal products in order for the MRTS to diminish?

11. A jeweler can potentially use two inputs in her handcrafted jewelry: copper or bronze. She finds that when she minimizes her costs, she uses either copper or bronze, but never both. What must her isoquants look like? What does this suggest about the relationship between copper and bronze?

12. Mad Max's Road Warriors fix potholes in interstate highways. Max's road crews fill potholes using workers and shovels in 1 to 1 correspondence. A worker with 1 shovel can fill 10 potholes in a day. A worker with 2 shovels can still only fill 10 potholes, as can 2 workers with 1 shovel.

a. Draw the production isoquant corresponding to filling 30 potholes.

b. Assume that production displays constant returns to scale and draw a few more isoquants.

c. If shovels rent for $5 and workers must be paid $25, draw several isocost lines.

d. If Mad Max has received a state contract to fill 30 potholes, what is the minimum cost at which it can fulfill the contract?

e. If the cost of renting a shovel suddenly rises from $5 to $6, what will happen to the composition of inputs that Mad Max uses to fill potholes? Why?

*13. Suppose that Manny, Jack, and Moe can hire workers for $12 per hour, or can rent capital for $7 per hour.

a. Write an expression for Manny, Jack, and Moe's total cost as a function of how many workers they hire and how much capital they employ.

b. Assume that Manny, Jack, and Moe wish to hold their total costs to exactly $100. Use your answer from (a) to find the equation for an isocost line corresponding to exactly $100 of costs. Rearrange your equation to isolate capital.

c. Graph the equation for the isocost line, putting labor on the horizontal axis and capital on the vertical axis.

d. What is the vertical intercept of the line you drew? The horizontal intercept? What does each represent?

e. What is the slope of the line you drew? What does it represent?

f. Suppose that bargaining with the local labor union raises wages. Manny, Jack, and Moe must now pay $14 per hour. What happens to the isocost line corresponding to $100 of expenditure? Explain. Show the new isocost line on your graph.

14. Miguel and Jake run a paper company. Each week they need to produce 1,000 reams of paper to ship to their customers. The paper plant's long-run production function is $Q = 4K^{0.75}L^{0.25}$, where Q is the number of reams produced, K is the quantity of capital rented, and L is the quantity of labor hired. For this production function, $MP_L = K^{0.75}/L^{0.75}$ and $MP_K = 3L^{0.25}/K^{0.25}$. The weekly cost function for the paper plant is $C = 10K + 2L$, where C is the total weekly cost.

a. What ratio of capital to labor minimizes Miguel and Jake's total costs?

b. How much capital and labor will Miguel and Jake need to rent and hire in order to produce 1,000 reams of paper each week?

c. How much will hiring these inputs cost them?

15. Use a diagram with one ordinary production isoquant and various isocost lines to show that a firm's cost of producing a given level of output in the long run will always be less than or equal to its cost of producing that same level of output in the short run. (*Hint:* To represent the short run, fix capital at one level, K_1. To do this, simply erase the portion of the isoquant that corresponds to capital levels higher than K_1.) Explain intuitively why this must be the case.

16. Fast-food restaurants like McDonald's are replacing cashiers with touch-screen ordering kiosks. Currently, the marginal product of another cashier is 48 customers served per hour; the marginal product of another kiosk is 32 customers served per hour. A cashier can be hired for a wage of $15; a kiosk rents for $12.

a. Is McDonald's currently minimizing the cost of serving its customers?

b. Show how McDonald's can improve its profits by changing its input mix.

17. Creekwood Lawn and Landscape is a small business that employs 20 minimum wage workers and 10 units of capital (in the form of mowers, spreaders, aerators, etc.)

to service 10 lawns. Creekwood is currently minimizing costs at $400 per hour, as depicted in the following diagram:

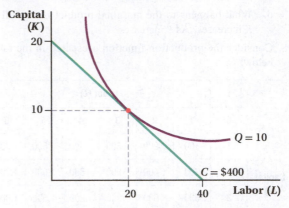

a. What is the minimum wage where Creekwood is located? The rental rate?

b. Suppose that the city government doubles the minimum wage in a bid to attract more unskilled workers. Draw a new isocost curve corresponding to $C = $400 that reflects this change. How will this impact Creekwood's cost of serving its customers?

c. Following protests of the wage increase by small business owners, the city government decides to compensate those owners by sending them a lump-sum subsidy. Creekwood, which was employing 20 workers, receives a check for exactly $200. Show that it is now possible for Creekwood to hire its original combination of inputs and serve its 10 customers at a cost of $400. Draw a new isocost line that reflects the effects of the subsidy.

d. The combined wage increase and subsidy can potentially have zero impact on Creekwood's costs. Does this mean Creekwood will once again resume hiring 20 workers and 10 units of capital?

18. In Bangladesh, where labor is relatively abundant, bricks are produced with a lot of labor and very little capital. In England, where labor is scarce, bricks are produced with a lot of capital and very little labor. Construct a graph to show that it is possible for both Bangladesh and England to share the same production technology, and then explain the difference in their chosen input mixes.

19. Determine whether each of the production functions below displays constant, increasing, or decreasing returns to scale:

a. $Q = 10K^{0.75}L^{0.25}$

b. $Q = (K^{0.75}L^{0.25})^2$

c. $Q = K^{0.75}L^{0.75}$

d. $Q = K^{0.25}L^{0.25}$

e. $Q = K + L + KL$

f. $Q = 2K^2 + 3L^2$

g. $Q = KL$

h. $Q = \min(3K, 2L)$

20. The graph below illustrates production isoquants for various levels of labor and capital. In the graph, supply the quantities Q_1, Q_2, and Q_3 so that the production function displays

    a.   Increasing returns to scale

    b.   Decreasing returns to scale

    c.   Constant returns to scale

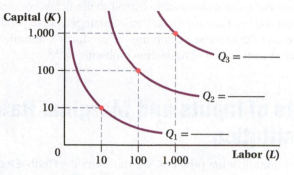

21. True or false: A production function that displays increasing returns to scale must also display increasing marginal returns to either labor or capital. Explain your answer and provide an example that supports your explanation.

22. Truffles are a tasty fungus traditionally located by trained pigs. Suppose the production function for truffles is given by $Q = 2K^{0.5}L^{0.5}$, where L is the number of pig handlers and K is the number of pigs.

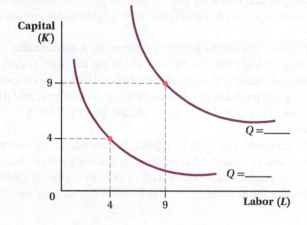

a.   Label the isoquants in the graph to reflect this production function.

b.   Suppose that an improvement in pig genetics results in technological change so that now $Q = 4.5K^{0.5}L^{0.5}$. Relabel your production isoquants to reflect this change.

c.   How must the technological change affect the cost of locating truffles? (Assume that wages and rents are constant.)

23. Cam's Cannolis produces delicious desserts. Cam's production function is depicted by the isoquants in the graph below. If labor and capital are both priced at $10 per unit,

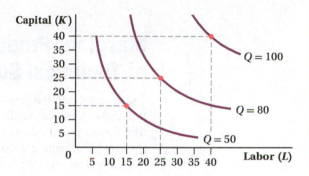

a.   Add appropriately sloped isocost lines to the graph to determine the combination of labor and capital that minimizes the cost of producing each level of output shown in the graph.

b.   Trace Cam's expansion path.

c.   Determine the total cost of producing each level of output shown in the graph.

d.   Create a new graph of Cam's total cost function, plotting output on the horizontal axis and total cost on the vertical axis.

Chapter 6 Appendix:
The Calculus of Cost Minimization

In the appendix to Chapter 4, we saw that calculus makes solving the consumer's optimization problem easier. The benefits of using calculus also extend to the firm's constrained optimization problem, cost minimization. Cost minimization is analogous to expenditure minimization for the consumer, and the exercise of solving the producer's optimization problem will serve as a refresher in constrained optimization problems.

Marginal Products of Inputs and Marginal Rate of Technical Substitution

To begin solving the firm's cost-minimization problem, we start with the Cobb–Douglas functional form (as we did in the Chapter 4 appendix). In this case, we use the production function that relates output (Q) to the amount of inputs capital (K) and labor (L): $Q = AK^{\alpha}L^{1-\alpha}$, where $0 < \alpha < 1$, and where the parameter for total factor productivity, A, is greater than zero. We have been relying almost exclusively on the Cobb–Douglas functional form throughout our calculus discussions because this functional form corresponds closely with the assumptions we make about the consumer and the producer. In the context of the producer, the Cobb–Douglas production function satisfies all the assumptions we've made about capital, labor, and firm output, while still yielding simple formulas. In addition, we have chosen a Cobb–Douglas function with another unique property: Because the exponents on K and L (α, $1 - \alpha$) sum to 1, the production function exhibits constant returns to scale.

Before we jump into the producer's cost-minimization problem, let's confirm that the Cobb–Douglas production function satisfies the assumptions about the marginal products of labor and capital and the marginal rate of technical substitution (MRTS). Specifically, we need to show first that the marginal products of labor and capital are positive, and that they exhibit diminishing marginal returns. Next, we will confirm that the MRTS is the ratio of the two marginal products.

Consider first the concept of the marginal product of capital, or how much extra output is produced by using an additional unit of capital. Mathematically, the marginal product of capital is the partial derivative of the production function with respect to capital. It's a partial derivative because we are holding the amount of labor constant. The marginal product of capital is

$$MP_K = \frac{\partial Q(K,L)}{\partial K} = \frac{\partial (AK^{\alpha}L^{1-\alpha})}{\partial K} = \alpha AK^{\alpha-1}L^{1-\alpha}$$

Similarly, the marginal product of labor is

$$MP_L = \frac{\partial Q(K,L)}{\partial L} = \frac{\partial (AK^{\alpha}L^{1-\alpha})}{\partial L} = (1-\alpha)AK^{\alpha}L^{-\alpha}$$

Note that the marginal products above are positive whenever both capital and labor are greater than zero (any time output is greater than zero). In other words, the MP_L and MP_K of the Cobb–Douglas production function satisfy an important condition of production—that output increases as the firm uses more inputs.

We also need to show that the assumptions about the diminishing marginal returns of capital and labor hold true; that is, the marginal products of capital and labor decrease as the amounts of those inputs increase, respectively, holding all else equal. To see this, take the second partial derivative of the production function with respect to each input. In other words, we are taking a partial derivative of each of the marginal products with respect to its input:

$$\frac{\partial^2 Q(K,L)}{\partial K^2} = \frac{\partial MP_K}{\partial K} = \frac{\partial(\alpha AK^{\alpha-1}L^{1-\alpha})}{\partial K} = \alpha(\alpha-1)AK^{\alpha-2}L^{1-\alpha} = -\alpha(1-\alpha)AK^{\alpha-2}L^{1-\alpha}$$

$$\frac{\partial^2 Q(K,L)}{\partial L^2} = \frac{\partial MP_L}{\partial L} = \frac{\partial[(1-\alpha)AK^{\alpha}L^{-\alpha})}{\partial L} = -\alpha(1-\alpha)AK^{\alpha}L^{-\alpha-1}$$

As long as K and L are both greater than zero (i.e., as long as the firm is producing output), both of these second derivatives are negative, so the marginal product of each input decreases as the firm uses more of the input. Thus, the Cobb–Douglas production function meets our assumptions about diminishing marginal returns to both labor and capital.

We also know from the chapter that the marginal rate of technical substitution and the marginal products of capital and labor are interrelated. In particular, the MRTS shows the change in labor necessary to keep output constant if the quantity of capital changes (or the change in capital necessary to keep output constant if the quantity of labor changes). The MRTS equals the ratio of the two marginal products. To show this is true using calculus, first recognize that each isoquant represents some fixed level of output, say, $\overline{Q}$, so that $Q = Q(K, L) = \overline{Q}$. Begin by totally differentiating the production function:

$$dQ = \frac{\partial Q(K,L)}{\partial K}dK + \frac{\partial Q(K,L)}{\partial L}dL$$

We know that dQ equals zero because the quantity is fixed at $\overline{Q}$:

$$dQ = \frac{\partial Q(K,L)}{\partial K}dK + \frac{\partial Q(K,L)}{\partial L}dL = 0$$

so that

$$\frac{\partial Q(K,L)}{\partial K}dK = -\frac{\partial Q(K,L)}{\partial L}dL$$

Now rearrange to get $-\dfrac{dK}{dL}$ on one side of the equation:

$$-\frac{dK}{dL} = \frac{\frac{\partial Q(K,L)}{\partial L}}{\frac{\partial Q(K,L)}{\partial K}} = \frac{MP_L}{MP_K}$$

The left-hand side of this equation is the negative of the slope of the isoquant, or the marginal rate of technical substitution.[6] Therefore,

$$MRTS_{LK} = \frac{MP_L}{MP_K}$$

In particular, we differentiate the Cobb–Douglas production function, $Q = AK^{\alpha}L^{1-\alpha}$, and set dQ equal to zero:

$$dQ = \frac{\partial Q(K,L)}{\partial K}dK + \frac{\partial Q(K,L)}{\partial L}dL = \alpha AK^{\alpha-1}L^{1-\alpha}dK + (1-\alpha)AK^{\alpha}L^{-\alpha}dL = 0$$

---

[6] Recall that isoquants have negative slopes; therefore, the negative of the slope of the isoquant, the MRTS, is positive.

Again, rearrange to get $-\dfrac{dK}{dL}$ on one side of the equation:

$$MRTS_{LK} = -\frac{dK}{dL} = \frac{(1-\alpha)AK^{\alpha}L^{-\alpha}}{\alpha AK^{\alpha-1}L^{1-\alpha}} = \frac{MP_L}{MP_K}$$

which simplifies to

$$MRTS_{LK} = \frac{(1-\alpha)}{\alpha}\frac{K}{L}$$

Thus, we can see that the marginal rate of technical substitution equals the ratios of the marginal products for the Cobb–Douglas production function. This also shows that the $MRTS_{LK}$ decreases as the firm uses more labor and less capital, holding output constant, as we learned in the chapter. Using calculus makes it clear, however, that the rate at which labor and capital can be substituted is determined by α, the relative productivity of capital.

Cost Minimization Using Calculus

Now that we have verified the usefulness of the Cobb–Douglas function for modeling production, let's turn to the firm's cost-minimization problem. Once again, we are faced with a constrained optimization problem: The objective function is the cost of production, and the constraint is the level of output. The firm's goal is to spend the least amount of money to produce a specific amount of output. This is the producer's version of the consumer's expenditure-minimization problem.

As we saw with the consumer's problem, there are two approaches to solving the cost-minimization problem. The first is to apply the cost-minimization condition that we derived in the chapter. At the optimum, the marginal rate of technical substitution equals the ratio of the input prices, wages (W) and capital rental rate (R). We just showed that the marginal rate of technical substitution is the ratio of the marginal products, so the cost-minimization condition is

$$MRTS_{LK} = \frac{MP_L}{MP_K} = \frac{W}{R}$$

For our Cobb–Douglas production function above, finding the optimum solution is easy using this relationship between the marginal rate of technical substitution and the input prices. We start by solving for K as a function of L using the equation for the marginal rate of technical substitution above:

$$\frac{MP_L}{MP_K} = \frac{(1-\alpha)}{\alpha}\frac{K}{L} = \frac{W}{R}$$

$$K = \left[\frac{\alpha}{(1-\alpha)}\frac{W}{R}\right]L$$

Next, plug K into the production constraint to solve for the optimum quantity of labor L^*:

$$\overline{Q} = \alpha AK^{\alpha}L^{1-\alpha} = A\left[\frac{\alpha}{(1-\alpha)}\frac{W}{R}L\right]^{\alpha}L^{1-\alpha}$$

$$\overline{Q} = A\left[\frac{\alpha}{(1-\alpha)}\frac{W}{R}\right]^{\alpha}L^{\alpha}L^{1-\alpha}$$

$$L^* = \left[\frac{(1-\alpha)}{\alpha}\frac{R}{W}\right]^{\alpha}\frac{\overline{Q}}{A}$$

Now solve for K^* by plugging L^* into the earlier expression for K as a function of L:

$$K^* = \left[\frac{\alpha}{(1-\alpha)}\frac{W}{R}\right]L^*$$

$$= \left[\frac{\alpha}{(1-\alpha)}\frac{W}{R}\right]\left[\frac{(1-\alpha)}{\alpha}\frac{R}{W}\right]^{\alpha}\frac{\overline{Q}}{A}$$

We can simplify this expression by inverting the term in the second set of brackets:

$$K^* = \left[\frac{\alpha}{(1-\alpha)}\frac{W}{R}\right]\left[\frac{\alpha}{(1-\alpha)}\frac{W}{R}\right]^{-\alpha}\frac{\overline{Q}}{A}$$

and combining the first and second terms:

$$K^* = \left[\frac{\alpha}{(1-\alpha)}\frac{W}{R}\right]^{1-\alpha}\frac{\overline{Q}}{A}$$

Thus, we have found that the cheapest way of producing $\overline{Q}$ units of output is to use $\left[\frac{\alpha}{(1-\alpha)}\frac{W}{R}\right]^{1-\alpha}\frac{\overline{Q}}{A}$ units of capital and $\left[\frac{(1-\alpha)}{\alpha}\frac{R}{W}\right]^{\alpha}\frac{\overline{Q}}{A}$ units of labor.

Now let's use a second approach to solve for the cost-minimizing bundle of capital and labor: the constrained optimization problem. In particular, the firm's objective, as before, is to minimize costs subject to its production function:

$$\min_{K,L} C = RK + WL \text{ s.t. } \overline{Q} = AK^{\alpha}L^{1-\alpha}$$

Next, write this constrained optimization problem as a Lagrangian so that we can solve for the first-order conditions:

$$\min_{K,L,\lambda} \mathcal{L}(K,L,\lambda) = RK + WL + \lambda(\overline{Q} - AK^{\alpha}L^{1-\alpha})$$

Now take the first-order conditions of the Lagrangian:

$$\frac{\partial \mathcal{L}}{\partial K} = R - \lambda(\alpha AK^{\alpha-1}L^{1-\alpha}) = 0$$

$$\frac{\partial \mathcal{L}}{\partial L} = W - \lambda[(1-\alpha)AK^{\alpha}L^{-\alpha}] = 0$$

$$\frac{\partial \mathcal{L}}{\partial \lambda} = \overline{Q} - AK^{\alpha}L^{1-\alpha} = 0$$

Notice that λ is in both of the first two conditions. Let's rearrange to solve for λ:

$$R = \lambda(\alpha AK^{\alpha-1}L^{1-\alpha})$$

$$\lambda = \frac{R}{\alpha AK^{\alpha-1}L^{1-\alpha}}$$

$$W = \lambda\left[(1-\alpha)AK^{\alpha}L^{-\alpha}\right]$$

$$\lambda = \frac{W}{(1-\alpha)AK^{\alpha}L^{-\alpha}}$$

Now set these two expressions for λ equal to one another:

$$\lambda = \frac{R}{\alpha AK^{\alpha-1}L^{1-\alpha}} = \frac{W}{(1-\alpha)AK^{\alpha}L^{-\alpha}}$$

How can we interpret λ in the context of the firm's cost-minimization problem? In general, the Lagrange multiplier is the value of relaxing the constraint by 1 unit. Here, the constraint is the quantity of output produced; if you increase the given output quantity by 1 unit, the total cost of production at the optimum increases by λ dollars. In other words, λ has a very particular economic interpretation: It is the marginal cost of production, or the extra cost of producing an additional unit of output when the firm is minimizing its costs. We can see that in our λ's above: It is the cost of an additional unit of capital (or labor) divided by the additional output produced by that unit. In Chapter 7, we develop other ways to find marginal costs, but it's good to keep in mind that marginal cost *always* reflects the firm's cost-minimizing behavior.

We can get another perspective on cost minimization by inverting the expressions for λ:

$$\frac{\alpha AK^{\alpha-1}L^{1-\alpha}}{R} = \frac{(1-\alpha)AK^{\alpha}L^{-\alpha}}{W}$$

This relationship shows us precisely what we know is true at the optimum, that $\frac{MP_K}{R} = \frac{MP_L}{W}$, which we can rearrange to get the cost-minimization condition:

$$\frac{W}{R} = \frac{MP_L}{MP_K} = MRTS_{LK}$$

To solve for the optimal bundle of inputs that minimizes cost, we can first solve for K as a function of L:

$$\frac{K^{\alpha}}{K^{\alpha-1}} = \frac{W(\alpha L^{1-\alpha})}{(1-\alpha)RL^{-\alpha}}$$

$$K = \left[\frac{\alpha}{(1-\alpha)}\frac{W}{R}\right]L$$

Plug K as a function of L into the third first-order condition, the constraint:

$$\overline{Q} - AK^{\alpha}L^{1-\alpha} = \overline{Q} - A\left[\frac{\alpha}{(1-\alpha)}\frac{W}{R}L\right]^{\alpha}L^{1-\alpha} = 0$$

Now solve for the cost-minimizing quantity of labor, L^*:

$$A\left[\frac{\alpha}{(1-\alpha)}\frac{W}{R}\right]^{\alpha}L^{\alpha}L^{1-\alpha} = A\left[\frac{\alpha}{(1-\alpha)}\frac{W}{R}\right]^{\alpha}L = \overline{Q}$$

$$L^* = \left[\frac{\alpha}{(1-\alpha)}\frac{W}{R}\right]^{-\alpha}\frac{\overline{Q}}{A} = \left[\frac{(1-\alpha)}{\alpha}\frac{R}{W}\right]^{\alpha}\frac{\overline{Q}}{A}$$

Substitute L^* into our expression for K as a function of L:

$$K^* = \left[\frac{\alpha}{(1-\alpha)}\frac{W}{R}\right]L^* = \left[\frac{\alpha}{(1-\alpha)}\frac{W}{R}\right]\left[\frac{(1-\alpha)}{\alpha}\frac{R}{W}\right]^{\alpha}\frac{\overline{Q}}{A}$$

To simplify, invert the second term and combine:

$$K^* = \left[\frac{\alpha}{(1-\alpha)}\frac{W}{R}\right]\left[\frac{\alpha}{(1-\alpha)}\frac{W}{R}\right]^{-\alpha}\frac{\overline{Q}}{A} = \left[\frac{\alpha}{(1-\alpha)}\frac{W}{R}\right]^{1-\alpha}\frac{\overline{Q}}{A}$$

So using the Lagrangian, we arrive at the same optimal levels of labor and capital that we found using the cost-minimization condition:

$$L^* = \left[\frac{(1-\alpha)}{\alpha}\frac{R}{W}\right]^{\alpha}\frac{\overline{Q}}{A}$$

$$K^* = \left[\frac{\alpha}{(1-\alpha)}\frac{W}{R}\right]^{1-\alpha}\frac{\overline{Q}}{A}$$

figure it out 6A.1

A firm has the production function $Q = 20K^{0.2}L^{0.8}$, where Q measures output, K represents machine hours, and L measures labor hours. If the rental rate of capital is $R = \$15$, the wage rate is $W = \$10$, and the firm wants to produce 40,000 units of output, what is the cost-minimizing bundle of capital and labor?

Solution:

We could solve this problem using the cost-minimization condition. But let's solve it using the Lagrangian, so we can get more familiar with that process. First, we set up the firm's cost-minimization problem as

$$\min_{K,L} C = 15K + 10L \text{ s.t. } 40,000 = 20K^{0.2}L^{0.8} \text{ or}$$

$$\min_{K,L,\lambda} \mathcal{L}(K,L,\lambda) = 15K + 10L + \lambda(40,000 - 20K^{0.2}L^{0.8})$$

Find the first-order conditions for the Lagrangian:

$$\frac{\partial \mathcal{L}}{\partial K} = 15 - \lambda(4K^{-0.8}L^{0.8}) = 0$$

$$\frac{\partial \mathcal{L}}{\partial L} = 10 - \lambda(16K^{0.2}L^{-0.2}) = 0$$

$$\frac{\partial \mathcal{L}}{\partial \lambda} = 40,000 - 20K^{0.2}L^{0.8} = 0$$

Solve for L as a function of K using the first two conditions:

$$\lambda = \frac{15}{4K^{-0.8}L^{0.8}} = \frac{10}{16K^{0.2}L^{-0.2}}$$

$$15(16K^{0.2}L^{-0.2}) = 10(4K^{-0.8}L^{0.8})$$

$$240(K^{0.2}K^{0.8}) = 40(L^{0.2}L^{0.8})$$

$$L = 6K$$

Now plug L into the third first-order condition and solve for the optimal number of labor and machine hours, L^* and K^*:

$$40,000 - 20K^{0.2}L^{0.8} = 0$$

$$20K^{0.2}(6K)^{0.8} = 40,000$$

$$20(6)^{0.8}K = 40,000$$

$$K^* \approx 477 \text{ machine hours}$$

$$L^* \approx 6(477) \approx 2,862 \text{ labor hours}$$

At the optimum then, the firm will use approximately 477 machine hours and 2,862 labor hours to produce 40,000 units. But once again, the Lagrangian provides us with one additional piece of information: the value of λ, or marginal cost:

$$\lambda = \frac{15}{4K^{-0.8}L^{0.8}} = \frac{15}{4(477^{-0.8})(2,862^{0.8})} \approx \$0.89$$

Therefore, if the firm wants to produce just one more unit of output—its 40,001st unit of output, to be precise—it would have to spend an additional $0.89.

The Firm's Expansion Path

So far, we have only solved the firm's cost-minimization problem for a specific quantity. In other words, we've assumed that the firm knows how much output it wants to produce and then decides how best to produce that quantity at the lowest cost. But it might make sense to expand our thinking about how the firm makes its production decisions. In particular, what if a firm wants to know how its optimal input mix varies with its output quantity? This is the firm's expansion path, and it's something we found graphically in the chapter. Recall that an expansion path shows the cost-minimizing relationship between K and L for all possible levels of output. Let's now find the expansion path using calculus.

Consider again the firm with the familiar Cobb–Douglas production function, $Q = AK^{\alpha}L^{1-\alpha}$, and rental cost of capital and wage equal to R and W, respectively. First, write out the constrained optimization problem and the Lagrangian. Note that, unlike before, we are not going to assume that Q is a fixed level of output. In the expansion path, quantity is a variable, and that is reflected in the way we set up the constrained optimization problem below:

$$\min_{K,L} C = RK + WL \text{ s.t. } Q = AK^\alpha L^{1-\alpha}$$

$$\min_{K,L,\lambda} \mathcal{L}(K,L,\lambda) = RK + WL + \lambda(Q - AK^\alpha L^{1-\alpha})$$

Take the first-order conditions for the Lagrangian:

$$\frac{\partial \mathcal{L}}{\partial K} = R - \lambda(\alpha AK^{\alpha-1}L^{1-\alpha}) = 0$$

$$\frac{\partial \mathcal{L}}{\partial L} = W - \lambda[(1-\alpha)AK^\alpha L^{-\alpha}] = 0$$

$$\frac{\partial \mathcal{L}}{\partial \lambda} = Q - AK^\alpha L^{1-\alpha} = 0$$

As we saw earlier, solving the first two conditions gives us the optimal value of capital K^* as a function of L^*:

$$K^* = \left[\frac{\alpha}{(1-\alpha)}\frac{W}{R}\right]L^*$$

What does this tell us? Given a set of input prices, we now know the cost-minimizing amount of capital at every quantity of labor. The combination of labor and capital then determines the quantity of output. So, what have we found? The expansion path! We could also solve for the optimal amount of labor for every quantity of capital, but it's easier to graph the expansion path with K^* as a function of L^*. Notice that any Cobb–Douglas production function with exponents α and $(1-\alpha)$ generates a linear expansion path with slope

$$\frac{\alpha}{(1-\alpha)}\frac{W}{R}$$

This linear expansion path is yet *another* useful property of the Cobb–Douglas functional form.

---

figure it out 6A.2

Using the information from Figure It Out 6A.1, derive the firm's expansion path.

Solution:

Because we've already solved the expansion path for the generalized Cobb–Douglas production function, we can plug in the parameters from the firm's cost-minimization

problem ($\alpha = 0.2$, $W = \$10$, $R = \$15$) into the equation for the expansion path we found above:

$$K^* = \left[\frac{\alpha}{(1-\alpha)}\frac{W}{R}\right]L^* = \frac{0.2(10)}{0.8(15)}L^* = 0.167L^*$$

Therefore, when minimizing costs, this firm will always choose a combination of inputs in which there is 6 times as much labor as capital, no matter what its desired output is.

Problems

1. For the following production functions,

   - Find the marginal product of each input.

   - Determine whether the production function exhibits diminishing marginal returns to each input.

   - Find the marginal rate of technical substitution and discuss how $MRTS_{LK}$ changes as the firm uses more L, holding output constant.

   a. $Q(K, L) = 3K + 2L$

   b. $Q(K, L) = 10K^{0.5}L^{0.5}$

   c. $Q(K, L) = K^{0.25}L^{0.5}$

2. A more general form of the Cobb–Douglas production function is given by

$$Q = AK^{\alpha}L^{\beta}$$

   where A, α, and β are positive constants.

   a. Solve for the marginal products of capital and labor.

   b. For what values of α and β will the production function exhibit diminishing marginal returns to capital and labor?

   c. Solve for the marginal rate of technical substitution.

3. Catalina Films produces video shorts using digital editing equipment (K) and editors (L). The firm has the production function $Q = 30K^{0.67}L^{0.33}$, where Q is the hours of edited footage. The wage is $25, and the rental rate of capital is $50. The firm wants to produce 3,000 units of output at the lowest possible cost.

   a. Write out the firm's constrained optimization problem.

   b. Write the cost-minimization problem as a Lagrangian.

   c. Use the Lagrangian to find the cost-minimizing quantities of capital and labor used to produce 3,000 units of output.

   d. What is the total cost of producing 3,000 units?

   e. How will total cost change if the firm produces an additional unit of output?

4. A firm has the production function $Q = K^{0.4}L^{0.6}$. The wage is $60, and the rental rate of capital is $20. Find the firm's long-run expansion path.

Costs

Ryanair is one of the largest and fastest-growing airlines in the world. It started flying in 1985 and, after an initial brush with financial problems in 1990, found its key to success: a cost structure so low that its European customers, accustomed to dowdy and expensive national carriers, can't help but fly Ryanair all over the continent.

Ryanair is cheap. They're famous for it. To save landing fees, it often skips a city's main airport, flying to secondary airports located far away from the main city. Flights to Paris, for example, arrive at Chalons-Vatry airport 91 miles (147 km) from downtown Paris. Its pilots load the legally mandated minimum requirement of fuel for each trip. The seats on its planes don't recline or have tray tables or seatback pockets. Ryanair has discussed squeezing in six more seats on each plane — by getting rid of all but one of the plane's bathrooms. You better check yourself in for your flight online, at least two hours early; it costs €55 (about $63 in 2019) to do so at the airport. (Ryanair doesn't employ a lot of desk agents.) These rules seem harsh until you realize that some of the airline's flights cost as little as €15 (about $17) each way.

Flying Ryanair isn't for everyone; comfort and customer service aren't its specialties. But the Ryanair example raises important points: Costs are key to firms' operations, and a firm's cost structure is a crucial factor in its production decisions and in determining whether it makes a profit. Costs play a crucial part in determining a firm's optimal output level, how much the firm should grow or shrink in response to changing market conditions, and how easily it can start producing another product if it wants to.

We began our look at a firm's production cost at the end of Chapter 6 when we introduced the expansion path (which shows how a firm's optimal mix of inputs varies with total output) and the total cost curve (which shows a firm's cost of producing particular quantities of output). These two concepts provide the foundation for understanding a firm's cost structure. It is vital for a firm to understand what its costs are and how they change as output changes. That's key for economists, too, who want to understand why producers act the way they do, and it is the key to explaining where supply curves come from (a topic we will explore in Chapter 8). In this chapter, we examine the nature of a firm's costs by considering how a firm's production function and level of output determine its costs, given the prices of its inputs. We also consider how a firm's costs vary between the short run and the long run. But first, we need to think about which costs actually matter when making decisions.

7.1 Costs That Matter for Decision Making: Opportunity Costs

accounting cost The direct costs of operating a business, including costs for raw materials, wages paid to workers, rent paid for office or retail space, and the like.

economic cost The sum of a producer's accounting and opportunity costs.

opportunity cost The value of what a producer gives up by using an input.

economic profit A firm's total revenue minus its economic cost.

accounting profit A firm's total revenue minus its accounting cost.

Economists define costs differently than many others do. Most people think about what we will call **accounting costs**, the *direct costs of operating a business, including costs for raw materials, wages paid to workers, rent paid for office or retail space, and the like.* **Economic costs**—the costs that economists pay attention to—are the *sum of a producer's accounting costs and something else: the producer's opportunity costs.* **Opportunity costs** are the *value of what a producer gives up by using an input,* whether that use is associated with an accounting cost or not. What the producer gives up is the return the input would earn in its next-best use: If a firm is using an input to do one thing (using the inventory of jet fuel for flying), it is giving up the ability to use the input for something else (selling the inventory of jet fuel at a profit to other companies). The lost value of this "something else" is the input's opportunity cost.

When contemplating the most cost-effective use of its inputs, it doesn't matter if Ryanair's accounting profit is positive. If its *economic* costs are large enough, its economic profit may be negative. Making decisions about the use of inputs using only accounting cost can lead to mistakes. Ryanair should use its jet fuel for flights only if that is the most profitable use for it. That is, the firm should consider its **economic profit** (*total revenue minus economic costs*) rather than its **accounting profit** (*total revenue minus accounting costs*). If the price of fuel goes up enough from the price Ryanair prepaid, Ryanair should fly less and sell their fuel to others to make more money.

The recognition that a firm's decisions about production must be based on economic cost (which takes into account a firm's opportunity costs) underlies *everything* we discuss about costs in the rest of this chapter and the rest of the book (and are the types of cost we referred to in Chapter 6). Unless otherwise stated, throughout this book when we mention a firm's costs, we are always talking about its economic costs (including opportunity costs).

🛠 Application: The Sharing Economy—A Story about Harnessing Opportunity Cost to Make Money

The growth of the "sharing economy," mostly made up of Internet-based platforms that link together people willing to lend their assets with people wanting to borrow them, has been one of the biggest changes in business in recent years. A prominent set of companies in this new space are platforms that specialize in housing, such as Airbnb, VRBO, HomeAway, and FlipKey. These platforms allow property owners to turn spaces that are not being used at the time into revenue.

Many vacation homeowners only use their homes for a fraction of the year. But they still must pay for the house or apartment—the mortgage, certain utilities, lawn maintenance, and so on—even when they aren't using it. Before sharing economy platforms came along, the story basically ended there. Some people loaned their vacation home to friends or family, but actually receiving income for its use during those periods when they couldn't was not easy.

When space-sharing platforms like Airbnb materialized, they made it a lot easier to find people who would be willing to rent an otherwise empty vacation home (or spare room). This raised the owner's opportunity cost for that space, because the owner could now rent it out rather than let the space sit empty, receiving nothing in return. Not surprisingly, many owners responded to this development by making their properties available a lot more of the time. Opportunity costs drove the decision. ∎

figure it out 7.1

Cooke's Catering is owned by Dan Cooke. For the past year, Cooke's Catering had the following statement of revenues and costs:

Revenues	$500,000
Supplies	$150,000
Electricity and water	$15,000
Employee salaries	$50,000
Dan's salary	$60,000

Dan has always had the option of closing his catering business and renting out his building for $100,000 per year. In addition, Dan currently has job offers from another catering company (offering a salary of $45,000 per year) and a high-end restaurant (at a salary of $75,000 per year). Dan can only work one job at any time.

a. What is Cooke's Catering's accounting cost?

b. What is Cooke's Catering's economic cost?

c. What is Cooke's Catering's economic profit?

Solution:

a. Accounting cost is the direct cost of operating a business. This includes supplies, utilities, and salaries:

$$\text{Accounting cost} = \$150,000 + \$15,000 + \$50,000 + \$60,000 = \$275,000$$

b. Economic cost includes both accounting cost and the opportunity costs of owner-supplied resources. Dan's opportunity costs include the rent he could earn on his building ($100,000) and the opportunity cost of his time. Because Dan could give up the store and earn a higher salary at the restaurant, we need to take into account the difference in the salary he could earn ($75,000) and the salary he currently earns ($60,000). Note that his offer with the caterer is not relevant because opportunity cost measures the value of the next best alternative, which is working at the restaurant. Therefore, economic cost is accounting cost + opportunity costs:

$$\text{Economic cost} = \$275,000 + \$100,000 + \$15,000 = \$390,000$$

c. Economic profit is equal to Total revenue − Economic cost = $500,000 − $390,000 = $110,000. Dan should continue to operate his catering business.

7.2 Costs That Do Not Matter for Decision Making: Sunk Costs

Unlike opportunity costs, which a firm must always consider when making production decisions, there are some costs that should *never* be taken into account when reaching such decisions. In Chapter 6, we learned that some of a firm's costs are **fixed costs (FC)**, *input costs that do not vary with the amount of output, even if it is zero.* Suppose you own a restaurant. Some of your fixed costs would be rent (if you have signed a lease), cookware, advertising expenses, and kitchen appliances such as refrigerators and ovens. (We often think of fixed costs as relating to capital inputs, but labor input costs can sometimes be a fixed cost, too. For example, if a security guard ensures the site is not broken into, whether the restaurant is open or not, the guard's wages are a fixed cost.) If you go out of business, even though you produce nothing, you still must pay those fixed costs. Of course, you might be able to recover some of these costs if you could sell the cookware and the ovens, or sublet the building to someone else. These refundable types of fixed costs are sometimes said to be *avoidable* because the firm can take action so that it does not have to pay them if it stops operating.

fixed cost (FC) An input cost that does not vary with the amount of output, even if it is zero.

sunk cost A cost that, once paid, cannot be recovered.

Some fixed costs, however, are not avoidable. A fixed cost that you cannot avoid is called a **sunk cost**, *a cost that, once paid, cannot be recovered*. For a restaurant, for example, money spent on advertising is a sunk cost. You already laid out the money, and there's no getting it back. If you've signed a long-term rental agreement and cannot sublet the building, the rent is a sunk cost, too. You cannot recover it even by shutting down.

One part of a firm's cost that is sunk is the difference between what the firm still owes on its fixed capital inputs (such as the equipment and cookware at your restaurant) and what the firm can resell this capital for. This difference should be relatively small for restaurant equipment, because most of it can be used easily by other restaurants.

But suppose you are a "miner" of the cryptocurrency Bitcoin. Solving a particular type of math problem faster than other people do is how Bitcoin miners make money. There is a unique kind of computer chip known as an ASIC chip that is specially designed to solve the math problems involved in Bitcoin mining. This special design makes them far better at mining than a standard server's CPU. Because of their design, though, they are *not* very good at doing most other tasks people want computers to perform. They're just good at Bitcoin mining. So if you mine a bunch of bitcoins and then decide to close up your mining operation, the only likely buyer is another miner. If a number of miners decide to stop at once — and, with a 75% drop in Bitcoin prices in early 2018, hundreds of thousands did — the ASICs you paid so much for will no longer be worth much. The cost of those ASICs is a sunk cost; you cannot recover it even by shutting down.

specific capital Capital that cannot be used outside of its original application.

As you can see from this last example, whether capital may be used by someone else is an important determinant of sunk costs. *Capital that cannot be used outside of its original application* is called **specific capital**. Expenditures on buildings or machines that are very specific to a firm's operations are likely to be sunk, because the capital has little value in another use.

Sunk Costs and Decisions

An important lesson about sunk costs is that once they are paid, *they should not affect current and future production decisions*. The reason is simple: Because they are lost no matter what you choose to do, they cannot affect the relative costs and benefits of current and future production decisions. Say you're bored at a concert and asking yourself, "Should I stay or should I go?" (Maybe you are over 60 years old and just want to go home and listen to your old Clash album?) Whether the ticket price was $1 or $1,000, that cost is sunk and cannot be recovered. The only thing that you should ask is whether you will have more fun staying for the second half of the concert or doing something else (going for a walk, taking a nap, or calling a friend). If the alternative would be more entertaining, then leave.

operating revenue The money a firm earns from selling its output.

operating cost The cost a firm incurs in producing its output.

To put this in a production context, let's go back to the restaurant example. Suppose you, as the owner, must decide between staying open for business or shutting down operations. Some of the restaurant's costs are sunk costs, including fixed costs that you cannot resell for what you paid. These costs are not recoverable and must be paid whether the restaurant remains open or is shut down. In thinking about staying open for business, you recognize the potential benefit from **operating revenue**, the *money a firm earns from selling its output* — in this case, meals and drinks. But there will also be **operating costs**, *costs a firm incurs in producing its output,* such as paying the waitstaff, purchasing ingredients, or turning on the heat or air conditioning.

If business falls off, then how should you decide whether to stay open for business or close your doors? Generally, the restaurant should stay open if the value of staying open is greater than the value of shutting down. But here's the important part: *Don't include the sunk costs when you add up those two sets of numbers*. You are going to lose your sunk costs whether you keep the restaurant open or not, so they are irrelevant to your decision about your restaurant's future. The choice between staying open and shutting down depends *only* on whether the firm's expected revenues are greater than its expected operating costs. If it costs more to stay open than you'll bring in, you should close the restaurant. It doesn't matter if you are facing $1 or $1 million of sunk costs.

When faced with actual choices that involve sunk costs, people and firms sometimes have a difficult time ignoring sunk costs. They commit what economists call the **sunk cost fallacy**, the *mistake of letting sunk costs affect forward-looking decisions*. The fallacy is that they act as if sunk costs matter (when they should be ignoring them). In making economic, financial, and life decisions, you want to avoid falling victim to this fallacy, but it's not hard to imagine scenarios where you might be tempted to do so.

sunk cost fallacy The mistake of letting sunk costs affect forward-looking decisions.

 ## Application: Gym Memberships

Everybody loves the gym, right? Economists Stefano DellaVigna and Ulrike Malmendier have studied the economics of the gym and how consumers behave.[1]

What they found probably won't surprise you: People are overly optimistic about how many times they'll go to the gym. Consumers who bought a membership that allowed unlimited visits ended up going to the gym just over 4 times per month, on average, making their average cost per visit about $17. They made this decision even though the same gym offered 10-visit passes for $100 (i.e., $10 per visit). For each member, it added up to an average overpayment of about $600 over the course of membership.

Consumers often purchase gym memberships with the hope that such behavior will induce them to work out more frequently. The fact that people then don't take full advantage of their memberships might, at first glance, seem like an irrational action. But the key point is that a gym membership is a sunk cost. In other words, when you're sitting on the couch watching TV and debating whether you should go work out, you're not inclined to consider how much you paid for your membership. It's sunk, after all. You will, on the other hand, consider the opportunity cost of going to the gym—maybe you'd rather spend more time studying economics or, more likely, watching your favorite show. Whatever the reason, the fact that your decision is based on opportunity cost, not sunk cost, makes it sound economics, even if it's not what your doctor would recommend. ∎

Application: Why Do Film Studios Make Movies That They Know Will Lose Money?

The feature film industry is a multibillion dollar enterprise. Blockbuster movies from franchises like *The Avengers* and *Star Wars* drive the business. A single major blockbuster movie can cost hundreds of millions of dollars, but there are no guarantees that people will like it enough to make back the costs. It is a risky business.

Sometimes while filming a movie, things go so wrong that the studio making the movie knows even before the film hits theaters that it will lose money. Yet, filmmakers often finish these movies and release them. Why they do this can be explained by the existence of sunk costs and their irrelevance to decision making.

One of the most infamous movie productions ever was *Waterworld*. You have probably never seen it—not many people did. It was nominated for four "Razzies" ("saluting the worst that Hollywood has to offer each year"), including worst picture, worst actor, and worst director.

[1] Stefano DellaVigna and Ulrike Malmendier, "Paying Not to Go to the Gym," *American Economic Review* 96, no. 3 (2006): 694–719.

Its losses on *Waterworld* made Universal Studios want to scream.

Waterworld is set in a future in which the ice caps have melted and water covers the earth. Kevin Costner stars as the Mariner, a mutant who can breathe under water. His job is to protect (from the evil Smokers on Jet Skis) a young girl who has what may be a map of land tattooed on her back. The movie was filmed almost entirely on and under water.

At the time, *Waterworld* was the most expensive movie ever made. By the end of production, costs totaled almost $175 million, even before marketing and distribution expenses, basically guaranteeing the producing studio, Universal, a loss no matter how well the film was received. It grossed only $88 million in the United States and about twice that amount overseas. Because studios get to keep only about half of total ticket sales, experts presume it flopped terribly.

Let's think through Universal's decision to complete the movie and release it. At the outset, the studio expected the movie to bring in $150 million of revenue (a 50% cut of an expected $300 million of global ticket sales), and the movie's budget (for a planned 96 days of filming) was $100 million.[2] As filming began, about $16 million of the $100 million in expected costs were sunk—including Kevin Costner's minimum guaranteed salary of $14 million.

Waterworld Economics as of June (in millions of dollars)			
Expected Profit	Expected Revenue	Expected Additional Cost	Sunk Cost
+50	+150	−84	−16

Things started to go wrong quickly. The filming location in Kawaihae Harbor on the Big Island of Hawaii was so windy that scores of the crew became seasick each day, and the medicine for it impaired their ability to use cameras and other equipment. Several divers suffered decompression sickness and embolisms from being underwater for too long, and a one-minute action scene in the movie ended up taking more than five weeks to film. Every additional day of filming added something like $350,000 to the film's cost. A few months into filming, the movie was now expected to take 120 days and cost $140 million. Of the $140 million, about $100 million was sunk. The movie remained on path to turn a small profit.

Waterworld Economics as of September (in millions of dollars)			
Expected Profit	Expected Revenue	Expected Additional Cost	Sunk Cost
+10	+150	−40	−100

Then the biggest accident struck. During a big storm, the "slave colony," a multi-ton part of a metal set located out in the harbor, sank 160 feet and had to be hauled upright at great expense. It took 21 days. At this late point in the filming, the expected total costs had now risen to $175 million, with $140 million of them already sunk (in some cases, quite literally) and $35 million still needed to complete the project.

---

[2] Movie accounting is both secretive and notoriously "flexible," so we present a stylized version of the movie's economics. For more information on movie economics and to learn some gory details about what went wrong in the filming and the various cost overruns, plus a fair amount of movie gossip, see Charles Fleming, "That Sinking Feeling," *Vanity Fair*, August 1, 1995, and "Fishtar? Why 'Waterworld,' with Costner in Fins, Is Costliest Film Ever," *Wall Street Journal*, January 31, 1996.

Waterworld Economics as of December (in millions of dollars)			
Expected Profit −25	Expected Revenue +150	Expected Additional Cost −35	Sunk Cost −140

By now, the studio had to know the movie would lose money. If the studio included sunk costs in its decision making, it would stop production. But that would be falling victim to the sunk cost fallacy. The studio could pay the additional $35 million of expected costs to complete the movie and earn an expected $150 million of revenue. Yes, it would lose the $140 million of sunk costs, but that would also be true if the studio canceled production instead. Canceling would avoid the incremental $35 million cost, but would forgo the $150 million in expected revenue. The correct decision—ignoring the sunk costs—came down to the choice between an incremental gain of $115 million ($150 million in revenue − $35 million in costs) by finishing the movie and an incremental loss of $115 million ($35 million in saved costs − $150 million in lost revenue) from shutting down.

To be sure, if Kevin Costner and the makers of the movie had had a crystal ball at the start of filming to see what terrible events would transpire and the massive costs that were to come, the decision would have been different. They could have halted production at a loss of only $16 million. But that would have been before the costs were sunk. Discovering the problems only after having sunk $140 million, on the other hand, meant that it made sense for the movie's producers to hold their noses and take the belly flop. ■

7.3 Costs and Cost Curves

We've seen that a firm considers its economic costs when making decisions about how much output to produce. Those economic costs include both accounting and opportunity costs so that the costs of all inputs are considered.

So now that we know what is included in costs, let's return to the costs of production like those we discussed previously in Chapter 6. A firm can have two types of costs: fixed costs (FC) and **variable costs (VC)**, the *cost of inputs that change as the firm changes its quantity of output*. Every cost is either a fixed or variable cost, so a firm's **total cost (TC)** is the *sum of its fixed and variable costs: TC = FC + VC*.

When a firm needs more of an input to make more output, the payment for that input counts as a variable cost. For every hamburger McDonald's makes, for example, it has to buy the ingredients. Payments for buns, ketchup, and beef are included in variable cost. Most labor costs are part of variable cost as well. When more workers are needed to make more hamburgers, when more doctors are needed to treat more patients, or when more programmers are needed to write more computer code, these additional workers' wages and salaries are added to variable cost. Some capital costs can be variable. If a construction firm has to rent more cranes to build more houses, for example, or the cranes wear out faster the more they are used, the extra rental payments or depreciation are variable costs.

variable cost (VC) The cost of inputs that change as the firm changes its quantity of output.

total cost (TC) The sum of a firm's fixed and variable costs: *TC = FC + VC*.

Flexibility and Fixed versus Variable Costs

There is an important relationship between how easy it is for a firm to change how much of an input it uses and whether the cost of that input is considered part of fixed or variable cost. When a firm can easily adjust the levels of inputs it uses as output changes, the costs of these inputs are variable. When a firm cannot adjust how much of an input it buys as output varies, the input costs are fixed.

Time Horizon   Over very short time periods, many costs are fixed because a firm cannot adjust these input levels over short spans of time even if the firm's output level changes. As the time horizon lengthens, however, firms have greater abilities to change the levels of all inputs to accommodate output fluctuations. In the long run, all inputs are flexible. This concept is related to the distinction between short- and long-run production functions in Chapter 6, in which capital inputs are fixed in the short run but flexible in the long run.

Let's return to your restaurant. On a given day, many of your costs are fixed: Regardless of how many customers come to eat, you pay for the building, the kitchen equipment, and the dining tables. You've scheduled the cooks and waitstaff, so you must pay them whether or not the restaurant is busy that day. The only costs that are variable are the food ingredients and the natural gas that heats the grill. If you produce no meals, you don't have to pay for those.

Over a month or two, more of the restaurant's input costs become variable. You can schedule fewer workers on typically slow days. You can also choose hours of operation excluding times that are sluggish, so you only pay for full lighting and air conditioning when you are open and expect to be busy. All those are variable costs now. But you still have a one-year lease to satisfy no matter what you produce, so that's a fixed cost. However, over longer horizons, even the building becomes a variable cost. Next year, you can terminate the lease if business is bad.

Other Factors   Other features of input markets can sometimes affect how easily firms may adjust their input levels, and thus determine their relative levels of fixed and variable costs.

One such factor is *the presence of active capital rental and resale markets*. These markets allow firms that need certain pieces of machinery or types of buildings only occasionally (like the construction firm that sometimes needs a crane to build houses) to pay for the input just when it's needed to make more output. Without rental markets, firms would have to buy such inputs outright and make payments whether they use the inputs or not. By making capital inputs more flexible, rental markets shift capital costs from fixed to variable.

A great example of how rental markets have changed what costs are considered fixed and variable comes from the airline industry. In the past, airlines owned virtually all their planes. Today, however, about one-half of commercial jet aircraft worldwide are leased. Sometimes airlines lease planes directly from Airbus or Boeing, but more often they use specialized aircraft-leasing companies such as GE Capital Aviation Services or International Lease Finance Corporation. These leasing companies buy planes from manufacturers and then lease them out under contract to airlines requiring extra capacity. If the capacity is no longer needed, the airline returns the plane to the leasing company, which typically then leases the plane to another airline that needs more capacity. This flexibility makes it less likely that airlines will be stuck paying for planes when they have low demand. An active resale market for capital can function the same way as a rental. If you buy a car for $20,000, but can resell it for $10,000 after five years, then it's like you leased the car at $2,000 per year for five years.

Labor contracts can affect the fixed versus variable nature of labor costs. Some contracts require that workers be paid a specified amount regardless of how much time they spend producing output. These payments are fixed costs. For example, in the past, U.S. automakers' contracts included "jobs banks" for laid-off workers. These provisions required that laid-off workers receive 95% of their regular salary, retain their health benefits, and continue to accrue pension benefits until reaching retirement age. Because of these contractual conditions, automakers' labor costs changed very little no matter what their output was. Jobs banks made autoworkers a fixed cost; they got paid whether or not they were building cars. This high-fixed-cost structure became one of many contributing factors to the troubles suffered by U.S. automakers during the financial crisis, and is why they abandoned the idea of the jobs bank.

Deriving Cost Curves

When producing output, the nature and size of a firm's costs are critically important in determining its profit-maximizing production behavior. To understand why firms act as they do, we have to recognize how their costs change with their level of output. *The mathematical relationship between a firm's production costs and its output is summarized* in a **cost curve**.

There are different types of cost curves depending on what kind of costs we relate to the firm's output, and all cost curves are measured over a particular time period. There can be hourly, daily, or yearly cost curves, for example. The specific period depends on the context, and as we discussed, so do what costs are fixed and what costs are variable.

Consider the example of Fleet Foot (FF), a running shoe company. In the short run, FF uses fixed inputs (such as machinery) and variable inputs (such as labor and materials) to produce shoes. **Table 7.1** shows the weekly costs for FF. These cost data are also shown graphically in **Figure 7.1**.

cost curve The mathematical relationship between a firm's production costs and its output.

- Fixed cost does not vary with output, so it is constant and the fixed cost curve is horizontal. And because fixed cost must be paid in the short run even if the firm chooses to not produce anything, fixed cost is the same at $Q = 0$ as it is at every other level of output. As shown in Table 7.1, FF's fixed cost is $50 per week, so the fixed cost curve *FC* in Figure 7.1 is a horizontal line at $50.

- Variable cost changes with the output level. Fleet Foot's variable cost rises as output increases because FF must buy more inputs. The relationship between the amount of variable inputs a firm must buy and its output means the slope of the *VC* curve is always positive. The shape of FF's particular *VC* curve in Figure 7.1

Table 7.1 Fixed, Variable, and Total Cost for Fleet Foot

Output Quantity Q (Pairs of Shoes/Week)	Fixed Cost *FC* ($/Week)	Variable Cost *VC* ($/Week)	Total Cost *TC* ($/Week)
0	50	0	50
1	50	10	60
2	50	17.5	67.5
3	50	22.5	72.5
4	50	25	75
5	50	30	80
6	50	37.5	87.5
7	50	47.5	97.5
8	50	60	110
9	50	75	125
10	50	100	150
11	50	150	200
12	50	225	275

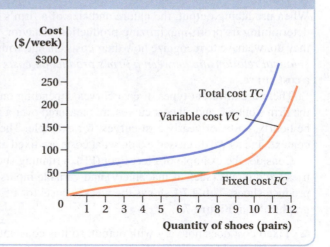

Figure 7.1 Fixed, Variable, and Total Costs

Plotting the values from Table 7.1 generates the fixed, variable, and total cost curves for Fleet Foot (FF). Because fixed cost is constant at $50 per week, even when $Q = 0$, the fixed cost curve is horizontal. The variable cost curve rises with output: At lower outputs, it increases with output at a diminishing rate, while at higher outputs, it begins to rise at an increasing rate. The total cost curve is the sum of the fixed and variable cost curves. It runs parallel to the variable cost curve and is greater than the variable cost curve by the amount of the fixed cost.

indicates that the *rate* at which FF's variable cost increases first falls and then rises with output. Specifically, the curve becomes flatter as weekly output quantities rise from 0 to 4 pairs of shoes, indicating that the additional cost of producing another pair of shoes is falling as FF makes more shoes. However, at quantities above 4 pairs per week, the *VC* curve's slope becomes steeper. At these output levels, the additional cost of producing another pair of shoes is rising. We talk more about why this is the case later in the chapter.

■ The total cost curve shows how a firm's total production cost changes with its level of output. Because all costs can be classified as either fixed or variable, the sum of these two components equals total cost. In fact, as is clear in Figure 7.1, the total and variable cost curves have the same shapes and are parallel to each other, separated at every point by the amount of fixed cost. Note also that when output is zero, total cost isn't zero; it is $50. Fleet Foot's fixed cost must be paid in the short run even when the firm produces no output.

7.4 Average and Marginal Costs

Understanding the total cost curve (and its fixed and variable cost components) is an important part of analyzing firms' production behavior. To see why, we introduce two other cost concepts that play a key role in production decisions: average cost and marginal cost. In our Chapter 6 analysis of a firm's production decisions, we took the firm's desired output level as given. In the next few chapters, we will see that average and marginal costs help determine a firm's desired output level.

Average Cost Measures

Average cost is fairly straightforward. It's just cost divided by quantity. Because there are three costs (total, fixed, and variable), there are three kinds of average cost: average fixed cost; average variable cost; average total cost. Each of these measures examines the *per-unit* cost at that level of output. We compute these measures in **Table 7.2** and illustrate them in **Figure 7.2**.

Table 7.2 Costs for Fleet Foot

(1) Output Quantity Q	(2) Fixed Cost FC	(3) Variable Cost VC	(4) Total Cost TC	(5) Marginal Cost MC ($=\Delta TC/\Delta Q$) ($=\Delta VC/\Delta Q$)	(6) Average Fixed Cost AFC ($=FC/Q$)	(7) Average Variable Cost AVC ($=VC/Q$)	(8) Average Total Cost ATC ($=TC/Q$)
0	50	0	50	—	—	—	—
1	50	10	60	10	50	10	60
2	50	17.5	67.5	7.5	25	8.75	33.75
3	50	22.5	72.5	5	16.67	7.5	24.17
4	50	25	75	2.5	12.5	6.25	18.75
5	50	30	80	5	10	6	16
6	50	37.5	87.5	7.5	8.33	6.25	14.58
7	50	47.5	97.5	10	7.14	6.79	13.93
8	50	60	110	12.5	6.25	7.5	13.75
9	50	75	125	15	5.56	8.33	13.89
10	50	100	150	25	5	10	15
11	50	150	200	50	4.55	13.64	18.18
12	50	225	275	75	4.17	18.75	22.92

Figure 7.2 Average Cost Curves

We can construct the average fixed, average variable, and average total cost curves for Fleet Foot using the values from Table 7.2. As FF makes more pairs of shoes, the average fixed cost per pair decreases. The average variable cost initially decreases slightly and then increases after 5 pairs. Average total cost, the sum of average fixed and average variable costs, is U-shaped and is separated from the average variable cost curve by the value of average fixed cost.

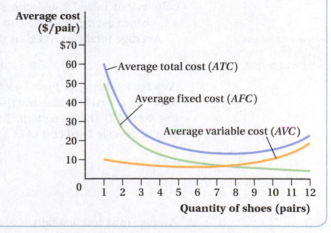

FREAKONOMICS

3D Printers and Manufacturing Cost

Star Trek is full of far-fetched technologies that we can only dream about — things like messages that travel faster than the speed of light; cloaking devices, transporters that beam humans from one place to another; and the "replicator" that reconstitutes matter to create items needed onboard the *Starship Enterprise*, such as food or spare parts.

As crazy as it sounds, though, the "replicator" is no longer science fiction. We don't call them replicators, but rather 3D printers. 3D printers take raw materials such as plastic or gold and convert them into forks and knives for your dining room table or eccentric sculptures for your living room. The new "Foodini" 3D printer can even print food, a Trek-kie's dream come true. If their cost falls enough, 3D printers could become as common as microwave ovens or toasters. Instead of going to the store to buy food or ordering a meal online, you could simply punch a few buttons and manufacture the desired items right in your own home.

As with many new technologies, their costs right now are extremely high. The fixed costs of a commercial-grade printer are in the hundreds of thousands of dollars. The variable costs, while not staggering (average variable cost is about $4 per cubic inch), are expensive enough that printed products can't compete with today's mass-produced offerings. Shapeways.com offers consumers the ability to order over 3 million 3D printer-made products, but they aren't cheap. A *SORRY!* gameboard piece will cost you $6.45, and a Cuisinart EasyPop Popcorn Maker handle will run you $7.28.

However, in 1910 it seemed just as unlikely that the assembly line would replace master craftsmen. Smartphones were science fiction 20 years ago. What was once conceivable only in the world of Star Trek might soon become a regular part of your daily life. You may have to wait a little longer, though, to acquire a transporter beam.

---

average fixed cost (AFC) A firm's fixed cost per unit of output.

Average fixed cost (AFC) is measured as the *fixed cost per unit of output*, or

$$AFC = FC/Q$$

Column 6 of Table 7.2 shows average fixed cost AFC for Fleet Foot (FF). AFC falls as output rises because the fixed cost is constant but gets divided by a larger and larger number (quantity). The fixed cost is spread over more and more units of output so the average fixed cost Fleet Feet pays per pair of shoes declines as quantity rises.

average variable cost (AVC) A firm's per-unit variable cost of production.

Average variable cost (AVC) measures the *per-unit variable cost of production*. It is calculated by dividing variable cost by the quantity of output:

$$AVC = VC/Q$$

Unlike average fixed cost, average variable cost can go up or down as quantity changes. In column 7 of Table 7.2, it declines until 5 units are produced, after which it rises, leading to a U-shaped average variable cost curve.

average total cost (ATC) A firm's total cost per unit of output.

Average total cost (ATC) is the *total cost per unit of output*:

$$ATC = TC/Q$$

Average total cost for Fleet Foot is shown in the last column of Table 7.2. For FF, average total cost at first falls and then rises as output rises. Firms' average total costs often exhibit this sort of U-shaped pattern. To see why, first note that average total cost (*ATC*) is the sum of average fixed cost (*AFC*) and average variable cost (*AVC*):

$$ATC = TC/Q = (FC + VC)/Q$$
$$= FC/Q + VC/Q$$
$$= AFC + AVC$$

Average total cost first falls as output rises because the dominant influence on average total cost is the rapidly declining average fixed cost. But as output continues to rise, average variable cost keeps increasing, first slowing the rate at which average total cost is falling and eventually causing average total cost to increase with output. These changes create a U-shaped average total cost curve.

Marginal Cost

Beyond average costs, the other key cost concept is **marginal cost (MC)**, a *firm's cost of producing one more unit of output*:

$$MC = \Delta TC / \Delta Q$$

where ΔTC is the change in total cost and ΔQ is a 1-unit change in output.

marginal cost (MC) A firm's cost of producing one more unit of output.

Fleet Foot's marginal cost is shown in column 5 of Table 7.2. It is the difference in total cost when output increases by 1 pair of shoes. But notice: Marginal cost also equals the difference in variable cost when one additional unit is produced. That's because, by definition, fixed cost does not change when output changes. Therefore, *fixed cost does not affect marginal cost*; only variable cost changes when the firm produces one more unit. This means marginal cost can also be defined as the change in variable cost from producing another unit of output:

$$MC = \Delta VC / \Delta Q \, (= \Delta TC / \Delta Q)$$

For this reason, marginal cost is not split into fixed and variable cost components, as is average cost. Marginal cost is only marginal variable cost.

Fleet Foot's marginal cost initially declines as output increases. After a certain output level (4 units in Table 7.2), marginal cost begins to rise, and at even higher output levels, it rises steeply. Why? Marginal cost may initially fall at low quantities because of complications in producing the first few units that can be fixed fairly quickly, or because having more scale allows workers to specialize in those tasks that they are best at performing. As output continues to increase, however, these marginal cost reductions stop and marginal cost begins to increase with the quantity produced, as seen in **Figure 7.3**. There are many reasons why it becomes more and more expensive to make another unit as output rises: Capacity constraints may occur, inputs may become more expensive as the firm uses more of them, it may be more difficult for the company to coordinate its operations, and so on.

The end-of-chapter appendix uses calculus to derive marginal costs from the total cost function.

Understanding the concept of marginal cost is critical: It is one of the most central concepts in all of economics, and *it is the* only *cost that matters for many of the key decisions a firm makes.*

Figure 7.3   Marginal Cost

Fleet Foot's marginal cost curve *MC* shows the additional cost of producing one more pair of shoes. It is U-shaped because marginal cost decreases initially and then increases at higher output levels.

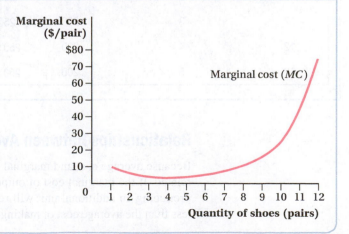

figure it out 7.2

Fields Forever is a small farm that grows strawberries to sell at the local farmers' market. It produces strawberries using 5 acres of land that it rents for $200 per week. Fields Forever also hires labor at a price of $250 per week per worker. The table below shows how the output of strawberries (measured in truckloads) varies with the number of workers hired:

Labor (workers/week)	Quantity of Strawberries (truckloads/week)
0	0
1	1
3	2
7	3
12	4
18	5

Calculate the marginal cost of 1 to 5 truckloads of strawberries for Fields Forever.

Solution:

The easiest way to solve this problem is to add several columns to the table above. We should add fixed cost, variable cost, and total cost. Fixed cost is the cost of land

that does not vary as output varies. Therefore, fixed cost is $200. Variable cost is the cost of labor. It can be found by multiplying the quantity of labor by the wage rate ($250). Total cost is the sum of fixed cost and variable cost.

Marginal cost is the change in total cost per unit increase in output, or $\Delta TC/\Delta Q$. When output rises from 0 truckloads to 1 truckload of strawberries, total cost rises from $200 to $450. Therefore, the marginal cost of the first truckload of strawberries is $450 − $200 = $250. As output rises from 1 to 2 truckloads, total cost rises from $450 to $950, so the marginal cost is $950 − $450 = $500. When the third truckload is produced, total cost rises from $950 to $1,950, so marginal cost is $1,950 − $950 = $1,000. Production of the fourth truckload pushes total cost to $3,200, so the marginal cost of the fourth truckload is $3,200 − $1,950 = $1,250. When production rises from 4 to 5 truckloads, total cost rises from $3,200 to $4,700, so the marginal cost of the fifth truckload is $1,500.

We could have also calculated the marginal cost of each truckload by looking at only the change in variable cost (rather than the change in total cost). Because the amount of land is fixed, Fields Forever can only grow more strawberries by hiring more labor and increasing its variable cost.

Labor/Week	Quantity of Strawberries (truckloads)	Fixed Cost, FC	Variable Cost, $VC = W \times L$	Total Cost, $TC = FC + VC$	Marginal Cost, MC
0	0	$200	$250 × 0 = $0	$200	—
1	1	200	250 × 1 = 250	450	$250
3	2	200	250 × 3 = 750	950	500
7	3	200	250 × 7 = 1,750	1,950	1,000
12	4	200	250 × 12 = 3,000	3,200	1,250
18	5	200	250 × 18 = 4,500	4,700	1,500

Relationships between Average and Marginal Costs

Because average cost and marginal cost are both derived from total cost, they are directly related. If the marginal cost of output is less than the average cost at a particular quantity, producing an additional unit will reduce the average cost because the extra unit's cost is less than the average cost of making all the units before it. (This relationship is the same as that between the average and marginal products of labor we learned about in Chapter 6.) Suppose, for example, that a firm is producing 9 units of output at an average cost of $100 per unit. If the marginal cost of the next unit is $90, the average cost will fall to ($900 + $90)/10 = $99, because the marginal cost of that extra unit is less than the average cost of the previous units.

This means that if the marginal cost curve is below an average cost curve at some quantity, average cost must be falling—that is, the average cost curve is downward-sloping. This is true whether we're talking about average total cost or average variable cost, because the marginal cost of producing another unit of output creates the same increment to both total and variable cost. This is also true even if, as is often the case, marginal costs are rising while they are below average costs. Producing another unit of output at a cost below the firm's current average will still bring down the average even if that marginal cost is rising with output. Just remember that the marginal cost curve is the cost at a specific output level—how much it costs to produce that specific unit—while average costs are averaging over all the previous units' costs, too.

When the marginal cost of the additional unit is above average cost, then producing it increases the average cost. Therefore, if the marginal cost curve is above an average cost curve at a quantity level, average cost is rising, and the average cost curve slopes up at that quantity. Again, this is true for both average total cost and average variable cost. This property explains why average variable cost curves and average total cost curves often have a U-shape. If marginal cost continues to increase as quantity increases, it eventually rises above average cost and begins pulling up the average variable and average total cost curves. You can see this relationship in **Figure 7.4**, which shows an average total cost curve, an average variable cost curve, and a marginal cost curve all derived from a single total cost curve.

The only point at which there is no change in average cost from producing one more unit occurs at the minimum point of the average variable and average total cost curves, where marginal and average cost are equal. These minimum points are indicated in Figure 7.4. (In the next chapter, we will see that the point at which average and marginal costs are equal and average total cost is minimized has a special significance in competitive markets.)

➡ The online appendix derives the relationship between marginal and average costs.

Figure 7.4   Relationship between Average and Marginal Costs

At lower quantities, when the marginal cost curve is below an average cost curve, the average cost curve is downward-sloping. At higher quantities, the marginal cost curve is above the average cost curve, and the average cost curve slopes upward. Therefore, the marginal cost curve intersects the average total and average variable cost curves at their minimums.

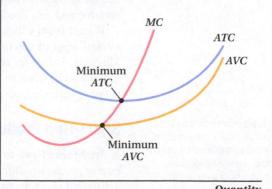

figure it out 7.3

Suppose a firm's total cost curve is $TC = 15Q^2 + 8Q + 45$, and $MC = 30Q + 8$.

a. Find the firm's fixed cost, variable cost, average total cost, and average variable cost.

b. Find the output level that minimizes average total cost.

c. Find the output level at which average variable cost is minimized.

Solution:

a. Fixed cost is a cost that does not vary as output changes. We can find FC by calculating total cost at 0 units of output:

$$TC = 15(0)^2 + 8(0) + 45 = 45$$

Variable cost can be found by subtracting fixed cost from total cost:

$$VC = TC - FC = (15Q^2 + 8Q + 45) - 45 = 15Q^2 + 8Q$$

Notice that, as we have learned in the chapter, VC depends on output; as Q rises, VC rises.

Average total cost is total cost per unit or TC/Q:

$$ATC = \frac{TC}{Q} = \frac{15Q^2 + 8Q + 45}{Q}$$
$$= 15Q + 8 + \frac{45}{Q}$$

Average variable cost is variable cost per unit or VC/Q:

$$AVC = \frac{VC}{Q} = \frac{15Q^2 + 8Q}{Q}$$
$$= 15Q + 8$$

b. Minimum average total cost occurs when $ATC = MC$:

$$15Q + 8 + \frac{45}{Q} = 30Q + 8$$
$$15Q + \frac{45}{Q} = 30Q$$
$$\frac{45}{Q} = 15Q$$
$$15Q^2 = 45$$
$$Q^2 = 3$$
$$Q = \sqrt{3} = 1.732$$

c. Minimum average variable cost occurs where $AVC = MC$:

$$15Q + 8 = 30Q + 8$$
$$15Q = 0$$
$$Q = 0$$

7.5 Short-Run and Long-Run Cost Curves

Earlier in this chapter, we discussed how fixed and variable costs change depending on the time horizon. Over longer periods of time, a firm can shift its input levels in response to changes in desired output, making even "heavy-duty" capital inputs such as factories more variable and less fixed.

Recall from Chapter 6 that we defined the short-run production function as having a fixed level of capital, whereas in the long-run production function, capital can adjust. The same is true for cost curves. Short-run cost curves relate production cost to the quantity of output when its level of capital is fixed. In the long-run cost curve, the capital inputs become variable costs just like labor.

Short-Run Production and Total Cost Curves

short-run total cost curve The mathematical representation of a firm's total cost of producing different quantities of output at a fixed level of capital.

A firm's **short-run total cost curve** is the *mathematical representation of the firm's total cost of producing different quantities of output at a fixed level of capital $\bar{K}$*. Just as there is a different short-run production function for every possible level of capital, so, too, is there a different short-run total cost curve for each capital level.

In Chapter 6, we saw that a firm's total cost curve (which relates cost and quantity of output) is related to its expansion path (which relates cost-minimizing input combinations to output). This relationship always holds, but in the short run the firm has only a fixed level of capital. Therefore, to examine how the firm minimizes its cost in the short run, we must examine the firm's expansion path only for that fixed amount of capital. Let's return to Ivor's Engines, the firm we dreamed up in Section 6.7 (Figure 6.14). **Figure 7.5** shows the same isoquants and isocost lines we used to construct Ivor's long-run expansion path. In the short run, Ivor's has a fixed capital level, and the expansion path is a horizontal line at that capital level. In the figure, we've assumed $\bar{K} = 6$. If the firm wants to adjust how much output it produces in the short run, it has to move along this line. It does so by changing its labor inputs, the only input it *can* change in the short run.

Suppose Ivor's Engines initially produces 20 units, as shown by the isoquant $Q = 20$, and that the cost of producing 20 engines is minimized when 6 units of capital are employed.

Figure 7.5 Long-Run and Short-Run Expansion Path for Ivor's Engines

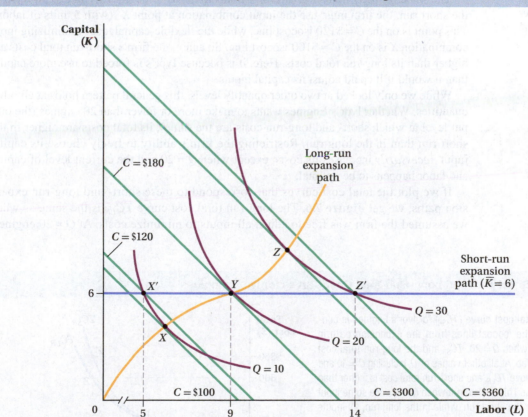

Along Ivor's Engines' long-run expansion path, the firm can change its level of capital. Along Ivor's short-run expansion path, capital is fixed at 6, and the expansion path is horizontal at $\bar{K} = 6$. Ivor's Engines can change its output quantity only by changing the quantity of labor used. At points X', Y, and Z', Ivor's Engines minimizes cost in the short run by using 5, 9, and 14 laborers to produce 10, 20, and 30 engines at a cost of $120, $180, and $360, respectively. At $Q = 20$, the cost-minimizing capital and labor combination, Y, is the same in the long run and short run, and production cost is the same ($180). At $Q = 10$ and $Q = 30$, production is more expensive in the short run than in the long run.

That is, the $Q = 20$ isoquant is tangent to the $C = \$180$ isocost line at point Y, when Ivor's capital inputs are 6. The labor input level that minimizes the cost of producing 20 engines is $L = 9$ units.

To see the difference between short-run and long-run cost curves, compare the points on the isoquants on the short-run (fixed-capital) expansion path to those on the long-run (flexible-capital) expansion path. For an output level of 20 engines, these are the same (point Y) because we have assumed that a capital level of $\bar{K} = 6$ was cost-minimizing for this quantity.

For the $Q = 30$ isoquant, however, the short-run and long-run input combinations are different. In the short run when capital is fixed at 6 units, if the firm wants to produce 30 units, it has to use the input combination at point Z', with 14 units of labor. But Z' is outside (i.e., further from the origin than) the $C = \$300$ isocost line that is tangent to the long-run, cost-minimizing input combination at point Z (which uses 11 units of labor). Instead, Z' is on the $C = \$360$ isocost line. In other words, it is more expensive for Ivor's Engines to produce 30 engines in the short run, when it cannot adjust its capital inputs. This is because Ivor's is forced to use more labor and less capital than it would if it could change all its inputs freely.

The same property holds true if Ivor's wants to make 10 engines. With capital fixed in the short run, the firm must use the input combination at point X' (with 5 units of labor). This point is on the $C = \$120$ isocost line, while the flexible-capital, cost-minimizing input combination X is on the $C = \$100$ isocost line. So again, the firm's short-run total costs are higher than its long-run total costs. Here, it is because Ivor's is forced to use more capital than it would if it could adjust its capital inputs.

While we only looked at two other quantity levels, this general pattern holds at all other quantities. Whether Ivor's Engines wants to make more or fewer than 20 engines (the output level at which short- and long-run costs are the same), its total costs are higher in the short run than in the long run. Restricting the firm's ability to freely choose its capital input *necessarily* increases its costs, except when $Q = 20$ and the current level of capital and labor happens to be optimal.

If we plot the total cost curves that correspond to these short- and long-run expansion paths, we get **Figure 7.6**. The long-run total cost curve TC_{LR} is the same as when we assumed the firm was free to adjust all inputs to minimize costs. At $Q = 20$ engines,

➡ The end-of-chapter appendix uses calculus to derive short-run and long-run cost curves.

Figure 7.6   Short-Run and Long-Run Total Cost Curves for Ivor's Engines

The short-run total cost curve (TC_{SR}) for Ivor's Engines is constructed using the isocost lines from the expansion path in Figure 7.5. At Y, when $Q = 20$, TC_{SR} and the long-run total cost curve (TC_{LR}) overlap. At all other values of Q, including $Q = 10$ and $Q = 30$, TC_{SR} is above TC_{LR}, and short-run total cost is higher than long-run total cost. This is also true when $Q = 0$ since some input costs are fixed in the short run, while in the long run, all inputs are flexible.

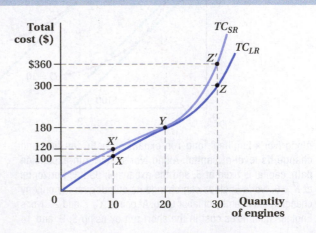

this curve and the short-run total cost curve TC_{SR} overlap because we assumed that capital was at the cost-minimizing capital level at this quantity. (We've labeled this point Y because it corresponds to the quantity and total cost combination at point Y in Figure 7.5.) For every other quantity, however, the short-run (fixed-capital) total cost curve is higher than the long-run (flexible-capital) total cost curve. Note that short-run total costs are positive when $Q = 0$ but zero in the long run because in the long run all inputs are flexible.

Short-Run versus Long-Run Average Total Cost Curves

From the total cost curves in Figure 7.6, we can construct Ivor's Engines' long-run and short-run average total cost curves as in **Figure 7.7**. The long-run average total cost curve is ATC_{LR} and the short-run average total cost curve $ATC_{SR,20}$. (We add the "20" subscript to remind us that capital was fixed at the level that minimized the costs of producing 20 units of output there.)

As with the total cost curves, the short- and long-run average total cost curves overlap at $Q = 20$ engines, because that's where the firm's fixed capital level of 6 units is also cost-minimizing. Here, long-run and short-run average total costs are $180/20 = $9.

Because average total cost divides these different total costs by the same quantity, average total cost must be higher in the short run, too. When Ivor's makes 30 engines with capital fixed at 6 units, its total cost is $360, and short-run average total cost is $12 per unit. When it makes 10 engines, short-run average total cost is $120/10 = $12 per unit as well. These points on the short-run average total cost curve $ATC_{SR,20}$ are labeled Z' and X' to correspond to the analogous points on the short-run total cost curve in Figure 7.6. The long-run average total costs at 10 and 30 units are labeled Z and X, and these match the similarly labeled points in Figure 7.6.

We've analyzed the distinction between long-run and short-run total and average total costs assuming that the short-run level of capital was fixed at 6 units (the level that minimized the cost of producing 20 engines). But suppose capital had been fixed at some other level instead. Say it was fixed at 9 units of capital, the level that minimizes the cost of producing 30 engines. (This is the capital level at point Z in Figure 7.6.)

The analysis would be the same as above. Long-run total and average total cost curves don't change because the firm will still choose the same capital inputs (resulting

Figure 7.7   **Short-Run and Long-Run Average Total Cost Curves for Ivor's Engines**

The short-run average total cost curve ($ATC_{SR,20}$) and the long-run average total cost curve (ATC_{LR}) are constructed using TC_{SR} and TC_{LR} from Figure 7.6. At Y, when $Q = 20$ and the cost-minimizing amount of capital is 6 units, the $ATC_{SR,20}$ and ATC_{LR} both equal $9. At all other values of Q, including $Q = 10$ and $Q = 30$, $ATC_{SR,20}$ is above ATC_{LR}, and short-run average total cost is higher than long-run average total cost.

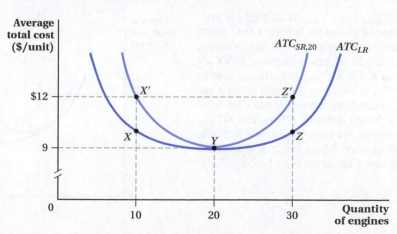

in the same costs) given its flexibility in the long run. However, the short-run cost curves do change because the fixed level of capital is different. Short-run total and average total cost curves will be above the corresponding long-run curves at every quantity except one. In this case, though, rather than overlapping at 20 units of output, it overlaps at $Q = 30$, because capital is now fixed at the cost-minimizing level for 30 engines. The logic behind why short-run total and average total costs are higher at every other quantity than 30 is the same: Not allowing the firm to change its capital with output raises the cost of producing any quantity except when the firm would have chosen that capital level anyway.

We can make the same comparisons with capital held fixed at 4 units, which minimizes the costs of producing 10 engines (corresponding to point X in Figure 7.6). Again, the same patterns hold. The short-run total and average total cost curves are higher at every quantity except $Q = 10$.

These other short-run average total cost curves are illustrated in **Figure 7.8** along with $ATC_{SR,20}$ and the long-run average total cost curve ATC_{LR} from Figure 7.7. $ATC_{SR,10}$ and $ATC_{SR,30}$ show short-run average costs when the firm has a fixed capital level for other output levels. As you can see in Figure 7.8, the long-run average total cost curve connects the locations (only one per fixed capital level) at which the short-run average total cost curves touch the long-run curve. If we drew out every such short-run average total cost curve, they would trace the long-run average total cost curve just like the three we have shown in the figure. Economists would say that the long-run average total cost curve forms an "envelope" of short-run average total cost curves as seen in Figure 7.8.

One interesting thing to notice about Figure 7.8 is that $ATC_{SR,10}$ and $ATC_{SR,30}$ do not touch ATC_{LR} at their lowest points. That's because even the output levels that minimize average total costs in the short run when capital is fixed (the low points on $ATC_{SR,10}$ and $ATC_{SR,30}$) can be produced more cheaply if capital inputs were flexible. In the one case where the short-run level of capital is fixed at the fully cost-minimizing level even if capital were flexible (the $ATC_{SR,20}$ curve), the two points are the same. For Ivor's Engines, this occurs at point Y, where output is 20 units.

Figure 7.8   Long-Run Average Total Cost Curve Envelops the Short-Run Average Total Cost Curves

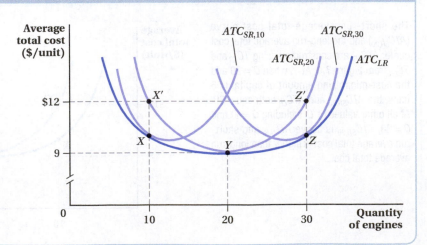

$ATC_{SR,10}$ and $ATC_{SR,30}$ show short-run average costs when the firm has a fixed capital level that minimizes the total costs of making 10 and 30 engines, respectively. With $\overline{K} = 4$ and $\overline{K} = 9$, $ATC_{SR,10}$ and $ATC_{SR,30}$ overlap ATC_{LR} at the cost-minimizing points X and Z, respectively. However, X and Z are not at the lowest points on $ATC_{SR,10}$ and $ATC_{SR,30}$ because the output levels that minimize $ATC_{SR,10}$ and $ATC_{SR,30}$ can be produced more cheaply if capital inputs are flexible.

figure it out 7.4

Go online for interactive, step-by-step help in solving the following problem.

Steve and Sons Solar Panels has a production function represented by $Q = 4KL$, where the $MP_L = 4K$ and the $MP_K = 4L$. The current wage rate (W) is \$8 per hour, and the rental rate on capital (R) is \$10 per hour.

a. In the short run, the plant's capital stock is fixed at $\bar{K} = 10$. What is the cost the firm faces if it wants to produce $Q = 200$ solar panels?

b. What will the firm wish to do in the long run to minimize the cost of producing $Q = 200$ solar panels? How much will the firm save? (*Hint:* You may have to review Chapter 6, to remember how a firm optimizes when both labor and capital are flexible.)

Solution:

a. If capital is fixed at $\bar{K} = 10$ units, then the amount of labor needed to produce $Q = 200$ units of output is

$$Q = 4KL$$
$$200 = 4(10)L = 40L$$
$$L = 5$$

Steve and Sons would have to hire 5 units of labor. Total cost would be

$$TC = WL + RK = \$8(5) + \$10(10) = \$40 + \$100 = \$140$$

b. In Chapter 6, we learned that in the long run, a firm minimizes costs when it produces a quantity at which the marginal rate of technical substitution of

labor for capital equals the ratio of the costs of labor (wage) and capital (rental rate): $MRTS_{LK} = W/R$. We know that

$$MRTS_{LK} = \frac{MP_L}{MP_K} = \frac{4K}{4L} = \frac{K}{L}$$
$$\frac{W}{R} = \frac{8}{10}$$

To minimize costs, the firm will set $MRTS_{LK} = W/R$:

$$10K = 8L$$
$$K = 0.8L$$

To produce $Q = 200$ units, we can substitute for K in the production function and solve for L:

$$Q = 200 = 4KL = 4(0.8L)(L)$$
$$200 = 3.2L^2$$
$$L^2 = 62.5$$
$$L = 7.91$$
$$K = 0.8L = (0.8)(7.91) = 6.33$$

To minimize cost, the firm will want to increase labor from 5 to 7.91 units and reduce capital from 10 to 6.33 units. Total cost will fall to

$$TC = WL + RK = \$8(7.91) + \$10(6.33)$$
$$= \$63.28 + \$63.30 = \$126.58$$

Therefore, the firm will save $\$140 - \$126.58 = \$13.42$.

Short-Run versus Long-Run Marginal Cost Curves

Just as the short- and long-run average total cost curves are related to the total cost curve, so are marginal costs over the two time horizons. Long-run marginal cost is the additional cost of producing another unit when inputs are fully flexible.

Every short-run average total cost curve has a corresponding short-run marginal cost curve that shows how costly it is to build another unit of output when capital is fixed at some particular level. A short-run marginal cost curve always crosses its corresponding short-run average total cost curve at the minimum of the average total cost curve.

While a long-run average total cost curve is the envelope of all the short-run average total cost curves, this isn't true for short- and long-run marginal cost curves. Let's look at the relationship between the two, step-by-step.

Figure 7.9 shows again the short- and long-run average total cost curves from Figure 7.8 and adds the short-run marginal cost curves corresponding to each short-run average total cost curve. ($MC_{SR,10}$ is the short-run marginal cost for $ATC_{SR,10}$, etc.)

Figure 7.9 Long-Run and Short-Run Marginal Costs

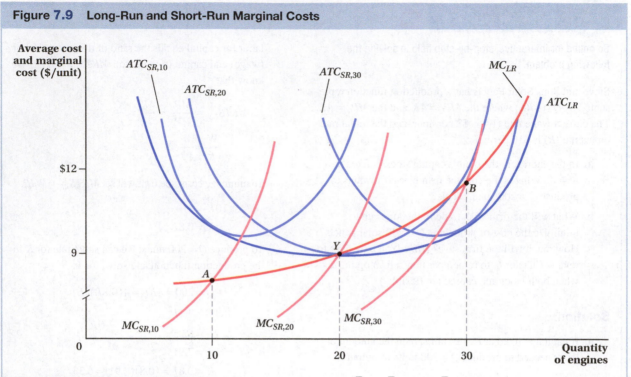

$MC_{SR,10}$, $MC_{SR,20}$, and $MC_{SR,30}$ are derived from $ATC_{SR,10}$, $ATC_{SR,20}$, and $ATC_{SR,30}$, respectively. The long-run marginal cost curve must intersect $MC_{SR,10}$, $MC_{SR,20}$, and $MC_{SR,30}$ at A, Y, and B, the points at which labor is cost-minimizing for $Q = 10$, $Q = 20$, and $Q = 30$ given $\bar{K} = 4$, $\bar{K} = 6$, and $\bar{K} = 9$. Therefore, A, Y, and B are the long-run marginal costs for $Q = 10$, $Q = 20$, and $Q = 30$, respectively, and the long-run marginal cost curve MC_{LR} connects A, Y, and B.

To figure out the long-run marginal cost, we know that in the short run with capital fixed, there is only one output level at which a firm would choose that same level of capital: the output at which the short-run average total cost curve touches the long-run average total cost curve. So, for example, if $Q = 10$, Ivor's Engines would choose a level of capital in the long run ($K = 4$) that is the same as that corresponding to short-run average total cost curve $ATC_{SR,10}$. Because the short- and long-run average total cost curves coincide at this quantity (but only at this quantity), so, too, do the short- and long-run marginal cost curves. In other words, because the firm would choose the same level of capital even if it were totally flexible, the long-run marginal cost *at this quantity* is the same as the short-run marginal cost on $MC_{SR,10}$. Therefore, to find the long-run marginal cost of producing 10 units, we can go up to the short-run marginal cost curve at $Q = 10$. This is point A in Figure 7.9 and represents the long-run marginal cost at an output level of 10 engines.

Likewise, the long-run marginal cost at $Q = 20$ is the value of $MC_{SR,20}$ when Ivor's Engines is making 20 engines. Therefore, the long-run marginal cost at $Q = 20$ can be found at point Y in Figure 7.9 (this is the same point Y as in Figures 7.7 and 7.8). Repeating this logic, long-run marginal cost when output $Q = 30$ is point B in the figure.

When we connect these long-run marginal cost points A, Y, and B, along with the similar points corresponding to every other output quantity, we trace out the long-run marginal cost curve MC_{LR}. Notice that, just as we have discussed, long-run marginal cost is below long-run average total cost when average total cost is falling (such as at point *A*), above long-run average total cost when average total cost is rising (such as at point *B*), and equal to long-run average total cost when average total cost is at its minimum (point *Y*).

7.6 Economies in the Production Process

Now that we understand long-run average total cost, let's examine how these average costs change as the firm size grows. Because all inputs are variable in the long run, we can consider how per-unit costs are affected as the firm alters its scale of operation—in other words, as the firm increases all its inputs by the same proportion.

Economies of Scale

We talked about returns to scale in Chapter 6. Remember that a production technology has increasing returns to scale if doubling all inputs leads to more than a doubling of output. If output less than doubles, there are decreasing returns to scale. If doubling all inputs exactly doubles output, its returns to scale are constant.

Economies of scale are the cost-based flip side of returns to scale. If doubling output causes cost to less than double, a firm has **economies of scale**: *total cost rises at a slower rate than output rises.* If doubling output causes cost to more than double, a firm has **diseconomies of scale**: *total cost rises at a faster rate than output rises.* If doubling output causes cost to double, a firm has **constant economies of scale**: *total cost rises at the same rate as output rises.*

Because economies of scale imply that total cost increases less than proportionately with output, they also imply that long-run average total cost falls as output grows. That is, the long-run average total cost curve is downward-sloping when there are economies of scale because total cost rises at a slower rate than quantity (remember, $ATC = TC/Q$). Similarly, diseconomies of scale imply an upward-sloping long-run average total cost curve because total cost rises more quickly than output. Constant economies of scale make the long-run average total cost curve flat.

Putting these together, we can see what the typical U-shaped, long-run average total cost curve implies about economies of scale. At low output levels (the left, downward-sloping part of the *ATC* curve), total cost rises more slowly than output does. As a result, average total cost falls, and the firm has economies of scale.

At the very bottom of the average total cost curve, where it is flat, average cost does not change, total cost rises proportionally with output, and marginal cost equals *ATC*. Here, average total cost thus increases at the same rate that output increases, and there are constant economies of scale.

At higher output levels (the right, upward-sloping part of the *ATC* curve, where *ATC* is rising), marginal cost is above average total cost, causing total cost to rise more quickly than output does. As a result, there are diseconomies of scale.

Economies of Scale versus Returns to Scale

Economies of scale and returns to scale are not the same thing. They are related, but there is a difference. Returns to scale describe how output changes when all inputs are increased by a common factor. But nothing says cost-minimizing firms must keep input ratios constant when they increase output. So, the measure of economies of scale, which is about how total costs change with output, does not impose constant input ratios. Returns to scale do.

economies of scale Total cost rises at a slower rate than output rises.

diseconomies of scale Total cost rises at a faster rate than output rises.

constant economies of scale Total cost rises at the same rate as output rises.

If a firm is able to change its input ratios when output changes, it can only improve its position or be the same—it can't do worse. So, it can have economies of scale but constant or even decreasing returns to scale. That is, even though the firm might have a production function in which doubling inputs would exactly double output, it might be able to double output without doubling its total cost by changing the proportion in which it uses inputs. Therefore, increasing returns to scale imply economies of scale, but not necessarily the reverse.[3]

 figure it out 7.5

Go online for interactive, step-by-step help in solving the following problem.

Suppose that the long-run total cost function for a firm is $LTC = 32,000Q - 250Q^2 + Q^3$ and its long-run marginal cost function is $LMC = 32,000 - 500Q + 3Q^2$. At what levels of output will the firm face economies of scale? Diseconomies of scale? (*Hint:* These cost functions yield a typical U-shaped, long-run average cost curve.)

Solution:

If we can find the output that minimizes long-run average total cost, we can determine the output levels for which the firm faces economies and diseconomies of scale. We know that when $LMC < LATC$, long-run average total cost is falling and the firm experiences economies of scale. Likewise, when $LMC > LATC$, the long-run average total cost curve slopes up and the firm faces diseconomies of scale. So, if we can figure out where the minimum $LATC$ occurs, we can see where economies of scale end and diseconomies begin.

Minimum average cost occurs when $LMC = LATC$. But we need to determine $LATC$ before we begin.

Long-run average total cost is long-run total cost divided by output:

$$LATC = \frac{LTC}{Q} = \frac{32,000Q - 250Q^2 + Q^3}{Q}$$
$$= 32,000 - 250Q + Q^2$$

Now, we need to set $LATC = LMC$ to find the quantity that minimizes $LATC$:

$$LATC = LMC$$
$$32,000 - 250Q + Q^2 = 32,000 - 500Q + 3Q^2$$
$$250Q = 2Q^2$$
$$250 = 2Q$$
$$Q = 125$$

Long-run average total cost is minimized and economies of scale are constant when the firm produces 125 units of output. Thus, at $Q < 125$, the firm faces economies of scale. At $Q > 125$, the firm faces diseconomies of scale. (You can prove this to yourself by substituting different quantities into the long-run average total cost equation and seeing if $LATC$ rises or falls as Q changes.)

 Application: **Who Killed the Mall: Amazon or Costco? E-Commerce or Economies of Scale?**

Hundreds of traditional department stores have closed across North America over the past couple of decades. Accompanying this has been the loss of tens of thousands of jobs, the shuttering of malls that relied on those department stores as their anchors, and the bankruptcy of some of the longest-lived and most famous names in retail.

---

[3] The only case in which the two concepts are the same is when it happens to be optimal for the firm to hold input ratios constant as output increases. (This would show up as an expansion path that is a straight line extending out from the origin.) In this case, the firm gets no extra cost reduction from changing the proportions in which it uses its inputs as its output changes.

What led to this collapse? Most people think it was the growth of online shopping. A study by Ali Hortaçsu and Chad Syverson[4] (one of the authors of this textbook) suggests that online shopping isn't the whole story behind the mall's collapse; in fact, it might not have even been the primary factor over most of the period involved.

Instead, it appears as if the growth of different, but still brick-and-mortar, retailing formats had an enormous effect. Specifically, evidence exists that warehouse clubs (places like Costco and Sam's Club) and "supercenters" (the groceries-plus-everything-else formats of some Target and Walmart stores) displaced a lot of sales at traditional department stores. For instance, while annual online retail sales increased by over $300 billion between 2000 and 2015, so did warehouse and supercenter sales. (In fact, throughout the 2000s, warehouse clubs and supercenter sales grew considerably more than online sales; it's only recently that the fast growth of online sales has caught up and begun to surpass supercenter sales growth.) There's also evidence in the timing of the changes: Job losses at department stores started exactly when warehouse club and supercenter employment took off, way back in 1999–2000. In addition, U.S. counties that saw larger increases in the number of warehouse club and supercenter stores experienced the closing of more local department stores.

So what was it about warehouse clubs and supercenters that allowed them to start pushing out department stores? A leading explanation for the success of these formats is their economies of scale. New technologies facilitated better order tracking, warehouse delivery, inventory, and checkout processes, which, in turn, allowed firms to operate at a low cost and a large scale. Although these same kinds of changes have occurred throughout the retail sector, they have been especially important in fostering the growth of warehouse clubs and supercenters. In fact, of the roughly 20% growth in the average retailer's size that the sector has witnessed over the past two decades, over half of it was due to warehouse clubs and supercenters.

Looking forward, online retail has some scale economies of its own that it might benefit from. And even if warehouse clubs and superstores expand more slowly in the future, the pressure on department stores might just shift to another source, rather than falling off altogether. ■

Economies of Scope

Many firms make more than one product. McDonald's sells Big Macs, Egg McMuffins, and french fries. Just as economies of scale indicate how firms' costs vary with the quantity they produce, *economies of scope* indicate how firms' costs change when they make more than one product. **Economies of scope** happen when the *simultaneous production of multiple products comes at a lower cost than if a firm made each product separately and then added up the costs.*

economies of scope The simultaneous production of multiple products comes at a lower cost than if a firm made each product separately and then added up the costs.

[4] Ali Hortacsu and Chad Syverson, "The Ongoing Evolution of U.S. Retail: A Format Tug-of-War," *Journal of Economic Perspectives* 29, no. 4 (2015): 89–112.

To be more explicit, let a firm's cost of simultaneously producing Q_1 units of Good 1 and Q_2 units of Good 2 be equal to $TC(Q_1, Q_2)$. If the firm produces Q_1 units of Good 1 and nothing of Good 2, its cost is $TC(Q_1, 0)$. Similarly, if the firm produces Q_2 units of Good 2 and none of Good 1, its cost is $TC(0, Q_2)$. Under these definitions, the firm is considered to have economies of scope if $TC(Q_1, Q_2) < TC(Q_1, 0) + TC(0, Q_2)$. In other words, producing Q_1 and Q_2 together is cheaper than making each separately.

We can go beyond just knowing whether or not economies of scope exist, and actually quantify them in a way that allows us to compare scope economies across companies. We call this measure *SCOPE*, and it's the difference between the total costs of single-good production $[TC(Q_1, 0) + TC(0, Q_2)]$ and joint production $[TC(Q_1, Q_2)]$ as a fraction of the total costs of joint production. That is,

$$SCOPE = \frac{[TC(Q_1, 0) + TC(0, Q_2)] - TC(Q_1, Q_2)}{TC(Q_1, Q_2)}$$

If *SCOPE* > 0, the total cost of producing Goods 1 and 2 jointly is less than making the goods separately, so there are economies of scope. The greater *SCOPE* is, the larger are the firm's cost savings from making multiple products. If *SCOPE* = 0, the costs are equivalent, and economies of scope are zero. And if *SCOPE* < 0, then it's actually cheaper to produce Q_1 and Q_2 separately. In other words, there are **diseconomies of scope**, meaning *the simultaneous production of multiple products comes at a higher cost than if a firm made each product separately.*

There are two important things to remember about economies of scope. First, they are defined for a *particular* level of output of each good. Economies of scope might exist at one set of output levels—for example, 100 units of Good 1 and 150 units of Good 2—but not at a different pair, like 200 units of each, for instance. (The specificity of economies of scope to particular output levels is shared with economies of scale. As we discussed earlier in this section, for example, a U-shaped average total cost curve embodies changing scale economies over different output levels—positive economies at low output levels, negative ones at higher output.) Second, economies of scope do not have to be related to economies of scale. A firm can have one without the other or both at the same time. In fact, it gets a bit difficult to even define economies of scale once there are multiple outputs. We don't need to go into why this is so; it's enough to recognize that scale and scope economies are different concepts.

Where Economies of Scope Come From

There are many possible sources of scope economies. They depend on the flexibility of inputs and the inherent nature of the products.

A common source of economies of scope is when different parts of a common input can be applied to the production of the firm's different products. Take a cereal company that makes two cereals, Bran Bricks and Flaky Wheat. The firm needs wheat to produce either cereal. For Bran Bricks, it needs mostly the bran, the fibrous outer covering of the wheat kernel, but for Flaky Wheat, the firm needs the rest of the kernel. Therefore, there are natural cost savings from producing both cereals together.

In oil refining, the inherent chemical properties of crude oil guarantee economies of scope. Crude oil is a collection of a number of very different hydrocarbon molecules; refining is the process of separating these molecules into useful products. It is physically impossible for a refining company to produce only gasoline (or kerosene, diesel, lubricants, or whatever petroleum product might be fetching the highest price at the time). While refiners have some limited ability to change the mix of products they can extract

diseconomies of scope The simultaneous production of multiple products comes at a higher cost than if a firm made each product separately.

from each barrel of crude oil, this comes at a loss of scope economies. That's why refineries always produce a number of petroleum compounds simultaneously.

The common input that creates scope economies does not have to be raw materials. For example, Google employees might be more productive using their knowledge about information collection and dissemination to produce multiple products (e.g., Google Earth, Google Docs, and YouTube) than to produce just the main search engine.

7.7 Conclusion

We've covered all sorts of concepts about firms' costs in this chapter: opportunity costs, fixed costs, variable costs, sunk costs, marginal costs, average costs, long-run and short-run costs, economies of scale and scope, and more. This information also allows us to connect what we learned in Chapter 6, which is how a firm optimally produces a *given* output quantity, to many of the analyses we will do in Chapters 8–11, when we look at how firms decide what output quantity to produce in the first place, or even whether to produce at all.

Summary

1. Economic cost includes **accounting cost** plus the **opportunity cost** of inputs. Opportunity cost is the value of the input's next-best use. Decisions should be made taking opportunity costs into account—that is, on the basis of **economic cost,** not accounting cost. **[Section 7.1]**

2. **Fixed cost** does not change when the firm's output does and must be paid even if output is zero. It can only be avoided by the firm completely shutting down and disposing of the inputs (an action that can be undertaken only in the long run). **Sunk costs** are fixed costs that can never be recovered even if the firm shuts down completely. Costs that are already sunk should not affect decisions going forward, because they have already been paid regardless of what choice is made in the present. **[Section 7.2]**

3. A firm's **total cost** can be split into fixed and variable components. **Variable costs** are costs that change with the output level. **[Section 7.3]**

4. Cost curves relate a firm's cost to its output quantity. Because fixed cost doesn't change as output changes, fixed cost curves are horizontal, and **total cost curves** are parallel to **variable cost curves** (separated by the amount of fixed cost). **[Section 7.3]**

5. Two additional important cost concepts are **average** and **marginal costs.** Average cost at a given output quantity equals the ratio of cost to output. **Average fixed cost** falls continuously as output increases. **Average variable cost** and **average total cost** tend to be U-shaped, falling initially, but then rising as output increases. Marginal cost is the additional cost of making one more unit of output. **[Section 7.4]**

6. In the short run, the firm's capital inputs are held constant along its expansion path, and all changes in output come from changing labor inputs. This means that, for all quantities except that quantity at which the fixed capital level is cost-minimizing, short-run total and average total costs must be higher than their long-run values. Every fixed capital level has its own short-run cost curves. The long-run average total cost curve is an "envelope" of all the short-run average total cost curves. Long-run marginal cost equals the short-run marginal costs at the quantities at which the fixed capital level is cost-minimizing. **[Section 7.5]**

7. **Economies of scale** describe the relative rate at which a firm's cost changes when its output changes. When cost increases at a slower rate than output, the firm has economies of scale. Average cost is falling and the long-run average total cost curve is downward-sloping when there are economies of scale. If cost increases at a faster rate than output, **diseconomies of scale** occur. Average total cost is rising and the long-run average total cost curve is upward-sloping in this case. If cost increases at the same rate as output, there are neither scale economies nor diseconomies, and long-run average total cost is constant. **[Section 7.6]**

8. **Economies of scope** describe how a firm's total cost changes with its product specialization. If producing two outputs jointly is cheaper than producing the same amount of the two outputs separately, then there are economies of scope. There are **diseconomies of scope** if it is instead more expensive. **[Section 7.6]**

Review Questions

1. What is the difference between a firm's accounting and economic costs? How do these costs relate to a firm's accounting and economic profits?

2. Define opportunity cost. How does a firm's opportunity cost relate to its economic cost?

3. What is the sunk cost fallacy?

4. Provide some examples of unavoidable fixed costs. How are these related to sunk costs? Describe why a firm should not consider sunk costs when making decisions.

5. Describe the relationship between fixed, variable, and total costs.

6. Why is a fixed cost curve horizontal? Why does a variable cost curve have a positive slope?

7. Name the three measures that examine a firm's per-unit cost at a given level of output.

8. Why does a firm's fixed cost not affect its marginal cost of producing an additional unit of a product?

9. Why is a firm's short-run total cost greater than its long-run total cost? Explain why this is also true for a firm's short-run and long-run *average* costs.

10. Describe the conditions under which a firm has economies of scale, diseconomies of scale, and constant economies of scale.

11. When does a producer face economies of scope? When does a producer face diseconomies of scope?

Problems

(Solutions to problems marked with an asterisk appear at the back of this book. Problems adapted to use calculus are available online.)

1. Chris owns his own business restoring antique cars. Last year, he restored 24 cars, which he sold for $1,100,000. The parts and supplies necessary for the restoration totaled $400,000. He paid $360,000 to his six employees and a salary of $110,000 to himself. The rent and utilities on his building were $80,000.

    Recently, Chris received an offer to work as Jay Leno's personal auto restorer, at a salary of $275,000. Chris also received a $180,000 offer to host a car-related reality TV show for the Discovery Channel. Chris can only work one job.

    a. What is Chris's accounting cost? His accounting profit?

    b. What is Chris's economic cost? His economic profit?

    c. Compare what Chris earns in his current job (both his salary and his company's accounting profit) to his best outside offer. Does the figure you calculated look familiar? Does it shed any light on the meaning of economic profit?

*2. Indicate whether the following statements are true or false, and then briefly explain your reasoning.

    a. It is possible for accounting and economic costs to be equal, but it is never possible for economic costs to be less than accounting costs.

    b. It is possible for a firm to show an economic profit without showing an accounting profit.

3. Who doesn't love kicking back after work with a snack and a good show? Everyone loves some free time . . . but, of course, time isn't free! In the past 10 years, ridesharing services like Uber have become wildly popular. People who need to get from A to B value the ability to connect with a driver rapidly, rather than waiting for a scarce taxi-cab. And ordinary people (with a nice enough car) can earn a few extra bucks giving rides, working as little or as much as they please. Today, an estimated 2 million people drive for Uber, often evenings and weekends after they're finished the day at a full-time job. Explain how the growth of Uber reflects the way in which ridesharing has altered the opportunity cost of leisure.

4. Philo T. Farmsworth is a corn farmer with a 40-acre tract of land. Each acre can produce 100 bushels of corn. The cost of planting the tract in corn is $20,000, and the cost of harvesting the corn is $10,000. In May, when corn is selling for $10 per bushel, Philo plants his crop. By September, the price of corn has fallen to $2 per bushel. What should Philo do? Explain, assuming that there are no costs involved with bringing the corn to market to sell.

5. Each year on January 1, millions of Americans, having made New Year's resolutions to lose weight and get in shape, purchase annual gym memberships. A CNN survey recently suggested that nearly 30% of all New Year's resolutions are abandoned by February 1; 80% by July. In other words, millions of people buy expensive gym memberships and then fail to use them. Does this indicate that they fell victim to the sunk cost fallacy? Or, does it suggest that they well understand the nature of sunk costs? Explain your answer.

6. In which of the following situations are costs sunk?

    a. A drug company spends $20 million to test the effectiveness of a new replacement drug for insulin, only to find out it is ineffective.

    b. AB-Inbev spends $15 million to develop and advertise a new mango-wheat beer that few people enjoy.

    c. A Kansas farmer wants to open a winery; she spends $600,000 to buy farmland only to discover that the weather is too extreme to grow finicky grapes. She can resell the land to a wheat farmer for $450,000.

d. Lockton, a risk-management company, pays a $10,000 signing bonus to a new employee who turns out to be unreliable.

e. You purchase a $150 ticket to a nighttime concert, only to have an instructor surprise you with a demanding assignment due the same evening.

7. Karam recently opened a bar and grill. The costs associated with his new business are as follows:

a. $300,000 to build the restaurant

b. $30,000 for a liquor license

c. $50,000 on furniture and kitchenware

d. 2 cooks who will each be paid $5,000 per month

e. 5 waiters who will each be paid $3 per hour plus tips

Which of Karam's costs are fixed, and which are variable? Explain.

*8. Amanda owns a toy manufacturing plant with the production function $Q = 100L - 3,000$, where L is hired labor hours. Assume that Amanda has no fixed costs.

a. Rearrange Amanda's production function to show how many workers Amanda would have to hire to produce a given level of output. In other words, isolate L on the left-hand side, expressing L as a function of Q.

b. Because Amanda has no fixed costs, all her costs derive from paying workers. In other words, $TC = w \times L$. Substitute your answer from (a) into this equation to find Amanda's total cost function.

9. Roy builds furniture in his North Carolina workshop. The cost of producing various numbers of bookstands is given in the table below:

Quantity (bookstands/week)	Total Costs	Fixed Costs	Variable Costs
0	300		
1	400		
2	480		
3	580		
4	700		
5	840		

Complete the table. Then graph the total, fixed, and variable cost curves.

10. A Toyota Corolla costs $18,700 and has average highway fuel economy of 36 miles per gallon (mpg). A Toyota Prius

costs $23,700 and offers average highway fuel economy of 50 mpg.

a. Assuming gas costs $2.75 per gallon, generate total cost equations as a function of miles driven for each of these cars. Identify the fixed and variable costs.

b. How many miles do you have to drive before the two cars have the same total cost?

c. You plan on holding on to your next car for 100,000 miles. You estimate that you can sell a used Corolla with 100,000 miles for $4,400; a used Prius with 100,000 miles is worth $7,800. If money is the only thing that matters to you, should you buy the Corolla or the Prius?

*11. Consider the costs for Gisela's cupcake business:

Quantity (batches)	Fixed Cost ($)	Total Cost ($)
1	50	75
2	50	85
3	50	102
4	50	127
5	50	165
6	50	210

Re-create the table above with columns showing Gisela's variable cost, average total cost, average fixed cost, and average variable cost.

12. Daniel's Midland Archers (DMA) makes children's wooden practice arrows. Draw a set of representative short-run cost curves for DMA. Include average variable cost, average fixed cost, average total cost, and marginal cost.

a. Suppose that Congress imposes a 39-cent excise tax on each children's wooden practice arrow DMA sells. Illustrate the effects of this tax on the cost curves of DMA. Which curves shift and which do not?

b. Suppose that the city where DMA produces arrows increases the annual property tax on DMA's factory from $80,000 to $150,000. Illustrate the effects of this tax on the cost curves of DMA. Which curves shift and which do not?

13. A firm's total cost curve is $TC = Q^3 - 60Q^2 + 910Q + 150$. Its marginal cost is $3Q^2 - 120Q + 910$.

a. Find the firm's fixed cost, variable cost, average total cost, and average variable cost.

b. Find the output level at which average variable cost is minimized.

14. You are the CEO of a major producer of funnel cakes. Your cost accountant has provided you with a table describing your cost structure, but you have inadvertently dripped cooking grease on it and most of the table is illegible. Reconstruct the table below, given the remaining legible numbers:

Q	TC	FC	VC	MC	AVC	AFC	ATC
0				—	—	—	—
1			17				
2				15			
3	101						
4					14.5		
5	122		67			11	
6							21

15. True or false: Average variable cost reaches its minimum point at a lower level of output than average total costs. Explain your answer, using a graph of average and marginal costs to illustrate.

16. Suppose a firm has the following production function: $Q = 2KL$. The marginal product of capital for this production function is $2L$, and the marginal product of labor is $2K$. If capital rents for $100 per unit per day, labor can be hired for $200 per unit per day, and the firm is minimizing costs,

    a. Find the total cost of producing 60 units of output.

    b. Suppose you want to determine the cost of producing the more general q units of output. Using the same set of procedures you followed in (a), but a more general Q instead of 60, find this firm's total cost function, which expresses total cost as a function of Q.

    c. Divide the total cost function you found in (b) by Q to determine this firm's average cost function.

17. You run a specialty bicycle company, which produces a limited quantity of extremely tricked out racing bikes. Consider the following graph, which illustrates the short-run average total cost curves corresponding to three possible plant sizes: small, medium, and large.

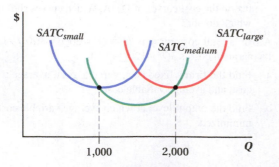

a. If you wanted to produce 900 bikes, which plant size should you choose, and why? What if you wanted to produce 1,100 instead?

b. If you wanted to produce 2,100 bikes, which plant size should you choose, and why? What if you wanted to produce just 1,900?

c. Darken the long-run average total cost curve your specialty bicycle company faces.

18. Suppose an increase in the minimum wage alters the cost of producing fast-food hamburgers. Show what happens to McDonald's long-run expansion path as a result of this wage increase. Does McDonald's alter its mix of inputs? What happens to McDonald's costs?

*19. A builder of custom motorcycles must choose between operating out of one garage or two. When the builder operates out of one garage, its average total cost of production is given by $ATC_1 = Q^2 - 6Q + 14$. If it operates out of two garages, its average total cost of production is given by $ATC_2 = Q^2 - 10Q + 30$. What does this firm's $LATC$ look like? Can you describe it as a function?

*20. Suppose that a firm has the following Cobb–Douglas production function: $Q = 12K^{0.75}L^{0.25}$.

    a. What must its long-run total cost curve look like? Its long-run average total cost curve?

    b. How do your answers to part (a) change if the firm's production function is $Q = KL$?

21. Peter's Pipers produces plumbing pipe. The long-run total cost of Peter's pipes is $LTC = 20,000Q - 200Q^2 + Q^3$, where Q is measured as thousands of feet of piping. The long-run marginal cost of Peter's pipes is given as $LMC = 20,000 - 400Q + 3Q^2$.

    a. Divide total cost by Q to obtain Peter's long-run average cost of producing pipe.

    b. Exploit the relationship between LMC and LAC to find the quantity where LAC is at a minimum.

    c. What is the lowest possible average cost at which Peter can produce pipe?

    d. Over what range of output does Peter's Pipers experience economies of scale? Over what range of output does Peter's Pipers experience diseconomies of scale?

22. Tyson Chicken produces both thighs and wings. When it produces 150 thighs and no wings, its total cost is $600. When Tyson produces 150 wings and no thighs, its total cost is $400. And when Tyson produces both 150 thighs and 150 wings jointly, its total costs are $900.

    a. Show that, for an output level of 150 thighs and 150 wings, Tyson experiences economies of scope.

    b. What is the likely source of Tyson's economies of scope?

Chapter 7 Appendix:
The Calculus of a Firm's Cost Structure

We saw in this chapter that firms face a multitude of costs—from opportunity costs and sunk costs to fixed and variable costs to marginal costs and more. These costs can be obtained directly from the firm's production function and its wage and rental rate for particular levels of output. But it is often helpful to have a more generalized form of a firm's costs that allows us to know its cost structure at any optimal input bundle. In this appendix, we use calculus to come up with total and marginal cost curves starting from the firm's production function.

Let's return to the firm with the Cobb–Douglas production function $Q = AK^\alpha L^{1-\alpha}$ with wages equal to W, the rental rate of capital equal to R, and the technology parameter A. Assume $0 < \alpha < 1$, and $A > 0$. The firm's total costs are

$$TC = RK + WL$$

This formula specifies the firm's total costs when the firm produces a specific quantity and thus knows its cost-minimizing bundle of capital and labor for that particular quantity. If the firm hasn't yet decided how much to produce, however, the firm would want to know its entire total cost curve—that is, what its total costs are at *any* quantity it chooses to produce. How can a firm find these costs? The firm wants to derive its total costs as a function of its demands for capital and labor. To do this, the firm first has to consider whether it is operating in the short or the long run. In the short run, capital is fixed at some level $\bar{K}$, and the firm's production function is $Q = A\bar{K}^\alpha L^{1-\alpha}$. Its demand for labor in the short run is then determined by how much capital the firm has. Finding the short-run demand for labor is as simple as solving for L in the production function:

$$L^{1-\alpha} = \frac{Q}{A\bar{K}^\alpha}$$

$$L = \left(\frac{Q}{A\bar{K}^\alpha}\right)^{\frac{1}{1-\alpha}}$$

Plugging this short-run demand for labor and the fixed amount of capital ($\bar{K}$) into the total cost equation, the firm faces short-run total cost:

$$TC_{SR} = R\bar{K} + WL$$

$$TC(Q)_{SR} = R\bar{K} + W\left(\frac{Q}{A\bar{K}^\alpha}\right)^{\frac{1}{(1-\alpha)}}$$

In the long run, the firm chooses the optimal amount of capital *and* labor, so its long-run demands for capital and labor look different. We know from the firm's cost-minimization problem in the Chapter 6 Appendix that at a fixed quantity $\bar{Q}$, the firm demands $L^* = \left[\frac{(1-\alpha)}{\alpha}\frac{R}{W}\right]^\alpha \frac{\bar{Q}}{A}$ and $K^* = \left[\frac{\alpha}{(1-\alpha)}\frac{W}{R}\right]^{1-\alpha}\frac{\bar{Q}}{A}$. At any level of Q, then, the firm demands $L^* = \left[\frac{(1-\alpha)}{\alpha}\frac{R}{W}\right]^\alpha \frac{Q}{A}$ and $K^* = \left[\frac{\alpha}{(1-\alpha)}\frac{W}{R}\right]^{1-\alpha}\frac{Q}{A}$, where Q is variable and not a fixed quantity.

These are the firm's long-run capital and labor demand curves. As with all demand curves, these are downward-sloping: As the wage (or rental rate) increases, the firm will want to purchase less labor (or capital), all else equal. Now that we have the firm's demands for both of its inputs, we can substitute them into the expression for total cost as a function of inputs to get the long-run total cost curve as a function of output:

$$TC_{LR} = RK + WL$$

$$TC(Q)_{LR} = \left[\frac{\alpha}{(1-\alpha)}\frac{W}{R}\right]^{1-\alpha}\frac{Q}{A} + W\left[\frac{(1-\alpha)}{\alpha}\frac{R}{W}\right]^{\alpha}\frac{Q}{A}$$

Notice that total cost increases as output and the prices of inputs increase, but that total cost decreases as total factor productivity A increases.

We can now also find the firm's generalized marginal cost curve by taking the derivative of the total cost curve with respect to quantity Q. But be careful before you do this! We have to again consider whether the firm is operating in the short run or the long run. In the short run, the cost of capital is a fixed cost and will not show up in the firm's marginal cost curve. Short-run marginal cost is only a function of the change in labor costs:

$$MC(Q)_{SR} = \frac{dTC(Q)_{SR}}{dQ} = \frac{d}{dQ}\left[RK + W\left(\frac{Q}{A\bar{K}^{\alpha}}\right)^{\frac{1}{1-\alpha}}\right]$$

$$= \frac{1}{(1-\alpha)}W\left(\frac{1}{A\bar{K}^{\alpha}}\right)^{\frac{1}{(1-\alpha)}}Q^{\frac{1}{(1-\alpha)}-1} = \frac{W}{(1-\alpha)}\left(\frac{1}{A\bar{K}^{\alpha}}\right)^{\frac{1}{(1-\alpha)}}Q^{\frac{\alpha}{(1-\alpha)}}$$

$$= \frac{W}{(1-\alpha)}\left(\frac{Q^{\alpha}}{A\bar{K}^{\alpha}}\right)^{\frac{1}{(1-\alpha)}}$$

As we would expect, marginal costs increase with output in the short run. Why? Because in the short run capital is fixed. The firm can only increase output by using more and more labor. However, the diminishing marginal product of labor means that each additional unit of labor is less productive and that the firm has to use increasingly more labor to produce an additional unit of output. As a result, the marginal cost of producing this extra unit of output increases as short-run production increases, all else equal.

In the long run, the firm can change both inputs, and its marginal cost curve reflects the firm's capital and labor demands. To get long-run marginal cost, take the derivative of long-run total cost with respect to Q:

$$MC(Q)_{LR} = \frac{dTC(Q)_{LR}}{dQ} = \frac{d}{dQ}\left[R\left[\frac{\alpha}{(1-\alpha)}\frac{W}{R}\right]^{1-\alpha}\frac{Q}{A} + W\left[\frac{(1-\alpha)}{\alpha}\frac{R}{W}\right]^{\alpha}\frac{Q}{A}\right]$$

$$= \frac{1}{A}\left[R\left[\frac{\alpha}{(1-\alpha)}\frac{W}{R}\right]^{1-\alpha} + W\left[\frac{(1-\alpha)}{\alpha}\frac{R}{W}\right]^{\alpha}\right]$$

Notice that this expression for marginal cost consists only of constants (A, α, W, and R). So, long-run marginal cost is constant for this production function. What is more, average total cost for this production function is exactly the same as marginal cost—you should be able to show this by dividing TC by Q. Both of these results (constant marginal cost and $MC = ATC$) are unique to firms with constant returns to scale. If these firms want to double output, they have to double labor and capital. This, in turn, doubles the firms' costs, leaving *average* total cost—total cost divided by total inputs—unchanged. If the firm does not face constant returns to scale, these results will not hold true. In particular, a firm with decreasing returns to scale would see increasing long-run marginal costs, while a firm with increasing returns to scale faces decreasing long-run marginal costs.

figure it out 7A.1

Let's revisit Figure It Out 7.4. Steve and Sons Solar Panels has a production function of $Q = 4KL$ and faces a wage rate of $8 per hour and a rental rate of capital of $10 per hour. Assume that, in the short run, capital is fixed at $\bar{K} = 10$.

a. Derive the short-run total cost curve for the firm. What is the short-run total cost of producing $Q = 200$ units?

b. Derive expressions for the firm's short-run average total cost, average fixed cost, average variable cost, and marginal cost.

c. Derive the long-run total cost curve for the firm. What is the long-run total cost of producing $Q = 200$ units?

d. Derive expressions for the firm's long-run average total cost and marginal cost.

Solution:

a. To get the short-run total cost function, we need to first find L as a function of Q. The short-run production function can be found by substituting $\bar{K} = 10$ into the production function:

$$Q = 4\bar{K}L = 4(10)(L) = 40L$$

Therefore, the firm's short-run demand for labor is

$$L = 0.025Q$$

Now plug $\bar{K}$ and L into the total cost function:

$$TC_{SR} = R\bar{K} + WL = 10(10) + 8(0.025Q)$$
$$TC_{SR} = 100 + 0.2Q$$

This is the equation for the short-run total cost curve with fixed cost FC equal to 100 and variable cost VC equal to $0.2Q$. Notice that the fixed cost is just the total cost of capital, $R\bar{K} = 10(10) = \$100$. The short-run total cost of producing 200 units of output is

$$TC_{SR} = 100 + 0.2(200) = \$140$$

b. Average costs are a firm's costs divided by the quantity produced. Hence, the average total cost, average fixed cost, and average variable cost measures for this total cost function are

$$ATC_{SR} = \frac{TC}{Q} = \frac{100 + 0.2Q}{Q} = \frac{100}{Q} + 0.2$$

$$AFC_{SR} = \frac{FC}{Q} = \frac{100}{Q}$$

$$AVC_{SR} = \frac{VC}{Q} = \frac{0.2Q}{Q} = 0.2$$

Marginal cost is the derivative of total cost with respect to quantity, or

$$MC_{SR} = \frac{dTC}{dQ} = 0.2$$

Marginal cost for Steve and Sons is constant and equal to average variable cost in the short run because the marginal product of labor is constant when capital is fixed.

c. In the long run, Steve and Sons solves its cost-minimization problem:

$$\min_{K,L} TC = 10K + 8L \text{ s.t. } Q = 4KL \quad \text{or}$$

$$\min_{K,L,\lambda} \mathcal{L}(K,L,\lambda) = 10K + 8L + \lambda(Q - 4KL)$$

The first-order conditions are

$$\frac{\partial \mathcal{L}}{\partial K} = 10 - \lambda(4L) = 0$$

$$\frac{\partial \mathcal{L}}{\partial L} = 8 - \lambda(4K) = 0$$

$$\frac{\partial \mathcal{L}}{\partial \lambda} = Q - 4KL = 0$$

To find the optimal levels of labor and capital, we need to set the first two conditions equal to solve for K as a function of L:

$$\lambda = \frac{10}{4L} = \frac{8}{4K}$$

$$40K = 32L$$

$$K = 0.8L$$

To find the firm's long-run labor demand, we plug this expression for K as a function of L into the production function and solve for L:

$$Q = 4KL = 4(0.8L)L = 3.2L^2$$

$$L^2 = 0.31Q$$

$$L = 0.56Q^{0.5}$$

To find the firm's long-run demand for capital, we simply plug the labor demand into our expression for K as a function of L:

$$K = 0.8L = 0.8(0.56Q^{0.5})$$

$$= 0.45Q^{0.5}$$

The firm's long-run total cost function can be derived by plugging the firm's long-run input demands L and K into the long-run total cost function:

$$TC_{LR} = RK + WL = 10(0.45Q^{0.5}) + 8(0.56Q^{0.5})$$

$$= 8.98Q^{0.5}$$

Therefore, the cost for producing 200 units of output in the long run is

$$TC_{LR} = 8.98(200)^{0.5} \approx \$127$$

d. We can also find the long-run marginal and average total costs for this firm:

$$MC_{LR} = \frac{dTC}{dQ} = 4.49Q^{-0.5}$$

$$ATC_{LR} = \frac{TC}{Q} = \frac{8.98Q^{0.5}}{Q} = 8.98Q^{-0.5}$$

Notice that marginal cost in this case decreases as output increases. Furthermore, $MC < ATC$ for all levels of output. This is because Steve and Sons' production function, $Q = 4KL$, exhibits increasing returns to scale at all levels of output.

Problems

1. A firm has a production function of $Q = 0.25KL^{0.5}$, the rental rate of capital is $100, and the wage rate is $25. In the short run, $\bar{K}$ is fixed at 100 units.

   a. What is the short-run production function?

   b. What is the short-run demand for labor?

   c. What are the firm's short-run total cost and short-run marginal cost?

2. Margarita Robotics has a daily production function given by $Q = K^{0.5}L^{0.5}$, where K is the monthly number of hours of use for a precision lathe (capital) and L is the monthly number of machinist hours (labor). Suppose that each unit of capital costs $40, and each unit of labor costs $10.

   a. In the short run, $\bar{K}$ is fixed at 16,000 hours. What is the short-run demand for labor?

   b. Given that $\bar{K}$ is fixed at 16,000 hours, what are total cost, average total cost, average variable cost, and marginal cost in the short run?

   c. What are the long-run demands for capital and labor?

   d. Derive total cost, average cost, and marginal cost in the long run.

   e. How do Margarita Robotics' marginal and average costs change with increases in output? Explain.

3. A firm has a production function given by $Q = 10K^{0.25}L^{0.25}$. Suppose that each unit of capital costs R and each unit of labor costs W.

   a. Derive the long-run demands for capital and labor.

   b. Derive the total cost curve for this firm.

   c. Derive the long-run average and marginal cost curves.

   d. How do marginal and average costs change with increases in output? Explain.

   e. Confirm that the value of the Lagrange multiplier you get from the cost-minimization problem in part (a) is equal to the marginal cost curve you found in part (c).

Supply in a Competitive Market

Raising chickens in urban areas is a new trend among fans of locally produced food. Suppose Ty is an aspiring urban farmer who must decide how many chickens to raise in his backyard. He might eat a few of the eggs and an occasional chicken himself, but he plans to sell most of his eggs at local markets. In essence, Ty is starting a firm, and he is facing the same production decisions that any firm faces. How many chickens Ty raises isn't going to noticeably affect the total supply of eggs or chicken in the market. Thousands of people raise chickens in their backyards, and there are also large farms that supply chickens and eggs to the market. How many chickens Ty raises *is* going to affect his profits, however. So, how should Ty—or any firm—make production decisions?

In Chapters 6 and 7, we learned how a firm chooses an input mix to minimize the cost of producing a particular amount of output and how this minimum cost changes with the output level. In this chapter, we explore how a firm chooses how much output to produce. In doing this, we move from talking about a firm's cost-minimizing behavior to a discussion of how a firm chooses an output level to maximize its profits. This choice gives us the supply curves we learned about in Chapters 2 and 3.

Although all firms use knowledge of marginal revenue, marginal costs, and prices to guide their actions, profit-maximizing behavior is different for different types of firms. We begin the chapter by explaining the different types of market structures within which firms operate and what competition truly means. For most of this chapter, we both focus on **perfect competition**, *a market (or industry) in which many firms produce an identical product and there are no barriers to entry*, and explore how firms behave in a perfectly competitive industry to maximize their profits.

perfect competition
A market (or industry) in which many firms produce an identical product and there are no barriers to entry.

8.1 Market Structures and Perfect Competition in the Short Run

To say more about how a firm makes its production decisions, it is useful to think about its **market structure**, *the competitive environment in which the firm operates*. There are four different types of markets that we explore in the next several chapters: perfect competition, monopolistic competition, oligopoly, and monopoly.

We categorize a market or industry using three primary characteristics:

- **Number of firms.** Generally, the more companies in the market, the more competitive it is.

- **Whether the consumer cares which company made the good.** In general, the more indistinguishable or identical the products are, the more competitive the market is.

- **Barriers to entry.** If new firms can enter a market easily, the market is more competitive.

market structure The competitive environment in which firms operate.

Table 8.1 Four Basic Market Structures

	Perfect Competition	Monopolistic Competition	Oligopoly	Monopoly
Number of Firms	Many	Many	Few	One
Type of Products Sold	Identical	Differentiated	Identical or differentiated	Unique
Barriers to Entry	None	None	Some	Many

Table 8.1 describes each market structure using these characteristics. They tell us a lot about the production decisions of firms in a given industry. For example, firms that can differentiate their products may be able to convince some consumers to pay a higher price for their products than for products made by their competitors. The ability to influence the price of their products has important implications for these firms' decisions. Only firms in a perfectly competitive market lack the ability to influence the price of their products; they take as given whatever price is determined by the forces of supply and demand at work in the wider market. A truly perfectly competitive market is rare but offers many useful lessons about how a market works (just as the supply and demand framework did before). In this chapter, we focus on perfectly competitive markets. In Chapters 9 and 10, we will look at monopoly and how monopolies can use different strategies to gain more profit, and in Chapter 11, we will examine market structures that fall in between perfect competition and monopoly.

Perfect Competition

Here's how the three primary market characteristics look in a perfectly competitive market (Table 8.1):

- **Number of Firms.** There needs to be a large number of firms so that no one firm has any impact on the market equilibrium price by itself. Thus, any one firm can change its behavior without changing the overall market equilibrium.

- **Types of Products Sold.** All firms produce an identical product. By identical, we don't just mean that all the firms make televisions or all the firms make smoothies. We mean the consumers view the output of the different producers as perfect substitutes and do not care who made it. This assumption is more accurate for nails or gasoline or bananas, but less accurate for smartphones or automobiles.

- **Barriers to Entry.** There are no barriers to entry. If someone decides she wants to start selling nails tomorrow, nothing prevents her from doing it.

The key economic implication of these three assumptions is that firms don't have a choice about what price to charge. If the firm charges a price above the market price, it will not sell any of its output. (We'll show you the math behind this result later in this section.) And because we assume that the firm is small enough relative to the industry that it can sell as much output as it wants at the market price, it will never choose to charge a price below the market price. For that reason, economists call perfectly competitive firms *price takers*. Their price is determined solely by the forces of supply and demand in the market, and they take that price as given when making decisions about how much to produce.

The classic example of a firm operating in a perfectly competitive market is a farmer who produces a commodity crop, such as soybeans. Because an individual farmer's output is tiny relative to total production for the entire market, the choice of how much to produce (or whether to produce at all) isn't going to create movements along the industry's demand curve. One farmer's decision to sell part or all of her soybean crop will not affect the price of soybeans. The *combined* effect of many soybean farmers' decisions *will* affect the market price, however, just as everyone in a city simultaneously turning on their faucets might cause water pressure throughout the city to drop. The key is that the city's water pressure won't fluctuate simply because one person decides to take a shower.

Note one important thing: A large number of firms in an industry does not automatically mean the industry is perfectly competitive. In the United States, for example, there are over 2,000 firms that sell ready-mixed concrete (the fluid form of concrete delivered to construction sites in the familiar barrel-shaped mixer trucks). The output of any one of these firms is small relative to all the concrete sold in a year. Still, these firms are probably not price takers; they choose the prices they charge for their products, despite their small size relative to the overall market because their products are not actually identical; you can't ship concrete very far because it's heavy and perishable. So, the concrete from a firm in one town can't be substituted easily for that of a firm in another town (or in some cases, a firm on the other end of the same town) even if the concrete mix is the same. This product differentiation makes the markets for these products less than perfectly competitive and gives concrete firms some market power—that is, the ability to set their own price. On the other hand, the outputs of perfectly competitive firms are perceived by consumers to be exactly the same and perfect substitutes: A soybean is a soybean is a soybean. The identity of the soybean's producer doesn't matter.

Why Perfectly Competitive Markets Are Important to Study, Even if Rare in Real Life

If firms have to meet such strict criteria to be considered perfectly competitive, you might wonder why we bother studying them. First, a few perfectly competitive markets exist, and it's useful to know how they work (maybe you've dreamed of farming soybeans). There are many more that are *almost* perfectly competitive, and the perfect competition model provides a fairly good idea about how these markets work, too.

Second, though, and more important, perfect competition is a benchmark against which economists measure the efficiency of other market structures. Perfectly competitive markets are, in a specific sense, the most efficient markets (as we see later in this chapter). In competitive markets, goods sell at their marginal costs, firms produce at the lowest cost possible, and combined producer and consumer surplus is at its largest. Comparing a market to the outcome under perfect competition is a way to measure how efficient a market is.

The Demand Curve as Seen by a Price Taker

Let's again think about Ty, the urban egg man. The price for a dozen Grade-A large eggs gets set by the market supply and demand. Panel a of **Figure 8.1** shows the perfectly competitive market for Grade-A large eggs. Quantity demanded equals quantity supplied at the equilibrium market price of $2.25 per dozen.

As a producer in this market, Ty can sell all the eggs his hens can produce as long as he is willing to sell them at $2.25 per dozen. He can't sell them for more than that price

---

Figure 8.1   Market and Firm Demand in Perfect Competition

(a) In the perfectly competitive market for Grade-A large eggs, farmers supply millions of dozens of eggs at a market price of $2.25 per dozen.
(b) Ty, an individual supplier of dozens of eggs in the market, must sell at the price set by the market. Hence, he faces a perfectly elastic demand curve, d, at the market price of $2.25 per dozen (we use lower case to denote the demand for an individual firm).

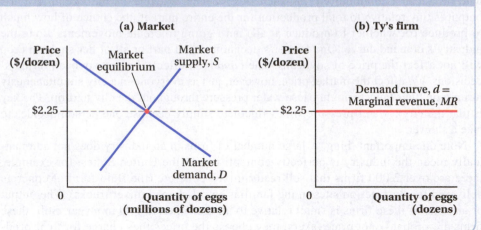

because, from a consumer's standpoint, a Grade-A large egg is a Grade-A large egg (perfect substitutes). If he insists on charging $2.30 per dozen, consumers will just buy other producers' identical eggs at the market price of $2.25 per dozen. At the same time, Ty has no incentive to lower his price below $2.25. He can already sell all the eggs he wants to at that price because his hens' output is such a tiny fraction of what is available on the market (you can see this by looking at the quantity axis for Ty's firm: He supplies dozens of eggs, while the market has *millions* of dozens of eggs)—he's not going to drive down the market price by selling a few more (or a few hundred more) dozen eggs, so why make less money?

This means the demand curve Ty (or any other egg farmer like him) faces personally is horizontal—that is, perfectly elastic—at a price of $2.25 (panel b of Figure 8.1). This logic holds for any firm in any perfectly competitive market: *The demand curve facing a firm in a perfectly competitive market is perfectly elastic at the market equilibrium price.*

8.2 Profit Maximization in a Perfectly Competitive Market

Any perfectly competitive firm thus sells at the price set by the market. Perfectly competitive firms then have one decision to make: the quantity to supply. Economists usually assume firms choose their actions—such as how much output to produce—to maximize profits. **Profit** is the *difference between a firm's revenue and its total cost*. What does it mean to maximize profit? A firm does this by choosing the output level at which the difference between its total revenue and its total cost is largest. In this section, we will see that a perfectly competitive firm maximizes its profit when it produces the quantity of output at which the marginal cost of production equals the market price.

profit The difference between a firm's revenue and its total cost.

Total Revenue, Total Cost, and Profit Maximization

There are two basic elements to profit: revenue and cost. In general, these are both affected by a firm's decisions about how much output to produce and the price it will charge for its output. Because perfectly competitive firms take the market price as given, we only need to focus on the choice of output.

Mathematically, let's denote the profit a firm makes as π. The profit function is total revenue TR minus total cost TC (each of which is determined by the firm's output quantity):

$$\pi = TR - TC$$

To figure out the level of output that maximizes profit, think about what happens to total cost and total revenue if the firm decides to produce one additional unit of output. Or, put differently, determine the firm's marginal cost and marginal revenue.

We know from Chapter 7 that marginal cost is the addition to total cost of producing one more unit of output:

$$MC = \Delta TC / \Delta Q$$

Marginal cost is always greater than zero—it takes more inputs to make more output.

Revenues equal the good's price times the quantity produced. A firm's **marginal revenue** is the *additional revenue it gets from selling one additional unit of output*:

$$MR = \Delta TR / \Delta Q$$

A perfectly competitive firm's marginal revenue is the market price for the good. To see why, remember that these firms can only sell their goods at the market price P. Therefore, the extra revenue they obtain from selling each additional unit of output is P. This is an extremely important concept, so we'll repeat it here: *In a perfectly competitive market, marginal revenue equals the market price; that is, $MR = P$*:

$$MR_{\text{perfectly competitive}} = \frac{\Delta TR}{\Delta Q} = \frac{\Delta (P \times Q)}{\Delta Q} = P \frac{\Delta Q}{\Delta Q} = P$$

Consider what this outcome implies. Total revenue is $P \times Q$. When a firm is a price taker, P does not change no matter what happens to Q. For a price taker, P is a constant, not a function of Q.

This fact means that a perfectly competitive firm's total revenue is proportional to its output. If output increases by 1 unit, total revenue increases by the price of the product. For this reason, a perfectly competitive firm's total revenue curve is a straight line from the origin, as shown in **Figure 8.2**. For example, if Ty sells another dozen eggs, his total revenue rises by the market price of $2.25. And if he keeps selling more eggs, each additional dozen increases total revenue by another $2.25.

As we'll see in Chapter 9, in market structures other than perfect competition, the price decreases as the quantity the firm produces increases. This introduces an additional factor into our marginal revenue calculation for firms in those other types of markets. The price reduction doesn't happen in perfectly competitive markets because a firm does not affect the market price with its output choice. *So remember, this case of marginal revenue equaling the market price is special: It only applies to firms in perfectly competitive markets.*

How a Perfectly Competitive Firm Maximizes Profit

Let's see how the firm maximizes profits. We know that total cost is always going to rise when output increases (as shown in Figure 8.2)—that is, marginal cost is always positive. Similarly, we know that the firm's marginal revenue here is constant at all quantities and equal to the good's market price. The key impact of changing output on the firm's profit depends on which of these marginal values is larger. If the market price (marginal revenue) is greater than the marginal cost of making another unit of output, then the firm can increase its profit by making and selling another unit, because revenues will go up more than costs. If the market price is less than

marginal revenue The additional revenue from selling one additional unit of output.

Figure 8.2 Profit Maximization for a Perfectly Competitive Firm

Because a perfectly competitive firm faces a constant market price, its total revenue curve is a straight line from the origin with a slope equal to marginal revenue, or the price. At the quantity Q^*, slope of the total revenue curve (price) equals the slope of the total cost curve (marginal cost), and the firm is maximizing profit.

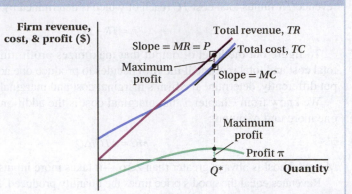

the marginal cost, the firm should not make the extra unit. The firm will reduce its profit by doing so because while its revenues will rise, they won't rise as much as its costs. The quantity at which the marginal revenue (price) from selling one more unit of output just equals the marginal cost of making another unit of output is the point at which a firm maximizes its profit. This point occurs at Q^* in Figure 8.2. There, the slope of the total revenue curve (the marginal revenue — here, the market price) equals the slope of the total cost curve (the marginal cost at Q^*). In mathematical terms, the profit-maximizing level of output occurs where marginal revenue (here, price) equals marginal cost:

$$\frac{\Delta TR}{\Delta Q} = \frac{\Delta TC}{\Delta Q}$$

$$MR = P = MC$$

> The appendix at the end of Chapter 9 uses calculus to solve the perfectly competitive firm's profit-maximization problem.

A firm should increase production as long as revenue increases by more than cost (i.e., when $MR = P > MC$). Conversely, a firm should decrease production if cost increases by more than revenue (i.e., when $MR = P < MC$).[1]

It should be clear from this discussion why cost plays such an important role in determining a firm's output (and this is true for a firm in any type of market structure): It is half of the firm's profit-maximization story. As cost changes, so does the firm's profit-maximizing output. In the next several chapters (which examine firms that are not perfectly competitive), we will learn how the firm's profit maximization is affected by the relationship between price and marginal revenue.

The analysis we've just completed shows that the output decision is fairly easy for the firm in a perfectly competitive market: It increases output until marginal cost equals the market price. If marginal cost rises with output — and in Chapter 7 we discussed the reasons why we might expect this — there will be a certain output level at which marginal cost rises to the market price. This is the profit-maximizing output level of a firm in perfect competition.

The $P = MC$ result is extremely useful because, by linking the market price to the firm's cost curve (or, more precisely, its marginal cost curve), we can determine how a competitive firm's output changes when the market price changes. Consider a firm with

---

[1] Technically, we have to say that $MR = P = MC$ implies profit maximization as long as marginal cost is rising at the quantity where that condition holds. If there were big economies of scale so that MC falls as output rises, the firm could make more profit by further expanding output until $MR = P = MC$ *and MC is rising*.

Figure **8.3** Profit Maximization for a Perfectly Competitive Firm Occurs Where $MR = P = MC$

At the initial market price P_1, the perfectly competitive firm is maximizing profit at Q_1^*, where $P = MC$. If price increases to P_2, the firm should increase output to Q_2^*. If, instead, price decreases to P_3, the firm is maximizing profit at Q_3^*.

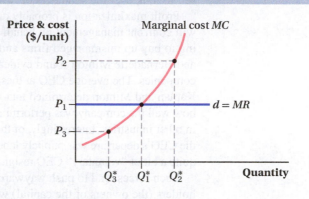

the marginal cost curve shown in **Figure 8.3**. If the market price is initially P_1, then the firm's demand and marginal revenue curve is horizontal at that price. The firm will maximize profit by setting $MR = P_1 = MC$ and producing an output of Q_1^*. If the market price increases to P_2, the firm should increase its production to output Q_2^*. The firm now faces a horizontal demand and marginal revenue curve at P_2, so it should produce up to the point where marginal cost equals the market price. If price rises to P_2 and the firm continues to produce only Q_1, it could be selling those units between Q_1 and Q_2^* at a marginal revenue level (the new market price P_2) that is higher than its marginal costs. These extra sales would raise the firm's profit.

If the market price instead decreases from P_1 to P_3, the firm should reduce its quantity to Q_3^*, which has a lower marginal cost equal to P_3. If the firm does not make this change, it will be producing those units between Q_3^* and Q_1 at a loss because marginal revenue for those units would be lower than marginal cost.

 Application: Do Firms Always Maximize Profits?

You've probably heard stories of CEOs who spend firm money on lavish offices, parties, or other perks. While these CEOs enjoy their spending sprees, it seems far-fetched to think that their behavior benefits the companies' shareholders by increasing profits.

Given such stories, can we really assume that firms maximize profits? It is easiest to see why a small firm would want to maximize profits: Because the manager is usually the owner of the firm, maximizing the firm's profits directly affects her personally. But larger firms are typically run by people other than the owners. As a result, their managers may be tempted to engage in behavior that does not maximize profits. These profit-killing actions don't have to be as blatant as the kind of stories that make the news. A manager might want to raise short-run profit if her compensation package is based on it, at the expense of reductions in future profit. These missed profits could be recognized only after the manager has left the company—or never missed at all, because it may be difficult to tell what profits *should* be. Or, managers might undertake mergers and acquisitions that increase management's power but cost the acquiring firm (and its shareholders) more than the acquisition is worth.

Although managers may sometimes take actions that aren't profit maximizing, there are mechanisms in place to punish that behavior. These include activist shareholders, a nosy financial press, and even the occasional academic economist who takes it upon herself to look over the shoulders of firms' managers and scrutinize their behavior.

Profit maximization is probably driven most directly by a strong board of directors who will confront management on behalf of the shareholders, or other companies that are willing to buy up mismanaged firms and replace their executives. Economists Steven Kaplan and Bernadette Minton found evidence of these forces at work among several large U.S. companies. The average CEO at these firms had been on the job less than seven years, and Kaplan and Minton determined that the likelihood a CEO stayed on the job was related to how well the company was performing relative to its industry competitors and to companies in other industries. Interestingly, of those CEOs who departed, the relationship held whether the CEO's departure was publicly labeled at the time as forced or unforced—suggesting that quite a bit of "voluntary" CEO resignations are anything but.[2]

Such forces tend to push wayward managers back toward maximizing profits, as shareholders (the owners of the capital) would desire. Even if these mechanisms fail, the competitive market itself pushes firms to maximize profit. In competitive markets, firms that maximize profits (or get as close to that as possible) should succeed where firms with profit-killing managers do not. Firms that maximize profits should attract capital more easily, have more money to invest, and take away market share from firms that don't. These are the benefits of perfect competition. ■

Measuring a Firm's Profit

A profit-maximizing firm in a perfectly competitive industry maximizes its profit by producing the quantity at which $P = MC$. But this doesn't tell us anything about the level of profit the firm is earning (or even if it is positive) at this point. To measure profit π, we subtract total cost TC from total revenue TR:

$$\pi = TR - TC$$

Panel a of **Figure 8.4** shows the firm's average total cost curve, its marginal cost curve, and its demand (marginal revenue) curve. The firm's total revenue equals the area of the rectangle with height P and base Q^*. Its total cost is the area of the rectangle with height ATC^* (ATC at the profit-maximizing level of output Q^*) and base Q^*. Because total revenue is greater than total cost at Q^*, the firm is earning a positive level of profit. Substituting the equations for TR and TC into the equation for profit, we see that

$$\pi = TR - TC$$
$$= (P \times Q) - (ATC \times Q)$$
$$= (P - ATC) \times Q$$

Therefore, the firm's profit can be seen in panel a of Figure 8.4 as the rectangle with height $(P - ATC^*)$ and base equal to the profit-maximizing quantity Q^*.

The profit equation tells us that profit $\pi = (P - ATC) \times Q$, and profit is positive only when $P > ATC^*$. If $P = ATC^*$, profit is zero, and when $P < ATC^*$, profit is negative. These scenarios are illustrated in panels b and c of Figure 8.4. Panel b shows that a firm earns zero profit when $P = ATC^* = MC$. In Chapter 7, we learned that $MC = ATC$ only when ATC is at its minimum. (Remember this fact! It will become very important to us toward the end of this chapter.) Panel c of Figure 8.4 shows a firm earning negative profit because $P < ATC^*$. The obvious question is, why would a firm produce anything at a loss? We answer that question in the next section.

[2] Steven N. Kaplan and Bernadette A. Minton, "How Has CEO Turnover Changed?," *International Review of Finance* 12, no. 1 (2012): 57–87.

Figure 8.4   Measuring Profit

Given a firm's marginal cost curve *MC*, average total cost curve *ATC*, and market price *P*, the firm's profit can be measured by the area of the rectangle with length Q^* and height $(P - ATC^*)$.

(a) A firm facing a market price above its average total cost curve at Q^* will earn a positive economic profit, $\pi > 0$.

(b) A firm facing a market price equal to its average total cost at Q^* earns zero economic profit.

(c) A firm with average total cost above the market price, at Q^*, will earn negative economic profit (loss), $\pi < 0$.

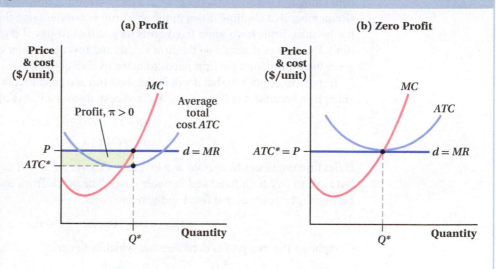

(a) Profit

(b) Zero Profit

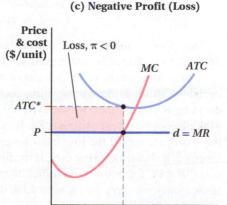

(c) Negative Profit (Loss)

figure it out 8.1

Suppose that consumers see haircuts as an undifferentiated good and that there are hundreds of barbershops in the market. The current market equilibrium price of a haircut is $15. Bob's Barbershop has a daily short-run total cost given by $TC = 0.5Q^2$. The associated marginal cost curve is $MC = Q$.

a. How many haircuts should Bob give each day if he wants to maximize profit?

b. If Bob maximizes profit, how much profit will he earn each day?

Solution:

a. Firms in perfect competition maximize profit by producing the quantity for which $P = MC$:

$P = MC$

$15 = Q$

b. If Bob gives 15 haircuts and charges $15 for each, his total revenue will be

$TR = P \times Q$

$= \$15 \times 15 = \$225$

We can use Bob's total cost function to find the total cost of producing 15 haircuts:

$TC = 0.5Q^2 = 0.5(15)^2 = \$112.50$

Since profit is $TR - TC$,

$\pi = \$225 - \$112.50 = \$112.50$ per day

If Profit Is Negative, Should a Firm Shut Down?

How does a perfectly competitive firm know if it is better off operating at a loss or shutting down and producing zero output? (Remember that shutting down in the short run is not the same thing as exiting the industry, because firms have some fixed costs they still must pay if they shut down in the short run.) The answer depends on the firm's costs and revenues under each scenario. **Table 8.2** gives the information the firm needs to make its decision.

If the firm decides to shut down in the short run and produce nothing, it will have no revenue. But, because it still must pay its fixed cost, its loss will exactly equal that fixed cost:

$$\pi_{\text{shut down}} = TR - TC = TR - (FC + VC)$$
$$= 0 - (FC + 0) = -FC$$

If the firm continues to operate at a loss in the short run, it will accumulate some revenue, but have to pay both fixed and variable costs. The profit from operating is the difference between total revenue and fixed and variable costs:

$$\pi_{\text{operate}} = TR - TC = TR - FC - VC$$

Comparing the two profits demonstrates which is better:

$$\pi_{\text{operate}} - \pi_{\text{shut down}} = TR - FC - VC - (-FC)$$
$$= TR - VC$$

Therefore, in the short run, a firm should operate as long as its revenue is greater than or equal to its *variable* cost, not its total cost ($TR \geq VC$). That's because fixed cost needs to be paid whether the plant operates or not, so it doesn't enter into the operate/shut-down decision. This was the excruciating decision faced by the *Waterworld* movie makers in deciding to release their movie even though they knew it would lose money (Chapter 7). Making enough revenue to cover the firm's variable cost is sufficient to justify operating in the short run, even if the firm can't cover its entire fixed cost, because it would lose more money if it shut down. However, if the firm has total revenue that is lower than its variable cost ($TR < VC$), the firm should shut down. It can't cover its variable cost at this point and loses money on every unit it sells. Like the old joke counsels, if you lose money on every unit, you can't make it up on volume.

The operate-or-shut-down decision can be summed up as follows:

Operate if $TR \geq VC$.

Shut down if $TR < VC$.

Figure 8.5 illustrates these rules. It shows a perfectly competitive firm's average total cost, average variable cost, marginal cost, and marginal revenue (market price) curves. In the case depicted, the firm is losing money because $TR < TC$, but it continues to operate because $TR > VC$. You can see this in the figure because TR is the area of a rectangle where P is the height and Q^* is the base ($TR = P \times Q$), and VC is the rectangle with height AVC^* (AVC at Q^*) and base Q^* ($VC = AVC \times Q$). Both TR and AVC contain Q^*, so this quantity cancels out and plays no role in the operate/shut-down decision. We can now rewrite the rules above in terms of the market price P facing the firm and its average variable cost AVC^* at the profit-maximizing (or in this case loss-minimizing) quantity:

Operate if $P \geq AVC^*$.

Shut down if $P < AVC^*$.

Table 8.2 Deciding Whether to Operate at a Loss or Shut Down in the Short Run		
	Shut Down	**Operate**
Revenue	None	Some (TR)
Cost	Fixed (FC)	Fixed (FC) + Variable (VC)
Loss	−FC	TR − FC − VC

Figure 8.5   Deciding Whether to Operate or Shut Down in the Short Run

At market price P, the firm earns a negative economic profit equal to the area of the rectangle with length Q^* and height $(P - ATC^*)$. Because price is above the firm's average variable cost AVC^* at the profit-maximizing quantity Q^*, however, the firm will continue to operate in the short run. That is because in doing so, the firm can at least cover its variable cost.

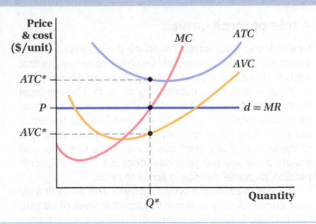

Therefore, the firm should keep operating as long as the market price is at least as large as its average variable cost at the quantity where price equals its marginal cost. Keep in mind that these rules apply to all firms in all industries in any type of market structure.

---

figure it out 8.2

Go online for interactive, step-by-step help in solving the following problem.

Cardboard boxes are produced in a perfectly competitive market. Each identical firm has a short-run total cost curve of $TC = 3Q^3 - 18Q^2 + 30Q + 50$, where Q is measured in thousands of boxes per week. The firm's associated marginal cost curve is $MC = 9Q^2 - 36Q + 30$. Calculate the price below which a firm in the market will not produce any output in the short run (the shut-down price).

Solution:

A firm will not produce any output in the short run at any price below its minimum AVC. How do we find the minimum AVC? We learned in Chapter 7 that AVC is minimized when $AVC = MC$. So, we need to start by figuring out the equation for the average variable cost curve and then solving it for the output that minimizes AVC.

AVC is equal to VC/Q. Remember that total cost is the sum of fixed cost and variable cost:

$$TC = FC + VC$$

Fixed cost is that part of total cost that does not vary with output (changes in Q have no effect on FC). Therefore, if

$TC = 3Q^3 - 18Q^2 + 30Q + 50$, then FC must be 50. This means that $VC = 3Q^3 - 18Q^2 + 30Q$. Because $AVC = VC/Q$,

$$AVC = VC/Q = \frac{3Q^3 - 18Q^2 + 30Q}{Q} = 3Q^2 - 18Q + 30$$

Next, we find the output for which AVC is at its minimum by equating AVC and MC:

$$AVC = MC$$
$$3Q^2 - 18Q + 30 = 9Q^2 - 36Q + 30$$
$$18Q = 6Q^2$$
$$18 = 6Q$$
$$Q = 3$$

This means that AVC is at its minimum at an output of 3,000 cardboard boxes per week. To find the level of AVC at this output, we plug $Q = 3$ into the formula for AVC:

$$AVC = 3Q^2 - 18Q + 30$$
$$= 3(3)^2 - 18(3) + 30 = 27 - 54 + 30 = \$3$$

Therefore, the minimum price at which the firm should operate is $3. If the price falls below $3, the firm should shut down in the short run and only pay its fixed cost.

A⁺ make the grade

A tale of three curves

One of the easiest ways to examine the diagrams of cost curves for a perfectly competitive firm is to remember that each of these cost curves tells only a part of the story.

What is the profit-maximizing output? The marginal cost curve: If you want to know the level of output that maximizes profit for any firm, you need to use the firm's marginal cost curve and equate marginal revenue and marginal cost. For a perfectly competitive firm *only,* you equate price and marginal cost because in perfect competition, marginal revenue is equal to price.

Is the firm earning a positive profit? The average total cost curve: Once you know the optimal level of output, you can use the average total cost curve to compare price and average total cost to determine whether a firm is earning a positive profit. Profit is measured as the rectangle with a base equal to output and a height equal to the difference between *P* and *ATC* at that quantity of output. If a perfectly competitive firm is earning a positive profit,

the story ends there. You don't even need to consider the firm's average variable cost curve.

Operate or shut down? The average variable cost curve: If a firm is earning a loss (negative profit) because its price is less than its average total cost, the decision of whether or not the firm should continue to operate in the short run depends entirely on the relationship between price and average variable cost. Look at the average variable cost curve to determine how these two variables compare at the profit-maximizing/loss-minimizing level of output. If price is greater or equal, the firm should continue to operate; if average variable cost is greater, the firm should shut down.

Knowing which curve is used to answer these questions makes it easier to analyze complicated diagrams and answer questions for homework, quizzes, and exams. Remember that each curve has its own role and focus on that curve to simplify your analysis.

8.3 Perfect Competition in the Short Run

We've just learned that a perfectly competitive firm maximizes its profit where $MR = P = MC$, and that the firm will operate in the short run (even at an economic loss) as long as price is greater than or equal to average variable cost, even if overall that means a negative profit. We can now take our analysis one step further and derive the short-run supply curve for a perfectly competitive firm.

A Firm's Short-Run Supply Curve in a Perfectly Competitive Market

Because the supply curve shows the quantity supplied at any given price, and the firm chooses to produce where $P = MC$, the short-run marginal cost curve *is* the firm's short-run supply curve. *There is one caveat:* Only the portion of the marginal cost curve above the minimum average variable cost will be on the firm's supply curve, because at any price below the minimum average variable cost, the firm would shut down and quantity supplied would be zero.

Figure 8.6 shows that the firm's short-run supply curve is the portion of its marginal cost curve *MC* that is at or above its average variable cost *AVC*, including the portion that is below its average total cost *ATC*. For prices below *AVC*, supply is zero, as shown in the figure. Keep in mind that we hold everything else constant except price and output when deriving the firm's supply curve.

Because of this relationship between marginal cost and the firm's short-run supply curve, anything that changes marginal cost will shift supply. As you may recall from Chapter 7, factors that shift the marginal cost curve include changes in input prices and technology. Note, however, that fixed cost does *not* affect a firm's marginal cost, and therefore changes in fixed cost do not shift the short-run supply curve. In the long run, as we know, no costs are fixed. Every cost is a marginal cost. Later in the chapter, we talk

---

Figure **8.6**   Perfectly Competitive Firm's Short-Run Supply Curve

Because a firm will only operate in the short run when the market price is above its average variable cost curve *AVC*, the perfectly competitive firm's short-run supply curve is the portion of the marginal cost curve *MC* above *AVC*. At prices below *AVC*, the firm shuts down, its quantity supplied is 0, and its supply curve is represented by the *y*-axis.

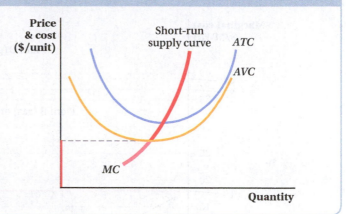

---

about how firms' long-run behavior in perfectly competitive markets differs from their short-run behavior.

Application: The Supply Curve of a Power Plant

Economists Ali Hortaçsu and Steven Puller published a detailed study of the Texas electricity industry.[3] Using data from this study, we can see how to construct the supply curve for a single electricity firm with several electricity plants (**Figure 8.7**). This, along with the supply curves of the other firms in the industry, is a building block of the industry supply curve that we construct later in the chapter.

The first and most important step in deriving the firm's supply curve is to determine its marginal cost curve. In the electric power generation industry, marginal cost reflects the firm's cost of producing one more megawatt of electricity for another hour (this amount of energy, called a *megawatt-hour* [MWh], would power about 1,000 homes for an hour). This marginal cost comes from the firm's variable cost of running its generators at its various power plants—this includes the labor cost of operating and maintaining generators, the cost of environmental permits, and, most important, the cost of fuel.

Our firm has three power plants. Plant A uses coal to power its generator and has a capacity of 200 megawatts (MW); Plants B and C use natural gas and each has a capacity of 25 MW. In this study, coal generators had generally lower costs to operate than natural gas generators.

The marginal cost of running Plant A's coal generator is $18 per MWh, and it is constant across the plant's production quantity up to 200 MW. The plant cannot produce quantities above this level, so the *plant's* marginal cost is, in effect, infinite at quantities greater than 200 MW. Plant B's natural-gas-fired generator has a constant marginal cost of $37 per MWh (up to its 25-MW capacity), and Plant C's natural gas generator has the highest constant marginal cost of $39 per MWh (up to its 25-MW capacity).

If the firm is generating 200 MW or less, only Plant A (its coal plant) will be on line (i.e., producing electricity) because that's the lowest-cost way of generating that quantity. Thus, the firm's marginal cost curve is flat at $18 per MWh for quantities from 0 to 200 MWh, as shown in Figure 8.7.

---

[3] Ali Hortaçsu and Steven L. Puller, "Understanding Strategic Bidding in Multi-Unit Auctions: A Case Study of the Texas Electricity Spot Market," *RAND Journal of Economics* 39, no. 1 (2008): 86–114.

Figure 8.7 **Marginal Cost Curve for an Electricity Firm (Firm 1)**

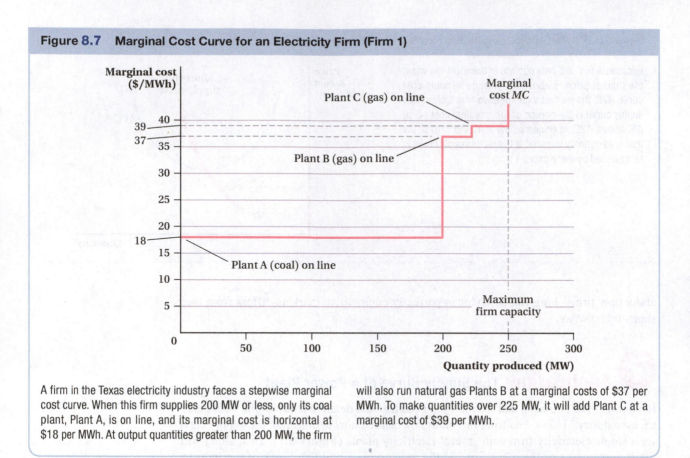

A firm in the Texas electricity industry faces a stepwise marginal cost curve. When this firm supplies 200 MW or less, only its coal plant, Plant A, is on line, and its marginal cost is horizontal at $18 per MWh. At output quantities greater than 200 MW, the firm will also run natural gas Plants B at a marginal costs of $37 per MWh. To make quantities over 225 MW, it will add Plant C at a marginal cost of $39 per MWh.

To generate quantities above 200 MWh, the firm has to use at least one of its other generators. If it wants to produce a quantity between 200 and 225 MWh, it only needs to run one of its natural gas plants, and it will put Plant B on line, the one with the smaller marginal cost of the two, $37 per MWh. Therefore, at a quantity of 200 MWh, the firm's marginal cost curve jumps up to $37 per MWh. It stays at this level up to the quantity of 225 MWh. To produce a quantity above 225 MWh, it needs to put Plant C on line (its natural gas generator with the $39 marginal cost), so the marginal cost curve jumps up to $39 per MWh. The firm's marginal cost remains at $39 per MWh up to the quantity of 250 MWh. At this point, the firm has exhausted its generating capacity and cannot produce any more electricity. Above 250 MWh, the firm's marginal costs effectively become infinite. Figure 8.7 reflects this as a vertical line extending off the graph at 250 MWh.

The portion of this marginal cost curve at or above the firm's average variable cost is its supply curve. We saw in Chapter 7 that a firm's total variable cost at any quantity is the sum of its marginal cost of producing each unit up to and including that quantity. Therefore, the firm's total variable cost of producing its first megawatt-hour is $18, and its average variable cost of producing that quantity is $18 per MWh. Its total variable cost of producing 2 MWh is $36, so its average variable cost is $36/2 = $18 per MWh. It's clear therefore that the average variable cost will be $18 per MWh at quantities up to 200 MWh. In other words, the marginal cost curve *is* the average variable cost curve up to that quantity. When marginal cost rises to $37 per MWh for the 201st MWh the firm produces, the *total* variable cost rises by $37 for 201 MWh, but the average variable cost only rises to ($18 × 200 MWh + $37)/201 MWh = $18.09 per MWh. By this logic, the firm's marginal cost curve will always be above its average variable cost curve at all quantities above 200 MWh. So, for this firm at least, its entire marginal cost curve is its supply curve. ■

The Short-Run Supply Curve for a Perfectly Competitive Industry

We know that an individual firm in a perfectly competitive market cannot affect the price it receives for its output by changing the level of its output, but the combined output decisions of all the firms in the market do — what is referred to as the *industry* supply curve. In this section, we look at how this combined output response is determined.

Before we begin, we must clarify what we mean by the firms' "combined" decisions. What we do *not* mean is "coordinated." Firms in a perfectly competitive market do not gather at an annual convention to determine their output levels for the year, or have an industry newsletter or website that serves the same function (which would, anyway, end up with an arrest for price fixing). Here, "combined" instead means aggregated — the total of all the individual firms' independent output decisions added together. An industry supply curve then indicates how much total output an industry supplies at any particular price.

It's easy to see how you can add up firms' short-run supply curves in an example. We assume that firms' combined output responses do not have any notable impact on *input* prices, so the industry short-run supply curve is the sum of firm-level short-run supply curves. Let's suppose that there are 100 firms in a perfectly competitive industry, each with the same short-run supply curve. Below a market price of $1 per unit, the firms do not operate because this is less than their average variable costs. For prices greater than or equal to $1 and less than $2, each firm supplies 1 unit of output. At any price equal to or above $2, each firm produces 2 units of output, but no more because of capacity limitations. (This is a contrived example, but it keeps things simple enough so that we can concentrate on the concepts rather than the arithmetic.)

To derive the industry short-run supply curve from these firm supply curves, we add up the individual firm outputs at each possible market price. At prices below $1, the industry supplies no output, again because none of its firms can cover its average variable cost at those prices. When the price is between $1 and $2, the industry produces 100 units of output — 1 unit from each of the 100 firms. When the price is at $2 or above, the industry quantity supplied is 200 units because each firm now makes 2 units. Therefore, the short-run supply curve for this industry is 0 units for prices below $1, 100 units for prices at or above $1 but below $2, and 200 units for prices $2 and higher.

The Short-Run Supply Curve: A Graphical Approach   If we use a graphical approach to construct the short-run industry supply curve, the firms' supply curves would look as they do on the left-hand side of **Figure 8.8**. There, we've drawn the short-run supply curve that each of the industry's 100 firms share. To build the industry short-run supply curve,

Figure 8.8   Deriving the Short-Run Industry Supply Curve When Firms Have the Same Costs

*Supply*Firm is the short-run supply curve of each firm in an industry with 100 firms. The short-run industry supply curve, *Supply*Industry, is the horizontal sum of the individual firms' supply curves.

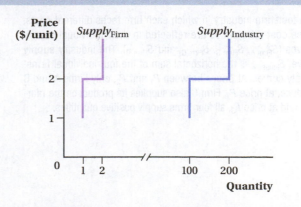

we horizontally add the firm's short-run supply curves: At any given price, we find the individual firms' outputs, add them up, and plot their sum to get the industry quantity supplied. These values yield the industry short-run supply curve on the right-hand side of the figure. Note how individual firms' supply curves are added up horizontally, not vertically, to obtain the industry supply curve, just as individual consumers' demand curves were horizontally added to obtain the market demand curve in Chapter 5.

In Figure 8.8, all industry firms have the same short-run supply curves (this is equivalent to saying they have the same cost curves). The analysis gets more complicated if firms in a perfectly competitive industry have different costs. In this case, the process for determining the industry supply curve is the same (we add up the supply curves of the individual firms), but there are additional ways in which the supply curves of individual firms can affect the shape of the industry supply curve.

To illustrate this point, suppose the industry (which still has 100 firms) has 50 firms with supply curves like those in Figure 8.8 and another 50 that have different supply curves. Let's say these other firms have higher costs and therefore will not produce any output at a market price less than $2. For prices greater than or equal to $2 and less than $3, they produce 1 unit of output, and at prices at or above $3, they produce 2 units. Now the industry supply curve is 0 units for prices under $1 because no firms can profitably produce below that price. For prices from $1 to just under $2, industry supply is 50 units; only the 50 low-cost firms can operate at these prices, and they produce 1 unit each. At prices at or above $2 and less than $3, the industry supplies 150 units: 100 units (50 firms times 2 units each) for the low-cost firms, and 1 unit for each of the 50 high-cost firms. At prices greater than or equal to $3, supply is 200 units because all firms now produce 2 units of output.

In general, the industry supply curve is the horizontal sum of the supply curves of the individual firms within it. The examples above use very simple "step-type" firm-level supply curves, like those in the electricity example. Conceptually, they are the same as the smooth curves that we're accustomed to. In that case, the firms' supply curves would look something like what we've drawn on the left-hand side of **Figure 8.9**. We're assuming there are four firms in the industry, with Firm A having the lowest costs, Firm B the next lowest, and so on. Again, the industry supply curve is the horizontal sum of the firms' supply curves. Only at prices above P_1 does any firm produce, so the industry supplies positive quantities only at price P_1 or higher. For prices between P_1 and P_2, the industry supply curve is the sum of Firm A's and Firm B's supply curves. At P_2, Firm C starts producing. The industry supply curve extends to the right by the quantity that C produces at P_2 when this happens, and Firm C's supply is also added to the industry supply curve above this price. Finally, Firm D starts producing at P_3, and again the industry supply curve extends horizontally as this output is added.

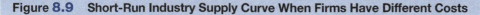

Figure 8.9   Short-Run Industry Supply Curve When Firms Have Different Costs

In a four-firm industry in which each firm faces different costs, these cost differences are reflected in their individual supply curves ($S_{Firm A}$, $S_{Firm B}$, $S_{Firm C}$, and $S_{Firm D}$). The industry supply curve, $S_{Industry}$, is the horizontal sum of the four individual firms' supply curves. At prices between P_1 and P_2, only Firms A and B produce; at price P_2, Firm C also supplies its product on the market; and at price P_3, all four firms supply positive quantities.

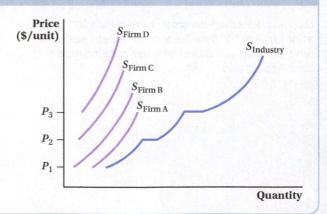

These examples make an interesting point: Industry output increases as price increases for two reasons. One is that individual firms' supply curves are often upward-sloping—an individual firm will tend to produce more as the market price rises. The other comes from the fact that some firms might have higher costs than others, so they only begin operating at higher price levels.

Producer Surplus for a Competitive Firm in the Short Run

The intersection of this short-run *industry* supply curve and the market demand curve determines the market equilibrium price. Each perfectly competitive firm then takes this price as given and chooses the quantity of output at which it maximizes profit (and chooses whether to operate at all). We showed how we can measure a firm's short-run profit earlier. Equally important is producer surplus, which we first learned about in Chapter 3. Remember that producer surplus is the vertical difference between the market price and the supply curve, which we now know reflects firms' marginal costs.

At all but the lowest market price levels, firms will sell some units of output at a price above their marginal cost of production. In the Application on Texas electricity generation, for example, Figure 8.7 shows that if the market price is at or above \$37 per MWh, the firm would be able to sell the electricity generated by its coal plant at a marginal cost of \$18 per MWh at a considerably higher price.

We can see this in a more general case in **Figure 8.10**, which shows the production decision of a particular firm. Profit maximization implies the firm will produce Q^*, the quantity where the firm's marginal cost equals the market price P. Notice that for all units the firm produces before Q^*, the firm's marginal cost of producing them is lower than the market price. The firm earns a markup for each of these units.

If we add up all these price-marginal cost markups across every unit of output the firm makes, we get the firm's producer surplus, the shaded area in panel a of Figure 8.10.

Figure 8.10 Producer Surplus for a Firm in Perfect Competition

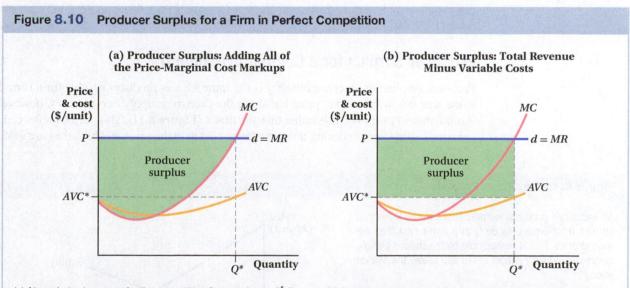

(a) At market price, a perfectly competitive firm produces Q^*. For each unit the firm produces below Q^*, the marginal cost MC is less than the market price, and the firm earns some producer surplus on that unit. As a result, total producer surplus is equal to the area below the demand curve and above MC.

(b) Producer surplus can also be calculated as a firm's total revenue minus its variable cost. A firm's total revenue is the entire rectangle with height P and length Q^*, and its variable cost is the rectangle with height AVC^* and length Q^*. Its producer surplus therefore is the area of the rectangle with height $(P - AVC^*)$ and length Q^*.

If this isn't clear, imagine slicing the shaded area into many tiny vertical slices, one for each unit of output. Each slice equals the difference between the price the unit sells for and the marginal cost of producing it. If we add up all the slices—that is, the price-cost gaps for all the units of output—we get the firm's producer surplus.

There's another way to compute producer surplus. First, remember from Chapter 7 that marginal cost involves only variable cost, not fixed cost. If we add up the firm's marginal cost for all the units of output it produces, we have its variable cost. And if we add up the firm's revenue for every unit of output it produces, we have its total revenue. That means the firm's total revenue minus its variable cost equals the sum of the price-marginal cost markups it earns on every unit it sells—that is, its producer surplus:

$$PS = TR - VC$$

In panel b of Figure 8.10, the firm's total revenue is the area of the rectangle with a height of P and a base of Q^*. Variable cost is output multiplied by average variable cost, so the firm's variable cost is the area of the rectangle with a base of Q^* and a height of AVC^* (AVC at the profit-maximizing level of output). The difference between these two areas is the shaded rectangle with base Q^* and height $(P - AVC^*)$. The area of this rectangle also equals the firm's producer surplus.

Producer Surplus and Profit

You're probably not going to be surprised when we tell you that producer surplus is closely related to profit. But it's important to recognize that producer surplus is *not* the same thing as profit. The difference is that producer surplus includes no fixed costs, while profit does. In mathematical terms, $PS = TR - VC$ and $\pi = TR - VC - FC$.

A new firm may operate with profit less than zero. It will never operate with producer surplus less than zero because that means each unit costs more to produce than it sells for, even without fixed costs. In fact, we can rewrite the firm's shut-down decision that we discussed above in terms of producer surplus: Operate if $PS \geq 0$ (i.e., if $TR \geq VC$) and shut down if $PS < 0$ ($TR < VC$).

Producer Surplus for a Competitive Industry

Producer surplus for an entire industry is the same idea as producer surplus for a firm. It is the area below the market price but above the short-run supply curve—now, however, it is the industry supply curve rather than the firm's (**Figure 8.11**). This surplus reflects the industry's gain from producing units at a lower cost than the price at which they are sold.

Figure 8.11   Industry Producer Surplus

An industry's producer surplus is the entire industry's surplus from producing units at a lower cost than the market price. This is represented by the shaded triangle above the industry supply curve and below the market price P.

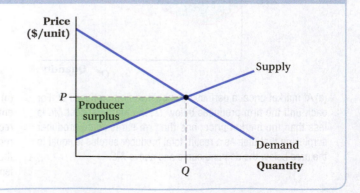

figure it out 8.3

Assume that the pickle industry is perfectly competitive and has 150 producers. One hundred of these producers are "high-cost" producers, each with a short-run supply curve given by $Q_{hc} = 4P$. Fifty of these producers are "low-cost" producers, with a short-run supply curve given by $Q_{lc} = 6P$. Quantities are measured in jars and prices are dollars per jar.

a. Derive the short-run industry supply curve for pickles.

b. If the market demand curve for jars of pickles is given by $Q^D = 6,000 - 300P$, what are the market equilibrium price and quantity of pickles?

c. At the price you found in part (b), how many pickles does each high-cost firm produce? Each low-cost firm?

d. At the price you found in part (b), determine the industry producer surplus.

Solution:

a. To derive the industry short-run supply curve, we need to sum each of the firm short-run supply curves horizontally. In other words, we need to add each firm's quantity supplied at each price. Since there are 100 high-cost firms with identical supply curves, we can sum them simply by multiplying the firm supply curve by 100:

$$Q_{hc} = 100Q_{hc} = 100(4P) = 400P$$

Similarly, we can get the supply of the 50 low-cost firms by summing their individual supply curves or by multiplying the curve of one firm by 50 (since these 50 firms are assumed to have identical supply curves):

$$Q_{lc} = 50Q_{lc} = 50(6P) = 300P$$

The short-run industry supply curve is the sum of the supply by high-cost producers and the supply of low-cost producers:

$$Q^S = Q_{hc} + Q_{lc} = 400P + 300P = 700P$$

b. Market equilibrium occurs where quantity demanded is equal to quantity supplied:

$$Q^D = Q^S$$
$$6,000 - 300P = 700P$$
$$1,000P = 6,000$$
$$P^* = \$6$$

The equilibrium quantity can be found by substituting $P = \$6$ into either the market demand or supply equation:

$$Q^D = 6,000 - 300P^* \qquad Q^S = 700P^*$$
$$= 6,000 - 300(6) \qquad = 700(6)$$
$$Q^* = 4,200 \text{ jars} \qquad Q^* = 4,200 \text{ jars}$$

c. At a price of $6, each high-cost producer will produce $Q_{hc} = 4P = 4(6) = 24$, while each low-cost producer will produce $Q_{lc} = 6P = 6(6) = 36$ jars.

d. The easiest way to calculate industry producer surplus is to graph the industry supply curve. Producer surplus is the area below the market price but above the short-run industry supply curve. In the figure below, this is the triangle with a base of 4,200 (the equilibrium quantity at a price of $6) and a height of $6:

$$PS = \frac{1}{2} \times \text{base} \times \text{height} = (0.5)(4,200)(\$6) = \$12,600$$

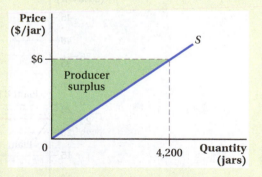

Application: Short-Run Industry Supply and Producer Surplus in Electricity Generation

Let's suppose that in the Application on the Texas electricity industry introduced earlier in this section, Firm 1 is in an industry with two other firms. (In reality, the Texas electricity industry comprises many firms, but we have chosen three to make it less complicated.) Like Firm 1, Firm 2 has both coal and natural gas plants, and it relies on its relatively low-cost coal plant up to its production capacity of 675 MW. To produce quantities above that, Firm 2 needs to also operate its natural gas generators. Firm 3, on the other hand, has only natural gas generators, though each has a different marginal cost. The three panels of **Figure 8.12** show each firm's marginal cost curve.

Figure 8.12 Differing Marginal Cost Curves across Electricity Producers

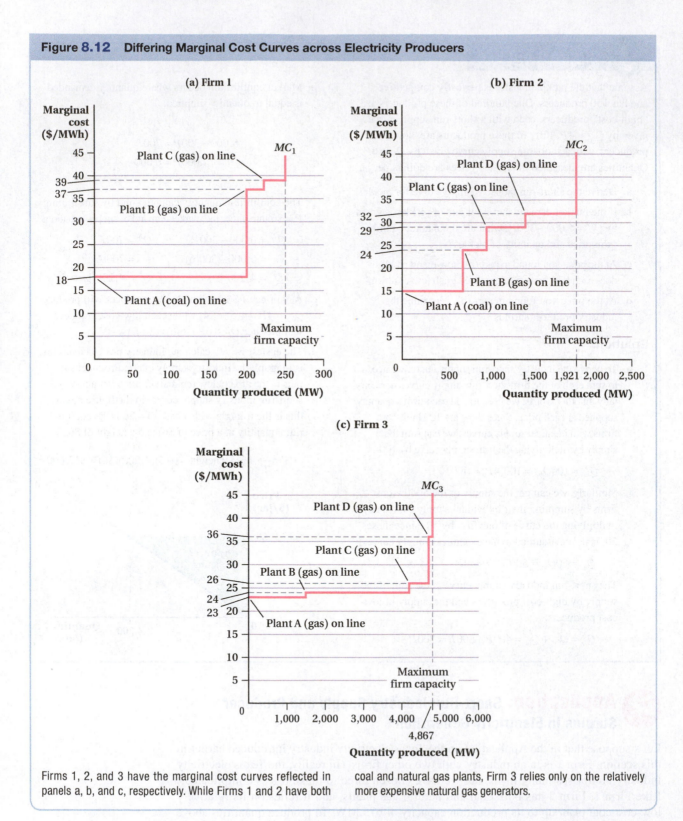

Firms 1, 2, and 3 have the marginal cost curves reflected in panels a, b, and c, respectively. While Firms 1 and 2 have both coal and natural gas plants, Firm 3 relies only on the relatively more expensive natural gas generators.

Figure 8.13   Short-Run Supply of Electricity in Texas

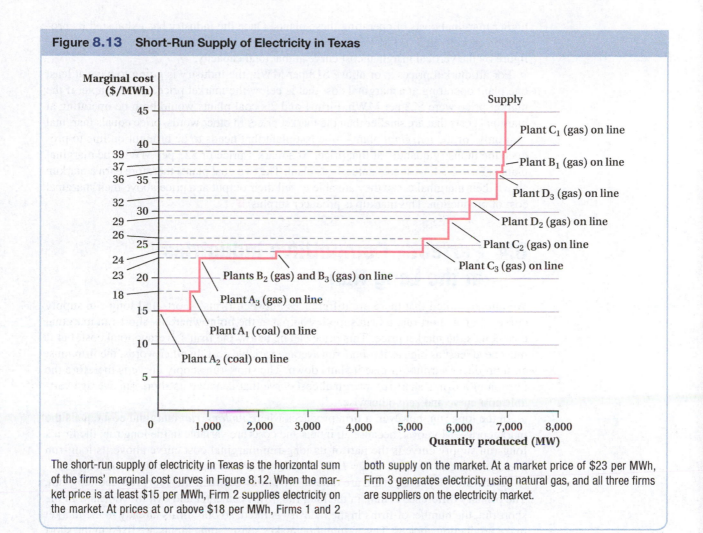

The short-run supply of electricity in Texas is the horizontal sum of the firms' marginal cost curves in Figure 8.12. When the market price is at least $15 per MWh, Firm 2 supplies electricity on the market. At prices at or above $18 per MWh, Firms 1 and 2 both supply on the market. At a market price of $23 per MWh, Firm 3 generates electricity using natural gas, and all three firms are suppliers on the electricity market.

We can construct the industry marginal cost curve by finding the horizontal sum of the three firms' individual marginal cost curves. This is demonstrated in **Figure 8.13**. As was true for Firm 1's marginal cost curve, the industry will rely first on generators with relatively cheaper marginal costs. In other words, the industry will first use all available coal generators. For the first 675 MW, only Firm 2's coal plant operates, because it has the lowest marginal cost of all the industry's plants ($15 per MWh). If a higher quantity is produced, Firm 1 brings its 200-MW coal plant on line, raising the industry's marginal cost to $18 per MWh. At quantities above 875 MW (the combined capacity of the industry's coal-fired plants), Firm 3, which has the lowest-marginal-cost natural gas plant, at $23 per MWh, also starts generating power. Once that plant's 1500-MW capacity is used up—that is, when the industry is producing more than 2,375 MW—the industry marginal cost curve shifts up again as more plants are brought on line. Notice that this next step up in the industry marginal cost curve (to $24 per MWh) actually reflects the total production capacity of two plants, one each from Firms 2 and 3, because both these firms have generators that operate at this same marginal cost. The horizontal summation of the three firms' supply curves continues as the industry must bring additional plants on line to produce higher and higher quantities, and the industry marginal cost curve shifts up to reflect the higher marginal costs of operating these plants. Once the industry has exhausted its production capacity at 7,038 MWh, its marginal costs become infinite. This is reflected in the figure by the vertical marginal cost curve at that total capacity.

For all market prices at or above $18 per MWh, the industry is going to have at least one plant operating at a marginal cost that is below the market price. For example, if the market price were $23 per MWh, Firm 1 and 2's coal plants would both be operating at marginal costs that are smaller than the market price. In other words, price equals marginal cost only for the *marginal* plant—the last plant that needs to be brought on line to produce the industry quantity at that price. At a market price of $23 per MWh, the marginal plant is Firm 3's lowest-cost natural gas plant. The two coal plants therefore earn a markup above their marginal costs; they are able to sell their output at a price above their marginal cost of production. This markup is producer surplus. ■

8.4 Perfectly Competitive Industries in the Long Run

We already noted that there are differences between firms' short- and long-run supply curves. In the short run, a firm supplies output at the point where its short-run marginal cost equals the market price. This price can be below the firm's average total cost, but it must be at least as high as its short-run average variable cost. In other words, the firm must earn producer surplus, or else it shuts down. The short-run supply curve is therefore the portion of a firm's short-run marginal cost curve that is above its short-run average variable cost curve and zero otherwise.

In the long run, however, a firm produces where its *long-run* marginal cost equals the market price. Moreover, because all inputs and costs are variable in the long run, the firm's long-run supply curve is the part of its long-run marginal cost curve above its long-run average total cost curve ($LATC = LAVC$ because there are no fixed costs in the long run).

At the industry level, there are other distinctions between the short run and long run. The primary difference is that, in the long run, firms can enter and exit the industry. In the short run, the number of firms in the industry is fixed, so only firms already in the market make production choices. This assumption makes sense; some inputs are fixed in the short run, making it difficult for new firms to start producing on a whim or for existing firms to avoid paying a fixed cost. In the long run, though, firms can enter or leave the industry in response to changes in profitability. In this section, we learn how this process works and what it implies about how competitive industries look in the long run.

Entry

Firms decide to enter or exit a market depending on whether they expect their action to be profitable. Think about a firm that is considering entering a perfectly competitive market. For simplicity, assume that all firms in the market, including this and any other potential entrants, have the same cost curves. (We look at what happens when firms have different costs later.)

Figure 8.14 shows the current market price and long-run cost curves for a typical firm in this industry. A profit-maximizing firm would produce the quantity where its long-run marginal cost curve equals the market price. We know that this quantity must be at a point where the firm's (long-run) marginal cost curve is at or above its (long-run) average total cost curve. If the market price is P_1, the firm's profit-maximizing quantity is Q^*, where LMC equals P_1. Notice that because P_1 is greater than the firm's minimum average total cost, the firm is making a profit of $(P_1 - LATC^*)$ on each unit of output.

Figure 8.14   Positive Long-Run Profit

In the long run, a perfectly competitive firm produces only when the market price is equal to or greater than its long-run average total cost $LATC^*$. Here, the firm produces Q^*, market price P_1 equals its long-run marginal cost LMC, and its long-run economic profit equals $(P_1 - LATC^*)$ per unit.

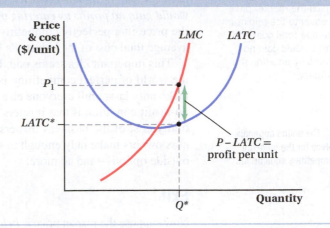

Because firms in this industry are earning positive profits, new firms—whether started anew by entrepreneurs or new divisions of companies already operating in different industries—will want to take advantage of this opportunity by entering the industry. With **free entry**, the *ability of a firm to enter an industry without encountering legal or technical barriers*—which doesn't have to mean "free" in the monetary sense (there can still be startup costs)—the market price will fall until it equals the minimum average total cost. Because the industry's short-run supply curve is derived from the sum of all industry firms' marginal cost curves, adding new firms would cause the industry to provide more output at any given price, as the supply from the new entrants is added to the industry total. In other words, entry shifts the short-run industry supply curve out from S_1 to S_2 (**Figure 8.15**). This outward shift lowers the market price from P_1 to P_2.

If P_2 is still above the minimum average total cost, an incentive remains for more firms to enter because they would make a profit. Entering firms would be making less profit than earlier entrants, but they're still better off entering the market than staying out. New entrants will shift the industry supply curve further out, lowering the market price even further.

This process continues until the last set of entrants drives down the market price to the minimum average total cost and there are no profits to be made by entering the industry. At this point, any potential entrant would be indifferent between entering the industry and

free entry The ability of a firm to enter an industry without encountering legal or technical barriers.

Figure 8.15   Entry of New Firms Increases Supply and Lowers Equilibrium Price

When firms in an industry are earning positive economic profits, new firms will enter, shifting the short-run industry supply curve out from S_1 to S_2 and lowering the market price from P_1 to P_2.

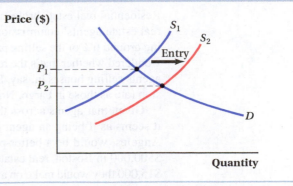

long-run competitive equilibrium The point at which the market price is equal to the minimum average total cost and firms would gain no profits by entering the industry.

➡ The online appendix solves for the long-run competitive equilibrium.

staying out. Entry ceases, and the market is in **long-run competitive equilibrium**, the *point at which the market price is equal to the minimum average total cost and firms would gain no profits by entering the industry*. The bottom line is that if there is free entry, the price in a perfectly competitive industry will be driven down toward the minimum average total cost of the industry's firms, and no firms will make a profit.

This important idea seems odd. If firms make no profit, why bother? The answer is that the world of perfect competition is tough. You may have a good idea, but the profit you make only lasts until everyone else enters and copies it. One thing to remember about this no-profit condition is that it refers to *economic* profit, not accounting profit. The opportunity cost of the business owners' time is included in the firms' costs. It means business owners make only enough to stay in business—that is, to be no worse off than their outside option—and no more.

Exit

free exit The ability of a firm to exit an industry without encountering legal or technical barriers.

Now suppose the market price is *below* the minimum average total cost instead. No firms will enter the industry because they would earn negative profits if they did. Furthermore, firms already in the industry are making negative profits, so this market situation isn't sustainable. If there is **free exit**, the *ability of a firm to exit an industry without encountering legal or technical barriers*, from the market, some of these firms will close up shop and leave the industry. Because we've assumed all firms in the market are the same, all firms are equally unprofitable and would prefer to exit. Which firms exit first? There are two ways to look at how firms make this decision. One is that a lucky few figure out they're losing money before the others, and they leave first. The other, probably more realistic possibility is that cost differences exist between firms and the highest-cost firms exit first. (We'll talk more about this case below.)

This exit from the industry shifts its supply curve in, raising the market price. Exit continues until the market price rises to minimum average total cost. At this point, exiting would not make any firms better off.

Free entry and exit are forces that push the market price in a perfectly competitive industry toward the long-run minimum average total cost. This outcome leads to two important characteristics of the long-run equilibrium in a perfectly competitive market. First, even though the industry's short-run supply curve slopes upward, the industry's *long-run* supply curve is horizontal at the long-run minimum average cost. Remember that a supply curve indicates the quantity supplied at every price. Long-run competitive equilibrium implies that firms produce where price is equal to minimum average total cost.

✈ Application: Entry and Exit at Work in Markets—Residential Real Estate

Residential real estate brokerage in the United States is a peculiar industry. For one thing, real estate agents' commissions are essentially the same everywhere, consistently hovering around 6% of the selling price, even though every city is a different market. Many have wondered whether that's the result of collusion among agents, but regardless of the reason, agents selling houses in, say, Boston, Massachusetts, charge essentially the same commission rate as those in Fargo, North Dakota.

Given that agents across the country are paid the same percentage of the sales price, it seems as if being an agent in a place with higher house prices, such as Boston or Los Angeles, would be a better-paying gig. With an average house selling for a little over $500,000 in Boston, real estate agents get around $30,000 per house. Compare this to the $15,000 they would make on a typical home in Fargo (where the average price is $250,000).

But it turns out that Boston agents pull in approximately the same average yearly salary as those in Fargo, despite the higher house prices. The same pattern holds across the United States: Regardless of house prices, agents' average salaries are roughly equal across cities.

Free entry can explain why this happens, according to economists Chang-Tai Hsieh and Enrico Moretti.[4] They found that more agents enter the expensive markets, so the typical Boston agent sells fewer homes over the course of the year than does the typical agent in Fargo. In other words, as housing prices increase, agents' productivity decreases, and the reduction in houses sold per year in high-house-price cities just about exactly counteracts the higher commission per house. So while average commissions *per house* might be twice as high in Boston as in Fargo, the typical Boston agent sells half the number of houses per year as the typical agent in Fargo. They end up making the same income.

It's not hard to become a real estate agent—spend maybe 30 to 90 hours in the classroom and pass a test, and you'll obtain your license. Therefore, in cities with high housing costs (and high commissions per house sold), more people choose to become real estate agents. Having more agents means each agent sells fewer houses, on average. This drives down agents' average yearly salaries until they are on par with those for agents in other lower-cost cities.

Not only did Hsieh and Moretti find this pattern across cities with different average house prices, they determined that it exists *within* cities over time as well. When housing prices increase in a city, so do the number of agents seeking to sell those houses, keeping average agent salaries from rising along with house prices. If prices fall, the opposite happens: Agents leave the market until the average productivity of those remaining rises to keep salaries at their original level. In this way, entry into and exit from the market keep the long-run average price for agents (i.e., their salaries) more or less constant. Although the constant commission rate still marks residential real estate brokerage as a peculiar business, free entry into the business explains why average salaries are the same. ■

Graphing the Industry Long-Run Supply Curve

Figure 8.16 shows how we can derive the industry long-run supply curve graphically. Suppose the industry (panel a) is currently in equilibrium at a price of P_1. Each firm in the industry (panel b) takes the price as given and maximizes profit by producing where $P_1 = LMC$. Because price equals long-run average total cost, all firms earn zero profit. This means that firms have no incentive to enter or exit the market, so the industry is in long-run competitive equilibrium at P_1.

Now suppose that the demand for the product rises as a result of a change in consumer tastes. This change increases the quantity demanded at each price and the demand curve shifts to D_2. Prices rise temporarily to P_2. As a result, each firm in the industry moves upward along its supply curve LMC to produce a higher quantity where $P_2 = LMC$. This increase in output gets reflected at the industry level as an increase in quantity to the level at the intersection of D_2 and S_1 in panel a. But even after this increase in output among existing industry firms, the market price is still above the firms' minimum $LATC$. As a result, new firms enter the market to take advantage of these economic profits. This shifts the industry quantity supplied at any given price, shifting the short-run industry supply curve to the right. Eventually, the industry returns to long-run equilibrium once the short-run supply shifts to S_2 and the market price falls back to long-run minimum average total cost (P_1). If we connect the two long-run equilibria, we have the industry's long-run supply curve S_{LR}, which is horizontal at P_1.

[4] Chang-Tai Hsieh and Enrico Moretti, "Can Free Entry Be Inefficient? Fixed Commissions and Social Waste in the Real Estate Industry," *Journal of Political Economy* 111, no. 5 (2003): 1076–1122.

Figure **8.16** Deriving the Long-Run Industry Supply Curve

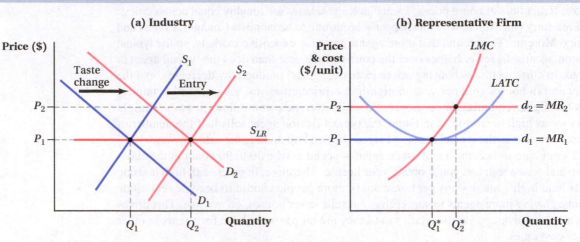

(a) The original long-run equilibrium for an industry is (P_1, Q_1) at the intersection of the long-run supply curve S_{LR} and the original demand curve D_1. After a change in tastes, demand increases to D_2, price increases to P_2, and firms earn positive economic profits in the short run. In the long run, new firms enter the industry, shifting the short-run supply curve to S_2 until it reaches the long-run equilibrium price P_1 at the new equilibrium quantity Q_2.

(b) At the long-run market price P_1, the representative firm earns zero economic profit and produces quantity Q_1^*. When market demand rises, the market price increases to P_2 and the firm's output increases to Q_2^*. At this combination, the firm earns positive economic profit. As entry into the industry occurs, the price falls back to P_1, and the firm reduces its output to Q_1^*. At this point, the firm earns zero economic profit.

FREAKONOMICS

The Not-So-Simple Economics of Blackmail

In 2006 a suspicious envelope arrived at Pepsi headquarters. The envelope wasn't laced with anthrax and didn't contain an explosive booby trap, but the contents *were* potentially deadly to Pepsi's main competitor, the Coca-Cola Corporation. The letter, sent by three Coke employees, offered to sell Coke's closely guarded secret recipe. No doubt, the senders believed Pepsi would greatly value the information and they would soon be rich beyond imagination. Instead, these employees found themselves behind bars, serving up to eight years on conspiracy charges after being caught in an FBI sting operation.

Although their fate must have come as a complete surprise, if the formula stealers had paid more attention to intermediate microeconomics, they might have ended up far better off.

PepsiCo and Coca-Cola have been entrenched in the Cola Wars for decades, and Coke's U.S. market share today is around 40% compared to Pepsi's 30%. In light of that fact, wouldn't Pepsi be desperate to weaken Coke by, say, buying Coke's secret formula and making it public? Most likely, the availability of the formula would cause dozens of new cola manufacturers to enter the market, making perfect

substitutes for Coke, much like generic drug manufacturers enter the market when a prescription drug goes off patent. One might imagine that the market for the Coke version of cola would start to look a whole lot like perfect competition (granted, the advertising-induced mystique surrounding the Coke brand would probably prevent truly perfect competition), and the price of Coke would plunge.

What would such a scenario do to Pepsi's profits? Coke and Pepsi are close substitutes. If the price of Coke falls, the demand for Pepsi falls and, along with it, Pepsi's profits. A (near) perfectly competitive market for Coke would likely be disastrous for Pepsi, not the boon that the formula stealers imagined. Thus, it is no surprise that the executives at Pepsi quickly delivered the letter to Coca-Cola, which then turned it, evidence of the employees' offer to sell Coke's secret formula, over to the FBI.

If the three renegade Coke employees had been better economists, what should they have done differently? For starters, they would have sent the letter not to Pepsi, but to a firm that was thinking of entering the cola market and would greatly value knowing Coke's formula. Crime doesn't always pay; good economic thinking definitely does.

Adjustments between Long-Run Equilibria

In theory, the long-run implication of perfect competition is clear: a price just high enough to cover firms' average total costs. Total industry quantity supplied adjusts through the free flow of firms in and out of the market. In reality, though, getting to the long run can take a long time. When changes in an industry's underlying demand or costs occur, some interesting events can occur while the industry transitions from the old long-run equilibrium to the new one.

A Demand Increase   Suppose an industry, such as cattle ranching, is in long-run equilibrium when the demand for its product unexpectedly rises. As before, let's say this change in demand derives from a change in consumer tastes. That is, at any price, consumers now want to eat more beef. This change shifts out the industry demand curve as we saw in Figure 8.16, which is replicated in panels a and b in **Figure 8.17**. In the short run,

Figure 8.17   Long-Run Adjustments to an Increase in Demand in a Perfectly Competitive Industry

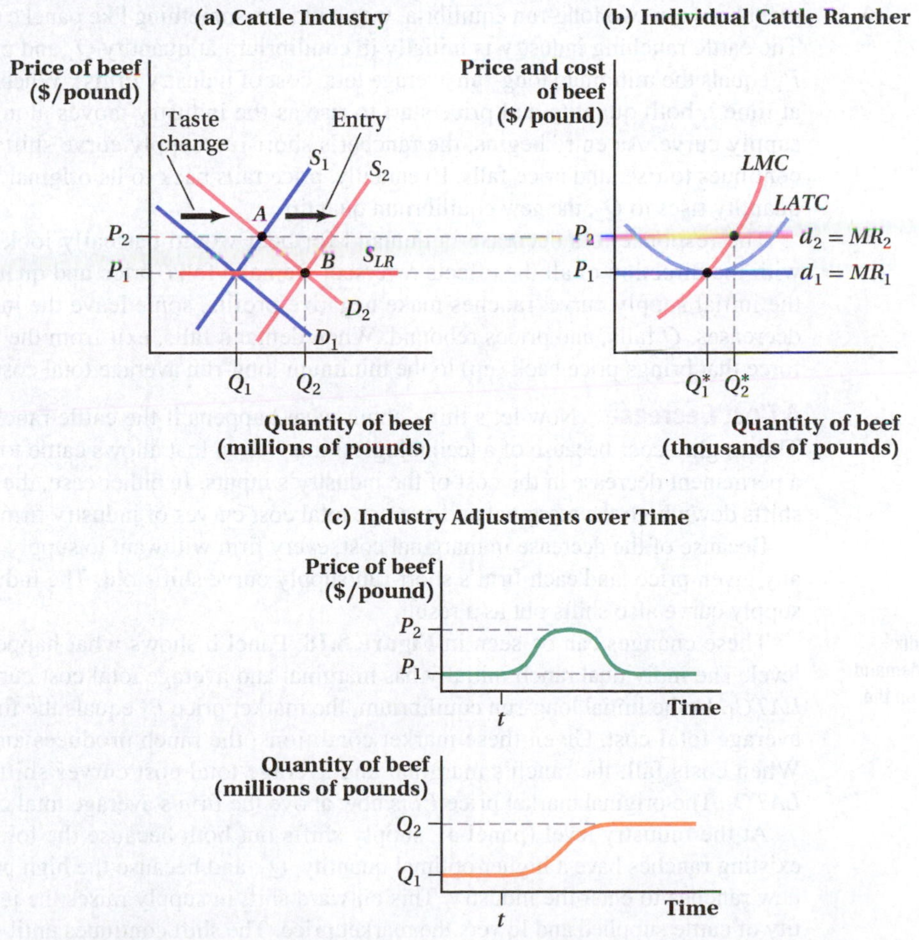

(a) As in Figure 8.16, an increase in the demand for beef will temporarily increase the market price from P_1 to P_2 and induce new ranchers to enter the market to capture the positive profits.
(b) An increase in demand leads to short-run economic profit for a perfectly competitive firm—here, a cattle ranch.

(c) An increase in demand leads to a short-run increase in price. Over time, new ranchers will enter the market, increasing equilibrium quantity to Q_2 and returning the market price to its long-run equilibrium P_1.

when entry is limited, the relevant industry supply curve is the short-run curve S_1. The initial short-term response to the demand increase is an increase in both equilibrium output and the market price to point A as the industry moves up its short-run supply curve.

During this short-run response, ranchers earn positive economic profits and producer surplus because the new price, P_2, exceeds the minimum long-run average total cost. Because price is above average cost, profit is positive, so new firms will enter the market. As new ranchers enter and existing ones expand, the industry's short-run supply curve keeps shifting out, from S_1 to S_2. With the demand curve now stable and fixed at its new level D_2, the entry raises industry output and lowers the market price, and consumers move along their demand curve until the market gets to point B, where the price is back to the minimum average cost level P_1. Total ranching output Q_2 is higher in this new long-run equilibrium because the demand for the industry's product is higher than before, but the price is back to the same old long-run equilibrium. The horizontal line connecting the two long-run equilibria is the industry's long-run supply curve because it reflects the industry's supply response once free entry and exit are accounted for.

If we were to plot the industry's output and market prices over time during this adjustment between two long-run equilibria, we would see something like panel c of Figure 8.17. The cattle ranching industry is initially in equilibrium at quantity Q_1 and price P_1 (where P_1 equals the minimum long-run average total cost of industry firms). When demand shifts at time t, both quantity and price start to rise as the industry moves along its short-run supply curve. As entry begins, the rancher's short-run supply curve shifts out, quantity continues to rise, and price falls. Eventually, price falls back to its original level P_1, while quantity rises to Q_2, the new equilibrium quantity.

The response to a decrease in demand for beef would basically look the same, but with the direction of all the effects reversed: Demand falls, price and quantity fall along the initial supply curve, ranches make negative profits, some leave the industry, supply decreases, Q falls, and prices rebound. When demand falls, exit from the industry is the force that brings price back (up) to the minimum long-run average total cost level.

A Cost Decrease   Now let's think about what happens if the cattle ranches' costs fall. This might occur because of a technological innovation that allows cattle to grow faster or a permanent decrease in the cost of the industry's inputs. In either case, the cost reduction shifts down both the marginal and average total cost curves of industry firms.

Because of the decrease in marginal cost, every firm will want to supply more output at any given price, and each firm's short-run supply curve shifts out. The industry short-run supply curve also shifts out as a result.

➡ The online appendix shows the effects of demand and production costs on the long-run equilibrium.

These changes can be seen in **Figure 8.18**. Panel b shows what happens at the firm level. The individual ranch initially has marginal and average total cost curves LMC_1 and $LATC_1$. In the initial long-run equilibrium, the market price P_1 equals the firm's minimum average total cost. Given these market conditions, the ranch produces an output of Q_1^*. When costs fall, the ranch's marginal and average total cost curves shift to LMC_2 and $LATC_2$. The original market price P_1 is now above the firm's average total cost.

At the industry level (panel a), supply shifts out both because the lower costs mean existing ranches have a higher optimal quantity, Q_2^*, and because the high price P_1 attracts new ranches to enter the industry. This outward shift in supply raises the industry's quantity of cattle supplied and lowers the market price. The shift continues until supply reaches S_2, at which point the market price of cattle has fallen to the new minimum average total cost level P_2.

If we plot the quantity and price changes over time in this case, as in panel c of Figure 8.18, we see that quantity rises and prices fall throughout the transition from the

Figure 8.18   Long-Run Adjustments to a Reduction in Costs in a Perfectly Competitive Industry

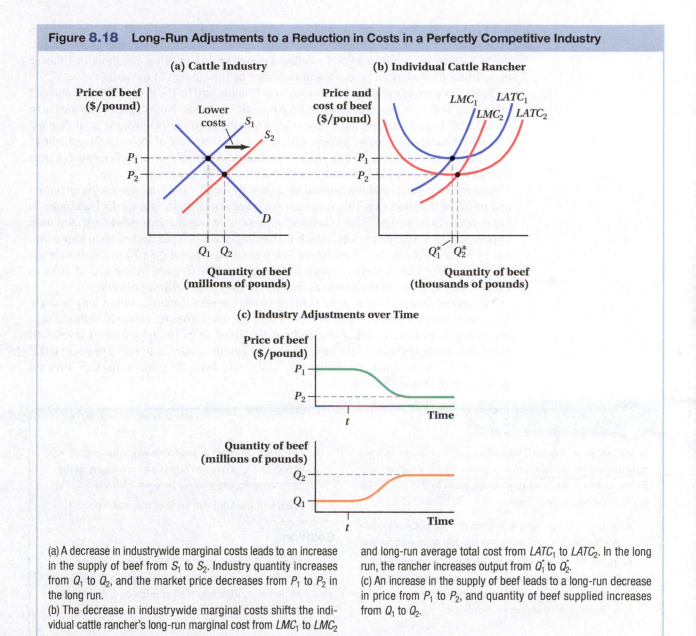

(a) A decrease in industrywide marginal costs leads to an increase in the supply of beef from S_1 to S_2. Industry quantity increases from Q_1 to Q_2, and the market price decreases from P_1 to P_2 in the long run.

(b) The decrease in industrywide marginal costs shifts the individual cattle rancher's long-run marginal cost from LMC_1 to LMC_2

and long-run average total cost from $LATC_1$ to $LATC_2$. In the long run, the rancher increases output from Q_1^* to Q_2^*.

(c) An increase in the supply of beef leads to a long-run decrease in price from P_1 to P_2, and quantity of beef supplied increases from Q_1 to Q_2.

high-cost to the low-cost long-run equilibrium. Here, unlike the response to the demand shift, there is a permanent drop in the long-run price. This happens because long-run costs have declined.

Application: Tariffs and the Decreased Demand for Soybeans

In the second year of the Trump administration, the president imposed 25% import tariffs on over 800 categories of products made in China. The Chinese government responded by imposing their own import tariffs on many American products. Tariffs are taxes that buyers must pay to purchase imported goods, so the Chinese tariffs acted much like the taxes on goods that we studied in Chapter 3. As discussed there, we can interpret a good-specific tax as a downward shift in a good's demand curve. In this case, we can think of Chinese demand for the American products shifting down by the amount of the tariff.

Soybeans were one of the products subject to Chinese tariffs. The drop in Chinese demand effectively shifted in the demand curve for American soybeans. Note that this demand curve includes all buyers, not just the Chinese, so while the tariff shifts down the total demand curve for American soybeans, it doesn't do so by the full amount of the tariff. Nevertheless, it was a substantial demand shift. In the year before the tariffs were implemented, China imported $13 billion of U.S. soybeans, fully half of all U.S. exports of the crop.

Our model predicts that the demand shift from the tariff would decrease soybean output and prices in the short run. This is exactly what happened. In the six weeks leading up to the imposition of the tariffs, as it became apparent that negotiations would not stop their imposition, U.S. soybean prices, which had averaged $10.20 per bushel up to that point, fell by about $2 per bushel. They stayed low thereafter, averaging $8.70 per bushel for the rest of the year. U.S. soybean exports to China basically stopped by the end of 2018 as Chinese buyers replaced their sources, mainly seeking out Brazilian growers.

Our model also predicts that if American farmers expect the tariffs to last long enough, low prices should cause many of them to stop growing soybeans. This will shift the supply of soybeans inward and, if demand remains fixed at its lower post-tariff level, will eventually bring soybean prices back up even as output continues to fall. Time will tell if this long-run prediction holds. Either way, at the very least, the outlook for U.S. soybean growers in 2018 was bleak. ∎

figure it out 8.4

Suppose that the market for cantaloupes is currently in long-run competitive equilibrium at a price of $3 per melon. A listeria outbreak in cantaloupe crops leads to a sharp decline in the demand for cantaloupes.

a. In the short run, what will happen to the price of a cantaloupe? Explain and use a graph to illustrate your answer.

b. In the short run, how will firms respond to the change in price described in part (a)? What will happen to each producer's profit in the short run? Explain, using a diagram to illustrate your answer.

c. Given the situation described in (b), what can we expect to happen to the number of producers in the cantaloupe industry in the long run? Why?

d. What will the long-run price of a cantaloupe be?

Solution:

a. As we can see in panel a of the diagram below, a decline in the demand for cantaloupes will lead to a fall in the equilibrium market price of cantaloupes (from $3 to P_2).

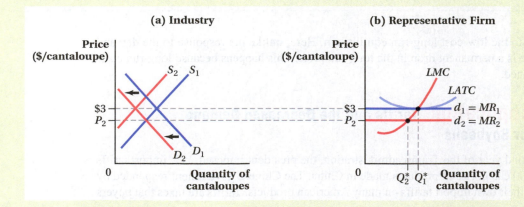

(a) Industry

Price ($/cantaloupe) vs. Quantity of cantaloupes. Curves S_2, S_1, D_2, D_1 with $3 and P_2 marked.

(b) Representative Firm

Price ($/cantaloupe) vs. Quantity of cantaloupes. Curves LMC, $LATC$, $d_1 = MR_1$, $d_2 = MR_2$ with $3 and P_2 marked; Q_2^*, Q_1^*.

b. As shown in panel b, when price declines to P_2, each firm moves along its long-run marginal cost curve to determine its output, which falls from Q_1^* to Q_2^*. Remember that, before the decrease in demand, the industry was in long-run competitive equilibrium so that, at a price of \$3 per cantaloupe, each firm was earning zero economic profit. Therefore, when price falls to P_2, it must be below the firm's average total cost. The drop in demand has led to an economic loss (or negative economic profit) for the firm.

c. If firms are incurring losses, we can expect some to exit the industry. Thus, the number of producers in the industry will fall, the quantity of cantaloupes will fall, and the price will rise.

d. The price of cantaloupes will continue to rise until it is once again at the minimum average total cost of \$3. At this point, the industry is in long-run competitive equilibrium and firms have no incentive to enter or exit the industry.

Long-Run Supply in Constant-, Increasing-, and Decreasing-Cost Industries

We saw above that the long-run supply curve of a perfectly competitive industry is horizontal, at a price equal to the minimum average total cost of its producers. However, that analysis made an implicit assumption that firms' total cost curves didn't change when total industry output did. That is, we assumed a **constant-cost industry**, an *industry whose firms' total costs do not change with total industry output*.

This might not always be the case, as for a firm in an **increasing-cost industry**, an *industry whose firms' total costs increase with increases in industry output*. This might occur because the price of an input rises in response to the industry's higher demand for that input. Suppose an industry requires special capital equipment that is in limited supply. When there is an increase in the industry's output, firms compete for this scarce capital, pushing up its price. This means that the higher industry output, the greater firms' average total costs will be, even in the long run. For this reason, the long-run supply curves of increasing-cost industries are upward-sloping. They're not as steeply sloped as the short-run supply curve for the industry because they account for entry and exit, but they're not horizontal either.

Shifts from one long-run equilibrium to another in response to a demand shift are similar to the case above for a constant-cost industry. The only difference is that entry only brings price back down to the new, higher long-run average total cost level.

A **decreasing-cost industry** is an *industry whose firms' cost levels decrease with increases in industry output*. This might be the case because there are some increasing returns to scale at the industry level, or in the production of one or more of the industry's inputs. The long-run supply curves for these industries are downward-sloping. Again, the short-run transition between long-run equilibria when demand for the industry's product increases looks like the constant-industry case, but now entry continues past the point where the market price is driven down to the old long-run average cost level. Instead, entry continues until the price falls all the way to the new, lower minimum average total cost.

constant-cost industry
An industry whose firms' total costs do not change with total industry output.

increasing-cost industry
An industry whose firms' total costs increase with increases in industry output.

decreasing-cost industry An industry whose firms' cost levels decrease with increases in industry output.

8.5 Producer Surplus, Economic Rents, and Economic Profits

Our analysis of perfect competition has shown that in the long run, perfectly competitive firms earn no economic profit.

Cost Differences and Economic Rent in Perfect Competition

In looking at long-run outcomes in perfectly competitive markets, however, we've assumed that all firms in an industry have the same cost curves. That's not usually true in real life. Firms differ in their production costs for many reasons: They face different prices for their inputs; they have various degrees of special know-how that makes them more efficient; they have a superior location; and so on. When there are cost differences between firms in a perfectly competitive industry, the more efficient producers earn a special type of return called **economic rent**, *returns to specialized inputs above what firms paid for them.*

economic rent Returns to specialized inputs above what firms paid for them.

We saw in Section 8.3 that cost differences among firms is one of the reasons why industry marginal cost curves (and therefore their short-run supply curves) slope up. Higher-cost firms produce only when the market price is high.

To see what happens in the long run when firms have different cost curves, let's first think about how output quantities vary when firms' costs do. If all firms have the same cost, their marginal cost curves are the same. Therefore, their profit-maximizing outputs are the same, too: the quantity at which the market price equals (their common) marginal cost. But if firms have different marginal cost curves, their profit-maximizing outputs will differ as well.

Consider an example in which the factors that cause these firms' costs to differ are specific fixtures of the firm; that is, these costs can't be influenced by the firm's actions or sold to other firms. For instance, the factors might involve access to special technologies no one else has or could use if they were sold. In any case, these factors affect only the cost structure of that particular firm. **Figure 8.19** shows the long-run marginal cost curves for three firms. Firm 1 has a high marginal cost shown by curve LMC_1, Firm 2 has a moderate marginal cost LMC_2, and Firm 3 has a low marginal cost LMC_3. Each firm's marginal cost curve intersects the market price at a different quantity of output. Firm 1's profit-maximizing output is the smallest, Q_1^*. The next largest is Firm 2, which produces Q_2^*. Finally, Firm 3 produces the highest output Q_3^*. Therefore, higher-cost firms produce less, and lower-cost firms produce more, when firms have different costs. This negative relationship between a firm's size (measured by its output) and its cost has been observed in many industries and countries.

Think about the industry's highest-cost firm, Firm 1. Assume that the market price exceeds Firm 1's minimum average total cost. As we discussed above, if all producers have the same cost curve, a perfectly competitive market in which price is above the minimum average total cost will attract new entrants. These entrants shift the industry supply curve out and reduce the price until it equals the minimum average total cost. That's exactly what would happen here, too: If the market price is above Firm 1's minimum average total

---

Figure 8.19 Firms with Different Long-Run Marginal Costs

Firms in the same industry with differing long-run marginal costs will produce different quantities of output at the market price. Because each firm maximizes profit where $P = LMC$, low-cost producers will produce a greater quantity of output (Q_3^*) than high-cost producers (Q_1^*).

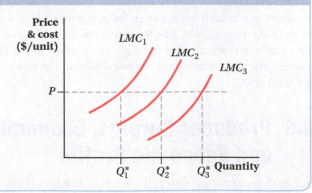

cost, the price is above all producers' minimum average total costs. Therefore, new firms will enter the market. If all of these firms have lower costs than Firm 1, the industry supply curve will shift out until the price falls to the minimum average total cost of Firm 1. If, on the other hand, some entrants have costs *above* Firm 1's cost, entry will occur until the supply curve shifts out only enough to lower the price to the minimum average total cost of the highest cost entrant.

In either case, the important thing to realize is that in a perfectly competitive market where firms have different costs, *the long-run market price equals the minimum average total cost of the marginal firm—the highest-cost firm remaining in the industry.* That highest-cost firm makes zero profit and zero producer surplus. The other firms have minimum average total costs that are lower than the minimum average total cost of the highest-cost firm, and therefore lower than the market price. They make a positive profit on every sale, and this profit is larger the lower their costs. It's just like what we saw in the earlier Application on electricity in Texas: The market price was determined by the marginal cost of the marginal producer, and the lower-cost generating plants could make extra producer surplus at that price. More firms with costs less than those of the highest-cost firm in the market don't enter because there are none. If anyone could make a positive margin over their average total cost on every sale, they would enter. Their entry would shift the industry supply curve out and drive down price enough so that the formerly highest-cost firm in the industry would no longer want to operate because the long-run price would be below its minimum average total cost. Entry would occur until there are no more firms left to enter that have costs below those of the industry's highest-cost firm. Note that if an existing low-cost firm can expand capacity at the existing low-cost level, that's a different form of entry, but is entry nonetheless.

The long-run outcome in an industry in which firms have different costs only occurs once all entry has stopped. All firms except the one on the margin (the one with the highest cost but still producing) sell their output at a price above their long-run average total costs, so they all earn producer surplus and economic rent. This surplus is tied to their special attributes that allow them to produce at a lower cost. As we said earlier, their lower cost could be the result of access to a special technology, better know-how of some sort or another, a better location, or a number of other possibilities. The greater this cost advantage is, the larger the producer surplus or economic rent.

Economic rents measure returns to specialized inputs above what the firms paid for them. Suppose a firm is a lower-cost firm because it was lucky enough to have hired a manager who is particularly smart at efficiently running it. If the firm only needed to pay this manager the same salary as every other firm was paying its manager (or, at least not so much more as to wipe out the cost advantage of the manager's ability), *and* if there is a limited supply of similarly exceptional managers, the manager's human capital earns economic rent for the firm. If the firm is instead lower-cost because it has a favorable location that makes servicing customers easier, like a gas station right off a busy highway, the location is the source of economic rent to the firm because not all firms can use that same location. What's important to recognize is that economic rents are determined by cost differences *relative* to other firms in the industry. That's because the profit earned by the scarce input depends on how much lower the firm's costs are than its competitors' costs. The larger the cost difference, the larger the rent.

Economic Profit Is Not the Same as Economic Rent
At this point, you might be a little confused: Earlier we said that perfectly competitive markets had zero economic profit in the long run, yet now we're saying that firms earn economic rents if they have different costs. Does the zero economic profit outcome only occur if all producers' costs are the same?

Firms in perfectly competitive industries make zero economic profit in the long run even if they have different costs. There is a distinction between economic profit and economic rent. Economic profit counts inputs' opportunity costs, and economic rent is included in the opportunity cost for inputs that earn them. This is because inputs that earn rents would still earn them if they were given to another firm. If we gave another firm the brilliant manager or the better location discussed above, it would lower that firm's costs. That other firm would therefore be willing to pay more for that rent-earning input. This willingness to pay for the economic rent inherent to the input raises the opportunity cost of the input to the firm that currently owns it—by using the input, they're giving up the ability to sell it to another firm. Once this opportunity cost is subtracted from the firm's revenue, its economic profit is no higher than if the input earned no rent at all.

In practice, this is often hugely important. If one firm has lower costs because it has better programmers and engineers than a different firm, the wages paid to the scarce talent may very well end up absorbing the advantage. The rent in such a case goes to the owner of the scarce resource itself (the workers) rather than to the firm.

 Application: Rents and Avocados from Mexico

Avocados from Mexico (AFM) is a consortium of avocado orchards in—you guessed it—Mexico. AFM first made a splash buying television ads during the Super Bowl, encouraging viewers, whose mouths might already have been stuffed with guacamole, to buy more avocados.

Suppose that avocado farming in Mexico is a perfectly competitive, price-taking industry. So, why advertise avocados to increase demand if it's just going to end up netting zero economic profit in the end? If you really understand how rents work, however, AFM's strategy makes sense.

In a perfectly competitive industry, the price is set by the costs of the marginal producer. When producers have different costs, this is reflected in an upward-sloping supply curve, with lower-cost farmers on the left side and increasingly higher-cost orchards as one moves along the supply curve toward higher quantities. The upward-sloping supply curve means that the market price will be higher than the production cost of some of the suppliers. Orchards with lower costs than the marginal orchard earn rents equal to this price–cost difference.

If AFM can shift out the demand curve for avocados, this will cause higher-cost producers who were formerly out of the market to start operating. The new marginal producer will have higher costs than the old marginal producer, and the market price of avocados will rise. Orchards earning rents before will see their rents rise further. The old marginal orchard will start earning rents itself, and a few of the higher-cost, but not highest-cost, entrants will also earn rents.

The rent comes from the cost advantage, so the sources of the rent are the sources of any cost advantage—here, that's likely to be the low-cost farmers' more favorable soil, local weather, or proximity to transportation facilities.

The marginal orchards would still be earning zero economic profits because the opportunity cost to a producer is what it could earn from selling its orchard to another owner. The sales price of the avocado orchard will reflect the rents it earns given market demand; the soil, weather, and location are inseparable from the orchard. If avocado demand increases, the orchard's sales price would also increase to reflect the increased rents from the higher market price. The same story works in reverse for a drop in demand, and similarly for cost changes. ∎

8.6 Conclusion

In this chapter, we learned about a firm's profit-maximizing behavior in a perfectly competitive industry. Perfectly competitive industries are characterized by having a large number of price-taking firms that produce identical products and by having few barriers to entry. A perfectly competitive firm maximizes its profits by producing where the market price (the same as marginal revenue in a perfectly competitive market) equals its marginal costs. We saw that a firm's supply curve is the portion of its marginal cost curve at or above its average cost curve and that individual firms' supply curves combine to form the market supply curve.

In the real world, most firms have some influence over the market price, and although many industries approach perfect competition, truly perfectly competitive industries are rare. Even so, the profit-maximization framework we developed here will prove useful as a simple foundation on which to build analyses of more complicated market structures. In Chapters 9 and 10, we will look at the type of firm that is most unlike the perfectly competitive firm—the monopoly that sells a unique product on the market. In Chapter 11, we will examine firms in monopolistic competition and oligopolies that share some characteristics with both monopolies and perfectly competitive firms.

Summary

1. An industry's **market structure** is characterized by the number of firms in the industry, the type of product sold, and the degree of barriers to entry. Given these criteria, there are four different types of market structures in an economy: perfect competition, monopolistic competition, oligopoly, and monopoly. **Perfectly competitive** industries feature a large number of firms selling identical products and have no barriers to entry. As a result of such characteristics, these firms are price takers, facing horizontal demand curves equal to their marginal revenue curves. **[Section 8.1]**

2. A firm aims to maximize its **profits**, the difference between its total revenue and its total costs. A perfectly competitive firm produces its profit-maximizing output when its marginal cost equals the market price. For a perfectly competitive firm, the market price also equals its **marginal revenue. [Section 8.2]**

3. Because firms will operate in the short run only when price is greater than or equal to the firm's average variable costs, a firm's short-run supply curve is the portion of its marginal cost curve at or above the average variable cost curve. For all prices below that, the firm's supply curve is vertical at the y-axis because quantity produced equals zero. **[Section 8.3]**

4. The industry supply curve is the horizontal sum of individual firms' supply curves; that is, the industry quantity supplied at any given price equals the sum of firms' quantities supplied at that price. Like a firm's supply curve, the industry supply curve generally slopes upward because of two factors. First, individual firms produce more as market prices rise; second, the quantity supplied by the industry will increase as firms operating with higher costs begin supplying at higher prices. **[Section 8.3]**

5. A firm's producer surplus equals its total revenue minus its variable cost, while a firm's profit is its total revenue minus its total cost. Graphically, the firm's and industry's producer surplus is the area below the market price but above the firm's or industry's short-run supply curve. **[Section 8.4]**

6. When a perfectly competitive industry is in **long-run competitive equilibrium,** firms earn zero economic profits. This is because perfectly competitive industries have no barriers to entry: Firms have **free entry** and **free exit** into and out of the industry, and will choose to enter or exit an industry when it is profitable to do so. Over time, changes in demand or in costs will change the long-run equilibrium quantity supplied. For **constant-cost industries,** the long-run supply curve is horizontal, while **increasing-cost industries** and **decreasing-cost industries** have upward- and downward-sloping supply curves, respectively. **[Section 8.4]**

7. While a perfectly competitive firm earns zero economic profits in the long run, it can earn positive **economic rents.** A firm earns positive rents when its costs are lower relative to those of other firms in the industry. **[Section 8.5]**

Review Questions

1. Economists categorize an industry by three criteria: the number of firms in the industry, the type of product sold, and barriers to entry. Using these three criteria, describe a perfectly competitive industry.

2. Why does a perfectly competitive firm face a horizontal demand curve?

3. Define a firm's profit.

4. What is the relationship between the market price and marginal cost when a perfectly competitive firm is maximizing its profit?

5. A firm operating at a loss will decide whether to shut down based on the relationship between the market price and the firm's average variable cost. When will a firm choose to operate? Why does a firm ignore its fixed cost when making this decision?

6. What is a perfectly competitive firm's short-run supply curve?

7. How do we use firms' short-run supply curves to create the industry short-run supply curve?

8. What happens to short-run industry supply when firms' fixed costs change?

9. Define producer surplus. What is the relationship between profit, producer surplus, and fixed costs?

10. Perfectly competitive industries have free entry and exit in the long run. When will firms decide to enter an industry? When will a firm exit an industry?

11. When do economists say that a market is in a long-run competitive equilibrium?

12. Economic rents are returns to scarce inputs above what firms paid for them. When will a firm earn economic rents?

13. Perfectly competitive firms earn zero economic profits in the long run. How can a firm earn zero economic profits and still yield positive economic rents?

Problems

(Solutions to problems marked with an asterisk appear at the back of this book. Problems adapted to use calculus are available online.)

1. Consider three industries: organic onion farming, aluminum production, and car production.

   a. Drawing on the characteristics of a competitive market outlined in the chapter, explain which of the industries named is most likely to be perfectly competitive. Be sure to explain why those industries you believe are less competitive fail to meet the criteria outlined in the chapter.

   b. The vast majority of industries are probably not perfectly competitive. Why then do you suppose economics courses emphasize the study of perfect competition as much as they do?

*2. Assume that soybean production is perfectly competitive. When we study the behavior of the firm, we assume that the demand faced by it is perfectly elastic. Yet in the marketplace, demand may be highly inelastic. Drawing on the determinants of the elasticity of demand outlined in Chapter 2, resolve this apparent paradox.

3. Nancy sells beeswax in a perfectly competitive market for $50 per pound. Nancy's fixed costs are $15, and Nancy is capable of producing up to 6 pounds of beeswax each year.

   a. Use that information to fill in the table below. (*Hint:* Total variable cost is simply the sum of the marginal costs up to any particular quantity of output!)

Quantity	Total Revenue	Fixed Cost	Variable Cost	Total Cost	Profit	Marginal Revenue	Marginal Cost
0	0	15				—	—
1							30
2							35
3							42
4							50
5							60
6							72

b. If Nancy is interested in maximizing her total revenue, how many pounds of beeswax should she produce?

c. What quantity of beeswax should Nancy produce in order to maximize her profit?

d. At the profit-maximizing level of output, how do marginal revenue and marginal cost compare?

e. Suppose that Nancy's fixed cost suddenly rises to $30. How should Nancy alter her production to account for this sudden increase in cost?

f. Suppose that the beeswax workers' union bargains for higher wages, making the marginal cost of producing beeswax rise by $8 at every level of output. How should Nancy alter her production to account for this sudden increase in cost?

4. The egg industry comprises many firms producing an identical product. Supply and demand conditions are indicated in the left-hand panel of the figure below; the long-run cost curves of a representative egg producer are shown in the right-hand panel. Currently, the market price of eggs is $2 per dozen, and at that price consumers are purchasing 800,000 dozen eggs per day.

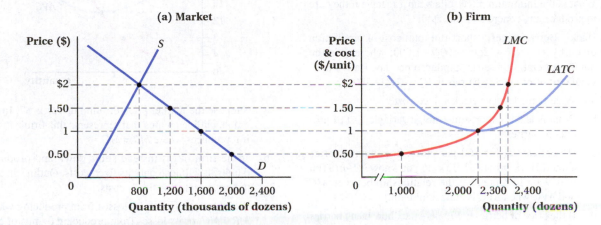

a. Determine how many eggs each firm in the industry will produce if it wants to maximize profit.

b. How many firms are currently serving the industry?

c. In the long run, what will the equilibrium price of eggs be? Explain your reasoning and illustrate your reasoning by altering the graphs above.

d. In the long run, how many eggs will the typical firm produce?

e. In the long run, how many firms will comprise the industry?

---

5. The diagram below depicts the revenues and costs of a firm producing vodka.

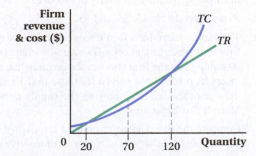

a. Why is total revenue represented as a straight line instead of a curve? What assumption of perfect competition does that linearity reflect?

b. What will the firm's profit be if it decides to produce 20 units of output? 120 units?

c. Suppose the firm is producing 70 units of output and decides to cut output to 60. What will happen to the firm's profit as a result?

d. Suppose the firm is producing 70 units of output and decides to increase output to 80. What will happen to the firm's profit as a result?

e. At an output level of 70, draw a line tangent to the total cost curve. Does your line look similar to the total revenue curve? What does the slope of the total revenue curve indicate? What does the slope of the total cost curve indicate?

6. Anthony's Bees is an Internet e-tailer that sells equipment to aspiring beekeepers. A complete starter kit in this competitive market sells for $900. Anthony's total costs are given by $TC = 3Q^3$, where Q is the number of starter kits he sells each month. The corresponding marginal cost of producing beehives is $MC = 9Q^2$.

a. How many starter kits should Anthony sell each year in order to maximize his profits?

b. How much profit will Anthony earn?

c. If Anthony were to sell one extra beehive each month, what would happen to his profits? One fewer? Are these results consistent with your answer to (a)?

7. Concrete blocks are produced by thousands of small producers in a perfectly competitive market. Each producer faces total costs of $TC = Q^3 - 6Q^2 + 20Q + 300$, where Q is the quantity of blocks, in hundreds. The corresponding marginal cost curve is given by $MC = 3Q^2 - 12Q + 20$. What is the minimum price sellers must receive if they are to produce any concrete blocks at all?

8. Hack's Berries faces a short-run total cost of production given by $TC = Q^3 - 12Q^2 + 100Q + 1,000$, where Q is the number of crates of berries produced per day. Hack's marginal cost of producing berries is $3Q^2 - 24Q + 100$.

a. What is the level of Hack's fixed cost?

b. What is Hack's short-run average variable cost of producing berries?

c. If berries sell for $60 per crate, how many berries should Hack produce? How do you know? (*Hint*: You may want to remember the relationship between MC and AVC when AVC is at its minimum.)

d. If the price of berries is $79 per crate, how many berries should Hack produce? Explain.

*9. Janis is one producer in the perfectly competitive pearl industry. Janis's cost curves are shown below. Pearls sell for $100, and in maximizing profits, Janis produces 1,000 pearls per month.

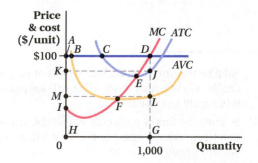

a. Find the area on the graph that illustrates the total revenue from selling 1,000 units at $100.

b. Find the area on the graph that indicates the variable cost of producing those 1,000 units.

c. Find the area on the graph that indicates the fixed cost of producing those 1,000 units.

d. Add together the two areas you found in (b) and (c) to show the total cost of producing those 1,000 units.

e. Subtract the total cost of producing those 1,000 units from the total revenue from selling those units to determine the firm's profit. Show the profit as an area on the graph.

10. The diagram below depicts the cost curves for a perfectly competitive jump drive producer that is currently operating at a loss.

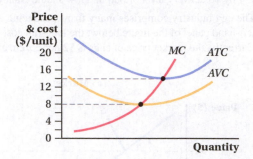

a. Suppose the market price of jump drives is $7. In the graph, outline an area that represents this firm's losses if it produces where $MR = MC$.

b. If the firm in (a) instead shuts down and produces 0 units, it will lose only its fixed costs. Outline an area that represents this firm's costs.

c. Which area is larger: its losses from producing where $MR = MC$, or its losses from producing 0 units of output? What should the firm do?

d. Do your answers to (a), (b), and (c) change if the price of jump drives is $11 rather than $7?

11. Marty sells flux capacitors in a perfectly competitive market. His marginal cost is given by $MC = Q$. Thus, the first capacitor Marty produces has a marginal cost of $1, the second has a marginal cost of $2, and so on.

a. Draw a diagram showing the marginal cost of each unit that Marty produces.

b. If flux capacitors sell for $2, determine the profit-maximizing quantity for Marty to produce.

c. Repeat part (b) for $3, $4, and $5.

d. The supply curve for a firm traces out the quantity that firm will produce and offer for sale at various prices. Assuming that the firm chooses the quantity that maximizes its profits [you solved for these in (b) and (c)], draw another diagram showing the supply curve for Marty's flux capacitors.

e. Compare the two diagrams you have drawn. What can you say about the supply curve for a competitive firm?

*12. Consider the following graph, which depicts the cost curves of a perfectly competitive seller of potatoes. Potatoes currently sell for $3 per pound.

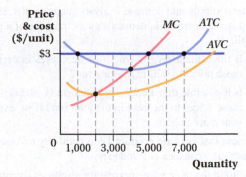

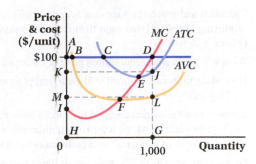

a.   To maximize profit, how many pounds of potatoes should this seller produce?

Suppose that the potato grower's bank ratchets up the interest rate applicable to the grower's adjustable-rate mortgage loan. This increases the size of the potato grower's monthly mortgage payment.

b.   Illustrate the change in the mortgage payment by shifting the appropriate cost curves.

c.   Which curves shift? Which do not? Why?

d.   How does the change in interest rates affect the grower's decision on how many potatoes to produce?

e.   What happens to the potato grower's profit as a result of the increased interest rate?

f.   How does the change in interest rates affect the shape and/or position of the grower's short-run supply curve?

13. Five hundred small almond growers operate areas with plentiful rainfall. The marginal cost of producing almonds in these locations is given by $MC = 0.02Q$, where Q is the number of crates produced in a growing season. Three hundred almond growers operate in drier areas where costly irrigation is required. The marginal cost of growing almonds in these locations is given by $MC = 0.04Q$.

a.   Find the individual supply curve for each type of almond grower. (*Hint:* Remember that the supply relationship expresses the quantity brought to market at various prices. Remember also that for a perfectly competitive firm, $P = MR$.)

b.   "Add up" the individual supply curves to derive the market supply curve.

c.   If the market demand for almonds is $Q^D = 105,000 - 2,500P$, what will the equilibrium price of almonds be? The equilibrium quantity?

d.   How many almonds will each type of almond grower produce at that price?

e.   Verify that the total production of all almond growers equals the equilibrium quantity you found in part (c).

14. Consider Janis the pearl producer with cost curves as shown next. Janis produces 1,000 pearls when the price of pearls is $100.

a.   What is the area of producer surplus earned by Janis if the price of pearls is $100?

b.   Explain why areas ADI and $ADLM$ must be equal.

15. For the past nine months, Iliana has been producing artisanal ice creams from her small shop in Chicago. She's just been breaking even (earning zero economic profit) that entire time. This morning, the state Board of Health informed her that it is doubling the annual fee for the dairy license under which she (and other ice cream makers) operates, retroactive to the beginning of her operations.

a.   In the short run, how will this fee increase affect Iliana's output level? Her profit?

b.   In the long run, how will this fee increase affect Iliana's output level?

c.   Suppose that instead of doubling the annual fee for a license, the state Board of Health required Iliana (and other ice cream makers) to treat every pint of ice cream to prevent the growth of bacteria. How would this regulation affect Iliana's production decision and profit in both the short and long run?

16. Martha is one producer in the perfectly competitive jelly industry. Last year, Martha and all her competitors found themselves earning economic profits.

a.   If entry and exit from the jelly industry are free, what do you expect to happen to the number of suppliers in the industry in the long run?

b.   Because of the entry/exit you described in part (a), what do you expect to happen to the industry supply of jelly? Explain.

c.   As a result of the supply change you described in part (b), what do you expect to happen to the price of jelly? Why?

d.   As a result of the price change you indicated in part (c), how will Martha adjust her output?

*17. The canola oil industry is perfectly competitive. Every producer has the following long-run total cost function: $LTC = 2Q^3 - 15Q^2 + 40Q$, where Q is measured in tons of canola oil. The corresponding marginal cost function is given by $LMC = 6Q^2 - 30Q + 40$.

a. Calculate and graph the long-run average total cost of producing canola oil that each firm faces for values of Q from 1 to 10.

b. What will the long-run equilibrium price of canola oil be?

c. How many units of canola oil will each firm produce in the long run?

d. Suppose that the market demand for canola oil is given by $Q = 999 - 0.25P$. At the long-run equilibrium price, how many tons of canola oil will consumers demand?

e. Given your answer to (d), how many firms will exist when the industry is in long-run equilibrium?

18. Suppose that the market for coffee-shop coffee is perfectly competitive. All producers have identical cost curves, and the industry is currently in long-run equilibrium, with each producer producing at its minimum long-run average total cost of $2 per cup.

a. A *Friends* reunion movie sparks a sudden increase in the demand for coffee-shop coffee. In the short run, what will happen to the price of a cup of coffee? Explain and illustrate with a graph.

b. In the short run, how will individual firms respond to this change in price? Is this price change good for firms? How do you know? Explain and draw a graph to illustrate your answer.

c. What can we expect to happen to the number of producers in the industry in the long run? What impact will this have on the market?

d. Will the change in quantity in the market be greater in the short run or the long run? What about the change in the quantity produced by individual sellers?

19. Suppose that the market for eggs is initially in long-run equilibrium. One day, enterprising and profit-hungry egg farmer Atkins has the inspiration to fit his laying hens with rose-colored contact lenses. His inspiration is true genius— overnight his egg production rises and his costs fall.

a. Will Farmer Atkins be able to leverage his inspiration into greater profit in the short run? Why?

b. Farmer Atkin's right-hand man Abner accidentally leaks news of the boss' inspiration at the local bar and grill. The next thing Farmer Atkins knows, he's being interviewed by *NBC Evening News*. What short-run adjustments do you expect competing egg farmers to make as a result of this broadcast? What will happen to the profits of egg farms?

c. In the long run, what will happen to the price of eggs? What will happen to the profits of egg producers (including those of Farmer Atkins)?

d. In the long run, who reaps the greatest benefit from Atkins's technological breakthrough: egg producers or egg consumers? Explain the role that competition plays in the distribution of those benefits in the transition between the short and long run.

20. General supply and demand analysis suggests that, in the short run, a decrease in demand causes the price of a good to fall.

a. Is the same assertion true (that decreases in demand cause prices to fall) in the long run?

b. Is it possible that a decrease in demand could actually cause prices to increase in the long run? If so, explain your reasoning.

21. Suppose that eggs are produced competitively and the egg industry is a constant cost industry.

a. Fill in the table with appropriate responses (increases, decreases, no change) in response to each of the following events:

Event	Short-Run Effect on Price	Long-run Effect on Price
Demand for eggs increases		
Cost of corn (an input into egg production) decreases		

b. Which event has a permanent effect on the price of eggs, and which does not?

c. How would your answer to (b) change if the egg industry were a decreasing cost industry?

*22. In western Kansas, corn can be grown in two ways—with or without irrigation. Dryland farmers, who do not irrigate their corn, have long-run average costs of $LAC_D = Q^2 - 20Q + 105$ and long-run marginal costs of $LMC_D = 3Q^2 - 40Q + 105$, where Q is measured in thousands of bushels. Farmers lucky enough to have water rights or river access have lower costs: Their long-run average cost is $LAC_I = Q^2 - 16Q + 67$ and their long-run marginal costs are $LMC_I = 3Q^2 - 32Q + 67$.

a. If the corn market is in long-run equilibrium, with both dryland and irrigated corn being grown, what must the price of corn be?

b. How much economic rent will farmers with access to irrigation earn?

c. Explain why irrigating farmers earn economic rents, but will still earn zero economic profits.

23. Heloise and Abelard produce letters in a perfectly competitive industry. Heloise is much better at it than Abelard: On average, she produces letters for half of the cost of Abelard's.

a. True or False: If Heloise and Abelard are both maximizing profit, the last letter that Heloise produces will cost half as much as the last letter written by Abelard. Explain your answer.

b. Suppose Heloise and Abelard both produce until their last letter costs them $5 to produce. True or False: Because the cost of their last letter is the same, nobody will earn any economic rent.

Market Power and Monopoly

I f you were in the market for a tablet computer when the iPad first came out, that was the only option. It didn't even come in a choice of colors. Apple couldn't have been happier. It had introduced a product that people literally lined up to buy—iPad was the only game in town. Other technology companies soon rushed their own tablets into production and distribution, but this took time. It also took considerable persuading to convince many wannabe iPad owners to abandon their plans and buy a different product when other tablets became available.

This sort of situation doesn't fit the perfectly competitive model of a firm's supply behavior we covered in Chapter 8. In a perfectly competitive market, a firm's output is so small relative to the total market that its choice of whether or how much to produce does not have a noticeable impact on the total supply in the market. But such was not the case for Apple when it introduced the iPad. After all, Apple *was* the market supply. By adjusting the number of iPads it produced for the market, the firm could cause movements along the market demand curve. If Apple produced only a few iPads, for example, the low quantity supplied would meet the demand curve at a high price, and quantity demanded would also be low. If it produced more, the quantity supplied would equal quantity demanded further down the demand curve, at a lower price. Therefore, Apple's choice of the quantity of iPads it supplied to the market gave the company effective control over the price at which the iPad sold.

In this chapter, we begin to look at firms' production choices when they have some ability to control the price at which their product sells. *A firm's ability to influence the market price of its product* is its **market power**. The most extreme version of market power is a **monopoly**, a *market that is served by only one firm*. Apple basically had a monopoly in the tablet computer market when the iPad first came out. A firm that has a monopoly is a **monopolist**, the *sole supplier and price setter of a good on the market*. A monopolist has the most market power because its decision about how much to supply completely determines the market price. As we saw in Chapter 8, a firm in a perfectly competitive market is a *price taker*; it has no market power because it has no influence over the market price.

Firms with market power do not behave in the same way as perfectly competitive firms do. They recognize that their supply decisions will influence the price at which they can sell their output, so such companies take this into account when choosing how much to produce and sell. We will learn how to measure the degree of market power and see that as a firm's market power falls, its supply behavior becomes more and more like that of a perfectly competitive firm.

market power A firm's ability to influence the market price of its product.

monopoly A market served by only one firm.

monopolist The sole supplier and price setter of a good on the market.

9.1 Sources of Market Power: Barriers to Entry

Some industries, like mobile phone companies and car manufacturers, for example, invariably end up with only a few companies and substantial market power. A key element of sustainable market power is that something must prevent competitors from entering when prices are high. A firm with market power can generate a substantial amount of producer

barriers to entry Factors that keep entrants out of a market despite the existence of a large producer surplus.

surplus and profit in a way that a competitive firm cannot. (Remember that producer surplus equals a firm's profit plus its fixed cost. In the long run, when fixed cost is zero, profit and producer surplus are equal.) As we saw in Chapter 8, however, producer surplus should be an irresistible draw for other firms to enter the market and try to capture some of it. **Barriers to entry** are the *factors that keep entrants out of a market despite the existence of a large producer surplus.* We start by thinking about the nature of these barriers.

Extreme Scale Economies: Natural Monopoly

natural monopoly A market in which it is efficient for a single firm to produce the entire industry output.

The existence of a *natural monopoly* is one barrier to entry. A **natural monopoly** is a *market in which it is efficient for a single firm to produce the entire industry output.* In this market, the cost curve of a firm exhibits economies of scale at any output level. In other words, the firm's long-run average total cost curve is always downward-sloping—the bigger the firm gets, the lower is its average total cost, even if it sells the entire market quantity itself.

In this situation, it is efficient (from a production standpoint) for society if a single firm produces the entire industry output; splitting output across more firms would raise the average total cost of production. Suppose a company could produce as large a quantity as it wants at a constant marginal cost of $10 per unit and has a fixed cost of $100. In this case, average total cost (total costs divided by output) declines across all quantities of output. In equation form,

$$TC = FC + VC = 100 + 10Q$$

so

$$ATC = \frac{TC}{Q} = \frac{100 + 10Q}{Q} = \frac{100}{Q} + 10$$

The larger the firm's quantity produced, Q, the lower is its average total cost. If all of the firms in an industry have this same cost structure, the lowest-total-cost way to serve industry demand is for one firm to produce everything. If more than one firm produces, the industry's average total cost of producing output is higher because each firm that operates has to pay the fixed cost of $100 to produce anything at all. Having only one firm in the industry saves the replication of those fixed costs. That's why it is more cost-effective from society's perspective to have only one producer in the industry. Furthermore, at a more practical level, it's difficult in these types of markets for new firms to enter and compete with the incumbent, because the incumbent's size usually gives it a cost advantage. Therefore, in markets with cost curves like this (high fixed cost and constant or slowly rising marginal cost), one firm will tend to become very large and dominate the industry with its low cost.

All that said, it is important to realize that even natural monopolies can disappear if demand changes sufficiently over time. Demand can rise so much that average total cost eventually rises enough to enable new firms to enter the market. This happened in a number of markets people used to consider natural monopolies, such as the markets for telephone and cable television service.

 Application: Natural Monopoly in Electricity Transmission

Electricity transmission is a classic example of a natural monopoly. Building a network of transmission lines, substations, meters, and so on to supply homes and businesses is a huge fixed cost. Once the network is built, the marginal cost of delivering another kilowatt-hour of electricity is almost constant. That means the average cost to deliver a kilowatt-hour on a network steadily falls (down to the marginal cost) as the quantity of delivered electricity rises. If even just two competing firms operated in the transmission market in a geographic area, two separate sets of power lines would run everywhere, and the combined fixed costs of the two firms would be an enormous waste of resources.

We might therefore expect a single firm to handle electrical transmission in a given market. And we often observe that. This used to mean a local monopoly utility that generated power and delivered it to customers. These utilities were typically regulated by the government to limit their ability to exercise the market power that their natural monopoly gave them. (Later in the chapter, we discuss why the government often regulates the behaviors of firms with market power whether their market power is the result of a natural monopoly or not.)

More recently, however, there has been a recognition that although electricity transmission might be a natural monopoly, electricity *generation* is not. As our power plant supply curve analysis from Chapter 8 showed, marginal costs in generation rise with output, eventually leading to increasing average costs at higher quantities. As a result, locations have restructured their electricity markets over the years so that a number of competing electricity generators sell their output to a regulated transmission monopolist. (Sometimes these transmission companies are even set up as nonprofit businesses.) The part of the industry that is the natural monopoly has been separated from the parts that are not. ∎

Switching Costs

A second common type of barrier to entry is the presence of consumer switching costs. If customers must give something up to switch to a competing product, this will tend to generate market power for the incumbent and make entry difficult. Think of a consumer who flies one airline regularly and has built up a preferred status level in the airline's frequent-flyer program. Even if a competing airline enters the market with lower prices, it may have a hard time convincing that person to fly with it, because the customer might lose her privileged status (shorter lines, upgrades, no checked-bag fees, etc.) on the current carrier. This lost status is a cost that inhibits the consumer's ability to switch to a competitor, raising the incumbent airline's market power.

For some products, the switching cost comes from technology. For example, once you buy a DIRECTV satellite dish and install it on your house, the only way to switch to the DISH Network is to get a new satellite dish and converter box installed. For other products, switching costs arise from the costs of finding an alternative. If you have your car insurance with one company, it can be very time consuming to research different competitors' rates to find out whether you could save money, and then fill out the paperwork required to actually switch. If you type in all your addresses with a photo service like Shutterfly for mailing holiday cards, switching to a new service would require you to enter them all once again.

Switching costs are not insurmountable barriers to entry. For example, some companies invest in making the switch as easy as possible as a way to convince people to go with their (often) cheaper product. But switching costs don't need to be insurmountable to be effective. To reduce the threat of competition and give the incumbent firm some market power, switching costs only need to be high enough to make entry costly, not impossible.

Perhaps the most extreme version of switching costs exists with a **network good:** a *good whose value to each customer increases with the number of other consumers who use the product.* With network goods, each new consumer creates a benefit for every other consumer of the good. Instagram is one example of a network good. If you are the only person in the world on Instagram, your account will not prove to be that much fun. If you're one of hundreds of millions with accounts, however, now you'll be talking (. . . to each other).

network good A good whose value to each consumer increases with the number of other consumers of the product.

The combination of large economies of scale (at or approaching natural monopoly levels) and network goods' attributes creates powerful entry barriers. Social networks like Facebook are prone to become monopolies because they both have major economies of scale in production (software is a high-fixed-cost, low-marginal-cost production process) and are network goods.

Product Differentiation

Even if firms sell products that compete in the same market, all consumers might not see each firm's product as a perfect substitute for other firms' versions. For example, all bicycle makers operate in what could be thought of as the same market, but not every potential bike buyer will see a $500 Trek as exactly the same thing as a $500 Cannondale. That means firms can price slightly above their competition without losing all their sales to their competitors. There is a segment of consumers who have a particular preference for one firm's product and will be willing to pay a premium for it (a limited premium, but a premium nonetheless). This *imperfect substitutability across varieties of a product* is called **product differentiation,** and it is another source of market power.

product differentiation Imperfect substitutability across varieties of a product.

In some industries, product differentiation can be spatial. When location matters, some sellers are in more convenient, appealing, or noticeable locations for certain customers than others. Those sellers will have some market power because even if their price is a bit higher than that of another more distant competitor, not all their customers will be willing to switch to the other seller. Likewise, their competitor has some customers who prefer its location, giving it some market power as well.

Product differentiation exists in one form or the other in most industries. Regardless of its specific source, it prevents new firms from entering the market and capturing most of the market demand just by pricing their version of the product slightly below the incumbents'. We will discuss product differentiation in greater detail in Chapter 11.

Absolute Cost Advantages or Control of Key Inputs

Another common barrier to entry is a firm's absolute cost advantage over other firms in obtaining a key input, meaning it has some special asset that other firms do not have — a secret formula or scarce resource. Controlling this input allows a firm to keep its costs lower than those of any competitor. To give an extreme example, suppose one firm owns the only oil well in town and can prevent anyone else from drilling a well. That would be a major advantage, because everyone else's cost of producing oil is infinite. The control of the input does not need to be that extreme, though. If a firm has one oil well whose production cost is substantially below that of everyone else's wells, that would be a cost advantage, too. These other firms would find it difficult to take away business from the low-production-cost firm, thus preserving its market power.

🔪 Application: Controlling a Key Input — The Troubled History of Fordlandia, Brazil

In the 1800s, there was no synthetic rubber. All rubber came from trees, and Brazil's rubber trees (*Hevea brasiliensis*) were the world's leading source. Rubber was one of Brazil's great exports.

In their natural state, the trees were often miles apart and hard to reach. In addition, because South American leaf-blight fungus (which attacks rubber trees in Brazil) could spread so easily from one tree to another, people could not plant the trees closer together.

In 1876 an Englishman named Henry Wickham stole 70,000 rubber seeds for the British, who then planted them in concentrated plantations in what is now Malaysia. The innovation of planting the trees close together in a place with no leaf-blight fungus dramatically reduced the cost of harvesting rubber, gave the British an absolute cost advantage over everyone else in the rubber industry, and conferred market power on British rubber producers. By the early 1900s, Britain's plantations in Asia met 95% of the world's demand for rubber. It was "the first worldwide monopoly of a strategic resource in human history."[1]

Rubber trees planted close together on a plantation in Malaysia.

Gavin Hellier/Alamy

In 1927 Henry Ford needed rubber for car tires and tried to copy the British approach. He set up a rubber plantation city in the Amazon and called it Fordlandia. Unfortunately, because Ford never consulted with any experts on rubber trees, the Fordlandia plantation rapidly fell prey to the leaf-blight fungus, culture clash, social unrest, and other ills. Repeated efforts to start new plantations all failed. As a result, Ford was unable to match the success of the British, and no rubber from Fordlandia was ever used in a Ford car.

Fordlandia ruins in Brazil.

Colin McPherson/Corbis Historical/Getty Images

Britain's market power from the absolute cost advantage of controlling this key input (rubber plants not threatened by the fungus) survived until the development of cheap synthetic rubber after World War II. It's still true, though, that if you travel from Brazil to Malaysia, the Malaysian government requires you to walk through a fungicide treatment at the airport and irradiates your luggage with ultraviolet radiation to kill any South American leaf blight you might be harboring. ■

Government Regulation

A final important form of entry barrier is government regulation. If you want to drive a cab in New York City, you need to have a medallion (a chunk of metal that is actually riveted to a car's hood to show that the New York Taxi & Limousine Commission has granted the cab a license to operate). The number of medallions is fixed; currently, there are just over 13,000 available. If you want to enter this industry, you need to buy a medallion from its current owner, and the price runs in the hundreds of thousands of dollars. That's a considerable entry barrier for a taxi driver.

Uber, a ridesharing service, created a way around this barrier (at least for now; the cab industry in New York City has been trying to limit Uber's ability to operate). An Uber driver can offer a service that is similar to a cab without having to buy a medallion. As a result, a medallion doesn't offer as much market power as it once did, and prices have fallen to reflect that. Medallion prices fell by as much as 70–80% in the five years after Uber's entry into New York City and other major U.S. cities like Boston, Chicago, and Philadelphia.

There are numerous other rules that prevent entry, such as licensing requirements in many occupations and industries. Note, however, that some regulatory barriers are intentional and probably good, as we discuss later in the chapter when we consider government

---

[1] Joe Jackson, *The Thief at the End of the World: Rubber, Power and the Seeds of Empire,* New York: Viking, 2008.

responses to monopoly. Examples include things like patents and copyrights, which explicitly give companies protection from entry by forbidding direct competitors.

Where There's a Will (and Producer Surplus), There's a Way

One important aspect to remember about barriers to entry is that they seldom last forever. If the producer surplus protected by entry barriers is large, competitors can often eventually find their way around even the most formidable barriers to entry. DuPont invented Nylon, the synthetic material, and patented it. In theory, this should have prevented entry. In reality, other companies figured out ways to develop competing, though not identical, synthetic fabrics that ultimately undermined the Nylon monopoly. Because there is no limit to the inventive capacity of the human mind, in the long run entrepreneurs and entrepreneurial firms will often find ingenious ways to encroach on other firms' protected positions.

9.2 Market Power and Marginal Revenue

Most firms have some sort of market power, even if they are not complete monopolists. The competitive market model is more of a useful starting point for studying market structures than it is a literal description of most industries.

A firm has market power if its individual demand curve is not flat. In a competitive market, firms are price takers. If they charge more than the market price, they lose all their demand. If their choice of output influences the price, they aren't price takers. Suppose the car manufacturer Tesla cuts production of all its vehicle models to one-fifth its current level. Prices would likely rise but not cut Tesla's demand to zero. So, Tesla's choice of output level can influence its price, and it is able to decide how many cars to make. That's the same idea we discussed with regard to Apple and the original iPad. We can describe the firm's decision in terms of choosing either its profit-maximizing price or its profit-maximizing level of output; either way, we (and the firm) obtain the same result.

Market Power and Monopoly

We made the argument that Apple was, effectively, a monopolist in the tablet computer market when it first introduced the iPad, but clearly we couldn't say the same about Tesla. It competes against other automakers. However, the basic lessons of this chapter apply whenever a firm has any market power, even if it isn't a pure monopolist. *The key element of our analysis in this chapter is that a firm with market power faces a downward-sloping demand curve.* In other words, its output level and price are interrelated. For a perfectly competitive firm, output level and price are not related.

We will see in Chapter 11 that **oligopoly** (*a market structure characterized by competition among a small number of firms*) and **monopolistic competition** (*a type of imperfect competition where a large number of firms have some market power, but each makes zero economic profit in the long run*) are other market types where individual demand curves slope downward. The difference between monopoly and these other two cases is that in an oligopoly and in monopolistic competition, the particular shape of the demand curve faced by any given firm (even though it still slopes down) depends on the supply decisions of the *other* firms in the market. In this chapter, we look at monopoly/market power in which there are no such interactions between firms. We will analyze how a firm in those kinds of markets chooses its production (or price) level *if other firms won't change their behaviors in response to its choices.* Having made this assumption, as long as the firm's

oligopoly Market structure characterized by competition among a small number of firms

monopolistic competition A type of imperfect competition where a large number of firms have some market power, but each makes zero economic profit in the long run.

FREAKONOMICS

Why Drug Dealers Want Peace, Not War

When it comes to gaining market power, monopolists have been extremely creative in the strategies they employ: lobbying governments for privileged access to markets, temporarily pricing below marginal cost to keep out rivals, and artificially creating entry barriers, just to name a few. But murder?

Can you imagine the CEO of Anheuser-Busch InBev ordering a hit man to take out the board of directors of Miller-Coors? No chance. Yet, not too long ago, when Prohibition laws made it illegal to produce and consume alcohol, such actions were commonplace among the "firms" that produced alcohol. For gangsters like Al Capone, violence was key to establishing and maintaining market power.

The crack cocaine trade offers a modern example of the same phenomenon. Because crack is illegal, crack markets function without legal property rights or binding contracts. Violence becomes a means of enforcing contracts and establishing market power for drug gangs. And because these gangsters are already working illegally, the costs of murder aren't nearly as high as they are in legal ventures. Researchers estimate that roughly one-third of *all* the homicides that occur in the United States—nearly 5,000 per year—are carried out by drug dealers fighting over property rights. But in a study based on the actual financial records of a Chicago gang over a three-year period, Steven

Levitt and Sudhir Venkatesh showed that gang leaders try to avoid excessive use of violence.[*] Why? Because it's bad for business! The shootings associated with a gang war scare away customers, reducing revenues by nearly 30%. During gang wars, the drug gang actually generated negative profits, on average.

Violence is one of the biggest costs of the illegal drug trade. Reducing this violence is one of the benefits touted by advocates of drug legalization. Simple economics suggests an alternative way to reduce the illegal drug trade and its effects. It is the high demand for drugs that makes drug sellers willing to take such extreme actions to establish market power. If the demand for illegal drugs were reduced, the ills associated with these markets would shrink, too. Several approaches along these lines have been tried—harsher punishments for users, education campaigns about drugs' health effects, and telling people to "Just Say No." These policies have met with mixed success, at best. Still, it's worth thinking about how to design better ways to reduce illegal drug demand, given the enormous benefits a sustained demand reduction would create.

[*]Steven D. Levitt and Sudhir Alladi Venkatesh, "An Economic Analysis of a Drug-Selling Gang's Finances," *Quarterly Journal of Economics* 115, no. 3 (August 2000): 755–789.

---

demand curve slopes downward, our analysis is the same whether this demand curve can be moved around by a competitor's actions (as in an oligopoly or monopolistically competitive market) or not (as in a monopoly). As a result, we sometimes interchange the terms "market power" and "monopoly power" even if the firm we are analyzing is not literally a monopolist. The point is that once the firm's demand curve is determined, its decision-making process is the same whether it is a monopoly, an oligopolistic firm, or a monopolistically competitive firm.[2]

Marginal Revenue

The key to understanding how a firm with market power acts is to realize that, because it faces a downward-sloping demand curve, it can only sell more of its good by reducing its price. This one fact enters into every decision such firms make. As we learn later in the chapter, because firms with market power recognize the relationship between output

---

[2] This similarity between the supply behavior of a monopolist and nonmonopoly firms that face downward-sloping demand curves is very handy, because it is often difficult to say definitively whether a firm is a monopolist or not. A key element of defining monopoly is deciding what the relevant market is, and drawing the boundaries can be arbitrary. Apple introduced the iPad, giving it a monopoly in the tablet market, but it was just one of many players in the market for computing devices. Fortunately, all that matters here is that the firm faces a downward-sloping demand curve for any reason.

and price, they will restrict output in a way that perfectly competitive firms won't. They do so to keep prices higher (and thereby make more money).

To see why, remember the concept of a company's marginal revenue, the additional revenue a firm earns from selling one more unit. At first, that just sounds like the price of the product. And as we saw in Chapter 8, for a firm with no market power, this is exactly the case; the price is the marginal revenue. If a hotdog vendor walking the stands at a football game (a "firm" that can reasonably be thought of as a price taker) sells another hotdog, his total revenue goes up by whatever price he sells the hotdog for. The price doesn't depend on how many hotdogs he sells; he is a price taker. He could sell hundreds of hotdogs and it wouldn't change the market price, so his marginal revenue is just market price P.

But for a seller with market power, the concept of marginal revenue is more subtle. The extra revenue from selling another unit is no longer just the price. Yes, the firm can get the revenue from selling one more unit, but because the firm faces a downward-sloping demand curve, the more it chooses to sell, the lower the price will be for *all* units it sells, not just that one extra unit. (*Important note:* We are assuming the firm makes the decision all at once and can't charge different prices to each customer. We will figure out what to do with differential pricing in Chapter 10.) This reduces the revenue the firm receives for the other units it sells. When computing the marginal revenue from selling that last unit, then, the firm must also subtract the loss it suffers on every other unit.

For example, consider Durkee-Mower, Inc., the Massachusetts firm that makes Marshmallow Fluff. Fluff has been around since 1920 and maintains a dominant position in the marshmallow creme market in the northeastern United States (you may have had some in a Fluffernutter sandwich, a s'more, or a Rice Krispies bar). This prominence in the market means that Durkee-Mower faces a downward-sloping demand curve for Fluff. If it makes more Fluff, its market price will fall, because the only way to get consumers to buy up the extra Fluff is to lower its price.

Table 9.1 shows how the quantity of Fluff produced this year varies with its price. As the quantity produced rises, the price falls because of the downward-sloping demand curve. The third column in Table 9.1 shows the total revenue for the year for each level of output. The marginal revenue of an additional unit of output (in this example, a unit is a million pounds) is shown in the last column. It equals the difference between total revenue at that level of output minus the total revenue had Durkee-Mower made one fewer unit.

If Durkee-Mower makes only 1 million pounds of Fluff, its price is $5 per pound, and its revenue is $5 million. Because total revenue would be zero if the firm didn't produce

Table 9.1 Marginal Revenue for Marshmallow Fluff

Quantity (millions of pounds) (Q)	Price ($/pound) ($P$)	Total Revenue ($ millions) ($TR = P \times Q$)	Marginal Revenue ($ millions) $\left(MR = \dfrac{\Delta TR}{\Delta Q} \right)$
0	6	0	—
1	5	5	5
2	4	8	3
3	3	9	1
4	2	8	−1
5	1	5	−3

anything, the marginal revenue of the first million pounds is $5 million. If Durkee-Mower makes 2 million pounds of Fluff instead, the market price falls to $4 per pound—the lower price makes consumers willing to buy another million pounds of Fluff. Total revenue in this case is $8 million. Therefore, the marginal revenue of increasing output from 1 to 2 million pounds is $3 million, or $3 per pound. Note that this is less than the $4 per pound price that it sells for at the quantity of 2 million pounds.

As we discussed earlier, the lower marginal revenue reflects the fact that a firm with market power must reduce the price of its product when it produces more. Therefore, the marginal revenue isn't just the price multiplied by the extra quantity, which would be ($4 per pound × 1 million pounds) = $4 million. It also subtracts the $1 million loss of revenue because the firm now sells the previous million units at a price that is $1 lower. Thus, the marginal revenue from producing 1 million more pounds of Fluff is $3 million: $4 million of revenue on the additional million pounds minus the $1 million lost from the price reduction on the initial million pounds sold.

If Durkee-Mower produces 3 million pounds, the market price drops to $3 per pound. Total revenue at this quantity is $9 million. The marginal revenue is now only $1 million. Again, this marginal revenue is less than the product of the market price and the extra quantity because producing more Fluff drives down the price that Durkee-Mower can charge for every unit it sells.

If the firm chooses to make still more Fluff, say, 4 million pounds, the market price drops further, to $2 per pound. Total revenue is now $8 million. That means in this case, Durkee-Mower has actually *reduced* its revenue (from $9 million to $8 million) by producing *more* Fluff, and marginal revenue is now negative (−$1 million) even though it sells the extra Fluff for $2 per pound. The problem is that the revenue loss due to the dropped price on all units outweighs the revenue gains from selling more. If Durkee-Mower insists on making 5 million pounds, the price drops to $1 per pound and total revenue falls to $5 million. Again, the marginal revenue of this million-pound unit is negative, −$3 million, because the revenue loss due to price reductions outweighs the extra units sold.

Why Does the Price Have to Fall for Every Unit the Firm Sells?
One thing about marginal revenue that can be confusing at first glance is why the seller has to lower the price on all its sales if it decides to produce one more unit. For instance, in the Marshmallow Fluff example, why can't Durkee-Mower sell the first million pounds for $5 per pound, and then the second million pounds for $4 a pound, the third million for $3 a pound, and so on? That way, marginal revenue would always equal the price.

The firm's decision here is not sequential. Durkee-Mower isn't deciding whether to sell a second million pounds after it has already sold its first million at $5 per pound. Instead, the firm is deciding whether to produce 1 million *or* 2 million pounds in this period. If it makes 1 million pounds, the price will be $5 per pound and revenue will be $5 million. The demand curve is at a specific point in time. We will discuss the reasons you might not be able to charge different prices to different people in more detail in Chapter 10. However, those reasons include not being able to identify the customers who are willing to pay more, and not being able to prevent the ones that buy cheap from reselling to other customers.

Marginal Revenue: A Graphical Approach
The idea that marginal revenue is different from the price is easy to see in a graph like **Figure 9.1**. On the downward-sloping demand curve, we can measure the total revenue TR (price × quantity) at two different points, x and y. At point x, the quantity sold is Q_1 and the price at which each unit is sold is P_1. The total revenue is price times quantity, seen in the figure as the rectangle $A + B$.

If the firm decides to produce more, say, by increasing output from Q_1 to Q_2, it will move to point y on the demand curve. The firm sells more units, but in doing so, the price

---

Figure 9.1 **Understanding Marginal Revenue**

For a firm with market power, the marginal revenue from producing an additional unit of a good is not equal to the good's price. When the firm decides to increase production from point x on the demand curve (quantity Q_1) to point y (Q_2), the price of the good decreases from P_1 to P_2. The firm's initial total revenue ($P_1 \times Q_1$) is equal to the area $A + B$. At the new production point, total revenue ($P_2 \times Q_2$) is equal to the area $B + C$. The firm's marginal revenue is the difference between the initial total revenue and the new total revenue, equal to $C - A$.

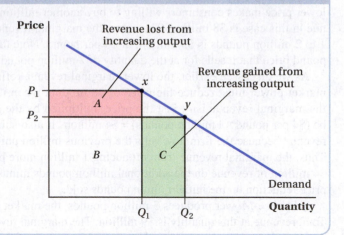

---

falls to P_2. The new total revenue is $P_2 \times Q_2$ or the rectangle $B + C$. Therefore, the marginal revenue of this output increase is the new revenue minus the old revenue:

$$TR_2 = P_2 \times Q_2 = B + C$$
$$TR_1 = P_1 \times Q_1 = A + B$$
$$MR = TR_2 - TR_1$$
$$MR = (B + C) - (A + B) = C - A$$

The area C contains the extra revenue that comes from selling more goods at price P_2, but this alone is not the marginal revenue of the extra output. We must also subtract area A, the revenue the firm loses because it now sells all units (not just the marginal unit) for the lower price P_2 instead of P_1. In fact, as we saw in the Fluff example, if the price-lowering effect from increasing output is large enough, marginal revenue could even be less than zero. In other words, selling more product could actually end up reducing a firm's revenue.

Marginal Revenue: A Mathematical Approach   We can compute the firm's marginal revenue using the logic we just discussed. As we saw, there are two effects when the firm sells an additional unit of output. Each of these will account for a component of the marginal revenue formula.

The first effect comes from the additional unit being sold at the market price P. In Figure 9.1, if we define $Q_2 - Q_1$ to be 1 unit, then this effect would be area C.

The second effect occurs because the additional unit drives down the market price for all the units the firm makes. To figure out how to express this component of marginal revenue, let's first label the change in price ΔP. In Figure 9.1, we're looking at the effect of a price cut, so $\Delta P < 0$. Let's also label the quantity before adding the incremental unit of output as Q and the incremental output as ΔQ. The second component of marginal revenue is therefore $\left(\dfrac{\Delta P}{\Delta Q}\right) \times Q$, the change in price caused by selling the additional unit of revenue times the quantity sold before adding the incremental unit. In Figure 9.1, this is area A. Note that because price falls as quantity rises—remember, the firm faces a downward-sloping demand curve—the term $\Delta P / \Delta Q$ is negative. This conforms to our logic above that this second component of marginal revenue is negative. It is the loss in revenue resulting from having to sell the non-incremental units at a lower price.

Putting together these components, we have the formula for marginal revenue (*MR*) from producing an additional quantity (Δ*Q*) of output (notice that we add the two components together even though the second represents a loss in revenue because Δ*P*/Δ*Q* is already negative):

$$MR = P + \left(\frac{\Delta P}{\Delta Q}\right) \times Q$$

This negative second component means that marginal revenue will always be less than the market price. If we map this equation into Figure 9.1, the first term is the additional revenue from selling an additional unit at price *P* (area *C*) and the second is area *A*.

➡ The end-of-chapter appendix derives a firm's marginal revenue using calculus.

Looking more closely at this formula reveals how the shape of the demand curve facing a firm affects its marginal revenue. The change in price corresponding to a change in quantity, Δ*P*/Δ*Q*, is a measure of how steep the demand curve is. When the demand curve is really steep, price falls a lot in response to an increase in output. Δ*P*/Δ*Q* is a large negative number in this case. This will drive down *MR* and can even make it negative. On the other hand, when the demand curve is flatter, price is not very sensitive to quantity increases. In this case, because Δ*P*/Δ*Q* is fairly small in magnitude, the first (positive) component *P* of marginal revenue plays a larger relative role, keeping marginal revenue from falling too much as output rises. In the special case of perfectly flat demand curves, Δ*P*/Δ*Q* is zero, and therefore marginal revenue equals the market price of the good. We know from Chapter 8 that when a firm's marginal revenue equals price, the firm is a price taker: Whatever quantity it sells will be sold at the market price *P*. This is an important insight that we return to below. Perfect competition is just the special case in which the firm's demand curve is perfectly elastic, so *MR* = *P*.

This connection between the slope of the demand curve and the level of a firm's marginal revenue is important in understanding how firms with market power choose the output levels that maximize their profits. We study this profit-maximization problem in detail in the next section, but it's useful to reflect a bit now on what the marginal revenue formula implies about it. Firms that face steep demand curves obtain small revenue gains (or even revenue losses, if *MR* is negative) when they increase output. This makes high output levels less profitable. Firms facing flatter demand curves obtain relatively large marginal revenues when raising output. This contrast suggests that (holding all else equal) having a steeper demand curve tends to reduce a firm's profit-maximizing output level. In the next section, we see that this is exactly the case.

We can apply the marginal revenue formula to any demand curve. For nonlinear demand curves, the slope Δ*P*/Δ*Q* is the slope of a line tangent to the demand curve at quantity *Q*. But the formula is especially easy for linear demand curves, because Δ*P*/Δ*Q* is constant. For any linear (inverse) demand curve of the form *P* = *a* − *bQ*, where *a* (the vertical intercept of the demand curve) and *b* are constants, Δ*P*/Δ*Q* = −*b*. The inverse demand curve itself relates *P* (the other component of marginal revenue) to *Q*, so if we also plug *P* = *a* − *bQ* and Δ*P*/Δ*Q* = −*b* into the *MR* formula above, we arrive at an expression for the marginal revenue of any linear demand curve:

$$MR = P + \left(\frac{\Delta P}{\Delta Q}\right) Q$$

$$= (a - bQ) + (-b)Q = a - 2bQ$$

So here, the marginal revenue curve looks just like the inverse demand curve but with twice the slope. It's only that simple for a linear demand curve, but the more general marginal revenue formula applies to any demand curve.

Figure 9.2 A Linear Demand Curve and Its Marginal Revenue Curve

A linear demand curve has a marginal revenue curve with the same vertical intercept and twice the slope. Here, the demand curve D is given by $P = 100 - 10Q$. The associated marginal revenue curve is therefore $MR = 100 - 20Q$. If $Q = 4$, for example, then $P = \$60$ and $MR = \$20$.

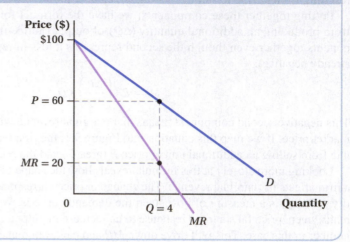

Figure 9.2 shows an example of a demand curve and its marginal revenue curve.[3] The demand curve in the figure is $P = 100 - 10Q$ and therefore the marginal revenue curve is $MR = 100 - 20Q$. If $Q = 4$, as shown, then the demand curve implies $P = \$60$ and $MR = \$20$.

figure it out 9.1

Suppose the demand curve is $Q = 12.5 - 0.25P$.

a. What is the marginal revenue curve that corresponds to this demand curve?

b. Calculate marginal revenue when $Q = 6$. Calculate marginal revenue when $Q = 7$.

Solution:

a. First, we need to solve for the inverse demand curve by rearranging the demand function so that price is on the left side by itself:

$$Q = 12.5 - 0.25P$$
$$0.25P = 12.5 - Q$$
$$P = 50 - 4Q$$

Thus, we know that the inverse demand curve is $P = 50 - 4Q$, with $a = 50$ and $b = 4$. Because $MR = a - 2bQ$, we know that $MR = 50 - 8Q$.

b. We can plug these values into our MR equation to solve for marginal revenue:

When $Q = 6$, $MR = 50 - 8(6) = 50 - 48 = 2$

When $Q = 7$, $MR = 50 - 8(7) = 50 - 56 = -6$

Note that, as we discussed above, MR falls as Q rises and can even become negative.

---

[3] If you know calculus, you can see that the multiplier of 2 comes from the derivative of the total revenue function. For a linear inverse demand curve $P = a - bQ$, the total revenue curve (the firm's revenue as a function of its quantity produced) that corresponds to it is $P \times Q$, or $aQ - bQ^2$. To find marginal revenue using the demand curve, we could compute the marginal revenue by taking the derivative of this total revenue function with respect to Q. Doing so gives $MR = a - 2bQ$.

9.3 Profit Maximization for a Firm with Market Power

Once you know how to compute marginal revenue, you can figure out the profit-maximizing output level for a firm with market power. At first glance, you might think it should produce until the marginal revenue hits zero and then stop. That's true only if there are no costs of production. A firm with market power should pay attention to its marginal revenue, but has to balance that against the production cost.

How to Maximize Profit

In Chapter 8, we discussed the two basic elements of firm profit — revenue and cost — and how each of these is determined by the firm's choice of how much output to produce. We saw that the profit-maximizing output was the one that set marginal revenue equal to marginal cost, and that marginal revenue for a perfectly competitive firm equals the market price, so maximizing profit meant producing the quantity at which price equals marginal cost. The firm should produce more if the additional revenue it would earn exceeds the additional cost and cut back on production if it's losing money on those extra units.

The same underlying logic works for firms with market power except that *marginal revenue no longer equals price*. To maximize its profit, a firm should choose its quantity where its marginal revenue equals its marginal cost:

$$MR = MC$$

If marginal revenue is above marginal cost, a firm, by producing more, can earn more revenue than the extra cost of production and increase its profit. If marginal revenue is below marginal cost, a firm can reduce its output, lose less revenue than it saves in cost, and again raise its profit. Only when these two marginal values are equal does changing output not increase profit.

Setting $MR = MC$ gives us the quantity, Q^*, that maximizes the firm's profit, and from that we figure out the profit-maximizing price. The height of the demand curve at that profit-maximizing quantity Q^* tells us the market price for the firm's output.

For a firm with market power, we can think of the firm choosing a profit-maximizing quantity as equivalent to choosing a profit-maximizing price. The demand curve ties together price and quantity, so picking one implies the other. The monopolist can either produce the profit-maximizing quantity of output and let the market determine the price (which will be the profit-maximizing price), or it can set the profit-maximizing price and let the market determine the quantity (which will be the profit-maximizing quantity).

An important factor to remember is that even though firms with market power have an ability to set any price for their output, that doesn't mean they can get away with it profitably. A firm with market power still is constrained by the demand curve. Customers will stop buying if the price gets too high, even if there aren't other competitors.

When Apple had market power as the only tablet producer, it could not charge whatever price it wanted. If Apple charged $20,000 for each iPad, almost no one would have bought one (even though it was the only tablet available). A monopolist doesn't lose business to direct competitors by raising the price for its product since a monopolist has no direct competitors. However, it loses business by driving its customers out of the market. A monopolist cannot charge anything it wants, but *will* charge a higher price than a more competitive firm.

▱ The end-of-chapter appendix uses calculus to solve the firm's profit-maximization problem.

Profit Maximization with Market Power: A Graphical Approach

We can apply the exact logic of the previous analysis to graphically derive the profit-maximizing output and price of a firm with market power, given the firm's demand and marginal cost curves. Let's assume we are again looking at the market for iPads and that marginal cost is constant at $200. Specifically, a firm with market power will follow these steps:

Step 1: Derive the marginal revenue curve from the demand curve. For a linear demand curve, this will be another straight line with the same vertical intercept that is twice as steep. In **Figure 9.3**, the marginal revenue curve is shown as *MR*.

Step 2: Find the output quantity at which marginal revenue equals marginal cost. This is the firm's profit-maximizing quantity of output. In Figure 9.3, Apple's profit-maximizing level of output is Q^*, or 80 million iPads.

Step 3: Determine the profit-maximizing price by locating the point on the demand curve at that optimal quantity level. To determine the price Apple should charge consumers to maximize its profit, just follow Q^* up to the demand curve and then read the price off the vertical axis. If Apple produces the profit-maximizing output level of 80 million, the market price will be $600. (Or equivalently, if Apple charges a price of $600, it will sell 80 million iPads.)

That's it. Once we have the firm's *MR* curve, we can use the profit-maximization rule $MR = MC$ to find the firm's optimal level of output and price.

Profit Maximization with Market Power: A Mathematical Approach

We can also solve for the profit-maximizing quantity and price mathematically, given equations for the firm's demand and marginal cost curves.

Suppose Apple's marginal cost of producing iPads is constant at $200, and the demand curve for iPads (where Q is in millions and P in dollars) is $Q = 200 - 0.2P$. How much

---

Figure 9.3 How a Firm with Market Power Maximizes Profit

Apple will maximize its profit from the iPad by producing where $MR = MC$. Therefore, Apple will sell 80 million iPads at a price of $600 each, well above Apple's marginal cost of $200 per iPad.

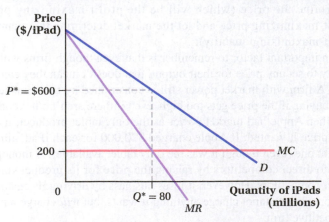

should Apple charge for iPads, and how many will it sell at that price? (Again, because of the equivalence of choosing price and choosing output level for firms with market power, we could ask how many iPads Apple should produce and at what price the iPads would sell, and the answer would be the same.)

We can figure this out using the same three-step process described above: Derive the marginal revenue curve, find the quantity at which marginal revenue equals marginal cost, and then determine the profit-maximizing price by computing the price at that quantity on the demand curve.

Step 1: Derive the marginal revenue curve from the demand curve. Let's start by obtaining the inverse demand curve by rearranging the demand curve so that price is a function of quantity rather than the other way around:

$$Q = 200 - 0.2P$$
$$0.2P = 200 - Q$$
$$P = 1,000 - 5Q$$

This is a linear inverse demand curve of the form $P = a - bQ$, where $a = 1,000$ and $b = 5$. Earlier we learned that $MR = a - 2bQ$ is the marginal revenue curve for this type of demand curve.[4] So for this demand curve, Apple's marginal revenue curve is

$$MR = 1,000 - 2(5Q) = 1,000 - 10Q$$

Step 2: Find the quantity at which marginal revenue equals marginal cost. Apple's marginal cost is constant at $200. Therefore, we just set the marginal revenue curve equal to this value and solve for Q:

$$MR = MC$$
$$1,000 - 10Q = 200$$
$$800 = 10Q$$
$$Q^* = 80$$

Thus, Apple's profit-maximizing quantity of iPads is 80 million.

Step 3: Determine the profit-maximizing price by locating the point on the demand curve at that optimal quantity level. Find the profit-maximizing price by plugging the optimal quantity into the demand curve. This tells us at what price the optimal quantity (80 million iPads) will be sold:

$$P^* = 1,000 - 5Q^*$$
$$= 1,000 - 5(80)$$
$$= 1,000 - 400 = 600$$

Given this demand curve and a constant marginal cost of $200 per iPad, then, Apple can maximize its profits by charging $600 per unit. It will sell 80 million iPads at this price. Notice that this price is well above Apple's marginal cost of $200, the price Apple would be charging in a perfectly competitive market. That's why firms like to have market power. The idea is simple: Reduce output. Raise prices. Make money.

---

[4] If we had a more complicated demand curve, we could compute the marginal revenue curve by using calculus. We would start with calculating total revenue by multiplying the inverse demand curve by Q. Then we would take the derivative with respect to Q to get the marginal revenue.

figure it out 9.2

Babe's Bats (BB) sells baseball bats for children around the world. The firm faces a demand curve of $Q = 10 - 0.4P$, where Q is measured in thousands of bats and P is dollars per bat. BB has a marginal cost curve that is equal to $MC = 5Q$.

a. Solve for BB's profit-maximizing level of output. Show the firm's profit-maximization decision graphically.

b. What price will BB charge to maximize its profit?

Solution:

a. To solve this problem, we should follow the three-step procedure outlined in the text. First, we need to derive the marginal revenue curve for BB bats. Because the firm faces a linear demand curve, the easiest way to obtain the marginal revenue curve is to start by solving for the firm's inverse demand curve:

$$Q = 10 - 0.4P$$
$$0.4P = 10 - Q$$
$$P = 25 - 2.5Q$$

For this inverse demand curve, $a = 25$ and $b = 2.5$. Therefore, since $MR = a - 2bQ$, we know that BB's MR curve will be

$$MR = 25 - 2(2.5Q) = 25 - 5Q$$

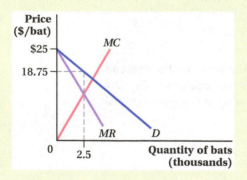

To solve for the profit-maximizing level of output, we can follow the profit-maximization rule $MR = MC$:

$$MR = MC$$
$$25 - 5Q = 5Q$$
$$10Q = 25$$
$$Q^* = 2.5$$

Therefore, BB should produce 2,500 bats. This profit-maximization decision is shown in the figure to the left. Profit is maximized at the output level at which the marginal revenue and marginal cost curves intersect.

b. To find BB's optimal price, we plug its profit-maximizing level of output ($Q^* = 2.5$) into its inverse demand curve:

$$P^* = 25 - 2.5Q^*$$
$$= 25 - 2.5(2.5)$$
$$= 25 - 6.25 = 18.75$$

BB should charge a price of $18.75 per bat. This is also demonstrated on the figure by following $Q^* = 2.5$ up to the demand curve and over to the vertical axis.

A Markup Formula for Companies with Market Power: The Lerner Index

We can take the logic we've just learned even further to come up with a rule-of-thumb for pricing that firms can use to determine profit-maximizing prices and output levels. Start with the definition of MR from above:

$$MR = P + \left(\frac{\Delta P}{\Delta Q}\right) \times Q$$

We know that the firm maximizes its profits by setting $MR = MC$, so plug that in:

$$MR = P + \left(\frac{\Delta P}{\Delta Q}\right) \times Q = MC$$

Now use a math trick and multiply the second term on the left side of the equation by P/P. This doesn't change the value of the equation, because multiplying by P/P is just another way of multiplying by 1. This changes our expression to

$$P + \left(\frac{\Delta P}{\Delta Q}\right) \times \frac{P}{P} \times Q = MC \quad \text{or} \quad P + \left(\frac{\Delta P}{\Delta Q} \times \frac{Q}{P}\right) \times P = MC$$

If the section in parentheses looks familiar to you, it's because it is the inverse of the elasticity of demand. Remember that in Chapter 2 we defined the price elasticity of demand E^D as $\frac{\Delta Q/Q}{\Delta P/P}$ or $\frac{\Delta Q}{\Delta P} \times \frac{P}{Q}$. The inverse of this value is $\frac{1}{E^D} = \frac{\Delta P}{\Delta Q} \times \frac{Q}{P}$. Substituting the inverse elasticity into the profit-maximization condition gives us

$$P + \left(\frac{\Delta P}{\Delta Q} \times \frac{Q}{P}\right) \times P = MC$$

$$P + \frac{1}{E^D} \times P = MC$$

A final bit of rearranging yields

$$P - MC = -\left(\frac{1}{E^D}\right) \times P \quad \text{or} \quad \frac{P - MC}{P} = -\frac{1}{E^D}$$

The left-hand side of this equation equals the firm's profit-maximizing **markup,** the *percentage of the firm's price that is greater than (or "marked up" from) its marginal cost*. What this equation indicates is that such a markup should depend on the price elasticity of demand that the firm faces. Specifically, as demand becomes more elastic—that is, as E^D becomes more negative, or equivalently, larger in absolute value—the optimal markup as a fraction of price falls. (If you can't quite see this in the equation, notice that elastic demand means a large negative number for E^D is in the denominator, making the right-hand side of the equation small.) On the other hand, as demand becomes less elastic, E^D becomes smaller in absolute value, indicating that the markup should be a larger fraction of price.

If we stop to think about these implications for a minute, they make perfect sense. When demand is quite inelastic, consumers' purchases of the firm's product are not sensitive to changes in price. This makes it easier for the firm to increase its profit by raising its price—it will sell fewer units, but not *that* many fewer, and it will make a higher margin on every unit it does sell. The firm should mark up its price more with less elastic demand. A firm facing relatively elastic demand, on the other hand, will suffer a greater loss in quantity sold when it raises its price, so high markups over cost benefit them less.

The measure of the markup given by the equation above has a special name: the *Lerner index* (after Abba Lerner, the economist who proposed it in 1934). As we just discussed, assuming the firm is trying to maximize its profit, the Lerner index tells us something about the nature of the demand curve facing the firm. When the index is high (i.e., when the markup accounts for a large fraction of the price), the demand for the firm's product is relatively inelastic. When the index is low, the firm faces relatively elastic demand. Because the ability to price above marginal cost is the definition of market power, the **Lerner index** is a *measure of a firm's markup and of its market power*. The higher it is, the greater the firm's ability to price above its marginal cost.

When demand is perfectly elastic—the firm faces a horizontal demand curve and any effort to charge a price higher than the demand curve will result in a loss of all sales—then

markup The percentage of the firm's price that is greater than (or "marked up" from) its marginal cost.

Lerner index A measure of a firm's markup and of its market power.

$E^D = -\infty$. As we see in the equation above, the Lerner index is zero in this case, which means the markup is also zero. The firm sells at a price equal to marginal cost, and the firm becomes a price taker.

When E^D lies between 0 and −1, that is, when the firm faces a demand curve that is inelastic, the Lerner index is greater than 1, implying $P - MC > P$, or $MC < 0$ which doesn't make sense. In other words, a firm should never operate at a point on its demand curve where demand is inelastic or unit elastic. That's because a price increase in that situation will raise the firm's revenue but reduce the quantity and therefore the cost. In other words, the firm is guaranteed to raise profit by increasing prices if demand is inelastic.

The Lerner index can range anywhere from 0 (perfect competition) to just under 1 (barely elastic—almost unit elastic—demand). It is a summary of the amount of market power a firm has. In comparing degrees of market power across firms, the firm with the highest Lerner index has the most market power; the firm with the second-highest Lerner index has the second-most market power, and so on.

Measuring the Lerner Index   Firms with market power know their profit-maximizing markups are tied to the price elasticities they face. The difficulty from a practical standpoint is that firms don't automatically know their Lerner index and ideal markup. So, they often spend considerable effort trying to learn about the shape of the demand and marginal revenue curves they face, because that tells them about the price elasticity of demand of their customers. Amazon has been sued over offering different prices to customers for the same products. In one prominent case, Amazon CEO Jeffrey Bezos apologized by insisting that Amazon was simply randomizing prices to develop a better sense of demand in its market. This chapter shows exactly why Amazon would do this. If a company knows the shape of its own demand curve, it can determine the most profitable price to charge using either the markup formula or the monopoly pricing method.

 Application: Market Power versus Market Share

Market power involves more than the size of a particular firm. For example, consider Dr. Brown's, a manufacturer of specialty sodas in the United States that produces a celery-flavored soda called Cel-Ray. Even though the sales of Coca-Cola are thousands of times larger than the sales of Cel-Ray, it turns out that Dr. Brown's has more market power than Coca-Cola by the economist's definition.

How can that be? The key factor to consider is the price elasticity of demand for the two products. Coca-Cola drinkers are, on average, fairly price-sensitive in the short run. The price elasticity of demand for a six-pack of Coke in a grocery store is around −4.1.[5] On the other hand, people who drink Cel-Ray must have a unique preference for the celery flavor. Whereas many substitutes exist for Coca-Cola, there really aren't many substitutes for Cel-Ray. Thus, Cel-Ray drinkers will likely be less price-sensitive than Coke drinkers. A reasonable estimate of the price elasticity of demand for a six-pack of Cel-Ray is about −2.

If we use these two elasticities to measure the Lerner index for each product, we indeed see that Cel-Ray has more market power than Coke:

$$\text{Lerner index for Coke} = -\frac{1}{E^D} = -\frac{1}{-4.1} = 0.244$$

$$\text{Lerner index for Cel-Ray} = -\frac{1}{E^D} = -\frac{1}{-2} = 0.5$$

Dr. Brown's Cel-Ray soda, a lock on its market since 1869.

[5] Jean-Pierre Dubé, "Product Differentiation and Mergers in the Carbonated Soft Drink Industry," *Journal of Economics and Management Strategy* 14, no. 4 (2005): 879–904.

Therefore, Cel-Ray's profit-maximizing price is a higher markup over its marginal costs than Coke's profit-maximizing price. In other words, Coca-Cola's pricing behavior is actually closer to the pricing behavior of a competitive firm than Cel-Ray's. It is not the size of the market or the firm's market share that determines or measures market power; it is the firm's ability to price above its marginal cost. ■

The Supply Relationship for a Firm with Market Power

We now know how to figure out the profit-maximizing quantity and price for a firm with market power, and we can do so for any given marginal cost and demand curves the firm might face. As you might imagine, we could sketch out all combinations of the firm's profit-maximizing quantities and prices implied by any possible set of marginal cost and demand curves.

That sounds a lot like a supply curve — it is, after all, a set of prices and the quantities produced — but it's not. Firms with market power don't have supply curves, strictly speaking. Their profit-maximizing price and quantity combinations are not supply curves because those combinations depend on the demand curve the firm faces. As we saw in Chapter 8, competitive supply curves exist completely independently of demand. They depend only on firms' marginal costs, because a perfectly competitive firm produces the quantity at which the market price (which the firm takes as given) equals its marginal cost. That's why a perfectly competitive firm's supply curve is a portion of its marginal cost curve, and a perfectly competitive industry's supply curve is the industry marginal cost curve. Neither of these supply curves is determined by anything having to do with demand; they are only about costs.

This strict relationship between costs and price isn't true for a firm with market power. Its optimal output level depends on not only the marginal cost curve, but also the firm's marginal revenue curve (which is related to the demand curve). Put another way, a supply curve gives a one-to-one mapping between the price and a firm's output. But for a firm with market power, even holding constant its marginal cost curve, the firm could charge a high price at a given quantity if it faces a steeper demand curve or a lower price at the same quantity if it faced a flatter demand curve. We'll see an example of this in the next section. Therefore, a simple mapping of price and quantity supplied is not possible for a firm with market power and there would be no supply curve.

9.4 How a Firm with Market Power Reacts to Market Changes

Given how profit-maximizing firms with market power should make production and pricing decisions, we can think through the effects of various market changes, much as we did with supply and demand in the competitive setting. Even though firms with market power do not have a supply curve, we will see that in some ways they react similarly to competitive firms, but sometimes quite differently.

Response to a Change in Marginal Cost

First think about the effect of an increase in marginal cost. In the iPad example, marginal cost was constant at $200 and the inverse demand curve was $P = 1,000 - 5Q$ (where Q is in millions). Suppose there's a fire in the plant that manufactures the screen on the iPad, raising the marginal cost of screens, and as a result, the marginal cost of the iPad increases from $200 to $250.

To determine the impact of this on the market, we follow the three-step method but with the new marginal cost curve:

Step 1: Derive the marginal revenue curve. The demand curve hasn't changed, so this is the same as before: $MR = 1{,}000 - 10Q$.

Step 2: Find the quantity at which $MR = MC$. The MC is now $250, so

$$1{,}000 - 10Q = 250$$
$$750 = 10Q$$
$$Q^* = 75$$

The new profit-maximizing quantity is 75 million units, down from 80 million.

Step 3: Determine the profit-maximizing price using the optimal quantity and the demand curve. The (inverse) demand curve is $P = 1{,}000 - 5Q$. Plugging in the new quantity, we have $P^* = 1{,}000 - 5(75) = \$625$. The new price will be $625, up from $600 before the fire.

We illustrate the change from the initial equilibrium to the new one in **Figure 9.4**.

A firm with market power responds to a cost shock in a similar way to how a competitive firm would. When marginal cost rises, prices rise and output falls. But in competition, a change in marginal cost is fully reflected in the market price, because $P = MC$. That doesn't have to be the case when the seller has market power. In the iPad example, the market price rose only $25 in response to a $50 increase in marginal cost. To maximize its profit, Apple does not pass along the full increase in its cost to its customers. The drop in quantity that results from the increase in cost is also smaller than the drop that would occur in a perfectly competitive market. Note, however, that the equilibrium quantity is still higher in a competitive market than one with market power, even after the cost increase. It's only the *change* in Q that is smaller.[6]

Figure 9.4   How a Firm with Market Power Reacts to an Increase in Marginal Cost

The initial quantity of 80 million is set by $MR = MC_1$ ($200) at point *a*. This quantity corresponds to a price of $600, as indicated at point *b*. After the fire, the marginal cost curve shifts up to $250 ($MC_2$). Because the fire only affects the supply side of the market, the consumer's willingness to pay does not change, and the demand and marginal revenue curves do not shift. Now marginal revenue equals marginal cost at point *c*, at a quantity of 75 million. Following that quantity up to the demand curve (at point *d*), we can see that the price of an iPad will rise to $625.

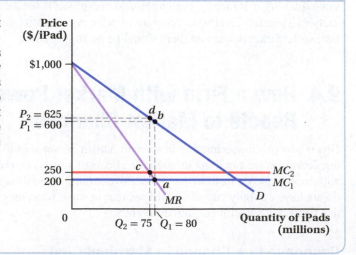

---

[6] Exactly how much of a cost change a firm with market power will pass along to its customers depends on the shapes of the marginal cost and marginal revenue curves. Here, the optimal pass-through is half of the cost change. In other situations, it could be more or less than that; in fact, there are conditions where the optimal pass-through is larger than the change in cost. The point is that is can be (and usually is) different than the dollar-for-dollar pass-through of perfect competition.

Response to a Change in Demand

Now suppose that instead of a cost shift, there is a parallel shift in the demand curve. Perhaps a revision of the iPad's OS doubles battery life, increasing demand and shifting out the demand curve. Specifically, let's say the new inverse demand curve is $P = 1,400 - 5Q$.

To figure out the impact, we again follow the three-step method. Because the demand curve has shifted, the marginal revenue curve changes as well. The new demand curve is linear, so we know how to derive the marginal revenue curve; we double the number in front of the quantity in the inverse demand curve. So,

$$MR = 1,400 - 2(5Q) = 1,400 - 10Q$$

Setting this equal to the marginal cost (which we'll assume is back at its original level of $200) implies

$$1,400 - 10Q = 200$$
$$10Q = 1,200$$
$$Q^* = 120$$

The quantity produced after the demand shift is now 120 million units, up from 80 million. Finally, we find the new price by plugging this quantity into the inverse demand curve:

$$P^* = 1,400 - 5Q^*$$
$$= 1,400 - 5(120)$$
$$= 800$$

The new price is $800, up from $600 before the demand shift.

An outward demand shift leads to an increase in both quantity and price in a market where the seller has market power, the same direction as in perfect competition. But again, the size of the changes differs.

 ## figure it out 9.3

Go online for interactive, step-by-step help in solving the following problem.

The Power Tires Company has market power and faces the demand curve shown in the figure below. The firm's marginal cost curve is $MC = 30 + 3Q$.

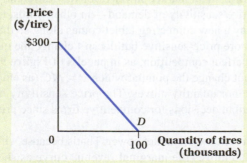

a. What is the firm's profit-maximizing output and price?

b. If the firm's demand changes to $P = 240 - 2Q$ while its marginal cost curve remains the same, what is the firm's profit-maximizing level of output and price? How does this compare to your answer for (a)?

c. Draw a diagram showing these two outcomes. Holding marginal cost equal, how does the shape of the demand curve affect the firm's ability to charge a high price?

Solution:

a. To solve for the firm's profit-maximizing level of output, we need to find the firm's marginal revenue curve. But we only have a diagram of the demand curve.

So, we will start by solving for the inverse demand function. The inverse demand function will typically have the form

$$P = a - bQ$$

where a is the vertical intercept and b is the absolute value of the slope $\left(= \left| \dfrac{\Delta P}{\Delta Q} \right| \right)$. We can see from the figure of the demand curve that $a = 300$. In addition, we can calculate the absolute value of the slope of the demand curve as $\left| \dfrac{\Delta P}{\Delta Q} \right| = \left| \dfrac{-300}{100} \right| = 3$. Therefore, $b = 3$.

This means that the demand for Power Tires is

$$P = 300 - 3Q$$

We know that the equation for marginal revenue (when demand is linear) is $MR = a - 2bQ$. Therefore,

$$MR = 300 - 6Q$$

Setting marginal revenue equal to marginal cost, we find

$$MR = MC$$
$$300 - 6Q = 30 + 3Q$$
$$270 = 9Q$$
$$Q^* = 30$$

To find price, we substitute $Q = 30$ into the firm's demand equation:

$$P = 300 - 3Q$$
$$= 300 - 3(30) = 210$$

The firm should produce 30,000 tires and sell them at a price of $210.

b. If demand changes to $P = 240 - 2Q$, marginal revenue becomes $MR = 240 - 4Q$ because now $a = 240$ and $b = 2$. Setting $MR = MC$, we find

$$240 - 4Q = 30 + 3Q$$
$$210 = 7Q$$
$$Q^* = 30$$

Even with changed demand, the firm should still produce 30 units if it wants to maximize profit. Substituting into the new demand curve, we can see that the price will be

$$P^* = 240 - 2Q^*$$
$$= 240 - 2(30) = 180$$

Here, the equilibrium price is lower even though the profit-maximizing output is the same.

c. The new diagram appears below. Because D_2 is flatter than D_1, the firm must charge a lower price. Consumers are more responsive to price.

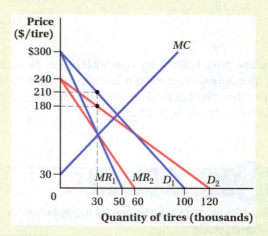

The Big Difference: Changing the Price Sensitivity of Customers

One type of market change to which firms with market power react very differently from competitive firms is a change in the price sensitivity of demand—in other words, making the demand curve steeper or flatter. Say a new competing tablet comes along so that consumers' demand for iPads becomes more price-sensitive but doesn't change the quantity demanded at the current price. With perfect competition, as in panel a of **Figure 9.5**, the flattening of the demand curve does not change the point at which $P = MC$ (as embodied in the supply curve), so neither price nor quantity moves. The price sensitivity of consumers does not impact the sellers' output decisions for competitive firms since price still equals marginal cost.

Things are different, however, for a seller with market power. That's because with market power, the rotation in demand also moves the marginal revenue curve as shown in panel b of Figure 9.5. Here, MR_2 intersects the marginal cost curve at a higher quantity

---

Figure 9.5   Responses to a Rotation in the Demand Curve

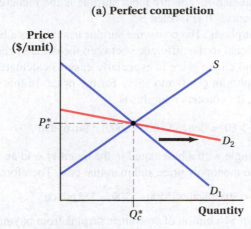

(a) Perfect competition

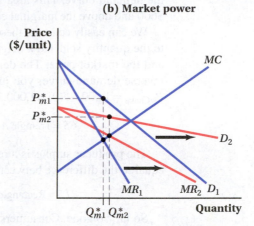

(b) Market power

(a) For a perfectly competitive market, a rotation in the demand curve from D_1 to D_2 does not change the equilibrium quantity Q_c^* and price P_c^*.

(b) For a firm with market power, a rotation in the demand curve from D_1 to D_2 rotates the marginal revenue curve from MR_1 to MR_2.

Prior to the rotation, the profit-maximizing quantity and price $\left(Q_{m1}^*, P_{m1}^*\right)$ occurred where $MR_1 = MC$. After the rotation, the firm is profit-maximizing at a higher quantity and lower price $\left(Q_{m2}^*, P_{m2}^*\right)$ where $MR_2 = MC$.

---

than did $MR_1\left(Q_{m2}^*\right.$ instead of $\left.Q_{m1}^*\right)$. Therefore, the firm's output rises as a result of the demand curve rotation and the price falls.

The opposite pattern holds when consumers become less price-sensitive and firms have market power: Output falls and price rises. Again, these changes wouldn't happen in perfect competition because suppliers' choices don't depend on the price sensitivity of demand.

9.5 The Winners and Losers from Market Power

Given that a firm with market power charges a price that is above its marginal cost, the market power benefits them. We can compute exactly how beneficial. We can also see how market power affects consumers (*Hint:* badly). We will use the same tools utilized to analyze competitive markets in Chapter 3—consumer and producer surplus. This approach allows us to directly compare markets in which firms have market power to those that are competitive.

Consumer and Producer Surplus under Market Power

Let's return to the original Apple iPad example. Apple had a marginal cost of $200 and an inverse demand curve of $P = 1,000 - 5Q$ (where Q was in millions). This demand curve implied a marginal revenue curve $MR = 1,000 - 10Q$. We set that equal to marginal cost to solve for Q and found that, to maximize profit, Apple should produce 80 million iPads and set its price at $600 per iPad.

We can compute the consumer and producer surplus when a firm has market power in the same way we computed these surpluses in a competitive market. The consumer surplus is the area under the demand curve and above the price. The producer surplus is the area below the price and above the marginal cost curve (in perfectly competitive firms, remember that marginal cost is the supply curve).

We illustrate these surpluses in **Figure 9.6**. Apple's profit-maximizing price and quantity occur at point *m*. The consumer surplus is the triangle above the price $600 and below the demand curve. This area is labeled *A*. The producer surplus is the rectangle below $600 and above the marginal cost curve. It is labeled *B*.

We can easily compute these surpluses. The consumer surplus triangle has a base equal to the quantity sold and a height equal to the difference between the demand choke price and the market price. The demand choke price is especially easy to calculate from an inverse demand curve; you just plug in $Q = 0$ and solve for the price. In this case, it's $P_{D\text{Choke}} = 1,000 - 5(0) = 1,000$. So, the consumer surplus is

$$CS = \text{Triangle } A = \frac{1}{2} \times 80 \text{ million} \times (\$1,000 - \$600) = \$16 \text{ billion}$$

The producer surplus is a rectangle with a base equal to the quantity sold and a height equal to the difference between the monopoly price and marginal cost. Therefore,

$$PS = \text{Rectangle } B = (80 \text{ million}) \times (\$600 - \$200) = \$32 \text{ billion}$$

So far, so good. Consumers earn $16 billion of consumer surplus from buying iPads, a fairly sizable sum, and Apple does well, making $32 billion of surplus.

Consumer and Producer Surplus under Perfect Competition

Now think about how the market would look if Apple behaved like a competitive firm and priced at marginal cost. The price would be $200 because marginal cost is constant at $200. Plugging $200 into the demand curve equation yields a quantity of 160 million. Therefore, in the competitive equilibrium, Apple would sell 160 million iPads at a price of $200 (point *c* in Figure 9.6). Note that because $P = MC$ and MC is constant, Apple would earn zero producer surplus in a competitive market.

With competition, then, iPad prices would be lower, the quantity sold would be higher, and Apple would make a lot less money (producer surplus would fall by $32 billion). It shows the standard result: The competitive market outcome has higher output and lower price than in a market where firms have market power.

Consumer surplus goes up under perfect competition but producer surplus goes down. In Figure 9.6, consumer surplus under perfect competition is the entire triangular area $A + B + C$ below the demand curve and above the competitive price of $200. The triangle's

---

Figure 9.6 Surplus from the Apple iPad

We can compute Apple's producer surplus, consumer surplus, and deadweight loss using the marginal cost curve, the demand curve, and the profit-maximizing output and price levels. Consumer surplus is the area of triangle *A*, equal to $\frac{1}{2} \times 80$ million $\times$ ($1,000 − $600) or $16 billion. The producer surplus, rectangle *B*, is (80 million) $\times$ ($600 − $200) or $32 billion. The deadweight loss is triangle *C* and can be calculated as $\frac{1}{2} \times$ (160 million − 80 million) $\times$ ($600 − $200) or $16 billion.

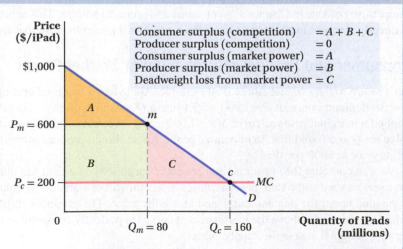

Consumer surplus (competition) $= A + B + C$
Producer surplus (competition) $= 0$
Consumer surplus (market power) $= A$
Producer surplus (market power) $= B$
Deadweight loss from market power $= C$

base is the competitive quantity of 160 million and its height is the difference between the demand choke price of $1,000 and the competitive price. This means consumer surplus under perfect competition is

$$CS = \frac{1}{2} \times 160 \text{ million} \times (\$1,000 - 200) = \$64 \text{ billion}$$

Recall that when Apple exercised its market power, consumer surplus was only $16 billion. In this example, consumers have 4 times the consumer surplus under competition than when Apple has market power. On the other side, by exploiting its market power, Apple moves from having no producer surplus to $32 billion of producer surplus. That's why firms want to use their market power whenever they can, even if it costs their customers a large amount of consumer surplus.

 ## Application: Ultra-Low-Cost Carrier Airlines

A fast-growing segment of the airline market is ultra-low-cost carriers (ULCCs). In the United States, airlines like Allegiant, Frontier, and Spirit Airlines (and others that didn't survive) base their business models off of what was arguably the original ULCC, Ryanair. As we discussed before, Ryanair takes low-cost consciousness to the highest degree so it can maintain shockingly low prices. When ULCCs enter a new airport market, they try to build traffic by aggressively undercutting fares offered by incumbent carriers. One way to think about this is that a ULCC's arrival moves an airport from a situation in which incumbents have market power to a situation that is closer to competition.

The impact is sometimes dramatic. Prices can fall by double-digit percentages on routes that the ULCC starts to fly, and the number of passengers flying the route goes up substantially. It's probably no coincidence that among the 25 busiest airports in the United States, the 5 that saw the biggest drops in average inflation-adjusted fares (for all airlines) from 2011 to 2017 were all airports at which a ULCC began to fly or substantially ramped up operations during that period. The lucky passengers were flying into and out of Chicago O'Hare (an average fare drop of 23% during the period), Newark Liberty International (average drop of 22%), Houston's George Bush Intercontinental (average drop of 21%), Dallas/Fort Worth International (average drop of 20%), and Las Vegas' McCarran (average drop of 20%).[7]

Passengers across the country have become familiar with these sorts of changes. They've gotten used to packing lighter luggage (to save on baggage fees), bringing their own food and small-size drinks onboard (there are no free snacks or beverages on a ULCC), and making do with less legroom. They're willing to go along with these changes because they can now fly for less than ever before. We suspect you can almost hear a collective cheer coming from students at schools in the cities where a ULCC has arrived in town. Thanks to competition from ULCCs, their consumer surplus is bound to rise, because returning home to visit mom and dad or heading off to a warm-weather locale for spring break just became more affordable. ∎

The Deadweight Loss of Market Power

Exercising market power can be great for firms and bad for consumers. Firms earn more producer surplus by restricting output and raising price, but this costs consumers a sizable chunk of their consumer surplus. That's not the only consequence of market power, though. Notice that, in the example above, the total surplus under market power of

---

[7] These numbers were taken from data compiled by the Bureau of Transportation Statistics of the U.S. Department of Transportation.

$48 billion ($16 billion consumer surplus + $32 billion producer surplus) is smaller than the total surplus under competition of $64 billion. That missing $16 billion of surplus has been destroyed by the firm's exercise of market power. No one gets it. It just disappears. In other words, it is the deadweight loss from market power.

The deadweight loss of market power can be seen in Figure 9.6. It is the area of triangle C whose base is the difference between the firm's output with market power and its output under perfect competition, and whose height is the difference between the prices under market power (P_m) and competition (P_c). We know from our comparison of the total surplus of the market power and competitive cases above that this area is $16 billion. We can confirm that value by calculating the area of triangle C:

$$DWL = \frac{1}{2} \times (160 \text{ million} - 80 \text{ million}) \times (\$600 - \$200) = \$16 \text{ billion}$$

The deadweight loss (DWL) is the inefficiency of market power. Note that this cost is exactly like the DWL from a tax or regulation we discussed in Chapter 3—a triangular area below the demand curve and above the marginal cost curve (supply curve, in Chapter 3). A firm with pricing power essentially puts a market power "tax" on consumers and keeps the revenue for itself. The DWL comes about because there are consumers in the market who are willing to buy the product (an iPad in this example) at a price above its cost of production, but who won't because the firm has hiked up prices to increase its profit. Just as with the DWL from taxes and regulations, the size of the DWL from market power is related to the size of the difference between the monopoly and competitive output levels. The more the firm withholds output to maximize profits, the bigger is the efficiency loss.

 The online appendix to Chapter 3 uses integration to calculate producer surplus and deadweight loss for firms.

---

figure it out 9.4

Let's return to our earlier problem regarding Babe's Bats (BB). Remember that BB faces an inverse demand curve of $P = 25 - 2.5Q$ and a marginal cost curve $MC = 5Q$. Calculate the deadweight loss from market power at the firm's profit-maximizing level of output.

Solution:

The easiest way to find deadweight loss is to use a diagram. Therefore, we should start by drawing a graph with demand, marginal revenue, and marginal cost:

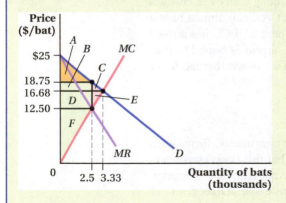

We know from our earlier problem that the profit-maximizing level of output is 2,500 bats sold at a price of $18.75.

To find the deadweight loss from market power, we need to consider the consumer and producer surplus and compare them with the competitive outcome. If BB participated in a competitive market, it would set price equal to marginal cost to determine its output:

$$P = MC$$
$$25 - 2.5Q = 5Q$$
$$25 = 7.5Q$$
$$Q^* = 3.33$$

Therefore, BB would sell 3,333 bats. Of course, the price will be lower at this level of output:

$$P^* = 25 - 2.5Q^*$$
$$= 25 - 2.5(3.33)$$
$$= 16.68$$

If the market were competitive, the bats would sell for $16.68 each. Consumer surplus would be areas $A + B + C$ (the area below the demand curve and above the competitive price), and producer surplus would be areas $D + E + F$ (the area below the competitive price but above the marginal cost curve). Total surplus would be areas $A + B + C + D + E + F$.

When BB exercises its market power, it reduces its output to 2,500 bats and increases its price to $18.75. In this situation, consumer surplus is only area A (the area below demand but above the monopoly price). Producer surplus is areas $B + D + F$ (the area below the monopoly price but above marginal cost). Total surplus under market power is $A + B + D + F$.

So, what happens to areas C and E? Area C was consumer surplus but no longer exists. Area E was producer surplus but also has disappeared. These areas are the deadweight loss from market power. We can calculate this area by measuring the area of the triangle that encompasses

areas $C + E$. To do so, we have one more important calculation to make. We need to calculate the height of the triangle, so we need to determine the marginal cost of producing 2,500 units:

$$MC = 5Q$$
$$= 5(2.5)$$
$$= 12.5$$

Now, we can calculate the area of the deadweight loss triangle:

$$DWL = \text{Areas } C + E = \frac{1}{2} \times \text{Base} \times \text{Height}$$
$$= \frac{1}{2} \times (3.33 - 2.5) \times (\$18.75 - \$12.50)$$
$$= \frac{1}{2} \times 0.83 \times \$6.25$$
$$= \$2.59375$$

Remember that the quantity is measured in thousands, so the deadweight loss is equal to $2,593.75.

Differences in Producer Surplus for Different Firms

One more important point about the implications of market power concerns how the slope of the demand curve influences the relative size of consumer and producer surplus in the market.

Consider two different markets: one with a relatively steep (inelastic) demand curve and one with a flatter (elastic) one. Each is served by a monopolist. To keep things simple, imagine that both firms have the same constant marginal cost curves, and that it just so happens each firm's profit-maximizing output is the same. We plot this case in **Figure 9.7**.

In the market in panel a of Figure 9.7, buyers aren't very price-sensitive, so the demand curve is steep. In the market in panel b, consumers are quite sensitive to prices, as reflected in the flatter demand curve. The figure also shows the marginal revenue curves in both markets. To maximize their profits, both firms choose quantity and price to set $MR = MC$. It is clear from looking at the figure that for the same-sized market (measured by the total quantity of the good that is produced, which we've set to be the same here), producer surplus is higher when the demand curve is steeper. That's because, as we pointed out earlier, a steeper demand curve raises the firm's profit-maximizing markup of price over marginal cost.

Firms with market power love to operate in markets in which consumers are relatively price-insensitive. If you're a consumer in that market, though, look out: Prices are going to be high.

Figure 9.7   Gains from Market Power under Different Demand Curves

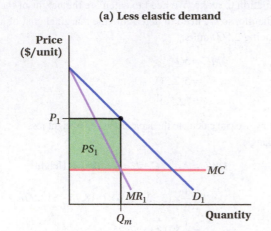

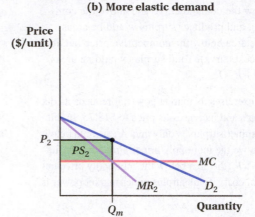

(a) When buyers are not very price-sensitive, the demand curve is steep. At $MR_1 = MC$, the producer supplies quantity Q_m at the relatively high price P_1, and generates the relatively large producer surplus PS_1.

(b) When buyers are price-sensitive, the demand curve is flat. At $MR_2 = MC$, the producer also supplies quantity Q_m, but at the relatively low price P_2, and generates the relatively small producer surplus PS_2.

9.6 Governments and Market Power: Regulation, Antitrust, and Innovation

We've seen the impact that market power can have on an industry—higher prices, smaller output, lower consumer surplus, and deadweight loss. The deadweight loss created by market power can justify government intervention in markets if such regulation can move the market toward a more competitive outcome and reduce deadweight loss. And, indeed, governments attempt to do this in several ways. After thinking about them, we will also explore the ways in which the government sometimes encourages market power and how this, too, can have an economic justification.

Direct Price Regulation

When a concern exists that firms in an industry have too much market power, governments sometimes directly regulate prices. Often, this occurs in markets considered to be natural monopolies. If there is no way to prevent the existence of a natural monopoly because of the nature of the industry's cost structure, the government will frequently allow only a single firm to operate but will limit its pricing behavior to prevent it from fully exploiting its market power. Governments have used this argument to justify regulating, at various times, the prices of electricity, natural gas, gasoline, cable television, local telephone service, long-distance telephone service, airfares, trucking, and many other products.

To understand the logic behind these actions, consider a typical natural monopoly case as shown in **Figure 9.8**. Let's suppose it is the market for electricity distribution, which we argued earlier may be a natural monopoly. With a demand curve of D, an unregulated electric company would produce at the point where marginal revenue equals marginal cost. This would lead to a price of P_m, substantially higher than the firm's marginal cost. The consumer surplus in this situation will be only the area A, rather than the area $A + B + C$, as would be the case if prices were instead set at P_c, a level equal to the firm's marginal cost.

Figure 9.8 Government Regulation of a Natural Monopoly

Before government regulation, the electric company produces at point m, where quantity is Q_m and price P_m is well above the firm's marginal cost curve. If the government sets a price cap at the level equal to the firm's marginal cost, the firm will produce at the perfectly competitive price (P_c) and quantity (Q_c). Consumer surplus under the regulation will expand from triangle A to the triangle $A + B + C$. However, since P_c falls below the firm's average total cost curve, the firm will be operating with negative profit, and the price cap is not a sustainable regulation.

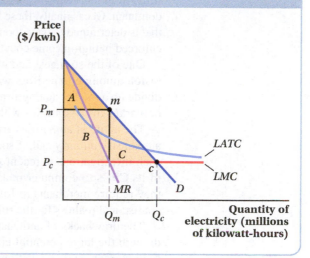

If the government imposes a price cap regulation that forbids the electric company from charging prices above P_c, output could equal its perfectly competitive level, and consumer surplus will equal area $A + B + C$. But there's a problem. P_c is below the firm's average total cost; if it sells every unit it produces at the regulated price, the firm will earn a negative profit, as it won't be able to cover its fixed cost. Therefore, a simple price regulation requiring competitive pricing is not a sustainable solution in regulating a natural monopoly. However, any regulation that would allow a price above marginal cost in order to permit the natural monopolist to recoup its fixed cost would also lead to a deadweight loss and less consumer surplus than the competitive case (though the deadweight loss may be smaller and the reduction in consumer surplus smaller than in the unregulated monopoly case).[8]

Aside from this problem, there are several other serious difficulties involved in using direct price regulations. First and foremost, only the company knows its true cost structure, so it's difficult to set the regulated price at the perfectly competitive level. The regulator is left to estimate them. Furthermore, the firm has an incentive to pretend its costs are higher than they really are, because this would justify a higher regulated price. In addition, companies that are regulated based on their cost often have no incentive to reduce their costs because the regulator would then reduce the regulated price, destroying any profit gained from the increase in efficiency.

Antitrust

Another approach governments use to address the effects of market power is **antitrust law** (sometimes called *competition policy* outside the United States), *laws designed to promote competitive markets by restricting firms from behaviors that limit competition.*

Antitrust laws are meant to promote competition in a market by restricting firms from certain behaviors that may limit competition, especially if the firm is an established and

antitrust law Laws designed to promote competitive markets by restricting firms from behaviors that limit competition.

[8] There is a way, at least theoretically, that regulation could achieve both the perfectly competitive outcome and allow the firm to pay its fixed costs. This would involve not just a per-unit price P_c, but also a lump-sum payment to the monopolist either from consumers or the government. Many regulated utilities have payment structures that try to replicate this in part, with a fixed monthly fee for service regardless of the quantity used plus an additional fee tied to the quantity the consumer purchases. However, these fee schedules are often only approximations to the true cost structure of the monopolist and can also be constrained by political considerations, so it is difficult to achieve perfectly competitive outcomes exactly.

substantial current player in the industry. In some cases, antitrust laws are used to prevent firms from merging with or acquiring other firms in order to stop them from becoming too dominant. Occasionally, these laws are even used to force the break-up of an established firm that is determined to have too much market power. Antitrust law tends to be strong and well enforced in high-income countries, but is often much weaker elsewhere in the world.

One of the strongest and most common prohibitions in antitrust law is the ban on collusion among competitors with regard to pricing and market allocation (agreements to divide up a market among firms). In the United States, for example, even discussing prices or market entry strategies with your competitors is a criminal act.

The antitrust authorities are also allowed to investigate whether a firm is monopolizing an industry unfairly and, if so, they can sue to change the behavior. There have been many such investigations in recent years—for example, those investigating Intel for its pricing of its CPUs to computer makers; American Express, Visa, and MasterCard for the rules they require merchants to follow when customers want to use credit cards to make purchases; and realtors for the rules they set about who is allowed to list houses for sale.

The drawbacks of antitrust enforcement as a way of preventing market power have to do with the large potential costs and uncertainties involved. The government should not fight mergers and acquisitions that would increase efficiency and make consumers better off, but only those that would harm them. The problem is that it's often difficult to tell those two cases apart ahead of time.

Promoting Monopoly: Patents, Licenses, and Copyrights

Even as the government tries to limit market power through regulation and antitrust policy, it sometimes *encourages* monopolies and helps them legally enforce their market power by conferring patents, licenses, copyrights, trademarks, and other assorted legal rights to exercise market power.

Why would the government do this if it cares about consumers and competitive markets? Pharmaceutical companies, for example, receive patent-based monopolies on all sorts of medicines, which raise the prices people pay. Radio stations and mobile phone companies license broadcast spectrum, which prohibits others from broadcasting. Copyright owners of a book or movie get 125 years of protection from anyone copying their work without obtaining approval and paying royalties in the United States. The Marvel superheroes have similar protection. You might have a great idea for using a superhero in your own movie, but the government has given Marvel (and its owner, Disney) the right to determine how Marvel characters are used commercially.

Collectively, all the monopolies created by the government add up to immense amounts of market power that inevitably lead to higher prices and lower quantities than would exist in a competitive market. The reason why it still might make sense for the government to do this is for the sake of encouraging innovation. Giving someone the exclusive right, at least temporarily, to the profits from innovation can provide a powerful incentive to create new things. Governments have decided that the consumer surplus created by these new goods can outweigh the deadweight loss from their producers having market power for a period of time. In some cases, innovation can be the upside of market power.

To see why, think about a company that invents a cure for the common cold. Demand for such a cure is the curve D in **Figure 9.9** and the marginal cost of production, say, is $5. Without a patent but with a competitive market of producers, consumer surplus would total $A + B + C$ but producer surplus would be zero.

But if developing a new drug has a high fixed cost, the firm will only try to find the cure if it thinks it can make some surplus. In theory, the government could try to subsidize the development cost (and it does subsidize many types of research and development), but all

Figure 9.9   Monopoly Power and Innovation

The government encourages innovation by giving companies monopolies on products. D represents the demand curve for the cure for the common cold. In a perfectly competitive market, the drug would be sold at a price equal to its marginal cost, $5, and consumer surplus would be $A + B + C$. However, at this price, the firm would be unable to recover the fixed cost of developing the drug and would choose not to invest in the cure for the common cold. By giving the firm a patent, the government allows it to recover the costs of innovation, and the firm produces at the monopoly price P_m and quantity Q_m. The consumer surplus is now the triangle A.

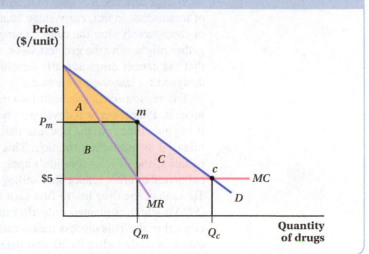

sorts of problems arise, such as trying to figure out what will work, avoiding corruption, and so on. Instead, the government makes a compromise. It promises the firm a monopoly on any drug it develops. The company realizes this means it can produce the quantity level Q_m (where $MR = MC$) and charge a price of P_m, giving it a producer surplus equal to area B from selling a new drug. Therefore, as long as the firm expects the fixed cost of discovering the drug to be smaller than the producer surplus B, it will set out to discover the cure for the common cold. Ultimately, this benefits consumers by giving them a consumer surplus equal to area A. This is lower than the consumer surplus consumers would get in a competitive market ($A + B + C$), but given that the firm would not have developed the drug in the first place if it had to charge a competitive price, consumers are better off with the more limited consumer surplus of A than none at all.

Overall, the economics of intellectual property protection suggest that it will tend to lead to innovations in just the types of goods that people like most. Goods with steeper demand curves tend to be those with the highest consumer surplus. Earlier in this chapter, we observed that the steeper demand curves are exactly those where monopoly profits are largest. So, a patent, license, or copyright that gives innovators a monopoly will tend to encourage innovation in exactly the types of goods that people value. The downside, of course, is that this will tend to lead to high prices as well.

Application: Patent Length and Drug Development

In the United States, as with most countries' patent systems, the monopoly right granted by the patent lasts for a certain period (20 years in the United States). This period begins when the patent application is filed, not when the application is approved or when the product is first sold. This timing detail is important in explaining what kinds of drugs are developed, and often it distorts development away from drugs that could have greater benefits than those that are actually brought to market.

Economists Eric Budish, Benjamin Roin, and Heidi Williams examined how this issue affected the development of cancer drugs.[9] Different drugs are designed to fight cancer

[9] Eric Budish, Benjamin Roin, and Heidi Williams, "Do Firms Underinvest in Long-Term Research? Evidence from Cancer Clinical Trials," *American Economic Review* 105, no. 7 (July 2015): 2044–2085.

at different stages of the disease. Some are more effective for early-stage cancers; others, later-stage cancers. It is easy to imagine that patients would benefit from this entire range of treatments. In fact, early-stage treatments may have even greater value if they can halt or considerably slow the cancer's progression. And a drug that could *prevent* cancer altogether might offer the greatest value of all. However, Budish, Roin, and Williams found that the cancer drugs actually developed and brought to market are disproportionately designed for late-stage treatments.

The reason for this is built into the designs of the patenting and drug development process. Pharmaceutical developers typically apply for a patent on a new drug just before it begins clinical trials, because that is when the drug's chemical compound must be released as public information. This compound could be easily copied by other companies if the developers didn't apply for a patent. At the same time, the pharmaceutical manufacturers cannot start selling the drug just because they've applied for a patent. To do that, the drug has to first earn the approval of the Food and Drug Administration (FDA), which is granted only after the drug has been shown to be safe and effective in clinical trials. This process means that a gap occurs between when a drug's patent application is made (when its 20-year patent clock starts ticking) and when the company can start making money off its monopoly power. The length of this gap depends on how long the drug's clinical trials last.

The length of that gap and how it varies across types of drugs are the key parts of the cancer drug story. The cancer drugs with the shortest clinical trials tend to be those designed to treat late-stage disease. The unfortunate reality is that most patients with late-stage cancer don't survive very long, so clinical trials for drugs to treat such late-stage cancers will show relatively quickly whether a new drug is effective. For example, one of the drugs in the study was a treatment for metastatic prostate cancer that increased expected patient survival from 12.8 months to 16.7 months. In this kind of situation, a drug only needs to be in clinical trials for a few years before it is clear that the drug is effective (in the sense that it is statistically shown to prolong life, even if only for a few months). The trial for this metastatic prostate cancer drug, for instance, lasted three years. Therefore, drugs like this tend to gain FDA approval relatively quickly, allowing the pharmaceutical company more time to sell the drug under patent protection.

The situation is different for early-stage cancer drugs. Because five-year survival rates for most early cancers are quite high, clinical trials for drugs that treat such cancers have to continue quite a while before it is clear if the drugs are effective or not. For these drugs, a longer gap thus exists between patenting and FDA approval. An example from the study involved another prostate cancer drug, but in this case one intended to treat the disease's early stages. This drug required an 18-year-long trial to prove that it was effective. By the time the drug received FDA approval, any patent on it would have expired. For drugs that might prevent cancer, some trials must span decades before their effects are confirmed.

Pharmaceutical companies are well cognizant of this issue. The length of time during which they can sell their drugs under patent protection will be longer for late-stage cancer treatments than early-stage treatments or preventive drugs. They respond to this incentive by developing many more late-stage cancer drugs, even though a lot of patients might, in fact, benefit from preventative or early-stage therapies. This disincentive really matters: Budish, Roin, and Williams estimated that the lost treatment options due to the underinvestment in preventative and early-stage cancer treatments cost the average U.S. cancer patient over a half year of life expectancy. Here, the incentives created by the patent system are literally a matter of life and death. ■

9.7 Conclusion

Unlike the perfectly competitive firms of Chapter 8, firms with market power don't just choose the quantity they supply at some fixed price determined by the market. Monopolies and other types of firms with market power have the ability to influence the prices of their goods. They produce at the profit-maximizing quantity where $MR = MC$. This production level is lower than the quantity a perfectly competitive market would produce, leading to a higher market price, more producer surplus, less consumer surplus, and deadweight loss. To raise consumer surplus and reduce deadweight loss, governments often intervene through direct price regulation and antitrust laws to reduce firms' market power. On the other hand, governments also sometimes encourage market power to promote product innovation, such as through the issuance of patents, trademarks, and copyrights.

Even though the firms we've studied in this chapter have the ability to set the price of their products, they are still limited in one important aspect of pricing. In particular, we assumed that if a firm increased the quantity it produces, this would lead to a decrease in the price on *every* unit of the good sold. But what if a firm could sell its product at different prices to different types of consumers? We will discuss this use of a firm's market power, a strategy broadly categorized as *price discrimination,* in Chapter 10.

Summary

1. Most firms have some **market power,** meaning that the firm's production decisions affect the market price of the good it sells. Firms maintain market power through **barriers to entry** into the market. These barriers include **natural monopolies,** switching costs, **product differentiation,** and absolute cost advantages of key inputs. **[Section 9.1]**

2. A monopoly is the sole supplier of a good in a market and represents the extreme case of a firm with complete market power. Monopolies and other firms with market power base their production decisions, in part, on their marginal revenue, the revenue from selling an additional unit of a good. Unlike perfectly competitive firms, these firms' marginal revenue falls as output rises. As a result, when a firm increases its production of a good, its marginal revenue falls, because it must sell all units of the good (not just the additional unit) at a lower price. **[Section 9.2]**

3. The profit-maximizing output level for a monopolist is found where marginal revenue equals marginal cost, $MR = MC$. A monopoly will charge a price above its marginal cost, meaning that the market price for a monopoly is higher than that for a perfectly competitive firm.

The **Lerner index** computes how much a firm should mark up its price; the more inelastic the demand for a product, the higher the firm's Lerner index and markup. **[Section 9.3]**

4. The changes in quantity supplied and price created by cost and demand shocks have the same direction, but different magnitudes, for firms with market power as for perfectly competitive firms. However, firms with market power respond differently to changes in consumers' price sensitivities — that is, rotations in the demand curve — than do perfectly competitive firms. **[Section 9.4]**

5. When a firm exercises its market power, it increases its producer surplus, decreases consumer surplus, and creates a deadweight loss. Producer surplus is greater when consumers are relatively price-insensitive and the demand curve is steep. **[Section 9.5]**

6. Governments often intervene to reduce the deadweight loss created by firms with market power. Direct price regulation and **antitrust laws** are aimed at reducing firms' market power. Conversely, governments also grant market power to firms through patents, copyrights, and other laws as a way of promoting innovation. **[Section 9.6]**

Review Questions

1. When does a firm have market power?

2. Name and describe three barriers to entry to a market.

3. What are the characteristics of a natural monopoly? Why is it efficient for society for a natural monopoly to produce all the output of an entire industry?

4. Describe the connection between the slope of the demand curve for a good and a firm's marginal revenue.

5. What is the profit-maximizing output level for a firm with market power?

6. Compare the consumer and producer surplus of perfectly competitive firms with that of firms with market power.

7. Why does the profit-maximizing strategy of a firm with market power create a deadweight loss?

8. Why do firms with market power have only demand—and not supply—curves?

9. Firms with market power respond differently to changes in consumers' price sensitivity than do perfectly competitive firms. Explain why this is true.

10. Name some regulations the government imposes on firms with market power.

Problems
(Solutions to problems marked an asterisk appear at the back of this book. Problems adapted to use calculus are available online.)

1. Consumers in Carlandia are willing to purchase up to 100,000 cars each year. Suppose the long-run average cost curve for auto producers in Carlandia looks like that shown in the figure below:

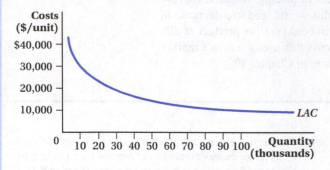

a. If the supply side of Carlandia's auto market has 10 identical firms operating, what is the lowest potential price that consumers might be able to purchase a car for?

b. If the supply side of Carlandia's auto market is served by a monopolist, what is the lowest potential price that consumers might be able to purchase a car for?

c. Conventional wisdom suggests that competition is preferred to a monopoly. Do your answers to (a) and (b) support this widely held view?

d. Suppose the car market in Carlandia is served by a monopolist. One day, fed up with the mediocre quality of the existing supplier's offerings, a resident decides to open a competing car company. What are the new company's chances of lasting in this industry? Explain your reasoning.

2. Identify and explain the sources of market power for each case listed below:

a. In the early 1990s, the DeBeers diamond cartel controlled almost all of the world's rough diamond production.

b. Microsoft's Word has a virtual monopoly in word processing, even though many claim that better word-processing programs exist.

c. Union Pacific dominates the rail shipping market in the north central United States.

d. In Louisiana, people must pass a licensing test before they can arrange flowers for a living.

e. There's a Starbucks on practically every busy corner, in every bookstore, and in every airport; customers willing to walk can find better coffee selling for less.

3. Indicate whether the following statements are true or false, and then explain your answers:

a. The marginal revenue from selling another unit of eggs can never be higher than the price of eggs.

b. Because the price a seller charges is always greater than $0, the marginal revenue from selling another unit must also be greater than $0.

*4. Consider the demand curve for otter food shown below:

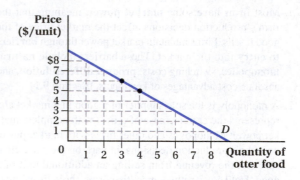

a. Indicate the area representing the total revenue Oscar, an otter food seller, would receive if he chose a price of $6.

b. On the same graph, indicate the area representing the total revenue Oscar the seller would receive if he chose a price of $5.

c. You should now have added two rectangles to your graph; however, because of some overlap, it actually appears that you've added three. One of the three is common to both scenarios above. The other two (smaller) rectangles are specific to scenario (a) or scenario (b). Label each rectangle with "A," "B," or "both" to indicate which scenario each rectangle belongs to.

d. Indicate what happens (gain or loss) to rectangle A as Oscar reduces his price from $6 to $5. Why?

e. Indicate what happens (gain or loss) to rectangle B as Oscar reduces his price from $6 to $5. Why?

f.   Calculate the area of rectangle *A* and the area of rectangle *B*. Then subtract the area of *A* from the area of *B*.

g.   Calculate the marginal revenue Oscar receives when he sells a 4th unit by subtracting the total revenue from selling 3 units from the total revenue from selling 4 units. Does your answer agree with the number you calculated in (f)? Explain.

5. In Cleveland, Clive sells 15 cloves at a price of $5 each. If Clive lowers his price by 10%, to $4.50 per clove, he will sell 16, or 6.67% more. In Dallas, Delores sells 15 cloves for $5 each. If Delores lowers her price by 2%, to $4.90, she will sell 16 cloves, or 6.67% more.

a.   Classify the demand curves that Clive and Delores face as elastic or inelastic.

b.   Determine the marginal revenue of the 16th unit for Clive. Then compute the marginal revenue of the 16th unit for Delores.

c.   How does the marginal revenue received by a seller depend on the price elasticity of demand? Explain your answer.

6. In this chapter, we noted that the marginal revenue a seller receives can be expressed as $MR = P + (\Delta P / \Delta Q) \times Q$.

a.   Using this formula as a starting point, show that marginal revenue can be expressed as $MR = P(1 + 1/E^D)$, where E^D is the price elasticity of demand.

b.   Using your knowledge about the price elasticity of demand, explain why the marginal revenue a firm with market power receives must always be less than the price.

c.   Using your knowledge of the price elasticity of demand, explain why the marginal revenue a perfectly competitive firm receives must be equal to the price.

*7. In a small college town, the demand for delivery pizza is given by $Q^D = 800 - 32P$, where Q^D measures the number of pizzas demanded each week.

a.   Use the demand function given above to derive the associated marginal revenue function. (In other words, express marginal revenue as a function of *Q*.)

b.   Calculate marginal revenue when $Q = 96$ and when $Q = 480$. How do they differ?

c.   At what quantity does $MR = 0$?

d.   What is special about the point at which marginal revenue is zero? (*Hint*: Graph the demand and marginal revenue curves.)

8. Juanita maintains the only greenhouse in isolated Point Barrow, Alaska, and therefore has a monopoly on the sale of fresh flowers. Her hired-gun statistician estimates that the elasticity of demand for her flowers is −0.5. Explain intuitively how you know that Juanita cannot be maximizing profits. (*Hint:* Think about total revenue and total costs.)

9. Consider the graph below, which illustrates the demand for Fluff. Fluff can be produced at a constant marginal and average total cost of $4 per case:

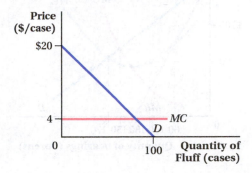

a.   Draw in a carefully constructed marginal revenue curve.

b.   Apply the $MR = MC$ rule to determine the profit-maximizing level of output. What price must the monopolist charge to maximize profit?

c.   Calculate the profit earned by the monopolist.

d.   The slope of the demand curve indicates that in order to sell one more unit, the price must fall by 20 cents. Verify that the seller cannot increase profit by reducing price and selling slightly more.

e.   The slope of the demand curve indicates that if the price of Fluff increases by 20 cents, consumers will buy one less unit. Verify that the seller cannot increase profit by increasing price and selling slightly less.

*10. Irwin is a monopoly seller of specialty bearings. Consider the graph on the next page, which illustrates the demand and marginal revenue curves for Irwin's 30-weight ball bearings, along with the marginal and average total costs of producing bearings.

a.   Find the monopolist's profit-maximizing level of output.

b.   Determine the price the monopolist should charge to maximize profit.

c.   Draw an appropriate rectangle on your graph to represent the total revenue the seller receives from selling the profit-maximizing quantity of bearings at the profit-maximizing price.

d.   Draw an appropriate rectangle on your graph to represent the total cost of producing ball bearings at the profit-maximizing quantity.

e.   The difference in the areas you drew in (c) and (d) represents profit. Calculate the profit Irwin earns from selling 30-weight ball bearings.

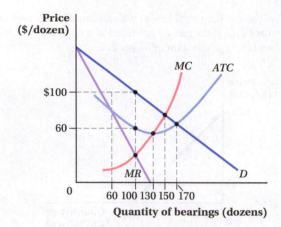

Quantity of bearings (dozens)

11. Suppose that econometricians at Hallmark Cards determine that the price elasticity of demand for greeting cards is −2.

    a. If Hallmark's marginal cost of producing cards is constant and equal to $1.00, use the Lerner index to determine what price Hallmark should charge to maximize profit.

    b. Hallmark hires you to estimate the price elasticity of demand faced by its archrival, American Greetings. Hallmark estimates that American's marginal cost of producing a greeting card is $1.22. You note that American's cards sell for an average of $3.25. Assuming that American Greetings is maximizing profit, calculate its price elasticity of demand.

12. In 2018 pop star Drake was downloaded twice as often as Cardi B. She, in turn, was downloaded twice as often as Bruno Mars. Yet, downloads for these artists all sold for the same price in Apple's iTunes store. Does this suggest that Apple is failing to maximize profits? (*Hint:* Make the reasonable assumption that the marginal cost of supplying a download is a constant $0.25. Then try to construct a graphical example in which very different demand curves produce the same price.)

13. Determine whether the italicized statement below is true or false. Then explain your answer. *A firm with market power will find that the quantity of output that maximizes revenue is lower than the quantity at which profits are maximized.*

14. Suppose that a monopolistic seller of designer handbags faces the following inverse demand curve: $P = 50 - 0.4Q$. The seller can produce handbags for a constant marginal and average total cost of $10.

    a. Calculate the profit-maximizing price for this seller.

    b. Suppose the government levies a $4 tax per unit on sellers of handbags. Calculate how this tax will affect the price the monopolist charges its customers.

    c. Who bears the burden of this tax?

15. The inverse demand for Harley Davidson motorcycles is given by $P = 40,000 - 10Q$, where P is the price in dollars and Q measures the number of units sold each month. Harley Davidson is currently producing motorcycles at a constant marginal and average cost of $16,000.

    a. Solve for the profit-maximizing price and quantity of Harley Davidson motorcycles.

    b. Heavy tariffs on imported steel drive up Harley's marginal and average cost by $2,000. How do these tariffs affect Harley's profit-maximizing price and quantity? How will the tariffs affect Harley's profits?

*16. Suppose that the demand for bentonite is given by $Q = 40 - 0.5P$, where Q is in tons of bentonite per day and P is the price per ton. Bentonite is produced by a monopolist at a constant marginal and average total cost of $10 per ton.

    a. Derive the inverse demand and marginal revenue curves faced by the monopolist.

    b. Equate marginal cost and marginal revenue to determine the profit-maximizing level of output.

    c. Find the profit-maximizing price by plugging the ideal quantity back into the demand curve.

    d. How would your answer change if demand increased to $Q = 55 - 0.5P$?

17. Consider the market for Pop Rocks depicted in the diagram below:

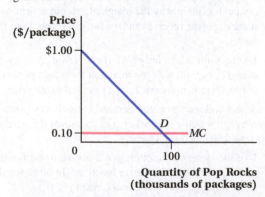

Quantity of Pop Rocks (thousands of packages)

    a. If the Pop Rock industry were competitive, what would the competitive price and quantity be?

    b. If the Pop Rock industry were competitive, what would the consumer and producer surpluses be, respectively?

    c. Suppose that gangland figure Tommy Vercetti monopolizes the Pop Rock market. To maximize his profit, what price and quantity would he choose?

    d. Calculate the consumer and producer surpluses of this Pop Rock monopoly.

    e. Compare your answers in (d) to (b). How big is the deadweight loss of monopoly?

18. The graph in Problem 10 depicts the market demand for 30-weight ball bearings. That particular market segment is monopolized by a single producer named Irwin. Referring to that graph:

    a. how do the monopolist's price and quantity compare to the price and quantity that would prevail under perfect competition?

    b. shade an area in the graph that represents the deadweight loss due to Irwin's monopoly.

*19. Suppose that a monopolistic seller of flux capacitors faces the inverse demand curve $P = 40 - 0.5Q$, and that the monopolist can produce flux capacitors at a constant marginal cost of $5.

    a. How many units will an unregulated monopolist sell?

    b. Suppose that the government imposes a price ceiling of $6. What does this price ceiling do to the monopolist's marginal revenue curve? Specifically, what is the marginal revenue of the 10th unit? The 68th? How about the 69th?

    c. How many units will a profit-maximizing monopolist sell when the price ceiling is in place? At what price?

    d. Compare the deadweight loss of unregulated monopoly to the deadweight losses with the price ceiling. Does the price ceiling improve social welfare?

20. Consider a small isolated town in which a brewery faces the following inverse demand: $P = 15 - 0.33Q$. The brewery can produce beer at a constant marginal and average total cost of $1 per bottle.

    a. Calculate the profit-maximizing price and quantity, as well as producer and consumer surplus and the deadweight loss from market power.

    b. If it were possible to organize the townsfolk, how much would they be willing to pay the brewery to sell beer at a price equal to its marginal cost?

    c. What is the minimum payment the brewery would be willing to accept to sell beer at a price equal to marginal cost?

    d. Is it possible for consumers and the brewery to strike a bargain that results in gains for both?

21. Consider the firm depicted in the following diagram:

    a. Is the firm a natural monopoly? How do you know?

    b. Will this firm earn a profit if it is not subject to regulation? How do you know?

    c. If the government requires the firm to charge no more than its marginal cost of production, how many units will be sold? At what price? What is the problem with the government capping prices at marginal cost?

    d. Suppose the government allows firms to charge no more than their average total costs of production. How many units will this firm sell? At what price? What is the problem with capping prices at average total cost?

    e. Evaluate the deadweight loss under each of the three pricing regimes above. Show each regime's deadweight loss as an area on the graph.

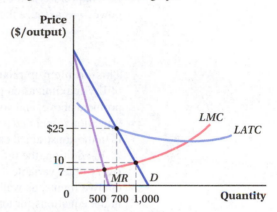

22. Five networks are vying to receive the pay-per-view broadcast rights to the World Series of Yahtzee. Each estimates that the inverse demand for watching this nail-biter of an event is given by $P = 100 - 0.01Q$. Each can provide the broadcast at a constant marginal cost of $1 per viewer.

    a. Calculate the deadweight loss of monopoly in the market for the televised Yahtzee tournament.

    b. Suppose that the governing body for the Yahtzee tournament plans to select one network at its discretion to air the tournament. How much will each network be willing to spend lobbying for the broadcast rights?

    c. Explain why, in this situation, the losses to society are much greater than just the deadweight losses of monopoly.

23. In the early days of navigation, sailors had a tough time figuring out exactly where they were. Pinpointing latitude was easy enough with a sextant, but because Earth was constantly spinning, pinpointing longitude by using celestial bodies was impossible. Anxious for a solution to this problem, the British government sponsored a contest with a prize of £20,000 (about $5 million in today's dollars) to the inventor who could devise a reliable method of calculating longitude. Once invented, the method would be made available to anyone who wanted to use it. Explain the advantages of such a system in maximizing social well-being relative to the traditional system of awarding patents.

Chapter 9 Appendix:
The Calculus of Profit Maximization

In Chapters 8 and 9, we saw that all firms—regardless of their degrees of market power—maximize their profits. In particular, the firm faces the optimization problem:

$$\max_{Q} \pi(Q) = TR(Q) - TC(Q)$$

This problem is relatively straightforward compared to the cost-minimization and utility-maximization problems we've focused on previously. Why? Look closely at the problem above, and you'll notice that there aren't any constraints on it. In fact, profit maximization is an *unconstrained* optimization problem and, as such, is much simpler to solve than the constrained optimization problems we've been dealing with so far.

In addition, the profit-maximization problem only has one choice variable: output, Q. Every other variable that factors into a firm's decisions—the quantities and prices of productive inputs, as well as the market price of the good—has already been accounted for in the equations for total revenue and total cost. How? First, total cost is determined only after a firm minimizes its costs, meaning it incorporates information about a firm's productive inputs. Next, consider total revenue, which is the product of price and quantity. For the perfectly competitive firm, price is constant, so given the market price, total revenue only varies with quantity. Firms with market power face variable prices, but we saw that those prices are a function of quantity sold. Therefore, total cost, total revenue, and—by extension—profit are all functions of quantity, holding all else constant.[10]

The Profit-Maximizing Condition

Let's begin by solving for the profit-maximizing condition. We take the first derivative of the profit-maximization problem above with respect to quantity Q to solve for the first-order condition:

$$\frac{d\pi}{dQ} = \frac{dTR}{dQ} - \frac{dTC}{dQ} = 0$$

$$\frac{dTR}{dQ} = \frac{dTC}{dQ}$$

$$MR = MC$$

What does this first-order condition tell us? As we saw in the chapter, *all* firms—firms with some market power, monopolists, and perfectly competitive firms inclusive—produce the profit-maximizing level of output when marginal revenue equals marginal cost.

We do need to check one more condition before considering this result conclusive. Producing where $MR = MC$ doesn't guarantee that the firm is maximizing its profit. It only guarantees that the profit function is at one extreme or another—the firm could actually

---

[10] We could be very explicit about these functions and always indicate profit, total revenue, and total cost as $\pi(Q)$, $TR(Q)$, and $TC(Q)$; however, this becomes a little cumbersome. So in this appendix, we'll just use π, TR, and TC and remind you now and then that each is a function of Q.

be *minimizing* its profit instead of maximizing it! To make sure we avoid this pitfall, we need to confirm that the second derivative of the profit function is negative:

$$\frac{d^2\pi}{dQ^2} = \frac{d^2(TR-TC)}{dQ^2} = \frac{d^2TR}{dQ^2} - \frac{d^2TC}{dQ^2} = \frac{dMR}{dQ} - \frac{dMC}{dQ} < 0$$

When will $\frac{dMR}{dQ} - \frac{dMC}{dQ} < 0$? This condition holds when

$$\frac{dMR}{dQ} < \frac{dMC}{dQ}$$

or when the *change* in marginal cost exceeds the *change* in marginal revenue. We have seen that marginal cost generally increases with output, while marginal revenue either is constant (for a price taker like the firms we saw in Chapter 8) or decreases as the quantity produced rises (for firms with market power, as we observed in Chapter 9). Therefore, this second-order condition generally is met because

$$\frac{dMR}{dQ} \leq 0 < \frac{dMC}{dQ}$$

The firm has to be careful about assuming this, however. If marginal cost is declining (which can be true of a firm with increasing returns to scale over the range that it is producing), we need to confirm that marginal revenue is decreasing at a faster rate than marginal cost:

$$\left|\frac{dMR}{dQ}\right| > \left|\frac{dMC}{dQ}\right|$$

If this condition does not hold for a firm experiencing increasing returns to scale, the firm is not maximizing its profit. In this context, the firm could increase its profit by producing more output.

Marginal Revenue

We know that all firms maximize profits when marginal revenue equals marginal cost. But what exactly is the marginal revenue of a firm? As we did in the past two chapters, we want to derive the relationship between marginal revenue and price. We'll do this first for firms in general and then look specifically at the case of a perfectly competitive firm.

We will start with the expression for total revenue:

$$TR = PQ$$

Note that, in general, price P is not fixed, but is instead a function of the quantity the firm produces.[11] To find marginal revenue, we take the derivative of the total revenue function with respect to Q using the product rule:

$$\frac{dTR}{dQ} = \frac{dPQ}{dQ} = P\frac{dQ}{dQ} + Q\frac{dP}{dQ}$$

[11] The one exception to the general rule that price is a function of output that we've seen so far is for firms in a perfectly competitive market—price takers. We'll come back to this special case shortly.

Equivalently,

$$MR = P + Q\frac{dP}{dQ}$$

What does this tell us about the relationship between marginal revenue and price? Because a firm with market power faces a downward-sloping demand curve, the good's price *decreases* as the quantity produced increases. Mathematically, $\frac{dP}{dQ} < 0$. Therefore, for a firm with market power,

$$MR < P$$

We can also see this result logically. P is the gain from selling an additional unit of the good at the new price. $Q\frac{dP}{dQ}$ is the loss from lowering the price on all previous units in order to sell the increased quantity. Therefore, the revenue from selling an additional unit of the good is less than the good's market price, because for every gain in revenue (P), there is a corresponding loss $\left(Q\frac{dP}{dQ}\right)$.

Let's work through a generic example to clarify this. Suppose a firm has the inverse demand curve $P = a - bQ$. (We discussed this particular inverse demand curve in footnote 3 in Chapter 9, but we'll go into more detail here.) To find marginal revenue, we first determine total revenue by multiplying P by Q:

$$TR = PQ = (a - bQ)Q = aQ - bQ^2$$

Now, we can take the derivative of total revenue to get marginal revenue:

$$MR = \frac{dTR}{dQ} = \frac{d(aQ - bQ^2)}{dQ} = a - 2bQ$$

As you can see, the marginal revenue curve derived from a linear demand curve is itself linear. It also has the same price intercept (in this case, a) and is twice as steep as the demand curve. As a result, it's clear that

$$a - 2bQ < a - bQ \quad \text{or}$$

$$MR < P$$

But what about the special case of the perfectly competitive firm? Unlike firms with market power, perfectly competitive firms are price takers that face horizontal demand curves. We know from above that the marginal revenue for any firm is

$$MR = P + Q\frac{dP}{dQ}$$

For a perfectly competitive firm, price remains fixed with changes in quantity, meaning $\frac{dP}{dQ} = 0$. Thus, $MR = P$ for all quantities of output.

Therefore, the profit-maximizing condition for the perfectly competitive firm is

$$MR = P = MC$$

This unique relationship is precisely what we showed in Chapter 8.[12]

---

[12] We can also show the relationship between price, marginal revenue, and marginal cost for the perfectly competitive firm by starting from profit maximization. For the perfectly competitive firm, $\pi = PQ - TC$. Taking the first-order condition with respect to Q gives us $P - MC = 0$ or $P = MC$ because price is independent of the quantity produced.

figure it out 9A.1

Let's reconsider the solution to Figure It Out 9.2 (p. 314) and use the calculus approach we learned here. Babe's Bats (BB) faces a demand curve of $Q = 10 - 0.4P$ and a total cost curve of $TC = 2.5Q^2$. BB's output, Q, is measured in thousands of baseball bats, and P in dollars per bat.

a. Solve for BB's profit-maximizing level of output using calculus.

b. What price will BB charge to maximize its profit?

Solution:

a. First, we need to set up Babe's profit-maximization problem:

$$\max_{Q} \pi = TR - TC = PQ - TC$$

Because Babe's Bats has some market power, its choice of Q affects the price. So, we need to use the demand curve for BB's bats to solve for price as a function of quantity, or the firm's inverse demand curve:

$$Q = 10 - 0.4P$$
$$0.4P = 10 - Q$$
$$P = 25 - 2.5Q$$

Substituting this expression for P and the total cost curve into the profit function, we find

$$\pi = TR - TC = PQ - TC$$
$$= (25 - 2.5Q)Q - 2.5Q^2$$
$$= 25Q - 2.5Q^2 - 2.5Q^2 = 25Q - 5Q^2$$

So, the firm's profit-maximization problem is

$$\max_{Q} \pi = 25Q - 5Q^2$$

The first-order condition for this problem is

$$\frac{d\pi}{dQ} = \frac{d(25Q - 5Q^2)}{dQ} = 0$$
$$25 - 10Q = 0$$
$$10Q = 25$$
$$Q^* = 2.5 \quad \text{or} \quad 2{,}500 \text{ bats}$$

b. Now we need to plug Q^* from (a) into the inverse demand curve to obtain the profit-maximizing price:

$$P^* = 25 - 2.5Q^* = 25 - 2.5(2.5) = \$18.75 \text{ per bat}$$

Babe's Bats is maximizing its profit when it sells 2,500 baseball bats at a price of $18.75 per bat.

A shortcut to solving is to begin with the profit-maximizing condition $MR = MC$, as we did in the chapter. In general, beginning with the profit-maximizing condition is easiest for firms with linear demand curves and simple cost functions. However, some firms have more complicated demand curves and total cost functions. For these firms, solving the profit-maximization problem directly using calculus may save you some work.

Now that we've worked through the calculus of profit maximization for a firm with market power, let's look at an example for a perfectly competitive firm.

figure it out 9A.2

Let's return to Figure It Out 8.1 and to Bob's Barbershop, the perfectly competitive firm with a daily total cost of $TC = 0.5Q^2$. Assume that the market price of a haircut is $15.

a. How many haircuts should Bob give each day if he wants to maximize his profit?

b. If the firm maximizes profit, how much profit will it earn each day?

Solution:

a. Bob's problem is to choose the quantity of haircuts that will maximize his profit or

$$\max_{Q} \pi = TR - TC = PQ - TC = 15Q - 0.5Q^2$$

Solving for the first-order condition gives

$$\frac{d\pi}{dQ} = \frac{d(15Q - 0.5Q^2)}{dQ} = 0$$

$$15 - Q = 0$$

$$Q^* = 15 \text{ haircuts}$$

Let's confirm that this is the same result that we get from choosing the quantity where $P = MC$. In the chapter, the question provided you with the marginal cost, but now we can solve for it by taking the first derivative of the total cost curve with respect to quantity, the firm's choice variable:

$$MC = \frac{dTC}{dQ} = \frac{d0.5Q^2}{dQ}$$

$$= 2(0.5Q) = Q$$

Now finding Bob's optimal quantity of haircuts per day is easy:

$$P = MC$$

$$P = Q$$

$$Q^* = 15 \text{ haircuts}$$

b. At 15 haircuts per day, Bob will earn

$$\pi = TR - TC = PQ - 0.5Q^2$$

$$= 15(15) - 0.5(15)^2 = \$225 - \$112.50 = \$112.50 \text{ per day}$$

Problems

1. Find marginal revenue for the firms that face the following demand curves:

   a. $Q = 1,000 - 5P$

   b. $Q = 100P^{-2}$

2. Suppose a firm faces demand of $Q = 300 - 2P$ and has a total cost curve of $TC = 75Q + Q^2$.

   a. What is the firm's marginal revenue?

   b. What is the firm's marginal cost?

   c. Find the firm's profit-maximizing quantity where $MR = MC$.

   d. Find the firm's profit-maximizing price and profit.

3. Suppose that American Borax is a monopolist and the worldwide demand for borax is $Q = 100 - P$, where Q is tons of borax and P is the price per ton. The total cost function for American Borax is $TC = 10Q + 0.5Q^2$.

   a. Write out the firm's total revenue as a function of Q.

   b. What is the profit function for American Borax?

   c. Find the firm's profit-maximizing quantity by applying calculus to the profit function.

   d. Find American Borax's profit-maximizing price and profit.

4. Suppose a firm faces the inverse demand curve $P = 600Q^{-0.5}$. The firm has the total cost curve $TC = 1,000 + 0.5Q^{1.5}$. Find the firm's profit-maximizing output, price, and profit.

5. Consider a firm in a perfectly competitive market with total costs given by

   $$TC = Q^3 - 15Q^2 + 100Q + 30$$

   a. What is this firm's marginal cost function? Over what range of output are the firm's marginal costs decreasing? Increasing?

   b. Suppose that the market price is \$52. What is this firm's profit-maximizing level of output? How do you know this is the profit-maximizing output? How much profit does this firm earn by producing the profit-maximizing output?

Pricing Strategies for Firms with Market Power

Y ou're probably aware of purchase situations where you can get a price discount if you show your student ID—movie theaters, gym memberships, train fare, or the like. It's nice of the sellers to give you a break while you're paying for school. Every bit helps. The sellers' motivation, though, isn't to encourage you to stay in school. Instead, it is often the sellers' simple attempt to extract more producer surplus from the market. Sure, you like receiving discounts and they make it more likely you will be able to consume goods that would otherwise be too expensive for you. But these discounts increase sellers' producer surplus and improve their bottom line.

We know from our study of market power in Chapter 9 that when a firm can influence its own price, it makes a higher profit than a perfectly competitive (i.e., price-taking) company. In this chapter, we will see that if a firm can charge different prices to different groups of customers (e.g., students and nonstudents), it can raise surplus and profit above even those earned by a standard monopolist (who charges everyone the same price). There are many ways in which firms with market power can charge different prices for the same good. This chapter explores the most common of these strategies and looks at how they affect producers and consumers in the market.

10.1 The Basics of Pricing Strategy

A **pricing strategy** is a *firm's plan for setting the price of its product given the market conditions it faces and its desire to maximize profit.* The pricing strategy for a perfectly competitive firm is that it just charges the equilibrium market price for its product. The pricing strategy for a firm with market power is to follow the three-step method of the last chapter and charge the price where marginal revenue equals marginal cost. Here, we explore a pricing strategy called **price discrimination,** the *practice of charging different prices to different customers for the same product.* If a firm with market power can price discriminate, it can earn greater economic profit than a single-price monopoly.

There are several pricing strategies a company with market power can use depending on its circumstances. These range from *direct price discrimination* to *indirect price discrimination* to *bundling* to *two-part tariffs* and beyond. The motivation for these strategies is straightforward: A company with market power charges a higher price for the units of output that provide consumers with greater consumer surplus. By adjusting the price, a firm extracts more producer surplus from each transaction.

pricing strategy A firm's plan for setting the price of its product given the market conditions it faces and its desire to maximize profit.

price discrimination The practice of charging different prices to different customers for the same product.

When a Firm Can Use a Pricing Strategy with Different Prices

All firms—from perfectly competitive to monopolistic and everything in between—have a pricing strategy. In this chapter, we discuss pricing strategies that can only be pursued by firms meeting two key requirements:

Requirement 1: The firm must have market power. A company must have market power to price discriminate. It's that simple.

Requirement 2: The firm must prevent resale and arbitrage. To take advantage of advanced pricing strategies, a firm must be able to prevent its customers from reselling its product among themselves. Otherwise, the customers able to buy the product at a low price could purchase a large number and resell them to other customers who would otherwise have had to buy the product from the firm at a higher price. *The practice of reselling a product at a price higher than its original selling price* is called **arbitrage.**

arbitrage The practice of reselling a product at a price higher than its original selling price.

You'll notice that these two requirements are repeated for emphasis in all the "When to Use It" features at the start of each section of this chapter. If a firm meets the two requirements, it can attempt to implement pricing strategies that make more profit than a single-price monopoly does. **Figure 10.1** provides an overview of these strategies.

The first pricing strategies we look at involve price discrimination. For price discrimination to be an option, a firm needs to have different types of customers with different price sensitivities of demand. The exact kind of pricing strategy the firm should use—the organizational foundation for this chapter—depends on the kind of information the firm possesses.

Figure 10.1   Overview of Pricing Strategies

A firm's optimal pricing strategy is determined by its characteristics, its product, and its consumers. In particular, a firm takes into account its degree of market power, whether the product can be resold, and its knowledge of its customers' demand for the product.

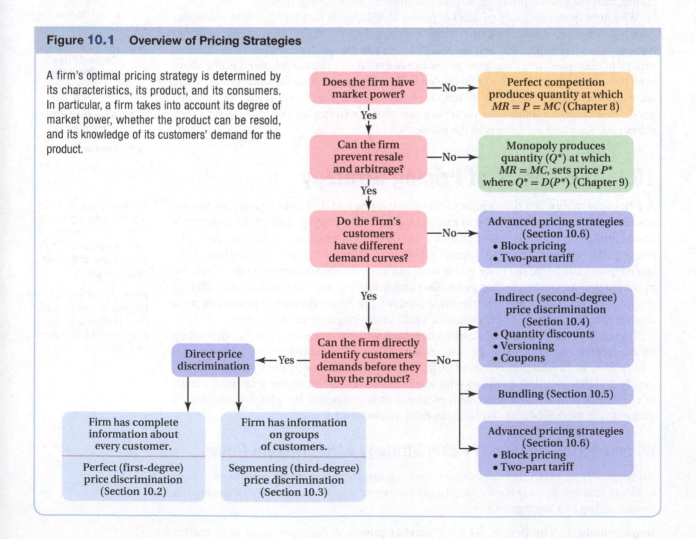

1. **If a firm can identify its customers' demands *before* they buy** (as can a store that requires students to show IDs when making purchases), it can practice **direct price discrimination,** *a pricing strategy in which firms charge different prices to different customers based on observable characteristics of the customers.* If the firm has complete, detailed information about each customer's own demand curve before she buys the product, it can practice *perfect price discrimination* (or as it's sometimes called, *first-degree price discrimination*) and charge every customer a different price (Section 10.2). If information about its customers is less detailed, a firm may be able to discriminate by customer group, as in *segmenting* (also called *third-degree price discrimination*) (Section 10.3).

2. **If a firm can identify its customers' differing demands only *after* they make a purchase,** it can try *indirect (second-degree) price discrimination,* which involves offering different pricing packages and then identifying the customer's type from the pricing package she chooses. These pricing packages can take the form of quantity discounts, different versions of the product at different prices, or coupons (Section 10.4). Under the right conditions, firms can also make a pricing package by bundling together different products (Section 10.5). In addition, firms can also pursue advanced pricing strategies such as block pricing and two-part tariffs (Section 10.6).

3. **If a firm's customers have the same demand curves,** there are still some pricing strategies that a firm can use to make more profit. These strategies, *block pricing* and *two-part tariffs,* involve offering different unit prices to the same customer for different quantities purchased or charging lump-sum fees on top of per-unit prices (Section 10.6).

> **direct price discrimination** A pricing strategy in which firms charge different prices to different customers based on observable characteristics of the customers.

10.2 Direct Price Discrimination I: Perfect (First-Degree) Price Discrimination

> **When to Use It** Perfect (First-Degree) Price Discrimination
>
> 1. *The firm has market power and can prevent resale.*
> 2. The firm's customers have different demand curves.
> 3. The firm has complete information about *every* customer and can identify each one's demand before purchase.

Let's start by looking at a firm that has market power, can prevent resale, and knows that its consumers differ in their willingness to pay and therefore have different demand curves.

First, consider the possibilities for a firm that has so much information about its customers before they buy that it literally knows each individual buyer's demand curve and can charge each buyer a different price equal to the buyer's willingness to pay. This is known as **perfect price discrimination** or **first-degree price discrimination,** *a type of direct price discrimination in which a firm charges each customer exactly his willingness to pay.*

Suppose a firm faces a market demand curve like the one labeled *D* in **Figure 10.2**. Panel a shows the outcomes for a perfectly competitive firm and a monopolistic firm. We know from Chapter 8 that in a perfectly competitive market, the equilibrium price (which

> **perfect price discrimination (first-degree price discrimination)** A type of direct price discrimination in which a firm charges each customer exactly his willingness to pay.

is the same as MR in that case) equals marginal cost MC and the firm produces quantity Q_c. Consumer surplus is the area under the demand curve and above the price, $A + B + C$. Because we assume that marginal cost is constant, there is no producer surplus.

In Chapter 9, we saw that a firm with market power facing demand curve D and with no ability to prevent resale produces the quantity where its marginal cost equals its marginal revenue, Q_m, and sets the price P_m for that quantity from its demand curve. It charges this single price to everyone in the market. This market power pricing has three outcomes relative to the competitive pricing: (1) There is now a producer surplus equal to the rectangle B (far better from the firm's perspective than the competitive outcome, no producer surplus); (2) there is now a deadweight loss equal to the triangle C, because quantity is below its competitive level; and (3) consumer surplus is reduced to area A.

If, however, the firm with market power can prevent resale and directly identify each and every customer's demand curve (panel b), the firm can charge every customer her willingness to pay for every unit (or, to guarantee she'd take the deal, just a bit below this level). This is perfect price discrimination, and the benefit to the firm is tremendous. For any unit of output where a customer's willingness to pay is greater than the firm's marginal cost of producing it, the firm captures the whole amount of available surplus. So, for example, a customer accounting for the portion of the demand curve at P_d pays that relatively high price, while another at P_f pays that relatively low price. In these and all other cases, even

---

Figure 10.2 Perfect (First-Degree) Price Discrimination

(a) Perfect competition and monopoly

Consumer surplus (competition) $= A + B + C$
Producer surplus (competition) $= 0$
Consumer surplus (market power) $= A$
Producer surplus (market power) $= B$
Deadweight loss from market power $= C$

(b) Perfect price discrimination

Consumer surplus $= 0$
Producer surplus $= E$
Deadweight loss from market power $= 0$

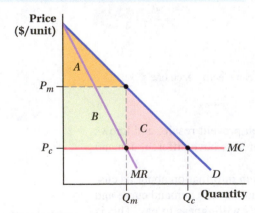

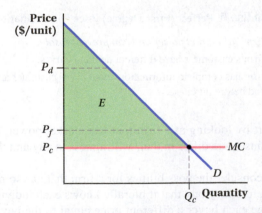

(a) A competitive market will set price equal to marginal cost, producing Q_c and selling at a price of P_c. Consumers will receive consumer surplus equal to $A + B + C$ and the firm will earn zero producer surplus. A single-price monopoly will sell quantity Q_m at a price of P_m and receive producer surplus equal to B. Consumers will receive consumer surplus equal to A and the deadweight loss from market power will be area C.

(b) If a firm with market power can identify each customer's demand curve, then it will charge each customer her willingness to pay and capture the entire surplus, E. For example, the firm will charge a customer willing to pay P_d exactly the price P_d and a customer willing to pay P_f the price P_f. The firm will sell up to the quantity Q_c, the perfectly competitive quantity where $P_c = MC$. There is no deadweight loss when a firm practices perfect price discrimination.

though the prices are different, customers pay the most they are willing to pay, and the firm gets the entire surplus (the area below demand and above marginal cost).

The firm sells Q_c to the various consumers at different prices depending on each buyer's willingness to pay. (Because the firm can prevent resale, customers aren't able to buy the product from another customer for a lower price than the firm offers.) The producer surplus the firm earns as a result equals the entire surplus in the market, $A + B + C$. This is the maximum amount of surplus that can be made from the market because no consumer will pay more than her willingness to pay (which rules out the area above the demand curve) and the firm must pay its costs (which eliminates the area below the marginal cost curve). A firm that can perfectly price discriminate has a great life.

Another interesting feature of perfect price discrimination is that, unlike the single-price market power outcome, there is no deadweight loss. It is efficient: The quantity sold (Q_c) is the same quantity that would be sold if the market were perfectly competitive. Who *keeps* the market surplus is very different in the two cases, however: Under perfect competition, the entire surplus goes to the consumers, while under perfect price discrimination, the entire surplus goes to the producer. Efficiency is not the same thing as fairness. (We will further discuss issues of market efficiency and distribution in Chapter 15.)

The online appendix demonstrates efficiency for firms that practice perfect price discrimination.

 figure it out 10.1

Go online for interactive, step-by-step help in solving the following problem.

A firm with market power faces an inverse demand curve for its product of $P = 100 - 10Q$. Assume that the firm faces a marginal cost curve of $MC = 10 + 10Q$.

a. If the firm cannot price discriminate, what is the profit-maximizing level of output and price?

b. If the firm cannot price discriminate, what are the levels of consumer and producer surplus in the market, assuming the firm maximizes its profit? Calculate the deadweight loss from market power.

c. If the firm has the ability to practice perfect price discrimination, what is the firm's output?

d. If the firm practices perfect price discrimination, what are the levels of consumer and producer surplus? What is the deadweight loss from market power?

Solution:

a. If the firm cannot price discriminate, it maximizes profit by producing where $MR = MC$. If the inverse demand function is $P = 100 - 10Q$, then the marginal revenue must be $MR = 100 - 20Q$. (Remember that, for any linear inverse demand function $P = a - bQ$, marginal revenue is $MR = a - 2bQ$.)

Setting $MR = MC$, we obtain

$$100 - 20Q = 10 + 10Q$$
$$90 = 30Q$$
$$Q^* = 3$$

To find the optimal price, we plug $Q = 3$ into the inverse demand equation:

$$P^* = 100 - 10Q^*$$
$$= 100 - 10(3)$$
$$= 100 - 30$$
$$= 70$$

The firm sells 3 units at a price of $70 each.

b. To find consumer and producer surplus, we need to start with a diagram showing the demand, marginal revenue, and marginal cost curves:

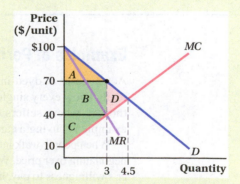

Consumer surplus is the area above price and below demand (area A). Producer surplus is the area above marginal cost but below the price (area $B + C$). (Note that we could just label these two areas as a large trapezoid, but it is easier to remember the formulas for the area of a rectangle and a triangle!) We can calculate the areas:

$$\text{Area } A = \frac{1}{2} \text{base} \times \text{height}$$
$$= \frac{1}{2} \times 3 \times (\$100 - \$70)$$
$$= 0.5(3)(\$30)$$
$$= \$45$$

Consumer surplus is $45.

$$\text{Area } B = \text{base} \times \text{height}$$

To get the height of areas B and C, we need the MC of producing a quantity of 3: $MC = 10 + 10Q = 10 + 10(3) = \$40$. So,

$$\text{Area } B = 3 \times (\$70 - \$40)$$
$$= 3(\$30)$$
$$= \$90$$

$$\text{Area } C = \frac{1}{2} \times \text{base} \times \text{height}$$
$$= \frac{1}{2} \times 3 \times (\$40 - \$10)$$
$$= 0.5(3)(\$30)$$
$$= \$45$$

Thus, producer surplus = area B + area C = $90 + $45 = $135.

The deadweight loss from market power is the loss in surplus that occurs because the market is not producing the competitive quantity.

To calculate the competitive quantity, we set $P = MC$:

$$100 - 10Q = 10 + 10Q$$
$$90 = 20Q$$
$$Q = 4.5$$

The deadweight loss can be seen on the diagram as area D:

$$\text{Area } D = \frac{1}{2} \times \text{base} \times \text{height}$$
$$= \frac{1}{2} \times (4.5 - 3) \times (\$70 - \$40)$$
$$= 0.5(1.5)(\$30)$$
$$= \$22.50$$

The deadweight loss from market power is $22.50.

c. If the firm practices perfect price discrimination, it will produce where $P = MC$. As we saw in part (b) above, this means that the firm will produce 4.5 units.

d. If the firm practices perfect price discrimination, consumer surplus will be zero because every consumer will be charged a price equal to his willingness to pay. Producer surplus will be the full area between the demand curve and the marginal cost curve (area $A + B + C + D$):

Producer surplus = area A + area B + area C + area D
$$= \$45 + \$90 + \$45 + \$22.50$$
$$= \$202.50$$

There is no deadweight loss when the firm perfectly price discriminates. The competitive output level is achieved ($Q = 4.5$). Producers end up with the entire surplus available in the market.

Examples of Perfect Price Discrimination

Actual cases of dyed-in-the-wool perfect price discrimination are rare because firms don't really know every single customer's willingness to pay for its product. There are instances, though, where sellers charge many different prices for the same product. One classic example is buying a car.

When people walk into a car dealership, the salesperson sizes them up and eventually begins negotiating over price. While the dealer doesn't have *complete* information about each customer's willingness to pay, haggling differently with every customer is a lot like perfect price discrimination—the auto dealer is trying to simultaneously learn about the customer's valuation of the car and arrive at a price as close as possible to that level. That's why you should think twice when you go to buy a car and the salesman asks you, "How much are you looking to spend on a car?" That's an invitation for you to give up your consumer surplus. Online sellers like Amazon keep detailed records of your purchase history that they use to estimate individual demand curves, which also seems closer to a perfect price discrimination environment.

Application: Perfect Price Discrimination in Tuition

Although you might not have realized it, you may have experienced something close to perfect price discrimination when you decided to go to college. Families in the United States applying for college financial aid are required to submit the Free Application for Federal Student Aid (FAFSA). This form requires them to report complete information about their family assets and income along with the student's assets and income. While this information is used by the government to determine how much subsidized federal aid a student is eligible for, it also gives the college an almost perfect understanding of each student's willingness to pay. This allows schools to produce an individually tailored financial aid plan that might supplement federal aid. But that is just another way of saying that they charge a different tuition price to each student, depending on how much they think the student can afford.

Economist Ian Fillmore has shown that this price discrimination has huge effects on the market.[1] He estimates the actual tuition paid at selective universities is almost $1,000 per year higher than it would be if schools couldn't use family financial information to determine financial aid (i.e., the student's effective price). However, as noted above, these price increases are partly counteracted by efficiency gains that (almost) perfect price discrimination allows. Fillmore demonstrates that colleges use high tuition rates paid by students from wealthy and high-willingness-to-pay families to subsidize students from poorer, low-willingness-to-pay families. This allows students from families with fewer financial resources to attend selective schools they would be priced out of if those schools had to charge all students the same price. In the end, whether you are a net gainer or loser from giving colleges your and your family's financial information depends on what exactly that information is. ∎

10.3 Direct Price Discrimination II: Segmenting (Third-Degree Price Discrimination)

> **When to Use It** Segmenting (Third-Degree Price Discrimination)
>
> 1. *The firm has market power and can prevent resale.*
> 2. The firm's customers have different demand curves.
> 3. The firm can directly identify specific *groups* of customers with different price sensitivities (but not the demand of every individual customer) before purchase.

Because it's rare for a firm to have the kind of comprehensive information about customers that it needs to practice perfect price discrimination, a firm can't generally capture *all* the market surplus using price discrimination. But it can still earn more profit than a regular monopolist by using a pricing strategy called **segmenting** (or **third-degree price discrimination**), a *type of direct price discrimination in which a firm charges different prices to different groups (segments) of customers based on the identifiable attributes of those groups.*[2]

segmenting (third-degree price discrimination)
A type of direct price discrimination in which a firm charges different prices to different groups (segments) of customers based on the identifiable attributes of those groups.

---

[1] Ian Fillmore, "Price Discrimination and Public Policy in the U.S. College Market," working paper, Washington University of St. Louis, 2018.

[2] Although third-degree discrimination sounds like a variant of first-degree discrimination, the truth is that these names were somewhat arbitrarily coined by economist E. H. Chamberlin back in the 1930s.

For this kind of pricing strategy to work, the company must be able to directly identify *groups* of customers — students, for example — who have systematically different demands than other buyers. This group-level demand identification is typically much easier than figuring out every individual customer's willingness to pay.

Think about a company that sells a clothing line emblazoned with your school logo. If the company knows that students typically don't have a lot of money and tend to be bargain hunters while their parents are less price-sensitive, the firm will want to charge students a lower price for its clothing and parents a higher price. To do this, the company needs to be able to identify which group a customer belongs to before the sale, and to prevent parents and faculty from pretending to be students to get the discount. One way the company can do this is by making the presentation of a student ID a condition of the lower price.

As with all forms of price discrimination, however, the company must be able to prevent resale. They can't sell school sweatshirts at a student discount just to have the students then turn around and sell them to visiting parents.

The Benefits of Segmenting: A Graphical Approach

If a firm is able to segment the market, let's explore how different the prices should be across the groups, and how much the company stands to gain by price discriminating compared to the standard one-price monopoly strategy.

To answer these questions, let's consider an example with two consumer groups, the market for entry into the prestigious Ironman 70.3 Cozumel Triathlon. This triathlon is a race that comprises a 1.2-mile swim, a 56-mile bike ride, and a 13.1-mile run. It may seem like a masochistic pursuit, but people pay serious money to enter this race.

There are two kinds of people who want to enter the Ironman Cozumel: people who live near Cozumel and people who fly in from somewhere else. The two groups' demand curves for entering the race are shown in **Figure 10.3**. Panel a shows the demand (D_T) for the participants traveling to Cozumel for the competition. The travelers mostly come

Figure 10.3 **Segmenting Entry Fees at the Ironman 70.3 Cozumel Triathlon**

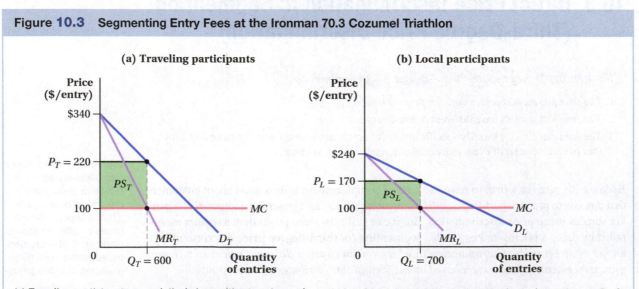

(a) Traveling participants are relatively insensitive to price and have an inelastic demand curve D_T. The number of traveling participants will be $Q_T = 600$, and each will pay a registration fee of $P_T = \$220$/entry. Producer surplus, PS_T, will be relatively large.

(b) Local participants have a relatively elastic demand curve D_L. A greater number of locals will register for the triathlon ($Q_L = 700$) at a lower price ($P_L = \$170$/entry). Producer surplus for locals, PS_L, is relatively small.

from the United States; have high incomes and expensive triathlon equipment; and must pay for a plane ticket, a hotel room, food, and a rental car. They don't care that much if the price of their registration for the race is a bit higher, because it's a small share of the total cost to them. In other words, the demand curve for the traveling participants is fairly inelastic. From the demand curve of out-of-town entrants (travelers) D_T, the organizers compute marginal revenue, labeled MR_T in panel a of Figure 10.3. Then from the point at which MR_T equals marginal cost MC, the organizers determine the optimal quantity of entries to sell to out-of-towners ($Q_T = 600$). At that quantity, the entry fee is $P_T = \$220$.

Panel b of the figure shows the local group's demand curve, D_L. The local residents' demand is more price-sensitive because they have many other activities they can pursue if the price of entering the race is too high. Thus, their demand curve is flatter and more elastic. These entrants' demand curve D_L in panel b implies a marginal revenue curve MR_L. The optimal number of entries for the organizer to offer to locals is $Q_L = 700$, the quantity at which marginal revenue from locals equals marginal cost. (The marginal cost is the same for either type of racer. It amounts, basically, to the cost of a number bib, some extra Gatorade, a finisher's medal, and a race T-shirt.) The price, determined from the locals' demand curve, is $P_L = \$170$, significantly lower than the $220 price for traveling entrants.

Preventing resale won't be a problem for the firm organizing the race as long as it can tell which athletes are from out of town and which are not. This is easy because out-of-town athletes have to pay their entrance fees with some form of identification that gives their address, and they have to prove who they are when claiming their bib numbers on race day.

The fundamental economic idea of segmenting is simple. If a firm can directly identify groups that have different demands and charge different prices to each, it can essentially treat each group as a separate market. The firm then establishes its profit-maximizing quantity for each one of these "markets" where $MR = MC$ and sets the corresponding single-price profit-maximizing price according to each market's demand curve. That's all there is to the strategy.

A firm following this pricing strategy will not earn as much producer surplus as one using perfect price discrimination (which would allow it to take the entire surplus from the market). However, it will earn more surplus than if it acted like a regular monopolist and charged the same price to everyone, because the strategy gives the firm some ability to charge a higher price to consumers with relatively inelastic demand and lower prices to consumers with relatively elastic demand.[3]

The Benefits of Segmenting: A Mathematical Approach

To do the same analysis of segmenting using mathematics, we start with the two distinct demand curves for the Ironman Cozumel. The demand curve of the traveling participants is given by $Q_T = 1,700 - 5P_T$, and the locals' demand curve is $Q_L = 2,400 - 10P_L$. As we said, the locals' demand is more sensitive to price than the travelers' demand: A $1 increase in the entry fee reduces the number of local entrants by 10, while it only decreases the number of traveling entrants by 5. We assume the marginal cost to the organizer of adding another triathlete to the race is a constant $100, no matter how many entrants there are.

The mathematical analysis of segmenting is done using the same steps as in the graphical analysis above. If the race organizers can identify the separate groups and prevent resale, they can compute the marginal revenue curves for each segment and solve for the monopoly prices separately for each group.

---

[3] Eventually, the actual Ironman Cozumel's foreign race demand became so high that it accounted for almost all of the race's demand curve, so the organizers abolished the local discount and chose to focus on the travel market.

We can follow the methods discussed in Chapter 9 to find the marginal revenue curves from linear demand curves. First, we determine the inverse demand curves by rearranging the demand function to express price in terms of quantity demanded. Doing so gives us the following equations:

For travelers:
$$Q_T = 1{,}700 - 5P_T$$
$$5P_T = 1{,}700 - Q_T$$
$$P_T = 340 - 0.2Q_T$$

For locals:
$$Q_L = 2{,}400 - 10P_L$$
$$10P_L = 2{,}400 - Q_L$$
$$P_L = 240 - 0.1Q_L$$

Next, we know that the marginal revenue curve will look like the inverse demand curve, but the coefficient on quantity will be twice as large. The marginal revenue curves for the two segments are

For travelers:
$$MR_T = 340 - 0.4Q_T \quad \text{and} \quad$$

For locals:
$$MR_L = 240 - 0.2Q_L$$

The organizers want to sell the quantities at which marginal cost ($100, the same for both groups of triathletes) equals its marginal revenue. Setting each marginal revenue equation above equal to marginal cost reveals the optimal number of entrants from each group:

For travelers:
$$MR_T = MC$$
$$340 - 0.4Q_T = 100$$
$$240 = 0.4Q_T$$
$$Q_T^* = 600$$

For locals:
$$MR_L = MC$$
$$240 - 0.2Q_L = 100$$
$$140 = 0.2Q_L$$
$$Q_L^* = 700$$

The last step is to find the entry fees that correspond to these quantities by plugging the quantities back into the inverse demand curve:

For travelers:
$$P_T^* = 340 - 0.2Q_T^*$$
$$= 340 - 0.2(600)$$
$$= 340 - 120$$
$$= \$220$$

For locals:
$$P_L^* = 240 - 0.1Q_L^*$$
$$= 240 - 0.1(700)$$
$$= 240 - 70$$
$$= \$170$$

Therefore, in a segmentation strategy, the race organizers sell 600 entries to out-of-towners for $220 each and 700 entries to locals at $170 each.

The total producer surplus the organizers earn is the difference between the price and the marginal cost for each segment times the number of entries sold to that segment. In Figure 10.3, those surpluses are rectangles PS_T for the segment of nonlocal triathletes and PS_L for the local triathletes. Using the results we computed above, we have

For travelers:
$$PS_T = (220 - 100) \times 600$$
$$= 120(600)$$
$$= \$72{,}000$$

For locals:
$$PS_L = (170 - 100) \times 700$$
$$= 70(700)$$
$$= \$49{,}000$$

for a combined producer surplus of $121,000 to the race organizer.

Above we contended that the price discriminating monopolist earns more producer surplus than the single-price monopolist. This makes intuitive sense, because a firm that segments the market can charge higher prices to more price-inelastic customers and capture more of their consumer surplus. We can prove this with the equations.

First, the marginal cost curve intersects the portion of the demand curve that is the sum of the local and nonlocal demand:

$$Q = 1,700 - 5P + 2,400 - 10P = 4,100 - 15P$$

The inverse demand curve at this intersection is then $P = \dfrac{4,100}{15} - \dfrac{Q}{15}$, and the marginal revenue curve has twice the slope, or $MR = \dfrac{4,100}{15} - \dfrac{2Q}{15}$. We set MR equal to the marginal cost to solve for the optimal number of participants under the single-pricing strategy:

$$\frac{4,100}{15} - \frac{2Q}{15} = 100$$
$$4,100 - 2Q = 1,500$$
$$Q^* = 1,300$$

Note that 1,300 is exactly the sum of the local and traveling participants under the previous pricing system. Single-price monopolists and those who segment differ in the prices they set, but not always in the quantity they provide. That doesn't mean the firm would be selling to the same group of individuals, however. The price will be lower than the segmented price for travelers (inducing more to buy than in the segmented case) and higher than the segmented price for locals (excluding some locals from buying). Just what is the price in this instance? Plug the quantity into the inverse demand curve:

$$P^* = \frac{4,100}{15} - \frac{1,300}{15} = \$186.67$$

Thus, although locals face a slightly higher price, the travelers get a bargain relative to the segmented outcome.

To calculate the producer surplus, we compute the difference between the price ($186.67) and marginal cost for the quantity sold (the constant marginal cost of $100 applies for all 1,300 participants):

$$PS = (186.67 - 100) \times 1,300$$
$$= 86.67(1,300) = \$112,671$$

If the monopolist organizers segment the market for triathlon entries, they earn $121,000 in producer surplus; if they must charge a single price, they earn $112,671. Just by segmenting the market, the monopolist organizers can increase their producer surplus by $8,329, or about 7%.

How Much Should Each Segment Be Charged?

Because the standard market power pricing rule applies in each segment, it also means that the Lerner index, the basic markup formula we derived in Chapter 9, applies in each market. Recall that this formula relates the price elasticity of demand at the optimal point to the markup of price over marginal cost:

$$\frac{(P - MC)}{P} = -\frac{1}{E^D}$$

If the firm sells the same good to both segments of the market, the marginal cost of producing for each segment is the same. In this case, the only reason to charge different prices to customers in different segments is because they have different demand elasticities. To see what the Lerner index implies for the ratio of the prices in the two segments (label them 1 and 2), first solve the Lerner index for price in each segment:

$$\frac{(P_1 - MC)}{P_1} = -\frac{1}{E_1^D}$$

$$P_1 - MC = -\frac{1}{E_1^D} \times P_1$$

$$P_1 + \left(\frac{1}{E_1^D} \times P_1\right) = MC$$

$$P_1\left(1 + \frac{1}{E_1^D}\right) = MC$$

$$P_1\left(\frac{E_1^D}{E_1^D} + \frac{1}{E_1^D}\right) = MC$$

$$P_1 = \left(\frac{E_1^D}{1 + E_1^D}\right) \times MC$$

Likewise,

$$P_2 = \left(\frac{E_2^D}{1 + E_2^D}\right) \times MC$$

Now, we can compute the ratio of these prices:

$$\frac{P_1}{P_2} = \frac{\left[E_1^D/(1 + E_1^D)\right] \times MC}{\left[E_2^D/(1 + E_2^D)\right] \times MC}$$

$$= \frac{\left[E_1^D/(1 + E_1^D)\right]}{\left[E_2^D/(1 + E_2^D)\right]}$$

As the demand in Segment 1 becomes less elastic relative to Segment 2 (i.e., E_1^D becomes smaller than E_2^D in absolute value), the ratio P_1/P_2 will rise. That is, the greater the difference in price sensitivities between the segments, the greater should be the ratio in their prices.

Returning to our Ironman Cozumel example, suppose we know that the elasticity of demand for travelers is −1.83 and the elasticity for locals is −2.43.[4] We can immediately determine what the ratio of prices should be by plugging these elasticities into the formula:

$$\frac{P_1}{P_2} = \frac{\dfrac{-1.83}{-1.83 + 1}}{\dfrac{-2.43}{-2.43 + 1}} = \frac{\dfrac{-1.83}{-0.83}}{\dfrac{-2.43}{-1.43}} = \frac{2.2}{1.7} = 1.29$$

In other words, the race organizer should set the price travelers face to be almost 1.3 times (i.e., 30% higher than) the price for locals. This is, in fact, the ratio between the $220 and $170 optimal entry fees we computed earlier.

---

[4] If you remember the calculation of elasticity from Chapter 2, you can verify these values.

A⁺ make the grade

Is it really price discrimination?

Always be careful about the distinction between *price discrimination,* when firms charge different prices for the same product, and *price differences*. It can be surprisingly difficult to tell them apart. Prices can differ across different customer groups if a firm with market power price discriminates, but prices can also differ across the groups if the marginal cost of supplying the groups differs, even in a perfectly competitive market.

For example, a bottle of Coca-Cola, which is basically just carbonated water plus syrup, is often less expensive than a bottle of carbonated water alone. Perhaps this price difference reflects price discrimination because the kinds of people who buy bottled water are less price-sensitive than the people who buy soda. But maybe the cost of bottling fancy carbonated water is greater than the cost of bottling soft drinks (e.g., a lot

more people buy soda than carbonated water and there might be some economies of scale). You can't tell just from the prices.

The only way to distinguish the difference between price discrimination and price differences due to costs in competitive markets (without actually being able to observe the firm's marginal cost) is to find something that changes the price elasticity of demand without changing the cost. Price discrimination implies that a firm with market power sets its price based on the elasticity of demand and the marginal cost of production. Price in a competitive market depends only on marginal cost. (This is related to a distinction we discussed in Chapter 9: how firms with market power react differently than competitive firms to rotations in demand.)

 figure it out 10.2

You manage a hair salon that has two locations: one in a large city in Ohio with several competing salons and another in a small city in Pennsylvania with less competition. In Ohio, your customer's price elasticity of demand is −3, while for your Pennsylvania customers it is −2. Assume that the marginal cost of producing a haircut is $30 regardless of location.

a. What are your salon's optimal markups and prices in each location?

b. Why do they differ?

Solution:

a. The Lerner index provides us with a formula for discerning the relationship between pricing and the price elasticity of demand:

$$\frac{(P-MC)}{P}=-\frac{1}{E^D}$$

Substituting for marginal cost (= $30) and the price elasticity of demand for Ohio customers (= −3),

we get

$$\frac{(P-\$30)}{P}=-\frac{1}{(-3)}$$
$$P=3(P-\$30)$$
$$2P=\$90$$
$$P=\$45$$

Repeating the same steps for Pennsylvania gives

$$\frac{(P-\$30)}{P}=-\frac{1}{(-2)}$$
$$P=2(P-\$30)$$
$$P=\$60$$

Customers in Ohio will be charged a price of $45 per haircut, while those in Pennsylvania will be charged a price of $60 per haircut.

b. Because demand is relatively more elastic in Ohio than in Pennsylvania (the absolute value of the price elasticity of demand is greater), customers in Ohio are more price-sensitive. Therefore, they will be charged a lower price.

Ways to Directly Segment Customers

There are many common ways firms directly segment customers for the purpose of price discrimination.

By Customer Characteristics   Firms sometimes price according to customer characteristics such as age (e.g., senior citizen discounts at the movies or child discounts at a hotel), gender, or whether the customer is a student or local resident. The basic idea is to identify the more price-sensitive customers and charge them less. Firms need to be careful when pricing based on consumer characteristics in certain countries because in some cases this may be prohibited by laws against discrimination based on age, gender, race, physical disabilities, and so on.

Segmenting can even be based on the user's species. Doctors and veterinarians sometimes use the same medicines. Drug makers recognize that Grandma's willingness to pay for the arthritis medication Lodine probably well exceeds her willingness to purchase Lodine for her arthritic dog Rover (and not only because Grandma's savings are larger than Rover's collection of buried rawhides). This difference in willingness to pay probably explains why a congressional investigation found that the price of Lodine for humans was almost 3 times higher than for dogs. Indeed, it determined that manufacturers priced almost every comparable medication significantly higher for people than for animals.[5]

Customer characteristics can also apply to firms or other corporate organizations in business-to-business transactions. Academic journals, for example, know that individuals are much more price-sensitive to subscription prices than libraries, so the publishers charge significantly more for institutional subscriptions than for individual ones. Elsevier, for example, one of the largest publishers of academic journals, charges individuals $142 for a year's subscription to the *International Journal of Industrial Organization* (don't all rush to order it at once), but the publisher charges libraries $2,702 for the same subscription.

By Past Purchase Behavior   Consumers reveal a lot about their willingness to pay when they buy other products, and many sellers use that information to segment customers. In industries like auto insurance or direct-broadcast satellite TV, where people don't like switching companies once they decide on a provider, existing customers tend to be less price-sensitive than potential new customers. If you enter all of your mailing addresses into an online photo service like Shutterfly to send out holiday cards, it would be a huge hassle to re-enter the same information should you decide to go with a competitor. As a result, it is common for firms in these industries to give discounts to new customers, such as reduced prices for new customers or the first three months of a subscription free. These are ways to price discriminate based on whether the customer has bought the product before.

For some other products, the price sensitivity of new customers is *lower* than that of past purchasers. For example, it is notoriously difficult to convince people to upgrade their software to a new version. When Microsoft releases a new version of Windows, the price of upgrading an older version is typically much lower than buying the new version outright. With this low price, Microsoft is trying to entice the more price-sensitive customers to purchase the new version.

---

[5] Minority Staff, Special Investigations Division, Committee on Government Reform, U.S. House of Representatives, "Prescription Drug Price Discrimination in the 5th Congressional District in Florida: Drug Manufacturer Prices Are Higher for Humans than for Animals," Prepared for Rep. Karen L. Thurman, http://lobby.la.psu.edu/010_Insuring_the_Uninsured/Congressional_Statements/House/H_Thurman_031600.htm.

FREAKONOMICS

Victoria's Not-So-Secret Price Discrimination

Sometimes price discrimination can end up being costly not just to consumers, but also to producers. In 1996 Denise Katzman of New York City sued Victoria's Secret for gender discrimination and sought millions of dollars in damages. In alleging gender discrimination, Katzman didn't object to the catalog's pages of scantily clad women. Rather, she pointed to the promotional coupon on the catalog's back page.

The problem? While Katzman's catalog offered her $10 off an order of $75, an almost identical catalog sent to a male friend offered him $25 off the same amount. Was her catalog out of date? Nope. The folks at Victoria's Secret were just engaging in a little "naked" price discrimination.

Although the company kept its reasons for the different promotions a secret, we can speculate on why it might have resorted to such price discrimination using economic reasoning. We know that price discrimination occurs when a company uses its market power to charge higher prices to people who are willing to pay more. In this case, Victoria's

Secret recognized that its practice of sending out catalogs gave it the opportunity to segment its customers and advertise different prices to different types of customers. They likely made the assumption that women might be willing to purchase $75 of fancy lingerie for a price of $65, but men are probably not as willing to shell out that much money. They might only pay $50 for the same order. Because most people don't end up reading through their friends' catalogs, this form of price discrimination would easily go undetected.

Katzman never did collect her millions in damages, however. The judge sanctioned her lawyer for filing a frivolous suit, ordering him to pay a portion of Victoria's Secret's legal fees. Not faring much better was Katzman's fellow New Yorker, Roy Den Hollander. In 2007 he brought suit against bars that sponsor Ladies' Nights, which Hollander termed "invidious." He lost his suit, and bars everywhere continue to advertise gender-based price discrimination with weekly Ladies' Nights.

By Location   Customers living in one area may have a hard time getting to another to take advantage of a lower price, or they might not even have knowledge of the prices in other locations. This often allows sellers to charge different prices in different locations, depending on the price sensitivity of local demand. For example, chain restaurants often charge higher prices at their airport locations than at their other stores, at least in part because travelers in a hurry, in an unfamiliar city, and (often) on an expense account tend not to be price-sensitive in their food and drink purchases.

Application: Segmenting by Location in the European Market for Cars

Car manufacturers like Volkswagen and BMW who do a lot of business in Europe sell the same car in many different countries. The customers in these countries have very different incomes and tastes in cars. Because the automakers in this market likely have some market power, this is an excellent opportunity for segmenting *if* the automakers can prevent their customers in one country from selling to those in another. Manufacturers could then segment their customers by country, selling the same car at different prices in each country using the price-discrimination methods we've been discussing. This practice would allow such manufacturers to earn higher profits and more producer surplus than they could by selling their cars at the same price everywhere.

It turns out the auto companies have many options for preventing resale across countries. First, they can print all manuals and documents only in the country's language. Swedish drivers don't want manuals in Greek, and vice versa. Second, they can forbid servicing a car in a country other than the one in which it was purchased. No one wants to get towed to Romania when their car experiences problems in Spain. Third, they can punish dealers who sell cars to people from a different country.

A VW Golf bought in Hannover, Germany, costs less than the same car bought in Portugal, but more than in Greece.

Economists Pinelopi Goldberg and Frank Verboven gathered evidence on car prices in Europe to investigate this issue.[6] They found that the price of the same car could vary substantially across countries. In 2015 the price of a base model VW Golf in Germany was almost 20% more expensive than in Greece, but about 20% lower than in Portugal.

Goldberg and Verboven concluded that some of the price differences across countries in Europe arose from differences in the taxation of autos, but that much of the price difference was due to basic direct price discrimination by segmenting. The auto firms were varying their markups depending on the conditions of local demand. VW Golf pricing patterns are consistent with the theory that demand in Germany is less elastic than in Greece but more elastic than in Portugal, so VW charges its German customers more than its Greek customers, and the Portuguese pay still more. ■

Over Time   One way to price discriminate in certain markets is to take advantage of the different kinds of people who buy a product at different times. When a new generation of computer CPUs first hits the market, for example, the new CPUs usually sell at a substantial premium, sometimes hundreds of dollars more than the last generation's chips. Yet only a few months later, they are available for a fraction of their original price. Maybe marginal cost fell that much, you say? Perhaps. But how about movies in first-run theaters that cost $10 but then cost only $4 when the same movie runs at a discount movie house several weeks later? Or, hardcover books that cost $26.95 while their paperback versions cost only $10.95, when the actual difference in production cost is only about a dollar? These are all cases in which the kinds of people who want the latest, greatest, most current version of a product — PC gamers, big movie fans, and active readers — tend to be less sensitive to price than the folks who enter the market later.

In other cases, demand can become less price-sensitive (more inelastic) over time, and price discrimination will lead to price increases over time. Many goods and services with initially uncertain quality share this feature. For example, tickets to a new play that hasn't been reviewed are often relatively inexpensive. But once local reviewers have given the play a "thumbs up," demand can become much more inelastic and the producers raise their price accordingly.

In either situation, a firm that prices the same good differently in two different time periods applies the basic segmentation rules and uses the standard monopoly pricing rule as it applies to the state of demand in each period.

However, there is one complication in pricing across time that is worth keeping in mind and that leads to our next section about different versions of the product. Technically, pricing across time isn't directly segmenting unless the seller tells the customer during what time period they can buy. If the customers are forward-looking, meaning that they consider what the seller might do in the future even as they decide whether to buy today, just offering different prices at different times and letting the customer decide when they want to buy is *not* actually directly segmenting the customers. The seller cannot prevent its customers from changing groups. In cases like this, the seller needs to consider how the different prices it plans to charge over time will affect the consumer's decision of when to buy. And it will limit their ability to price discriminate too dramatically. We call this indirect price discrimination and discuss it next.

[6] Pinelopi K. Goldberg and Frank Verboven, "Cross-Country Price Dispersion in the Euro Era: A Case Study of the European Car Market," *Economic Policy* 19, no. 40 (October 2004): 484–521.

10.4 Indirect (Second-Degree) Price Discrimination

When to Use It Indirect (Second-Degree) Price Discrimination

1. *The firm has market power and can prevent resale.*
2. The firm's customers have different demand curves.
3. The firm cannot directly identify which customers have which type of demand before purchase.

A firm with market power can use direct price discrimination to increase its producer surplus above the amount it could earn by charging only a single price. The key is to charge higher prices to customers with relatively inelastic demand and lower prices to those with more elastic demand. However, being able to directly observe a customer's elasticity before he buys (as required with direct price discrimination) is often difficult. A firm might know that its customers have different price sensitivities, but frequently can't tell which group any particular customer belongs to.

Even without this knowledge, a firm can still earn extra producer surplus through price discrimination by using a pricing strategy called **indirect price discrimination,** also known as **second-degree price discrimination,** a *pricing strategy in which customers pick among a variety of pricing choices offered by the firm.*

There are many different kinds of indirect price-discrimination techniques a company can use. The principle that underlies all of them, however, is the need to set up the pricing options and let the customers sort themselves into the "right" choice; that is, to purchase the option meant for their group rather than another option for a different group. For example, airlines choose ticket rules and prices so that business travelers with inelastic demand pay more, on average, for their tickets than leisure travelers with relatively more elastic demand. At the same time, however, the airline wants to keep business travelers from deciding that tickets meant for them are too expensive and instead buying up cheaper tickets intended for leisure travelers.

> **indirect price discrimination (second-degree price discrimination)** A pricing strategy in which customers pick among a variety of pricing choices offered by the firm.

Indirect Price Discrimination through Quantity Discounts

The most basic type of indirect price discrimination is the **quantity discount,** a *pricing strategy in which customers who buy larger quantities of a good pay a lower per-unit price.* For quantity discounting to work, customers who purchase larger quantities of a product need to have relatively more elastic demands than consumers who buy smaller quantities. If the consumers in the market do not have these elasticity characteristics, the firm would be trying to find a way to raise prices on the people who buy greater quantities, the opposite of a quantity discount.

> **quantity discount** A pricing strategy in which customers who buy larger quantities of a good pay a lower per-unit price.

To illustrate the idea, let's say there are two types of customers at the online brokerage house E*TRADE. One type of customer is not very interested in trading stocks. Because of this, these customers don't have a big incentive to shop across different online brokers in search of lower commission rates (the fees paid to a brokerage firm to facilitate a trade). Thus, their demands are relatively inelastic with respect to the commission charged. The demand curve for uninterested traders is D_u in panel a of **Figure 10.4**. The other type of customer is obsessed with trading stocks. These people trade many times each day and are very sensitive to the commission rate. Thus, their demands are relatively elastic with respect to the commission. The demand curve for these obsessed traders is shown as D_o in

---

Figure 10.4 Quantity Discounts at E*TRADE

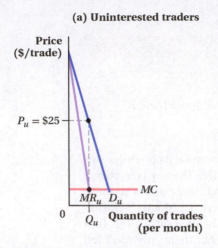
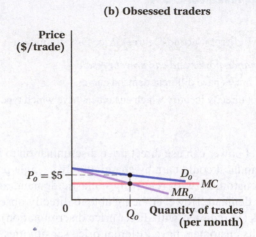

(a) Uninterested traders

(b) Obsessed traders

(a) The online brokerage company E*TRADE has two types of customers: uninterested traders and obsessed traders. Uninterested traders have a relatively inelastic demand curve D_u. E*TRADE would like to charge uninterested traders the profit-maximizing commission rate $P_u = \$25$ per trade and sell quantity Q_u trades per month.

(b) Obsessed traders have a relatively elastic demand curve D_o. E*TRADE would like to charge them the lower commission rate $P_o = \$5$ per trade. Although E*TRADE cannot directly identify which group any particular trader belongs to, it can set different prices for the two groups using a quantity discount by requiring traders to make at least Q_o trades per month to get a reduced commission rate.

---

panel b. The marginal revenue curves for each group are MR_u and MR_o, respectively. The marginal cost is the same for both groups.

E*TRADE would like to charge higher commissions to the uninterested traders with an inelastic demand than to the obsessed traders with the more elastic demand. This third-degree price discrimination (segmenting) would bring E*TRADE more producer surplus, but the company cannot pursue this strategy because it cannot tell which type of trader each person is when she signs up for an account. What E*TRADE *does* know, however, is what the demand curves of the two groups look like, even if it can't identify to which group any given trader belongs. Based on the demand curve D_u, for example, E*TRADE would want to set its standard profit-maximizing quantity and price (commission per trade) for uninterested traders where MR_u equals MC: For Q_u trades per month, E*TRADE would charge uninterested traders $25 per trade. For obsessed traders, E*TRADE would like to follow the same procedure and charge them a price of $5 per trade; at that commission, the obsessed traders would make Q_o trades per month.

If E*TRADE could segment the market, it would charge each group P_u and P_o per trade, and at those prices, each group would make Q_u and Q_o trades per month. However, E*TRADE can't directly assign different commission rates to different traders. And it can't just offer new customers a choice of whether to pay $25 or $5 commissions no matter how much or little they trade because every customer would choose the cheaper option. But E*TRADE can still do something to take more of the traders' surplus for itself. Rather than offer all customers a $5 per trade commission, E*TRADE can tie that commission rate to a requirement that the customer make at least Q_o trades per month. For customers who do not want to make at least Q_o trades per month, E*TRADE can offer a $25 per trade commission plan that allows them to trade as little or as much as they'd like in one month.

Incentive Compatibility   The plan to charge uninterested traders a higher commission than obsessed traders is logical, but for such a plan to work well, E*TRADE needs to make sure that the uninterested trader won't want to switch from her $25/$Q_u$ package to the $5/$Q_o$ package designed for the obsessed traders. That is, the $5 commission deal can't be so good that the uninterested trader will make extra trades just to obtain the lower price. This is the essence of any kind of successful indirect price-discrimination strategy: The firm must set its prices so that a customer doesn't try to fake her demand type and buy the package meant for another customer type. E*TRADE has to be sure that the uninterested trader's consumer surplus is bigger with the $25 per trade package than with the $5 package that requires a purchase of at least Q_o trades. The offers need to be internally consistent so that each type of buyer actually chooses the offer designed for it.

Incentive compatibility is the term for the *requirement under an indirect price-discrimination strategy that the price offered to each consumer group is chosen by that group.* In this example, the two packages are incentive-compatible if:

1. An uninterested trader prefers the $25 package to the $5 package (and she will make this choice if the $25 package gives her greater consumer surplus than the $5 package).

2. An obsessed trader prefers the $5 package because it offers her more consumer surplus than the $25 package.

Let's see whether this set of offers is incentive-compatible. First, we need to show that the uninterested trader's consumer surplus from trades at $25 each is greater than her surplus from making Q_o trades at $5 each. Finding the consumer surplus from the first offer is familiar territory. As shown in **Figure 10.5**, at a price of $25 per trade, an uninterested

incentive compatibility
The requirement under an indirect price-discrimination strategy that the price offered to each consumer group is chosen by that group.

Figure 10.5   Incentive Compatibility

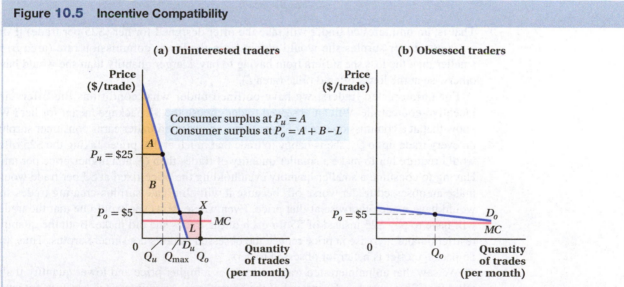

(a) Before offering a quantity discount to obsessed traders, E*TRADE needs to ensure that its pricing strategy is incentive-compatible. At $P_u = \$25$ per trade, uninterested traders make Q_u trades and receive surplus A. At the quantity and price offered to obsessed traders (Q_o, P_o), their surplus is reduced by area L but increases by area B. Uninterested traders will choose to pay $25 per trade if area L is greater than area B.

(b) Under the pricing policy for uninterested traders, obsessed traders would have to pay both a higher price $(P_u = \$25 > P_o = \$5)$ and make fewer trades per month $(Q_o > Q_u)$. Therefore, the quantity discount is incentive-compatible for these traders.

trader makes quantity Q_u trades, and the consumer surplus is the area under the uninterested trader's demand curve and above the $25 price. This is triangle A in panel a.

Finding the uninterested trader's consumer surplus for the $5 package offer is a bit trickier. The first thing we need to do is put the $5 package's price and quantity combination in the diagram showing the demand for trades of an uninterested trader. Call this point X, as shown in panel a. Notice that point X lies *above* the uninterested trader's demand curve. That means if an uninterested trader were to make trade number Q_o (at a commission of $5), she would actually lose consumer surplus by doing so. At a price of $5, an uninterested trader really only wishes to purchase Q_{max} trades, the quantity demanded at that price.

The fact that Q_{max} is less than Q_o implies that the uninterested trader's willingness to pay for the trades between Q_{max} and Q_o is lower than the $5 she would have to pay for them. In fact, all trades for which her demand curve (indicating her willingness to pay) lies below $5 will result in a loss of consumer surplus. In panel a, these surplus-destroying trades are those between Q_{max} and Q_o, and the total consumer surplus lost is the area labeled L. That area is the downside for an uninterested trader accepting the lower-commission offer. There is an upside, however. The first Q_{max} trades she conducts create consumer surplus, area $A + B$ in the figure. This consumer surplus is quite a bit larger than her surplus under the $25 per trade offer (area A) because the price is so much lower. The net consumer surplus an uninterested trader gets from taking the $5 package offer is therefore area A + area B − area L.

Comparing the uninterested trader's consumer surpluses from the two offers, we can now see that she will choose the $25 per trade offer over the $5 package offer if

$$\text{Area } A > \text{area } A + \text{area } B - \text{area } L$$

$$0 > \text{area } B - \text{area } L$$

$$\text{Area } B < \text{area } L$$

That is, an uninterested trader will take the offer designed for her ($25 per trade) if the extra consumer surplus she would obtain from the lower commission rate (area B) is smaller than the loss she suffers from having to buy a larger quantity than she would have otherwise at the lower offered price (area L).

For uninterested traders, we have outlined under what conditions the offers are incentive-compatible. Will an obsessed trader choose the $5 package meant for her? We know that at a commission rate of $5 per trade, an obsessed trader earns consumer surplus on every trade up to Q_o; she is happy to trade that much at that price. Taking the $25 offer would require her to make a smaller quantity of trades than Q_o at a higher price per unit. Having to consume a smaller quantity even holding the price fixed at $5 per trade would make an obsessed trader worse off, because it will eliminate surplus-creating trades she would have made otherwise at that price. Even worse, however, would be that the trader will have to pay $25 instead of $5 for each of the trades she did make. Both the quantity restriction and increase in price reduce the obsessed trader's consumer surplus. Thus, the $5 package offer is better for obsessed traders.

We saw that an uninterested trader also faces a higher price and lower quantity if she takes the $25 per trade offer instead of the $5 package. An uninterested trader is not automatically worse off by taking the $25 offer, as is an obsessed trader, because if an uninterested trader faced a price of $5 per trade but was able to choose how many trades she makes, she will not opt to complete Q_o trades. She will only choose to make Q_{max}, the quantity of trades demanded at a price of $5 per trade. Any trades between Q_{max} and Q_o destroy consumer surplus for an uninterested trader because the price is higher than her willingness to pay. It is the potential consumer surplus-destroying trades tied to the $5 package that make it likely an uninterested trader would prefer the $25 offer.

figure it out 10.3

Suppose you are a pricing analyst for MegaDat Corporation, a firm that recently developed a new software program for data analysis. You have two types of clients who use your product. Type A's inverse demand for your software is $P = 120 - 10Q$, where Q represents users and P is in dollars per user. Type B's inverse demand is $P = 60 - 2Q$. Assume that your firm faces a constant marginal cost of $20 per user to install and set up this software.

a. If you can tell which type of buyer is buying the product before a purchase is made, what prices will you charge each type?

b. Suppose instead that you cannot tell which type of buyer the client is until after the purchase. Suggest a possible way to use quantity discounts to have buyers self-select into the pricing scheme set up for them.

c. Determine whether the pricing scheme you determined in part (b) is incentive-compatible.

Solution:

a. To maximize profit, set $MR = MC$ for each type. Therefore, we first need to solve for the marginal revenue curves for each type. Because we have linear inverse demand curves, we know that the MR curves will have the same vertical intercept but twice the slope. This means that $MR = 120 - 20Q$ for Type A buyers and $MR = 60 - 4Q$ for Type B buyers. Now set $MR = MC$ to find the profit-maximizing quantity for each type:

For Type A:	**For Type B:**
$120 - 20Q_A = 20$	$60 - 4Q_B = 20$
$20Q_A = 100$	$4Q_B = 40$
$Q_A^* = 5$	$Q_B^* = 10$

At these quantities, the prices will be

For Type A:	**For Type B:**
$P_A^* = 120 - 10Q_A^*$	$P_B^* = 60 - 2Q_B^*$
$= 120 - 10(5)$	$= 60 - 2(10)$
$= \$70$	$= \$40$

b. The firm could charge $70 per user for a package where the buyer can purchase any quantity she wishes and a price of $40 for any buyer willing to purchase 10 or more units.

c. This plan is incentive-compatible for Type B users. They are willing to continue to purchase $Q = 10$ at a price of $40 each.

For a Type A consumer, we need to consider the amount of consumer surplus she receives under each scheme. We can do this with the help of a diagram showing the Type A demand curve and the two prices, $70 and $40.

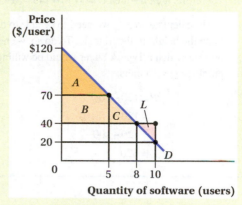

At a price of $70, a Type A buyer would choose to purchase 5 units. Consumer surplus would equal area A, the area below the demand curve but above price.

If a Type A buyer were to opt to purchase the other package (10 units at a price of $40 each), her consumer surplus would be the area above the price and below demand (area $A + B + C$), but she would also lose consumer surplus because she would be buying units that she values less than the price of $40. This would be area L in the diagram.

Thus, opting for the quantity discount would change the Type A buyer's consumer surplus by area B + area C − area L. The $40 10-unit package would be incentive-compatible only if area $L >$ area B + area C. Let's calculate those values:

$$\text{Area } B = \text{base} \times \text{height}$$
$$= (5)(\$70 - \$40)$$
$$= (5)(\$30)$$
$$= \$150$$

To calculate area C, we need to determine the base of the triangle. This means that we need to know the quantity at which the Type A buyer's willingness to pay is exactly $40:

$$P = 120 - 10Q$$
$$40 = 120 - 10Q$$
$$10Q = 80$$
$$Q = 8$$

$$\text{Area } C = \frac{1}{2} \times \text{base} \times \text{height}$$
$$= (0.5)(8 - 5)(\$70 - \$40)$$
$$= (0.5)(3)(\$30)$$
$$= \$45$$

Therefore, area B + area C = \$150 + \$45 = \$195.

To calculate area L, we need to be able to determine the height of the triangle. To do so, we need the price at which a Type A buyer would be willing to purchase $Q = 10$ units:

$$P = 120 - 10Q$$
$$= 120 - 10(10)$$
$$= 120 - 100$$
$$= \$20$$

$$\text{Area } L = \frac{1}{2} \times \text{base} \times \text{height}$$
$$= (0.5)(10 - 8)(\$40 - \$20)$$
$$= (0.5)(2)(\$20)$$
$$= \$20$$

So, we know that area B + area C = \$150 + \$45 = \$195 and area L = \$20.

Because area A + area B > area L, the \$40 10-unit pricing scheme is not incentive-compatible for Type A buyers. These buyers will want to receive the quantity discount and will purchase 10 units at a price of \$40 each. Thus, this pricing scheme would not be successful at making the buyers self-select into the pricing scheme established for their types.

Indirect Price Discrimination through Versioning

versioning A pricing strategy in which the firm offers different product options designed to attract different types of consumers.

Airline tickets are a classic example of what we call **versioning,** a *pricing strategy in which the firm offers different product options designed to attract different types of consumers.* Airlines have a group of business travel customers who are not very sensitive to prices and a group of leisure travelers who are highly sensitive to price. Airlines want to charge different prices to the two passenger groups, but they can't tell who is flying on business when a customer buys a ticket. So, the airlines instead offer different versions of the product (tickets on a given flight) available at different prices. The cheaper version, with many restrictions, is intended for leisure travelers who buy generally well in advance of the travel date, stay over a Saturday night, and book a round-trip flight. The more expensive version has fewer restrictions and is intended for business travelers who generally don't like spending a weekend away from home, often need to buy their tickets at the last minute, and may choose to purchase a one-way flight for each segment to provide them with added flexibility. By offering two versions of tickets for a given flight, the airline attempts to make the two types of customers sort themselves (and by doing so, the airline captures more producer surplus).

For this scheme to work, the airlines need to make sure the prices of each version are incentive-compatible. If the airline sets the prices for each group based on the markup formula it would use with direct price discrimination, the restricted-travel version might be too cheap relative to the ticket with fewer restrictions. In this case, business travelers might actually bite the bullet and start planning trips earlier or stay at their destination over the weekend.

Versioning and Price-Cost Margins   With versioning, the different versions' marginal costs do not need to be the same. All that is necessary for versioning to work is for the markup of price over marginal cost to be bigger for the versions bought by customers with less elastic demand.

Consider the example of an automaker like Toyota, which sells a lot of midsize sedans. Some of Toyota's buyers in this segment will not be very price-sensitive. Maybe they are status-conscious, or just have a particular taste for cars with many fancy features.

Others will be more price-sensitive. If Toyota was able to tell which type of customer was which when he or she walked through the door, Toyota could just use direct price discrimination and charge different prices according to the strategy we discussed in Section 10.3. In reality, however, it's not always easy to tell what type of customer comes through the door at any particular time. So, Toyota uses indirect price discrimination and designs different versions of the car that it can sell at different markups, hoping to induce buyers to segment themselves based on their price sensitivity and taste for features.

For example, Toyota makes the Camry, one of the highest-selling cars in the world. It sells, nicely equipped, for about $29,000 in the United States. But Toyota also makes the Lexus ES 350, which is built on the same platform and in the same plant as the Camry. It is similar in many respects to the Camry but is more luxurious. Think of the ES 350 as being a Camry but with a bigger engine, a nicer sound system, a fancier multimedia interface, and a moonroof. The ES 350 sells for around $39,000.

Although those extra options raise Toyota's marginal cost of producing an ES 350, it's unlikely that this increase in marginal cost would amount to $10,000 per car. Toyota charges more than the cost difference because the different versions split its customers into groups based on their price sensitivities. The Lexus group has less elastic demand, so Toyota's markup over marginal cost can be higher, just like the Saturday-night stay splits an airline's customers into leisure and business travelers.

To be incentive-compatible, Toyota can't make the deal for the cheap version so good that it convinces the luxury customers to purchase Camrys instead. Quantitatively, think of it in the following way. Suppose there are just two types of customers whose willingness to pay for each car is listed in **Table 10.1**.

Notice that both consumers believe the Lexus is worth more than the Camry. It's not that Toyota has made a version one group likes and the other doesn't. The budget consumers value a Lexus more than a Toyota, but not very much more: $33,000 versus $30,000. The luxury consumers, however, value the ES 350 *a lot* more than the Camry: $44,000 versus $33,000.

If Toyota prices the Camry at $28,000 and the Lexus ES 350 at $38,000, the budget consumers get $2,000 of consumer surplus from buying the Camry and −$5,000 from buying the Lexus (it costs more than they value it), so they will buy the Camry. The luxury consumers get $5,000 of surplus from buying the Camry and $6,000 from the Lexus, so they go with the Lexus. Each group chooses the version designed to take advantage of the nature of their demand curves. That means these prices are incentive-compatible.

If Toyota priced the Lexus at $41,000 rather than $38,000, the budget consumers would still buy the Camry. The status consumers, however, would get more consumer surplus from buying the Camry ($5,000) than from buying the Lexus ($3,000), so they would also decide to buy the Camry. That $3,000 price increase for the Lexus would cause Toyota to lose $10,000 (losing a sale of a $38,000 Lexus at the old price for a $28,000 Camry instead) for each luxury consumer. By charging the group with the less elastic demand too high a price, Toyota would not be setting incentive-compatible prices and its attempt at indirect price discrimination would fail.

One detail that is important to note is that it is not the mere existence of customers with inelastic demand that allows Toyota (or any other firm) to indirectly price discriminate with versioning. What is required is a *difference* in the demand elasticities across customer groups. If all consumer groups had the same price elasticities of demand, even if relatively inelastic, then there's no need to price discriminate.

Table 10.1 Consumer Valuations for Camrys and ESs

	Toyota Camry	Lexus ES 350
Budget consumer	$30,000	$33,000
Luxury consumer	$33,000	$44,000

Automakers offer cars with different paint colors, for example, but there is rarely price discrimination based on paint color because the price sensitivities of people who like blue cars and silver cars are no different.

There is virtually no limit to the kinds of versioning a company can implement to get its customers to self-select into groups based on their price sensitivities. Now that you understand this kind of price discrimination, you will see it everywhere you look.

10.5 Bundling

When to Use It Bundling

1. *A firm has market power and can prevent resale.*
2. A firm sells a second product and consumers' demand for that product is negatively correlated with their demand for the first product.

bundling A pricing strategy in which the firm sells two or more products together at a single price.

Another indirect price-discrimination strategy that firms with market power can use to increase their producer surplus over the standard monopoly pricing surplus is called **bundling,** a *pricing strategy in which the firm sells two or more products together at a single price.*

When you subscribe to cable or satellite television, for example, you are buying a bundled good. You pay a single monthly fee for service, and the cable or satellite company delivers a number of networks together. You don't pick and choose every channel individually. For your $45 per month, you get, say, 90 channels rather than paying $6 per month for ESPN, $4 a month for MTV, and so on.

Sometimes, things can be bundled just because people prefer buying things together (think about left and right shoes). This sort of bundling occurs because the goods are strong complements to each other (i.e., one good raises the marginal utility of the other), and is not a price-discrimination strategy. However, in this chapter, we're interested in ways that companies can use bundling as a way to price discriminate. To explain how bundling can be a strategic pricing decision, we first need to clear up a common misconception. Bundling will generally *not* allow a company with market power in one product to leverage its market power into a second product. To illustrate what we mean, let's look at a specific example.

Take a cable company providing TV channels to your home. To make it easy, let's say there are only two cable networks: the sports network ESPN and truTV, a channel that specializes in reality TV shows. (ESPN is among the most watched cable networks, and truTV definitely is not.) Why would the cable company force you to buy both as a bundle for some price rather than just sell them separately?

At first glance, people tend to think it's a way for the cable company to leverage market power/high demand for ESPN to force people to pay more for the lesser product (truTV). But this "forcing it down their throat" argument usually does not make sense. To see why, suppose there are two customers (Madison and Dakota) in the market. Both like ESPN a lot and truTV less, as reflected in **Table 10.2**. Madison values ESPN at $9 per month and Dakota values it at $10 per month. Madison values truTV at $1 per month, while Dakota values it at $1.50. For simplicity, let's assume the marginal cost of supplying the networks is zero.

Does the cable company raise its producer surplus by bundling the prized ESPN with truTV? If it sells the channels

Table 10.2 Positively Correlated Valuations per Subscriber-Month

	ESPN	truTV	Bundle
Madison	$9.00	$1.00	$10.00
Dakota	$10.00	$1.50	$11.50

separately, it would have to price each channel at the lower of the two customers' valuations for each channel ($9.00 for ESPN and $1.00 for truTV). Otherwise, the company would sell to only one of the customers and would lose the revenue from the other.[7] Thus, it sells ESPN for $9 per month and truTV for $1 per month, earning a total surplus of $20 per month $(2 \times \$9) + (2 \times \$1)$ from selling the channels separately.

Now suppose the cable company sells the channels as a bundle. The combined value the customers put on the bundle ($10.00 per month for Madison and $11.50 for Dakota) means the company will again set the price at the lower valuation so it won't lose half of the market. It therefore prices the bundle at $10 and sells it to both customers. This yields a surplus of $(2 \times \$10)$, or $20 per month, the same amount it earned selling the networks separately. Bundling has not raised the firm's surplus.

Furthermore, if the company combines ESPN with something customers don't actually want at all (say, e.g., that the valuation on truTV was zero or even negative), then the amount that customers would be willing to pay for that network plus ESPN would be that much lower. As a general matter, then, a company can't make extra money by attaching a highly desired product to an undesired one.

But a bundle can increase producer surplus in a particular situation. Suppose that, instead of the valuations being given in Table 10.2, the two valuations for truTV are switched. Both customers value ESPN far more, but now Madison has a higher valuation for truTV ($1.50 per month) than does Dakota ($1.00). The key condition that has changed, as will become clear in a minute, is that the *willingness to pay for the two goods is now negatively correlated across the consumers*. This means that one of the customers has a higher willingness to pay for one channel than the other customer, but a lower willingness to pay for the other channel. In our example, Madison has lower willingness to pay for ESPN than Dakota but greater demand for truTV, as shown in **Table 10.3**.

With this change, the firm receives more producer surplus using the bundling strategy. If the cable company sells the channels separately, the calculation is the same as before (ESPN for $9 per month, truTV for $1), and it earns a total of $20 of surplus per month. If the firm bundles the channels, however, it can sell the package to both customers for $10.50 per month. This earns the company $(2 \times \$10.50)$ or $21 of producer surplus per month, more than the $20 per month from selling the channels separately.

The reason why bundling works in the second scenario is the negative correlation between the two customers' willingness to pay. Dakota values one part of the bundle (ESPN) more than Madison, while Madison values truTV more than Dakota. If the cable company wants to sell to the entire market, it can only set a price equal to the smaller of the two customers' willingness to pay, whether pricing separately or as a bundle. In the first example with positively correlated demand (when Dakota had a higher willingness to pay for both channels), the lower of the customers' valuations for the bundle ($10 per subscriber for Madison) is smaller by $1.50 than the larger valuation ($11.50 per month for Dakota) because it reflects Madison's lower valuations for both channels. Therefore, if the cable company wants to sell the channels as a bundle, it must offer Dakota a discount that embodies the fact that Madison has a lower willingness to pay for both channels. As a result, the cable company does no better than having sold the channels separately.

Table 10.3 Negatively Correlated Valuations per Subscriber-Month			
	ESPN	**truTV**	**Bundle**
Madison	$9.00	$1.50	$10.50
Dakota	$10.00	$1.00	$11.00

---

[7] In reality, most network owners like Disney, which owns ESPN and History, do not own the cable company, so they actually bundle the channels they sell to the cable company that then passes along that bundle to you. The point is the same, however.

With a negative correlation of demands across customers, there is less variation (only $0.50) in each customer's willingness to pay for the bundle: $10.50 per month for Madison and $11.00 per month for Dakota. This reduced variation means the cable company doesn't need to give as large a discount to Dakota to sell to both customers. Bundling has reduced the difference in total willingness to pay across the customers. What's important is that the smaller of the two combined valuations is larger when the channel demands are negatively correlated. Madison will pay $10.50 instead of only $10, which allows the company to raise its price. In this way, bundling allows sellers to "smooth out" variations in customers' demands, raises the prices sellers can charge for their bundled products, and increases the amount of surplus they can extract.

Mixed Bundling

mixed bundling A type of bundling in which the firm simultaneously offers consumers the choice of buying two or more products separately or as a bundle.

pure bundling A type of bundling in which the firm offers the products only as a bundle.

The previous example shows why a firm might choose to sell two products as a bundle instead of separately. Sometimes, however, firms let the consumer make the choice. This indirect pricing strategy, a *type of bundling in which the firm simultaneously offers consumers the choice of buying two or more products separately or as a bundle,* is called **mixed bundling**. An Extra Value Meal at McDonald's includes a sandwich, fries, and a drink for one price. McDonald's also offers these three menu items individually. This is where mixed bundling acts as a form of indirect price discrimination because the firm offers different choices and lets customers sort themselves in ways that increase producer surplus.

Mixed bundling is a lot like the bundling strategy we've just discussed (a *type of bundling in which the firm offers the products only as a bundle,* often called **pure bundling**). It is useful in the same type of situations, but is better than pure bundling when the marginal cost of producing some of the components is high enough relative to some consumers' willingness to pay that it makes sense to let those customers opt out of buying the entire bundle.

Returning to our cable network example, let's suppose there are four customers and that they value the networks according to **Table 10.4**. The willingness to pay is negatively correlated across the networks, so we know bundling can work as a pricing strategy.

Now suppose instead of marginal costs being zero, the marginal cost of supplying ESPN is $6.00 per month and truTV is $1.00 per month. Therefore, the marginal cost of producing the bundled package is $7.00. If the cable company sells the bundle for $12.15 (the minimum valuation of the bundle across the customers), it will sell the bundle to all four customers. Subtracting costs, this will net a per-customer producer surplus of $5.15 per month for a total of ($4 \times \$5.15$), or $20.60.

But look more closely at Penny and Sheldon. Their relative values for the two channels are extreme. Penny really values ESPN and barely values truTV, while the opposite is true for Sheldon. And crucially, the value they put on one of these channels is *below* the marginal cost of supplying it: truTV for Penny and ESPN for Sheldon. As we will see, in these cases it makes sense for the cable company to try to split these customers off from the bundle, because it does not want to supply channels to customers whose value for them is low relative to the the cost of providing them.

Figuring out the right mixed bundling strategy is complicated by the incentive compatibility constraint, so we'll take it one step at a time.

Table 10.4 Negatively Correlated Valuations When the Marginal Cost Exceeds the Valuation for Some Customers			
	ESPN (*MC* = $6)	truTV (*MC* = $1)	Bundle (*MC* = $7)
Penny	$12.00	$0.50	$12.50
Leonard	$11.00	$1.15	$12.15
Raj	$9.00	$3.15	$12.15
Sheldon	$5.00	$7.75	$12.75

Given the issues we just discussed, the cable company would like to end up selling the bundle to Leonard and Raj, only ESPN to Penny, and only truTV to Sheldon. Because both Leonard and Raj value the bundle at $12.15 per month, that's a reasonable starting point for thinking about the price of the bundle. If this is the price of the bundle, however, the company can't charge Sheldon his full $7.75 valuation for truTV. If it tried to, Sheldon would choose the bundle instead because it would give him 60 cents more consumer surplus ($12.75 – $12.15) than if he bought only truTV (consumer surplus of zero if priced at $7.75). A price of $7.75 for truTV is therefore not incentive-compatible. To set an incentive-compatible price for truTV, the cable company has to leave Sheldon with at least 60 cents of consumer surplus per month. Thus, the incentive-compatible price for the purchase of truTV alone would be $7.75 – $0.60, or $7.15 per month. And because Leonard and Raj value truTV at less than $7.15, both will buy the bundle rather than take the truTV-only option, so incentive compatibility holds in the other direction, too.

We can do the same type of calculations with ESPN and Penny. The cable company can't charge $12.00 for ESPN alone, because Penny would opt for the bundle to get 35 cents ($12.50 – $12.15) of consumer surplus rather than zero from buying ESPN at $12.00. So, the company has to leave Penny with at least 35 cents of surplus from buying just ESPN. The highest price that will achieve this is $12.00 – $0.35, or $11.65. Again, offering this option won't move Leonard and Raj away from the bundle, because both value ESPN at less than $11.65.

Thus, with these three prices—ESPN alone for $11.65, truTV alone for $7.15, and the bundle for $12.15—the cable company will sell two bundles (to Leonard and Raj) to earn a producer surplus (subtracting out the marginal costs) of $5.15 per month for each bundle. Additionally, it will sell ESPN alone to Penny to earn a surplus of $11.65 – $6.00 = $5.65 and truTV alone to Sheldon for a surplus of $7.15 – $1.00 = $6.15. The total monthly producer surplus from using mixed bundling is therefore $(2 \times \$5.15) + \$5.65 + \$6.15 = \$22.10$. That is more than the $20.60 per month the cable company would make by using pure bundling.

Producer surplus has increased because the cable company has saved itself the trouble of delivering a product to a customer who values it at less than it costs to produce.

 figure it out 10.4

Fit Club, Inc. is a health club that offers two types of equipment: weight machines and a swimming pool. There are currently three customers (Abdul, Betty, and Chris), whose willingness to pay for using each type of equipment per month is listed in the table below:

	Willingness to Pay (per month)	
	WEIGHT MACHINES	**INDOOR POOL**
Abdul	$60	$50
Betty	$50	$125
Chris	$25	$140

The weight room and swimming pool each have a constant marginal cost of $20 per month. In the case of the pool, the marginal cost is the price of the water and chemicals used, while the marginal cost of the weight machines is the cost of cleaning and maintaining them. Each customer is considering monthly access to each type of equipment, and the firm has to decide what type of membership package to offer the customers.

a. What price will the firm charge for each product if it wishes to sell a health club membership to all three customers? What is the firm's producer surplus if it sells separate access to the weight room and the pool room at these prices?

b. What price will the firm charge for a bundle of access to both the weight room and the swimming pool if it wishes to sell the bundle to all three customers? How much producer surplus will Fit Club, Inc. earn in this case?

c. Suppose the firm is considering offering its customers a choice to either purchase access to the weight room and the swimming pool separately at a price of $60 for the weight machine and $140 for the pool, or to purchase a bundle at a price of $175. Which option will each customer choose? How much producer surplus will Fit Club, Inc. earn in this situation?

Solution:

a. To sell access to the weight machines to all three customers, the health club must charge a price no greater than $25, the lowest willingness to pay of the customers (Chris). For the same reason, the price for the pool will be $50.

At these prices, the firm's producer surplus for its sales of access to the weight machines will be

$$\text{Producer surplus for weight machine} = (\text{price} - \text{marginal cost}) \times \text{quantity}$$
$$= (\$25 - \$20) \times 3$$
$$= (\$5)(3) = \$15$$

For access to the pool, producer surplus will be

$$\text{Producer surplus for the pool} = (\$50 - \$20) \times 3$$
$$= (\$30)(3) = \$90$$

Total producer surplus will be $15 + $90 = $105.

b. To determine the price of the bundle, we need to calculate each buyer's willingness to pay for the bundle. This is done simply by summing the customers' willingness to pay for each product as shown in the table below:

	Willingness to Pay (per month)		
	WEIGHT MACHINES	**INDOOR POOL**	**BUNDLE**
Abdul	$60	$50	= $60 + $50 = $110
Betty	$50	$125	= $50 + $125 = $175
Chris	$25	$140	= $25 + $140 = $165

So, the maximum price the health club can charge for its bundle (and still sell to all three buyers) is $110. It will sell three bundles at this price. Therefore, its producer surplus will be

$$\text{Producer surplus for bundle} = (\text{price} - \text{marginal cost}) \times \text{quantity}$$
$$= (\$110 - \$40) \times 3$$
$$= (\$70)(3) = \$210$$

c. We need to compare each buyer's willingness to pay to the prices set for purchasing access to each room separately and the price of the bundle.

Abdul will only purchase a weight machine membership. His willingness to pay for the pool is below the price of $140. The same is true for the bundle, which he values only at $110. Therefore, the health club will only sell Abdul access to the weight machines.

Betty will not be willing to buy either membership separately, because her willingness to pay for each is below the set price. However, Betty's willingness to pay for the bundle ($175) is exactly equal to the price, so she will purchase the bundle.

Chris will only purchase access to the indoor pool. His willingness to pay for weight machines is only $25, far below the price of $60. Likewise, Chris is willing to pay at most $165 for the bundle. Thus, the health club will only be able to sell pool access to Chris.

Total producer surplus will therefore be

$$\text{Producer surplus for weight machines} = (\text{price} - \text{marginal cost}) \times \text{quantity}$$
$$= (\$60 - \$20) \times 1$$
$$= \$40$$
$$\text{Producer surplus for the pool} = (\$140 - \$20) \times 1$$
$$= \$120$$
$$\text{Producer surplus for bundle} = (\$175 - \$40) \times 1$$
$$= \$135$$

Total producer surplus when the health club offers customers a choice of bundling or separate prices is $40 + $120 + $135 = $295.

10.6 Advanced Pricing Strategies

When to Use It Block Pricing and Two-Part Tariffs

1. *The firm has market power and can prevent resale.*
2. The firm's customers may have either identical or different demand curves.

In the previous sections, we analyzed pricing strategies based on price discrimination, the ability of a firm to charge more for units of output sold to those willing to pay more and, as a result, extract producer surplus by departing from the single-price monopoly pricing discussed in Chapter 9. In this section, we look at how firms with market power can achieve that goal not by charging a given price per unit, but by varying unit prices offered to the same customer or charging lump-sum fees on top of per-unit prices. We return to our discussion of quantity discounts.

Block Pricing

We call the *practice of reducing the price of a good when the customer buys more of it* **block pricing.** You see this sort of thing all the time. Buying a single 12-ounce can of Pepsi might cost $1, but a six-pack of 12-ounce cans costs only $2.99. However, unlike indirect price discrimination (such as quantity discounts), block pricing does not require that buyers have different demand curves and price sensitivities. All buyers of Pepsi may, in fact, have the same demand curve, but Pepsi could still gain producer surplus from providing buyers with an option to buy a larger quantity of soda at a lower price.

block pricing The practice of reducing the price of a good when the customer buys more of it.

Figure **10.6** Block Pricing

D is the demand curve of an individual consumer of Walmart's photo cards. Under monopoly pricing, Walmart sells at the point on the demand curve corresponding to the quantity where $MR = MC$ ($Q^* = 100$ photo cards, $P^* = \$0.25$ per card). When Walmart can prevent resale, it can use a block pricing strategy instead. It could still sell the first 100 at a price of $0.25 per card, while charging a lower price of $0.20 each for the next 25 photos purchased (for a total quantity of 125 cards) and $0.10 each for the next 50 cards (for a total of 175 cards). Producer surplus increases from area A to $A + C$ to $A + C + E$, respectively, and consumer surplus increases by area B and area $B + D$, respectively.

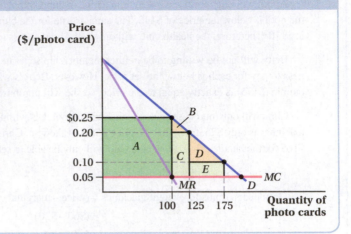

Consider **Figure 10.6**, which shows a demand curve for Walmart's photo holiday cards. Here, we assume this is the demand curve of just one customer (or we could suppose all customers have this same demand curve), so the firm is not trying to price discriminate across customers with different types of demand, as would be the case if Walmart offers quantity discounts. If Walmart follows the pricing rule for firms with market power in Chapter 9, it will pick the quantity at which marginal revenue equals marginal cost and charge a price equal to the height of the demand curve at that quantity. In the figure, the monopoly quantity is 100 cards and the price is 25 cents per card. Walmart's producer surplus from pricing at that point equals the area of rectangle *A*.

But say Walmart doesn't have to charge a single price per card. It could offer the first 100 holiday cards for sale at 25 cents each, but then offer as many as 25 more cards (numbers 101 to 125) at a lower per-unit price of 20 cents each. The customer will take advantage of this offer because the incremental purchase at the lower price yields an additional consumer surplus equal to the area of triangle *B*. Walmart is better off, too, because it adds an additional amount of producer surplus equal to the area of rectangle *C*.

➡ The online appendix finds profit-maximizing block prices.

Walmart could keep offering discounted prices on larger quantities. For example, it could offer the next 50 cards, up to the 175th photo card, for 10 cents each. Again, the consumer will take the deal because the consumer surplus from that block of cards (area *D* in the figure) is positive. Walmart also comes out ahead because it earns producer surplus *E*. Note that the price strategy we just described could also be expressed in the following way: 100 units are $25, 125 units are $30, and 175 units are $35. Even if all customers have this same demand, all will opt to purchase 175 cards at a price of $35 and Walmart still increases its producer surplus. (This is why block pricing is different from the quantity discounts we observed when discussing indirect price discrimination. Here, no customer sorting needs to occur for Walmart to gain producer surplus.)

A block-pricing strategy like this raises more producer surplus for a firm than does the conventional single-price monopoly strategy because it allows a firm to better match the prices of different quantities of its output to consumers' valuations of those quantities. For the first set of units that customers buy — the units for which customers have a high willingness to pay — the firm charges a relatively high price. With block pricing, the firm doesn't have to completely give up selling a large number of units by charging that initial high price. Block pricing lets it sell additional units of its product, those for which consumers have lower willingness to pay, at lower prices.

This example shows how block pricing can work for even a single customer type, though if there were lots of identical customers, the firm would need to be able to prevent resale to avoid being undercut by its own customers.

Two-Part Tariffs

Another pricing strategy available to firms with market power and identical consumers is the **two-part tariff,** a *pricing strategy in which the payment has two components.* One component is a standard *per-unit price.* The second is a *fixed fee* that must be paid to buy any amount of the product at all, no matter how large or how small.

For example, a membership at warehouse clubs like Costco and Sam's Club has this structure. You might pay, say, $50 a year for a membership and then gain access to as much as you want to buy at the club's famously lower unit prices. A video game system such as Microsoft's Xbox is similar to a two-part tariff, too. The cost of the console itself is the fixed fee and the cost of the individual games represents the per-unit price.

To see the advantage of using a two-part tariff for a firm with market power, consider the market in **Figure 10.7**. It shows the demand for mobile phone service offered by the firm, the marginal revenue curve corresponding to demand, and the firm's constant marginal cost.

The firm's conventional single-price monopoly profit-maximizing quantity is found where marginal revenue equals marginal cost. The quantity at which this condition holds is 3 GB per month, and the price at which consumers are willing to purchase that quantity is $20 per GB. At the price of $20 per GB, the consumer surplus is area *A* and the firm's producer surplus is rectangle *B*.

Now suppose instead that the firm uses the following two-part tariff pricing structure. First, it reduces the per-unit price all the way to marginal cost, $10 per GB. This change increases the number of units it sells from 3 GB to 6 GB, but drives per-unit profit to zero. However, the firm knows that each customer will buy a quantity of 6 GB per month at this price and have a consumer surplus equal to area *A + B + C* as a result. Knowing that this consumer surplus represents the willingness of the consumers to pay above the market price, the firm will set a fixed fee to try to capture that consumer surplus. Therefore, the firm decides to set the fixed-fee portion of the two-part tariff equal to *A + B + C*. This fee is not per GB; it's a fixed monthly fee for any consumer who wants to buy *any* number of units at $10 per GB.

two-part tariff A pricing strategy in which the payment has two components, a per-unit price and a fixed fee.

Figure 10.7   Two-Part Tariff

As a single-price monopolist, a mobile phone service will sell 3 GB of mobile service per month at a price of $20 per GB. Using a two-part tariff, however, the firm can increase its producer surplus from rectangle *B* to the triangle *A + B + C*. To do this, it will charge the per-unit price of $10 per GB, where *D = MC*, and set a fixed fee equal to the consumer's surplus at this quantity, the area *A + B + C*. Under this pricing scheme, the firm will sell 6 GB of mobile service per month.

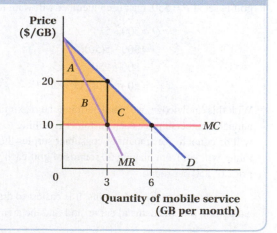

Under this two-part tariff pricing structure, a unit price of $10 per GB leads the consumer to buy 6 GB. This part of the price structure doesn't make the phone company any money, because its marginal cost of delivering service is also $10 per GB. However, the company is also charging the fixed fee $A + B + C$. And importantly, the consumer is willing to pay that, because if she uses 6 GB, she will enjoy consumer surplus equal to the same area. The company has set the size of the fixed fee so that the consumer is no worse off (in fact, it could make her strictly better off if it charged just a touch less than $A + B + C$) than if she bought nothing. By using a two-part tariff, the firm captures the *entire* surplus in the market for itself, as opposed to only area B under standard market power pricing.

Again, if you apply this insight to a market with many identical customers, the ability to prevent resale would be crucial for making the pricing strategy work. If the phone company can't prevent resale, one customer could pay the fixed fee, buy up a huge amount of GB at marginal cost, sell off these extra GB at a small markup to other consumers who did not pay the fixed fee, and make lots of money. For example, if the consumer could rig her phone so other people would pay her $6 per GB to stream off it when she wasn't using the phone, this would defeat the company's strategy.

 figure it out 10.5

You have been hired as an intern at the Golden Eagle Country Club Golf Course. You have been assigned the task of creating the pricing scheme for the golf course, which typically charges an annual membership fee and a per-use cost to its customers. Each of your customers is estimated to have the following demand curve for rounds of golf per year:

$$Q = 300 - 5P$$

If Golden Eagle can provide rounds of golf at a constant marginal cost of $50 and charges that amount per round of golf, what is the most that members would be willing to pay for the annual membership fee?

Solution:

This pricing scheme, with an annual membership fee and a per-unit price, is a two-part tariff. If the price per round of golf is set at $P = \$50$, then each member will want to play

$$
\begin{aligned}
Q &= 300 - 5P \\
&= 300 - 5(50) \\
&= 300 - 250 \\
&= 50 \text{ rounds per year}
\end{aligned}
$$

With this knowledge, we can determine the maximum annual membership fee each customer is willing to pay. This will be equal to the amount of consumer surplus the customer will get from playing 50 rounds of golf each year at a price of $50 per round.

To calculate consumer surplus, it is easiest to draw a diagram, plot the demand curve, and find the area of consumer surplus. To simplify matters, let's rearrange the demand function into an inverse demand function:

$$
\begin{aligned}
Q &= 300 - 5P \\
5P &= 300 - Q \\
P &= 60 - 0.2Q
\end{aligned}
$$

The vertical intercept is 60 and the consumer surplus is the area below the demand curve and above the price of $50, area A. We can calculate the area of triangle A:

$$
\begin{aligned}
\text{Area of } A &= \frac{1}{2} \times \text{base} \times \text{height} \\
&= \frac{1}{2} \times 50 \times (\$60 - \$50) = 0.5(50)(\$10) \\
&= \$250
\end{aligned}
$$

If the golf course set the price of a round of golf at $50, the consumer would purchase 50 rounds per year. This gives the golfer a consumer surplus equal to $250. Therefore, customers would be willing to pay up to $250 for an annual membership.

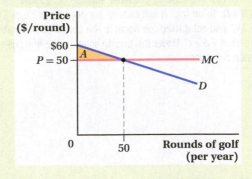

Figure 10.8   Two-Part Tariff with Different Customer Demands

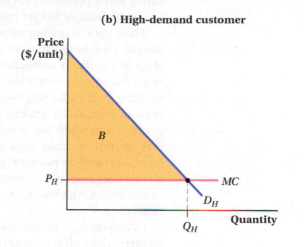

(a) Low-demand customer

(b) High-demand customer

(a) For low-demand customers, the firm would want to sell a quantity of Q_L, charge a per-unit price of P_L and a fixed fee equal to the consumer surplus A. Because this is much lower than the consumer surplus for high-demand customers (B in panel b), such a pricing strategy will leave a lot of surplus to the high-demand customers in the market.

(b) For high-demand customers, the firm would want to sell a quantity of Q_H, and charge a per-unit price of P_H and a fixed fee equal to B. Because this fixed fee is higher than the consumer surplus for low-demand customers, low-demand customers won't buy anything.

Being able to capture the entire surplus in the market is great if you're running a firm, but it's important to realize that a firm can attain this extreme result only if its customers have the same demand curve. The problem is much more complicated when there are customers with different demand curves.

For this more advanced two-part tariff pricing case, consider a firm that faces two kinds of customers whose demand curves for the firm's product are depicted in **Figure 10.8**. Panel a shows the demand curve of the firm's relatively low-demand customers, while panel b shows the demand of the firm's relatively high-demand customers. If the firm tries to use a two-part tariff where it sets the unit price at marginal cost MC and the fixed fee at equal to area A, it will capture all the surplus from the relatively low-demand customers in panel a but leave a lot of surplus to the relatively high-demand customers in panel b, because area A is much smaller than area B. If the firm instead sets the fee at equal to area B to capture the surplus of the high-demand customers, low-demand customers won't buy at all. This is not necessarily better than the first strategy. If the firm has a lot of low-demand customers, this could represent a big loss for the firm, even if the reduction in profit from losing any given low-demand customer might be small. So, neither approach is perfect. Computing the profit-maximizing two-part tariff when consumers have different demands is a mathematical challenge beyond the scope of this book, but it usually entails a unit price above the firm's marginal cost.

10.7 Conclusion

We explored a number of different ways in which firms with market power, under the right conditions, can increase the producer surplus they earn above and beyond the surplus they can earn by following the standard, one-price market power pricing rule we focused on in

Chapter 9. These pricing strategies are all around us; after learning about such strategies in this chapter, you will start to recognize them in practice. You may also find yourself wondering why a particular firm isn't using one of these strategies. Just remember that certain conditions must be met for price discrimination to work.

These various pricing strategies work in different ways, but there are some common threads. First, none will work unless the firm has market power. Therefore, any firm operating in a perfectly competitive market cannot use these strategies because it is a price taker. Second, the firm must prevent resale. Without the ability to prevent resale, doing anything besides the single-price monopoly pricing in Chapter 9 is futile. Third, while price-discrimination strategies differ in the specifics of their mechanisms and the types of markets in which they are applicable, all of these methods work on the basic principle that the firm can make more producer surplus if it can adjust the price it charges so that consumers end up paying higher prices for those units of its output that provide them with greater consumer surplus. Price discrimination also works by charging higher prices to consumers with less elastic demand and lower prices to consumers with more elastic demand.

Other pricing strategies, such as block pricing and two-part tariffs, can be used even in markets where all consumers have the same demand. These strategies work by allowing consumers to buy relatively large quantities at a low price on the margin, but then grab back producer surplus for the firm through higher up-front payments.

In the next chapter, we will examine firms with degrees of market power that fall between perfect competition and monopoly. We will find that these firms' decisions are not made in a vacuum (where they only consider their own costs and their customers' demands), but are also based on the decisions made by other firms in the same market. Although many may choose to follow the pricing strategies discussed in this chapter, each firm has to take into account how its competitors may react to such a move before determining if the strategy increases its producer surplus.

Summary

1. By using **pricing strategies,** a firm with market power can extract more producer surplus from a market than it can from following the monopoly pricing rule of Chapter 9 (where the firm produces the quantity at which marginal revenue equals marginal cost, and then charges the price at which buyers would consume that quantity). It can only do so, however, if the situation satisfies certain criteria. A crucial factor is that in addition to market power, the firm has to be able to prevent resale among customers. If the firm can prevent resale, the amount of information it has on its customers determines what kind of pricing strategy it can follow. **[Section 10.1]**

2. When customers differ and the firm has sufficient information about its customers' demands to charge every person a different price, **perfect** or **first-degree price discrimination** is possible. This strategy of **direct price discrimination** allows the firm to capture the entire surplus in the market for itself. It is very rare to have this kind of information, however. **[Section 10.2]**

3. If the firm has different types of customers and can directly identify at least two groups whose price elasticities of demand differ, it can charge different prices to the two groups and earn more producer surplus. The profit-maximizing direct price-discrimination strategy in this case is to follow the single-price monopoly pricing rule separately for each group. There are many ways to directly separate customers, including customer characteristics, geography, past purchase behavior, the timing of the purchase, and so on, a practice known as **segmenting,** or **third-degree price discrimination. [Section 10.3]**

4. If the company knows that there are different types of customers but cannot directly identify which group a customer belongs to before the purchase, it must rely on **indirect (second-degree) price discrimination.** This involves designing choices that induce customers to sort themselves into groups. **Quantity discounts** can be used if customers who demand a higher quantity also have a more elastic demand. **Versioning** a product can also work. The key additional requirement for indirect price discrimination is that the pricing structure has to be **incentive-compatible,** meaning that each consumer group wants to take the offer designed specifically for it. **[Section 10.4]**

5. If a company sells multiple products and consumers' demands for the products are negatively correlated, it can sell the products together as a bundle and increase producer surplus beyond what it could earn by selling the products separately. Sometimes, particularly if the marginal cost of producing one of the products exceeds the value that a customer places on that product, the company may be better off using **mixed bundling,** which gives customers the choice of buying individual products at high prices or a bundle of products at a discount. **[Section 10.5]**

6. Even when there are not different types of customers, a firm can use advanced pricing strategies like **block pricing** (a discount for buying extra quantity) or a **two-part tariff** (a fixed fee paid up-front in addition to a price per unit of the good) as a way to capture more producer surplus than it could earn with standard monopoly pricing. However, each of these strategies is much more complicated to implement when there are many consumers with different demand curves. **[Section 10.6]**

Review Questions

1. What are the two requirements of price discrimination?

2. Why is producer surplus maximized under perfect price discrimination?

3. What are the two types of direct price discrimination?

4. What are some ways that a firm can segment its customers?

5. Contrast direct price discrimination and indirect price discrimination.

6. What is incentive compatibility? Why is it necessary for an indirect price discrimination strategy to be incentive-compatible?

7. Provide an example of product versioning.

8. What are the differences between the following three pricing strategies: block pricing, segmenting, and quantity discounts?

9. What is the difference between mixed bundling and pure bundling?

10. What are the two component prices of a two-part tariff?

Problems

(Solutions to problems marked with an asterisk appear at the back of this book. Problems adapted to use calculus are available online.)

1. There are seven consumers, each of whom is hungry for exactly one Butterfinger. The consumers' maximum willingness to pay is given in the table below:

Consumer (age, gender)	Maximum Willingness to Pay
Marge (34, female)	$2
Homer (38, male)	4
Lisa (6, female)	5
Maggie (2, female)	6
Ned (46, male)	1
Krusty (55, male)	3
Bart (9, male)	7

a. Given that each consumer wants one and only one Butterfinger, draw the demand curve for Butterfingers.

b. If Butterfingers are priced at $7, only one will be sold. Who buys that Butterfinger? Label the point at $7 on the demand curve with the name of that buyer.

c. If Butterfingers are priced at $6, a second buyer will be priced into the market. Who is that buyer? Label the point at $6 on the demand curve with the name of that buyer.

d. Continue to label each point on the demand curve with the name of the buyer represented by that point.

e. Suppose that you are a monopoly seller of Butterfingers, which you can produce at a constant marginal and average total cost of $2. Suppose you charge every customer the same price for Butterfingers. What price should you set to maximize your profit? How many Butterfingers will you sell? Calculate your profit. Calculate the consumer surplus received by the buyers. Calculate the deadweight loss.

f. Suppose that every customer that comes into your Butterfinger store has their maximum willingness to pay displayed in neon on their foreheads. You decide to use this information to increase your profit by practicing first-degree price discrimination. How many Butterfingers will you sell? Calculate your profit. Calculate the consumer surplus received by the buyers. Calculate the deadweight loss.

g. Where does the consumer surplus go when you begin price discriminating?

h. What happens to the deadweight loss?

2. Rich Uncle Pennybags is the only seller of board games in Atlantic City, New Jersey. The inverse demand curve for board games is given by $P = 40 - 0.5Q$, where Q is in

hundreds of games per month. Rich Uncle Pennybags' marginal cost of producing board games is $7 + 0.1Q$.

a. If Rich Uncle Pennybags cannot price discriminate, what is his profit-maximizing level of output? What is his profit-maximizing price?

b. How much consumer surplus will buyers of board games receive? How much producer surplus will end up in Uncle Pennybags' pockets? How much dead-weight loss is created by the board game monopoly?

c. Suppose Uncle Pennybags is a magnificent salesman, able to discern perfectly his customers' willingness to pay. If he leverages this information to begin perfectly price discriminating, how many board games will he sell?

d. How much surplus will buyers receive from a perfectly price discriminating Uncle Pennybags? How much producer surplus will Uncle Pennybags capture? What will the deadweight loss due to monopoly be?

*3. Every passenger on a flight departs from point A and arrives at point B. Yet few of those passengers will pay the same price for that flight, because airlines are master price discriminators.

a. Enumerate and explain at least three ways in which airlines may end up charging different passengers different prices for the same flight.

b. First-degree price discrimination requires information about customers' individual price sensitivity. Where do airlines obtain the information they need to appropriately price each seat?

c. One requirement to implement first-degree price discrimination is the ability to prevent resale. Explain why airlines don't have to worry about that. Are there other businesses you can think of where resale simply isn't possible?

4. Many textbooks are now available in two versions, a high-priced "domestic" version and a low-priced "international" version. Each version generally contains exactly the same text, but slightly altered homework problems.

a. Why would a textbook publisher go to the trouble of producing two versions of the same text?

b. Discuss whether the publisher's strategy would be more effective if it made the alterations secret, or if it announced them boldly.

c. The production of international versions of textbooks was concurrent with the explosion of the Internet. Explain why this is likely to be more than just a coincidence.

5. Consider the problem faced by the Butterfinger seller in Problem 1.

a. Assume that the seller is able to prevent resale between customers. In the real world, why is the seller *still* unlikely to be able to perfectly price discriminate?

b. Because of the reason you just indicated, the Butterfinger seller decides to segment her customers into two groups, each of which will be charged a different price. In order to maximize profit, should the seller sort by gender or by age?

c. Based on your answer to (b), determine who is in each group, and indicate (1) the price the seller should set for each group, (2) the total profit received by the seller, (3) total consumer surplus, and (4) the dead-weight loss.

d. Is this pricing strategy (segmenting) more profitable to the seller than perfectly price discriminating? Is this pricing strategy more profitable than charging every consumer the same price?

e. What happens to consumer surplus and deadweight loss when a single-price monopolist begins segmenting in this way?

*6. Promoters of a major college basketball tournament estimate that the demand for tickets on the part of adults is given by $Q_{Ad} = 5,000 - 10P$, and that the demand for tickets on the part of students is given by $Q_{St} = 10,000 - 100P$. The promoters wish to segment the market and charge adults and students different prices. They estimate that the marginal and average total cost of seating an additional spectator is constant at \$10.

a. For each segment (adults and students), find the inverse demand and marginal revenue functions.

b. Equate marginal revenue and marginal cost. Determine the profit-maximizing quantity for each segment.

c. Plug the quantities you found in (b) into the respective inverse demand curves to find the profit-maximizing price for each segment. Who pays more, adults or students?

d. Determine the profit generated by each segment and add them together to find the promoter's total profit.

e. How would your answers change if the arena where the event was to take place had only 5,000 seats?

7. Kip's Auto Detailing has locations in two distant neighborhoods, Uptown and Downtown. Uptown customers' demand is given by $Q_{UT} = 1,000 - 10P$, where Q is the number of cars detailed per month; Downtown customers' demand is $Q_{DT} = 1,600 - 20P$. The marginal and average cost of detailing a car is constant at \$20.

a. Determine the price that maximizes Kip's profit if he prices uniformly in both markets. How many customers will he serve at each location? What will his profits be?

b. Suppose Kip decides to charge different prices at each location. What price should he establish in each location? What will his profits be?

c. How big are the gains to Kip's differential pricing scheme?

8. You are the owner of a nail salon. Your female customer's price elasticity of demand for manicures is −2.5; your male customer's price elasticity of demand for manicures is −1.2. The marginal cost of manicuring a customer's nails is $12.

   a. If you segment the market by gender, what price should you charge women? What price should you charge men?

   b. Explain intuitively why you should charge each group a different price.

9. Movie theaters often charge substantially less for afternoon showings than for evening showings. Explain how theaters use time of day to segment their customers into low-elasticity and high-elasticity groups.

10. Owners of a Florida restaurant estimate that the elasticity of demand for meals is −1.5 for senior citizens and −1.33 for everyone else.

    a. The restaurant is considering offering a senior citizen discount. Use Lerner indices to determine how big (in percentage terms) that discount should be. (*Hint:* Determine the ratio of the senior citizens' price to the price for everyone else.)

    b. Suppose that the restaurant owners discover seniors tend to demand more attention from their waiters and send back more food as unsatisfactory, to the extent that the marginal cost of serving a senior is twice as high as serving an adult. Accounting for these costs, how large should the senior citizen discount be? (*Hint:* Refer back to the example in the text, but don't cancel out marginal costs!)

    c. Were your results in part (b) surprising? Explain them, intuitively.

11. A local golf course's hired-gun econometrician has determined that there are two types of golfers, frequent and infrequent. Frequent golfers' annual demand for rounds of golf is given by $Q_F = 24 - 0.3P$, where P is the price of a round of golf. In contrast, infrequent golfers' annual demand for rounds of golf is given by $Q_I = 10 - 0.1P$. The marginal and average total cost of providing a round of golf is $20.

    a. If the golf course could tell a frequent golfer from an infrequent golfer, what price would it charge each type? How many times would each type golf? How much profit would the golf course generate?

    The greens manager has difficulty telling frequent from infrequent golfers, so she decides to use second-degree price discrimination (quantity discounts) to make different types of golfers self-select into the most profitable pricing scheme. The course sets a price for individual rounds of golf, but also offers a quantity discount for members willing to buy a rather large quantity of rounds in advance. The course's owners hope that frequent golfers will self-select into the discounted plan, and that infrequent golfers will choose to buy individual rounds.

    b. What price should the golf course set for individual rounds of golf? Why?

    c. If the course wishes to maximize profit, what price and minimum quantity should it establish for the discounted plan?

    d. Which plan will generate the greatest consumer surplus for frequent golfers, the individual-round plan or the discount plan? Illustrate your answer by showing and measuring the areas of surplus on frequent golfers' inverse demand curves.

    e. Which plan will generate the greatest consumer surplus for infrequent golfers, the individual-round plan or the discount plan? Illustrate your answer by showing the areas of surplus on infrequent golfers' inverse demand curves.

    f. Based on your answers to (d) and (e), will the plan be successful in making golfers self-select into the most profitable plan for the golf course?

    g. Suppose that each type of golfer came to the course with the word "frequent" or "infrequent" tattooed on his or her forehead. Is this information of any value to the golf course owner? (In other words, can the owner earn any more profits by segmenting than it did with its quantity discount plan?)

12. Carolina Atlantic sells specialty paper to commercial clients. Some clients are intensive users who are price-sensitive; their demands are given by $P = 8 - 0.1Q$, where Q is the number of reams of paper desired per week. Other clients are less-intensive users of paper and have inverse demands given by $P = 10 - 0.2Q$. Let $MC = 0$.

    a. Carolina Atlantic attempts to separate more-intensive and less-intensive buyers by implementing a quantity discount plan. What price should Carolina Atlantic set for each group? How should the quantity discount plan be structured?

    b. Show that the quantity discount plan you outlined in (a) is not incentive-compatible.

    c. Suppose instead that intensive users had inverse demands given by $P = 8 - (1/15)Q$. Determine the structure of the quantity discount and show that the plan is incentive-compatible.

    d. Why did the quantity discount plan outlined in (b) fail, while the quantity discount plan outlined in (c) succeeded?

*13. Rockway & Daughters Piano Co. wishes to sell a piano to everyone. But some consumers are budget-conscious, and others are not, and unfortunately, Rockway cannot tell which is which. So, Rockway produces a premium line of pianos that it markets under the Rockway name, and a similar line of pianos that it markets under the Dundee name. Although the cost of producing these pianos is quite similar, all consumers agree that Rockway pianos are of higher quality than Dundee pianos, and would be willing to pay more for a Rockway. Budget-conscious consumers feel that Dundee pianos are worth $6,000 and Rockways are worth $8,000. Performance artists believe that Dundee pianos are worth $7,000 and Rockways are worth $12,000.

a. Suppose Rockway & Daughters prices its Dundee pianos at $5,000 and its Rockway pianos at $10,500. Are these prices incentive-compatible — that is, will more price-conscious consumers purchase the Dundee line, while more performance-oriented players choose the Rockway? Explain.

b. How much must Rockway & Daughters reduce the price of its Rockway line in order to achieve incentive compatibility?

c. Suppose instead that Rockway & Daughters tries to achieve incentive compatibility by raising the price of its Dundee line. Can it do this? And if so, how?

d. If you ran Rockway & Daughters Piano Co., which method would you use to achieve incentive compatibility: the one you outlined in (b), or the one you outlined in (c)? Why?

14. London's Market Bar has a unique pricing system where a computer sets the price based on demand. When demand picks up, the computer begins to gradually reduce prices. This pricing strategy is puzzling to those who have studied supply and demand. Celene Berman, the assistant manager, says a group of "young city-boy types" recently kept asking why prices "were going the wrong way around." Explain, using your knowledge of block pricing, why the owner's strategy of reducing prices as sales increase might actually lead to increased profit for the bar.

*15. Microsoft sells two types of office software, a word processor it calls Word, and a spreadsheet it calls Excel. Both can be produced at zero marginal cost. There are two types of consumers for these products, who exist in roughly equal proportions in the population: authors, who are willing to pay $120 for Word and $40 for Excel, and economists, who are willing to pay $50 for Word and $150 for Excel.

a. Ideally, Microsoft would like to charge authors more for Word and economists more for Excel. Why would it be difficult for Microsoft to do this?

b. Suppose that Microsoft execs decide to sell Word and Excel separately. What price should Microsoft set for Word? (*Hint:* Is it better to sell only to authors, or to try to sell to both authors and economists?) What price should Microsoft set for Excel? What will Microsoft's profit be from a representative group of one author and one economist?

c. Suppose that Microsoft decides to bundle together Word and Excel in a package called Office, and not

offer them individually. What price should Microsoft set for the package? Why? How much profit will Microsoft generate from a representative group of one author and one economist?

d. Does bundling allow Microsoft to generate higher profit than selling Word and Excel separately?

16. Three consumers, John, Kate, and Lester, are in the market for two goods, dates and eggs. Their willingness to pay for dates and eggs is given in the table below:

	Dates (1 package)	Eggs (1 dozen)
John	$0.60	$2.00
Kate	$1.30	$1.30
Lester	$2.00	$0.60

a. If you are a local farmer who can produce dates and eggs for free, what is the optimal price for dates and eggs if you price them individually? How much profit will you generate?

b. If you bundle dates and eggs together, what price should you set for a bundle containing one package of dates and a dozen eggs? How much profit will you generate?

c. Is there any advantage to mixed bundling in this case? Why or why not?

d. Suppose that the cost of producing dates and eggs rises to $1.00 per package and $1.00 per dozen, respectively. Now is there any advantage to mixed bundling? Why or why not? Explain your answer with a numerical illustration.

e. What accounts for the change in optimal strategy when costs change?

*17. Elario makes delicious cupcakes that he mails to customers across the country. His cupcakes are so delicious that he has a great degree of pricing power. Elario's customers have identical demands for cupcakes. A representative customer's demand is shown in the diagram below. Elario can make a cupcake for a constant marginal and average total cost of $0.50.

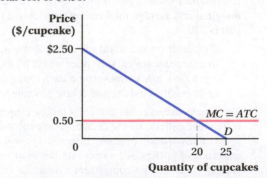

a. If Elario is an ordinary monopolist, what price should he charge for cupcakes? How many will each customer order? How much profit will Elario earn? How much consumer surplus will the buyer get?

b. Suppose that Elario decides to offer a quantity discount according to the following terms: The first 10 cupcakes can be bought for $1.50 each; any cupcake over 10 will be offered at a discounted price. What discount price will maximize Elario's profit from this pricing scheme? (*Hint:* Draw a new demand curve for Elario's customers' demand, but because his customers have already purchased 10, begin your demand curve at the 11th unit. Alternatively, shift the vertical axis to the right by 10 units.)

c. How many cupcakes will customers order at full price? How many at the discounted price?

d. What will Elario's profit be? How does this scheme compare to the profit he earned as an ordinary monopolist?

e. Suppose that Elario gets super greedy and decides to implement a three-tiered pricing system. What three prices should he choose to maximize his profit? At what quantities will the price points change? What will his profit be?

f. Suppose Elario decides to charge $2.40 for the first cupcake, $2.30 for the second, and so on. How many cupcakes will he sell, and what will his profit be?

g. What happens to consumer surplus as Elario adds more price points? Where does it go?

18. Consider the demand for cupcakes in Problem 17. Suppose Elario decides to sell cupcakes only in packages of 20.

a. How much would customers be willing to pay to obtain a 20-pack of Elario's cupcakes? (*Hint:* Remember that the value of each cupcake is given by the corresponding point on the demand curve. Add up those values for cupcakes 1–20.)

b. How much profit will Elario earn from each customer?

c. How does the profit from this scheme compare to the profit Elario earned in part (f) of Problem 17?

19. Many gyms offer a mixed two-part tariff pricing scheme. One can join the gym and then have daily access at a very low cost (often, free); alternatively, one can choose not to join and pay a higher daily fee (perhaps $10 or $15). Explain the rationale for this dual pricing scheme. What must be true of the gym's customers' demands?

20. The most popular movie streaming service is Netflix. Netflix members pay a monthly fee and are then entitled to stream as many hours of programming as they wish. You've been hired by Netflix to determine the profit-maximizing monthly fee. You estimate that each customer's inverse demand for streaming is given by $P = 0.56 - 0.0112Q$, where Q is measured in hours of streaming time. What is the most you should charge for a monthly Netflix membership? (You may assume Netflix can provide an hour of streaming at essentially zero marginal cost.)

21. Nathan sells gourmet hot dogs. His customers have identical inverse demands, given by $P = 5 - 0.25Q$. Nathan can produce hot dogs at a constant marginal and average cost of $1.

a. If Nathan operates as a single-price monopolist, what price should he set? How many units will he sell? What will his profits be?

b. Suppose Nathan decides to create a hot dog club where members pay an annual enrollment fee and are then entitled to buy as many hot dogs as they wish at a fixed price. If Nathan chooses a fixed price of $2.00 per hot dog, what is the maximum membership fee he will be able to charge his customers? How much profit will Nathan earn from each customer? (*Hint:* Add Nathan's profits from selling hot dogs to the membership fee.) How do Nathan's profits compare to what he earned in (a)?

c. If Nathan chooses a fixed price of $1.00, what membership fee will he be able to charge his customers? What will his overall profits be?

d. Can Nathan increase his profits by charging a super-high admission fee and giving away hot dogs to members for free?

e. Generalize a rule about the per-unit price and membership fee that will maximize profits for a seller implementing a two-part tariff.

22. Revisit the Netflix membership fee issue discussed in Problem 20. Suppose you learn that there are actually two types of Netflix user: intensive users and casual users. Intensive users comprise 20% of all viewers and have inverse demand:

$$P_I = 0.6 - 0.01Q_I$$

where Q is measured in hours of streaming time. Casual users comprise 80% of all viewers and have inverse demand:

$$P_C = 0.4 - 0.02Q_C$$

You are tasked with choosing the optimal monthly membership fee. Netflix remains committed to allowing unlimited streaming once this fee has been paid. (You may assume Netflix can provide an hour of streaming at essentially zero marginal cost.)

a. What fee will you charge?

b. Would your answer change if intensive users comprised 25% of all viewers?

23. Identify the pricing strategy each seller uses in the following items:

a. A local bar hosts "Ladies' Night" at which women pay half-price.

b. A local tire store offers Firestone tires at $160 each, or $400 for a set of 4.

c. The Sands, a local country club, charges \$4,000/year to join, plus a \$30 greens fee each time you play a round of golf.

d. Charmin Ultra toilet paper is sold only in 12-roll packages.

e. At Denny's, you can order a bacon and egg breakfast, but you can also order bacon and eggs individually.

f. Lie-Nielsen Toolworks sells a handplane made of ordinary cast iron, but for a premium price you can buy the same plane in beautiful cast bronze.

24. For each situation below, identify an appropriate pricing strategy the firm could use to increase profits, if any:

a. All Krispy Kreme customers have identical demands.

b. Some movie buffs like action movies and love spy thrillers; others love action movies and like spy thrillers. Unfortunately, DVD movie seller Best Buy cannot tell who is who.

c. AMC theaters know that working professionals have a less elastic demand for movie tickets than students and senior citizens.

d. Some buyers of toner cartridges don't print very often, only printing documents that are very important. Other buyers print frequently and purchase many toner cartridges; those buyers are quite price-sensitive.

e. McGraw-Hill, a publisher of college textbooks, knows there is a very active secondary market in used textbooks.

Imperfect Competition

I n previous chapters, we studied the two ends of the market power spectrum: perfect competition and monopoly. In perfect competition, a firm has no market power because it is only one of many producers in the market, the price is driven down to marginal cost, and output is relatively high. In a monopoly, one firm has market power because it is the only producer of a good in the market, price is greater than marginal cost, and output is lower. We also learned about the many pricing strategies that firms with market power can use to earn greater economic profit.

Between these two ends of the spectrum are lots of industries that are neither perfectly competitive nor monopolistic. Coke and Pepsi dominate the cola market together. Nintendo, Sony, and Microsoft dominate console video games. These companies compete but are hardly perfectly competitive. Yet they aren't stand-alone monopolies either. The *industry structure between perfect competition and monopoly* is known as **imperfect competition**.

This chapter introduces this important but sometimes complicated market structure. We begin by looking at several types of **oligopoly**, a *market structure characterized by competition among a small number of firms*. Because there are many possible ways in which oligopolistic firms compete, no single model of oligopoly exists that is applicable to every situation. Having a few competitors in an industry—rather than many or only one—can lead to many possible price and output outcomes. It's not as simple as just picking the one where price equals marginal cost or the like. We might observe many outcomes, depending on the market circumstances.

With oligopolies, firms have some market power, but not necessarily monopoly power, and there is some competition, but not perfect competition. We need to be a little more specific about aspects of the market before we can figure out what prices they will charge, how much each company will produce, and how much profit each firm will earn. Just knowing how many companies are in the market is not enough to know what will happen in an oligopolistic market. Industries with, say, four major firms can look extremely different from each other. Other factors that have an effect on price and quantity decisions in an oligopoly include: (1) whether the companies make identical products (as in an oil oligopoly) or products that are slightly different from one another (like Coke and Pepsi); (2) how intensely the companies compete; and (3) whether they compete with one another by choosing the prices they charge or the quantities they produce.

In this chapter, we present five of the most common models of how oligopolies behave, plus one additional model called **monopolistic competition**, a *type of imperfect competition where a large number of firms have some market power, but each makes zero economic profit in the long run.* Whenever you have this many models as possible explanations for market behavior, it's important to determine which one is appropriate for a specific case. This decision isn't always obvious in practice, so we discuss some ideas for determining which model is most appropriate for various real-world situations.

imperfect competition The industry structure between perfect competition and monopoly.

oligopoly A market structure characterized by competition among a small number of firms.

monopolistic competition A type of imperfect competition where a large number of firms have some market power, but each makes zero economic profit in the long run.

11.1 What Does Equilibrium Mean in an Oligopoly?

Before we introduce the different models of oligopoly, we need to lay some groundwork. Specifically, we have to expand on the idea of what an equilibrium is for these industries. The concept of equilibrium in perfect competition and in monopoly is easy. It means a price at which the quantity of the good demanded by consumers equals the quantity of the good supplied by producers. That is, the market "clears." The market is stable with no excess supply or demand, and the consumers and producers do not want to change their decisions.

The problem with applying this idea of equilibrium to an oligopolistic industry is that each company's action influences what the other companies want to do. To achieve an outcome in which no firm wants to change its decision means determining more than just a price and quantity for the industry as a whole. It has to apply to each firm individually, too.

An equilibrium in an oligopoly starts with the same idea as in perfect competition or monopoly: The market clears. However, it adds a requirement that no company wants to change its behavior (its own price or quantity) once it knows what other companies are doing. In other words, each company must be doing as well as it can *conditional* on what other companies are doing. Oligopoly equilibrium has to be stable not only in equating the total quantities supplied and demanded, but also must be stable among the individual producers in the market.

An *equilibrium in which each firm is doing its best conditional on the actions taken by other firms* is called a **Nash equilibrium**. It is named after Nobel laureate John Nash (who was also the subject of the award-winning book and movie titled *A Beautiful Mind*). The Nash equilibrium concept is even more central in the next chapter when we study game theory, which explores the strategic interaction among firms. For our purposes in this chapter, though, the following example will help clarify what is and what is not a Nash equilibrium in an oligopoly.

Nash equilibrium An equilibrium in which each firm is doing its best conditional on the actions taken by other firms.

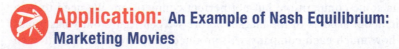

Application: An Example of Nash Equilibrium: Marketing Movies

Major superhero action movies like Disney's *Black Panther* or Warner Brothers' *Wonder Woman* are amazingly expensive to make. By the time the studios have paid for the CGI, the actors, and everything else, they're looking at a bill of around $180 million.[1] But on top of these production costs, Disney and Warner Brothers each then had to pay many more millions of dollars on advertising and marketing the films so people would watch their movies.

Let's suppose Disney and Warner Brothers are the only two movie companies that make superhero feature films, and that their advertising influences people's choices of what movie to see. Advertising doesn't increase the overall number of movies people watch, just which movie they do.

Now think of both studios planning to release the next installments in these series, *Black Panther* 2 and *Wonder Woman* 2, on the same summer weekend. Furthermore, let's assume that the cost of production is still $180 million and the cost of advertising is

---

[1] Industry reports estimate *Black Panther* cost $200 million to make, whereas *Wonder Woman* cost $150 million.

$70 million. If both studios advertise and compete with each other, their marketing efforts will cancel out. As a result, the two will split the market, and each will bring in, let's say, $500 million of revenue. Subtracting the $180 million production cost and the $70 million advertising cost, that leaves $250 million of profit to each studio.

If, on the other hand, the studios could somehow agree not to advertise at all, they would again split the market, but this time each would save the $70 million in advertising costs. In this case, the studio profits would be greater at $320 million each.

Disney and Warner Brothers would prefer the second, higher-profit outcome. The problem is that, due to the nature of advertising's influence on moviegoers, if only one studio advertises and the other doesn't, then the studio that advertises will get a larger share of the audience and the other one will be left with less. Suppose, for example, that the studio engaged in advertising would earn $800 million of revenue, and the other would earn only $100 million. The firm advertising its film therefore earns a profit of $550 million ($800 million of revenue minus the $180 million production cost and the $70 million in advertising). The other studio, the one that doesn't advertise, *loses* $80 million ($100 million of revenue minus the $180 million production cost).

Table 11.1 lays out these scenarios. The table's four cells correspond to the four possible profit outcomes if each firm pursues the strategy described at the top of each column and the start of each row: Both firms advertise (upper left), neither firm advertises (lower right), Warner Brothers advertises and Disney doesn't (upper right), or vice versa (lower left). Profit is measured in millions of dollars. The number before the comma in each cell is Warner Brothers' profit if both studios take the actions that correspond to that cell. The number after the comma is Disney's profit.

Look at the table and contemplate where equilibrium might occur in this industry. At first glance, you may expect that, because they could maximize their joint profits by agreeing not to advertise, the studios should just collaborate and earn $320 million each. This is not a Nash equilibrium, however. Here's why: Suppose a studio applied this reasoning and actually held off from advertising because it believed its profit would be higher. Once the first studio decides not to advertise, however, the other studio has a strong incentive to advertise. The other studio can now earn far more profit by advertising than by going along with the don't advertise plan. Recall that the Nash equilibrium means both companies are doing the best they can, *given what the other is doing*. Because one studio can earn a higher profit by advertising when the other doesn't, agreeing not to advertise is not a Nash equilibrium.

To make this scenario concrete, let's say Disney has decided not to advertise. Looking at the profits in Table 11.1, you can see that if Warner Brothers goes along, it will earn $320 million in profit. If it instead abandons the agreement and chooses to advertise, however, it will earn $550 million. Clearly, Warner Brothers will do the latter. You can also see in the table that it works the other way, too: If Warner Brothers chooses not to advertise, Disney does better by advertising (also earning $550 million instead of $320 million).

Table 11.1 An Advertising Game*

		DISNEY	
		Advertise	**Don't Advertise**
WARNER BROTHERS	**Advertise**	250, 250	550, −80
	Don't Advertise	−80, 550	320, 320

*Outcomes are measured in millions of dollars of profit.

Therefore, any agreement to hold off from advertising is not stable because both parties have an incentive to cheat on it. Even if one of them sticks to the agreement, the other will earn more profit by sabotaging it. Because each studio will earn higher profit by advertising when the other does not, an outcome in which neither studio advertises cannot be a Nash equilibrium. Agreeing not to advertise is not a Nash equilibrium.

Our analysis so far has established that if one studio *doesn't* advertise, the other studio wants to advertise. What is a studio's optimal action if the other studio *does* advertise? The answer may be found in Table 11.1. If Disney advertises, Warner Brothers earns $250 million by advertising and loses $80 million by not advertising. A similar situation holds for Disney's best response to Warner Brothers. Therefore, advertising is each studio's best response to the other's choice to advertise.

This means that choosing to advertise is a studio's best course of action regardless of whether the other studio advertises or not. Because this is true for both Disney *and* Warner Brothers, the only Nash equilibrium in this case is for both studios to advertise. It is stable because each company is doing the best it can *given what the other is doing.*

prisoner's dilemma
A situation in which the Nash equilibrium is an outcome that is somehow worse for all involved than another (unstable) outcome.

Notice that this is true even though it means the studios' profits in the Nash equilibrium will be $250 million each—lower than the $320 million each would earn if they could both hold off from advertising. *A situation in which the Nash equilibrium is an outcome that is somehow worse for all involved than another (unstable) outcome* is known as a **prisoner's dilemma** in game theory. We will look at such situations in more detail in the next few sections and in the next chapter. ■

11.2 Oligopoly with Identical Goods: Collusion and Cartels

Model Assumptions Collusion and Cartels

- Firms make identical products.
- Industry firms agree to coordinate their quantity and pricing decisions, and no firm deviates from the agreement even if breaking it is in the firm's best self-interest.

collusion Economic behavior in which all the firms in an oligopoly coordinate their production and pricing decisions to collectively act as a monopoly to gain monopoly profits to be split among themselves.

In the next several sections, we examine several different models of imperfect competition. They give very different answers about the way in which firms make decisions, so it's important to know which model is the right one to use. A box at the start of each section lists the conditions an industry must meet for that model to apply. In the first model, *all the firms in an oligopoly coordinate their production and pricing decisions to collectively act as a monopoly to gain monopoly profits to be split among themselves.* This economic behavior is known as **collusion**. The *organization formed when firms collude* is often called a **cartel**.[2]

cartel The organization formed when firms collude.

If the companies in an oligopoly can successfully collude, figuring out the oligopoly equilibrium is easy. The firms act collectively as a single monopolist would, and the industry equilibrium is the monopoly equilibrium (output is the level for which $MR = MC$ and the price is determined by the demand curve, as we saw in Chapter 9).[3] Don't try

---

[2] Sometimes the term "cartel" is reserved for a joint monopoly behavior when the firms involved have a public agreement, whereas "collusion" is used to refer to this behavior when it is done in secret. Both describe the same economic behavior, however.

[3] While determining the market equilibrium price, total quantity, and total profits in a cartel is easy, it's not always easy (either for economists studying cartels or the firms in the cartels themselves) to figure out how the cartel's quantity and profits will be divided among its members. We discuss this problem later in the section.

this at home, though. Cartels and collusion violate the law in most every country of the world, and in the United States, it is a criminal offense that has landed many executives in prison. We discussed in Chapter 9 that governments enforce antitrust laws because of monopolies' potential to harm consumers. That explains why collusion has to be done in secret. Interestingly, the secrecy itself makes it more difficult for cartels to maintain a stable equilibrium.

 # FREAKONOMICS

Apple Always Wins, or Does It?

In the months leading up to the launch of the iPad, Apple was also preparing to open the iBooks Store, which would allow users to buy and read books on mobile devices. But Apple faced a dilemma. It would be difficult for the iBooks Store to succeed unless it could match the $9.99 price point of Amazon's Kindle, its major competitor. This price, thought by some to be less than marginal cost, had served Amazon well in building a customer base for e-books, but the price made it challenging for a new entrant like Apple to successfully compete.

Amazon's low price point was a concern for book publishers as well. They feared that cheap e-books would hurt sales of their more expensive print copies and, over the longer term, influence the public's expectations regarding book prices. Amazon's growing market power also posed the threat that Amazon might start directly competing with publishers.

The major publishers had already begun engaging in talks, meeting in private dining rooms in New York City restaurants to discuss ways to force Amazon to price above $9.99. Before one of their meetings, David Young, then chairman and CEO of Hachette Book Group, told a fellow publisher, "I hate [Amazon's] bullying behavior and will be happy to support a strategy that restricts their plans for world domination." The publishers started implementing their strategy. They coordinated on raising the wholesale price of e-books and introducing "windowing," which delayed e-book versions of new releases to protect hardcover sales. After one particular correspondence regarding these tactics, Young advised another publishing executive that "it would be prudent for you to double delete this from your email files."

Eddy Cue, Apple's Senior Vice President of Internet Software and Services, learned of the publishers' discontent with Amazon's price point, and he began requesting meetings with the major publishers to encourage them to join the iBooks Store. Cue assured the publishers that Apple would price books higher than Amazon. After the first of his meetings, he reported to Apple's then-CEO Steve Jobs that the publishers were "ecstatic" about the prospect of Apple's entry into the industry.

Over the next several weeks, the publishers and Apple crafted a contract that featured a market-wide transition from a wholesale model to an agency model (whereby the publisher rather than the retailer sets the retail price) and a clause that guaranteed Apple would hold the lowest prices on the market. These changes would effectively drive e-book prices upward while securing Apple's competitive position in the market.

Amazon responded by also moving to an agency model in the following months. Soon thereafter, e-book retail prices increased an average of 14.2% per unit and 42.7% for *New York Times* bestsellers. Publishers sold fewer e-books through Amazon, as might have been expected, though estimates of the magnitude of this decrease varied. On the whole, however, the collusion between Apple and the publishers appeared to be a massive success. Not only had it raised prices, it seriously eroded Amazon's monopoly. Before the price-fixing scheme, Amazon held about 90% of the e-book market. A year-and-a-half after the kickoff of the iBooks Store, when the scheme was in full effect, this share was closer to 60%.

Once again, it seemed as if the old Apple magic had worked: The company revolutionized yet another market by entering it. Maybe that would have been the case had things stayed the way they were. But any cheers of victory among Apple and the publishers quickly faded when the U.S. government sued them for collusion. The presiding judge announced her decision just over a year later: Apple was guilty. The words the judge used were scathing. "To adopt Apple's theory, a fact-finder would be confronted with the herculean task of explaining away reams of documents and blinking at the obvious." Several states and private plaintiffs sought more than $800 million in damages. Apple managed to soften the blow by appealing and reaching a $450 million settlement in case its appeal fell through, but it lost the most important gain the scheme had rendered: its ability to control e-book prices.

The Instability of Collusion and Cartels

The firms in an oligopoly would love to collude. They could earn more profit. Adam Smith, the eighteenth-century philosophy professor and one of the fathers of the discipline of economics, recognized this. He wrote in *The Wealth of Nations*, "People of the same trade seldom meet together, even for merriment and diversion, but the conversation ends in a conspiracy against the public, or in some contrivance to raise prices."

But colluding is harder than it looks. Each member of a cartel has an incentive not to go along. Although firms in a market might be able to come to some initial agreement over a bargaining table, collusion turns out to be unstable—not an equilibrium.

Think about an industry in which there are two firms, Firm A and Firm B, that want to collude. To keep things simple, say both firms have the same constant marginal cost c. If the two firms act collectively as a monopolist, we can follow the monopoly method from Chapter 9 to determine the market equilibrium. Each firm will operate where marginal revenue equals marginal cost. It's not stable, though, because each will want to increase its output at the other's expense.

Suppose the inverse market demand curve for their product is $P = a - bQ$, where P is the price per unit and Q is the quantity produced. We know from Section 9.2 that the marginal revenue curve corresponding to this linear inverse demand curve is $MR = a - 2bQ$. The firms will produce a quantity that sets their marginal revenue equal to their marginal cost c:

$$MR = MC$$

$$a - 2bQ = c$$

Solving this equation for Q gives $Q = (a - c)/2b$. This is the industry's output when its firms collude to act like a monopolist. If we plug this back into the demand curve equation, we find the market price at this quantity: $P = (a + c)/2$.

This is the industry's *total* production in the collusive monopoly outcome. Any combination of the individual firms' outputs that adds to this total will result in the monopoly price and profit. Of course, the firms have to decide how to split this profit. Because both firms have the same costs, splitting seems reasonable. Each firm produces half of the output, $Q/2 = (a - c)/4b$, and they split the monopoly profit equally. Later in this section, we discuss why collusion is even more unstable when firms have different costs.

Cartel Instability: A Mathematical Analysis   To see why collusion is unstable, let's work though an example with specific numbers. Suppose the inverse demand curve is $P = 20 - Q$ and $MC = \$4$. Setting $MR = MC$, as above, the total industry output in a collusive equilibrium will be $Q = 8$ units, and the monopoly price will be $P = \$12$. Assuming that Firms A and B split production evenly, each makes 4 units under collusion. This outcome is shown in **Figure 11.1**.

Collusion and cartels fall apart for the same reason that Disney and Warner Brothers can't agree to stop advertising in our earlier example. It's in each company's interest to expand its output once it knows the other company is restricting output. Each company has the incentive to cheat on the collusive agreement. In other words, collusion is *not a Nash equilibrium*.

Think about either company's output choice in our example. Will Firm A want to stick with the output of 4 (half the monopoly output of 8) if Firm B decides to produce 4? If Firm A decides to increase its output to 5 instead of 4, then the total quantity produced in the industry would increase to 9. This higher output level lowers the price from \$12 to \$11 (the demand curve in Figure 11.1 slopes down so price falls when quantity rises).

Once Firm A cheats and increases its output, the industry is no longer at the monopoly quantity and price level, and total industry profit will fall because of overproduction.

Figure 11.1 Cartel Instability

A cartel would like to operate as a monopoly, restricting output to 8 (where $MR = MC$) and selling each unit at a price of $12 for an industry profit of $($12 - $4) \times 8 = 64. If production and profit are shared equally between two firms, each firm earns a profit of $($12 - $4) \times 4 = 32. However, Firm A may earn a greater profit by cheating on the agreement and producing another unit, which raises total output in the market and lowers price to $11 per unit. At this price and output, Firm A earns a profit of $($11 - $4) \times 5 = 35. So, each firm has an individual incentive to cheat, and collusion is not stable.

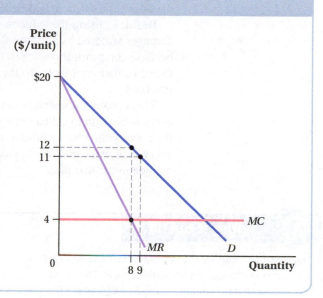

Total profit drops from $Q \times (P - c) = 8 \times (12 - 4) = 64 at the monopoly/cartel level to $9 \times (11 - 4) = 63 after Firm A increases its output on the sly.

Although the profit of the industry as a whole falls, Firm A, the company that violates the agreement, earns more than with collusion. Its profit under collusion was $32 (half of the monopoly profits of $64). But now its profit is $5 \times (11 - 4) = 35. The extra sales from increasing production more than make up for the lower prices caused by the increase in production.

A Nash equilibrium requires each firm to be doing the best it can given what the other firm is doing. This example shows that one firm can do better by violating the collusive agreement if the other firm continues to uphold it, so collusion is not a Nash equilibrium. In fact, the cheating firm can do better still by producing more than 5 units. If one firm sticks to the collusive agreement and makes 4 units, the profit-maximizing output for the other firm is 6 units. At this quantity, the price is $20 - (4 + 6) = 10, and the cheating firm's profit is $6 \times (10 - 4) = 36. (Test this out for yourself. Notice that the cheating firm's profit only starts to fall if it produces 7 or more units.) Both firms face the same incentives to cheat. That's why collusion is difficult.

Increasing the Number of Firms in the Cartel

This example was for a two-firm cartel. If more firms are involved, the difficulties of holding an agreement together get even worse. Consider the above example, but now with four firms instead of two. In a collusive agreement, each firm would make 2 units (one-fourth of the total quantity of 8) and earn $16 (one-fourth of the monopoly profit of $64). If three of the firms abide by the cartel and make 2 units, but the fourth decides to cheat and make 3, price would again fall to $11. The company that cheated on the agreement would earn a profit of $3 \times (11 - 4) = 21. The $5 increase in profit from cheating here is even larger than the $3 increase when there were only two firms. And the cheater would want to expand production even more. If the other firms remain at the collusive output (2 units per firm), the cheater will increase its profit by producing both a 4th and 5th unit. However, producing a 6th unit would reduce the cheater's profit. (To see this, consider the prices that would occur when total output is 8, 9, and 10 units and calculate the cheating firm's profits at those prices.) Because profit falls when the cheating firm produces 6 units, its profit-maximizing output, conditional on the others' production, will be 5 units.

Besides raising the value to cheating, having more firms in a cartel also reduces the damages suffered by any firm that continues to abide by the collusive agreement. This is because the profit losses caused by the cheating will be spread across more firms. This factor further contributes to the difficulty of maintaining collusion when more firms are involved.

This cheating problem is familiar to cartels everywhere. Each firm in the cartel wants every *other* firm to collude, thereby raising the market price, while it steals away business from everyone else by producing more output, thus lowering the market price. Because every firm in a cartel has this same incentive to cheat, it's difficult to persuade anyone to collude in the first place.

---

figure it out 11.1

Suppose that Squeaky Clean and Biobase are the only two producers of chlorine for swimming pools. The inverse market demand for chlorine is $P = 32 - 2Q$, where Q is measured in tons and P is dollars per ton. Assume that chlorine can be produced by either firm at a constant marginal cost of $16 per ton and there are no fixed costs.

    a. If the two firms collude and act like a monopoly, agreeing to evenly split the market, how much will each firm produce and what will the price of a ton of chlorine be? How much profit will each firm earn?

    b. Does Squeaky Clean have an incentive to cheat on this agreement by producing an additional ton of chlorine? Explain.

    c. Does Squeaky Clean's decision to cheat affect Biobase's profit? Explain.

    d. Suppose that both firms agree to each produce 1 ton more than they were producing in part (a). How much profit will each firm earn? Does Squeaky Clean now have an incentive to cheat on this agreement by producing another ton of chlorine? Explain.

Solution:

    a. If the firms agree to act like a monopoly, they will set $MR = MC$ to solve for the profit-maximizing output:

$$MR = MC$$
$$32 - 4Q = 16$$
$$4Q = 16$$
$$Q = 4$$

and each firm will produce 2 tons. To find the price, we substitute the market quantity ($Q = 4$) into the inverse demand equation:

$$P = 32 - 2Q = 32 - 2(4) = \$24 \text{ per ton}$$

Each firm will earn a profit of $(\$24 - \$16) \times 2 = \$16$.

    b. If Squeaky Clean cheats and produces 3 tons, Q rises to 5 and price falls to $22. Squeaky Clean's profit will be equal to $(\$22 - \$16) \times 3 = \$18$. Therefore, Squeaky Clean does have an incentive to cheat on the agreement because its profit would rise.

    c. If Squeaky Clean cheats, the price in the market falls to $22. This reduces Biobase's profit, which is now $(\$22 - \$16) \times 2 = \$12$.

    d. If both firms agree to limit production to 3 tons, $Q = 6$ and $P = \$20$. Therefore, each firm earns a profit of $(\$20 - \$16) \times 3 = \$12$. If Squeaky Clean tries to produce 4 tons of chlorine, Q rises to 7 and P falls to $18. Therefore, Squeaky Clean's profit will be $(\$18 - \$16) \times 4 = \$8$. Thus, Squeaky Clean does not have an incentive to cheat on this agreement because its profit would fall.

What Makes Collusion Easier?

Although collusion isn't an especially stable form of oligopoly, there are some conditions that make it more likely to succeed. The first circumstance an aspiring cartel needs is a way to detect and punish cheaters. We just saw that each company in a cartel has the private incentive to produce more output (or charge a lower price) than at the collusive level. If the other firms in a cartel have no way of knowing when a member cheats—and no form of punishment to inflict when they discover someone is cheating—little chance exists that an agreement will hold. That's why collusion is more likely to work when firms can closely observe the transaction quantities and prices of other firms. Such transparency limits the ability of potential cheaters to cut secret, lower-price deals with customers. If a firm cheats, the cartel needs to have some way to enforce the agreement or punish the cheater. Because collusion is generally illegal, the cartel can't really take the cheaters to court, but it might be able to take other actions that reduce the profits of firms that stray from the agreement, such as shutting them out of a share of future cartel profits.

Second, a cartel may find it easier to succeed if there is not much variation in marginal costs across its members. To maximize profit, a monopoly (or a cartel trying to act like a monopoly) wants to use the lowest-cost production method. This desire complicates any scheme to share the monopoly profit among the cartel members and leaves open more opportunities to cheat. Within OPEC, for example, if Saudi Arabia can pump its oil out of the ground for about $4 a barrel, while in Nigeria it costs about $20 per barrel, OPEC would need to explain to Nigeria that the most efficient production strategy would be to sell only Saudi Arabian oil and none from Nigeria.

Third, cartels are more stable when firms take the long view and care more about the future. Think of staying in a cartel (i.e., choosing not to cheat on a collusive agreement) as trading off a short-term opportunity cost to earn a long-term gain. The short-term opportunity cost is giving up the higher profit a firm could obtain by cheating on the agreement. The long-term benefit is that, if the cartel can avoid dissolving into competition, it stands to make monopoly profits. The more the firm values those future monopoly profits relative to the quick hit of additional profit from cheating, the more it will abide by the collusive agreement. Impatient companies, like those in danger of bankruptcy and therefore in desperate need of profit today, are more likely to cheat.

 ## Application: Cartel Bots?

Most people's idea of a cartel is a group of businesspeople who get together to plan out the manipulation of a market. These meetings are often set in either a literal or, more likely these days, figurative "smoke-filled room." Either way, people are involved.

The advent of artificial intelligence (AI) and other algorithmic business practices, however, has recently raised another concern. What if collusion isn't the result of people actually deciding to act in a particular way, but rather because pricing algorithms built into software "decide" to raise prices? Suppose competing companies wrote pricing software that effectively operationalized the command, "If our competitors raise prices, raise our price." It isn't difficult to imagine that the market could fall into a cartel-like outcome without any humans agreeing with one another to actually take the step of increasing prices. How could antitrust authorities prosecute a case where people never made a collusive deal? You can't put an algorithm in jail.

Perhaps we could make even *using* such cartel-spurring algorithms illegal and subject the installers to penalties. But a while a strategy to "price high if they price high" is transparent and easy to track, most pricing algorithms are much more complex. They could plausibly lead to cartel-like outcomes in ways that no one, possibly even their creators, might have imagined. Several AI bots given no other guidance than to set prices to maximize profits might quickly discover for themselves that the best way to do this is to collude. (They would also be fairly good at quickly detecting any cheating behavior, raising the stability of the collusive outcome.)

Policymakers and economists have yet to settle on a recommended course of action. But technological trends make it likely that these sorts of situations will occur with increasing frequency in the future. ■

11.3 Oligopoly with Identical Goods: Bertrand Competition

> **Model Assumptions** Bertrand Competition with Identical Goods
>
> - Firms sell identical products.
> - The firms compete by choosing the price at which they sell their products.
> - The firms set their prices simultaneously.

In the previous section, we learned that the collusion/cartel model of oligopoly in which firms behave like a monopoly is unlikely to hold in reality because coordination is not an equilibrium and the agreement will likely break down. We need a model in which firms compete against one another. The first such model is as simple as it gets: Firms sell the same product, and consumers compare prices and buy the product with the lowest price. This *oligopoly model in which each firm chooses the price of its product* is called **Bertrand competition**, after Joseph Bertrand, the nineteenth-century French mathematician and economist who first wrote about it. When firms are selling identical products, as we're assuming here, Bertrand oligopoly has a particularly simple equilibrium: $P = MC$, just like perfect competition. In later sections of this chapter, we see how circumstances change when firms sell products that are not identical.

Bertrand competition Oligopoly model in which each firm chooses the price of its product.

Setting Up the Bertrand Model

To set up this model, let's suppose a market with only two companies in it exists. They sell the same product and have the same marginal cost. For example, suppose there are only two stores in a city, a Walmart and a Target, and these stores are located next to each other. They both sell the latest Nintendo Switch and each firm's marginal cost is $300 per console. This includes the wholesale price the firm has to pay Nintendo as well as miscellaneous selling costs, such as stocking the consoles on shelves, checking customers out, and so on.

We need one further assumption: Consumers don't view either store differently in terms of service, atmosphere, or the like. If consumers value these characteristics separately from the consoles, then in a way the products would no longer be identical and we would need to model the firms' behavior using the model of differentiated products discussed later in the chapter.

With only two companies in a market, it might seem as if there would be a lot of market power and high markups over cost. But suppose the customers in this market have a simple demand rule: Buy the console from the store that sells it at the lowest price. If both stores charge the same price, consumers flip a coin to determine where they buy. This rule means, in effect, that the store charging the lowest price will garner all the demand in the market. If both stores charge the same price, each store gets half the demand.

Suppose the total demand in the market is for Q consoles. Let's denote Walmart's price as P_W and Target's price as P_T. The two stores then face the following demand curves:

Demand for Nintendo Switches at Walmart:

$$Q, \quad \text{if } P_W < P_T$$

$$Q/2, \quad \text{if } P_W = P_T$$

$$0, \quad \text{if } P_W > P_T$$

Demand for Nintendo Switches at Target:

$$Q, \quad \text{if } P_T < P_W$$

$$Q/2, \quad \text{if } P_T = P_W$$

$$0, \quad \text{if } P_T > P_W$$

Each store chooses its price to maximize its profit, realizing that it will sell the number of units according to the demand curves above. We've assumed the total number of consoles sold, Q, doesn't depend on the price charged. The price only affects which store people buy from. (We could alternatively have allowed Q to depend on the lowest price charged; all the key results discussed below would remain the same.)

Nash Equilibrium of a Bertrand Oligopoly

Remember that in a Nash equilibrium, each firm is doing the best it can given whatever the other firm is doing. So to find the equilibrium of this Bertrand model, let's first think about Target's best response to Walmart's actions. (We could do this in the reverse order if we wanted.) If Target believes Walmart will charge a price P_W for Nintendo Switches, Target will sell nothing if it sets its price above P_W, so we can probably rule that out as a profit-maximizing strategy. Target is left with two options: Match Walmart's price and sell $Q/2$ units, or undercut Walmart and sell Q. Because all it has to do is undercut Walmart by *any* amount, dropping its price just below P_W will only reduce its per-unit margin by a tiny amount, but the store will double its sales because it will take the whole market instead of splitting it.

As an example, suppose $Q = 1{,}000$ and Target thinks Walmart will charge $P_W = \$325$. If Target also charges $P_T = \$325$, it will sell 500 consoles at a profit of $25 each (the $325 price minus the $300 marginal cost). That's a total profit of $12,500. But if Target charges $324.99, it will sell 1,000 Nintendo Switches at a profit of $24.99 each. This is a profit of $24,990—almost double what it was at $175. Target has a strong incentive to undercut Walmart's expected price.

Of course, things are the same from Walmart's perspective: It has the same incentive to undercut whatever price it thinks Target will choose. If it believes Target is going to charge $P_T = \$324.99$ for a Nintendo Switch, Walmart could price its consoles at $324.98 and gain back the entire market. But then Target would have the incentive to undercut *this* expected price, and so on.

This incentive for undercutting would only stop once the price each store expects the other to charge falls to the level of the stores' marginal costs ($300). At that point, cutting prices further would let a store gain the entire market, but that store would be selling every Switch at a loss.

The equilibrium of this Bertrand oligopoly occurs when each store charges a price equal to its marginal cost—$300 in this example. Each obtains half of the market share, and each store earns zero economic profit. The stores would like to charge more, but if either firm raises its price above marginal cost by even the smallest amount, the other firm has a strong incentive to undercut it. And dropping prices below marginal cost would only cause the stores to suffer losses. Thus, the outcome isn't great for the firms, but neither firm can do better by unilaterally changing its price. This is the definition of a Nash equilibrium.

In the identical-good Bertrand oligopoly, one firm cannot increase its profit by raising its price *if* the other firm still charges a price equal to its marginal cost. If the firms could somehow figure out a way to coordinate changes in their actions so that they both raised prices together, they would raise their profits. However, the problem with this strategy, as we saw earlier, is that collusion is unstable. Once the firms are charging prices above marginal cost, a firm can raise its profits by unilaterally changing its action and lowering its price just slightly.

The Bertrand model of oligopoly shows that even with a small number of firms, competition can still be extremely intense under the right conditions. *In fact, the market outcome of Bertrand competition with identical goods is the same as that in a perfectly competitive market: Price equals marginal cost.* This super-competitiveness occurs because either firm can steal the whole market away from the other by dropping price only slightly. The strong incentive to undercut the price leads both firms to drop their prices to marginal cost.

This example had only two firms, but the result would be the same if there were more. The intuition is the same: Every firm's price-cutting motive is so strong that the only equilibrium is for them to all charge a price equal to marginal cost and split the market evenly.[4] The strong assumptions of the Bertrand model with identical products are rare, but some online markets approximate this condition. Where comparing across merchants is really easy, the lowest-priced seller can take the lion's share of the market and these markets often end up with all firms charging the same low price, as the model predicts.

11.4 Oligopoly with Identical Goods: Cournot Competition

Model Assumptions Cournot Competition with Identical Goods

- Firms sell identical products.
- Firms compete by choosing a quantity to produce.
- All goods sell for the same price—the market price, which is determined by the sum of the quantities produced by all the firms in the market.
- Firms choose quantities simultaneously.

When firms sell identical goods, the Bertrand competition model results in the same equilibrium that we find in a perfectly competitive market, where price equals marginal cost. Because consumers care only about the price of the good (the product is identical across firms), each firm faces a demand that is perfectly elastic. Any increase in a firm's price results in it losing all its market share. The demand for the product will go to the firm offering the lowest price.

---

[4] This again assumes all firms in the market have the same marginal cost. If firms have different marginal costs in an identical-product Bertrand oligopoly, then the equilibrium is for the lowest-cost firm to charge a price just under the *second-lowest* cost in the market and take the whole market.

But firms often face capacity constraints, and that limits how much demand they can fill in the short run. With capacity constraints, if a firm undercuts another's price, it can only steal as many customers as it has available capacity.

In this case, there won't be as much pressure for a firm to respond to price cuts because each firm will not lose all its customers even if it sets its price higher than that of a competitor. In fact, if the capacity of the low-price company is small enough, its competitor may not feel the need to cut prices much at all. This avoids the price-cutting spiral we saw in the Bertrand model. In this situation, the critical issue is for a firm to determine how much capacity it has and thus what quantity it can produce.

Setting Up the Cournot Model

We raise the idea of capacity constraints to motivate another major model, **Cournot competition**, an *oligopoly model in which each firm chooses its production quantity* (named after its first modeler, Augustin Cournot—yet another nineteenth-century French mathematician and economist).

In Cournot competition, firms produce identical goods and choose a quantity to produce rather than a price at which to sell the good. Individual firms do not control the price of their goods as they do in the Bertrand model. First, all firms in the industry decide how much they will produce; then based on the quantity produced by all firms, the market demand curve determines the price at which all firms' output will sell. In Chapter 9, we learned that when dealing with a monopolist, the price-quantity outcome is the same whether a firm sets the price of its product or the number of units of output it produces. In an oligopoly, however, the market outcome differs depending on whether the firm chooses to set its price or its quantity.

To be more specific, let's say there are two firms in a Cournot oligopoly, Firm 1 and Firm 2. (There can be more; we keep it at two for the sake of simplicity.) Each has a constant marginal cost of c, and both firms independently and simultaneously choose their production quantities q_1 and q_2. The good's inverse demand curve is

$$P = a - bQ$$

where Q is the *total* quantity produced in the market: $Q = q_1 + q_2$.

Firm 1's profit π_1 is the quantity q_1 it produces times the difference between the market price P and its production costs c, or

$$\pi_1 = q_1 \times (P - c)$$

Substituting the inverse demand equation for P, we find that

$$\pi_1 = q_1 \times [a - b(q_1 + q_2) - c]$$

Similarly, Firm 2's profits are given by the equation

$$\pi_2 = q_2 \times [a - b(q_1 + q_2) - c]$$

These two profit equations make clear that the firms in this oligopoly strategically interact. Firm 1's profit is not just a function of its own quantity choice q_1, but also of its competitor's quantity q_2. Likewise, Firm 2's profit is affected by Firm 1's output choice. The logic is that each firm's production choice, through its influence on the market price P, affects the other firm's profit.

An example of an industry that is like the Cournot model is the crude oil industry. Crude oil is a commodity; consumers are indifferent about oil from different sources. The price of oil is set on a worldwide market, and it depends on the total amount of oil supplied at a given time. Therefore, it's realistic to assume that oil producers, even those such as

Cournot competition
Oligopoly model in which each firm chooses its production quantity.

Saudi Arabia or Iran with large oil reserves, do not choose the price of their outputs. They just choose how much to produce. Oil traders observe these production decisions for all oil producers, and they bid oil's market price up or down depending on how the total quantity produced (the market supply) compares to current demand. This price-setting process derives from the demand curve that connects total output to a market price.

Equilibrium in a Cournot Oligopoly

Finding the equilibrium for a Cournot oligopoly will be easier to follow using an example. Suppose for simplicity that only two countries pump oil, Saudi Arabia and Iran. Both have a marginal cost of production of $20 per barrel. Also assume that the inverse demand curve for oil is $P = 200 - 3Q$, where P is in dollars per barrel and Q is in millions of barrels per day.

Finding the equilibrium for the Cournot model is similar to doing so for a monopoly, but with the one change noted above: The market quantity Q is the sum of the quantities produced in Saudi Arabia q_{SA} and Iran q_I, rather than just the monopolist's output: $Q = q_{SA} + q_I$. After recognizing this difference, we follow the same steps used to solve for a monopoly's profit-maximizing output. That is, we find each country's marginal revenue curve and then the quantity at which marginal revenue equals marginal cost.

Let's examine Saudi Arabia's profit maximization first. As we learned in Section 9.2, we can more easily find a firm's marginal revenue curve by starting with its inverse demand curve. Therefore, we start by writing the inverse demand curve equation in terms of the quantity choices of each country:

$$P = 200 - 3Q = 200 - 3(q_{SA} + q_I) = 200 - 3q_{SA} - 3q_I$$

Because the slope of the marginal revenue curve is twice the slope of the inverse demand function, Saudi Arabia's marginal revenue curve is[5]

$$MR_{SA} = 200 - 6q_{SA} - 3q_I$$

Saudi Arabia maximizes profit when it produces the quantity at which its marginal revenue equals its marginal cost:

$$200 - 6q_{SA} - 3q_I = 20$$

We can solve this equation for Saudi Arabia's profit-maximizing output:

$$q_{SA} = 30 - 0.5q_I$$

This outcome differs from the monopoly outcome: If Saudi Arabia were a monopoly, setting marginal revenue equal to marginal cost would result in a single quantity Q because its quantity supplied q_{SA} would be the market quantity supplied Q. In this example, however, Saudi Arabia's profit-maximizing output depends on the competitor's output q_I. Similarly, Iran's profit-maximizing q_I depends on q_{SA} because it faces the same market demand curve and has the same marginal cost:

$$q_I = 30 - 0.5q_{SA}$$

This result shows that one country's output choice effectively decreases the demand for the other country's output. That is, the demand curve for one country's output is shifted

---

[5] The inverse demand curve for Saudi Arabia, in a diagram with quantity, q_{SA}, on the horizontal axis and price on the vertical axis, has a slope of $\Delta P / \Delta q_{SA} = 3$. This means that only the coefficient on q_{SA} is used to determine the slope of the marginal revenue curve. The slope of the marginal revenue curve is $\Delta MR / \Delta q_{SA} = 6$.

by the amount of the other country's output. If the Saudis expect Iran to produce, say, 10 million barrels per day (bpd), then Saudi Arabia would effectively be facing the demand curve

$$P = 200 - 3q_{SA} - 3q_I = 200 - 3q_{SA} - 3(10) = 170 - 3q_{SA}$$

If it expected Iran to pump out 20 million bpd, Saudi Arabia would face the demand curve

$$P = 200 - 3q_{SA} - 3(20) = 140 - 3q_{SA}$$

In Cournot competition, the demand remaining for a firm's output given competitor firms' production quantities is called the **residual demand curve**. We just derived Saudi Arabia's residual demand curves for two of Iran's different production choices, 10 and 20 million bpd.

In effect, a firm in a Cournot oligopoly acts like a monopolist, but one that faces its residual demand curve rather than the market demand curve. Like any regular demand curve, there's a *marginal revenue curve corresponding to the residual demand curve* (it's called . . . wait for it . . . the **residual marginal revenue curve**). The firm produces the quantity at which its residual marginal revenue equals its marginal cost. That's why Saudi Arabia's optimal quantity is the one that sets $200 - 6q_{SA} - 3q_I = 20$. The left-hand side of this equation is Saudi Arabia's residual marginal revenue (expressed in terms of any expected Iranian output level, q_I). The right-hand side is its marginal cost.

How does the profit-maximizing output of one country change with the other country's expected production? In other words, what role do strategic interactions play in a Cournot oligopoly? This can be seen in **Figure 11.2**, which shows Saudi Arabia's residual demand, residual marginal revenue, and marginal cost curves. (The Iranian case would be the same, just with the two countries' labels switched.) The residual demand RD_{SA}^1 and residual marginal revenue RMR_{SA}^1 curves correspond to an Iranian output level of 10 million bpd. In other words, if Saudi Arabia expects Iran to produce 10 million bpd, Saudi Arabia's optimal output quantity is 25 million bpd. If it expects Iran to produce 30 million bpd, Saudi Arabia's residual demand and marginal revenue curves shift in to RD_{SA}^2 and RMR_{SA}^2, to $P = 110 - 3q_{SA}$ and

residual demand curve In Cournot competition, the demand remaining for a firm's output given competitor firms' production quantities.

residual marginal revenue curve A marginal revenue curve corresponding to a residual demand curve.

Figure 11.2   Optimal Quantity Choices

Saudi Arabia's optimal production quantity is dependent on Iran's production quantity. If the Iranian output level is 10 million bpd, Saudi Arabia's optimal output is 25 million bpd, where its residual marginal revenue curve intersects its marginal cost. If Iranian output increases to 30 million bpd, Saudi Arabia's residual demand and residual marginal revenue curves shift to RD_{SA}^2 and RMR_{SA}^2. As a result, Saudi Arabia's optimum output decreases to 15 million bpd.

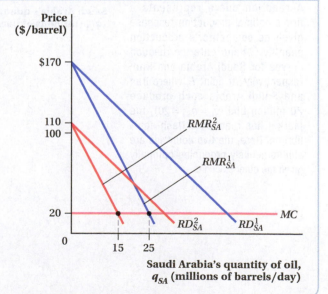

$MR = 110 - 6q_{SA}$, respectively. The Saudis' optimal quantity then falls to 15 million bpd. At Iranian output levels higher than 30 million bpd, Saudi Arabia's residual demand and marginal revenue curves would shift in further and its optimal quantity would fall.

Each competitor's profit-maximizing output depends on the other's output and in an opposite direction: If a firm expects its competitor to produce more, it will reduce its production. Although this kind of interaction seems to create a hopeless chicken-and-egg problem, we can still pin down the specific production quantities for each country if we return to the concept of Nash equilibrium: Each producer does the best it can, taking the other producer's action as given.

For a Cournot oligopoly, the equation for each country's profit-maximizing output is described given the particular output choice of the other country. The equation for q_{SA} gives Saudi Arabia's best response to any production level q_I that Iran might choose. Likewise, the q_I equation gives Iran's best response to any Saudi production decision. In other words, when both equations hold simultaneously, each country is doing the best it can given the other country's action. So, the Nash equilibrium is the combination of outputs that make both equations hold.

Cournot Equilibrium: A Graphical Approach

We show this situation graphically in **Figure 11.3**. Saudi Arabia's output is on the vertical axis and Iran's output is on the horizontal axis. The curves illustrated are examples of a **reaction curve**, a *function that relates a firm's best response to its competitor's possible actions. In Cournot competition, this is the firm's best production response to its competitor's possible quantity choices.* Because both reaction curves are downward-sloping, a firm's optimal output falls as the other producer's output rises.

Reaction curve *SA* shows Saudi Arabia's best response to any production choice of Iran—it shows the points at which $q_{SA} = 30 - 0.5q_I$. If it expects Iran to produce no oil ($q_I = 0$), for example, the profit-maximizing Saudi response is to produce $q_{SA} = 30$ million bpd. This combination occurs at point A. The optimal q_{SA} falls as Iranian production rises. If Iran produces $q_I = 10$, then Saudi Arabia maximizes its profit by producing

reaction curve A function that relates a firm's best response to its competitor's possible actions. In Cournot competition, this is the firm's best production response to its competitor's possible quantity choices.

Figure 11.3   Reaction Curves and Cournot Equilibrium

A reaction curve represents a firm's optimal production response given its competitor's production quantity. *SA* and *I* are the reaction curves for Saudi Arabia and Iran, respectively. At point *E*, where Iran and Saudi Arabia each produce 20 million bpd ($q_I = q_{SA} = 20$), the market has reached a Nash equilibrium. Here, the two countries are simultaneously producing optimally given the other's actions.

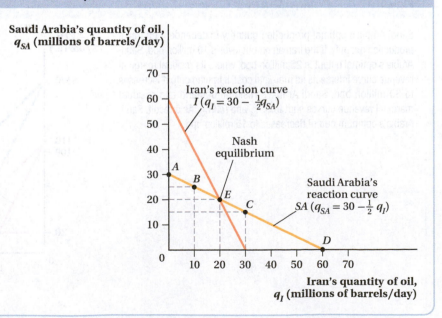

$q_{SA} = 30 - 0.5(10) = 25$ million bpd (point B). If $q_I = 30$, then the optimal q_{SA} is 15 million bpd (point C). Saudi Arabia's optimal production continues to fall as Iran's production rises until it hits zero at $q_I = 60$ million bpd (point D). At any q_I greater than 60 million bpd, the market price is below $20 per barrel (see the demand curve). Because this price is below the marginal cost of production, it wouldn't be profitable for Saudi Arabia to pump any oil if Iran produced 60 million bpd.

Line I is the corresponding reaction curve for Iran's profit-maximizing quantity $q_I = 30 - 0.5q_{SA}$. It's essentially the same as SA, except with the axes flipped. Just as Saudi Arabia's profit-maximizing output falls with Iran's production choice, Iran's optimal production decreases with expected Saudi production q_{SA}. The optimal q_I is 30 million bpd if $q_{SA} = 0$, and it falls toward 0 as q_{SA} rises toward 60 million bpd.

Each country realizes that its actions affect the desired actions of its competitor, which, in turn, affect its own optimal action, and so on. This back-and-forth strategic interaction is captured in firms' reaction curves and is why the equilibrium is found where reaction curves intersect. The intersection of the two reaction curves at point E shows the quantities at which both competitors are simultaneously producing optimally given the other's actions. That is, point E is the Nash equilibrium of the Cournot oligopoly—the mutual best response. If one country is producing at point E, the other country would only reduce its profits by unilaterally producing at some other point. At this equilibrium, each country produces 20 million bpd, and total output is 40 million bpd.

Cournot Equilibrium: A Mathematical Approach

Instead of finding the Cournot equilibrium graphically, we algebraically solve for the output levels that equate the two reaction curves. One way to do this is to substitute one equation into the other to get rid of one quantity variable and solve for the remaining one. For example, if we substitute Iran's reaction curve into Saudi Arabia's reaction curve for q_I, we find

 The online appendix finds the equilibrium for Cournot competition using calculus.

$$q_{SA} = 30 - 0.5q_I = 30 - 0.5(30 - 0.5q_{SA})$$
$$= 30 - 15 + 0.25q_{SA}$$
$$0.75q_{SA} = 15$$
$$q_{SA} = 20$$

Thus, the equilibrium output for Saudi Arabia is 20 million bpd. If we substitute this value back into Iran's reaction curve, we find that $q_I = 30 - 0.5q_S = 30 - 0.5(20) = 20$. Iran's optimal production is also 20 million bpd. Equilibrium point E in Figure 11.3 has the coordinates (20, 20), and total industry output is 40 million bpd.

The equilibrium price of oil at this point can be found by plugging these production decisions into the inverse market demand curve. Doing so gives $P = 200 - 3(q_{SA} + q_I) = 200 - 3(20 + 20) = \$80$ per barrel. Each country's profit is 20 million bpd $\times$ ($\$80 - \$20$) = $\$1,200$ million = $\$1.2$ billion per day, so the industry's total profit is $\$2.4$ billion per day.

 figure it out 11.2

Go online for interactive, step-by-step help in solving the following problem.

OilPro and GreaseTech are the only two firms that provide oil changes in a local market in a Cournot duopoly (a two-firm oligopoly). The oil changes performed by the two firms are identical, and consumers are indifferent about which firm they will purchase an oil change from. The market inverse demand for the oil changes is $P = 100 - 2Q$, where Q is the total number of oil changes (in thousands per year) produced by the two firms, $q_O + q_G$. OilPro has a marginal cost of $12 per oil change, while GreaseTech has a marginal cost of $20. Assume that neither firm has any fixed cost.

a. Determine each firm's reaction curve and graph it.

b. How many oil changes will each firm produce in Cournot equilibrium?

c. What will the market price for an oil change be?

d. How much profit does each firm earn?

Solution:

a. Start by substituting $Q = q_O + q_G$ into the market inverse demand curve:

$$P = 100 - 2Q = 100 - 2(q_O + q_G) = 100 - 2q_O - 2q_G$$

From this inverse demand cure, we can derive each firm's marginal revenue curve:

$$MR_O = 100 - 4q_O - 2q_G$$
$$MR_G = 100 - 2q_O - 4q_G$$

Each firm will set its marginal revenue equal to its marginal cost to maximize profit. From this, we can obtain each firm's reaction curve:

$$MR_O = 100 - 4q_O - 2q_G = 12$$
$$4q_O = 88 - 2q_G$$
$$q_O = 22 - 0.5q_G$$

$$MR_G = 100 - 2q_O - 4q_G = 20$$
$$4q_G = 80 - 2q_O$$
$$q_G = 20 - 0.5q_O$$

These reaction curves are shown in the figure in answer b.

b. To solve for equilibrium, we need to substitute one firm's reaction curve into the reaction curve for the other firm:

$$q_O = 22 - 0.5q_G$$
$$q_O = 22 - 0.5(20 - 0.5q_O) = 22 - 10 + 0.25q_O = 12 + 0.25q_O$$
$$0.75q_O = 12$$

$$q_O = 16$$
$$q_G = 20 - 0.5q_O = 20 - 0.5(16) = 20 - 8 = 12$$

Therefore, OilPro produces 16,000 oil changes per year, while GreaseTech produces 12,000.

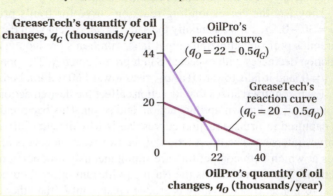

c. We can use the market inverse demand curve to determine the market price:

$$P = 100 - 2Q = 100 - 2(q_O + q_G) = 100 - 2(16 + 12)$$
$$= 100 - 56 = 44$$

The price will be $44 per oil change.

d. OilPro sells 16,000 oil changes at a price of $44 for a total revenue $TR = 16,000 \times \$44 = \$704,000$. Total cost $TC = 16,000 \times \$12 = \$192,000$. Therefore, profit for OilPro is $\pi = \$704,000 - \$192,000 = \$512,000$.

GreaseTech sells 12,000 oil changes at a price of $44 for a total revenue of $TR = 12,000 \times \$44 = \$528,000$. Total cost $TC = 12,000 \times \$20 = \$240,000$. Thus, Grease Tech's profit is $\pi = \$528,000 - \$240,000 = \$288,000$.

Note that the firm with the lower marginal cost produces more output and earns a greater profit.

Comparing Cournot to Collusion and to Bertrand Oligopoly

Let's compare this equilibrium in a Cournot oligopoly ($Q = 40$ million bpd at $P = \$80$) and profit ($2.4 billion per day) to the outcomes in other oligopoly models we've analyzed. These results are described in **Table 11.2**.

Table 11.2 Comparing Equilibria across Oligopolies

Oligopoly Structure	Total Output (million bpd)	Price ($ per barrel)	Industry Profit (per day)
Collusion	30	$110	$2.7 billion
Bertrand (identical products)	60	20	0
Cournot	40	80	2.4 billion

Collusion Let's first suppose Saudi Arabia and Iran can actually get their acts together and collude to behave like a monopolist. In that case, they would treat their separate production decisions q_I and q_{SA} as a single total output, $Q = q_{SA} + q_I$. Following the normal marginal-revenue-equals-marginal-cost procedure, we would find that $Q = 30$ million bpd. Presumably, the two countries would split this output evenly at 15 million bpd because they have the same marginal costs. This is less than the total Cournot oligopoly production of 40 million bpd that we just derived. Furthermore, because monopoly production is lower, the price is higher, too: Plugging this monopoly quantity into the demand curve, price becomes $P = 200 - 3(30) = \$110$ per barrel. We also know that total industry profit must be higher in the collusive monopoly outcome. In this case, it's 30 million bpd × ($110 – $20) = $2.7 billion per day (or $1.35 billion for each country). This total is $300 million per day higher than the Cournot competition outcome. At the collusive monopoly equilibrium, output is lower than at the Cournot equilibrium, and price and profit are higher.

Bertrand Oligopoly with Identical Products Next, let's consider the Nash equilibrium if the two countries competed as in the Bertrand model with identical products. In this case, we know that price will equal marginal cost, so $P = \$20$. Total demand at this price is determined by plugging $20 into the demand curve: $P = 20 = 200 - 3Q$, or $Q = 60$ million bpd. The two countries would split this demand equally, with each selling 30 million bpd. Because both countries sell at a price equal to their marginal cost, each earns zero profit. At the Bertrand equilibrium, output quantity is higher than at the Cournot equilibrium, price is lower, and there is no profit.

Summary To summarize then in terms of total industry output, the lowest is the collusive monopoly outcome, followed by Cournot, then Bertrand:

$$Q_m < Q_c < Q_b$$

The order is the opposite for prices, with Bertrand prices the lowest and the collusive price the highest:

$$P_b < P_c < P_m$$

Similarly, profit is lowest in the Bertrand case (at zero), highest under collusion, with Cournot in the middle:

$$\pi_b < \pi_c < \pi_m$$

Therefore, the Cournot oligopoly outcome is something between those for a monopoly and Bertrand oligopoly (for which the outcome is equivalent to perfect competition). And, unlike the collusive and Bertrand outcomes, the price and output in the Cournot equilibrium depend on the number of firms in the industry.

What Happens if There Are More Than Two Firms in a Cournot Oligopoly?

These intermediate outcomes are for a market with two firms. If more than two firms are in a Cournot oligopoly, the total quantity, profits, and price remain between the monopoly and perfectly competitive extremes. However, the more firms there are, the closer these outcomes get to the perfectly competitive case, with price equaling marginal cost and economic profits being zero. Having more competitors means that any single firm's supply decision becomes a smaller and smaller part of the total market. Its output choice therefore affects the market price less and less. With a very large number of firms in the market, a producer essentially becomes a price taker. It therefore behaves like a firm in a perfectly competitive industry, producing where the market price equals its marginal cost.

Cournot versus Bertrand: Extensions

The fact that the intensity of competition changes with the number of firms in the market is a nice feature of the Cournot model. This prediction is more in line with many people's view of oligopoly than the Bertrand model's prediction that anything more than a single firm leads to a perfectly competitive outcome. The downside of the Cournot framework is that it's a bit more of a stretch than usual to assume that companies can only compete in their quantity choices and have no ability to charge different prices. Oil seems a very special case.

Economists David Kreps and José Scheinkman examined this scenario in more detail and showed (using math that's a bit beyond our level here) that even if firms actually set their prices instead of quantities, the industry equilibrium will still look like a Cournot model as long as the firms first choose their production capacity before they set prices. The firms are then constrained to produce at or below that capacity level once they make their price decisions.[6]

As an example of a market described by the Cournot model, imagine that a few real estate developers in a college town build student apartments that are identical in quality and size. Once these developers have constructed their apartment buildings, they can charge whatever price the market will bear for the apartments, but their choice of prices will be constrained by the total number of apartments they have built. If, for some reason, the developers want to charge a ridiculously low rent of, say, $50 per month, they would probably not be able to satisfy all the quantity demanded at that low price because they only have a fixed number of apartments to rent. If the developers first choose the number of apartments in their buildings and then sell their fixed capacity at whatever prices they select, Kreps and Scheinkman show that the equilibrium price and quantity (which, as it turns out, will equal the developers' capacity choice in this case) will be much like those in a Cournot oligopoly.

This result means that in industries where there are large costs of investing in capacity so that firms don't change their capacity very often, the Cournot model will probably be a good predictor of market outcomes even if firms choose their prices in the short run. (In the long run, the firms could both change their capacity by building more apartment buildings and alter the prices they choose.)

---

[6] David M. Kreps and José A. Scheinkman, "Quantity Precommitment and Bertrand Competition Yield Cournot Outcomes," *Bell Journal of Economics* 14, no. 2 (1983): 326–337.

11.5 Oligopoly with Identical Goods but with a First-Mover: Stackelberg Competition

Model Assumptions Stackelberg Competition with Identical Goods

1. Firms sell identical products.
2. Firms compete by choosing a quantity to produce.
3. All goods sell for the same price (which is determined by the sum total of quantities produced by all the firms combined).
4. Firms do *not* choose quantities simultaneously. One firm chooses its quantity first. The next firm observes this and then chooses its quantity.

The Cournot model gave us a way to analyze oligopolistic markets that are somewhere between collusion/monopoly and Bertrand/perfect competition. As in most oligopoly models, equilibrium in the Cournot model came from firms rationally thinking through how other firms in the market are likely to behave in response to their production decisions.

Importantly, the Cournot model also relies on another assumption whose implications we didn't consider much, namely, that the firms choose simultaneously. That is, each firm chooses its optimal quantity based on what the firm believes its competitor(s) *might* do. If it expects its competitor(s) to produce some other quantity, its own optimal action changes—that was the logic of the reaction curve.

If you more fully contemplate this situation, though, each company has an incentive to try to choose its output level first and force its competitors to be the ones who have to react. The first firm to make its decision could increase its output and say, "Oh well, I have already made more than Cournot says I am supposed to produce. What are you going to do about it?"

An *oligopoly model in which firms make product decisions sequentially*—first one, then another, then (if there are more than two firms) another, and so on—is referred to as **Stackelberg competition**. (Heinrich Freiherr von Stackelberg was an early-twentieth-century German economist who first analyzed this type of oligopoly.) Because the competitor's reaction curve slopes downward in this model, the competitor, seeing the high quantity the original firm is producing, would want to reduce its output. Therefore, this creates a **first-mover advantage**, an *advantage gained in a Stackelberg competition by the initial firm in setting its production quantity*. The firm that moves first is sometimes called the Stackelberg leader. To see how sequential competition changes things, let's revisit our oil producers, Saudi Arabia and Iran.

The market inverse demand for oil was $P = 200 - 3Q$, and both countries had a constant marginal cost of $20 per barrel. Each firm produced where marginal revenue equaled marginal cost:

$$MR_{SA} = 200 - 6q_{SA} - 3q_I = 20$$
$$MR_I = 200 - 6q_I - 3q_{SA} = 20$$

In Cournot competition, we rearranged these equations to solve for each country's reaction curve:

$$q_{SA} = 30 - 0.5q_I$$
$$q_I = 30 - 0.5q_{SA}$$

Stackelberg competition
Oligopoly model in which firms make production decisions sequentially.

first-mover advantage
The advantage gained in a Stackelberg competition by the initial firm in setting its production quantity.

We know that these formulas give the best output each country can choose, taking as given the other country's output level. Plugging one reaction curve into the other gave us the Nash equilibrium, in which each country produced 20 million bpd at a market price of $80 per barrel.

Stackelberg Competition and the First-Mover Advantage

Now suppose Saudi Arabia is a Stackelberg leader: It chooses its quantity first. Iran's incentives remain unchanged. It still has the same residual demand and reaction curve, and the reaction curve continues to show Iran's best response to any choice by Saudi Arabia. In Stackelberg competition, however, Iran will know with certainty what Saudi Arabia's production decision is before it makes its own. Iran reacts optimally to any production choice that Saudi Arabia makes by plugging this value for q_{SA} into its reaction function. Importantly, *Saudi Arabia realizes Iran will do this before it makes its first move.*

Because Saudi Arabia knows that Iran's output is going to be a function of whatever Saudi Arabia chooses first, the Saudis want to take that impact into account when they make their *initial* production decision. In this way, Saudi Arabia can take advantage of being the first mover. To do so, it plugs Iran's best response function into its own demand and marginal revenue curve equations. The fact that the Saudi marginal revenue curve changes means that Saudi Arabia will no longer have the same reaction curve it had in the Cournot model. In that model, Saudi Arabia faced the demand curve

$$P = 200 - 3(q_{SA} + q_I)$$

Now that it is a first-mover in a Stackelberg oligopoly, Saudi Arabia's demand is

$$P = 200 - 3q_{SA} - 3q_I = 200 - 3q_{SA} - 3(30 - 0.5q_{SA}) = 200 - 3q_{SA} - 90 + 1.5q_{SA}$$

Do you see what happened? We substituted Iran's reaction function ($q_I = 30 - 0.5q_{SA}$) directly into the Saudi demand curve. We did this because Saudi Arabia recognizes that, by going first, its output choice affects its demand (and therefore its marginal revenue) both directly and indirectly through its effect on Iran's production decision. The direct effect is captured by the term $-3q_{SA}$ in the equation; this effect is the same as in the Cournot model. The indirect effect comes from the impact of Saudi Arabia's output choice on Iran's production response, embodied in the equation's second q_{SA} term ($1.5q_{SA}$).

We can further simplify this demand curve:

$$P = 110 - 1.5q_{SA}$$

We know from Chapter 9 that Saudi Arabia's marginal revenue curve is then $MR_{SA} = 110 - 3q_{SA}$. Setting this equal to marginal cost ($20 per barrel) and solving for q_{SA} give Saudi Arabia's profit-maximizing output in this Stackelberg oligopoly:

$$MR_{SA} = 110 - 3q_{SA} = 20$$
$$3q_{SA} = 90$$
$$q_{SA} = 30$$

As the first-mover, Saudi Arabia finds it optimal to produce 30 million bpd, 10 million more than the Cournot oligopoly output (20 million bpd).

Next, we need to see how Saudi Arabia's decision affects Iran's optimal production level. To do this, we plug Saudi Arabia's output level into Iran's reaction curve:

$$q_I = 30 - 0.5q_{SA} = 30 - 0.5(30) = 15$$

Iran now produces 15 million bpd, rather than 20 as in the Cournot case. By moving first, Saudi Arabia gets the jump on Iran, leaving Iran no choice but to drop its output level from 20 to 15 million bpd.

Therefore, total production is 45 million bpd in the Stackelberg case. This is more than the output produced in the Cournot oligopoly (40 million). And, because production is higher, the market price must be lower under sequential production decisions than under Cournot's simultaneous-decision framework. Specifically, the price is $200 - 3(30 + 15) = \$65$ per barrel (instead of the Cournot equilibrium price of $80).

Profit changes, too. For Saudi Arabia, profit is $30 \times (65 - 20) = \$1,350$ million/day, $150 million more than its $1,200 million/day profit in the (simultaneous-move) Cournot oligopoly. Such an outcome shows us the advantage of being the first mover. Iran, on the other hand, makes a profit of only $15 \times (65 - 20) = \$675$ million/day, well below its Cournot profit level of $1,200 million/day. In the next chapter on game theory, we will discuss the role of first-mover advantage in strategic decision making in more detail, but you can already see why firms might want to enter a market early.

Although it's somewhat abstract, the idea of Stackelberg competition in which one firm moves first and obtains an advantage that leads later firms to adjust their strategy and reduce their output is very true to life, as we will see in the next chapter.

---

figure it out 11.3

Go online for interactive, step-by-step help in solving the following problem.

Consider again the case of the two oil change producers Oil-Pro and GreaseTech from Figure It Out 11.2. Recall that the market inverse demand for the oil changes is $P = 100 - 2Q$, where Q is the total number of oil changes (in thousands per year) produced by the two firms, $q_O + q_G$. OilPro has a marginal cost of $12 per oil change, while GreaseTech has a marginal cost of $20.

a. Suppose this market is a Stackelberg oligopoly and OilPro is the first-mover. How much does each firm produce? What will the market price of an oil change be? How much profit does each firm earn?

b. Now suppose that GreaseTech is the first-mover in this Stackelberg oligopoly. How much will each firm produce, and what will the market price be? How much profit does each firm earn?

Solution:

a. We need to start by reconsidering the demand for OilPro's product. It is going to move first and we assume that it knows from previous experience that GreaseTech's output is a function of OilPro's output. Thus, we need to substitute GreaseTech's reaction curve, from the illustration in prior Figure It Out 11.2, into the market inverse demand curve to solve for the inverse demand for OilPro.

GreaseTech's reaction curve is $q_G = 20 - 0.5q_O$. Substituting this into the inverse market demand curve, we get

$$P = 100 - 2Q = 100 - 2(q_O + q_G) = 100 - 2q_O - 2q_G$$
$$= 100 - 2q_O - 2(20 - 0.5q_O) = 100 - 2q_O - 40 + q_O = 60 - q_O$$

So, the inverse demand curve for OilPro oil changes is $P = 60 - q_O$. This means that the marginal revenue curve for OilPro is

$$MR_O = 60 - 2q_O$$

Setting $MR = MC$ will provide us with OilPro's profit-maximizing output:

$$MR_O = 60 - 2q_O = 12$$
$$2q_O = 48$$
$$q_O = 24$$

Now that we know q_O, we can substitute it into GreaseTech's reaction curve to find q_G:

$$q_G = 20 - 0.5q_O = 20 - 0.5(24) = 20 - 12 = 8$$

OilPro will produce 24,000 oil changes, while GreaseTech will only produce 8,000. Using the inverse market demand, we can determine the market price:

$$P = 100 - 2(q_O + q_G) = 100 - 2(32) = 100 - 64 = \$36$$

OilPro's profit will be $\pi_O = (\$36 - \$12) \times 24,000 =.$ \$576,000. GreaseTech's profit will be $\pi_G = (\$36 - \$20) \times 8,000 = \$128,000$.

b. If GreaseTech is the first-mover, we can use OilPro's reaction curve (from the figure in prior Figure It Out 11.2) to find the inverse market demand for Grease-Tech. OilPro's reaction curve is $q_O = 22 - 0.5q_G$. Substituting into the market inverse demand, we get

$$P = 100 - 2q_O - 2q_G = 100 - 2(22 - 0.5q_G) - 2q_G$$
$$= 100 - 44 + q_G - 2q_G$$
$$= 56 - q_G$$

This is the inverse demand for GreaseTech's oil changes. Its marginal revenue is therefore

$$MR_G = 56 - 2q_G$$

Setting $MR = MC$, we can see that

$$MR_G = 56 - 2q_G = 20$$
$$2q_G = 36$$
$$q_G = 18$$

To find OilPro's output, we substitute q_G into OilPro's reaction curve:

$$q_O = 22 - 0.5q_G = 22 - 0.5(18) = 22 - 9 = 13$$

So, when GreaseTech is the first-mover, OilPro only produces 13,000 oil changes, while GreaseTech produces 18,000. We can determine the price using the inverse market demand:

$$P = 100 - 2(q_O + q_G) = 100 - 2(31) = \$38$$

GreaseTech's profit will be $\pi_G = (\$38 - \$20) \times 18,000 = \$324,000$. OilPro's profit will be $\pi_O = (\$38 - \$12) \times 13,000 = \$338,000$.

11.6 Oligopoly with Differentiated Goods: Bertrand Competition

Model Assumptions Bertrand Competition with Differentiated Goods

1. Firms do *not* sell identical products. They sell differentiated products, meaning consumers do not view them as perfect substitutes.
2. Each firm chooses the price at which it sells its product.
3. Firms set prices simultaneously.

Every model of imperfect competition that we've looked at so far—collusion, Bertrand, Cournot, and Stackelberg—has assumed that the industry's producers all sell the same product. Often, however, a more realistic description of an industry is a set of firms that make similar but not identical products. When consumers buy cars, breakfast cereals, or even light bulbs, they must choose between competing versions and brands, each with its own unique features, produced by a small number of companies. A *market in which multiple varieties of a common product type are available* is called a **differentiated product market**.

differentiated product market A market in which multiple varieties of a common product type are available.

It is often possible to treat the differentiated products as interacting in a single market, even when it seems as if each one could be considered its own separate market. The key is to explicitly account for the way consumers are willing to substitute among the products.

To see how a Bertrand oligopoly works with differentiated products, think back to the Bertrand model we studied in Section 11.3. There, two companies (Walmart and Target in our example) competed by setting prices for an identical product (the Nintendo Switch). Now, however, instead of thinking of the firms' products as identical as we did in Section 11.3, we assume that consumers view the products as being somewhat distinct. Even though a game console is the same regardless of where customers buy it, the stores offering such a product may have, for example, different locations and customers might care about travel costs. The specific source of the product distinction isn't important. Regardless of its source, any differentiation counts that helps the stores exert more market power and earn more profit. When products are identical, the incentive to undercut price is so intense that firms compete the market price right down to marginal cost and earn zero economic profit as a result. That is not how it works in the differentiated-product Bertrand model, as we see in the following example.

Equilibrium in a Differentiated-Products Bertrand Market

Suppose there are two main manufacturers of snowboards, Burton and K2. Because many snowboarders view the two companies' products as similar but not identical, if either firm cuts its prices, it will gain market share from the other. But because the firms' products aren't *perfect* substitutes, the price-cutting company won't take all the business away from the other company just because it sets its price a bit lower. Some people are still going to prefer the competitor's product, even at a higher price.

This product differentiation means that each firm faces its own demand curve, and each product's price has a different effect on the firm's demand curve. So, Burton's demand curve might be

$$q_B = 900 - 2p_B + p_K$$

As you can see, the quantity of boards Burton sells goes down when it raises the price it charges for its own boards, p_B. On the other hand, Burton's quantity demanded goes up when K2 raises its price, p_K. In this example, we've assumed that Burton's demand is more sensitive to changes in its own price than to changes in K2's price. (For every \$1 change in p_B, there is a 2-unit decrease in quantity demanded; this ratio is 1-to-1 — and positive — for changes in p_K.) Our assumption is a realistic one in many markets.

K2 has a demand curve that looks similar, but with the roles of the two firms' prices reversed:

$$q_K = 900 - 2p_K + p_B$$

The responses of each company's quantity demanded to price changes reflect consumers' willingness to substitute across varieties of the industry's product. But this substitution is limited; a firm can't take over the entire market with a 1 cent price cut, as it can in the identical-products Bertrand model.

To determine the equilibrium in a Bertrand oligopoly model with differentiated products, we follow the same steps we used for all the other models: Assume each company sets its price to maximize its profit, taking the prices of its competitors as given. That is, we look for a Nash equilibrium. To keep things simple, we assume that both firms have a marginal cost of zero.[7]

---

[7] We assume zero marginal cost in this example because the concept of marginal cost is a little different when firms choose prices rather than quantities. Remember that marginal cost is the change in total cost driven by changing output by 1 unit: $MC = \Delta TC/\Delta Q$. As in all other market structures, a firm in a differentiated-product Bertrand oligopoly maximizes profit by setting its marginal revenue equal to its marginal cost. But the expression for marginal revenue in a Bertrand setup is the change in revenue resulting from small *price* changes, or $MR = \Delta TR/\Delta P$, rather than from small *quantity* changes, or $MR = \Delta TR/\Delta Q$. Therefore, the profit-maximizing price in a differentiated-products Bertrand oligopoly sets this price-based marginal revenue equal to a price-based marginal cost: $\Delta TR/\Delta P = \Delta TC/\Delta P$. We could go through some extra algebra to tie the two together, but it's easier for our purposes here to just assume that marginal costs are zero.

Burton's total revenue is

$$TR_B = p_B \times q_B = p_B \times (900 - 2p_B + p_K)$$

Notice that we've written total revenue in terms of Burton's price, rather than its quantity. This is because in a Bertrand oligopoly, Burton chooses the price it will charge rather than how much it will produce. Writing total revenue in price terms lets us derive the marginal revenue curve in price terms as well. Namely, marginal revenue is

$$MR_B = 900 - 4p_B + p_K$$

(Recall that the marginal revenue curve of a linear inverse demand curve is just the inverse demand curve with the quantity coefficient doubled. The same logic holds when marginal revenue is expressed in terms of price.) We can solve for Burton's profit-maximizing price through the usual step of setting this marginal revenue equal to the marginal cost (zero in this case). Doing so and rearranging gives

$$MR_B = 900 - 4p_B + p_K = 0$$
$$4p_B = 900 + p_K$$
$$p_B = 225 + 0.25p_K$$

Notice how this again gives a firm's (Burton's) optimal action as a function of the other firm's action (K2's). In other words, this equation describes Burton's reaction curve. But here, the actions are price choices rather than quantity choices as in the Cournot model.

K2 has a reaction curve, too. It looks similar to, but is a little different than, Burton's because K2's demand curve is slightly different. Repeating the same steps as above, we have

$$MR_K = 900 - 4p_K + p_B = 0$$
$$4p_K = 900 + p_B$$
$$p_K = 225 + 0.25p_B$$

An interesting detail to note about these reaction curves in the Bertrand differentiated-product model is that a firm's optimal price *increases* when its competitor's price increases. If Burton believes K2 will charge a higher price, for instance, Burton wants to raise its price. That is, the reaction curves are upward-sloping. This is the opposite of the quantity reaction curves in the Cournot model (review Figure 11.3). There, a firm's optimal response to a competitor's output change is to do the opposite: If a firm expects its competitor to produce more, then it should produce less.

Differentiated Bertrand Equilibrium: A Graphical Approach   **Figure 11.4** plots Burton's and K2's reaction curves. The vertical axis shows Burton's optimal profit-maximizing price; the horizontal axis represents K2's optimal profit-maximizing price. The positive slope of Burton's reaction curve indicates that Burton's profit-maximizing price rises when K2 charges more. The positive slope of K2's reaction curve indicates that K2's profit-maximizing price rises when Burton charges more. If Burton expects K2 to charge $100, then Burton should price its boards at $250 (point *A*). If instead Burton believes K2 will price at $200, then it should price at $275 (point *B*). A K2 price of $400 will make Burton's optimal response $325 (point *C*), and so on. K2's reaction curve works the same way.

The point where the two reaction curves cross, *E*, is the Nash equilibrium. There, both firms are doing as well as they can given the other's actions. If either were to decide on its own to change its price, that firm's profit would decline.

Differentiated Bertrand Equilibrium: A Mathematical Approach   We can algebraically solve for this Nash equilibrium as we did in the Cournot model—by finding the point at which the reaction curve equations equal one another. Mechanically, that means we substitute one reaction curve into the other, solve for one firm's optimal price, and then use it to solve for the other firm's optimal price.

➡ The online appendix finds the equilibrium for differentiated Bertrand competition using calculus.

Figure 11.4   Nash Equilibrium in a Bertrand Market

This shows Burton and K2's reaction curves. At point *E*, when each company sells 600 snowboards at a market price of $300 per snowboard, the market is at a Nash equilibrium, and the two companies are producing optimally.

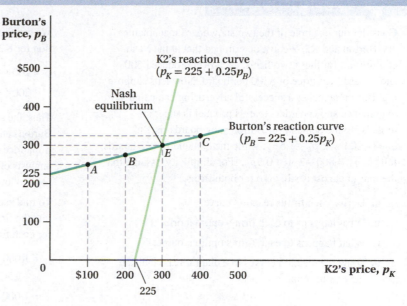

First, we plug K2's reaction curve into Burton's and solve for Burton's equilibrium price:

$$p_B = 225 + 0.25 p_K$$
$$p_B = 225 + 0.25 \times (225 + 0.25 p_B)$$
$$p_B = 225 + 56.25 + 0.0625 p_B$$
$$0.9375 p_B = 281.25$$
$$p_B = 300$$

Substituting this price into K2's reaction curve gives its equilibrium price:

$$p_K = 225 + 0.25 p_B = 225 + (0.25 \times 300) = 225 + 75 = 300$$

In equilibrium, both firms charge the same price, $300. This isn't too surprising. After all, the two firms face similar-looking demand curves and have the same (zero) marginal costs. Interestingly, the particular implication of the identical-products Bertrand oligopoly that we looked at in Section 11.3 (that both firms charge the same price in equilibrium) holds here. The difference is that the price no longer equals marginal cost. Instead, equilibrium prices are above marginal cost ($300 is a lot more than zero).

To figure out the quantity each firm sells, we plug each firm's price into its demand curve equation. Burton's quantity demanded is $q_B = 900 - 2(300) + 300 = 600$ boards. K2 also sells $q_K = 900 - 2(300) + 300 = 600$ boards. Again, the fact that both firms sell the same quantity is not surprising because they have similar demand curves and charge the same price. Total industry production is therefore 1,200 boards, which is two-thirds of what it would be if both firms charged their marginal costs (each firm in that case would make 900 boards, meaning total production of 1,800 boards). In the Bertrand model where the firms produce differentiated products, each firm earns a profit of $600 \times (300 - 0) = \$180,000$.

In this example, both firms had demand curves that were mirror images of each other. If instead the firms had different demand curves, we would go about solving for equilibrium prices, quantities, and profits the same way, but these probably wouldn't be the same for each firm.

figure it out 11.4

Consider our example of the two snowboard manufacturers, Burton and K2. We just determined that at the Nash equilibrium for these two firms, each firm produced 600 snowboards at a price of $300 per board. Now let's suppose that Burton launches a successful advertising campaign to convince snowboarders that its product is superior to K2's, so the demand for Burton snowboards rises to $q_B = 1,000 - 1.5p_B + 1.5p_K$, while the demand for K2 boards falls to $q_K = 800 - 2p_K + 0.5p_B$. (For simplicity, assume that the marginal cost is still zero for both firms.)

a. Derive each firm's reaction curve.

b. What happens to each firm's optimal price?

c. What happens to each firm's optimal output?

d. Draw the reaction curves in a diagram and indicate the equilibrium.

Solution:

a. To determine the firms' reaction curves, we first need to solve for each firm's marginal revenue curve:

$$MR_B = 1,000 - 3p_B + 1.5p_K$$
$$MR_K = 800 - 4p_K + 0.5p_B$$

By setting each firm's marginal cost equal to marginal revenue, we can find the firm's reaction curve:

$$MR_B = 1,000 - 3p_B + 1.5p_K = 0$$
$$3p_B = 1,000 + 1.5p_K$$
$$p_B = 333.33 + 0.5p_K$$

$$MR_K = 800 - 4p_K + 0.5p_B = 0$$
$$4p_K = 800 + 0.5p_B$$
$$p_K = 200 + 0.125p_B$$

b. We can solve for the equilibrium by substituting one firm's reaction curve into the other's:

$$p_B = 333.33 + 0.5p_K$$
$$p_B = 333.33 + 0.5(200 + 0.125p_B)$$
$$= 333.33 + 100 + 0.0625p_B$$
$$p_B = 433.33 + 0.0625p_B$$
$$0.9375p_B = 433.33$$
$$p_B = \$462.22$$

We can then substitute p_B back into the reaction function for K2 to get the K2 price:

$$p_K = 200 + 0.125p_B$$
$$= 200 + 0.125(462.22) = 200 + 57.78 = \$257.78$$

Thus, the successful advertising campaign means that Burton can increase its price from the original equilibrium price of $300 (which we determined in our initial analysis of this market) to $462.22, while K2 will have to lower its own price from $300 to $257.78.

c. To find each firm's optimal output, we need to substitute the firms' prices into the inverse demand curves for each firm's product. For Burton,

$$q_B = 1,000 - 1.5p_B + 1.5p_K = 1,000 - 1.5(462.22)$$
$$+ 1.5(257.78)$$
$$= 1,000 - 693.33 + 386.67 = 693.34$$

For K2,

$$q_K = 800 - 2p_K + 0.5p_B = 800 - 2(257.78) + 0.5(462.22)$$
$$= 800 - 515.56 + 231.11 = 515.55$$

Burton now produces more snowboards (693.34 instead of 600), while K2 produces fewer (515.55 instead of 600).

d. The reaction curves are shown in the diagram below:

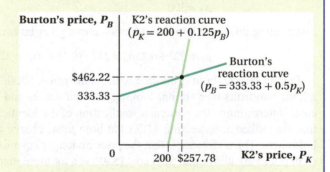

Application: Computer Parts—Differentiation Out of Desperation

Bertrand competition with identical products is extremely intense. In equilibrium, firms set price equal to marginal cost and earn no profit. This is a situation that most firms want to avoid. And, as we just saw, firms can earn profits if their products are differentiated. This gives firms a huge incentive to try to differentiate their products from their competitors' products, even if an outsider to the market might not believe any important differences really exist among them.

This sort of behavior was documented by economists Glenn Ellison and Sara Ellison in an online market for computer chips.[8] In this market, high-tech customers who like to build their own computers shop for CPUs and memory chips using an online price search engine that tracks down and lists the products of various electronic parts retailers.

Ellison and Ellison documented how some computer parts retailers in the market used a little economic know-how to get away with setting their prices above marginal cost. Those firms realized that the key to getting more producer surplus was to differentiate their products, thus shifting the structure of competition from a Bertrand oligopoly with identical products to one with differentiated products.

Just how could these firms differentiate what were otherwise identical computer chips? They couldn't do this the way K2 and Burton can with the snowboards they sell, by varying designs, materials, and so on. So, they turned to slightly more, well, creative methods—methods that Ellison and Ellison categorized as "obfuscation."

Ellison and Ellison found that online firms rely on two primary means of obfuscation. In the first, the firm lists a cheap but inferior product that the price search engine displays at the beginning of its listings. Customers click on this product and are redirected to the firm's website, where the company then offers a more expensive product upgrade. Once one firm undercuts its competitors with this "loss leader" strategy, all firms will list similarly cheap products or risk having their product listing buried deep in the last pages of the listings. As a result, it becomes more time consuming for the customer to compare the prices of the product "upgrades," and the firm can charge a price higher than marginal cost without the risk of being priced out.

Another common strategy is the use of product add-ons. As with the first method, firms list artificially cheap products that bait consumers into visiting their website. This time, instead of upgraded products, customers are offered product add-ons, such as additional screws to fasten the chip to the circuit board or a snazzy mouse pad. Often, these products are added on automatically; that is, to purchase only the original product, the consumer has to unselect a number of additional products. Although the product the consumer initially selected may be selling at or even below marginal cost, the add-ons often sell at inflated prices—the mouse pad one online firm offered cost nearly $12 according to Ellison and Ellison. This practice allows the firm to sell the entire bundle of products at a price above marginal cost.

Obfuscation methods such as these are part of the reason the Bertrand model with identical products that we first studied is so unusual in the real world. Even products that aren't obviously differentiable can be made to stand out through some clever strategies devised by the firms selling them. Given that firms selling such products would otherwise expect to earn something close to nothing, they have a massive incentive to figure out differentiation strategies, and thus try to reduce competition. ∎

---

[8] Glenn Ellison and Sara Fisher Ellison, "Search, Obfuscation, and Price Elasticities on the Internet," *Econometrica* 77, no. 2 (2009): 427–452.

11.7 Monopolistic Competition

Model Assumptions Monopolistic Competition

- Industry firms sell differentiated products that consumers do not view as perfect substitutes.
- Other firms' choices affect a firm's residual demand curve, but the firm ignores any strategic interactions between its own quantity or price choice and that of its competitors.
- There is free entry into the market.

monopolistic competition A market structure characterized by many firms selling a differentiated product with no barriers to entry.

In the models we've studied thus far, we haven't considered the possibility that other firms might want to enter markets in which firms are earning positive economic profits. Presumably, other firms exist that would like a piece of such action. If there are no barriers to entering a market like the snowboard market, an additional firm will cause Burton and K2's profits to decline. We saw in the Cournot model that adding more firms to the industry drove the equilibrium closer to perfect competition. In this section, we look at our last model of imperfect competition, and see what happens when there is entry into a market with differentiated products. **Monopolistic competition** is a *market structure characterized by many firms selling a differentiated product with no barriers to entry*. This term might sound like an oxymoron—competitive monopoly?—and in a way it is, but the term reflects the basic tension between market power and competitive forces that exists in these types of markets.

Every firm in a monopolistically competitive industry faces a downward-sloping demand curve, so it has some market power and every firm follows the monopoly pricing rule. That's where the "monopolistic" comes from. What is *competitive* about such markets is that there are no restrictions on entry as exist in monopoly markets—any number of firms can come into the industry at any time. This means that the firms in a monopolistically competitive industry, despite having market power, earn zero economic profit. (If they were making a profit, more firms would enter to acquire some of it. Entry only stops when profit is driven to zero for every firm in the market.)

Many markets are monopolistically competitive. For example, there are hundreds of fast-food restaurants in Chicago. Some differences between them exist, but basically people view such restaurants as largely interchangeable. Because travel is costly, though, each restaurant has a bit of market power in its local neighborhood. So, a restaurant does have some ability to set its own prices. At the same time, however, there's little to stop a new restaurant from opening. If people in a neighborhood become more enthralled with eating out, an existing restaurant might be able to raise its prices and earn economic profit for a brief period, but if the trend lasts, it is likely that a new restaurant will open up to grab some of that profit.

Keep in mind that, although monopolistic competition is categorized as "imperfect competition" along with oligopoly, there are differences between these two market structures. One is that oligopoly markets have barriers to entry, while monopolistically competitive markets do not. However, the key distinction between oligopoly and monopolistic competition is the assumption about strategic interaction. In an oligopoly, firms know that their production decisions affect their competitors' optimal choices, and all oligopolistic firms take this feedback effect into account when making their decisions. On the other hand, in monopolistic competition, firms do not worry about the production decisions of their competitors because the impact of any competitor on another is assumed to be too small for these firms to be concerned about.

Equilibrium in Monopolistically Competitive Markets

To analyze monopolistically competitive markets, let's look at a single company with market power—say for a moment that, for some reason, a city has only one fast-food restaurant. In this city, that restaurant has a monopoly on fast food. The firm faces a downward-sloping demand curve for meals served per day, as in **Figure 11.5**. We'll label this demand D_{ONE} (for one firm). The figure also shows the marginal revenue curve that corresponds to this demand, as well as the firm's average total and marginal cost curves.

Because the restaurant in Figure 11.5 is a monopolist, it produces where its marginal revenue equals marginal cost, Q^*_{ONE}. The price it charges is P^*_{ONE}. In addition to the marginal cost of production, however, the restaurant has to pay a fixed cost equal to F (this fixed cost is the reason why the firm's average total cost curve is U-shaped). The monopolist restaurant's profit is shown by the shaded rectangle: the difference between the price and the average total cost at the quantity produced, multiplied by that quantity. Because average total cost includes both variable and fixed costs, the average total cost at Q^*_{ONE}—that is, ATC^*—fully reflects all the firm's production costs.

Now suppose another restaurateur notices this firm's profit and decides to compete and open a second, slightly different fast-food restaurant. The new restaurant may differ in location, type of food served, anything that differentiates it from the existing restaurant.

The key to understanding monopolistically competitive markets is to recognize what happens to the demand curve(s) of the market's existing firm(s) when another firm enters. We know that when more substitutes for a good are available, the demand curve for the initial good becomes more elastic (less steep). Having another restaurant open up means that more substitution possibilities now exist for consumers. Instead of there being one firm with a demand curve, as in Figure 11.5, the entry of a second firm means each restaurant now has a demand curve that is a bit flatter than the monopolist firm's demand curve. And, because the demand is being split across two firms, not only is the monopolist firm's demand curve flatter, but it has shifted in as well. **Figure 11.6** shows this change from one

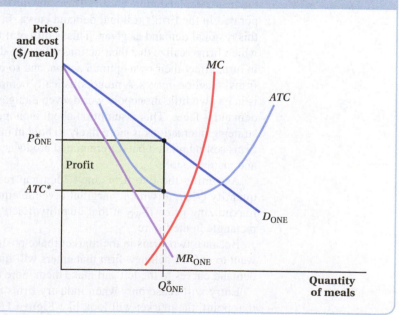

Figure 11.5   Demand and Cost Curves for a Monopoly

A monopolist restaurant has demand D_{ONE}, marginal revenue MR_{ONE}, average total cost ATC, and marginal cost MC. The restaurant produces where marginal revenue equals marginal cost, at quantity Q^*_{ONE}. The restaurant's profit, represented by the shaded rectangle, is the difference between the firm's price P^*_{ONE} and average total cost ATC^*, multiplied by Q^*_{ONE}.

Figure 11.6 Effect of Firm Entry on Demand for a Monopolistically Competitive Firm

When a second restaurant enters the market, the original restaurant's demand curve shifts left from D_{ONE} to the more elastic residual demand curve D_{TWO}, and the marginal revenue curve MR_{ONE} shifts to MR_{TWO}. The restaurant now sells quantity Q^*_{TWO} at price P^*_{TWO} and earns profit represented by the shaded rectangle.

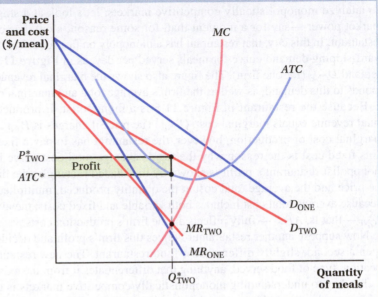

to two firms, as the initial (monopolist) firm's demand curve (now it is a residual demand curve) shifts from D_{ONE} to D_{TWO}. Notice how D_{TWO} is both flatter than D_{ONE} and to the left of it. The marginal revenue curves also shift accordingly. (The figure illustrates only what's going on for one of the two firms in the market; the picture is exactly the same for the other firm.)

Even after entry, however, both firms are essentially monopolists over their own residual demand curves. Each individual firm's demand curve reflects the fact that (1) it is splitting the market with another firm and (2) the presence of a substitute product makes the firm's demand more elastic. The competitor's presence *is* accounted for, but it is incorporated in the firm's residual demand curve. In monopolistic competition, the firm takes this residual demand as given. This is different from the oligopoly models we covered, in which firms realize that their actions affect the desired actions of their competitors, which, in turn, affect their own optimal action, and so on. This strategic interaction is captured in firms' reaction curves. A monopolistically competitive firm, on the other hand, acts as if it is in its own little monopoly world, even though its competitors' actions affect the residual demand it faces. This assumption about monopolistically competitive firms' ignorance of strategic interactions is more likely to hold in industries where there are a large number of firms selling related but differentiated products, such as car washes, self-storage facilities, and mattress stores.

Assuming the two firms have identical residual demand curves, both produce the quantity Q^*_{TWO} at which marginal revenue equals marginal cost and charge the profit-maximizing price P^*_{TWO} at that quantity. Each firm earns the profit given by the shaded rectangle in the figure.

Because two firms in the market make positive economic profit, still more firms will want to enter. Each new firm that enters will further shift the other individual companies' demand curves to the left and make them more elastic (flatter).

Entry will cease only when industry firms are no longer making economic profit. At that point, the market will look like **Figure 11.7**. When there are N firms in the market, each firm's residual demand curve eventually shifts back to D_N. Faced with this demand

Figure **11.7** Long-Run Equilibrium for a Monopolistically Competitive Market

In a monopolistically competitive market with N firms, firms face long-run demand D_N, marginal revenue MR_N, marginal costs M_C, and average total cost ATC. At the long-run equilibrium, the firm's quantity is Q_N^*, price P_N^* is equal to average cost ATC^*, and each firm earns zero economic profit.

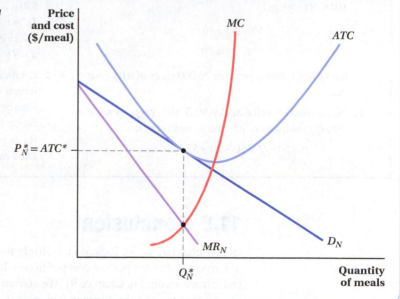

curve, the firm produces the quantity Q_N^* at which marginal revenue equals marginal cost, charges a price of P_N^*, and earns zero economic profit.

Economic profit equals zero at this point because the firm's average total cost curve and its demand curve are tangent at Q_N^* and P_N^*. When price equals average total cost, profit is zero. The firm is just covering its costs of operation (variable and fixed) at this point.

Here's an important point about monopolistically competitive markets: Even though entry occurs until profits are zero, the entry process does not ultimately lead to a perfectly competitive outcome in which price equals marginal cost (because there are fixed costs). Firms in a monopolistically competitive market face a downward-sloping demand curve, so marginal revenue is always less than price. At the profit-maximizing output, marginal cost will equal marginal revenue, which means that marginal cost will also be less than price. Free entry ensures that this markup over marginal cost is just enough to cover the firm's fixed cost, and no more.

 figure it out 11.5

Sticky Stuff produces cases of taffy in a monopolistically competitive market. The inverse demand curve for its product is $P = 50 - Q$, where Q is in thousands of cases per year and P is dollars per case.

Sticky Stuff can produce each case of taffy at a constant marginal cost of $10 per case and has no fixed cost. Its total cost curve is therefore $TC = 10Q$.

a. To maximize profit, how many cases of taffy should Sticky Stuff produce each month?

b. What price will Sticky Stuff charge for a case of taffy?

c. How much profit will Sticky Stuff earn each year?

d. In reality, firms in monopolistic competition generally face fixed costs in the short run. Given the information above, what would Sticky Stuff's fixed costs have to be in order for this industry to be in long-run equilibrium? Explain.

Solution:

a. Sticky Stuff maximizes its profit by producing where $MR = MC$. Since the demand curve is linear, we know from Chapter 9 that the MR curve will be linear with twice the slope. Therefore, $MR = 50 - 2Q$. Setting $MR = MC$, we get

$$50 - 2Q = 10$$
$$Q = 20$$

Sticky Stuff should produce 20,000 cases of taffy each year.

b. We can find the price Sticky Stuff will charge by substituting the quantity into the demand curve:

$$P = 50 - Q = 50 - 20 = \$30 \text{ per case}$$

c. Total revenue for Sticky Stuff will be $TR = P \times Q = \$30 \times 20,000 = \$600,000$. Total cost will be $TC = 10Q = (10 \times 20,000) = \$200,000$. Therefore, Sticky Stuff will earn an annual profit of

$$\pi = TR - TC = \$600,000 - \$200,000 = \$400,000.$$

d. Long-run equilibrium occurs when firms have no incentive to enter or exit. Therefore, firms must be earning zero economic profit. From (c), we know that Sticky Stuff is earning a profit of \$400,000. In order for its profit to be zero, Sticky Stuff must face annual fixed costs equal to \$400,000.

11.8 Conclusion

In this chapter, we've looked at multiple models of imperfect competition—that middle ground between perfect competition (which we studied in Chapter 8) and monopoly (which we studied in Chapter 9). We started with the reminder that the number of firms in a market is only one of many factors that can determine market prices, quantities, and producer profits. So, it's no surprise that there are different models of imperfect competition, each of which offers different predictions about market outcomes. Which model is the most applicable to any market situation requires some judgment on the part of the economist. Are the products essentially identical, or slightly or completely differentiated? Are the firms setting prices or quantities? Are firms making their choices simultaneously or in sequence? Are there barriers to entry or is entry into the market free? These and other questions need to be considered when choosing the imperfect competition model most applicable to the industry being analyzed. In the next chapter, we will examine how individuals and firms may act strategically to achieve a greater outcome (such as increased utility or higher profits).

Summary

1. In oligopolistic markets, each firm makes production decisions conditional on its competitors' actions. The resulting market equilibrium is known as a **Nash equilibrium**, one of the cornerstones of economic game theory. A Nash equilibrium occurs when each firm is doing its best given the actions of other firms. **[Section 11.1]**

2. Oligopolistic firms may be able to form cartels, in which all participating firms coordinate their production decisions and act collectively as a monopoly. The resulting market quantity and price are equal to those from a monopoly, and industry profit is maximized. While collusive behavior allows firms to capture monopoly profits, **collusion** and **cartels** are rarely stable because every firm has the incentive to increase its own profit by producing more (pricing lower). **[Section 11.2]**

3. In **Bertrand competition**, products are identical and firms compete on price. Each firm simultaneously sets the price of its good, and consumers then choose to purchase all

the quantity demanded from whichever firm has the lowest price, even if the price is only one penny lower. The Bertrand model shows that only two firms need to be in a market to achieve the perfectly competitive market outcome where price equals marginal cost. This result arises because firms in these situations have such a strong incentive to try to undercut the prices of their rivals. Market output is equal to the competitive level of output and firm profits are zero. **[Section 11.3]**

4. In contrast to firms in Bertrand competition, firms in **Cournot competition** simultaneously choose the quantity of a good to produce, and not the price at which the good sells. The Cournot equilibrium price is generally above the price in Bertrand competition, but below the monopoly price. The Cournot output is less than the Bertrand level of output, but greater than the output generated by a cartel. Firms in a Cournot oligopoly earn greater profits than those

in the Bertrand model, but less than the monopoly profit. **[Section 11.4]**

5. In **Stackelberg competition,** firms make production decisions sequentially. Because the first firm in an industry can make production decisions independently of other firms and may be able to capture larger profits, a **first-mover advantage** exists for these firms. **[Section 11.5]**

6. In the Bertrand model with differentiated products, consumers in these markets are willing to substitute across goods, but do not consider them identical, or perfect substitutes. As a result, small differences in prices do not lead to all demand being satisfied by the producer with the lowest price (as in the Bertrand oligopoly with identical products). **[Section 11.6]**

7. **Monopolistic competition** is a market structure in which firms sell differentiated products, and firms have some characteristics of both monopolies and perfectly competitive firms. Because there are no barriers to entry in a monopolistically competitive market, economic profit is driven to zero through the entry of firms. **[Section 11.7]**

Review Questions

1. Name some different forms of imperfect competition.

2. Define Nash equilibrium. Why do firms in oligopoly situations reach Nash equilibria?

3. Why are collusions and cartels often unstable?

4. What is the market equilibrium in Bertrand competition with identical goods?

5. Contrast Bertrand and Cournot competition. Why do they reach different market equilibria?

6. What does the residual demand curve tell us about a firm's output in Cournot competition?

7. How can reaction curves be used to find a firm's equilibrium in Cournot competition?

8. What causes the first-mover advantage in Stackelberg competition?

9. Contrast the market equilibria in Betrand competition with identical products and with differentiated products.

10. What are the characteristics of a monopolistically competitive firm?

11. When will firms enter a monopolistically competitive industry? At what point will firms stop entering a monopolistically competitive industry?

12. Why do firms in monopolistic competition not reach the perfectly competitive equilibrium?

Problems

(Solutions to problems marked with an asterisk appear at the back of this book. Problems adapted to use calculus are available online.)

1. In 1969, tobacco companies were the largest single product advertisers on television. That same year, the Surgeon General of the United States released a report linking smoking to adverse health consequences. Shortly thereafter, the federal government banned cigarette companies from advertising on television. Suppose you were an executive at a tobacco company at that time. Read Section 11.1 carefully, then explain how you might react to the federal government's advertising ban, and why.

2. Suppose you and a rival are the only producers of oysters in an isolated town. Every morning you both dive for oysters that you will sell in the market that afternoon. Each morning, you both have a choice of bringing up 10 or 20 dozen oysters; each dozen you bring up has a marginal cost of $10. If 20 dozen oysters are brought to market in total, they will sell for $35 each. If 30 dozen oysters are brought to market, they will sell for $25 each. If 40 dozen oysters are brought to market, they will sell for $20 each. The following table shows the profit you and a rival can expect to earn based on your choice of bringing up 10 or 20 dozen oysters each:

		Your Rival	
		10 dozen	**20 dozen**
You	**10 dozen**	250, 250	150, 300
	20 dozen	300, 150	200, 200

a. Verify that the profits represented in the table above are accurate.

b. Where is the Nash equilibrium in the game you and your rival play?

c. Is the Nash equilibrium one that you and your rival would agree to if you were to discuss production before diving each day? If not, explain why that agreement is unlikely to be honored.

d. Draw a parallel between the game described in this problem and the advertising game Disney and Warner Brothers played in Table 11.1.

*3. Because cooking soufflés is incredibly difficult, the supply of soufflés in a small French town is controlled by two bakers, Gaston and Pierre. The demand for soufflés is given by $P = 30 - 2Q$, and the marginal and average total cost of producing soufflés is $6. Because baking a soufflé requires a great deal of work and preparation, each morning Gaston and Pierre make a binding decision about how many soufflés to bake.

a. Suppose that Pierre and Gaston agree to collude, evenly splitting the output a monopolist would make and charging the monopoly price.

   i. Derive the equation for the monopolist's marginal revenue curve.

ii. Determine the profit-maximizing collective output for the cartel.

iii. Determine the price Pierre and Gaston will be able to charge.

iv. Determine profits for Pierre and Gaston individually, as well as for the cartel as a whole.

b. Suppose that Pierre cheats on the cartel agreement by baking one extra soufflé each morning.

   i. What does the extra production do to the price of soufflés in the marketplace?

   ii. Calculate Pierre's profit. How much did he gain by cheating?

   iii. Calculate Gaston's profit. How much did Pierre's cheating cost him?

   iv. How much potential profit does the group lose as a result of Pierre's cheating?

c. Suppose that Gaston, fed up with Pierre's behavior, also begins baking one extra soufflé each morning.

   i. How does the extra production affect the price of soufflés in the marketplace?

   ii. Calculate Gaston's profit. How much did he gain by cheating?

   iii. Calculate Pierre's profit. How much did Gaston's cheating cost him?

   iv. How much potential profit does the group lose as a result of Pierre's and Gaston's cheating?

   v. Demonstrate that it is in neither Pierre's nor Gaston's best interest to cheat further on their agreement.

4. Consider the soufflé bakers Gaston and Pierre, described in Problem 3. Suppose Gaston and Pierre are each faced with the choice of baking 3 or 4 souffles each morning.

a. Calculate the profits each would earn based on the decision each makes. Insert those numbers into the table below, with Gaston's number on the left and Pierre's on the right.

		Pierre	
		Bake 4 Souffles	**Bake 3 Souffles**
Gaston	**Bake 4 Souffles**	____, ____	____, ____
	Bake 3 Souffles	____, ____	____, ____

b. Explain how the profits Gaston earns are conditional on the decision Pierre makes.

c. Draw parallels between this problem and the advertising game Disney and Warner Brothers play in Table 11.1.

5. Suppose in Problem 3 that Gaston can produce soufflés at a constant marginal cost of $5, but Pierre produces soufflés for $7. Together, they collude to produce 3 units each.

a. How much profit will each producer earn? What will be the total profit of the cartel?

b. Gaston observes that he is a more efficient producer than Pierre, and suggests that if they are going to produce 6 units, the cartel's interests are better served if Gaston produces all of the soufflés.

   i. If Gaston produces and sells all the soufflés and Pierre produces nothing, what happens to the profit of the cartel?

   ii. Is Pierre likely to agree not to produce any soufflés?

   iii. Suppose Gaston offers to pay Pierre not to produce any soufflés. How much would Gaston potentially be willing to offer? What is the minimum offer that Pierre should accept?

   iv. Suppose that the deal in part (iii) is reached for Pierre's minimum price. What happens to Pierre's profit if he cheats on his agreement with Gaston and increases his output from zero soufflés to 1? What happens to Gaston's profit?

   v. Compare Pierre's incentive to cheat under this arrangement with the incentive that exists when they split production equally. Also compare Gaston's vulnerability to Pierre's cheating under both arrangements. Why might this cartel choose to use the less profitable method of each member producing 3 units to the potentially more profitable method of having Gaston produce everything?

6. The Organization of Petroleum Exporting Countries (OPEC) is a cartel that attempts to keep oil prices high by restricting output. As part of that process, each member nation is assigned a production quota; most members have nationalized their oil industry so that the government controls overall production. However, member nations routinely exceed their production targets. Read "What Makes Collusion Easier" in Section 11.2; then explain why OPEC often has difficulty keeping output low and prices high. Do you think that violators are more likely to emerge from politically stable countries or unstable countries? From monarchies or democracies?

7. Suppose that the inverse market demand for pumpkins is given by $P = \$10 - 0.05Q$. Pumpkins can be grown by anyone at a constant marginal cost of $1.

a. If there are lots of pumpkin growers in town so that the pumpkin industry is competitive, how many pumpkins will be sold, and what price will they sell for?

b. Suppose that a freak weather event wipes out the pumpkins of all but two producers, Linus and Lucy.

Both Linus and Lucy produced bumper crops and have more than enough pumpkins available to satisfy the demand at even a zero price. If Linus and Lucy collude to generate monopoly profits, how many pumpkins will they sell, and what price will they sell for?

c. Suppose that the predominant form of competition in the pumpkin industry is price competition. In other words, suppose that Linus and Lucy are Bertrand competitors. What will be the final price of pumpkins in this market — in other words, what is the Bertrand equilibrium price?

d. At the Bertrand equilibrium price, what will be the final quantity of pumpkins sold by both Linus and Lucy individually, and for the industry as a whole? How profitable will Linus and Lucy be?

e. Would the results you found in parts (c) and (d) be likely to hold if Linus let it be known that his pumpkins were the most orange in town, and Lucy let it be known that hers were the tastiest? Explain.

f. Would the results you found in parts (c) and (d) hold if Linus could grow pumpkins at a marginal cost of $0.95?

8. Andres and Julian have the only liquor licenses in a small resort town. The inverse demand for mimosas (a favorite adult breakfast drink) is given by $P = 8 - 0.5Q$. Mimosas can be produced at a constant average and marginal cost of $2.

a. Adam Smith once wrote, "People of the same trade seldom meet together . . . but the conversation ends in a conspiracy against the public, or in some contrivance to raise prices." Suppose Andres and Julian were to follow Smith's advice and conspire to raise prices to the level a monopolist would charge. What price should they agree to set in order to maximize profits?

b. Suppose both Andres and Julian each have two choices: charge the price you found in (a), or charge $1 less. Fill in the prices each may choose to charge. Then determine the profits each will earn given the choice each makes, and put them in the table below, with Andres's profits before the comma and Julian's after it.

		Julian	
		Price from (a):	$1 less:
Andres	Price from (a):	___,___	___,___
	$1 less:	___,___	___,___

c. Draw parallels between this problem and the advertising game Disney and Warner Brothers play in Table 11.1.

9. Suppose that three grocery stores sell Bubba's Gourmet Red Beans and Rice. Bullseye Market is able to acquire, stock, and market them for $2.00 per package. OKMart can acquire, stock, and market them for $1.98 per package. SamsMart can acquire, stock, and market them for $1.96 per package.

a. If the three competitors are located in close proximity to one another, so the cost of going to a different store to purchase red beans and rice is negligible, and if the market for prepackaged gourmet red beans and rice is characterized by Bertrand competition, what will the prevailing market price be?

b. Where will customers buy their red beans and rice? Bullseye Market, OKMart, or SamsMart? What does your answer suggest about the potential rewards to small improvements in efficiency via cost-cutting?

c. Suppose that each day, equal numbers of customers begin their shopping at each of the three stores. If the cost of going to a different store to purchase red beans and rice is 2 cents, is the Bertrand result likely to hold in this case? Where will customers purchase red beans and rice? Where will they not purchase them?

*10. The platypus is a shy and secretive animal that does not breed well in captivity. But two breeders, Sydney and Adelaide, have discovered the secret to platypus fertility and have effectively cornered the market. Zoos across the globe come to them to purchase their output; the world inverse demand for baby platypuses is given by $P = 1,000 - 2Q$, where Q is the combined output of Sydney (q_S) and Adelaide (q_A).

a. Sydney wishes to produce the profit-maximizing quantity of baby platypus. Given Adelaide's choice of output, q_A, write an equation for the residual demand faced by Sydney.

b. Derive Sydney's residual marginal revenue curve.

c. Assume that the marginal and average total cost of raising a baby platypus to an age at which it can be sold is $200. Derive Sydney's reaction function.

d. Repeat steps (a), (b), and (c) to find Adelaide's reaction function to Sydney's output choice.

e. Substitute Sydney's reaction function into Adelaide's to solve for Adelaide's profit-maximizing level of output. Then use your answer to find Sydney's profit-maximizing level of output.

f. Determine industry output, the price of platypus, and the profits of both Sydney and Adelaide.

g. If Adelaide were hit by a bus on her way home from work, and Sydney were to become a monopolist, what would happen to industry quantity, price, and profit?

11. Suppose that two firms are Cournot competitors. Industry demand is given by $P = 200 - q_1 - q_2$, where q_1 is the output of Firm 1 and q_2 is the output of Firm 2. Both Firm 1 and Firm 2 face constant marginal and average total costs of $20.

    a. Solve for the Cournot price, quantity, and firm profits.

    b. Firm 1 is considering investing in costly technology that will enable it to reduce its costs to $15 per unit. How much should Firm 1 be willing to pay if such an investment can guarantee that Firm 2 will not be able to acquire it?

    c. How does your answer to (b) change if Firm 1 knows the technology is available to Firm 2?

12. Consider the demand for boccie balls shown in the diagram below. Demand is given by $P = 80 - Q$. Boccie balls can be produced at a constant marginal and average total cost of $20.

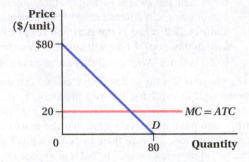

    a. If the boccie ball industry were perfectly competitive, what quantity would be sold, and what price would prevail in the market?

    b. Suppose that the boccie ball industry were a monopoly. Draw in a marginal revenue curve and determine the profit-maximizing quantity.

       i. Divide the monopoly (one-firm) quantity by the competitive quantity to determine the proportion of competitive output that a monopolist provides. Present your answer in reduced fractional form.

       ii. Determine the price and draw a dot on the demand curve indicating the monopolist's price and quantity.

    c. Suppose the boccie ball industry were a Cournot duopoly, with two firms. Use the procedures developed in this chapter to determine the industry output.

       i. Divide the duopoly quantity by the competitive quantity to determine the proportion of competitive output that a duopoly provides. Present your answer in reduced fractional form.

       ii. Determine the price and draw a dot on the demand curve indicating the duopoly's price and quantity.

    d. Hypothesize as to the fraction of competitive output that would be sold if the boccie ball industry had

three identical Cournot competitors. Then check your answer by deriving reaction functions for a three-firm oligopoly and solving for each firm's output.

    e. In general, what fraction of the competitive output level will be brought to market if there are N identical firms in the industry?

    f. What happens to the quantity sold as more competitors are added to the industry? The price? What happens to consumer surplus and deadweight loss? Does this provide support for the government's desire to ensure competitive industries rather than monopolies or small oligopolies?

13. Two organic emu ranchers, Bill and Ted, serve a small metropolitan market. Bill and Ted are Cournot competitors, making a conscious decision each year regarding how many emus to breed. The price they can charge depends on how many emus they collectively raise, and demand in this market is given by $Q = 150 - P$. Bill raises emus at a constant marginal and average total cost of $10; Ted raises emus at a constant marginal and average total cost of $20.

    a. Find the Cournot equilibrium price, quantity, profits, and consumer surplus.

    b. Suppose that Bill and Ted merge and become a monopoly provider of emus. Furthermore, suppose that Ted adopts Bill's production techniques. Find the monopoly price, quantity, profits, and consumer surplus.

    c. Suppose that instead of merging, Bill considers buying Ted's operation for cash. How much should Bill be willing to offer Ted to purchase his emu ranch? (Assume that the combined firms are only going to operate for one period.)

    d. Has the combination of the two ranches discussed above been good for society or bad for society? Discuss how the forces of monopoly power and increased efficiency tend to push social well-being in opposite directions.

*14. The market for nutmeg is controlled by two small island economies, Penang and Grenada. The market demand for bottled nutmeg is given by $P = 100 - q_P - q_G$, where q_P is the quantity Penang produces and q_G is the quantity Grenada produces. Both Grenada and Penang produce nutmeg at a constant marginal and average cost of $20 per bottle.

    a. Verify that the reaction function for Grenada is given by $q_G = 40 - 0.5q_P$. Then verify that the reaction function for Penang is given by $q_P = 40 - 0.5q_G$.

    b. Find the Cournot equilibrium quantity for each island. Then solve for the market price of nutmeg and for each firm's profit.

    c. Suppose that Grenada transforms the nature of competition to Stackelberg competition by announcing its production targets publicly in an attempt to seize a first-mover advantage.

  i. Grenada must first decide how much to produce, and to do this, it needs to know the demand conditions it faces. Substitute Penang's reaction function into the market demand curve to find the demand faced by Grenada.

  ii. Based on your answer to the problem above, find the marginal revenue curve faced by Grenada.

  iii. Equate marginal revenue with marginal cost to find Grenada's output.

  iv. Plug Grenada's output into Penang's reaction function to determine Penang's output.

  v. Plug the combined output of Grenada and Penang into the market demand curve to determine the price. How do the industry quantity and price compare to those under Cournot competition?

  vi. Determine profits in Grenada and Penang. How do the profits of each compare to profits under Cournot competition? Is there an advantage to being the first-mover?

15. Two farmers, Tito and Helen, supply a chain of islands with kale. The inverse demand for kale in the islands is given by $P = 60 - 0.5Q$, where Q is the combined output of Tito (q_T) and Helen (q_H), measured in 10-pound bunches. Tito grows kale at a constant marginal and average cost of \$12 per bunch; Helen grows kale at a constant marginal and average cost of \$10 per bunch.

  a. Suppose this market is a Stackelberg oligopoly and Tito is the first-mover. How much will he and Helen produce? What will the market price of kale be? How much profit will each farmer earn?

  b. Now suppose that Helen is the first-mover in this Stackelberg oligopoly. How much will each farmer produce? What will the market price of kale be? How much profit will each farmer earn?

  c. Quantify the value to Helen of being the first-mover in this Stackelberg game.

16. In each case below, identify the type of competition and determine if there is likely to be a first-mover advantage.

  a. Saudi Arabia, a major oil producer, announces its annual oil production target to the world.

  b. L.L.Bean and Land's End sell nearly identical outerwear via mail order. Each is anxious to publish its fall catalog; once that catalog is published, the firm cannot change its prices without undertaking another costly mailing.

17. August and François are the only sellers of sparkling water at a market in a small, rural French town. They obtain their sparkling water for free from wells in their backyards and transport it to the market in wheelbarrows; neither has access to motorized transportation. Identify the type of oligopoly (Cournot, Bertrand, Stackelberg) that is the best fit for each situation below and explain your reasoning:

  a. August and François both live 4 hours' walk from the market.

  b. August and François both live half a block from the market.

  c. August lives a long walk away, but is an early riser who always arrives at 8:00 A.M.; François lives quite close and never shows up until 8:30.

18. Internet users in a small Colorado town can access the Web in two ways: via their television cable or via a digital subscriber line (DSL) from their telephone company. The cable and telephone companies are Bertrand competitors, but because changing providers is slightly costly (waiting for the cable repairman can eat up at least small amounts of time!), customers have some slight resistance to switching from one to another. The demand for cable Internet services is given by $q_C = 100 - 3p_C + 2p_T$, where q_C is the number of cable Internet subscribers in town, p_C is the monthly price of cable Internet service, and p_T is the price of a DSL line from the telephone company. The demand for DSL Internet service is similarly given by $q_T = 100 - 3p_T + 2p_C$. Assume that both sellers can produce broadband service at zero marginal cost.

  a. Derive the cable company's reaction curve. Your answer should express p_C as a function of p_T.

  b. Derive the telephone company's reaction curve. Your answer should express p_T as a function of p_C.

  c. Combine reaction functions to determine the price each competitor should charge. Then determine each competitor's quantity and profits, assuming that the average total costs are zero.

  d. Suppose that the cable company begins to offer slightly faster service than the telephone company, which alters demands for the two products. Now $q_C = 100 - 2p_C + 3p_T$ and $q_T = 100 - 4p_T + p_C$. Show what effect this increase in service has on the prices and profit of each competitor.

19. Consider two Bertrand competitors in the market for brie, François and Babette. The cheeses of François and Babette are differentiated, with the demand for François' cheese given by $q_F = 30 - p_F + p_B$, where q_F is the quantity François sells, p_F is the price François charges, and p_B is the price charged by Babette. The demand for Babette's cheese is similarly given as $q_B = 30 - p_B + p_F$. Assume that the marginal cost of producing cheese is zero.

  a. Find the Bertrand equilibrium prices and quantities for these two competitors.

  b. Now consider a situation in which François sets his price first and Babette responds. Follow procedures similar to those you used for Stackelberg quantity competition to solve for François's profit-maximizing price, quantity, and profit.

c. Solve for Babette's profit-maximizing price, quantity, and profit.

d. Was François's attempt to seize the first-mover advantage worthwhile?

20. There are only three big tobacco companies, but they produce dozens of brands of cigarettes. Compare and contrast Bertrand competition with undifferentiated and differentiated products to explain why the big three tobacco companies devote many resources to support so many different brands instead of each producing just a single type of generic cigarette. Do you think supporting all these different brands is good for society, or bad?

21. Consider a monopolistically competitive industry. A graph of demand and cost conditions for a typical firm is depicted in the diagram below:

a. Is this firm generating producer surplus? Is this firm earning a profit? How can you reconcile your answers?

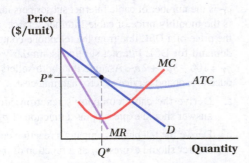

b. Do you expect any entry into or exit from this industry to occur? Explain.

c. Suppose that the government reduces annual licensing fees, causing the fixed cost of the typical firm to fall. Make appropriate shifts of all curves that might be affected. What happens to producer surplus? What happens to profit? Do you expect the fall in fixed costs to cause entry into or exit from this industry? Explain.

d. Shift the demand and marginal revenue curves to reflect the entry/exit you indicated in (c). Find the new equilibrium.

e. Continue to reduce fixed cost. What happens to the demand curve as fixed cost continues to fall? What happens to producer surplus and profit?

f. Find the equilibrium as fixed cost falls to zero.

22. Sally sells brilliant economics lectures to knowledge-seeking students. (This industry is monopolistically competitive: There are at least two other brilliant lecturers Sally competes with.) The inverse demand

for Sally's lectures is given by $P = 60 - 0.5Q$, where Q measures the number of lectures Sally gives each week. The total cost of her delivering lectures is given by $TC = 4Q + F$, where F represents her fixed costs. The marginal cost of each lecture is therefore $4.

a. To maximize profit, how many lectures should Sally deliver each week?

b. What price will Sally charge for her lectures?

c. How much producer surplus will Sally earn?

d. What must Sally's fixed costs be for the industry to be in long-run equilibrium? If Sally's fixed costs were lower than this, what would you expect to happen to the demand for Sally's lectures in the long run?

23. One big question economics ponders is how to produce the greatest material well-being using the fewest resources. Compare and contrast perfect competition and monopolistic competition in achieving that end. (*Hint:* You may want to consider a particular monopolistically competitive industry such as clothing or restaurant meals, and imagine what that industry would look like if it were perfectly competitive instead.) How does your answer depend on your definition of material well-being?

24. When competition between firms is based on quantities (Cournot competition), the reaction functions we derive tell us that when Firm A increases its output, Firm B's best response is to cut its own. However, when competition between firms is based on price (Bertrand competition), reaction functions tell us that Firm B's response to a cut in Firm A's price (which will lead to an increase in the quantity A sells) should be a corresponding cut in B's price (and a corresponding increase in its own output). Reconcile these two results.

*25. Suppose that the market demand for rose hips is given by $P = 100 - Q$. There are two firms, A and B, producing rose hips, each at a constant marginal and average total cost of $5. Fill in the table below for each market structure.

	Collusive Monopoly	Cournot Oligopoly	Bertrand Oligopoly	Stackelberg Oligopoly (A is first-mover)
A's Quantity				
B's Quantity				
Industry Quantity				
Price				
A's Profit				
B's Profit				
Industry Profit				

Game Theory

When Amazon first came out with its e-book reading device, the Kindle, it priced the books at $9.99, below the royalties that Amazon had to pay the publishers. Analysts figured that Amazon's plan was to lose money on the books in order to sell more Kindle devices at high margins. As we discussed in Chapter 11's Freakonomics box, however, Apple soon thereafter released the iPad equipped with its own e-book reader as well as many other capabilities. Competition between the devices drove Amazon to cut the price of its Kindle significantly. Next, Amazon created a Kindle app for the iPad that allowed iPad users to purchase and read their Kindle books on their Apple devices. Then, to compete directly with Apple's iPad, Amazon released its own tablet device, the Fire, at a price considerably lower than the iPad. Each of these decisions entailed strategic considerations by Apple and Amazon. When deciding what to do, the companies needed to think through the moves they could make and the countermoves their competitor would likely undertake in response.

In the previous chapter, we looked at various ways in which firms make price and quantity decisions in industries in which they have some market power but also face some competition. We discussed how market equilibrium in these situations requires more than just quantity supplied equaling quantity demanded. Each individual firm must also be unwilling to change its price or output decisions once it knows its competitors' price or output decisions. In other words, the point at which quantity demanded equals quantity supplied must also be a Nash equilibrium.

The firm interactions we covered in the last chapter, just like the interactions between Amazon and Apple, are more complicated than those in perfectly competitive or monopolistic markets. These market structures involve many possible market outcomes because of strategic interactions between imperfectly competitive firms. Each firm's actions affect not only its own payoff but also the other firms' payoffs. Because every firm takes this interconnectedness into account when planning what to do, decision making can become quite complex.

Being able to understand what might happen when economic actors interact strategically, as they do in oligopoly markets, is the purpose of **game theory**, *the study of strategic interactions among two or more economic actors*, and is the focus of this chapter. Game theory concerns behavior when several players make decisions knowing their actions affect others, others' actions affect them, and they are trying to anticipate the actions of others. These are **strategic decisions**, *actions made based on the anticipation of others' actions*.

Game theory applies to *real* games, too. Playing chess well involves choosing your moves based on how you believe your opponent will respond. In poker, if you raise the bet, you're contemplating whether the other players believe you have good cards and will therefore fold, or believe you are bluffing and will call your bet. In this chapter, we learn that game theory can be used to better understand all kinds of economic decisions, such as when movies are released, what products companies choose to produce, how to deter the entry of competitors, and many others. Truth be told, we already used a fair amount of game theory in the previous chapter. The oligopoly models—collusion, Bertrand,

game theory The study of strategic interactions among two or more economic actors.

strategic decision An action made based on the anticipation of others' actions.

Cournot, Stackelberg, and differentiated-product Bertrand—are all specific applications of game theory.

In this chapter, we study three basic categories of games. First are **simultaneous games**, *in which participants choose their actions at the same time without knowing their opponents' strategies*. Examples of simultaneous games include Chapter 11's Cournot and Bertrand models, in which firms choose quantities or prices simultaneously. Next, we look at **repeated games**, a *series in which the players play the same simultaneous game over and over*. Our discussion in Chapter 11 about how collusion could be stable in some circumstances even though every colluding firm has an incentive to cheat on the agreement can be explained by considering the collusive model as a repeated game. Finally, we look at **sequential games**, *games where one player moves first and other players observe this action before making their decisions*. These games are like the Stackelberg oligopoly we analyzed in Chapter 11.

Being comfortable with these three basic types of game structures gives us a useful tool for understanding many economic scenarios. That said, there are many other, more advanced areas of game theory we won't cover in this chapter, such as situations in which some players have information that other players do not. These are known as games with asymmetric information; we discuss the role of asymmetric information in economic decision making in Chapter 16. Another set of games we won't cover are *cooperative games*, in which players are able to make binding commitments to one another and can form coalitions that play as a single unit. We instead focus on *noncooperative games*, in which it's every player for herself, which we think is the most relevant given the nature of competition between firms (and customers).

Several themes emerge as we apply game theory to understand the strategic interactions producers and consumers engage in every day. First, understanding game theory is all about being able to see the world through the eyes of the other guy. A player must anticipate what her opponents will do and plan for it. A second theme is that much of game theory (at least the kind we study in this chapter) rests on the view that opponents are rational; that is, they know what's good for them. If that isn't true (and who hasn't had to deal with some irrational bozo, on occasion?), what a player should do may vary quite a lot from the standard game-theoretical approach.

A final theme evokes something we discussed while analyzing oligopoly in Chapter 11. How you set up the rules of the game—who gets to move first, or who starts with what—can make a big difference in the outcomes that game theory predicts.

12.1 What Is a Game?

Every game, no matter how simple or complex, shares three common elements: players, strategies, and payoffs. We describe what each of these concepts means in the context of game theory to lay the groundwork for our analysis in the rest of the chapter.

Players are *participants in an economic game who must decide on actions based on the actions of others*. They are the decision makers. They face situations in which outcomes they care about are affected by both their own choices and the choices of others. Players in economic games can be firms (and their managers), consumers, workers, or many other entities. Regardless of their role, however, by definition, all players make choices.

A **strategy** is a *player's plan of action for a game*. Generally, the strategy a player chooses to pursue depends on the anticipated actions of other players. That is, the strategy a player chooses depends on what strategies she *thinks* her competitors will use. Strategies can be simple, such as "I'll redesign my product this year no matter what my competitor does," or more complex, such as "If the other firm keeps its price high for the next three

---

simultaneous games Games in which participants choose their actions at the same time without knowing their opponents' strategies.

repeated games A series in which the players play the same simultaneous game over and over.

sequential games Games where one player moves first and other players observe this action before making their decisions.

player A participant in an economic game who must decide on actions based on the actions of others.

strategy A player's plan of action for a game.

months, I'll raise my price. Otherwise, I will keep prices low and try to take some market share from it." In fact, instead of being dependent on the actions of an opponent, a strategy can even be random: "I'll flip a coin. If it comes up heads, I'll charge a low price, and if it comes up tails, I'll charge a high price."

Payoffs are the *outcomes players receive from playing the game.* For consumers, the payoff may be measured in terms of utility or consumer surplus. For firms, payoffs generally represent producer surplus or profits. Most of the time, one player's payoff depends on the strategies that both the player and her opponents choose. The fact that the players' actions affect each other's payoffs and that they know about this effect ahead of time is what makes game theory *game* theory. When only the player's own choices affect her payoffs, that is called a *single-agent problem.* A monopolist choosing an output level given the demand and marginal cost curves it faces or the consumer's utility-maximization problem are examples of single-agent problems. Once a player's payoffs are affected by others' choices, however, it's a game. The player now has an incentive to understand what motivates her opposing players. The better she can understand her opponents' motivations, the better the choices she can make in response.

These are the three common elements of games, and you need to understand them to be able to predict the likely outcomes of strategic interactions. But a key to forming those predictions—that is, to pinning down a game's equilibrium outcome—is to understand how players' strategies intertwine. The next section deepens our knowledge of strategies before we move on to analyzing various types of games.

payoffs The outcomes the players receive from playing the game.

Dominant and Dominated Strategies

Predicting behavior in games is about finding a player's **optimal strategy**—the *action that has the highest expected payoff.* This can be difficult because a particular strategy may be optimal for a player if her opponent chooses one action, but not optimal if her opponent chooses another action (this is another way of saying her optimal strategy must be a best response to the other player's chosen strategy). Some situations, though, don't entail that level of complexity; we start by talking about those simpler situations.

A strategy that is always the best thing for a player to do is called a **dominant strategy**, a *winning strategy for a player, regardless of her opponents' strategies.* Strategies that are never the right thing to do are called **dominated strategies**, *losing strategies for a player, regardless of her opponents' strategies.*

Let's think back to our example from the last chapter: the advertising decisions of Warner Brothers and Disney with regard to their superhero movies. **Table 12.1** (a reprint of Table 11.1) is an example of a **payoff matrix**, a *table that lists the players, strategies, and payoffs of an economic game.* The first (left) payoff always belongs to the row player; the second (right) payoff always belongs to the column player. Thus, Warner Brothers'

optimal strategy The action that has the highest expected payoff.

dominant strategy A winning strategy for a player, regardless of her opponents' strategies.

dominated strategy A losing strategy for a player, regardless of her opponents' strategies.

payoff matrix A table that lists the players, strategies, and payoffs of an economic game.

Table 12.1 An Advertising Game*

		DISNEY	
		Advertise	**Don't Advertise**
WARNER BROTHERS	**Advertise**	250, 250	550, −80
	Don't Advertise	−80, 550	320, 320

*Outcomes are measured in millions of dollars of profit.

choices are shown on the left (the rows of the payoff matrix) and its payoffs are listed in red, before the comma. Disney's choices are listed along the top of the table (the columns of the payoff matrix) and its payoffs are in blue, after the comma.

In Chapter 11, we saw that this game is a prisoner's dilemma: Even though Warner Brothers and Disney could both make higher profits if they agreed not to advertise, each had such a strong individual incentive to advertise that they both ended up committing to a full advertising budget.

The expression "prisoner's dilemma" comes from the classic example often used to introduce people to the concept behind this type of game. In the example, two suspected conspirators are brought in by the police and interviewed in separate rooms. If neither confesses, the district attorney will only have enough evidence to convict them on a lesser charge, and they will quickly go free. If both confess, they will be convicted of a serious crime and severely punished. If one confesses but not the other, the one who confesses will get a lighter sentence for cooperating, and the other will receive an especially harsh sentence. Although it is clear the prisoners would be best off if they could coordinate on remaining silent, the payoff structure of the game is set up so that each has the unilateral incentive to confess. This makes the game's Nash equilibrium unappealing (at least to the suspects): Both confess and receive severe sentences. Here, Warner Brothers and Disney are the prisoners and advertising is akin to confessing.

The reason for such an outcome is that in this game, the "Advertise" strategy is a *dominant strategy* for both companies. That is, Warner Brothers makes more profit by advertising *Wonder Woman* 2 whether Disney advertises *Black Panther* 2 or not. If Disney does not advertise, Warner Brothers earns $550 million if it advertises instead of $320 million if it doesn't. If Disney *does* advertise, Warner Brothers earns $250 million if it also advertises, but loses $80 million if it doesn't. If we do a similar analysis for Disney's response to Warner Brothers' advertising decisions, we arrive at the same result.

On the other side of the coin, the "Don't Advertise" strategy is never the best thing to do. In other words, it is a dominated strategy because "Advertise" is a dominant strategy. (When one strategy is dominant, all other strategies must be dominated.) There is never a situation in which Disney's or Warner Brothers' payoffs are larger from choosing "Don't Advertise" than from choosing "Advertise."

The notion of dominated strategies is useful for finding the equilibrium in a game. Because a dominated strategy is not a player's best choice under any circumstances, it makes no sense for a player to ever choose such a strategy. So, the first thing to do when analyzing any game is to go through the payoff matrix and eliminate all the dominated strategies as possible equilibrium outcomes for *all* players. In the game represented in Table 12.1, this process eliminates the "Don't Advertise" row for Warner Brothers because Warner Brothers can always achieve a higher payoff from advertising, so it will not select this strategy. Likewise, we want to eliminate the "Don't Advertise" column for Disney for the same reason. Note that not every game has dominated strategies. If a game has dominated strategies, however, as does this Warner Brothers–Disney game, it is much easier to find the game's equilibrium outcome once the dominated strategies have been ruled out as possibilities.

After crossing out this row and column, a look at the remaining square shows there's only one possible strategy for rational players to pursue: Both Warner Brothers and Disney end up advertising and earning $250 million each. Notice that we are sure of this outcome even though both companies must make their decisions simultaneously. That is, they do not know what action the other company will take before making their own choices, but they can anticipate that a rational competitor would never use dominated strategies such as "Don't Advertise."

12.2 Nash Equilibrium in Simultaneous Games

In Chapter 11, we had to expand the concept of equilibrium to apply it to market outcomes in oligopolistic industries. Because each oligopolistic firm's price and quantity decisions influence those of its competitor, equilibrium in oligopolies requires more than just an equilibrium price and quantity for the industry as a whole. The stable market equilibrium *also* requires that no firm in the industry wants to change its decision *given* the choices its competitors are making.

A Nash equilibrium is a natural concept for determining the likely outcome of a game. In a Nash equilibrium, no player wants to unilaterally change her strategy given whatever strategies the other players are choosing. That is, the players are all doing the best they can, given the others' actions.

Lots of dominated strategies in a game, as in the Warner Brothers–Disney example above, make finding a Nash equilibrium easy. However, in most games, eliminating dominated strategies alone won't completely pin down Nash equilibria. That's because the conditions that must hold in a Nash equilibrium are not as stringent as those that define dominant and dominated strategies. A dominant strategy is *always* the best thing for a player to do, no matter what an opponent does. But a Nash equilibrium only requires that an action is the best thing a player can do *given the action the opponent happens to be taking.* Therefore, a game can have a Nash equilibrium even if it has no dominated or dominant strategies. Finding the equilibrium in these more general cases can still be straightforward if there aren't too many players or possible actions.

The first step to finding a Nash equilibrium in any game is to lay out the game's players, strategies, and the payoffs that result from each combination of strategies. Table 12.1 does this for the Warner Brothers–Disney game. This particular way of organizing the economic content of a game is called the **normal form**, the *common organization of an economic game into its players, strategies, and the payoffs in a payoff matrix.* Putting a game into normal form makes it easier to determine what its equilibria are.

Let's do an example with a new game. Two competing magazines, *I'm Famous Weekly* and *Look at Me! Magazine*, are considering what cover story to use for their next issue. They each have the same two choices, which we'll label new reality show (RS) and celebrity interview (CI). We assume that neither magazine can observe its competitor's cover choice until the issue where the cover story appears hits the newsstands, so both magazines must make their choices simultaneously. In addition, say some readers only like stories about new reality shows, others only like celebrity interviews, and the readers who prefer celebrity interviews outnumber those who like reality show articles. If a magazine is the only one offering a particular type of story, it will secure all those readers. If both offer the same story, they will split the same group of readers between them, but *Famous* will receive a larger share than *Me!* because a majority of readers prefer *Famous*, all else equal.

The profits (in thousands of dollars, net of expenses of course) that each magazine earns depend on its own choice for a cover story as well as its competitor's choice. These choices and their payoffs are shown in **Table 12.2**. As before, the red number before the comma in each cell is the payoff to *I'm Famous Weekly*, and the blue number after the comma is the payoff to *Look at Me! Magazine*.

To zero in on the game's Nash equilibrium, let's first consider *Famous*'s best responses to *Me!*'s possible actions. If *Me!* chooses an RS cover story (left column), then *Famous*'s best action is to choose a CI cover. This is because it will earn a $500,000 payoff by choosing CI but only $300,000 by choosing RS. To keep track of this best response, we'll put

normal form The common organization of an economic game into its players, strategies, and the payoffs in a payoff matrix.

Table 12.2 Choosing a Cover Story*

		Look at Me! Magazine's Cover Story	
		Reality Show (RS)	Celebrity Interview (CI)
I'm Famous Weekly's Cover Story	Reality Show (RS)	300, 0	400, 400 ✓
	Celebrity Interview (CI)	✓ 500, 300 ✓	✓ 450, 200

*Payoffs are measured in thousands of dollars of profit.

a check next to *Famous*'s payoff in the bottom left cell. If *Me!* runs a CI cover, *Famous*'s best response is still to choose CI because it earns $450,000 instead of $400,000. Because that is *Famous*'s best response in this situation, we put another check next to the $450. We can see that choosing a celebrity interview as its cover story is a dominant strategy for *Famous*; no matter what *Me!* does, *Famous* makes more money by going with the CI cover.

Now let's do the same exercise for *Me!* If *Famous* chooses a reality show cover, then *Me!* should choose a celebrity interview cover, because it will make $400,000 of profit rather than $0. We put a check next to the $400 payoff in the upper-right cell to indicate that this is a best response for *Me!*. However, if *Famous* chooses a CI cover, *Me!* is better off choosing an RS cover. It will make $300,000 instead of $200,000 by doing so, because it will have the reality show readers all to itself rather than splitting the set of celebrity interview fans. Another check goes next to the $300 payoff for *Me!* in the lower-left corner.

Looking at the pattern of checks (i.e., the pattern of best-response strategies), we can see several things right away. First, *Famous* will choose a celebrity interview for its cover because this is a dominant strategy. Why? Remember that a dominant strategy is the best strategy for a player to follow no matter what the other player does. Because choosing a celebrity interview cover results in higher payoffs (profits) for *Famous* no matter what *Me!* does (note the check marks for *Famous*'s payoffs in Table 12.2), the celebrity interview is a dominant strategy for *Famous*. And, because a reality show cover is never the best option for *Famous*, RS is a dominated strategy.

Me! Magazine, on the other hand, has no dominant strategy: If *Famous* chooses an RS cover, then *Me!* is better off choosing CI. If *Famous* instead chooses a CI cover, *Me!* will earn a higher profit by choosing a reality show cover. Thus, *Me!*'s best strategy changes with the choice made by *Famous*; no one strategy is best under all circumstances, so *Me!* has no dominant strategy. It also has no dominated strategy because both strategies (RS and CI) can each be a best strategy for *Me!*, depending on *Famous*'s action.

Second, even though we can't eliminate many possible outcomes by getting rid of dominated strategies, there is still a Nash equilibrium to the game. In fact, we can see that *Famous* choosing a CI cover story and *Me!* choosing an RS cover are a mutual best response—both players have checks by their payoffs in this cell. Therefore, such a scenario is a Nash equilibrium. As is true of Nash equilibria in general, even if you gave either magazine the ability to unilaterally change its strategy choice, once one magazine knew what the other was doing, it wouldn't want to switch because doing so would only reduce its profit. That stability is a primary reason why the Nash equilibrium is useful for predicting the outcomes of games.

A⁺ make the grade

The check method

Solving games can be challenging and complicated. But there are ways to simplify games that will make you a Nash equilibrium expert in no time!

To begin, always look at each player's decision-making process separately. Suppose you are trying to solve a game with two players, "Row" and "Column," each of whom can take one of two actions: "A" or "B."

Let's start by considering how Row should form her strategy:

- First, ask, *"If Column chooses action A, what is the best action for Row to take?"* Then place a check mark next to the payoff for that action for Row. Row's payoffs should always be to the left of the comma in payoff matrices.

- Next, ask, *"If Column chooses action B, what is the best action for Row to take?"* Then place a check mark next to that option.

Second, repeat the exercise from Column's perspective:

- First, ask, *"If Row chooses A, what is the best action for Column to take?"* Check mark that payoff. (Remember that Column's payoffs should always be to the right of the comma in payoff matrices.)

- Next, ask, *"If Row chooses B, what is the best action for Column to take?"* Another check mark.

Once you have finished looking at the game from both players' perspectives, consider all the boxes in the payoff matrix. Do any have two check marks? If so, those are Nash equilibria. However, if none have double check marks, then the game does not have a Nash equilibrium (at least in pure strategies, covered later in this section).

The following sample game illustrates this method at work. (We print the payoff matrix in black ink rather than red and blue, so you can see what a matrix will look like on an assignment or exam.)

First, we examine Row's choices. If Column chooses action A, Row is better off choosing A (100 > 50). If Column chooses action B, Row is once again better off choosing action A (125 > 75). Therefore, we place check marks next to both of Row's payoffs from choosing A.

Next, we consider Column's choices. If Row chooses action A, Column is better off choosing B (100 > 50). If Row chooses action B, however, Column is better off choosing A (100 > 75). We place check marks next to these payoffs.

Note that there is only one box in the payoff matrix in which two check marks appear: Row selecting A and Column choosing B. This is the Nash equilibrium of the game.

You can also use this method to find dominant and dominated strategies for each player. A dominant strategy is a strategy that is best for a player *no matter what action the other player takes*. Consider Row's decision we described above. If her answer to both questions is the same (always choose action A no matter what action Column takes or always choose B no matter what action Column takes), that strategy is a dominant strategy. You can then cross out the alternative (dominated) strategy, allowing you to reduce the game to fewer options. Then repeat the process for Column. Crossing out can only occur when there are dominated strategies. When using the check method, dominated strategies are indicated by rows or columns without any check marks.

Remember that following dominant strategies will lead to a Nash equilibrium but not all Nash equilibria involve dominant strategies. Here is an easy way to tell the difference (again using our example from above):

Row: *"Column, I don't care what you do! **No matter what action you take,** I am always better off choosing action A."* (In other words, Row has a dominant strategy.)

Column: *"Row, your choice influences my best option. **Given that you are choosing action A,** I am better off choosing action B."* (Column has no dominant strategy, but choosing B when Row chooses A is the best response.)

Practice these steps, and game theory will no longer be a mystery to you!

Column

		A	B
Row	A	✓ 100, 50	✓ 125, 100 ✓
	B	50, 100 ✓	75, 75

figure it out 12.1

Go online for interactive, step-by-step help in solving the following problem.

Two grocery stores in a small city are considering ways to update their stores. Each store can build a new store, remodel its existing store, or leave its store in its current condition. The game is shown below. Food4U's payoffs a re listed before the comma and Grocery Mart's after.

Payoffs listed are the stores' annual profits in thousands of dollars.

a. Are there any dominant strategies for either Food4U or Grocery Mart? Explain.

b. Are there any dominated strategies for either Food4U or Grocery Mart? Explain.

c. Solve for any Nash equilibria.

		Grocery Mart		
		Build New Store	**Remodel Existing Store**	**Leave Store as Is**
Food4U	**Build New Store**	200, 200	300, 400	400, 150
	Remodel Existing Store	400, 300	450, 450	300, 175
	Leave Store as Is	150, 300	175, 350	350, 300

Solution:

a. A dominant strategy is a strategy that is best for a player no matter what strategy its opponent follows. Let's begin with the decision for Food4U. If it believes that Grocery Mart will build a new store, Food4U will remodel its existing store ($400,000 > other payoffs when Grocery Mart builds a new store). If Food4U believes that Grocery Mart will remodel its existing store, it will also remodel its existing store ($450,000 > other payoffs). But, if Food4U believes that Grocery Mart will leave its store as it currently stands, Food4U will build a new store ($400,000 > other payoffs). Because no strategy is the best to follow no matter what action Grocery Mart takes, Food4U does not have a dominant strategy.

Now, let's examine the decision for Grocery Mart. If Grocery Mart believes that Food4U will build a new store, its best strategy would be to remodel its existing store ($400,000 > other payoffs). If Grocery Mart thinks that Food4U will remodel its

store, Grocery Mart's best strategy is to also remodel its own store ($450,000 > other payoffs). And, if Grocery Mart believes that Food4U will leave its own store as it is, Grocery Mart will still want to remodel its own store ($350,000 > other payoffs). Therefore, remodeling its store is a dominant strategy for Grocery Mart because it is the best strategy for Grocery Mart to follow regardless of the strategy Food4U chooses.

b. When Food4U believes that Grocery Mart will either build a new store or remodel its current store, Food4U's best strategy is to remodel its own store. When Food4U believes that Grocery Mart will leave its own store in its current state, Food4U is better off building a new store. This means that under no circumstances is it better for Food4U to leave its store as is. Thus, "Leave Store As Is" is a dominated strategy for Food4U. Because "Remodel Existing Store" is a dominant strategy for Grocery Mart, the other two strategies must be dominated strategies for Grocery Mart.

c. Using the check method (shown in the table below), we can see that the Nash equilibrium occurs when Food4U and Grocery Mart both remodel their stores. This makes sense because "Remodel Existing Store" is a dominant strategy for Grocery Mart, and when Grocery Mart remodels its store, Food4U is also better off remodeling its own store.

		Grocery Mart		
		Build New Store	Remodel Existing Store	Leave Store as Is
Food4U	**Build New Store**	200, 200	300, 400 ✓	✓ 400, 150
	Remodel Existing Store	✓ 400, 300	✓ 450, 450 ✓	300, 175
	Leave Store as Is	150, 300	175, 350 ✓	350, 300

Multiple Equilibria

Predicting likely outcomes of a game can be fairly easy when there's only one Nash equilibrium, as there is with prisoners' dilemmas or with the magazine cover story game we just analyzed. Because of the mutual-best-response logic of the Nash equilibrium, it's likely that the players will end up following the Nash equilibrium strategies. But the best option becomes more difficult to figure out if there is more than one Nash equilibrium, which happens fairly often.

Let's revisit Warner Brothers and Disney, but this time we look at their choice of when to release their next movies. Suppose that both companies currently have superhero movies ready for distribution, so now they must decide when these movies should open in theaters around the country.

Both companies want to take advantage of certain periods of the year when people have especially high demand for watching movies. Let's simplify things by saying the companies basically have three periods from which to choose their opening date. One is the Memorial Day weekend (which we'll call May). This is traditionally a big movie-going time of the year and, as such, is an appealing option for an opening date. The second possibility is the time around Christmas and New Year's (which we'll call December). This is also typically a high-demand period of the year, though not quite as high as Memorial Day. Finally, there is mid-March, usually a low-demand period.

Warner Brothers and Disney both understand these demand patterns. And if either were a monopolist, it could easily rank its opening date choices: May is best, then December, then March. But they're not monopolists. Their profits from choosing a particular opening date will depend on the *other* company's choice as well. This is, then, a game theory problem. The two companies realize that if they both choose the same opening date, it will be a disaster. They'll split the superhero feature market down the middle rather than having the whole market to themselves (though at different times in the year).

So, how will Warner Brothers and Disney balance these opposing considerations? **Table 12.3** shows the specifics of the game they are playing, including the payouts that both companies would receive for any possible set of opening date strategies.

Table 12.3   Selecting a Release Date*

Warner Brothers' Opening Date Choice		Disney's Opening Date Choice		
		May	**December**	**March**
	May	100, 100	✓ 600, 400 ✓	✓ 600, 200
	December	✓ 400, 600 ✓	0, 0	400, 200
	March	200, 600 ✓	200, 400	−100, −100

*Payoffs are measured in millions of dollars of profit.

If either company chooses a May opening when the other does not, the May opener makes $600 million. If either company opens by itself in December, its movie will make $400 million. Finally, if either company has a March opener to itself, it makes $200 million.

If both companies open their movies in the same month, however, neither fares so well. In fact, we assume they'll earn lower profit regardless of the opening date (although they'll lose more if they open during worse times of the year). If they both choose to open in May, they make only $100 million each. If both movies open in December, each company earns zero profit. And if both firms opt to open in March, they will each incur a $100 million loss.

To find the Nash equilibrium for this game, we apply our box-check method to mark each player's best-response strategies. First, let's do it for Warner Brothers. If Disney chooses a May opening date, Warner Brothers' best response is to choose a December opening ($400 million > $200 million > $100 million). This outcome is shown in the middle cell of the left column. If Disney chooses December, then May is Warner Brothers' best response (top cell of middle column). May is also Warner Brothers' best response if Disney chooses a March opening date (top cell of right column). We've put checks next to the payoffs for all of Warner Brothers' best responses. (Remember that Warner Brothers' numbers are in red and to the left of the comma.)

Everything for Disney's optimal responses is just a mirror image, so we can check off its best responses in the same manner. If Warner Brothers chooses a May opening date, Disney should choose December ($400 million is its largest payoff possible; top cell of middle column). If Warner Brothers chooses either a December or March opening date, Disney earns more profit by choosing May ($600 million is its largest payoff possible; middle and bottom cells of the left column).

Now we've identified each firm's best response to any possible strategy its competitor might pursue. Notice that a March opening is a dominated strategy for both players. That is, it is *never* optimal to open in March regardless of what the competitor might do. So, we can ignore any outcomes that involve either firm opening in March. That simplifies the game to the four squares in the upper left of the game table. These are shown by themselves in **Table 12.4**.

Look at the mutual best responses, where there are two checks in the same box. There are two of them: Either Warner Brothers picks December and Disney chooses May, or the other way around. Both outcomes are Nash equilibria of the game. This game shows the difficulty of predicting the outcome of games with multiple equilibria. We can narrow down the possibilities—no rational company would choose a March date, for example, and both companies would avoid opening their movies in the same period—but we cannot say precisely what the one outcome will be. We know that one company would likely pick May and the other December, but given the information in the table, we have no basis to determine what company chooses which date.

Later in the chapter, we will see that changes in the structure of the game, such as changes in the sequence of moves or modest shifts in payouts, can lead to different outcomes than the multiple Nash equilibria shown here. For the time being, however, we've gone as far as game theory can take us with this game.

Table 12.4 Selecting a Release Date (Simplified Game)*

		Disney's Opening Date Choice	
		May	**December**
Warner Brothers' Opening Date Choice	**May**	100, 100	✓ 600, 400 ✓
	December	✓ 400, 600 ✓	0, 0

*Payoffs are measured in millions of dollars of profit.

Mixed Strategies

We have been focusing on games in which a player makes a choice between different actions, choosing the specific strategy that maximizes her payoff. A *strategy in which the player chooses a particular action with certainty* is known as a **pure strategy**. However, it may not always be in the player's best interest to follow a pure strategy. In some situations, a *strategy in which the player randomizes her actions*, or **mixed strategy**, may be the best choice.

As an example of a game that can be played using a mixed strategy, think of a soccer game in which a player is taking a penalty kick. You've probably seen this on TV, or perhaps done it yourself on the field. The kicker faces the goalie, alone, and kicks the ball from close range. The distance is so close, in fact, that the goalie just dives to one side or the other and prays that it's the right way. It turns out that penalty kicks can be analyzed using game theory. There are two players (the kicker and the goalie), with each having a set of strategy choices ("kick left" or "kick right" for the kicker, "dive left" or "dive right" for the goalie), and payoffs that depend on the chosen strategies of both players. This game is shown in **Table 12.5**.

Let's assume we're considering a pivotal penalty kick: If the goalie picks the same side as the kicker, the goalie's team wins, and if the players choose opposite sides, the kicker's team wins. We can assign payoffs of 1 to the winner and 0 to the loser. That's what is illustrated in the table. Note that, because the kicker and goalie face each other, a kicker choosing to kick to the right will hope that the goalie dives to the left—that is, the goalie's *own* right. To avoid confusion, we set up the table so a dive by the goalie toward where the kicker kicks the ball is considered to be the same direction choice—that is, both choose right or both choose left.

Let's use our check method again. The kicker always wants to do the opposite of what the goalie does: If the goalie chooses left, the kicker's best response is to choose right. If the goalie dives right, the kicker wants to kick left. However, the goalie always wants to match the kicker's choice: If the kicker chooses left, the goalie's best response is to go left, and to go right if the kicker chooses right. Putting checks by all these responses gives us the situation in the table.

Notice what has happened: *There is no box with two checks in it*. That's because no set of strategies exists such that both players simultaneously choose the best response to the other's choice. Given what one player chooses, the other player will want to switch. Our check method therefore doesn't indicate any pure-strategy Nash equilibrium to the game, at least in the way we have been defining a Nash equilibrium. In pure strategies, a Nash equilibrium always needs two checks in a box. Up to now, the games we've analyzed have had at least one (and sometimes more) pure-strategy equilibria,

pure strategy A strategy in which the player chooses a particular action with certainty.

mixed strategy A strategy in which the player randomizes her actions.

Table 12.5 A Mixed-Strategy Game: Penalty Kicks in Soccer

		Goalie	
		Left	**Right**
Kicker	**Left**	0, 1 ✓	✓ 1, 0
	Right	✓ 1, 0	0, 1 ✓

such as both firms choosing to advertise, magazines selecting different cover stories, or film studios ensuring their films are not released at the same time.

The Nash equilibrium that exists in the penalty-kicks game involves *randomizing* across different strategies, that is, sometimes choosing one option (kick right) and at other times choosing another (kick left). Suppose the kicker, rather than simply choosing left or right as a strategy to follow all of the time, formed a strategy like "I will kick right 80% of the time and kick left 20% of the time." The goalie could have a similar strategy of diving one way or the other with a set probability. These randomized actions are mixed strategies. In mixed strategies, the randomization pattern (whether the probability mix is 80/20, 50/50, or anything else) is itself a strategy, just as kicking left for certain is a strategy.

Although the 80/20 right/left strategy example above is a mixed strategy, it is not a Nash equilibrium strategy. Think about it: If the kicker is going right 80% of the time, then the goalie's best response is to always go right. But the kicker's best response to a goalie diving right every time is to kick *left* all of the time. But if the kicker always goes left, the goalie also wants to go left all the time. If they want to switch once they know what the other player is doing, it's not a Nash equilibrium.

The only mixed-strategy Nash equilibrium in this game is for both the kicker and goalie to go left and right exactly half of the time. If the kicker randomly kicks to the right half of the time and to the left the other half, the goalie gets the same payoff whether she jumps left or right, so she is happy to randomize between the two. And if the goalie splits 50/50, the same is true of the kicker. Therefore, this is a mutual best response.

The strange thing about a mixed-strategy Nash equilibrium is that, given the fact that they are using the optimal probabilities, both players are indifferent between the actions they randomize over. If they weren't indifferent, they would prefer to play a pure strategy, where they would kick (dive) one direction all of the time. To arrive at a mixed-strategy equilibrium, each player needs to pick the probability of taking each action so that the player's *opponent* is indifferent between her own actions. By choosing a 50/50 split between kicking right and left, the kicker leaves the goalie equally well off whether she chooses to dive left or dive right. As a result, there is no way for the goalie herself to do better than dive right 50% of the time and dive left 50% of the time. This is one of the most confusing and counterintuitive results in all of economics, so if it seems bizarre, you are not alone in thinking so.

 The online appendix solves for mixed-strategy equilibria.

Application: Random Mixed Strategies in Soccer

One of this book's authors, Steven Levitt, researched whether soccer players used mixed strategies when they take penalty kicks as we just described. Along with his coauthors Pierre-André Chiappori and Tim Groseclose, Levitt collected data on all the penalty kicks during a three-year period in the French and Italian elite soccer leagues.[1]

They classified kickers' and goalies' choices into one of three strategies: left, right, and center. This is a bit more complicated than the left/right example, but the logic of the analysis was the same: The Nash equilibrium theory says that kickers and goalies should randomize across the choices in a way that makes the observed success rates of any direction choice the same.

This is just what Levitt, Chiappori, and Groseclose found in the actual data. The kickers and goalies seem to randomize their choices almost perfectly. The success rate was

[1] Pierre-André Chiappori, Tim Groseclose, and Steven Levitt, "Testing Mixed-Strategy Equilibria When Players Are Heterogeneous: The Case of Penalty Kicks in Soccer," *American Economic Review* 92, no. 4 (September 2002): 1138–1151.

basically identical no matter which way they went. Chalk up a victory for game theory! It predicted very well the behavior of these players—who certainly had a lot at stake in the games they were playing and therefore had great incentive to optimize their behavior.

The funny side story of this research involves one hapless player who didn't quite figure out how randomized strategies work. When we talk about mixed strategies involving randomizing across strategies with certain probabilities, we mean *randomizing*. It's more than just making sure that one-third of the kicks occur in each direction, because you also need to ensure that a given strategy does not depend on the strategy the kicker chose before (for the same reason a coin that always comes up heads, tails, heads, tails, heads, tails, etc. would be highly suspect even though each outcome happens 50% of the time).

This kicker and goalie are playing more than one kind of game.

Evidently, truly randomizing was too difficult for this player. So, he followed a set pattern for his kicks: first left, then center, then right, then back to left, and so on. He figured that mixing equally across the three choices would be enough to make goalies randomize in response. But it didn't take too long for the goalies to recognize his system. They started blocking virtually all his kicks. This player may not know microeconomics, but he still learned (the hard way) that in soccer, there is no pure-strategy Nash equilibrium. ■

What If My Opponent Is an Idiot? The Maximin Strategy

In game theory, the idea of Nash equilibrium is based on players rationally considering all the possible payoffs and coldly calculating their optimal best responses to their opponent's choices. You can probably imagine, then, that the notion of players making systematic errors (errors that are nonrandom and occur over and over again in the same direction) poses a big problem for predicting the outcomes of games by looking for Nash equilibria. If a player cannot trust her opponents to at least do what's in the opponents' best interests, how should she act?

In Chapter 18, we will look at some of the new economic research on behavioral economics, the branch of economics that argues people don't always behave rationally and often make various systematic errors in judgment.

We have a lot to say about irrationality in Chapter 18, but now is a good time to bring up a type of strategy known in game theory as the **maximin strategy** (short for "maximize the minimum"), *whereby the player minimizes her exposure to loss.* Maximin is a conservative strategy because the player is not going for the highest payoff. Therefore, maximin can be useful in games in which one or more players might be irrational. The idea of the maximin strategy (and the origin of its name) is that a player takes actions that minimize the damage to her in the worst-case scenario—maximizing her minimum payoff. In other words, if an opponent chooses the exact strategy that would punish a player as much as possible (even if it hurts the opponent, too), in what way can the player respond that will minimize the damage? A maximin strategy limits the game's downside; instead of looking for the best outcome given an opponent's actions, the player just tries to minimize her exposure to losses.

maximin strategy A strategy in which the player minimizes her exposure to loss.

Let's go back to our earlier example in which two magazines are choosing a cover story for their next issue. We saw that a celebrity interview (CI) cover story was a dominant strategy for *I'm Famous Weekly*, and that the Nash equilibrium had *Look at Me! Magazine* going with a reality show (RS) cover as a best response. The payoffs are shown in **Table 12.6** (which is the same as Table 12.2).

Table 12.6 Choosing a Cover Story Using a Maximin Strategy*

		Look at Me! Magazine's Cover Story	
		RS	CI
I'm Famous Weekly's Cover Story	RS	300, 0	400, 400 ✓
	CI	✓ 500, 300 ✓	✓ 450, 200

*Payoffs are measured in thousands of dollars of profit.

But suppose for a minute that *Me!*'s management believes its competitor isn't just *Famous* but also dumb—so dumb it can't even tell that CI is its dominant strategy. If the *Famous* editorial board goes with the reality show cover (because they're irrational, confused, or in a hurry), and *Me! Magazine* proceeded with an RS cover, too, it would be disastrous for *Me!* because its profit would be zero. (Remember, both magazines are making these cover story decisions simultaneously.) If *Me!* goes with a CI cover instead, the worst it can do is make $200,000 if *Famous* opts for a CI cover (as it rationally should), and the best it can do is $400,000 if *Famous* acts irrationally and does an RS cover.

If *Me!* is risk-averse enough, it will choose to go with a celebrity interview cover even though the Nash equilibrium suggests a reality show. This choice (choosing a CI cover) is a maximin strategy for *Me!*: It chooses the strategy that maximizes its minimum possible outcome, by raising it from $0 under RS to $200,000 under CI. The outcome of the game in this case is not a Nash equilibrium or profit-maximizing equilibrium, however. *Me!* could do better (earning $300,000) by unilaterally changing its cover from CI to RS *if it knew for sure* that *Famous* was going to choose CI. *Me!* is giving up that best response in order to avoid what it considers to be a potential disaster should *Famous* be too dumb to do the rational thing.

Something of interest to note about this sort of situation is that a firm might realize it can influence its competitor's behavior by seeming to be crazy. The mere threat of irrational behavior—if it's credible enough—can be used in some cases to manipulate an opponent's actions in a player's favor.

Application: Fun in the Sun: Wine Making for Irrational Billionaires

Ah, owning a vineyard—the sun, the hills, the natural beauty. Sniffing wine out of one of those big glasses while sitting in Tuscany or Napa Valley, talking about vintages and "a hint of black currants"—such activities have an appeal to rich people throughout the world. It seems just about every wealthy celebrity who retires decides to go into wine making. Examples include moviemaker Francis Ford Coppola, tire magnates Leonard and Brooks Firestone, golfer Greg Norman, and many others.

If you simplify the business of wine making, you can think of two basic types of product: high-end wine and cheap (jug) wine. A person who has made lots of money, say, running a successful tire company is probably not better equipped to make high-end wine than a big winemaker with extensive experience like Gallo. From a pure profit perspective, the payoffs from choosing a type of wine for the celebrity and for Gallo to produce might look something like those illustrated in **Table 12.7.**

If both the celebrity and Gallo decide to produce the same type of wine, Gallo will make a bigger profit because of its relative expertise. In fact, the celebrity might be expected to lose money if both make high-end wine because the market is a bit smaller and the costs are higher. Both Gallo and the celebrity will be profitable if they make different types of wine.

Let's look at the players' best responses, shown by the checks. We can see that the Nash equilibrium has Gallo making high-end wine and the celebrity producing cheap wine.

In fact, making high-end wine is a dominated strategy for the celebrity: No matter what type of wine Gallo chooses to make, the celebrity's profit is greater when producing cheap wine.

If the celebrities think like game theorists, they'll realize this. So, Gallo ought to be able to count on celebrities making cheap wine, in which case Gallo should make high-end wine. There's only one problem. Celebrities may not act rationally to maximize their profits. Or, to be more generous, their wine-making dream is driven by something besides profit. The hobbyists want to make high-end, award-winning wines (the kind they are accustomed to drinking, naturally), and they are willing to give up a lot of money in lost profit for this bragging right.

If Gallo suspects that the celebrities might be committed to producing high-end wine because of irrationality or motives other than profit, it might make sense for Gallo to go with a maximin strategy. In this case, that would be to produce cheap wine. The worst it could do in this case is make $30,000 per acre. If Gallo makes high-end wines instead, its profit could fall as low as $5,000 per acre if the celebrity also chooses to produce the "good stuff."

This example comes straight from microeconomic research done by Fiona Scott Morton and Joel Podolny.[2] Their study of the wine industry documents an extremely large amount of entry into the high-end market segment—presumably from rich amateur vintners—despite extremely low profits in that segment. It makes sense, then, that the big winemakers place their main focus on mass market wines instead. They can avoid competition with wineries that just don't care about losing money. Sometimes the toughest competitor is the one who doesn't care about losing. ■

Table 12.7 Choosing a Wine to Produce*

		Celebrity's Wine-Making Choice	
		High-End	Cheap
Gallo's Wine-Making Choice	High-End	5, –10	✓ 60, 15 ✓
	Cheap	✓ 50, 5	30, 10 ✓

*Payoffs are measured in thousands of dollars of profit per acre of vineyard.

12.3 Repeated Games

You now know how to find the Nash equilibrium (or equilibria) in a game where the players make simultaneous moves. One of the examples we went over was the prisoner's dilemma Warner Brothers and Disney faced in choosing whether to advertise (Table 12.1). Both firms would be better off if they could coordinate so that neither company advertises, but each firm has the individual incentive to advertise, so the firms are stuck making lower profits than they would if they could coordinate their decisions.

Now consider a perfectly sensible question: Would it matter if these firms played this prisoner's dilemma game twice in a row? The basic problem in a prisoner's dilemma is that neither firm has the individual incentive to cooperate with the other, even though both would be better off if they could jointly agree to do so. If players know they are going to end up in the same situation again (and perhaps again and again), they might have a better chance of coordinating their actions in a mutually beneficial way. In this section, we examine this issue and learn how to analyze repeated games that are more general than prisoner's dilemmas.

[2] Fiona M. Scott Morton and Joel M. Podolny, "Love or Money? The Effects of Owner Motivation in the California Wine Industry," *Journal of Industrial Economics* 50, no. 4 (December 2002): 431–456.

Finitely Repeated Games

When a simultaneous game is played multiple times, a player's strategy includes the actions they take across all the games. If a game is played twice, players' strategies will involve what they do in both Periods 1 and 2, and they can differ across periods.

So, let's analyze the Warner Brothers–Disney prisoner's dilemma played twice—first for one pair of movies (*Wonder Woman 2* vs. *Black Panther 2*) and then for a second pair (*Wonder Woman 3* vs. *Black Panther 3*)—to see if they can reach a different outcome than they did in the single-game version.

To answer this question, we first have to figure out how to think about strategy in games that are played more than once. The way to do this—not only for repeated prisoner's dilemmas like the one here, but also for any game with multiple rounds of play—is to use **backward induction**, the *process of solving a multistep game by first solving the last step and them working backward*. Once you determine what happens in the last period of the game, you next ask what players would do in the period before the final one, given that they know how all the other players will act in the last period. (They know because they can analyze the game's last period just as you can.) You repeat this process for as many steps as there are in a game, working backward one step at a time, until you can solve for the outcome in the first period. At that stage, you'll have determined the players' optimal strategies at all points in the game.

In our example game here, there are only two periods, so backward induction is easy. First, we know that no matter what happened in the first period, the second period is the end. So, when the two players get to the second and final period, they will be facing the normal one-shot prisoner's dilemma.

Unfortunately for the firms, the fact the final period is a one-shot prisoner's dilemma means that, despite our speculation that it might be possible to cooperate, cooperation in both periods (or either period, for that matter) is *not* a Nash equilibrium. Here's why. Suppose Warner Brothers knows for sure that Disney will agree not to advertise in both periods. Warner Brothers' best response in the last period, because it's just a one-shot prisoner's dilemma, is to cheat on the agreement and advertise. (After all, Disney can't do anything to punish them for cheating. It's the end of their interaction.) The logic works the other way, too: Disney will also advertise in the second period, no matter what.

Now you can probably see how the situation unravels. Both players realize *in the first period* that they will both end up cheating in the second. It's going to be every firm for itself. But if they know this is how things will go down, there's no point cooperating (by not advertising) in the first period. If a studio violates the first-period agreement and advertises, there can't be any special punishment in Period 2—it already knows what's going to happen. So, the first period becomes essentially another one-shot prisoner's dilemma, and we know the outcome of that from our discussion above: Both players cheat (advertise).

As long as everyone knows when the game will end, repeated play doesn't help players solve their cooperation problems in prisoner's dilemmas. In every period, the Nash equilibrium remains the same as it was in the one-period setup. Even if you played it 52 consecutive times, the *Wonder Woman* final period will still be a one-shot game in which both firms go with their dominant strategies and advertise. In the 51st period, the firms realize that period 52 will be a cheatfest, so Period 51 becomes a one-shot game in which both firms advertise. And the process unravels all the way back to the first period.

Not every game played across multiple periods is a repeated prisoner's dilemma like this one. But the use of backward induction is a standard technique that can be applied to determine equilibria in other types of multiple-period games. We look at examples of multiple-period games later in the chapter.

backward induction The process of solving a multi-step game by first solving the last step and then working backward.

Infinitely Repeated Games

The prisoner's dilemma conundrum isn't completely hopeless, though. There is a way out (or, more specifically, a possible way to cooperate). The problem with the repeated game scenario we just discussed is that everyone knows when the last period is, so they know that everyone will cheat in the last period. This knowledge causes everything before the last period to unravel. But, if the players don't know for sure when the last period is or they consider playing the game over and over, forever, it goes differently.

The first thing you have to do in this seemingly odd game is specify a strategy for every period. This could become massively complex, given all the different orders in which a player could take actions. To make things easy, let's consider the following simple strategy: Warner Brothers does not advertise in the first period and continues not to advertise as long as Disney doesn't break the agreement and advertise. If Disney ever advertises, Warner Brothers abandons the deal and advertises from that point forward, forever. Disney's strategy is the mirror image of this: Don't advertise at first and stick to the agreement as long as Warner Brothers doesn't advertise, but switch to advertising from then on if Warner Brothers ever advertises.

With this set of strategies, a Nash equilibrium when the game is played forever, or perhaps more realistically, where the game could end in any particular period, but the players never know when exactly the last period will come, the analysis changes.

Because there is no final period in this game that the players can predict precisely, we can't use backward induction. The way to think about Nash equilibria in this case is to weigh what a player could gain at any given point from trying something different from her current strategy. The logic of this approach comes straight from the definition of a Nash equilibrium: A player is doing as well as possible given the actions of the other players. If we can show that *any* change of strategy would make the player worse off, we know that sticking with the current strategy is a best response. If we can show this same thing for all the players, we know the strategies result in a Nash equilibrium.

Let's try that here. Suppose Warner Brothers decides to break with the cooperative "Don't Advertise" strategy and starts advertising even though Disney hasn't advertised. We know that Warner Brothers will experience a short-term gain in this period because even though Warner Brothers advertises, Disney does not—remember, we're holding the actions of the other player fixed, so Disney will be playing the cooperative strategy of not advertising. This strategy is shown in the upper-right payoff box of **Table 12.8** (a reprint of Table 12.1): Warner Brothers will make $550 million during this period and Disney will lose $80 million.

Warner Brothers pays a price for its cheating ways, however. When it violates the agreement, Disney stops cooperating in the future. Having chosen to advertise this period, Warner Brothers will have to duke it out with Disney from that point forward. Both firms will advertise all future films, and each studio will earn $250 million each time the game is played.

Warner Brothers' payoff from cheating that one time is that it earns $550 million in the current period. In the next and every following period, it earns $250 million. Let's allow for a firm to care somewhat less about future payoffs than current payoffs. We embody this discounting of the future with the

Table 12.8	The Single-Period Payoffs of an Infinitely Repeated Advertising Game*	

		Disney	
		Advertise	**Don't Advertise**
Warner Brothers	**Advertise**	250, 250	550, −80
	Don't Advertise	−80, 550	320, 320

*Payoffs are measured in millions of dollars of profit.

variable d. (We will discuss the origin and impact of the discount rate and how to compute a "present value" for future payments in Chapter 14.) This variable is a number between 0 and 1, and it shows what a payoff in the next period is worth in the current period. That is, the firm views $1 in the next period as being worth $$d$ today. If $d = 0$, the player doesn't care at all about the future: Any payoff in the next period (or following periods) is considered worthless today. If $d = 1$, the player makes no distinction between future payoffs and today's payoffs; they are all equally valuable. A higher d means the player cares more about the future, making the value of future payments greater.[3]

Let's write down Warner Brothers' payoff if it decides to break from the "Don't Advertise" strategy and advertise in the current period:

Payoff from breaking away:

$$550 + d \times (250) + d^2 \times (250) + d^3 \times (250) + \dots$$

Notice how payoffs further in the future are discounted more and more, because d is a per-period discount. What we have to do is compare this to the payoff Warner Brothers receives by sticking with the "Don't Advertise" strategy and earning $320 million in this and every future period:

Payoff from sticking with the "Don't Advertise" strategy:

$$320 + d \times (320) + d^2 \times (320) + d^3 \times (320) + \dots$$

The analysis is the same for Disney's choice of adhering to the "Don't Advertise" strategy or reneging and surprise advertising in one period. If we can show that the payoff from sticking with the strategy is greater than the payoff from breaking away, we know that the outcome of pursuing the cooperative "Don't Advertise" strategy is a Nash equilibrium. This is true if

$$320 + d \times (320) + d^2 \times (320) + d^3 \times (320) + \dots > 550 + d \times (250) + d^2$$
$$\times (250) + d^3 \times (250) + \dots$$
$$70 \times (d + d^2 + d^3 + \dots) > 230$$
$$(d + d^2 + d^3 + \dots) > 23/7$$

To solve for d, we can use a simple math trick, $d + d^2 + d^3 + \dots = d/(1-d)$ for any d between zero and one ($0 \leq d < 1$), and substitute it into the equation above:

$$\frac{d}{(1-d)} > 23/7, \quad d > 23/30 = 0.77$$

This means that as long as Warner Brothers and Disney care enough about the future—as long as they view $1 in the next period to be worth at least as much as $0.77 in this period—they can earn higher expected profits by cooperating and not advertising than they could by unilaterally deviating and advertising today, setting off a cheating battle forever after. In other words, both firms cooperating (i.e., not advertising) is a Nash equilibrium in this game.

This "caring about the future" condition makes sense. Choosing to cooperate is about skipping a big payoff (profit) right now that the firm could earn by cheating on the agreement in order to get a stream of higher payoffs (profits) in the future by cooperating. This can be seen in **Figure 12.1**, which shows Warner Brothers' and Disney's payoffs in each

---

[3] When a game might end in any given period with some probability p, and that's the reason why the players don't care as much about the future, then we can think of $d = 1 - p$. The larger the chance that the game ends after today, the less the players care about future payoffs.

Figure 12.1   Payoffs from Cooperating and Cheating

In the repeated advertising game between Warner Brothers and Disney, if a firm chooses to continue cooperating by sticking with the "Don't Advertise" strategy, it earns a steady payoff of $320 million per period. If it instead breaks away from the agreement by advertising, it earns a larger $550 million payoff in that period but a lower $250 million payoff every period after that.

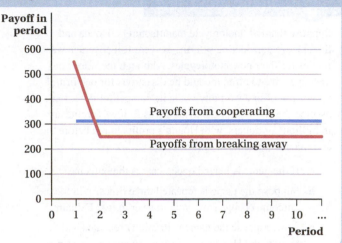

period for the two options. Cooperating by sticking with "Don't Advertise" leads to a steady payoff of $320 million per period. Breaking away from the agreement by advertising leads to a larger $550 million payoff in the first period but a lower $250 million payoff every period after that. The more players care about the future—the larger d is—the more willing they are to sustain those future cooperative payouts. If this isn't quite clear to you, suppose $d = 0$, meaning that neither Warner Brothers nor Disney cares about future payoffs at all. Then the only relevant payoffs for both firms are those of the one-period prisoner's dilemma, and we know in such a case that advertising is a dominant strategy for both firms. There's no reason to cooperate when you don't care about the future, which is where the benefit from cooperating is earned.

By the way, the strategy we analyzed here—*in which cooperative play ends permanently when one player cheats*—is called the **grim trigger** or **grim reaper strategy**. Like a visit from the grim reaper, the punishment for deviating from cooperation, never cooperating again, is permanent for both players. In an alternative strategy, known as **tit-for-tat**, the *player mimics her opponent's prior-period action in each round*. If the opponent cooperated last period, then the player cooperates this period. If the opponent cheated instead, then the player cheats until her opponent cooperates again (allowing the player to punish the opponent's cheating for one period in the process). The outcome of the tit-for-tat strategy is a little more complicated to work through than that of the grim trigger strategy, but a tit-for-tat strategy can also support cooperation as a Nash equilibrium in an infinitely repeated game if firms care sufficiently about the future. Tit-for-tat is also appealing because it closely matches the types of actions we often see in the real world. For example, gas stations situated across the road from each other will often engage in price wars in which each reduction in price by one station is quickly matched by the other. This situation is like the noncooperative breakdown in a repeated prisoner's dilemma—both stations would prefer coordinating on higher prices, but each has the incentive to cut prices to sell a higher quantity. However, quite often if one station relents and actually raises its price in an attempt to start cooperating, the other station will follow suit rather than insisting on the grim reaper strategy of keeping prices low forever.

Now we've identified the factors that can make coordination in a prisoner's dilemma a Nash equilibrium: The players cannot determine when the game will end, and the players have to care sufficiently about future payoffs.

grim trigger or **grim reaper strategy** A strategy in which cooperative play ends permanently when one player cheats.

tit-for-tat A strategy in which the player mimics her opponent's prior-period action in each round.

figure it out 12.2

Suppose that two motorcycle manufacturers, Honda and Suzuki, are considering offering 10-year full coverage warranties for their new motorcycles. Although the warranties are expensive to offer, it could be disastrous for one firm if it does not offer a warranty while its competitor does. Let's assume the payoffs for the firms are as follows (profits are in millions of dollars, with Honda's profits in red before the comma and Suzuki's in blue after it):

a. If the game is played once, what is the outcome?

b. Suppose the game is repeated three times. Will the outcome change from your answer in (a)? Explain.

c. Now, suppose the game is infinitely repeated and Suzuki and Honda have formed an agreement to not offer warranties to their customers. Each firm plans the use of a grim trigger strategy to encourage compliance with the agreement. At what level of d would Honda be indifferent about keeping the agreement versus cheating on it? Explain.

		Suzuki	
		OFFER WARRANTY	**DON'T OFFER WARRANTY**
Honda	**OFFER WARRANTY**	20, 20	120, 10
	DON'T OFFER WARRANTY	10, 120	50, 50

Solution:

a. We can use the check method to solve for the Nash equilibrium in a one-time game:

		Suzuki	
		OFFER WARRANTY	**DON'T OFFER WARRANTY**
Honda	**OFFER WARRANTY**	✓ 20, 20 ✓	✓ 120, 10
	DON'T OFFER WARRANTY	10, 120 ✓	50, 50

The Nash equilibrium occurs when both firms offer a warranty. Note that this is not the best cooperative outcome for the game, but it is the only stable equilibrium.

b. If the game is played for three periods, there would be no change in the players' behavior. In the third period, both firms would offer warranties because that is the Nash equilibrium. Knowing this and using backward induction, players will opt to offer warranties in both the second and first periods as well.

c. Honda's expected payoff from cheating and offering a warranty would be the 120 million from the first period (when cheating) and 20 million for each period after that (because Suzuki will also start offering warranties):

$$\text{Expected payoff from cheating} = 120 + d \times (20) + d^2 \times (20) + d^3 \times (20) + \ldots$$

Honda's expected payoff from following the agreement is earning 50 million each period throughout time:

$$\text{Expected payoff from following agreement} = 50 + d \times (50) + d^2 \times (50) + d^3 \times (50) + \ldots$$

Therefore, Honda will be indifferent between these two options when the payoff streams are equal:

$$120 + d \times (20) + d^2 \times (20) + d^3 \times (20) + \ldots = 50 + d \times (50) + d^2 \times (50) + d^3 \times (50) + \ldots$$

$$d \times (30) + d^2 \times (30) + d^3 \times (30) + \ldots = 70$$

$$d + d^2 + d^3 + \ldots = \frac{7}{3}$$

Because $d + d^2 + d^3 + \ldots = \dfrac{d}{(1-d)}$ for any $0 \leq d < 1$,

$$\frac{d}{(1-d)} = \frac{7}{3}$$

$$d = 0.7$$

Therefore, Honda will be indifferent between following the agreement or cheating if $d = 0.7$.

Multiple Equilibria in Infinitely Repeated Games   The weird aspect of infinitely repeated games is that there are usually a whole range of possible Nash equilibria. Suppose Warner Brothers and Disney are playing tit-for-tat strategies in the game above. We mentioned that following this strategy can sustain cooperation, period-after-period, in equilibrium. But suppose for some reason, every once in a while, one of the firms advertises. The competitors might go through a cycle of punishment as a result, but with tit-for-tat, it's possible that the two studios could return to cooperation afterward. Thus, an equilibrium with cooperation part of the time, but not all of the time, also exists. In fact, any outcome that is at least as good for the players as the one-shot cheating payoff has the potential to work as an equilibrium in this infinitely repeated game. The idea that many equilibria exist in repeated games and that anything meeting a minimum threshold could, in principle, work as a Nash equilibrium is known as the folk theorem. The folk theorem holds even in much more complicated games than we will cover in this book.

12.4 Sequential Games

There are many situations in which players do not have to make their moves at the same time, as we've been assuming so far. Instead, they take actions in turn. In sequential games, one firm moves first and the next firm gets to see what the first mover did.

The normal-form matrix that we've been using for simultaneous games doesn't work for sequential games because it does not provide us with a way to keep the timing of actions separate from the choice of actions. Instead, we plot sequential games in what's called the **extensive form** or **a decision tree**, a *representation of a sequential game that shows both the choice and timing of players' actions* (Figure 12.2). The sequence of the game flows from left to right. Each node in an extensive form game represents a choice, and the player listed at that node is the one choosing what action to take. The payoffs to every possible sequence of strategies are listed at the far right.

extensive form or **decision tree** Representation of a sequential game that shows both the choice and timing of players' actions.

Figure 12.2 revisits the Warner Brothers–Disney release date game we presented earlier in Table 12.3 (which we repeat as **Table 12.9** for convenience) as a game in which

---

Figure 12.2   Decision Tree for Choosing a Release Date

In this sequential game, Warner Brothers chooses a release date first at node *A*. If Warner Brothers chooses a May release date, Disney will choose a December release date at node *B*; if Warner Brothers chooses December or March, Disney will choose May at nodes *C* and *D*, respectively. Unlike the simultaneous game outcome in Table 12.3, the companies reach a single Nash equilibrium at node *B*. Here, Warner Brothers releases *Wonder Woman 2* in May, and Disney releases *Black Panther 2* in December.

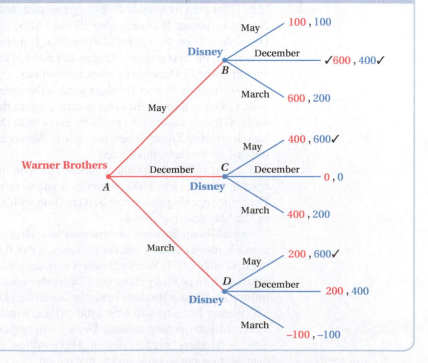

Table 12.9 Selecting a Release Date*		Disney's Opening Date Choice		
		May	**December**	**March**
Warner Brothers' Opening Date Choice	**May**	100, 100	✓ 600, 400 ✓	✓ 600, 200
	December	✓ 400, 600 ✓	0, 0	400, 200
	March	200, 600 ✓	200, 400	−100, −100

*Payoffs are measured in millions of dollars of profit.

both firms make their decisions at the same time. Now let's say that Warner Brothers finishes *Wonder Woman 2* first and gets to choose a release date before Disney chooses one for *Black Panther 2*.

Depending on two firms' choices, the firms earn the payoffs listed on the far right. [As in the normal form game, the first number listed in each pair (red) is Warner Brothers' profit, and the second number (blue) is Disney's profit.] If you look at these payoffs for a minute, you can see that we've just transformed the normal form game payoffs in Table 12.9 into extensive form for this sequential game. When one firm moves first, however, as Warner Brothers does here, the outcome of the game is completely different. When the game was a simultaneous-move game, we found that there were two pure strategy Nash equilibria: (1) Warner Brothers releases in May for a profit of $600 million, and Disney releases in December for a profit of $400 million and (2) Warner Brothers releases in December for a profit of $400 million, and Disney releases in May for a profit of $600 million. Now consider what happens in a sequential game.

Just as we did in the repeated simultaneous games in Section 12.3, we use backward induction to find Nash equilibria in sequential games. Suppose Warner Brothers picks May. That puts us at node *B* in the game tree, and Disney must now choose an opening date in response. If Disney also chooses May, it will make $100 million. If it chooses December, its profit will be $400 million. If it chooses March, it will earn $200 million. Therefore, the best response Disney can make is to choose December, and we put a check next to Disney's December payout in the figure.

Now suppose Warner Brothers picks a December opening instead, putting the game at node *C*. Going through the same process, we see that if Disney chooses May, it earns $600 million. It now makes zero profit by going with December and earns $200 million with a March opening. Disney's best response to Warner Brothers' choice of December is to open in May, so we check this choice.

Finally, if Warner Brothers chooses to open its film in March (node *D*), Disney will open in May. It earns $600 million by doing so instead of earning only $400 million with a December opening and losing $100 million with a March opening. Again, we put a check by the May opening choice.

Once Warner Brothers understands how Disney will respond in the last stage for each possible move taken by Warner Brothers, it can figure out the best choice to begin with at the first node (*A*). If Warner Brothers chooses a May opening, it knows that Disney maximizes its own profit by choosing a December opening and Warner Brothers will earn $600 million. If Warner Brothers opens in December, Disney will respond by opening in May, and Warner Brothers will earn $400 million. Finally, Warner Brothers earns $200 million with a March opening because Disney will respond with a May opening. It is clear that Warner Brothers' highest payout, $600 million, occurs when it chooses a May opening date, and we put a check next to that payoff.

That's it; we have an equilibrium of the sequential game. *Wonder Woman 2* opens in May and *Black Panther 2* opens in December. Warner Brothers earns $600 million in profit and Disney makes $400 million. In the simultaneous-move game, we had multiple equilibria; either firm could open in May and the other in December. But when the firms act sequentially, the firm that chooses first gets the lucrative May slot. The sequential structure eliminates the multiple equilibria problem that can occur with simultaneous games. The outcome is still a Nash equilibrium, though. Taking the other player's action as given, each player is doing the best it can once its turn rolls around.

A⁺ make the grade

Backward induction and trimming trees

Solving sequential games requires you to work backward, using a technique that game theorists call *backward induction*. It may seem a little strange to start with the second player when you know that the second player must wait until the first player makes her move. After all, the whole point of a sequential game is that the *order* of plays is important, and often the first player has a first-mover advantage. So, why would we start solving the game from the end and work backward?

Remember that we assume all players know the strategies available to every player in the game and the payoffs that accompany every possible outcome. Before Player 1 decides her strategy, she must consider what Player 2 is likely to do. After all, Player 1's payoff is determined both by her choice and that of her opponent. When we are solving the game, we want to think like the players. Therefore, to determine the best strategy for Player 1 to use, we must first examine what Player 2 is likely to do given every possible choice that Player 1 might choose. While it seems like we are acting as if Player 2 is moving first, in reality we are just putting ourselves in Player 1's shoes as she considers her best strategy, and that begins with predicting Player 2's moves.

There is another useful step, called "trimming the branches," that you can take to simplify sequential games. (This term comes from the idea that the extensive form of a game is often referred to as a "decision tree.") Trimming the branches is very similar to removing dominated strategies in a normal-form game. Basically, this method allows you to narrow the solution options by eliminating any branches that represent any actions that Player 2 would never take.

We can use backward induction to solve the game shown in Figure A. Remember, we are trying to think like Player 1 — who is moving first — in considering what Player 2 will do. Look at node *B*, where Player 1 has selected "up." What will Player 2 do? He will choose "down," because his payoff is greater. Not only can we add a check mark to that payoff, but we can also eliminate "up" as an option at node *B* (because Player 2 will not choose it). Therefore, we can trim (mark out) that branch as shown in Figure B. Now, consider what Player 2 will do if Player 1 chooses "down" (node *C*). Here, Player 2 will choose "up," so we can put a check mark next to that payoff and mark out the "down" branch at node *C*.

Figure B

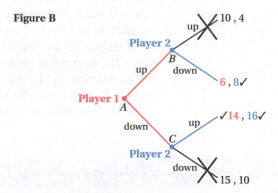

The final step we must take is choosing Player 1's best strategy. She knows that, given Player 2's expected moves, she is only left with two options (those not trimmed from the tree): Choose "up" and earn a payoff of 6, or choose "down" and earn a payoff of 14. Therefore, she will choose "down" and we can place a check mark by her payoff.

Backward induction and trimming the tree greatly simplify even the most complex sequential games. The trick is to place yourself in the first player's shoes by considering the actions that will be chosen by the second (third, fourth, etc.) player. Sometimes it is beneficial to do things backward!

Figure A

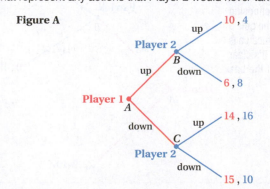

It's important to realize that we just arbitrarily picked Warner Brothers as the first-mover in playing this game. Look at the structure of the game's payouts. If Disney were able to choose first, the equilibrium would be reversed: Disney would open in May (earning $600 million) and Warner Brothers would open in December (earning $400 million). This outcome raises the key questions about who gets to move first. It seems like everyone should try to move first. We think through these issues in the next section.

Another Sequential Game

Let's close this section by considering another sequential game. Here's how it works:

Suppose that Danica and Patrick are two contestants on a game show called "Play or Pass." They flip a coin to decide who goes first, and Danica wins. The rules are simple: Danica decides if she wants to play or pass. If Danica chooses "Play," the game ends and she receives a payoff of 1, and Patrick receives a payoff of −10. However, if Danica chooses "Pass," then Patrick gets a turn. If Patrick chooses "Play," he receives a payoff of 12 and Danica receives a payoff of 0. If Patrick chooses "Pass," however, both players receive a payoff of 11. This sequential game is shown in **Figure 12.3**. Danica's decision occurs at node *A*, and Patrick's at node *B*.

Before we solve for the equilibrium of this game, let's look at all the possible payoffs. One outcome—which occurs if both Danica and Patrick call "Pass"—results in high payoffs for both players, with each getting 11. The other two outcomes are lopsided: If Danica calls "Play" immediately, the game ends with her earning a payoff of 1 and Patrick losing 10. If Danica instead calls "Pass" and Patrick responds with "Play," the game ends with Patrick earning 12 and Danica obtaining nothing. You might think that a game structure like this gives the players a strong incentive to get to the pass/pass outcome, so that both can receive a positive payoff. Check the figure using backward induction to see if this prediction is correct.

This equilibrium wasn't obvious from an initial look at the game's structure and payoffs. The example shows how backward induction can provide help beyond intuition alone when determining the outcomes of sequential games. The example also demonstrates the value of actions that players might take to change the structure of a game in a favorable way. We talk about these sorts of actions in the next section.

Figure 12.3   Sequential "Play or Pass" Game

In the "Play or Pass" game, Danica must first decide whether to choose "Play" or "Pass" (node *A*). If Danica calls "Play," she earns a payoff of 1 and Patrick loses 10. If Danica decides to opt for "Pass," Patrick can call "Play" and earn 12 or call "Pass" and earn 11 (node *B*). Because the higher payoff comes from choosing "Play," Patrick will choose that. Knowing that Patrick will choose "Play" if he gets a turn, Danica will call "Play" at node A and earn 1. (If for some reason Danica calls "Pass," she knows she will earn a payoff of 0.) Faced with this choice, it's clear that Danica does better by calling "Play" and ending the game right off the bat. Therefore, the equilibrium payoffs are 1 for Danica and −10 for Patrick.

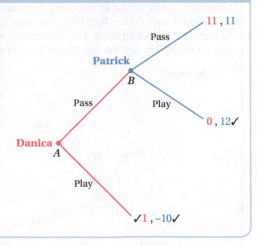

figure it out 12.3

Two firms, GamesRUs (GRU) and PlayThings Incorporated (PTI), are considering a new television advertising campaign for their Christmas gift registries. Because television advertising is expensive, each firm earns greater profit ($50 million) when it does not advertise. If both choose to advertise, very few new customers are gained and each firm earns only $30 million profit. However, if one firm advertises while the other does not, the firm choosing to advertise gets the majority of customers, earning a profit of $70 million, while its competitor only earns $20 million profit.

a. Create a table showing the normal form of this game.

b. List all Nash equilibria.

c. If this game is played sequentially and GRU makes its decision before PTI, what will the outcome be?

d. Is there a first-mover advantage in this case? Explain.

Solution:

a. The normal form is shown below (payoffs are in millions of dollars with GRU's profits before the comma and PTI's after):

		PTI	
		ADVERTISE	**DON'T ADVERTISE**
GRU	**ADVERTISE**	30, 30	70, 20
	DON'T ADVERTISE	20, 70	50, 50

b. We can use the check method to determine the Nash equilibria. If GRU believes that PTI will advertise, its best move is to also advertise ($30 million > $20 million). If GRU believes that PTI will not advertise, its best move is to advertise ($70 million > $50 million). Therefore, advertising is a dominant strategy for GamesRUs because it is the best strategy no matter what strategy PlayThings Inc. follows. Note, too, that because PTI's payoffs are the same as those of GRU's, advertising is also a dominant strategy for PTI. Therefore,

we end up with the following:

		PTI	
		ADVERTISE	**DON'T ADVERTISE**
GRU	**ADVERTISE**	✓ 30, 30 ✓	✓ 70, 20
	DON'T ADVERTISE	20, 70 ✓	50, 50

Because advertising is a dominant strategy for both firms, the outcome of this game is found in the upper-left portion of the payoff matrix and each firm earns a profit of $30 million. This is the Nash equilibrium because neither firm has an incentive to change its strategy given the strategy of the other.

c. The extensive form of this game (with GamesRUs moving first) is shown in the figure below:

Using backward induction, we can see that, when GRU chooses to advertise, PTI will also choose to advertise (because $30 million > $20 million). If GRU chooses not to advertise, PTI will still choose to advertise (because $70 million > $50 million). Therefore, if GRU understands how PTI will respond to its strategy, it will also choose to advertise (because $30 million > $20 million).

d. No first-mover advantage exists in this case because both firms have dominant strategies. A dominant strategy is the best strategy to follow *no matter what your opponent does*. Therefore, it is irrelevant if one firm makes its decision before the other firm; each firm will always choose its dominant strategy: to advertise.

12.5 Strategic Moves, Credibility, and Commitment

There's something not very satisfying about the equilibrium of the play or pass bargaining game. There was a big payoff for both players (11, 11) available later in the game, yet because each player followed his own self-interest, the equilibrium ended up with one player receiving something small (Danica earned a payoff of 1) and the other really getting hurt (Patrick lost 10). With this kind of result from the quick-exit equilibrium, you might think that both players would have an incentive to avoid it.

In this section, we discuss ways in which players can avoid such poor outcomes in certain kinds of sequential games. The key is for players to use **strategic moves**, defined by Nobel Laureate Thomas Schelling in his wonderful book *The Strategy of Conflict* as *actions taken early in a game to influence the ultimate outcome in a way that benefits the player.*[4]

strategic moves Actions taken early in a game to influence the ultimate outcome in a way that benefits the player.

FREAKONOMICS

Game Theory in Track Cycling Competitions

Usain Bolt ran 100 meters in 9.58 seconds—not quite as fast as a cheetah (which would take about 5.8 seconds to run that far), but still, faster than any other human who has ever lived. As a reward for his extreme speed, Bolt earned eight Olympic gold medals between 2008 and 2016, and yearly earnings totaling over $30 million.

Jason Kenny, the 2016 Olympic gold medalist in the track cycling individual sprint, probably won't impress you quite as much as Usain Bolt. The event he won involves two cyclists racing three laps around a 250-meter track. In the finals, it took Kenny well over a minute to complete the first lap. To put this into perspective, that's about how long it would take you to run that same distance! But don't strap on your bike helmet and buy a ticket to the next Olympic Games just yet.

It's not that Jason Kenny can't bike faster than this. In a full sprint, he travels at frighteningly high speeds — nearly 50 miles per hour. Kenny goes extremely slowly at the start of the race because he understands game theory.

Here is the problem. The racer who is behind, counterintuitively, has an inherent advantage over the racer who is in front because of *drafting* — the act of riding behind another cyclist and taking advantage of the reduction in air resistance in that cyclist's wake. It requires less physical effort to draft off another rider than to ride in front. The faster the rider in front goes, the greater the advantage that accrues to the rider who is behind because of the ability to draft.

This means the riders are not at an equilibrium when one leads and rides quickly; if a rider does that, he will surely lose as the other rider drafts behind him for the race and then "slingshots" past him at the end. Instead, the riders creep around the track until one suddenly tries to make a breakaway, hoping that the head start he gets is enough to offset the disadvantage of allowing the other rider to draft. The longer the riders wait, the more the scales tip toward the rider in front, so eventually one of the riders starts to sprint. That is when things get exciting. Unless, of course, you are an economist, in which case the application of game theory in the first few laps is what gets your adrenaline flowing.

Jamie Squire/Getty Images

No, please, YOU first.

---

[4] Strategic behavior is an incredibly rich area of study in microeconomics; we simply don't have the room to do a full overview in this book. We will touch on a few of the more common concepts and leave it to you to dig further through one of the many books on the topic if you're interested.

Examples of such actions include side payments, commitments, and reputation building, and their purpose is to alter the payoffs of a game to change its outcome in a way that is favorable for the player taking the action.

Side Payments

One of the simplest types of strategic behavior is a **side payment**, *a type of bribe that influences the outcome of a strategic game*. It is a promise of a payment from one player to an opposing player conditional on the choice the opponent makes, and it is aimed at compelling the opponent to choose the strategy that is in the player's best interest.

Think about side payments in the context of the "Play or Pass" game. The essence of the problem is that Danica chooses to play right away in the game because she knows that if she doesn't, Patrick's best choice is to choose "Play" and leave her, Danica, with nothing. But note how much Patrick's "best" choice hurts him: Because "Play" is Patrick's best choice at node B, Danica has no choice but to choose to play at node A, end the game early, and cause Patrick to lose 10. Patrick could avoid this poor outcome he could convince Danica that he will choose "Pass" at node B if given the opportunity to do so (i.e., so Danica will not immediately end the game at node A by choosing to play). Moreover, Danica would *like* to be convinced that Patrick will choose "Pass" at node B because then she would earn 11 rather than the measly 1 she gets in the Nash equilibrium.

How might Danica get Patrick to commit to choosing "Pass" at node B? She could make a side payment. Suppose Danica, instead of choosing to play right away, ending the game, and receiving a payoff of 1, makes the following take-it-or-leave-it offer to Patrick: "If you promise to choose to 'Pass' if I choose to 'Pass,' I'll give you a payment of 2. That way, you will definitely earn 13: your payoff at node B from choosing 'Pass,' plus my payment to you of 2. If you refuse this offer and stick with choosing 'Play' at node B, you will force me to choose to play, and you will lose 10."

How does this side payment of 2 affect the game's outcome? As **Figure 12.4** shows, Patrick's payoff from "Pass" at node B is now 13 instead of 11. Because this is more than he would get by choosing to play, he'll now want to choose to pass instead. Danica is fine with this: she gets a payoff of 9 (the original payoff of 11 minus the side payment of 2), which is better than the 1 she would have received by choosing to play.

side payment A type of bribe that influences the outcome of a strategic game.

Figure 12.4 **A Side Payment Can Alter the Nash Equilibrium**

In the original sequential "Play or Pass" game (Figure 12.3), Danica chose "Play" and received a payoff of 1. If Danica instead offers Patrick a side payment of 2 if Patrick will call "Pass" when it is his turn, the equilibrium changes. Now when Danica passes to Patrick, Patrick will also call "Pass." In the new Nash equilibrium, Danica and Patrick earn payoffs of 9 and 13, respectively, more than they would have earned without the side payment.

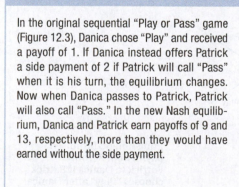
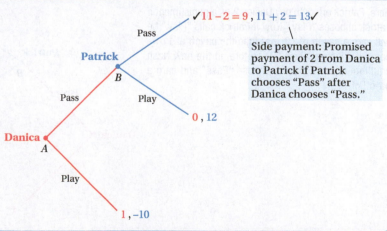

Side payment: Promised payment of 2 from Danica to Patrick if Patrick chooses "Pass" after Danica chooses "Pass."

Effective use of side payments, then, can alter the game in beneficial ways for both players. In this game, the players have figured out how to take some of the extra payment they receive in the coordinated outcome and split it in a way that creates incentives for them to coordinate.

Somewhat amazingly, just having the *ability* to make side payments can sometimes work, even if no money ever changes hands. Suppose, for example, that Patrick proposes the side payment this time. Before the game starts, he promises Danica that if he chooses "Play" at node *B*, he will give Danica a payment of 2 as a punishment to himself for hurting her. This promised punishment reduces Patrick's payoffs from "Play" at node *B* from 12 to 10 (**Figure 12.5**) and changes his node *B* best option from "Play" to "Pass." Realizing that the side payment punishment makes "Pass" Patrick's best option, Danica now faces the following node *A* options: Choose "Play" and receive 1, or choose "Pass" and receive 11. Danica now chooses "Pass." Patrick responds by choosing "Pass" at node *B*, and both earn 11.

Note that no side payment actually needs to be made: The punished option (Patrick choosing "Play") was never chosen because the punishment makes "Pass" the better choice for Patrick. This promised punishment encourages Danica to choose "Pass" at node *A* because it eliminates Danica's worry about what Patrick will do at node *B*. With the punishment in place, Patrick is better off by also selecting "Pass."

In fact, if Patrick wants to send a *really* strong message, he could promise to pay Danica the full payment of 12 if he chooses "Play." The key is that the side payment must be large enough to make "Play" a lower-paying choice than "Pass" for Patrick.

Commitment

Side payments do not always work. In our "Play or Pass" game, we assumed that Danica and Patrick would have no difficulty in sticking to the choice encouraged by the promised side payment. But, in real life, a player might have incentives to renege on side-payment agreements. By their very nature, side payments may often be secret. Players may find it difficult to ask a court to enforce these types of contracts. Therefore, firms often use other strategic moves to try to achieve better game outcomes.

Let's think about this some more by returning once again to the simultaneous-game version of the movie-release-date problem for Warner Brothers and Disney. In this version, we drop the March choice because it is a dominated strategy, so in **Table 12.10**, we're looking again at the game from Table 12.4.

Figure 12.5   **Using a Side Payment as Punishment for Noncooperation**

Here, Patrick offers to pay Danica 2 as a punishment if Patrick chooses "Play." Now if Patrick calls "Play," he will earn a payoff of 10, less than the payoff of 11 he earns if chooses "Pass." Therefore, in the new Nash equilibrium, both players choose "Pass" and earn a payoff of 11.

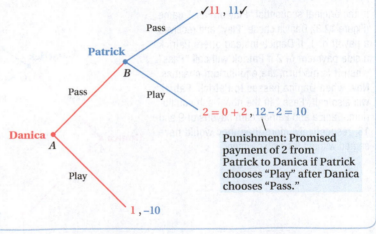

✓11 , 11✓

Pass

Patrick

B

Pass   Play

$2 = 0 + 2$, $12 - 2 = 10$

Punishment: Promised payment of 2 from Patrick to Danica if Patrick chooses "Play" after Danica chooses "Pass."

Danica

A

Play

1 , −10

Each studio would like to signal convincingly that it is releasing its movie in May to force its competitor into a December release. At the same time, the studios need to be careful to not *both* choose a May release. In Section 12.4, we saw that if one of the companies can move first, then it will take advantage of its first-mover status and choose May, forcing the other to open in December. It's a simultaneous-move game where each firm is trying to get a first-mover advantage.

Table 12.10 Selecting a Release Date*		Disney's Opening Date Choice	
		May	**December**
Warner Brothers' Opening Date Choice	**May**	100, 100	✓ 600, 400 ✓
	December	✓ 400, 600 ✓	0, 0

*Payoffs are measured in millions of dollars of profit.

One possible approach to gaining first-mover advantage might be for one studio to issue a strong threat: "We're going to release our movie in May regardless of when you release yours." By doing this, the threat-issuing firm hopes its opponent, worried about making only the tiny profit that would come with a simultaneous opening, will relent and open in December. But simply threatening to open in May doesn't change the fact that if the other firm actually *does* open in May, the firm making the threat would want to switch to December if given the opportunity. In other words, "opening in May no matter what" is a **noncredible threat**, *a threat made in a game that is not rational for the player to actually follow through on and, as such, is an empty threat.* No one will believe a studio threatening to open in May no matter what because it doesn't make rational sense for the firm to make that choice: Opening in May is not a best response when the other studio chooses May.

The key to making a successful strategic move toward an exclusive May opening is a **credible commitment**, *a choice (or a restriction of choices) that guarantees a player will take a particular future action if certain conditions occur that transform the game.* A firm not only needs to threaten to open in May, it also needs to take actions ahead of time that would make it costly for it to *not* do so and thus signal to the firm's opponent that the firm will carry out its threat.

Suppose Warner Brothers funds an early national advertising campaign for *Wonder Woman 2* with "Opening This May" all over the ads and leaks word to the media during production that it expects the film to be a "summer blockbuster." Suppose Warner Brothers even signs contracts for distribution that incorporate huge penalty payments to theaters if the movie does not arrive on screens in May. Or, perhaps Warner Brothers creates copies of the movie that will erase themselves after the summer so that *Wonder Woman 2* can never be viewed again (yes, this is a stretch, but we are making the point of what counts as a credible move).

Each of these actions gives Warner Brothers a way to credibly commit to a May opening and thus change its payoffs. If the payoff changes from this commitment are large enough, Warner Brothers can alter the basic structure of the game. As long as Warner Brothers makes less than $100 million if it opens in December, opening in May will become a dominant strategy for Warner Brothers, as you can see in **Table 12.11**. Suppose that Warner Brothers makes commitments that will cost it $301 million if *Wonder Woman 2* opens in December. Subtracting 301 from Warner Brothers' payoffs in the "December" row changes its payoffs to 99 in the lower left and −301 in the lower right. Now, no matter what Disney does, Warner Brothers is better off if it chooses May.

Once Warner Brothers has made its threat to open in May credible, Disney's best response is to choose a December release date. Therefore, Warner Brothers has achieved what it wanted (forcing Disney to choose a December opening) by *limiting* its own options ahead of time. By making a December choice so unappealing as to be impossible, Warner Brothers effectively commits itself to take its threatened action (opening in May).

noncredible threat A threat made in a game that is not rational for the player to actually follow through on and, as such, is an empty threat.

credible commitment A choice (or a restriction of choices) that guarantees a player will take a particular future action if certain conditions occur that transform the game.

Table 12.11 A Credible Commitment to Releasing the Film in May*

		Disney's Opening Date Choice	
		May	**December**
Warner Brothers' Opening Date Choice	**May**	✓ 100, 100	✓ 600, 400 ✓
	December	400 − 301 = 99, 600 ✓	0 − 301 = −301, 0

*Payoffs are measured in millions of dollars of profit.

What is so compelling about this strategic move is that on its face it looks irrational. Imagine explaining to your boss that she should make the movie erase itself after the summer. "You took microeconomics for *that*?!" you hear, as security escorts you to your desk to box up your possessions. But, by taking these seemingly detrimental actions, you have actually helped the studio earn $200 million more profit ($600 million instead of $400 million) than it may have earned without them (because the studio could have ended up with a December opening while its competitor chose May). "Nicely done, kid," your boss says as you move into a corner office.

 figure it out 12.4

MagicPill Inc. has developed a new wonder drug for curing obesity that has been approved by the Food and Drug Administration. If the drug is released for sale, a competitor, GenDrug, will attempt to copy the formula and steal all of MagicPill's customers by offering the wonder drug at a lower price. (Assume there are no patent laws at this time.) The extensive form of the game is shown below (payoffs represent profits in millions of dollars):

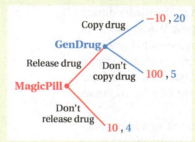

a. Should MagicPill release this new wonder drug for sale? Explain.

b. Would your answer to (a) change if GenDrug promised not to copy the new drug? Explain.

c. Would your answer to (a) change if GenDrug signed a contract with MagicPill promising to pay $10 million if it copies the drug? Explain.

d. How would your answer to (a) change if patent laws protect MagicPill's exclusive right to produce its new wonder drug?

Solution:

a. No. MagicPill will not release the drug. Using backward induction, we can see that if the drug is released, GenDrug will choose to copy it (because it can earn $20 million profit rather than $5 million). Knowing this, MagicPill is better off not releasing the drug (because it can earn $10 million rather than losing $10 million).

b. No. GenDrug's promise would not be credible. The incentive ($15 million additional profit) is large enough that MagicPill cannot believe the promise by GenDrug.

c. No. The payment of $10 million by GenDrug will not change GenDrug's incentive for copying the drug ($20 million − $10 million > $5 million). Furthermore, the payment of $10 million would not be enough to induce MagicPill to release the drug (−$10 million + $10 million < $10 million).

d. Yes. If the patent prohibited GenDrug from copying the wonder drug, we can ignore the "Copy Drug" option in the game. In this case, MagicPill will want to release the drug because $100 million > $10 million.

Application: Dr. Strangelove and the Perils of Secrecy

Stanley Kubrick's classic black comedy *Dr. Strangelove or: How I Learned to Stop Worrying and Love the Bomb* is set in the midst of the Cold War and the nuclear arms race between the United States and the Soviet Union.

In real life, the military consulted extensively with game theorists in the realm of nuclear deterrence. For example, two Nobel Laureate game theorists mentioned in this chapter, John Nash and Thomas Schelling, worked for a time at RAND Corporation analyzing various facets of the Cold War conflict.

The movie mocks the game theory basis of nuclear deterrence. The plot features a rogue U.S. general who, convinced that water fluoridation is a Communist conspiracy to "sap and impurify all of our precious bodily fluids," orders his bomber squadron to launch a nuclear attack on the Soviets. The president orders his top commander to stop the bombers, but the commander says it's impossible; to establish a credible commitment to fight back against a Soviet attack, the bombers cannot be recalled once they pass the point of no return. The president calls the Soviet premier to plead with him not to respond with a massive retaliation, but discovers that, unfortunately, the Soviets have recently installed a doomsday machine that automatically responds to any attack by launching a world-destroying nuclear barrage. Further, the doomsday machine has been programmed to consider any attempt to shut it down as sabotage, thereby also triggering an automatic launch. The Soviets believed this was the only way the machine would act as a credible commitment to respond to an attack.

But, the Soviets had been keeping the machine a secret for the prior six months. The president's game theory advisor, Dr. Strangelove (thought by some to be a parody of John von Neumann, one of the inventors of game theory), asks the Soviet ambassador incredulously, "The whole point of the doomsday machine is lost if you keep it a secret! WHY DIDN'T YOU TELL THE WORLD, EH?" The ambassador answers, "It was to be announced at the Party Congress on Monday. As you know, the premier loves surprises."

We're not sure this is the message that Stanley Kubrick wanted to deliver by making this movie, but it's still right: If you have a doomsday machine, make it credible, and TELL PEOPLE. ■

Entry Deterrence: Credibility Applied

One of the most common applications of strategic moves in microeconomics relates to incumbents trying to deter new competitors from entering their industry.

We have seen repeatedly throughout the past several chapters that firms earn higher profits if they are able to prevent other firms from entering their market. Preventing entry isn't always easy, though. One reason, as with Warner Brothers' threat to open in May no matter what, is the issue of credibility.

Think of the iPad when it was the only tablet on the market and Apple was, in a way, a monopolist. Now suppose another company comes along—Samsung, say—that threatens to enter the market with its own tablet computer.

We can think of this as a sequential game. The extensive form of the game is shown in **Figure 12.6**. The payoffs are profits in billions of dollars.

First, Samsung decides whether to enter the market. If it doesn't enter, the game is over. Samsung earns a profit of zero and Apple earns the monopoly profit of $2 billion (Samsung's payoffs are listed in red, first in every payoff pair). If Samsung enters the market, however, then Apple must decide how to react. If Apple fights Samsung's entry by starting a price war, Samsung will lose $0.5 billion and Apple will earn only $0.8 billion. If Apple

Figure 12.6   An Entry Game*

Samsung uses backward induction to decide whether to enter the tablet market currently dominated by Apple. If Samsung chooses to enter the market, Apple's optimum strategy is to not fight a price war, and Samsung earns $0.5 billion in profit, higher than the zero profit it earns when it doesn't enter the market. Because Samsung knows that Apple's threat to enter a price war is not credible, Samsung will enter the tablet market.

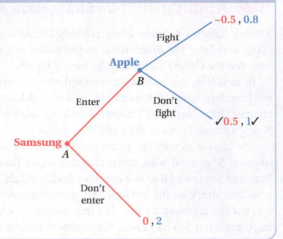

*Payoffs are in billions of dollars of profit.

doesn't fight, Samsung will earn $0.5 billion and Apple $1 billion—less than the monopoly profit, but more than it would by engaging in a price war.

It might seem as though Apple could crush a new entrant like the Samsung Galaxy Note anytime it wants by just threatening to start a price war. In a price war Samsung will lose money if it enters so Samsung should look ahead and realize that, leading them not to enter, right?

Not so fast. Samsung will also consider the credibility of a price-war threat. They won't automatically believe Apple will start a price war just because Apple says it will. Look what a price war does to Apple: If Samsung enters, Apple earns only $0.8 billion by fighting but earns $1 billion by going along. Because Samsung knows this about them, Apple's threat is not credible. By using backward induction, then, Samsung realizes its choices are between entering and earning $0.5 billion (knowing Apple will back down if faced with entry) or not entering and earning nothing. Samsung will therefore call Apple's bluff and enter, and Apple won't fight when it does.

From our previous discussion, we know that the only way Apple can deter entry is by initiating a strategic move that somehow makes the threat to fight credible. One classic maneuver discussed by business strategists is the use of excess capacity. Under this strategy, the incumbent (Apple) builds all the capacity it would need *if* Samsung were to enter and there was a price war—remember that with low prices, quantity sold would go up significantly. The strategy is to build this capacity *before* entry ever occurs.

This strategy wouldn't affect Apple's payoffs much in the event of an actual price war, because it's going to be fully utilizing the capacity it has already built. But the fact that Apple has so much capacity also tends to reduce its price (and profits) if it remains a monopolist, or if Samsung enters and Apple rolls over (since its output would be greater because of its capacity). This output effect of the extra capacity occurs because it greatly lowers Apple's marginal cost, causing its optimal price to fall. A closely related interpretation of this effect is that if the two firms operate in a Cournot oligopoly, Apple's extra capacity is used to raise its output, thus lowering the market price.

Let's suppose Apple invests in extra capacity at an earlier date, and this investment lowers its profit to $1.2 billion in the monopoly case with no entry (because the extra factory capacity sits idle) and to $0.6 billion if Samsung enters and Apple chooses not to fight.

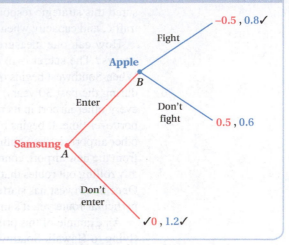

Figure 12.7 Excess Capacity to Create a Credible Threat

To lend credibility to its threat of a price war, Apple invests in extra capacity before Samsung decides whether to enter the tablet market. Apple's profit as a monopolist decreases to $1.2 billion, a profit that is still higher than Apple's equilibrium payoff in Figure 12.6. With this credible threat, however, if Samsung chooses to enter the market, Apple will choose to fight, earning $0.8 billion. Because Samsung will lose $0.5 billion under this strategy, Samsung will choose not to enter the market.

This investment would change the game tree from the one shown in Figure 12.6 to the one in **Figure 12.7** because Apple's threat to fight is now credible.

The strategic use of overcapacity affects the game's payoffs in a way that helps Apple. Now, if Samsung enters, Apple makes more profit by fighting ($0.8 billion) than not ($0.6 billion). Samsung realizes that Apple will definitely fight and chooses to not enter, because zero profit is better than losing $0.5 billion. Apple remains a monopolist, earning $1.2 billion instead of the $1 billion it would have made as a duopolist in the original equilibrium (Figure 12.6). Apple has therefore made its threat to start a price war credible by making a strategic move (early capacity investment choices).

Again, strategic considerations have made seemingly irrational actions beneficial. Imagine trying to explain this strategy to the boss: "We need to build a series of factories that we will never use to create massive excess capacity for making iPads."

"Wait, what? Why would we pay for factories we don't need?" the boss asks.

"So we can credibly prove that our profit will be lower if Samsung enters the market and we don't try to fight them," you say.

Somewhere in the accounting department, someone reads this plan and feels their blood pressure rise. "Now the economist wants us to pay for factories that we won't even use!" But, the logic is absolutely right—those unused factories will make the company an extra $200 million in profit.

Application: Incumbent Airlines' Responses to Threatened Entry by Southwest

While economists rightfully pay a lot of attention to theories about strategic behavior in response to entry threats, actually testing these theories is difficult. By nature, most market data are about firms already operating in a market. But entry threats come from firms that aren't yet in a market. Rarely can economists actually observe data that measure this potential for entry before it ever happens.

Two of this book's authors (Austan Goolsbee and Chad Syverson)[5] figured out a way around this problem in a study testing for strategic behavior among incumbents in the

---

[5] Austan Goolsbee and Chad Syverson, "How Do Incumbents Respond to the Threat of Entry? Evidence from the Major Airlines," *Quarterly Journal of Economics* 123, no. 4 (2008): 1611–1633.

passenger airline industry. Goolsbee and Syverson measured how incumbents responded when Southwest Airlines threatened to offer service on the incumbents' routes. They measured this strategic response by tracking what happened to incumbents' fares, passenger traffic, and capacity when Southwest Airlines loomed as a potential competitor.

How can one measure the threat of entry in this industry before actual entry ever occurs? The secret is in understanding the way Southwest expands its route network. When Southwest begins operating in a new airport (and it has entered a lot of new airports during the past 30 years), it does not immediately offer service from that new airport to every other airport in its route network. Instead, it ramps up its operations at the new airport over time. It begins by offering service between the new airport and only a handful of other airports in the Southwest network. It then gradually adds flights to more destinations from the new airport, connecting more of the dots in its network. It's this practice of gradually rolling out routes that allows one to observe entry threats before entry actually occurs. Once Southwest has started operating in that new airport, even if it hasn't started flying a particular route yet, it's much more likely to do so soon.

An example of this principle in action occurred in spring 2019, when Southwest began flying to Hawaii. Southwest's service to and from Hawaii began with nonstop flights to only two locations. Hawaiian Airlines, a major incumbent carrier, had a new competitor to deal with as a result. Routes between Hawaii and those two cities were cases of Southwest actually entering markets. But the route-rollout process meant this actual entry on two routes was accompanied by Southwest threatening entry into several other routes to other cities in its network. For example, if you're Hawaiian management, you recognize that even though Southwest hasn't actually started flying from Hawaii to Los Angeles (a route on which you are a primary incumbent), now that Southwest has operations in Hawaii, it's much more likely that Southwest will start flying this route. Similarly, if you're in the boardroom at Alaska Airlines, you now view Southwest's entry into the Seattle-to-Hawaii route — one in which you are a major incumbent — as much more likely than before. In this way, Southwest's start in Hawaii in spring 2019 coincided with entry threats felt by Hawaiian on its Hawaii-to-Los Angeles route and Alaska on its Seattle-to-Hawaii route. Similar entry threats were noticed by other incumbent airlines on their own routes to Hawaii. Therefore, if incumbents on these routes were going to make any strategic moves in response to this threatened entry, they should have done so around this time.

Goolsbee and Syverson tested for strategic behavior by looking at how incumbents like Hawaiian and Alaska behaved on hundreds of routes like these that Southwest similarly threatened to enter as it expanded into roughly 20 new airports over a 12-year period.

The data indicate that incumbents did indeed engage in strategic behavior on routes when Southwest loomed as a potential competitor. **Table 12.12** illustrates how incumbents' average fares changed on threatened routes around the time Southwest entered the new airport. It shows incumbents' average fares on threatened routes relative to what they were on those same routes more than two years before Southwest entered the new airport.

By the quarter in which Southwest entered the new airport, incumbents had already dropped their fares by 17% on the routes that Southwest threatened. Incumbents continued to drop fares after Southwest was in the new airport, on average, to levels 21% below their prior levels. This is a fairly substantial fare cut. It can be compared to the total 28% fare cut (again, relative to fares more than two years prior) that incumbents made when Southwest finally did enter those routes it was threatening. In other words, about two-thirds of incumbents' total pricing response to competition from Southwest occurred before Southwest actually started flying on their routes.

Goolsbee and Syverson hypothesized that these strategic responses to threatened entry were attempts by the incumbent airlines to build up loyalty among their flyers on the threatened routes, especially highly valuable frequent-flyer/business customers. This would make it more difficult for Southwest to steal those customers away if and when it began flying the route. This motive is consistent with the finding in the data that incumbents dropped fares more on threatened routes that were likely to have had a smaller share of leisure flyers. Certainly, it's true that flyers responded to these preemptive price cuts. Incumbents saw increased passenger traffic on the threatened routes when they dropped their fares.

One interesting thing to note is that the incumbents actually began cutting prices before Southwest started operating in the new airport—by 12% in the prior year, for example. This makes sense when you think about when incumbents would actu-

Table 12.12 Incumbent Airlines' Responses to Southwest's Threat of Entry

Period	Relative Fare Change
2 + years before Southwest starts operating at the new airport	0
1–2 years before Southwest starts operating at the new airport	−6%
Less than 1 year before Southwest starts operating at the new airport	−12%
Quarter Southwest starts operating at the new airport	−17%
After Southwest has begun operating at the new airport, but before it has started flying the route	−21%
After Southwest has begun operating at the new airport, and it has started flying the route	−28%

ally recognize an entry threat. Southwest doesn't just show up one day at a new airport saying, "We've got a plane parked outside. . . . Who wants to buy a ticket?" They have to lease gates, hire staff, and (of course) sell tickets before ever starting operations at a new airport. This process can take over a year. Incumbents therefore know Southwest is coming and can respond strategically before Southwest actually starts operating in the new airport.

However, in many cases, Southwest was simply a tide that the incumbents weren't going to be able to stop, no matter how aggressively they responded to the entry threat. But don't think this necessarily means that the incumbent's efforts were futile. By cutting fares early, it may have been able to keep business flyers whom it otherwise would have lost to Southwest. While the incumbent would have preferred that Southwest had never shown up, it may have been making the best of a tough competitive situation. ■

Reputation

One last example of a strategic behavior a player might undertake to deter the entry of a rival is to establish a reputation. Reputations themselves can be sources of commitment to a game-playing strategy.

Suppose Apple is facing potential entry not just by Samsung, but by scores of potential tablet makers. Apple could benefit from establishing a reputation for aggressively fighting any entry in any market. If Apple *didn't* fight the entry by Samsung, such behavior may leave them open to even more new entrants like HTC, Xiaomi, or Amazon. Thus, Apple may incur the costs of fighting Samsung (even though doing so could harm its current profit) in order to promote its reputation as a fighter to deter future entrants. In this case, its desire to establish and then preserve a tough reputation becomes a commitment device itself.

Tobacco companies tried this strategy in their response to lawsuits by their former (and sometimes still current) customers. These suits were often for relatively small sums of money. Many of the smokers suing figured they could get the tobacco companies to settle the cases, essentially paying them off to avoid the high costs of a full trial.

But the companies realized that settling one case would encourage more cases. Other smokers would observe the settlement and then file suit in hopes of obtaining their own.

While going to trial in any one case would be a money-loser for the tobacco companies, settling could open the door to billions of dollars in future settlement costs.

The companies therefore tried to establish a reputation for fighting any lawsuit with everything they had. They might pay millions in legal fees to fight a $1,000 lawsuit. While this practice seems irrational at first glance, the hope was that developing such a reputation would effectively commit them to fight any suit in the future, thereby cutting off the "entry" of new plaintiffs before they even filed papers.

Ultimately, though, the cigarette companies' strategy fell apart. The lawsuits grew so numerous and so massive that the companies reached a multi-billion dollar settlement with the federal government and numerous state governments, the Tobacco Master Settlement Agreement, to shield them from further lawsuits.

But, a reputation for being crazy can be valuable. Return to the case of Apple facing entry by Samsung. Suppose Apple could convince Samsung that, regardless of the profit implications, it was just crazy enough to ignite a self-destructive price war for tablets, no matter what Samsung does. This could work to Apple's advantage. If Apple were so combative as to actually *enjoy* fighting for its own sake—even if it's costly in profit terms—it might be able to convince a rational potential entrant like Samsung to stay out of the market. In the spirit of our earlier discussion of the maximin strategy, Samsung might find that avoiding a vicious price war with a rabid competitor is a lower-risk option than hoping for a rational response to its entry.

12.6 Conclusion

Thinking through your opponent's likely responses before you make your decisions remains the essence of strategic thinking and the basis of game theory. Game theory gives us a formal way to think about how companies and people should act in these environments. To figure out the equilibrium in an oligopolistic market in which firms must interact strategically with each other, we need to understand the exact rules of the game (Who are the players? What are their payoffs? Are they making decisions simultaneously or sequentially?). Once we understand the game and how it's being played, we can figure out what the equilibrium should be. It's more difficult to predict outcomes in markets with small numbers of players who interact strategically, but it is important and—as the example of the iPad and the Samsung Galaxy Note indicate—very common in the real world.

Even in situations in which people choose their actions strategically, there are often some obvious equilibria that the games will gravitate toward. These can vary a lot depending on whether the games involve repeated interactions or if the decisions become sequential and one player moves followed by the other one, and so on.

As long as you (or a firm or a government) are thinking about how your opponent will react when you are making your decisions, you are using game theory. It will not only improve your chess game, it will make you a better economist.

Summary

1. **Game theory** is the study of what happens when economic actors—like the firms and consumers we've studied up until this point—behave strategically. Every game features three key elements: **players, strategies**, and **payoffs**. **Dominant strategies** are always the best action for players to take regardless of their opponents' actions, while **dominated strategies** are never the best action. Identifying

any dominant and dominated strategies in a game makes solving for the Nash equilibria easier. **[Section 12.1]**

2. In **simultaneous-move games**, a player must choose her strategy without first knowing her opponent's choice. The mutual-best-response concept of Nash equilibrium is a natural way to predict the outcomes of such games. Depending on the particular structure of the strategies and payoffs,

games can have one, multiple, or even **mixed-strategy** Nash equilibria. Players may also vary their strategies if faced with an irrational or erratic opponent. In addition, players may be interested in using a **maximin strategy** to minimize their losses in a game. **[Section 12.2]**

3. The outcome of a one-shot simultaneous game differs from the outcome of a **repeated simultaneous game. Backward induction** is used to find the equilibria of multi-stage games. When applied to a repeated prisoner's dilemma, backward induction reveals that cooperation is still not an equilibrium when a repeated game has a known final stage (regardless of how many stages there are). However, when the actors

play an infinite game or do not know with certainty which is the final round, cooperation can be an equilibrium. **[Section 12.3]**

4. In **sequential games**, players take actions in turn, meaning that one player sees the other's action before choosing her own strategy. As with other multistage games, backward induction can be used to find the equilibria of sequential games. **[Section 12.4]**

5. Players often use strategic moves to ensure that their later outcomes are favorable. Economic actors may strategically use **side payments, credible commitments**, and **reputation**. **Entry deterrence** is one of the most common applications of strategic moves in microeconomic analysis. **[Section 12.5]**

Review Questions

1. What are the three common elements of an economic game?

2. What differentiates game theory from single-agent problems?

3. How does the existence of multiple Nash equilibria complicate the solution to an economic game?

4. How can a payoff matrix be used to find a player's optimal strategy?

5. Why might a player pursue a mixed strategy?

6. Why is the maximin strategy considered a conservative strategy?

7. Define backward induction. How can backward induction be used to solve a strategic game?

8. Compare the grim trigger and tit-for-tat strategies.

9. Why do we use decision trees—instead of normal-form matrices—to solve sequential games?

10. How can side payments be beneficial to both players in a two-player game?

11. Describe the relationship between credibility and entry deterrence to a market.

12. What are some ways in which a company uses its reputation to its advantage?

Problems (Solutions to problems marked with an asterisk appear at the back of this book. Problems adapted to use calculus are available online.)

*1. Consider the game below:

		Duvall		
		Stop	Drop	Roll
	Hammer	4, 14	9, 6	5, 3
Earl	**Anvil**	8, 2	6, 12	1, 7
	Stirrup	11, 5	16, 3	9, 8

a. Who are the players in this game?

b. What strategies are available to Duvall?

c. If Earl plays "Hammer" and Duvall plays "Roll," then what is Earl's payoff?

d. If Earl plays "Stirrup" and Duvall plays "Drop," what is Duvall's payoff?

2. Consider the following game:

		Fireman Sam		
		Stop	Drop	Roll
	Try on Costume	12, 7	8, 6	5, 2
	Look for Adventure	11, 16	6, 1	21, 8
Mr. Benn	**Hesitate**	1, 3	4, 2	9, 4
	Open the Door	2, 8	11, 5	8, 7

a. Find each player's dominant strategy, if any.

b. Find any dominated strategies.

3. For each of the following games,

a. Find each player's dominant strategy, if any, and

b. Use dominance to find the Nash equilibrium. Each game contains only one Nash equilibrium.

i.

		MacBeth	
		Clean Spot	Listen to Wife
MacDuff	**Slay King**	10, 2	8, 4
	Roll Head	6, 4	4, 5

ii.

		Ferris	
		Twist	Shout
Elvis	**Bump**	2, 8	4, 5
	Grind	4, 4	6, 2

iii.

		Billy	
		Bottle of Red	Bottle of White
Julia	**Steak**	5, 2	8, 4
	Chicken	6, 1	7, 3

iv.

		Stanley		
		Don't Touch This	Sound Bells	Wave Hands
Robert	Stop	2, 8	9, 7	1, 4
	Collaborate	8, 6	11, 4	7, 2
	Listen	7, 7	4, 3	6, 2

4. Dominance can be a very useful and intuitive way to find the likely outcome of a game. Consider, for example, the following game between Bobbi and Gary:

		Gary		
		Left	Center	Right
Bobbi	High	4, 4	7, 5	5, 2
	Middle	8, 3	2, 4	1, 12
	Low	10, 6	9, 1	4, 3

a. Are there any dominant strategies in this game?

b. Finding the likely outcome of this complex game appears difficult. Can you simplify the game by finding a strategy that Bobbi should never reasonably play? Redraw the game with that strategy eliminated. (*Hint:* Look for dominated strategies.)

c. In your simplified game, find a strategy that Gary should never reasonably play. (Again, look for dominated strategies.) Did that strategy appear to be unreasonable in the original game? Redraw the simplified game.

d. In your twice-simplified game, find a strategy that Bobbi should never reasonably play and redraw the game with that strategy removed from consideration.

e. Eliminate the one strategy remaining that Gary is unlikely to use. The only outcome remaining is the likely outcome of the game.

5. Use the check method to find the Nash equilibrium or equilibria (if any) in each of the following games:

a.

		Jada	
		Starbucks	Peets
Will	Starbucks	5, 5	0, 0
	Peets	0, 0	6, 6

b.

		Chuck	
		Straight	Swerve
Ren	Straight	0, 0	4, 2
	Swerve	2, 4	3, 3

c.

		Reggie	
		Swing Early	Swing Late
Rocket	Fastball	40, 60	90, 10
	Changeup	70, 30	25, 75

d.

		KISS-FM		
		Country	Pop	Rock and Roll
KNBU Radio	Country	2, 4	5, 1	4, 5
	Pop	4, 7	4, 5	2, 6
	Rock and Roll	5, 5	8, 6	3, 3

6. Consider the game below:

		Ethel	
		Left	Right
Fred	Up	100, 50	130, 8
	Down	150, 6	−10,000, 4

a. What is the Nash equilibrium in this game?

b. Explain why this game might reasonably end up at a non-equilibrium outcome. Whose play is likely to be responsible for that happening?

7. Each day, you and a friend play odds/evens to see who gets the last doughnut. On command, you each extend either one or two fingers. If the sum of the fingers is odd, you get the doughnut. If the sum of the fingers is even, your friend gets the doughnut.

a. Let the payoffs from winning be 1, and from losing, 0. Fill in the payoff matrix below:

		You	
		One Finger	Two Fingers
Friend	One Finger		
	Two Fingers		

b. Find the pure-strategy Nash equilibria in this game, if any.

c. If you always play one finger, how will your friend respond? How much can you expect to win, on average?

d. If you always play two fingers, how will your friend respond? How much can you expect to win, on average?

e. If you mix one finger and two fingers 50:50, and your friend does the same, what fraction of the time will you emerge victorious? How much can you expect to win, on average? Does mixing give you a higher average payout than playing a pure strategy?

f. Suppose your day-by-day mixture is as follows: 1, 2, 1, 2, 1, 2, 1, 2. Will your 50:50 mixture give you a higher payout than playing a pure strategy? Why or why not?

g. Economist Avinash Dixit claims that there is no better way to surprise your opponent than to surprise yourself. Suggest an easy way to randomize your play that gives you a 50:50 mix overall, but that does so in an unpredictable fashion.

8. You are one of two member nations of OOEC: the Organization of Otter Exporting Countries, a cartel designed to artificially restrict otter output in an attempt to generate monopoly profits. Demand conditions are such that various combinations of output yield the profits in the payoff matrix below:

		Other Country	
		Produce 1,000 Otters	Produce 2,000 Otters
Your Country	Produce 1,000 Otters	$500, $500	$250, $700
	Produce 2,000 Otters	$700, $250	$400, $400

   a. If your country is able to successfully collude with the other country, how many otters will each country produce, and how much profit will each earn?

   b. What is the equilibrium outcome in this game if it is only played once? Is the equilibrium outcome a good one for your country?

*9. Refer to Problem 8. It seems realistic to assume that the game could continue indefinitely — after all, the world will need otters 50 years from now just as badly as it does today. But time is money, so a dollar of profit a year from now is only valued as much as d received today, where d (the discount rate) is some amount less than $1.

   Assume that you adopt a grim trigger strategy whereby your country pledges to produce 1,000 otters as long as the other country produces 1,000 otters. But should the other country ever produce 2,000 otters, you will respond by producing 2,000 otters, forever and ever. After you announce your strategy, the other country pledges to abide by the grim trigger strategy.

   a. What stream of profits will you generate if both countries adopt such a grim strategy? (Don't forget to discount each year's future profits by the appropriate multiple of d.) Express your answer as a sum.

   b. Suppose your country decides to take advantage of the other country's pledge to reduce output by expanding your own output in the first year. What stream of profits can you expect to generate? Again, be sure to discount appropriately, and express your answer as a sum.

   c. Suppose $d = 0.5$. Are you better off cheating on your agreement, or abiding by it? How does your answer change if $d = 0.99$? What about $d = 0.01$?

   d. At what level of d are you indifferent between cheating on or abiding by the agreement?

10. Consider the Organization of Otter Exporting Countries playing a repeated game as described in Problems 8 and 9. Assume, however, that your opponent is playing a tit-for-tat strategy rather than a grim trigger.

   a. What stream of profits will you generate if you always cooperate and your opponent follows the tit-for-tat strategy?

   b. What stream of profits will you generate if you defect once against an opponent playing a tit-for-tat strategy?

   c. Assume that $d = 0.5$. Is it worthwhile to defect once against such an opponent? And if it's worthwhile to defect once, should it be worthwhile to defect more than once should the game last that long?

   d. What value for d makes defecting worthwhile? How does the value of defecting change as d changes?

11. You and a classmate (let's call him Dave) discover that your economics teacher has been secretly talking about notions such as "love," "fairness," and "decency." Desperate to preserve his reputation in the community of economists, he tries to buy your silence in the following way. "You two sit silently at a table. I'll put down a hundred-dollar bill. You can take the bill, or pass the decision to Dave. Before Dave decides, I'll put another hundred-dollar bill on the table. If he passes, I'll add yet another bill to the table and you can have another turn. The game will end when someone takes the money, or when the $500 in my wallet is gone, whichever comes first." You both agree to keep quiet about your instructor's transgressions for the chance to play the game, and as your teacher indicated, you get the first turn.

   a. Suppose that each of you has passed twice, and your instructor has just put the last $100 bill on the table. It is your turn: What should you do?

   b. Suppose that you have passed twice, and Dave has passed once. Your instructor has just put the fourth $100 bill on the table. What should Dave do: Take the money or pass? Why?

   c. Suppose that you and Dave have each passed once. Your instructor has just put the third $100 bill on the table. What should you do: Take the money or pass? Why?

   d. Suppose that you have passed once. Your instructor has just put the second $100 bill on the table. What should Dave do: Take the money or pass? Why?

   e. Your instructor has just laid the first $100 bill on the table. It is your turn. Should you take the money or pass? Why?

   f. What is the likely outcome of this game? Does your instructor pay the entire $500 for your silence?

12. Consider the situation the economics professor faces in Problem 11, but now let's suppose that Dave makes you the following offer: "Let's really soak this guy. I'll pass on turns 2 and 4 if you'll go halves on the 500 bucks with me." Should this offer fundamentally alter the outcome of the game? (*Hint:* Think about this problem using backward induction!)

13. Trim the branches in the following game tree to solve the game depicted:

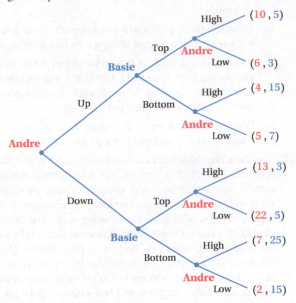

*14. Your little twin sisters (whom you lovingly refer to as Thing 1 and Thing 2) are driving you crazy! You've baked them a lovely birthday cake, but they won't stop fighting over who gets the biggest slice. To settle the dispute, you draw on a time-honored ritual: You ask Thing 1 to cut the cake, and Thing 2 to choose which piece she wants.

a. Draw the extensive form of this game. Let Thing 1's strategies be "Cut Evenly" or "Cut Unevenly"; depending on what's on the platter, Thing 2's strategies might include "Take Big Slice," "Take Small Slice," or "Take Equal Slice." Assign payoffs to Thing 1 and Thing 2 that grow with the size of the slice they receive.

b. Use backward induction to find the equilibrium outcome for this game. Is the equilibrium consistent with your experience?

c. After the rules are announced, Thing 2 says, "It's not fair! I want to be the one who gets to cut the cake, not the one that chooses the slice!" Is Thing 2's complaint valid — in other words, is there a first-mover advantage in this game?

15. Crazy Eddie and Loopy Larry are two electronics merchants who sell plasma TVs at either a high price or a low price. If they both charge a high price, they will each earn high profits. If one charges a high price while the other charges a low price, the low-price seller will get all the business and earn a huge profit. If they both charge low prices, their customers get great deals and the merchants each earn a modest profit.

a. Draw the extensive form of the game between Crazy Eddie and Loopy Larry. Assume that Crazy Eddie

moves first and can choose a high price or a low price. Loopy Larry then follows with a high price or a low price.

b. Find the equilibrium outcome in the battle between Crazy Eddie and Loopy Larry.

c. In a series of wild TV commercials, Crazy Eddie announces, "Crazy Eddie will not be undersold! Find a better price, and I will match it!" Loopy Larry responds with the same offer. Redraw the game these two cutthroat competitors play, but give each player the chance to match his competitor's price if he prices high and his competitor prices low.

d. Find the equilibrium outcome in the battle between Crazy Eddie and Loopy Larry. Has the price-matching guarantee been good for consumers? Is price matching indicative of intense competition?

16. After years of training, Sara has landed a contract playing professional lacrosse. Eager to leverage her pro status by bringing in endorsements, she asks Jenny MacGuire to be her personal manager. Jenny has offered Sara a choice of two payment plans. Sara can engage Jenny's services for a flat fee of $100,000. Alternatively, Sara can pay Jenny 15% of all endorsement revenue.

Sara estimates that if Jenny expends modest effort ($20,000 worth) in her job, she will generate $600,000 in endorsement revenue for Sara. But if Jenny expends high effort ($50,000 worth), she'll bring in $1 million in endorsements. On the day Sara and Jenny are to sign their agreement, Jenny tells Sara, "I am 100% dedicated to you, and will always work as hard as humanly possible on your behalf no matter what payment plan you choose."

a. Sara has a choice of payment plans; Jenny has a choice of effort levels. Determine the relevant payouts for all of the possible outcomes, and draw the extensive form of the game Sara and Jenny are playing.

b. Find the equilibrium outcome to this game. Will Sara choose the flat fee or the 15% plan? Will Jenny expend modest effort or high effort?

c. Is Jenny's promise believable?

d. Discuss the implications of the type of payment scheme on the incentives and payoffs each player faces. Then, extend your analysis by discussing paying workers an annual salary versus paying them a certain amount for each finished product they produce (called "piece-rate compensation").

17. Abel, Brenda, and Carlos are members of the Human Resources Management Club at their university. The club plans to bring a motivational speaker to campus with money earned selling doughnuts at the local farmers' market. If the club sells doughnuts on three weekends, it will be able to afford a terrific speaker and Abel, Brenda, and Carlos will each get 100 units of happiness. If the club sells doughnuts on two weekends, it will be able to

afford an above-average speaker that brings each member 70 units of happiness. If the club sells doughnuts on just one weekend, it will be able to bring in their college's personnel director to speak and each member will receive 25 units of happiness. If the club doesn't sell doughnuts at all, nobody will receive anything.

Abel is scheduled to sell doughnuts the first weekend, Brenda the second, and Carlos the third, after which the farmers' market closes down for winter. Working at the farmers' market costs the worker 40 units of happiness. On the scheduled day, each worker must choose between staffing the doughnut stand or sleeping in.

a. Draw the extensive form of this game, with Abel moving first, Brenda second, and Carlos third.

b. Solve for the equilibrium outcome of this game. What does each player do? What kind of speaker does the club bring in?

c. Is there an advantage to being the first-mover in this game? Explain why or why not.

18. Two graduate students are engaged to each other, and both are working on their master's thesis — Kristen in political science and Michael in music education. Because both have incomes that are tied to their academic achievement, and because they plan to marry and share household income, each wants the other to complete their thesis. But Kristen is having a motivational crisis: She doesn't want to complete her thesis.

		Kristen	
		Complete Thesis	Don't Complete
Michael	Complete Thesis	11, 6	8, 8
	Don't Complete	7, 2	4, 4

a. How do the payoffs in the table reflect Kristen's motivational crisis? Explain.

b. What is the Nash equilibrium in this game?

c. Michael would like Kristen to complete her thesis. He tells Kristen, "If you don't complete your thesis, then I'm not going to complete mine." Explain, using the numbers from the payoff matrix, why this threat is not immediately credible.

d. Suppose that Kristen believes Michael's threat. Explain, referring to the payoffs in the table above, why this threat should be sufficient to motivate Kristen to complete her thesis.

19. Consider the game played by Michael and Kristen in Problem 18 above. Suppose that Michael decides not to threaten Kristen, but instead decides to promise her a monetary reward if she completes her thesis.

a. How many points' worth of money must Michael pay Kristen to convince her to complete her thesis?

b. How many points' worth of money is Michael willing to spend in order to convince Kristen to complete her thesis?

c. Based on your answers to (a) and (b), can Michael and Kristen work out a mutually beneficial trade in which Michael gives Kristen money and she completes her thesis?

20. Assume that two clothing manufacturers, Lands' End and L.L. Bean, market their goods strictly by mail order. Each produces an essentially identical field coat. The cost of producing such a coat is exactly $100. Because the field coats are perfect substitutes, customers will flock to the seller that offers the lowest price. If both firms offer identical prices, each receives half the customers.

For simplicity, assume that the two firms have the choice of pricing at whole-dollar prices of $103, $102, or $101. Market demand at $103 is 100 coats; at $102, 110 coats; and at $101, 120 coats. The profit each firm would earn at various prices is shown in the payoff matrix below:

		L.L. Bean		
		$103	$102	$101
Lands' End	$103	$150, $150	$0, $220	$0, $120
	$102	$220, $0	$110, $110	$0, $120
	$101	$120, $0	$120, $0	$60, $60

a. What is the equilibrium outcome of the game Lands' End and L.L. Bean are playing?

b. Is collusion between Lands' End and L.L. Bean likely to last?

c. If Lands' End and L.L. Bean were allowed to quote prices in cents rather than whole dollars, what would the likely outcome of this game be?

d. Suppose that in hopes of raising prices above equilibrium, L.L. Bean decides to announce the price for its field coat early in the summer. Will that strategic move be successful for L.L. Bean? Why or why not?

21. Consider the following game, played by Player 1 (P1) and Player 2 (P2).

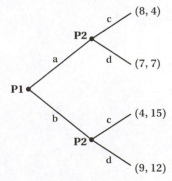

a. Use induction to find the equilibrium in this game.

b. Suppose that Player 2 wishes to change the outcome of the game to one better for Player 2. Can Player 2 achieve this by making a promise to Player 1? If so, what must that promise be? Is the promise believable?

c. Can Player 2 achieve an outcome preferable to the equilibrium by making a commitment? If so, what would Player 2 have to commit to?

d. Can Player 2 achieve an outcome preferable to the equilibrium by issuing a threat to Player 1? If so, what must that threat be?

22. There are two ice cream vendors, Ben and Jerry, on a crowded strip of beach. There are five permissible locations for ice cream vendors to locate, cleverly named positions 1, 2, 3, 4, and 5. Position 1 is at the far north end of the beach, Position 5 at the far south end, and Position 3 in the middle, while Positions 2 and 4 are midway between their respective neighbors. Each location may accommodate more than one vendor. There are 1,000 beachgoers scattered uniformly across the beach (200 at each position) who will buy from the closest vendor.

a. Fill in the payoff matrix below with payouts reflecting the number of customers each vendor receives. (Example: If Ben is at Position 1 and Jerry is at Position 4, Ben will get 400 beachgoers at locations 1 and 2, and Jerry will get 600 of the beachgoers at Positions 3, 4, and 5.)

b. Find the Nash equilibrium or equilibria in this game. Where are Ben and Jerry likely to end up locating?

23. In the 1960s, tobacco producers engaged in fierce battles for market share. The major weapon in that war was advertising—advertising that was designed not to attract new smokers, but to lure smokers away from competing brands. Consider the following scenario: There are two tobacco sellers, Phillip and R. J., each of whom can choose to advertise on TV (at a cost of $20 million) or not. There are $100 million of pre-advertising profits available to the two firms. If they both adopt the same budget, they will split the market evenly. If one chooses a high budget while the other chooses low, the high-budget firm will steal half the other's customers and capture $75 million of pre-advertising profit; the other will earn $25 million. The firms' net profits (after advertising expenses are considered) are illustrated in the payoff matrix below:

		R. J.	
		Advertise	**Don't Advertise**
Phillip	**Advertise**	$30, $30	$55, $25
	Don't Advertise	$25, $55	$50, $50

a. Verify that the payoffs in the table reflect the story told above.

b. What is the Nash equilibrium in this game? Is the equilibrium outcome a good one for anybody?

c. Suppose that Phillip and R. J. promise each other that they will not advertise. Is such a promise credible? Explain.

d. In 1971 the federal government banned cigarette advertising on TV. Initially, tobacco companies protested vehemently. Referring to the game table above, discuss whether Big Tobacco's protests were genuine.

		Jerry				
		Position 1	**Position 2**	**Position 3**	**Position 4**	**Position 5**
Ben	**Position 1**					
	Position 2					
	Position 3					
	Position 4					
	Position 5					

Factor Markets

In Chapter 6, we saw how a firm like Samsung chooses the mix of labor and capital inputs they use to produce their desired output. We know that, given the prices of labor and capital and its production function, a firm minimizes its production costs by hiring the input mix that equates the marginal rate of technical substitution to the input price ratio.

But we need to think more about what variables determine those input prices in the first place. This chapter does that by examining **factor markets**, the *markets for inputs such as labor, intermediate goods, and land (called factors of production) that are used to produce outputs*. (We will analyze the capital market in Chapter 14.)

In many ways, factor markets are like all the other product markets we've studied so far. There is demand. There is supply. And there is an equilibrium price that equates the quantity demanded and quantity supplied. But the "product" in the factor market is now an input (such as employees) used by someone else to produce an output (such as head-phones). The prices that matter are now the wage rate in the case of labor, or the prices of material, service, energy, or land inputs in other cases. Although these similarities mean factor markets work in the same basic way as product markets, the stories behind the demand and supply curves are a bit different. (Even so, we'll see in these stories some connections to the markets we've already studied.)

We begin by analyzing perfectly competitive factor markets. As with the perfectly competitive output markets we studied in Chapter 8, all market participants are price takers who are so small relative to the entire market that their choices of how much of a factor to supply or demand will not change the market price. Thus, market participants behave as if that price is fixed. Even though all or even most factor markets do not exactly fit this assumption, the perfectly competitive case is a useful benchmark against which to compare actual market outcomes.

13.1 Demand in a Perfectly Competitive Factor Market

We start our analysis of factor markets by looking at the market for labor inputs. The labor market is probably the most important factor market. In most economies, about 60%–70% of the money spent on inputs is paid to workers. Once we understand how the labor market works, the analysis of any factor market follows the same pattern.

factor markets Markets for inputs such as labor, intermediate goods, and land (called factors of production) that are used to produce outputs.

The Firm's Demand for Labor

The demand side of the labor market comprises all firms that need to hire workers to help produce their output. We begin by looking at a single firm's demand for labor. After that, we add up such demands across all firms to obtain the total market demand for labor.

Let's think about a company (say, Samsung) that needs to hire workers/buy labor services to produce an output like smartphones. As with our analysis of other markets, we make some simplifying assumptions.

To make our analysis simpler, we assume all labor units are the same: An employee-hour is an employee-hour, no matter who that employee is, what she does at work, or what her wage is. For now, we won't worry about these differences, and we'll just say that Samsung buys "labor" at a single wage.

Another simplifying assumption we make is that Samsung chooses the short-run amount of labor to hire. Because we are looking at the short run, Samsung's capital inputs are fixed (see Chapter 6). The firm therefore wants to hire the optimal amount of labor to work with its fixed amount of capital. Later in this chapter, we study long-run labor demand, which describes hiring when firms can also change their capital inputs.

To start, think about the tradeoffs Samsung faces when it hires more labor. Adding more workers (or having its existing workers work more hours) allows Samsung to make more smartphones. The amount of additional production from a 1-unit increase in labor is the marginal product of labor, MP_L. In our example, the MP_L is the extra number of smartphones Samsung can make with 1 additional unit of labor. Samsung doesn't just want to make smartphones, though; it needs to sell them. The extra revenue that those additional smartphones yield when they are sold is their marginal revenue, MR. Therefore, the total benefit to Samsung of hiring 1 more unit of labor is the number of phones that worker makes times the extra revenue earned by selling the phones. This value is *the marginal product of labor times the marginal revenue*, called the **marginal revenue product of labor**, or MRP_L. Thus, $MRP_L = MP_L \times MR$.

Samsung's cost of hiring that additional unit of labor is the wage (set by the market). In a perfectly competitive market, the firm can hire as much labor as it would like at the market wage W.

Consider how this benefit (the MRP_L) and cost (W) change with the amount of labor Samsung hires. We know the cost W is fixed and thus unaffected by the amount of labor hired. On the other hand, as we learned in Chapter 6, a firm's production exhibits diminishing marginal returns to labor and capital. Thus, labor's marginal revenue product falls as Samsung hires more workers (remember, capital inputs are fixed in the short run, so more and more people are using the same amount of capital). If the output market is perfectly competitive, we know from Chapter 8 that MR is constant and equal to the market price of the product. In this case, since MR is constant but MP_L falls as more labor is hired, MRP_L must drop. If instead the firm has some market power (as Samsung probably does with smartphones), we know from Chapter 9 that marginal revenue falls as output rises. Because more labor must be hired to produce more output, MR will fall. This drop in MR reinforces the negative effect on MP_L of hiring more labor, further causing MRP_L to fall when more labor is hired.

The Firm's Labor Demand: A Graphical Approach

The changes in labor's marginal revenue product as hiring changes are shown in **Figure 13.1**. Samsung's marginal revenue product curve MRP_L (measured in dollars) falls as it hires more labor, and the wage it pays to the extra workers stays constant.

We now have all the elements we need to describe Samsung's demand for labor. Think about Samsung's tradeoff between its benefit (MRP_L) and cost (W) of hiring more labor. At relatively low levels of hiring, labor's marginal revenue product is high because MP_L is still large. As a result, $MRP_L > W$. Samsung wants to hire any unit of labor for which this

marginal revenue product of labor (MRP_L) The marginal product of labor times the marginal revenue.

Figure **13.1** Samsung's Labor Hiring Decision

Given market wage W, a firm optimally hires the quantity of labor l^*, where $MRP_L = W$. If Samsung hired less labor than l^* so that $MRP_L > W$, it could increase its profits by hiring more because the firm's benefit from that labor (MRP_L) would be greater than its cost (W). If, on the other hand, Samsung hired more labor than l^*, it would be paying for labor with a benefit less than its cost, and could do better by reducing hiring. Only when $MRP_L = W$ can Samsung do no better.

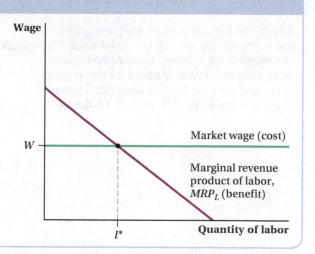

is true because that labor unit's benefit is greater than its cost. In Figure 13.1, this is true for all quantities of labor less than l^*.

Samsung will not want to hire any unit of labor for which $MRP_L < W$, as is the case for labor levels above l^*, because the benefit of those additional units of labor MRP_L is less than their cost W. In fact, Samsung wants to hire exactly l^*. Hiring less labor than l^* means there is room to hire additional people whose benefit exceeds their cost. Hiring more labor than l^* means Samsung has some people that cost more than their MPR_L. The relationship between the marginal revenue product and the wage at l^* is key because it reflects what must be true at the optimal level of hiring: A firm is employing the optimal amount of labor when the marginal revenue product of labor equals the wage:

$$MRP_L = W$$

Demand curves show the quantity demanded of a good as its price changes. Here, the good is labor and the price is the wage. We just saw that the MRP_L curve gives the quantity demanded at each price. If the wage changes, the amount of hiring the firm wants to do changes with it. You can see this in **Figure 13.2**. If the market-determined wage rises from W to W_1, fewer units of labor have a marginal revenue product that is greater than the wage, so Samsung hires only l_1^*, where $MRP_L = W_1$. If the wage falls to W_2, Samsung hires l_2^*, where $MRP_L = W_2$. Samsung wants to hire the quantity of labor such that the marginal revenue product of labor equals the wage. In other words, *the MRP_L curve is Samsung's labor demand curve*. Like the other demand curves we've seen, it slopes down. Figure 13.2 also shows Samsung's **choke wage**, *the wage at which a firm won't want to hire any labor*, which is where the curve crosses the vertical axis, and the maximum amount of labor Samsung would hire if it were free to do so (because MRP_L equals zero), where the curve crosses the horizontal axis.

We've been using Samsung as an example, but this outcome is true for any firm. Its labor demand curve is its MRP_L curve because the MRP_L curve shows how much labor the firm wants to hire at any given wage.

choke wage The wage at which a firm won't want to hire any labor.

Figure 13.2   The Marginal Revenue Curve Is the Labor Demand Curve

Because the MRP_L curve shows the quantity of labor that a firm will hire at any given market wage, it is also the firm's labor demand curve. At market wage W, Samsung hires l^* units of labor. If the market wage were higher, like at W_1, Samsung would hire l_1^* instead. At a lower wage like W_2, Samsung hires a larger quantity, l_2^*.

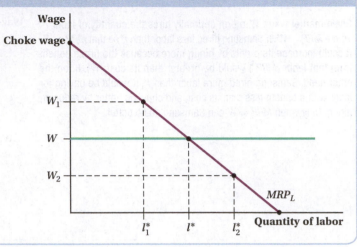

 figure it out 13.1

Go online for interactive, step-by-step help in solving the following problem.

Victoria's Tours, Inc. is a travel company that offers guided tours of nearby mountain biking trails. Its marginal revenue product of labor is given by $MRP_L = 1{,}000 - 40l$, where l is the number of tour-guide-weeks it hires (a tour-guide-week is the amount of work done by one tour guide working one full-time week) and MRP_L is measured in dollars per tour-guide-week. The going market wage in the city where Victoria's Tours is located is $600 per tour-guide-week.

a. What is the optimal amount of labor for Victoria's Tours to hire?

b. Above what market wage would Victoria's Tours not want to hire anyone?

c. What is the most labor Victoria's Tours would ever hire given its current marginal revenue product?

Solution:

a. Victoria's Tours' optimal amount of labor is that which equates the marginal revenue product of labor and the wage:

$$MRP_L = W$$
$$1{,}000 - 40l = 600$$
$$400 = 40l$$
$$l^* = 10$$

Victoria's Tours' optimal quantity of labor is 10 tour-guide-weeks.

b. Victoria Tours will not want to hire any workers at all if the wage is higher than the marginal revenue product of the first unit of labor. That (choke) wage, which we label W_{choke}, is given by setting l in the MRP_L equation to zero:

$$W_{choke} = 1{,}000 - 40(0)$$
$$W_{choke} = 1{,}000$$

If the wage rises to or above $1,000 per tour-guide-week, Victoria's Tours will not demand any labor.

c. Given the MRP_L curve, there is an amount of labor at which the marginal revenue product becomes zero. Any more hiring, even if the wage is zero, will only reduce revenue. This maximum amount of hiring, l_{max}, sets $MRP_L = 0$:

$$1{,}000 - 40l_{max} = 0$$
$$1{,}000 = 40l_{max}$$
$$l_{max} = 25$$

The most labor Victoria's Tours would hire with its current MRP_L curve is 25 tour-guide-weeks.

There is another interpretation of the optimal hiring condition that can be seen if we break MRP_L into its two components, MP_L and MR:

$$MRP_L = MP_L \times MR = W$$

Rearranging this condition gives

$$MR = \frac{W}{MP_L}$$

We see that at the firm's optimal hiring level, marginal revenue equals the wage divided by the marginal product of labor. The ratio on the right side reflects the cost of hiring an additional unit of labor (in dollars) divided by the number of units of output that additional labor produces. For Samsung, it's the number of dollars (or, perhaps more accurately, Korean won) Samsung has to spend to make each incremental smartphone — the marginal cost of that smartphone. In other words, Samsung (and firms in general) wants to hire labor until marginal revenue equals marginal cost. This is exactly the profit-maximizing output quantity choice we discussed in Chapter 9. This equivalence implies that producing the profit-maximizing quantity also means that the firm hires the optimal amount of labor.

This connection between the output a firm makes and its optimal labor hiring implies that labor demand is a **derived demand**, *a demand for one product (such as labor) that arises from the demand for another product (a firm's output)*. This connection to the firm's output is one conceptual way in which factor markets are distinct from markets for regular goods. When consumers are buying the typical kinds of goods we've been dealing with in this text, they're seeking to maximize their utility directly. When firms buy factors, they're doing so as part of making profits by selling something else.

derived demand
A demand for one product (such as labor) that arises from the demand for another product (a firm's output).

Shifts in the Firm's Labor Demand Curve

Like any other demand curve, the labor demand curve holds everything else constant about demand except for price (in this case, the wage). Changes in any other variable that affects labor demand show up as shifts in the labor demand curve rather than movements along it.

To understand some of those other variables, think of the separate components of the labor demand (MRP_L) curve: the marginal product of labor and marginal revenue. Forces that change either component will shift labor demand.

We saw in Chapter 6 that the MP_L depends on both the production function and the amount of capital the firm has. Changes in the production function from changes in total factor productivity (also known as *technical change*) will shift MP_L and, therefore, the labor demand curve. Increases in productivity increase MP_L and increase the quantity of labor demanded at each wage, thus shifting labor demand out. (Decreases in productivity have the opposite effects and shift labor demand in.)

Shifts in capital can also shift the MP_L curve, but remember for now that we are looking at labor demand in the short run when capital is fixed. We will see how changes in a firm's capital affect the firm's long-run demand for labor later in the chapter.

The relationship between shifts in marginal revenue and shifts in labor demand results from the fact that labor demand is a derived demand. If the demand for Samsung's smartphones falls (as a result of changing tastes, improvements in the availability of substitutes, etc.), the price of Samsung's smartphones will fall, and their marginal revenue will fall along with it. As shown in **Figure 13.3**, this decrease in marginal revenue shifts Samsung's MRP_L curve in from $MRP_{L,\text{high}}$ to $MRP_{L,\text{low}}$ (where "high" and "low" denote the level of smartphone demand). Because Samsung is a wage taker, it faces a fixed market wage of W per hour. Therefore, Samsung's quantity of labor demanded falls from l_{high}^* to l_{low}^*. This outcome is intuitive: If fewer people want Samsung smartphones or have lower

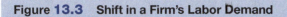

Figure 13.3   Shift in a Firm's Labor Demand

When a firm's labor demand curve (the MRP_L curve) shifts while the market wage stays constant, the firm's optimal quantity of labor changes. If Samsung's MRP_L curve shifts in from $MRP_{L,high}$ to $MRP_{L,low}$ (due to a drop in demand for its smartphones, say), its quantity of labor demanded will fall from l^*_{high} to l^*_{low}.

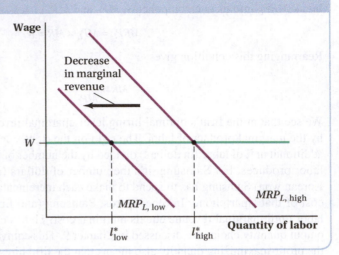

willingness to pay for them, Samsung won't want to hire as many workers. In general, any variable that shifts the firm's marginal revenue curve shifts the labor demand curve.

Market Labor Demand Curve

That's how labor demand is determined at the firm level. To analyze how the labor market as a whole works, we have to add up the labor demand of all firms in the economy.

In Chapter 5, we learned that a product's market demand curve is the horizontal sum of individual consumers' demand for that product. That's true here, too. The market demand for labor is the horizontal sum of all firms' labor demand curves. To compute it, we pick a wage level and add up all firms' quantity of labor demanded at that wage to get market quantity demanded at that wage. Then we repeat the process for every possible wage. The market labor demand curve must slope down because every individual firm's labor demand curve slopes down.

The only aspect of market labor demand that can be a bit tricky has to do with the relationship between the market wage and the price of the output that firms are hiring the labor to make. When we looked at how the firm-level quantity of labor demanded changes with the market wage, we held everything else constant, including all components of the firm's MRP_L. But for market-level labor demand, there's a natural feedback loop between the market wage and the MRP_L of industry firms. A drop in the market wage—because it would reduce all industry firms' costs—will also lead to a reduction in the price of the industry output. This price drop reduces the firms' marginal revenue, shifting their MRP_L curves in. (An *increase* in the market wage would raise the output price and shift firms' MRP_L curves out.) This means firms' total response to a change in the market wage will be smaller in size than it would if there weren't a connection between the market wage and the output price.

Figure 13.4 illustrates how this works. At the initial market wage and output price, an industry firm has a labor demand curve of MRP_{L1}. Given a market wage W_1, it hires l^*_1 units of labor, as shown in panel a. If the market wage falls from W_1 to W_2, all industry firms' costs fall and so does the output price. This reduction in marginal revenue shifts the firm's labor demand curve to MRP_{L2}. Now that the market wage is W_2, the firm hires l^*_2 labor units. Had there been no change in output price associated with the wage drop, the firm would have hired l^*_{NC} (on MRP_{L1}) instead. At the market level, this feedback between the market wage and the output price implies that a wage drop from W_1 to W_2 increases

Figure 13.4   **Industry Labor Demand**

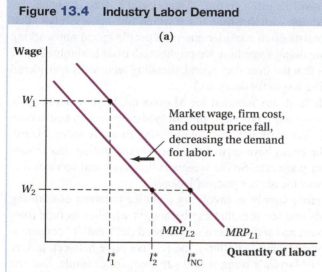

(a)

In panel a, which shows outcomes for an industry firm, the firm has a labor demand curve of MRP_{L1} at the initial market wage and output price. Given market wage W_1, it hires l_1^* units of labor. A fall in the market wage from W_1 to W_2 reduces all industry firms' costs and thus the output price. The lower price reduces marginal revenue and shifts in the firm's labor demand curve to MRP_{L2}, implying

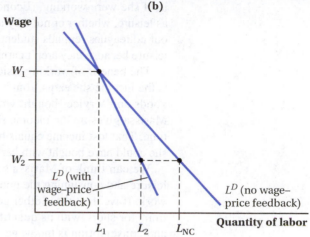

(b)

that at W_2 the firm hires l_2^* instead of l_{NC}^*. At the industry level in panel b, which sums the responses of firms like the one shown in panel a, this feedback between the market wage and the output price implies that a wage drop from W_1 to W_2 increases the industry's quantity of labor demanded from L_1 to only L_2 instead of the no-feedback increase of L_1 to L_{NC}.

the quantity of labor demanded from L_1 to L_2 instead of from L_1 to L_{NC}, as would be the case without the feedback loop. Therefore, the feedback between the market wage and output price makes the market labor demand curve steeper—less sensitive to wage changes—than it would be without the feedback, as shown in panel b.

13.2 Supply in a Perfectly Competitive Factor Market

In a perfectly competitive market, labor supply at the firm level is straightforward. Because the firm can hire as much labor as it wants at the market wage, it faces a perfectly elastic supply of labor at the market wage. All shifts in the firm's labor demand will show up as changes in the quantity of labor hired rather than changes in the wage. The supply of labor available to firms in the labor market depends on the collective willingness of people to work. A person's willingness to work depends on his age, family situation, health, and many other factors. As with any supply curve, we hold all these other things constant and focus on the effect of the wage on the quantity of labor supplied. To understand what market-level labor supply looks like, then, we have to understand how people's willingness to work changes when the wage changes.

Work, Leisure, and Individual Labor Supply

A key to grasping how wages affect people's labor supply is to understand how they think about leisure time. For just about everyone, leisure is a good, just like cell phones or massages. Consuming more of it raises people's utility.

If leisure is a good, its price involves using up time. The price of leisure is what a person (call her Marissa) could be doing with that time if she weren't being leisurely—that is, if she were working. (Economists often consider any time people spend not working as leisure, whether or not they are doing something we might think of as leisurely. One of our colleagues reminds students that the time they spend attending lectures is considered leisure because they aren't earning wages for doing so.)

The benefit of working, aside from any inherent joy Marissa might get from her job, is the income she earns from it—or more precisely, the utility she obtains by consuming goods and services bought with her work income. By choosing to enjoy more leisure, Marissa gives up the income she could have earned had she worked during that leisure time. That lost income equals her wage rate. So the wage and the goods and services that she could have bought with her income are her price of leisure.

We can think of Marissa's labor supply as involving a choice between consuming leisure and consuming the goods and services that can be bought with her income from work. If we treat those other goods and services as a single good (let's call it "consumption" for short, with its quantity measured in dollars), the relative price between leisure and consumption is the wage. If Marissa's wage is $30 per hour, for example, and she chooses to take one more hour of leisure (i.e., work one hour less), she gives up $30 in consumption.

We can describe the work–leisure choice using the set of tools we utilized in Chapter 4: Marissa has a utility function that depends on both the amount of leisure time she spends and the consumption she enjoys from her work income. She maximizes her utility subject to a budget constraint for which the relative price of leisure and consumption is her wage rate. This is illustrated in **Figure 13.5**, which looks at Marissa's choice of how many hours to work in a day. (We could easily look at consumption–leisure choices over different

---

Figure 13.5   The Consumption–Leisure Choice

An increase in the wage from W_1 to W_2 shifts the budget constraint from BC_1 to BC_2, and the optimal consumption–leisure bundle changes from A to B. The substitution effect of the wage increase, which decreases leisure and increases consumption because leisure has become relatively more costly, accounts for the shift from bundle A to A', the tangency of U_1 and BC'. The shift from A' to B is the income effect.

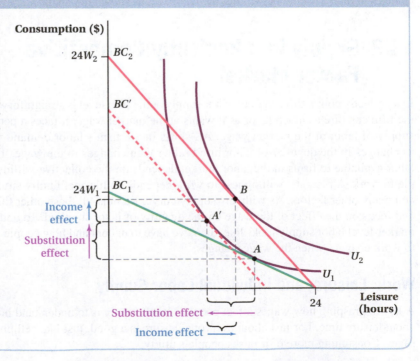

periods than a day—say, a week or a year—if we wanted to; the analysis would be qualitatively the same.)

The most leisure Marissa could take in a day is 24 hours. If she does, she won't earn any wages that day, and her consumption will be $0. Therefore, we know the budget constraint must include the point for 24 hours of leisure and $0 of consumption. This is the budget constraint's horizontal intercept. If she instead chooses to take no leisure and work the entire 24-hour period, she will maximize her consumption at $24 \times W_1$, where W_1 is her wage. Thus, another point on the budget constraint BC_1 is 0 hours of leisure and $24W_1$ of consumption, the vertical intercept of the constraint. Because Marissa must give up W_1 of consumption for each hour of leisure she takes, the budget constraint's slope is $-W_1$.

An indifference curve U_1 from Marissa's utility function for consumption and leisure is shown in the figure. Marissa's optimal consumption and leisure bundle is at the tangency of U_1 and the budget constraint BC_1, point A.

Suppose the wage rises to W_2. This rotates the budget constraint around the horizontal intercept (a different wage doesn't change the fact that Marissa can take at most 24 hours of leisure in a day), as shown in Figure 13.5. At any other leisure choice, however, Marissa can now have a higher level of consumption. The increase in wage shifts Marissa's optimal consumption–leisure bundle to the tangency of indifference curve U_2 and the new budget line BC_2, point B.

Income and Substitution Effects of a Change in Wages

A higher wage has two effects on Marissa's consumption and leisure choices. First, leisure now has a higher price relative to consumption; working one less hour has become more expensive for Marissa in terms of forgone consumption. This substitution effect pushes her to choose less leisure (i.e., work more) and consume more goods and services. (If her wage were to fall instead, it would make leisure relatively cheaper and she would choose to work fewer hours.)

But there is another effect of an increase in the wage that we hinted at before. For any given level of work—or equivalently, any given level of leisure time—it raises Marissa's income. This means there is also an income effect of a wage increase, not just a substitution effect. For Marissa as with most people, leisure is a normal good, so she will consume more of it as her income rises—the opposite of the substitution effect.

These two effects are the same ones we saw for price changes in Chapter 4. As we did there, we can decompose the total change in consumption and leisure into the separate influences of the substitution and income effects. To do so, remember that we need to figure out what Marissa's optimal consumption–leisure bundle would be if the relative prices had changed but her income hadn't (i.e., if the substitution effect of the wage change applied but the income effect didn't). We can do this by finding a budget constraint that is parallel to the new post-wage-increase budget constraint but is tangent to the original indifference curve U_1. This is the dashed line BC' in Figure 13.5. The tangency point A' shows the bundle Marissa would choose at the new relative price but without the income effect; in other words, it isolates the influence of the substitution effect. The difference in the bundles A and A' reflects the substitution effect of the wage increase on Marissa's consumption and leisure choices. The difference between A' and B reflects the income effect of the higher wage.

The substitution effect makes Marissa's labor supply curve, which shows how much she is willing to work at any given wage level, slope up. This shape is how we usually think of supply curves for anything: The higher the price of the good (here, the wage), the higher the quantity of the product (work hours) the producer (Marissa) will supply.

Backward-Bending Supply Curves

The net effect of a wage change on how much she is willing to work is the combination between the income and substitution effects. In principle, at least, if the income effect is large enough, there would be a negative relationship between wages and how much Marissa is willing to work, and her labor supply curve would no longer slope up. An example of this outcome is shown in **Figure 13.6**. At wages below W_{BB}, the substitution effect dominates; increases in the wage will make Marissa willing to work more. Above W_{BB}, however, the income effect begins to dominate, and the quantity of work she is willing to supply falls as wages rise. Economists call labor supply curves with this negative slope *backward-bending* labor supply curves.

Economists have found examples of backward-bending labor supply curves in certain markets. Economic historian Dora Costa gathered surveys on the work habits of thousands of U.S. men working in the 1890s and found that low-wage workers spent more hours per day working than those earning high wages.[1] Specifically, workers in the lowest wage decile (those being paid wages in the lowest 10% of all observed wage rates) averaged 11.1 hours of work per day, but those in the top wage decile (the top 10% of wage rates) worked only 8.9 hours per day. Workers in the highest-wage group worked 5% fewer hours than those being paid the median wage, who in turn worked 14% less than those in the lowest-wage group. In other words, the daily labor supply curve appeared to exhibit backward-bending patterns. (Interestingly, using other data, Costa also showed that the pattern had reversed itself by the 1990s. While workers in that period across the wage scale spent, on average, less time per day working than a century before, now those at the high end of the scale worked more.)

The net effect of wage changes on labor supply is the sum of the substitution and income effects. As explained in the Application below, economists have found evidence of backward-bending labor supply behavior among certain workers at certain times.

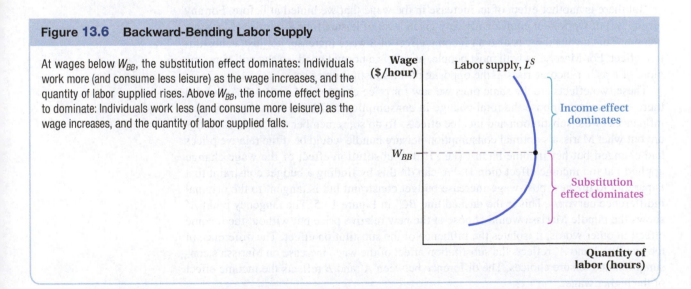

Figure 13.6   Backward-Bending Labor Supply

At wages below W_{BB}, the substitution effect dominates: Individuals work more (and consume less leisure) as the wage increases, and the quantity of labor supplied rises. Above W_{BB}, the income effect begins to dominate: Individuals work less (and consume more leisure) as the wage increases, and the quantity of labor supplied falls.

[1] Dora L. Costa, "The Wage and the Length of the Work Day: From the 1890s to 1991," *Journal of Labor Economics* 18, no. 1 (2000): 156–181.

Application: Tiger Woods's Backward-Bending Labor Supply Curve

Tiger Woods was once, and perhaps still is, the most recognizable face in professional golf. Over his career he has won 81 PGA tour events and picked up 15 Majors (so far). He has lent his name to product endorsement campaigns for which he has taken home tens of millions of dollars. But it isn't just his athletic skill that separates him from the average American laborer: He is probably one of the rare set of workers who face week-to-week wages on the backward-bending portion of his labor supply curve. In other words, as his wages increased, he actually decreased the number of tournaments in which he played.

PGA rules allow each golfer to elect which and how many events to play in, meaning the athlete considers the labor–leisure tradeoff separately for each tournament event. With tournament payoffs in the millions of dollars for just four rounds of golf, who wouldn't play? Indeed, most golfers do. Generally, around 100 players sign up for any given event. This doesn't even include the over 1,000 hopefuls who play in brutal qualifying rounds, vying for just 25 spots on the PGA Tour.

Tiger Woods supplying labor.

Andrew Redington/Getty Images

Given the opportunity, these hopefuls would gladly play every tournament, but as economists Otis Gilley and Marc Chopin discovered, players like Tiger Woods didn't.[2] Gilley and Chopin looked at how low- and middle-income PGA players responded to increases in their wages and compared this result to the effects of wage increases on high-income players. Whereas low-level players entered more events as their event winnings increased, golfers at the top of their game decreased their tournament play as their wages increased. Top golfers were operating on the backward-bending portion of their labor supply curves. In particular, for every $10,000 to $20,000 increase in their per-event average winnings, high-income players entered one less tournament. For these select players, the income effect dominated the substitution effect, and, faced with the leisure–labor tradeoff, they elected to consume more leisure.

Workers in other fields — including some economists — often spend their leisure time on the golf course. But for a professional golfer, a day on the green is work, not leisure. So just what does a PGA player do on his day off? Gilley and Chopin found that married golfers took more days off than did single golfers. Drawing on their own experiences as family men, the two hard-working economists concluded that golfers must be taking off work to spend more quality time with their wives and kids. The example of Tiger Woods, however, shows that not all predictions of economic theory hold up in the real world. ∎

Market-Level Labor Supply

The market-level labor supply curve shows the total amount of labor all workers are willing to supply at every possible wage. In other words, it is the horizontal sum of every worker's labor supply curve. To construct it, we fix a wage, figure out each worker's quantity of labor supplied at that wage, and add up those quantities. Once we've done this for every possible wage, we have found the market-level labor supply curve.

We discussed earlier how it is possible that individual workers' labor supply curves can be backward-bending. In principle, the market-level labor supply curve can be backward-bending, too. However, most available evidence suggests that at the market

[2] Otis W. Gilley and Marc C. Chopin, "Professional Golf: Labor or Leisure," *Managerial Finance* 26, no. 7 (2000): 33–45.

Figure 13.7 Labor Market Equilibrium

The labor market equilibrium wage, W^*, equates the market quantity demanded (as determined by the labor demand curve L^D) and the market quantity supplied (as determined by the labor supply curve L^S). The sum of all firms' labor hiring when the wage is W^* will be L^*.

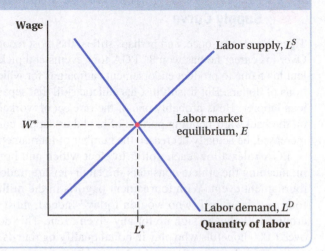

---

level, the substitution effect dominates so there is no backward bend. Backward-bending labor supply is unlikely at the market level because, even if an individual like Marissa hits the point where her quantity of labor supply will fall if her wage rises higher, there are usually many other people willing to supply more labor at those high wages (whether that's because they add more hours to the number they're already working or, if they weren't working before, decide to start working) to counteract the income effects of Marissa and those like her who cut back on their work hours. Thus, although an individual's labor supply may sometimes bend backward, the market labor supply curve usually slopes up because the total quantity of labor supplied by all workers increases as the wage rises.

13.3 Labor Market Equilibrium

The labor market reaches equilibrium when the wage equates the quantity of labor demanded by firms and the quantity of labor supplied by workers, as shown in **Figure 13.7**. L^D is the market labor demand curve and L^S is the market labor supply curve. The equilibrium wage is W^* and the equilibrium quantity of labor is L^*.

This market equilibrium relates to our analysis of labor demand at the firm level. Recall that the firm takes the wage as given and hires labor until its marginal revenue product of labor equals the market-equilibrium wage W^*. (This is the situation shown in Figure 13.1, with W equal to W^*.)

By definition of market equilibrium, the sum of *all* firms' hiring when the wage is W^* will be L^*. In other words, if every firm hires up to the point where W^* equals its MRP_L — which generally varies across firms because they have different production functions, have amounts of capital, and face different demands for their output markets — the total amount of hiring when added across all firms will be L^*.

13.4 The Labor Market in the Long Run

Our labor market analysis up to this point has been for the short run when the firm's level of capital is fixed. Let's look at what happens when the firm can change its capital level.

Earlier, we learned that changes in the amount of capital a firm has alter the marginal product of labor MP_L and thus shift the short-run labor demand curve. An increase in capital raises MP_L, increases the quantity of labor demanded at each wage, and shifts out the firm's short-run labor demand curve. Decreases do the reverse.

Suppose that there is a permanent drop in the market equilibrium wage, as shown in **Figure 13.8**. The firm initially has a short-run demand for labor given by MRP_{L1}. Given that the firm's MRP_L equals the initial wage W_1 at point a, the firm hires the quantity of labor l_1. In the short run, if the wage drops to W_2 and the firm's stock of capital is fixed, the firm will hire more labor until MRP_{L1} equals the lower wage, at point b, resulting in the quantity of labor l_2.

In the long run, however, this is not the *total* effect of the lower wage. The increase in labor hired to l_2 also raises the firm's marginal product of capital because, as we saw in Chapter 6, for most production functions, having more of one input raises the marginal product of the other. The increase in the marginal product of capital gives the firm an incentive to purchase more capital. When it does, the additional capital, in turn, raises the firm's marginal product of labor, and thus its marginal revenue product of labor. The increased MRP_L increases the amount of labor the firm demands at each wage and shifts out the firm's short-run labor demand curve to MRP_{L2}, the marginal revenue product curve of the firm at its new, higher capital level. Because the wage W_2 and the firm's new short-run labor demand curve MRP_{L2} are equal at point c, the firm hires l_3.

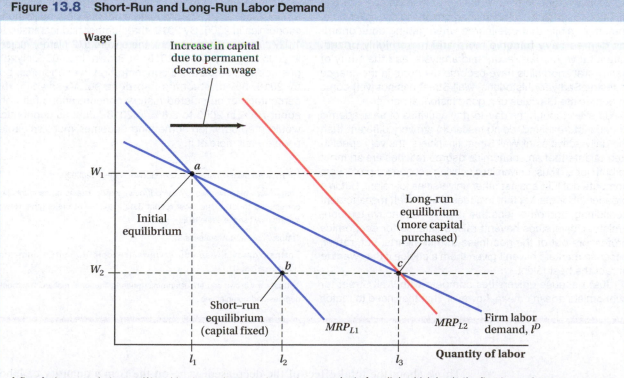

Figure 13.8   Short-Run and Long-Run Labor Demand

A firm facing a market wage W_1 and having a short-run demand for labor given by MRP_{L1} initially hires labor quantity l_1 (point a). The short-run effect of a permanent drop in the market equilibrium wage from W_1 to W_2 will cause the firm to hire more labor until MRP_{L1} equals W_2. This is labor quantity l_2 (point b). In the long run, the increase in labor hired to l_2 raises the firm's marginal product of capital, which leads the firm to purchase more capital and, in turn, raises the firm's marginal revenue product of labor. This shifts out the firm's short-run labor demand curve to MRP_{L2}, and the firm hires additional labor until $W_2 = MRP_{L2}$. This is labor quantity l_3 (point c). The long-run labor demand curve, l^D, runs through points a and c.

FREAKONOMICS

Competition in the Market for Economists

Twenty years ago, the average salary for academic economists was $58,730. The comparable number for historians was only a little bit lower — about $50,800.[1] Nowadays, an economics teacher can expect to earn $114,820 per year on average. That is almost a doubling — great news for budding economists. Time has not been quite as kind to historians. Their average salaries have increased to only $82,900 a year.[2] The wages of historians have just barely been ahead of inflation.

What explains the divergence in wages between academic economists and historians? Ironically, it likely has little or nothing to do with academics. Rather, the reasons for economists' rising salaries are two changes that took place on Wall Street. The first change is that Wall Street salaries, which were already high, have skyrocketed over the past two decades. According to the U.S. Department of Labor, employees in "Financial Investment and Related Activity" working in New York City earned an average pay of $422,459 in 2017.[3] The second change is that, over time, the set of skills that one learns when getting an economics degree have become more and more highly prized. Quantitative models, economic analysis, and the study of behavioral anomalies have become the norm in the finance industry. Sadly for historians, Wall Street has not (yet) come to appreciate the value of a good historical narrative.

So even though the day-to-day activities of an academic economist (teaching, doing research) are very different than the daily activities of Wall Street financiers, the very specialized talents that an economics degree teaches are an input to both jobs. Thus, universities seeking economics professors compete not just against other universities for talent, but in a broader labor market that includes Wall Street, management consulting, and other jobs that might be attractive to economists. Universities haven't raised salaries for economics professors out of the goodness of their hearts, but, rather, because markets haven't given them a choice if they want to attract the best talent.

Just because universities compete with Wall Street for economists doesn't mean, however, that they need to match Wall Street salaries dollar for dollar. For many people, being a professor is a much more attractive job (fewer hours, more freedom, less stress, the joy of interacting with students, among other perks). Thus, all else being equal, most economics PhDs are willing to take a large (but not infinitely large) salary hit to go into academics.

The good news for you — should you choose to major in economics — is that all the evidence suggests that the market rewards for economists will only grow. Firms are increasingly coming to appreciate the value and importance of "Big Data" and are desperate to find people capable of teasing insights from these data. "Data scientist" is one of the fastest growing job categories in America today, and many of these jobs are going to economists.

And if you need any additional evidence of the power of economics, you need look no further than the trends in college major choices. At the University of Wisconsin–Madison, for instance, 321 undergraduate students were majoring in economics in 2005. By 2018, that number had increased to 1,027.[4] As for history majors, there were 572 history majors in 2005 and only 286 in 2018. At Brown, in 2005, only 4% of students completed a concentration in economics; but by 2018, 8% of students had done so. Meanwhile, the percentage of completed history concentrations fell from about 7.5% in 2005 to 3.8% in 2018.[5] Just as economics would predict, when something becomes more valuable, people want more of it.

[1] http://www.bls.gov/news.release/history/ocwage_12202000.txt

[2] http://www.bls.gov/news.release/pdf/ocwage.pdf. The numbers in this box correspond to 2017, the most recent data available at press time. Newer reports may use the same URL.

[3] https://labor.ny.gov/stats/ins.asp

[4] https://dataviz.wisc.edu/#/views/TrendsinStudentEnrollments/Homepage?:iid=1

[5] http://www.brown.edu/about/administration/institutional-research/factbook/degrees-and-completions

Think about the total effect of the decreased wage on the firm's quantity of labor demanded: At wage W_1, the firm demanded the quantity of labor l_1. When the wage fell to W_2, once it had enough time to adjust its amount of capital, the firm ended up demanding quantity l_3. Therefore, the curve running through points a and c in Figure 13.8, l^D, is the firm's long-run labor demand curve. It shows the firm's desired hiring at any wage level once the firm is able to fully adjust its capital inputs. The long-run labor demand curve is the firm's quantity of labor demanded when the time horizon is long enough that the firm's capital inputs are completely flexible.

The long-run labor demand curve is flatter than the short-run curve because in the long run, the quantity of labor demanded increases as the quantity of capital increases. This raises labor's marginal revenue product relative to what it would be had capital remained constant, counteracting some of the drop in the MRP_L in the short run. At a practical level, firms' decisions about hiring labor are more responsive to wage changes in the long run than in the short run. Decreases in wages boost hiring more than they would in the short run, and increases in wages have larger negative effects on hiring.

13.5 Other Perfectly Competitive Factor Markets

We have looked specifically at labor markets as our example of factor markets. But there are other important factor markets, too. Capital is one of the more prominent of these. Because capital markets involve elements of timing and uncertainty, we discuss the market for capital in the next chapter when we introduce these topics. However, any other inputs firms use in production, such as intermediate materials (steel and fiberglass to make cars, leather to make shoes, etc.), business services, energy, and land, are bought and sold in factor markets. These markets have many similarities to the labor market.

Demand in Other Factor Markets

The markets for factors other than labor and capital operate, for the most part, just as the labor market does.

The demand for any factor is similar to that for labor:

1. A firm's demand for any factor is given by the marginal revenue product of that factor.

2. A factor's marginal revenue product falls as more of it is bought because of its diminishing marginal product (and because of falling revenue, too, if the market for the firm's output isn't perfectly competitive).

3. A price-taking firm will optimally buy the quantity of a factor that equates its marginal revenue product to its market price.

4. Total market demand for a factor is the horizontal (i.e., quantity) sum of the firm-level demands.

Supply in Other Factor Markets

The supply of a factor comes from producers or owners of those factors.

Intermediate Goods   Many factors are outputs of firms. *Products that are made specifically to be used as factor inputs into the production of another good* are called **intermediate goods**. Examples of intermediate goods include steel, advertising, mining equipment, and accounting services. The supply of an intermediate good is like the supply of any other product. It slopes upward because as the market price increases, producers of the factor are willing and able to supply more of their good to the factor market. The equilibrium price of intermediate goods (as with labor) is the price at which the quantity demanded equals the quantity supplied.

intermediate good
A product that is made specifically to be used as a factor input into the production of another good.

✈ Application: Smartphones, Coltan, and Conflict Minerals

Inside of all smartphones are complex electronics that use small amounts of rare materials. One of those materials is tantalum, a chemical element used to make tantalum capacitors, which are very heat-resistant but can still hold an electric charge. These capacitors are in virtually every smartphone in the world.

Producing tantalum requires extracting it from columbite—tantalite (coltan) ore mined in various places around the world. Therefore, coltan is a factor used in the production of mobile phones, and the demand for coltan is a demand derived from the demand for smartphones.

As the demand for smartphones has grown dramatically over time, so has the demand for the tantalum in coltan. This shift out in the coltan demand curve has raised coltan prices, as shown in **Figure 13.9**. Initially, demand for tantalum (in the form of coltan ore) is D_1, leading to a market price for coltan of P_1^* and a quantity of Q_1^*. As demand for smartphones rises, the marginal revenue product of tantalum to phone makers—and therefore the demand for coltan ore—shifts out. This shift in demand to D_2 raises coltan's market price and quantity to P_2^* and Q_2^*, respectively.

The supply curve for coltan S is upward-sloping because it is increasingly costly on the margin to mine more coltan. This is true for several reasons, and one big reason involves the political geography of where coltan deposits are located. At low levels of coltan demand, more easily attainable supplies of coltan from Canada and Australia are able to meet the needs of the market. But as demand has shifted out, miners have expanded production by going into places that are more difficult and expensive to mine, such as remote and war-torn parts of the Democratic Republic of the Congo and Rwanda, and environmentally sensitive areas in the Brazilian jungle.

Sadly, some of the costs of obtaining more coltan aren't borne by just the miners, but also by the people of these regions, who have suffered additional social and environmental problems as a result of coltan mining. (These additional costs not borne by the producers are called *externalities*; we discuss externalities in detail in Chapter 17.) Coltan users like Apple and suppliers like China's Huayou Colbalt Company are collaborating to build

---

Figure 13.9   Market for Coltan

An increase in the demand for smartphones shifts out the demand for coltan from D_1 to D_2. This raises the equilibrium price and quantity of coltan from P_1^* and Q_1^* to P_2^* and Q_2^*. The supply curve for coltan S slopes upward because it is increasingly costly on the margin to mine more coltan.

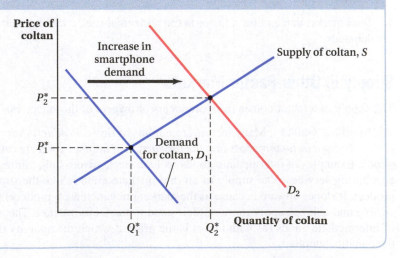

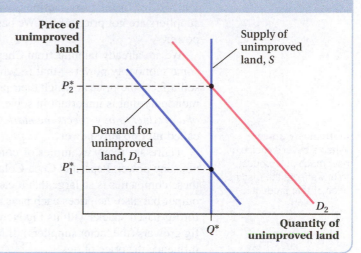

Figure 13.10 Market for Unimproved Land

The supply of unimproved land is fixed at Q^*. Therefore, any changes in demand end up changing only the price of land. For example, an increase in the demand for unimproved land from D_1 to D_2 raises the equilibrium price of land from P_1^* to P_2^* with no change in quantity.

a system that will certify which Congo mines value worker safety and don't use child labor, and then electronically track shipments from those mines to try to ensure they aren't mixed with ore from more problematic producers. ■

Land   One factor market that is a bit different from the labor and intermediate goods markets is the market for **unimproved land**, *the physical space on which economic activity (such as agriculture, housing, manufacturing, or office space) takes place.* The difference is that unlike most other factors, the supply of unimproved land is close to fixed. The land area of the earth is what it is (with sea levels rising, it may even be shrinking).

The fixed supply of unimproved land does not pose a problem for our standard supply and demand analysis; it just means that the supply curve is vertical. Thus, any changes in the demand for unimproved land affect only the equilibrium price of land—there can be no changes in quantity. This is shown in **Figure 13.10**.

Note that the supply of land *for any particular use*, however, is not fixed. If the prices of crops rise, for example, you can expect people to begin to cultivate some land that wasn't formerly farmed. Likewise, if crop prices fall, some farmland will be transformed into other uses such as housing or industry. And, if the demand to live in an area rises, land that was once a farm or logging forest will be converted to housing, commercial, or industrial use.

unimproved land The physical space on which economic activity (agriculture, housing, manufacturing, etc.) takes place.

13.6 Imperfectly Competitive Factor Markets: Monopsony, a Monopoly in Factor Demand

We've restricted our attention so far to perfectly competitive factor markets. Individual demanders of factors—firms—choose how much of the factors to buy while taking their price as given, an equilibrium price that is determined in the factor markets by the forces of supply and demand. Suppliers of factors do the same: They take their price as given and decide what quantity to supply at that price.

As we have learned in earlier chapters, perfectly competitive markets are rare in the real world. In the next sections, we look at what happens when factor demanders or suppliers are not price takers. We begin by looking at cases in which buyers have market power.

We are already familiar from Chapters 9–11 with how markets work when sellers have some monopoly power—that is, when they recognize their decision about how much to sell affects the price at which their products will be sold. There is a buyer-side analogy to monopoly that is important in some factor markets. *When a buyer's choice of how much of a product to buy affects the market price of that product*, this is a type of market power called **monopsony power**.

There are many examples of concentrated buyers who are likely to have some monopsony power. Pepsi and Coca-Cola, Target and Walmart, Apple and Samsung—each of these companies is so large that it can influence not only the prices buyers will pay for its output but also the prices each pays to its factor suppliers. Nabisco dominates the market for fig-based snacks with its Fig Newtons cookies and it buys figs from a large number of fig growers (the factor suppliers). If Nabisco decides to make fewer Fig Newtons, this will influence the price of figs.

monopsony power
When a buyer's choice of how much of a product to buy affects the market price of that product.

Marginal Expenditure

To make things more concrete, let's think about the market for oil workers in the Athabasca Oil Sands (AOS), which are located in a remote area of northern Alberta, Canada. If you live and work in this region, it's likely you work in oil production and have limited ability to change jobs unless you leave the area. At the same time, only a few large companies account for most of the oil production and employment there.

These facts imply that employers in the AOS region have some monopsony power. Because each company accounts for a considerable share of the total market demand for labor, the more labor it hires, the higher the wage will rise. Note that just as we discussed regarding the relationship between monopoly and market power, a firm can have monopsony power without being literally the only buyer. The key is that it is not a price/wage taker when it hires. We know from our analysis earlier in this chapter that in a competitive factor market, oil companies would hire workers until the marginal revenue product of those oil workers equaled the market wage. That wage would be set by market-level supply and demand, and firms would take it as given. However, a monopsonist like Syncrude (one of the biggest oil companies operating in Alberta) is a buyer with market power. Because its hiring is such a large part of market labor demand, it influences the wage. In other words, it faces an upward-sloping (not horizontal) labor supply curve. The more people Syncrude hires, the higher the wage it has to pay. As a result, a monopsonist like Syncrude faces a dilemma that is similar to that dealt with by a monopolist.

We can think about Syncrude's decision in terms of **marginal expenditure**, *ME*, the *incremental amount spent to buy one more unit of labor*. Buyers with no market power can buy as many units as they want without affecting the price. For them, marginal expenditure is just the market price (the wage) irrespective of the quantity they buy. This isn't so for monopsonists, however. If Syncrude wants to hire more labor, the increase in quantity demanded is large enough to require the market wage to rise to bring the additional labor into the market. This means Syncrude's marginal expenditure (*ME*) when it buys an incremental unit of labor isn't just the higher wage for that one worker. It is that wage *plus* the incremental wage increase it has to pay to all its other nonincremental workers.

marginal expenditure (ME) The incremental amount spent to buy one more unit of labor.

This is easier to understand in an example. Suppose hiring 1,000 employees would cost Syncrude a wage of $50,000 per employee, while hiring 1,100 employees would raise the wage to $60,000 per employee (here, we're treating the marginal unit of labor as being 100 employees). Syncrude's total payroll for employing 1,000 workers would then be $50 million (1,000 × $50,000), while its payroll for hiring 1,100 workers would be $66 million (1,100 × $60,000). Therefore, its marginal expenditure (*ME*) for 1 incremental unit of labor (100 employees) is not just the $6 million it pays to hire 100 extra workers ($60,000 × 100) but $16 million ($66 million for 1,100 workers − $50 million for 1,000 workers). Syncrude's extra hiring requires the company to pay an extra $10 million ($10,000 to each of its 1,000 nonincremental workers) beyond the $6 million it has to pay the extra hires. Therefore, just as marginal revenue differs from the price for a monopoly supplier, marginal expenditure differs from the price (wage) for a monopsony buyer. The direction of the difference is opposite, though: While marginal revenue is always less than the price for a monopolist, marginal expenditure is always more than the price for a monopsonist.

We can mathematically express marginal expenditure for a monopsonist as the price plus the amount that prices would change from increasing quantity times the quantity:

$$ME = P + (\Delta P/\Delta Q) \times Q$$

If this looks familiar, it is because it's very much like the definition of marginal revenue from Chapter 9. The difference is that for monopoly power and marginal revenue, $\Delta P/\Delta Q$ is negative because it depends on the downward-sloping demand curve. Here, for monopsony power and marginal expenditure, $\Delta P/\Delta Q$ is positive because it is tied to the upward-sloping supply curve. Notice that for a buyer who faces a flat supply curve—that is, a buyer who has no monopsony power and therefore takes the factor's purchase price as given—$\Delta P/\Delta Q$ is zero and $ME = P$, as we saw earlier.

When Syncrude hires labor as a monopsonist, it faces an upward-sloping supply curve of labor. This means Syncrude's *ME* on labor is always greater than the wage, and Syncrude's labor *ME* curve will always be above the labor supply curve it faces, as shown in **Figure 13.11**. For a linear supply curve like L^S, as depicted in the figure, the *ME* curve will be twice as steep as the supply curve, just like marginal revenue is for the demand curve (see Chapter 9).

Factor Demand with Monopsony Power

We saw earlier in the chapter that price-taking buyers purchase a factor until its marginal revenue product equals its price (which equals the input's price). This means we can express the optimal amount of inputs for a price-taking buyer as the quantity that equates the marginal revenue product to the marginal expenditure: $MRP = ME$. This same expression holds true for a monopsonist like Syncrude as well as for a competitive firm. It's just a matter of defining *ME*. If a monopsonist buys more of an input than the $MRP = ME$ amount, then the additional amount the monopsonist spends to buy those inputs will exceed the revenues it earns from them. If the firm buys fewer inputs than the $MRP = ME$ quantity, then by buying more of the input, it could raise revenues by a greater amount than its expenditures on the inputs. Only when $MRP = ME$ is the monopsonist buying the profit-maximizing amount of inputs.

While the competitive and monopsony cases have the same $MRP = ME$ rule for input demand, *ME* is different for a monopsonist than for a price-taking buyer. For a price taker, $ME = P$. For a monopsonist, $ME = P + (\Delta P/\Delta Q) \times Q$, which is always greater than P. Therefore, for the same *MRP* and input supply curves, a monopsonist will buy fewer

Figure 13.11 A Monopsonist's Hiring Decision

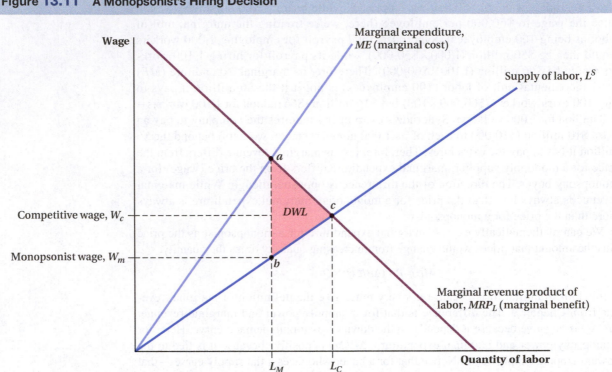

A monopsonist faces an upward-sloping supply curve L^S, implying that its marginal expenditure curve, ME, is above the supply curve. It hires labor quantity L_M at point a, where its marginal expenditure (its marginal cost of labor) equals its MRP_L (its marginal benefit of labor). It pays a wage W_m at point b, the height of the supply curve at that quantity of labor L_M. A set of perfectly competitive firms facing the same supply curve would hire the labor quantity L_C and pay a wage W_c. The deadweight loss of monopsony, area DWL, arises because there will be some workers who would work for wages that are lower than the marginal revenue product they create for the firm, but are not hired because doing so would raise overall wages too much. The deadweight loss is due to the labor that is not sold in the monopsonist market, which would be sold in the competitive market. This lost social surplus equals DWL, the area between the MRP_L and labor supply curves for labor units between L_M and L_C.

inputs than a price-taking firm, because a monopsonist's marginal expenditure on a factor will equal its marginal revenue product at a lower quantity of the factor. Because Syncrude knows it drives up the wage by hiring more workers, it holds back a little. Hiring an incremental unit of input is more expensive for it than for a price-taking firm. In this way, a monopsonist restricts purchases just as a monopolist restricts sales.

Equilibrium for a Monopsony

To find the equilibrium of a market when a buyer has monopsony power, we follow the same three-step procedure that we did in the monopoly power case, but looking at the supply curve rather than the demand side. Specifically:

1. Derive the ME curve from the supply curve facing the buyer.

2. Find the quantity at which ME equals the marginal revenue product to determine the optimal quantity.

3. Jump down to the supply curve at that quantity to determine the price paid for the factor.

Figure 13.11 shows this analysis for Syncrude. Syncrude's marginal revenue product curve for labor is MRP_L, and the labor supply curve it faces is L^S. We first plot the marginal expenditure curve, ME, that corresponds to the supply curve. It is, as we know, above L^S, and because L^S is linear, it is twice as steep. Second, we find the optimal quantity of labor for Syncrude to hire by identifying where the ME curve intersects MRP_L. This intersection is at point a in the figure and the quantity is L_M. Third, we find the wage Syncrude pays by reading off the level of the supply curve at quantity L_M. This is point b, and the corresponding wage W_m is what Syncrude has to pay workers to make them willing to supply Syncrude with its desired quantity of labor L_M.

The monopsony quantity L_M and wage W_m are different than those that would be found if Syncrude's labor demand (embodied in MRP_L) was instead the demand of a set of perfectly competitive buyers. In that case, the equilibrium wage and quantity of labor would be identified by point c, the intersection of the market demand and supply curves — quantity L_C and wage W_c. Monopsony results in a smaller quantity of the input hired and at a lower price than would be found in a competitive market. The workers here do not get paid their marginal product. They get paid less. And the amount less — the equivalent of the "markup" in the monopolist producer case — depends on the labor supply elasticity facing the particular firm.

Just as with monopoly power, monopsony creates a deadweight loss, DWL. This arises because there will be some workers who would work for wages less than the marginal revenue product they create for the firm, but they aren't hired because it would raise overall wages too much. In the Syncrude case shown in Figure 13.11, the units of labor that have social value but are not sold are those between L_M and L_C. The total size of the deadweight loss from this unsold labor is the total surplus they would have created had they been sold. Any given unit of labor has a surplus equal to the vertical distance between the labor demand curve (the value of the labor to Syncrude) and the labor supply curve (which shows what workers must be paid to be willing to work). If we add up the surplus of all the labor that is unsold in the monopsony market but would be sold in the competitive market, this is the triangular area labeled DWL in the figure. This triangle is the deadweight loss of monopsony power.

 Application: The Rookie Pay Schedule in the NBA

One fairly prominent example of monopsony power at work in the labor market is the market for young players in the National Basketball Association. The NBA is a monopsony because it is the only buyer of professional basketball services in the United States, and its teams coordinate their hiring to sustain this single-buyer structure. The collective bargaining agreement between the NBA and its players uses the monopsony power of the league to impose artificially low salaries on rookies for their first contract.

Great players like James Harden, LeBron James, and Stephen Curry, for example, were not allowed to make more than the maximum salary specified in a rookie contract during their early years in the league, even though their true value was much higher. Analysts at 82games.com, for example, estimated that in LeBron James's third season, his fair salary in a competitive market would have been $27.4 million. Instead, his contract allowed him to be paid only $4.6 million. While that's not pocket change, it's a whole lot less than he was worth, and what he would have been paid if the NBA didn't coordinate the rookie hiring decisions of its teams. ■

---

 figure it out 13.2

Richland Uranium Mining operates a mine in a remote area. Because of its location, it has monopsony power in the labor market. Its marginal revenue product of labor curve is $MRP_L = 800 - 10L$, where L is the total number of miners it hires and MRP_L is measured in thousands of dollars per miner. The labor supply curve of local miners is $W = 10L - 100$, where W is the wage.

a. What is Richland's marginal expenditure curve for labor?

b. What quantity of labor does it want to hire, and what wage will it pay?

c. What would the quantity of labor and wage be if Richland's marginal revenue product curve belonged to a perfectly competitive set of mines?

Solution:

a. Because the labor supply curve is linear, we know the marginal expenditure curve has twice the slope of the labor supply curve:

$$ME = 20L - 100$$

b. Richland will want to hire the quantity of labor that equates its marginal revenue product of labor with its marginal expenditure:

$$MRP_L = ME$$
$$800 - 10L = 20L - 100$$
$$30L = 900$$
$$L_m = 30$$

Richland's optimal amount of labor to hire is 30 miners.

To find the wage it must pay, we substitute the quantity of labor into the labor supply curve:

$$W_m = 10L_m - 100$$
$$W = 10(30) - 100 = 300 - 100$$
$$W_m = 200$$

Richland must pay a wage of $200,000 per miner to hire 30 miners.

c. A competitive market would hire labor until MRP_L equaled the wage from the labor supply curve. The competitive quantity of labor would therefore be

$$MRP_L = W$$
$$800 - 10L = 10L - 100$$
$$20L = 900$$
$$L_c = 45$$

A competitive set of mines would hire 45 miners.

The wage can be found using the supply curve:

$$W_c = 10L_c - 100$$
$$W = 10(45) - 100 = 450 - 100$$
$$W_c = 350$$

The wage in a competitive market would be $350,000 per miner.

13.7 Imperfectly Competitive Factor Markets: Monopoly in Factor Supply

We covered markets with monopoly power extensively in Chapters 9 and 10. The concepts we explored there apply equally to factor markets in which sellers have market power. Consider, for example, the world's best tax accountant who helps companies use loopholes to reduce their tax burden. If that accountant has market power (maybe because he knows tricks other accountants don't), then he will restrict sales relative to a competitive market because he knows that he drives down the price of his service by selling too much of it. He may also try to price-discriminate. We've analyzed each of these types of scenarios in the earlier chapters on market power. It's important to see that the market power of factor suppliers is the same as the market power of a supplier of any good or service.

Labor Markets and Unions

Perhaps the most studied holders of market power in factor markets are labor unions. Unions coordinate the labor supply actions of their members so that these workers act together as a monopoly seller of labor. In this way, unions are like cartels, coordinating their members' market behavior to arrive at an outcome that is jointly better for all members. Unions face the same cartel stability issues that we discussed previously: problems with free-riding, accommodating new market entrants, and so on, but when they are able to handle these successfully, they can substantially raise the wages earned by their members.

The analysis of a union's effect on a labor market is similar to the standard monopoly model with which we're already familiar. The union faces a demand for its product, the labor of its members. This is L^D in **Figure 13.12**. The union's coordinating role gives it market power, so the demand curve for its members' labor is downward-sloping. As its members supply a greater quantity of labor, the wage they earn will fall. Therefore, the union's marginal revenue—that is, the extra wages earned by its members when they supply an incremental unit of labor—is less than the wage rate. The union's marginal revenue curve is MR in the figure. The marginal cost curve MC in this case reflects the value of the members' leisure time, because that's what they give up when they supply a greater quantity of labor.

Everything to this point is exactly as it was in our earlier monopoly models. What might be a bit unusual for a union relative to other sellers with market power, though, is the objective it is trying to maximize with its supply choices. We know a profit-maximizing seller with market power will sell the quantity at which its marginal revenue equals its marginal cost. If a union did this, it would maximize the difference between the wages its members earn and their total opportunity cost of working. This outcome is shown at point a in Figure 13.12. The resulting quantity of labor is L_1, the wage is W_1, and the total "profit" for the union's members is the trapezoidal area below W_1, above MC, and between $L = 0$ and $L = L_1$. (The difference between their wage and their lost value of leisure can be thought of as the surplus created by the members' labor supply that they keep.)

This analysis may describe some unions' labor supply decisions. However, some economists believe such an objective may not describe many unions' goals. In part, this is because it is difficult for unions to measure their members' opportunity costs of working. While a firm with market power probably has a good idea about its marginal costs of production so it can know when it is maximizing profit, a union can't really measure this analog to its marginal cost. Instead, economists often believe that unions maximize the total earnings of their members—that is, the wage their members earn times their total quantity of labor supplied. This objective is easily measurable—it's just every member's wage earnings, added up—and is a tangible target for union members and leadership.

Total wage earnings are maximized when the union's marginal revenue (its marginal wage earnings when it adds another member) equals zero. This is when $MR = 0$, because at that point supplying any additional labor would reduce revenue (total earnings). This occurs at point *b* in Figure 13.12. If unions seek this objective, their quantity of labor supplied will be L_2 and the wage W_2. This higher labor quantity and lower wage result in a smaller "profit" than L_1 and the wage W_1 (as we know it must, because profit is maximized only when $MR = MC$). However, the $MR = 0$ objective results in a larger total amount of wage payments to the union's members; that is, $(L_2 \times W_2) > (L_1 \times W_1)$.

Regardless of whether it seeks to maximize its members' "profit" or total wage payments from their labor supply, the union will supply a lower quantity of labor at a higher wage than would be obtained in a competitive market. A competitive market equilibrium would be at point *c*, the intersection of the labor demand and labor supply (here, *MC*) curves. At this point, the competitive market wage is W_c and quantity of labor is L_c. The

Figure 13.12   A Union's Labor Supply Decision

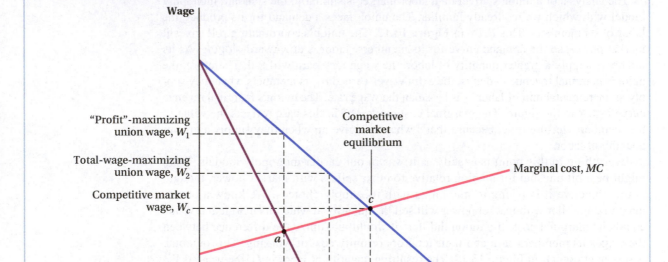

If, like a typical profit-maximizing seller with market power, the union aims to maximize total "profit" for union members, it will supply the quantity of labor L_1 at point *a*, where the marginal cost curve and marginal revenue curve intersect. At this quantity, the wage will be W_1, the wage indicated by the labor demand curve, L^D. If the union instead aims to maximize total wage earnings, it would sell at point *b*, where the union's marginal revenue equals 0. At this point, the quantity of labor supplied would be L_2 and the wage would equal W_2. Point *c* represents the competitive market equilibrium, where the labor demand and marginal cost curves intersect. The competitive market wage is W_C and quantity of labor is L_C. Thus, regardless of the union's goal, it will supply a smaller quantity of labor to the market at a higher wage than in the competitive equilibrium.

wage premium the union earns its members by coordinating their labor supply decisions is the difference between W_c and, depending on the union's objective, W_1 or W_2. As noted, however, this wage premium comes with a restriction in employment relative to that in a competitive labor market.

Application: Longshore Workers' Wage Premium

About 5 million people in the United States work in the transportation and warehousing sector. The firms that operate in this sector, including trucking companies, railroads, airlines, overseas and inland shippers, pipelines, parcel services, and the U.S. Postal Service, all have as their primary task moving people and goods from where they are to where they need to be. This sector plays a crucial role in our dynamic, globalized, and just-in-time economy.

In the latest data, the average annual earnings in the transportation and warehousing sector were $49,226, very close to the overall average earnings in the U.S. private sector.

There's a group of workers in this sector who do considerably better than this, however. The longshore workers (those who load and unload cargo at seaports), who are members of the International Longshore and Warehouse Union (ILWU) and work at one of the 29 largest ports on the U.S. West Coast, have average annual earnings that tip into six figures. About half make more than $100,000 a year, and around 15% make over $150,000. Pay starts at $29.49 an hour ($58,940 per year if full-time) for an ILWU member with no previous experience or trade skills who works the daytime shift, and it goes up from there. On top of this, health care is free for all ILWU members.[3]

How does this group of workers command pay that can be two to three times that of other employees in the sector? One possible explanation is that they are more experienced or skilled, on average, and the higher pay reflects the fact that their human capital makes them more productive. This is likely part of the story. Many longshore workers are skilled in trades that are very valuable; a crane operator who is careless or unskilled is both destructive and dangerous. But the market power of the ILWU is probably also an important factor.

Some features of the market environment in which the ILWU works have made it a particularly powerful seller. For one, an explosion of shipping through West Coast ports has greatly increased the demand for longshore workers. West Coast container traffic rose sixfold over the past 35 years as global trade expanded and Asian countries became manufacturing powerhouses. Every year, goods worth about $400 billion come in through the ports of Los Angeles and Long Beach alone. Second, there aren't many substitutes for a port. When goods are on a ship, they need to be taken off and sent inland, and there's really only one way to do that. You can't move a port to a

A longshore worker on the job.

Jane Tyska/The Oakland Tribune/ZUMA Press/Newscom

---

[3] Many of the figures in this application were taken from Chris Kirkham and Andrew Khouri, "How Longshoremen Command $100K Salaries in Era of Globalization and Automation," *Los Angeles Times*, March 1, 2015. The sector-level wage and earnings data are from the U.S. Bureau of Labor Statistics.

lower-wage country the way you could move a factory, and it's not easy to build new ones. Given that the ILWU operates in all major ports on the West Coast, shipping companies have no real choice but to cut a deal with it. Third, the ILWU has a history of accommodating technological changes that increase efficiency even if they require less labor, as long as its members share in the accompanying profit gains. This has increased the size of the pie that the company and union bargain over, giving ILWU's "customers" less reason to balk. ■

13.8 Bilateral Monopoly

The models of factor market power we've looked at in this chapter, whether that power is exercised on the seller's or buyer's side, are extremely useful when one side of the market is concentrated or particularly powerful, and the competitive model's assumptions that factor buyers or sellers are price takers are unlikely to apply.

There are many markets, though, where even the one-sided market power models don't fit the situation well. These are markets in which both the supply and demand sides are concentrated. For example, consider the automobile industry. Each of the small number of giant automakers accounts for billions of dollars in sales, and that probably means each company has some monopsony power over its suppliers. On the other hand, four mega-suppliers of tires — Goodyear, Michelin, Cooper, and Bridgestone — account for the vast majority of tire sales. These firms almost surely have some market power on the supply side of this market.

The market structure that exists when there is a major concentration of market power on both sides of the market is called a **bilateral monopoly**. ("Monopoly-monopsony" is probably a more accurate term, but no one uses it.) Our models of market power above assume that only one side of the market has pricing power. In the case of bilateral monopoly, there is no single, obvious model to use for figuring out what will happen in a factor market or what either party should do. It could be anything between the monopoly outcome and the monopsony outcome, and that's a large range indeed. What happens in these situations comes down to negotiation and bargaining power. The game theory tools we learned in Chapter 12 can be helpful to predict outcomes in such situations.

> **bilateral monopoly** The market structure that exists when there is major concentration of market power on both sides of a market.

13.9 Conclusion

In this chapter, we have studied markets for factors, goods that firms use as inputs into production. These markets are in many ways like the other markets we've looked at in this book, markets in which demand and supply interact to determine an equilibrium quantity and price. What's a bit unique is that the demand for factors is a derived demand; the demand for them depends on the demand for the outputs that firms make with the factors. The story behind factor supply can be a bit different, too, with labor supply arising from people's decisions about labor–leisure tradeoffs and the supply of unimproved land being fixed. We sometimes also have special names for factor prices — wages for labor, rent for land. But in the end, the basic mechanics of factor markets are nearly the same as those for other markets, and so the lessons we've learned from them serve us well in understanding factor prices and quantities.

Summary

1. **Factor markets** are markets for inputs that are used to produce outputs. One of the most important factor markets is the labor market. The **marginal revenue product of labor** is the marginal product of labor times the marginal revenue. In perfectly competitive factor markets, a firm employs the optimal amount of labor when the marginal revenue product of labor equals the wage. As the wage increases, the optimal amount of labor hired decreases, and the opposite is true when the wage decreases. Labor demand is an example of a **derived demand**, a demand for one product that results from the demand for another product. **[Section 13.1]**

2. Changes in the production function and the amount of capital a firm has can shift the marginal product of labor curve and, in turn, the labor demand curve. Likewise, changes in demand for the output good can shift the marginal revenue curve, shifting the labor demand curve. The market demand for labor is the horizontal sum of all firms' labor demand curves. **[Section 13.1]**

3. An individual's labor supply involves a choice between consuming leisure and consuming the goods and services that can be bought with income from work. As a result, the relative price of leisure and consumption is the individual's wage rate. The net effect of a wage change on labor supply is the sum of the substitution effect and the income effect. In general, the substitution effect dominates so that a higher wage encourages a person to work more. In principle, however, above a certain wage, the income effect can dominate so that the quantity of work a person is willing to supply falls as wages rise. This phenomenon can give rise to a backward-bending labor supply curve. **[Section 13.2]**

4. The labor market reaches equilibrium when the wage equates the quantity of labor demanded by firms and the quantity of labor supplied by workers. In the long run, the firm is able to adjust its capital inputs, and consequentially,

the labor demand curve is flatter than it is in the short run. **[Sections 13.3 and 13.4]**

5. **Intermediate goods** are products that are made specifically to be used as factor inputs into the production of another good, and the supply of an intermediate good is like the supply of any other product. Meanwhile, the supply curve for **unimproved land**, land that is not designated for any specific use, is vertical because the supply is essentially fixed. **[Section 13.5]**

6. **Monopsony power** exists when a buyer's choice of how much to buy affects the market price of what it purchases. **Marginal expenditure**, the incremental expenditure from buying one more unit of a product, is equal to the price for buyers with no market power, but is always higher than the price for a monopsonist. The monopsonist buys the profit-maximizing amount of an input when the marginal revenue product of the input equals the marginal expenditure on it. In a monopsony, a smaller quantity of the input is purchased at a lower price than would be purchased in a competitive market. **[Section 13.6]**

7. The concepts that applied to monopolists in previous chapters also apply to sellers with market power in factor markets. Labor unions are among the most well-known holders of market power in factor markets. If unions acted as standard profit-maximizing sellers, they would supply the amount of labor that would equate marginal revenue and marginal cost. Some economists, however, believe that unions instead maximize total wage earnings, in which case they supply labor until their marginal revenue equals zero. Either way, the union supplies a lower quantity of labor at a higher wage than would be obtained in a competitive market. **[Section 13.7]**

8. A **bilateral monopoly** is the market structure that exists when there is major concentration of market power on both sides of the market, and the one-sided market power models don't fit this situation well. **[Section 13.8]**

Review Questions

1. What two terms are equal when a firm in a perfectly competitive market is employing the optimal amount of labor? How can this condition be rearranged so that the marginal cost of labor to the firm is on the right side of the equation?

2. What happens to the optimal amount of labor hired when the wage increases in a perfectly competitive market? When the wage decreases?

3. Name two components of the labor demand curve that can change, thus shifting the curve.

4. How is the market demand for labor computed?

5. What is the relative price of leisure and consumption?

6. Are firms' decisions about hiring labor more responsive to wage changes in the short or the long run?

7. What is the marginal expenditure for a monopsonist?

8. Does a monopsonist buy fewer or more inputs than a price-taking firm when the two have the same *MRP* and input supply curves?

9. How do unions maximize total earnings?

10. What do we call a market structure that exists when there is a major concentration of market power on both sides of the market?

Problems

(Solutions to problems marked with an asterisk appear at the back of this book. Problems adapted to use calculus are available online.)

1. Tessa's Techs is a small, competitive firm that provides online and telephone support for people with computer problems. The marginal product of labor (measured in numbers of support requests fulfilled per shift) is given in the table below:

Units of Labor	MP_L	MRP_L
1	14	
2	12	
3	10	
4	8	
5	6	

   a. If Tessa's charges $6 for each service call, calculate the marginal revenue product of labor for Tessa's Techs.

   b. Suppose Tessa can hire workers for $60 per four-hour shift. Explain why, if Tessa currently has just one employee, she isn't maximizing her profits. How much will her profits increase if she hires a second worker?

   c. Suppose Tessa can hire workers for $60 per four-hour shift. Explain why, if Tessa hires five employees, she isn't maximizing her profits.

   d. Determine the optimal number of employees for Tessa to hire.

*2. Offer two explanations why, at below profit-maximizing levels of output, a firm is likely to find that its MRP_L is greater than the prevailing market wage. What happens to the firm's MRP_L as output expands, and why? Does your answer depend on whether the firm has market power?

3. Consider the situation facing Tessa, the owner of Tessa's Techs in Problem 1.

   a. Draw Tessa's demand curve for labor. Then, draw the supply curve for labor that Tessa faces. (*Hint:* Remember that the demand for labor equals the marginal revenue product of labor.)

   b. On your graph, indicate the profit-maximizing quantity of labor for Tessa to hire.

   c. Suppose that Microsoft releases a particularly bug-prone version of Windows that causes the demand for service calls to increase. The increase in demand for service calls drives up the market price of a service call from $6 to $10. Draw Tessa's new demand for labor, and determine the number of workers Tessa should hire.

   d. Does the change you illustrated in (c) help explain why the demand for labor is called a derived demand?

4. The *real wage* a firm pays its employees measures the number of units of output the firm must sell in order to pay an employee's dollar wage.

   a. If employees at a whipped cream factory earn $21 per hour and whipped cream sells for $3 per carton, determine the real wage the workers are being paid. In what units is your answer expressed?

   b. Express the real wage more generally as a function of the dollar wage and the firm's output price.

   c. To maximize profits, a firm should hire labor until the marginal revenue product of labor equals the dollar wage. Show that a competitive firm should hire workers until the marginal product of labor is equal to the real wage.

*5. The house painting industry is highly competitive on both the input and output side. The marginal product of labor faced by a typical firm in the industry is given by $MP_L = 25 - l$, where l is the number of workers hired and MP_L is measured in square feet painted per hour. Firms typically charge their clients $10 per 25 square feet painted.

   a. Determine the marginal revenue product of labor faced by the typical firm.

   b. At what wage will firms not want to hire any workers at all?

   c. If workers worked for free, how many workers would the typical firm hire? Explain intuitively why the firm should not hire any more.

   d. If the prevailing market wage for house painters is $20 per hour, how many workers should the typical firm hire?

   e. Suppose a new paint formulation requires fewer coats, increasing workers' marginal products to $MP_L = 35 - l$. How will this new paint affect the hiring decisions of employers?

*6. Jawbats produces wooden baseball bats used by professional athletes. Jawbats's short-run production function is given by $Q = 2L^{0.5}$. The associated marginal product of labor is $MP_L = 1/L^{0.5}$.

   a. If the inverse demand for Jawbats's bats is $P = 100 - 0.5Q$, find the marginal revenue product of labor.

   b. Jawbats can hire workers for $18 per hour. How many workers should Jawbats hire?

   c. What will Jawbats bats sell for in the market? How many will Jawbats sell?

   d. Show that hiring one more worker beyond the optimal level you found in (b) will be bad for Jawbats.

7. Consider Tessa, from Tessa's Techs, as given in Problem 1. Tessa is struggling to find workers in a tight labor market.

a.   Suppose that the struggle to find qualified workers is due to Tessa's location in an isolated Idaho town. If the tight labor market drives the going wage for online support workers up to $84 for a four-hour shift, how should Tessa adjust her hiring?

b.   Suppose the tight labor market is due to exploding demand across the entire tech sector, and as a result it affects all tech support firms, not just Tessa. If the increased cost of hiring qualified support personnel drives up the price of a service call from $6 to $7, how will Tessa adjust her hiring?

c.   Explain how the feedback of wages into prices causes labor demand to be less elastic than it would otherwise be.

8.   Crazy Eddie is the world's worst politician. At a recent political rally, he told the crowd, "This country was founded on hard work. If elected, I plan to encourage that work by raising income taxes." Is it possible that Crazy Eddie is right—that *increasing* income taxes could cause people to work more? Explain your answer, being sure to mention income and substitution effects.

9.   Consider Jillian, whose backward-bending labor supply curve is shown in the figure below. Above $50 per hour, increases in wages cause Jillian to work less and enjoy more leisure. That implies that leisure is a normal good. *True or false: It must then be the case that below $50 per hour, leisure is an inferior good.* Explain your answer.

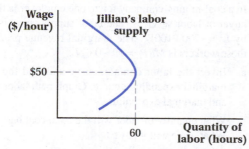

10.   Tobin works at a ball-bearing assembly factory; he likes spending his paycheck, but he also likes lounging on his patio. His indifference curves are shown below:

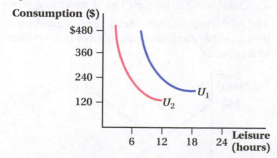

a.   Tobin is currently making $20 per hour. Add Tobin's budget constraint to the graph. How many hours will Tobin spend working? Lounging on his patio?

b.   Things are looking rough in the ball-bearing industry. Tobin's boss, Mr. McGuire, explains why: "One word: plastics." Then, McGuire slashes his pay in half. Add Tobin's new budget constraint to the graph. Does Tobin work more or less after the pay cut?

c.   Break the total effect of the wage cut into substitution and income effects.

d.   Is leisure a normal or inferior good for Tobin? Explain why you can determine the answer to this question without answering part (c).

e.   Graph Tobin's labor supply. Is its shape interesting?

11.   The market for nurses is highly competitive on both the supply and demand sides. Suppose a hospital is trying to determine how many nurses to hire.

a.   Graph the hospital's supply and demand for labor to illustrate how the hiring decision will be made.

b.   Suppose that a relative scarcity of nurses drives up the market wage nurses receive. Illustrate this increase in the market wage in your graph.

c.   Does the increase in the market wage for nurses reduce the demand for nurses? Explain.

d.   Show what happens to the demand for nurses and the hiring of nurses when a new type of medical equipment enables them to serve more patients each hour.

12.   Indicate whether the following statement is true or false, and explain your answer: *Because firms can substitute capital for labor in the long run, the demand for labor must be less elastic in the long run than in the short run.*

13.   Pete's Pools digs swimming pools for wealthy Seattle residents. Pete currently pays his workers the going wage, $10 per hour. The labor market he faces is depicted below:

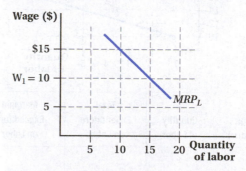

a.   How many workers does Pete hire at $10 per hour?

b.   Seattle recently increased its minimum wage to $15. How will Pete adjust his hiring in the short run?

c.   As Pete adjusts his hiring, what will happen to the productivity of Pete's capital? In the long run, how will Pete adjust his capital?

d.   As Pete adjusts his capital, what happens to the productivity of his employees? Illustrate the effects of the shift in capital in your graph. How will Pete adjust his hiring?

e.   Connect your initial and final wage–labor points to create Pete's long-run demand for labor.

*14.   In Glutonia, there are 1,000 bakers who buy flour to bake into bread. The marginal revenue product of flour faced by each baker is $MRP_F = 60 - 0.01Q$, where Q is the quantity of flour used by each baker. The flour market in Glutonia is perfectly competitive.

a.   Each baker's inverse demand for flour is simply his or her marginal revenue product for flour. Add up the demands of all 1,000 bakers to find the market demand for flour. (*Hint:* Solve each baker's MRP_F equation for Q, then multiply by 1,000.)

b.   The market supply of flour is given by $Q_S = 150,000P$. Solve for the market price of flour.

c.   At the price you found in (b), how many units of flour to bake into bread will each baker choose to purchase?

d.   Verify that the total amount demanded by all 1,000 bakers equals the equilibrium quantity in the market.

e.   Suppose that a decrease in the price of bread reduces the marginal revenue product of flour to $MRP_F = 60 - 0.02Q$. Find the new market price and quantity, as well as the quantity purchased by each baker.

15.   Tilda grows Brussels sprouts and is a monopsony buyer of labor in her small town. The labor supply she faces is given in the following table and shown in the accompanying graph.

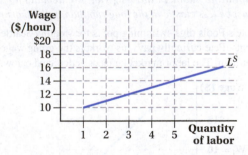

Wage ($/hour)	Quantity of Labor	Total Expenditure on Labor	Marginal Expenditure on Labor
$10	1		
$11	2		
$12	3		
$13	4		
$14	5		

a.   Calculate Tilda's total expenditure on labor if she wants to hire one worker, and fill in the appropriate cell in the table. Then, figure out how much Tilda would have to spend to hire two workers, three workers, and so on.

b.   Calculate Tilda's marginal expenditure on labor for the first worker, the second worker, and so on. Fill in the marginal expenditure column in the table.

c.   Carefully graph the values from the Marginal Expenditure on Labor column in the graph provided.

d.   Describe how the marginal expenditure curve you graphed behaves, relative to the labor supply curve.

16.   Suppose that the government of a small equatorial country requires all coconut producers to sell their output to the government. According to the text, a monopsony buyer's marginal expenditure is given by $ME = P + (\Delta P/\Delta Q) \times Q$, where Q is the quantity of coconuts and P is the market price of coconuts.

a.   Show that the marginal expenditure faced by the government is $ME = P \times (1 + 1/\varepsilon_s)$, where ε_s is the elasticity of supply of coconuts. [*Hint:* Multiply and divide $(\Delta P/\Delta Q) \times Q$ by the same variable.]

b.   Show that the government's marginal expenditure on coconuts will always be greater than or equal to the price of coconuts.

c.   Use the formula you derived to explain why, if the buyer's side were competitive, marginal expenditure would equal price.

17.   In a coal-mining company town, one employer is the sole buyer of labor services. The labor supply curve is given by $L^S = -700 + 100W$. The marginal revenue product of those workers is $MRP_L = 19 - 0.02L$.

a.   Invert the labor demand curve and find the firm's marginal expenditure curve. Graph both labor supply and marginal expenditure.

b.   What quantity of labor will the local coal baron hire? What wage will it pay?

c.   What would the quantity of labor hired and the wage be if there were lots of mining firms competing for workers?

d.   Calculate the deadweight loss of monopsony power.

18.   The following diagram shows the marginal revenue product of labor and the supply of labor in the production of lemongrass.

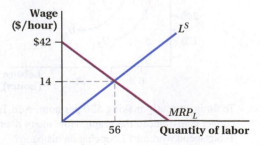

a. Express the marginal revenue product of labor in the lemongrass industry mathematically.

b. Express the supply of labor in the lemongrass industry mathematically.

c. If lemongrass production were competitive in both input and output markets, how many workers would be hired and what wage would they be paid?

d. A ruthless lemongrass producer drives all other lemongrass producers out of town with dire threats. That producer becomes a monopsonistic buyer of labor. Find the marginal expenditure curve facing that employer. Then, graph the marginal expenditure curve.

e. How many units of labor will a monopsonistic lemongrass producer hire? How much will the workers be paid?

f. By how much does employment fall when the labor market goes from competitive on the buyer's side to monopsonistic?

g. Calculate the deadweight loss of monopsony and illustrate it on the graph. Is eliminating competition on the buyer's side of the labor market a good thing for society, or a bad thing?

*19. In a tourist-destination city, the market for ATM fillers is perfectly competitive. The demand for ATM fillers is given by $L^D = 200 - 5W$, where L^S is the number of workers desired and W is their wage. On the supply side of the market, the marginal cost of providing ATM fillers is given by $MC = 0.5L$.

a. Find the inverse demand for ATM fillers. Then, equate supply and demand for ATM fillers to find the equilibrium quantity of ATM fillers hired in a competitive market.

b. Find the equilibrium wage of ATM fillers.

c. Tired of exploitation by large bank systems, ATM fillers decide to unionize and sell their services collectively. Derive the marginal revenue curve faced by the newly formed ATM fillers' union.

d. Suppose the ATM fillers' union decides to maximize profits. Equate marginal revenue and marginal cost to determine how many ATM fillers will be employed. What wage will they be paid?

e. The unemployment rate is the percentage of workers who are willing to work at a given wage but who are not actually working. Determine how many workers would like to work at the union wage; then calculate the unemployment rate created by unionization.

20. Suppose that the employment of elevator mechanics is controlled on the supply side by a union. Is it better for the union to attempt to maximize the profits of its membership, or to maximize the total wages its members receive? Is it better for society if the union attempts to maximize its profits, or the total wages its members receive? Explain your answer using a graph.

*21. An oil-well fire is raging in Texas. The Texas state government is trying to hire International Well Control, a famed oil-well firefighting firm. Explain why the models of the labor market developed in this chapter are unable to predict how much Texas will eventually pay to put out the horrific blaze.

Investment, Time, and Insurance

P eloton is a fitness company that sells not just a stationary bike, but also live video exercise class streaming. Apparently quite a few folks have paid $2,000 for the bike and $40 a month for livestreamed instructors who encourage them to grind it out. This market potential has caught the eye of enthusiastic investors, who have been throwing hundreds of millions of dollars at the company, which is now valued in the billions.

The economics behind Peloton's business contains two interesting features that have been missing from our analyses to this point. The first is the element of *time*. Before Peloton became a high-flying company, it struggled for several years trying to design a better bike, get the instructors necessary to offer a slate of popular classes, and convince investors it was a viable business. It spent vast amounts before it ever started getting a payback. The second feature is *uncertainty*. Peloton was offering a product combination that had never existed. Starting out, no one knew for sure whether demand would ultimately be high enough to pay back all those upfront costs. (Their potential investors appeared even more skeptical.) Yet despite this, Peloton managers had to make hugely consequential decisions without a sure sense of how things would turn out.

The inherent elements of time and uncertainty that Peloton faced are involved in all sorts of decisions firms and consumers face every day. In this chapter, we explore economic decisions involving time and uncertainty. We pay particular attention to two types of decisions, those involving investment over time, and insurance for uncertainty.

Investment is *the purchase of capital in the present with the intent of reaping future benefits*. A retail firm's construction of a new store is an example of investment. The firm pays the up-front costs of building it in order to earn future profits from sales over the store's lifetime.[1] We will learn how payoffs that occur at different times can be valued on an equal basis, and discuss how to account for the riskiness that might be associated with future payoffs from capital investment. We will also see how interest rates, which play a critical role in evaluating capital investment decisions, are determined in the investment capital market.

Insurance is *a payment from one economic actor to another with the aim of reducing the risk facing the payer*. Consumers and firms buy all types of insurance to reduce the risks they face. We explore why they are willing to do so and how much they are willing to pay to reduce risks.

investment The purchase of capital in the present with the intent of reaping future benefits.

insurance A payment from one economic actor to another with the aim of reducing the risk facing the payer.

---

[1] The words "investment" and "investing" are often used in casual conversation to describe individuals and firms saving money through banks, brokers, and other financial institutions. This isn't exactly what economists usually mean when they use these words; the economic definition implies the purchase of some sort of capital with the hope of a future payoff. As we see later in the chapter, however, savings and investment (by the economic definition) are, in fact, linked. This connection results from the functioning of capital markets. Essentially, savers provide funds that investors use to purchase capital. The investors compensate the savers by paying back some of the investment's returns.

14.1 Present Discounted Value Analysis

Decisions about costs and benefits that occur at different times add a layer of complexity beyond the conventional situation where everything happens at once. When things happen simultaneously, it's easy to compare whether the benefits outweigh the costs. But, consider a capital investment decision that involves a $1,000 cost now that pays off $1,200 in five years. Or, suppose an investment involved costs of $500 now, and again one and two years from now, and paid benefits of $400 one, two, three, and four years from now. We need to evaluate costs and benefits that occur at different times (and to evaluate future benefits that might be risky, too). This chapter gives us the tools to do that. The first tool is the concept of **present discounted value (PDV)**, *a mathematical concept that allows us to compare costs and benefits over time in a way that puts all present and future financial values on equal footing.*

present discounted value (PDV) A mathematical concept that allows us to compare costs and benefits over time in a way that puts all present and future financial values on equal footing.

Interest Rates

Interest rates play a key role in present discounted value analysis by giving us a way to value future money versus today money. You've probably dealt with these topics in your personal finances (savings accounts, car loans, student loans, mutual fund or stock holdings, etc.), but let's do a quick review.

interest A periodic payment made by individuals or firms tied to an amount of assets borrowed or lent.

    Interest is *a periodic payment made by individuals or firms tied to an amount of assets borrowed or lent.* **Principal** is *the amount of assets on which interest payments are made.* The **interest rate** is *the amount of interest paid, expressed as a fraction of the principal.* Interest rates are quoted on a per-period basis—yearly, monthly, or even daily—so the payment of interest is a *flow payment,* paid out per unit of time. If a savings account has $100 in it (the principal) at a 4% annual interest rate, it pays $4 of interest at the end of the year. That is, $I = A \times r$, where I is the amount of interest paid, A the principal (think "A" for assets), and r the interest rate.

principal The amount of assets on which interest payments are made.

interest rate The amount of interest paid, expressed as a fraction of the principal.

    When interest paid in one period is added to the principal, and the interest rate in the next period is applied to the sum, this is called **compounding** or **compound interest**. If our savings account pays a 4% interest rate that is compounded annually, an initial principal deposit of $100 earns $4 interest after one year and the principal the next year becomes $104. The interest in the second period is then computed based on this new principal, making it $104 × 0.04 = $4.16. Notice how this interest payment is slightly more than the first period's interest payment because the interest rate has been applied to a higher principal level. The third-period interest is $108.16 × 0.04 = $4.33, raising the principal to $112.49 after three periods. If the account holder leaves the account untouched, this process continues. Principal growth accelerates over time because the interest rate keeps getting applied to larger and larger amounts of principal.

compounding or **compound interest** When interest paid in one period is added to the principal, and the interest rate in the next period is applied to the sum.

    You can see how compounding works. Starting with an amount of principal A and an interest rate r, our principal after one time period would be $A + (A \times r) = A \times (1 + r)$. (In the example above, $A = \$100$ and $r = 0.04$.) After two periods, the principal would grow to

$$A \times (1+r) \times (1+r) = A \times (1+r)^2$$

After three periods, the principal would become

$$A \times (1+r)^2 \times (1+r) = A \times (1+r)^3$$

Repeating this type of calculation shows that the value of the account after t periods, V_t, will be

$$V_t = A \times (1+r)^t$$

Figure 14.1 Compound Interest

Compounding is used to plot the growth of an initial principal amount of $100 over 30 years at interest rates of 2%, 4%, and 6%. While higher interest rates lead to faster growth, each of the lines has the same basic shape and becomes steeper over time.

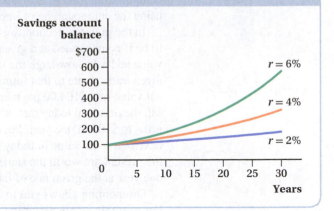

Figure 14.1 uses this formula to plot how an initial principal amount of $100 would grow over 30 years. The bottom line traces the account balance growth when the interest rate is 2%, the middle line shows the case of a 4% interest rate, and the top line assumes a 6% rate. Higher interest rates lead to faster growth—no surprise there. Each of the lines has the same basic shape, however, with the lines growing steeper as time goes on. This is because the compounding process—in which present-period interest is computed on not just the last period's principal but also on the interest it earned—accelerates the growth of the account balance.

Notice that because of compounding, the same gap in interest rate levels can imply very different balances after extended periods. With a 2% interest rate, for example, the balance after 30 years is $100×(1.02)^{30} = $181.14. With a 4% interest rate, it's $100×(1.04)^{30} = $324.34, or $143.20 higher. With a 6% interest rate, the 30th-year balance is $574.35.

Also, because of compounding, the number of periods it takes the balance to double is less than you might think. There's a handy rule-of-thumb for approximating how long it will take for a balance growing at any constant interest rate to double. It's referred to as the "Rule of 72" or the "Rule of 70" depending who you ask. To use it, simply divide 72 (or 70) by the per-period interest rate. The quotient will be the approximate number of periods until the balance doubles.[2]

An account compounding at 4% per year should double every 72/4 = 18 years. It should take about 72/6 = 12 years for a sum to double at a 6% rate, and 72/2 = 36 years for the principal to double at the 2% rate.

Present Discounted Value

As we discussed in the chapter's introduction, a fundamental feature of capital investment decisions is that their costs and benefits are incurred and earned at different times. Typically, investment decisions involve spending money in the present to earn benefits in later periods. A project costing $1,000 today and paying $1,001 in 50 years is a bad idea, even without inflation, as we will see. We need a way to adjust expenditures and payoffs that

---

[2] It works because the size of initial value A growing at a constant rate r over a time period t is $X = Ae^{rt}$. If we replace X with $2A$ (meaning it doubles) and take the natural log of both sides of the equation, we have $rt = \ln 2$. Since $\ln 2 \approx 0.70$, substituting and solving give $t \approx 0.70/r$. So the Rule of 70 is more accurate but more numbers divide evenly into 72, so some people use that instead.

happen at different times so that they can be compared on a consistent basis. Present discounted value (PDV) analysis (sometimes called just present value analysis) does that by using the compounding of interest rates in reverse.

In the previous section, we figured out how large an initial principal value would grow to be if compounded at a given interest rate. Present discounted value takes a future dollar value and asks how large the initial principal would have to be today in order to grow at a given interest rate to that future value. For example, let's say we wanted to know the present value of a $104.00 payment one year from now at an interest rate of 4%. At 4% interest, the principal today that would give you $104 in one year is $100; at 4%, the $100 will grow to $104 in one year. So, at 4% interest, the *present* discounted value (PDV) of $104 next year—its value in today's dollars—is $100. The $104 in the future and the $100 in the present are worth the same amount because $100 today can be used to create $104 in one year at the given rate of interest (4%).

Discounting allows you to compare payments that happen more than one period apart. For example, again assuming a 4% interest rate, the PDV of $108.16 in two years (what we saw above would be the account balance after two years) is $100. The PDV of $112.49 in three years at 4% is also $100.

Present discounted values use interest rates and compounding to compare payments happening at different times. You discount future values so that they can be put in terms of equivalent present-period dollars. This lets us compare an investment's costs and benefits, regardless of when they are paid, on an equal footing. With that, we can ask whether a particular investment is a good idea or compare a number of different investment choices to see which is best.

The interest rate matters a lot for the calculation because it tells you how much you should care about the future compared to today. A $104 payment that will occur in one year has a PDV of $100 at a 4% rate. At a 6% rate, though, we would need to find what initial principal today would grow at a 6% rate to be exactly $104 after one year. This is easy using the formula from above:

$$A \times (1+r) = A \times (1+0.06) = \$104$$

$$A = \frac{\$104}{1.06} = \$98.11$$

In other words, the PDV of $104 is $98.11 when the interest rate is 6%. If we did the same exercise with a 2% interest rate, we would find that the PDV of $104 at this rate is $101.96.

The PDV of a given future value is *always* inversely related to the interest rate. That is, the higher the interest rate, the smaller the initial principal needs to be to grow to the same future value. Therefore, a particular future-period payment has a lower PDV when the interest rate is higher.

All we had to do to compute the PDVs above was reverse the equation for the future account balance under compounding. We solved for the initial principal that would be needed to grow to that future value. That's what a present discounted value is. We saw above that any initial principal A growing at interest rate r for t periods will grow to a value of

$$V_t = A \times (1+r)^t$$

A PDV reinterprets V_t as the future payment that needs to be expressed in present value terms. A, as the initial principal, is the PDV. That is,

$$PDV = \frac{V_t}{(1+r)^t}$$

We can use this equation to find the present discounted value of any payment V_t that occurs t periods in the future. This equation plays a central role in much of what we do in this chapter. Knowing how to calculate PDV is practical, too. If you go to buy a car and the salesperson tells you that you can either buy the car for $20,000 or lease it for $2,000 down and $500 per month, you need to figure out the PDV of the payments to determine which option is the better deal.

The present value equation has some important implications. First, PDVs are proportional to the future value being discounted. If V_t were twice as high, its PDV would be, too.

Second, just as we noted above, higher interest rates imply lower PDVs for fixed values of V_t and t. The intuition is that higher interest rates reduce the initial value necessary to grow to future value V_t.[3]

Finally, the PDV of any particular value V_t is smaller the further into the future that it occurs. The PDV of $104 one year from now is greater than the PDV of $104 in two years, which is itself greater than the PDV of $104 three years from now, and so on.

🪓 Application: The Curious Case of Col. Polubotok and His Missing Trillions

Colonel Pavlo Polubotok was a Cossack military leader born in 1660 who hailed from what we know of as Ukraine. The Ukranians view him as a hero in their effort for independence. In addition to being a military leader, Polubotok was a rich man.

The story goes that in 1723, Polubotok was summoned to discuss Ukranian matters with the Russian tsar Peter the Great in St. Petersburg. Before leaving, he deposited two barrels containing 200,000 *chevronet* gold coins at the Bank of England for safe keeping. Once Polubotok arrived in St. Petersburg, Peter had him jailed for treason, where he died the next year. Polubotok's will decreed that the gold should be given to a sovereign and independent Ukraine.

Fast-forward to 1990. With the collapse of the Soviet Union, Ukraine was preparing to become a sovereign and independent state and Ukranian lawmaker Roman Ivanychuk publicly called for the Bank of England to finally deliver Colonel Polubotok's deposit *plus interest* (supposedly he had been promised a rate of 7.5%). Ivanychuk calculated that at £17 trillion ($29 trillion)—a value that exceeded the combined GDP of the entire world for that year.

Although it seemed an insane amount, Ivanychuk was merely applying the logic of compound interest: The original gold deposit was worth about £10 million in 1990 pounds.[4] At an interest rate of 7.5% compounded for 267 years, the value would around 250 million times its value at the start.

$$V_{1990} = V_{1723} \times (1+r)^{267}$$
$$= £10\,\text{m} \times (1.075)^{267}$$
$$\approx £10\,\text{m} \times 250\,\text{m} = £25\,\text{trillion}$$

---

[3] An important detail when calculating PDVs is to make sure the interest rate r matches the period t. That is, if t is expressed in years, annual interest rates should be used. If t is instead, say, months, then monthly interest rates should be used (and if necessary, converted from whatever time basis they were originally expressed in).

[4] Chevronet gold coins weighed about 3.5 g each and the value of gold at the time was £4.25 per ounce. That would make the deposit of 700 kg in gold worth more than £100,000 in 1723. That was more than £10 million in 1990 terms according to the Bank of England's handy inflation calculator (going back to 1209): https://www.bankofengland.co.uk/monetary-policy/inflation/inflation-calculator.

So maybe Ivanychuk even *under*stated the value of the colonel's gold.

The only problem was that the Bank of England could find no official record of the deposit or the interest rate. They refused to pay, leaving us with one of the most important lessons of nation building and of financial history: If you plan on bequeathing a fortune on your future nation, don't forget to give them the receipt.[*] ∎

Present Discounted Value of Payment Streams   It's easy to extend the PDV method beyond one-off payments to *payment streams*—collections of payments that happen at different times. To compute the PDV of an entire stream, we just apply the present value discounting equation to each of the stream's elements and then add them together.

Suppose you earn a scholarship that will pay $1,000 in each of four installments: The first installment arrives today, and then the next three come one, two, and three years from today. The PDV of the scholarship is the sum of the PDVs of each installment. So, for any generic annual interest rate r, the scholarship's PDV is

$$PDV = \$1,000 + \frac{\$1,000}{(1+r)} + \frac{\$1,000}{(1+r)^2} + \frac{(\$1,000)}{(1+r)^3}$$

The first $1,000 payment is not discounted because it occurs in the present period. (This is what the PDV formula implies, too. If $t = 0$—that is, the payment happens 0 periods from now, or today—then the denominator of the first installment in the PDV equation is 1.) The second installment is discounted by $(1 + r)$, because it occurs in one year (we left the $t = 1$ implicit in that term). The third installment, which happens in two years, is discounted by $(1 + r)^2$. The final installment is discounted by $(1 + r)^3$ because that payment doesn't come for three years.

The interest rate affects the PDV of a stream of payments in the same way that it affects a single payment. For $r = 0.04$ (a 4% interest rate), for example, the scholarship's $PDV = \$1,000 + \$961.54 + \$924.55 + \$889.00 = \$3,775.09$. This present value is less than the simple $4,000 sum of the payments because of discounting. Payments in the future are not equivalent to the same dollar-sized payment in the present. For $r = 0.06$, the scholarship's PDV is lower, at $3,673.01. For $r = 0.02$, the PDV is higher, $3,883.88.

Special Cases of PDVs   There are some commonplace payment stream patterns that have general PDV formulas that are worth learning. One is a constant payment that is made for a set number of periods. For example, a car loan might require a payment of $400 per month for 60 months. Fixed-rate mortgages also have this type of payment pattern. Let's call the regular per-period payment M. The PDV of a set of regular payments M made for T periods (starting one period from now) is

$$PDV = \frac{M}{(1+r)} + \frac{M}{(1+r)^2} + \cdots + \frac{M}{(1+r)^T} = M \times \sum_{t=1}^{T} \frac{1}{(1+r)^t}$$

If we simplify the series of terms with $1/(1 + r)^t$ for various t, we end up with

$$PDV = \left(\frac{M}{r}\right) \times \left[1 - \left(\frac{1}{(1+r)^T}\right)\right]$$

The PDV of this stream of payments is proportional to the regular payment M. That means if you borrow twice as much at the same terms (interest rate and repayment length), your regular payment will be twice as high. The payment stream's PDV is negatively related to the interest rate, but not proportionately. Specifically, changes in r have the largest effect on the PDV at low interest rates; their influence declines in size as r climbs. Finally, the PDV of the payment stream grows with T. This is no surprise;

[*]https://www.nytimes.com/1990/07/24/world/evolution-in-europe-ukraine-s-glittering-hopes.html

the longer the payments last, the greater the total value of those payments. This formula also shows the familiar tradeoff facing many borrowers: When borrowing a fixed amount of money (i.e., a given PDV), a borrower can often lower his payment M by agreeing to a longer payback term T.

An interesting special case of this formula occurs when T goes to infinity, meaning a payment of M every period, forever. (This type of arrangement is called a *perpetuity*.) The PDV of this perpetual stream can be expressed as

$$PDV = \frac{M}{(1+r)} + \frac{M}{(1+r)^2} + \frac{M}{(1+r)^3} + \ldots$$

This may look like it's infinitely large, but it's not because the $(1+r)^t$ values in the denominator grow fast enough with time that the PDV of payments in the far distant future is basically worth zero. You can see the result of this property by plugging a large number for T into the PDV formula. For instance, if the final payment occurs 500 years from now, this makes the expression $(1+r)^{500}$ in the denominator very large. With an interest rate of 4%, you would divide the 500th-year payment by more than 325 million to compute its value in today's terms. Its PDV is therefore basically zero.

When T goes to infinity, the PDV formula above simplifies to

$$PDV = \frac{M}{r}$$

This says that the PDV of any regular payment occurring forever equals the payment divided by the interest rate. If the interest rate is 5%, the PDV of a payment M is 20 times the payment $\left(\frac{M}{0.05} = 20 \times M \right)$. If the interest rate is 10%, the PDV is $10 \times M$; for $r = 2\%$, the PDV is $50 \times M$.

While you may believe that the idea of a payment occurring infinitely seems unrealistic, there are actually a few investment choices or financial instruments that pay off forever. One of the best known is a type of bond, called a consol, issued by the government of the United Kingdom. Consols pay a constant interest payment forever to whoever holds the bond. They don't sell for infinite prices.

British government debt aside, the perpetuity PDV formula is useful as a shorthand way to approximate PDVs. It's not easy to compute the PDVs of even steady payment streams in your head, but if you can assume the payments continue forever, you can approximate it (if a payment stream ends before "forever," the PDV will be a little less than the approximation).

To see an example, suppose you are talking to a friend who is thinking about buying a business. She is confident the business can earn a profit of $100,000 per year for the foreseeable future. The business costs $1.2 million. If the interest rate is 10% (and expected to be constant), should she buy? Not at that price: Even if the business paid that $100,000 profit forever, the PDV of the business is

$$PDV = \frac{M}{r}$$

$$= \frac{\$100,000}{0.10}$$

$$= \$1 \text{ million}$$

The business's earnings can't justify the $1.2 million asking price. On the other hand, if the interest rate is 5%, then the PDV of the business would be, at most, $100,000/0.05 = $2 million, which would make the $1.2 million price worth considering.

figure it out 14.1

Suppose that Emmy is going to turn 21 exactly one year from today, and she wants to throw a spectacular party. Emmy would like to have $1,000 to spend, and wants to set aside enough money today to fund her $1,000 party in a year.

a. If interest rates are 6%, how much does Emmy have to set aside today?

b. If interest rates are 9%, how much does Emmy have to set aside today?

c. What happens to the amount she needs to set aside as interest rates change? Explain.

Solution:

a. We can use the present discounted value (PDV) formula to determine the amount that Emmy needs to set

aside today to have $1,000 one year from now if the interest rate is 6%:

$$PDV = \frac{V}{(1+r)} = \frac{\$1,000}{1+0.06} = \frac{\$1,000}{1.06} = \$943.40$$

b. If the interest rate rises to 9%, Emmy will need to set aside

$$PDV = \frac{V}{(1+r)} = \frac{\$1,000}{1+0.09} = \frac{\$1,000}{1.09} = \$917.43$$

to fund her party.

c. As the interest rate rises, the present value of $1,000 falls. This is because Emmy's current funds will grow more quickly at a higher interest rate. Therefore, she will not need to set as much aside to fund her party.

14.2 Evaluating Investment Choices

Now that we've covered the basics of present discounted value analysis, we can apply that framework to evaluate investment choices.

Net Present Value

In Section 14.1, all the payments had the same sign. But there are many cases in which some payments are benefits and others are costs. Investment projects, for example, usually have up-front costs and then pay benefits in the future. You can evaluate them the same way. Benefits enter the PDV calculation with positive signs, costs with negative signs. You still add up the individual terms of the payment stream to get the PDV.

Let's suppose you go skiing a few times a year and are considering buying your own skis to save the hassle and cost of renting them. You have found a pair you like that costs $500, and you expect to use them for the next three years. You figure out that you typically spend $200 a year on rental skis. Thus, there are three $200 benefit payments: one a year from now, another in two years, and a third in three years. (For simplicity, assume that the $200 benefit comes in one payment at the end of the season.) The payoff structure of the skis purchase is shown in **Table 14.1**.

The first thing to do is figure out the present discounted value of the investment in your own pair of skis. Applying the PDV formula, we have

$$PDV = -\$500 + \frac{\$200}{(1+r)} + \frac{\$200}{(1+r)^2} + \frac{\$200}{(1+r)^3}$$

The first term is the cost of buying the skis. It happens in the present period, so it is not discounted. Because it is a cost to the decision maker rather than a benefit, it is negative. The other terms account for the future benefits of buying

Table 14.1 Payoff Structure of the Skis Purchase

Period	Costs	Benefits
0	$500	$0
1	0	200
2	0	200
3	0	200

Figure 14.2   The PDV of Purchasing a Pair of Skis

The present discounted value (PDV) of an investment in your own pair of skis is plotted against the interest rate r. In this case, buying skis yields positive returns up until $r = 9.7\%$. At interest rates higher than 9.7%, you should continue to rent skis rather than purchasing your own pair.

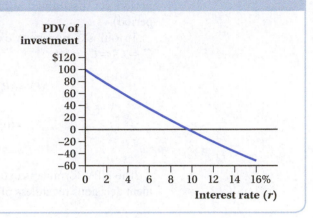

the skis. They have positive signs and are discounted based on how far into the future they occur.

As we have seen in our examples, the PDV of this potential investment also depends on the interest rate. If $r = 4\%$, the PDV of buying the skis is $55.02:

$$PDV = -\$500 + \frac{\$200}{(1+r)} + \frac{\$200}{(1+r)^2} + \frac{\$200}{(1+r)^3}$$

$$= -\$500 + \frac{\$200}{(1+0.04)} + \frac{\$200}{(1+0.04)^2} + \frac{\$200}{(1+0.04)^3}$$

$$= -\$500 + \$192.31 + \$184.91 + \$177.80 = \$55.02$$

This positive number implies that at a 4% interest rate, the skis' future benefits outweigh their cost in present value terms, so buying them is a worthwhile idea. However, if r is higher than 4%, the PDV is less than $55.02. In fact, if r is high enough, the net PDV will be negative. At a 10% interest rate, for example, the PDV is −$2.63; that is, buying the skis creates a *loss* of $2.63 in present value terms. At an interest rate of 10%, the present value of the skis' future benefits does not make up for their up-front costs. **Figure 14.2** plots the PDV of this example investment versus r. You can see that the skis' PDV becomes negative at an interest rate just below 10%, at 9.7% to be exact, and continues to drop at higher interest rates.

Net present value (NPV) analysis is *the use of the present discounted value to evaluate the expected long-term return on an investment* (as we just did in our skis example). It is a method of evaluating investment projects that puts all of an investment project's future cost and benefit flows on a common basis, so they can be compared apples-to-apples. If the PDV of a project's benefits outweighs the PDV of its costs, the project's NPV (the sum of these PDVs) will be positive, and the investment is worthwhile. If the PDVs of the costs are greater than the benefits, the project's NPV is negative, and the investment is not worthwhile.

net present value (NPV) analysis The use of the present discounted value to evaluate the expected long-term return on an investment.

This procedure gives us the generic formula for computing the NPV of any investment decision. Label the periods spanned by the investment project 0, 1, 2, . . . , T, where 0 is the current period and T is the last period in which any costs or benefits associated with the project occur. $B_0, B_1, \ldots, B_T$ are the investment's benefits in the respective periods and $C_0, C_1, \ldots, C_T$ are the costs. The NPV formula is

$$NPV = (B_0 - C_0) + \frac{(B_1 - C_1)}{(1+r)} + \frac{(B_2 - C_2)}{(1+r)^2} + \cdots + \frac{(B_T - C_T)}{(1+r)^T}$$

where $B_t - C_t$ is the net benefit in any particular period t (costs and benefits in the same period get discounted at the same rate so you can just compute the *net* benefit each period).

In our ski purchase example, $T = 3, B_0 = \$0, B_1 = B_2 = B_3 = \$200, C_0 = \$500,$ and $C_1 = C_2 = C_3 = \$0$:

$$NPV = (B_0 - C_0) + \frac{(B_1 - C_1)}{(1+r)} + \frac{(B_2 - C_2)}{(1+r)^2} + \cdots + \frac{(B_T - C_T)}{(1+r)^T}$$

$$= (0 - \$500) + \frac{(\$200 - 0)}{(1+0.04)} + \frac{(\$200 - 0)}{(1+0.04)^2} + \cdots + \frac{(\$200 - 0)}{(1+0.04)^3}$$

$$= -\$500 + \$192.31 + \$184.91 + \$177.80 = \$55.02$$

The NPV formula is extremely useful and can be used to evaluate all sorts of investment decisions regardless of the timing of their positive or negative payouts.

The Key Role of Interest Rates in Determining NPV

For payment streams with both positive and negative terms, the value of the interest rate r can determine whether the net present value NPV is positive or negative. This is because the interest rate, through its discounting role, determines how important future payoffs are relative to those occurring nearer to the present time period. As r rises, more distant payoffs become relatively less important. Mathematically speaking, this is because the term $(1+r)^t$ in the denominator grows larger with t.

This characteristic means that investment projects tend to become less appealing in NPV terms when the interest rate is higher. Investment projects typically have up-front costs with their benefits realized later on. Higher interest rates reduce the present discounted value of those future benefits relative to the investment's current and earlier costs, driving down the investment's NPV.

So where does the interest rate come from? Well, think of it as the opportunity cost of investing. Consider households or firms that are deciding whether to put financial capital toward a potential investment project. They face a choice. They can invest and earn the investment's returns, or they could instead lend their funds on the financial market to other investors implementing their own projects. A household could do this by holding assets in, say, a mutual fund rather than building an addition to their house. Firms can also use financial markets to offer their uncommitted funds to others. If the firm or household chooses to undertake an investment project, it is giving up the return it could have made by lending to others through the financial market. That rate of return is the interest rate r. That's why r captures the opportunity cost of investing. The higher the market interest rate is, therefore, the more a household or firm gives up by investing. NPV analysis, by putting all payments on a common present value basis using the market interest rate, implicitly accounts for this opportunity cost. The higher opportunity costs of investment implied by higher interest rates are the reason investments with a typical "up-front-costs-for-future-returns" payment stream pattern have NPVs that fall as interest rates rise. (These financial markets are very closely related to the market for capital, which we discuss below. Financial markets are the money-based side of capital markets, because capital is bought and sold using funds allocated through financial markets. This connection is the reason the interest rate is the price that matters for the supply and demand of both productive capital and the financial capital used to buy and sell it.)

✈ Application: Replacing Planes

In November 2018, United Airlines took delivery of a Boeing 787-10 Dreamliner, becoming the first airline in the world to fly all three variants of the 787, the 787-8, -9, and the newest and largest, -10. The delivery marked roughly the halfway point of Boeing meeting United's 52-plane Dreamliner order. The new planes would allow United to offer new routes, but a large part of the airline's plans for them was to use them to replace their older, less fuel-efficient Boeing 767-300s.

When deciding whether and when to purchase the new aircraft, United Airlines' management team considered two options.[5] They could buy the replacement planes at about $175 million each, or they could keep their existing 767-300s and pay higher costs for fuel. Experts estimate that the Dreamliners are 20% more fuel efficient than 767-300s, which consume 1,600 gallons of fuel per hour. Therefore, at an expected jet fuel cost of about $4.75 per gallon over the life of the plane, each 787 Dreamliner would save about $1,520 per hour ($1,600 \times 0.20 \times \$4.75$) in fuel costs. Adding to that some extra maintenance costs associated with the older planes, that's an operating cost difference of around $1,600 per hour. What should the management team have done?

Let's start the analysis by laying out the payment flows. If United opted to buy new planes, it would have to pay $175 million per plane immediately and operating costs C per year thereafter.

If United did not buy the new planes, it would pay operating costs C plus the additional $1,600 per hour in fuel costs. Long-haul planes like the Dreamliner and the 767 might fly as many as 4,400 hours per year, so this amounts to an extra operating cost of about $7 million per year for each 767. Furthermore, the 767-300s weren't going to last forever. Even if it didn't buy the Dreamliners right away, United would have to buy new planes eventually. A realistic estimate would be that United could push back the new plane purchase by 10 years. That means that in the 10th year, United would spend an additional $175 million (assuming the price did not change over this period). After that purchase, United's annual expenditures would again equal C, the same as they would have been if the airline had bought the new planes immediately.

United had to decide which of these cost streams would be smallest. **Table 14.2** shows the difference between the two payment streams over the relevant horizon.

Table 14.2 Cost Profiles for United Airlines' Investment Decisions

Year	Costs if New Plane Bought ($ millions per plane)	Costs if Old Plane Kept ($ millions per plane)	Net Cost Difference if New Plane Bought ($ millions per plane)
0	$-(C+175)$	$-(C+\$7)$	−168
1	$-C$	$-(C+\$7)$	$7
2	$-C$	$-(C+\$7)$	$7
...	...	...	...
9	$-C$	$-(C+\$7)$	$7
10	$-C$	$-(C+\$7+\$175)$	$182
11	$-C$	$-C$	0
12	$-C$	$-C$	0
...	...	...	...

---

[5] This example is based on an actual decision United faced at the time. We picked the dollar values in the example to be realistic, but we don't know what United actually paid. Furthermore, to keep things simple, we've ignored many other aspects of the plane-replacement problem that matter in real life, such as flyers' willingness to pay to fly on newer aircraft, the interactions between United's plane choice and its contracts with its unions, and so on.

Table 14.3 United Airlines' NPV of Buying New Planes

Year	Buying New Plane ($ millions)	Buying New Plane, Growing Costs ($ millions)	Buying New Plane, Lower *r* ($ millions)
0	−168	−168	−168
1	6.67	7.13	6.80
2	6.35	7.27	6.60
3	6.05	7.41	6.41
4	5.76	7.55	6.22
5	5.48	7.69	6.04
6	5.22	7.84	5.86
7	4.97	7.99	5.69
8	4.74	8.14	5.53
9	4.51	8.30	5.36
10	111.7	115.9	135.4
11	0	0	0
...	...	...	...
NPV =	−$6.5	$17.2	$21.9

Looking at the difference in costs makes it clear that buying the new planes is an investment: United pays an up-front cost (the $168 million difference between the purchase cost and the higher fuel costs), but it saves the additional fuel costs of $7 million per year plus the $175 million cost of purchasing a new plane when the 767-300s are retired after 10 years. Following the 10th year, United has new planes and there is no longer any difference in operating costs.

Suppose the interest rate United faces is 5%. We first compute the PDV of each year's net payment. These PDVs are given in the first column of **Table 14.3**. Their sum is the per-plane NPV of buying new planes right away. The fact that the sum is −$6.5 million indicates that buying new planes causes a net *loss* to United of $6.5 million per plane. In other words, in net present value terms, United's additional cost of buying the new planes immediately at $175 million each is too high relative to the money the airline would save in lower fuel costs and by being able to put off buying new planes for another 10 years. Therefore, United should choose to keep the 767-300s in its fleet for the time being; otherwise, the airline is setting itself up for a net loss of $6.5 million per plane.

Under what circumstances might United have found it beneficial to replace the 767-300s? We consider two such cases: fuel costs that increase by 7% per year and a lower interest rate.

Suppose United anticipates that the additional operating costs of the 767-300s increase by 7% per year (so it is $7 million in the first year, $7.49 million in the second year, etc.), perhaps because fuel prices rise or because the aging 767-300s require ever-more maintenance attention. The NPV analysis for this case is shown in the second column of Table 14.3. Notice how the present value of the fuel cost difference actually rises over time rather than falls. This is because the 7% cost growth rate is higher than the 5% interest rate. With growing costs, the NPV of purchasing a new plane is now positive ($17.2 million), implying that United should replace the 767-300s with Dreamliners immediately. This makes sense: If the 767-300s are becoming more costly over time, this raises the return of replacing them earlier.

As a final case, let's suppose again that the fuel cost difference is fixed at $7 million per year, but that United faces a lower interest rate of 3%. This lower interest rate means that the future cost savings won't be discounted as much, nor will the savings from not having to purchase new planes 10 years from now. Both of these factors raise the value of buying the new planes right away, and that's exactly what we see in the third column of Table 14.3. The NPV of purchasing now is $21.9 million per plane.

When United received its first Dreamliner, interest rates were at historical lows, and it was plausible that fuel prices and maintenance costs for the 767-300s could continue to rise. This suggests that United was indeed saving money by replacing the planes with Dreamliners immediately rather than waiting 10 more years. ■

NPVs versus Payback Periods

You may have heard of investments getting evaluated in terms of **payback periods**, *the length of time required for an investment's initial costs to be recouped in future benefits without discounting future flows*. For our ski purchase example above, the payback period is three years. The total benefits obtained after two years ($200 + $200 = $400) are less than the $500 up-front cost, but the $600 in total benefits recovered after three years is greater.

 Payback periods are easy to compute but they are misleading because they don't discount future money by an interest rate. They treat future payments as equivalent to current payments in dollar terms. The skis, for example, would be considered worthwhile in payback period terms as long as three years is an acceptable period to the person making a decision about the investment. At high enough interest rates, however, the purchase will have a negative NPV. You would do better by not buying the skis and earning interest on the $500 instead. If you had used the payback period method as an evaluation standard when interest rates are high, you would mistakenly buy the skis. For this reason, while payback periods are a handy "first-pass" way to think about investments, they can lead to wrong decisions. NPV is better.

payback period The length of time required for an investment's initial costs to be recouped in future benefits without discounting future flows.

 figure it out 14.2

Go online for interactive, step-by-step help in solving the following problem.

Marty owns a travel agency and is considering the purchase of a flux capacitor. Owning the capacitor will enable Marty to earn $100,000 per year selling trips through time. Marty plans to hold on to the capacitor for three years. He estimates that at the end of three years, he will be able to resell the flux capacitor for $250,000.

a. If the flux capacitor is priced at $475,000 and interest rates are 7%, calculate the net present value of the investment.

b. Is the flux capacitor a wise investment for Marty? Explain.

Solution:

a. Net present value is the present value of the benefits minus the present value of the costs for each period. We must account for three factors in this calculation: the price Marty must pay initially, the

revenue he earns each of the three periods, and the amount he will receive from selling the capacitor at the end of the three years. Therefore,

$$NPV = -\$475,000 + \frac{\$100,000}{1.07} + \frac{\$100,000}{(1.07)^2}$$
$$+ \frac{\$100,000}{(1.07)^3} + \frac{\$250,000}{(1.07)^3}$$

Note that the cost of $475,000 is occurring now, so it is not discounted (and it enters the equation with a minus sign), while the benefits (the annual revenue and the sale price) occur in the future and thus must be discounted.

Calculating, we get

$$NPV = -\$475,000 + \$93,457.94 + \$87,343.87 + \$81,629.79$$
$$+ \$204,074.47 = -\$8,493.93$$

b. No, this is not a wise investment for Marty because the NPV is negative.

14.3 The Correct Interest Rate to Use, and Capital Markets

In everything we've done to this point, we've talked about "the" interest rate r. But real financial markets have many different interest rates. Which one should investors use to evaluate net present values?

Nominal versus Real Interest Rates

Because investments' costs and benefits occur at different times, price inflation can affect the net value of an investment, a fact we've ignored so far. When prices change over time, they create their own discounting effect: A future payment doesn't have the same purchasing power as an equal-sized payment in the present. If there is inflation (rising prices), a future payment of $1,000 will buy fewer goods and services than a payment of $1,000 today. The further the payment is in the future, the more prices will likely have increased, and the larger is this purchasing power gap. Because firms and households care about real purchasing power, they need to adjust for these gaps when evaluating investments.

nominal interest rate
Rate of return expressed in raw currency values without regard for how much purchasing power those values hold.

real interest rate Rate of return expressed in terms of purchasing power.

Economists account for inflation in these situations by drawing a distinction between nominal and real interest rates. A **nominal interest rate** is a *rate of return expressed in raw currency values without regard for how much purchasing power those values hold*. A **real interest rate** is a *rate of return expressed in terms of purchasing power* (also called *inflation-adjusted interest rates*), the amount of goods and services that the payment can purchase. If the growth rate in the price level has reduced a future payment's purchasing power because a dollar buys less in the future than it does in the present, real interest rates take that into account.

As long as inflation rates aren't wildly high, the basic rule is that the real interest rate, r, is approximately the nominal interest rate, i, minus the inflation rate, π:[6]

$$r \approx i - \pi$$

Once we have computed the real interest rate, we use it as the interest rate r in PDV and NPV calculations. This will automatically take into account the discounting effects of price changes over the lifetime of the investment as well as the other reasons future payments are discounted.

Using the Correct Rate

To find the proper interest rate to use in NPV calculations, it's helpful to recall that the interest rate captures the opportunity cost of investing. It is an opportunity cost because resources used to purchase capital cannot be otherwise saved to earn interest. NPV analysis asks whether an investment's future payoffs are worth the current costs by comparing

---

[6] This became known as the Fisher rule, in honor of the early-twentieth-century Yale economist Irving Fisher. It derives from the fact that any principal amount A earning a nominal interest rate of i will be worth $A \times (1+i)$ in non-inflation-adjusted terms. If the inflation rate over the period is π, then money that could buy A worth of goods at the beginning of the period can buy $A/(1+\pi)$ at the end of the period. So, the real value of the principal at the end is $A \times (1+i)/(1+\pi)$. The real interest rate is the percentage change in purchasing power over the initial principal's purchasing power: $r = [(A(1+i)/(1+\pi)) - A]/A = (1+i)/(1+\pi) - 1 = (i - \pi)/(1+\pi)$. If π isn't very high, that's approximately equal to $i - \pi$.

those future payoffs to what would have been earned by simply saving the funds and earning interest. Discounting future flows in an NPV analysis puts them on comparable terms with the possible interest earned on savings.

This means that the interest rate used to compute NPVs should be the alternative rate of return that is forgone if the investment is made. If a firm is considering whether to build a new store, for example, it is in essence deciding between building the store or saving the funds in the financial market and earning the market rate. However, we will discuss how even this "correct" interest rate needs to be modified if there is uncertainty about the future payoffs.

14.4 Evaluating Risky Investments

That's how to analyze investment choices using net present value analysis. But up to this point, we have ignored risk. In real life, firms and consumers face a lot of uncertainty when making investment decisions. Sometimes investments flop. In this section, we discuss the ways to analyze NPVs while taking uncertainty into account, including situations in which investors have the option of waiting to gather more information before deciding to invest.

NPV with Uncertainty: Expected Value

The basic way to incorporate risk into NPV investment analysis is to compute NPV as an *expected value*, that is, by weighting each payoff by the probability that it happens. Risky payouts give a combination of two things: amounts and probabilities that they happen.

Think about a risky investment that will pay an uncertain benefit in one year. **Table 14.4** shows the possible benefits along with the probabilities of their occurrence. Looking at these possible outcomes, we see that the investment could perform poorly and earn no return with a small probability (0.2, or 20%), do very well and deliver a $2 million payout with a small probability (0.2), or, most likely, yield a modest $1 million payout with higher probability (0.6).[7]

We use the concept of **expected value**, *the probability-weighted average payout*, to evaluate the situation. The expected value of any uncertain outcome is the sum of the product of each possible outcome/payment and the probability of that outcome/payment. In general terms, for an uncertain outcome with N possible payments,

$$\text{Expected value} = (p_1 \times M_1) + (p_2 \times M_2) + \ldots + (p_N \times M_N)$$

Table 14.4 Analyzing a Risky Investment

Benefit Payout	Probability of Payout
$0	0.2
$1 million	0.6
$2 million	0.2

expected value The probability-weighted average payout.

[7] Many factors can affect these probabilities in actual investment choices. Sometimes probabilities are objectively defined; that is, they are verifiably exact. An example is the outcome of flipping a coin: Everyone knows there is exactly a 50% chance of either a head or tail. Another example is a state lottery game that promises 10% of all cards are winners. You know that 1 out of every 10 cards will be a winner. In most real-world investment scenarios, however, probabilities are not objective, but subjective. That is, they are determined by the decision maker's judgment rather than set in stone by the fact that a coin has only two sides or that an accounting firm has verified the lottery's procedures. With subjective probabilities, knowing which factors affect the possible outcomes helps a decision maker. We're not going to worry about the distinction between the two types of probabilities here—we keep it simple and assume all the probabilities we discuss are objectively defined—but it's worth remembering the difference in practical situations.

where $p_1, p_2, \ldots p_N$ are, respectively, the probabilities of payments 1, 2, and so on, and $M_1, M_2, \ldots M_N$ are the payments themselves. So, in our example investment above, the expected benefit payout is

$$\text{Expected benefit payout} = (0.2 \times \$0) + (0.6 \times \$1 \text{ million}) + (0.2 \times \$2 \text{ million})$$
$$= \$0 + \$0.6 \text{ million} + \$0.4 \text{ million}$$
$$= \$1 \text{ million}$$

For payment flows that are guaranteed—that is, for which there is no uncertainty—computing expected value is easy. Because the payment is certain, its probability is 1 (or 100% if you prefer). Therefore, the expected value is just 1 times the guaranteed payment. An investment with a $1 million guaranteed payout has an expected payout value of $1 million.

Using expected value, then, all of the NPV calculations hold up exactly the same way as before, but you just need to multiply outcomes by their probabilities.

Risk and the Option Value of Waiting

Evaluating an investment using expected value provides a natural way to incorporate risk into the NPV calculation. One way risk can influence decisions is by creating an incentive to postpone investments and gather more information. The **option value of waiting** is *the value created if an investor can postpone the investment decision until the uncertainty about an investment's return is wholly or partially resolved.* This incentive arises if waiting will resolve some of the uncertainty about the investment before deciding whether to go forward with the investment. (The name refers to the fact that an investor's option to postpone an investment decision is conceptually related to financial options—contracts that give someone the right, but not the obligation, to buy or sell an item.)

option value of waiting
The value created if an investor can postpone the investment decision until the uncertainty about an investment's return is wholly or partially resolved.

Let's use an example to see how this operates. You want to get a new, high-tech television and there is an emerging battle over advanced television formats between mythical formats 16K and Hyper-3D HD systems, but you don't have enough money or space to be able to buy both. It's not clear what the future of TV broadcasting will be; maybe channels will eventually be broadcast in 16K, or maybe they'll decide to go with Hyper-3D instead. This is what economists call a "standards war": It's likely only one format will succeed in becoming the standard technological platform in the market. The other will probably die off. Suppose the battle is expected to be settled one year later. Therefore, if you buy the wrong television, within a year, you won't be able to see your favorite shows using it. If you choose correctly, everything will be fine.

Let's apply some numbers to see how this uncertainty affects the NPV and the option value of buying a television. Suppose the interest rate is 5%; 16K TVs cost $1,350; and Hyper-3D TVs cost $1,200. Furthermore, each type of television gives its owner $150 per year of value forever if his or her favorite shows are broadcast in that format and $0 if not (i.e., if the TV's format has lost the standards war).

Given this information, the value of a 16K television in the first year is $-\$1,350 + \$150 = -\$1,200$. For every year following that, a 16K TV offers a $150 benefit if that is the format that channels are broadcast in. Using the formula we discussed above, the total PDV of this infinite stream of $150 benefits is $\$150/0.05 = \$3,000$. The Hyper-3D television has a first-year value of $-\$1,200 + \$150 = -\$1,050$ and a per-year $150 benefit after that, if the Hyper-3D format becomes the standard. In this case, the PDV of the Hyper-3D's infinite stream of $150 benefits is also $3,000.

Finally, suppose analysts believe that 16K has a 75% chance of winning the standards war and Hyper-3D has a 25% chance.

Now we have everything we need to compute the net present value (NPV) of buying each television today. If you purchase a 16K TV, the first year's payouts include the price you pay for the television ($1,350) and the $150 benefit you receive from it for that year. After that, starting next year, there is a 75% chance 16K will win the standards war and you will receive a $150 annual benefit forever ($PDV = \$3,000$). On the other hand, there is a 25% chance Hyper-3D will win the standards war and your 16K TV will become worthless. Therefore, the NPV of buying the 16K now is

$$16K \ NPV_{now} = (-\$1,350 + \$150) + 0.75 \times (\$3,000/1.05) + 0.25 \times (\$0/1.05)$$
$$= -\$1,200 + 0.75 \times \$2,857.14 + 0.25 \times \$0$$
$$= -\$1,200 + \$2,142.86 + \$0 = \$942.86$$

Notice that this NPV calculation is an *expected* value — we've weighted each cost and benefit by the probability that it occurs. The payments in the first year, the $1,350 outlay to buy the television and the $150 benefit you receive from it, are guaranteed, so they are multiplied by 1. For future payouts, we multiply the $3,000 PDV benefit stream received if 16K TV wins the standards war by the 75% probability that 16K does, in fact, win the war. Similarly, we multiply the $0 benefit stream that occurs if 16K loses by the 25% chance that this outcome occurs. Both of these future benefit streams effectively occur one year in the future, so we must also discount their value by $1 + r$, or 1.05 in this case. Given all this, the NPV of buying the 16K TV is $942.86.

We calculate the NPV of buying the Hyper-3D television in the same way. The differences are that the price of the television is only $1,200 and the probabilities are reversed. There is only a 25% chance that Hyper-3D becomes the standard in 2017 and you receive the $3,000 PDV of future benefits. There is a 75% chance it loses and future benefits are zero:

$$Hyper\text{-}3D \ NPV_{now} = (-\$1,200 + \$150) + 0.25 \times (\$3,000/1.05) + 0.75 \times (\$0/1.05)$$
$$= -\$1,050 + 0.25 \times \$2,857.14 + 0.75 \times \$0$$
$$= -\$1,050 + \$714.29 + \$0 = -\$335.71$$

The NPV of buying the Hyper-3D television is −$335.71.

So, we see that the NPV of buying the 16K is $942.86, while the NPV of buying the Hyper-3D is negative, −$335.71. These calculations indicate that if you *had* to choose your television in 2016, you would buy a 16K.

But, if you could wait a year before deciding whether to buy, you could find out which platform wins the standards war and then buy that one, sure that you'll have a supply of programs available (and the $3,000 of benefit they give you) in the future. To find the value of waiting, we need to compute the NPV of that plan *today*. We compute it today, even though following through with the plan means you wouldn't actually buy anything until next year, because we need to compare the NPVs of this wait-until-next-year plan on an even basis to the NPVs of buying now that we calculated above.

This wait-a-year NPV, NPV_{wt+1} (the "w" indicates the value of waiting), is

$$NPV_{wt+1} = 0.75 \times (-\$1,200/1.05) + 0.75 \times (\$3,000/1.05^2) + 0.25 \times (-\$1,050/1.05) + 0.25 \times$$
$$(\$3,000/1.05^2)$$
$$= 0.75 \times (-\$1,142.86) + 0.75 \times (\$2,721.09) + 0.25 \times (-\$1,000.00) + 0.25 \times (\$2,721.09)$$
$$= -\$857.15 + \$2,040.82 - \$250.00 + \$680.27 = \$1,613.94$$

Here, in the 75% chance 16K TV wins the standards war, you buy that type of machine. It delivers a net benefit of −$1,200 next year (its $1,350 cost plus its $150 benefit) and gives you a $150 per year benefit forever after (PDV = $3,000). From the perspective of today, however, the first of these payment flows occurs one year in the future and therefore must be discounted by 1.05, and the second payment occurs in two years and must be discounted by 1.05^2. If Hyper-3D wins, which has a 25% chance of happening, you buy that type of machine next year, instead, losing $1,050 the first year and earning the $3,000 lifetime benefit after that. When we add together all of these probability-weighted costs and benefits, we end up with the wait-a-year plan having a NPV of $1,613.94.

So, while the NPV of buying the 16K TV in 2016 was positive ($942.86), waiting one more year before buying yields an even higher NPV ($1,613.94). The extra value comes from eliminating the chance that you buy a losing television that ends up providing no future benefit. By not buying until next year, you *guarantee* yourself the $3,000 PDV of future benefits of the television, rather than rolling the dice and hoping you happen to choose the right format. This ability to choose after you see what happens is what creates the option value of waiting; you can eliminate the worst possible outcomes that could have happened had you made your investment earlier. There is a cost to waiting, however: You delay any benefit of the investment in a television by a year. (This is fully taken into account in the calculations because we computed NPV_{wt+1} from the perspective of today, thereby accounting for the lost $150 in benefits that buying a television early would have provided.) In this case, at least, the amount of uncertainty is great enough that it's very valuable to wait to eliminate it. The option value of waiting is the difference between the NPV of the wait-a-year policy and the NPV of buying a 16K TV now: $1,613.94 – $942.86 = $671.08.

Option values of waiting arise in many real-world investment decisions because uncertainty is common. Recognizing the value that waiting creates can be one of the most important considerations in evaluating investment options.

---

 figure it out 14.3

Alex is a house flipper: He buys old houses that appear to be bargains, rehabs them, and then puts them back on the market for resale. Alex recently discovered a lovely Victorian home that he is considering for rehab. There is a 0.2 probability that Alex will lose 10% on the deal, a 0.7 probability that he will gain 8% on the deal, and a 0.1 probability that he will gain 20%.

a. Calculate Alex's expected return from the project.

b. Suppose that, in a different neighborhood, there is a bungalow selling for the same price. Alex estimates that there is a 0.3 probability that he will gain 3%, a 0.5 probability that he will gain 5.8%, and a 0.2 probability that he will gain 9%. Calculate Alex's expected return from this project.

c. Assume that Alex has only enough money to flip one house. If he bases his decision solely on expected return, is it clear which project Alex will prefer? If not, is there an additional factor that might tip the balance?

Solution:

a. Remember that expected value $= (p_1 \times M_1) + (p_2 \times M_2) + (p_3 \times M_3)$. Substituting the numbers for the Victorian, we find

Expected return $= (0.2 \times -10) + (0.7 \times 8) + (0.1 \times 20)$
$= -2 + 5.6 + 2 = 5.6\%$

b. Substituting the numbers for the bungalow, we find

Expected return $= (0.3 \times 3) + (0.5 \times 5.8) + (0.2 \times 9)$
$= 0.9 + 2.9 + 1.8 = 5.6\%$

c. The expected return for the two investments is the same. If this is the only basis of comparison, neither the Victorian nor the bungalow is obviously superior. However, there is no chance he will lose money on the bungalow, while he faces a 0.2 probability of experiencing a 10% loss on the Victorian. Some investors (perhaps including Alex) may be willing to give up a small chance at a higher return if they know that the worst outcome is less costly, as is the case with the bungalow. This preference is characteristic of *risk aversion*, which we discuss more below.

14.5 Uncertainty, Risk, and Insurance

Expected value gives us a way to think about risks in the context of investment. But, as we see in this section, when we use expected value analysis, we are implicitly assuming that people aren't especially afraid of risk. For example, in expected value terms, a 1% chance of $100 million is worth just as much as having $1 million in cash. In this section, we explore what happens when people do not like taking risks and see why insurance is valuable to these people and how risk changes investment decisions.

Expected Income, Expected Utility, and the Risk Premium

To understand what we mean by people not liking risk, think about a person and the utility he gets from consuming the goods he can buy with his income. Our analysis in Chapter 4 explains what bundle of goods a person picks given the goods' prices and the person's income, but when trying to figure out a consumer's distaste for risk, we don't need to keep track of exactly what goods are in that bundle. All we need to know is the total amount of utility this person enjoys at any given income level.

We plot the relationship between utility and income for a random guy named Adam in **Figure 14.3**. Adam's income is shown on the horizontal axis, and his utility from consuming the goods he buys with that income level is on the vertical axis. Utility rises with income, as we would expect, because the more income he has, the more stuff he can buy. However, the curve becomes less steep as his income rises. That is, Adam has diminishing marginal utility of income. The bump in utility he would enjoy from an increase in income of, say, $10,000 to $15,000 is more than the extra utility he'd experience from moving from an income of $1,000,000 to $1,005,000. It turns out that if diminishing marginal utility holds, Adam will be sensitive to risk and willing to pay to eliminate or reduce uncertainty.

To make the relationship between risk and diminishing marginal utility as clear as possible, consider a specific example. Suppose most of Adam's income comes from a country store he owns, and that the only important uncertainty his business faces is whether the store is destroyed by a tornado (causing Adam's income to take a big hit).

Figure 14.3 **A Risk-Averse Individual Will Pay to Avoid Risk**

Adam faces a 50% probability of an income of $100,000 (point *B*) and a 50% probability of an income of $36,000 (point *A*). Therefore, his expected income is $68,000 and his expected utility is 8 (point *C*). A certain income of $64,000 also gives Adam a utility of 8 (point *E*). Because Adam is risk-averse, he is willing to give up as much as $4,000 in expected income (the distance from point *C* to point *E*) to have a certain income of $64,000 instead of his uncertain income.

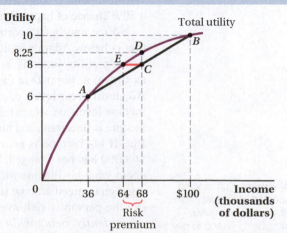

We assume the utility, U, that Adam enjoys from goods purchased with his income is given by the function

$$U = \sqrt{I}$$

where I is Adam's income in thousands of dollars. This utility function is plotted in Figure 14.3, and it exhibits diminishing marginal utility of income.

Now suppose that Adam's income is $100,000 in a year there is no tornado and only $36,000 if there is a tornado. The utility levels corresponding to these incomes are shown as points B and A, respectively, in Figure 14.3. With $100,000 in income, Adam's utility is $U = \sqrt{100} = 10$; with $36,000 in income, it's $U = \sqrt{36} = 6$.

Let's say the probability of a tornado is ridiculously high, 50%, to make the math easy. This is where the uncertainty comes from.

Following a basic expected value calculation, we first compute Adam's expected income for the year. There's a 50% chance his store blows down, giving him an income of $36,000. There's a 50% chance of no tornado, and his income is $100,000. Applying the formula for computing expected values, we find that Adam's expected income is $68,000:

$$\text{Expected income} = (0.5 \times \$36,000) + (0.5 \times \$100,000)$$
$$= \$18,000 + \$50,000$$
$$= \$68,000$$

Similarly, we can compute his expected utility:

$$\text{Expected utility} = (0.5 \times 6) + (0.5 \times 10)$$
$$= 3 + 5$$
$$= 8$$

We plot these expected income and utility levels at point C. Notice how this point is halfway along the straight line connecting A and B, the income-utility combinations in the tornado and no-tornado cases. This isn't a coincidence. Adam's expected income and utility values will be somewhere on that same line for *any* probability of a tornado. Where exactly on the line the point will be depends on the probability that each event (tornado or no tornado) occurs. The higher the probability of a tornado, the closer Adam's expected income and utility will be to the tornado income–utility point A. (If a tornado happens 100% of the time, point A is the expected income and utility.) If the probability of a tornado is low, Adam's expected income and utility will be near point B. The expected values shown at point C happen to be at the halfway point on the AB line because the tornado has a 50% chance of happening.

Notice another important thing about point C: It's at an expected utility level, 8, that is below Adam's utility function at that same actual level of income. According to Adam's utility function, an income level of $68,000 gets him utility of $U = \sqrt{68} = 8.25$, as shown at point D in Figure 14.3. So the same expected income, $68,000, can give Adam different levels of expected utility depending on the riskiness of the underlying income levels on which the expectation is based. Due to the chance of tornado, Adam's income is uncertain, and his $68,000 in expected income delivers an expected utility of 8. But, if his income is *guaranteed* to be $68,000, even though his expected income of $68,000 has not changed, his expected utility would be 8.25. In words, the uncertainty about what his income will be reduces Adam's expected utility. If a person prefers having a guaranteed amount to having a risky but equivalent-in-expected-value amount, we say the person is **risk-averse**: *suffering an expected utility loss from uncertainty, or equivalently, being willing to pay to have that risk reduced.* Uncertainty reduces the utility of a risk-averse person like Adam.

risk-averse Suffering an expected utility loss from uncertainty, or equivalently, being willing to pay to have that risk reduced.

A related way to see how uncertainty reduces expected utility is to ask what guaranteed income would offer Adam the same expected utility level as his uncertain income. *The guaranteed income level at which an individual would receive the same expected utility level as from an uncertain income* is sometimes referred to as the **certainty equivalent**. In our example it is shown at point E in Figure 14.3. The certainty equivalent in this example is $64,000, because $U = \sqrt{64} = 8$. Adam derives the same expected utility from a guaranteed $64,000 income as he does from having a 50% chance of a $36,000 income and a 50% chance of a $100,000 income. Another way to put this is that Adam is willing to give up $4,000 in expected income ($68,000 – $64,000) in exchange for eliminating his income uncertainty. This income difference is called the **risk premium**—*the compensation an individual would require to bear risk without suffering a loss in expected utility.* It's the extra amount of expected income (here, $4,000) Adam must receive to make him as well off when his income is uncertain as when it is guaranteed.

Notice how these relationships we've just pointed out—that for risk-averse individuals, expected utility falls as a given expected income becomes more uncertain, and that risk-averse individuals are willing to give up expected income to reduce uncertainty—are, graphically speaking, a consequence of the diminishing marginal utility of income. That is, the fact that point C (or any point on the AB line) is below the income-utility curve is a direct consequence of the fact that there is diminishing marginal utility of income. Diminishing marginal utility causes this curve to be concave as income rises, ensuring that any uncertain combination of income-utility outcomes will have an expected utility below that of an equivalent expected income that is guaranteed.

certainty equivalent The guaranteed income level at which an individual would receive the same expected utility level as from an uncertain income.

risk premium The compensation an individual would require to bear risk without suffering a loss in expected utility.

Insurance Markets

A world full of uncertainties and risk-averse people creates demand for insurance. We all understand the basic idea of insurance, but economists define it specifically as when one economic actor pays another to reduce the payer's economic risk. The details of the insurance–risk aversion connection are important to understand, and we'll go through them in a moment, but the basic idea is simple. If someone is risk-averse, he will pay to have his risks reduced. That's what insurance does: It reduces risk by paying the policyholder when things would otherwise be bad (his car is stolen, he becomes sick and needs to pay a lot of medical bills, etc.). In exchange for this, the policyholder pays a premium to the insurer each year and makes do with a little less income (by the amount of the premium) in exchange for help against the possibility of something bad.

The Value of Insurance   The loss in expected utility Adam experiences due to the uncertainty of his income and his willingness to give up some expected income to reduce this loss suggest a way to make him better off. Suppose someone or some company offers him an insurance contract to reduce his uncertainty and that it involves the following arrangement. If Adam's store blows down, the insurer will pay him a sum of money. This will reduce his losses in the bad situation. In exchange, Adam makes a payment to the insurer—a policy premium—if there isn't a tornado. This premium reduces his income in a good situation; there's no tornado, but Adam has to do without the money he paid for the premium. By reducing Adam's uncertainty, however, the insurance contract raises Adam's expected utility for any given expected income level. Note that the arrangement does not raise Adam's expected utility by increasing his expected income; in fact, the insurance policy could very well reduce his expected income. Nevertheless, he benefits because less uncertainty translates into greater expected utility.

We can see this benefit more explicitly in some examples. A straightforward policy would have the insurer pay Adam $32,000 if a tornado destroys his store, while having

Adam pay the insurer a $32,000 premium if there is no tornado. Under such a policy, Adam's income is $68,000 regardless of whether a tornado occurs. If there's a tornado, his income is $36,000 and his payout from the insurer is $32,000, and $36,000 + $32,000 = $68,000; if no tornado occurs, his income is $100,000 and his insurance premium is $32,000, and $100,000 − $32,000 = $68,000. As we saw above, that guaranteed income of $68,000 yields Adam an expected utility of 8.25, greater than the expected utility of 8 he would receive without an insurance policy and the same *expected* income of $68,000. With this policy, all uncertainty has been eliminated for Adam; he ends up equally well off no matter what event happens (tornado or no tornado). *An insurance policy that leaves the insured individual equally well off regardless of the outcome* is **complete insurance** or **full insurance**.

complete insurance or **full insurance** An insurance policy that leaves the insured individual equally well off regardless of the outcome.

Even partial insurance is valuable, however. Suppose that the policy instead pays Adam $20,000 if there is a tornado in exchange for a $20,000 premium in the case of no tornado. This makes his income $36,000 + $20,000 = $56,000 in the case of a tornado and $100,000 − $20,000 = $80,000 if no tornado occurs. This policy keeps Adam's expected income at $68,000 ($0.5 × $56,000 + 0.5 × $80,000 = $68,000), but gives him an expected utility of 8.21 ($0.5 × \sqrt{56} + 0.5 × \sqrt{80} = 3.74 + 4.47 = 8.21$). While this is less than the expected utility of 8.25 from having a guaranteed $68,000 in income, it is higher than Adam's expected utility of 8 without a policy.

Insurance is a good deal for Adam, but what's in it for the insurer? An insurance policy basically shifts Adam's risk to the insurer: The insurer does not know for certain what its profit from the policy will be. However, insurers don't typically suffer a loss as a result of this transfer because they issue a large number of policies like Adam's. By adding together all these risks from all the policies they issue, insurers greatly reduce the uncertainty of their profits.

To see why adding risks together helps an insurer, suppose that an insurer has sold policies to thousands of people exactly like Adam, each of whom owns a store that delivers income to the storeowner but also has a 50% chance of blowing down. Although it is uncertain if any particular store is going to blow down, because the insurer covers thousands of such stores, in a given year that insurer can expect almost exactly half of its covered stores to blow down. Thus, rather than having high uncertainty over the claims it will have to pay, the insurer actually has low uncertainty. The insurer doesn't make big profits half the time and lose big money the other half; instead, it knows it's going to almost surely have to pay claims on about half its stores while collecting premiums from the other half. This **diversification**—*a strategy to reduce risk by combining uncertain outcomes*—is one of the key functions of insurance markets. An important part of making diversification work is that risks being added together must be at least partially unrelated. If instead they were highly correlated with one another—for instance, if all the insured stores were tightly packed together in the same location so that if one blew down, they all would—the insurer couldn't diversify away the risk. Half the time no stores would blow down, and half the time all the stores would blow down. The insurer would be left with a risk just as uncertain as Adam's, but bigger in financial terms.

diversification A strategy to reduce risk by combining uncertain outcomes.

Insurers can benefit from offering to take away policyholder's risks in another way. Remember that risk aversion creates a willingness to pay to remove or reduce risk. Insurers can design policies to capture some of this value. Both of the example policies we discussed above have the same expected profit for the insurer: zero. The payment the insurer makes to Adam in case of a tornado equals the policy premium he pays in the absence of a tornado, and both outcomes happen with equal probability. (For example, $0.5 × −$32,000 + 0.5 × $32,000 = −$16,000 + $16,000 = $0.$) *An insurance policy with expected net payments equal to zero*—that is, when the expected premiums equal the expected payouts—is said to be **actuarially fair**.

actuarially fair Description of an insurance policy with expected net payments equal to zero.

But we've just seen how insurance has value for consumers like Adam; in real life, insurers design policies to capture some of this value. Consider the following policy: The insurer pays Adam $20,000 if there is a tornado, while Adam pays a $24,000 premium if no tornado occurs. Adam's expected utility under this policy is 8.10 ($0.5 \times \sqrt{56} + 0.5 \times \sqrt{76} = 8.10$). The policy raises his expected utility relative to the level it would be without the policy. Adam's expected income under the policy is $(0.5 \times \$56,000) + (0.5 \times \$76,000) = \$66,000$. This is $2,000 less than his expected income of $68,000 without the policy, but Adam is willing to give up this $2,000 because his expected utility is higher with the policy than without it. As we saw above, in fact, Adam is willing to give up as much as $4,000 in expected income to purchase a policy that would remove all of his income uncertainty.

From the insurer's point of view, Adam's $2,000 drop in expected income is its expected profit from the policy: There is a 50% chance it will have to pay Adam $20,000 and a 50% chance it will not have to pay Adam anything, but will earn a $24,000 premium, yielding an expected profit of $(0.5 \times \$24,000) - (0.5 \times \$20,000) = \$2,000$. While this outcome from Adam's policy is uncertain, again, if the insurer sells thousands of such policies to unrelated risks, it can expect to earn profits of nearly $2,000 per policy without much uncertainty around that total.[8] The more competition, the more the terms of policies will be tilted in the favor of policyholders and toward being actuarially fair.

The Degree of Risk Aversion

Given the connection between diminishing marginal utility of income (reflected in how curved the utility-income relationship is) and risk aversion, it should be clear that the greater the curve in a consumer's utility function, the more risk-averse he is.

Figure 14.4 demonstrates this in an example. The figure's two panels show portions of the utility-income functions for two consumers with different degrees of curvature.

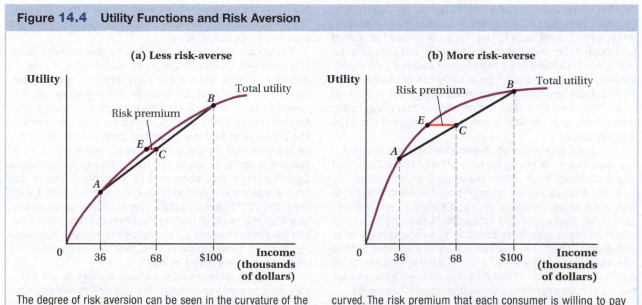

Figure 14.4   Utility Functions and Risk Aversion

The degree of risk aversion can be seen in the curvature of the utility curve. A consumer who is less risk-averse (panel a) has a utility function that is fairly straight, while a consumer who is more risk-averse (panel b) has a utility function that is highly curved. The risk premium that each consumer is willing to pay (distance *CE*) varies with his degree of risk aversion. The greater the level of risk aversion, the more curvature of the utility function, and the larger the risk premium.

[8] Insurers often make money one other way. They invest the premia paid by their policyholders and earn interest on those investments during the time between when they collect the premia and have to pay out claims.

The consumer in the left panel (a) has relatively little curvature; his marginal utility of income drops relatively slowly as his income rises. The consumer in the right panel (b) has a relatively large amount of curvature and a marginal utility of income that falls quickly as his income rises.

Suppose that these consumers faced a situation like Adam's, with a 50% chance of a $36,000 income and a 50% chance of a $100,000 income. The utility-income points corresponding to these outcomes are shown at points A and B in both panels. The consumers' expected incomes and utilities again occur at the midpoints of the AB lines, point C in each panel. The figure also shows the certainty equivalents for the consumers, point E.

The horizontal distances between points C and E in each panel — that is, the expected income consumers are willing to give up in order to have their risky expected incomes at point C replaced by the guaranteed income at point E — are the consumers' respective

FREAKONOMICS

Insurance for Subway Fare Evaders

If you ride the subway in Stockholm, you might see an odd site: a dog jumping up and down, over and over, just beyond the turnstiles where you enter the station. You might at first think that the poor dog has gone crazy, but that is not the case. It is simply well-trained. The dog has been taught the precise location of the sensors that, when triggered, open the gate to let passengers out of the subway. A creative Stockholm commuter who doesn't want to pay the subway fare has trained his pooch to squeeze under the turnstile and then jump up and down until the sensor is activated and the gate opens, allowing his master to enter the subway free of charge.

Not many fare dodgers are this creative, but in one way or another, over 40,000 commuters a day find a way to slip through the gates in Stockholm, saving the cost of a $100 monthly pass.

There are, however, risks associated with fare dodging. If you are caught just once, you face a fine of about $160. That might not happen very often, but when it does, it stings.

Enter Planka.nu, an enterprising Swedish non-profit with a rather odd mission. It doesn't want to end poverty, save polar bears, or build hospitals. Rather, its mission is to get as many people as possible to evade subway fares in Sweden. (The name Planka.nu roughly translates to "free ride.now" – keep this in mind when reading Chapter 17 on public goods.) If you visit the non-profit's website, you will see instructions teaching commuters how to fare dodge.

By far the most interesting thing it's done, however, is to use economic thinking to further its mission. Most people are risk-averse — even fare dodgers, it turns out — and are willing to pay to avoid unexpected negative income shocks. With that in mind, Planka.nu has created an insurance plan designed especially for those who sneak into the subway. For only $11 a month, Planka.nu will pay any fines a

commuter receives if caught. If being a cheat doesn't bother you, you are much better off buying the insurance ($11) than the monthly subway pass ($100).

It turns out that a combination of plenty of people unbothered by cheating and a low detection rate of fare evaders has made the insurance plan a profit maker for Planka.nu. The non-profit earns about $7,500 a month after paying the fines its members accrue.

The people who run the Stockholm subway understandably hate this insurance program. But what can they do about it? In India, when a company offered a similar product, the transit authorities pressured the government into passing a law that made such an insurance program illegal. Another way to fight Planka.nu would be to use economics. The only reason that this insurance program can profitably be offered is that the detection rates of cheaters are so low. The fine if you are caught is $160. If Planka.nu can make a profit offering insurance for $11 a month, it means that the average insured person is caught less than once a year: 12 months × $11 a month = $132 a year in insurance premiums, less than the price of getting caught just once. Assuming that the typical insured person takes the subway, say, once per day, and sneaks in every time, that means the detection rate per trip is less than 1 in 365!

Essentially, Stockholm's subway system is not trying very hard to catch evaders. If the authorities want to stop this cheating behavior, they need to make the marginal cost greater than the marginal benefit by hiring more people to check that riders on trains actually have tickets. It is estimated that fare dodging costs Stockholm Transport about $27 million in lost revenue per year. No wonder, then, that Stockholm Transport recently announced they would double the number of ticket checks they would conduct.

risk premia. Notice how the risk premium of the more risk-averse consumer in the right panel is larger than that for the less risk-averse consumer. This reflects the fact that the degree of a consumer's risk aversion is tied to the curvature in his utility function (or equivalently, the rate at which his marginal utility of income falls as his income grows). When there is more curvature, the expected utility loss due to any given amount of income uncertainty is larger. Consumers with highly curved utility functions have a greater willingness to pay to have risk reduced.

If the curve stays straight, we call the consumers *risk-neutral*. If it curves up (which can happen), then we say that person is *risk-loving*. A risk-lover would actually pay money to have a chance to gamble on a big payoff rather than take the certainty equivalent.

figure it out 14.4

The Hotel California faces a risk that it will suffer a fire causing a $200 million loss with a probability of 0.02. The owner of the firm, Don Glenn, has a utility function of $U = W^{0.5}$, where W is the owner's wealth (as measured by the value of the hotel in millions of dollars). Suppose that the initial value of the hotel is $225 million ($W = 225$).

    a. What is Don Glenn's expected loss?

    b. What is Don Glenn's expected utility?

    c. What is Don Glenn's risk premium?

Solution:

    a. The expected loss is calculated by multiplying the probability of a loss by its dollar amount:

        Expected loss = 0.02 × $200 million = $4 million

        Another way to calculate the loss is to compute Don Glenn's expected wealth and subtract it from his wealth if there were no fire:

Expected wealth = (0.98 × $225 million) + (0.02 × $25 million)

                 = $220.5 million + $0.5 million = $221 million

    Therefore, his expected loss is $225 million – $221 million = $4 million.

    b. Without a loss, Don has $225 million. With a loss, he has $225 million – $200 million = $25 million. His utility

without a loss (when $W = 225$) is $U = W^{0.5} = (225)^{0.5} = 15$. His utility with a loss (when $W = 25$) is $U = W^{0.5} = (25)^{0.5} = 5$.

    Because a 0.02 probability of a fire exists, there is a 0.98 probability that no fire will occur. Therefore, Don Glenn's expected utility is

        Expected utility = (0.98 × 15) + (0.02 × 5)

                    = 14.7 + 0.1 = 14.8

    c. With no insurance, Don Glenn has an *expected* utility of 14.8. There is a guaranteed wealth level that would deliver a certain utility of 14.8, however. If an insurance policy could guarantee him that wealth level or higher, Don Glenn would be willing to purchase it. Therefore, we must first determine how much guaranteed wealth would offer him a utility level of 14.8:

$$U = W^{0.5} = 14.8$$
$$W = (14.8)^2 = 219.04$$

Thus, a certain wealth of $219.04 million would provide Don Glenn with a guaranteed utility of 14.8.

    From part (a) above, his expected wealth without insurance is $221 million. But he's willing to accept a guaranteed wealth of only $219.04 million to ensure he receives the same expected utility as in the case without insurance. Therefore, the risk premium is $221 million – $219.04 million = $1.96 million.

14.6 Conclusion

Deciding how to invest and whether to invest remains one of the central issues of any business and a great many individual decisions, too. To make such decisions rationally, there must be a way to compare future payoffs to current costs, and to make that comparison, you need to use the interest rate and discounting.

When investments are risky, there is an additional layer of complication that requires you to know how to quantify risks and compare payoffs and costs. Given the way most people value income, individuals are often especially sensitive to risks and that characteristic is the foundation of most insurance markets.

We've only scratched the surface of these issues here. If we've piqued your interest, the field of finance deals with the issue of how time and uncertainty shape various markets.

Summary

1. Using **compound interest rates, present discounted value (PDV)** allows consumers to compare the costs and benefits of an investment over time in a consistent way by putting the future benefits of a given investment into its present-day dollar value. [**Section 14.1**]

2. **Net present value (NPV)** analysis incorporates the PDVs of both the costs and benefits of an investment to arrive at a summary measure of the investment's return. The concept of a **payback period,** the length of time before an investment's initial costs are recouped in future benefits, provides another way of determining the net benefits of a given investment. The weakness of payback periods is that, unlike NPV analysis, they do not discount future cash flows. [**Section 14.2**]

3. The **real interest rate** captures the difference between an investment's **nominal interest rate** expressed in currency values and the inflation rate. The equilibrium interest rate,

as with any good's price, equates the quantities supplied and demanded of a good, which in this case is capital. [**Section 14.3**]

4. Investing can be a risky and uncertain undertaking. Evaluating investments using **expected value**—or the expected outcome of an investment—is one way to include risk in NPV analysis. For risky investments, there is often an **option value of waiting,** that is, waiting to invest may eliminate some or all of the uncertainty. [**Section 14.4**]

5. A **risk-averse** person gains more utility from a set amount of income than from the equivalent amount in expected value from an uncertain income. Because it reduces the policyholder's risk, **insurance** increases the individual's expected utility. Through practices such as **diversification** and by designing policies to capture some of the policy's value to the consumer, insurers also benefit from selling insurance policies. [**Section 14.5**]

Review Questions

1. Provide an example of an investment.

2. What is the benefit of using present discounted value analysis?

3. When will an investment's net present value be positive? Given its sign, should you invest in this project?

4. What advantage does net present value analysis have over the use of payback periods to evaluate investment decisions?

5. What is the approximate relationship between an investment's nominal interest rate and its real interest rate?

6. How can expected value be used to evaluate risky investments?

7. What is the value of insurance to a risk-averse consumer?

8. Why do we consider diversification a key function of insurance markets?

Problems   (Solutions to problems marked with an asterisk appear at the back of this book. Problems adapted to use calculus are available online.)

1. Imagine that you have $100 of ill-gotten gains stashed in an offshore bank account. Lest the IRS get too nosey, you plan to leave that account idle until your retirement in 45 years.

   a. If your bank pays you 3% annual interest, what will your account balance be upon retirement?

   b. If your bank pays you 6% interest, what will your account balance be upon retirement?

   c. Does doubling the interest rate double your accumulated balance at retirement? More than double it? Less? Explain your answer.

2. Suppose that when you were one year old, your grandmother gave you a shiny silver dollar. Your parents put that silver dollar in a savings account with a guaranteed 9% interest rate, and then promptly forgot about it.

    a. Use the Rule of 72 to *estimate* how much that account will grow to by the time you are 65.

    b. Calculate *exactly* how much you will have in that account using the formula for compound interest.

    c. How close are your answers to (a) and (b)?

3. Evie is a 20-year-old social media influencer who earns lots of income from her YouTube channel. She brags to her friends, "I'm going to be a millionaire by the time I'm 40," but seems to spend money as fast as it comes in.

    a. If interest rates are currently 9%, how much should Evie set aside today to guarantee her millionaire status by 40?

    b. How much should Evie set aside if she decides she wants to reach millionaire status by 30 instead of 40?

    c. Does the amount Evie must set aside double when she decides she needs to achieve millionaire status twice as quickly?

*4. You are writing the great American novel and have signed a contract with the world's most prestigious publisher. To keep you on schedule, the publisher promises you a $100,000 bonus when the first draft is complete, and another $100,000 following revisions. You believe that you can write the first draft in a year and have the revisions done at the end of the second year.

    a. If interest rates are 5%, what is the value today of the publisher's future payments?

    b. Suppose the publisher offers you $80,000 after the first draft and $125,000 following revisions. Is this a better deal than the original offer?

5. A state lottery makes the following announcement: "Frederick Carbuncle has just won $100 million! We'll pay Frederick $10 million each year for the next 10 years!"

    a. Has Frederick really won $100 million? Explain.

    b. Many state lotteries allow winners to choose a single payment instead of a series of annual payments. "We'll offer you the present value of your annual payments, Frederick," the lottery commissioner says. "And because we're feeling generous, we'll use a really high interest rate when we calculate how much that prize will be. Congratulations, Fred!" Comment on the generosity of the lottery commissioner.

6. You have just purchased a Kia with a $20,000 price tag. The dealer offers to let you pay for your car in five equal annual installments, with the first payment due in a year.

    a. If the dealer finances your purchase at an interest rate of 10%, how much will your annual payment be?

    b. How much would your payment be if you had purchased a $40,000 Camry instead of a $20,000 Kia?

    c. How much would your payment be if you arranged to pay in 10 annual installments instead of 5? Is your payment cut in half? Why or why not?

    d. How much would your payment fall if you paid $10,000 down at the time of purchase?

7. Many college graduates feel as if their student loan payments drag on forever. Suppose that the government offers the following arrangement: It will pay for your college in its entirety, and in return you will make annual payments until the end of time.

    a. Suppose the government asks for $6,000 each year for all of eternity. If interest rates currently sit at 4%, what is the present value of the payments you will make?

    b. Your college charges $140,000 for four years of quality education. Should you take the government up on its offer to pay for your college? What if your college charges $160,000?

8. As a New Year's gift to yourself, you buy your roommate's 1976 Ford Pinto. She has given you the option of two payment plans. Under Plan A, you pay $500 now, plus $500 at the beginning of each of the next two years. Under Plan B, you would pay nothing down, but $800 at the beginning of each of the next two years.

    a. Calculate the present value of each plan's payments if interest rates are 10%. Should you choose Plan A or Plan B?

    b. Recalculate the present value of each plan's payments using a 20% interest rate. Should you choose Plan A or Plan B?

    c. Explain why your answers to (a) and (b) differ.

9. Ricardo is considering purchasing an ostrich, which he can graze for free in his backyard. Once the ostrich reaches maturity (in exactly three years), Ricardo will be able to sell it for $2,000. The ostrich costs $1,500.

    a. Suppose that interest rates are 8%. Calculate the net present value of the ostrich investment. Does the NPV indicate that Ricardo should buy the ostrich?

    b. Suppose that Ricardo passes on the ostrich deal and invests $1,500 in his next-best opportunity: a safe government bond yielding 8%. How much money will he have at the end of three years? Is this outcome better or worse than buying the ostrich?

    c. Calculate the net present value of the ostrich if interest rates are 11%. Does the NPV method indicate that Ricardo should buy the ostrich?

    d. If Ricardo passes on the ostrich deal and invests in a government bond yielding 11%, how much money will he have at the end of three years? Is this outcome better or worse than buying the ostrich?

    e. Based on your answers to (b) and (d), how well does the NPV method capture the concept of opportunity cost?

*10. Marian currently makes $40,000 a year as a tow truck driver. She is considering a career change: For a current expenditure of $30,000, she can obtain her florist's license and become a flower arranger. If she makes that career change, her earnings will rise to $48,000 per year. Marian has five years left to work before retirement (you may safely assume that she gets paid once at the end of each year).

   a. Calculate the net present value of Marian's investment in floriculture if interest rates are 10%.

   b. Assume that in terms of job satisfaction, floriculture and tow truck driving are identical. Should Marian change careers?

   c. Compare the present value of Marian's earnings as a tow truck driver to the present value of Marian's earnings as a florist. Is the difference large enough to justify spending $30,000?

   d. Does the method you used in part (a) give an identical answer to the method you used in part (c)? Explain.

11. You are currently driving a gas-guzzling Oldsmobuick that you expect to be able to drive for the next five years. A recent spike in gas prices to $5 per gallon has you considering a trade to a fuel-efficient hybrid Prius. Your Oldsmobuick has no resale value and gets 15 miles per gallon. A new Prius costs $25,000 and gets 45 miles per gallon. You drive 10,000 miles each year.

   a. Calculate your annual fuel expenditures for the Prius and the Oldsmobuick.

   b. Assume that the interest rate is 7%. Calculate the present value of your costs if you continue to drive the Oldsmobuick for another five years. Assume that you purchase a new Prius at the end of the fifth year, and that a Prius still costs $25,000. Also assume that fuel is paid for at the end of each year. (Carry out your cost calculations for only five years.)

   c. Calculate the present value of your costs if you purchase a new Prius today. Again, carry out your cost calculations for only five years.

   d. Based on your answers to (b) and (c), should you buy a Prius now, or should you wait for five years?

   e. Would your answer change if your Oldsmobuick got 30 miles per gallon instead of 15?

12. Whiskey makers have an unusual business model: They make a product today, and then let it sit in barrels in a warehouse for 20 years before they sell it. Suppose that it takes $12 of resources to produce a bottle of whiskey today. How much will the whiskey maker have to charge for a bottle of whiskey in 20 years in order to make spending that $12 a wise investment? (Assume the whiskey maker faces market interest rates of 6%.)

13. You have $832.66 in a savings account that offers a 5.25% interest rate.

   a. If you leave your money in that account for 20 years, how much will you have in the account?

   b. Suppose that inflation is expected to run at 3.25% for the next 20 years. Use the real interest rate to calculate the inflation-adjusted amount your account will contain at the end of the 20-year period.

   c. The amount you calculated in (b) is smaller than the amount you calculated in (a). Explain exactly what the amount you calculated in (b) tells you, and why the difference arises.

14. Mariq really likes M&Ms. Currently, he has $100, which, at the market price of $1 per bag of M&Ms, translates to 100 bags. He's considering putting that money in the bank so next year he can afford even more M&Ms.

   a. Suppose that Mariq can earn 7% interest on any money he saves. In one year, how many dollars will he have? How many M&Ms will he be able to afford?

   b. The real rate of return is calculated by using goods and services rather than dollars. Calculate Mariq's real rate of return by dividing next year's possible M&M count by this year's. In percentage terms, how many more M&Ms can Mariq enjoy?

   c. Suppose Mariq can save at 7%, but that over the course of the year, the price of a bag of M&Ms increases by 3%, to $1.03. If Mariq saves his money today, how many bags of M&Ms will Mariq be able to afford next year? What is his real rate of return?

   d. What happens to Mariq's real rate of return if the price of a bag of M&Ms increases by 10%, to $1.10, over the next year?

   e. Using your results from (b), (c), and (d), develop a formula that relates the nominal interest rate, the real interest rate, and the inflation rate (percentage increase in prices). Your formula may be an approximation.

15. Mel is a risk-neutral investor concerned about the future availability of gas. He is considering purchasing a gallon of gas today and placing it in storage for 10 years as a hedge against future gas price increases.

   a. If today's price of gas is $4.00 per gallon, and the future price of gas is $6.00 per gallon, is placing a gallon of gas in storage a good idea? Assume that the market interest rate is 4%.

   b. Suppose that Mel is uncertain of the future price of gas. He estimates that there is a 0.1 probability that gas will continue to sell for $4.00 per gallon, a 0.4 probability that gas will sell for $5 per gallon, and a 0.5 probability that gas will sell for $6.80 per gallon. Should Mel place a gallon of gas in storage today? Will your answer be the same if Mel is risk-averse?

16. You are romantically interested in Chris, but have always wanted to date the president of the Economics Club. As it turns out, Chris is battling Pat for control of the Econ Club.

That battle should be decided in a year, and you estimate the odds of Chris winning at 60%. Attracting Chris and kindling a relationship will involve $1,000 of effort on your part; if Chris wins the presidency, you will receive benefits worth $2,200 (assume you receive these benefits one year after beginning the relationship). If Chris loses the election, you receive nothing.

a. Assume an interest rate of 10%. Calculate the net present value of building a relationship with Chris today. Notice that the costs of kindling a relationship today are certain, but the benefits are uncertain.

b. Considering only your answer to (a), should you initiate a relationship with Chris at this time? Assume you are risk-neutral in formulating your answer.

c. Calculate the net present value of waiting until the presidency is decided to build a relationship with Chris. Note that both the costs and benefits of kindling a relationship are uncertain at this point, but that the two will be certain in one year.

d. Based on your answers to both (a) and (c), should you initiate a relationship with Chris today, or should you wait to initiate the relationship until the presidency is determined?

*17. You are considering the purchase of an old fire station, which you plan to convert to an indoor playground. The fire station can be purchased for $200,000, and the playground will generate lifetime profits (excluding the cost of the building) of $700,000. (Assume that those profits are all realized one year after opening.) However, there is a 20% chance that the city council will rezone the district to exclude establishments such as yours; a hearing is scheduled for the coming year, and if your building is rezoned, your profit will be zero. Assume that there is no other building currently under consideration.

a. Assume an interest rate of 10%. Calculate the net present value of opening the playground today. Note that the cost of purchasing the building today is certain, but the benefits are uncertain.

b. Calculate the net present value today of opening the playground in one year, after the zoning issues have been decided. Note that the benefits of opening the playground are uncertain today, but will be certain in one year.

c. Based on your answers to (a) and (b), should you open the playground today, or should you wait until the zoning commission reaches its decision?

*18. Speedy Steve is a traveling salesman. His utility function is given by $U = I^{0.5}$, where U is his utility and I is his income. Steve's income is $900 each week, but if Steve is caught speeding while making his rounds, he will receive a hefty fine. There is a 50% chance he will be caught speeding in any given week and pay a fine of $500.

a. Calculate Steve's expected income and expected utility.

b. Suppose that Steve's boss offers him a position in online sales that eliminates the risk of being caught speeding. What salary would provide Steve with the same utility he expected to receive as a traveling salesman?

c. Suppose instead that Steve was given the opportunity to purchase speeding ticket insurance that would pay all of his fines. What is the most Steve would be willing to pay to obtain this insurance? Explain how you arrived at this number.

d. If the company issuing the insurance referred to in (c) convinces Steve to pay the amount you indicated, will the insurer earn a profit? If so, how much profit will it earn?

19. Danielle is a farmer with a utility function of $U = I^{0.5}$, where U is Danielle's utility and I is her income. If the weather is good, she will earn $100,000. If there is a hailstorm, she will earn only $50,000. The probability of a hailstorm in any given year is 30%.

a. What is Danielle's expected income if she is uninsured? Her expected utility?

b. Suppose a crop insurer makes the following offer to Danielle: In years when there is no hailstorm, Danielle pays the insurer $16,000. In years when there is a hailstorm, the insurer pays Danielle $34,000. What is Danielle's expected income? Her expected utility?

c. Comment on the following statement, referring to your answers to parts (a) and (b): "The insurance agreement in (b) reduces Danielle's expected income. Therefore, it must make her worse off."

d. Suppose instead the insurer offers Danielle the following: In years when there is no hailstorm, Danielle pays the insurer $10,000; in years when there is a hailstorm, the insurer pays Danielle $20,000. How does Danielle's expected income and expected utility compare to the uninsured outcome in (a) and the insured outcome in (b)?

20. Perry the picker has stumbled across a piece of pottery in an antique shop. Because of its style, he believes it might be by Frog Woman, a famous Hopi artist. If he buys the pot for $3,000, he will be able to resell it for $4,500, provided it is a genuine Frog Woman pot. If it is not genuine, he will be forced to unload it for only $1,000. Perry estimates that there is a 2/3 chance the pot is genuine.

a. If Perry bases his decision on expected monetary value, should he buy the pot?

b. Perry's utility depends on his wealth: Specifically, $U = W^{1/4}$. Compute Perry's utility at the possible levels of *final wealth* he might experience.

c. If Perry bases his decision to buy on expected utility, what should he do?

d. Suppose Perry spends a little bit too much time in the hotel bar, and buys the pot without doing the math first. At breakfast the next morning, Penny, another picker, notices the pot and decides to make an offer for it. What is the minimum Penny would have to offer to convince Perry to sell. (Remember — Perry still doesn't know whether the pot is genuine; an offer from Penny removes all risk.)

e. What is Perry's risk premium?

21. A classmate offers to play the following game: He will roll a 10-sided die; if it comes up between 1 and 9, he will pay you $10; if it comes up a 10, he will pay you $110.

a. If you are risk-neutral, and base all decisions on expected monetary value, what is the most you will pay to play this game?

b. Your classmate Risa has a utility function that depends on wealth. Specifically, $U = W^2$. If Risa bases her decisions on expected utility, what is the most she would pay to play this game? What can you ascertain about Risa's attitude toward risk?

General Equilibrium

Almost every local government has an economic development office whose job is to attract businesses to settle there. Although there are a lot of reasons people love where they live, economic vitality matters, too.

The easiest way for a locale to prosper would be to find itself sitting on a pile of money. That's basically what happened in towns like Midland, Texas; Williston, North Dakota; Stavanger, Norway; and Aberdeen, Scotland. They found they were sitting on giant pools of oil.

Life isn't that simple, however. As these places got rich from their natural resources, other problems surfaced. Companies and workers in the sectors that exploited the resources prospered, but this drove up the cost of living for everyone else. Services and other products became scarce and expensive. Businesses had to raise wages to keep from losing their workers to the natural resource sector. Local manufacturers, also having to raise pay to keep workers, found it harder to compete with companies located in places without oil booms. Housing grew difficult to find and more expensive.

These sort of effects from a boon of natural resources are so common that economists have a shorthand name for them: Dutch Disease (named after the experience in the Netherlands following the discovery of natural gas). They are perfect examples of the ways in which one market can affect a completely different market. Throughout most of this textbook, we've examined how markets function in isolation. Each market has its own demand side that reflects consumers' tastes and its own supply side driven by producers' costs, production technologies, and market power. The two sides combine in a self-contained unit to determine an equilibrium price and quantity for that market.

In earlier chapters, we talked about substitutes and complements, the cross-price elasticity of demand, and other topics that involve the interaction of markets for different goods, but we largely ignored how other markets can indirectly affect the ones we're dealing with. Ignoring cross-market effects simplified our analysis, but at a cost. Most markets in the real world are interconnected. What happens in one (such as oil in Texas) can affect outcomes in another (like trucking in Texas). Sometimes cross-market spillovers can be so large that ignoring them causes us to miss critical parts of the story.

In this chapter, we stop ignoring these cross-market effects and think explicitly about how the market-clearing process in one market affects the process in other markets. Economists refer to this as **general equilibrium analysis,** *the study of market behavior that accounts for cross-market influences and is concerned with conditions present when all markets are simultaneously in equilibrium.*

General equilibrium holds when all markets are in equilibrium at the same time. Taking explicit account of the way each market operates on its own while recognizing the influences of market spillovers is the key to understanding general equilibrium effects. What we've done up to this point is called **partial equilibrium analysis,** *the determination of equilibrium in a particular market assuming there are no cross-market spillovers.* General equilibrium analysis is more complicated because there are more "moving parts" to keep track of. You might think it's unlikely that all those markets would manage to achieve equilibrium at the same time, but one of the most

general equilibrium analysis The study of market behavior that accounts for cross-market influences and is concerned with conditions present when all markets are simultaneously in equilibrium.

partial equilibrium analysis Determination of the equilibrium in a particular market that assumes there are no cross-market spillovers.

fundamental results of microeconomic theory is that everything at play *will* come together under the right circumstances.

General equilibrium analysis also deals with conceptual questions about how well markets allocate goods. It asks whether market outcomes in general equilibrium are desirable. Of course, defining "desirable" can get sticky, so economists are fairly specific about what standards apply to that term. We will illustrate these standards for you and clarify what conditions must be true for markets to meet them.

15.1 General Equilibrium Effects in Action

General equilibrium analysis has two parts. One part describes the mechanics of market interactions and illustrates how various market features affect the size and direction of equilibrium effects in all these markets. This branch of general equilibrium analysis describes markets *as they are*. The other part asks whether economy-wide market equilibria are efficient or equitable (and how to define those terms). You could say this type of analysis focuses on markets *as they ought to be*. People will never fully agree on the ideal of how markets ought to behave, but general equilibrium analysis at least gives us a way to describe how it can work.

These two approaches use somewhat different frameworks for thinking about general equilibrium, and are in some respects independent of each other. In Section 15.1, we start with the first approach: how general equilibrium effects work in markets and what market features influence these mechanisms.

Can the use of corn to make biofuel lead to an increase in the price of wheat?

An Overview of General Equilibrium Effects

Members of the United States Congress like ethanol. Not the drink (although they might like that, too), but the renewable fuel. Since the oil crises of the 1970s, the U.S. government has subsidized the production of ethanol. This support includes direct cash subsidies, protection from foreign imports, and mandates for use as a fuel. What are the general equilibrium effects?

Most ethanol in the United States is made from corn. Therefore, the ethanol mandate is, in effect, a mandate to use corn. Such a mandate therefore shifts the demand curve for corn outward. We know from our analyses in earlier chapters how a mandate would affect the equilibrium price and quantity in the corn market. The increase in demand should drive up prices and induce more production: Producers would plant more corn and less of substitute crops like wheat, soybeans, or rice. The increase in demand moves the market up its supply curve (because marginal costs rise with the added production) and raises the equilibrium price and quantity of corn.

Yet corn isn't likely to be the only commodity crop affected by an ethanol-from-corn mandate. General equilibrium suggests that the markets for related crops would be affected, even though the mandate doesn't include these other crops. We would expect an increase in the price of corn to raise the demand for corn substitutes like wheat, rice, and soybeans.

These cross-market effects don't stop there. Higher corn demand also increases the demand for the inputs farmers use to produce it. Those inputs may have upward-sloping supply curves of their own, so the increased demand for corn may also drive up the prices of farm machinery, fertilizer, and farmland. Furthermore, the increased demand for substitutes like wheat would also help drive up the cost of the inputs used to make the substitutes.

All these spillover effects on other markets then bounce back and influence the corn market itself. **Figure 15.1** depicts this feedback loop. Panel a shows the corn market. In the absence of a mandate, the market is in equilibrium with demand curve D_{c1} and supply curve S_{c1}, and the equilibrium quantity and price are Q_{c1} and P_{c1}. The direct effect of the mandate is to increase the demand for corn from D_{c1} to D_{c2}. In a partial equilibrium analysis, we'd expect this to increase the quantity and price of corn to Q_{c2} and P_{c2}, respectively, and we'd be done.

A general equilibrium analysis, however, recognizes that because wheat and corn are substitutes, an increase in the demand for corn will affect the wheat market as shown in panel b. Before the mandate, wheat supply and demand are at S_{w1} and D_{w1}. The higher corn price caused by the mandate causes people to shift, say, from corn-based breakfast cereals to wheat-based cereals, thus increasing the demand for wheat from D_{w1} to D_{w2}, and raising wheat quantities and prices to Q_{w2} and P_{w2}.

Because wheat is a substitute for corn, higher wheat prices cause the demand for corn to increase, and there is a secondary outward shift in corn demand, from D_{c2} to D_{c3}. This raises the quantity and price of corn to Q_{c3} and P_{c3}. Higher corn prices, in turn, shift out wheat demand *again*, from D_{w2} to D_{w3}, raising wheat quantity and price to Q_{w3} and P_{w3}, and so on.

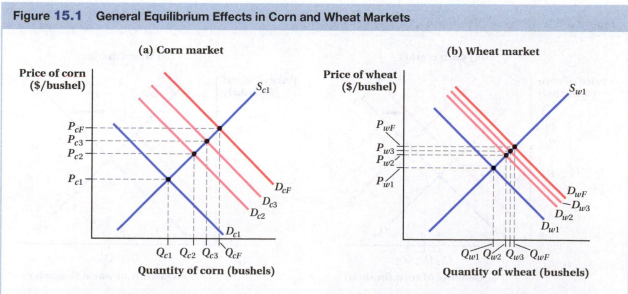

Figure 15.1   General Equilibrium Effects in Corn and Wheat Markets

(a) Corn market

(b) Wheat market

(a) Before an ethanol-from-corn mandate, the corn market is in equilibrium at (Q_{c1}, P_{c1}), where the initial demand curve D_{c1} and supply curve S_{c1} intersect. The direct effect of the mandate shifts demand out to D_{c2}. Because the mandate also increases the price of wheat, however, the demand for corn continues to shift out until general equilibrium is reached at (Q_{cF}, P_{cF}), where D_{cF} intersects S_{c1}.

(b) Wheat, a substitute good for corn, is at an initial equilibrium of (Q_{w1}, P_{w1}), where the initial demand curve D_{w1} and supply curve S_{w1} intersect. When the mandate increases corn prices, the demand for wheat increases to D_{w2}. The subsequent increases in corn prices continue to shift out the demand for wheat until general equilibrium is reached at (Q_{wF}, P_{wF}), where D_{wF} intersects S_{w1}.

This feedback eventually slows down and stops. The size of the secondary feedback effect is smaller than the initial demand shift from D_{c1} to D_{c2}, the third shift is smaller than the second, and so on until the markets settle at a stable point. In the corn and wheat markets in Figure 15.1, the final demand curves after all the feedback effects are shown by D_{cF} for corn and D_{wF} for wheat.

Therefore, the general equilibrium effect of the mandate in the corn market is to increase quantity from Q_{c1} to Q_{cF} and price from P_{c1} to P_{cF}. These changes are considerably larger than the quantity and price increases to Q_{c2} and P_{c2} that a partial equilibrium analysis implies. When the links between two markets are strong, as they are between corn and wheat, the gap between the partial and general equilibrium outcomes in the corn market is larger. Moreover, in a partial equilibrium analysis, the effect of the ethanol-from-corn mandate on wheat quantities and prices, which increase from Q_{w1} and P_{w1} to Q_{wF} and P_{wF}, is completely ignored.

We can also analyze the supply-side links between industries, such as the spillovers created when two markets use common inputs. (We examine this case in detail in a later quantitative section.) In this case, higher corn demand causes the supply of wheat to fall because farmers shift some of their production from wheat to corn. This decrease in supply shifts the supply of wheat inward, and with no change in wheat demand (we ignore demand spillovers like those we just discussed to focus on supply-side links), the equilibrium quantity of wheat falls and its price rises. **Figure 15.2** illustrates this scenario. The decrease in wheat supply from S_{w1} to S_{w2} and the resulting increase in its price feed back, in turn, to the corn market and shift the supply of corn from S_{c1} to S_{c2} because this raises the price of inputs into corn production.

Figure 15.2 **Supply-Side Input Links across Industries**

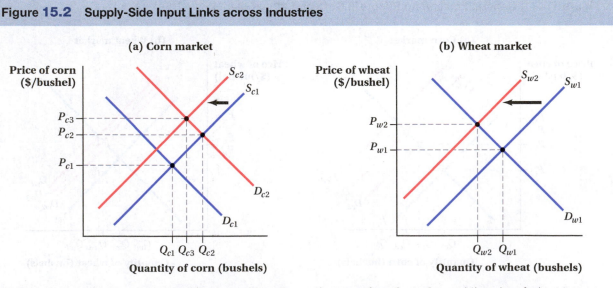

(a) Corn market

(b) Wheat market

(a) The increase in the demand for corn shifts demand from D_{c1} to D_{c2}. As a result, the quantity of corn increases from Q_{c1} to Q_{c2}, and the price of corn increases from P_{c1} to P_{c2}.
(b) The increased demand for corn causes farmers to shift some of their production from wheat to corn. Consequently, the supply of wheat shifts in from S_{w1} to S_{w2}. The quantity of wheat

decreases from Q_{w1} to Q_{w2}, and the price of wheat increases from P_{w1} to P_{w2}. The resulting increase in the wheat price feeds back, in turn, to the corn market, shifting the supply of corn from S_{c1} to S_{c2}, reducing the quantity of corn to Q_{c3} and raising its price to P_{c3}, because of increases in the price of inputs into corn production.

   With that overview of how general equilibrium works, the next two subsections put actual numbers to the two cases to make the process of determining general equilibrium effects clear.

Quantitative General Equilibrium: The Corn Example with Demand-Side Market Links

Let's put some specific numbers on the types of processes discussed above to get a better feel for analyzing general equilibrium effects. To simplify, assume that wheat and corn are the only two goods in the world. In this world, general equilibrium is the set of wheat and corn prices that simultaneously equate supply and demand in both markets.

   In this section, we look at the cross-market general equilibrium effects that arise because of demand-side links between the wheat and corn markets (i.e., because consumers' preferences for wheat and corn are interrelated). In the next section, we look at how supply-side links between the markets (the production of wheat and corn is interrelated) drive the general equilibrium effects.

   Let's suppose the supply of wheat is $Q_w^s = P_w$, where Q_w^s is the quantity of wheat supplied (in millions of bushels) and P_w is the price of wheat (in dollars per bushel). This supply curve has the typical upward slope: The quantity of wheat supplied increases as wheat prices rise. Similarly, corn supply is $Q_c^s = P_c$, where Q_c^s is the quantity of corn supplied (in millions of bushels) and P_c is the price of corn (in dollars per bushel). This supply curve also slopes upward; the quantity of corn supplied increases as corn prices rise.

   Now let's say wheat demand is given by the equation $Q_w^d = 20 - P_w + P_c$. This equation tells us that, as with a standard demand curve, the quantity of wheat demanded decreases as wheat prices rise. But notice that the quantity of wheat demanded is also affected by corn prices P_c: When they increase, so does Q_w^d. This second effect reflects the fact that wheat is a substitute for corn. Therefore, higher corn prices cause consumers to shift some corn purchases toward wheat. This raises the quantity of wheat demanded at any given wheat price and shifts out the wheat demand curve. We assume corn demand is given by the equation $Q_c^d = 20 - P_c + P_w$. Thus, corn is a substitute for wheat; higher wheat prices shift out the demand for corn.

   The fact that wheat and corn are substitutes for each other in this example is what creates general equilibrium effects. If we had assumed that wheat demand and corn demand were only a function of their own prices (while keeping the same supply curves that we assumed above), no cross-market effects would occur. Changes in wheat prices wouldn't shift the demand for corn, and there would be no general equilibrium impact.

Finding Equilibrium Prices   To find the general equilibrium in this two-good economy, we need to find prices that equate supply and demand in both markets. We start with the wheat market. Substituting the supply and demand curves above into the partial equilibrium condition that the quantity of wheat supplied must equal the quantity demanded, we have

$$Q_w^s = Q_w^d$$
$$P_w = 20 - P_w + P_c$$

We can rearrange this equation to express the equilibrium wheat price in terms of the price of corn:

$$P_w = 10 + \frac{P_c}{2}$$

Repeating the same steps for corn (equating the quantity supplied and demanded and solving for the corn price in terms of the wheat price) gives

$$P_c = 10 + \frac{P_w}{2}$$

These equations look similar to each other because we set up the example so that the two markets have identically shaped supply and demand curves.

The two equations for wheat and corn prices make clear that each market's equilibrium price depends on the other's. That is the essence of general equilibrium. We can find the prices that put both markets in equilibrium by substituting $P_c = 10 + \frac{P_w}{2}$ for P_c in $P_w = 10 + \frac{P_c}{2}$ and solving for P_w:

$$P_w = 10 + \frac{P_c}{2}$$

$$= 10 + \frac{\left(10 + \frac{P_w}{2}\right)}{2}$$

$$\frac{3P_w}{4} = 15$$

$$P_w = \$20$$

The general equilibrium price for wheat, then, is $20 per bushel.

To find corn prices in general equilibrium, we substitute the wheat price $P_w = 20$ into the equation for the price of corn:

$$P_c = 10 + \frac{P_w}{2}$$

$$= 10 + \frac{20}{2} = \$20$$

Corn prices are also $20 per bushel. That corn and wheat prices are the same occurs only because we assumed the two markets have identically shaped supply and demand curves.

Finding Equilibrium Quantities Given the equilibrium prices of $20 per bushel, we can calculate the general equilibrium quantities of wheat and corn by substituting $P_w = 20$ and $P_c = 20$ into the supply or demand curve equations for wheat and corn:

	For wheat	For corn
Supply	$Q_w^s = P_w$	$Q_c^s = P_c$
	$Q_w^s = 20$	$Q_c^s = 20$
Demand	$Q_w^d = 20 - P_w + P_c$	$Q_c^d = 20 - P_c + P_w$
	$Q_w^d = 20 - 20 + 20$	$Q_c^d = 20 - 20 + 20$
	$Q_w^d = 20$	$Q_c^d = 20$
Equilibrium Q	$Q_w^s = Q_w^d = Q_w = 20$	$Q_c^s = Q_c^d = Q_c = 20$

The general equilibrium quantities for wheat and corn are therefore both 20 million bushels.

This is the initial general equilibrium in the economy (akin to quantities and prices $Q_{c1}, Q_{w1}, P_{c1},$ and P_{w1} in our example in the previous section).

General Equilibrium Effects   Now suppose the ethanol-from-corn mandate increases the demand for corn by 12 million bushels at any given set of corn and wheat prices. The demand curve for corn becomes

$$Q_c^d = 32 - P_c + P_w$$

This is reflected in the shift of corn demand from D_{c1} to D_{cF} in **Figure 15.3**.

We know that prices have to change—if they stayed at \$20, consumers would demand 32 million bushels but producers would supply only 20 million. To determine the new general equilibrium price in the corn market, repeat the steps above using the new corn demand curve.

Because the supply and demand curves for wheat are not directly affected by the mandate, the equation for the price of wheat in terms of corn remains the same $\left(P_w = 10 + \dfrac{P_c}{2}\right)$. But the equation for the equilibrium price of corn, which was $P_c = 10 + \dfrac{P_w}{2}$, changes because of the new corn demand curve. Setting $Q_c^s = Q_c^d$, we now have

$$P_c = 32 - P_c + P_w$$

$$= 16 + \frac{P_w}{2}$$

Again, we can solve for the general equilibrium wheat price by plugging one price equation into the other. This gives

$$P_w = 10 + \frac{P_c}{2}$$

$$= 10 + \frac{\left(16 + \dfrac{P_w}{2}\right)}{2}$$

Figure 15.3   The Effects of a Ethanol-from-Corn Mandate on the Markets for Corn and Wheat

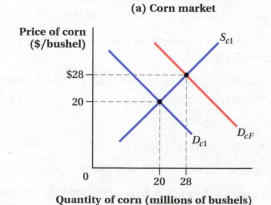
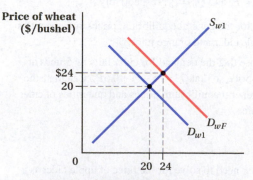

(a) Before the mandate, the corn market supplies 20 million bushels of corn at a price of \$20 per bushel, where D_{c1} intersects S_{c1}. When the demand for corn shifts out to D_{cF}, corn's price increases to \$28 per bushel, and its quantity increases to 28 million bushels.

(b) Wheat, a substitute good for corn, is at an initial equilibrium of 20 million bushels at \$20 per bushel, where initial demand curve D_{w1} and supply curve S_{w1} intersect. When the mandate increases corn prices, the demand for wheat increases to D_{wF}. The wheat market now supplies 24 million bushels of wheat at a price of \$24 per bushel, where D_{wF} intersects S_{w1}.

$$\frac{3}{4}P_w = 18$$

$$P_w = \$24$$

The price of wheat is now \$24 per bushel. Substituting this price back into the new price of corn equation shows that the new equilibrium corn price is $P_c = 16 + \frac{24}{2} = \$28$ per bushel.

We then plug these prices into the supply or demand curves to obtain the new general equilibrium quantities:

$$Q_c^d = 32 - 28 + 24 = 28 \text{ million bushels of corn}$$
$$Q_w^d = 20 - 24 + 28 = 24 \text{ million bushels of wheat}$$

Summing Up   We've just seen how an increase in the demand for corn leads not only to higher corn prices and quantities, as we would expect from a partial equilibrium analysis that just looks at what happens in the corn market, but also to higher wheat prices and quantities. Not surprisingly, the price increase is greater for corn (an \$8 per bushel, or 40% increase) than for wheat (a \$4 per bushel, or 20% increase). But notice that wheat prices rose even though the increase in corn demand did not directly affect the supply or demand curve for wheat. The general equilibrium effect would not have shown up in the partial equilibrium approach of previous chapters.

---

 figure it out 15.1

Apple cider and orange juice are substitutes. Suppose that the demand for cider is given by $Q_c = 20 - P_c + 0.5P_o$, and that the demand for orange juice is given by $Q_o = 20 - P_o + 0.5P_c$, where Q_c and Q_o are measured in millions of gallons and P_c and P_o are the prices per gallons. The supplies of cider and orange juice are given by $Q_c = P_c$ and $Q_o = P_o$, respectively.

a. Solve for the general equilibrium prices and quantities of apple cider and orange juice.

b. Suppose that the demand for cider falls by 5 units at every price so that $Q_c = 15 - P_c + 0.5P_o$. Calculate the new general equilibrium prices and quantities of cider and juice.

Solution:

a. We first need to solve for the price of apple cider as a function of orange juice by setting quantity demanded and quantity supplied equal in the cider market:

$$20 - P_c + 0.5P_o = P_c$$
$$2P_c = 20 + 0.5P_o$$
$$P_c = 10 + 0.25P_o$$

Then we follow the same step for the orange juice market so that the price of juice is expressed as a function of the price of cider:

$$20 - P_o + 0.5P_c = P_o$$
$$2P_o = 20 + 0.5P_c$$
$$P_o = 10 + 0.25P_c$$

To solve for P_c, we can substitute in the equation we just derived for P_o:

$$P_c = 10 + 0.25P_o = 10 + 0.25[10 + 0.25P_c] = 10 + 2.5 + 0.0625P_c$$
$$0.9375P_c = 12.5$$
$$P_c = \$13.33$$

This means that P_o is

$$P_o = 10 + 0.25P_c = 10 + 0.25(13.33) = 10 + 3.33 = \$13.33$$

Because $Q_c = P_c$ and $Q_o = P_o$, $Q_c = 13.33$ million gallons and $Q_o = 13.33$ million gallons.

b. When the demand for cider falls, both the markets for apple cider and orange juice will be affected. We will need to follow the same steps used in part (a) to solve for the new equilibrium prices and quantities.

First, we solve for the price of cider as a function of the price of juice:

$$15 - P_c + 0.5P_o = P_c$$

$$2P_c = 15 + 0.5P_o$$

$$P_c = 7.5 + 0.25P_o$$

Because the supply and demand for juice are not affected initially, we know from part (a) that

$$P_o = 10 + 0.25P_c$$

Therefore, we can substitute P_o into the equation for P_c:

$$P_c = 7.5 + 0.25P_o = 7.5 + 0.25[10 + 0.25P_c] = 7.5 + 2.5 + 0.0625P_c$$

$$0.9375P_c = 10$$

$$P_c = 10.67$$

Substituting for P_c and solving for P_o, we get

$$P_o = 10 + 0.25P_c = 10 + 0.25(10.67) = 10 + 2.67 = 12.67$$

Because $Q_c = P_c$ and $Q_o = P_o$, $Q_c = 10.67$ million gallons and $Q_o = 12.67$ million gallons.

 ## Application: The General Equilibrium of Carmageddon

In July 2011 residents of metropolitan Los Angeles prepared for disaster. Residents stocked up on food so they wouldn't have to leave their houses for the weekend. Hospitals enacted emergency procedures to ensure they would have enough staff. Local news stations planned for live coverage.

It wasn't an earthquake, a flood, or a military attack. They were preparing for "Carmageddon," a weekend-long construction project during which 10 miles of the 405 freeway, one of the busiest highway stretches in America, would completely shut down.

The city government hoped that when the entire project was finished (which would take more than just a single weekend), it might lessen congestion and commute times on the notoriously busy Los Angeles freeways. To this end, officials planned to build an additional lane and add a carpool lane to encourage people to share their commutes with coworkers. How successful were these measures and were they worth the hassle?

Probably not. The traffic analytics company INRIX measured average speeds on the reconstructed highway and found they are no faster than before the project. INRIX rated Los Angeles the most congested city in the United States in 2017, and it pointed to the reconstructed stretch of the 405 as the country's sixth-worst congested stretch of highway. (Other parts of the 405 were ranked second and third.) Regular commuters on the route complain bitterly about suffering through years of construction for nothing.

Had Angelenos read a study by economists Gilles Duranton and Matthew Turner, they might not have been surprised by this outcome. The study's results indicate that the construction project was unlikely to make much difference to commuters. The reason: general equilibrium effects.[1]

Over the past 20 years, as the U.S. roadway system expanded, the average number of cars on the road in metropolitan areas nearly doubled. Using this fact as a jumping-off point, Duranton and Turner examined the effects of increasing the number of highways and major roadways on traffic in urban areas. In particular, they looked at the effect of the number of lane-kilometers in an area on vehicle-kilometers traveled. Lane-kilometers are the product of a road's length and its number of lanes, capturing the road's total

---

[1] Gilles Duranton and Matthew A. Turner, "The Fundamental Law of Road Congestion: Evidence from US Cities," *American Economic Review* 101, no. 6 (October 2011): 2616–2652.

vehicle-carrying capacity. Vehicle-kilometers are the product of the number of vehicles on the road and the average distance a vehicle travels.

What they found would resonate with commuters on the 405: The elasticity between vehicle-kilometers traveled and lane-kilometers is approximately 1.03. That is, for every increase in roads' traffic-carrying capacity, there was a *one-for-one* increase in how much people drove. So, for every 10% the 405 expansion added to the highway's capacity, the number of cars grew by 10%, too. Thus, even as measures are taken to improve congestion, the traffic that commuters face seems to hold steady.[2]

Why doesn't the density of cars on the road decrease as the number of roads increase? When Los Angeles decided to expand the 405 to improve traffic, the city was relying on a partial equilibrium analysis. Unfortunately, this problem involves general equilibrium effects — an increase in roadways in an area has effects beyond just the direct impact. The Duranton and Turner study documents that expanding the supply of roadways encourages more businesses and people to move to the area. This increase in demand for roadways continues until traffic in the area converges to its "natural" equilibrium level (of "terrible").

Taking these findings to heart before starting on the rebuild might have saved L.A. commuters a lot of blood, sweat, and tears. But there was one unexpected benefit of Carmageddon on area traffic: Because most people stayed home that weekend, those who did take to the roads faced practically empty roadways for a couple of days. ∎

Quantitative General Equilibrium: The Corn Example with Supply-Side Market Links

In the example just covered, the link between the corn and wheat markets was on the demand side. The two products were substitutes, so the change in one good's price affected the demand for the other. Supply-side links can create general equilibrium effects as well. Corn production and wheat production, for example, use common inputs (fertilizer, land, farm workers).

Again, let's start with a simple setup. The demand curve for wheat is $Q_w^d = 20 - P_w$, and the demand curve for corn is $Q_c^d = 20 - P_c$. Notice that the demand-side links between the markets are now gone. Only a good's *own* price affects its quantity demanded. There is no demand-side interaction between markets.

But the supply curves are now $Q_w^s = 2P_w - P_c$ for wheat and $Q_c^s = 2P_c - P_w$ for corn. You can see the connections between the two markets in these new supply curve equations. The quantity supplied of each good increases as its own price increases and decreases as the other good's price increases. This relationship captures the notion that when one good's price increases, production shifts toward that good, allocating scarce resources away from production of the other good (such as replanting wheat fields with corn).

We can solve for the general equilibrium prices and quantities using the same steps we followed in the demand-side market links analysis. (Here, we skip some of the details because we've already done these types of calculations.) Setting $Q_w^s = Q_w^d$ and solving for the price of wheat in terms of the corn price give

$$P_w = \frac{20}{3} + \frac{P_c}{3}$$

---

[2] For a look at a different approach to reducing congestion, see the Application: Would Higher Driving Taxes Make Us Happier Drivers? on pages 607–608.

Again, the symmetry of how we've set up these markets will result in a similar solution for corn prices: $P_c = \dfrac{20}{3} + \dfrac{P_w}{3}$. If we solve this system of equations, we find that $P_w = \$10$ per bushel and $P_c = \$10$ per bushel. If we substitute these prices into the supply and demand curves, we find that the quantities of both wheat and corn in this general equilibrium are 10 million bushels.

Now again, suppose there is a 12 million bushel increase in the quantity demanded of corn at all prices because of the ethanol mandate so that $Q_c^d = 32 - P_c$. The equation expressing the wheat price as a function of the corn price is the same as above $\left(P_w = \dfrac{20}{3} + \dfrac{P_c}{3} \right)$ because the supply and demand curves for wheat are not directly affected. The equation for the price of corn changes, though. It's now $P_c = \dfrac{32}{3} + \dfrac{P_w}{3}$.

When we solve this equation and the one for wheat prices above, we find that $P_w = \$11.50$ and $P_c = \$14.50$ per bushel. Plugging these prices into the supply or demand curves shows that the equilibrium wheat quantity is 8.5 million bushels and the equilibrium quantity of corn is 17.5 million bushels.

Summing Up   As in our previous example, an increase in corn demand leads to increases in both corn and wheat prices in general equilibrium. Such is true in markets like this one where there are supply-side interactions between markets, just as it was in the market with demand-side links.

With supply-side links, higher corn prices move production from wheat to corn, thus decreasing the quantity of wheat supplied at every price and shifting in wheat's supply curve. Because the demand curve for wheat does not change, wheat prices rise. Also, just as in the case of demand-side links, the price increase is larger for the good receiving the direct demand shift (corn).

However, notice that these similarities do not necessarily mean that demand-side market links create the same general equilibrium effects as supply-side connections. While the prices of all goods go up in both cases, the implications for quantities differ. In the demand-side link case above, the general equilibrium quantities of both goods increased in response to the demand shift for corn. In the supply-side case we just discussed, though, while equilibrium corn quantities rose, wheat quantities fell.

The quantity results are different because with the demand-side connection between the two markets, the increase in the demand for corn also increased the demand for wheat. Because the supply curves in both markets were fixed, these increases in demand led to increases in both quantities. With supply-side connections, however, the increased demand for corn resulted in a decrease in the supply of wheat, lowering its equilibrium quantity. These opposing predictions about the quantity changes in the wheat market give us a way to test whether the general equilibrium corn and wheat price increases are caused by demand-side or supply-side cross-market effects. If the two goods are substitutes, then demand-side linkages imply that wheat *quantities* rise in response to the increased corn demand. If wheat quantities fall, on the other hand, this suggests supply-side links are more important.[3]

---

[3] A full analysis would test between the two possibilities while controlling for other influences on the amount of wheat and corn production, but a look at the raw numbers is still instructive. U.S. corn acreage increased 9% between 2005 and 2018, while wheat acreage fell by about 18% over the same period. This is consistent with the observed higher wheat prices resulting more from supply-side than demand-side spillovers.

FREAKONOMICS

Memories of Mutton

You've probably never eaten mutton and you're probably glad. Mutton is the meat of mature sheep. It's stronger in flavor than lamb, gamier, with a considerably chewier consistency. Even mutton's supporters admit that it is an acquired taste. There was a time, however, when more mutton was consumed than turkey, cheese, cocoa, or rice! Why did mutton disappear? The answer is one that you would never guess.

The man who spelled doom for mutton went by the name of Wallace Hume Carothers. Carothers was a small, bespectacled man who lived in Wilmington, Delaware. He didn't care much about mutton; his passion was complex chemical compounds, especially a class of molecules known as polyamides. He worked obsessively, sometimes to the point where he had to be institutionalized. Indeed, his great discovery in February 1935 came shortly after his release from a mental hospital.

Carothers didn't discover a substitute for mutton. Nor did he discover something bad about mutton that drove it out of fashion. Rather, his discovery was nylon.

Nylon was a miracle fabric that revolutionized women's fashion. The demand for nylon skyrocketed. By the 1940s, "nylon riots" — at which hundreds to thousands of women lined up at department stores in the hope of procuring nylon stockings — became commonplace. In a single incident, 40,000 women queued outside a store in Pittsburgh for the chance to buy 1 of only 13,000 pairs of stockings!

More and more women switched to nylon stockings, abandoning wool ones. The demand for wool plunged, driving down its price. In response, farmers raised many fewer sheep. Farmers had never exclusively raised sheep for mutton; they raised them for their wool. Being able to sell the slaughtered animals as mutton simply generated a bit of profit on the side. Fewer sheep meant there was now little mutton to be had. This scarcity might have transformed it into a rare delicacy. For whatever reason, that never happened. Nowadays in the United States, mutton is most commonly reserved for dog and cat food.

The impact of one market on another is exactly what we mean by general equilibrium. But the effects of general equilibrium are not always as subtle as the link between mutton and nylon. Just a few years after nylon was introduced, a new material called polyester hit the streets, which held up better than nylon against water, most chemicals, light, and heat. Nylon's dominance was soon eclipsed by that of polyester, which today is 10 times more prevalent in the marketplace. While mutton lovers may have believed justice was served when nylon fell from its place of preeminence, nylon's decline did not signal the return of mutton. Polyester, like nylon, was a substitute for wool, meaning there was even less mutton to go around.

Application: Did the United States Catch the Dutch Disease?

The introduction to this chapter discussed how the discovery of natural resources in a local area can have less than favorable general equilibrium effects. Many economists believe the effects of this "Dutch Disease" are particularly harsh for some manufacturers in newly wealthy areas, because they frequently end up having to pay considerably higher costs for space and workers while still competing with rival manufactures in other areas whose costs haven't risen.

Recent research by economists Hunt Allcott and Daniel Keniston examined in detail whether manufacturers "caught" the Dutch Disease in areas of the United States that experienced significant finds in oil and gas reserves over the past half-century.[4] They used highly detailed data from the U.S. Census Bureau to study manufacturing companies in areas with big discoveries during and after the local oil and gas boom.

They did indeed find evidence of Dutch Disease. As oil and gas activity increased, the operations of local manufacturers who produced goods sold mostly in other locations contracted. However, they also determined that the overall effects were more

[4] Hunt Allcott and Daniel Keniston, "Dutch Disease or Agglomeration? The Local Economic Effects of Natural Resource Booms in Modern America," *Review of Economic Studies* (April 2018): 695–731.

complex than that. A substantial segment of local manufacturers *grew*. These were specialized producers that made goods used as inputs by the local oil and gas industries. In fact, the growth of these specialized manufactures was large enough that it typically canceled out the contraction of other local manufacturers. As a result, no net change occurred, on average, in the size of the local manufacturing sector after oil and gas discoveries.

Because they had compiled such an extensive sample of data, Allcott and Keniston were also able to explore the effects of a natural resource boom in certain areas where it had long since faded. They found that the combination of a boom's neutral effects on overall manufacturing plus the expansions due to oil and gas led to persistently higher wages and employment in boom areas. It therefore appears that, on balance, although there might be some sniffles along the way, U.S. boom communities were able to avoid the worst of Dutch Disease. ∎

15.2 General Equilibrium: Equity and Efficiency

The second branch of general equilibrium analysis deals with conceptual—some might even say philosophical—questions of how well markets allocate goods. That is, it asks whether market outcomes in general equilibrium are "desirable." People argue over what should count as desirable, however, so economists get fairly specific about the standards for well-functioning markets. In this section, we will talk about these standards and whether markets can meet them.

Standards for Measuring Market Performance: Social Welfare Functions

One way economists often try to think about the overall desirability of market outcomes is to use a **social welfare function,** *a mathematical function that combines the utility levels of the individuals in a society to obtain a single overall measure of an economy's performance*. That way, we can compare various market outcomes (i.e., distributions of utilities across all individuals in the economy) to one another. If one outcome has a higher value than another according to the social welfare function, the higher-valued outcome is considered more desirable.

The ranking of various market outcomes depends on the particular form of the social welfare function one chooses to use to evaluate outcomes in the first place. For example, a function that explicitly penalizes inequalities in individuals' utility levels will rank certain market outcomes differently than a function that ranks outcomes based only on average utility levels. Choosing a social welfare function is therefore a bit of a philosophical exercise; it depends on one's notion of what sort of outcomes are desirable in the first place. Thus, social welfare functions can be thought of as ways to rank economic outcomes once you have decided what features are desirable (such as the amount of equality or whether particular groups of individuals have systematically higher or lower utilities).

Once you pick the social welfare function, it automatically implies how bad inequality is for society. But, given the subjectivity of a social welfare function choice, economists don't have any hard-and-fast rules about the particular form a social welfare function should take. That said, they use some versions more commonly than others because they're easy to work with or because they succinctly capture elements of various philosophies about what is desirable in terms of the distribution of utilities across individuals.

social welfare function
A mathematical function that combines the utility levels of the individuals in a society to obtain a single overall measure of an economy's performance.

The Utilitarian Social Welfare Function

One common type of social welfare function just adds together the utility levels U of everyone in the economy equally:

$$W = U_1 + U_2 + \ldots + U_N$$

where W is the value of the social welfare function, the grand total of all utility in a society. The subscripts denote individuals; there are a total of N people in this economy. This **utilitarian social welfare function** is *a mathematical function that computes society's welfare as the sum of every individual's welfare.* That seems easy enough. But note that a utilitarian society will be one with relatively little concern about how equally utility is distributed among individuals. Raising anyone's utility a given amount has the same total welfare effect for society regardless of how well off that person already was. In fact, a utilitarian function would say there's no harm in driving any particular individual's utility down to zero as long as someone else experiences an equal-sized utility gain, even if that person is already better off than everyone else in the economy.

utilitarian social welfare function A mathematical function that computes society's welfare as the sum of every individual's welfare.

The Rawlsian and Egalitarian Social Welfare Functions

The utilitarian social welfare function's relative indifference to utility inequality has led some people to propose the use of other social welfare functions.

The **Rawlsian social welfare function** is *a mathematical function that computes society's welfare as the welfare of the worst-off individual.* It's named for political philosopher John Rawls who argued on the grounds of social justice that a society should strive to maximize the utility of its worst-off member. In mathematical terms, the Rawlsian social welfare function says that

$$W = \min[U_1, U_2, \ldots, U_N]$$

Rawlsian social welfare function A mathematical function that computes society's welfare as the welfare of the worst-off individual.

In words, society's welfare W is the minimum of all the utilities in society. Only the utility of the least well-off individual matters; the utility levels of all other individuals in the society do not matter at all. The Rawlsian utility function is an extreme example of an **egalitarian** welfare function, *the belief that the ideal society is one in which each individual is equally well off.*

egalitarian The belief that the ideal society is one in which each individual is equally well off.

The Drawbacks of Social Welfare Functions

Although social welfare functions can be useful, they may prove difficult to use as practical standards for evaluating market outcomes, especially because different functions might give varied answers about what makes for desirable outcomes. For example, consider how differently a utilitarian society and an egalitarian society would think about taxing the rich to give to the poor. As we mentioned above, how one would evaluate the result of such policies is going to depend on subjective judgments about how worthwhile inequality reductions are in the first place.

Furthermore, even if everyone agreed on the type of social welfare function to use, combining individuals' utility levels mathematically—which is the point of a social welfare function—is conceptually dicey, as we discussed in Chapter 4 because they require us to compare and combine utility levels across people.

figure it out 15.2

Arnold, Bruce, and Sylvester are residents of a tiny commune in Peru. Arnold currently has a utility level, U_A, of 55 utils; Bruce's utility, U_B, is 35 utils; and Sylvester's utility, U_S, is 10 utils. Angelina, the benevolent ruler of the commune, is considering enacting a new policy that will increase Arnold's utility by 10 utils and decrease Sylvester's by 5.

a. If Angelina believes the social welfare function is given by $W = U_A + U_B + U_S$, should she enact the change?

b. If Angelina believes the social welfare function is given by $W = \min[U_A, U_B, U_S]$, should she enact the change?

c. If Angelina believes the social welfare function is given by $W = U_A \times U_B \times U_S$, should she enact the change?

Solution:

a. To determine if Angelina should enact the policy, we must calculate the social welfare before and after the change.

Before:

$$W = U_A + U_B + U_S = 55 + 35 + 10 = 100$$

After:

$$W = U_A + U_B + U_S = 65 + 35 + 5 = 105$$

Because welfare is increased after the change, Angelina should enact the policy.

b. Before:

$$W = \min(U_A, U_B, U_S) = \min(55, 35, 10) = 10$$

After:

$$W = \min(U_A, U_B, U_S) = \min(65, 35, 5) = 5$$

In this case, Angelina should not enact the new policy because welfare is reduced.

c. Before:

$$W = U_A \times U_B \times U_S = 55 \times 35 \times 10 = 19,250$$

After:

$$W = U_A \times U_B \times U_S = 65 \times 35 \times 5 = 11,375$$

Again, because welfare falls as a result of the new policy, Angelina should not enact it.

Standards for Measuring Market Performance: Pareto Efficiency

The difficulties with trying to use social welfare functions to evaluate how well markets are working have led economists to use a criterion that everyone can understand and agree on: Pareto efficiency.

Pareto efficiency is *an economic allocation of goods in which the goods cannot be reallocated without making at least one individual worse off.* As an example, say that in one small economy, Larry has a laptop, Moe has a TV, and Curly has a used Buick Enclave. If there is no way to reshuffle the goods among the three guys that makes no one worse off and at least one person better off, then the economy is Pareto-efficient. If a reshuffling of the goods could make one or more better off without making anyone worse off, then the economy isn't Pareto-efficient. So, for example, if Larry would happily swap his laptop for Curly's Buick and Curly would also like to make this swap, then the initial allocation of goods wasn't Pareto-efficient. These sorts of trades are not possible in a Pareto-efficient allocation because someone (the one who is made worse off) will refuse. Under Pareto efficiency, *someone* would be made worse off by any rearrangement of goods, whether it's a simple two-person, two-good swap, or something a lot more complicated.[5]

What this means for general equilibrium is that a Pareto-efficient economy should not have a lot of something for nothing—what economists call "free lunches" or "$20 bills lying on the sidewalk" (figuratively or literally). In this way, Pareto efficiency is a fairly intuitive concept of efficiency.

Note that Pareto efficiency doesn't imply it is fair or that it maximizes some social welfare function. Pareto-efficient allocations can exist even with large differences in individuals' utility levels. In fact, as long as marginal utilities are positive, giving one person everything in the economy and everyone else nothing is Pareto-efficient because any rearrangement of goods from the starting allocation requires making at least one

Pareto efficiency An economic allocation of goods in which the goods cannot be reallocated without making at least one individual worse off.

---

[5] Note that this doesn't mean *no one* could be made better off by a reshuffling of goods from a Pareto-efficient allocation. In fact, it's likely an individual or set of individuals would be made better off. But this would come at the expense of others.

person worse off (the person who has everything to start with), violating the Pareto efficiency condition.

That's why it is important to remember what a weak standard Pareto efficiency holds markets to. A Pareto-efficient outcome (sometimes called a Pareto equilibrium) might violate our norms for equality but still serve as a useful benchmark because we are interested in knowing whether voluntary trade in markets could eliminate any free lunches that might exist in an initial distribution of resources.

Looking for Pareto Efficiency in Markets

Now that we've defined Pareto efficiency as a standard to measure market outcomes, let's see how market outcomes compare to Pareto-efficient outcomes. This is an extremely important question to economists: Markets are the most common way for the world to allocate trillions of goods to billions of people. We would like to know, for lack of a better phrase, whether markets are any good at it. But to answer that question, we need to compare market equilibria to standards such as Pareto efficiency.

We start by giving away the ending: Under a certain set of assumptions about the market environment, the outcomes from a free market *are* Pareto-efficient. Economists have speculated about this possibility for as long as there have been economists. Adam Smith's famous notion of an *invisible hand* (the unseen force in markets that tends to create socially beneficial results even though market participants act only in their individual best interests) essentially made the point that market outcomes can be efficient. It wasn't until the mid-twentieth century, however, that the Pareto efficiency result was proven mathematically. (The highly technical proof is beyond the scope of this chapter and won the two people who proved it—Ken Arrow and Gerard Debreu—a Nobel Prize.) We will cover the economic intuition behind it in a moment.

The market efficiency result is a big reason why economists tend to look favorably on markets: Markets have a natural tendency to arrive at efficient outcomes under a certain set of assumptions. (You are already familiar with some of these assumptions, such as perfect competition and price-taking behavior among suppliers and consumers.) The chances that *all* of these assumptions actually hold in any real-world market are small, however, so real markets may not be Pareto-efficient.

If real markets aren't completely efficient, economists still seem to favor market solutions more often than the general public because the market efficiency proof shows exactly what must hold for markets to be efficient. That is, whatever makes markets work or fail isn't mysterious. We *know* what factors gum up the works, and often this suggests what kinds of policies would remove the gum.

Therefore, economists of most political orientations tend to think that markets have the potential to create the greatest amount of benefits for the greatest number of people. What they are more likely to disagree on is how much intervention (such as government actions to reduce market power) is necessary to make markets run smoothly.

Efficiency in Markets—Three Requirements

Now it's time to look at the details of what must be true if markets are operating efficiently. Three basic conditions must all hold for an efficient economy:

exchange efficiency A Pareto-efficient allocation of a set of goods across consumers.

1. **Exchange efficiency** is a *Pareto-efficient allocation of a set of goods across consumers.* It holds if no consumer can be made better off in her consumption without making someone worse off. The term *exchange* comes from the fact that we don't worry about what products are made or how, or who buys them so long as people can trade (exchange) goods or services if they want to.

2. **Input efficiency** is *a Pareto-efficient allocation of inputs across producers*. It holds if inputs are allocated to producing the goods in the economy in such a way that making a higher quantity of one good means a smaller quantity must be made of at least one other good.

input efficiency A Pareto-efficient allocation of inputs across producers.

3. **Output efficiency** is *a mix of outputs that simultaneously supports exchange and input efficiency*. The first two conditions take the set of goods produced in the economy as a predetermined starting point, and then evaluate efficiency in how they are allocated among consumers (exchange efficiency) and producers (input efficiency). Output efficiency deals with *which* goods are produced and in what quantities. It holds when the mix and amount of goods that the economy produces cannot be changed without making some consumer or producer worse off.

output efficiency A mix of outputs that simultaneously supports exchange and input efficiency.

We study each of these three conditions separately, in detail, below and then show how they are interrelated in an efficient general equilibrium.

15.3 Efficiency in Markets: Exchange Efficiency

Before we begin our examination of the various aspects of an efficient general equilibrium with a discussion of *exchange efficiency,* we introduce an extremely handy tool for analyzing market efficiency named after the Irish economist Francis Edgeworth. The **Edgeworth box** is *a graph of an economy with two economic actors (consumers or producers) and two goods that is used to analyze market efficiency.*

Edgeworth box Graph of an economy with two economic actors and two goods that is used to analyze market efficiency.

The Edgeworth Box

Suppose there are two consumers—we'll call them Jerry and Elaine—each of whom has his or her own preference for two goods, bowls of cereal and pancakes. Let's also suppose that there are a total of 10 bowls of cereal and 8 pancakes that can be split between them. We want to figure out in what Pareto-efficient ways we can distribute these goods between Jerry and Elaine.

To do this analysis, we use an Edgeworth box. An Edgeworth box utilizes the fact that when there is a fixed total number of goods to be split between two individuals, giving one more unit of a good to one person necessarily means the other person gets one less unit. In our case, for example, if Elaine gets one more bowl of cereal, Jerry must get one less. A point within or on the sides of the Edgeworth box shows the distribution of two goods (like cereal and pancakes) between two people (like Jerry and Elaine). Basically, you read Jerry's situation upside down on the graph.

Figure 15.4 illustrates how the Edgeworth box works in our example. The horizontal sides of the box measure 10 bowls of cereal; the vertical sides measure 8 pancakes. The lower-left-hand corner represents one consumer (we'll say Elaine here, though we could just as easily have picked Jerry) who receives 0 units of both goods. If we give Elaine one more bowl of cereal, we move her allocation 1 unit to the right. If we give her one more pancake, we move Elaine's allocation 1 unit up.

The upper-right-hand corner represents Jerry when he receives 0 units of both goods. Note that if Jerry receives no goods, Elaine receives all of both goods—10 bowls of cereal and 8 pancakes. If we give Jerry one more bowl of cereal, his allocation moves 1 unit to the left (one less bowl for Elaine). If we give him one more pancake, we move Jerry's allocation down 1 unit (one less pancake for Elaine).

To get accustomed to working with the Edgeworth box, let's do some quick examples. Consider an initial allocation at point *A* in Figure 15.4. At point *A*, Elaine has 3 bowls of cereal and 6 pancakes, and Jerry has the rest of the goods: 7 bowls of cereal and

Figure 15.4   A Consumption Edgeworth Box

This Edgeworth box plots specific allocations of cereal (10 bowls total, shown on the horizontal axes) and pancakes (8 total, shown on the vertical axes) between two consumers, Jerry and Elaine. If Jerry consumes 7 bowls of cereal and 2 pancakes, Elaine consumes 3 bowls of cereal and 6 pancakes (point *A*). If Jerry consumes one less bowl of cereal at point *B*, then Elaine's consumption of cereal increases by 1 bowl to 4 bowls of cereal. At point *C*, Jerry now eats one more pancake, decreasing Elaine's consumption of pancakes by 1 pancake to 5 pancakes.

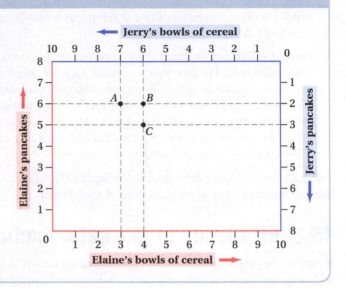

2 pancakes. If we change the allocation by giving Elaine another bowl of cereal and taking one from Jerry, we are at point *B*; Elaine has 4 bowls of cereal and 6 pancakes and Jerry has 6 bowls of cereal and 2 pancakes. If we change the allocation from point *B* by taking away a pancake from Elaine and giving it to Jerry, we move to point *C* (Elaine has 4 bowls of cereal and 5 pancakes and Jerry has 6 bowls of cereal and 3 pancakes). Any change in the allocation that moves one of the consumers in a certain direction will move the other consumer by the same amount but in the opposite direction. As a result, the Edgeworth box allows us to see simultaneously the effects of changes in goods allocations on both consumers. It's like a game board where each person's side is the opposite of the other.

Gains from Trade in the Edgeworth Box

To analyze whether allocations are efficient, we need to know consumers' preferences. In Chapter 4, we learned that indifference curves show consumers' preferences. To see the gains from trade, we add Elaine's and Jerry's indifference curves to the Edgeworth box (**Figure 15.5**).

Elaine's preferences for bowls of cereal and pancakes are represented by indifference curves U_{E1}, U_{E2}, U_{E3}, and so on. Each shows combinations of cereal and pancakes that make Elaine equally well off. Indifference curves farther away from Elaine's origin depict more of each good, so they represent higher utility levels. Jerry's preferences are represented by indifference curves U_{J1}, U_{J2}, U_{J3}, and so on. Jerry's indifference curves may look odd, but just remember that you read Jerry's situation upside down. His origin is in the upper right corner so they're normal indifference curves, bowed toward the origin. Indifference curves farther away from Jerry's origin show higher utility levels.

Now that we've laid out Jerry's and Elaine's preferences, we can use them to determine an efficient allocation of the two goods. Start at an arbitrary allocation, point *A*, and ask if we can reshuffle who gets what to make both Elaine and Jerry better off. (Remember the definition of Pareto efficiency: There is no possible way to reallocate who gets what without making at least one individual worse off than before.) At allocation *A*, such a reshuffling is possible. Let's see why.

Elaine and Jerry each have indifference curves that pass through point *A*, U_{E3} and U_{J3}. We know from our analysis in Chapter 4 that any allocation giving Elaine quantities of cereal and

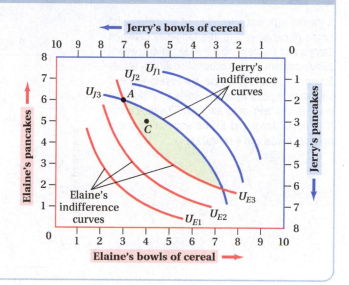

Figure 15.5   Edgeworth Box with Two Sets of Indifference Curves

By including Jerry's and Elaine's indifference curves, we can determine the efficient allocation of bowls of cereal and pancakes. Point *A* is an inefficient allocation because any point in the shaded area, including point *C*, will yield higher utilities for both Jerry and Elaine.

pancakes that are above and to the right of U_{E3} will give her a higher utility than at point *A*. Similarly, any allocation that raises Jerry's utility will be below and to the left of U_{J3}. Knowing this, we can figure out the allocations that make *both* Elaine and Jerry better off, or at least make one of them better off without making the other worse off. These are the allocations in the shaded area in Figure 15.5. Any distribution of goods in this area must be on indifference curves (not drawn to keep the graph uncluttered) that correspond to higher utility levels for both Elaine and Jerry. Any change that moves the allocation of goods from *A* to somewhere in the shaded area makes both Elaine and Jerry better off. For example, if Jerry traded one of his bowls of cereal to Elaine for one of her pancakes, we'd be at point *C* inside the shaded area, and Jerry and Elaine would both have higher utility levels than at the initial allocation (point *A*).

Remember that a Pareto-efficient allocation is one that, if changed in any way, would make at least one person worse off. Because there is a set of allocations that would make both Jerry and Elaine better off (the shaded area), point *A* is not Pareto-efficient. (Reallocations that make at least one person better off without making anyone worse off are sometimes referred to as *Pareto-improving reallocations* or just *Pareto improvements*.[6])

If the existence of a shaded area like that in Figure 15.5 means an allocation isn't Pareto-efficient, you might think that only allocations *without* shaded areas *are* Pareto-efficient, and you'd be right. To see what this would look like, let's think about another allocation that is inside the shaded area, point *C*.

Although *C* gives both Jerry and Elaine higher utility levels than *A*, they could still make mutually beneficial trades from there. Look at **Figure 15.6**. Indifference curves U_{E4} and U_{J4} are Elaine and Jerry's indifference curves that pass through *C*. The area that U_{E4} and U_{J4} enclose are cereal and pancake allocations that would make both Elaine and Jerry better off than they are with allocation *C*. Therefore, allocation *C* can't be Pareto-efficient either. But notice that this area is smaller than the corresponding area for allocation *A*. We're closing in on Pareto efficiency.

To find a Pareto-efficient allocation, we need to find situations where there is no area between Jerry's and Elaine's indifference curves—when we reach indifference curves for

---

[6] While we've only drawn a two-consumer, two-good case in Figure 15.5, these concepts extend to any number of people consuming allocations of any number of goods. It's just that we haven't figured out how to draw in 4-, 5-, or higher-dimensional hyperspace yet. We're working on it, though; wish us luck.

Figure 15.6   **Closing In on Pareto Efficiency for Elaine and Jerry**

A Pareto-efficient allocation of pancakes and bowls of cereal occurs at a tangency between Jerry's and Elaine's indifference curves, where Jerry's marginal rate of substitution MRS_{CP} equals Elaine's MRS_{CP}. In this case, the Pareto-efficient allocation is point D, where Elaine's indifference curve U_{E5} is tangent to Jerry's indifference curve U_{J5}. Here, Jerry and Elaine each consume 5 bowls of cereal and 4 pancakes.

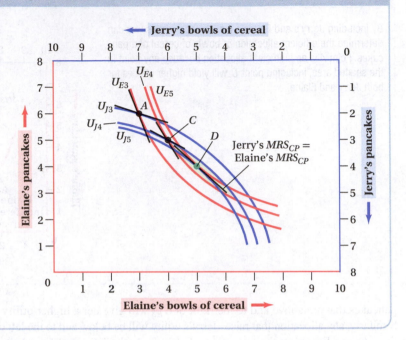

Elaine and Jerry that meet at a single point, point D in Figure 15.6. Notice that Elaine's and Jerry's indifference curves that pass through this point, U_{E5} and U_{J5}, are tangent to each other. Also notice that we can't change the allocation even slightly without making either Jerry or Elaine worse off by going below and to the left of U_{E5}, or above and to the right of U_{J5}. Allocation D, therefore, is Pareto-efficient.

We've shown that exchange efficiency is achieved when two consumers' indifference curves are tangent. Only at such a tangency are there no mutually beneficial gains from trade. This tangency condition offers an interpretation for what must be true for exchange efficiency to hold. Recall from Chapter 4 that the slope of an indifference curve at any point reflects the marginal rate of substitution (MRS) between goods at that point. That means at a common tangency like point D, the slopes of both Jerry's and Elaine's indifference curves are the same. (Remember, the slope of a curve at a particular point equals the slope of a line tangent to the curve at that point.) Thus, at point D, Jerry and Elaine have the same MRS between cereal and pancakes. At any point that *isn't* a Pareto-efficient allocation, consumers have a different MRS for the goods. At points A and C in Figure 15.6, the difference in the slopes of Elaine and Jerry's indifference curves is clear.

To understand why the MRSs need to be equal, think for a moment about what it would mean if they weren't. One consumer would have a higher marginal utility from consuming one of the goods than the other consumer. When marginal utilities for the same good are unequal across consumers, each could give a unit of her low-marginal-utility good to the other. She would be getting rid of what is, for her, a relatively low-value item, but she would receive in return the good for which she has a higher marginal utility. The same would be true of the consumer receiving the unit, so both individuals would be better off. Only when marginal utility ratios are equal across the two consumers—that is, when exchange efficiency has been achieved—would there not be a mutual benefit from trade.

In allocation A in Figure 15.6, Elaine would be willing to trade 3 pancakes for 1 bowl of cereal. That is, her MRS_{CP} (marginal rate of substitution of cereal for pancakes) and the absolute value of the slope of her indifference curve is 3. Jerry would trade 3 bowls of cereal for 1 pancake, or equivalently, one-third of a pancake for a bowl of cereal. So,

Jerry's $MRS_{CP} = 1/3$. Elaine therefore has a relatively high marginal utility from cereal at allocation A; she'd be willing to give up 3 pancakes to get 1 bowl. Jerry feels the opposite. He would enjoy another pancake so much he would be willing to part with 3 bowls of cereal for it. Clearly, both would benefit from making a trade to get them to point C, which we know Elaine and Jerry like better than A. Mutually beneficial trade between Elaine and Jerry could continue like this until they get to D. At that point, their marginal rates of substitution are equal, and neither would want to trade. Further exchange would necessarily make one of them worse off than at D, where their MRSs are equal.

Prices and the Allocation of Goods
Up to this point, we've talked about the allocation of goods as if magical economists shuffle goods among consumers. In reality, consumers choose how much of each good to consume given the prices they face. In Chapter 4, we learned that a utility-maximizing individual consumes the product bundle at which her MRS between goods equals the ratio of those goods' prices. (This optimal consumption bundle is located where the indifference curve is tangent to the budget line.)

In Elaine and Jerry's case, then, we know that they will both consume amounts where $MRS_{CP} = \dfrac{P_C}{P_P}$. We also just saw that Elaine's and Jerry's MRS_{CP} will be equal in a Pareto-efficient allocation. Thus, it must be that Pareto efficiency in a market implies

$$\text{Elaine's } MRS_{CP} = \text{Jerry's } MRS_{CP} = \frac{P_C}{P_P}$$

In other words, an efficient market will result in the goods' price ratio equaling consumers' marginal rates of substitution for those goods.

If an initial allocation is not efficient, consumers will be willing to sell those goods that have (for them) marginal utilities below the market price. They can then use the proceeds to buy their high-marginal-utility goods. There will be individuals whose relative marginal utilities for those goods are the reverse and who will be willing to be on the other side of those transactions. In this way, we don't need magical economists to reshuffle goods among people to get everyone's MRSs to match. Prices drive people to do it themselves.

The Consumption Contract Curve
The key condition of exchange efficiency that consumers have equal marginal rates of substitution—that is, their indifference curves are tangent to one another—is true at more than one location in this Edgeworth box. In **Figure 15.7**, we've drawn a more extensive set of Elaine's and Jerry's indifference curves, showing several tangencies. If we connect these tangencies and all those in between (remember, there are indifference curves running through every point in the box), *every allocation on the line is Pareto-efficient*—they all meet the equal-MRS test. Called the **consumption contract curve,** *this curve shows all possible Pareto-efficient allocations of goods across consumers.*

consumption contract curve Curve that shows all possible Pareto-efficient allocations of goods across consumers.

Looking at the contract curve emphasizes the distinction between efficiency and equity that we mentioned earlier. While all allocations along the contract curve are efficient, they have very different implications for Jerry's and Elaine's respective utility levels. Some—those toward the lower-left corner of the Edgeworth box—imply low utility for Elaine and high utility for Jerry. Those toward the upper right, on the other hand, will be good for Elaine and bad for Jerry.[7]

---

[7] In fact, the lower-left and upper-right corners of the Edgeworth box—the actual origins themselves—can also be on the contract curve. At either origin, either Elaine or Jerry will be consuming everything, and the other will be consuming nothing. If Elaine's and Jerry's marginal utilities of a good are always positive, there is no way that a good can be moved from one of them to the other without making whoever of the pair was consuming everything worse off. Allocations where one person gets everything and everyone else receives nothing can be Pareto-efficient.

Figure 15.7 A Consumption Contract Curve

The consumption contract curve connects every point of tangency between Jerry's and Elaine's indifference curves for bowls of cereal and pancakes. Each point on the contract curve represents a Pareto-efficient allocation of bowls of cereal and pancakes between Jerry and Elaine.

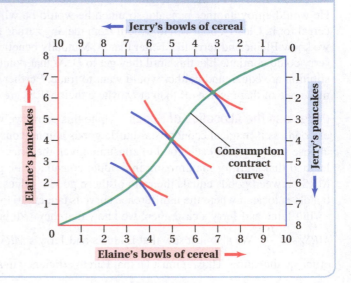

 figure it out 15.3

Go online for interactive, step-by-step help in solving the following problem.

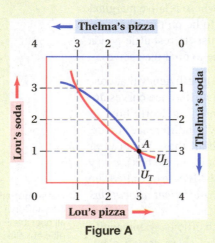

Figure A

Consider the Edgeworth box above (Figure A), which depicts the amount of soda and pizza available to two consumers, Thelma and Lou.

a. Suppose that Thelma and Lou are initially at point *A*. How much soda does each have? How many slices of pizza?

b. Suppose that Thelma and Lou's child Ted takes 2 slices of pizza from Lou and gives them to Thelma,

then takes 2 sodas from Thelma and gives them to Lou. Find and plot the new allocation in the Edgeworth box. Label the allocation with a large "B." Does such a reallocation represent a Pareto improvement? Explain your answer.

c. Suppose that Ted had reallocated 1 slice of pizza and 1 soda instead of 2 of each. Would such a reallocation represent a Pareto improvement? Explain your answer, using indifference curves to illustrate it.

Solution:

a. At point *A*, Thelma has 3 sodas and Lou has 1 soda. Thelma has 1 slice of pizza, while Lou has 3 slices of pizza.

b. If Ted takes 2 slices of pizza from Lou and gives them to Thelma, Lou will end up with 1 slice, while Thelma will have 3. If Ted takes 2 sodas from Thelma and gives them to Lou, Thelma will be left with 1 soda and Lou will have 3 sodas. This allocation can be represented at point *B* in Figure B. A Pareto improvement occurs when at least one individual is made better off without making anyone worse off. Because point *B* is on the same indifference curves as point *A*, neither Thelma nor Lou is better off. Therefore, this is not a Pareto improvement.

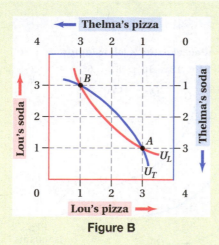

Figure B

c. If Ted takes 1 slice of pizza from Lou and gives it to
Thelma, both Lou and Thelma will end up with 2 slices
each. If Ted also takes 1 soda from Thelma and gives it
to Lou, both Thelma and Lou will be left with 2 sodas
each. This allocation can be represented by point C in
Figure C. A Pareto improvement occurs when at least

one person is made better off without harming another
person. In this case, point C is on a higher indifference
curve for both Thelma and Lou, implying that they are
both better off with this new allocation. Therefore, it is
a Pareto improvement. Moreover, as drawn below, the
allocation at point C is also Pareto-efficient.

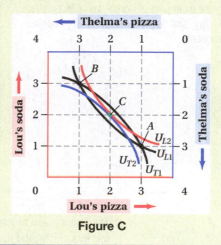

Figure C

15.4 Efficiency in Markets: Input Efficiency

Exchange efficiency shows what conditions must hold on the demand side of a market
for the market to be efficient. Efficiency is also important on the production side of the
economy, especially the efficiency with which inputs are allocated across the production
of various goods and services. An input can be used to make one product or another, but
not both simultaneously. So, which product should it be used to make? That is, how do we
answer questions such as how much steel should be used to make cars instead of kitchen
knives and surgical instruments, or how many workers should work in which industries?
Questions like these lie at the heart of the second market efficiency condition of general
equilibrium, *input efficiency.*

Many of the tools we used to analyze exchange efficiency are also useful in analyzing
input efficiency. We saw that in exchange efficiency, goods are consumed where consumers' indifference curves are tangent to one another. Similarly, input efficiency requires an
allocation of inputs across producers where their *isoquants* are tangent to each other. The
reasoning is similar to the exchange efficiency case. At locations where producers' isoquants are tangent to each other, no input can be transferred from one producer to another
without at least one experiencing a loss in output.

Because of the similarity of the two problems, we use an Edgeworth box for our analysis. It's just like the one we used for Elaine and Jerry, except with two producers instead of
two consumers. And rather than allocating two goods between consumers, we look at how
two inputs are allocated between the producers.

Figure 15.8 shows how 20 units of labor (horizontal axes) and 12 units of capital (vertical axes) are allocated between Cereal, Inc. (CI) and Pancake, Inc. (PI). CI's origin, which
denotes where it is using 0 units of capital and labor, is at the lower-left-hand corner of the box.
Increases in CI's use of inputs are represented by movement to the right (labor) and up (capital).
CI's isoquants—Q_{C1}, Q_{C2}, Q_{C3}, and so on—show the combinations of labor and capital that

Figure 15.8 A Production Edgeworth Box

An Edgeworth box can be used to determine the efficient input allocation between two firms. In this case, Cereal, Inc.'s and Pancake, Inc.'s labor inputs are on the horizontal axes and their capital inputs are shown on the vertical axes. Q_{C1}, Q_{C2}, and Q_{C3} are examples of Cereal, Inc.'s isoquants, and Q_{P1}, Q_{P2}, and Q_{P3} are examples of Pancake, Inc.'s isoquants.

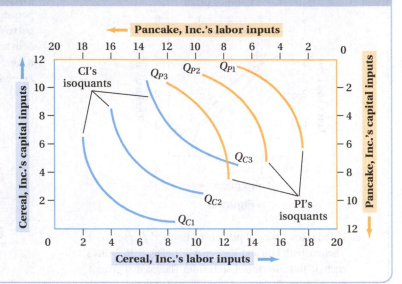

produce a given amount of output. PI's origin, which denotes where it is using 0 units of capital and labor, is at the upper-right-hand corner of the box. Increases in PI's use of inputs are represented by movements to the left (labor) and down (capital). PI's isoquants—Q_{P1}, Q_{P2}, Q_{P3}, and so on—show the combinations of labor and capital that produce a given amount of output.

The connection between the analysis of Elaine's and Jerry's consumption bundles and the analysis of Cereal, Inc.'s and Pancake, Inc.'s input use is direct. CI's isoquants look "normal." PI's isoquants also look normal if we remember that we're looking at them upside down with the upper right as the origin. Start at an arbitrary allocation of inputs between the two firms, point F in **Figure 15.9**. At this point, CI is using 14 units of labor and 4 units of capital, which means that PI is using 6 units of labor and 8 units of capital. CI's isoquant Q_{C1} and PI's isoquant Q_{P1} pass through point F and enclose an area. If they use input combinations in this highlighted area, both firms can make more output than they are able to with input allocation F. Because both firms can make more output with the same total inputs, F cannot be a Pareto-efficient allocation of inputs.

At input allocation G, where CI's and PI's isoquants Q_{C2} and Q_{P2} are tangent, there is no way to move labor and capital from one firm to the other and raise output for at least one of the firms without reducing the other firm's output. Therefore, G is a Pareto-efficient allocation of inputs. This tangency condition also indicates that firms could not trade inputs for mutual gain.

There are more similarities between input and exchange efficiency. Exchange efficiency implies that consumers' marginal rates of substitution—the slopes of their indifference curves—are equal. Input efficiency implies equal slopes of producers' isoquants. As you may recall from Chapter 6, this slope is called the marginal rate of technical substitution (MRTS), the ratio of inputs' marginal products. For example, the MRTS between labor and capital is the ratio of the marginal product of labor to the marginal product of capital,

$MRTS_{LK} = \dfrac{MP_L}{MP_K}$. In our example, input efficiency requires that

$$\text{CI's } MRTS_{LK} = \text{PI's } MRTS_{LK} = \frac{MP_L^{CI}}{MP_K^{CI}} = \frac{MP_L^{PI}}{MP_K^{PI}}$$

We can see this common $MRTS_{LK}$ slope in Figure 15.9.

Figure **15.9**   Edgeworth Box with Two Sets of Isoquants

A Pareto-efficient allocation of capital and labor inputs occurs at a tangency between Cereal, Inc.'s and Pancake, Inc.'s isoquants, where Cereal, Inc.'s marginal rate of technical substitution ($MRTS_{LK}$) equals Pancake, Inc.'s $MRTS_{LK}$. Point F shows a possible allocation of labor and capital between Cereal, Inc. and Pancake, Inc. Because it lies on the intersection of isoquants Q_{C1} and Q_{P1}—and not at the tangency—F is an inefficient allocation. G, which is located at the tangency between Q_{C2} and Q_{P2}, is a Pareto-efficient input allocation.

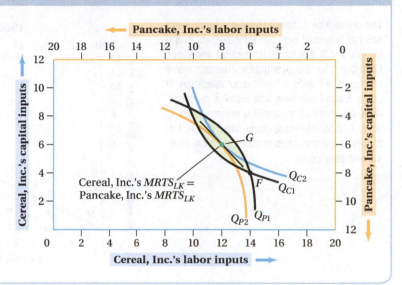

We also learned in Chapter 6 that cost-minimizing firms set their MRTS equal to the ratio of the input prices (wages and rental rates in the cases of labor and capital). Putting this all together, input efficiency implies

$$\text{CI's } MRTS_{LK} = \text{PI's } MRTS_{LK} = \frac{MP_L^{CI}}{MP_K^{CI}} = \frac{MP_L^{PI}}{MP_K^{PI}} = \frac{W}{R}$$

where W is the wage rate and R the capital rental rate.

Finally, a similarity exists between input and exchange efficiency in terms of the set of efficient allocations. In the exchange efficiency case, the collection of efficient goods allocations, the consumption contract curve, connects all common tangencies of the consumers' indifference curves. The **production contract curve** is *the curve that shows all Pareto-efficient allocations of inputs across producers*. It connects all common tangencies of producers' isoquants and contains all efficient allocations of inputs across producers (**Figure 15.10**).

Just as different locations on the contract curve can imply very different total utility levels for Elaine and Jerry, different locations on the production contract curve correspond to disparate production quantities of cereal and pancakes. In the lower left, Cereal, Inc. uses few inputs and does not make much cereal, while Pancake, Inc. stays busy. The opposite is true in the upper-right corner with high cereal and low pancake production.

production contract curve Curve that shows all Pareto-efficient allocations of inputs across producers.

The Production Possibilities Frontier

The production contract curve generates a useful idea. Think about what various input allocations across the two firms imply with regard to the tradeoffs between the *output* of either good. Imagine running along the production contract curve from the lower-left corner in Figure 15.10 to the upper-right corner, but instead of thinking about what each point corresponds to in terms of inputs, consider what each point means for cereal and pancake output.

Figure 15.10 A Production Contract Curve

The production contract curve connects every point of tangency between Pancake, Inc.'s and Cereal, Inc.'s isoquants for capital and labor. Each point on the production contract curve represents a Pareto-efficient input allocation. At points *H* and *I*, relatively little cereal is produced, while relatively more pancakes are produced. At point *J*, no pancakes are made, while Cereal, Inc. produces the maximum amount of cereal given the available inputs.

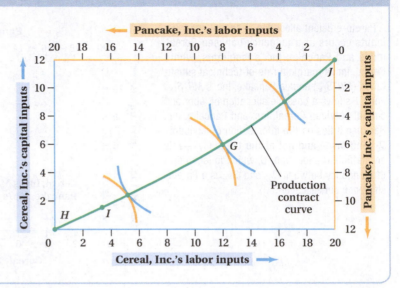

At the very lower-left-hand corner, no inputs are used to make cereal, so cereal production is zero. Pancake output, however, is maximized at this location. This combination is plotted as point *H* on **Figure 15.11**. (For comparison, we've labeled the corresponding input combination in Figure 15.10.) Pancake production is positive; cereal output is zero.

Now move up and to the right along the production contract curve to input allocation *I* in Figure 15.10. This move shifts inputs from pancake to cereal production. The corresponding effect on output is traced by the movement from point *H* to point *I* in Figure 15.11. Cereal output increases while pancake output falls. As we continue in the same direction along the production contract curve, cereal production rises further as pancake production drops more. When we reach the upper-right-hand corner of the Edgeworth box, we hit maximum cereal output and zero pancake output (point *J*).

We just traced out all the possible combinations of the cereal and pancakes that could be made with inputs efficiently allocated across producers. The level of output for any particular good depends on how many inputs are applied to its production, but whatever level this is, as long as the input allocation is on the production contract curve, efficiency tells us we cannot increase the output of the other good without decreasing

Figure 15.11 A Production Possibilities Frontier

The production possibilities frontier (PPF) plots all possible output combinations of cereal and pancakes that can be made if inputs are allocated efficiently. Points *H*, *I*, *G*, and *J* all lead to efficient outputs. Point *F*, which lies within the PPF, results from an inefficient allocation of inputs across producers.

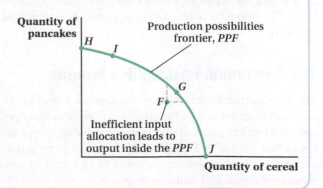

figure it out 15.4

Suppose that there are 10 units of capital available in a small economy and 20 units of labor. Those inputs can be used to produce food and clothing.

    a. If the $MRTS_{LK}$ in the clothing industry is 4, and the $MRTS_{LK}$ in the food industry is 3, is the economy productively efficient? Explain your answer.

    b. If you indicated in part (a) that the economy was not productively efficient, suggest a reallocation of labor and capital that will lead to a Pareto improvement.

Solution:

    a. Production efficiency requires that the MRTS between labor and capital be equal across industries.

Therefore, the economy is not productively efficient because the $MRTS_{LK}$ for clothing is greater than the $MRTS_{LK}$ for food.

    b. To become equal, the $MRTS_{LK}$ in the clothing industry must fall, while the $MRTS_{LK}$ in the food industry must rise. This means that the clothing industry should use more labor and less capital, while the reverse is true for the food industry. As the clothing industry uses more labor and less capital, the MP_L will fall and the MP_K will rise, decreasing the $MRTS_{LK}$. Likewise, as the food industry uses less labor and more capital, the MP_L will rise and the MP_K will fall, increasing $MRTS_{LK}$. This Pareto improvement will move the economy toward productive efficiency.

---

the output of the first. *The curve that connects all possible efficient output combinations of two goods*, curve *HJ* in Figure 15.11, is called the **production possibilities frontier (PPF)**. Again, efficiency doesn't necessarily imply equality. Depending on the location on the production possibilities frontier, the proportions of two goods here can vary dramatically.

    Inefficient input allocations will lead to cereal and pancake outputs that are inside the PPF. For example, the inefficient input allocation given by point *F* in Figure 15.9 might correspond to the output combination at point *F* in Figure 15.11. At point *F*, more of both goods could be made with the same total amount of inputs. The possible combinations of outputs that would be an improvement over point *F* (and that are attainable given the total amount of inputs available) are those contained within the wedge-shaped area in Figure 15.11. This area corresponds to the outputs that could be made by input combinations within the shaded area between Q_{C1} and Q_{P1} in Figure 15.9. Points on the PPF curve itself, rather than inside it, correspond to the outputs produced by efficient combinations of inputs along the production contract curve. For example, Point *G* in Figure 15.11 shows the output that corresponds to the efficient input allocation *G* in Figure 15.9.

production possibilities frontier (PPF) Curve that connects all possible efficient output combinations of two goods.

15.5 Efficiency in Markets: Output Efficiency

We've described what must be true if exchange and input efficiency hold, and we've seen a lot of parallels between the two cases: common tangencies, consumer and production contract curves, and so on. But we haven't drawn a direct connection between the two types of efficiency.

    If you think about it, though, a connection must exist. Producers use inputs to make goods that consumers buy. There should be a link between the efficient allocation of inputs for making different outputs and the efficient allocation of these outputs across consumers. The link is *output efficiency,* which involves the choice of how many units of each product the economy should make. Understanding the requirements for output efficiency requires us to see the inherent tradeoff between the production of various goods. We describe this tradeoff first and then show how it ties together the three efficiency conditions.

The Marginal Rate of Transformation

The production possibilities frontier, which we showed was related to the production contract curve, illustrates how much of one output must be given up to obtain one more unit of another. *The tradeoff between the production of any goods on the market* is called the **marginal rate of transformation (MRT)**.

marginal rate of transformation (MRT)
The tradeoff between the production of any goods on the market.

The MRT from pancakes to cereal, for example, is the slope of the production possibilities frontier in Figure 15.11. At point *H*, the frontier is relatively flat, so the MRT is small. In other words, few pancakes have to be given up to produce one more box of cereal. This is true because we've assumed inputs have diminishing marginal products. When they use all inputs to make pancakes, the inputs have relatively low marginal products in pancake production, but relatively large marginal products in cereal production. At this point, shifting just a few inputs from pancake to cereal production will have a modest impact on total pancake production but a noticeable impact on cereal production.

The opposite is true near point *J*, where the inputs' marginal products in pancake production are high and low in cereal production. The MRT from pancakes to cereal is therefore very high. Intermediate MRT levels exist at points toward the middle of the production possibilities frontier, like *G*.

This logic shows how the marginal rate of transformation is related to inputs' marginal products. We can pin down this relationship with the following thought experiment. Suppose we want to increase cereal production. To do so, we take 1 unit of labor, a worker, say, who was making pancakes at Pancake, Inc., and instead have her start working at Cereal, Inc. By doing this, we lose the marginal product of labor at Pancake, Inc., MP_L^{PI}, but gain the marginal product of labor at Cereal, Inc., MP_L^{CI}. The ratio of these two values — the amount of pancake production that we give up to produce more cereal — is the definition of the marginal rate of transformation, or MRT. Therefore,

$$MRT_{PC} = \frac{MP_L^{PI}}{MP_L^{CI}}$$

That is, the marginal rate of transformation from pancakes to cereal is the ratio of labor's marginal product in pancake production to its marginal product in cereal production.

Similarly, with a different input, moving a unit of capital from Pancake, Inc. to Cereal, Inc. will lead to the conclusion that the MRT is also the ratio of capital's marginal products at the two firms:

$$MRT_{PC} = \frac{MP_K^{PI}}{MP_K^{CI}}$$

We can see this equivalence another way. First, remember two things from above: The production contract curve connects all equal-marginal-rate-of-technical-substitution points, and every point on the production contract curve corresponds to a point on the production possibilities frontier. Therefore, it must be the case that firms' marginal rates of technical substitution are equal at any point on the frontier. Next, realize that because the MRTS is the ratio of the marginal products of inputs, $\frac{MP_L^{PI}}{MP_K^{PI}} = \frac{MP_L^{CI}}{MP_K^{CI}}$ at every point on the PPF. We can rearrange this equation to show that on the PPF, $\frac{MP_L^{PI}}{MP_L^{CI}} = \frac{MP_K^{PI}}{MP_K^{CI}}$.

That is, the ratios of an input's marginal product across firms are the same for all inputs on the PPF, which is the same as saying that the MRT on the PPF is related to inputs' marginal products.

So, we've defined the marginal rate of transformation MRT and shown that it is related to inputs' marginal products, and through these marginal products, the MRT is related to firms' marginal rates of technical substitution. They play a role linking exchange and input efficiency.

First, suppose they didn't—that the consumption and production sides of the market have independently come to efficient allocations. To give a specific example, say Elaine and Jerry are at an exchange-efficient allocation on the contract curve where the marginal rate of substitution between pancakes and cereal is 1.5: Each is willing to give up one-and-a-half pancakes to have one more bowl of cereal. (Equivalently, each would have to receive one-and-a-half pancakes to make up for the loss of 1 bowl of cereal.)

Suppose, as well, that the economy's production side has arrived at an efficient input allocation on the production possibilities frontier—where the marginal rate of transformation from pancakes to cereal is 1. That is, 1 pancake must be given up to make another bowl of cereal.

As it turns out, these outcomes result in a mismatch between consumers' willingness to substitute one good for the other and firms' abilities to switch from producing one to the other. To *consume* one more bowl of cereal, Elaine and Jerry are both willing to give up 1.5 pancakes for 1 bowl of cereal. But to *produce* one more bowl of cereal, society needs to only give up 1 pancake for 1 bowl of cereal. So, this economy has a disconnect. Because Elaine and Jerry's relative preferences for cereal are stronger than the relative costs of making cereal, we would want producers to allocate additional inputs toward cereal making. This example shows that exchange and input efficiency can both exist, but there could still be a missing link that keeps the economy from being completely efficient: This missing link is *output efficiency*.

Output efficiency exists when the tradeoffs on the consumption and production sides of an economy are equal. The tradeoff on the consumption side is the marginal rate of substitution. The tradeoff on the production side is the marginal rate of transformation. Output efficiency therefore requires $MRS = MRT$. In our example above, if Elaine and Jerry were at an efficient allocation where their common MRS was equal to the MRT, then output efficiency would exist.

Figure 15.12 shows the production possibilities frontier from Figure 15.11 with a consumer's indifference curves plotted with it. It doesn't really matter whose indifference curves we plot—Jerry's or Elaine's—because exchange efficiency means they both have the same MRS. That is, their indifference curves have the same slope at any efficient allocations.

The outcome in the example above, where Elaine's and Jerry's MRS is 1.5, and the MRT is 1, is point *M*. Exchange efficiency holds at this point because Elaine and Jerry

---

Figure 15.12 **Achieving Output Efficiency**

Output efficiency occurs at the tangency between the consumers' indifference curves and the production possibilities frontier, where the marginal rate of substitution MRS equals the marginal rate of transformation MRT. Point *M* shows a possible output combination of pancakes and cereal. Because it lies on the intersection of the PPF and the indifference curve U_M—not at the tangency—*M* is an inefficient output combination. *N*, which is located at the tangency between the PPF and U_N where $MRS = MRT = 1.25$, is an efficient output allocation.

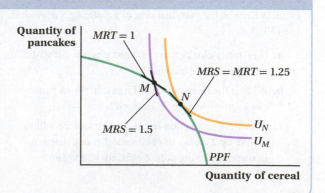

have the same MRS. Input efficiency also holds because the output combination is on the production possibilities frontier. But output efficiency does not hold because the indifference curve U_M that goes through output combination M cuts inside the PPF. This configuration establishes two important facts. First, output combinations above and to the right of U_M are preferable to those on U_M. Second, any output combination on or inside the PPF is feasible — that is, it can be produced with the available inputs. Thus, U_M and the PPF border a set of output combinations that are both (1) preferred to M and (2) possible to produce. This cannot be an efficient outcome because we are able to make Elaine and Jerry better off without using more inputs.

We can shift some production from pancakes to cereal until they reach output combination N, where the indifference curve U_N is tangent to the PPF. Therefore, $MRS = MRT$ (we've assumed both are 1.25 in the figure), and we arrive at output efficiency. We know this is the efficient output mix because no other feasible output combination exists that would give Elaine and Jerry higher utility. Thus, output efficiency is also marked by a tangency condition.

Another way to think about the $MRT = MRS$ condition is as a statement of the classic principle that marginal benefits should equal marginal costs. As we discussed earlier, the MRS between goods equals the goods' price ratio. Under perfect competition, as we saw in Chapter 8, a profit-maximizing firm will produce a quantity at which its marginal cost equals the good's price. For complete efficiency to hold in our cereal and pancakes example, the marginal rate of substitution must equal not only the ratio of the goods' prices but also the ratio of the goods' marginal costs of production: $MRS_{CP} = \dfrac{P_C}{P_P} = \dfrac{MC_C}{MC_P}$. Because the marginal cost of production equals the price of an input divided by the marginal product of that input (essentially, it's how much you have to spend on an extra amount of input to raise output by 1 unit), $MC_C = \dfrac{W}{MP_L^C}$ and $MC_P = \dfrac{W}{MP_L^P}$. Therefore, $\dfrac{MC_C}{MC_P} = \dfrac{MP_L^P}{MP_L^C}$. Earlier, we showed that this ratio of the marginal products of labor is also equal to the MRT. (We would arrive at the same answer if we used the marginal products of capital because these ratios are equivalent.) Saying that output efficiency implies $MRT = MRS$ is the same as saying that it equates the ratio of consumers' marginal utilities of goods to the marginal costs of producing those goods.

---

figure it out 15.5

In Ecoland, producers make both televisions and clocks. At current production levels, the marginal cost of producing a clock is $50 and the marginal cost of producing a television is $150.

a. How many clocks must Ecoland give up if it wishes to produce another television?

b. What is the marginal rate of transformation from clocks to televisions in Ecoland?

c. At current production levels, consumers are willing to give up 2 clocks to obtain another television. Is Ecoland achieving output efficiency? Explain.

Solution:

a. Because the marginal cost of producing a television is 3 times that of producing a clock, Ecoland must give up 3 clocks for each television it produces.

b. The marginal rate of transformation (MRT) measures how much of one output must be given up to obtain one more unit of another. Therefore, the MRT from clocks to televisions is 3.

c. Because consumers are only willing to trade 2 clocks for a television, the marginal rate of substitution (MRS) is 2. However, output efficiency requires that $MRS = MRT$. Therefore, Ecoland is not achieving output efficiency.

15.6 Markets, Efficiency, and the Welfare Theorems

The links between the marginal rate of transformation, marginal rate of substitution, and input and output prices have implications for the ability of markets to create efficient outcomes.

In our discussions of exchange, input, and output efficiencies, we acted as if it would be easy to shift input and output allocations through some basic interventions. But the examples were oversimplified — two inputs, two outputs, two firms, and two consumers. We also had full knowledge of firms' production functions and consumers' utility functions (because we made them up).

The real economy is vastly more complicated. Trying to centrally coordinate the allocations of inputs to production and consumption bundles to consumers, while also getting the optimal output mix, would be astronomically difficult. When governments have embraced that kind of central planning of the economy on a large scale, it has failed spectacularly. For example, the government of Venezuela has directly tried to dictate prices in markets for certain basic consumer goods like milk, sugar, meats, toilet paper, and soap. This has resulted in shortages, rationing, long lines for goods, and smuggling (not to mention violence and malnutrition). Although Venezuelan officials have blamed these problems on many sources (including Venezuelan citizens' overeating and the hoarding of Venezuela's "parasitic bourgeoisie"), these are the classic symptoms of misallocation in a managed economy.

Do the harsh realities of this complexity mean that our Pareto-efficient outcomes are only theoretical fantasies? Perhaps not. As we suggested earlier in discussing the relationship between exchange efficiency and utility-maximizing behavior, markets and prices might achieve efficiency even in the absence of an all-knowing, omnipotent economic controller.

In the section on exchange efficiency, we learned that if consumers maximize their utility (taking goods' prices as given), they will end up with the same marginal rates of substitution. Markets can meet the exchange efficiency condition in this way.

On the production side, for any given set of input prices, profit-maximizing firms will choose their input mix so that their marginal rate of technical substitution (MRTS) equals the input price ratio. This outcome equates firms' MRTS levels, the condition for input efficiency.

Barring some specific kinds of market failures we will discuss in the next two chapters, market prices alone create two of the three efficiency conditions. The final link, output efficiency, ties together these two conditions. One way to think about output efficiency's $MRS = MRT$ condition is that it sets the ratio of goods' prices equal to their marginal costs of production. If the goods are produced by a perfectly competitive industry, price will equal marginal cost. Therefore, the price and cost ratios are equal, satisfying output efficiency while preserving input and exchange efficiency. Decentralized, competitive markets can achieve all three efficiency conditions.

This is the ending we gave away at the start of our discussion of efficiency — markets can create efficient outcomes, even in the absence of interventions and forced allocations, by letting prices do the work: Input prices equate marginal rates of technical substitution in production, and output prices lead to the optimal output mix among producers and cause consumers to equate their marginal rates of substitution. The result, that *perfectly competitive markets in general equilibrium distribute resources in a Pareto-efficient way*, is called the **First Welfare Theorem**. It formalized Adam Smith's notion of the "invisible hand."

First Welfare Theorem
Theorem stating that perfectly competitive markets in general equilibrium distribute resources in a Pareto-efficient way.

The First Welfare Theorem comes with a lot of conditions. A big one is that firms and consumers take as given all the prices of goods and inputs. In other words, there is no market power. Market power prevents markets from reaching an efficient outcome because the output price ratio, which is now set by producers rather than taken as given, no longer needs to equal the marginal cost ratio. As a result, market power supports markups that drive a wedge between the two ratios and create output inefficiency. If firms or individuals have market power in buying goods, this, too, will create inefficiencies.

The First Welfare Theorem relies on other assumptions we shouldn't ignore. These include the absence of *asymmetric information*, *externalities*, and *public goods*. We discuss exactly what these are and why they can lead to market failures in Chapters 16 and 17.

Application: Output Efficiency among Manufacturing Firms in India

We learned how the output-efficient product mix reflects both cost (marginal rate of transformation or MRT) and demand (marginal rate of substitution or MRS) factors, and how well-functioning markets can lead firms to produce that optimal mix. In reality, those cost and demand factors are constantly changing. When changes occur, prices in competitive markets should change accordingly and spur firms to switch to the new optimal product mix.

Economists have documented a lot of evidence that firms, when choosing what products to make, do respond to market signals. In one study, however, a group of economists found that these sorts of product mix shifts are slower and less frequent among firms in India than in other economies.[8] As a result, India may lag behind other countries in output efficiency.

The study looks at the products made by over 4,000 Indian manufacturing firms and tracks their production of about 2,000 separate products. (To give you an idea of the level of detail this involves, example products from the iron and steel industry include welded steel tubular poles, stranded wire, and malleable iron castings.) Some of the firms made only one product, but many manufactured multiple products.

The results show an interesting contrast. In some ways, Indian firms' production choices look a lot like those in more developed countries. Bigger firms, on average, make a larger variety of products than smaller firms, for example. And when firms grow, they often do it by adding products. However, the results also show that overall product turnover—the frequency with which firms add new products or drop old ones—is significantly lower in India. For example, this "product churn" rate is less than two-thirds that computed using comparable U.S. data. What's particularly interesting is that this lower product turnover does not seem to occur because Indian firms are less likely to start making new products. Instead, they are less likely to drop old ones.

What might this result say about output efficiency in India? As costs and tastes change, the efficient quantity of certain products will rise while others will fall. If markets are working well, prices should change to reflect the new costs and tastes, and firms should respond to these price changes by shifting what they manufacture. More firms will begin making products whose markets are growing. Those making products for which the markets are shrinking will shut down or cut back on the manufacture of such products. This shift allows the inputs used to make those dying products to be put toward making ascending products instead. (Or, it might also be that a product itself isn't dying, but there is a

---

[8] Pinelopi K. Goldberg, Amit K. Khandelwal, Nina Pavcnik, and Petia Topalova, "Multiproduct Firms and Product Turnover in the Developing World: Evidence from India," *Review of Economics and Statistics* 92, no. 4 (November 2010): 1042–1049.

cost change that makes particular firms much less capable of manufacturing the product than before. In this case, those firms can shut down such product lines and allow more able firms to pick up the lost production.)

In India, firms appear reluctant to stop manufacturing products whose consumption levels (and likely profitability) are shrinking. Too many resources are devoted to making low-marginal-utility goods, upsetting the $MRT = MRS$ condition and output efficiency.

The study's authors speculate that the tight regulations on when and how firms can change the level and location of employment (part of the extensive Indian regulatory structure often referred to as the "License Raj") make it costly for firms to shut down existing production lines, even if they are making a faltering product or one that is a bad match for their abilities. As a result, the product mix becomes skewed away from the efficient combination and firms make too many things that people don't value very much. That is why the market isn't making India output efficient. ■

As we come to the end of our analysis of general equilibrium efficiency, remember: Efficiency does not imply equality nor does it have to match anyone's concept of fairness. Efficient markets can (and do) lead to unequal outcomes. That doesn't automatically imply that any effort to increase equity will necessarily harm efficiency but, in practice, it is often the case.

It is theoretically possible to change how equitable market outcomes are while still ensuring that the outcome is efficient. This result is a prediction of the **Second Welfare Theorem,** which says that (under the same assumptions made for the First Welfare Theorem) *any Pareto-efficient equilibrium in a perfectly competitive market can be achieved by choosing the right initial allocation of goods.* What this means is that, if we want efficient outcomes that are also equitable (by whatever standard we judge this), we can get to those outcomes by being careful about how we initially allocate goods and inputs across consumers and producers. Imagine, for example, shuffling the allocation of goods among consumers along the contract curve from an undesirably unequal market outcome to a point we feel is more equitable. By doing that, we're changing the allocation in a way that preserves efficiency while moving toward the outcome.[9] We could also do similar reshufflings in the input market and along the production possibilities frontier, preserving overall efficiency while obtaining a particular outcome we prefer.

Achieving this goal is not easy. First, there is the practical issue of how society would gather enough information about preferences and production technologies to know what the exact transfers should be. Second, the necessary reallocations would have to be what are called **lump-sum transfers,** *transfers to or from an individual where the size of the transfer cannot be affected in any way by the individual's choices.* These are the sort of reach-in-and-reshuffle reallocations we imagined a magic wand–waving economist making in our earlier discussions. In reality, lump-sum transfers are almost never used (and we could probably drop the "almost") because it is difficult to legislate taxes or subsidies that bear absolutely no relation to people's actions.[10]

Second Welfare Theorem Theorem stating that any given Pareto-efficient equilibrium can be achieved by choosing the right initial allocation of goods.

lump-sum transfer Transfer to or from an individual where the size of the transfer cannot be affected in any way by the individual's choices.

[9] Even this precise placement isn't necessary. What is required is that our intervention puts the allocation somewhere on the line that is tangent to consumers' indifference curves at an equitable efficient point. Trade among consumers at the market price (as those with low-marginal-product goods trade with others for high-marginal-product goods) will move any initial allocation on this line to the efficient point.

[10] Lump-sum taxes are also treacherous for politicians. People tend to really despise lump-sum taxes, probably because they feel (correctly) that there is nothing they can do to mitigate the burden of the tax and they are unfair. Indeed, capitation taxes (sometimes called "head taxes")—which are levied on each person regardless of her actions or status—are banned by the U.S. Constitution. Margaret Thatcher's ouster as the United Kingdom's prime minister was in large part driven by negative popular reaction toward her party's institution of a local tax system that approximated a lump-sum tax structure.

In reality, governments must try to achieve equity through transfers (taxes and subsidies) that depend on individuals' actions, such as taxes on income and payroll (which depend on how much you work), sales (how much you buy), and property (how valuable your home is), and subsidies like social security payments (which depend on how much you worked in the past and currently), Medicare (how many health services you consume), and so on. The problem is that these kinds of transfers also change the relative prices of the actions or goods that are taxed or subsidized. This creates wedges between the costs of goods and services and the post-tax or post-subsidy prices that consumers face, creating losses in efficiency (just as market power does).

This doesn't mean seeking more equitable outcomes is wrong. It just says that there will likely be some inefficiency introduced when trying to promote it.

15.7 Conclusion

In this chapter, we saw that all markets are interconnected: What happens in any given individual market affects countless other markets. Take a simple trip to the grocery store to purchase chocolate chip cookie dough ice cream. Before that single container of ice cream could make it into your hands, a Wisconsin dairy farmer milked cows, Brazilian processors distributed sugarcane, and the cacao plant was harvested. And that's just three of the many markets that contributed to the production of the ice cream. Many more markets—such as the market that produced the ice cream packaging—were also involved. This coming together of individual markets to produce a single good, and how they jointly influence one another, is one example of general equilibrium in action.

General equilibrium allows us to consider a wide variety of concepts that partial equilibrium cannot address. Issues about the desirability of economic outcomes can be explored using the conditions for exchange, input, and output efficiencies. If certain conditions are met, we saw that the free market will generate an efficient outcome without any intervention. In reality, however, these conditions are often not met. We've already extensively discussed in Chapters 9–11 one of these breaks in conditions, market power. In Chapters 16 and 17, we look at more ways in which market failures can lead to inefficient outcomes.

Summary

1. In this chapter, we've stepped outside our normal approach of looking at markets in isolation and have instead specifically contemplated how markets are interrelated. This recognition of markets' interrelatedness and explicit accounting for its effects is called **general equilibrium analysis.** It focuses on what is necessary for all markets to be in equilibrium simultaneously and what happens when they are. [Section 15.1]

2. General equilibrium analysis allows us to consider fundamental questions about whether market outcomes are desirable. Social welfare functions (functions that summarize the utility levels of every individual in society) are one tool that economists use to make such judgments, but they have several drawbacks. As a result, economists often instead focus on Pareto efficiency as a criterion. A market is **Pareto-efficient** if resources cannot be reallocated without making at least one person worse off. Individual markets must have three types of efficiency to create economy-wide efficiencies: **exchange efficiency, input efficiency,** and **output efficiency**. [Section 15.2]

3. **Edgeworth boxes** display a simple model economy with two consumers and two goods, and allow for an analysis of exchange efficiency. A Pareto-efficient allocation occurs at the tangency point between two consumers' indifference curves. The **consumption contract curve** represents all such Pareto-efficient allocations between any two individuals' consumption of two goods. [Section 15.3]

4. Input efficiency considers the production side of the economy, and occurs where two firms' isoquants are tangent, or where the firms' marginal rates of technical substitution are equal. The **production contract curve** maps out these efficient allocations across two producers, while the **production possibilities frontier (PPF)** looks at the possible output combinations of two goods given efficient production. [Section 15.4]

5. Output efficiency links the concepts of exchange and input efficiency, and exists when the tradeoffs on the consumption and production side of the economy are equal. The tradeoff between the production of any two goods is the **marginal rate of transformation (MRT),** equal to the slope of the production possibilities frontier. When the marginal rate of transformation equals the marginal rate of substitution (the consumption tradeoff), a market has achieved output efficiency. **[Section 15.5]**

6. Under certain conditions, markets can lead to efficiency without any interventions being necessary. The **First Welfare Theorem** shows how markets can result in Pareto-efficient distributions of goods. The **Second Welfare Theorem** states that every Pareto-efficient allocation is a general equilibrium outcome for some initial allocation. While the conditions that lead to market efficiency may not always hold in the real world, the market efficiency result is nevertheless a powerful finding that strengthens our understanding of both market efficiencies and market failures. **[Section 15.6]**

Review Questions

1. Describe the two branches of general equilibrium analysis.

2. Social welfare functions combine the utility levels of everyone in society into a single index. List three types of social welfare functions and discuss what they mean.

3. How do economists generally define efficiency in a market?

4. What are the three requirements of an efficient market?

5. What can the Edgeworth box be used to examine? What does an Edgeworth box plot?

6. What is the relationship between consumers' marginal rates of substitution and the goods' prices in an efficient market? How can this relationship be seen in an Edgeworth box?

7. How does the consumption contract curve relate to Pareto efficiency?

8. What does input efficiency imply about the relationship between the marginal rate of technical substitution and input prices? How can this relationship be seen in an Edgeworth box?

9. How does the production contract curve relate to Pareto efficiency?

10. How does the production possibilities frontier relate to the marginal rate of transformation?

11. What conditions are required for the First Welfare Theorem to hold?

12. What does the Second Welfare Theorem predict?

Problems

(Solutions to problems marked with an asterisk appear at the back of this book. Problems adapted to use calculus are available online.)

1. Peanut butter has always been thought to be a delicious, wholesome food. That is, until the FDA releases its Food Defect Guidelines that set maximum allowable amounts of rodent excreta that may be present in every jar (surprisingly, the maximum is not zero!). Following this release, the demand for peanut butter falls.

   a. What is the immediate effect on the price of peanut butter and the quantity consumed?

   b. Peanut butter and jelly are complements. What is the residual effect on the price of jelly?

   c. What effect does the change in the price of jelly you indicated in part (b) have on the demand for peanut butter?

   d. Does the demand effect you indicated in part (c) tend to push peanut butter prices and quantities back toward their original values, or farther away from them?

*2. Following a renewable fuels mandate the demand for yellow corn, the key ingredient in ethanol, skyrockets.

   a. What is the immediate effect of the increase in demand on the price and quantity of yellow corn?

   b. Yellow corn and white corn (the key ingredients in corn tortillas) are substitutes in production. As a result

   of the changes in the market for yellow corn, what happens to the supply of white corn?

   c. How does the changing supply of white corn affect its market price?

   d. As the price of white corn changes, what effect does that change have on the supply of yellow corn? Indicate the likely effects on both the price and quantity of yellow corn produced.

   e. Does the change in the price of white corn tend to push yellow corn prices and quantities back toward their initial values, or farther away from them?

*3. The following statements describe supply and demand conditions in the markets for cheese and wine, respectively.

   - The demand for cheese is given by $Q_c^d = 30 - P_c - P_w$, where Q_c^d is the quantity of cheese demanded each week in ounces, P_c is the price of a pound of cheese, and P_w is the price of a bottle of wine.

   - The demand for wine is given by $Q_w^d = 30 - P_c - P_w$.

   - The supply of cheese is given by $Q_c^s = P_c$.

   - The supply of wine is given by $Q_w^s = P_w$.

a. Are wine and cheese linked on the supply side of the market, or on the demand side?

b. Equate supply and demand in the cheese market, and simplify to express the price of cheese as a function of the price of wine.

c. Equate supply and demand in the wine market, and simplify to express the price of wine as a function of the price of cheese.

d. Substitute the expression for the price of wine you found in (c) into the equation you found in (b) to solve for the price of cheese.

e. Plug the price you calculated in (d) into the expression you derived in (c) to solve for the price of wine.

f. Plug the prices of wine and cheese you found in (d) and (e) back into either the supply or demand functions for wine and cheese to find the equilibrium quantities of wine and cheese that will be sold.

4. Consider the wine and cheese problem you solved in Problem 3. Suppose the demand for wine changes so that at every price, 10 fewer bottles are demanded.

a. Hold the price of cheese constant, and calculate the partial equilibrium effects of the change in the demand for wine. What happens to the price? What happens to the quantity?

b. Plug the new price of wine into the demand for cheese. Does the shock to the wine market cause the demand for cheese to increase or decrease?

c. Calculate the effect of the change in demand for cheese on the price of cheese and the quantity of cheese sold.

d. Plug the new price of cheese into the demand for wine. Does it cause the demand for wine to increase or decrease? Does the wine market get pushed farther from its initial equilibrium, or back toward it? How will these changes in the wine market feed back into the cheese market?

e. Following the steps taken in Problem 3, but using the new cheese demand function, solve for the new general equilibrium price and quantity of both wine and cheese.

f. How do the final general equilibrium price and quantity of wine you calculated in (e) compare to the partial equilibrium effects you calculated in part (a)?

5. Suppose that lettuce and tomatoes are goods that are related on the demand side of the market, and that both markets are in equilibrium. George and Janet are analyzing the effect of an increase in the demand for tomatoes. George is using a partial equilibrium framework, and Janet is using a general equilibrium framework.

a. True or False: George will predict a larger increase in the price of tomatoes than Janet will. Explain.

b. True or False: George will predict a larger increase in the quantity of tomatoes sold than Janet will. Explain.

c. True or False: The answers to parts (a) and (b) depend on whether lettuce and tomatoes are complements or substitutes. Explain.

6. In the central United States, farm ground is devoted to corn and beans as far as the eye can see. The supply of beans (in millions of bushels) is given by $Q_b^s = 2P_b - P_c$. The supply of corn is given by $Q_c^s = P_c - P_b$. Let the demand for beans be given by $Q_b^d = 30 - P_b$, and the demand for corn be given by $Q_c^d = 30 - P_c$.

a. Solve for the general equilibrium price and quantity of both beans and corn. (*Hint:* If you have trouble with this step, follow the procedures outlined in Problem 3.)

b. Suppose there is a shock to bean demand so that the quantity demanded at each price increases by 8 million bushels. The new demand for beans can be written as $Q_b^d = 38 - P_b$. Solve for the new general equilibrium price and quantity of beans and corn.

c. What happens to the price of beans and the quantity sold as a result of the demand increase?

d. What happens to the price of corn and quantity sold as a result of the increase in the demand for beans? Explain.

7. Bob, Carol, and Ted are residents of a tiny commune in darkest Peru. Bob currently has a utility level (U_b) of 55 utils, Carol's utility (U_c) is 35 utils, and Ted's utility (U_t) is 10 utils. Alice, the benevolent ruler of the commune, has discovered a policy that will allow her to redistribute utility between any two people she chooses in a util-to-util transfer.

a. If Alice believes the social welfare function is given by $W = \min(U_b, U_c, U_t)$,

  i. Recommend a transfer that will improve social welfare, if any such transfers are possible.

  ii. What is the highest level of welfare that the commune can achieve, and how must utility be divided among Bob, Carol, and Ted?

b. If Alice believes the social welfare function is given by $W = U_b + U_c + U_t$,

  i. Recommend a transfer that will improve social welfare, if any such transfers are possible.

  ii. What is the highest level of welfare that the commune can achieve, and how must utility be divided among Bob, Carol, and Ted?

c. If Alice believes the social welfare function is given by $W = U_b \times U_c \times U_t$,

  i. Recommend a transfer that will improve social welfare, if any such transfers are possible.

  ii. What is the highest level of welfare that the commune can achieve, and how must utility be divided among Bob, Carol, and Ted?

8. Dante and Naia get utility from having money. Dante's utility function is $U_d = 10M^{1/3}$; Naia's utility function

is $U_n = 10M^{1/2}$. Dante currently has $1,000; Naia has $400.

a. The Rawlsian social welfare function values egalitarianism. Compute the value of the Rawlsian social welfare function for Dante and Naia.

b. A transfer program will take $100 from Dante and transfer it to Naia. Does this transfer program improve welfare under a Rawlsian social welfare function?

c. Suppose, instead, the program described in (c) will take $100 from Naia and transfer it to Dante. Evaluate the effect of this program on social welfare for both of the social welfare functions.

d. If a transfer from Dante to Naia results in a decrease in Rawlsian social welfare, then why does a transfer from Naia to Dante not increase social welfare?

e. Here's another social welfare function that places some value on egalitarianism: $W = U_d + U_n - 0.3(|U_d - U_n|)$. Dante's and Naia's utilities are added together, but as the difference between their utilities increases, social welfare declines. Compute the value of this social welfare function for Dante and Naia, and then evaluate the transfer described in (b). Would a society that values egalitarianism in this way make the same recommendation regarding this transfer as a Rawlsian society? Explain.

9. Abel, Baker, and Charlie are identical triplets with identical tastes. The utility they get from consuming various amounts of bacon, eggs, and cheese is summarized in the following table:

# of Units Consumed	Utility from Bacon	Utility from Eggs	Utility from Cheese
1	100	60	80
2	155	110	135
3	175	150	183
4	190	180	210
5	200	200	225

Thus, if Abel has 4 pieces of bacon and 3 eggs, his total utility will be $190 + 150$, or 340.

a. Suppose that Abel initially has 5 pieces of bacon, Baker has 5 eggs, and Charlie has 5 pieces of cheese. Assuming that bacon, eggs, and cheese all trade one-for-one in the marketplace, suggest a series of Pareto-improving trades that will raise everyone's overall utility.

b. What allocation does each end up with when all gains are exhausted?

c. Show that once all gains are exhausted, if we force Abel to trade any of his goods for any of Baker's goods, neither will be made better off, and at least one will be made worse off.

*10. Consider the Edgeworth box diagram below, which illustrates the amount of peaches and cream in the refrigerator of Billy Joe and Bobby Sue:

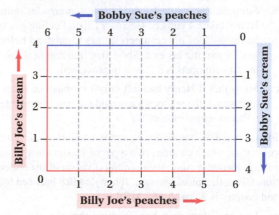

a. How many peaches do Billy Joe and Bobby Sue have in their fridge?

b. How much cream do Billy Joe and Bobby Sue have in their fridge?

c. Suppose that Billy Joe pulls 5 peaches and 1 pint of cream out of the fridge, and says, "You can have the rest" to Bobby Sue. Illustrate this allocation of peaches and cream by placing a point in the Edgeworth box. Label the point A.

d. Bobby Sue pulls the remaining peaches and cream out of the refrigerator, and comments, "Hey—I'm a bit long on cream and short on peaches here. Give me a couple of your peaches and take one of my creams." Represent this reallocation of peaches and cream by placing a second point in the Edgeworth box. Label the point B.

e. Billy Joe happens to find a couple of extra peaches behind last night's gnocchi leftovers, and proudly proclaims, "Finders, keepers!" Represent the effects of Billy Joe's discovery by altering your Edgeworth box. Assume that Bobby Sue acknowledges and respects the "finders, keepers" rule.

11. Consider the Edgeworth box below, which represents the amount of tea and crumpets available to Eliza and Henry:

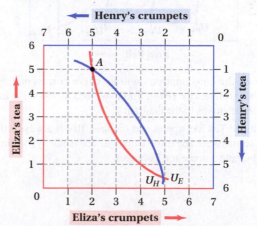

a. Suppose that Eliza and Henry are currently at point A. How many servings of tea and how many crumpets are each enjoying?

b. Suppose that while Eliza is using the powder room, Henry takes 4 cups of tea from Eliza. Feeling guilty, he leaves 2 of his crumpets on her nightstand before hastily making his exit. Show that this reallocation of tea and crumpets is a Pareto improvement.

c. Show that if Henry had left only 1 crumpet on Eliza's nightstand, the reallocation would not have represented a Pareto improvement.

12. Johnny and June are divorcing and must divide their music collection, which contains two types of music: country and folk. A mediator suggests an initial division of the collection. Given the initial division, Johnny's MRS between folk and country is 3, and June's MRS is 1.

a. Use an Edgeworth box to show that the allocation of music is inefficient. Be sure to draw indifference curves for both Johnny and June, and to show their respective marginal rates of substitution at the initial allocation.

b. Suggest a general reallocation that could potentially make both parties better off. Explain who would have to give up folk music and who would have to give up country.

c. After some reallocation, Johnny's MRS and June's MRS are equal. Show that the allocation is Pareto-efficient.

13. Consider the following Edgeworth box diagram that illustrates the preferences of Ed and Peggy for fish and chips:

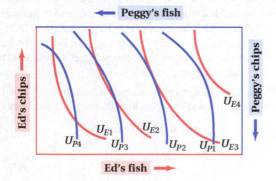

Draw the consumption contract curve corresponding to these preferences. (*Hint:* You may need to add some indifference curves to the diagram.)

14. Bill and Ted like apples and oranges. Bill is always willing to substitute 1 apple for 1 orange. Ted is always willing to substitute 1 apple for 2 oranges.

a. Assume that there are 10 apples and 10 oranges to split between Bill and Ted. Construct an appropriately sized Edgeworth box for them.

b. Draw indifference curves for both Bill and Ted in your Edgeworth box. Draw Bill's indifference curves with thick lines and Ted's with thin lines. (*Hint:* Remember that both Bill and Ted believe that apples and oranges are perfect substitutes!)

c. Demonstrate that any initial allocation of apples and oranges in which Bill and Ted each have some apples and some oranges is Pareto-inefficient.

d. Find a few Pareto-efficient allocations; then shade the consumption contract curve. [*Hint:* You showed in part (c) that both parties having both goods couldn't be efficient!]

15. Sydney and Simon both like coffee and pie. Their utility functions are identical: $U_{\text{Simon}} = U_{\text{Sydney}} = C^{1/2}P^{1/2}$, where C is the number of cups of coffee and P is the number of slices of pie.

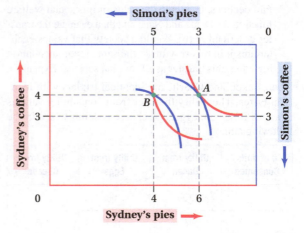

Sydney's and Simon's allocations of coffee and pie are illustrated in the accompanying Edgeworth box. The current allocation of coffee and pie occurs at point A: Simon has 2 cups of coffee and 3 slices of pie; Sydney has 4 cups of coffee and 6 slices of pie.

a. Is the current allocation of coffee and pie Pareto-optimal? How do you know?

b. Suppose that the social welfare function is given by $W = U_{\text{Simon}} \times U_{\text{Sydney}}$. Show that the allocation at A is less socially desirable than the allocation at B.

c. Is the allocation at B Pareto-optimal?

d. Comment: Just because an allocation is Pareto-efficient doesn't mean it must produce the most welfare; just because a different allocation produces a lot of welfare doesn't mean it is Pareto-efficient.

*16. The Edgeworth box below shows how castaways Tom and Hank are allocating labor and capital to the production of two goods, food and clothing:

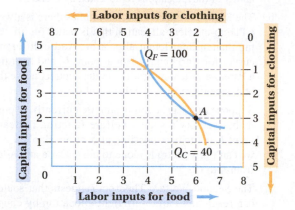

The economy is currently at point *A*.

a. How many units of labor and capital are being used in the production of each good?

b. How many units of food are being produced? Clothing?

c. Suggest a simple reallocation of labor and capital between food and clothing that will enable Tom and Hank to enjoy more food and clothing than they currently produce.

17. In Milwaukee, labor (*L*) and capital (*K*) are used in combination to produce both motorcycles and beer. In the motorcycle industry, the $MRTS_{LK}$ is 1; in the beer industry, the $MRTS_{LK}$ is 3.

a. Is the economy productively efficient? Explain how you know.

b. If, in (a), you indicated that the economy is not productively efficient, suggest a reallocation of labor and capital that can lead to a Pareto improvement—both more motorcycles *and* more beer!

*18. Consider the production contract curve in the graph below that illustrates efficient allocations of labor and capital to the production of two goods, guns and roses:

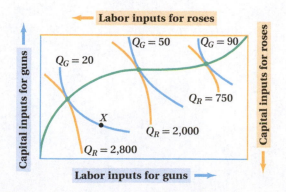

a. Use the information in the production contract curve to draw the production possibilities frontier for guns and roses. Put roses on the horizontal axis and guns on the vertical axis. Assume that when all resources are devoted to gun production, 100 guns can be produced; when all resources are devoted to rose production, 3,000 roses can be grown.

b. Locate point *X* in the Edgeworth box. Draw a corresponding point *X* on your production possibilities frontier. Be as accurate as possible in locating this point.

19. Consider the production possibilities frontier depicted below, which shows the different combinations of guns and roses an economy can produce when it uses all its inputs efficiently:

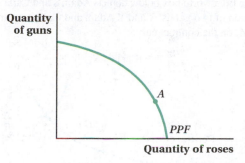

a. If the MRT_{GR} at point *A* is 2.0, and the marginal product of labor in the gun industry is 12, what must the marginal product of labor be in the rose industry?

b. If the MRT_{GR} at point *A* is 2.0 and the marginal product of capital in the gun industry is 6, what must the marginal product of capital in the rose industry be?

20. The economy of Nashville is producing both guitars and Cadillacs. The production possibilities frontier for guitars and Cadillacs is shown in the accompanying figure, along with an indifference curve showing the utility of a representative consumer. The economy is currently operating at point *A*, where it is both productively efficient and efficient in exchange. If, at *A*, the marginal utility of another guitar is 10, and the marginal utility of another Cadillac is 5, while the marginal product of labor in the guitar industry 10, what must the marginal product of labor be in producing Cadillacs?

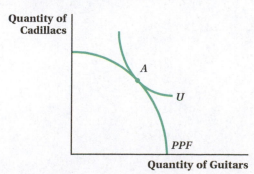

21. In Switzerland, the marginal cost of producing a chocolate is $2, and the marginal cost of producing a watch is $20.

    a. How many chocolates must Swiss producers give up if they wish to produce another watch?

    b. What is the marginal rate of transformation from chocolates to watches in Switzerland?

    c. The marginal utility of a Swiss watch to consumers is currently 30; the marginal utility of a chocolate is currently 10. What is Swiss consumers' marginal rate of substitution between chocolate and watches?

    d. Is Switzerland achieving output efficiency? Explain and then illustrate your answer with a carefully constructed graph.

22. The Edgeworth box below depicts Adam's and Carla's allocation of two goods, X and Y. Adam and Carla are currently at A, on the contract curve.

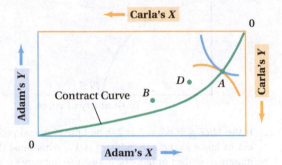

a. When allocating goods, Pareto efficiency seems like a property we should be pleased with. But is Pareto efficiency everything? Comment critically on the desirability of the allocations represented by A and B.

b. The Second Welfare Theorem implies there is always a Pareto-efficient allocation that is better for all people than an inefficient allocation. Add indifference curves for Carla and Adam at point B, and then find a Pareto-efficient allocation on the contract curve that both would prefer. Label that point C.

c. Suppose that Carla and Adam are currently at point A, but society's social welfare function indicates point C is the best possible allocation. Explain why we can't rely on trade alone to move Carla and Adam from A to C.

d. The Second Welfare Theorem suggests that society can reach any Pareto-efficient allocation by choosing an appropriate redistribution and then letting individuals trade. Suppose the government decided to redistribute the initial allocation of X and Y in hopes of achieving the socially optimal allocation at C. Explain why redistributing to allocation B might eventually produce that allocation, but redistributing to allocation D would not.

Asymmetric Information

Almost everybody ends up thinking about a used car at some point in their life. People buy over 35 million used cars and small trucks in the United States each year, more than double the number of new vehicles purchased.[1] And all of those buyers must contemplate the quality of the used cars under their consideration. If buying from an individual, they wonder why that person is selling the car. If buying from a dealer, they wonder if the car was a rental or was abused by a series of reckless drivers who might not have owned the car. Or, perhaps the car was repossessed from an owner who never did any maintenance.

The analyses we've done up until this point don't fully capture the economics of situations like these. That's because in the topics we've analyzed so far, we assumed that economic decision makers have all the relevant information about the markets in which they operate. Consumers know all the attributes of the goods. Firms know their marginal costs, how productive their employees are, and so on. That is, we've described markets with **complete information**—*a situation where all market participants know everything important for making economic decisions.*

In the real world, however, information is often neither free nor commonly shared among all parties in a transaction. **Asymmetric information**[2] is the economist's term for *a situation where there is an imbalance of information across participants in an economic transaction*—where one side knows things the other side doesn't. It takes an extra set of tools to understand these types of situations.

Asymmetric information can have a profound impact on markets—an impact that is often quite negative. Indeed, if the information gaps are large enough, a market may *completely shut down* even if everyone would benefit from trade if it occurred. Interestingly, the people who suffer from such market failure include not only those with an information disadvantage, but also those who have the information. We'll explain why below. Given that asymmetric information can destroy the large gains in consumer and producer surplus that occur in markets, many institutions exist to lessen the problem, and we will talk about these institutions in this chapter as well.

complete information A situation where all market participants know everything important for making economic decisions.

asymmetric information A situation where there is an imbalance of information across participants in an economic transaction.

16.1 The Lemons Problem and Adverse Selection

One common form of asymmetric information in markets is the **lemons problem,** *an asymmetric information problem that occurs when a seller knows more about the quality of the good to be sold than the buyer does*. The used car example cited in the introduction is one such case. It is, in fact, the origin of the problem's name, because poor-quality cars

lemons problem An asymmetric information problem that occurs when a seller knows more about the quality of the good he is selling than does the buyer.

---

[1] U.S. Department of Transportation. *National Transportation Statistics.*

[2] Economic situations with *symmetric information*—meaning that all participants in a transaction share the same knowledge—include both cases of complete information and cases in which market participants don't have full knowledge, but are *equally* ignorant.

are sometimes referred to as "lemons." The issue was first formalized by the economist George Akerlof and is partly why he won the Nobel Prize.[3]

To understand the lemons problem, consider the following example (overly simplified, though it makes clear the central issue). Suppose there are two types of used cars: good ones ("plums") and bad ones ("lemons"). Half of all used cars are plums, and the other half are lemons. Potential buyers value plum cars at $10,000, but lemons at nothing. Sellers value their plum cars at $8,000 and also value lemons at nothing.

Observable Quality

Clearly, if buyers and sellers can observe the quality of the car, then sellers will sell the plum cars they value at $8,000 to the buyers who value the car at $10,000, and any price between the two values will make them both better off. Lemons have no value to either their current owners or potential buyers, so none will sell and no one will be worse off.

When quality is fully observable to everyone, buyers and sellers in the market are at least as well off—and many are better off—because of the transactions in the used car market. This is the way in which well-functioning markets work and raise the welfare of the markets' participants.

Unobservable Quality

But now consider what happens under asymmetric information, when sellers know if their cars are plums or lemons, but buyers do not. All that buyers know is that half of used cars available for sale are plums and half are lemons. They realize the probability that any particular car is a plum is 50%.

Because the buyers value a plum at $10,000 and a lemon at $0, and a car here has a 50% chance of being either, the most they would be willing to pay for a used car is $(\$10,000 \times 0.50) + (\$0 \times 0.50) = \$5,000$. Anything more than that and they will be worse off in expectation: Any one car only has an expected value of $5,000.

Now think about the owner of a plum deciding whether to sell it. This seller values the car at $8,000, but because buyers can't know for sure whether or not this car is a plum, the seller can't get more than $5,000 for it. Therefore, the seller won't sell a plum car, only a lemon. But that's the problem: Buyers aren't stupid. They recognize that the owners of good cars won't sell when the price is $5,000, so buyers know that any used car available for sale *must* be a lemon. Because buyers don't want lemons for $5,000, they are not willing to buy any used car that is actually offered for sale.

This is the tragedy of the lemons problem. We have a situation in which we know that if everyone had access to complete information, lots of cars would change hands and many people would be better off (because buyers value the plum cars more than their former owners did). With enough asymmetric information, however, no sales take place. There is a *market failure*. All those potential gains from exchange are destroyed because one side knows more than the other.

Adverse Selection

This example brings up two important points about asymmetric information and the lemons problem. First, the existence of quality differences is not, by itself, the cause of the market failure. With complete information on both sides, higher-quality products would

[3] George Akerlof, "The Market for 'Lemons': Quality Uncertainty and the Market Mechanism," *Quarterly Journal of Economics* 84, no. 3 (August 1970): 488–500. Akerlof earned the right to name the problem—he actually called it the "Lemons Principle"—by virtue of being the first to formalize it. It is good that he chose the name as modestly as he did; it's easier to remember how to correctly spell "lemons" than "Akerlof."

have higher prices and lower-quality products would have lower prices. (Here, those prices would be between $8,000 and $10,000 for high-quality cars and $0 for lemons.) Consumers with a high valuation for quality would pay for it and no problem would exist for the market. Every buyer who would be willing to pay more for a good than it is worth to the seller would be able to buy it. The market will efficiently allocate goods.

The lemons problem arises when buyers and sellers have different information about quality. This asymmetry leads to poor-quality goods being disproportionately put up for sale. That is, the average quality of items *that are offered for sale* is lower than the average quality of all such items, *including those not for sale*. This is exactly what happened in the simple example above: The average value of used cars to buyers was $5,000, but the average value of those offered for sale was $0. This prevented mutually beneficial trades from happening that otherwise would have if everyone had had full information.

A situation where there are stronger incentives for "bad" types of a product to be involved in a transaction than "good" types of the product is called **adverse selection** (so named because the selection of types in the market tilts adversely toward those of bad quality). In our used car case, lemons are the "bad" types. They are disproportionately likely to be put up for sale because buyers can't tell the difference between lemons and good cars. This makes the price that buyers are willing to pay for a used car of uncertain quality too low to induce owners of good cars to sell. The sellers who *are* willing to offer their cars for sale at this price must, therefore, have lemons. Adverse selection on the buyers' side of the market can also cause problems. We'll see that below in our discussion of the insurance market.

The second important point in this example is that information asymmetry harms not only the less-informed participants but also those who have *more* information. Both sides lose because information asymmetries keep sales from taking place that would have benefited both buyers and sellers. Paradoxically, rather than their information edge being an advantage for the sellers, it ends up hurting them.

Could sellers get around this problem by telling potential buyers that their car is indeed a plum? The problem is that lemon sellers have an incentive to lie about the quality of their cars and try to pass them off as plums. If buyers recognize this incentive to lie, then a seller saying the car is a plum won't be informative about its true quality. Without additional information, a buyer won't be able to tell a plum *seller* (claiming a high-quality car) from a lemon *seller* (also claiming a high-quality car) any better than he can tell a plum from a lemon. But if there is a way to *credibly* convey the truth to buyers, it could fix the problem, as we discuss below.

The specific example we ran through above was, as we said, purposely simplistic. Lemons problems usually don't completely destroy markets. After all, we see plenty of cars purchased in the used car market in the real world. However, adverse selection can still reduce trade to a level below what is economically efficient. The vicious cycle of uncertain quality still reduces buyers' willingness to pay, leading in turn to low-quality cars being disproportionately offered for sale, further reducing buyers' willingness to pay and exacerbating adverse selection, and on and on. In our simple example, this feedback process was so strong that buyers were unwilling to pay for *any* car brought to market, since it was sure to be a lemon. But real-world factors can slow down the adverse-selection feedback before it spins a market into oblivion.

For example, in reality there is a much broader distribution of quality among used cars than the two-type distribution in our example. Furthermore, buyers and sellers don't all share the same value for each quality type. These factors tend to diminish the disastrous effect of information asymmetries on markets. There will be disproportionately more "worse" types offered for sale, and the amount of trade will still be inefficiently low, but some cars will be bought and sold.

adverse selection A situation where there are stronger incentives for "bad" types of a product to be involved in a transaction than "good" types of the product.

Adverse selection is why, when considering buying a used car, you are likely to have the type of concerns about quality discussed in the introduction to this chapter. You recognize, for example, that the late-model Kia you are considering is likely to be of lower quality than the average late-model Kia, because owners satisfied with their current Kias are less likely to put them on the market. This holds down your willingness to pay for such cars, reinforcing in turn the reluctance of owners of good-quality Kias to sell them.

Other Examples of the Lemons Problem

Potential lemons problems abound in the economy. We've discussed the most well-known example—used cars—but "lemons" can exist in any market where the quality of a product is better known by the seller than by the buyer. Online sales might be especially vulnerable to lemons issues: Transactions are not face-to-face, and potential buyers typically cannot physically inspect the product beforehand.

Adverse selection is common in services and factor (input) markets, too. People seeking to remodel their homes confront the lemons problem, for example. It is difficult to judge the quality of workmanship to expect from a contractor. This concern might make homeowners reluctant to offer adequate compensation to contractors who bid on a job. But this reluctance would, in turn, reduce the likelihood of a high-quality (but expensive) contractor taking the job, making it more likely that a contractor who would take a job at this lower pay level would turn out to be incompetent.

In input markets, lemons problems can show up in used capital goods sales. Trucks, machine tools, and even buildings are often bought from sellers who know more about their quality than buyers. Labor markets can have their own adverse selection issues. Suppose workers differ in, and know, their "quality"—which could be their willingness to work hard, their honesty, or their knowledge of the tasks necessary for the job. If a firm could readily observe the quality type of any worker, it could pay him his marginal product (which would be higher for higher-quality workers), and everything would be fine. But if the employer can't easily differentiate good workers from bad ones, it will only be willing to offer a wage equal to an average of the marginal products of the different worker types. This result can make higher-quality workers less likely to apply for a job, and lower-quality workers will be adversely selected in the applicant pool.

Mechanisms That Mitigate Lemons Problems

Because lemons problems can destroy so much economic value, many real-world mechanisms have been developed to lessen information asymmetries. We start again with the used car market, but the lessons we draw from this can be much more general. The fixes work in one of three ways: by giving buyers the ability to observe a car's quality before any transaction; by punishing sellers who try to sell cars they know are lemons without admitting those problems to prospective buyers; by reducing adverse selection with an increased number of high-quality used cars brought to market. Note that the second and third sets of mechanisms don't allow buyers to observe a car's qualities directly. Instead, the second set creates incentives for sellers to be truthful about quality, and the third set incentivizes owners to put good-quality used cars on the market. We'll discuss some examples of each type of mechanism in this section.

Reducing Asymmetric Information Directly   There are several ways potential buyers can learn about the quality of a used car. Buyers can hire a trusted mechanic who is not affiliated with the seller to inspect the car before agreeing to purchase it, for example. Owners can make their cars' ownership and maintenance records available. (Sellers may voluntarily take the initiative to close the information gap because, as we said before, even the parties with more information lose when the lemons problem causes market failure.)

Some companies have made a successful business model out of reducing information asymmetries. AutoCheck and CarMax specialize in providing information about used cars. Customers can type a car's unique vehicle information number (VIN) into either company's website and immediately see the ownership history of the car, and sometimes the maintenance records, too. This is valuable information for buyers, but sellers also benefit from the service. In fact, a large fraction of AutoCheck and CarMax searches are paid for not by buyers, but instead by auto dealers who have bought subscriptions that allow their customers to do background searches on cars that they are considering.

Incentives for Truthful Quality Reporting The second set of mechanisms reduce the lemons problem by making it costly for sellers to be dishonest about their cars' quality. These can work even if they don't actually give the buyer all the information about a car that the seller knows.

One mechanism is for the government to make it illegal to knowingly pass off a lemon as a plum car and to punish sellers who do so. In some locations, disclosure requirements are in place, for example, if a seller has engaged in certain kinds of suspect practices in the past.

But there are nongovernmental approaches, too. A classic example of this type of mechanism is reputation, a potential buyer's perception of a seller. Businesses that operate honestly (by selling good-quality cars or, when selling lower-quality cars, by disclosing this and selling at an appropriately discounted price) will develop a reputation for doing so. This makes consumers more likely to do business with them. Dishonest dealers, on the other hand, will suffer when word gets out about their practices.

Reputation incentives work best when a business expects to operate for a long time, because a good reputation pays off in increased business in the future. A "fly-by-night" seller may be willing to cheat to make a quick buck today, knowing he will have moved on to something else before his loss of reputation would really matter.

Warranties can also reduce adverse selection. High-quality car sellers can communicate the value of their cars to buyers by offering to fix any problems that occur after the sale, or even return the buyer's money if she is unsatisfied. Just as with reputation, warranties don't solve the lemons problem by getting rid of the asymmetric information. They instead give sellers an incentive to be truthful about the quality of their cars. It's expensive — too expensive — for a seller to offer a warranty on a car he knows is a lemon. The seller has, as they say, "put his money where his mouth is." Recognizing this, if a buyer sees that a car will be sold under warranty, she can reasonably infer that it is a higher-quality car. Cars without warranties are likely to be of lower quality. (And that's fine, again as long as the price reflects their lower quality.[4])

Well-designed legislation and regulation can also counteract adverse selection. Most states have "lemon laws." As the name suggests, these laws focus on conditions that must be met in auto sales. The laws essentially mandate short-term warranties for dealer-sold used cars under specified age and mileage limits. These warranty mandates help keep low-quality cars out of the market. Note that it is not necessarily efficient to keep low-quality used cars from being sold altogether. There may be people who would prefer inferior cars as long as these cars are priced appropriately. What's important is not that low-quality cars are removed from the market, but rather that all potential buyers recognize them as such.

---

[4] The fact that warranties are relatively less expensive to offer for good cars rather than bad ones, and therefore act as an effective way for buyers to distinguish between cars of otherwise unobservable quality, means that warranties are what economists call *signals*. Signals are a particular type of solution to asymmetric information problems that we will discuss in more detail later in the chapter.

Increasing the Average Quality of Cars Placed on the Market   The lemons problem can be lessened if something reduces adverse selection. Bringing more plums onto the market, even if the quality of individual cars is still unobservable, can do this. Raising the average quality of cars available increases buyers' willingness to pay for used cars. This increase in demand further encourages owners of higher-quality used cars to sell. In the end, the amount of trade in the market rises, making both buyers and sellers better off.

Leasing programs are one way to make this happen. With a lease, a buyer, or "lessee," takes ownership of a car for a set period of time, with the option to return the car to the seller (the "lessor") at the end of the contract period. By encouraging the return of vehicles at a predetermined date regardless of their quality, leasing can increase the number of higher-quality cars on the used car market and reduce the adverse selection of only the lemon owners putting their vehicles up for sale.

Beyond Used Cars   The used car example shows generally how the lemons problem, while potentially very damaging to markets, also offers powerful incentives for people and firms to take actions that limit its reach. It's easy to find similar mechanisms at work in other markets with asymmetric information.

For instance, we see similar mechanisms at work in home repair services and labor market examples, discussed earlier. In home repair, referral networks enable homeowners to learn more about contractors' performance and specialties before they hire them. Angie's List is a company that compiles grades on contractors from their previous clients. Homeowners can use these grades when considering which contractor to hire. (Such information is valuable. Over a million people have purchased memberships allowing them to view these grades.) Angie's List and other business-rating organizations like the Better Business Bureau also enhance the benefits to contractors of preserving a good reputation.

Referrals and reputations play a key role in labor markets, too. Job applicants will often list references on their résumés. Firms then check with these references and previous employers about a potential employee's performance. Other institutions — schools, trade associations, and so on — act as third parties that certify competence at various tasks. There are even "warranties" of sorts in labor markets. Employees are frequently hired on a provisional or intern basis at pay rates below their position's typical pay, making it relatively easy to terminate such employees after an introductory period.

These examples can help markets. In some cases, these mechanisms are so effective that they remove the effects of information asymmetries on trading. Nevertheless, it's important to remember that even then, the lemons problem still influences those markets.

---

 figure it out 16.1

Go online for interactive, step-by-step help in solving the following problem.

Suppose that consumers value a high-quality used laptop computer at a price of $400, while they value a low-quality used laptop at $100. The supply of high-quality laptops is $Q_H = P_H - 100$, while the supply of low-quality laptops is $Q_L = 2P_L - 50$. Potential buyers cannot tell the difference between high-quality and low-quality laptops when purchasing one.

a. Assume that buyers believe there is a 50% probability that a used laptop will be of high quality. What would be the price that buyers are willing to pay for any used laptop?

b. If the price determined in (a) is offered in the market for used laptops, how many high-quality laptops will be made available in the market? How many low-quality laptops will be available in the market? Are buyers correct in their assumption that 50% of the used laptops available for sale are of high quality? Explain.

c. What would you expect to happen over time as information about the true odds of buying a high-quality used laptop becomes known? Explain.

Solution:

a. If buyers expect that 50% of the used laptops available are of high quality (meaning that the other 50% are of low quality), then the expected value of a laptop is equal to

$$0.50 \times \$400 + 0.50 \times \$100 = \$200 + \$50 = \$250$$

Therefore, $250 would be the most that buyers are willing to pay for a used laptop.

b. If the price of a used laptop is $250, then the quantity supplied of high-quality laptops is $Q_H = P_H - 100 = 250 - 100 = 150$. The quantity supplied of low-quality used laptops is $Q_L = 2P_L - 50 = 2(250) - 50 = 500 - 50 = 450$.

Therefore, there will be 600 used laptops for sale (150 of high quality and 450 of low quality).

The probability of buying a used laptop of high quality is not 50%, but actually equal to $150/600 = 0.25$ or 25%. Because of asymmetric information, buyers are not willing to pay a very high price for a used laptop. Therefore, the owners of high-quality laptops will be reluctant to sell them, while the owners of low-quality laptops will be eager to sell them. This changes the proportion available in the market.

c. Over time, buyers will adjust their expected value of used laptops. This will further reduce the price buyers are willing to pay. Owners of high-quality used laptops will be even less inclined to sell them, reducing even more the proportion of high-quality used laptops available. Ultimately, it is possible that the market could end up with only low-quality used laptops available.

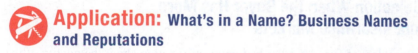 ## Application: What's in a Name? Business Names and Reputations

For many companies, reputation is one of their most important assets—an asset that can take a lot of time, effort, and resources to build. (You could even think of reputation as a type of capital input.) In markets where asymmetric information is a potential problem, a good reputation is a very valuable thing. But reputations can be fragile, too. As Warren Buffett once said, "It takes 20 years to build a reputation and five minutes to ruin it."

Most companies' reputations are embodied in their names. For customers, a company's name may summarize not just what products the company sells, but also the way it sells those products: whether the products are delivered honestly, on time, and with a promise to refund the price or replace them if the customer is not completely satisfied.

This close tie between a company's name and its reputation implies that when something isn't right—when a company has earned a sufficiently bad reputation for one reason or another—it might change its name altogether. The hope is that by breaking the link between its products and its name, the company can put its customers' minds at ease, limiting the damage a poor reputation has done to its profits. Such a company essentially prefers no reputation to a bad one.

A pair of studies by economist Ryan McDevitt determined exactly that.[5] Examining the records of thousands of plumbing companies in Illinois, McDevitt showed that name changes are not so unusual. Over the course of just one year, about 1 in 12 plumbing companies changed its name. With regard to names and reputation, a strong predictor of an eventual name change is a large number of customer complaints to the Better Business Bureau. Name-changing companies averaged fully seven times more complaints as did name-keepers. And for a given number of complaints, companies that had been in business longer were less likely to change their name, suggesting an

[5] Ryan C. McDevitt, "Names and Reputations: An Empirical Analysis," *American Economic Journal: Microeconomics* (2011), and "'A' Business by Any Other Name: Firm Name Choice as a Signal of Firm Quality," *Journal of Political Economy* (2014).

established company might try to weather a string of bad customer service outcomes (why throw the reputation baby out with the complaint bathwater?), whereas a newer business might simply decide to start over.

McDevitt also found that even among name-keepers, the particular *type* of name a company chooses reveals something about its reputation. According to the data he compiled for the Chicago area, about 20% of the plumbing companies have a name that starts with either a number or the letter "A," usually multiples of them (A-AAAA Sewer & Drains and AAAA Scott's Plumbing are good examples). Such a name choice puts these companies early in alphabetical order, making them more quickly visible in listings. McDevitt demonstrated that these "A" plumbers receive systematically more complaints and worse ratings on Angie's List and Yelp than do other plumbers. It appears they are willing to trade off a solid reputation and a more traditional (but difficult to find) business name for the higher visibility this kind of name will yield when would-be customers make relatively uninformed searches.

These issues extend well beyond plumbers. For example, ValuJet Airlines changed its name to AirTran after a deadly crash amidst reports of lax maintenance. The Weinstein Company dropped the name of its founder, Harvey Weinstein, after many allegations of sexual assault were lodged against him in the media. The name change wasn't enough, however; the company was forced to file for bankruptcy just a few months later. ■

Adverse Selection When the Buyer Has More Information: Insurance Markets

In the lemons problem above, the seller had more information about the quality of the good than the buyer. But information asymmetries where buyers know more than sellers can cause problems, too. Insurance markets are one example.

In insurance markets, buyers may know more about their riskiness than the company does. Think about what insurance is: a good that compensates a policyholder when some event occurs. Depending on the type of insurance, these events could involve the policyholder getting sick, being in a car accident, dying, and so on. Individuals expecting such events to be more likely will obviously assign a greater value to being insured. If you know you need expensive braces for your teeth, for example, you highly value dental insurance because it will help pay for your orthodontia.

But this means that buyers are adversely selected in insurance markets. From the standpoint of insurance companies, potential customers differ in "quality" because they have different likelihoods of making big claims on their policies. Risky drivers are more likely to make claims on their auto insurance policies; unhealthy individuals are more likely to make health insurance claims.

Just as with the "seller-side" lemons problems discussed earlier, having different types of customers is not a problem in and of itself. If insurance companies can observe potential policyholders' true riskiness, they can then charge them different policy premiums. Higher risk policyholders will pay higher premiums. There would be no economic efficiency loss in this world: Risky customers pay more and get coverage.

The adverse selection problem occurs when the customer knows more about their expected claim behavior than insurers do. Insurance companies realize that the riskiest customers will be those most likely to buy insurance; they will purchase more insurance than low-risk individuals. After all, such customers have the most to gain from being insured. If the insurance companies can't differentiate the good risks (those customers unlikely to submit many claims) from the bad, they have to charge premiums high enough to account for the large fraction of riskier customers.

The vicious cycle starts again: The high premiums price some low-risk customers out of the insurance market. These low-risk buyers don't want to pay high premiums for a policy they are unlikely to need. That, in turn, makes the high-risk individuals an even greater share of those seeking insurance. This necessitates that the insurance company charge an even higher premium, and so on. In a worst-case scenario, that can result in the destruction of a market, as in the used car example discussed above.

Adverse selection on the buyers' side of a market can therefore be as damaging as adverse selection on the sellers' side. Just as happened in the previous cases, the party with more information can be hurt, not just the party with less information. In particular, low-risk insurance customers could lose the ability to buy insurance if they cannot convince insurers that they are, in fact, less risky. At the same time, insurance companies suffer from adverse selection because it makes it more difficult for them to write policies for a consumer segment that they would very much prefer to insure, if they could see everyone's true risk type. (There's another asymmetric information problem in insurance markets when insurers cannot observe all the actions of their policyholders: Once someone is insured against a particular event, he is less likely to take steps to prevent that event from occurring. Someone who has auto insurance may not drive as carefully, for example. This type of problem is called *moral hazard*. We will discuss moral hazard problems later in this chapter.)

Mitigating Adverse Selection in Insurance

As we saw in the markets with seller-side lemons problems, market institutions have arisen to mitigate adverse selection in insurance.

Group Policies   One example is the writing of group insurance policies. These are general policies written for all members of a specified group, often defined as employees of particular firms. In the United States, most people get their health insurance this way, for example. Group insurance helps with adverse selection because by tying insurance to employment status, the insurance company removes much of the link between individuals' riskiness and their insurance purchases. It pools together a wider range of risk types. The good risks are added to the bad, reducing the correlation between individuals seeking to buy health insurance and their chances of falling ill. This is in many ways similar to the way in which leasing reduces the lemons problem in the used car market by breaking the tie between a car's quality and its likelihood of being resold. (It also doesn't hurt, from the insurance company's perspective, that unhealthy people are less likely to be employed. This, too, reduces adverse selection.)

Screening   A second tactic for reducing adverse selection is screening. Insurance companies vet the likelihood of potential customers submitting claims by observing as many risk factors as possible. People seeking life insurance, for example, typically have to complete a medical questionnaire and submit to blood and urine tests, and sometimes a full medical exam. Once his risk is known by both the buyer and seller, the customer might have to pay higher premiums that match his riskiness or be denied coverage at any price. For example, life insurance premiums are higher for smokers, diabetics, or those with high blood pressure. Screening for risk factors isn't constrained to direct influences on expected claims. If you have purchased auto insurance, in addition to asking questions about your driving habits and running a records check for moving violations and accidents, the insurer may have asked you to supply an academic transcript to take advantage of a good-student discount. Even though academic performance is not directly related to driving, in the data, good academic performance is historically linked to lower accident rates. The insurer wants to account for as many observable risk factors

FREAKONOMICS

Online Ratings and Information Asymmetries

British food once had a less than stellar reputation, but those days are long past. London, in particular, is known as one of the best food cities around, with many top chefs and some of the best restaurants in the world calling the city their home. A little while ago, a formerly unknown establishment called the Shed at Dulwich rose to prominence, achieving the distinction of being London's top-rated restaurant (out of over 15,000) at the frequently consulted TripAdvisor website. Foodies around the world were abuzz with interest in the formerly obscure hotspot a few miles south of central London, trying to figure out how to get a reservation.

That reservation was going to be more difficult than they imagined. The Shed at Dulwich didn't have any seats available, because it wasn't actually a restaurant. Instead, it was Oobah Butler's backyard garden shed in south London's Dulwich neighborhood. It served no food and hosted no customers. Butler made up the "restaurant" as part of an experiment to see how easily online rating sites could be manipulated and how much of an effect they would have on their users. After creating the sham eatery's website (featuring pictures of fake menu items created from household materials like shaving cream and dishwasher tablets), Butler and his friends started posting dozens upon dozens of rave reviews on TripAdvisor, extolling the excellence of the fake restaurant's food and atmosphere. Eventually, the site's scoring algorithm named the Shed at Dulwich the best restaurant in London, transforming it into a gourmet sensation. Butler topped off the whole project by hosting for dinner, on a single night, a small number of guests who believed they had scored a real reservation at the now-famous (and unreal, though his guests didn't know it) restaurant. The menu consisted of surreptitiously microwaved frozen dinners and cheap wine served in mugs. The diners reported enjoying the experience immensely.

How could a vaporware eatery become a real sensation? If everyone already knew how good or bad (or real) each business was, online reviews like those on TripAdvisor wouldn't matter. But, especially in big cities, potential customers can't possibly know the quality of every restaurant, spa, and dentist's office. Information asymmetries exist. As a result, a profile on a commonly visited review site like TripAdvisor or Yelp with quite a few five-star reviews really helps a business's reputation — and a lot of one-star reviews really hurt. Online reviews matter.

One impact of online reviews is to produce better customer service. When the cost to customers of acquiring information on quality falls, firms have an incentive to serve clients better. But better customer service is hard work . . . maybe there is an easier way to attract customers. That is what economists Dina Mayzlin, Yaniv Dover, and Judith Chevalier set out to explore by looking at data on online hotel reviews.[*]

The authors examined hotel reviews posted at both TripAdvisor, where anyone can post a review, and Expedia.com, where only those who have booked at least one night at a hotel over the last six months can post a review. Because its posts are not restricted to known customers, it is easier to create a fake review on TripAdvisor (as the Shed at Dulwich episode attests). It seems as if the hotels themselves started to leave reviews at this site, and not only positive reviews for their business, as Oobah Butler did for his "shed," but negative reviews for competing hotels. The authors found that hotels with neighboring hotels close by saw an increase of 1.9 percentage points in their share of negative reviews on TripAdvisor as compared to Expedia.com. The worst offenders were independent, privately owned hotels. If your hotel is located next to another one fitting this description, you can expect an average of six more negative reviews on your TripAdvisor page, but no difference on Expedia.

Ultimately, too many fake reviews mean potential customers will not know which reviews to trust, and a review website could lose its usefulness (and therefore your sources of income). When a hotel pens a scathing but false review against its next-door neighbor, that business is hurting not just its neighbor's reputation, but the review site's reputation as well. That is exactly why Expedia won't let you post a review unless you purchase a reservation. TripAdvisor, while not restricting its reviews to those of verifiable customers, uses machine learning along with more old-fashioned investigative techniques to suss out fake reviews, and punish with demotion any establishment that makes or solicits them.

[*]Dina Mayzlin, Yaniv Dover, and Judith Chevalier, "Promotional Reviews: An Empirical Investigation of Online Review Manipulation," *American Economic Review* 104, no. 8 (August 2014): 2421–2455.

as possible and adjust premiums to these factors accordingly. (Of course, all these relationships between observable risk factors and actual policy claims hold *on average*, not individual-by-individual.)

Denying Coverage   Insurers can also try to head off adverse selection directly by outright denying coverage to individuals with certain risk factors. Health insurance policies were previously allowed to not cover conditions that already existed at the time a policy was purchased. If you could buy insurance *after* you became ill, many consumers would not buy it beforehand. Insurers would pay out massive claims while receiving little premium revenues. If this happened often enough, no one—healthy or unhealthy—might be able to obtain coverage.

This problem explains the economics behind the combination of the "preexisting condition" and original "mandate" rules in the Affordable Care Act (aka Obamacare, or the ACA) and the Massachusetts health care insurance law on which it was patterned. The ACA as initially written included provisions that both prevented health insurers from denying anyone coverage and mandated that everyone must buy health insurance. The cannot-deny provision was, and still is, broadly popular among Americans. Before the ACA, there were a lot of people who wanted to buy health insurance but couldn't because of a previously existing condition. The mandate, on the other hand, was not popular (it was, in fact, eliminated with the passage of a new tax law, effective 2019). Although controversial, a mandate helps solve what could otherwise be extreme adverse selection problems. The mandate is a lot like a government-driven form of the benefits from group insurance we discussed above. Requiring everyone to buy insurance solves the adverse selection problem by eliminating adverse selection entirely. Under a mandate, the average insurance customer must have the average insurance risk in the population. That's why states require all drivers to get auto insurance. Without a mandate, the cannot-deny provision means people can wait until they actually need insurance to purchase it because, well, insurers cannot deny them coverage. This poses an enormous potential adverse selection problem. It's one reason why virtually every state mandates that all drivers must purchase insurance if they drive a car.

Summing Up   These mechanisms and others like them moderate adverse selection in insurance markets for the same reasons that the seller-side mechanisms discussed earlier arose: In the absence of such mechanisms, asymmetric information between parties in the market could destroy considerable gains from exchange.

 Application: Adverse Selection in Credit Cards

Buyer-side adverse selection is common in lending markets. People who pose bigger credit risks in ways that are hard for lenders to observe may be more apt to apply for credit for several reasons. Their risky financial behavior may have put them in dire need of funds. In such cases, when lenders offer funding, the typical borrowers applying for a loan won't have the average credit risk for potential borrowers in that market. They will instead be systematically more risky. If the lender tries to raise the interest rate at which it lends the money to make up for this extra risk, it will drive away less risky borrowers, making the pool of potential borrowers even riskier.

Economists Sumit Agarwal, Souphala Chomsisengphet, and Chunlin Liu tested this idea using a series of experiments in the credit card market.[6] The experiment called for a

---

[6] Sumit Agarwal, Souphala Chomsisengphet, and Chunlin Liu, "The Importance of Adverse Selection in the Credit Card Market: Evidence from Randomized Trials of Credit Card Solicitations," *Journal of Money, Credit and Banking* 42, no. 4 (June 2010): 743–754.

large financial institution to use direct mail to offer new credit cards to potential customers. The offers varied randomly in their financial terms, with some more favorable than others. Agarwal, Chomsisengphet, and Liu found that customers who returned an application for a card were significantly worse credit risks than those who received a mailing but did not submit an application. This suggests that adverse selection was occurring in the market, even though the set of borrowers targeted for the solicitations were considered part of a low-risk population overall. Furthermore, when the researchers evaluated the credit risks of respondents to the various offers, they determined that those who responded to the higher-interest-rate offers (i.e., the offers that are more expensive for the borrower) were systematically riskier than those who responded to lower-rate offers. Not only was there adverse selection in the market, it worsened when the offered terms of credit were less favorable for borrowers.

Agarwal, Chomsisengphet, and Liu then followed the credit histories of those borrowers for whom the bank approved cards. Even though approval meant the cardholders had to pass the bank's credit screening process, they found that those who applied for and received the cards with the worst terms were the most likely to miss their payments once they started using the cards.

Even among a pool of customers considered "good" credit risks, adverse selection exists in the credit card market. Raising cards' rates to try to recoup the losses from a riskier set of cardholders only serves to make the problem worse. The existence of this issue in the market implies that there are potential borrowers out there who can't find credit because they aren't able to distinguish themselves from more risky borrowers in the eyes of card issuers. ■

16.2 Moral Hazard

moral hazard A situation that arises when one party in an economic transaction cannot observe another party's behavior.

Another information asymmetry that can cause problems in markets is **moral hazard,** *a situation that arises when one party in an economic transaction cannot observe another party's behavior.* That last word—"behavior"—is key. Moral hazard is about how one party *acts* once an economic relationship has been entered into; that is, after an insurance policy has been sold, a contract has been signed, an employee has been hired, and so on.

A stark example of a moral hazard problem is fraud. Suppose you pay a mechanic to do scheduled maintenance on your car like changing the oil, and he pockets the money without doing it, hoping that you will not notice. He's relying on the fact that his action is unobservable. If you literally cannot see whether the work has been done, it's difficult to rely simply on the car's performance to determine the quality of the work. A lack of improvement in the car's performance might indicate nothing was done, but there are also genuine reasons why no performance improvement might be observed even if the mechanic did the work as specified.

Fraud aside, numerous moral hazard situations are less malicious but still potentially damaging to markets. Insurance markets again offer many such cases. We talked about adverse selection in insurance, which deals with the unobservable riskiness of people seeking insurance coverage. Moral hazard is different. Moral hazard has to do with the effect insurance coverage has on individuals' behaviors once they have it: specifically, that they will make fewer efforts to avoid having to make claims once they are already covered. Moral hazard is therefore a concern to insurers after a policy has been purchased.

An Extreme Example of Moral Hazard

An example will make this clear. (It's exaggerated to make the point.) Suppose movie producers could buy "box office insurance" that guaranteed them a specified gross revenue for a particular film if box office receipts did not reach this level. Producers wanting more coverage — that is, a higher minimum revenue guarantee — could obtain it for a higher premium.

Such policies would have a value. Movie revenues are unpredictable. Producers might prefer to have a more certain income flow for planning purposes among many other reasons, and they tend to avoid making risky movies entirely. Insurance companies could find selling such policies appealing in principle as well: If the insurers spread their risk over enough movies, they could earn enough premium revenue from the successful movies that didn't need to cash in their policies to both pay claims on disappointing movies and make a profit.

There's a moral hazard, though. Consider the decisions a producer faces once she buys the insurance. Suppose the movie hadn't yet been shot when the policy was purchased. Now the producer is guaranteed the insured gross revenue, no matter what. So, the producer will want to make as low-cost a film as possible: *The Stuff I Found in My Pocket: Part 2.* (Now in 3D!) The producer will have spent virtually nothing on the film but will have earned a guaranteed amount of revenue. Even if the insurance contract was signed after filming, the producer would still have no incentive to spend resources marketing it.

It's a somewhat absurd example to make a point. These forces operate in many markets. **Figure 16.1** shows one way to think about how moral hazard works more generally. This graph plots a potential policyholder's marginal benefit and the marginal cost of taking actions that increase the chance of a "good" outcome occurring.

What we mean by "good" outcomes depends on the particular situation. This could include a movie doing well at the box office, a driver not getting into an accident, a person not falling into ill health, and so on. Importantly, however, actions that raise the likelihood of such good outcomes are not costless to the potential policyholder. Those actions may involve financial cost, such as hiring a decent cast and crew and designing a solid marketing plan for a movie, and almost always involve effort, such as driving with care and resisting the temptation to text friends while behind the wheel, and eating well and exercising regularly. The cost in terms of the money and effort required to take more of these sorts of actions is shown in Figure 16.1 as marginal cost *MC*. We assume that this marginal cost rises with the amount of actions already taken. Such an assumption is realistic; making initial efforts to put together a decent movie or to not drive recklessly is probably not too difficult and thus not too costly, but after having implemented the easier actions, taking further actions to improve outcomes becomes increasingly arduous and costly.

Figure 16.1   Moral Hazard in the Insurance Market

In a market without insurance, a potential policyholder would take actions to improve the potential for a good outcome up to A^*, where the marginal benefit of further action, MB, equals the marginal cost of further action, MC. If instead the policy offers full insurance, MB shifts to MB_{FI}, and the policyholder does not take any action (makes zero effort) to make the good outcome more likely. If the policy offers partial insurance, MB shifts to MB_{PI}, and the policyholder takes action level A_{PI}^*.

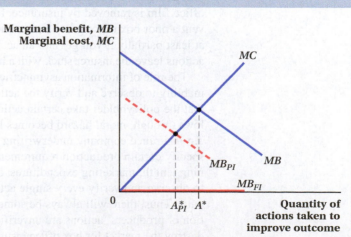

The benefit of such actions is the gain that the potential policyholder obtains when a good outcome occurs. Thus, the marginal benefit of the actions is the incremental increase in the good outcome (or the probability of the outcome) that taking further action creates. In Figure 16.1, these marginal benefits are shown as MB. We assume they decrease as the amount of action taken increases, because it's likely that the actions taken to create a good outcome have diminishing returns.

In a market with no insurance, the potential policyholder would take actions up to point A^*. Here, his marginal benefit of taking further action just equals his marginal cost of doing so; taking any more or less action than this level would only reduce his net benefit. Action levels less than A^* would decrease his expected benefit more than it saves him in cost. Actions beyond A^* would cost more than they are worth in benefit.

Now suppose he obtains insurance against bad outcomes. If the movie is a flop, he gets in a car accident, or needs medical care due to unhealthy behavior, the policy will kick in. If the policy offers *full insurance* — that is, the policy pays off enough so that the policyholder is just as well off as he would have been had the good outcome occurred instead of the bad one — then there is *no* marginal benefit to taking actions that make the good outcome more likely. The policyholder is going to be just as well off regardless of what outcome happens. In this case, the marginal benefit curve shifts to MB_{FI} (for full insurance) in Figure 16.1. This curve lies along the horizontal axis because with full insurance there is no marginal benefit to taking actions that make the good outcome more likely. In this case, even the simplest actions involve a marginal cost greater than their marginal benefit, so the policyholder takes no action. This outcome is terrible for the insurer, because it makes it much more probable that the insurer will have to pay a claim on the policy.

Even without full insurance, the existence of a policy that pays off in case of a bad outcome will reduce the policyholder's marginal benefit of taking actions to make good outcomes more likely — whatever payouts the insurance company makes mean that any bad outcome won't be as bad as it would have been without the insurance. In situations of *partial insurance,* the marginal benefit curve might shift to something like MB_{PI} in Figure 16.1. In this case, the policyholder still takes actions to raise the likelihood of a good outcome occurring, but takes fewer actions than he would have if he had no insurance. Specifically, he takes action level A_{PI}^*, where his marginal cost equals his now lower marginal benefit of action. Therefore, bad outcomes are more likely than they would have been if he weren't insured.

These cases exemplify the moral hazard problem in insurance: Being insured against a bad outcome actually leads the insured party to act (or not act) in ways that increase the probability of the bad outcome. If the loss associated with having a low-performing box office film is removed by insurance, for example, the policyholder has no motive to prevent a poor box office gross from occurring. Or, if you know your car repairs will be paid at least partially if you get into an accident, you may be less careful when driving. These actions leave the insurer stuck with a higher likelihood of having to pay a claim.

The role of information asymmetries in the moral hazard problem involves the insurer's inability to observe and verify the actions of the policyholder. If the insurer could specify that the policyholder take certain actions and is able to observe that the policyholder follows through, moral hazard becomes less of a problem (more on this in the next section). An insurance company underwriting a movie's box office receipts, for example, might specify certain production requirements: cast and crew members, minimum budget, running length, marketing expenditures, and so on. But as a practical matter, it is impossible to observe and verify every single action taken by a producer that affects a movie's revenue. Thus, there will always be some moral hazard problem. Because such a large fraction of producers' actions are unverifiable, the problem is so difficult that it would likely destroy the market for box office insurance altogether.

figure it out 16.2

Anastasia and Katherine own a café. Because of their equipment and business, they run a risk of loss due to small kitchen fires. This risk can be mitigated by taking precautions such as purchasing fire extinguishers or by increasing the training and awareness of the café's employees. Assume that the marginal cost of these precautions can be represented by $MC = 80 + 8A$, where A is equal to the actions taken to mitigate the risk of a fire. Likewise, the marginal benefit of these precautions is $MB = 100 - 2A$.

a. If the café has no insurance, what would be the optimal level of precautions for Anastasia and Katherine to take?

b. Suppose the café has insurance that reduces the marginal benefit of taking precautions to $MB = 90 - 4A$. What happens to the optimal level of precautions? Explain why this is the case.

Solution:

a. With no insurance, the optimal level of precautionary actions would occur where $MB = MC$:

$$100 - 2A = 80 + 8A$$
$$10A = 20$$
$$A = 2$$

b. Once the insurance is in place, the marginal benefit of taking precautions falls to $MB = 90 - 4A$. The optimal level of precautions also falls:

$$MB = MC$$
$$90 - 4A = 80 + 8A$$
$$12A = 10$$
$$A = 0.83$$

The optimal level of precautionary actions falls when insurance is available. If a fire occurs, the café's owners will experience a smaller loss as a result of the insurance coverage. Therefore, the owners' incentives to try to prevent a loss are reduced.

Examples of Moral Hazard in Insurance Markets

Moral hazard problems abound in real-world insurance markets. The United States' National Flood Insurance Program, for example, encourages homeowners to build—and sometimes *rebuild*—too close to water. This program is administered by the U.S. government. It covers damages to homes caused by flooding (private insurance rarely covers such losses). The program's provisions do not do a good job of matching premiums to risk, however. Even policyholders with large prior claims can obtain coverage relatively cheaply. As you might expect, knowing one's beach house will be fully insured in case of a storm surge doesn't do much to discourage the construction of beach houses in vulnerable locations. There are several cases where benefits were paid out on properties that had been destroyed by storms multiple times, and then rebuilt each time in the same location. A Government Accountability Office report calculated that 1% of the properties covered by the program had experienced repetitive losses, accounting for 25 to 30% of total claim costs.[7]

Auto insurers are always concerned about their policyholders' unobserved driving habits. Insurance is usually priced by the period (per six-month term) rather than the intensity of driving. Sometimes rough premium adjustments for mileage are made, but they are based on the policyholders' reported "typical" mileage numbers, not actual use. Additionally, there is no adjustment for aggressive driving, like jackrabbit starts and stops or tailgating, which are associated with an increased probability of being in an accident. Once covered, then, the driver doesn't bear the full marginal cost he imposes on the insurance company when driving more miles or more aggressively. Drivers therefore have too little incentive to avoid actions that raise the likelihood of their being in an accident.

[7] Government Accountability Office, "National Flood Insurance Program: Continued Actions Needed to Address Financial and Operational Issues," Statement of Orice Williams Brown, September 2010.

Unemployment insurance, while offering some financial relief to workers who have lost their jobs by partially replacing their lost wages, can also reduce unemployed individuals' incentives to look for work. While unemployment benefits are tied to the recipient actively looking for work, the agencies that administer the program cannot fully observe recipients' true efforts to find employment. The intensity of the job search and the individual's effort in interviews are difficult to monitor.

Moral Hazard Outside Insurance Markets

Moral hazard problems aren't restricted to insurance markets. They arise between lenders and borrowers in financial markets, too. Lenders often loan funds to borrowers to use for a particular purpose. Suppose a borrower asks for a loan to invest in new equipment for a business. Once he has the money, however, he may find expenditures on other items more appealing. Perhaps he would like some fancy antique furniture for his office. If the borrower uses the loan for the antiques and then skimps on equipment, and the lender can't fully observe how the funds are used, there is moral hazard. By spending part of the loan on unproductive antiques and shortchanging actual investment, the borrower reduces the probability that he will be able to repay the loan. This is bad news for the lender, and it results from the lender's inability to observe exactly how the borrower uses the loaned funds.

Discussions about policy responses to the financial crisis of 2008 have involved moral hazard concerns. Governments around the world bailed out banks and other financial institutions in an effort to stave off a collapse of the financial system. There is concern, however, that knowing the government will step in during a crisis will encourage excessive risk-taking by banks in the future. If their bets do not pay off, the banks will probably be covered anyway, so why not take the risk? This scenario, while taking place outside the insurance market, is in many ways similar to the moral hazard problem facing insurers. Here, taxpayers are the insurance company. If financial institutions know they will be bailed out by the government if things go badly, they are in essence insured against such outcomes. They therefore take fewer actions to avoid bad outcomes (such as engaging in less risky behavior) as a result.

Unobserved actions play an important role in labor markets, too. Employers cannot typically observe all of the actions of their employees. Employees may wish to engage in work-time messaging of friends or surfing the Internet, actions that are not in the firm's best interest. This presents employers with the difficulty of figuring out how to induce employees to do their jobs even when some of the workers' activities cannot be monitored. These employer–employee relationships apply at all ends of the manager–worker hierarchy: from those between foreman and line workers to those between shareholders and the firm's CEO. There is actually a special class of economic analyses — called *principal–agent relationships* — that deal with these sorts of issues. We will discuss them in more detail later in this chapter.

Lessening Moral Hazard

Just as with adverse selection and the lemons problem, some market mechanisms have been developed to reduce moral hazard. One possibility for insurance markets that we hinted at above is the insurer's specifying certain actions that must be taken by the policy-holder as a condition of coverage. For example, commercial property insurance companies may require smoke detectors and firefighting equipment to be installed and maintained in the buildings they insure. These insurers may then send inspectors to verify compliance with such regulations. Many life insurance policies include an exemption from paying benefits if the policyholder commits suicide.

These approaches seek to head off moral hazard problems directly, by specifying and monitoring what the policyholder does. That is, these methods recognize that while the actions of the policyholder might not be perfectly observable, key behaviors that greatly impact the insurer's payoff can be specified by contract (assuming that the insurer maintains the ability to monitor and verify the policyholder's actions).

A related approach is for insurers to give policyholders incentives to take actions that reduce risk. Homeowners typically get a break on their policies if they install smoke detectors or dead-bolt locks. Life insurance policy rates drop for those who quit smoking. Auto insurance policies offer discounts to drivers who maintain a clean driving record. Insurers can also reduce moral hazard by structuring policies that align policyholders' incentives with those of the insurer. This is done by giving insured individuals some "skin in the game." That is, they directly tie together the policyholders' and insurer's payoffs. Insurers could impose a deductible, for example, that requires customers to make the initial payment out of their own pocket before the insurance company pays anything. They could mandate a copayment system whereby the customer pays a portion of any charge; that is, the insurance company is only responsible for part of it.

These and other practices reduce the impact of moral hazard on insurance markets, preserving much of the economic gains from their existence. It's important to remember, however, that even when damped by these institutions, moral hazard can still affect the structure of the markets in which it is a factor.

16.3 Asymmetric Information in Principal–Agent Relationships

Principal–agent relationships are *economic transactions that feature information asymmetry between a principal and her hired agent, whose actions the principal cannot fully observe.* More specifically, they exist whenever one party (the principal) hires another (the agent) to perform some task, and the principal has an asymmetric information problem because she cannot fully observe the agent's actions (or, sometimes, the information the agent possesses). When this information asymmetry is combined with the fact that the principal's and agent's individual self-interests are usually not perfectly aligned, things get interesting.

There are many principal–agent relationships. One of the most common, and the one on which we focus in this section, is between an employer and employee. An employer would like the employee to perform certain tasks. The employee likes to be paid for working, but might not prefer to work as hard or work at the same tasks as the employer would like him to.

The divergence in an employer's preferences (let's call our employer Yvonne) and those of her employee (let's call her Jean) is not in and of itself a problem. The two could write an employment contract with Jean's pay contingent on her completing a set of tasks or conveying certain information specified by Yvonne. Jean would then have strong incentives to do as Yvonne wished, and Yvonne would have to pay Jean enough for her to do it. The problem lies in the fact that, because of the information asymmetry, the principal (Yvonne) can't know for sure if the agent (Jean) did what she requested. Yvonne must instead infer what Jean did using only imperfect information about Jean's job performance. For example, Yvonne can't know exactly how hard Jean worked just from looking

principal–agent relationships Economic transactions that feature information asymmetry between a principal and her hired agent, whose actions the principal cannot fully observe.

at total sales. Maybe Jean didn't work hard, but other factors caused sales to be high. Or, maybe Jean did work hard but other factors caused sales to be low. While sales are likely to be correlated with Jean's effort, they are also influenced by unrelated factors. Sales make an imperfect measure for Yvonne to gauge Jean's actual level of effort.

This logic carries over to other types of principal–agent relationships. A company's shareholders — the principals in this case — want the CEO to maximize the value of the company. But the CEO might want to use company resources to pay for personal perks like a big corporate jet. If it's not clear whether such expenses are justified — corporate jets do save time, after all — shareholders can't be certain that management is acting fully in their interest.

The moral hazard problems facing insurers and their policyholders can also be cast as principal–agent relationships. Insurance companies (the principals) want policyholders (agents) to take actions to reduce risks. Because insurance companies typically can't observe all these actions, a principal–agent problem exists.

What can the principals do in these situations? The principals must set up incentives to make it in the agents' *own best interests* to take the actions that the principals want.

Principal–Agent and Moral Hazard: An Example

Take a simple example. Suppose the daily profit of a small mobile phone store is uncertain but is higher when the store's only employee, Joe, works harder. If Joe works hard, the store's daily profit is $1,000 with 80% probability and $500 with 20% probability. Alternatively, when Joe just sits around texting his friends and does not work hard, the probabilities reverse: a 20% chance of a $1,000 profit and 80% chance of $500. Joe doesn't like to work hard; he has to be paid at least $150 before he's willing to do so. Otherwise, he's going to spend the entire day texting his friends.

How should the store's owner (Selena, the principal) structure Joe's (the agent's) compensation? Remember, the root of the principal–agent problem is that the owner can't directly observe the employee's effort. Either it's costly to monitor Joe all day or Joe's effort involves some dimension that is not readily apparent. Otherwise, Selena could simply require Joe to work hard and only pay him $150 if he does. Joe would accept this deal because he is being paid enough to compensate him for his cost of effort, and Selena also likes this deal because inducing Joe to work hard raises her expected profit from $600 ($0.2 \times \$1,000 + 0.8 \times \$500$) to $900 ($0.8 \times \$1,000 + 0.2 \times \$500$), a $300 increase that exceeds the $150 wage.

When Joe's effort is unobservable, however, she can't tie his pay to how hard he works. Offering Joe a flat wage of $150 doesn't work. Because he faces a cost of working hard but would take home the same pay regardless of whether he exerts any effort, he might as well just settle for the money and not work hard.

What Selena *can* do, however, is tie Joe's pay to something she knows is related to Joe's effort: namely, the store's profit. Because Joe can affect the likelihood that profits (and therefore his wages) are high by working hard, this offers him an incentive to exert effort. Of course, the extra wages he expects to earn have to be high enough to compensate him for the extra effort.

Suppose Selena offers the following deal: Joe gets $255 if the store's profits are high (i.e., $1,000) and $0 if profits are low ($500). Now think about Joe's tradeoffs. If he works hard, he has an 80% chance of earning $255 and a 20% chance of earning nothing. His expected earnings are $204 ($0.8 \times 255 + 0.2 \times 0$). However, he also suffers an effort cost of $150, so his net gain from working hard is $54. If Joe chooses to be lazy, he will have an 80% chance of earning nothing and a 20% chance of earning $255, yielding expected earnings of $51. By being lazy, Joe pays no effort cost, so his net gain from being lazy is $51. Under this compensation plan, Joe prefers working hard to being lazy.

Selena also prefers this new contract. If Joe works hard, the store's expected profit will be $300 higher. Selena expects to pay Joe $204 ($0.8 \times 255 + 0.2 \times 0$) if he works hard, so it raises her expected profit minus the wages she has to pay by $96.

Selena (the principal) can, in fact, give Joe (the agent) incentives to work hard even if she can't observe his work level. The key is to pay him much more when observable events occur that are correlated with his unobservable effort (i.e., when the profit is high because Joe works hard). By tying the agent's compensation to outcomes that the principal likes, the principal aligns the agent's incentives on the margin with her own.

More General Principal–Agent Relationships

The Selena–Joe example is simple: It has only two outcomes (high or low profits) and two choices for the agent (high or low effort). However, its insights hold in more general settings with multiple possible outcomes and a range of agent choices. The optimal compensation structure fully aligns the marginal incentives of the agent with those of the principal. In other words, principals want to design compensation structures that make agents face the same incentives the principals would face if they were making the agents' choices for them. When this is not the case, the principals' and agents' incentives are misaligned and can lead to inefficient outcomes.

You might wonder, if principal–agent situations are so common, especially in employment relationships, why pay-for-performance (or maybe pay-for-outcome is more accurate) isn't the norm. Certainly, many people in sales professions have their pay tied directly to outcomes related to their performance through commissions. Some workers also get paid piece rates, where they are compensated a set amount per unit of work they complete (e.g., per dress sewn). But many people are paid a fixed hourly wage or even an annual salary. This might mean there is no principal–agent dynamic involved in those jobs, but it could also mean other "levers" are available to tie job outcomes to compensation for those workers. Annual bonuses, promotions, stock options, deferred compensation, and threats of being fired all serve as ways that employers can give workers the incentives to perform as the employer wishes. So, when you are looking for evidence of principal–agent relationships, be sure to consider the full range of tools the principal has available to induce the agent to behave in a way (unobservable by the principal) that results in the best outcome for the principal.

🛩 Application: The Principal–Agent Problem in Residential Real Estate Transactions

Home sellers face an asymmetric information problem when they hire a real estate agent. An agent typically knows more about the state of the housing market than does a home seller. Indeed, the agent's extra information is one of the reasons why people want to hire a real estate agent.

In addition to this information gap, in the United States, contracts in the industry typically give agents very weak marginal incentives to get the highest price for the houses they sell. Most agents are paid a commission that is a small fraction of the selling price of the home. Typically, the total commission on a sale is around 6%, but after the buyer's agent and the brokerage for which the agent works receive their shares of the commission, the seller's agent takes home only about 1.5% of the sales price.

You might think that linking compensation to the outcome the seller would desire (a higher sales price) fits the optimal principal–agent compensation plans we just discussed, but this is true only to a limited extent. The problem is that the agent's incentive to get a higher price for his client *on the margin* is far less than the homeowner's. By taking actions that raise the sales price by $1,000, the agent would only earn an extra $15, while the owner would earn $940. The owner's marginal incentives are over 60 times larger than the agent's.

The combination of the information gap and the misaligned incentives can create distortions, as two of this book's authors (Steven Levitt and Chad Syverson) pointed out in their study of real estate transactions.[8] Because agents bear much of the cost of selling a house (hosting open houses, buying ads, showing the home to potential buyers, etc.), but gain much less from a higher price, the agents have an incentive to convince the homeowner to sell more quickly at a lower price. For example, while most homeowners would wait two extra weeks if they could get an offer that is $10,000 higher (that's worth an extra $9,400 to the sellers), agents may not be willing to pay two extra weeks' worth of selling costs for an incremental commission increase of only $150. And, because sellers know less than agents about the likely offers forthcoming on their houses, sellers are susceptible to being convinced to swiftly accept a lower offer.

To test this theory, we compared house-sales outcomes in the typical principal–agent setting described above to those that happen when the real estate agent *is* the homeowner. In the second case, the principal and agent are the *same person*, so there is no principal–agent problem. By comparing the two outcomes, we measured the distortions created by the asymmetric information and misaligned incentives in the principal–agent relationship between the seller and real estate agent.

The results confirmed the prediction. When real estate agents sell their own houses, they keep their homes on the market longer and sell them for a higher price than comparable non-agent-owned homes. (In fact, agents earn, on average, an extra 3.7% in terms of sales price and wait 10 days longer to do so.) This suggests that agents are able to convince sellers to accept early offers that they themselves take a pass on. ■

16.4 Signaling to Solve Asymmetric Information Problems

We talked earlier in the chapter about the ways in which sellers of high-quality goods can convince buyers of this fact. One involved offering warranties. The notion was that, since low-quality products are especially expensive to warranty (because they break more often), the very fact a seller offers a warranty suggests that he or she is likely selling a high-quality product.

signaling A solution to the problem of asymmetric information in which the knowledgeable party alerts the other party to an unobservable characteristic of the good.

It turns out this basic idea applies across many economic settings, enough to have its own name: **signaling,** *a solution to the problem of asymmetric information in which the knowledgeable party alerts the other party to an unobservable characteristic of the good.* It's one way in which asymmetric information problems can be solved in markets.

Signaling was first formalized by economist Michael Spence in the early 1970s; he won the Nobel Prize for his seminal work in this area.[9] The basic idea of signaling is

---

[8] Steven D. Levitt and Chad Syverson, "Market Distortions When Agents Are Better Informed: The Value of Information in Real Estate Transactions," *Review of Economics and Statistics* 90, no. 4 (November 2008): 599–611.

[9] Michael Spence, "Job Market Signaling," *Quarterly Journal of Economics* 87, no. 3 (August 1973): 355–374.

that there is some action, the "signal," that conveys otherwise unknown information about the signal sender. For the signal to be meaningful — that is, for the receiver to actually be able to learn something about the signal sender — the net economic benefit of sending the signal must vary across different "types" of senders. That is, sending the signal must be less costly for some types of senders than others. In the warranty example, sending the signal of providing a warranty is less costly for producers of high-quality products than for producers of low-quality products. This difference makes it more likely that high-quality products will have a warranty, allowing consumers to infer something about a product's quality, which would be otherwise unobservable at the time of purchase.

The Classic Signaling Example: Education

Signaling can have surprisingly powerful effects. Even if a signal is inherently worthless — that is, if the action itself has no economic value of its own other than as a signal — the information it conveys can make a big difference for equilibrium prices and quantities. To see how this can happen, consider *the* classic signaling example: the well-documented fact that college graduates earn more, on average, than workers with only high school diplomas.

Suppose that going to college does *absolutely nothing* to improve your productivity on a job. (This is not what labor economists have found, but it will show how powerful signaling can be on its own.) Let's assume that productivity is a function of personal organization, perseverance, and the ability to concentrate and learn new things quickly. Employers would like to find workers with these qualities. They want to hire productive workers and pay them more. But the problem of asymmetric information gets in the way. Employers cannot tell from an interview and résumé if a potential employee has these characteristics.

Highly productive workers would like to convince potential employers they would be good hires. Applicants, however, can't just say, "Hey, I'm very productive." Anyone could make such a claim. Productive workers need some sort of way to prove it.

That's what a college degree can offer. College is costly, and, importantly, it's more costly for some than others. It's costly in a monetary sense, but also because securing a diploma requires a lot of effort. To expend the necessary effort, a student has to have certain qualities, like being organized, a willingness to persevere, and the ability to concentrate. The same attributes that characterize productive workers make it easier for them to finish college. College may be difficult, but it's even harder for people without those attributes. If you want to be recognized as a productive worker, then, a good way to demonstrate this to potential employers is by completing a college degree. It sends a **signal,** *a costly action taken by an economic actor to indicate something that would otherwise be difficult to observe.* Here, the signal is aimed at employers with the intent of demonstrating your productivity.

signal A costly action taken by an economic actor to indicate something that would otherwise be difficult to observe.

The signal in this example won't be meaningful if unproductive workers also receive college degrees. Employers can't distinguish between high- and low-productivity workers in that case. This is why it's important that the signal be more costly for low-productivity workers. If the gap is large enough, low-productivity workers won't obtain college degrees.

When more productive workers finish college and less productive workers don't, employers can tell the difference between them. These employers are willing to pay the college graduates more, because they are more productive. We end up with the empirical fact we talked about earlier: College graduates earn more pay, even if they didn't learn anything in school.

Signaling: A Mathematical Approach

Let's use some specific numbers to make this result clearer. Suppose there are two types of workers: high-productivity and low-productivity. Each year of higher education costs high-productivity workers the equivalent of $25,000. This includes the monetary cost equivalent of going to class, finishing assignments, studying for exams, and so on. For low-productivity workers, each year of higher education costs the equivalent of $50,000 because of the higher cost of effort they face when attending school. Therefore, we can write the total costs of going to college as

$$C_H = \$25,000y$$
$$C_L = \$50,000y$$

where y is years in college, and C_H and C_L are the costs of attending school for high- and low-productivity workers, respectively.

Let's suppose that, over the course of a worker's lifetime, a high-productivity worker produces $250,000 worth of value for employers, while a low-productivity worker produces $125,000 of value. Because of the production of this extra value, employers are willing to pay high-productivity workers up to $125,000 more in wages.[10]

To be willing to pay high-productivity workers more, however, employers need to be able to tell them apart from low-productivity workers. Suppose for a moment that employers use completion of a college degree as a way to do that. That is, employers pay workers for whom $y \geq 4$ extra wages to the tune of $125,000 over the course of their lifetime. For employers to use this payment strategy, only high-productivity workers better be finishing college. Otherwise, employers would face the prospect of paying extra wages to workers who weren't creating the extra value to justify the higher wage.

So, we need to first check whether only the high-productivity workers will choose to finish college. Compare the cost and benefit of completing four years of college for each type of worker. For high-productivity workers, finishing college — that is, receiving at least $y = 4$ years of higher education — costs $100,000:

$$C_H = \$25,000y = \$25,000 \times 4 = \$100,000$$

Low-productivity workers face a larger cost of finishing college, $200,000:

$$C_L = \$50,000y = \$50,000 \times 4 = \$200,000$$

The benefit to each worker of finishing college is actually the same. Employers pay a total premium of $B = \$125,000$ in wages for completion of a college degree. Remember, because employers can't tell directly how productive a worker is, they are trying to rely on college completion to make the distinction.

Therefore, the net benefit (NB) to completing college for high-productivity workers is

$$NB_H = B - C_H = \$125,000 - \$100,000 = \$25,000$$

while for low-productivity workers, it is

$$NB_L = B - C_L = \$125,000 - \$200,000 = -\$75,000$$

High-productivity workers are $25,000 better off if they finish college, so they do. Low-productivity workers are actually worse off because the cost of finishing is higher for them. They will not choose college.

Signaling: A Graphical Approach

With this example, we've shown that the employers' strategy makes sense. They pay a wage premium to college graduates on the expectation that they will be high-productivity workers, even though the employers

---

[10] Wages will be exactly $125,000 more if there is enough competition among firms for workers. For simplicity, we assume that outcome holds here, but it isn't necessary to make signaling work.

can't observe productivity directly. Their expectation turns out to be correct because low-productivity workers aren't willing to pay the extra costs that completing college requires of them.

This outcome can be seen in **Figure 16.2**, which shows workers' costs and benefits of college as a function of the number of years in college. Low-productivity workers' costs are shown by curve C_L; they increase $50,000 for every year of schooling. High-productivity workers' costs are shown by curve C_H. They are lower because these workers only pay a total cost of $25,000 per year. The wage premium (benefit) of college to both types of workers is shown by curve B. Workers with fewer than four years of college receive no wage premium. Those with four or more years, however, earn a premium of $125,000, which is why the wage premium jumps from 0 to $125,000 at $y = 4$.

For low-productivity workers, no amount of college creates a positive net benefit. Going for fewer than four years offers no wage premium but imposes costs. Attendance for exactly four years results in a wage premium of $125,000, but this isn't worth the $200,000 cost. And, more than four years only raises costs further without any additional wage premium. For high-productivity workers, however, four years of college does make sense. The four years costs them $100,000, but earns them a wage premium of $125,000, leading to a $25,000 net benefit. In this example, in fact, high-productivity workers don't just have an incentive to finish college, they have an incentive to finish it in only four years, as more schooling creates extra costs without the benefit of extra pay.

This demonstrates the potential power of signaling. Here, something that has no real benefit to society (because we assumed education does not enhance worker productivity) actually determines how much income each worker earns. The productive workers pay to go to college, but society gets nothing economically useful in return. A college degree doesn't make these workers *more* productive, because they were already more productive before attending college. Yet, using a degree as a signal allows productive workers to indicate their productivity to employers, so these workers are paid more. However, four years of college is a rather expensive signal! If these workers could somehow find a cheaper way to signal their greater productivity, society would be better off.

Figure 16.2   Education as a Signal on the Job Market

The benefits of a signal of education on the job market are shown using the relative costs and benefits of a four-year degree to low-productivity and high-productivity workers. Low-productivity workers' costs increase by $50,000 for every year of college, as shown by C_L. High-productivity workers' costs, represented by C_H, are lower at $25,000 per year. At four years of college, the wage premium jumps from $0 to $125,000. In this market, high-productivity workers will attend exactly four years of college because the benefits of college outweigh the costs. Low-productivity workers will not attend college because the costs of education outweigh the benefits.

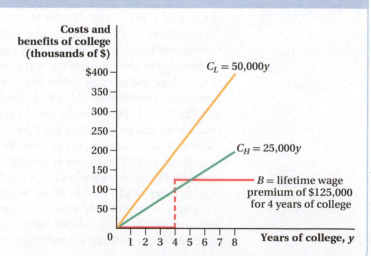

Economists sometimes use "money burning" as a shorthand phrase to refer to the wasteful expenditure of resources for the purposes of sending a signal. In fact, *literally* burning money can itself be a signal in some cases. Suppose wealth were imperfectly observable (perhaps it's difficult to show people all your assets at once or to convince them of their value), and that a person wished to signal his wealth to another. He could do so by starting a cash bonfire. While burning money is obviously costly, it is less costly—relatively speaking—for wealthier people. Therefore, wealthy individuals could show they are rich by demonstrating that they literally have money to burn.

Education and Productivity   As we said, economists have found a lot of evidence that, in reality, college (and more years of education in general) does have positive effects on actual on-the-job productivity. Students aren't wasting all their tuition and effort just to prove that they will make good employees. There is some evidence, however, that *part* of the wage differences between workers with different education levels comes from signaling effects. For example, evidence exists of what is called the "sheepskin effect"—students with four years of college and a degree to show for it earn higher wages than students who have also finished four years of college but who did not receive a degree because they were just short of some graduation requirement. If time in school is what confers skills that are useful in the labor force, and employers pay workers based on which of those skills they observe in workers, then whether a student actually holds a degree shouldn't affect his pay. The fact that having the degree does affect a worker's pay suggests that signaling is at work; employers are, in part, relying on the existence of the degree itself to determine how much to pay workers.

This sheepskin effect has shaped the recent debate about college costs and whether the actual productivity benefits of higher education are overstated. After all, if tuition levels double, not because college has actually made graduates more productive, but instead because students are trying harder to signal their abilities by going to highly regarded (and more expensive) colleges, this situation is like an arms race among students. That is, it is a situation where competitors just try to stay ahead of their competition without any real improvement in rank. In this example, students spend large amounts without any real change in their job market prospects because they're sending the same signal as before, but it's now more expensive. In addition, the increased spending does not provide any additional benefits to society in the form of more productive workers.

Other Signals

Signaling is present in all sorts of economic situations beyond this example. Buying an engagement ring for a fiancée can signal one's commitment to getting married. If, as sometimes happens, the woman keeps the ring should the wedding be called off, only men expecting the wedding to occur will be willing to pay for the ring. The ring, as with attending college and offering warranties, allows men to substitute "expensive talk" regarding their (imperfectly observed) true feelings for what would otherwise be cheap talk.

The choices people make about the products they use or the ways in which they live their lives can be signals. They may want to inform family, friends, neighbors, or even strangers about some aspect of their personalities that would otherwise be difficult to convey. Some monks take vows of poverty. This, in part, signals their devotion. Dressing up to go to work can be a signal of one's commitment to and seriousness about a job. Consumption patterns can be used to signal income or wealth to one's social network.

These examples only scratch the surface of the wide span of signaling that occurs in our society. They also indicate both the frequency of asymmetric information in economic interactions as well as the power signaling can have to reduce it.

Application: Advertising as a Signal of Quality

Firms use advertising to send all kinds of messages about their products: newer, cheaper, cooler—you name it, there's an ad saying it. But many economists argue that sometimes the message about the product isn't what's *in* the ad; instead, it's simply that the ad *exists*. In other words, the mere fact a company advertises a product sends a signal that there is something desirable about the product.

The argument for advertising as a signal goes something like this. Advertising is costly, but it's really costly for unsuccessful companies that make products consumers don't like. The only firms that can afford to advertise are those that make things consumers want to buy. By advertising, companies are effectively saying to consumers, "Our product is so excellent and will reap such great profits for us that we can afford to spend all this money advertising it. Companies that make poor products aren't able to do that." All that's needed for this signaling effect to work is for the company to spend money on advertising. And the ad doesn't even need to offer any specific information about the product.

Perhaps one of the best examples of an "all-signal, no information" ad was online brokerage firm E*TRADE's Super Bowl ad a number of years ago—Super Bowl advertising rates continue to be the most expensive worldwide. The E*TRADE ad opened with two oddly dressed men sitting in lawn chairs in an open garage. Between them, a chimpanzee in an E*TRADE T-shirt stood on a bucket, dancing to the tune of "La Cucaracha" as the men clapped (badly) to the beat. After 25 seconds, the screen went dark, with a simple message then appearing, "We just wasted 2 million bucks. What are you doing with your money?"

The ad was widely considered a success. Evidently, millions of people thought, "E*TRADE must be some kind of trading firm if it can afford to waste its money on a Super Bowl ad like that." Signal sent; signal received. ∎

 ## figure it out 16.3

Last year, Used Cars "R" Us sold very few cars and ended up with a large economic loss. The owner, Geoffrey, has developed two strategies to help the dealership sell more vehicles in the coming year by signaling that it deals in only high-quality used vehicles:

- Change the name of the dealership to Quality Used Cars "R" Us.

- Offer a 60-day bumper-to-bumper warranty for every car sold.

Which of these two strategies is the best signal of high quality? Explain.

Solution:

To be a good signal of quality, a signal must be cheaper for high-quality producers and more expensive for low-quality producers. Therefore, the best signal is the 60-day warranty. If the cars sold at Used Cars "R" Us are truly of high quality, the warranty will not be very expensive for the dealership to offer. On the other hand, if Used Cars "R" Us only sold lemons, the warranty would be very expensive and negate the benefit of increased sales. Thus, consumers can be more confident that a dealership offering a warranty has higher-quality products than those that do not.

A name change for the dealership would just be "cheap talk." Any dealership can alter its name, and the cost of doing so will not vary across high-quality sellers and low-quality sellers.

16.5 Conclusion

In this chapter, we've studied markets in which asymmetric information exists — one party knows more than the other about the goods or services being traded. We saw that asymmetric information can have big impacts on how well markets operate. Under complete information, for example, buyers and sellers in a market engage in mutually beneficial exchanges and partake of the economic surplus created by these exchanges. In the extreme, asymmetric information can cause markets to seize up completely, because buyers and sellers are so afraid of making a decision that will result in a poor economic outcome for them. Such a freeze on market exchanges harms not just the parties with the information disadvantage, but also those with the advantage. This potential for economic harm explains why so many economic institutions have come about to reduce the effects of information asymmetries.

We've looked at numerous examples of the ways in which asymmetric information can show up in markets: adverse selection, moral hazard, and principal–agent problems, and we've discussed the steps consumers and firms take to try to reduce their impact. We covered a lot of ground, but it's important to remember that we really only scratched the surface of this interesting area of economics.

In the next chapter, we study more ways that the well-functioning markets we studied in the earlier parts of this book may fail to deliver outcomes that are socially optimal. Specifically, we investigate the roles of externalities and public goods.

Summary

1. The **lemons problem,** a common feature of markets like the used car market, exists when the seller knows more about the quality of a good than does the buyer. The existence of lemons on the market results in **adverse selection** in the market; low-quality goods are more likely to be put on the market than high-quality goods because consumers cannot differentiate between the two types of goods before buying them. The same type of adverse selection problem occurs in markets where buyers have more information than sellers, such as the insurance market. **[Section 16.1]**

2. When one party in an economic transaction cannot observe the *behavior* of the other party, **moral hazard** arises. Moral hazard is especially common in insurance markets, because once insured against a bad outcome, the insured party is more likely to act in ways that increase the probability of that bad outcome. Clauses specifying the actions

that must be taken by a policyholder in order to be covered are designed to mitigate moral hazard. **[Section 16.2]**

3. Information asymmetry in the workplace and other economic arenas can lead to **principal–agent problems**. In this case, the principal hires an agent whose actions the principal cannot fully observe. To ensure that the agent acts in the principal's best interest, the principal must create incentive structures that align the interests of the agent with the principal's own best interests. **[Section 16.3]**

4. One way to solve information asymmetry is through the use of **signaling,** in which one party in a transaction communicates information that is not immediately observable. A common example of signaling is education, which enables employers to distinguish relatively high-productivity workers from low-productivity workers. **[Section 16.4]**

Review Questions

1. Contrast market situations with complete and asymmetric information. What is an example of a market with complete information?

2. What characteristics of a market can create the lemons problem?

3. Define adverse selection. Why does the lemons problem result in adverse selection?

4. How can warranties reduce the lemons problem in an economic market?

5. How can insurance companies mitigate the problems of adverse selection?

6. What is moral hazard? Describe the example of moral hazard in the insurance market.

7. How can insurance providers use incentives to reduce moral hazard in the insurance market?

8. What market characteristics can create problems in a principal–agent relationship?

9. How can principals reduce the problems associated with principal–agent relationships?

10. How can signaling be used to reduce asymmetric information in a market?

11. How can education be used as a signal in the job market?

12. Name two examples of signals other than education. How do these examples reduce asymmetric information?

Problems
(Solutions to problems marked with an asterisk appear at the back of this book. Problems adapted to use calculus are available online.)

1. Car buyers value a high-quality used car at $16,000 and a low-quality used car at $8,000. The supply of high-quality cars is given by $Q_H = -200 + 0.05P_H$; the supply of low-quality cars is given by $Q_L = -200 + 0.1P_L$. Potential buyers cannot tell the difference between high-quality and low-quality cars when purchasing one.

    a. Assume that buyers believe there is a 75% chance that a used car will be of high quality. What would be the price buyers are willing to pay for a used car of unknown quality?

    b. If the price you found in (a) is offered in the market for used cars, how many high-quality cars will be offered for sale? How many low-quality cars? What will be the overall proportion of high-quality cars offered for sale? Does it match buyers' expectations?

    c. What is likely to happen when the true proportion of high-quality cars becomes known? Describe the impact on the price of a used car and the quantity of high-quality used cars offered for sale. What is the logical conclusion of this process?

2. In Problem 1, we discovered that imperfect information about the quality of used cars caused fewer high-quality cars to be offered for sale than people expected. Thinking in discrete steps,

    a. How does this change in the proportion of high-quality cars affect the expected value of a used car of unknown quality?

    b. How does this change in expected value subsequently alter the number of high-quality and low-quality cars offered for sale?

    c. Briefly describe the logical conclusion of this process.

*3. In an isolated town, there are two distinct markets for cars. Buyers will pay up to $12,000 for a high-quality car or $8,000 for a low-quality car. There are 100 high-quality cars for sale, and the sellers have a minimum acceptable price of $11,000. There are also 100 low-quality cars for sale at a minimum acceptable price of $5,000. The supply of automobiles is perfectly inelastic above the reservation price.

    a. If there is perfect information, how many high-quality and how many low-quality cars will be sold?

    b. Suppose that the quality of a car is known to the seller, but not the buyer. What price will prevail in the marketplace if buyers correctly estimate the chance of acquiring a low-quality car at 50%? What happens to the number of high-quality cars for sale at that price?

    c. After sellers make all adjustments, what will the equilibrium price of cars be? What proportion of those cars will be high-quality cars?

    d. What happens to your answers to (a), (b), and (c) if sellers of high-quality cars have a reservation price of $9,500 instead of $11,000?

4. In the 1960s, Yale University began offering students an alternative to taking out student loans. Instead, students could attend Yale in exchange for a specified percentage of their earnings over a significant length of time. Yale used historical data to determine the percentage so that the program would pay for itself—large payments from high earners would offset the smaller payments from low earners.

    a. If you were planning on becoming a Wall Street financier, would you be more likely to take out loans or enroll in the Yale program? Why?

    b. If you were planning on becoming a missionary, would you be more likely to take out loans or enroll in the Yale program? Why?

    c. The tuition program turned out to be a financial disaster for Yale. Do your answers to (a) and (b) shed light on why? Explain.

    d. What kind of information problem did the Yale program suffer from?

5. Toyota regularly takes its own cars in trade for new models. It then subjects them to a rigorous inspection process, fixing defects as it goes, and offers them for sale with an extended warranty. Explain how these procedures help Toyota deal with the adverse selection problem.

*6. Two types of individuals are seeking health insurance: skydivers and groundhuggers. Skydivers have a 75% chance of suffering an injury in a given year; groundhuggers have a 25% chance of suffering an injury. All injuries require a $4,000 surgery to repair.

    a. You run a health insurance company, and believe there are equal numbers of skydivers and groundhuggers in the population. Unfortunately, you can't, at first glance, distinguish a skydiver from a groundhugger.

How much of a premium would you have to collect from each individual if you were to just cover your expected payouts for surgeries?

b. At the premium you set in (a), who thinks insurance looks like a great deal? Who thinks it looks like a poor deal?

c. Describe the likely reaction of skydivers and ground-huggers when informed of your premiums. What are the implications for who decides to buy insurance? What are the implications for the premiums you must charge?

d. Smokers have a greater risk of illness than nonsmokers, in the same way skydivers have a higher risk of injury than groundhuggers. Explain why both smokers and nonsmokers remain in the pool of the insured in the real world, but only the skydivers in this problem obtained insurance.

7. To assist in ensuring adequate and affordable health care for all, the federal government has mandated that health insurers provide health insurance to all, regardless of their physical condition. Insurers may not reject coverage for preexisting health problems.

a. Explain why this mandate, standing alone, creates the potential for adverse selection problems.

b. A second part of the original ACA legislation that guaranteed coverage for preexisting conditions required all people to obtain health insurance. Explain how this mandate reduced the potential for adverse selection.

c. Recent changes to the tax law rolled back the individual mandate discussed in (b) in 2019. What impact do you expect this rollback to have on health insurance premiums? Do you expect health insurance markets to unravel in the way Akerlof described the unraveling of the used-car market?

8. The federal government would like everyone to have access to health insurance. Currently, the government allows insurance companies to test an applicant's smoking status (they can test a blood sample for nicotine), but does not allow insurers to use the results of any genetic tests. Explain why these seemingly inconsistent provisions are both consistent with the government's goal.

9. Auto insurer Progressive Insurance recently implemented a new program. Policyholders who agree to voluntarily install a Snapshot telematics device in their car receive a small discount on their car insurance premium. The Snapshot device records distance, time of day, speed, and hard braking activity in much the same way as an airplane's black box, and reports that information to Progressive. Customers with good driving habits receive a substantial discount on their insurance; those with bad habits may see their premiums increase.

a. Explain how the Snapshot device helps Progressive overcome adverse selection.

b. Explain how the Snapshot device helps Progressive overcome moral hazard.

10. After a probationary period of six years, during which they teach, research, and serve on committees, university professors who meet acceptable standards are given tenure. Tenure offers these professors tremendous job security.

a. Explain why a tenure system makes universities susceptible to a moral hazard problem.

b. Explain why the problems of moral hazard caused by tenure are likely to be greater than the problems of adverse selection.

11. Suppose that, to deal with adverse selection problems, a new federal lemons law requires all used car dealerships to provide a one-year warranty for each car they sell. Explain how this new law, designed to reduce adverse selection, might increase the problem of moral hazard.

*12. Harry is dating Sally. Because he is devastated at the thought of being dumped, he spends considerable resources making himself attractive to her: expensive haircuts, ballroom dancing classes, a gym membership, and so on. Harry's marginal cost of making himself attractive to Sally is given by MC in the graph below. Sally, of course, appreciates his efforts: The marginal benefit Harry receives from his efforts (which account for the probability of being dumped) is shown as MB.

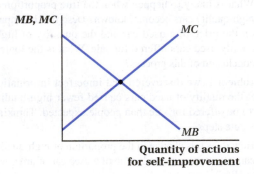

a. On the graph, determine the optimal amount of resources Harry should expend making himself more attractive to Sally.

b. Harry marries Sally. The marriage contract raises the cost of exiting a relationship, and thus, for any given level of Harry's expenditure, Sally is less likely to dump Harry. Illustrate the effects of the marriage contract in the accompanying graph by shifting the appropriate curve in the appropriate direction.

c. "Harry has really let himself go since we got married. He burps too much, seldom shaves, and never takes out the trash." Is this commonly heard statement consistent with the illustration you have drawn?

d. What kind of problem does this illustrate: adverse selection or moral hazard?

e. A "covenant marriage" is one that is virtually impossible to exit for a given period of time. Illustrate the effects of a covenant marriage on your graph, and comment on the predictions your graph holds for the quality of relationships fostered by covenant marriages.

13. Divorce is often very costly to all parties involved. Recently, Safeguard Guaranty Corporation began offering divorce insurance that helps defray the financial hit imposed by a divorce. Divorce benefits are distributed as a lump sum to both former partners and are available after a mandatory 48-month waiting period.

   a. Using a graph similar to Figure 16.1, show how the existence of divorce insurance may create a moral hazard problem.

   b. How does Safeguard Guaranty deal with the problem of adverse selection? Explain.

14. Consider the graph below, which demonstrates the costs and benefits of theft-proofing one's home. The marginal costs increase as more precaution is taken: It's cheap to install good locks, but more difficult to install invisible laser intruder-detection systems. The marginal benefit declines as more precaution is taken: If I am a burglar, adding a guard dog isn't going to provide much deterrence if you already have an electric fence and 30 locks on each door and window.

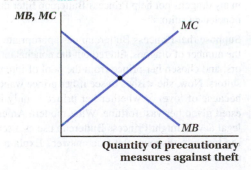

**Quantity of precautionary
measures against theft**

   a. Determine the optimal amount of precaution the homeowner would take if theft insurance were unavailable.

   b. Suppose the homeowner can obtain an insurance policy that covers half of any losses he might suffer. Assuming that the marginal benefit curve represents dollar losses to the homeowner, shift the marginal benefit curve by an appropriate distance and determine what happens to the homeowner's optimal amount of care.

   c. Suppose that the insurance company decides to institute a deductible: The homeowner pays the first $1,000 of losses, and after that the insurance company splits the losses with the homeowner 50-50. Shift the marginal benefit curve by an appropriate amount (be sure to indicate the magnitude of the shift in an appropriate fashion). What effect does the deductible have on the precautions taken by the homeowner?

15. Simon, a self-made millionaire, owns the world's most extensive collection of artisan garden gnomes. His collection is very attractive to thieves, so Simon takes costly measures to protect his investment. The marginal benefit of these measures is $MB = 5,000 - 5A$, where A represents the quantity of theft prevention actions taken. The marginal cost of these actions is $MC = 1,000 + 3A$.

   a. If Simon has no insurance, what is the optimal number of precautionary measures for him to take to protect his valuable gnome collection?

   b. Suppose Simon insures his collection and the insurance contract covers half of all losses so that the marginal benefit is now $MB = 2,500 - 2.5A$. What happens to Simon's optimal level of precautions? Explain why this is the case.

   c. What would Simon's optimal level of precaution be if he insured his collection fully against losses?

*16. After years of training, Sara has landed a contract playing professional lacrosse. Eager to leverage her pro status by bringing in endorsements, she asks Jenny MacGuire to be her personal manager. Jenny has offered Sara a choice of two payment plans. Sara can engage Jenny's services for a flat fee of $100,000. Alternatively, Sara can pay Jenny 15% of all endorsement revenue.

   Sara estimates that if Jenny expends modest effort ($20,000 worth) in her job, she will generate $600,000 in endorsement revenue for Sara. But if Jenny expends high effort ($50,000 worth), she will bring in $1 million in endorsements.

   a. Suppose Sara agrees to the flat-rate plan. What can Sara expect to receive if Jenny expends modest effort? If Jenny expends high effort? What can Jenny expect to receive in either case? Explain the associated principal–agent problem. Who is the principal? Who is the agent?

   b. For both possible effort levels, determine the rewards to Jenny and Sara if Sara chooses the 15% plan. What happens to the principal–agent problem if Sara chooses this plan?

17. The board of directors of a major corporation is trying to determine how to structure the salary of the new CEO. One option is for the board to offer the new CEO a flat salary of $1 million per year. A second option is to offer a profit-sharing plan with a base salary of $200,000 plus 10% of the firm's profit. If the CEO puts a lot of effort into the job, she will generate a $10 million profit for the firm. If the CEO exerts modest effort, the corporation will earn $7 million in profit. Expending a lot of effort costs the CEO $500,000; expending modest effort costs her $300,000.

   a. Draw the extensive-form game tree for the game played between the board and the CEO. (See Chapter 12 on game theory for assistance in constructing this game.) Assume that the board moves first, choosing the type of salary offer. Assume that the CEO moves second, choosing her effort level. Be sure to enumerate payoffs to the board (and the shareholders they represent) and the CEO.

b. What is the equilibrium outcome for this game? What kind of contract should the board offer? What level of effort should the CEO choose?

18. Consider the questions faced by the board and the CEO in Problem 17. Assume that, as before, expending modest effort costs the CEO $300,000. But assume now that expending high effort costs the CEO $750,000.

a. Draw the extensive form for this game and find the equilibrium. (Again, for assistance in constructing this game, see Chapter 12 on game theory.) Does the change in the cost of high effort alter the outcome? Explain.

b. Demonstrate that the directors cannot improve their outcome by changing the base salary in the profit-sharing plan.

c. What is the minimum share of the firm's profit that will induce the CEO to expend high effort?

19. Most workplaces are subject to federal minimum wage guidelines, but restaurants are not. Currently, restaurant owners are required to pay waiters and waitresses only $2.13 per hour, provided that those servers are eligible to receive tips.

a. Explain how this pay scheme (low minimum plus tips) resolves a principal–agent problem for restaurant owners.

b. Explain how this pay scheme may backfire by creating a different principal–agent problem for restaurant owners.

20. Princess Buttercup has a multitude of potential suitors. She wishes to separate them into two groups—those who are truly interested in her hand in marriage, and those who are only interested because she's convenient, pretty, and rich. Let's call these two groups "interested" and "nonchalant," respectively. In an attempt to separate the two groups, Princess Buttercup devises a plan under which potential suitors must slay dragons before coming to the castle to court her.

• Those who slay the requisite number of dragons, $\bar{D}$, will be allowed to court her.

• Those who do not slay the requisite number of dragons will only be allowed to court Princess Buttercup's ugly half-sister, Princess Poison Ivy.

• To a member of either group, the benefit to courting Princess Buttercup is equal to $1,000.

• To a member of either group, the benefit to courting Princess Poison Ivy is $64.

• To a member of the "interested" group, who pursue their goal with unbridled passion, the cost of passing Princess Buttercup's test is given as D^2, where D is the number of dragons slain.

• To a member of the "nonchalant" group, who pursue their goal halfheartedly, the cost of passing Princess Buttercup's test is given as D^3, where D is the number of dragons slain.

a. Princess Buttercup wants to sort the interested suitors from the nonchalant suitors. What is the *minimum* number of dragons Princess Buttercup can ask potential suitors to slay if she wants them to separate into groups? (You can round to an appropriate integer.)

b. Suppose that Princess Buttercup asks suitors to slay *three fewer* dragons than you indicated in your answer to (a). Why will asking suitors to slay this many dragons not help Princess Buttercup filter out the nonchalant suitors?

c. What is the *maximum* number of dragons Princess Buttercup can ask potential suitors to slay if she wants to be able to distinguish between interested and nonchalant suitors? (Again, you may round your answer to an appropriate integer.)

d. Suppose that Princess Buttercup asks potential suitors to slay *three more* dragons than you indicated in your answer to (c). Why will asking suitors to slay this many dragons not help Princess Buttercup filter out the nonchalant suitors?

e. Suppose that Princess Buttercup has appropriately set the number of dragons, filtered out the nonchalant suitors, and chosen her prince from the pool of interested suitors. Now, she wishes to see if her prince wants her because of love, or whether her prince is only interested given her vast fortune. What modern American legal device might Princess Buttercup use as a screening tactic to discover the true answer? Explain your response.

*21. Suppose that there are two types of workers in the world: Charlie Hustles, who are high-productivity workers, and Lazy Susans, who are low-productivity workers. The market would pay $70,000 (this and all numbers in this question are in present value terms) to hire a Charlie Hustle, but only $20,000 to hire a Lazy Susan. The problem, of course, is that a firm cannot tell on sight whether a job applicant is a Charlie or a Susan. One way to attempt to separate the Chucks and the Suzies is to require a college degree. It is easy for a Charlie Hustle to obtain a degree (the degree takes four years to complete and costs $40,000 in total). It is harder for a Lazy Susan to obtain a degree (six years and a cost of $60,000). Assume that a college education adds nothing to either worker's productivity.

a. If the company, operating blindly with no degree requirements, were to pay an average wage of $45,000, what would most of its applicants look like?

b. Suppose that the company announces that it will pay $70,000 to those with college degrees, and $20,000 to those without. What is the net benefit of a college education to a Charlie? To a Susan? Does the degree requirement allow the firm to filter out low-quality applicants?

c. Suppose that a new federal subsidy to assist low-productivity workers reduces the cost of obtaining a degree to $46,000. What is the net benefit of a college education to a Charlie? To a Susan? Does the degree requirement allow the firm to filter out low-quality applicants?

d. In light of your answers to (b) and (c), discuss the following assertion: *To be effective, a signal must be costly, but it must be more costly for a low-productivity applicant.*

e. Colleges and universities have been accused of practicing grade inflation. In fact, some colleges have actually outlawed awarding a grade of "F." Given your answer to (d), discuss the impact of this practice on the signaling value of a college diploma. Is this practice good for students? Does your answer depend on the quality of the student? Explain.

*22. Peacocks, with their fabulous tails, live wild in the jungle. There, a tail is a detriment—it slows the birds in flight and presents an excellent handle for a predator to grab hold of. Nevertheless, males continue to grow them because peahens love bling, and the more, the better.

a. Explain the value of a long tail as a signal, focusing on the general principle that signals must be costly to a strong bird, but even more costly to a weak bird.

b. Peahens would receive the same information if all peacocks cut their tails in half. In light of this truth, explain why the signal is socially costly.

c. Suppose all male peacocks agreed to cut their tails in half. Explain why such an agreement is unlikely to last, and why the disintegration of the agreement makes all peacocks worse off.

23. In the late 1800s "wildcat banks," which were easy to charter and largely unregulated, sprang up across the American West. Some new banks chose to operate out of simple and inexpensive wooden structures, but others built elaborate buildings out of stone, with lots of gilding and other adornment.

a. Explain how the variety of building types that sprung up can be attributed, at least in part, to the potential for moral hazard.

b. Explain how the building choices of bankers in late 1800s America illustrate the inherent wastefulness of signaling.

Externalities and Public Goods

For people living in most major cities in the world, air pollution is a fact of life. Ozone, particulates, and general "crud" in the air result from economic activities like driving cars and operating factories. This pollution imposes a significant cost on the health of people who must live with it. Some studies estimate the damages in terms of health costs at more than $225 billion per year in the United States alone.[1]

Over the past 50 years, the United States has sought to reduce air pollution by setting limits on emissions by cars and by industries. In recent years, however, the baseline level of pollution on the West Coast (the level that would exist even if there were no domestic polluters) has risen significantly. Experts believe that a significant cause of the increase in baseline pollution comes from polluted air that originates in coal-burning power plants in Asia (primarily China), blows across the Pacific on the jet stream, and settles on the West Coast of the United States.

In this example, economic transactions take place between the power-producing plants and their customers in China, but they are not the only ones affected by those transactions: Inhabitants of the U.S. West Coast experience increased air pollution.

That's more than bad luck for the United States—it is a market failure. As we learned in Chapter 3, in efficient markets, every transaction that would benefit society does take place. It is this condition—that transactions make *society* better off as a whole, not just the parties directly involved in a transaction—that fails in the power plant example. The power plant in Asia looks at its costs and sets prices as the production and cost chapters here advise. The consumers of power take into account their costs and benefits. Neither considers the costs their transactions impose on West Coast residents in North America. An efficient market would take all costs into account, but because West Coasters are not part of the transaction, such costs do not enter into the firms' cost calculations and output decisions.

In Chapter 16, we saw that an imbalance of information between the participants in a transaction can lead to an inefficient market outcome (the production and consumption of too much or too little of a good), which reduces welfare by decreasing the surplus available to consumers and producers in a market. Asymmetric information is one source of market failure. In this chapter, we look at two other sources of market failures: *externalities* (such as pollution in our example) and *public goods* (which we discuss in detail later in the chapter). In addition to seeing why and how the existence of externalities and public goods cause market failures, we examine government policies that aim to eliminate market failures.

---

[1] World Bank, Institute for Health Metrics and Evaluation, *The Cost of Air Pollution: Strengthening the Economic Case for Action*, 2016.

left: Shi zhongwei/Imaginechina/AP Images; right: DSP/steinphoto/istock/E+/Getty Images

The pollution emitted by this coal-burning power plant in Changchun City in northeast China ends up in the air over Los Angeles and other West Coast cities and towns.

17.1 Externalities

externality A cost or benefit that affects a third party not directly involved in an economic transaction.

As we learned in the introduction, **externalities** are *costs or benefits that affect a third party not directly involved in an economic transaction*. **Negative externalities** (such as increased West Coast pollution) are *costs imposed on a third party not directly involved in an economic transaction*. **Positive externalities** are *benefits conferred on third parties who are not directly involved in an economic transaction*. A classic example of a positive externality involves bees. The bees in a beekeeper's hives not only produce honey for the beekeeper to sell but also help pollinate the crops and flowers on neighboring properties, a beneficial service for which neighbors often do not pay the beekeeper.

negative externality A cost imposed on a third party not directly involved in an economic transaction.

A free market usually does not produce the optimal quantity of goods with externalities present. Instead, the market will produce too much of those goods with negative externalities and not enough of the goods with positive externalities.

positive externality A benefit conferred on a third party not directly involved in an economic transaction.

Why Things Go Wrong: The Economic Inefficiencies from Externalities

external marginal cost The cost imposed on a third party when an additional unit of a good is produced or consumed.

Externalities create inefficient outcomes because society's overall benefit or cost from a transaction is different from the private benefit or cost to the consumer and producer involved in the transaction. We will regard **external marginal cost** as the *cost imposed on a third party when an additional unit of a good is produced or consumed*, and **external marginal benefit** as the *benefit conferred on a third party when an additional unit of a good is produced or consumed*.

external marginal benefit The benefit conferred on a third party when an additional unit of a good is produced or consumed.

When there are no externalities in a market, society's cost and benefit and private cost and benefit are the same. No external marginal costs or benefits exist. When there are externalities, though, there is a **social cost,** the *cost of an economic transaction to society as a whole, equal to the private cost plus the external cost*, as well as a **social benefit,** the *benefit of an economic transaction to society as a whole, equal to the private benefit plus the external benefit*. As we see in the next sections, incorporating social cost and benefit alters our analysis of market outcomes, including the optimal quantities and prices.

social cost The cost of an economic transaction to society as a whole, equal to the private cost plus the external cost.

social benefit The benefit of an economic transaction to society as a whole, equal to the private benefit plus the external benefit.

Negative Externalities: Too Much of a Bad Thing

To begin our study of negative externalities, let's look at the air pollution created by fossil-fuel-fired power plants when they generate electricity (**Figure 17.1**). Firms in a competitive industry decide how many megawatt hours (MWh) to produce by following the basic method presented in Chapter 8: Their optimal output is the point where price P (which, in a competitive market equals marginal revenue and is represented by the demand curve) equals the industry's marginal cost (MC_I).[2] Note, however, that this marginal cost is *private* marginal cost. It is not *social* marginal cost because it does not include any of the external costs that the industry's output imposes on other people. The power plant doesn't pay those costs. The industry produces Q_{MKT} MWh of electricity and the equilibrium market price per MWh is P_{MKT}.

Now let's assume that as the industry produces Q_{MKT}, it also produces particulates, ozone, and other pollutants that cause health and environmental damage to others. To make things easier, say the per-unit external marginal cost of pollution is constant and fixed at EMC.[3] External marginal cost is summarized by EMC in Figure 17.1.

To obtain the social marginal cost, we add together MC_I and EMC and come up with the curve SMC. Including the cost of the externality, society as a whole has a higher marginal cost of producing electricity than the industry alone (the SMC curve is above the MC_I curve). Considering all costs, the maximum total surplus occurs at Q^* and price P^*,

---

Figure 17.1   Negative Externalities in a Competitive Electricity Market

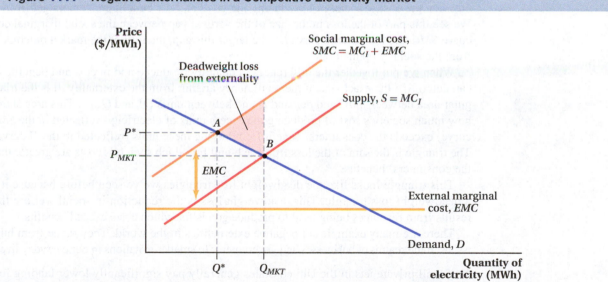

The social marginal cost of electricity (SMC) equals the industry's private marginal cost (MC_I) plus the external marginal cost (EMC). The socially optimal quantity of electricity, Q^*, is found at point A, the intersection of the social marginal cost curve (SMC) and D. In a competitive market, however, production occurs at point B (Q_{MKT}, P_{MKT}), where $MC_I = S = D$. Because the industry does not take into account the external marginal cost (EMC), it produces a quantity of electricity Q_{MKT} that is higher than the socially optimal quantity (Q^*). This results in a deadweight loss equal to the shaded triangle.

---

[2] Of course, power plants do not produce in a perfectly competitive market. We could do this exercise for a single firm with market power following the normal monopoly rule of setting output at the level for which marginal revenue equals marginal cost. Here, too, the external marginal cost would not be included in the firm's decision, leading to an inefficient level of output. Assuming a competitive industry makes the analysis simpler, though, so we will stick with that.

[3] In reality, external marginal cost can rise or fall as Q rises; the analysis is the same.

where price (demand) equals social marginal cost. Because we've now included the cost of the externality, the price is higher than that in the competitive market equilibrium, and the quantity produced is lower. When the production of a good creates a negative externality and its external cost is ignored by producers, the market produces more than the socially optimal level of output.

The pollution externality and the market inefficiency it creates arise because the power companies in the industry do not pay pollution costs. They pay only private production costs, such as expenditures for fuel, labor, physical capital, and so on. They ignore the external costs that society must bear because of the pollution the industry generates. (In the real world, power companies can be required to pay some of these external costs. We discuss how this is accomplished later in the chapter.) If the firms in the industry had to pay both of these costs, the industry would choose to generate a smaller quantity of electricity.

The inefficiency comes about because at point A, every person who buys electricity values it at least as much as it costs society to produce the electricity (including the pollution costs). The industry produces at point B, however, and the portion of the demand curve between points A and B represents consumers who value the electricity they want to purchase less than it costs society to produce. They buy the electricity only because the market price is lower that it would be if that price included the true cost of the product.

The size of the inefficiency depends on how many people buy electricity who otherwise wouldn't if the price represented the true social cost. This is reflected in the difference between Q^* and Q_{MKT}. The size of the inefficiency also depends on the discrepancy between the cost to society of producing the good and the benefit consumers get from it. We see this part of the loss in the size of the vertical gap between the social marginal cost curve SMC and the demand curve D: The larger this gap, the further the market outcome is from the socially optimal one.

When we put together the differences in quantity produced and in cost and benefit, we can determine the exact size of the inefficiency arising from the externality. It is the triangular area between SMC and demand D and between units Q^* and Q_{MKT}. This area shows how much society's cost of producing the excess units of electricity (reflected in the SMC curve) exceeds the consumers' benefit from buying these units (reflected in the D curve). The triangle is the sum of the loss from each unit for which society's costs are greater than the consumers' benefits.

This triangle looks like the deadweight loss triangles we've seen before because it *is* a deadweight loss triangle. This deadweight loss is the reduction in social welfare that results from resources being used to produce goods for which costs exceed benefits.

There are many examples of negative externalities in the world. They range from huge issues in the realms of businesses and governments to smaller irritations in our everyday lives.

■ Small private jets in the United States generally pay significantly lower landing fees than large commercial airplanes do, but they crowd the airspace and lead to flight delays for others. Because the private jets do not have to pay the full cost of their flights (such as the higher costs of congestion), this is a negative externality.

■ When individuals decide not to get vaccinated (or decide not to vaccinate their children), they and their children become carriers who can give the disease to others. When doctors overprescribe antibiotics for patients, bacteria develop resistance to the medicine. Because both these actions impose costs on third parties, they have negative externalities.

■ When you go to a sporting event and the person in front of you is wearing a big hat that blocks your view, she is not including the external marginal cost in that decision.

Remember that, without incorporating external cost into production decisions, firms will supply too much of goods that have negative externalities and sell them for too low a price.

figure it out 17.1

Go online for interactive, step-by-step help in solving the following problem.

Assume that notebook paper is sold in a perfectly competitive industry. The industry short-run supply curve (or marginal cost curve) is $P = MC = 2Q$, where Q is measured in millions of reams per year. The inverse demand for notebook paper is $P = 40 - 8Q$.

a. Find the equilibrium market price and quantity sold.

b. Suppose that, in their production processes, paper manufacturers have been dumping waste in nearby streams. The external marginal cost is estimated to be $0.50 for each ream produced. Calculate the socially optimal level of output and price for the paper industry.

Solution:

a. First, rearrange the inverse supply and demand equations to put them in terms of quantity supplied and quantity demanded:

$$P = 2Q \qquad\qquad P = 40 - 8Q$$
$$Q^S = 0.5P \qquad\quad 8Q = 40 - P$$
$$\qquad\qquad\qquad Q^D = 5 - 0.125P$$

Market equilibrium occurs where $Q^D = Q^S$:

$$0.5P = 5 - 0.125P$$
$$0.625P = 5$$
$$P = \$8$$

When $P = \$8$,

$$Q^S = 0.5P = 0.5(8) = 4$$
$$Q^D = 5 - 0.125P = 5 - 0.125(8) = 5 - 1 = 4$$

Paper will sell for $8 per ream, and 4 million reams will be sold each year.

b. The social marginal cost is equal to the industry marginal cost plus the external marginal cost:

$$SMC = MC + EMC$$
$$= 2Q + 0.50$$

To find the socially optimal price and quantity, we equate the social marginal cost with the inverse demand:

$$2Q + 0.50 = 40 - 8Q$$
$$10Q = 39.50$$
$$Q^* = 3.95$$

The socially optimal level of output is 3.95 million reams of paper each year.

The socially optimal price can be found by substituting the optimal quantity into either the social marginal cost or inverse demand curves:

$$P^* = 2Q + 0.50 = 2(3.95) + 0.50 = \$7.90 + 0.50 = \$8.40$$
$$= 40 - 8Q = 40 - 8(3.95) = 40 - 31.60 = \$8.40$$

Therefore, the socially optimal price is $8.40 per ream.

Positive Externalities: Not Enough of a Good Thing

A positive externality exists when economic activity has a spillover benefit enjoyed by third parties who are not directly engaged in the activity. Just as negative externalities create a gap between private marginal cost and social marginal cost (equal to the external marginal cost), positive externalities create a gap between private benefit (as summarized by the demand curve) and social benefit. The social benefit is represented by the social demand curve, which is the sum of the buyers' private benefit (the demand curve) and the external marginal benefit.

We can explore positive externalities by looking at the decision about how many years of education to get. People generally benefit from acquiring more education, and we express that in a demand curve. There is also a cost (sometimes a huge one!) to spending more years in school that includes not only tuition, books, and supplies, but also the opportunity cost of not being able to take a job that pays a salary while you are busy in school (which is often much more than the tuition). Evidence suggests, however, that the more people in a city who have advanced educations, the better the pay and job prospects of *other* people living in their area. One possible explanation for this link is that the more education you have, the more likely you are to start companies and hire other people. If true, there is a positive externality from your decision to spend additional years in school. The social benefit of that extra education is greater than the private benefit. It should come as no surprise then that in a circumstance like this, the free market will lead people to obtain fewer years of education than would be socially optimal.

To see why, consider the market for college degrees that is represented in **Figure 17.2**. To keep it simple, assume all college degrees are of equal value and the market for education is perfectly competitive.

The number of students getting a college degree will be at the point where the private marginal benefit of the college degree (measured by the demand curve) equals the private marginal cost of obtaining the degree (point *B*). Left to its own devices, the free-market equilibrium occurs where Q_{MKT} college degrees are produced and consumed, and the price of a college degree is P_{MKT} (where $MC = P = MR$ for a competitive market).

The external marginal benefit *EMB* from each person obtaining a college degree is shown by the *EMB* curve.[4] The social demand curve *SD* is the private marginal benefit (demand curve) plus the external marginal benefit. *SD* measures the marginal benefit of college degrees to society as a whole, rather than only students. In Figure 17.2, $SD = D + EMB$.

The socially optimal number of college degrees occurs at point *A*, the intersection of the marginal cost curve and the social demand curve *SD*. At this point, Q^* degrees are awarded at a price of P^*. In the free-market outcome (point *B*), however, the quantity

Figure 17.2   Positive Externalities in the Market for College Degrees

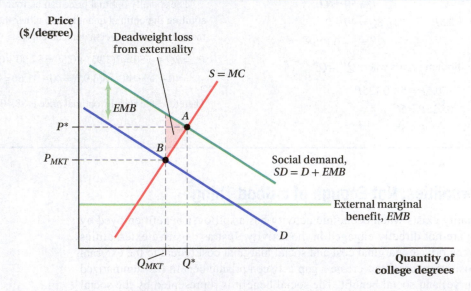

The social demand for college degrees (*SD*) equals the private marginal benefit curve (*D*) plus the external marginal benefit (*EMB*). The socially optimal number of college degrees, Q^*, is found at point *A*, the intersection of the marginal cost curve $S = MC$ and *SD*. In an unregulated market for college degrees, production occurs at point *B* (Q_{MKT}, P_{MKT}), where $D = S = MC$. Because the market does not take into account the external marginal benefit (*EMB*), it ends up producing fewer college degrees Q_{MKT} than the socially optimal quantity (Q^*), resulting in a deadweight loss equal to the shaded triangle.

---

[4] Again, for convenience, we assume that the *EMB* is flat—the same external marginal benefit per additional college degree—but it could be rising or falling with the number of degrees awarded without significantly altering the analysis.

of degrees Q_{MKT} is too low and creates a deadweight loss equal to the shaded triangle in Figure 17.2. For all the potential degrees between Q_{MKT} and Q^*, the social demand curve lies above the marginal cost curve, but the private demand curve is below marginal cost. As a result, some people choose not to seek degrees even though society as a whole would prefer that they did. Those potential students do not consider the external marginal benefit when deciding to obtain a college degree—for them, the private benefit is not great enough to convince them that a college degree is worth it, even though the social benefit actually makes getting that degree optimal from a societal standpoint. The bottom line is that when a good has a positive externality associated with it, the market will likely provide too little of the good because the external marginal benefit is ignored.

Later in the chapter, we talk in detail about how governments can encourage greater production and consumption in markets with positive externalities. For now, just note that states and countries tend to subsidize college education to persuade their citizens to get more education than they would choose to acquire on their own.

Another classic example of positive externalities includes the research and development (R&D) undertaken by companies in many industries. These firms spend money to come up with new and better products, but often the discoveries they make help other firms improve their own products and come up with new ideas. Apple created the iOS operating system for iPhones and iPads through their own R&D and, in turn, this creation enabled app developers to create programs they could sell for a profit. For example, Epic Games (a computer game developer) created its popular Fortnite game, which has been downloaded by tens of millions of iPhone and iPad users. Without Apple's R&D, Epic would not have been able to make so much money. Because Apple does not fully take account of the social demand curve when producing its R&D, it likely produces less R&D than society would like it to. The same is true for scientific research of many kinds, especially basic science research. Firms won't produce enough R&D if they can't fully recover or capture the social benefits of the R&D production.

Positive externalities are also attached to activities that make things safer for others or that improve the value of other people's property. Thus, companies that spend money on cybersecurity help make the Internet safer for everyone, and people who invest in the appearance of their homes raise property values for the whole neighborhood.

 ## Application: Device-Finding Apps and Positive Externalities

One morning in 2017, a Port Orange, Florida, homeowner awoke to, rather than from, a nightmare. His home had been burglarized while he slept. The two thieves took many valuables from inside the house, including the keys to both his pickup and Corvette convertible. They helped themselves to the vehicles in the driveway for use as getaway cars.

As stunned as he was by all that had happened inside his home, the homeowner was still able to do some quick thinking that stopped what could have turned out to be an even worse crime spree. He realized his iPad was one of the items the burglars had pilfered. So, he used the "Find My iPad" app to locate the device. As it happened, the iPad was at a hotel the next town over. Police rushed to the hotel and found the burglars and their loot. They recovered the stolen property, and they couldn't have made the arrests a minute too soon. The burglars admitted to police that they had just gotten started; their plan was to commit several more armed robberies later that day. Find My iPad saved the day.[5]

---

[5] Katie Kustura, "Burglars Hit New Smyrna Beach's Venezia Neighborhood," *The Daytona Beach News-Journal*, August 15, 2017, http://www.news-journalonline.com/news/20170818/teens-arrested-in-volusia-burglary-spree.

Millions of tablet computers, smartphones, and other electronic devices are stolen every year. A number of apps exist that help owners track down their devices when stolen, like the Find My iPad feature used by the burglary victim. However, many device owners (most, according to some surveys) have not configured their devices so they can be located remotely. Why aren't more people taking advantage of this ability? Externalities are one big reason.

Because thieves can't usually tell which devices have location-detecting software installed, the apps do not directly deter thefts. Once the device is stolen, however, the apps increase the likelihood that the thief will be caught. Still, the software indirectly plays a role in deterring device thefts. As more device owners install the software, thieves realize that the likelihood of being caught when stealing any given device increases. Thus, every time someone installs Find My iPad or a similar app on his or her phone, it reduces the chance that *any* device (the installer's, yours, and everyone else's) will be stolen.

These findings imply that the social benefit of installing software that can locate a stolen device is likely to be large relative to the private benefit. Most of the software's theft-deterring properties apply to all devices, not just those with the software installed. The private benefit is the increased likelihood that the device on which the feature is installed will be recovered and returned, while the social benefit is an overall reduction in theft. In other words, Find My iPad has a positive externality: When device owners install the anti-theft software, they do not partake in many of the benefits created for all other device owners. As a result, the actual number of installed apps is likely to fall below the optimal level. ■

17.2 Correcting Externalities

Left to its own devices, a free market with negative externalities produces more than the welfare-maximizing quantity (and less than optimal if there are positive externalities). As a result, the free market generates a deadweight loss when externalities exist.

But society is not necessarily doomed to live with this inefficiency. Just as we saw in Chapter 16—that asymmetric information's potential welfare losses give incentives for institutions to remedy them—the same is true for externalities. Governments or the economic actors in these markets may implement one of several interventions that can reduce the inefficiencies externalities create.

Externality fixes come in two basic types: those that work through their effect on price and those that work through their effect on quantity. Both steer the market away from the inefficient outcome of the private market (in which only private marginal costs and benefits are considered) toward the more efficient outcome (which include social marginal costs and benefits in the decisions).

To understand the mechanisms, we will focus on the case of the negative externality from pollution.

The Efficient Level of Pollution

efficient level of pollution The level of emissions necessary to produce the efficient quantity of the good tied to the externality.

Before considering how to correct for an externality, we need to consider how the government chooses its efficiency target. The goal is to set the total level of pollution at the efficient level. The **efficient level of pollution** is the *level of emissions necessary to produce the efficient quantity of the good tied to the externality.* That's the level resulting from the quantity where demand equals marginal *social* cost.

We can also think about the efficient amount of pollution (or any negative externality) as the level that balances its costs and benefits. Pollution's costs—the health and environmental consequences—are easy to grasp. Its "benefits," though, may be harder to imagine. They derive from the fact that some pollution is an automatic by-product of the production of goods, for example, electricity. To ban pollution would mean banning the production of all these goods and would create a loss for society. The "benefit" from pollution then simply reflects the benefit of the goods that require pollution to supply. (It is for this reason that market efficiency does not generally mean the level of a negative externality must be driven to zero.)

We can see how the efficient level of pollution is determined in **Figure 17.3**. In reality, the marginal cost of pollution (MC_P) likely rises with the level of pollution. The incremental damage of more pollution may be modest at low levels, but the severity of the damage grows as the pollution increases. This is reflected in the shape of curve MC_P in Figure 17.3.

The marginal benefit of pollution (MB_P), on the other hand, is likely to be high at low levels because *some* positive level of pollution is necessary to make goods. But the marginal benefit will fall as pollution output increases (and as output of the good increases). These factors are reflected in curve MB_P in Figure 17.3.

A different way to think about the marginal benefit curve MB_P is to consider how much it would cost a firm to reduce the level of pollution it creates. Just as the MB_P curve shows the marginal benefit from more pollution, it also reflects the flip-side: the marginal cost of *cutting* pollution, also called *pollution abatement*. Every unit of pollution a producer cuts entails a lost marginal benefit—giving up the sale of something that they could make (but would generate that extra unit of pollution). As more cuts in the amount of pollution are made (i.e., as we move from right to left along the horizontal axis in the figure), the marginal cost of cutting pollution rises. Therefore, MB_P also reflects the marginal cost of cutting pollution, which economists often call the **marginal abatement cost (MAC)**, the *cost of reducing emissions by 1 unit*. This is shown in Figure 17.3 by indicating that MB_P and MAC are equal. We can think of it either way.

marginal abatement cost (MAC) The cost of reducing emissions by 1 unit.

The efficient level of pollution is where its marginal benefit equals its marginal cost, or Q_{poll} in Figure 17.3. If something's marginal benefit is higher than its marginal cost, produce more; if its marginal cost is greater than its marginal benefit, produce less. The maximum benefit occurs where the two are equal.

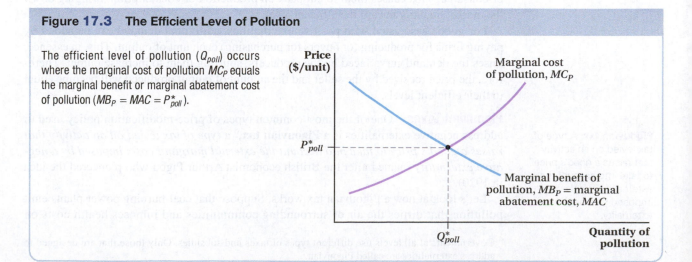

Figure 17.3 The Efficient Level of Pollution

The efficient level of pollution (Q_{poll}) occurs where the marginal cost of pollution MC_P equals the marginal benefit or marginal abatement cost of pollution ($MB_P = MAC = P^*_{poll}$).

If we want to think of the marginal benefit curve as being the marginal abatement cost curve instead, we can interpret optimal pollution in terms of emissions cuts. Emissions should be cut whenever the marginal cost of a reduction in the level of emissions (as reflected by the MAC curve) is less than the reduced harm (as reflected by MC_P). This will be true at any pollution levels greater than Q_{poll}^*. On the other hand, if marginal abatement costs are greater than the marginal cost of the pollution, which will be the case at pollution levels less than Q_{poll}^*, then pollution cuts should be scaled back. These considerations are balanced at the optimal pollution level Q_{poll}^*.

The optimal "price" of pollution is equal to the marginal cost of pollution (and marginal benefit) at the optimal quantity, or P_{poll}^* in Figure 17.3. If pollution were tradable (which, as we see later, it can be), at P_{poll}^* polluters would be willing to purchase the right to pollute up to the level Q_{poll}^*. For levels of pollution below Q_{poll}^*, the price Q_{poll}^* is lower than the value from being able to pollute more (measured by the marginal benefit of pollution). At the same time, those harmed by pollution would still be willing to sell an amount of pollution rights equal to Q_{poll}^*, because at this price they are being more than compensated for the harm they suffer ($P_{poll}^* > MC_p$).

In principle, an efficient level of pollution could result from either price or quantity mechanisms. If regulators could impose the socially optimal price in a market, for instance, the quantity (of either the good or the externality) at that price would also be at its optimal level. Similarly, if regulators could specify the socially optimal quantity, the price at that quantity would be the optimal price. In practice, however, we will see that one approach may be easier than the other to enact, depending on the nature of the externality and the information available to regulators.

Using Prices to Correct Externalities

One way to view the failure of the free market in the presence of externalities is that the market participants do not consider the correct, society-wide costs and benefits when they make their decisions. If we could modify prices so the private cost matched the social cost or so the private benefit matched the social benefit, then producers and consumers would make the choice that results in a welfare-maximizing price and quantity.

For goods tied to negative externalities, price-based mechanisms apply additional costs by making firms or consumers pay an extra amount for each unit of the good they produce or consume. This causes them to cut back on production or consumption, bringing down the market quantity toward the efficient level.

For goods associated with positive externalities, additional demand can be added by paying firms for producing (or buyers for purchasing) each unit of output. This, in essence, raises the demand curve faced by the producers, spurring them to increase output. Therefore, the price received by the seller and the amount of output produced will become equal to their efficient levels.

Pigouvian Taxes   One of the most common types of price-modification policy used to address negative externalities is a **Pigouvian tax,**[6] *a type of tax levied on an activity that raises a good's price to take into account the external marginal costs imposed by a negative externality* (named after the British economist Arthur Pigou who pioneered the idea in 1920).[7]

Let's look at how a Pigouvian tax works. Suppose that coal-burning power plants emit pollution that dirties the air of surrounding communities and imposes health costs on

Pigouvian tax A type of tax levied on an activity that raises a good's price to take into account the external marginal costs imposed by a negative externality.

---

[6] Governments at all levels use different types of taxes and subsidies. Only those that are designed to address externalities are called Pigouvian.

[7] Arthur C. Pigou, *The Economics of Welfare*, London: Macmillan, 1920.

the people living in those areas. A Pigouvian tax on electricity generated by these plants would bring equilibrium in the electricity market toward an efficient level of output and price (**Figure 17.4**).

Because the electricity industry's private marginal costs MC_I are not the same as the social marginal costs SMC, we get overproduction: The power company generates Q_{MKT} when the optimal quantity is Q^*.

Now, let's say that a government could impose a tax T per MWh on electricity production equal to the external marginal cost EMC of pollution. This would increase the private marginal cost of supplying energy, and shift MC_I up to $MC_I + T$. Because $T = EMC$, the industry's marginal cost curve is now the same as the social marginal cost curve SMC. The old marginal cost curve MC_I intersected the demand curve at the price P_{MKT}. At that price, the industry's output was Q_{MKT}. If the size of the tax is chosen so that the tax-inclusive marginal cost curve $MC_I + T$ intersects the demand curve at the efficient price P^*, the industry's output falls to the efficient quantity Q^*.

The Pigouvian tax raises the electricity industry's marginal cost by an amount equal to the external damages its production causes. This exactly aligns the industry's private incentives with society's. In effect, the Pigouvian tax "internalizes" the pollution externality. That is, the tax forces the industry to take into account the external damage of its operations when it decides how much electricity to generate. This process results in the efficient market outcome.

In reality, there are all kinds of Pigouvian taxes. One of the rationales for placing taxes on cigarettes and alcohol, and for recent calls to impose a tax on soda, arises from the external costs (from secondhand smoke, drunk driving, obesity, health expenses, etc.) that consumers of these goods do not otherwise bear.

Figure 17.4   A Pigouvian Tax Corrects for a Negative Externality

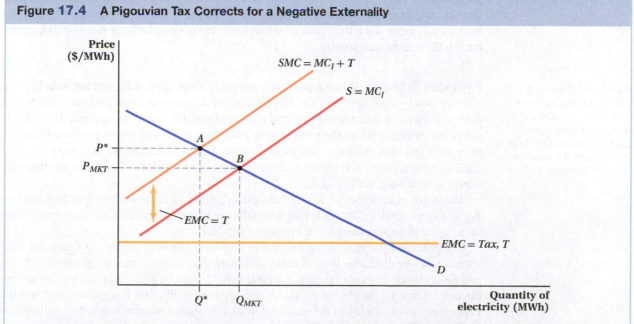

In an unregulated market, the power industry overproduces quantity Q_{MKT} at price P_{MKT} (point B). A Pigouvian tax (T) equal to the external marginal cost EMC shifts the supply curve (S) up from marginal cost $S = MC_I$ to the social marginal cost curve (SMC). Now, the industry produces at point A, where SMC intersects demand (D), and supplies the socially efficient quantity Q^* MWh at price P^*.

🔪 Application: The Social Cost of Carbon

One of the most important economic numbers in policy debates about climate change is the social cost of carbon (SCC). The SCC is the negative externality that will result from one additional unit of carbon dioxide emissions through its effects on climate change. Another way to describe the SCC is that it is how big the Pigouvian tax would have to be to lead to the socially optimal amount of carbon dioxide emissions.

Many environmental economists have tried to measure the social cost of carbon. It isn't easy; there is a lot of uncertainty about how the climate works, the types and magnitudes of economic effects that climate change will have, and how much people today should weigh the welfare of future generations. All these factors need to be taken into account to arrive at an estimate. That's why the estimates have varied widely, from less than $20 per metric ton to over $600 per metric ton.

A recent estimate by the Nobel Prize–winning economist William Nordhaus has received a lot of attention.[8] Using the latest version of a large model of the climate and the economy, he computes a SCC of about $36 per metric ton (in 2018 dollars). To put that in perspective, a typical car produces about 5 metric tons of carbon dioxide per year. Therefore, if Nordhaus's calculation was used to establish a climate change Pigouvian tax, it would be about $180 per year for a typical car.

You might be thinking, "Well, it's not as if $180 a year is nothing, but I would still keep driving if this was the tax. How is that going to stop my carbon emissions?" The answer is that it won't stop your carbon emissions, nor should it. You derive a benefit from being able to drive around; that's why you would pay the tax. Without a carbon tax, you would add to the climate change problem without paying for the damage you are doing. If a tax is imposed (and it is set at the true social cost of carbon dioxide emissions), you would pay for exactly the amount of damage you do. You will balance this cost against the benefit you obtain from your car and drive the optimal amount from a social perspective. This will be less than the amount you drove when there was no tax and you did not pay for your negative externality, but it will be more than nothing. ∎

Pigouvian subsidy A subsidy paid for an activity that can be used to decrease a good's price (paid by the buyer) to take into account the external marginal benefits.

Pigouvian Subsidy   When a positive externality does exist, a **Pigouvian subsidy** — *a subsidy paid for an activity that can be used to decrease a good's price (paid by the buyer) to take into account the external marginal benefits* — may be applied. The subsidy raises the effective price (the market price plus the subsidy) at which producers can sell their products, thus making it profit-maximizing for them to increase their outputs to the socially optimal level. You would analyze the subsidy in much the same way as other subsidies, as discussed in Chapter 3.

There are many types of actual subsidies that are at least supposed to be based on Pigouvian principles. Tax credits for education or to buy hybrid cars and energy-efficient home appliances are examples of Pigouvian subsidies.

One practical problem facing Pigouvian taxes and subsidies is how to figure out their correct size. Realistically, it's difficult to estimate the exact external marginal cost of carbon pollution or the exact external marginal benefit from more college degrees, so setting the correct rate for the Pigouvian tax or subsidy is also difficult. If a government sets the Pigouvian tax or subsidy at the incorrect level, the market price and quantity will still be inefficient. We discuss this problem in greater detail below.

[8] William D. Nordhaus, "Revisiting the Social Cost of Carbon," *Proceedings of the National Academy of Sciences* 114, no. 7 (2017): 1518–1523.

figure it out 17.2

Go online for interactive, step-by-step help in solving the following problem.

Refer to Figure It Out 17.1 on page 599. Suppose the government places a $0.50 tax on each ream of paper sold.

a. What price would buyers pay, and what price would sellers receive (net of the tax)?

b. How many reams of paper would be sold?

Solution:

a. To solve this problem, we can use the method we learned in Chapter 3, where we consider that the price paid by buyers, P_b, is equal to the price received by sellers, P_s, plus the tax: $P_b = P_s + T$. Therefore, $P_b = P_s + 0.50$. We can rewrite the demand curve and the supply curve (the industry marginal cost curve) from Figure It Out 17.1:

$$Q^D = 5 - 0.125P_b \quad \text{and} \quad Q^S = 0.5P_s$$

Because $P_b = P_s + 0.50$, we can substitute this expression into the demand curve for P_b:

$$Q^D = 5 - 0.125P_b = 5 - 0.125(P_s + 0.50)$$
$$= 5 - 0.125P_s - 0.0625 = 4.9375 - 0.125P_s$$

Now that the supply and demand equations are both written in terms of P_s, we can solve $Q^D = Q^S$:

$$4.9375 - 0.125P_s = 0.5P_s$$
$$0.625P_s = 4.9375$$
$$P_s = \$7.90$$
$$P_b = P_s = +0.50 = \$7.90 + \$0.50 = \$8.40$$

Note that this is the socially optimal price we found in Figure It Out 17.1.

b. To solve for the quantity sold, we can substitute the buyer's price ($P_b = \$8.40$) into the demand curve or the seller's price ($P_s = \$7.90$) into the supply curve:

$$Q^D = 5 - 0.125P_b = 5 - 0.125(8.4) = 5 - 1.05 = 3.95$$
$$Q^S = 0.5P_s = 0.5(7.9) = 3.95$$

This is the socially optimal quantity.

 **Application: Would Higher Driving Taxes Make Us Happier Drivers?**

Imagine you were the only driver on the road. You could go fast, ignore stop lights and stop signs, and make left turns without first checking for oncoming traffic—all with no worry that you'd hit another car. Having other drivers on the road creates negative externalities. The research company INRIX recently estimated that road congestion costs Americans over $300 billion a year in fuel costs and lost productivity.[9] That doesn't even account for the fender benders and other accidents generated by having other cars on the road. Most mistakes that drivers make, such as swerving out of a lane or running a stop sign, only cause a crash if there is another car present to hit.

Some locations have become very creative, in economic terms, in an attempt to limit the negative externality of drivers. London, for example, institutes a Pigouvian tax—a £11.50 (about $15) toll—on drivers who enter the city's central district during the workweek. The island city-state of Singapore applies a Pigouvian tax to the car itself. The average excise tax paid when you buy a new car in Singapore is in excess of 100% of the market price of the car (you're looking at about $80,000 for a modest sedan). Other cities with congestion taxes include Stockholm and Milan, and similar taxes have been proposed by local governments in New York City and Chicago. The point of these charges is to reduce the social costs of wasted time, pollution, and injuries and deaths from crashes.

[9] Graham Cookson, *INRIX Global Traffic Scorecard*, INRIX Research, Kirkland, WA, February 2018.

The development of autonomous vehicles (AVs) has many people thinking about how moving to a world where most cars are autonomous would affect the negative externalities of congestion. On the one hand, simulations indicate that a given number of AVs can move more quickly and with fewer collisions on a given network of roads than can vehicles driven by humans. On the other hand, not having to pay attention while being in a car might make "driving" less costly for people, raising the demand for travel and tending to increase congestion. What size the optimal Pigouvian tax should be in this world will depend on the relative size of these competing considerations.

One scenario that people have contemplated is whether AV-facilitated ridesharing services might tend toward monopoly. Basically, everyone in a given market would be driven around by one company's robot cars. We aren't sure if such would be the case, but if things do end up that way, then it's not clear Pigouvian taxes will be needed to solve the congestion problem. The reason is that any congestion externality a monopolist rideshare company imposes would be an imposition on *itself*. Thus, the company will take into account how adding vehicles to the market would negatively affect the efficiency with which its existing vehicles operate (both through its operating costs and its customers' willingness to pay for its rides). It would, as economists say, "internalize the externality." It will operate an efficient number of vehicles. ■

Quantity Mechanisms to Correct Externalities

Quantity-based interventions have the same goal as price-based mechanisms: to move a market with externalities toward the efficient outcome. They just use a different lever.

quota A regulation mandating that the production or consumption of a certain quantity of a good or externality be limited (negative externality) or required (positive externality).

Quotas   The simplest of the quantity-based approaches is to set a **quota,** a *regulation mandating that the production or consumption of a certain quantity of a good or externality be limited (negative externality) or required (positive externality).* Limiting quotas are also called caps (and required quotas are called floors). By regulating the amount of output, the cap also regulates the amount of the externality associated with producing the output. As you would expect, with negative externalities, the quantity restriction must be set below the free-market equilibrium quantity to match the socially efficient quantity.

In **Figure 17.5**, we look once again at the market for electricity production and see that the pollution externality leads to excessive production at Q_{MKT} and an inefficient market outcome. Suppose the government enacts a law mandating that the production of electricity can be no greater than Q^*. With this law in place, the private MC_I curve becomes vertical at that quantity level. The private MC_I curve now intersects the demand curve at point A, and the private decision matches the socially efficient one.

Examples of quotas used to reduce externalities in real life include restrictions on the amount of pollution factories can emit, the amount of noise neighbors can make, or the number of tourists that can visit a fragile site in a day. Hunting and fishing licenses limit the number of fish or animals a person can take because of the negative externality of overfishing and overhunting.

We see fewer real-world mandates for positive externalities that require people to supply a minimum quantity that is higher than the free-market equilibrium output. However, they do exist. People are required by law to attend school until age 16 in most states. Many states mandate vaccines for infectious diseases for any child who attends school or auto liability insurance for anyone who drives a car. Each of these is a quantity-based way to promote more of an activity that has a positive externality on others.

Practically speaking, however, the use of quotas creates complications. First, as with setting Pigouvian taxes, it is difficult to determine what the socially optimal amount of the quotas should be.

Figure 17.5   The Effects of a Quota on a Market with a Negative Externality

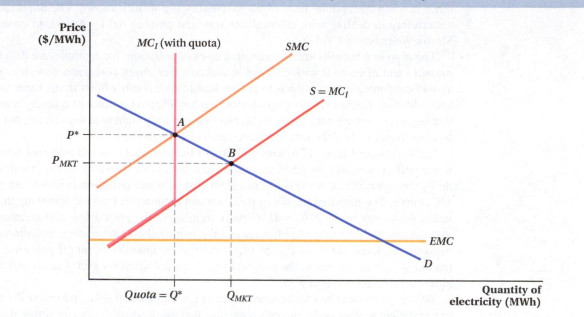

In an unregulated market, the power industry overproduces the quantity of electricity (Q_{MKT}) at price P_{MKT} (point B). When the government enacts a quota limiting production to Q^*, the private marginal cost curve MC_I becomes vertical at Q^*, intersecting the social marginal cost SMC and demand D at the socially optimal quantity Q^* and price P^* (point A).

Second, the government often wants to influence the total amount of an externality produced by an industry, but can only set quotas on a firm-by-firm basis. For example, it might be much more expensive to reduce pollution emitted from old power plants and much cheaper to reduce pollution from newer plants. Under these conditions, enacting a rule that says each plant must hit the same target level will not be the most cost-effective way to accomplish the goal of less pollution. (In the next section, we will discuss how granting permits and allowing permit holders to buy and sell them can solve this complication.)

Third is the question of the distribution of costs and benefits. A Pigouvian tax, for example, generates revenues for the government (or costs the government in the case of subsidies). With quotas and mandates, the benefits or costs are left with the market participants. With licensing, the government receives some revenue, while market participants incur some cost but also reap some benefits.

Government Provision of a Good   Another type of quantity intervention in the case of positive externalities occurs when the government actually provides the product itself. Basic scientific research has a large positive externality and little private sponsorship, so the federal government subsidizes it through tax credits and research funding. Governments also perform research directly, as does the United States at the National Institutes of Health and a system of federal labs around the country.

Price-Based versus Quantity-Based Interventions with Uncertainty

We saw above that, as a matter of principle, quantity and price mechanisms can be equally effective at addressing externalities. In reality, though, there are situations in which one type of market intervention might be preferred to the other.

A particularly important situation in which one mechanism might be preferred to the other is when the optimal level of the externality is not fully known. The importance of uncertainty in dealing with externalities was first pointed out by American economist Martin Weitzman in 1974.[10]

The marginal benefits and the marginal costs of pollution, for example, are difficult to measure and often shift with changes in technologies, input costs, and new discoveries about how damaging pollution is to human health. As a result, efforts to intervene in markets with externalities are generally inexact, so any Pigouvian taxes or quantity mandates that regulators set are not exactly right. Not being exactly right is always costly, but it can be even more costly if the wrong intervention is used.

Let's consider **Figure 17.6**, which illustrates the marginal cost and marginal benefit of water pollution caused by fertilizer runoff from farms (measured in parts per million, or milligrams per liter of water). The marginal cost of water pollution is illustrated by the MC_P curve. The marginal benefit of pollution and the marginal cost of removing this pollution are shown by the $MB_P = MAC$ curve (remember the prior discussion underscoring that the marginal benefit of pollution and the marginal cost of abating pollution really measure the same thing). In Figure 17.6, the efficient quantity of runoff pollution in the market Q^*_{poll} is found where the marginal benefit of pollution is exactly equal to the marginal cost of pollution (point A).

Before we examine how uncertainty can affect the ability of a regulation to move the market to its efficient level of pollution, let's remember that the deadweight loss occurring when the pollution level is not at the efficient level equals the area between the marginal benefit of pollution (alternatively, the marginal abatement costs) and the marginal cost of pollution for each of the units of pollution between the efficient level of pollution and the current level of pollution.

Figure 17.6   When Quantity Mechanisms Are Preferable to Price Mechanisms

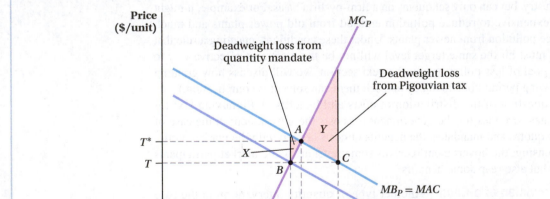

$MB_P = MAC$ and MC_P are the marginal benefit (marginal abatement cost) and marginal cost of pollution curves for farmers' fertilizer use. The efficient level of water pollution is quantity Q^*_{poll} of fertilizer runoff. If government regulators incorrectly estimate farmers' marginal abatement costs at $MAC_e < MAC$, the quantity-based intervention would reduce pollution to $Q_{poll\,B} < Q^*_{poll}$, while the Pigouvian tax would increase pollution to $Q_{poll\,C} > Q^*_{poll}$. Because MAC is flat relative to MC_P, the quantity-based intervention is preferable to the price mechanism, as seen by comparing the resulting deadweight losses from the two interventions ($X < Y$).

[10] Martin Weitzman, "Prices vs. Quantities," *The Review of Economic Studies* 41, no. 4 (1974): 477–491.

If the level of pollution is too high (to the right of Q^*_{poll}), pollution costs society more (as seen by the MC_P curve) than its value (in terms of output produced along with the pollution, reflected in the MB_P curve). If the level of pollution is inefficiently low (i.e., the level lies to the left of Q^*_{poll}), there are units of pollution that provide greater value (in terms of the output that would be produced along with the pollution) than their cost to society.

Now suppose the regulator does not know exactly what farmers' marginal abatement costs are, and so is unsure about the true marginal benefits of water pollution. Can we say whether the regulator would be better off choosing a quantity- or price-based mechanism to reduce the pollution to its efficient level?

For example, suppose the regulator mistakenly estimates farmers' marginal abatement costs as being lower than they really are, shown by curve $MB_{P_e} = MAC_e$ in Figure 17.6. If these were the true abatement costs, the optimal level of pollution would be $Q_{poll\,B}$ because the marginal cost of pollution is equal to the estimated marginal benefit of pollution at point B. The regulator could achieve a pollution level of $Q_{poll\,B}$ in two ways: by limiting the quantity of fertilizer used so that total runoff pollution is $Q_{poll\,B}$, or by setting a tax on runoff at price T.

If the regulator uses a quota, the amount of pollution will be limited to $Q_{poll\,B}$, lower than the socially optimal level Q^*_{poll}. In this case, the deadweight loss from incorrectly mandating the quantity is the triangle X in Figure 17.6. This area reflects the pollution for which the true marginal benefit is higher than the marginal cost to society. This pollution does not occur, however, because of the quantity restriction at the wrong pollution level.

If the regulator instead uses a Pigouvian tax equal to T, farmers will reduce their fertilizer use from where it would be without any tax until their marginal abatement cost equals the tax (at point C). Additional cuts in the level of pollution beyond this point would be more expensive (in terms of forgone output) than simply paying the pollution tax. So, this incorrect tax (due to the mis-estimate of marginal abatement costs) results in the farmers polluting an amount, $Q_{poll\,C}$, that is greater than the optimal level. The deadweight loss from this mistake by the regulator is area Y. Comparing area Y (caused by setting the wrong price) to the deadweight loss of area X (caused by setting the wrong quantity), it's clear that setting the wrong tax creates a much bigger loss, even though both the quantity restriction and tax were not far from their optimal values in absolute terms. Note that the optimal tax level would be T^*, which would result in the efficient level of pollution Q^*_{poll}.

This result, that price-based mechanisms led to larger inefficiency losses, is *not* always true, and it is not a consequence of the regulator believing that abatement costs were lower than they actually were. If the regulator were instead mistaken in the other direction—that is, it thought abatement costs were higher than they really were—we'd find the same result. (Though in that case, pollution will be above the optimal level under a quantity-based intervention and below it with a Pigouvian tax.)

The reason why the deadweight losses are so much larger with price mechanisms in this example is because in this case the marginal abatement curve is relatively flat and the marginal cost of pollution curve is relatively steep. The flat MAC curve implies that farmers' abatement choices are very sensitive to the price of abatement (in other words, the tax), so being just a little wrong on setting a Pigouvian tax leads to wild swings in the amount of pollution the farmers create. These large swings, in turn, cause big inefficiency losses because the marginal cost of pollution is so sensitive to the amount of pollution (as shown by the steep MC_P curve). Therefore, when faced with cases in which farmers' abatement choices are sensitive to a tax and the marginal cost of pollution is likely to rise rapidly with pollution, regulators should favor quantity-based interventions. That way, if they're wrong about how much tweaking the market needs, damages will be limited.

If the situation were reversed, with a steep marginal abatement cost curve and a flat marginal cost of pollution curve, the price mechanism would cause smaller inefficiency losses than the quota. This case is shown in **Figure 17.7**.

Figure 17.7 **When Price Mechanisms Are Preferable to Quantity Mechanisms**

If government regulators incorrectly estimate farmers' marginal abatement costs at $MAC_e < MAC$, the quantity-based intervention would reduce pollution to $Q_{poll_B} < Q^*_{poll}$, while the Pigouvian tax would increase pollution to $Q_{poll_C} > Q^*_{poll}$. Because MAC is steep relative to the marginal cost of pollution MC_P, the price mechanism is preferable to the quantity mechanism, as seen by comparing the resulting deadweight losses from the two interventions ($Y < X$).

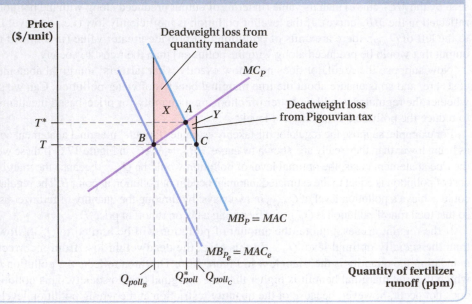

In Figure 17.7, the optimal level of pollution from fertilizer runoff occurs at point A, where the marginal cost of pollution equals the marginal benefit of pollution (or marginal abatement cost), and the efficient level of pollution is Q^*_{poll}. Once again, suppose the regulator believes that farmers' abatement costs are lower than they really are, shown by curve $MB_{P_e} = MAC_e$. If regulators use a quantity-based intervention, they will set the quantity mandate at Q_{poll_B}, pollution will be Q_{poll_B} instead of Q^*_{poll}, and area X will be the deadweight loss from inefficiency. If a Pigouvian tax is used instead, regulators will set it at T. Farmers will produce a quantity of pollution Q_{poll_C}, and the deadweight loss from the inefficient level of pollution will be area Y.

Figure 17.7 shows that when the marginal abatement cost curve is steep relative to the marginal cost of pollution curve, setting incorrect Pigouvian taxes is less costly than setting incorrect quantity mandates. The relative insensitivity of abatement to the level of the tax means that being a little wrong about the optimal tax won't have much effect on the actual level of pollution. But setting the wrong quantity will be very costly. Regulations that force producers to undertake unnecessarily high abatement will be expensive relative to the marginal costs of pollution it saves. Similarly, mandating too little abatement will mean that some pollution cuts with benefits that would far outweigh their costs won't be made.

Therefore, when regulators are uncertain about the optimal level of an externality, the choice of quantity- or price-based market interventions should depend on what the regulator perceives are the relative sensitivities of the marginal cost of pollution and the marginal abatement cost (or marginal benefit of pollution).

A Market-Oriented Approach to Reducing Externalities: Tradable Permits Markets

Trying to mandate the total amount of an externality in a market by restricting each firm's quantity individually or determining the correct tax rate is difficult. Worse, it may lead to costly errors if producers differ in their costs of changing output levels. It would be optimal for firms that could do this more cheaply to make a larger share of the necessary quantity adjustments. But it can be very difficult for a regulator to know what each firm's costs are and set quantity restrictions or taxes appropriately.

In these cases, allowing firms to jointly determine how best to reduce an externality to its optimal level can work by using **tradable permits,** *government-issued permits that allow a firm to emit a certain amount of pollution during production and that can be traded to other firms.* No firm can pollute without one. After the permits are allocated among firms, they can be traded, allowing some firms to emit a greater amount of pollution than others. In essence, a market for pollution emissions develops. Such systems are sometimes called "cap-and-trade" programs for this reason: The government sets a cap on pollution emissions, issues an amount of permits equal to this cap, and then firms trade the rights to pollute among them. For example, the United States regulates sulfur dioxide (SO_2) using a system of tradable permits.

tradable permit A government-issued permit that allows a firm to emit a certain amount of pollution during production and that can be traded to other firms.

A competitive tradable permits market will arrive at a price per permit that equates the marginal cost of pollution abatement across all firms. If the permit price was above a firm's marginal abatement cost (alternatively, its marginal benefit of polluting), the company could make a profit by reducing its pollution by an extra unit and selling the permit for that extra pollution to someone else. If permit prices were instead below its marginal benefit of pollution, the firm could raise its profits by buying a permit and going ahead with polluting that extra unit. Only when the permit price equals the marginal abatement cost of the firm would it not want to change its pollution level. Because this logic holds for every firm, each firm's level of pollution must equate that firm's marginal abatement cost to the permit price. (This is similar to the logic in a perfectly competitive market where all firms produce a quantity that equates their marginal cost to the output price.)

This is an important result; it means that the total amount of abatement in the industry (as set by the government cap) is done efficiently. If one firm has a lower marginal abatement cost than another, it should reduce pollution more. A permits market ensures that all firms have the same marginal abatement cost, so no reshuffling of pollution reduction across firms would lower the total cost of reducing pollution.

Moreover, if the government sets the total number of permits to the efficient level of pollution, then (by definition of the efficient level) the permit price will equal the marginal benefit of pollution reduction. Therefore, a competitive permits market ends up with each firm cutting pollution to the point where its cost of doing so equals society's benefit from those cuts.

The permits market achieves the total emissions cuts necessary for efficiency at the lowest possible cost, and it does so without the regulator having to determine which firm cuts how much. It works because permits trading allows firms that face lower abatement costs to shoulder more of the emissions-cutting burden and be compensated for it by selling their permits. High-abatement-cost firms prefer to buy these permits because it's cheaper for them than cutting emissions directly. It is the way some people advocate the world could confront the problem of carbon pollution and climate change—rather than imposing a carbon tax, nations could agree to a global cap requiring permits that could then trade on the open market.

17.3 The Coase Theorem: Free Markets Addressing Externalities on Their Own

Now we know how, in theory, the government can use taxes, subsidies, or quotas to solve externality problems and help the market get to the efficient market price and quantity when markets fail to do so. Sometimes, though, individuals can solve the externality problem themselves. The reason this may be possible (and the conditions it requires) lie at

Coase theorem States that if negotiation costs are low enough, negotiation among market participants will lead to the efficient market outcome regardless of who holds the property rights.

the heart of the **Coase theorem,** which states that *if negotiation costs are low enough, negotiation among market participants will lead to the efficient market outcome regardless of who holds the property rights.* The Coase theorem was developed by Nobel Prize–winning economist Ronald Coase in 1960.[11]

To understand what this means, let's consider the market for business school naming rights. Over the past few decades, a large number of business schools have sold the right to name their school after a wealthy benefactor. The University of Michigan's Ross School of Business, New York University's Stern School of Business, and UCLA's Anderson School of Management are just a few of many such examples. (In fact, two of the authors, Austan Goolsbee and Chad Syverson, work at the University of Chicago Booth School of Business, named in honor of alumnus and benefactor David Booth.)

Universities have the right to sell the naming rights to their business schools, but an externality may be involved with a naming decision. Often other alumni or students may want their school to only retain the name of the university and not include a benefactor. Thus, their utility can fall if the school sells its naming rights. Because they aren't directly involved in the transaction between the school and its donor, this utility loss is a negative externality.

At first glance, it would seem as if the critics of this practice might be out of luck. A school has the right to sell its name, a donor has the right to buy it, and unless the law for some reason gives others a right to decide whether to sell a school's naming rights, the people who don't favor the sale of the naming rights had better get used to disappointment.

The Coase theorem, however, says this is not correct. In certain situations, it doesn't matter who has the "property rights" in the transaction—that is, who, legally, gets to make the decision (in this case, the school and the donor). The Coase theorem asserts that if market participants can negotiate, they will reach a deal that yields the economically efficient outcome regardless of the allocation of these decision rights.

To understand why and under what conditions this negotiation can take place, consider the case of the Wisconsin School of Business at the University of Wisconsin. In the mid-2000s, the university considered selling the school's naming rights, just as many of its competitors had done. However, some alumni felt strongly that the school should not change its name. *Legally*, there was nothing they could do. If the university wanted to sell the school's name, it could, with or without alumni approval. But the Coase theorem points us to the answer. If the alumni value the university *not* naming the school after a donor more than the donor values naming the school, they can prevent this event from happening.

And this is exactly what happened. In 2007, a group of 13 alumni jointly pledged an $85 million gift to guarantee that the school would remain the "Wisconsin School of Business" for at least 20 years. The school had the legal right to sell its name, but didn't because, in effect, the externality that it would have imposed on its alumni was larger than the value the university would receive from renaming the school. The alumni ended up paying the university not to impose that negative externality on them.

If the valuations were reversed, and the university valued selling the school's name more than the alumni valued keeping the name the same, then the "efficient" outcome would be changing the name and the Coase theorem indicates that's what would happen.

One concept that's important to understand here is that the Coase theorem predicts the same outcome even if the property rights were allocated differently. Suppose for some

[11] Ronald H. Coase, "The Problem of Social Cost," *Journal of Law and Economics* 3 (1960): 1–44.

reason that the school's alumni had the right to veto any proposed name changes. If the university valued selling its name more than the alumni valued not selling it, the university could sell the name but then compensate the alumni for their losses, making both the university and alumni better off. If, instead, the alumni felt more strongly than the university, the name wouldn't be sold.

The upshot is that, in the end, the resource (here, the right to name the school) is allocated to its highest-value use no matter who retains the property rights. If the university values a renaming more than the alumni value the status quo, the name ends up being sold regardless of whether the university or the alumni have decision rights over the renaming. If, instead, the alumni care more about not changing the name, the name doesn't change, again regardless of which party has the decision rights.

This example shows that when negative externalities are present, the third party incurring an external cost may be willing to pay those generating the externality to stop. (Of course, this will only occur when the external cost borne by the third party is greater than the value of the externality to those generating it.) Likewise, those generating an externality may pay for the right to impose external costs on third parties. These payments allow the efficient outcome to be reached through negotiation.

The property rights only matter in that they affect who pays whom to reach the efficient outcome. Suppose again that the alumni derive a greater value from the name remaining the "Wisconsin School of Business" than the university does from selling the naming rights. These values tell us that the efficient outcome will be for the name to remain unchanged, regardless of which party initially owns the property rights. But whether the alumni will actually have to pay the university to not rename the school *does* depend on the assignment of property rights. If it's the university's decision to make, then the alumni will pay the university. If alumni are given the right to approve any name change, however, no money would change hands (and the name still wouldn't change). Either scenario yields the efficient outcome, although in the first case the alumni pay up (as they did in reality), and in the second case they don't. Note that the Coase theorem is not about fairness. The negotiated outcome might be terribly unfair to one of the parties. It is only about whether the outcome is efficient.

We must also be careful not to oversimplify the negotiation process and rely too much on Coase-type negotiations to sort out externality problems. The assumption that the involved parties (those creating the externality and those suffering from it) can bargain without costs incurred is critically important. If negotiation is costly—if, for instance, lawyers become involved in negotiating the dispute, or it's hard to contact all living alumni to solicit their opinion—the Coase theorem may not work.

It can also be difficult to organize such a negotiation when there are multiple parties involved. The Wisconsin School of Business alumni managed to coordinate their actions, but it would be difficult to get millions of people living on the West Coast of North America to agree on a contract to pay factories in China to stop burning dirty coal, for example. The Coase theorem would predict that it doesn't matter whether the law gives the factories the right to pollute as much as they want or requires them to obtain the permission of all breathers of air before they can burn their coal. However, when negotiation isn't easy, the Coase theorem will fail, and we're back to the role of government to deal with externalities.[12]

---

[12] Asymmetric information can also cause problems for the predictions of the Coase theorem. If negotiating parties have private information about their valuations of an externality (or its absence), they won't be anxious to share them with the other negotiating parties. As we saw in Chapter 16, if information asymmetries are bad enough, negotiations might break down, even if an agreement would be efficient given full information.

figure it out 17.3

Green Acres Fertilizer Company is located near Lucy's Dry Cleaning Service. In its production process, Green Acres emits noxious odors that are absorbed by the clothing that Lucy is cleaning. The result is that Lucy has lost many customers over time. Lucy estimates that the odors cost her business $10,000 per year. Green Acres can eliminate its odors by altering its production process at a cost of $12,000 per year.

a. If Green Acres has the right to emit the odors, what will the socially optimal outcome be? How will it be reached? Will any money change hands?

b. If Lucy has the right to odor-free air, what will the socially optimal outcome be? How will it be reached? Will any money change hands?

Solution:

a. The socially optimal outcome will occur when Green Acres emits the odor. The cost of eliminating the emissions ($12,000 per year) is greater than the external cost of the odor ($10,000 per year). If Green Acres has the right to emit the odors, it will continue to do so. Lucy does not value clean air enough to purchase that right from Green Acres, so no money will change hands.

b. The socially optimal outcome will still be for Green Acres to emit the odor. The optimal outcome is determined by the relative values that Green Acres and Lucy place on the resource (air). Because Green Acres values the air more highly, it should use the resource and emit the odor. However, because Lucy has a right to odor-free air, Green Acres will have to purchase the right to emit odors from her. Assuming that this transaction can be done without cost, Green Acres will have to pay Lucy between $10,000 and $12,000 for that right.

Application: Sometimes the Coase Theorem Takes a While

Hoyt Bleakley and Joseph Ferrie looked at a particular market to test whether the Coase theorem held. It did; the efficient allocation was arrived at through negotiation and exchange among individuals. But in the case Bleakley and Ferrie studied, it took a while to achieve this outcome.[13] And when we say, "a while," we mean about 150 years.

Bleakley and Ferrie's study examined the results of the "first" settlement of large parts of the U.S. state of Georgia (meaning after the expropriation and eviction of its original Native American inhabitants). When these lands were opened to new settlement in the early 1800s, the state used lotteries to allocate different-sized plots to settlers. Some lucky settlers randomly received large plots; others received small ones. Because the smallest plots were too small to be farmed efficiently (a problem that would only get worse later as optimal farm sizes grew), the plots imposed a type of negative externality on each other. One plot's existence made another plot too small for efficient farming.

The Coase theorem implies that a process of negotiation and land sales would allow owners of small plots to sell their land to those with nearby larger plots (or to another owner of a small plot who could then combine them) so that efficient-sized farms could be created. The economic gains from greater farming efficiency would be more than enough to compensate the owners of small plots for giving up the opportunity to eke out a living on an undersized farm. (If farmers differed in their agricultural ability, then perhaps the relatively untalented owner of a large plot would sell to a more talented farmer who had a small plot. Either way, efficient farm size would be obtained.)

[13] Hoyt Bleakley and Joseph Ferrie, "Land Openings on the Georgia Frontier and the Coase Theorem in the Short- and Long-Run," working paper, 2014.

Bleakley and Ferrie showed that this is exactly what happened . . . after about 150 years. They found that even 50 years after the lottery, farm sizes were almost perfectly predicted by the corresponding plot sizes from the lottery. In other words, hardly any changes in plot boundaries had occurred in a half century. Land values indicated that these farms were, in fact, undersized, so it was clear an externality was still at work. As time unfolded, however, farm boundaries gradually started to change. Finally, about 150 years after the lottery, farm sizes were no longer related to the lottery's initial plot sizes, and plots appeared to have reached efficient size.

It took so long for the Coase theorem to work because negotiations were complicated and expensive. For one thing, if a plot for sale was the right size but too far away from the farmer's current plot, it wouldn't make sense for the farmer to purchase it, even if the current owner was looking to sell. Other types of negotiation costs were also involved, everything from asymmetric information problems to family squabbles. Working through all of that took time—a long time. Bleakley and Ferrie's results offer striking evidence of just how long it can take to reach an efficient solution. ■

The Coase Theorem and Tradable Permits Markets

One area in which the Coase theorem has impacted the real world is in the design of government strategies to combat pollution. As we demonstrated earlier in the chapter, tradable permits can move a market with a negative externality to the socially optimal outcome, often at a lower cost than quantity mechanisms such as quotas.

The Coase theorem says that it shouldn't matter who gets the initial permits to pollute (i.e., the quota allotments) as long as the firms are allowed to trade freely and bargaining costs are low. Thus, the government can reach an efficient amount of pollution by setting up a market for tradable permits.

By enabling trades, the market for permits allows the most efficient reduction in emissions while sparing the government the trouble of determining how to allocate the reductions across firms. The government can achieve the efficient *total* level of emissions by issuing the optimal number of permits to the firms in an industry and allowing them to trade among themselves to reach the right outcome. Firms that face lower abatement costs will reduce emissions further. It gives them a way, through permit sales, to be compensated for their additional abatement costs. High-abatement-cost firms, at the same time, prefer to buy these permits because it's cheaper for them than cutting emissions directly.

Externalities, uncorrected, cause markets to become inefficient. But tradable permits markets *create a new market* for the externality itself. Externalities are essentially extra, unpriced "products" tied to market transactions. Polluters don't consider the external costs of their emissions because they don't have to pay those costs. However, by creating a market for pollution, tradable permits markets actually put a price on pollution. Because the permits market makes polluting firms face this price, polluters consider the social implications of their production activity. Price mechanisms (such as Pigouvian taxes) that are used to address externalities serve the same purpose: They put a price on an externality that normally doesn't have one, causing market participants to be aware of the externality's effects.

We can therefore think of externalities as resulting from missing markets. The fundamental problem is that, in the absence of intervention, there is no way to do for externalities what markets do for regular goods: Provide a value for their costs and benefits to society through the price mechanism. The Coase theorem basically implies that, if you can create a market for the externality, the market's supply and demand mechanism will lead to the efficient outcome.

17.4 Public Goods

So far in this chapter, we have looked at market failures in which markets end up with an inefficient level of output as a result of externalities (or unclear property rights). There is another type of good for which markets can fail to deliver the socially optimal level of output. **Public goods** are *goods that are accessible to anyone who wants to consume them and that remain just as valuable to the consumer even as other people consume them* (such as national defense, a fireworks display, or clean air). For example, when you watch a fireworks display from your backyard, it doesn't matter for your utility if your neighbors watch, too. And the individuals mounting the fireworks display can't stop people from watching it, even if they wanted to. As a result, public goods have distinctive properties that make it difficult for markets to deliver them at efficient levels. Note that a public good does not automatically imply something provided by the government (though governments often do provide public goods because private markets may provide too few of them).

Public goods are similar in some ways to positive externalities: They can provide external benefits to individuals other than those who purchase them. For example, if you pay for beautiful landscaping in your yard, you may not consider the benefits received by your neighbors when making your purchases. This leads to an output that is smaller than is socially optimal because the full benefits are not considered. Put simply, if the true social benefits were taken into account, there would probably be better fireworks shows and nicer yards.

Public goods have two important properties. One is that they are **nonexcludable,** *a defining property of a public good which means that consumers cannot be prevented from consuming the good.* All people who want to use the good have access to it. Nonexcludable means you can't monitor or limit the use of a good by any particular user. In the instance of the fireworks display, you can't keep people from looking up at the sky; therefore, the fireworks are nonexcludable.

The second property of public goods is that they are **nonrival,** meaning *one person's consumption of the good does not diminish another consumer's enjoyment of the same good.* A different way to think of a good being nonrival is that the marginal cost of providing the good to another consumer is zero. For example, a weather forecast is a nonrival good. The value of the forecast to a consumer is unaffected by how many other people also receive the same forecast. The fact that your neighbor checked her weather app does not in any way diminish or eliminate the utility you derive from receiving the same information. Any good that many people can consume independently without using it up or degrading it is a nonrival good. In contrast, if a consumer buys a rival (regular, private) good, then someone else cannot buy that exact good. If you purchase a taco to eat, no one else will be able to eat it. A taco is a **private good,** meaning it is both *rival (one person's consumption affects the ability of another to consume it) and excludable (individuals can be prevented from consuming it).* **Table 17.1** shows the different types of goods that exist categorized by rivalry and excludability.

- An example of a rival, excludable good is a gallon of gasoline. Because the gasoline is rival, another person can't consume the same gallon you bought. Gasoline is also excludable because producers can keep you from consuming the gasoline unless you purchase it.

- A **common resource** is *a special class of economic good that is rival but nonexcludable, whose value to the individual consumer decreases as others use it, and that all individuals can access freely.* (Common resources can suffer from a special and often damaging type of externality called the *tragedy of the commons*, which we discuss in

public good A good that is accessible to anyone who wants to consume it, and that remains just as valuable to a consumer even as other people consume it.

nonexcludability A defining property of a public good which means that consumers cannot be prevented from consuming the good.

nonrival Defining property of a public good meaning one person's consumption of the good does not diminish another consumer's enjoyment of the same good.

private good A good that is rival (one person's consumption affects the ability of another to consume it) and excludable (individuals can be prevented from consuming it).

common resource A special class of economic good that is rival but nonexcludable, whose value to the individual consumer decreases as others use it, and that all individuals can access freely.

Table 17.1 Examples of Goods by Characteristics

	Excludable *Individuals can be kept from consuming.*	**Nonexcludable** *Individuals cannot be kept from consuming.*
Rival *One individual's consumption affects another's consumption.*	**Private good:** tacos, gasoline, paper	**Common resource:** shared property, fisheries, interstate highways
Nonrival *One individual's consumption has no effect on another's consumption.*	**Club good:** satellite TV services, private parks, movies	**Public good:** fireworks display, mosquito abatement, national defense

more detail later in this section.) An example of a common resource is the stock of a particular fish, like bluefin tuna. This good is rival because fish that are caught by one boat cannot be caught by another. However, this good is nonexcludable because it is hard to stop someone from fishing if he has set his mind to it.

- An example of a nonrival good that is excludable is a satellite TV broadcast of a football game. This good is nonrival because anyone can receive the satellite transmission without taking away the ability of other consumers to watch the same event. However, this good is excludable because consumers must pay a subscription fee to receive the show's unscrambled signal. *Nonrival, excludable goods* are sometimes referred to as **club goods.**

club goods Nonrival and excludable goods.

- An example of a nonrival, nonexcludable good might be mosquito control, which is often performed by spraying public waterways with pesticides. This good is nonrival because one person's enjoyment of a mosquito-free backyard does not impact another person's enjoyment of the same situation. Because eliminating mosquitoes benefits everyone regardless of who paid for it, mosquito abatement is also nonexcludable. *Nonrival, nonexcludable goods* are sometimes referred to as **pure public goods.**

pure public good Nonrival and non-excludable goods.

The Optimal Level of Public Goods

Before we can see why markets provide inefficient levels of public goods, we have to define what the efficient level of output is for these types of goods. It's a little different from the efficiency conditions we've discussed before.

Efficiency generally occurs when a market produces the quantity for which the marginal cost of producing the good just equals the marginal benefit society receives from the good. For a competitive market without externalities, that quantity is also where quantity supplied equals quantity demanded. As we saw earlier in this chapter, in markets with externalities present, we need to be sure that all external costs and benefits are considered when determining the efficient output. Efficiency in these markets thus occurs at the output for which social demand (which measures social marginal benefit) is equal to social marginal cost.

With public goods, the marginal benefit from the good is not the benefit for just one consumer because more than one person can consume the good simultaneously. A public good is nonrival, so to value the good, we have to add up the marginal benefits of everyone who consumes it. The **total marginal benefit** curve is the *vertical sum of the marginal benefit curves of all of a public good's many consumers.* This total marginal benefit (MB_T)

total marginal benefit The vertical sum of the marginal benefit curves of all of a public good's consumers.

is what equals marginal cost when a public good is being provided at its optimal level. In equation form, the total marginal benefit is written

$$MB_T = \Sigma MB_i$$

The summation symbol Σ denotes that the good's marginal benefits are added over all consumers (whom we've indexed with i) of that good.

There is no "sum of marginal costs" condition because you don't have to pay more as additional people consume the good. Whether made for one consumer or all consumers, the marginal cost of 1 unit is the same.

Figure 17.8 shows the public goods efficiency condition for a simple example in which the public good is consumed by two people. The marginal benefit curves of each person are illustrated in the figure as MB_1 and MB_2. The total marginal benefit of the public good, shown as curve MB_T, is the vertical sum of the individual marginal benefit curves. MC is the marginal cost of producing the good.

Efficiency requires that the public good be provided at point A, where $MB_T = MC$, with a quantity of Q_{Pub}^*. It's important to realize that this is the quantity of the public good that *both* individuals consume. Because it is nonrival, they don't have to split Q_{Pub}^* between them. They consume Q_{Pub}^* units of the good simultaneously.

The free market will get the wrong amount of this for the same reasons we saw things go wrong in markets with externalities. The market yields production up to the point where the good's *private* marginal cost equals individuals' *private* marginal benefits. However, that is not where the *combined* marginal benefits of multiple consumers equal the good's marginal cost. If individuals could buy the public good themselves at marginal cost, each would buy the quantity at which *her own* marginal benefit equals its marginal cost. Looking at Figure 17.8 again, Person 1 would buy Q_1, where $MB_1 = MC$. Similarly, Person 2 would buy Q_2.

Figure 17.8   Efficiency in the Market for a Public Good

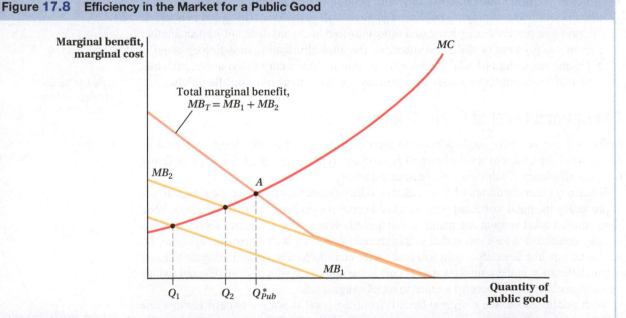

The two consumers of a public good have marginal benefit curves MB_1 and MB_2. At the efficient point, both consumers consume Q_{Pub}^* of the public good, where their total marginal benefit curve (MB_T) intersects the marginal cost curve (MC). If the two consumers privately bought the good, each would consume less than the optimal level at quantities Q_1 and Q_2, where MB_1 and MB_2 each intersect MC.

Therefore, although both individuals would be willing to pay for some quantity of the public good, neither would, by herself, pay for the efficient quantity because her individual marginal benefit is less than the joint marginal benefit. The inefficiency arises in a way that is similar to how inefficiency arises with a positive externality: Individuals paying privately for a public good don't consider everyone else's benefit from the good. This is one reason why private markets fail to produce the efficient quantity of public goods. Left to their own devices, private markets don't supply enough national defense, mosquito control, clean air, fireworks displays, and the like.

In addition to not taking into account the total marginal benefit of the good and thus having less of it available than is socially optimal, there is the issue of free-riders. The **free-rider problem** is *a source of inefficiency resulting from individuals (free-riders) consuming a public good or service without paying for it.* For example, electronics manufacturers, shoe manufacturers, and car manufacturers want people to be able to try out their products before purchase, and there are retailers that provide those services. In many cases, however, online retailers, who don't have to provide (or pay for) free trials and other services, can offer lower prices than "brick-and-mortar" stores. The online retailers are free-riding on the services provided by the brick-and-mortar stores. The problem with this is that if enough people try out a product in a retail store and then go online to buy it at a lower price (a practice sometimes called "showrooming"), offline retailers will stop providing try-out services. The free market ends up generating too little of the try-out information (which benefits consumers and producers) because it has become a public good.

> **free-rider problem** A source of inefficiency resulting from individuals consuming a public good or service without paying for it.

figure it out 17.4

Jasmine and Casey are neighbors in a rural area. They are considering the joint installation of a large fountain near their joint property line so that each can enjoy its beauty and also improve the value of their property. Jasmine's marginal benefit from the fountain is $MB_J = 70 - Q$, where Q measures the diameter of the fountain (in feet). Casey's marginal benefit from the fountain can be represented as $MB_C = 40 - 2Q$. Assume that the marginal cost of producing the fountain is constant and equal to $80 per foot (in diameter).

a. Find an equation to represent the total marginal benefit of the fountain.

b. What is the socially optimal size of the fountain?

c. Show that if either Jasmine or Casey had to build a fountain by themselves, neither would find even the smallest fountain worth building.

Solution:

a. The total marginal benefit is the vertical summation of Jasmine's and Casey's individual marginal benefit curves:

$$MB_T = MB_J + MB_C = (70 - Q) + (40 - 2Q) = 110 - 3Q$$

b. The socially optimal size of the fountain occurs where MB_T equals the marginal cost of producing the fountain:

$$MB_T = MC$$
$$110 - 3Q = 80$$
$$3Q = 30$$
$$Q = 10$$

The optimal size of the fountain is 10 feet in diameter.

c. Jasmine's marginal benefit is $MB_J = 70 - Q$. If the smallest possible fountain was zero feet in diameter ($Q = 0$), Jasmine's marginal benefit would only be $70, while the marginal cost would be $80. Therefore, Jasmine would not find even the smallest fountain to be worth the cost. Likewise, the marginal benefit of a zero-foot fountain for Casey will be $MB_C = 40 - 2Q = 40, which is also less than the $80 marginal cost.

Solving the Free-Rider Problem

A common solution to the free-rider problem in the fireworks and online retailer cases, and in paying for public goods more generally, is for an entity like the government or the manufacturer to compel people to pay their share through a tax or retailer fee. This is why the most expensive and broad-scoped public goods such as national defense, "rule-of-law" goods (e.g., court systems, police services), and national transportation infrastructure—items for which free-riding might be the most severe—are paid for through taxation.[14]

Other solutions are also possible. Beneficiaries of a public good can form an organization that compels members to pay their share of the public good's costs. The tricky issue in such situations is convincing potential members to *voluntarily* form a group that may *compel* them to pay for something they'd rather not pay for at all. Condo owners, for example, often form a condo association to pay for maintaining a pool and other common areas because free-rider problems will develop among the owners if they don't.

As economist Mancur Olson pointed out in 1965, the likelihood of solving the free-rider problem depends on how large the public good's benefits are per potential member of the group who would enjoy the good.[15] If each potential member's gain from cooperative action—his benefit from having the efficient level of the public good available—would be large, it is more likely that a cooperative group will form. When the benefit-per-potential-member ratio is low, success at forming a group is less likely. Because each member of the group only benefits a little from the public good, less is lost trying to free-ride. The incentive to free-ride makes it difficult to hold a group together. (This is a lot like the logic we discussed in Chapter 11 about why it's easier for a small number of firms to form a stable cartel than it is for a large number of firms to do the same thing.)

It's important to realize that the benefit per member of a public good might not be closely correlated with the *total* benefit of the good. It's quite possible a public good that would offer an enormous total benefit may not end up being provided because the size of its potential group is also large, making the benefit per person too small to overcome free-riding. At the same time, a public good with a much smaller total benefit might be provided if it benefits only a select group who enjoy a large benefit per member. This effect may explain why special interest groups successfully lobby for programs that jointly benefit their members despite imposing a much larger collective cost on everyone else. Each member of the special interest group enjoys large gains by paying lobbyists to put forward the group's agenda and encourage legislators to vote favorably for its programs. The lobbying can be thought of as a public good for the members. Even though the program imposes a very large collective cost on everyone outside the special interest group, the cost borne by any one person is too small to overcome free-riding, and no one mounts a concerted effort to stop the legislation.

The Tragedy of the Commons

tragedy of the commons
The dilemma that common resources create when everyone has free access and the resource is used more intensively than it would be if privately owned, leading to a decline in its value for everyone.

A common resource (a type of public good that is rival but nonexcludable) isn't a pure public good, but it presents a similar kind of inefficiency. The **tragedy of the commons** is *the dilemma that common resources create when everyone has free access and the*

---

[14] Note that the government, having raised the necessary revenues through taxes to pay for the public good, does not necessarily need to itself produce the public good to achieve efficiency. In principle, the government could use the tax revenue to pay private entities to provide the public good. The U.S. interstate highway system, for example, was paid for with public funds but built by private contractors.

[15] Mancur Olson, *The Logic of Collective Action: Public Goods and the Theory of Groups*, Cambridge, MA: Harvard University Press, 1965.

FREAKONOMICS

Is Fire Protection a Public Good?

When a small trash fire sparked a fire at a house just outside of South Fulton, Tennessee, firefighters rushed to the scene. But instead of putting out the blaze, the firefighters stood by and simply let the house burn to the ground.*

Why didn't they do anything? To understand why, we have to first understand how the South Fulton fire department is funded. Residents in the city of South Fulton pay taxes to fund the fire department, so the city itself has fire coverage. It's inefficient for the rural areas outside South Fulton to maintain their own fire department. So, the South Fulton fire department offers fire coverage — for a $75 yearly fee per household — to these surrounding areas. The South Fulton government can't force the people in the outlying areas to pay; it's up to the rural homeowners to voluntarily cough up the $75. As you can imagine, many of them do not pay. "After all," they figure, "what's the chance my house will catch fire? And if it does catch fire, will the fire department actually just let it burn? No way."

It turns out, however, that South Fulton Fire Chief David Wilds thinks more like an economist. To the non-economist, fighting rural house fires regardless of the fee seems like the neighborly thing to do. But the local fire chief recognized an important fact: that without an enforced yearly fee, firefighting would be a nonexcludable good — that is, no individual or family could be kept from enjoying fire protection. The time and effort the fire department put into preventing fires, fighting those that do arise, and watchfully waiting when there isn't a fire benefit everyone in an area, whether it's their house on fire or not.

Some homeowners would like to enjoy the benefits of this nonexcludable good but only pay if their house catches on fire. (This is also related to the adverse selection problem in insurance markets that we discussed in Chapter 16.) Such a practice wouldn't provide much of a budget for the fire department to work with, though. The South Fulton fire department thus requires all rural homeowners to pay their fire coverage service fee ahead of time if they want the department to answer their calls.

We know why the firefighters didn't put out the blaze — it was a matter of public goods. But why did they bother showing up at all? The answer also involves the public good aspect of firefighting. The firefighters had an obligation to the homeowners' neighbors who *had* paid their fee. That's why they arrived at the scene, watching the house burn down, but were prepared to put out any fire that crossed the border to the neighbors' yards. And, in fact, firefighters did stop the fire from crossing into a neighboring yard while ignoring the still roaring fire on the original property.

Despite the economic rationale behind this fire department's policy, they still took a lot of heat for its decision. Letting the house burn garnered Fire Chief Wilds national attention, and the media did not appreciate the economic logic of his decision. In response to this public uproar, it only stands to reason that Wilds would succumb to political pressure and abandon the policy. If you think that's what happened, then you underestimated Wilds. Just a little over a year later, he allowed another house to burn to the ground, ensuring his spot in the Freakonomics Hall of Fame.

South Fulton, Tennessee, firefighters allowed this man's home to burn down to prevent rural areas from free-riding on South Fulton's fire protection services.

WPSD Local 6/AP Images

*"No Pay, No Spray: Firefighters Let Home Burn," October 6, 2010, http://www.nbcnews.com/id/39516346/ns/us_news-life/t/no-pay-no-spray-firefighters-let-home-burn/, and "Firefighters Let Home Burn over $75 Fee — Again," December 7, 2011, http://usnews.nbcnews.com/_news/2011/12/07/9272989-firefighters-let-home-burn-over-75-fee-again.

resource is used more intensively than it would be if privately owned, leading to a decline in its value for everyone.

A reservoir of water, public forests, public airwaves, and even public restrooms are all examples of common resources. The key element is that the common resource is nonexcludable: Anyone can use or take from it, and those who use it cannot be monitored easily. Because access to the resource is shared by all comers, common resources are also called *common-pool* or *common-property resources*.

We can think of the tragedy of the commons as a problem caused by a negative externality. No single user takes into account the negative externality she imposes on others by using the common resource, leading everyone to consume too much of it. The externality involved with a common resource arises because of the combination of open access and depletion through use. When deciding how much of the common resource to consume, everyone considers only her own cost of use. But this use depletes the resource for all other users. Because individuals don't consider the cost they impose on others when making their decisions about how much of the common resource to consume, they end up using too much of the resource. And, because everyone accessing the resource creates this same externality with her own use, the total usage of the resource exceeds the social optimum. This outcome is analogous to the market quantity being higher than the efficient level in our earlier negative externality examples. Without controls, people draw too much water from aquifers, overfish the ocean, cut down too many trees on public lands, jam the airways with too many communications devices and broadcasts, and so on.

The Petrified Forest National Park in Arizona, for example, is a surreal landscape full of fallen ancient trees that have been petrified into rock. It is a common resource for everyone to enjoy, yet many visitors steal small pieces of petrified wood to keep as a souvenir. The parks service estimates that it loses about 12 tons per year in theft. Each thief thinks, "I can take just a small piece . . . it won't make any difference" and doesn't take into account the fact that removal of one piece of wood reduces the value of the park for others. Without controls—park ranger patrols, heavy fines and punishments, and so on—this attitude would easily lead to a dwindling of the resource. This happened to the original Plymouth Rock, in Massachusetts, the supposed landing spot of Mayflower immigrants in 1620. So many people chipped off a piece of the rock that by 1835 it dwindled to less than half its original size and had to be moved behind a fence to prevent it from disappearing completely.

In some cases, the consequences of this overuse can be severe: Instead of preserving a sustainable fishing stock, for example, overfishing can drive an entire population of fish to extinction. It's not that fishers prefer to drive their prey to extinction; in fact, they prefer to have a steady supply available. But the overfishing happens because of the externality and the open access to the fishing stock.

Remedies for the Tragedy of the Commons   Because the tragedy of the commons is just a special form of negative externality, any of the solutions we described in the previous section can be used to try to fix it, and they are indeed applied in many actual situations. For example, governments use price-based mechanisms (Pigouvian taxes) to charge individuals for the external damage they do to the common resource. They charge fees for each unit of the common resource an individual consumes (such as an entrance fee to a national park). Governments also set quantity restrictions (quotas) on the rate at which common resources can be extracted, such as limits on the amount of fishing, hunting, or logging, for example. These interventions can be used by governments or other organized public or private regulatory bodies. In fact, as with other types of public goods, users of common resources have incentives to join together to self-regulate use of the resource.

Another way to fix the tragedy of the commons externality involves defining property rights and facilitating negotiation among those who share the common resource, as laid out in the Coase theorem. For the airwaves, for example, the government auctions off spectrum and says that whoever buys it is the only one allowed to broadcast at that frequency. Granting sole control of one part of the resource to one party eliminates the negative externality. The person in control gets all the benefit and pays all the cost of using the resource, so she doesn't have an incentive to overuse it.

17.5 Conclusion

Throughout the book, we have seen that an economy relies on free, competitive markets to provide optimal outcomes for producers and consumers: Firms produce and consumers buy up to the point at which the marginal benefit of the product equals the marginal cost of producing it. When there are externalities or public goods involved, however, this process doesn't work.

When one economic actor's purchase or production decision imposes costs or benefits on other economic actors that are not included in the transaction, those imposed costs and benefits are not taken into account by the decision maker, and free-market outcomes can lead the economy far away from its optimum. There will be too many products with negative externalities and too few products with positive externalities. Common resources and public goods are a bit different from externalities, but the markets for them show many of the same pathologies: overconsumption (of common resources) and underprovision (of public goods).

There are many ways to mitigate or even get rid of the problems associated with market failures. Governments can impose Pigouvian taxes or subsidies on markets with externalities to bring the private costs and benefits in line with the true costs and benefits to society. For common resource and public goods problems, governments can impose quantity restrictions or mandates or even provide a product themselves. However, governments aren't the only entities that may correct for these market failures. The Coase theorem indicates that, if negotiation costs are low enough, the private sector may itself come up with a closer-to-optimal solution.

The key to this chapter is understanding why some markets may not always work as efficiently as the standard economic models predict. In the last chapter of this book, we examine situations in which economic actors (consumers and producers) may not appear to be the rational, utility- and profit-maximizing agents we have modeled throughout this text.

Summary

1. **Externalities** impose costs or benefits on a third party not directly involved in an economic transaction. Without market intervention, both **negative** and **positive externalities** result in inefficient market outcomes. In an efficient market, firms produce where the market demand for the good equals the social marginal cost. **[Section 17.1]**

2. Regulators can use quantity- or price-based interventions to fix externalities and push the market equilibrium toward the efficient outcome. **Pigouvian taxes** (or **subsidies**) are a tax (or subsidy) on the production or consumption of a good. The simplest form of a quantity-based intervention is a **quota.** Whether a price-based intervention like a Pigouvian tax or a quantity-based intervention like a quota should be used depends on the relative steepness of the **marginal abatement** and **external marginal cost** curves. **[Section 17.2]**

3. The **Coase theorem** predicts that in the absence of transaction costs, negotiation among economic actors will lead to efficient outcomes regardless of who holds the property rights, and is used as the basis for a frequently used strategy to combat pollution: **tradable permits. [Section 17.3]**

4. All **public goods** are characterized by two properties. First, public goods are **nonrival,** meaning one consumer's enjoyment of the good does not diminish another's enjoyment of it. Second, public goods are **nonexcludable,** meaning once a public good is on the market, it is impossible to prevent people from consuming it. Because of these two properties, public goods create a **free-rider problem** in which consumers want to freely consume, or free-ride, the public good that others have provided. **Common resources** are a special class of public goods that are rival but nonexcludable. The **tragedy of the commons** affects common resources, which are used more intensively than users would prefer if they could coordinate their actions. **[Section 17.4]**

Review Questions

1. Contrast negative and positive externalities. Provide an example of each type of externality.

2. Why does an unregulated market overproduce goods with negative externalities?

3. How can the external marginal benefit and external marginal cost curves be used to find the efficient level of an externality?

4. Why are the marginal benefit and marginal abatement cost of pollution considered equivalent?

5. How do regulators use Pigouvian taxes to produce efficient outcomes?

6. Describe how tradable pollution permits can be used to address pollution.

7. Compare and contrast Pigouvian taxes and quantity-based solutions to externalities. What are some of the advantages and disadvantages of each?

8. What is the main prediction of the Coase theorem?

9. What are the two defining properties of public goods?

10. When is a public good being produced efficiently?

11. Why does the free-rider problem arise?

12. What types of solutions can address the tragedy of the commons?

Problems

(Solutions to problems marked with an asterisk appear at the back of this book. Problems adapted to use calculus are available online.)

*1. Kansas City is famous for its barbecue. But good barbecue comes at a cost: Pit masters have to bear the costs of producing slow-roasted pulled pork and beef briskets. There is also an external cost: Every time a pit master roasts another rack of ribs, it offends the sensibilities of nearby animal lovers. Consider the graphical representation below of a typical pit master in the competitive barbecue industry:

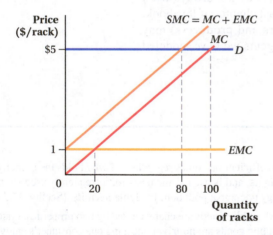

a. What is the market price of barbecue?

b. How much psychic damage (external cost) do animal lovers suffer for each rack roasted?

c. If our pit master accounts only for her private costs, how many racks will she roast? How much total damage will animal lovers suffer?

d. If our pit master feels sympathy for animal lovers and wholly considers their feelings in her decision about how many racks to produce, how many racks will she roast?

e. Does the decision to consider animal lovers' feelings eliminate the damage they suffer from transactions in the rib market?

f. Cutting output *below* the level you determined in (d) clearly benefits animal lovers. Who is hurt by such a decision? Explain why such a cut in output would not be Pareto-efficient, that is, there is another allocation that would make someone better off without making anyone worse off.

2. Jill sells bouquets of flowers that she grows in her backyard. Jill's marginal cost of producing bouquets is given by $MC = 0.25Q$, where Q is the number of bouquets she makes. Jill can sell all the bouquets she wishes at the local farmers' market for $6 per bouquet. Unfortunately, Jill's floriculture aggravates the allergies of her next-door neighbor, Cooper: Every bouquet that Jill grows produces 50 cents' worth of sneezes.

a. Jill wants to maximize her profit. Determine the profit-maximizing quantity of bouquets.

b. Assume that Jill produces the quantity of bouquets you determined in (a). Add up the cost of the last bouquet to Jill and the cost that bouquet imposes on Cooper, and compare your answer to the $6 worth of benefit the last bouquet creates for the buyer. Is producing the last bouquet a good thing for society?

c. From society's standpoint, is Jill overproducing or underproducing bouquets?

d. Suppose that Jill marries Cooper. Determine the social marginal cost of producing bouquets by adding the 50 cents' worth of damage each bouquet causes Cooper to Jill's private marginal cost. Express your answer as an equation.

e. Determine how many bouquets Jill should produce if she fully considers the costs she imposes on her new husband. Explain why it makes a difference if Cooper is just a neighbor or is Jill's husband.

3. The craft beer industry is highly competitive. The industry short-run supply curve is given by $P = 1 + 0.5Q$, where Q is measured in millions of barrels. The inverse demand for craft beer is $P = 10 - Q$.

   a. Find the equilibrium market price and quantity of craft beer sold.

   b. The brewing process creates an unpleasant aroma that adversely affects the property values of nearby residents. Beer economists estimate these external marginal costs to be $EMC = 0.5Q$. Calculate the socially optimal level of output and price for craft beer.

*4. Gasoline brings great benefit to those who buy it, but burning it also creates external costs. Consider the following graph, which shows the demand for gasoline, the private marginal cost of producing gasoline, and the social marginal cost of producing gasoline.

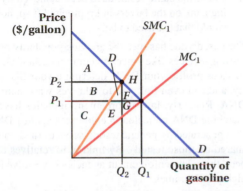

   a. Suppose that buyers and producers of gasoline do not consider the external marginal costs they impose on others. Determine the equilibrium quantity and price; then use the letters in the diagram to fill in the appropriate spaces in the table below:

	External Marginal Costs Not Considered	External Marginal Costs Considered
Consumer Surplus		
Producer Surplus		
External Damage (–)		
Total net value to society		

   b. Suppose that conscientious sellers, out of the sheer goodness of their hearts, decide to incorporate external marginal costs into their production decisions. Determine the new quantity (*Hint*: Use the social marginal cost curve) and price, then use the letters in the diagram to fill in the appropriate spaces in the table above. (Be sure to remember that producer surplus is the area above *private* marginal cost and below the price, out to the relevant quantity.)

   c. Producers rarely do something out of the goodness of their hearts and are likely to consider only their private marginal costs. Compare total surplus in both cases to determine the deadweight loss of the externality when external marginal costs are not considered.

5. A number of competing bakeries in a trendy downtown neighborhood produce fresh cookies. The demand for cookies in that neighborhood is $P = 16 - 0.25Q$, where Q is the dozens of cookies baked each day. The industry marginal cost for these competing bakeries is $MC = 2 + 0.25Q$.

   a. Solve for the equilibrium price and quantity of cookies in the neighborhood.

   b. Who doesn't love the smell of fresh-baked cookies? Downtown residents and passersby receive $2 worth of benefit from every dozen of cookies baked. Show that bakers are producing fewer cookies than is socially desirable. Then show that cookies are underpriced.

6. You've just acquired a sweet new ride and are trying to determine how to protect your wheels from theft. You're considering purchasing the Club, a large steel bar that locks to your steering wheel and prevents car thieves from easily driving away. Alternatively, you're considering installing LoJack, a hidden electronic device that allows law enforcement agencies to locate your car should you notify them of its theft.

   a. Re-read the Application: Device-Finding Apps and Positive Externalities. Then explain why the Club is more likely to directly deter thefts than LoJack is.

   b. LoJack customers must agree not to display any window stickers or other signs that indicate their cars are LoJack-equipped. Why do you suppose the company that created LoJack insists on this agreement?

   c. Support the argument that car drivers are probably buying the socially ideal quantity of the Club and other club substitutes, but that too few drivers are probably installing LoJack.

7. Goods that are accompanied by *negative* externalities are priced lower than is socially ideal. But, oddly, goods that are accompanied by *positive* externalities are *also* priced lower than is socially ideal. Explain this apparent paradox.

8. The private demand for drive-in movies is given by $P = 20 - 0.1Q$. The industry marginal cost of showing drive-in movies is given by $MC = 0.1Q$.

   a. Graph the private demand and marginal cost curves, and determine the price and quantity of movies that will be shown.

   b. Drive-in movies can be viewed imperfectly from outside the fence. The external marginal benefits received by such viewers are given by $EMB = 2 - 0.01Q$. Graph the external marginal benefit curve and then use that information to graph the social demand curve.

c. Suppose that all drive-in movies are nationalized and shown for the public good. The Movie Czar chooses the price and quantity of movies that bring the greatest benefit net of costs to all viewers, regardless of the vantage point from which they view the movie. Determine the optimal price and quantity of drive-in movies.

d. Indicate the deadweight loss created by the positive externality as an area on your graph and calculate its value. (*Hint:* You'll need to determine how much external marginal benefit the very last unit of output created when drive-ins were privately run.)

e. Can government-run movies potentially improve on the private market outcome when a positive externality exists?

*9. The inverse demand for leather is given by $P = 50 - 0.5Q$. The industry supply of leather is determined by its marginal cost: $MC = 0.45Q$. Unfortunately, the production of leather causes noxious chemical residue to leach into groundwater supplies. The external marginal cost caused by these residues grows with the amount of output and is measured as $EMC = 0.05Q$.

a. Suppose that the government wishes to reduce the externality to efficient levels by imposing a restriction on quantity (a quota). What maximum level of output should it set for leather production? What price would prevail in the marketplace once this quota is in place?

b. Suppose that the government wishes to reduce the externality to efficient levels by levying a tax on leather production. How high would that tax need to be? What is the resulting net price paid by buyers once the tax is in place? How much leather is bought and sold with the tax in place?

10. Consider the market for smelted kryptonite depicted below. A by-product of kryptonite smelting is the release of clouds of toxic blackish-yellow smoke. Each ton of toxic smoke emitted causes nearby residents' health-care expenditures to rise; the external marginal costs associated with the toxic exhaust are depicted as EMC on the graph below:

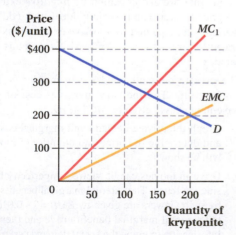

a. On the diagram, *carefully* graph the social marginal cost curve associated with the kryptonite industry. Precision matters!

b. Without any environmental regulation, how much kryptonite is produced?

c. From society's standpoint, how much kryptonite should be produced?

d. Regulators can achieve the efficient level of kryptonite production by imposing a tax on kryptonite production. To achieve the efficient level of production, how big should that tax be?

e. Draw an industry supply curve that reflects the tax you determined in part (d). Show that private producers, forced to internalize their externality by the tax, produce the socially optimal amount.

f. Could the same result have been achieved by assessing a tax on the buyers of kryptonite? If so, how much would that tax need to be?

11. The past decade has seen the growing popularity of genetic testing services like Ancestry.com and 23andMe. Those services profile your DNA, determine your likely ancestry, and can even link you to relatives who share similar DNA. Recently, law enforcement agencies have begun matching DNA collected in cold cases against DNA profiles generated by genetic testing services (and voluntarily shared by those tested). By linking to relatives of a suspect, those law enforcement agencies have solved several high-profile crimes.

a. Identify the externality described in this problem.

b. Using the terminology developed in the chapter, explain why markets are over- or underproviding DNA testing services.

c. What is the appropriate government policy to remedy the over- or underprovision of DNA testing services—quotas, taxes, subsidies, or cap-and-trade? Explain why each choice is appropriate or inappropriate.

*12. In Paris, hundreds of small bakeries produce bread for sale to their customers at a marginal cost of $MC = 2 + 0.1Q$. The inverse demand for bread is given by $P = 10 - 0.1Q$, where P is in euros per loaf and Q is loaves per hour. The baking of bread also creates a positive externality: There is nothing quite like the smell of fresh-baked bread. Tourists and residents receive external marginal benefits given by $EMB = 2 - 0.02Q$.

a. Find the quantity of bread produced in Paris in the absence of any government intervention.

b. To achieve a socially optimal output, the government can use a price-based intervention. Determine the ideal measure the government should use to achieve this goal. Specify both the type of policy and its magnitude.

13. Consider the diagram below, which depicts the external marginal cost of each ton of sulfur dioxide emitted by power plants, and the marginal abatement cost of eliminating that pollution.

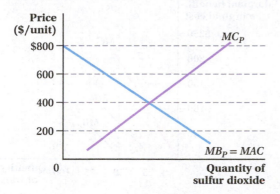

Price
($/unit)

a. Explain why the marginal abatement cost (or marginal benefit of pollution) curve slopes downward.

b. Find the efficient level of pollution and indicate it on your graph.

c. Firms, which care little about the damage imposed on people hundreds or thousands of miles away, have little incentive to produce the optimal amount of pollution on their own. Explain how, if regulators tax the producer $400 for each ton of pollutant emitted, power producers will have an incentive to cut emissions to exactly the socially optimal level.

d. Explain why a tax of $600 for each ton of pollutant emitted is too high a tax, and $200 per ton is too low a tax.

14. Brimstone is a caustic by-product of the production of fairy dust. The external marginal cost caused by inhalers of brimstone is indicated in the graph here as MC_P. The marginal abatement costs to fairy dust producers $(MB_P = MAC)$ are indicated as well. Suppose that regulators overestimate the damage that brimstone causes; their best guess of the harm is shown as MC_{Pe}.

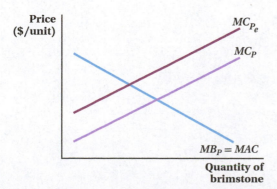

Price
($/unit)

a. Show (graphically) that if regulators attempt to achieve what they believe to be an efficient amount of brimstone, it doesn't matter whether they attempt to limit the quantity of brimstone, or set what they believe to be an efficient tax.

b. Show graphically that the elasticities of the marginal abatement cost and marginal cost of pollution are irrelevant in this special case to the choice of a quantity or price intervention.

c. Show that the results you demonstrated in (a) and (b) also hold if regulators *underestimate* the amount of marginal pollution cost brimstone causes.

15. The Pigouvian tax works by forcing polluters to pay for the costs they impose on others, to "internalize the externality." Explain how the cap-and-trade system also forces polluters to internalize the externality.

*16. Al regularly rehearses accordion music on his back deck with members of his musical troupe, the Starland Polka Band. Practicing on his deck saves him the $500 per year it would take to rent a rehearsal space. Unfortunately, practicing on his deck keeps his neighbor, Marcy, awake at night. The value of Marcy's lost sleep is $600 per year.

a. Is it efficient for Al to rehearse on his back deck? Explain your answer.

b. If the law says that it is illegal for Al to rehearse on his back deck, will Al end up practicing there? What might Marcy do to try to stop him?

c. Suppose that the law says it is legal for Al to rehearse on his back deck.

   i.   How much is Marcy willing to pay to get him to stop?

   ii. What is the minimum amount of money Al is willing to accept in exchange for his silence?

   iii. If possible, craft a bargain between Marcy and Al that results in his silence. Show that the bargain (if possible) makes both parties better off.

d. Given your answers to (b) and (c), does the outcome of this conflict depend on the law? Is the outcome consistent with your answer to (a)?

e. Suppose that instead of doing $600 damage to one neighbor, Al does $1 damage to 600 neighbors. Are those 600 neighbors as likely to be able to convince him to stop as easily as Marcy can? Explain.

17. Assume that everyone agrees global warming is both real and caused by humans. Give two major reasons why bargaining in the spirit of Coase is unlikely to resolve the problem of excess carbon emissions.

*18. Two dairy farmers, Ben and Jerry, share a common pasture. Each has a choice of grazing 1 or 2 cows on the pasture. If 2 cows graze on the pasture, each will give 1,000 gallons of milk each year, which may be sold for $1 each at the local farmers' market. If 3 cows graze on the pasture, the grass will be thinner, and each will give

750 gallons of milk. If 4 cows graze on the pasture, the grass will have little chance to recover, and each cow will only give 400 gallons of milk.

a. What is the efficient number of cows to keep on the common pasture: 2, 3, or 4? Explain.

b. If Jerry keeps 1 cow in the pasture, how many should Ben keep? (Assume that the only thing that concerns Ben is revenue received at the farmers' market.)

c. If Jerry keeps 2 cows in the pasture, how many should Ben keep?

d. Repeat your analysis for Jerry. What outcome are we likely to see: 2, 3, or 4 cows in the pasture?

e. What strategies might be useful in preventing overgrazing on the commons?

19. Classify each of the following goods using these terms: nonrival, nonexcludable, private good, club good, public good, and common resource.

   a. Hamburger

   b. Lighthouse

   c. Flood control

   d. Swimming pool

   e. Park

   f. Broadcast television

   g. Cellular telephone service

   h. Computer software

20. Using the appropriate terminology, explain why public radio stations, which rely on contributions from listeners, always seem to be in financial jeopardy.

21. A home-team baseball victory produces benefits for residents (in terms of hometown pride) that is both nonrival and nonexcludable. The graph below depicts the marginal benefits that Beatrice, Edward, and Charlotte (the residents of a very tiny town indeed) receive from home-team wins. The graph also depicts the marginal costs of achieving each victory.

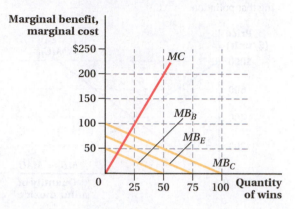

a. Draw the total marginal benefit received by hometown residents. Graph your result carefully.

b. Determine the socially optimal number of wins. Indicate this amount on your graph.

22. There are two consumers of mosquito abatement, a public good. Dash's benefit from mosquito abatement is given by $MB_D = 100 - Q$, where Q is the quantity of mosquito abatement. Lilly's benefit is given by $MB_L = 60 - Q$.

a. Calculate the total marginal benefit, MB_T.

b. Suppose that mosquito abatement can be provided at a marginal cost of $MC = 2Q$. Find the optimal level of mosquito abatement.

c. How much benefit do Dash and Lilly enjoy at the optimal level of mosquito abatement? (Assume Dash and Lilly do not have to bear any of the cost personally, but that abatement is provided by the government at no direct cost to the recipient.)

Behavioral and Experimental Economics

Imagine you run the Centers for Disease Control and Prevention (CDC) located in Atlanta, Georgia. Your job is to keep America safe. Suddenly, an unusual disease breaks out in Florida. Your best scientists estimate that 600 Americans were exposed to the disease and will die if the government does not act. Your staff presents you with two possible programs to address the crisis. Within each program, you'll have to choose one of two response plans. Which would you choose for each of the following?

- Program 1 offers two possible responses to the crisis, each of which costs the same. Because of resource constraints, you can choose only one. Response A is a sure thing: It will definitely save 200 people. Response B is risky. It has a one-third chance to save all 600 people but a two-thirds chance to save no one. Which do you pick?

- Program 2 also offers two possible responses, each of which costs the same. Again, you can choose only one. With Response C, 400 people will die for certain. With Response D, there is a one-third chance that no one will die and a two-thirds chance that all 600 infected people will die. Again, ask yourself, what would you choose?

If you choose Response A for Program 1, did you choose Response C for Program 2? You should have, because both responses are the same; they are only described differently. In either case, 200 people live and 400 people die with certainty. Similarly, B and D are the same outcomes with different wording. With each response, there is a one-third chance to save everyone and a two-thirds chance to save no one.

In a famous study, economic researchers asked people which response they would pick.[1] When presented with Program 1, 72% of the people chose Response A: Better to save 200 lives for certain with this option than gamble on saving more lives and risk saving no one with Response B. But when offered Program 2, 78% of the same people picked Response D. Their reasoning? How can you pick a response (C) in which 400 people die for sure when you can take a chance to save everyone? Remember that Responses A and C are the same: Response A saves 200 lives for certain (and thus 400 people die for certain), and in Response C, 400 people die for certain (and 200 people live for certain). By manipulating how these alternatives were framed, Amos Tversky and Daniel Kahneman (now a Nobel laureate) were able to alter the choices dramatically.

This outcome should not happen in a standard economic model. When we have thought about utility functions, costs, risks, and the like in the previous 17 chapters, how the choices are described is not supposed to matter. You prefer one bundle of goods to a second bundle or you don't. A standard economic model cannot explain why framing the problem in terms of lives saved versus lives lost should matter. Nor can it easily explain why companies price items in 99-cent increments, or why a consumer would buy 1 Nike shirt priced at $25, but instead purchase 3 if the shirt is marked down by 50% from $50. In building economic models, economists assume that the agents behave rationally and

---

[1] Amos Tversky and Daniel Kahneman, "The Framing of Decisions and the Psychology of Choice," *Science* 211, no. 4481 (1981): 453–458.

realize that in the disease example 200 lives are saved with Responses A and C, and that in both cases the price of the Nike shirt is $25.

In recent years, economists have increasingly come to accept that, as great a job as standard economic models can do in explaining the world, they sometimes fail badly when human psychology plays an important role in people's decision making.

The nature of these models' failures matters. If people and firms sometimes make mistakes and act differently from perfectly rational, self-interested agents, but those mistakes are random (i.e., not predictable), then the standard economic models may be fine. But if the mistakes are *systematic,* that is, if people repeatedly act differently from the model in predictable ways, then the flaws are more serious. It is claims of systematic departure from rational economic decision making that motivate the rising prominence of **behavioral economics,** the *branch of economics that incorporates insights from human psychology into models of economic behavior.*

Like the field of behavioral economics itself, this chapter is a bit different from the conventional microeconomics we've presented thus far. Instead of laying out specific models and showing you how to solve and apply them, this chapter examines some of the ways that economists and psychologists have expanded traditional economic models in an effort to better explain real-world behaviors. The first half of the chapter presents an overview of some of the common psychological biases and mistakes people make that have emerged from behavioral economics research and why they might pose a problem for traditional models. In addition, we learn how fully rational, self-interested market participants might take advantage of such biases in a well-functioning market. These biases include the susceptibility to framing (the bias we saw in our disease example), overconfidence, being overly oriented to the present, an inability to ignore sunk costs, and other economic taboos.

In the second half of the chapter, we discuss the new ways economists have begun to test these behavioral economic models using actual experiments rather than traditional statistical methods like econometrics. We conclude the chapter and the book with a discussion of what behavioral economics means for the future of microeconomics.

18.1 When Human Beings Fail to Act the Way Economic Models Predict

The actors who populate the economic models mostly worry about only one thing: getting the most they can for themselves. Firms maximize profit; consumers maximize utility. They make rational tradeoffs, and evaluating those tradeoffs often requires some stout computational ability.

Critics of the "normal" economic models have mockingly used the term *Homo economicus* to describe the creature that inhabits the economic world. *Homo economicus* is like a regular human being (*Homo sapiens*), except able to solve any complicated economic problem, *never* makes a mistake, and knows how to maximize anything. In other words, *Homo economicus* doesn't seem much like *Homo sapiens* at all.

In this section, we explore five of the most important ways in which behavioral economics says *Homo economicus* differs from *Homo sapiens.*[2]

Systematic Bias 1: Overconfidence

One psychological bias that behavioral economists say real people suffer from is **overconfidence,** a *belief that one's skill and judgment are better than they truly*

behavioral economics Branch of economics that incorporates insights from human psychology into models of economic behavior.

overconfidence A belief that one's skill and judgment are better than they truly are, or that better outcomes are more likely to happen than their true probability.

[2] If you develop an interest in behavioral economics, the books *Misbehaving: The Making of Behavioral Economics* by Richard H. Thaler and *Thinking, Fast and Slow* by Daniel Kahneman offer solid introductions to the field.

are, or that better outcomes are more likely to happen than their true probability. Overconfident people will systematically make mistakes in a rational economic model that assumes they have realistic expectations and base their decisions strictly on them.

When asked in surveys, 93% of American college students say that they are above-average drivers. Indeed, most people believe they are outstanding on many dimensions, not just behind the wheel. Other studies have found that people overestimate their intelligence, sense of humor, and many other qualities. On at least one Internet dating site, 77% of listed individuals (about equal fractions for men and women) rated themselves as having either "very good" or "above-average" physical attractiveness. In fairness, perhaps they don't believe their attractiveness is superior, but are just saying this so they can get a first date and then wow that person with their above-average sense of humor.

Two economic settings in which overconfidence can play an important role are stock markets and futures markets. Every time someone makes a trade in one of these markets — selling 100 shares of Google, say, or a thousand barrels of oil — there must be another trader willing to take the other side of the transaction and buy the shares. The buyer must believe the value will rise, the seller that it won't. One of them is wrong. If the person on one side of the trade believes that the other has better information or better judgment, he probably won't want to make the trade. But if each trader thinks he is smarter than everyone else, he will want to make more trades.

Likewise, company managers confident in their own abilities will be inclined to make bigger investments and take more risks on the overconfident view that they will succeed.

How Economic Markets Take Advantage of Overconfident People   Having a psychological bias opens a person up to being taken advantage of in the marketplace by more rational players. The health club industry keenly understands and takes advantage of people who suffer from overconfidence bias. When individuals sign up for a health club, they tend to be far too optimistic about the prospects of sticking to their exercise goals; they use the health club much less, on average, than they expect to at the outset. Aware of this, health clubs tailor their offerings to exploit such over-optimism. For example, suppose individuals who work out frequently are willing to pay $100 a month for a health club membership, but a membership is only worth $20 a month to those who work out infrequently. Having just made a New Year's resolution to be more fit in the upcoming year, overly optimistic consumers believe they will go to the gym frequently over the next year. And, indeed, some people will stick to their resolution for the entire year. Most, however, will be heavy users of the gym for only a few months (or days).

In light of this, rational health club owners detected a business strategy. They could have priced their product the way most goods are priced: per unit like a gallon of milk or a ticket to the movie. But health clubs don't price that way — they don't usually allow customers to pay, say, $10 for each visit to the club. Instead, health clubs usually require customers to sign a long-term contract that involves a big up-front payment, sometimes with a very short trial period.

If every customer overconfidently believes he will be a heavy gym user after a week of working out, he might be willing to make an up-front payment of $1,200 for a membership that allows him unlimited use of the gym for two years. That type of contract extracts a lot more revenue from overly optimistic consumers than charging them per visit. Consumers may be willing to pay huge up-front fees even though they would be better off paying very high prices per trip to the gym given how infrequently they will end up going. Behavioral economics researchers have documented exactly this situation for health club businesses.[3]

---

[3] Stefano DellaVigna and Ulrike Malmendier, "Paying Not to Go to the Gym," *American Economic Review* 96, no. 3 (2006): 694–719.

Systematic Bias 2: Self-Control Problems and Hyperbolic Discounting

Another psychological bias highlighted by behavioral economics is people's strong desire to have things NOW and the difficulties that poses for self-control. We addressed discounting the future in Chapter 14, where we learned about net present value, and in Chapter 12's discussion of repeated games. In those discussions, we used a simple discounting framework in which people discount the future by a set percentage each period, such as 10% per year (i.e., they view a payment of $1 a year from today as equivalent to $0.90 today). Behavioral economists argue that although people may think that way about decisions well into the future, they seem to value immediate payoffs by much more than the basic discount rate would suggest. This behavior is called **hyperbolic discounting** — the *tendency of people to prefer immediate payoffs to later payoffs, even if the later payoff is much greater.*

hyperbolic discounting
The tendency of people to prefer immediate payoffs to later payoffs, even if the later payoff is much greater.

One way to understand this is to think about a person deciding to buy a Ronco Smart Juicer as seen on TV. It costs either $200 up-front or four (easy) monthly payments of $65 each. Either way, Ronco sends the juicer to the consumer upon purchase; there's no four-month delay if you choose the installment payment plan. A fully rational consumer (one who conforms to economic models' assumptions of rationality) buying the juicer would do a net present value calculation discounting at a discount rate of, say, 5% per month (this is a really high number, but it makes our point easier to see than if we use a lower discount rate). The cost of the juicer in one payment is $200. The four undiscounted payments of $65 total $260, but the NPV of the four payments is $65/(1.05) + 65/(1.05)^2 + 65/(1.05)^3 + 65/(1.05)^4 = \$230.49$. Because the NPV of the four payments ($230.49) is higher than the up-front cost ($200), the consumer should pay for the juicer in full upon purchase.

However, because hyperbolic discounters heavily value the present, they have a huge discount rate for that first period. Another way to say this is they need to earn a much higher interest rate to make it worth their while to postpone their instant gratification. In our example, let's say our hyperbolic discounting consumer discounts the first month at 25% and the remaining three months at 5%. The calculation then involves an NPV of $65/(1.25) + 65/(1.25)(1.05) + 65/(1.25)(1.05)^2 + 65/(1.25)(1.05)^3 = \$193.61$, less than the $200 up-front cost. Someone who really wants the juicer now will therefore opt for the installment plan because it allows her to acquire the product and keep more of her money today. The hyperbolic discounter's very high discount rate in the first period makes paying the full $200 immediately very painful because that individual wants to keep such a sum available to buy other things (and to buy them NOW).

Note that hyperbolic discounting is different than just having a high discount rate. Regular discounting applies the same discount rate between periods. For example, consumers who discount the future in the regular way apply the same discount rate between now and one period in the future as they do between one period in the future and two periods in the future. (In the Ronco example, this rate was 5% per month.) Hyperbolic discounting specifically applies different discount rates between now and the near future (25% in the Ronco example) and between two future periods (5%).

One of the problems this dual-discount aspect of hyperbolic discounting raises is that consumers stop being **time-consistent,** which refers to *consistencies in a consumer's preferences in a given economic transaction, whether the economic transaction is far off or imminent.* That is, consumers may want to do something now, but then when they get to next year (Year 2), they won't be inclined to stick with the plan they initially set up. When a decision is off in the distance, waiting an extra month doesn't seem like a big deal for a hyperbolic discounter. But, after a year passes, and that same wait is between today and

time-consistent
Consistencies in a consumer's preferences in a given economic transaction, whether the economic transaction is far off or imminent.

month from now, the waiting feels much more costly. What people *think* they will do two years from now, and what they *actually* do, no longer match up, even if the world two years from now ends up being exactly how they predicted it.

When people are not time-consistent, analyzing their behavior gets complicated. The person you are today is different from the person you will be tomorrow, and that fact turns self-control issues into a game theory battle between two different people. "*Today* you" wants to save a lot of money next year, but "*next year* you" would rather spend the money and put off saving one more year. If you understand that you are like this, "today you" (who wants to save next year) can take an action that commits "next year you" to save. You could sign up with your employer to automatically take money out of your salary for a retirement account starting next year. You could write out a check to an organization you do not like and hand it to a friend who promises to mail it to the organization if you don't follow your plan (and who will rip up the check if you do). People use less extreme versions of these sorts of commitment devices all the time. Smokers might throw away their cigarettes, or dieters their ice cream, so their future selves won't be tempted.

How Economic Markets Take Advantage of People with Self-Control Problems

Because hyperbolic discounters put so much weight on the present, they make choices they regret in the long run, such as not studying hard enough for their final exams, or not saving enough for the future.

Clever marketers often try to take advantage of people's propensity for impulsiveness. Furniture stores let you sit on the futon and offer "no money down" purchases that end up costing more over time. Credit card companies send out offers of 0% interest for the first 30 days, low minimum payments on your monthly bill, and "free" balance transfers from other cards. In each case, the cards make it as easy as possible for consumers to obtain money or reduce the costs of borrowing right now in exchange for higher costs they will have to pay in the future.

As you might imagine, if you build an economic model in which some people or firms are hyperbolic discounters who put great weight on the present and others are fully rational economic agents who discount at "normal" rates, after a while, the rational discounters often end up with all the money (because they are patient and keep building their savings year after year), and those who "want it now" end up broke (because they want everything right away and spend all their money each year). So, if you believe you are prone to impulsive hyperbolic discounting behavior, watch out. Try to find ways to commit to your financial plans and avoid temptations.

Systematic Bias 3: Falling Prey to Framing

Another systematic bias in decision making is that people often make incompatible (and thus irrational) decisions depending on how a decision or problem is framed. The disease treatment program example at the opening of the chapter was a case in point, but there are many types of framing biases.

One is the **endowment effect,** the *phenomenon whereby simply possessing a good makes it more valuable to the owner; that is, the owner must be paid more to give up the good than she would have paid to buy it in the first place.* For example, a professor decides to give every student in class a gift. Half of the class gets coffee mugs and the other half gets chocolate bars. The gifts are of equal average value and distributed randomly, so some students who prefer candy will end up with mugs and vice versa. Conventional economic models tell us that allowing the students to trade in a free market will increase total welfare (we discussed this in Chapter 15). Because there are an equal number of identically

endowment effect The phenomenon whereby simply possessing a good makes it more valuable; that is, the possessor must be paid more to give up the good than she would have paid to buy it in the first place.

valuable gifts and because they were randomly assigned, something like half the students should want to swap gifts (because we expect half the students to prefer candy and half to prefer mugs).

When researchers tested this and similar scenarios in real life, however, that's not what happened. When behavioral economist Richard Thaler tried this experiment, only 15% of students (instead of around 50% as the theory predicts) were willing to trade what they had been given initially, regardless of what item that was. As soon as the students received the mug or the candy, they felt it was more valuable to them. Indeed, when asked if they would sell the coffee mug back to the experimenter at the retail price, many people refused to do so, even though they had never chosen in the past to buy such a coffee mug at the store. (Presumably, having passed on the mug at the store means they valued the mug less than its retail price.) Their perception of the utility they would obtain from the mug had been altered by their ownership of the mug. That is the endowment effect. In another example of this effect, the online news site Business Insider approached 14 people who had just bought lottery tickets and offered to buy their tickets at twice the price they paid. Almost 80% refused.[4]

loss aversion A type of framing bias in which a consumer chooses a reference point around which losses hurt much more than gains feel good.

The endowment effect is a special case of a broader pattern of behavior known as **loss aversion,** *a type of framing bias in which a consumer chooses a reference point around which losses hurt much more than gains feel good.* Falling below that point (which is perceived by the person as suffering a loss) hurts worse than rising above it (perceived as a gain) feels good. So, for instance, if a restaurant raises prices and the consumer's reference point is what he paid for the meal last time, he suffers a large drop in utility relative to how good he feels when the restaurant lowers its prices by the same amount. The reference point, of course, may be totally arbitrary.

This is not true for the traditional consumer model from economics; in it, consumers just care about the bundle of goods they are able to buy. A small price increase lowers those consumers' utility levels by essentially the same amount as a small price reduction increases their utility levels. What makes loss aversion different is that consumers' choices depend on where they start. When a loss-averse person is just above the reference point, the consumer will be very risk-averse. A little below the reference point, the consumer may act risk-loving in order to try to get back to the reference point.

anchoring A type of framing bias in which a person's decision is influenced by the specific pieces of information given.

Another framing bias is **anchoring,** *a type of framing bias in which a person's decision is influenced by the specific pieces of information given.* When asked what percentage of countries in the United Nations were in Africa, for example, people responded with a smaller number, on average, if the question was "Is it more than 10%?" rather than "Is it more than 65%?"[5] In a market transaction, anchoring bias means that a consumer's willingness to pay for a kayak, say, is higher if he first sees several high-priced items that frame the kayak purchase and raise his willingness to pay. Thus, the presentation of the products and their prices influences a consumer's choice, whereas conventional demand theory says that the willingness to pay comes straight from the consumer's tastes. Framing and labeling are not supposed to matter.

mental accounting A type of framing bias that occurs when people divide their current and future assets into separate, nontransferable portions, instead of basing purchasing decisions on their assets as a whole.

Last, there is **mental accounting,** *a type of framing bias that occurs when people divide their current and future assets into separate, nontransferable portions, instead of basing purchasing decisions on their assets as a whole.* In traditional consumer behavior theory, a consumer makes rational decisions about savings or buying various products

---

[4] Immanuel Ocbazghi and Sara Silverstein, "Why Most People Refuse to Sell Their Lottery Tickets for Twice What They Paid," *Business Insider,* October 23, 2018, https://www.businessinsider.com/powerball-tickets-winning-numbers-regret-avoidance-behavioral-economics-2017-8

[5] Amos Tversky and Daniel Kahneman, "Judgment under Uncertainty: Heuristics and Biases," *Science* 185, no. 4157 (1974): 1124–1130.

based on income, prices, and other factors that are part of that person's utility function. In contrast to this rational consumer, some behavioral economists claim that people make mental accounts in which they divide up their money and their purchases. Instead of considering "savings" as one big category, for example, people keep mental accounts for college money, vacation money, and retirement money, and act as if moving funds between these accounts is difficult or impossible. For consumption, they may have mental accounts for monthly spending on gasoline, clothing, and food instead of one account for "consumption."

Mental accounting can also apply to different sources of income. If a person finds a $20 bill on the floor and goes out and spends this windfall, but saves most of a $20 tip she receives at work, that's mental accounting. The standard economic model says that a $20 bonus is a $20 bonus whether it comes from the floor or from a grateful customer.

How Markets Take Advantage of People Who Fall Prey to Framing   The number of ways a clever marketer can use a person's framing bias to make money is almost unlimited. Some cynics might even say that knowing how to do this is the very *definition* of clever marketing.

To take advantage of people with the endowment effect bias, a firm might offer a money-back guarantee. Before buying a product, the fully rational consumer isn't always sure whether he will like it, so the option to return it and get back his money has value — the guarantee makes it more likely that he will buy the product to try it out. After buying the product, though, a customer with an endowment bias will experience an exaggerated increase in the product's value to him, so he will be very unlikely to return it for a refund, even if he is not fully satisfied.[6]

To take advantage of people with an anchoring bias, a firm might artificially inflate the base price of a good and then advertise a "50 percent off" sale. By anchoring in the consumer's mind the idea that the good is worth the original inflated price, the half-price good looks like a bargain, even though the "50 percent off" price is what the good normally would have sold for anyway.

A buyer who is a mental accountant must beware of the tactic often used by salespeople in car showrooms across the world: "How much do you want to pay for a car?" Once you put an amount of money into a mental account, you can be fairly sure that a smart seller will find a way to withdraw it for you.

Systematic Bias 4: Paying Attention to Sunk Costs

An important theme in economics is to ignore sunk costs when making decisions. Money already spent that cannot be recovered shouldn't matter. Rational decision makers think at the margin and only consider opportunity costs. (To review these ideas, see Chapter 7.)

In reality, however, behavioral economists say that people often fall prey to the **sunk cost fallacy,** the *mistake of allowing sunk costs to affect decisions*. A classic example of the sunk cost fallacy comes from an experiment published in 1985 by psychologists Hal Arkes and Catherine Blumer.[7] The researchers worked out a deal with the theater at

sunk cost fallacy The mistake of allowing sunk costs to affect decisions.

---

[6] Note that there are other explanations for why producers give money-back guarantees that don't rely at all on behavioral economics. When asymmetric information is available (Chapter 16), a producer who makes a high-quality good can use a money-back guarantee to signal that the good is of high quality. It is more costly for a company that makes low-quality goods to offer a money-back guarantee, because more consumers will return the low-quality good, so providing the guarantee up-front is a credible sign that a product is indeed well made. Contrasting views of economic behavior like this lie at the heart of the vigorous debate over behavioral economics among economists.

[7] Hal R. Arkes and Catherine Blumer, "The Psychology of Sunk Cost," *Organizational Behavior and Human Decision Processes* 35, no. 1 (1985): 124–140.

Ohio University so that when a person arrived at the ticket window and asked to buy a season ticket (for 10 plays), the buyer was randomly assigned a price for the season ticket. A third of the buyers paid the full price of $15 per play for the season ticket. A second group paid $13 per play, and a third group paid just $8 per play.

Given that the ticket holders all had tickets in hand on the morning of a performance, how much people paid for the tickets had no bearing on the size of the marginal benefit from attending the plays. The price of the ticket was a sunk cost, and the marginal cost of attending was just the value of their time; there was no additional expense. And yet, in the first half of the season, the people who had paid full price attended about 25% more of the plays than did the groups that received discounts. Behavioral economists argued this happened because the high-price group felt a greater obligation to attend so that they could get their money's worth from the tickets. People just can't seem to ignore sunk costs, even though, rationally, they should.[8]

Companies and governments have made similar sunk cost mistakes. One example involves the Concorde supersonic jet, which was jointly developed by the British and French governments. The joint venture began in the early 1960s, amidst great optimism. Plans went quickly awry, however. Ultimately, development costs ended up being 6 times higher than projected, cost overruns that were anticipated far in advance. By virtually all accounts, the right course of action would have been to stop the project, but the governments forged ahead because there was "too much invested to quit," as described in Allan Teger's 1980 book on the subject.[9] Ultimately, only 20 of the airplanes were ever made and eventually the program died.

Application: The Sunk Cost Fallacy and Professional Athletes

Star professional athletes are paid millions of dollars. The teams they play for are willing to offer these kinds of salaries because of fans' willingness to pay to watch games. The better players are at what they do—the more their performances thrill fans and help their teams win—the more they play, and the more they are paid.

At least that's how it's supposed to work. But there is some evidence that the relationship between playing time and pay is a little more complicated—that certain players get more playing time just because they are paid more, even if they aren't that good. The reason seems to be that teams fall prey to the sunk cost fallacy.

A study by economist Quinn Keefer finds this type of behavior at play in the National Football League (NFL).[10] New players to the league are typically assigned to teams through an annual draft, where teams take turns choosing which new players they want to add to their rosters. There are seven rounds in the draft, and each team is granted one pick per round.

As you might guess, the last player picked in one round is basically about as talented as the first player in the next round; after all, they were chosen right after one another.

[8] It is worth noting that the standard economic model better predicts the theatergoers' behavior in the second half of the season than in the first half. In the second half of the season, there were no differences in attendance according to the price paid for the tickets, so any sunk cost fallacy effect disappeared. Indeed, all three groups appear to have figured out that they just don't like going to the theater that much: Attendance fell to about two plays in the second half of the season, regardless of the price paid for the tickets.

[9] Allan I. Teger, *Too Much Invested to Quit*, Oxford: Pergamon Press, 1980.

[10] Quinn A. W. Keefer, "The Sunk-Cost Fallacy in the National Football League: Salary Cap Value and Playing Time," *Journal of Sports Economics* 18, no. 3 (2015) 282–297.

Their playing statistics look almost identical, but their salaries aren't. The last pick in an earlier round typically receives a salary considerably higher than the player chosen immediately after, in the first pick of the later round. This gap is the largest between the first and second rounds of the draft, where the last first-round pick gets paid, on average, 35% more than the first second-round pick.

Once the team commits to a contract, how much the player is paid shouldn't affect playing time. Prior salary commitments are sunk costs. Playing time should be determined by how much a player will contribute to the team's performance. Equal-quality players should play the same amount.

They don't. The last first-round draft pick plays about 5 more games a season than the first second-round pick. That's more than a quarter of the NFL's 16-game season. It seems as if the teams believe that if they are paying so much more for a first-rounder, he should play more than a (cheaper) second-rounder, even though their impact on the team's success is the same.

Big-salary hires help teams when players fulfill their potential, but the gap in playing time between equivalent players in different draft rounds illustrates how such purchases can also lead teams to place undue weight on sunk costs. If NFL team managers were thinking like economists, they would realize that using the players who would most help the team, irrespective of what they had paid for those players, is the right choice. ∎

How Markets Take Advantage of Loss-Averse People Attentive to Sunk Costs   At the most basic level, the market will make those who are suffering from the sunk cost fallacy end up taking the hit. In the Application above, for example, it's the stubborn NFL teams who suffer: They're stuck losing games they might have won if they signed equally good players for less money. Market participants who do not suffer from the sunk cost bias can end up benefiting from the mistakes of people who do.

Systematic Bias 5: Fairness and Generosity

Economic models are premised on rational, self-interested consumers and firms. Perhaps one of the most basic challenges to this assumption is that people often engage in acts of generosity and selflessness. Parents sacrifice for their children; volunteers work long hours for various causes; people seem to care about fairness as much as their own personal benefit; and so on. Economists have tried to introduce non-self-interested behavior into the standard model by adding a taste for generosity (called the "warm glow of giving") into the utility function or by letting a parent's utility depend on not only his own consumption but also that of his children. But these methods seem like a bit of a dodge. They fail to address the fundamental issue that, by frequently helping others at no benefit to themselves, people don't always appear to act as rational economic agents.

One specific form of generosity that people seem to exhibit is an inherent preference for fairness. That is, people will sometimes take costly actions that aren't profitable from a standard cost–benefit standpoint (at least one that ignores social returns or losses of such actions) in order to get to an outcome that would be viewed as more fair.

Consider, for instance, individuals' responses in the following game, often called the "ultimatum game." One player, the *proposer*, is given an amount of money by the experimenter and then instructed to offer whatever portion of it she wishes to an anonymous second player, the *recipient*. The recipient then decides whether to accept or reject this offer. If the recipient accepts the offer, each player gets the portion of money specified in the proposer's offer. If the recipient instead rejects the offer, *neither* player gets anything.

The traditional models we have been working with throughout this book would predict that the proposer will offer a minimal amount, say, 1 cent, the recipient will accept this offer, and the proposer will end up with virtually all the initial money. We can use backward induction to see why. Think about the recipient's choice of whether to accept an offer once it has been made. Because the recipient gets nothing if he rejects the offer, he should be willing to accept any offer greater than zero—something, no matter how small, is better than nothing. Knowing this will be the case, the proposer should offer the recipient a tiny but positive amount (1 cent), keeping almost all of the cash for herself.

It turns out, however, that people who play this game in lab experiments deviate far from the outcomes predicted by backward induction. On average, proposers offer between 40% and 50% of their endowment, and recipients frequently reject offers that are below 20% of the endowment. It seems that recipients see low offers as being somehow unfair, and they are willing to give up some cash of their own (whatever was offered to them by the proposer) to punish the proposer for their selfishness. Proposers, sensing this, make more generous offers at the outset to avoid getting nothing from an angry recipient rejecting the offer.[11]

How Markets Take Advantage of Generous People   Sadly, this scenario is fairly obvious. In principle, the more selfless or generous a party is, the more the purely selfish actor could collect from them. The more subtle answer that comes from the research on fairness and generosity is that many of people's selfless behaviors are tied to reciprocity. Over the long run, people who constantly take advantage of others' generosity without paying back their debts may be excluded or shunned. That kind of long-run strategic thinking makes the underlying principle a bit more complicated.

 Application: Does Psychology Affect Animal Decisions, Too?

You learned about the lab experiments in the ultimatum game and the ways in which people seem to embrace fairness and not just operate selfishly. Scientists have wondered if this behavior derives uniquely from human psychology or culture and if, in contrast, animals act only in their self-interest. Researchers Darby Proctor, Rebecca Williamson, Frans de Waal, and Sarah Brosnan set out to explore this question with chimpanzees.[12] They conducted a standard ultimatum game with chimpanzees, except rather than money, they gave proposer chimpanzees tokens that could be exchanged for bananas. (The chimps had already been trained to understand what the tokens could be used for and how the ultimatum game worked in their context.)

The chimpanzees matched human behavior in one respect. Proposer chimps offered something near an even split nearly 75% of the time, suggesting they valued fairness. However, unlike human recipients, recipient chimps never rejected an offer, no matter how small it was. Not rejecting lopsided offers seems to indicate these recipient chimps *didn't* care about fairness. But if that's the case, why did the proposers often make even-split offers?

It turns out that the recipients did value fairness; they just chose to express it in a different way than their human counterparts. Rather than reject offers they saw as unfair, chimp recipients sometimes responded to these entreaties with threats, such as spitting water at the proposer or pounding on the barrier separating the two chimps. The high number of

---

[11] See Ernst Fehr and Klaus M. Schmidt, "Theories of Fairness and Reciprocity: Evidence and Economics Applications," in *Advances in Economics and Econometrics: Theory and Applications, Eighth World Congress,* vol. 1, New York: Cambridge University Press, 2003, 208–257. It gives an excellent summary of both the theory and data on fairness-related concerns. And yes, one of the world's leading expert on fairness is, indeed, named Fehr.

[12] Darby Proctor, Rebecca A. Williamson, Frans B. M. de Waal, and Sarah F. Brosnan, "Chimpanzees Play the Ultimatum Game," *Proceedings of the National Academy of Sciences* 110, no. 6 (February 5, 2013): 2070–2075.

offers with close to even splits, especially later on in the experiment as the proposers became familiar with the recipients' typical reactions, suggests that the proposing apes understood the point of these threats, even if their offers were never rejected.

Sarah Brosnan and Frans de Waal, two of the authors in the original chimpanzee study, conducted a second, somewhat similar experiment with pairs of female capuchin monkeys.[13] Each of the two monkeys had its own cage, but the cages were made of plastic, so each could see what was happening in the other's area. In one

Video still of the experiment at the Yerkes National Primate Research Center, courtesy Frans de Waal.

"Tasteless cucumbers. No fair. Grapes, we want sweet grapes."

version of the experiment, both of the monkeys would receive a cucumber slice if they gave the researcher a token. In another version, one monkey would get a cucumber slice for a token, while the other would get a grape (capuchins like grapes a lot more than cucumbers). In a third version, one monkey would get a cucumber slice for a token, while the other received grapes without even having to exchange a token.

The researchers found that in the second and third versions of the experiment, the "cucumber monkeys" would sometimes refuse to accept the cucumber when the researcher offered it to them. (A video of the experiment shows one particularly irate monkey throwing its cucumber slice at the researcher.) In other cases, the cucumber monkeys refused to even hand over the token in the first place. It's almost unheard of for monkeys to refuse food, and the unusual behavior was most pronounced when the other monkey received grapes for "free." The cucumber monkeys, unhappy with what they viewed as unfair treatment, were willing to express a preference for fairness, even if it meant giving up food they would normally eat. ∎

18.2 Does Behavioral Economics Mean Everything We've Learned Is Wrong?

At this point, you may be wondering why you bothered reading 17 chapters on economic models only to find out that behavioral economics says people don't, in fact, behave the way the models predict they will. It may seem that we could have simply avoided studying difficult models and theories that don't work and instead just read a book on behavioral economics.

That's not quite right, though. First of all, the behavioral anomalies we've discussed in this chapter do not invalidate the economic models you've learned. They show us that some people, under certain circumstances, act in a way that the basic models might miss. But the foundational models you learned actually do a remarkably good job of describing how the economic world works *most* of the time. When describing something as complex as human behavior, that is still an important advance. Second, in many areas in which behavioral economics seems to give a different answer, simple adjustments to the basic economic model often provide perfectly viable alternative explanations. As an example,

---

[13] Sarah F. Brosnan and Frans B. M. de Waal, "Monkeys Reject Unequal Pay," *Nature* 425 (September 18, 2003): 297–299.

think about behaviors that the basic, rational consumer decision-making model might have a hard time explaining, such as people becoming addicted to products that are bad for them, like smoking cigarettes. Yet, Nobel laureate Gary Becker has developed conventional economic models to explain such seemingly irrational behaviors. His "rational addiction" model (developed with Kevin Murphy) is just a variant of the consumer behavior theory we studied in Chapters 4 and 5.[14] In it, consumers think about the lifetime costs of becoming addicted and balance that against the utility they get from smoking, knowing that starting now will make it hard to stop in the future. This theory can explain why addiction rates respond to prices, for example, in a better way than an explanation based on the belief that people become addicted because they just can't help themselves.

Third, as we emphasized in the previous section, people and firms that have systematic biases can lose out to people in the marketplace who are not biased. Markets can weed out systematic biases, and economic actors that participate repeatedly in markets often recognize and adjust for their behavioral biases or just exit the marketplace completely. Once biased participants are gone, remaining participants exhibit less irrationality than might a random survey respondent.

It is important for economists and businesses to test how people behave as thoroughly as they can. This desire to better understand the behavior of consumers, customers, suppliers, and producers has led to the rise of another new field of economics: experimental economics.

18.3 Testing Economic Theories with Data: Experimental Economics

The unorthodox results emanating from behavioral economics research in recent years have placed even more significance on the issue of how economists can test models of behavior. Testing some predictions seems fairly easy. For example, demand theory predicts that people buy less of a good when its price increases (in other words, that demand slopes downward). So just check it, right? Well, real-world complications often get in the way of testing even the most basic predictions from the models. Even if you had data on the prices and quantities of, say, chicken nuggets across different cities, you couldn't really say that supply-and-demand theory predicts that the markets with higher prices will have lower quantities demanded. The theory predicts that *holding all else equal,* when prices are higher, consumers will want less of a good. A comparison of two markets only sheds light on this question if all else is equal between the two markets, and in the real world, that's a big "if."

To help get around the messiness of the real world, economists have developed a large number of data, statistical, and analytical techniques to test economic theories — techniques such as how to use shifts in a market's supply curve to statistically trace out its associated demand curve and so on. These techniques are part of **econometrics,** the *field that develops and uses mathematical and statistical techniques to test economic theory.* But even the best econometric techniques still rely on some strong assumptions to get around the potential complications of the real world, to say nothing of the difficulties inherent in most data.

Dissatisfied with empirical data methods like econometrics, some economists have turned to **experimental economics,** a *branch of economics that relies on experiments to illuminate economic behavior.*

econometrics Field that develops and uses mathematical and statistical techniques to test economic theory.

experimental economics Branch of economics that relies on experiments to illuminate economic behavior.

[14] Gary S. Becker and Kevin M. Murphy, "A Theory of Rational Addiction," *Journal of Political Economy* 96, no. 4 (August 1988): 675–700.

Lab Experiments

Lab experiments, *tests of an economic theory in a laboratory setting,* allow an economist to control all aspects of a test and explain precisely what was done. Typically, the experimenter asks groups of subjects, often undergraduates, to take part in the same activity, but with one element of the activity altered for one group. For instance, to test if demand curves slope downward, an experimenter might bring students into a lab, give them each $30, and then randomly assign each student to one of three groups. Each group would then be given the chance to buy coffee mugs embossed with their school's mascot, but one group would face a price of $3 per mug, the second $5 per mug, and the third $10 per mug. Everything but the price is the same in this experiment, so a comparison of the quantities purchased by the groups traces out a demand curve and allows the experimenter to test whether it slopes downward (spoiler alert: It does).

Experiments that randomly assign participants to a treatment group allow researchers to test for influences such as mental accounting errors, overconfidence, the endowment effect, and the other biases we talked about earlier in the chapter.

As helpful as economic laboratory experiments are, they are not without shortcomings or controversy. Economic experiments suffer from some important weaknesses that are missing in most scientific applications of the experimental method. First, unlike chemicals or even lab mice, humans know that when they participate in an experiment, their behavior is being watched. Not surprisingly, critics believe that participants in economic experiments tend to act differently because they are being observed. One factor that tends to distort participants' behavior is that subjects in lab experiments exhibit a strong tendency to act in ways they think will please the experimenter or make themselves look good. For example, college students repeatedly make choices in experiments that are more socially desirable, cooperative, or morally "proper," and shy away from taking actions that will make them look selfish or simply maximize their personal gains. This distortion leads some critics of such economic experiments to question whether lab experiments really tell us about people's behavior in actual markets and whether the experiments truly show that individuals make systematic mistakes in their decision making.

A second issue with the typical lab experiment is that the stakes of the experiment are often much different than in real life. Undergraduates don't get much money to participate in experiments so the stakes at risk in the typical test are low. Low stakes make it cheap for participants to act in ways that are against their own self-interest. Furthermore, sometimes experiments involve really complex or tedious tasks that hardly seem worth doing for so little, whereas in the real world, if you could make a million dollars completing some tedious calculations, you might do it.

A third issue with lab experiments is that students are frequently asked to perform tasks in the lab that they have never done before, such as participating in auctions with randomized and strange rules, or abstract games with complicated payoff functions. Novices at these tasks probably do much worse than experts who would have practiced or benefited from work experience.

Finally, although an experimenter can control the experiment, he cannot control the personal baggage brought by the participants. For instance, experimenters regularly design experiments as one-shot games so that the choice made by a lab subject can be dictated exclusively by the direct payoff and not by any future considerations. But in real life, people do not seem to be able to assume away their cultural norms. The Freakonomics box on the next page describes how differently people from varying cultures play the same lab games, highlighting the difficulties of designing experiments that truly hold everything else equal.

lab experiment Test of an economic theory in a laboratory setting.

FREAKONOMICS

Going to the Ends of the World (Literally) to Test Economic Theory

The great majority of economics lab experiments are done with college students. This is a perfect example of the principles of economics at work: Students are plentiful and willing to participate in experiments for relatively low wages. This makes it cheap and easy to run experiments on campus, and economic researchers have responded by running lots of them. When researchers have looked beyond students to other subject pools like CEOs, professional soccer players, and dealers at flea markets, the results have generally been similar to those obtained from students. It is also the case that Americans and Europeans tend to make similar choices in many lab experiments.

The fact that lab results are robust (i.e., they hold up) across different groups of subjects is good news for lab experiments because it means that what we find in one particular experiment is more likely to generalize to other settings. One characteristic that is shared by virtually all the subjects who have been part of experiments, however, is their *culture*. Americans, whether they are college students, CEOs, or pro athletes, have grown up with a shared culture. European culture differs from American culture, but both of them are closer to each other than to many non-Western cultures. Do the lab experiments on economic behavior yield similar results when conducted in other places?

A collaborative team of economists and anthropologists set out to answer this question.* The team gathered together anthropologists who had spent their careers living with and studying indigenous societies in many different parts of the world. These were small-scale societies that had virtually no contact with the modern world.

The Lamalera cooperate in whaling and in games, while the Hadza, a hunting and gathering tribe, display more self-interest and less cooperation in games.

Despite the potential pitfalls of lab experiments, they remain a useful economic tool. After all, the analysis of real market data without experiments suffers from shortcomings as well. But be wary of assuming that what happens in the lab will automatically happen in real markets. Instead, when faced with data generated from a lab experiment, consider the various biases we've discussed and contemplate how they might distort any interpretation of the lab results.

Natural Experiments and Field Experiments

Responding to some of the criticisms of lab experiments, economists have tried using experiments in the real world instead of the lab to test their theories, in the hope that they can merge some of the control features of lab experiments with the real stakes and context of the marketplace.

One type of real-world experiment is known as a **natural experiment,** a *randomization or near-randomization that arises by happenstance.* It is a situation where, by

natural experiment A randomization or near-randomization that arises by happenstance.

These groups included hunter-gatherers in Tanzania, nomadic herders in Mongolia, and whale hunters in Indonesia. The anthropologists learned how to carry out certain experimental games and then scattered to the far reaches of the world to conduct them. The results obtained from these different groups were all over the map. Some groups behaved more like *Homo economicus* than Westerners; others deviated even further from economic predictions than American college students do. Members of some cultures exhibited remarkable altruism. Others were the epitome of selfishness.

And yet, from this wild mishmash of findings, a simple yet profound pattern emerged: How people played these experimental games was systematically related to the norms that existed in their cultures. For instance, the Lamalera of east Indonesia subsist by hunting whales, an activity that requires high degrees of cooperation across large numbers of hunters to succeed. Not surprisingly, the Lamalera played the games in a cooperative way, with players frequently passing up chances to act in a way that would benefit them to the detriment of the other players.

In contrast, the Hadza, hunters and gatherers in Tanzania, were very self-interested and uncooperative toward one another. It is said that the Hadza abandoned traditional garb for Western-style blue jeans because the deep pockets of the jeans allowed them to more effectively hide the spoils of their hunting and gathering from the prying eyes of their neighbors. The Hadza in the lab experiments did not cooperate much with the other players and instead looked out for themselves.

Perhaps the most remarkable example of culture permeating the lab came from the Au and Gnau peoples of Papua New Guinea. When playing a lab game that involved splitting a pie between themselves and another player, the Au and Gnau often offered the bigger slice of the pie to their opponent (something that virtually never happens with American students), and the opponent frequently refused to accept this bigger slice (again, not common with American students). It turns out that the Au and Gnau are competitive gift-giving societies in which accepting a gift today obligates the recipient to provide a more generous gift to the giver in the future. Thus, a gift is a mixed blessing in this culture. Even though the lab experiment was explicitly described as a one-shot game and played anonymously, so there was no chance that the recipient of the big slice of the experimental pie could be obligated to make a more generous repayment in the future, the Au and Gnau apparently brought such powerful cultural norms into the lab that they participated in the experiment as if it were a typical, real-life gift exchange.

These experiments teach us an important lesson about lab experiments. Although it might seem as if the experimenter gets to choose the game that is played and the context of the experiment, in practice, experimental subjects bring their own contexts with them when they enter the lab. In particular, when people enter a lab, they are not able to instantly abandon life lessons about what society expects and the rules-of-thumb that serve them well in the real world.

[*]Joseph Henrich, Robert Boyd, Samuel Bowles, Colin Camerer, Ernst Fehr, Herbert Gintis, and Richard McElreath, "In Search of Homo Economicus: Behavioral Experiments in 15 Small-Scale Societies," *American Economic Review Papers and Proceedings* 91, no. 2 (May 2001): 73–78.

chance, something happens that allows the researcher to learn about an economic question of interest. When the United States passed the Clean Air Act and its amendments, for example, it set up pollution thresholds for counties in the United States. If a county had a pollution level above the threshold, it faced stringent anti-pollution requirements. If the county fell below the threshold, even by a small amount, the anti-pollution requirements did not apply. For counties just a tiny bit above and just a tiny bit below the threshold, the Clean Air Act provided a natural experiment on the impact of environmental regulation and researchers documented its effects on pollution, industrial activity, health, infant mortality, and so on (and it appears as if regulation matters a lot). An obvious problem with natural experiments is that they are hard to find. A second weakness is that it is not always straightforward to generalize from a specific natural experiment to other settings of economic interest.

The other type of real-world experiment is the **field experiment,** a *research method that uses randomizations, just as in the lab, but does so in real-world settings.* Ideally, research subjects are making decisions as part of their everyday lives, unaware that they

field experiment A research method that uses randomizations, just as in the lab, but does so in real-world settings.

are part of an experiment. Consequently, it is possible to make strong inferences about behavior from field experiments without having to worry about how the artificiality of the lab might be distorting the results.

Clever firms have long engaged in field experiments, and you have unknowingly been part of these experiments throughout your life. Online merchants constantly conduct field experiments, by changing around the order in which goods are presented for some customers, altering the descriptions of goods to see which lead to more sales, and perhaps playing with the prices offered to different recipients. Economists have increasingly turned to field experiments to answer questions as diverse as whether paying high school students for good grades leads to better outcomes, the best way to incentivize people to lose weight, and which movies will be box-office hits.

18.4 Conclusions and the Future of Microeconomics

In this chapter, we have addressed a group of topics collectively known as *behavioral economics*. The claims and predictions of behavioral economics often contradict the findings of the economic models we learned in the earlier chapters of this book. Behavioral economics describes economic decision makers (firms, consumers, governments) that make systematic and fundamental errors based on psychological biases — propensity to overconfidence, mental accounting, susceptibility to framing, sunk cost fallacies, and others. The actions predicted by behavioral economics leave biased agents open to being taken advantage of by all sorts of rational economic actors, as we have also tried to emphasize. But in some sense, the behavioral economics ideas we studied in this chapter provide a critique of the traditional microeconomics we outlined in all the previous chapters.

With that critique has come a renewed emphasis on how we test theories. The use of data to test economic theories is the realm of econometrics, and a full discussion of econometric techniques is beyond the scope of this book. We have, however, introduced some of the new ways in which economists and companies go about testing economic theories outside of econometrics by using experiments in the lab and in the field. The results from those experiments sometimes suggest the importance of behavioral economics critiques and sometimes seem to verify the usefulness of the main economic models we've studied.

We, the authors, strongly believe in the importance and insight of microeconomics. We recognize that the traditional models, while extremely powerful, are far from perfect. The goal of every economist should be to understand actual economic behavior. If that means discovering where the limits of our discipline lie, then we should commit to finding those limits.

In the end, microeconomics is one of humanity's most useful and important intellectual contributions. What you have learned about the subject in this course can serve you extremely well in life if you will let it.[15] One cannot help but be struck by the thought that if the rest of the world knew as much about economics as you now do after completing microeconomics, we would all be a lot better off.

The goal of academics is to disseminate knowledge through teaching and writing. You can help spread that knowledge through your actions. We hope you have enjoyed the ride and that you will use what you've learned for the rest of your life.

---

[15] Thus, we suggest keeping your book for future reference! Of course, you'll have to analyze that suggestion using your skills of economic analysis and consider the incentives of all parties involved.

Summary

1. The traditional economic models of the previous chapters assume that economic actors such as consumers and firms are fully rational and self-interested agents who maximize their well-being without making systematic errors. **Behavioral economics** argues that the conventional models do not take into account psychological biases in human behavior, and that these systematic biases affect the decisions made by parties in an economic transaction. Such biases include **overconfidence, time inconsistency,** susceptibility to framing, attention to sunk costs, and possibly altruistic behavior. Markets tend to take advantage of people suffering from psychological biases and drive them out (or take their money). **[Section 18.1]**

2. Even if we accept the existence of systematic human psychological biases, the fundamental microeconomics of the preceding chapters is still incredibly valuable and relevant to the real world. **[Section 18.2]**

3. Economists have moved into a new realm of testing economic theories using **lab, natural,** and **field experiments** rather than purely **econometric** data analyses. Experiments allow economists to test only the economic theory of interest, holding all else equal. **[Section 18.3]**

4. Microeconomics is perhaps the most important and useful thing you will ever learn in your life. **[Section 18.4]**

Review Questions

1. Differentiate *Homo economicus* and *Homo sapiens.*

2. Define overconfidence.

3. What does hyperbolic discounting lead consumers to prefer?

4. Why is time consistency important in economic models?

5. How does the endowment effect contradict aspects of conventional economic theory?

6. What is the importance of the reference point in loss aversion?

7. Describe one example of anchoring.

8. How does mental accounting affect individuals' consumption decisions?

9. How do economists attempt to account for altruism in economic models?

10. In the opinion of the authors of this textbook, what tends to happen to irrational or biased actors in the market system?

11. Lab experiments allow economists to test economic theory while holding all other variables constant. What are some downfalls of lab experiments?

12. Contrast natural and field experiments. What are some advantages of each?

Problems

(Solutions to problems marked with an asterisk appear at the back of this book. Problems adapted to use calculus are available online.)

1. AJ pays full price to view *The Avengers* at the multiplex. After three minutes of viewing, he realizes that the movie is worse than anything he could be watching on TV at home. Yet he stays to the end, "because I paid $9 for the ticket." What behavioral bias has AJ fallen victim to? Explain.

2. Connor and Marie are in a relationship with each other, a relationship punctuated by constant bickering and mistrust. "Connor," Marie's friends tell her, "is a jerk. Why on earth don't you leave him?" To which Marie responds, "Silly, we've been together for 9 years! I can't just throw away those years!" Explain how Marie has fallen victim to the sunk cost fallacy.

3. A Google search for "New Year's Resolutions" results in more than 219 million hits. Year after year, exercising and losing weight rank among the top resolutions. To accomplish these goals, many people pay high fees to join a gym in early January. Unfortunately, 80% of New Year's resolutions are abandoned by June, and most new gym members fail to work out more than a few times.

    a. What behavioral anomaly causes people to pay high fees to join a gym that they won't use?

    b. Does this evidence provide support for or against the sunk cost bias? Explain your reasoning.

*4. In a recent survey, two-thirds of respondents indicated that they were not saving enough for retirement. What behavioral bias can explain the willingness of individuals to knowingly underfund their future standard of living? Explain.

5. Subscription boxes are all the rage these days. Subscribers pay a small fee and receive a box each month containing music, clothing, electronics, food — you name it! A teenager named Juliette signed up for a subscription makeup box, telling her mother, "It won't cost you much at all. I'll just send back any items that I don't want; you only pay for the items you keep!" Explain why Juliette is likely to buy more makeup from the subscription service than she would if she just shopped in a store. Describe, in your explanation, at least two systematic biases the subscription box service is exploiting.

*6. Economist Dean Karlan has created stickk.com, a non-profit entity that he calls a "commitment store." Individuals attempting to achieve a goal (to lose weight, to quit smoking, to write daily in a journal, etc.) authorize stickk.com to charge them a prespecified amount if they fail to reach their goal (as determined by a third-party referee).

   a. What behavioral bias is stickk.com designed to help overcome?

   b. Should they fail, subscribers are given the option of donating the fees to a charity they support or to an organization that they despise. Why might allowing the subscribers to direct their losses to a favorite charity weaken their resolve?

7. You are considering becoming a hedge-fund manager, and you will make your living by charging your clients a fee for managing their money. You are considering two payment schemes: a "no-load" scheme whereby you charge each client an annual fee that is a relatively high percentage of the amount of money you manage for them, or a "front-load" scheme in which you charge investors a very large one-time fee for each dollar they invest, followed by a very low annual fee.

   a. If your investors are overconfident in your ability to generate abnormally high returns, which scheme can potentially generate the highest profit for you? Explain.

   b. If your investors are a group of very conservative pessimists, which scheme can potentially generate the highest profit for you? Explain.

*8. Economics professor Alan is at his wit's end. Each year, before his first microeconomics exam, he tells his students that they'll need to memorize the formula for the price elasticity of demand. Yet time after time, students fail to accurately regurgitate the formula on their exams. Alan is considering two options to motivate a better performance: Option A is to tell his students, "If you correctly write the formula, I'll give you three extra credit points." Option B is to tell students, "I'm giving you three extra credit points on this exam. But if you don't correctly write the formula, I will take back those extra credit points."

   a. If Alan's students are completely rational, will they be more motivated by Option A or Option B to memorize the formula? Or, will both options motivate them equally?

   b. If Alan's students are swayed by the endowment effect, which scheme is likely to be most effective in motivating them to memorize the formula? Explain your answer.

   c. Discuss the interplay of the endowment effect and framing bias inherent in this problem.

9. Where are you more likely to see racial discrimination: in the highly competitive financial services industry, or in the tobacco industry (where four firms control about 99% of the market share)? Explain your answer, drawing on your knowledge of market structures from Chapters 8, 9, and 11.

10. On the popular TV show *Who Wants to Be a Millionaire* contestants answer a series of multiple-choice trivia questions of increasing difficulty. With each question, their earnings grow; contestants are free to quit the game and keep their winnings at any point before a question is asked. As the game progresses, some lucky contestants find themselves with $500,000, which they can keep or wager on one last question. If they get the question correct, they go home with 1 million dollars; if they miss the question, they leave with only $50,000.

    Explain why someone might wager $500,000 of game show winnings on a 1-in-4 chance of $1 million, but why that same someone might be reluctant to wager $500,000 of retirement savings on the same 1-in-4 chance. What bias is at work?

11. Brick and mortar retailer JCPenney was well known for its weekly sales, in which certain clothes, shoes, jewelry, and home goods would be heavily advertised at discount prices. In 2012, struggling to compete against Internet retailers, then JCPenney CEO Ron Johnson announced that there would be no more weekly sales—instead, all prices would be permanently reduced and JCPenney would trumpet their "everyday low prices."

    JCPenney's experiment was a colossal failure; its sales plummeted. Within a year, Johnson was fired, and JCPenney was once again marking up prices on its products, so the store could immediately mark them down for the appearance of a discount. Explain the behavioral anomaly that JCPenney exploits when it does this.

12. "The most heartfelt gifts are anonymous ones." Explain this statement, drawing on your knowledge of utility functions that account for behavioral traits.

13. Consider the ultimatum game, a two-player game often played in experimental economics labs. In the ultimatum game, one player is given an amount of money and then instructed to give some arbitrary portion of it to an anonymous second player. The second player has the option of accepting the offer or rejecting it. If the second player rejects the offer, neither player gets anything.

    a. According to traditional economic theory (which assumes that individuals are self-interested utility maximizers), what should the first player offer the second?

    b. What does traditional economic theory suggest the second player should be willing to accept?

    c. In experimental settings, the first player often offers the anonymous second player about 50% of the initial amount. Is this result consistent with theory? Can we easily attribute this anomaly to something other than an innate sense of fairness? Explain.

14. Consider the dictator game, a two-player game often played in experimental economics labs. In the dictator game, one player (the dictator) is given an amount of money and then instructed to give some arbitrary portion of it to an

anonymous second player. The second player must accept whatever the first player offers, if anything.

a. According to traditional economic theory, what should the first player offer the second?

b. In experimental settings, the average offer given to the second player is about 30% of the initial amount. Explain how such an offer might not be motivated by an innate sense of fairness.

15. One way of stating the Coase theorem is that "in the absence of transactions costs, the property right to an activity will be acquired by the party that values it most." This suggests that if environmentalists initially value a wetlands more than a developer (who wants to convert that wetlands into a subdivision), then if the developer happens to acquire that land, environmentalists can save the wetlands by simply purchasing the wetlands from her. Explain how the existence of endowment effects may interfere with the process of bargaining and may potentially result in a less-than-optimal allocation of resources.

16. Identical twins Jo and Jerri have identical preferences; both love to go to football games, and both are looking forward to their alma mater's homecoming. Jo bought her ticket in advance; Jerri plans to buy hers at the gate. On the day of the big game, a blizzard strikes. Explain, using the theories of behavioral economics, why Jerri is more likely to stay home than Jo. What bias is at work? Explain.

17. Jameel is offered two sets of choices.

Choice A. Take a $100 check that can be cashed today, or a $200 certified check that can be cashed in two years.

Choice B. Take a $100 certified check that can be cashed in six years, or a $200 check that can be cashed in eight years.

a. Put yourself in Jameel's shoes. Which option would you choose from Choice A? From Choice B?

b. Jameel chooses the $100 check in Choice A and the $200 check in Choice B. Explain how Jameel's choices are not time-consistent.

c. Which systematic bias has Jameel fallen victim to?

18. Siblings Sacha and Simon *love* basketball—and there's nothing better for a basketball fan than March Madness! If they had the chance to attend an NCAA tournament game today, each would value an Elite Eight game at $1,000, a Final Four game at $1,600, and a Championship game at $1,800. A benevolent aunt offers Sacha and Simon one ticket each to a game of their choosing: Elite Eight, Final Four, or Championship. But there's the hitch; the benevolent aunt is slightly controlling! The siblings can attend an Elite Eight game this year, but if they choose a Final Four game, they'll have to wait one year, and if they want to see the Championship game, they'll have to wait for *two* years.

a. Suppose Sacha discounts each year of waiting at 10%. Which option will she choose today?

b. Suppose Simon discounts hyperbolically so that something a year away is always discounted at 30%, while horizons beyond the first year are discounted at 10%. Which option will Simon choose today?

c. Next year, Simon and Sacha's aunt tells them, "You've waited so patiently. If you'd like to see the Final Four game today, you can. Or, you can wait and see next year's Championship game." What will Simon and Sacha do?

d. Explain why Sacha's preferences are time-consistent, but Simon's aren't.

19. You have just graduated from college and receive two job offers doing identical work. Firm A offers you $40,000 per year and informs you that your coworkers will make the same. Firm B offers you $38,000 per year and informs you that your coworkers will make $35,000.

a. Which job offer does economic theory predict you will take?

b. When experimental subjects were asked which job would make them happier, well over half indicated that they preferred Firm B. Can you think of a systematic bias that might lead people to prefer a job that pays less for identical work? Explain.

Math Review Appendix

Section 1: Math Concepts and Basic Skills

There is no doubt that economics is about ideas. These economic ideas can be conveyed in a variety of languages—from words to the use of algebraic equations and graphs. We've used all these methods in the text. The appendices scattered throughout the book and online add yet another language: calculus.

Sometimes it's easier to express and understand economic ideas using mathematical symbols rather than words. The material we present here reviews the algebra and geometry concepts we use in the text, as well as the calculus that the material in the appendices relies on. You have likely encountered most of these concepts and techniques before in your high school or college algebra or calculus classes, but we compile them here in a way that is most relevant to your study of economics. We will begin with a discussion of lines and curves, which are crucial to economic ideas such as utility and income, among others, and will set the foundation for the rest of our review.

Lines and Curves   Functions describe the relationships between input variables and outputs, and may be written generically as $y = f(x)$, where x is some input and y the output. One function crucial to our study is that of the line, which we commonly write in the form $y = mx + b$, and which we've graphed on the x-y plane—the Cartesian plane—in **Figure A.1** below. As in our generic function, x and y are inputs and outputs, respectively.

We can learn a lot from this functional form of the line, which is known as the *slope-intercept* form for reasons that will soon become clear. The line's slope, m, describes the change in y from a given change in x, and can be written mathematically as

$$m = \frac{\Delta y}{\Delta x} = \frac{y_2 - y_1}{x_2 - x_1}$$

where Δ represents the change in a variable, and (x_1, y_1) and (x_2, y_2) are two points on the line.

Figure A.1   Slope and Intercept of a Line

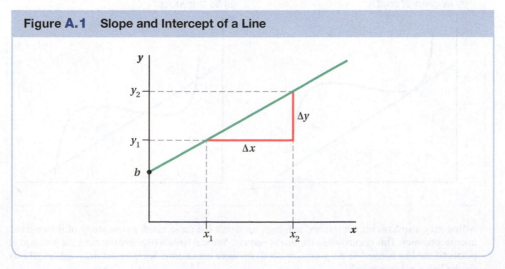

The slope tells us two important pieces of information about the line. First, it describes how flat or steep the line is. In other words, we can answer the question: If x increases by one unit, by how much does y change? The slope also tells us whether the relationship between x and y is negative or positive. An upward-sloping line, as in Figure A.1, has a positive slope, meaning that when x increases, so does y. A negative slope indicates that an increase in x results in a decrease in y, creating a downward-sloping line. A flat, horizontal line has a slope equal to zero; as x changes, there is no corresponding change in y. On a vertical line, x doesn't change at all, even as y increases or decreases. As a result, we describe a vertical line's slope—which is equal to infinity—as undefined.

The form $y = mx + b$ holds one final piece of information about the line: b, or the y-intercept. You can clearly see this in Figure A.1—it's where the line intersects the y-axis. In this case, the y-intercept is positive, but the line could also have a negative intercept and intersect the y-axis below the x-axis, or have a y-intercept equal to zero.[1]

We have described the equation for the line using the slope-intercept form, but a line can be expressed in any way that demonstrates the relationship between the input x and its output y. You might also see a line written in the standard form of a line, $mx - y = -b$, or even as $x = \dfrac{(y - b)}{m}$. In fact, we'll see that last form a lot throughout our study of economics: It's how we typically write supply and demand functions.

By definition, the slope of a straight line is constant; the slope will be the same no matter where you measure the change in x and y. But, the relationship between x and y may be more complicated. In contrast to the line, a curve can have different slopes at different points along it. Because a curve can have an almost infinite number of shapes and curvatures, there are no standard functional forms for curves.

Tangency   The point at which a given line and curve just touch—without intersecting or overlapping—is the tangent point. It describes the point at which the slope of the line is equal to the slope at the particular point on the curve. This concept of tangency is particularly useful in the study of microeconomics, which relies on tangencies in optimization problems such as profit and utility maximization.

Graphically, a tangent point is easy to see. Point A in panel a of **Figure A.2** is a tangent point between the curve and a line. How can we tell this is a tangency? At A, the curve just

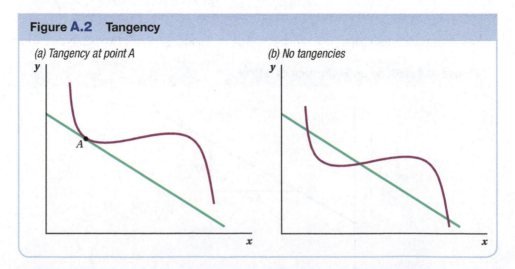

Figure A.2   Tangency

(a) Tangency at point A

(b) No tangencies

figure it out A.1

A line has a slope of −2 and an intercept of 10.

a. Write the line in slope-intercept form.

b. Graph the line on a Cartesian plane.

c. Draw a curve tangent to the line.

Solution:

a. The slope-intercept form of a line can be expressed as $y = mx + b$, where m is the slope and b is the intercept. The slope-intercept form corresponding to $m = -2$ and $b = 10$ therefore is $y = -2x + 10$.

b. To graph the equation $y = -2x + 10$ on the Cartesian plane, we can calculate the coordinates of the intercepts and connect these points. Because the equation is in slope-intercept form, we already know that the intercept along the y-axis occurs at point (0, 10). (Another way to solve for this is to plug $x = 0$ into the equation for the line. Note that when $x = 0$, $y = -2(0) + 10 = 10$.)

To get the x-axis intercept, we can substitute $y = 0$ into the equation for the line: $0 = -2x + 10$. Rearranging this equation, we see that $2x = 10$ or $x = 5$. We therefore know that (5, 0) is another point along this line. Next, we connect these points to illustrate the line in the x-y plane.

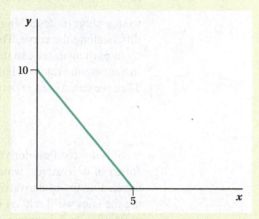

c. A curve tangent to the line $y = -2x + 10$ is included in the figure below. Note that, for this example, the tangency occurs at only one point on the line we graphed in the previous part of this problem. We could have drawn a curve that is tangent to the line at more than one point.

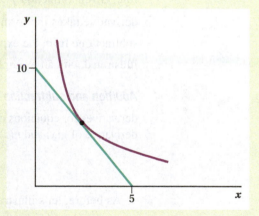

touches the line without crossing it. In this case, this is the only point at which the slope of the curve equals the slope of the line, and is therefore tangent to the line.

Not all lines and curves are tangent to each other. Panel b illustrates an example of a curve and a line that, while intersecting, have no tangencies.

Section 2: Calculus Review

The basic algebraic concepts we just reviewed are used throughout the book. We'll turn now to calculus, which we use in the appendices to further our understanding of economic concepts. If you've taken calculus before, this section will be purely review. If you haven't taken calculus, you might be able to pick up a few tricks. This section is *not* a substitute for a background in calculus. If you want to apply calculus to economics, it's important to start with the solid foundation that an entry-level course in calculus provides.

First Derivatives We have already seen that slopes are incredibly important to our study of economics. We can find the slope of a line using the formula $m = \dfrac{\Delta y}{\Delta x} = \dfrac{y_2 - y_1}{x_2 - x_1}$. We had to stop short of describing the slope of a curve, since a curve's slope, unlike that of a line, differs along the curve. This is where calculus can help us.

In particular, we can describe the slope of a curve (or a line) using a *derivative*, or the instantaneous rate of change of a function at a given point. Take the function $y = f(x)$. Then we can write the derivative in the equivalent forms

$$f'(x) = \frac{df(x)}{dx} = \frac{dy}{dx}$$

Solving for first derivatives is easiest to demonstrate using examples of a few basic forms of derivatives, which we outline below. The rules we present are by no means an exhaustive list of derivatives rules. For that, you should consult a calculus text. But, these are the ones we'll rely on in the calculus appendices, and which you'll probably encounter most often in the context of economics.

Derivative of a constant: Take the function $f(x) = c$, where c is a constant. Then $\dfrac{df(x)}{dx} = 0$. Why? We know that a line of this form is horizontal at $y = c$. Since a horizontal line has a slope equal to zero, its derivative must also equal zero.

Power rule for derivatives: Perhaps the rule that we will most often rely on is the power rule. Given a function $f(x) = cx^{\alpha}$, where c is again some constant as is the exponent α, the derivative takes the form $\dfrac{df(x)}{dx} = c\alpha x^{\alpha-1}$. In words, you multiply x by its exponent and subtract one from the exponent you began with to find the derivative. This is perhaps best illustrated with an example. Take $f(x) = 3x^4$. Then, $\dfrac{df(x)}{dx} = 3(4)x^{4-1} = 12x^3$.

Addition and subtraction rules for derivatives: We can rely on the rules above to find the derivatives for equations of the form $f(x) = g(x) + h(x)$. To solve for $\dfrac{df(x)}{dx}$, simply take the derivative of $g(x)$ and $h(x)$ separately:

$$\frac{df(x)}{dx} = \frac{dg(x)}{dx} = \frac{dh(x)}{dx}$$

As before, let's illustrate this with a simple example. Take the function $f(x) = x^2 + 10$. Then, $\dfrac{df(x)}{dx} = \dfrac{d(x^2)}{dx} + \dfrac{d(10)}{dx} = 2x + 0 = 2x$.

Note that this rule applies whether you are adding or subtracting, since subtraction is simply the addition of a negative number. In other words, if $f(x) = g(x) - h(x)$, $\dfrac{df(x)}{dx} = \dfrac{dg(x)}{dx} - \dfrac{dh(x)}{dx}$.

Second Derivatives We've found the derivative of a function, but sometimes we need to find the derivative of the derivative, or the *second* derivative:

$$f''(x) = \frac{d^2 f(x)}{dx^2} = \frac{d^2 y}{dx^2}$$

What does the second derivative tell us about a function? While the first derivative describes the slope of a function, the second derivative describes a function's curvature. A function's curvature is said to be convex (as shown in **Figure A.3**, panel a) or concave (panel b). Note that a function may be convex over some values of x, and concave over others, such as in panel c.

Figure A.3   Convexity and Concavity

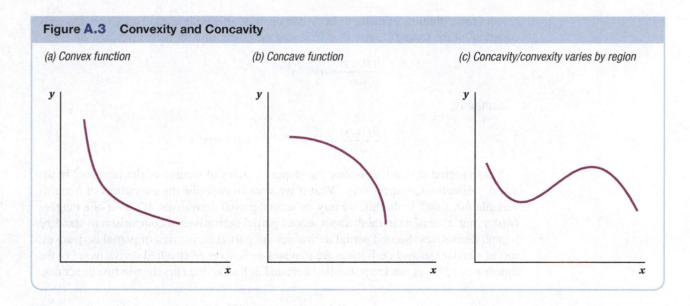

(a) Convex function

(b) Concave function

(c) Concavity/convexity varies by region

Over some range of x, a curve is said to be convex if the second derivative with respect to x is greater than zero, meaning that

$$\frac{d^2 f(x)}{dx^2} > 0$$

It is concave when

$$\frac{d^2 f(x)}{dx^2} < 0$$

These two rules we've presented may seem to be a bit of hand-waving, but the intuition behind them is clear. Consider first the meaning of a function's first derivative: A positive (or negative) first derivative indicates that a function is increasing (or decreasing) over that region. Similarly then, the second derivative tells us whether the slope, as measured by its first derivative, is increasing or decreasing over that region. A positive second derivative indicates that the slope increases with higher values of x (panel a), which we call *convexity*; a negative second derivative means that the slope decreases with higher values of x (panel b), which we call *concavity*.[2]

Partial Derivatives   Above we found first and second derivatives for single-variable equations. Sometimes, however, we will need to find the slopes or curvatures of a multi-variable equation. In this case, we apply partial derivatives.

Consider the function $z = f(x, y)$ where x and y are both inputs into the function that maps output z. Given this function, we can now find two partial first derivatives: the first derivative of z with respect to x, or $f_x(x, y) = \dfrac{\partial f(x, y)}{\partial x} = \dfrac{\partial z}{\partial x}$, and the first derivative of z with respect to y, or $f_y(x, y) = \dfrac{\partial f(x, y)}{\partial y} = \dfrac{\partial z}{\partial y}$.

Calculating partial derivatives is actually quite simple when you know how to calculate a standard derivative. To find $\dfrac{\partial f(x, y)}{\partial x}$ you simply take the first derivative of $f(x, y)$ with

---

[2] Note that in panel a, the slope is increasing since it is becoming less negative as we move to the right. Similarly, the slope in panel b is decreasing since it is becoming more negative as we move to the right.

respect to x, holding y constant. Let's demonstrate this with a standard Cobb–Douglas equation[3] of the form $f(x, y) = x^\alpha y^{1-\alpha}$. Using the power rule for derivatives, we get

$$\frac{\partial f(x, y)}{\partial x} = \alpha x^{\alpha-1} y^{1-\alpha}$$

Similarly,

$$\frac{\partial f(x, y)}{\partial y} = (1 - \alpha)x^\alpha y^{1-a-1} = (1 - \alpha)x^\alpha y^{-\alpha}$$

These partial derivatives isolate the slopes (or rates of change of the function) in the x and y directions, respectively. What if we want to describe the curvatures of a multi-variable function? To do this, we rely on second partial derivatives. It's a bit of a tongue-twister, but it's easiest to think about second partial derivatives in comparison to standard second derivatives: Second partial derivatives are partial derivatives of partial derivatives, just as standard second derivatives are standard derivatives of standard derivatives. For the function $z = f(x, y)$, we are primarily interested in finding the curvature in two directions:

$$f_{xx}(x, y) = \frac{\partial^2 f(x, y)}{\partial x^2} = \frac{\partial^2 z}{\partial x^2} \text{ and}$$

$$f_{yy}(x, y) = \frac{\partial^2 f(x, y)}{\partial y^2} = \frac{\partial^2 z}{\partial y^2}$$

Using the Cobb–Douglas function from above, we get

$$\frac{\partial^2 f(x, y)}{\partial x^2} = \alpha(\alpha - 1)x^{\alpha-2} y^{1-a}$$

$$\frac{\partial^2 f(x, y)}{\partial y^2} = -\alpha(1 - a)x^\alpha y^{-a-1}$$

There is actually, in this case, another type of second partial derivative that we could calculate. Known as a cross partial derivative, it calculates the first partial derivative with respect to x, and the second partial derivative with respect to y, or vice versa:

$$f_{xy}(x, y) = \frac{\partial^2 f(x, y)}{\partial x \partial y} = \frac{\partial^2 z}{\partial x \partial y} \text{ and}$$

$$f_{yx}(x, y) = \frac{\partial^2 f(x, y)}{\partial y \partial x} = \frac{\partial^2 z}{\partial y \partial x}$$

While it is useful to be aware of these cross partial derivatives, we will not rely on them for the analyses in this book.

One application of partial derivatives that we will use, however, is total differentiation. Total differentiation gives us the *total* change in a function, or the combined change in both the x and y directions. This comes up often in our study of economics: Sometimes we need to describe movements along a curve when two variables change simultaneously,

---

[3] You will see Cobb–Douglas functions a lot in your study of economics—it is one of the most common functional forms for a variety of economics concepts, including utility and production functions. We won't go into much detail about its properties here, but it is useful to see basic calculus techniques applied to this very common set of functions. In the calculus appendices, we'll assume $0 < \alpha < 1$ for the purposes of solving economics problems. But to solve first and second partial derivatives, we don't actually need to make this assumption, and so we don't make it here. The exponent α could be negative or positive, fractional or a whole number, and the rules we present here still apply.

as do a firm's capital K and labor L inputs in Chapter 6. To totally differentiate a multi-variable function, we solve

$$df(x, y) = \frac{\partial f(x, y)}{\partial x} dx + \frac{\partial f(x, y)}{\partial y} dy$$

Let's break down what each part of this equation tells us. The two partial derivatives $\left(\frac{\partial f(x, y)}{\partial x} \text{ and} \frac{\partial f(x, y)}{\partial y} \right)$ indicate the *rate* of change in the x and y directions, respectively. Likewise, dx and dy are the changes in x and y. Combining these as we do in the equation above gives us the *total* change of the function with respect to all variables.

Unconstrained Optimization Problem   In many ways, what we have been building up to in this math review is the last mathematical concept we will look at here: basic, or unconstrained, optimization. (For a consideration of *constrained* optimization, see the Appendix to Chapter 4.) In solving an optimization problem, we will rely on the derivative techniques we have learned thus far.

Begin with a function of the form $y = f(x)$. We will first solve for what is known as the first-order condition. To do this, we set the first derivative equal to zero:

$$\frac{df(x)}{dx} = 0$$

What does this tell us? Remember first that $\frac{df(x)}{dx}$ is the slope of the function $f(x)$, examples of which are shown in **Figure A.4**. When this slope is zero, the line tangent to the curve is horizontal. This means that the curve must be at either a maximum (panel a) or a minimum (panel b).

We actually don't yet know whether the first-order condition we found has given us a maximum or a minimum. We just know that we have found an optimum. To learn whether we have maximized or minimized the function, we need to return to our second piece of derivative knowledge: second derivatives. Specifically, we need to take the second derivative of the function, and test whether it is negative or positive:

When $\frac{d^2 f(x)}{dx^2} < 0$, the curve is concave, and the point is a maximum.

When $\frac{d^2 f(x)}{dx^2} > 0$, the curve is convex, and the point is a minimum.

Figure A.4   Optima

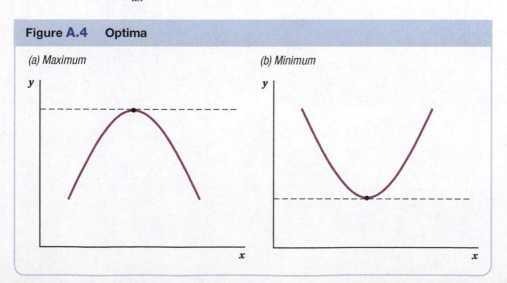

(a) Maximum

(b) Minimum

figure it out A.2

Optimize the function of one variable $y = 5x^2 - 100x$. Use the second derivative to determine if the point is a maximum or a minimum.

Solution:

First, solve for the first-order condition by setting the first derivative equal to zero. In this case,

$$\frac{df(x)}{dx} = \frac{d(5x^2 - 100x)}{dx}$$

$$= 5(2)x^{2-1} - 100$$

$$= 10x - 100 = 0$$

Solve for x to find the optimum:

$$10x - 100 = 0$$

$$x = 10$$

Again, the first-order condition only tells us that we have optimized the function. To tell if this is a maximum or a minimum, we take the second derivative:

$$\frac{d^2 f(x)}{dx^2} = \frac{d(10x - 100)}{dx} = 10 > 0$$

Because $\frac{d^2 f(x)}{dx^2} > 0$, we see that this is a minimum.

Solutions to Review Questions

CHAPTER 1

1. Microeconomics looks at the specific economic actions of consumers and producers, whereas macroeconomics is a broader examination of the combined economic behavior of all consumers and producers in an economy.
2. Most of you make multiple consumption decisions each day, from the coffee you buy in the morning to the classes, textbooks, and notebooks you purchase for your education.
3. Consumption and production decisions interconnect to determine the market price and supply. This is because producers produce the goods and services that consumers consume.
4. Microeconomics relies on tools for graphs and mathematics in addition to empirical methods to explore microeconomic theories and phenomena.
5. Computers have made using empirical analysis easier and faster. In economic terms, the relative price of empirical analysis has decreased.

CHAPTER 2

1. The supply and demand model assumes that (a) supply and demand are in a single market, (b) all goods in the market are identical, (c) all goods sell for the same price and everyone in the market has the same information, and (d) there are many consumers and producers in the market.
2. A complement is a good that is purchased and used *in combination with* another good. A substitute is a good that can be used *in place of* another good.
3. We assume that there is no change in any other factors that may also affect how much of a good a consumer buys. The downward slope reflects the fact that consumers demand less of a good as its price increases.
4. A change in quantity demanded is a movement along the demand curve that occurs because of a change in the good's own price, while a change in demand reflects a shift of the entire demand curve caused by a change in a determinant of demand other than the good's price.
5. The inverse demand curve expresses the price of a product as a function of quantity demanded. The inverse supply curve expresses the price of a product as a function of quantity supplied. Expressing price as a function of quantity makes the demand and supply choke prices more explicit.

6. The upward slope of the supply curve reflects the fact that holding all else equal, producers supply more of a good as its price increases.
7. A change in quantity supplied is a movement along the supply curve that occurs because of a change in the good's own price, while a change in supply reflects a shift of the entire supply curve caused by a change in a determinant of supply other than the good's price.
8. The market equilibrium occurs at the intersection of supply and demand curves for a good. At equilibrium, the quantity supplied by producers equals the quantity demanded by consumers.
9. When the market price is too low, there is excess demand (shortage) for a good because consumers demand more of the good than producers are willing to supply at the relatively low price.
10. A demand shift causes equilibrium price and quantity to change in the same direction. More specifically, an outward shift in demand increases both price and quantity, while an inward shift in demand decreases price and quantity.
11. A supply shift causes equilibrium price and quantity to change in opposite directions. More specifically, an outward shift in supply decreases price but increases quantity; an inward shift in supply increases price but decreases quantity.
12. When both supply and demand shift, the direction of change in either quantity or price is determined by the relative magnitudes and directions of the shifts.
13. If supply and demand both increase, quantity increases; if both supply and demand decrease, quantity decreases. The effect on price is unknown: It depends on the relative magnitudes of the supply and demand shifts.
14. The slope of a supply or demand curve relates changes in the level of prices to changes in the level of quantity demanded or supplied. Elasticity represents the *responsiveness* of quantities to prices. More specifically, we express elasticity as the percentage change in quantity for a given percentage change in price.
15. The magnitude of each is as follows: inelastic $E < 1$, elastic $E > 1$, unit elastic $E = 1$, perfectly elastic $E = 0$, and perfectly inelastic $E = \infty$.
16. Normal goods have positive income elasticities; luxury goods have income elasticities greater than 1; and inferior goods have negative income elasticities.
17. When a good has a positive cross-price elasticity with another good, that good is a substitute for the other good. When a good has a negative cross-price elasticity with another good, that good is a complement for the other good.

CHAPTER 3

1. Consumer surplus is the difference between the price consumers would be willing to pay for a good and the price they actually have to pay. Producer surplus is the difference between the price at which producers would be willing to sell their good or service and the price they actually receive.

2. The demand choke price is the price at which quantity demanded is reduced to zero. Consumer surplus is equal to the area of the triangle, with its base equal to the quantity sold and its height the difference between the market price and the demand choke price.

3. The supply choke price is the price at which quantity supplied is reduced to zero. Producer surplus is equal to the area of the triangle, with its base equal to the quantity sold and its height the difference between the market price and the supply choke price.

4. An inward shift of the supply curve reduces consumer surplus and has an ambiguous effect on producer surplus. An outward shift of the supply curve increases consumer surplus, while also having an ambiguous effect on producer surplus.

5. An inward shift of the demand curve reduces producer surplus and has an ambiguous effect on consumer surplus. An outward shift of the demand curve increases producer surplus, while also having an ambiguous effect on consumer surplus.

6. A price ceiling sets the highest price that can be paid legally for a good. If this price is set below the equilibrium price, consumers will demand more of the good than producers are willing to supply, resulting in excess demand for the good.

7. A price floor sets the lowest price that can be paid legally for a good. If this price is set above the equilibrium price, producers will supply more of the good than consumers are willing to buy, resulting in excess supply for the good.

8. Deadweight loss is the reduction in total surplus that results from a market inefficiency. A large price elasticity indicates that supply or demand is sensitive to price. As a result, the resulting deadweight loss in a market with a large price elasticity will be relatively large.

9. A nonbinding price ceiling is set at a level above equilibrium price, and a nonbinding price floor is set at a level below equilibrium price.

10. A quota directly regulates the *quantity* of a good or service that can be provided, unlike a price floor or price ceiling that directly regulates the *price* of a good or service.

11. A tax causes quantity to decrease and the price that consumers pay to increase. A tax wedge occurs because the price suppliers receive for the good is lower than the price consumers pay by the amount of the tax.

12. The tax wedge reduces both consumer and producer surplus in the market, creating the deadweight loss of a tax.

13. The tax incidence is who—the producers or consumers—actually bears the burden of a tax. The tax incidence is determined by the elasticity of supply and demand.

14. A subsidy is the opposite of a tax—it is a payment by the government to a buyer or seller of a good or service.

15. A subsidy increases both producer and consumer surplus.

16. In a market with a subsidy, more people purchase the good or service than would have in the competitive market. The resulting deadweight loss derives from these people who would not have purchased the good in the competitive market.

CHAPTER 4

1. Completeness and rankability mean that consumers can make comparisons across all consumption bundles. "More is better" describes the assumption that for most goods, consuming more of the good benefits the consumer. Transitivity implies that if a consumer prefers good A to good B and good B to good C, then the consumer also prefers good A to good C. Finally, consumers prefer variety, meaning that the more a consumer has of a particular good, the less she is willing to give up something else to get more of that good.

2. Utility provides a measure of how satisfied a consumer is with a consumption bundle. The utility function describes the relationship between a consumer's satisfaction level, or utility, and what the consumer actually consumes.

3. An indifference curve shows the combination of all the different consumption bundles at a given utility level. In other words, given a utility level, it shows all the consumption bundles among which a consumer is indifferent.

4. The marginal rate of substitution of X for Y reveals the willingness of a consumer to give up good X for good Y while still being left equally well off.

5. The negative of the slope of the indifference curve is equal to the consumer's MRS_{XY}, or how much of good X he is willing to give up to receive more of good Y. As you move along a consumer's indifference curve in the standard case, the curvature of the indifference curve reflects the change in the consumer's relative preferences for the two goods. In particular, as the consumer gains more of good X, he is willing to give up less of good Y—a characteristic of the indifference curve that stems from our assumption that consumers prefer variety.

6. Indifference curves that are relatively steep indicate that the consumer is willing to give up a large quantity of good Y to get another unit of good X. Relatively flat indifference curves imply that the consumer would require a large increase in good X to be willing to give up a unit of good Y.

7. Perfect substitutes are goods that a consumer can trade for another good, in fixed units, and receive identical levels of utility. Indifference curves for perfect substitutes are straight lines.

8. Perfect complements are goods whose utility levels depend on being used in fixed proportion with one another. Indifference curves for perfect complements are L-shaped.

9. Consumers make utility-maximizing decisions based on the goods' prices and the consumers' incomes.

10. We make three assumptions before defining the economic model that incorporates a consumer's budget constraint: (a) Each good has a fixed price and unlimited quantity, (b) the consumer's income is fixed, and (c) the consumer cannot save or borrow.

11. A consumer's budget constraint is the curve that describes the entire set of consumption bundles a consumer can purchase when spending his entire income.

12. The slope of the budget constraint is equal to the negative of the ratio of the two prices, $-P_x/P_y$. Any nonproportional change in the goods' prices would affect the slope.

13. The consumer's optimal, or utility-maximizing, consumption bundle occurs at the point of tangency between his budget constraint and his indifference curve.

14. At the point of tangency between the consumer's budget constraint and her indifference curve, the ratio of the goods' marginal utilities equals the ratio of the goods' prices.

CHAPTER 5

1. The income effect describes the change in a consumer's consumption choice given a change in the purchasing power of the consumer's income. In describing this change, we hold the goods' prices fixed.

2. We characterize a good as normal when consumption of the good rises with income. Luxury goods are a class of normal goods whose income elasticity is greater than 1. In contrast to normal goods, the consumption of an inferior good decreases when income rises.

3. The income expansion path connects the optimal bundles of two goods for one consumer, while the Engel curve shows the relationship between the quantity of a good consumed and a consumer's income. While both the Engel curve and the income expansion path contain the same information, the income expansion path allows us to understand how

two goods' relative quantities change with income. The Engel curve isolates the impact of income changes on the consumption of a single good.

4. Holding the consumer's income constant, we can draw his demand curve by connecting the utility-maximizing quantities of a good at different prices of the good. When the price of a good increases, the consumer's demand for the good decreases, creating a downward-sloping demand curve.

5. The demand for pizza will shift in response to changes in the consumer's income or preferences, as well as the price of other goods. Three possibilities of shifts in the demand for pizza are listed below:

   a. **Increase in the consumer's income:** If pizza is a normal good, then an increase in the consumer's income will shift out his demand for pizza.

   b. **Decrease in the consumer's relative preference for pizza:** If the consumer's relative preference for pizza decreases—say, he starts preferring the substitute good, Chinese take-out—then his demand for pizza will shift in.

   c. **Increase in the price of another good:** If the price of a good such as Chinese take-out increases, then the consumer's demand for pizza will shift out. If the price of a complement of a good—like the beverage the consumer prefers to have with his pizza—increases, then the consumer's demand for pizza will shift in.

6. Both the income and substitution effects stem from a change in the prices of two goods. While the substitution effect is the change in a consumer's consumption choices that results from a change in the *relative prices* of the two goods, the income effect describes the change resulting from the consumer's *purchasing power.*

7. We can isolate income and substitution effects using three basic steps. Take a consumer with initial utility-maximizing bundle A.

   a. A change in the goods' prices rotates the budget constraint. The new optimal bundle (B) is at the tangency of the new budget constraint to a new indifference curve.

   b. The line that is parallel to the new budget constraint but tangent to the original indifference curve gives you point A'. The substitution effect is the movement from A to A'.

   c. The income effect is the movement from A' to the new optimal bundle B.

8. The direction of the substitution effect is the same for both normal and inferior goods, but the income effect differs between the two types of goods. If a normal good's price decreases, the change in consumption due to the income effect is an increase in consumption of the good. If an inferior good's price decreases, the change in consumption due to the income effect is a decrease in consumption of the good.

9. A Giffen good is a good for which price and quantity demanded are positively related. In other words, if the price of the good decreases, the consumer demands *less*—not more—of the good.

10. A complement is a good that is purchased and used in combination with another good. A substitute is a good that can be used in place of another good.

11. If the price of a good (X) decreases, consumers will buy more X. If the demand for a second good (Y) increases, too, that indicates that consumers want to consume X and Y together: They are complements. If the price of good X decreases and consumers respond by demanding less Y, consumers are substituting X for Y; the goods are substitutes.

12. The shape of the indifference curve reveals information about the degree of two goods' substitutability. The less curved the indifference curve, the more substitutable the two goods are.

13. The market demand is the horizontal sum of all individuals' demand curves for a good.

14. For a given change in price, the change in quantity demanded by the market as a whole must be at least as great as the change in quantity demanded by an individual consumer. As a result, the market demand curve must be at least as flat as an individual's demand curve.

CHAPTER 6

1. In the short run, a firm's capital is fixed, while in the long run, a firm can change its quantities of both labor *and* capital inputs.

2. A production function shows the relationship between a firm's inputs (capital and labor) and its output quantity.

3. Fixed costs don't depend on how much output a firm produces — they are the same whether the firm produces 1 unit of output or 1 million units of output or even zero units of output. Variable costs depend on how much the firm produces: As output increases, variable costs increase.

4. In the long run, the firm can adjust the level of each of its inputs. In the short run, at least one input is fixed and cannot be adjusted by the firm.

5. A producer's isoquants share many of the same characteristics as a consumer's indifference curves. Isoquants farther from the origin are associated with higher output levels. Isoquants cannot cross because if two isoquants did, it would imply that the same quantities of inputs yield two different quantities of output.

6. The marginal rate of technical substitution is the rate at which the firm can trade one input (X) for another (Y) holding output constant, and is equal to the marginal product of input X over the marginal

product of input Y. For the standard case, the MRTS implies a curved isoquant. As you move down and to the right along the isoquant, the marginal product of labor becomes low relative to the marginal product of capital.

7. The curvature of the isoquant demonstrates the degree of substitutability between capital and labor. A nearly straight isoquant implies that the MRTS is nearly constant along the isoquant, implying that the two inputs are close substitutes for each other in the production process. A more curved isoquant indicates that capital and labor are poor substitutes for each other in the production process.

8. An isocost line is the curve that shows all the input combinations that yield the same cost. Since the slope of the isocost line is the negative ratio of wages to the capital rental rate, $-W/R$, we can use the slope to determine the cost tradeoff of substituting labor for capital (or vice versa).

9. In reaction to an increase in the price of one input (say, labor), the firm will substitute away from units of that input to another (in this case, capital) *in the long run*.

10. Returns to scale refer to the change in the amount of output in response to a proportional change in all the inputs. Constant returns to scale indicate that a proportional change in all inputs changes the quantity of output by that same proportion. Increasing returns to scale mean that a proportional change in all inputs changes the quantity of output more than proportionately. Finally, decreasing returns to scale imply that a proportional change in all inputs changes the quantity of output less than proportionally.

11. Technological change, A, enters the production function as a scale factor: $Q = Af(K, L)$. This type of technological change implies that after an improvement in technology, the firm produces extra output using the same level of productive inputs as prior to the change.

12. The expansion path plots the optimal input combinations for each output quantity. The total cost curve plots the output quantities from the expansion path against the total cost of the productive inputs.

CHAPTER 7

1. Accounting costs include the direct costs of operating a business, while a firm's economic costs are its accounting costs plus its opportunity costs. A firm can calculate its profits in one of two ways: as accounting profits equal to its total revenue minus its accounting costs, or as economic profits equal to its total revenue minus its economic costs.

2. Opportunity cost is the value of what a producer gives up by using an input. A firm's opportunity

costs are what differentiate the calculation of its accounting costs from that of its economic costs. Specifically, opportunity costs are included in economic cost but not in accounting cost.

3. A firm that lets its sunk costs affect its operating decisions has committed the sunk cost fallacy. In the forward-looking perspective, firms — and people — shouldn't allow costs that have already been paid and cannot be recovered to affect their decisions in the present.

4. Fixed costs include expenditures on overhead such as the cost of the building or plant, insurance, or operating permits. Once paid, these fixed costs are sunk — they cannot be recovered; they should not be considered when making production decisions; that would be committing the sunk cost fallacy as we saw in Question 3 above.

5. A firm's total cost is equal to the sum of its fixed and variable costs.

6. A firm's fixed costs are constant no matter what its output level is, resulting in a horizontal fixed cost curve. The variable cost curve is positively sloped— as production increases, the associated variable costs increase.

7. Average fixed, average variable, and average total cost curves calculate a firm's fixed, variable, and total costs as costs per unit.

8. Since a firm's fixed cost does not vary with the level of output, fixed cost does not affect its marginal cost of producing an additional unit of output. That marginal cost is dependent only on the firm's variable cost.

9. In the short run, a firm has fixed costs on capital, while in the long run, the firm can vary both its capital and labor inputs. As a result, short-run total cost may be greater than long-run total cost. Since average cost is calculated as the total cost per unit of output, the same relationship holds true for a firm's short-run and long-run average costs.

10. Economies of scale look at the way a firm's costs increase with output. A firm with economies of scale has costs that increase at a slower rate than the increase in output. With diseconomies of scale, the firm's costs increase at a faster rate than the increase in output. Constant economies of scale indicate that the firm's costs increase at the same rate as the increase in output.

11. Economies of scope look at how a firm's costs change when it produces more than one product. Economies of scope exist when a firm can produce more than one product simultaneously at a lower cost than producing the products separately. Diseconomies of scope indicate that a firm produces more than one product simultaneously at a higher cost than producing the products separately.

CHAPTER 8

1. A perfectly competitive industry has no barriers to entry, and features many firms selling identical products.

2. Perfectly competitive firms are price takers. As a result, the demand curve facing a perfectly competitive firm is horizontal; no matter what quantity the firm produces, the market price at which the firm sells its product stays constant.

3. A firm's profit is the difference between its revenue and its total cost.

4. At its profit-maximizing output, the perfectly competitive firm's marginal cost equals the market price.

5. A firm will stay in operation so long as the market price is at least as large as the firm's average variable cost at its profit-maximizing level. In the short run, fixed costs need to be paid whether the firm stays in operation or not; because of this, the firm's fixed costs will not enter into its operating decisions.

6. The portion of the short-run marginal cost curve above the minimum average variable cost is the perfectly competitive firm's supply curve. At any price below the minimum average variable price, the firm shuts down, and supply goes to zero.

7. The short-run industry supply is the horizontal sum of the short-run supply curve of all individual firms in the industry. This industry supply curve represents the combined decisions of all firms in the industry.

8. In the short run, fixed costs do not affect firms' operating decisions, and any changes in fixed costs do not affect the short-run industry supply.

9. Producer surplus is the aggregation of price-marginal cost markups across every unit of output that the firm makes, or the revenue a firm makes above and beyond its variable cost. A firm's profit is its producer surplus minus its fixed cost.

10. Firms enter a perfectly competitive industry when the market price is above minimum long-run average total cost, or when firms in the industry earn positive economic profits. Conversely, a firm exits the industry when the market price is below minimum long-run average total cost, or when the firm earns negative economic profits.

11. Long-run competitive equilibrium occurs when price is equal to the firm's minimum average total cost. In other words, in the long run, there is no entry or exit into the industry, and firms earn zero economic profits.

12. A firm earns economic rents when it has lower costs than other firms in its industry.

13. Economic profits incorporate a firm's opportunity costs. Once opportunity costs are included, all firms — even those earning positive economic rents — earn zero economic profits in perfect competition.

CHAPTER 9

1. A firm that can influence the price at which it sells its product holds market power.
2. Industries with market power have barriers to entry that prevent new firms from entering the market:
   a. Natural monopolies—or markets in which it is efficient for a single firm to produce the entire industry output—serve as effective barriers to entry to other firms.
   b. A switching cost makes it less likely a consumer will switch from one business or product to another, since the consumer will have to give up something in order to make the switch.
   c. Differentiation among products creates an imperfect substitutability across otherwise similar products. As a result, new entrants to the market cannot gain customers simply by selling their product at a lower price.
   d. A firm's control of key inputs (absolute cost advantage) also will prevent entry into the market.
3. Natural monopolies face economies of scale at all output levels. This means that the larger the firm is, the lower its average total costs. Splitting industry output among different firms would increase average total costs, making it most efficient for one firm to produce the entire industry output.
4. Just as the demand curve shows the relationship between a good's price and its quantity, the marginal revenue curve shows the relationship between a good's marginal revenue and its quantity. The marginal revenue curve of a linear demand curve is also very similar to a demand curve on other dimensions: Its vertical intercept is identical, and its slope is twice the slope of the demand curve.
5. A profit-maximizing firm produces where marginal revenue equals marginal cost.
6. A perfectly competitive firm faces a market price equal to its marginal cost, and thus does not earn producer surplus. A firm with market power is able to price above its marginal cost; as a result, it earns producer surplus, at the expense of some of the consumer surplus that would benefit buyers under perfect competition.
7. The deadweight loss represents the inefficiency of market power: There are consumers who demand the product at a price above its marginal cost but below the higher price set by the firm with market power. The resulting loss in surplus from these consumers who do not purchase the product under monopoly is the deadweight loss.
8. Firms with market power face a set of profit-maximizing prices and quantity combinations, but these combinations do not, strictly speaking, form a supply curve. These price–quantity combinations depend on the firm's demand curve, while a supply curve by its formal definition exists independent of its associated demand curve.
9. In perfect competition, suppliers' production decisions are independent of the price sensitivity of demand. This is not true for decisions made by firms with market power. A change in the price sensitivity of demand rotates the demand curve, thereby rotating the firm's marginal revenue curve. The firm's profit-maximizing price–quantity combination is now at the intersection of the new marginal revenue curve and the marginal cost curve.
10. Governments use a variety of regulations to restrict market power and decrease deadweight loss, including:
    a. direct price regulations that set the price that a firm may charge in a market.
    b. antitrust laws that restrict firms from behaviors that limit competition in a market.

CHAPTER 10

1. In order for a firm to price-discriminate, it must have market power and be able to prevent resale or arbitrage of its product.
2. Under perfect price discrimination, the producer charges each individual customer the price equal to his willingness to pay for the product. As a result, the producer captures all available surplus of the market, maximizing his producer surplus.
3. Direct price discrimination encompasses two types of price discrimination. We discussed the first—perfect or first-degree price discrimination—in our answer to Question 2 above. The second, segmenting or third-degree price discrimination, is the practice of charging different prices to different groups of customers based on identifiable group characteristics.
4. Segmenting may be based on one of a variety of characteristics, including customer characteristics such as age or gender, past purchasing behavior, location, and overtime.
5. Direct price discrimination hinges on the firm's ability to distinguish customers' demand for the product before purchase. In indirect price discrimination, the firm doesn't have this knowledge; instead, it allows customers to choose among a variety of offered prices, effectively having customers sort themselves into groups based on their demand for the product.
6. Incentive compatibility dictates that the price offered to each consumer group must be chosen by that group. Without incentive compatibility, the firm using indirect price discrimination will not be maximizing its producer surplus.

7. A firm that offers different product options designed to attract different types of customers is using yet another pricing strategy — versioning. An airline that offers business class and coach tickets, for example, is betting on versioning to maximize its producer surplus.

8. When segmenting, the firm uses its knowledge of characteristics of specific groups of customers to charge different prices to the groups. Quantity discounting is a form of indirect price discrimination in which firms charge a lower per-unit price to customers who buy larger quantities. Similar to a quantity discount, block pricing reduces the price of a good when the customer buys more of the good. Unlike both segmenting and quantity discounts, however, block pricing does not depend on customers having different demand curves and price sensitivities; the firm still earns surplus by offering all customers the option of purchasing a greater quantity at a lower price.

9. A firm that uses mixed bundling offers consumers the choice of buying two or more products separately or as a bundle, while pure bundling is a type of bundling in which the firm offers the products only as a bundle.

10. A firm using a two-part tariff breaks the product's price into two components: the standard per-unit price and a fixed fee that must be paid to buy any amount of the product at all.

CHAPTER 11

1. Imperfectly competitive markets have characteristics between those of perfectly competitive and monopolistic markets. Oligopolies and monopolistic competition are two examples of imperfectly competitive markets.

2. Nash equilibrium is an equilibrium in which each firm does the best it can conditional on the actions its competitors take. Since oligopolies are in a stable equilibrium where no firm wants to change its behavior when it learns of its competitors' market behavior, we say that oligopolies reach a Nash equilibrium.

3. A member of a cartel often has a strong incentive to cheat on its collusive agreement to gain more of the market and thus increase its profit. As a result, cartels are extremely unstable.

4. The market outcome of Bertrand competition is identical to that of perfect competition: At equilibrium, price equals marginal cost and quantity equals the competitive market quantity. This is because all firms have a strong incentive to continue to cut prices to gain more of the market. Firms will

continue to slash prices until all firms charge a price equal to the marginal cost of production.

5. Firms in Bertrand competition set their *prices* simultaneously. In contrast, firms in Cournot competition choose *quantities* simultaneously and sell their products at the same market price. As a result, the equilibrium in Bertrand competition is the result of price cutting; as we saw in Question 4, this outcome is equivalent to the perfectly competitive equilibrium. The Cournot equilibrium is based on quantity decisions, and firms in Cournot competition are in equilibrium at the point where their reaction curves intersect.

6. The residual demand curve depicts the demand remaining for a firm's output given its competitor firms' outputs.

7. In Cournot competition, the reaction curve shows a firm's best production response to its competitor's possible quantity choices. The Cournot equilibrium occurs at the intersection of the two firms' reaction curves.

8. Unlike in Cournot competition, firms in Stackleberg competition do not choose quantities simultaneously but instead choose sequentially. As a result, the firm that chooses first has the first-mover advantage. This first-mover decides the optimal quantity it should produce, and all other firms in the market must react to the first firm's quantity choice.

9. Firms in a Bertrand market with differentiated products hold some market power. As a result, they can price above the perfectly competitive market price that Bertrand oligopolies with identical products face in equilibrium.

10. Three primary characteristics mark a monopolistically competitive firm:
    a. Firms sell differentiated products that consumers do not consider perfect substitutes.
    b. Other firms' choices affect a firm's residual demand curve. However, the firm makes production decisions ignoring the interactions between its own quantity or price choice and its competitors'.
    c. As with a perfectly competitive market, there is free entry into the market.

11. Firms will enter a monopolistically competitive market when firms in the market earn positive economic profits. Entry will continue until economic profits are driven to zero.

12. Firms in monopolistic competition are not price takers, but instead face a downward-sloping demand curve. As a result, a monopolistically competitive firm charges a price above its marginal revenue (and, likewise, its marginal cost), and the market never reaches the perfectly competitive equilibrium.

CHAPTER 12

1. All economic games have three common elements:
   a. Players, or the decision makers in a game
   b. Strategies, or a player's plan of action in a game
   c. Payoffs, or the outcome of a game
2. Unlike single-agent problems, game theory is concerned with situations in which a player's actions affect her opponents' choices and payoffs, and not just her own.
3. In games with multiple Nash equilibria, just as with all games with Nash equilibria, firms' best responses depend on competitor firms' decisions. As a result, we can narrow down the possible outcomes but cannot determine the final outcome of the game prior to its being played.
4. The payoff matrix incorporates information about all three elements of a game—its players, their possible strategies, and the associated payoffs—and therefore can be used to eliminate dominant strategies as possible equilibrium outcomes and to find the players' mutual best responses or the strategy that will lead to the Nash equilibrium or equilibria.
5. In some situations, it may be best for the player to choose actions randomly from the set of available pure strategies and therefore to pursue a mixed strategy. One example would be in a game in which a pure strategy does not lead to a mutual best response (i.e., two checks using the check-box method).
6. A player using a maximin strategy is not going for the greatest payoff, but rather is choosing the conservative strategy of minimizing her losses.
7. Backward induction is the process of reasoning backward from the end of a game to the beginning in order to determine the optimal sequence of actions. To use backward induction, we solve first for the game's final step, and then proceed backward to the game's beginning, finding the optimal play at each step along the way.
8. A player using a grim trigger strategy cooperates with her opponent so long as her opponent is also cooperative. If her opponent cheats, then the player responds by cheating for the rest of the game. In tit for tat, the player instead mimics her opponent's actions. When the opponent cooperates, so does she; when the opponent cheats, the player cheats in the next period.
9. Unlike a normal-form matrix, a decision tree incorporates information about the timing of decisions, a piece of information that is key to the outcome of a sequential game.
10. In some games, a player may offer a side payment to his opponent. This payment is designed to ensure the opponent chooses the strategy optimal to the player, and provides both with a greater outcome than they would receive in a game without side payments.
11. Entry deterrence relies on credibility. Without it, the claim a firm makes about its actions once new firms enter is simply an empty threat. With credible commitment, a firm's threat can deter entrance, and allows the firm to earn greater profits than it would in a market with more firms.
12. A reputation—for fighting lawsuits, for aggressively competing against new entrants, or for being unpredictable or crazy, among other actions—signals a commitment to a game-playing strategy. That commitment encourages opponents to play strategies they otherwise wouldn't, to the benefit of the player with the reputation, such as preventing new entrants to a market.

CHAPTER 13

1. When the firm is hiring optimally, the marginal benefit of producing an additional unit of output (its marginal revenue) is equal to its marginal cost. To produce more units of output, the firm must use more labor; the marginal cost of one additional unit is the wage the firm pays the extra labor, divided by the number of additional units of output that labor generates. So, when the firm hires optimally, $MR = W/MP_L$. Multiply both sides of the equation by the marginal product of labor to get $MR \times MP_L = W$. This states that the firm, when hiring optimally, hires until the marginal revenue product of labor ($MR \times MP_L$) equals the wage (W)—the marginal cost of labor to the firm.
2. In a perfectly competitive market, as the wage increases, the quantity of labor demanded by firms decreases, and less labor is hired. As the wage decreases, the quantity of labor demanded by firms increases, and more labor is hired.
3. The labor demand curve *is* the firm's marginal revenue product of labor curve. So, anything that changes either the marginal product of labor or the marginal revenue of the firm's output will change the demand for labor. The demand for labor will increase if the marginal product of labor increases due to a technological improvement or an increase in the firm's physical capital. The demand for labor will also increase if the marginal revenue associated with various output levels increases due to an increase in the demand for the firm's output.
4. To compute the market demand for labor, add up the quantity of labor all firms demand at each possible wage. In other words, the market demand for labor is the horizontal sum of all firms' labor demand curves.
5. When a worker chooses to spend an hour at leisure, he gives up the opportunity to consume the goods and services he could have purchased with an hour's

worth of earnings. So, the relative price of leisure and consumption is the worker's wage.

6. A decrease in the wage makes less-productive workers more affordable and leads to an increase in hiring. Those additional workers make capital more productive. In the short run, capital is fixed; but in the long run, the firm will hire more capital. The additional capital raises the marginal product of labor and leads the firm to hire even more workers. So, the firm's decision about how much labor to hire is more responsive in the long run than in the short run.

7. The marginal expenditure for a monopsonist is the additional expenditure that is incurred when the monopsonist purchases one more unit (in this chapter, one more unit of labor). Because the buyer is a monopsonist—a large buyer—each extra unit purchased drives up the price that must be paid for all units. So, the additional expenditure incurred by the firm includes the price of the last unit, P, plus the increase in the price that must be paid ($\Delta P/\Delta Q$) on all the other units purchased, Q. In equation form, $ME = P + (\Delta P/\Delta Q) \times Q$.

8. A monopsonist buys fewer inputs than a price-taking firm when the two have the same MRP and input supply curves. A price-taking firm is so small it can buy all the inputs it wants without driving up the price of those inputs. But a monopsonist has such a large share of the market for inputs that, as it hires more, it drives up their price, making hiring less desirable.

9. Unions are a monopoly seller of labor. Like any monopoly seller, a union can maximize its total revenue (the total earnings of its members, in this case) by offering for sale the quantity of labor where its marginal revenue equals zero.

10. A market structure that exists when there is a major concentration of market power on both sides of the market is called a bilateral monopoly.

CHAPTER 14

1. Investment is defined as the purchase of capital now with the intent of reaping future benefits from that capital. Examples of investment include the purchase of stocks and bonds, as well as economic transactions such as a retail firm's investment in a new store or a manufacturing company's purchase of a new production technology.

2. Present discounted value (PDV) analysis uses interest rates and compounding to put all payments in terms of equivalent present-period dollars. The advantage of PDV analysis is that it enables us to compare payments that occur across different time periods.

3. An investment's net present value will be positive when the PDV of its benefits outweighs the PDV of its costs. This suggests that the investment is worthwhile.

4. While payback periods are a relatively simple way to compare an investment's initial costs to its future benefits, they do not discount an investment's future payouts by an interest rate. As a result, payback period analysis is less reliable than NPV analysis, which considers the *present-day value* costs and benefits of an investment.

5. An investment's nominal interest rate expresses rates of return in raw currency values, while the real interest rate expresses rates of return in terms of purchasing power. The real interest rate approximately equals the nominal interest rate minus the inflation rate.

6. Expected value takes into account the uncertainty associated with an investment by using the probability that an investment payout will occur. More specifically, it is equal to the sum of the product of each possible payout and the probability that such a payout will occur.

7. Insurance benefits a risk-averse consumer because it reduces the uncertainty associated with a given investment or situation. This reduction in uncertainty increases the policyholder's expected utility.

8. Because insurance companies insure many consumers, the companies can rely on diversification to reduce their own risk, as well as to earn net profits on their insurance policies. Diversification reduces the risk to an insurer by combining uncertain (and unrelated) outcomes across all policyholders. As a result, the insurer will most likely only have to pay claims on a portion of its insurance policies, while collecting premiums from all those remaining.

CHAPTER 15

1. General equilibrium analysis describes economic markets in two distinct ways. The first describes economic markets as they are in the real world. The second branch of general equilibrium analysis aims to describe markets as they ought to exist, and attempts to define what constitutes an efficient or equitable market.

2. We looked at three types of social welfare functions: utilitarian, Rawlsian, and egalitarian. A utilitarian social welfare function is simply the total sum of every individual's welfare. In the Rawlsian worldview, social welfare is determined by the utility of the worst-off individual and therefore the social welfare function is equal to the minimum utility level across individuals. The egalitarian social welfare function posits that the ideal society is one in which every individual is equally well off.

3. Most economists consider a market's efficiency using the concept of Pareto efficiency. A Pareto-efficient allocation is one in which you could not reallocate the goods without making at least one individual worse off than before.

4. In order for an economy to be considered efficient, it must exhibit exchange, input, and output efficiency.

5. The Edgeworth box can be used to examine market efficiency, including exchange, input, and output efficiency. It plots the allocation of two goods (products or inputs) between two economic actors (either consumers or firms).

6. Two goods are allocated efficiently when the consumers' marginal rates of substitution are equal to the ratio of the goods' prices. A Pareto-efficient allocation can be found at the tangency between the two consumers' indifference curves.

7. The contract curve is the line that shows the collection of all possible Pareto-efficient allocations.

8. An economy exhibits input efficiency when the two firms' marginal rates of technical substitution equal the ratio of the wage rate to the capital rental rate. An efficient input allocation can be found at the tangency between the two firms' isoquants.

9. Similar to the contract curve for consumers, the production contract curve is the line that shows the collection of all possible Pareto-efficient input allocations.

10. The marginal rate of transformation is the tradeoff between how much of one output must be given up to gain an additional unit of the other output. This can be seen on the production possibilities frontier—which connects all possible Pareto-efficient output combinations—as the slope of the production possibilities frontier at a given point.

11. The First Welfare Theorem relies on many conditions that often do not hold in the real world. The first assumption is that firms operate in a perfectly competitive market. The theorem also relies on the absence of market power and of several concepts explored in the next chapter—asymmetric information, externalities, and public goods.

12. The Second Welfare Theorem predicts that every Pareto-efficient allocation is a general equilibrium outcome for some initial allocation.

CHAPTER 16

1. In a market with complete information—such as a perfectly competitive market—all parties in an economic transaction know the relevant information. Markets with asymmetric information are perhaps more common. These are markets in which one party knows more than the other party in the economic transaction.

2. The lemons problem arises in markets in which the seller knows more about the quality of the good than does the buyer.

3. Adverse selection is the offering of a disproportionately high number of low-quality to high-quality goods on the market. In a market with the lemons problem, buyers cannot tell the difference between low- and high-quality goods prior to purchase, and the price they are willing to pay for high-quality goods is below the price at which sellers are willing to part with high-quality goods; therefore, adverse selection results.

4. Warranties serve as a signal to potential buyers that a product is of relatively high quality. This is because the seller of a low-quality good isn't going to offer a warranty—it's too expensive for him to offer a warranty on a product he knows is a lemon.

5. In the insurance market, buyers (potential insurance holders) know more about their likelihood to file claims than do the insurance companies. A variety of solutions to this asymmetric information problem that results in adverse selection of buyers into the insurance market include:
   a. Group policies, which pool together a group of people with a wide array of risks.
   b. Screening, which vets potential insurance holders for the likelihood that they will file claims.
   c. Denying coverage, such as what happens to people with preexisting health conditions in the health insurance market.

6. Moral hazard arises when one party in an economic transaction cannot observe the other party's behavior. Moral hazard is a particular problem in insurance markets where policyholders, once insured, make fewer efforts to avoid the bad outcomes that insurance will now cover.

7. Insurance companies take a range of actions to mitigate moral hazard. They may specify certain actions that a policyholder must take in order to be covered, such as installing smoke detectors. Practices such as good driver policies give policyholders incentives to take actions to reduce risk. Lastly, deductibles, copayments, and coinsurance directly connect the policyholder's payoff to the insurer's payoff.

8. Two main market characteristics combine to create principal–agent problems. First, the principal (e.g., employer) must be unable to fully observe the agent's (e.g., employee's) actions. Second, the self-interests of the principal and agent must not align.

9. Principals want to align their agents' incentives with their own. To do so, principals can compensate agents in such a way that they face the same incentives the principals would face if they were making the agents' choices for them. Payment

structures such as commissions, piece rates, and annual bonuses are designed with this goal in mind.

10. Signaling is a situation in which a knowledgeable party communicates an unobservable characteristic to the other party. This communication of information can resolve the asymmetric information problem in many markets.

11. In the classic signaling model, education is a costly action that has no impact on an individual's productivity yet can reveal information about that worker to potential employers. Because it is too costly for low-productivity workers to pursue, only high-productivity workers obtain a degree. On the job market, that degree serves as a signal of the individual's productivity to potential employers.

12. Signals may be used in all facets of life. Purchasing an engagement ring would signal your commitment to marriage. Parking an expensive car in your driveway would let your neighbors know of your wealth. And wearing a nice suit to work gives your employer an idea of just how seriously you take your job.

CHAPTER 17

1. Negative externalities, like pollution, impose costs on third parties not directly involved in the economic transaction. Positive externalities confer benefits on third parties. Factors such as education and increased immunizations provide benefits to people beyond those directly involved.

2. In an unregulated market, firms pay only the private cost of the good. For a good with a negative externality, this private cost does not equal the social cost of the good, since the external marginal cost of the good is positive. As a result, firms face lower costs than the social cost and overproduce the good.

3. The efficient production level of an externality occurs at the intersection between the social marginal cost curve (equal to the private marginal costs plus external marginal costs) and the social demand curve (equal to the private marginal benefits plus external marginal benefits).

4. The marginal benefit of a pollution curve allows us to consider how much it would cost a firm to reduce the level of pollution it creates and therefore is equivalent to the marginal cost of cutting pollution, also known as the marginal abatement cost.

5. A Pigouvian tax is a tax that equals the external marginal cost imposed by an externality. This tax rate shifts marginal costs up to the social marginal cost, resulting in efficient production on the market.

6. The holder of a government-issued tradable permit has two options: The firm may emit a certain level of pollution allowed by the permit, or the firm may trade its permit to another firm in the industry. By restricting the number of tradable permits issued, the government puts a cap on the amount of pollution that a given industry can produce. At the same time, since permits may be traded, the policy allows pollution across individual firms to vary and effectively creates a market for pollution.

7. In a market where the optimal level of the externality is known, a price-based mechanism such as a Pigouvian tax or a quantity-based mechanism such as a quota or tradable permits market will produce the same efficient result. But when the optimal level is unknown, a deadweight loss is produced. Depending on market characteristics, a Pigouvian tax or a quantity-based mechanism will prove more optimal. In particular, the deadweight loss from regulation is minimized in a market with a relatively flat marginal abatement cost curve when a quantity regulation is imposed. A Pigouvian tax is more optimal in a market with a relatively steep marginal abatement cost curve.

8. The Coase theorem predicts that economic parties will reach the optimal level of an externality if they can costlessly negotiate with one another, regardless of who holds the property rights.

9. Public goods are nonexcludable and nonrival. This means that anyone can access and use the good (nonexcludable), and that any one person's consumption of the good does not diminish another consumer's enjoyment of it (nonrival).

10. When produced efficiently, a public good's total marginal benefit—the vertically combined marginal benefit curves of all its individual consumers—equals its marginal cost.

11. A free-rider is an individual who uses a good or service without paying for it. Since a public good is nonexcludable and nonrival, the free-rider problem arises.

12. The tragedy of the commons is the phenomenon whereby anyone can use a common resource without restraint. As a result, that common resource is used more intensely than it would if it were privately held. As with other negative externalities, Pigouvian taxes or quantity-based mechanisms are one set of solutions to the tragedy of the commons. Another solution is to grant property rights to an individual, transforming the resource from one that is commonly held to one that is privately held.

CHAPTER 18

1. *Homo economicus,* unlike *Homo sapiens,* follows the principles and predictions of economics exactly. He knows what he wants and how to get it, and can solve any and every economic problem he faces (no matter how complicated) with no mistakes.

2. Overconfidence—a trait that afflicts the average human but not *Homo economicus*—is a person's belief that his skill level or judgment is better than it, in fact, is.

3. Hyperbolic discounting leads consumers to prefer payoffs in the present to future payoffs, even if the future payoff is of greater monetary value.

4. A *time-inconsistent* person's actions differ across time. The choice he makes today is different from the choice he makes in the future and that fact makes self-control issues like a game theory battle between two different people. As a result, it is difficult to analyze his behavior using traditional economic theory and models.

5. The endowment effect states that an individual's perception of the value of an object is altered by owning the good. In other words, the pain a person suffers from giving up the object is greater than the pleasure he experienced when receiving it—a fact not taken into consideration in traditional economic models.

6. Nominal loss aversion refers specifically to the instance when individuals care about the nominal—not inflation-adjusted—value of their loss, whereas loss aversion in the standard economic model assumes that consumers respond to real variables.

7. Anchoring is the tendency to base a decision on the specific pieces of information that were given. As one possible example, a shopper who first looks at high-end designer dresses may be more likely to pay a high price for the dress she eventually purchases than the person who first checks out the bargain rack.

8. Mental accounting describes a bias in which individuals divide their current and future assets into separate, nontransferable portions. Mentally apportioning income into separate purchasing and saving categories may affect how much a person spends and what he spends it on.

9. Economists account for the "warm glow" of altruism by incorporating generosity into the utility function, or allowing a person's utility to depend on not only his own consumption but also the consumption of other people, such as his children.

10. Irrational or biased actors tend to lose out to more rational, economically sound market participants. As a result, people who exhibit economic biases are often weeded out of the market.

11. Laboratories differ from real life in several key ways that make lab experiments potentially problematic. First, individuals' behaviors tend to change when they know they are being watched by an experimenter. Second, the stakes of economic games played in the lab are much lower than those played in real life. In addition, participants are often asked to perform tasks in the lab that are foreign to them, and in real life, people do not assume away their cultural norms. Even so, lab experiments allow experimental economists to test and gain insights into many economic theories.

12. A natural experiment is a situation in which, by chance, something happens that allows the researcher to learn about an economic question. A field experiment uses randomization, just as in the lab, but is carried out in real-world settings. Both natural and field experiments allow economists to examine economic actors in their natural environments, and field experiments, like lab experiments, give economists a degree of control over the way in which the theory is tested.

Solutions to Select End-of-Chapter Problems

CHAPTER 2

3. a. We begin with the demand equation and substitute the given values for P_C and I:

$$Q_O^D = 75 - 5P_O + P_C + 2I$$
$$Q_O^D = 75 - 5P_O + 5 + (2 \times 10)$$

This simplifies to

$$Q_O^D = 100 - 5P_O$$

To find the inverse demand curve, we want to rearrange terms to express P as a function of Q:

$$5P_O = 100 - Q_O^D$$
$$P_O = 20 - 0.2Q_O^D$$

The choke price can be found by solving for the price that corresponds to a quantity demanded of zero:

$$P_O = 20 - (0.2 \times 0) = 20$$

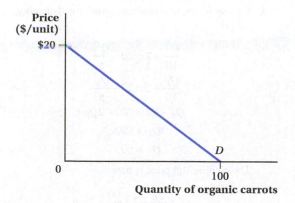

b. Substitute 5 for P_O in the demand function to find Q_O^D:

$$Q_O^D = 100 - 5P_O = 100 - 5(5) = 75$$

Substitute 10 for P_O in the inverse demand function to find Q_O^D:

$$P_O = 20 - 0.2Q_O^D$$
$$10 = 20 - 0.2Q_O^D$$
$$10 = 0.2Q_O^D$$
$$50 = Q_O^D$$

c. We begin with the demand equation and substitute the given values for P_C and I:

$$Q_O^D = 75 - 5P_O + P_C + 2I$$
$$Q_O^D = 75 - 5P_O + 15 + (2 \times 10)$$

This simplifies to

$$Q_O^D = 100 - 5P_O$$

To find the inverse demand curve, we want to rearrange terms to express P as a function of Q:

$$5P_O = 110 - Q_O^D$$
$$P_O = 22 - 0.2Q_O^D$$

We can substitute 10 for the price of organic carrots to find the quantity demanded:

$$10 = 22 - 0.2Q_O^D$$
$$0.2Q_O^D = 12$$
$$Q_O^D = 60$$

We find the choke price by finding the price that would make quantity demanded equal to zero:

$$P_O = 22 - 0.2Q_O^D$$
$$P_O = 22 - (0.2 \times 0) = 22$$

The demand for organic carrots has changed because the entire curve has shifted to the right.

d. The demand for organic carrots has increased, shifting the demand curve to the right. This shows that the two goods are substitutes for one another, because an increase in the price of conventional carrots has led to a higher quantity of organic carrots demanded at any given price.

e. There is a positive coefficient (+2) on the variable for income. This means that an increase in income will shift the demand for organic carrots to the right. As a consequence, we know that organic carrots are a normal good.

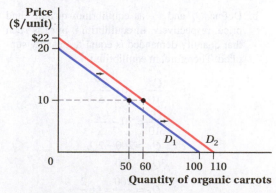

4. a. Since tea and coffee are the classic examples of substitutes, as the price of tea increases, the demand for coffee is likely to increase.

   b. An increase in the price of doughnuts decreases the quantity demanded of doughnuts. Because doughnuts and coffee are complements, this will likely decrease the demand for coffee.

   c. A decrease in the price of coffee will decrease the quantity demanded of coffee via a movement along the demand curve.

   d. The Surgeon General's announcement will likely increase the number of people who are interested in drinking coffee and, thus, increase the demand for coffee.

   e. Heavy rain will decrease the supply of coffee. This can be shown as an inward shift of the supply curve. As a result, the equilibrium price increases and the equilibrium quantity decreases. This adjustment is accomplished via a movement along the demand curve.

10. a. The inverse supply is

$$P = \frac{Q^S}{10}$$

   whereas the inverse demand is

$$P = 20 - \frac{1}{5}Q^D$$

   The graph is shown at the right.

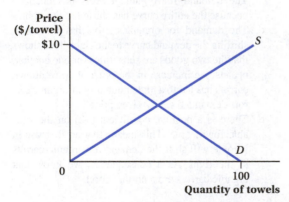

   Price ($/towel)
   $10
   S
   D
   0   100
   Quantity of towels

   b. Define Q_E and P_E as equilibrium quantity and price, respectively. In equilibrium, price is such that quantity demanded is equal to quantity supplied. Therefore, in equilibrium,

$$\frac{Q^S}{10} = 20 - \frac{Q^D}{5}$$

$$\frac{Q_E}{10} = 20 - \frac{Q_E}{5}$$

$$Q_E = 200 - 2Q_E$$

$$3Q_E = 200$$

$$Q_E = \frac{200}{3} = 66\frac{2}{3}$$

The equilibrium price is then

$$P_E = \frac{Q_E}{10} = \frac{\frac{200}{3}}{10} = \frac{20}{3} = 6\frac{2}{3}$$

   c. The new supply function is

$$Q^S = 10P - 20$$

   Hence, the new inverse supply function is

$$P = \frac{1}{10}Q^S + 2$$

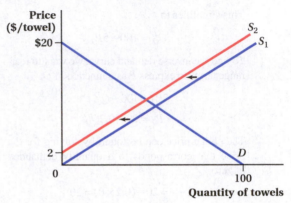

   Price ($/towel)
   $20
   S_2 S_1
   2
   D
   0   100
   Quantity of towels

   d. Solving for the new equilibrium price and quantity, we get

$$\frac{Q^S}{10} + 2 = 20 - \frac{Q^D}{5}$$

$$\frac{Q_E}{10} + 2 = 20 - \frac{Q_E}{5}$$

$$Q_E + 20 = 200 - 2Q_E$$

$$3Q_E = 180$$

$$Q_E = 60$$

The equilibrium price is now

$$P_E = \frac{Q_E}{10} + 2 = \frac{60}{10} + 2 = 8$$

The decrease in supply has lowered the equilibrium quantity to 60 and raised the equilibrium price to 8.

   e. If the quantity of towels demanded at any given price is 25 less than before, this means that the demand equation becomes $Q^D = 75 - 5P$ and the inverse demand is $P = 15 - 0.2Q^D$.

   Therefore, in equilibrium,

$$\frac{Q^S}{10} = 15 - \frac{Q^D}{5}$$

$$\frac{Q^E}{10} = 15 - \frac{Q^E}{5}$$

$$Q^E = 150 - 2Q^E$$

$$3Q^E = 150$$

$$Q^E = 50$$

The equilibrium price is now $P_E = \dfrac{Q^S}{10} = \dfrac{50}{10} = 5$.

The decrease in demand has lowered both the equilibrium price and quantity. This is in contrast to the decrease in supply that lowered the equilibrium quantity and raised the equilibrium price.

15. a. In equilibrium, $Q^S = Q^D$ so that

$$Q^D = 100 - P = -20 + 2P = Q^S$$
$$100 - P = -20 + 2P$$
$$P_E = 40$$

The equilibrium price for pillows is 40.

b. The equilibrium quantity is

$$Q_E = 100 - P_E = 60$$

c. The equilibrium quantity using the supply equation is

$$Q^S = -20 + 2P_E = 60 = Q_E$$

Hence, $Q^S = Q^D = Q_E$, just like what was obtained in (b).

d. The elasticity of supply or demand can be calculated using the expression

$$E = \frac{1}{\text{slope of the inverse demand curve}} \times \frac{P}{Q}$$

Note that $P = 40$ and $Q = 60$ at the equilibrium point. The slope of the demand curve is -1 so that

$$E_D = \frac{1}{-1} \times \frac{40}{60} = -\frac{2}{3}$$

whereas the slope of our supply curve is 0.5, so

$$E_S = \frac{1}{0.5} \times \frac{40}{60} = \frac{4}{3}$$

The elasticity of demand lies within the interval $-1 < E_D < 0$. Hence, the demand is inelastic. The coefficient of elasticity of supply indicates that supply is elastic. Out of the two, the supply is more elastic.

e. Inverting the demand function, we get

$$Q^D = 100 - P$$
$$P = 100 - Q^D$$

Inverting the supply function yields

$$Q^S = -20 + 2P$$
$$P = 0.5Q^S + 10$$

At the equilibrium, we get

$$100 - Q^D = \frac{Q^S}{2} + 10$$

$$100 - Q_E = \frac{1}{2}Q_E + 10$$

$$\frac{3}{2}Q_E = 90$$

$$Q_E = 60$$

$$P_E = 100 - Q_E = 40$$

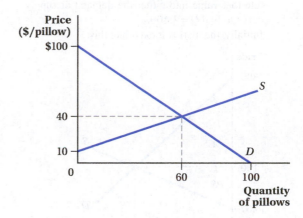

Therefore, the equilibrium point coincides with our previous answer. Since the equilibrium point is the same and since the slopes of both curves are also unchanged, the elasticities will correspond to the previously derived coefficients in part (d).

19. a. The elasticity of demand at any point can be calculated as $(\Delta Q/\Delta P) \times (P/Q)$. $\Delta Q/\Delta P$ is the slope of the demand curve. But we are given the slope of the *inverse* demand curve, $\Delta P/\Delta Q$. So, the elasticity of demand can be rewritten as $(1/(\Delta P/\Delta Q)) \times (P/Q)$, or $(1/\text{slope}) \times (P/Q)$, where "slope" is the slope of the inverse demand curve. Thus, for Jo, the elasticity of demand at point A is $(1/(-3)) \times (3/1) = -1$. The elasticity of demand at point B is $(1/(-4/3)) \times (2/1.5) = -1$. The elasticity of demand at point C is $(1/(-1/3)) \times (1/3) = -1$. So, at all points on Jo's demand curve, the elasticity of demand is -1; Jo's demand is unit elastic.

b. At point Q, Kyle's elasticity of demand is $(-1) * (3/1) = -3$; demand is elastic. At point R, Kyle's elasticity of demand is $(-1) * (1/3) = -1/3$; demand is inelastic. So, Kyle's elasticity of demand varies at different points on his demand curve.

c. Jo has a demand curve where the slope changes from point to point, but the elasticity doesn't. Kyle has a demand curve where the slope is always the same, but the elasticity changes from point to point. So, we can conclude that slope and elasticity are related (the formula for elasticity includes the slope of the demand curve), but are most definitely not the same.

CHAPTER 3

5. a. The equation for the new demand curve is $Q^D = 7,000 - 20P$. (Note that the intercept increases by 1,000, reflecting the change in demand.)

   b. $Q^D = Q^S$ implies that $7,000 - 20P = 30P - 2,000$, or $50P = 9,000$. Solving for P, $P = \$180$. Substitute that value into either the demand or supply curve to find $Q = 3,400$.

   c. Initially, the market looked like this:

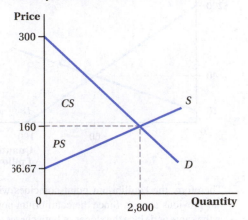

   We found the initial demand choke price by setting $Q^D = 0$ in the original demand curve. If $Q^D = 6,000 - 20P$, then $Q^D = 0$ implies that $0 = 6,000 - 20P$, or $20P = 6,000$, or $P = 300$. We found the supply choke price the same way, by setting $Q^S = 0$: If $Q^S = -2,000 + 30P$, then $Q^S = 0$ implies that $0 = -2,000 + 30P$, or $30P = 2,000$, or $P = 66.67$.

   Calculate the consumer surplus as the area under the demand curve and above the price: $\frac{1}{2} \times (300 - 160) \times 2,800$, or \$196,000. Producer surplus is the area above the supply curve and below the price: $\frac{1}{2} \times (160 - 66.67) \times 2,800$, or \$130,666.67.

   After the demand shift, the market looked like this:

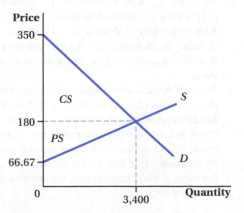

We found the new demand choke price by setting $Q^D = 0$ in the new demand curve. If $Q^D = 7,000 - 20P$, then $Q^D = 0$ implies that $0 = 7,000 - 20P$, or $20P = 7,000$, or $P = 350$.

Calculate the consumer surplus as the area under the demand curve and above the price: $\frac{1}{2} \times (350 - 180) \times 3,400$, or \$289,000. Producer surplus is the area above the supply curve and below the price: $\frac{1}{2} \times (180 - 66.67) \times 3,400$, or \$192,666.67.

So, as a result of the demand change, consumer surplus increased by $\$289,000 - \$196,000$, or \$93,000. Producer surplus increased by $\$192,666.67 - \$130,666.67$, or \$62,000.

8. a. The cost to consumers in lost surplus is

$$\text{Areas } A \text{ and } B = (0.5 - 0) \times (\$4 - \$3) +$$
$$\frac{1}{2} \times (1 - 0.5) \times (\$4 - \$3) = \$0.75$$

   Since the quantity is measured in millions of pounds, the cost to consumers is \$750,000.

   b. The cost to taxpayers is

$$(1.5 - 0.5) \times \$4 = \$4$$

   Therefore, the cost to taxpayers is \$4,000,000.

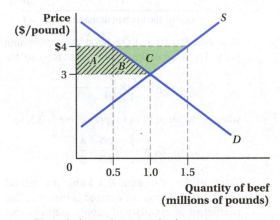

Quantity of beef
(millions of pounds)

   c. The gain in producer surplus is

$$\text{Areas } A, B, \text{and } C = \text{Cost to consumers} + \frac{1}{2} \times (1.5 - 0.5)$$
$$\times (\$4 - \$3) = \$1.25$$

   Thus, producers gain \$1,250,000.

   d. The loss to society is

$$\$4,000,000 + \$750,000 - \$1,250,000 = \$3,500,000$$

   e. The gain of producers from the scheme is \$1,250,000. Therefore, compensating the producers marginally above their gain should suffice. It costs consumers and taxpayers collectively \$2.2 million instead of \$4.75 million; the scheme is better for all parties concerned.

15. a. The inverse demand function is

$$Q^D = 20 - 2P$$

$$P = 10 - 0.5Q^D$$

The inverse supply curve is

$$Q^S = 4P - 10$$

$$P = 2.5 + 0.25Q^S$$

The equilibrium price is

$$Q^D = 20 - 2P = 4P - 10 = Q^S$$

$$6P = 30$$

$$P^* = \$5$$

The equilibrium quantity is

$$20 - (2 \times 5) = 10 \text{ gallons of ice cream}$$

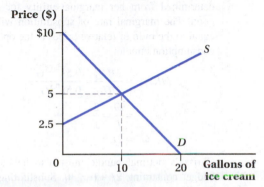

b. The demand curve shifts inward by the amount of the tax. See graph at right.

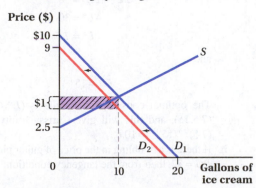

c. The buyers face a new price $P_S + TAX$, and sellers sell at P_S:

$$Q^D = 20 - 2 \times (P_S + 1) = 4P_S - 10 = Q^S$$

$$6P_S = 28$$

$$P_S \approx 4.67$$

Hence, buyers pay $5.67 and sellers sell at $4.67. The quantity sold is

$$(4 \times \$4.67) - 10 = 8.68$$

d. After the $1 tax, buyers pay $5.67 for a gallon of ice cream. After the buyers send in the tax, the sellers only end up with $4.67 per gallon sold. Therefore, of the $1 going to the government, approximately 67% of it is coming out of consumers' pockets because their price went up by 67 cents per gallon. The price realized by the suppliers goes down by approximately 33 cents per gallon. The incidence of this tax is 67% on the buyers and 33% on the seller. Hence, buyers bear a proportionately greater burden of the tax. This happens when demand is relatively inelastic when compared to supply, which in this case is relatively elastic.

e. Before the tax, the demand choke price is $10 per gallon of ice cream. Hence, the consumer surplus is

$$\frac{1}{2} \times (10 - 0) \times (\$10 - \$5) = \$25$$

After the tax, the demand choke price is $9 per gallon of ice cream. Hence, the consumer surplus is

$$\frac{1}{2} \times (8.68 - 0) \times (\$10 - \$5.67) \approx \$18.79$$

Or if you reduce the choke price and use the gross price of $4.67, the consumer surplus is still

$$\frac{1}{2} \times (8.68 - 0) \times (\$9 - \$4.67) \approx \$18.79$$

f. Before the tax, the supply choke price is $2.50 per gallon of ice cream. Hence, the producer surplus is

$$\frac{1}{2} \times (10 - 0) \times (\$5 - \$2.50) \approx \$12.50$$

After the tax, the producer surplus is

$$\frac{1}{2} \times (8.68 - 0) \times (\$4.67 - \$2.50) = 0.5 \times 8.68 \times \$2.17 \approx \$9.42$$

g. The tax revenue raised by the government is

$$\$1 \times 8.68 \approx \$8.68$$

h. Due to the tax, quantity falls by 1.33 units. The tax creates a deadweight loss of

$$0.5 \times \$1 \times 1.33 \approx \$0.67$$

16. a. At equilibrium, the price elasticity of demand is $(-0.5) \times (6/7)$ or $-3/7$. The elasticity of supply is $2 \times (6/7)$, or $12/7$.

b. The share of the tax born by consumers $= E_s /$ $(|E_d| + E_s)$. This equals $(12/7)/((3/7) + (12/7))$, or $(12/7)/(15/7)$, which is 0.8. The share of the tax born by producers $= |E_d|/(|E_d|+E_s)$. This equals $(3/7)/((3/7)+(12/7))$, or $(3/7)/(15/7)$, which is 0.2.

c. Buyers bear 80% of the burden of the $1 tax, so the price buyers pay should rise by 80 cents, from $6 to $6.80. Sellers bear 20% of the burden of the $1 tax, so the price buyers pay should fall by 20 cents, from $6 to $5.80.

CHAPTER 4

6. *A* and *B* are two bundles on the same indifference curve U_1, so any bundle that lies along the straight line joining *A* and *B* will lie on a higher indifference curve. Bundle *C*, consisting of 3 peaches and 2 apples, is such a bundle so John will choose bundle *C* over bundle *A*.

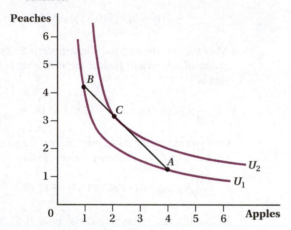

7. a.

$$U(1,2) = (1)(2) = 2$$
$$U(2,1) = (2)(1) = 2$$
$$U(5,2) = (5)(2) = 10$$

b.

Bundle	Quantity of X	Quantity of Y	Utility
A	2	2	4
B	10	0	0
C	1	5	5
D	3	2	6
E	2	3	6

From the table, $U(D)=U(E)>U(C)>U(A)>U(B)$; we thus have the ranking (> denotes strictly preferred, ~ denotes indifferent)

$$D \sim E > C > A > B$$

c.

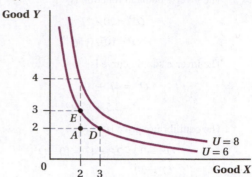

The "more is better" assumption is satisfied.

19. a. Chrissy's marginal rate of substitution can be determined from her marginal utility for each good. The marginal rate of substitution will be equal to the ratio of relative prices at the optimal consumption bundle:

$$MRS_{LG} = \frac{MU_L}{MU_G} = \frac{0.5L^{-0.5}G^{0.5}}{0.5L^{0.5}G^{-0.5}}$$
$$= \frac{G}{L} = \frac{2}{1}$$
$$G^* = 2L^*$$

Chrissy's optimal bundle must also lie on her budget constraint, $2L+G=30$. Substituting the relation from the tangency condition yields

$$2L^*+2L^* = 30$$
$$4L^* = 30$$
$$L^* = 7.5$$

and

$$G^* = 15$$

The optimal consumption bundle is $(L^*,G^*) = (7.5,15)$, and this will give Chrissy utility $U = (7.5)^{0.5}(15)^{0.5} = 10.6$.

b. If there is a doubling in the price of guitar picks to $PG = \$2$, then from the tangency condition:

$$MRS_{LG} = \frac{P_L}{P_G}$$
$$\frac{G}{L} = \frac{2}{2}$$
$$G^* = L^*$$

Chrissy will want to consume the two goods in equal quantities. In order to maintain utility at $U = 10.6$,

$$U(L,G) = L^{0.5}G^{0.5}$$
$$10.6 = L^{0.5}G^{0.5}$$

with $G^* = L^* = k$

$$10.6 = k^{0.5}k^{0.5}$$
$$10.6 = k$$

Chrissy will consume the bundle $(L^*, G^*) =$ $(10.6, 10.6)$, which at the new price for guitar picks will cost

$$(2)(10.6) + (2)(10.6) = \$42.40$$

Chrissy will require income $I' = \$42.40$ in order to maintain the same level of utility.

CHAPTER 5

7. a. When the price of a movie ticket is \$10, Tyler sees 6 movies in the theater.

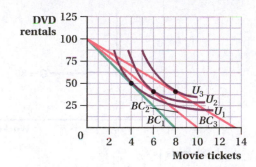

b–e.

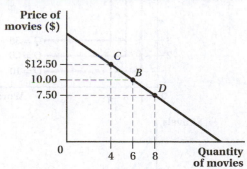

12. a.

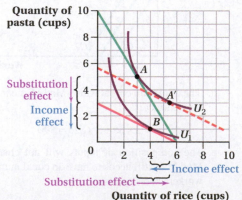

b. The two effects seem to be equivalent in magnitude for pasta with a decrease of 2 cups of pasta for each effect. As far as rice, the substitution effect dominates the income effect; in particular, the substitution effect leads to a 2-cup increase in rice consumption, whereas the income effect causes rice consumption to fall by 1 cup.

15. a. The implication of the optimal bundle is that Yoshi's income is at least \$600. In addition, assuming well-behaved indifference curves implies that Yoshi's income is greater than \$600. As a result of the tax and the rebate, the intercepts in the two axes change. The intercept of the horizontal axis, after the tax and the rebate, lies to the left of $Y/3$. The intercept of the vertical axis, after the tax and the rebate, lies above Y. The graph is indicated on the right. As shown, Yoshi's consumption of soda will decrease and his consumption of the composite good will increase.

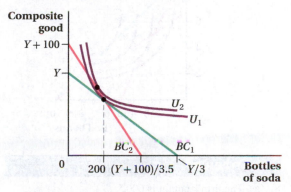

b. Notice that Yoshi's initial bundle is still affordable, but that Yoshi chooses a different bundle. Therefore, Yoshi must be better off at his new bundle than his initial bundle (or he would have simply purchased the initial bundle again).

c. Since Yoshi cuts back on soda, the government raises less than \$100 in revenue. At the same time, the government spends \$100 subsidizing Yoshi. The government is therefore worse off.

16. a. Gaston's demand for red beans

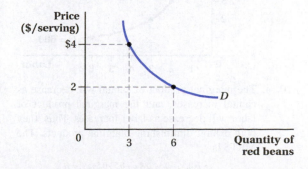

b.

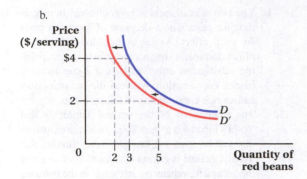

c. When the price of rice increases to $3, the demand for red beans decreases.

d. The changes in prices and quantities are consistent with the definition of complements.

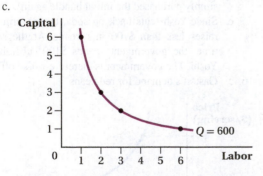

CHAPTER 6

8. a. The firm's output is 600.

b. Output of 600 can also be achieved with either 3 units of capital and 2 units of labor, 2 units of capital and 3 units of labor, or 1 unit of capital and 6 units of labor.

c.

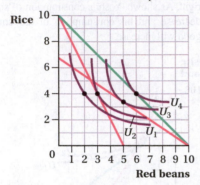

10. a. The marginal product of capital will decrease as capital increases, and the marginal product of labor will decrease as labor increases. Thus, they both exhibit diminishing marginal products. The MRTS is

$$(2K^{0.5}L^{-0.5})/(2K^{-0.5}L^{0.5}) = K/L$$

As labor increases, this value will diminish. Therefore, the marginal rate of substitution is diminishing.

b. For a given amount of labor, the marginal product of capital is constant. For a given amount of capital, the marginal product of labor is constant. Hence, neither input exhibits diminishing marginal returns. The MRTS is

$$4K/4L = K/L.$$

As labor increases, the MRTS will diminish.

c. In both (a) and (b), the production function displays a diminishing MRTS. Yet in (b), both inputs were characterized by a constant marginal product. So, a diminishing rate of substitution can be found even when marginal product is not diminishing.

12. a. **Shovels**

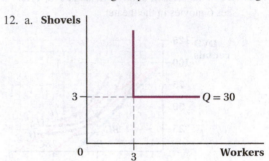

b. **Shovels**

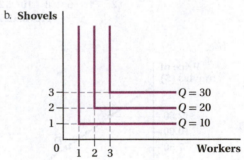

c. **Shovels**

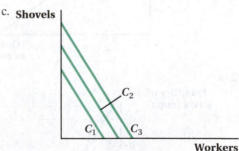

d. The minimum cost at which Mad Max can fulfill the contract is

$$3 \times \$5 + 3 \times \$25 = \$90$$

e. The composition of inputs will not change as Mad Max still needs to have an equal number of workers and shovels.

13. a. The cost function is
$$\$12 \times L + \$7 \times K$$

b.
$$\$100 = \$12 \times L + \$7 \times K$$
$$K = \frac{100}{7} - \frac{12}{7}L$$

c.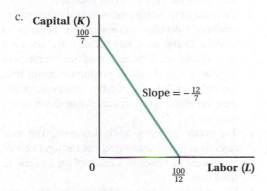

d. The vertical intercept indicates the quantity of capital that can be rented with \$100 if no labor is hired. The horizontal intercept indicates the quantity of labor that can be hired with \$100 if no capital is rented.

e. The slope is the (negative) ratio of the price of labor (wage) and the rental price of capital. The isocost line has a slope of $-\frac{12}{7}$.

f. In this case, the isocost function rotates inward as shown:
$$K = \frac{100}{7} - 2L$$

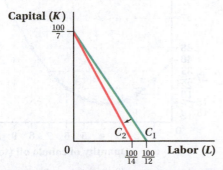

The new isocost line is steeper; the slope is –2.

CHAPTER 7

2. a. True. Economic costs include both accounting costs and the opportunity cost. Conditional on the opportunity cost equaling zero, accounting and economic costs may be equal, but since the opportunity cost cannot be negative, the economic costs are at least as high as the accounting costs.

b. No, it is not possible. The economic profit is the total revenue minus the economic cost, whereas the accounting profit is the total revenue minus the accounting costs. Since economic cost is at least as large as the accounting cost, it is not possible to make an economic profit without making an accounting profit.

8. a. Begin by putting L on the left-hand side:
$$100L = 3000 + Q$$
$$L = 30 + 0.01Q$$

b. $TC = w(30 + 0.01Q) = 30w + 0.01Qw$

11.

Q (batches)	Variable Cost (\$)	Average Total Cost (\$)	Average Fixed Cost (\$)	Average Variable Cost (\$)
1	25	75	50	25
2	35	42.5	25	17.5
3	52	34	16.67	17.33
4	77	31.75	12.5	19.25
5	115	33	10	23
6	160	35	8.33	26.67

19. A builder will be indifferent between the two choices when
$$ATC_1 = ATC_2$$

Thus, the quantity Q at which the builder of custom motorcycles is indifferent is
$$Q^2 - 6Q + 14 = Q^2 - 10Q + 30$$
$$Q = 4$$

For $Q < 4, ATC_1$ is less, whereas for $Q > 4, ATC_2$ is less. Hence, the $LATC$ is
$$\begin{cases} Q^2 - 6Q + 14, \text{ for } Q \le 4 \\ Q^2 - 10Q + 30, \text{ for } Q > 4 \end{cases}$$

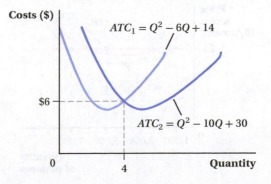

20. a. This Cobb–Douglas production function exhibits constant returns to scale. Hence, the long-run average cost curve is horizontal, whereas the long-run total cost curve is a straight upward-sloping line.

b. Now the production function exhibits increasing returns to scale. The long-run average cost curve is downward-sloping and the total cost curve's slope is positive, but as output increases, the slope declines.

CHAPTER 8

2. The number of available substitutes is a key determinant for the elasticity of demand. Although there may not be a lot of substitutes for soybeans, there are many substitutes for soybeans from any one individual producer. The more narrowly the product is defined, the greater the elasticity due to more substitutes being available.

9. a. The rectangle *ADGH* represents the total revenue when selling 1,000 units at $100 each.

b. The variable cost at 1,000 units is represented by the area *MLGH*.

c. The fixed cost of producing 1,000 units is equal to the area *KJLM*.

d. The total cost of producing 1,000 units is shown by the area *KJGH*.

e. The profit from producing 1,000 units is represented by the area *ADJK*.

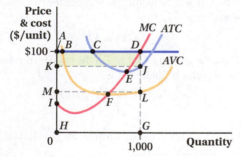

12. a. The seller should produce at the level of output where *MR* equals *MC*, which occurs at 5,000 pounds of potatoes.

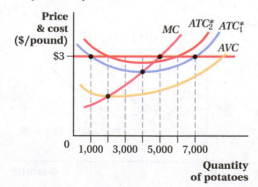

b. An increase in the mortgage payment increases the fixed cost of production, shifting the average total cost curve up.

c. Only the average total cost curve shifts. The average variable cost curve remains unchanged since the mortgage payment does not alter the variable cost. Similarly, the marginal cost curve is not affected by the increase in the fixed cost.

d. The change in interest rates has no effect on the producer's decision of how many potatoes to produce in the short run because *MC* does not shift. (However, if the increased interest rate will increase the total cost of production above total revenue, leading to a negative economic profit, then the potato grower would shut down in the long run.)

e. The potato grower's profit decreases. The total revenue remains unchanged but the total cost of production increases as a result of the increase in fixed cost.

f. The grower's short run supply is the *MC* curve above *AVC*. Since neither the *MC* curve nor the *AVC* curve shifted, the short run supply curve is unaffected.

17. a. The long-run average total cost of producing canola oil is

$$LATC = \frac{LTC}{Q} = Q^2 - 15Q + 40$$

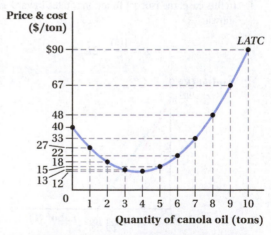

b. The long-run equilibrium price of canola oil is approximately $12, which is the minimum of the *LATC* curve.

c. Each firm will produce the quantity of canola oil that corresponds to the minimum point on the *LATC* curve, that is, 4 tons of canola oil.

d. Using the demand function, we get

$$Q^D = 999 - 0.25P = 999 - 0.25 \times 12 = 996$$

At the long-run equilibrium price, consumers will demand approximately 996 tons of canola oil.

e. Since each representative firm supplies 4 tons of canola oil, the number of suppliers in the long-run equilibrium will be

$$\frac{996}{4} = 249$$

22. a. With two types of producer in the market, the price will be determined by the costs of the marginal producer—in this case, the dryland producer. If the price was below dryland farmers' minimum long-run average cost of production, they would exit the market. If the price was above dryland farmers' minimum LAC, there would be positive profits that would induce entry. So, in equilibrium, the price must be equal to the producers' minimum average cost.

But what is the minimum average cost for a dryland farmer? At its minimum point, $LAC_D = LMC_D$. We can thus find the quantity where that is true and then see what the actual LAC is. Set

$$LMC_D = LAC_D$$
$$3Q^2 - 40Q + 105 = Q^2 - 20Q + 105$$
$$2Q^2 = 20Q$$
$$2Q = 20$$
$$Q = 10$$

At $Q = 10$, $LAC_D = 10^2 - 20(10) + 105 = 5$. So, the minimum long-run average cost of dryland corn is $5 per bushel. Because the corn market is in equilibrium, the price must equal the marginal farmer's minimum LAC, so corn must be selling for $5 per bushel.

b. At the market price of $5 per bushel, the optimal output for irrigating farmers can be found by equating LMC_I and P:

$$LMC_I = P$$
$$3Q^2 - 32Q + 67 = 5$$
$$3Q^2 - 32Q + 62 = 0$$

This can be solved by the quadratic formula; the profit-maximizing level of Q is 8.12 thousand bushels.

The average cost of producing 8.12 thousand bushels for an irrigating farmer is

$$LAC_I = Q^2 - 16Q + 67$$
$$LAC_I = (8.12)^2 - 16(8.12) + 67$$
$$LAC_I = \$3.01$$

Thus, the irrigating farmer earns rents of $5 - \$3.01 = \$1.99$ per bushel. Given output of

8.12 thousand bushels, the rents earned by irrigating farmers are 8,120($1.99), or $16,158.

c. The rents exist because of water access. That valuable water access has an opportunity cost: It could be sold or rented to someone else. So, Farmer A with water access could lease his ground to Farmer B, where it would fetch a premium of up to $16,158 per year over what land without water access rents for. Because of the expensive lease, Farmer B's costs would then be identical to those of dryland farmers; Farmer B would earn zero profits. And Farmer A would capture the rent, even if he didn't farm.

Therefore, if Farmer A decides to farm instead of leasing his ground to someone else, his economic profits should account for the opportunity cost of renting his ground to someone else. Once that's done, Farmer A earns positive rents, but zero economic profits.

CHAPTER 9

4. a., b. and c.

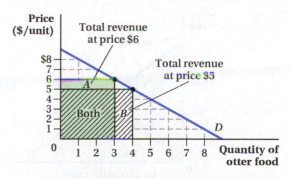

d. As Oscar reduces his price from $6 to $5, the rectangle A represents the loss. This is the revenue lost from decreasing the price.

e. As Oscar reduces his price from $6 to $5, the rectangle B represents the gain. This is the revenue gained from decreasing the price and selling more units.

f. The area of rectangle A is

$$(\$6 - \$5) \times 3 = \$3$$

The area of rectangle B is

$$\$5 \times (4 - 3) = \$5$$

Subtracting area A from area B, we obtain $5 - \$3 = \$2$.

g. The marginal revenue from selling a 4th unit is

$$MR = TR_B - TR_A = (\$5 \times 4) - (\$6 \times 3) = \$2$$

Therefore, the result corresponds to the value obtained in (f).

7. a. Invert the demand curve to find P as a function of Q: $P = 25 - (1/32) \times Q$. The MR curve has the same vertical intercept as the inverse demand curve, but twice the slope. So, $MR = 25 - (1/16) \times Q$.

    b. When $Q = 96$, $MR = 25 - (1/16) \times (96)$, or 19. When $Q = 480$, $MR = 25 - (1/16) \times (480)$, or -5. MR is positive when quantities are relatively low; it is negative at high quantities.

    c. To find the quantity where $MR = 0$, plug 0 into the expression for MR:

    $$0 = 25 - (1/16) \times Q$$
    $$(1/16) \times Q = 25$$
    $$Q = 25 \times 16$$
    $$Q = 400$$

    d. $MR = 0$ at the midpoint of the demand curve, where the elasticity of demand $= -1$.

10. a. The monopolist will maximize its profit by producing the level of output at which $MR = MC$, that is, 100 dozen bearings.

    b. The monopolist should charge $100 per dozen to maximize profit.

    c.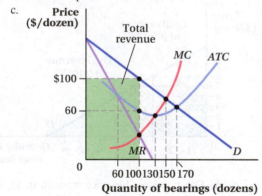

    d.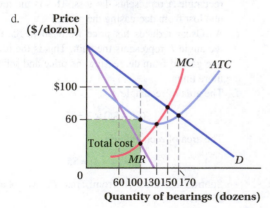

    e. The profit is

    $$\pi = TR - TC = (100 \times \$100) - (100 \times \$60) = \$4,000$$

16. a. The inverse demand curve is

    $$Q = 40 - 0.5P$$
    $$P = 80 - 2Q$$

    The marginal revenue is

    $$MR = 80 - 4Q$$

    b. $$MR = 80 - 4Q = 10 = MC$$
    $$4Q = 70$$
    $$Q = 17.5$$

    The profit-maximizing level of output is 17.5 tons of bentonite.

    c. The profit-maximizing price is

    $$17.5 = 40 - 0.5P$$
    $$0.5P = 40 - 17.5$$
    $$P = \$45$$

    d. If demand increased to $Q = 55 - 0.5P$, the inverse demand curve will be $P = 110 - 2Q$, and the associated marginal revenue curve would be $MR = 110 - 4Q$. The profit-maximizing quantity is:

    $$MR = 110 - 4Q = 10 = MC$$
    $$100 = 4Q$$
    $$Q = 25$$

    The profit maximizing price is $P = 110 - 2(25) = \$60$.

19. a. The marginal revenue is $40 - Q$:

    $$MR = 40 - Q = 5 = MC$$
    $$Q = 35$$

    The unregulated monopolist constant will sell 35 flux capacitors.

    b. The price ceiling is also the marginal revenue for the first 68 units; that is, $MR = 6$ because consumers are willing to pay $6 or more. Therefore, the marginal revenue for the 10th unit and the 68th unit is $6. However, selling the 69th unit requires reducing the price to $5.50. Thus, the total revenue from selling 68 units is $6 \times 68 = \$408$, and the total revenue from selling 69 units is $5.50 \times 69 = \$379.50$. Therefore, the marginal revenue of the 69th unit is $408 - \$379.50 = -\$28.50$.

    c. The monopolist will sell the first 68 units at a price of $6 since the marginal revenue exceeds the marginal cost. The monopolist will not sell the 69th unit because the marginal cost is greater than the marginal revenue.

d. As shown in the diagrams below, the price ceiling indeed reduces the deadweight loss.

Case 1: Unregulated Monopoly

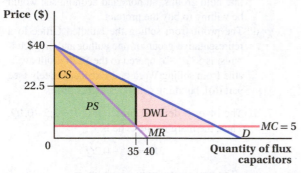

Case 2: Price Ceiling

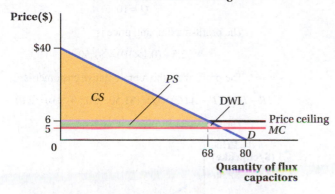

CHAPTER 10

3. a.
  - Airlines sort passengers into first class (very expensive tickets), business class (not quite as expensive), and coach/economy (lowest prices). They offer a slightly higher level of service and a bit more space to the higher-class passengers.
  - Airlines give economy/coach passengers the option of paying more for extra legroom, aisle seats, or exit row seating.
  - Airlines charge an extra fee for those who wish to check a bag rather than simply travel with a carry-on.
  - Airlines often charge extra for weekday travel (which business travelers, who have deeper pockets, prefer).
  - Airlines often charge more for last-minute tickets, which indicate urgent travel rather than more price-sensitive leisure travel.

  b. Generally, the customer reveals his or her willingness to spend through the upgrades and options

he or she selects at the time the reservation is made.

  c. Fortunately for airlines, the Transportation Security Administration (TSA) has outlawed the transfer of airline tickets from one passenger to another. Often we see price discrimination in services, because while it is easy to transfer goods from person to person, it is generally difficult to transfer services like education or haircuts.

6. a. The inverse demand for adults is

$$P = 500 - 0.1Q$$

Hence, the marginal revenue is

$$MR = 500 - 0.2Q$$

The inverse demand for students is

$$P = 100 - 0.01Q$$

Hence, the marginal revenue is

$$MR = 100 - 0.02Q$$

  b. The profit-maximizing quantity for adults is

$$MR = MC$$
$$500 - 0.2Q = 10$$
$$Q = 2,450$$

The profit-maximizing quantity for students is

$$100 - 0.02Q = 10$$
$$Q = 4,500$$

  c. The profit-maximizing price for adults is

$$P_{Ad}^* = 500 - 0.1Q_{Ad}^* = 500 - (0.1 \times 2,450) = \$255$$

The profit-maximizing price for students is

$$P_{St}^* = 100 - 0.10Q_{St}^* = 100 - (0.01 \times 4,500) = \$55$$

Adults pay more.

  d. The profit from adults is

$$TR - TC = (\$255 \times 2,450) - (\$10 \times 2,450) = \$600,250$$

The profit from students is

$$TR - TC = (\$55 \times 4,500) - (\$10 \times 4,500) = \$202,500$$

Hence, the total profit is \$802,750.

  e. Given that the capacity is 5,000, continue to sell 2,450 tickets to adults at \$255, which maximizes profit in that segment. Sell the remaining 2,550 tickets for as much as the student segment will bear, \$74.50. So, students should pay \$74.50 = $100 - (0.01 \times 2,550)$. Profit in the student segment would be $(\$74.50 \times 2,550) - (\$10 \times 2,550) = \$164,475$. The total profit in this case would be $\$164,475 + \$600,250 = \$764,725$.

13. a. The price-conscious consumers will buy the Dundee pianos because their valuation exceeds the price of lower-quality pianos; the price of Rockway pianos exceeds the valuation of the higher-quality pianos by these customers. Thus, for budget-conscious customers, incentive compatibility is sustained. However, the net gain for performance-oriented consumers from buying Dundee pianos is $2,000, whereas for Rockway pianos it is $1,500. Therefore, the incentive compatibility condition is violated, as performance-oriented consumers would rather choose the Dundee pianos.

Consumer Valuations for Dundee and Rockway		
	Dundee (Budget Line)	**Rockway (Premium Line)**
Budget Consumer	$6,000	$8,000
Luxury Consumer	$7,000	$12,000

Consumer Surplus at $5,000 for Dundee and $10,500 for Rockway		
	Dundee (Budget Line)	**Rockway (Premium Line)**
Budget Consumer	$1,000	−$2,500
Luxury Consumer	$2,000	$1,500

b. The price of Rockway pianos should be reduced by at least $500, but by less than $3,500.

c. Yes, incentive compatibility can be achieved by raising the price of Dundee pianos from $5,000 to at least $5,501 (but not higher than $6,000). Then budget-conscious consumers will still buy Dundee pianos and performance-oriented professionals will choose the Rockway pianos.

d. Either plan would create incentive compatibility, but the one described in part (c) would do so by raising prices, rather than lowering them. Raising prices would be the better option.

15. a. It may be difficult for Microsoft to be able to observe a customer's demand type before purchase.

b. Word should cost $120 so that only authors buy it, and Excel should cost $150 so that only economists purchase it. The profit is $120+$150=$270, since ATC and MC are zero. To sell Word to both groups, the price must equal the maximum willingness to pay of the group that values Word less than Excel; that is, $50. Hence, Word would be sold to both groups and the profit would be $50+$50=$100; that is, $20 less than if the price were set at $120. Similarly for Excel, if the price were set at $40 so

that both groups would be willing to buy it, the profit would be $80 instead of $150.

c. The price for Microsoft Office should be $160 so that both groups, authors and economists, would be willing to buy the product.

d. The profit from selling the bundled Office to a representative group of one author and one economist is $320. Compared to the $270 profit available from selling Word and Excel separately [see part (a)], bundling generates higher profit.

17. a. The inverse demand function is $P = 2.5 - 0.1Q$. Thus, the marginal revenue is

$$MR = 2.5 - 0.2Q$$

The profit-maximizing quantity is

$$MR = 2.5 - 0.2Q = 0.5 = MC$$
$$Q = 10$$

The profit-maximizing price is

$$2.5 - (0.1 \times 10) = \$1.50$$

The profit from the representative customer is

$$TR - TC = (P - ATC) \times Q = (\$1.50 - \$0.50) \times 10 = \$10$$

The consumer surplus is area A.

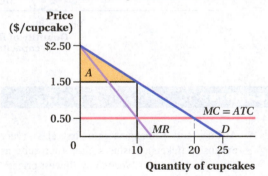

Thus, the consumer surplus is

$$\frac{1}{2} \times (\$2.50 - \$1.50) \times 10 = \$5$$

b. and c. The demand function does not change. Consider the "discounted" part of the demand function.

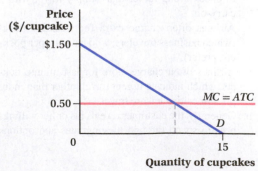

The new inverse demand function is $P = 1.5 - 0.1Q$. Thus, the marginal revenue is

$$1.5 - 0.2Q$$

The profit-maximizing quantity is

$$MR = 1.5 - 0.2Q = 0.5 = MC$$

$$Q = 5$$

The profit-maximizing price is

$$1.5 - (0.1 \times 5) = \$1$$

At full price, each consumer will order 10 cupcakes and at the discounted price 5 cupcakes.

d. The profit from this two-tiered pricing plan is

$$\$10 + (\$1 - \$0.50) \times 5 = \$12.50$$

Having introduced the discounted price for cupcakes, Elario has increased his profit by $2.50.

e.

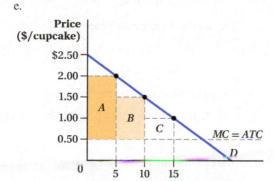

To implement a three-tiered pricing system, simply split the demand curve above marginal cost into four equal parts, as shown in the graph above. Elario will set the price points as follows: $2 for the first 5 units, $1.50 for the next 5, and $1 for any quantity more than 10. Consumers will purchase 15 units in all. Elario will earn $5 \times (\$2 - \$0.50) = \$7.50$ (shown as area A) on the first 5 units sold; he will earn $5 \times (\$1.50 - \$0.50) = \$5$ (shown as area B) on units 6 through 10, and $5 \times (\$1 - \$0.50) = \$2.50$ (shown as area C) on the remaining 5 units. Elario's total profit will be $15. He earns more profit with a three-tiered pricing system than he did with a two-tiered system.

f. Elario is essentially adopting a 20-tiered pricing system. He will sell one cupcake at $2.40, the next at $2.30, and so on, working his way down the customer's demand curve one unit at a time. He will stop cutting the price when it dips below his cost of production: In total, he will sell 20 cupcakes and the price of the last cupcake will be $0.50.

Accounting for his cost of production, he will earn a profit of $\$1.90 + \$1.80 + \cdots + \$0.10 + \$0$. This all adds up to $19.00 profit.

g. The consumer surplus decreases and is captured as profit by Elario. The pricing strategy should eliminate all deadweight loss as well, captured as profit by Elario.

CHAPTER 11

3. a. i. The marginal revenue is $MR = 30 - 4Q$.
   ii. The profit-maximizing collective output for the cartel solves the condition $MR = MC$; that is,

$$30 - 4Q = 6$$

$$4Q = 24$$

$$Q = 6$$

   iii. The price Pierre and Gaston will be able to charge is

$$P = 30 - 2Q = 30 - (2 \times 6) = \$18$$

   iv. Pierre and Gaston split the output equally; hence, each of them gets

$$(P - ATC) \times Q = (\$18 - \$6) \times 3 = \$36$$

   The profit for the cartel is $72.

   b. i. The extra production of soufflés decreases the price in the marketplace; that is,

$$P = 30 - 2Q = 30 - (2 \times 7) = \$16$$

   ii. Pierre's profit is now

$$(P - ATC) \times Q = (\$16 - \$6) \times 4 = \$40$$

   Hence, Pierre gained $4 by cheating.
   iii. Gaston's profit is now

$$(P - ATC) \times Q = (\$16 - \$6) \times 3 = \$30$$

   Guston thus lost $6.
   iv. The profits are now $\$40 + \$30 = \$70$. Therefore, as a result of Pierre's cheating, the group loses $2 of potential profit.

   c. i. The extra production of soufflés decreases the price further in the marketplace; that is,

$$P = 30 - 2Q = 30 - 2(8) = \$14$$

   ii. Gaston's profit is now

$$(P - ATC) \times Q = (\$14 - \$6) \times 4 = \$32$$

   Hence, Gaston gains $2 compared to the previous scenario.
   iii. Pierre's profit is now

$$(P - ATC) \times Q = (\$14 - \$6)4 = \$32$$

   Pierre thus loses $8 compared to the previous scenario.
   iv. The group's profits are $\$32 + \$32 = \$64$. Therefore, they lose in total $8 of potential profit.

v. If they decide to continue cheating, the price of soufflés will decrease, which will result in a reduction of profit for both individuals. More specifically, if one cheats further, the total output rises to 9. The price becomes

$$P = 30 - 2Q = 30 - 2(9) = \$12$$

The profit for the cheater is now

$$(P - ATC) \times Q = (\$12 - \$6) \times 5 = \$30$$

Hence, neither Pierre nor Gaston has an incentive to cheat as the cheater's profit falls from $32 to $30.

10. a. The inverse demand is

$$P = 1,000 - 2(q_S + q_A)$$

The residual demand faced by Sydney is

$$P = (1,000 - 2q_A) - 2q_S$$

b. The residual marginal revenue is

$$MR_S = (1,000 - 2q_A) - 4q_S$$

c.

$$MR_S = 1,000 - 2q_A - 4q_S = 200 = MC$$

$$q_S = 200 - 0.5q_A$$

d. The residual marginal revenue for Adelaide is

$$MR_A = 1,000 - 4q_A - 2q_S$$

Thus,

$$MR_A = 1,000 - 4q_A - 2q_S = 200 = MC$$

$$q_A = 200 - 0.5q_S$$

e. Adelaide's reaction function as a function of Sydney's quantity is

$$q_A = 200 - 0.5q_S = 200 - 0.5(200 - 0.5q_A)$$

$$0.75q_A = 100$$

$$q_A = 133.33$$

Because both firms have a constant marginal cost of $200, the profit-maximizing level of output for Sydney is also 133.33.

f. The output of the industry is 266.66. Thus, the price is

$$P = 1,000 - 2(q_S + q_A) = 1,000 - 2(266.66) = \$466.66$$

Both Sydney and Adelaide earn the same profit, which is equal to

$$(P - ATC) \times Q = (\$466.66 - \$200) \times 133.33 \approx \$35,556$$

Total industry profit is equal to $71,111.11.

g. If Sydney becomes a monopolist, she would set the price so that the marginal cost equals the marginal revenue, that is,

$$MR = 1,000 - 4Q = 200 = MC$$

$$Q = 200$$

The price is

$$P = 1,000 - 2Q = 1,000 - 2 \times 200 = \$600$$

The profit is now

$$(P - ATC) \times Q = (\$600 - \$200) \times 200 = \$80,000$$

Therefore, the quantity sold decreases, price increases, and so does the profit for the industry as a whole.

14. a. The reaction function for Grenada is

$$MR_G = 100 - q_P - 2q_G = 20 = MC$$

$$q_G = 40 = 0.5q_P$$

The reaction function for Penang is

$$MR_P = 100 - 2q_P - q_G = 20 = MC$$

$$q_P = 40 - 0.5q_G$$

b. The equilibrium quantity for Grenada is

$$q_G = 40 - 0.5q_P = 40 - 0.5(40 - 0.5q_G) = 20 + 0.25q_G$$

$$= 26.67$$

The equilibrium quantity for Penang is

$$q_P = 40 - 0.5q_G = 40 - (0.5 \times 26.67) = 26.67$$

The market price is then

$$P = 100 - q_P - q_G = \$46.67$$

The profit for Grenada is

$$(P_G - ATC_G) \times Q_G = (\$46.67 - \$20) \times 26.67 = \$711.11$$

The profit for Penang is

$$(P_P - ATC_P) \times Q_P = (\$46.67 - \$20) \times 26.67 = \$711.11$$

c.
   i. The demand faced by Grenada is

$$P = 100 - q_P - q_G = 100 - (40 - 0.5q_G) - q_G = 60 - 0.5q_G$$

   ii. The marginal revenue for Grenada is

$$MR_G = 60 - q_G$$

   iii. Grenada's output is

$$MR_G = 60 - q_G = 20 = MC$$

$$q_G = 40$$

   iv. Penang's output is

$$q_P = 40 - 0.5q_G = 40 - (0.5 \times 40) = 20$$

v. The price is

$$P = 100 - q_P - q_G = 100 - 20 - 40 = \$40$$

The industry quantity is greater compared to the Cournot competition, and the price is lower.

vi. The profit for Grenada is

$$(P_G - ATC_G) \times Q_G = (\$40 - \$20) \times 40 = \$800$$

The profit for Penang is

$$(P_P - ATC_P) \times Q_P = (\$40 - \$20) \times 20 = \$400$$

Grenada's profit is greater in the Stackelberg competition, whereas the profit for Penang is smaller in the Stackelberg competition. Therefore, the first-mover is better off.

25.

	Collusive Monopoly	Cournot Oligopoly	Bertrand Oligopoly	Stackelberg Oligopoly (A is first-mover)
A's Quantity	23.75	31.67	47.50	47.50
B's Quantity	23.75	31.67	47.50	23.75
Industry Quantity	47.50	63.33	95	71.25
Price	$52.50	$36.67	$5	$28.75
A's Profit	$1,128.13	$1,002.70	$0	$1,128.13
B's Profit	$1,128.13	$1,002.70	$0	$564.06
Industry Profit	$2,256.25	$2,005.40	$0	$1,692.19

The Collusive Monopoly Case

Firms produce exactly the same output and sell it at the price where $MC = MR$, that is,

$$MR = 100 - 2Q = 5 = MC$$
$$Q = 47.50$$

Thus, each firm produces 23.75 units of output. The monopolistic price is

$$P = 100 - Q = \$52.50$$

Both Firm A and Firm B generate the same profit, which is equal to

$$(P - ATC) \times Q = (\$52.50 - \$5) \times 23.75 = \$1,128.13$$

The profit for the industry is $2,256.25.

The Cournot Oligopoly Case

The inverse demand function is

$$P = 100 - q_A - q_B$$

The residual marginal revenue for Firm $i = \{A, B\}$ is

$$MR = 100 - 2q_A - q_B$$

Therefore, the reaction function for Firm i is

$$100 - 2q_A - q_B = 5$$
$$q_A = 47.5 - 0.5q_B$$

Therefore, the output produced by Firm A and Firm B is

$$q_1 = 47.5 - 0.5q_2 = 47.5 - 0.5(47.5 - 0.5q_1) = 23.75 + 0.25q_1$$
$$q_A = 31.67 = q_B$$

The output for the industry is 63.33. The price is

$$P = 100 - q_A - q_B = \$36.67$$

Both firms earn the same profit, which is equal to

$$(P - ATC) \times Q = (\$36.67 - \$5) \times 31.67 = \$1,002.70$$

Hence, the profit for the industry is

$$\$1,002.70 \times 2 = \$2,005.40$$

The Bertrand Oligopoly Case

Both firms will sell the product at the marginal cost of $5 and each will produce exactly the same quantity, that is,

$$5 = 100 - 2q_i$$
$$q_i = 47.50$$

Since firms sell output at the marginal cost, each firm's profit is $0; thus, the industry profit is also equal to $0.

The Stackelberg Oligopoly Case

The reaction function for Firm B is

$$100 - q_A - 2q_B = 5$$
$$q_B = 47.5 - 0.5q_A$$

Assuming that Firm A is the first-mover, the inverse demand function faced by Firm A is

$$P = 100 - q_A - q_B = 100 - q_A - 47.5 + 0.5q_A = 52.5 - 0.5q_A$$

Equating the marginal revenue with marginal cost, the quantity produced by Firm A is

$$MR = 52.5 - q_A = 5$$
$$q_A = 47.50$$

Thus, Firm B produces

$$q_B = 47.5 - 0.5q_A = 47.5 - 0.5 \times 47.5 = 23.75$$

The industry quantity is 71.25. The price is

$$P = 100 - q_A - q_B = \$28.75$$

Firm A generates a profit of

$$(P_A - ATC_A) \times Q_A = (\$28.75 - \$5) \times 47.50 = \$1,128.13$$

Firm B generates a profit of

$$(P_B - ATC_B) \times Q_B = (\$28.75 - \$5) \times 23.75 = \$564.06$$

Thus, the industry's profit is $1,692.19.

CHAPTER 12

1. a. The players are Duvall and Earl.
   b. Duvall's strategies are "Stop," "Drop," and "Roll."
   c. If Earl plays "Hammer" and Duvall plays "Roll," Earl's payoff is 5.
   d. If Earl plays "Stirrup" and Duval plays "Drop," Duvall's payoff is 3.

9. a. The sum should equal

$$500 + d \times 500 + d^2 \times 500 + \ldots$$

   b. The sum should equal

$$700 + d \times 400 + d^2 \times 400 + \ldots$$

   c. If $d = 0.5$, the sum from part (a) is equal to

$$500 + d \times 500 + d^2 \times 500 + \ldots = 500 + \left(\frac{500d}{1-d}\right)$$
$$= \left(\frac{500}{1-d}\right) = \$1,000$$

   If you decided to cheat, you would get

$$700 + d \times 400 + d^2 \times 400 + \ldots = 700 + \left(\frac{400d}{1-d}\right)$$
$$= 700 + 400 = \$1,100$$

   Thus, when $d = 0.5$, you should cheat. If $d = 0.99$, plugging 0.99 into the calculations above, we see that abiding gives us a payout of $50,000; cheating yields a payout of $40,300. Therefore, you should abide. If $d = 0.01$, abiding gives a payout of $505.05; cheating yields a payout of $704.04. You should cheat.

   d. Setting both sums from parts (a) and (b) equal to each other, we get

$$500 + d \times 500 + d^2 \times 500 + \ldots = 700 + d \times 400 + d^2$$
$$\times 400 + \ldots$$
$$\left(\frac{500}{1-d}\right) = 700 + \left(\frac{400d}{1-d}\right)$$
$$500 = 700(1-d) + 400d$$
$$d = \frac{2}{3}$$

   At $d = \frac{2}{3}$, you are indifferent between cheating or abiding by the agreement.

14. a.

   b. The equilibrium outcome for this game is (2, 2) or (Cut Evenly, Equal Slice), so Thing 1 and Thing 2 take equal slices. The reason is that in the case of an uneven split, the second-mover will always choose the larger piece. Thus, the first-mover knows that she will end up with a smaller piece if she doesn't cut evenly. Therefore, her best move is to cut the cake evenly.
   c. Given the discussion in (b), the equilibrium outcome of this game will always be for the cutter to cut even slices, no matter who is the first-mover. Therefore, there is no first-mover advantage here.

CHAPTER 13

2. If a firm can increase profit by expanding output, then the benefit from hiring another worker (marginal revenue product) exceeds the cost of hiring another worker (the wage rate). Also, since the marginal product of labor typically declines as more workers are hired, it will be larger at low levels of output. If the marginal revenue product of labor is equal to the wage at the profit-maximizing point, then it will be above the wage at output levels below that point. This relationship is true regardless of whether the firm has market power. It stems from the assumption of diminishing marginal product of labor.

5. a. $MRP_L = \left[\frac{(25-l)}{25}\right] \times 10$

   b. Firms will not want to hire any workers at all when the wage is higher than the MRP_L of the first worker; that is, when the wage is higher than $9.60 per hour.
   c. The firm would not want to hire workers to the point where marginal product is negative. At 25 workers, marginal product is zero. So 25 workers would be the maximum they would allow on the job, even if painters worked for free.
   d. Zero. There is no quantity of labor at which marginal product would be 50 square feet, which is what it would have to be in order to pay a wage of $20.
   e. With this innovation, the marginal revenue product of labor would become $[(35 - l)/25] \times 10$. At any given wage rate, the quantity of labor hired would be greater than before.

14. a. The inverse demand is:

$$P = 60 - 0.01Q$$

   Solve for Q to find the demand equation for each individual baker:

$$0.01Q = 60 - P$$
$$Q = 6,000 - 100P$$

Multiply by 1,000 to find the demand for the market as a whole:

$$Q^D = 6,000,000 - 100,000P$$

b. The market price can be found by setting quantity supplied equal to quantity demanded:

$$150,000P = 6,000,000 - 100,000P$$

$$250,000P = 6,000,000$$

$$P = 24$$

c. Use the individual demand from part (a) to find the amount of flour each baker will buy at a price of $24:

$$Q = 6,000 - 100(24) = 3,600 \text{ units of flour}$$

d. According to the market demand from part (a), the market quantity will be:

$$Q^D = 6,000,000 - 100,000(24) = 3,600,000$$

This number is consistent with each of the 1,000 bakers buying 3,600 units each:

$$3,600 \times 1,000 = 3,600,000$$

e. The inverse demand is the marginal revenue product of labor:

$$P = 60 - 0.02Q$$

Convert this to a demand equation by solving for Q:

$$0.02Q = 60 - P$$

$$Q = 3,000 - 50P$$

This is the demand for each individual baker. To find the demand for the market as a whole, multiply by 1,000:

$$Q^D = 3,000,000 - 50,000P$$

The market price can be found by setting quantity supplied equal to quantity demanded:

$$150,000P = 3,000,000 - 50,000P$$

$$200,000P = 3,000,000$$

$$P = 15$$

The market quantity will be 3,000,000 − 50,000(15) = 2,250,000.
Each of the 1,000 bakers will purchase 3,000 − 50(15) = 2,250 units of flour.

19. a. Begin with the demand function, and solve for W:

$$l = 200 - 5W$$

$$5W = 200 - l$$

$$W = 40 - 0.2l$$

Then, set the wage equal to marginal cost:

$$40 - 0.2L = 0.5l$$

$$40 = 0.7l$$

$$l \approx 57$$

Fifty-seven ATM fillers would be employed in a competitive market.

b. $W = 40 - 0.2(57) = 28.60$

c. Using the rule that the marginal revenue curve has twice the slope of the labor demand curve if the latter is linear, we find:

$$MR = 40 - 0.4l$$

d. If $MR = MC$, then:

$$40 - 0.4L = 0.5l$$

$$40 = 0.9l$$

$$l \approx 44$$

$$W = 40 - 0.2(44) = 40 - 8.8 = 31.20$$

Forty-four workers would be hired at a wage of $31.20.

e. Use the wage in the supply (marginal cost) equation to find the number of workers willing to work at a wage of $31.20:

$$MC = 0.5l = W$$

$$l = 2W$$

$$l = 2(31.20) \approx 62$$

Sixty-two workers would be willing to work at this wage, but only 44 will be employed. The unemployment rate is:

$$\frac{(62 - 44)}{62} = \frac{18}{62} = 29\%$$

21. This is a case of bilateral monopoly. International Well Control may be the only firm Texas is willing to use, giving the firm a measure of monopoly power. Also, the State of Texas has some measure of monopsony power because it is one of a handful of government entities needing to purchase this service. Consequently, negotiating skills and bargaining power play a significant role in determining the amount Texas will pay.

CHAPTER 14

4. a. The value of the publisher's future payments is

$$\frac{\$100,000}{1.05} + \frac{\$100,000}{1.05^2} = \$185,941$$

b. Considering the second offer, the value becomes

$$\frac{\$80,000}{1.05} + \frac{\$125,000}{1.05^2} \approx \$189,569$$

Hence, this is a better deal than the original one, as $189,569 > $185,941. The net present value of the loss in payments of the first year (20,000/1.05) is more than compensated for by the net present value increase in payments offered in the second year (25,000/1.05^2).

10. a. The net present value of Marian's investment is

$$-\$30,000 + \frac{\$8,000}{1+0.10} + \cdots + \frac{\$8,000}{(1+0.10)^5} = -\$30,000$$
$$+ \$30,326.29 = \$326.29$$

b. The net present value of Marian's investment is $326.29.
   Therefore, Marian should change careers.

c. The present value of Marian's earnings as a tow truck driver is

$$\frac{\$40,000}{1+0.10} + \cdots + \frac{\$40,000}{(1+0.10)^5} = \$151,631.47$$

The present value of Marian's earnings as a florist is

$$\frac{\$48,000}{1+0.10} + \cdots + \frac{\$48,000}{(1+0.10)^5} = \$181,957.76$$

The difference of $181,957.76 − $151,631.47 = $30,326.29 is large enough to justify spending the $30,000.

d. The methods used in parts (a) and (c) give precisely the same answer, $326.29:

$$\frac{\$48,000}{1+0.10} + \cdots + \frac{\$48,000}{(1+0.10)^5} - \frac{\$40,000}{1+0.10} + \cdots + \frac{\$40,000}{(1+0.10)^5} - \$30,000$$

$$= -\$30,000 + \frac{\$8,000}{1+0.10} + \cdots + \frac{\$8,000}{(1+0.10)^5} = \$326.29$$

17. a. The NPV is

$$-\$200,000 + 0.80 \times \frac{\$700,000}{(1+0.10)} + 0.20 \times \frac{\$0}{(1+0.10)}$$

$$= \$200,000 + \frac{\$560,000}{(1.10)} = \$309.090.91$$

b. The net present value today of opening the playground in one year is

$$\frac{-\$200,000}{1.10} + \frac{\$700,000}{(1+0.10)^2} = \$396,694.21$$

c. The NPV in part (b) is greater than the NPV in (a). Therefore, you should wait until the zoning commission reaches its decision.

18. a. Steve's expected income is

$$\$900 - 0.50 \times \$500 = \$650$$

His expected utility can be found as follows. Half the time, he will receive 900$^{0.5}$, or 30. The other half of the time, he will receive 400$^{0.5}$, or 20:

$$U = 0.5 \times 30 + 0.5 \times 20 = 25$$

b. A salary of $625 would provide Steve with the same utility he expected to receive as a traveling salesman because 625^{0.5}$ = 25.

c. Steve gets exactly the same utility from a risk-free $625 a week as he does from a risky job where his earnings average $650. Given that he is expected to pay, on average, $250 to the traffic court each week anyway, he would be willing to pay an extra $25 in weekly earnings to avoid the uncertainty (since $900 − $250 = $650). Therefore, he should be willing to pay up to $275 for speeding ticket insurance.

d. The insurance company would break even if the insurer charges Steve $250 each week. If the insurer can charge him the $275 he is willing to pay, it will earn a $25 profit.

CHAPTER 15

2. a. The price and quantity of yellow corn increase.

b. The supply of white corn decreases because farmers shift some of their production from white corn to yellow corn.

c. The market price of white corn increases.

d. As a result of the increase in the price of white corn, the supply of yellow corn decreases as the farmers now shift some of their production back toward white corn. The price of yellow corn increases and the quantity decreases.

e. The increase in the price of white corn tends to push yellow corn prices further away from its initial value (as both shifts, the increase in demand and the decrease in the supply of yellow corn, push prices upward, whereas the quantity is pushed back toward its initial value).

3. a. Wine and cheese are linked on the demand side of the market.

b. $$Q_c^d = 30 - P_c - P_w = P_c = Q_c^s$$
   $$P_c = 15 - 0.5P_w$$

c. $$Q_w^d = 30 - P_c - P_w = P_w = Q_w^s$$
   $$P_w = 15 - 0.5P_c$$

d. $$P_c = 15 - 0.5P_w = 15 - 0.5(15 - 0.5P_c) = 7.5 + 0.25P_c$$
   $$0.75P_c = 7.5$$
   $$P_c = \$10$$

e. $$P_w = 15 - 0.5P_c = 15 - 0.5 \times 10 = \$10$$

f. $$Q_w = 30 - P_c - P_w = 30 - 10 - 10 = 10$$
   $$Q_c = 30 - P_c - P_w = 30 - 10 - 10 = 10$$

CHAPTER 16

3. a. If there is perfect information, 100 high-quality cars and 100 low-quality cars will be sold.
   b. If the quality of the car is not known to the buyer, the expected value of a used car to a buyer is

$$\$12,000 \times \frac{1}{2} + \$8,000 \times \frac{1}{2} = \$10,000$$

   No high-quality cars will be offered for sale at that price as it is below the minimum acceptable price of $11,000.
   c. No high-quality cars will be offered for sale, and the equilibrium price will range between $5,000 and $8,000, depending on the negotiation skills of buyers and sellers of low-quality cars.
   d. If there is perfect information, the answer to part (a) does not change. Similarly, the market price for a used car will remain the same, $10,000, as buyers' valuation has not changed. Given the reservation price of $9,500 of the high-quality sellers, 100 high-quality cars will be offered for sale as the price for a car exceeds the reservation price of high-quality car sellers. Moreover, 100 low-quality cars are also offered for sale at $10,000. All in all, the equilibrium price will be $10,000 and the proportion of high-quality cars to all cars will be $\frac{1}{2}$.

6. a. The expected surgery cost for any given sky-diver is $0.75 \times \$4,000$, or $3,000. The expected surgery cost for any given groundhugger is $0.25 \times \$4,000$, or $1,000. Since there are equal numbers of skydivers and groundhuggers in the population, the insurer expects to pay out $0.5 \times \$3,000 + 0.5 \times \$1,000$, or $2,000. So, to cover those costs, the insurer needs to charge a premium of $2,000.
   b. Each skydiver expects $3,000 of injuries each year, but is charged only $2,000 to insure against those injuries: As it turns out, insurance is a great deal! Each groundhugger expects only $1,000 of injuries each year, but gets charged $2,000 to protect against them: For that person, insurance is a lousy deal!
   c. Groundhuggers will likely decide to simply pay their injury costs out-of-pocket rather than pay twice as much for insurance. The pool of the insured will only contain skydivers; the premium for an injury policy will eventually be $3,000.
   d. One obvious answer is that it is easy for insurers to test individuals to determine whether they are smokers or not; that allows insurers to charge high rates to smokers and low rates to nonsmokers. There is no such test for skydivers; in this

problem, everyone was grouped together, which caused the market to unravel. Beyond that, in the real world, many nonsmokers remain in the pool of the insured due to group insurance coverage provided through their employer—in other words, the insured receive insurance as part of their compensation, rather than having to pay their premiums out of their own pocket.

12. a.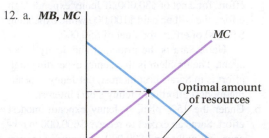
    b. There is a shift-in of the marginal benefit curve (to the left), which leads to a smaller optimal quantity of actions for self-improvement.

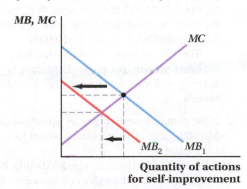

   c. Yes, it is consistent with the illustration. The quantity of actions for self-improvement decreased.
   d. It is a moral hazard problem, as Harry's behavior is likely to change with the change in incentives.
   e. The marginal benefit curve is a horizontal line with an optimal amount of actions for self-improvement at 0.

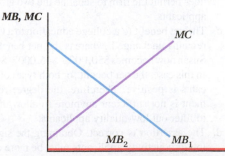

16. a. If Jenny expends modest effort, Sara can expect to receive $600,000 in revenue, but will spend $100,000 on Jenny's services, for a net of $500,000. If Jenny expends high effort, Sara can expect to receive $1 million in revenue, but will spend $100,000 on Jenny's services, for a net of $900,000.

   If Jenny expends modest effort, she will be paid $100,000 while expending $20,000 of effort, for a net of $80,000. If Jenny expends high effort, she will be paid $100,000 while expending $50,000 of effort, for a net of $50,000.

   Here, Sara is the principal and Jenny is her agent. The problem is that Jenny expending high effort is in Sara's best interest, but Jenny expending modest effort is in Jenny's best interest.

   b. Under the 15% plan, if Jenny expends modest effort, Sara can expect to receive $600,000 in revenue, but will spend $90,000 on Jenny's services, for a net of $510,000. If Jenny expends high effort, Sara can expect to receive $1 million in revenue, but will spend $150,000 on Jenny's services, for a net of $850,000.

   If Jenny expends modest effort, she will be paid $90,000 while expending $20,000 of effort, for a net of $70,000. If Jenny expends high effort, she will be paid $150,000 while expending $50,000 of effort, for a net of $100,000.

   The 15% payment scheme makes the principal agent problem disappear: Expending high is not only in Sara's best interest, but it is also in Jenny's.

21. a. If the company were to pay an average wage of $45,000, most of its applicants would look like Lazy Susan.

   b. The market is willing to pay $70,000 to those who signal ability through a college degree. Otherwise, the pay offered will be $20,000 now that this requirement is in place. Thus, the net benefit of obtaining a degree is the $50,000 difference minus the cost of a degree. For Charlie Hustle, this difference is +$10,000 ($50K minus $40K). For Lazy Susan, the net benefit is −$10,000 ($50K minus $60K). Therefore, the degree requirement does permit the firm to separate the two groups of applicants.

   c. The net benefit to a college education to a Charlie remains unchanged, whereas the net benefit to a Susan now becomes $50,000 − $46,000 = $4,000. In this case, the net benefit for both types of applicants is positive. Therefore, the degree requirement is not sufficient anymore to allow the firm to filter out low-quality applicants.

   d. The assertion is correct. Obtaining the signal to low-productivity applicants must be more costly; otherwise, the filtering will not be possible.

e. Grade inflation is definitely a bad practice for students as it bridges the qualitative differences among students in a way that makes it almost impossible to differentiate the level and potential of students. A B or a B+ student who is pushed in the A range prevents the appropriate sorting and inhibits the efficient functioning of merit. This is bad for high-quality students who would like to distinguish themselves. It also is bad for both types of students because this signal then becomes an "arms race" (as explained in the chapter) of who will be able to (get into and) graduate from the most prestigious (most expensive) institutions of higher learning.

22. a. The signal is costly to both types of birds because it represents an expense in terms of being slower in flight and thus susceptible to predators. However, it is even more expensive to a weak bird given that he is already more likely to fall victim to a predator's attack.

   b. If the same signal could be achieved at a lower cost (represented by the lower danger of being caught by predators when the tails are half as long), then any growing of tails longer than that is just a waste of resources from society's point of view.

   c. Such agreement is unlikely to last as peacocks have an incentive to cheat and grow their tails in order to signal greater attractiveness to peahens. Therefore, the scheme would break apart, which would result in peacocks growing their tails long. Such a signal would be costly as peacocks would be slower in flight and more susceptible to predators.

CHAPTER 17

1. a. The market price is $5, where marginal benefit equals marginal cost.

   b. The external cost is $1 regardless of the number of racks roasted.

   c. The intersection of the marginal benefit curve (demand) and the marginal cost curve determines the number of racks. Thus, 100 racks will be roasted. Animal lovers will suffer damage of $1 for each rack, for a total damage of $100.

   d. Incorporating the external costs would lead the pit master to produce 80 racks.

   e. The total damage suffered by animal lovers will be $80. Some of the damage is eliminated, but not all.

   f. Cutting the level of output further would hurt the pit master, who would be foregoing profits. Such a cut is not Pareto-optimal, because although the output cut would reduce damage to the animal lovers by \$1 per rack roasted, below 80 units any output cut will cost the pit master more than \$1 in lost profit.

4. a. The equilibrium price is P_1 and quantity is Q_1.

	External Marginal Costs Not Considered	External Marginal Costs Considered
Consumer Surplus	$A+B+D+F$	
Producer Surplus	$C+E+G$	
External Damage (–)	$D+E+F+G+H$	
Total net value to society	$A+B+C-H$	

b. The new quantity is Q_2 and price is P_2.

	External Marginal Costs Not Considered	External Marginal Costs Considered
Consumer Surplus	$A+B+D+F$	A
Producer Surplus	$C+E+G$	$B+C+D+E$
External Damage (–)	$D+E+F+G+H$	$D+E$
Total net value to society	$A+B+C-H$	$A+B+C$

c. As indicated in the table above, when external costs are ignored by producers, total net value is lower by area H. Thus, H is the deadweight loss.

9. a. The SMC is $MC + EMC = 0.45Q + 0.05Q = 0.5Q$. The efficient output level can be found where $MB = SMC$:

$$50 - 0.5Q = 0.5Q$$
$$Q* = 50$$

Thus, the government should set the quota at 50 units. The price that prevails in the marketplace once this quota is in place is

$$P = 50 - 0.5Q* = 50 - 0.5 \times 50 = \$25$$

b. At the efficient level of production, $Q* = 50$, the external damage can be calculated as $0.05Q$, or \$2.50. If government imposes a \$2.50 tax on producers, their private marginal costs will be given as

$$MC = 0.45Q + 2.50$$

Producers will find the profit-maximizing level of output where $MB = MC$, or where

$$50 - 0.5Q = 0.45Q + 2.50$$

Solving, we get 50 units for Q, the profit-maximizing level of output. The prevailing market price can be found by substituting $Q = 50$ into the MB curve:

$$P = 50 - 0.5(50) = \$25$$

Buyers will pay \$25. Sellers will receive that amount less the tax, or \$22.50.

12. a. Without any government intervention, the quantity of bread produced is

$$P = 10 - 0.1Q = 2 + 0.1Q = MC$$
$$0.2Q = 8$$
$$Q = 40$$

b. Ideally, society would like producers to consider all the benefits their activity creates, both internal and external. Thus, the total social benefit is given as

$$SD = P + EMB = 10 - 0.1Q + 2 - 0.02Q = 12 - 0.12Q$$

So, the magnitude of a price-based intervention is

$$12 - 0.12Q = 2 + 0.1Q = MC$$
$$0.22Q = 10$$
$$Q \approx 45.45$$

Producers are under producing relative to the welfare-maximizing quantity of 45.45. The government can use a price-based intervention to encourage them to produce more. In this case, the appropriate intervention is to subsidize production. At the ideal quantity, bread baking creates an external marginal benefit of

$$EMB = 2 - 0.02(45.45) = \$1.09$$

If the government offers producers a subsidy of \$1.09 per loaf, producers' marginal cost becomes

$$MC = 2 + 0.1Q - 1.09$$

Equating MC and MB yields

$$2 + 0.1Q - 1.09 = 10 - 0.1Q$$
$$Q = 45.45$$

A subsidy of \$1.09 encourages producers to produce the socially optimal amount.

16. a. No. Rehearsing on the deck brings Al \$500 of benefits, but costs Marcy \$600 in lost sleep. Society loses \$100 of welfare as a result of Al's rehearsals.

b. If rehearsals are illegal, Marcy can simply call the police to put an end to Al's rehearsals. No rehearsals will take place.

c. i. Marcy is willing to pay Al up to \$600 per year to rehearse elsewhere.

ii. The minimum amount of money that Al is willing to accept is $500.

iii. Let us assume that Marcy pays Al $550 for silence. Al is better off taking the offer, as he gains $50 (= $550 − $500) and Marcy is better off paying him as $600 − $550 = $50.

d. The outcome does not depend on the law. When rehearsing is illegal, Marcy calls the police. When rehearsing is legal, Marcy pays Al to rehearse elsewhere. No matter what the law states, society gets the same efficient outcome.

e. It will be more difficult for the neighbors to organize and to gather the amount that would compensate Al for the rent. Neighbors will try to avoid chipping in and free-ride. Thus, even though it is not efficient for Al to rehearse on his back deck, that may be the outcome for society.

18. a.

Number of cows	2	3	4
Total gallons of milk each year	2,000	2,250	1,600

The efficient number of cows is 3.

b. If Ben keeps 1 cow, that cow will produce 1,000 gallons of milk and Ben will earn $1,000. If Ben keeps 2 cows, each will produce 750 gallons of milk and Ben will earn $1,500. Ben will keep 2 cows.

c. If Ben keeps 1 cow, that cow will produce 750 gallons of milk and Ben will earn $750. If Ben keeps 2 cows, each will produce 400 gallons of milk and Ben will earn $800. Ben will keep 2 cows.

d. Following similar reasoning, Jerry's best choice is to keep 2 cows regardless of how many cows Ben grazes. So, both Ben and Jerry will keep 2 cows on the pasture. Relative to what is socially ideal (3 cows), Ben and Jerry keep too many cows and the pasture is overgrazed.

e. It could be useful to restrict the number of cattle grazed on some specific area or to charge a tax for grazing. An alternative would be to sell the pasture to Ben or Jerry, who will then have a private incentive to graze the socially ideal number of cows.

CHAPTER 18

4. This behavioral bias is known as the hyperbolic discounting bias. People place relatively more importance on current time periods rather than future periods when making economic decisions; that is, people choose to consume more today than save for retirement.

6. a. The site stickk.com helps individuals to overcome the hyperbolic discounting problem that leads to time inconsistency. Having specified their goals, individuals have an incentive to consistently achieve them in order to avoid incurring the penalty.

b. If we assume that individuals are altruistic or generous, or exhibit warm glow, failing to meet their goals does not cost them as much since the fee is donated to an organization they hold in high regard. It is, therefore, more likely that individuals will "stick" to their commitment if they identify a charity they despise, since they will be more inclined to work hard to avoid the cost (ill-feeling) of having to contribute to it.

8. a. Both Option A and Option B should motivate them equally—in either case, a student with a perfect paper who correctly recalls the formula will receive a score of 103; a student with a perfect paper who cannot recall the formula will only receive a score of 100.

b. Option B will more strongly motivate students—they will be more motivated to avoid losing the points that have already been given to them (in Option B) than they will to gain those same points in Option A.

c. By framing the extra credit as a potential loss of an endowment rather than a potential gain, Alan can better motivate his students.

Glossary

accounting cost The direct costs of operating a business, including costs for raw materials, wages paid to workers, rent paid for office or retail space, and the like. (p. 224)

accounting profit A firm's total revenue minus its accounting cost. (p. 224)

actuarially fair Description of an insurance policy with expected net payments equal to zero. (p. 514)

adverse selection A situation where there are stronger incentives for "bad" types of a product to be involved in a transaction than "good" types of the product. (p. 565)

anchoring A type of framing bias in which a person's decision is influenced by the specific pieces of information given. (p. 636)

antitrust law Laws designed to promote competitive markets by restricting firms from behaviors that limit competition. (p. 325)

arbitrage The practice of reselling a product at a price higher than its original selling price. (p. 340)

asymmetric information A situation where there is an imbalance of information across participants in an economic transaction. (p. 563)

average fixed cost (AFC) A firm's fixed cost per unit of output. (p. 234)

average product The total quantity of output divided by the number of units of input used to produce it. (p. 187)

average total cost (ATC) A firm's total cost per unit of output. (p. 234)

average variable cost (AVC) A firm's per-unit variable cost of production. (p. 234)

backward induction The process of solving a multistep game by first solving the last step and then working backward. (p. 434)

bad A good or service that provides a consumer with negative utility. (p. 108)

barriers to entry Factors that keep entrants out of a market despite the existence of a large producer surplus. (p. 298)

behavioral economics Branch of economics that incorporates insights from human psychology into models of economic behavior. (p. 632)

Bertrand competition Oligopoly model in which each firm chooses the price of its product. (p. 388)

bilateral monopoly The market structure that exists when there is major concentration of market power on both sides of a market. (p. 486)

block pricing The practice of reducing the price of a good when the customer buys more of it. (p. 367)

budget constraint A curve that describes the entire set of consumption bundles a consumer can purchase when spending all income. (p. 110)

bundling A pricing strategy in which the firm sells two or more products together at a single price. (p. 362)

cartel The organization formed when firms collude. (p. 382)

certainty equivalent The guaranteed income level at which an individual would receive the same expected utility level as from an uncertain income. (p. 513)

change in demand A shift of the entire demand curve caused by a change in a determinant of demand other than the good's own price. (p. 17)

change in quantity demanded A movement *along* the demand curve that occurs as a result of a change in the good's price. (p. 17)

change in quantity supplied A movement *along* the supply curve that occurs as a result of a change in the good's price. (p. 19)

change in supply A shift of the entire supply curve caused by a change in a determinant of supply other than the good's own price. (p. 19)

choke wage The wage at which a firm won't want to hire any labor. (p. 463)

club goods Nonrival and excludable goods. (p. 619)

Coase theorem States that if negotiation costs are low enough, negotiation among market participants will lead to the efficient market outcome regardless of who holds the property rights. (p. 614)

collusion Economic behavior in which all the firms in an oligopoly coordinate their production and pricing decisions to collectively act as a monopoly to gain monopoly profits to be split among themselves. (p. 382)

commodities Goods traded in markets where consumers view different varieties of the good as essentially interchangeable. (p. 13)

common resource A special class of economic good that is rival but nonexcludable, whose value to the individual consumer decreases as others use it, and that all individuals can access freely. (p. 618)

complement A good that is purchased and used in combination with another good. (pp. 14, 163)

complete information A situation where all market participants know everything important for making economic decisions. (p. 563)

complete insurance or **full insurance** An insurance policy that leaves the insured individual equally well off regardless of the outcome. (p. 514)

compounding or **compound interest** When interest paid in one period is added to the principal, and the interest rate in the next period is applied to the sum. (p. 494)

constant economies of scale Total cost rises at the same rate as output rises. (p. 245)

constant returns to scale A production function for which changing the amount of capital and labor by some multiple changes the quantity of output by exactly the same multiple. (p. 200)

constant-cost industry An industry whose firms' total costs do not change with total industry output. (p. 287)

consumer surplus The difference between the price consumers would be willing to pay for a good (as measured by the height of their demand curves) and the price they actually have to pay. (p. 51)

consumption bundle A set of goods or services a consumer considers purchasing. (p. 92)

consumption contract curve Curve that shows all possible Pareto-efficient allocations of goods across consumers. (p. 543)

corner solution A utility-maximizing bundle located at the "corner" of the budget constraint where the consumer purchases only one of two goods. (p. 123)

cost curve The mathematical relationship between a firm's production costs and its output. (p. 231)

cost minimization A firm's goal of producing a specific quantity of output at minimum cost. (p. 189)

Cournot competition Oligopoly model in which each firm chooses its production quantity. (p. 391)

credible commitment A choice (or a restriction of choices) that guarantees a player will take a particular future action if certain conditions occur that transform the game. (p. 447)

cross-price elasticity of demand The ratio of the percentage change in one good's quantity demanded (say, good X) to the percentage change in the price of another good Y. (p. 44)

deadweight loss (DWL) The difference between the maximum total surplus that consumers and producers could gain from a market and the combined gains they actually reap after a price regulation. (p. 62)

decreasing returns to scale A production function for which adjusting all inputs by the same multiple changes output by *less* than that multiple. (p. 201)

decreasing-cost industry An industry whose firms' cost levels decrease with increases in industry output. (p. 287)

demand choke price The price at which quantity demanded is zero; the vertical intercept of the inverse demand curve. (p. 16)

demand curve The relationship between the quantity of a good that consumers demand and the good's price, holding all other factors constant. (p. 15)

demand The combined amount of a good that all consumers in a market are willing to buy. (p. 12)

derived demand A demand for one product (such as labor) that arises from the demand for another product (a firm's output). (p. 465)

differentiated product market A market in which multiple varieties of a common product type are available. (p. 402)

diminishing marginal product The reduction in the incremental output obtained from adding more and more labor. (p. 185)

direct price discrimination A pricing strategy in which firms charge different prices to different customers based on observable characteristics of the customers. (p. 341)

diseconomies of scale Total cost rises at a faster rate than output rises. (p. 245)

diseconomies of scope The simultaneous production of multiple products comes at a higher cost than if a firm made each product separately. (p. 248)

diversification A strategy to reduce risk by combining uncertain outcomes. (p. 514)

dominant strategy A winning strategy for a player, regardless of her opponents' strategies. (p. 421)

dominated strategy A losing strategy for a player, regardless of her opponents' strategies. (p. 421)

durable good A good that has a long service life. (p. 206)

econometrics Field that develops and uses mathematical and statistical techniques to test economic theory. (p. 642)

economic cost The sum of a producer's accounting and opportunity costs. (p. 224)

economic profit A firm's total revenue minus its economic cost. (p. 224)

economic rent Returns to specialized inputs above what firms paid for them. (p. 288)

economies of scale Total cost rises at a slower rate than output rises. (p. 245)

economies of scope The simultaneous production of multiple products comes at a lower cost than if a firm made each product separately and then added up the costs. (p. 247)

Edgeworth box Graph of an economy with two economic actors and two goods that is used to analyze market efficiency. (p. 539)

efficient level of pollution The level of emissions necessary to produce the efficient quantity of the good tied to the externality. (p. 602)

egalitarian The belief that the ideal society is one in which each individual is equally well off. (p. 536)

elastic A price elasticity with an absolute value greater than 1. (p. 39)

elasticity The ratio of the percentage change in one value to the percentage change in another. (p. 35)

empirical Using data analysis and experiments to explore phenomena. (p. 8)

endowment effect The phenomenon whereby simply possessing a good makes it more valuable; that is, the possessor must be paid more to give up the good than she would have paid to buy it in the first place. (p. 635)

Engel curve A curve that shows the relationship between the quantity of a good consumed and a consumer's income. (p. 143)

equilibrium price The only price at which quantity supplied equals quantity demanded. (p. 20)

excess demand The difference between the quantity demanded and the quantity supplied at a price ceiling. (p. 60)

excess supply The difference between the quantity supplied and the quantity demanded at a price floor. (p. 66)

exchange efficiency A Pareto-efficient allocation of a set of goods across consumers. (p. 538)

expansion path A curve that illustrates how the optimal mix of inputs varies with total output. (p. 208)

expected value The probability-weighted average payout. (p. 507)

experimental economics Branch of economics that relies on experiments to illuminate economic behavior. (p. 642)

extensive form or **decision tree** Representation of a sequential game that shows both the choice and timing of players' actions. (p. 439)

external marginal benefit The benefit conferred on a third party when an additional unit of a good is produced or consumed. (p. 596)

external marginal cost The cost imposed on a third party when an additional unit of a good is produced or consumed. (p. 596)

externality A cost or benefit that affects a third party not directly involved in an economic transaction. (p. 596)

factor markets Markets for inputs such as labor, intermediate goods, and land (called factors of production) that are used to produce outputs. (p. 461)

feasible bundle Any combination of goods on or below the budget constraint that the consumer has the income to purchase. (p. 111)

field experiment A research method that uses randomizations, just as in the lab, but does so in real-world settings. (p. 645)

final good A good that is bought by a consumer. (p. 181)

First Welfare Theorem Theorem stating that perfectly competitive markets in general equilibrium distribute resources in a Pareto-efficient way. (p. 553)

first-mover advantage The advantage gained in a Stackelberg competition by the initial firm in setting its production quantity. (p. 399)

fixed cost (FC) An input cost that does not vary with the amount of output, even if it is zero. (pp. 202, 225)

fixed inputs Inputs that cannot be changed in the short run. (p. 182)

free entry The ability of a firm to enter an industry without encountering legal or technical barriers. (p. 279)

free exit The ability of a firm to exit an industry without encountering legal or technical barriers. (p. 280)

free-rider problem A source of inefficiency resulting from individuals consuming a public good or service without paying for it. (p. 621)

game theory The study of strategic interactions among two or more economic actors. (p. 419)

general equilibrium analysis The study of market behavior that accounts for cross-market influences and is concerned with conditions present when all markets are simultaneously in equilibrium. (p. 523)

Giffen good A good for which a fall in price leads the consumer to want *less* of the good. (p. 160)

grim trigger or **grim reaper strategy** A strategy in which cooperative play ends permanently when one player cheats. (p. 437)

hyperbolic discounting The tendency of people to prefer immediate payoffs to later payoffs, even if the later payoff is much greater. (p. 634)

imperfect competition The industry structure between perfect competition and monopoly. (p. 379)

incentive compatibility The requirement under an indirect price-discrimination strategy that the price offered to each consumer group is chosen by that group. (p. 357)

income effect The change in a consumer's consumption choices that results from a change in the purchasing power of the consumer's income. (pp. 140, 151)

income elasticity of demand The ratio of the percentage change in quantity demanded to the corresponding percentage change in consumer income. (p. 44)

income elasticity The percentage change in the quantity consumed of a good in response to a given percentage change in income. (p. 141)

income expansion path A curve that connects a consumer's optimal bundles at each income level. (p. 143)

increasing returns to scale A production function for which changing all inputs by the same proportion changes output *more* than proportionately. (p. 201)

increasing-cost industry An industry whose firms' total costs increase with increases in industry output. (p. 287)

indifference curve The combination of all the different consumption bundles that provide a consumer with the same utility. (p. 96)

indifferent The special case in which a consumer derives the same level of utility from each of two or more consumption bundles. (p. 95)

indirect price discrimination (second-degree price discrimination) A pricing strategy in which customers pick among a variety of pricing choices offered by the firm. (p. 355)

inelastic A price elasticity with an absolute value less than 1. (p. 39)

infeasible bundle Any combination of goods above or to the right of the budget line that the consumer cannot afford to purchase. (p. 111)

inferior good A good for which quantity demanded decreases when income rises. (pp. 44, 141)

input efficiency A Pareto-efficient allocation of inputs across producers. (p. 539)

insurance A payment from one economic actor to another with the aim of reducing the risk facing the payer. (p. 493)

interest A periodic payment made by individuals or firms tied to an amount of assets borrowed or lent. (p. 494)

interest rate The amount of interest paid, expressed as a fraction of the principal. (p. 494)

interior solution A utility-maximizing bundle that contains positive quantities of both goods. (p. 123)

intermediate good A good that is used to produce another good. (p. 181)

intermediate good A product that is made specifically to be used as a factor input into the production of another good. (p. 476)

inverse demand curve A demand curve written in the form of price as a function of quantity demanded. (p. 16)

inverse supply curve A supply curve written in the form of price as a function of quantity supplied. (p. 19)

investment The purchase of capital in the present with the intent of reaping future benefits. (p. 493)

isocost line A curve that shows all the input combinations that yield the same cost. (p. 193)

isoquant A curve representing all the combinations of inputs that allow a firm to make a particular quantity of output. (p. 190)

lab experiment Test of an economic theory in a laboratory setting. (p. 643)

learning by doing The process by which a firm becomes more efficient at production as it produces more output. (p. 203)

lemons problem An asymmetric information problem that occurs when a seller knows more about the quality of the good he is selling than does the buyer. (p. 563)

Lerner index A measure of a firm's markup and of its market power. (p. 313)

long run In production economics, the amount of time necessary for all inputs into production to be fully adjustable. (p. 182)

long-run competitive equilibrium The point at which the market price is equal to the minimum average total cost and firms would gain no profits by entering the industry. (p. 280)

loss aversion A type of framing bias in which a consumer chooses a reference point around which losses hurt much more than gains feel good. (p. 636)

lump-sum transfer Transfer to or from an individual where the size of the transfer cannot be affected in any way by the individual's choices. (p. 555)

luxury good A good with an income elasticity greater than 1. (pp. 44, 142)

marginal abatement cost (MAC) The cost of reducing emissions by 1 unit. (p. 603)

marginal cost (MC) A firm's cost of producing one more unit of output. (p. 235)

marginal expenditure (ME) The incremental amount spent to buy one more unit of labor. (p. 478)

marginal product The additional output that a firm can produce by using an additional unit of an input (holding use of the other input constant). (p. 185)

marginal rate of substitution of X for Y The rate at which a consumer is willing to trade off one good (the good on the horizontal axis, X) for another (the good on the vertical axis, Y) and still be left equally well off. (p. 98)

marginal rate of technical substitution ($MRTS_{XY}$) The rate at which the firm can trade input X for input Y, holding output constant. (p. 190)

marginal rate of transformation (MRT) The tradeoff between the production of any goods on the market. (p. 550)

marginal revenue product of labor The marginal product of labor times the marginal revenue. (p. 462)

marginal revenue The additional revenue from selling one additional unit of output. (p. 261)

marginal utility The extra utility a consumer receives from a 1-unit increase in consumption. (p. 93)

market equilibrium The point where the demand and supply curves cross. (p. 20)

market power A firm's ability to influence the market price of its product. (p. 297)

market structure The competitive environment in which firms operate. (p. 257)

markup The percentage of the firm's price that is greater than (or "marked up" from) its marginal cost. (p. 313)

maximin strategy A strategy in which the player minimizes her exposure to loss. (p. 431)

mental accounting A type of framing bias that occurs when people divide their current and future assets into separate, nontransferable portions, instead of basing purchasing decisions on their assets as a whole. (p. 636)

microeconomics The branch of economics that studies the specific choices made by consumers and producers. (p. 1)

mixed bundling A type of bundling in which the firm simultaneously offers consumers the choice of buying two or more products separately or as a bundle. (p. 364)

mixed strategy A strategy in which the player randomizes her actions. (p. 429)

monopolist The sole supplier and price setter of a good on the market. (p. 297)

monopolistic competition A market structure characterized by many firms selling a differentiated product with no barriers to entry. (p. 408)

monopolistic competition A type of imperfect competition where a large number of firms have some market power, but each makes zero economic profit in the long run. (pp. 302, 379)

monopoly A market served by only one firm. (p. 297)

monopsony power When a buyer's choice of how much of a product to buy affects the market price of that product. (p. 478)

moral hazard A situation that arises when one party in an economic transaction cannot observe another party's behavior. (p. 574)

Nash equilibrium An equilibrium in which each firm is doing its best conditional on the actions taken by other firms. (p. 380)

natural experiment A randomization or near-randomization that arises by happenstance. (p. 644)

natural monopoly A market in which it is efficient for a single firm to produce the entire industry output. (p. 298)

necessity good A normal good for which income elasticity is between zero and 1. (p. 142)

negative externality A cost imposed on a third party not directly involved in an economic transaction. (p. 596)

net present value (NPV) analysis The use of the present discounted value to evaluate the expected long-term return on an investment. (p. 501)

network good A good whose value to each consumer increases with the number of other consumers of the product. (p. 299)

nominal interest rate Rate of return expressed in raw currency values without regard for how much purchasing power those values hold. (p. 506)

noncredible threat A threat made in a game that is not rational for the player to actually follow through on and, as such, is an empty threat. (p. 447)

nonexcludability A defining property of a public good which means that consumers cannot be prevented from consuming the good. (p. 618)

nonrival Defining property of a public good meaning one person's consumption of the good does not diminish another consumer's enjoyment of the same good. (p. 618)

normal form The common organization of an economic game into its players, strategies, and the payoffs in a payoff matrix. (p. 423)

normal good A good for which quantity demanded rises when income rises. (pp. 44, 140)

oligopoly A market structure characterized by competition among a small number of firms. (p. 379)

oligopoly Market structure characterized by competition among a small number of firms (p. 302)

operating cost The cost a firm incurs in producing its output. (p. 226)

operating revenue The money a firm earns from selling its output. (p. 226)

opportunity cost The value of what a producer gives up by using an input. (p. 224)

optimal strategy The action that has the highest expected payoff. (p. 421)

option value of waiting The value created if an investor can postpone the investment decision until the uncertainty about an investment's return is wholly or partially resolved. (p. 508)

output efficiency A mix of outputs that simultaneously supports exchange and input efficiency. (p. 539)

overconfidence A belief that one's skill and judgment are better than they truly are, or that better outcomes are more likely to happen than their true probability. (p. 632)

own-price elasticities of demand The percentage change in quantity demanded for a good resulting from a percentage change in the price of that good. (p. 44)

Pareto efficiency An economic allocation of goods in which the goods cannot be reallocated without making at least one individual worse off. (p. 537)

partial equilibrium analysis Determination of the equilibrium in a particular market that assumes there are no cross-market spillovers. (p. 523)

payback period The length of time required for an investment's initial costs to be recouped in future benefits without discounting future flows. (p. 505)

payoff matrix A table that lists the players, strategies, and payoffs of an economic game. (p. 421)

payoffs The outcomes the players receive from playing the game. (p. 421)

perfect competition A market (or industry) in which many firms produce an identical product and there are no barriers to entry. (p. 257)

perfect complement A good from which the consumer receives utility dependent on its being used in a fixed proportion with another good. (p. 105)

perfect price discrimination (first-degree price discrimination) A type of direct price discrimination in which a firm charges each customer exactly his willingness to pay. (p. 341)

perfect substitute A good that a consumer can trade for another good, in fixed units, and receive the same level of utility. (p. 104)

perfectly elastic A price elasticity that is infinite; any change in price leads to an infinite change in quantity demanded or supplied. (p. 39)

perfectly inelastic A price elasticity that is equal to zero; there is no change in quantity demanded or supplied for any change in price. (p. 39)

Pigouvian subsidy A subsidy paid for an activity that can be used to decrease a good's price (paid by the buyer) to take into account the external marginal benefits. (p. 604)

Pigouvian tax A type of tax levied on an activity that raises a good's price to take into account the external marginal costs imposed by a negative externality. (p. 604)

player A participant in an economic game who must decide on actions based on the actions of others. (p. 420)

positive externality A benefit conferred on a third party not directly involved in an economic transaction. (p. 596)

present discounted value (PDV) A mathematical concept that allows us to compare costs and benefits over time in a way that puts all present and future financial values on equal footing. (p. 494)

price ceiling The highest price that can be paid legally for a good or service. (p. 60)

price discrimination The practice of charging different prices to different customers for the same product. (p. 339)

price elasticity of demand The percentage change in quantity demanded resulting from a given percentage change in price. (p. 35)

price floor (or **price support**) A price regulation that sets the lowest price that can be paid legally for a good or service. (p. 66)

pricing strategy A firm's plan for setting the price of its product given the market conditions it faces and its desire to maximize profit. (p. 339)

principal The amount of assets on which interest payments are made. (p. 494)

principal–agent relationships Economic transactions that feature information asymmetry between a principal and her hired agent, whose actions the principal cannot fully observe. (p. 579)

prisoner's dilemma A situation in which the Nash equilibrium is an outcome that is somehow worse for all involved than another (unstable) outcome. (p. 382)

private good A good that is rival (one person's consumption affects the ability of another to consume it) and excludable (individuals can be prevented from consuming it). (p. 618)

producer surplus The difference between the price producers actually receive for their goods and the cost of producing them (measured by the height of the supply curve). (p. 53)

product differentiation Imperfect substitutability across varieties of a product. (p. 300)

production contract curve Curve that shows all Pareto-efficient allocations of inputs across producers. (p. 547)

production function A mathematical relationship that describes how much output can be made from different combinations of inputs. (p. 184)

production possibilities frontier (PPF) Curve that connects all possible efficient output combinations of two goods. (p. 547)

production technology The processes used to make, distribute, and sell a good. (p. 17)

production The process by which a person, company, government, or non-profit agency uses inputs to create a good or service for which others are willing to pay. (p. 181)

profit The difference between a firm's revenue and its total cost. (p. 260)

public good A good that is accessible to anyone who wants to consume it, and that remains just as valuable to a consumer even as other people consume it. (p. 618)

pure bundling A type of bundling in which the firm offers the products only as a bundle. (p. 364)

pure public good Nonrival and nonexcludable goods. (p. 619)

pure strategy A strategy in which the player chooses a particular action with certainty. (p. 429)

quantity discount A pricing strategy in which customers who buy larger quantities of a good pay a lower per-unit price. (p. 355)

quota A regulation mandating that the production or consumption of a certain quantity of a good or externality be limited (negative externality) or required (positive externality). (p. 608)

quota A regulation that sets the quantity of a good or service provided. (p. 69)

Rawlsian social welfare function A mathematical function that computes society's welfare as the welfare of the worst-off individual. (p. 536)

reaction curve A function that relates a firm's best response to its competitor's possible actions. In Cournot competition, this is the firm's best production response to its competitor's possible quantity choices. (p. 394)

real interest rate Rate of return expressed in terms of purchasing power. (p. 506)

repeated games A series in which the players play the same simultaneous game over and over. (p. 420)

residual demand curve In Cournot competition, the demand remaining for a firm's output given competitor firms' production quantities. (p. 393)

residual marginal revenue curve A marginal revenue curve corresponding to a residual demand curve. (p. 393)

returns to scale A change in the amount of output in response to a proportional increase in all the inputs. (p. 200)

risk premium The compensation an individual would require to bear risk without suffering a loss in expected utility. (p. 513)

risk-averse Suffering an expected utility loss from uncertainty, or equivalently, being willing to pay to have that risk reduced. (p. 512)

Second Welfare Theorem Theorem stating that any given Pareto-efficient equilibrium can be achieved by choosing the right initial allocation of goods. (p. 555)

segmenting (third-degree price discrimination) A type of direct price discrimination in which a firm charges different prices to different groups (segments) of customers based on the identifiable attributes of those groups. (p. 345)

sequential games Games where one player moves first and other players observe this action before making their decisions. (p. 420)

short run In production economics, the period of time during which one or more inputs into production cannot be changed. (p. 182)

short-run total cost curve The mathematical representation of a firm's total cost of producing different quantities of output at a fixed level of capital. (p. 238)

side payment A type of bribe that influences the outcome of a strategic game. (p. 445)

signal A costly action taken by an economic actor to indicate something that would otherwise be difficult to observe. (p. 583)

signaling A solution to the problem of asymmetric information in which the knowledgeable party alerts the other party to an unobservable characteristic of the good. (p. 582)

simultaneous games Games in which participants choose their actions at the same time without knowing their opponents' strategies. (p. 420)

social benefit The benefit of an economic transaction to society as a whole, equal to the private benefit plus the external benefit. (p. 596)

social cost The cost of an economic transaction to society as a whole, equal to the private cost plus the external cost. (p. 596)

social welfare function A mathematical function that combines the utility levels of the individuals in a society to obtain a single overall measure of an economy's performance. (p. 535)

specific capital Capital that cannot be used outside of its original application. (p. 226)

Stackelberg competition Oligopoly model in which firms make production decisions sequentially. (p. 399)

strategic decision An action made based on the anticipation of others' actions. (p. 419)

strategy A player's plan of action for a game. (p. 420)

subsidy A payment by the government to a buyer or seller of a good or service. (p. 83)

substitute A good that can be used in place of another good. (pp. 14, 162)

substitution effect The change in a consumer's consumption choices that results from a change in the relative prices of two goods. (p. 151)

sunk cost A cost that, once paid, cannot be recovered. (p. 226)

sunk cost fallacy The mistake of letting sunk costs affect forward-looking decisions. (pp. 227, 637)

supply choke price The price at which no firm is willing to produce a good and quantity supplied is zero; the vertical intercept of the inverse supply curve. (p. 18)

supply curve The relationship between the quantity supplied of a good and the good's price, holding all other factors constant. (p. 18)

supply The combined amount of a good that all producers in a market are willing to sell. (p. 12)

tax incidence Who *really* bears the burden of a tax. (p. 80)

theories and models Explanations of how things work that help us understand and predict how and why economic entities behave as they do. (p. 2)

time-consistent Consistencies in a consumer's preferences in a given economic transaction, whether the economic transaction is far off or imminent. (p. 634)

tit-for-tat A strategy in which the player mimics her opponent's prior-period action in each round. (p. 437)

total cost (TC) The sum of a firm's fixed and variable costs: (p. 229)

total cost curve A curve that shows a firm's cost of producing particular quantities. (p. 208)

total effect The total change effect in a consumer's optimal consumption bundle as a result of a price change. (p. 152)

total factor productivity growth (technological change) An improvement in technology that changes the firm's production function such that it gets more output from the same amount of inputs. (p. 203)

total marginal benefit The vertical sum of the marginal benefit curves of all of a public good's consumers. (p. 619)

tradable permit A government-issued permit that allows a firm to emit a certain amount of pollution during production and that can be traded to other firms. (p. 613)

tragedy of the commons The dilemma that common resources create when everyone has free access and the resource is used more intensively than it would be if privately owned, leading to a decline in its value for everyone. (p. 622)

transfer Surplus that moves from producer to consumer, or vice versa, as a result of a price regulation. (p. 61)

two-part tariff A pricing strategy in which the payment has two components, a per-unit price and a fixed fee. (p. 369)

unimproved land The physical space on which economic activity (agriculture, housing, manufacturing, etc.) takes place. (p. 477)

unit elastic A price elasticity with an absolute value equal to 1. (p. 39)

utilitarian social welfare function A mathematical function that computes society's welfare as the sum of every individual's welfare. (p. 536)

utility A measure of how satisfied a consumer is. (p. 93)

utility function A mathematical function that describes the relationship between what consumers actually consume and their level of well-being. (p. 93)

variable cost (VC) The cost of inputs that change as the firm changes its quantity of output. (p. 229)

variable inputs Inputs that can be changed in the short run. (p. 182)

versioning A pricing strategy in which the firm offers different product options designed to attract different types of consumers. (p. 360)

welfare economics The area of economics concerned with the economic well-being of society as a whole. (p. 94)

References

Acemoglu, Daron, and Amy Finkelstein. "Input and Technology Choices in Regulated Industries: Evidence from the Health Care Sector." *Journal of Political Economy* 116, no. 5 (2008): 837–880.

Agarwal, Sumit, Souphala Chomsisengphet, and Chunlin Liu. "The Importance of Adverse Selection in the Credit Card Market: Evidence from Randomized Trials of Credit Card Solicitations." *Journal of Money, Credit and Banking* 42, no. 4 (June 2010): 743–754.

Aguiar, Mark, and Mark Bils. "Has Consumption Inequality Mirrored Income Inequality?" *American Economic Review* 105, no. 9 (September 2015): 2725–2756.

Akerlof, George. "The Market for 'Lemons': Quality Uncertainty and the Market Mechanism." *Quarterly Journal of Economics* 84, no. 3 (August 1970): 488–500.

Allcott, Hunt, and Daniel Keniston. "Dutch Disease or Agglomeration? The Local Economic Effects of Natural Resource Booms in Modern America." *Review of Economic Studies* (April 2018): 695–731.

Arkes, Hal R., and Catherine Blumer. "The Psychology of Sunk Cost." *Organizational Behavior and Human Decision Processes* 35, no. 1 (1985): 124–140.

Becker, Gary S., and Kevin M. Murphy. "A Theory of Rational Addiction." *Journal of Political Economy* 96, no. 4 (August 1988): 675–700.

Berry, Steven, James Levinsohn, and Ariel Pakes. "Differentiated Products Demand Systems from a Combination of Micro and Macro Data: The New Car Market." Journal of Political Economy 112, no. 1, Part 1 (February 2004): 68–105.

Black, Dan A., Seth Sanders, and Lowell Taylor. "The Economic Reward for Studying Economics." *Economic Inquiry* 41, no. 3 (2003): 365–377.

Bleakley, Hoyt, and Joseph Ferrie. "Land Openings on the Georgia Frontier and the Coase Theorem in the Short- and Long-Run." Working paper, 2014.

Brosnan, Sarah F., and Frans B. M. de Waal. "Monkeys Reject Unequal Pay." *Nature* 425 (September 18, 2003): 297–299.

Brown University, Office of Institutional Research. Degrees Awarded by Brown University (2006–2015). http://www.brown.edu/about/administration/institutional -research/factbook/degrees-and-completions

Budish, Eric, Benjamin Roin, and Heidi Williams. "Do Firms Underinvest in Long-Term Research? Evidence from Cancer Clinical Trials." *American Economic Review,* 105, no. 7 (July 2015): 2044–2085.

Chiappori, Pierre-André, Tim Groseclose, and Steven Levitt. "Testing Mixed-Strategy Equilibria When Players Are Heterogeneous: The Case of Penalty Kicks on Soccer." *American Economic Review* 92, no. 4 (September 2002): 1138–1151.

Coase, Ronald H. "The Problem of Social Cost." *Journal of Law and Economics* 3 (1960): 1–44.

Cookson, Graham. *INRIX Global Traffic Scorecard*, INRIX Research, Kirkland, WA, February 2018.

Costa, Dora L. "The Wage and the Length of the Work Day: From the 1890s to 1991." *Journal of Labor Economics* 18, no. 1 (2000): 156–181.

DellaVigna, Stefano, and Ulrike Malmendier. "Paying Not to Go to the Gym." *American Economic Review* 96, no. 3 (2006): 694–719.

Dubé, Jean-Pierre. "Product Differentiation and Mergers in the Carbonated Soft Drink Industry." *Journal of Economics and Management Strategy* 14, no. 4 (2005): 879–904.

Duranton, Gilles, and Matthew A. Turner. "The Fundamental Law of Road Congestion: Evidence from US Cities." *American Economic Review* 101, no. 6 (October 2011): 2616–2652.

Dwyer, Gerald P., Jr., and Cotton M. Lindsay. "Robert Giffen and the Irish Potato." *American Economic Review* 74, no. 1 (1984): 188–192.

Ellison, Glenn, and Sara Ellison. "Search, Obfuscation, and Price Elasticities on the Internet." *Econometrica* 77, no. 2 (2009): 427–452.

Fehr, Ernst, and Klaus M. Schmidt. "Theories of Fairness and Reciprocity: Evidence and Economics Applications." in *Advances in Economics and Econometrics: Theory and Applications, Eighth World Congress*, vol. 1, New York: Cambridge University Press, 2003, 208–257.

Fillmore, Ian. "Price Discrimination and Public Policy in the U.S. College Market." Working paper, Washington University of St. Louis, 2018.

Fleming, Charles. "That Sinking Feeling." *Vanity Fair,* August 1, 1995.

Fleming, Charles. "Fishtar? Why 'Waterworld,' with Costner in Fins, Is Costliest Film Ever." *Wall Street Journal,* January 31, 1996.

Gilley, Otis W., and Marc C. Chopin. "Professional Golf: Labor or Leisure." *Managerial Finance* 26, no. 7 (2000): 33–45.

Goldberg, Pinelopi K., and Frank Verboven. "Cross-Country Price Dispersion in the Euro Era: A Case Study of the European Car Market." *Economic Policy* 19, no. 40 (October 2004): 484–521.

Goldberg, Pinelopi K., Amit K. Khandelwal, Nina Pavcnik, and Petia Topalova. "Multiproduct Firms and Product Turnover in the Developing World: Evidence from India." *Review of Economics and Statistics* 92, no. 4 (November 2010): 1042–1049.

Goolsbee, Austan, and Chad Syverson. "How Do Incumbents Respond to the Threat of Entry? Evidence from the Major Airlines. *Quarterly Journal of Economics* 123, no. 4 (2008): 1611–1633.

Government Accountability Office. "National Flood Insurance Program: Continued Actions Needed to Address Financial and Operational Issues." Statement of Orice Williams Brown, September 2010.

Harford, Tim. *The Logic of Life: The Rational Economics of an Irrational World*. New York: Random House, 2008. 18–21.

Henrich, Joseph, Robert Boyd, Samuel Bowles, Colin Camerer, Ernst Fehr, Herbert Gintis, and Richard McElreath. "In Search of Homo Economicus: Behavioral Experiments in 15 Small-Scale Societies." *American Economic Review Papers and Proceedings* 91, no. 2 (2001): 73–78.

Hortaçsu, Ali, and Steven L. Puller. "Understanding Strategic Bidding in Multi-Unit Auctions: A Case Study of the Texas Electricity Spot Market." *RAND Journal of Economics* 39, no. 1 (2008): 86–114.

Hortacsu, Ali, and Chad Syverson. "The Ongoing Evolution of U.S. Retail: A Format Tug-of-War." *Journal of Economic Perspectives* 29, no. 4 (2015): 89–112.

Hsieh, Chang-Tai, and Enrico Moretti. "Can Free Entry Be Inefficient? Fixed Commissions and Social Waste in the Real Estate Industry." *Journal of Political Economy* 111, no. 5 (2003): 1076–1122.

Huang, K. S., and B. Lin. Estimation of Food Demand and Nutrient Elasticities from Household Survey Data, Technical Bulletin 1887, Food and Rural Economic Division, Economic Research Service, U.S. Department of Agriculture, August 2000.

Jackson, Joe. *The Thief at the End of the World: Rubber, Power and the Seeds of Empire*. New York: Viking, 2008.

Jensen, Robert. "The Digital Provide: Information (Technology), Market Performance, and Welfare in the South Indian Fisheries Sector." *The Quarterly Journal of Economics* 122, no. 3 (2007): 879–924.

Jensen, Robert T., and Nolan H. Miller. "Giffen Behavior and Subsistence Consumption." *American Economic Review* 98, no. 4 (2008): 1553–1577.

Kahneman, Daniel. *Thinking, Fast and Slow*. New York: Farrar, Straus and Giroux, 2011.

Kaplan, Steven N., and Bernadette A. Minton. "How Has CEO Turnover Changed?" *International Review of Finance* 12, no. 1 (2012): 57–87.

Keefer, Quinn A. W. "The Sunk-Cost Fallacy in the National Football League: Salary Cap Value and Playing Time." *Journal of Sports Economics* 18, no. 3 (2015) 282–297.

Kirkham, Chris, and Andrew Khouri. "How Longshoremen Command $100K Salaries in Era of Globalization and Automation." *Los Angeles Times*, March 1, 2015. http://www.latimes.com/business/la-fi-dockworker-pay-20150301-story.html.

Kreps, David M., and José A. Scheinkman. "Quantity Precommitment and Bertrand Competition Yield Cournot Outcomes." *Bell Journal of Economics* 14, no. 2 (1983): 326–337.

Kustura, Katie. "Burglars Hit New Smyrna Beach's Venezia Neighborhood." *The Daytona Beach News-Journal*, August 15, 2017, http://www.news-journalonline.com/news/20170818/teens-arrestedin-volusia-burglary-spree

Levitt, Steven, and Chad Syverson. "Market Distortions When Agents Are Better Informed: The Value of Information in Real Estate Transactions." *Review of Economics and Statistics* 90, no. 4 (2008): 599–611.

Levitt, Steven D., and Sudhir Alladi Venkatesh. "An Economic Analysis of a Drug-Selling Gang's Finances." *Quarterly Journal of Economics,* 115, no. 3 (August 2000): 755–789.

Martinez, Jose. "Uber Prices Are Surging Because of Snow and People Aren't Happy." November 15, 2018, https://www.complex.com/life/2018/11/uber-prices-are-surging-because-of-the-snow-and-people-arent-happy/

Mayzlin, Dina, Yaniv Dover, and Judith Chevalier. "Promotional Reviews: An Empirical Investigation of Online Review Manipulation." *American Economic Review* 104, no. 8 (August 2014): 2421–2455.

McDevitt, Ryan C. "Names and Reputations: An Empirical Analysis." *American Economic Journal: Microeconomics* 3(3) (2011): 193–209.

McDevitt, Ryan C. "'A' Business by Any Other Name: Firm Name Choice as a Signal of Firm Quality." *Journal of Political Economy* 122, no. 4 (2014): 909–944.

Minority Staff, Special Investigations Division, Committee on Government Reform, U.S. House of Representatives. "Prescription Drug Price Discrimination in the 5th Congressional District in Florida: Drug Manufacturer Prices Are Higher for Humans than for Animals." Prepared for Rep. Karen L. Thurman, http://lobby.la.psu.edu/010_ Insuring_the_Uninsured/Congressional_Statements/ House/H_Thurman_031600.htm

MSNBC.com. "No Pay, No Spray: Firefighters Let Home Burn." October 6, 2010. http://www.nbcnews .com /id/39516346/ns/us_news-life/t/no-pay-no-spray -firefighters-let-home-burn/

MSNBC.com. "Firefighters Let Home Burn over $75 Fee—Again." December 7, 2011. http://usnews.nbcnews .com /_news/2011/12/07/9272989-firefighters-let-home -burn-over-75-fee-again

Murphy, S. M., C. Davidson, A. M. Kennedy, P. A. Eadie, and C. Lawlor. "Backyard Burning." *Journal of Plastic, Reconstructive & Aesthetic Surgery* 61, no. 2 (2008): 180–182.

Nevo, Aviv. "Measuring Market Power in the Ready-to-Eat Cereal Industry." *Econometrica* 69, no. 2 (2001): 307–342.

Nordhaus, William D. "Revisiting the Social Cost of Carbon." *Proceedings of the National Academy of Sciences* 114, no. 7 (2017): 1518–1523.

Ocbazghi, Immanuel, and Sara Silverstein. "Why Most People Refuse to Sell Their Lottery Tickets for Twice What They Paid." *Business Insider*, October 23, 2018, https:// www.businessinsider.com/powerball-tickets-winning -numbers-regret-avoidance-behavioral-economics-2017-8

Olson, Mancur. *The Logic of Collective Action: Public Goods and the Theory of Groups.* Cambridge, MA: Harvard University Press, 1965.

PayScale. College Salary Report, 2015–2016. http:// www.payscale.com/college-salary-report/majors-that -pay-you-back/bachelors

Pigou, Arthur C. *The Economics of Welfare.* London: Macmillan, 1920.

Proctor, Darby, Rebecca Williamson, Frans B. M. de Waal, and Sarah F. Brosnan. "Chimpanzees Play the Ultimatum Game." *Proceedings of the National Academy of Sciences* 110, no. 6 (February 5, 2013): 2070–2075.

Rosen, Sherwin. "Potato Paradoxes." *Journal of Political Economy* 107, no. 6 (1999): S294–S313.

Scott Morton, Fiona M., and Joel M. Podolny. "Love or Money? The Effects of Owner Motivation in the California Wine Industry." *Journal of Industrial Economics* 50, no. 4 (December 2002): 431–456.

Spence, Michael. "Job Market Signaling." *Quarterly Journal of Economics* 87, no. 3 (August 1973): 355–374.

Teger, Allan I. *Too Much Invested to Quit.* Oxford: Pergamon Press, 1980.

Tversky, Amos, and Daniel Kahneman. "Judgment under Uncertainty: Heuristics and Biases." *Science* 185, no. 4157 (1974): 1124–1130.

Tversky, Amos, and Daniel Kahneman. "The Framing of Decisions and the Psychology of Choice." *Science* 211, no. 4481 (1981): 453–458.

U.S. Department of Labor, Bureau of Labor Statistics. Occupational Employment and Wages in 1999 on the New Standard Occupational Classification System. December 20, 2000. http://www.bls.gov/news.release /history /ocwage_12202000.txt

U.S. Department of Labor, Bureau of Labor Statistics. Occupational Employment and Wages—May 2014. March 25, 2015. http://www.bls.gov/news.release/pdf/ ocwage.pdf

U.S. Department of Transportation, Bureau of Transportation Statistics. National Transportation Statistics. http://www.rita.dot.gov/bts/sites/rita.dot.gov.bts/ files/publications/national_transportation_statistics/ index.html

Waldfogel, Joel. "The Deadweight Loss of Christmas." *American Economic Review* 83, no. 5 (1993): 1328–1336.

Weitzman, Martin. "Prices vs. Quantities." *The Review of Economic Studies* 41, no. 4 (1974): 477–491.

World Bank, Institute for Health Metrics and Evaluation. *The Cost of Air Pollution: Strengthening the Economic Case for Action*, 2016.

Index

Note: Page numbers followed by f indicate figures; those followed by t indicate tables; those followed by n indicate footnotes.